A.D.Page

Philips' New World Atlas

A.D.Page

NEW WORLD ATLAS

George Philip
London·Melbourne·Milwaukee

Edited by
B.M. Willett, B.A., Cartographic Editor, George Philip and Son Ltd
Consultant Cartographer Harold Fullard, M.Sc.
Maps prepared by George Philip Cartographic Services Ltd
under the direction of A.G. Poynter, M.A.,
Director of Cartography

Fifth Edition 1983

British Library Cataloguing in Publication Data

Philips' new world atlas. — 5th ed.
  1. Atlases, British
  912   G1021
ISBN 0 540 05439 9

© 1983 George Philip & Son, Ltd

Printed in Great Britain by George Philip Printers Ltd

Acknowledgements
The Landsat images in *The Earth from Space* were provided by: Canada
Center for Remote Sensing, Ottowa; Eros Data Center, US Geological
Survey, South Dakota; National Air Survey Center, Maryland, USA.

Title-page illustration Savannah country in the Samburu Game
Reserve, Kenya (Bruce Coleman Ltd)

Preface

The **New World Atlas** has been designed to provide a compact and convenient reference book which is easy to handle and consult.

The maps in the atlas are arranged in continental sections; each is introduced by a physical and a political map of the whole continent and these are followed by regional maps at medium scales and larger-scale maps of the more densely-populated areas. The contents list to the atlas as a whole not only gives a complete list of maps but also includes an outline map of each of the continents showing the areas covered by the large-scale map pages. This will help the reader to find the page required very quickly. The location of a specific place can, of course, be found via the index, where place names are listed alphabetically and the map page number and geographical coordinates for each entry are given.

The name forms on the maps are those that are used locally, or that have been transcribed according to the accepted systems. In the case of China, the Pinyin system for romanization, which is being increasingly used in the west, has been accepted. Well-known and well-used forms (often English conventions) for foreign place names are cross-referenced to the local form in the index and are often given alongside the local form on the map.

Where there are rival claims to territory, international boundaries are drawn to indicate the *de facto* situation. This does not denote international recognition of these boundaries but shows the limits of administration on either side of the line. Boundaries crossing disputed areas in the eastern Mediterranean have been specifically identified.

The maps are preceded by a series of satellite photographs, or, more accurately, images of the earth. These are false-colour images and have been obtained from the Landsat satellites of the American space agency NASA which have been circling the globe for many years. The images are all on the scale of 1:1M so they are easily compared and each is accompanied by a locational map and a brief descriptive text. There is also a short introduction on how the Landsat images are produced. To date the information from the satellites is mainly used for specialized purposes and research is concentrated in these areas. Before the end of the century, however, it is likely that satellite information will be used to compile and revise the kind of maps that make up the bulk of this atlas.

Contents

The Earth from Space

World Maps 1-128

The Abbey of Baume-les-Messieurs in the Jura, France (Bruce Coleman Ltd)

Europe

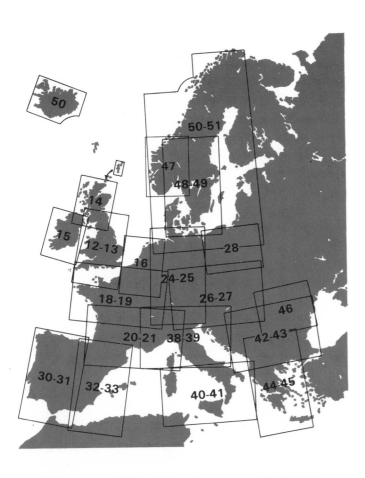

Asia

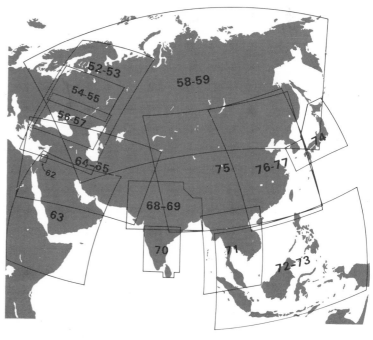

The monastery of Lamayuru Gonpa in Ladakh, Kashmir (Bruce Coleman Ltd)

Africa

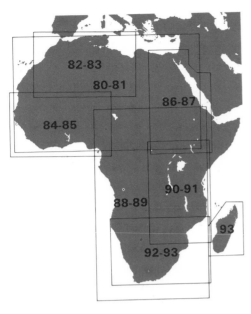

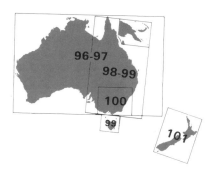

Australasia

Opposite below Ox-bow loop on the Luangwa River, Zambia
(Bruce Coleman Ltd)

Below The Twelve Apostles, Victoria, Australia (Bruce Coleman Ltd)

The Americas

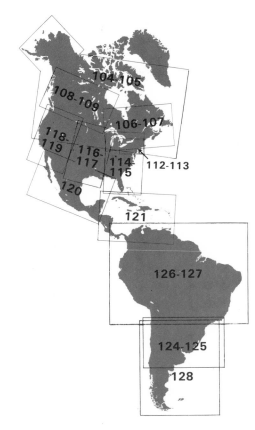

Index

Mt Ausengate, Peru (Bruce Coleman Ltd)

Landsat Images — Introduction

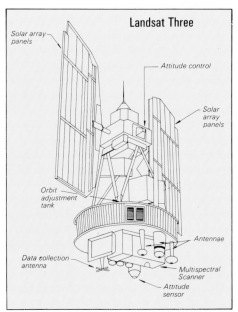

Landsat Three

The National Aeronautics and Space Administration (NASA) of the United States established its Earth Resources Survey Programme in 1965. It has developed the space programmes of Gemini, Apollo, Skylab and Landsat. The first Landsat was launched in 1972 and the fourth in 1982. The satellite is put into orbit and gathers its information by "remote sensing", that is viewing the Earth from a great height and signalling what it sees back to Earth.

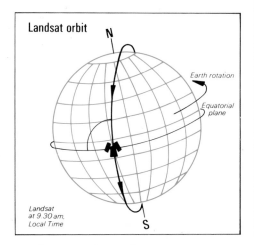

Landsat orbit

The Landsat spacecraft circles the Earth at a height of 919km and nearly crosses the Poles, cutting the Equator at 9° from a rightangle. It weighs 959kg. It takes 103 minutes to complete a revolution of the Earth and crosses the Equator at the same local time, about 9.30 in the morning, always therefore on the sunlit side of the Earth. It circles the Earth fourteen times a day and on the fifteenth orbit is overhead, 159km west of its original point. It returns to the original point eighteen days later. When Landsat 2 and 3 were working together this "same image" period was reduced to nine days. The instruments on board record a view of the Earth along its path to a width of 185km and an area of approximately 35,000km² per scene. The fourth Landsat was launched in 1982, flies at an altitude of 705km and has a sixteen day cycle.

Landsat carries a number of instruments and the one responsible for the images on the following pages is the Multi Spectral Scanner (MSS). The word "image" is used rather than photograph because they are not produced by a camera or are they true in colour. On board the spacecraft a

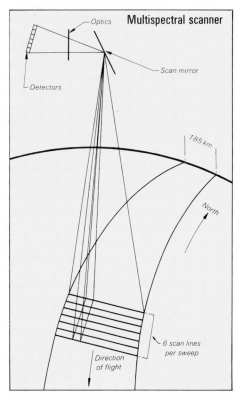

Multispectral scanner

mirror oscillates slightly, scanning a swathe of the Earth at rightangles to the orbit path. The light from the ground is broken down through filters into four selected parts of the spectrum, two of visible light and two in the infra-red. The intensity in each of these bands for a small area of the Earth is measured and converted into a signal which is sent to the Earth receiving station. If the satellite is out of sight the material is recorded and transmitted when it is in contact with a ground station.

Four black and white images are made for each of the spectral bands by reproducing the intensity for the given area on a grey scale. To produce the false colour images in the following pages, the black and white images of the two visible bands and the longer infra-red are passed through colour filters.

In such a false colour image, growing vegetation being highly reflective in the near infra-red appears in shades of red. Water areas appear as black if clear and deep, but if it has sediment in it, it will be blue. This can be seen at the mouths of rivers and along coastal bays. Soils and rocks appear bluish but can range through yellow and browns; where there is a high water content, as in peats, they will be black. Cities and principal roads which can be detected on the image will be white to blue-grey. These are only indications of the colour for their actual hue can be affected by the angle of illumination of the sun on the original scene, the atmospheric conditions, the season in the vegetational growth cycle and minor variations in the image processing and printing.

Landsat false colour

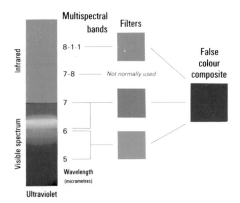

On each of the following pages are presented a false colour image of part of the Earth at a scale of 1:1 000 000 (1cm = 10km), a map of the same area and a brief description. The map is normally at a scale of 1:2 500 000 (1cm = 25km) but if it is at a smaller scale the image area is shown on the map by a red square.

Some applications of Landsat

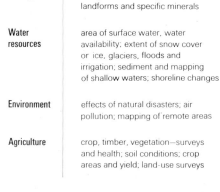

Geology	recognition of rock types, landforms and specific minerals
Water resources	area of surface water, water availability; extent of snow cover or ice, glaciers, floods and irrigation; sediment and mapping of shallow waters; shoreline changes
Environment	effects of natural disasters; air pollution; mapping of remote areas
Agriculture	crop, timber, vegetation—surveys and health; soil conditions; crop areas and yield; land-use surveys

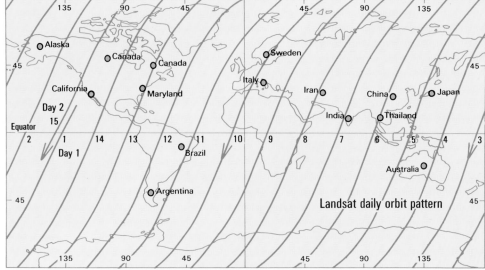

Landsat daily orbit pattern

● Ground receiving station

Southwest Iceland

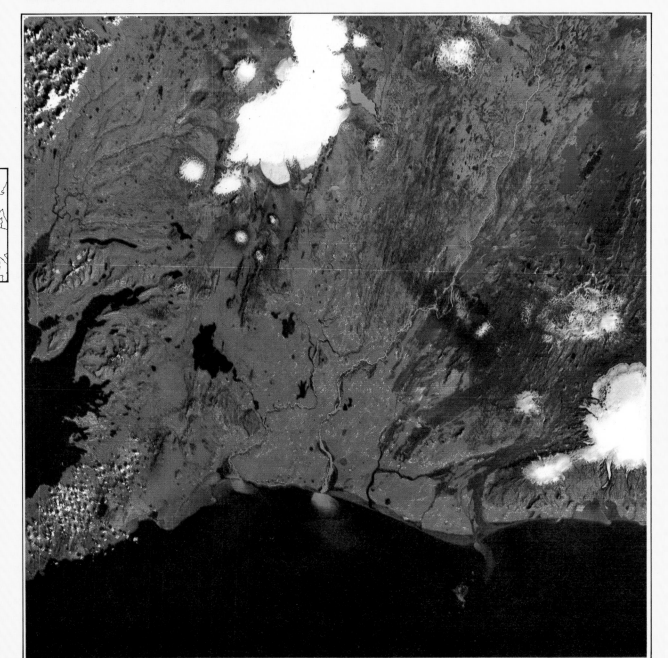

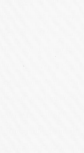

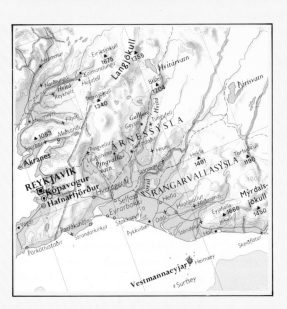

Iceland lies across the Mid-Atlantic Ridge, a great divide in the Earth's crust being forced apart at the rate of a few centimetres per year. The Ridge runs southwestwards across the image, following the lie of the hills and the Hvita valley. It is here that molten lava has poured out across the Earth's surface in volcanic eruptions. The older, dormant cones are topped with ice-caps, but the active Mt. Hekla and the new volcanoes on Heimaey and Surtsey can also be seen. The dark grey lands are bare or thinly-vegetated volcanic rock, but glaciers, rivers and wind have spread soils taken from them across the coastal lowlands. Here, where most Icelanders live, the Arctic climate just allows grass to grow in Summer. *(Image taken in August)*

The Norwegian Fjords

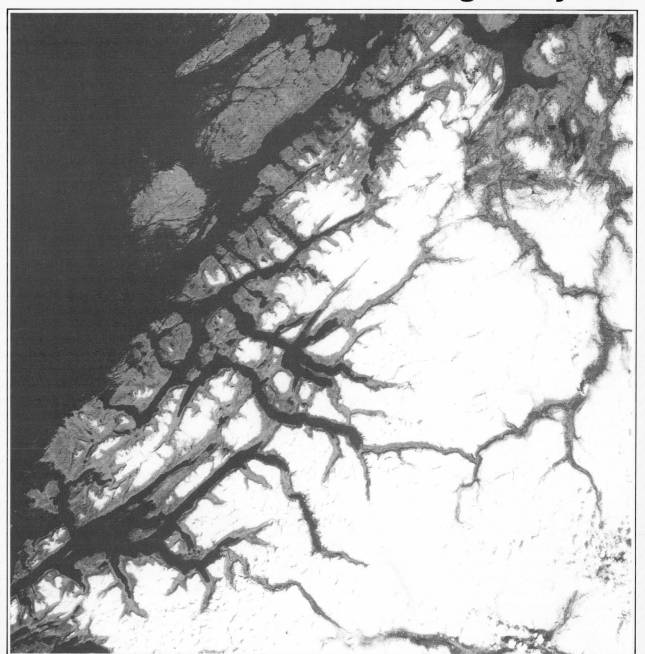

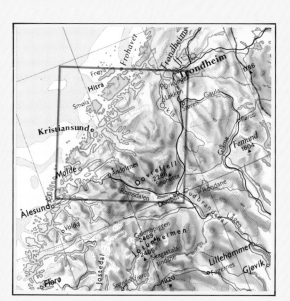

At the end of a long Norwegian winter, the snow has receded to the high moors or *fjeld,* revealing in this image a two-tone red fringe to the coastline. The brighter red traces the *strandflat,* a shelf of lowland hugging the seashore, just wide enough to hold towns and villages, graze cattle and sheep, or grow a few crops. The darker red identifies the spruce and pine of the higher slopes and offshore islands. Viewed from space, the long, thin, black fingers of the sea reach inland. The high, steep-sloping walls of these sea-inlets, or *fjords,* are ancient river-valleys, widened and deepened by glaciers, then later filled by the sea. *(Image taken in May)*

Copenhagen

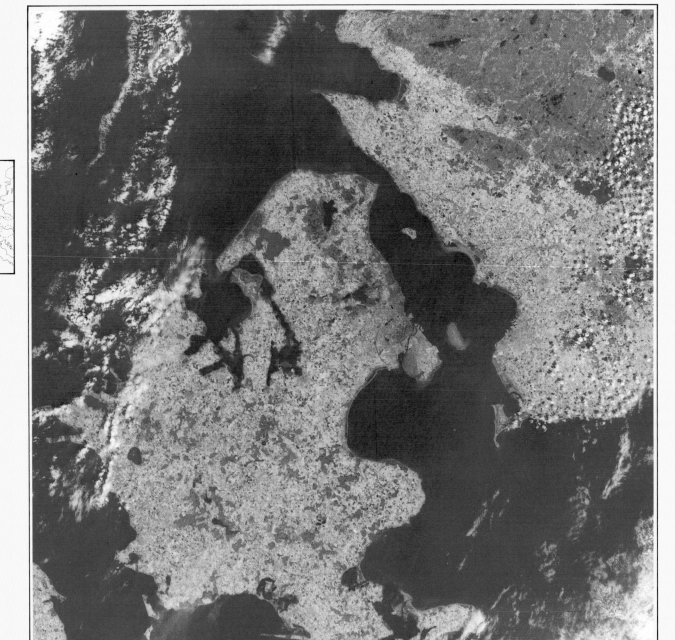

When the last ice-cap retreated at the end of the Ice Age, it left behind a fertile soils cover overlying Denmark and Southern Sweden, then a continuous plain. The sea-level later rose to separate the two countries and leave Sjælland as an island. Most of the land is now intensively farmed, the fine mosaic texture reflecting the variety of uses to which the land is given at any one time – generally shared between livestock and the crops grown to feed them. Only the larger towns are visible, most notably Copenhagen, which grew up as a port on this important neck of the sea. Moving north-eastwards through Sweden, the character of the land suddenly changes as a fault-line is crossed. The forests and lakes of Scandinavia begin here. *(Image taken in September)*

The Lake Belt of Central Sweden

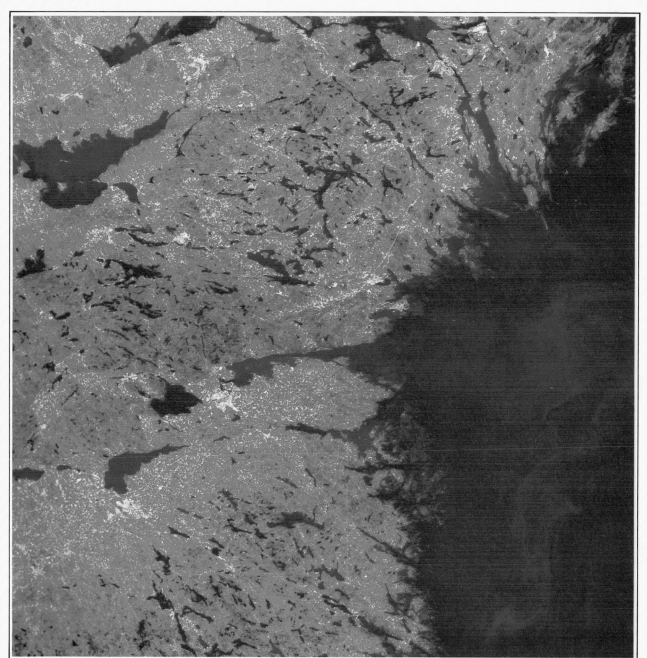

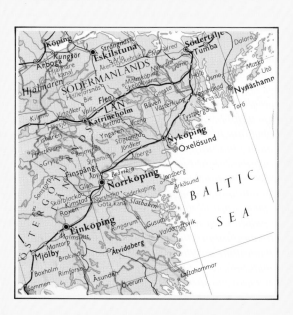

The Lake Belt of Sweden is a region of lowland in a land of mostly inhospitable uplands, and the nation's historic and industrial heart. It is peppered with small towns, a number of which can easily be picked out in this view. A combination of complex faulting and the gouging action of the great ice-cap that once obliterated Northern Europe produced a heavily-cracked surface now containing a myriad of lakes. With the region having once been under sea as well as ice, the variable soil cover has made for a diverse and charming landscape of forest, meadow, moor and farmland. *(Image taken in July)*

London

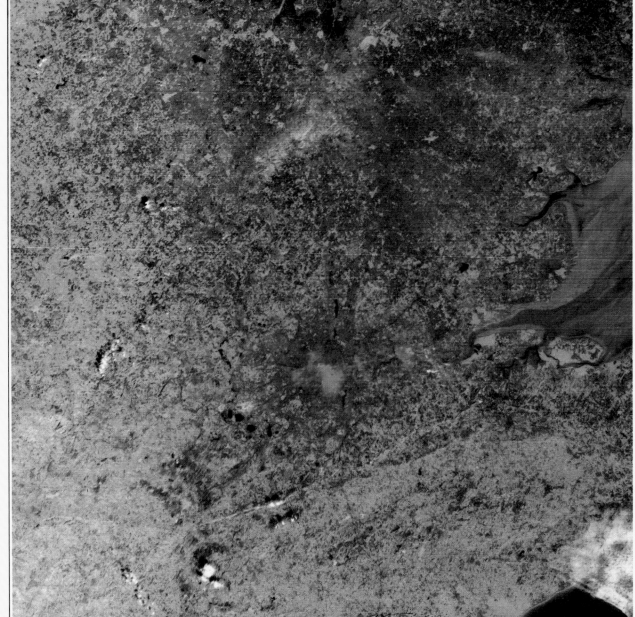

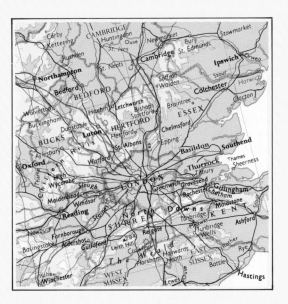

The London Basin, framed within the angle made by the Chiltern Hills and North Downs, comprises 11% of the land area of the United Kingdom, but it is inhabited by some 17 million people, nearly a third of the population, with London itself the established metropolitan core of the country. North of the Thames estuary mudflats is the level, predominantly agricultural countryside of East Anglia, mostly dark-brown ploughed fields just ahead of the growing season, speckled with the pink of occasional grassland. To the south and west, the colours – and use of land – are reversed, apart from in North Kent, where orchards, vegetables and hops supply the London market. *(Image taken in March)*

East Midlands, England

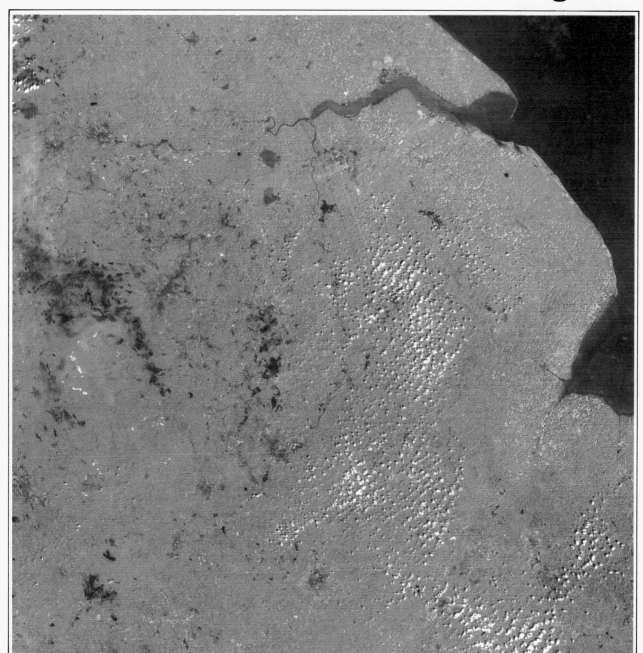

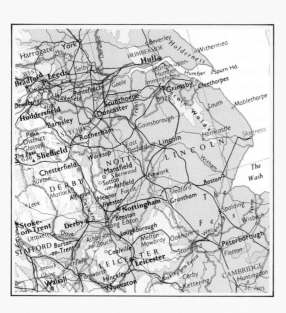

A good part of the industrial heartland of England is covered by this image. From Birmingham to Leeds, from Manchester to Hull, famous manufacturing towns and cities blot the landscape, some so closely packed they begin to merge together, others large enough to exhibit the lighter grey ring of their tree-lined suburbs. To the east, there is farming country, some of the richest in England. Cereals are grown across the flat Lincolnshire countryside; market-gardening occupies the lush Fenland bordering the Wash. Further inland, moving into the pastures of the Midlands, obtrusive dark grey patches appear here and there. They identify the heathlands of Cannock Chase and Sherwood Forest, and the open moorland of the Peak District. *(Image taken in June)*

Paris

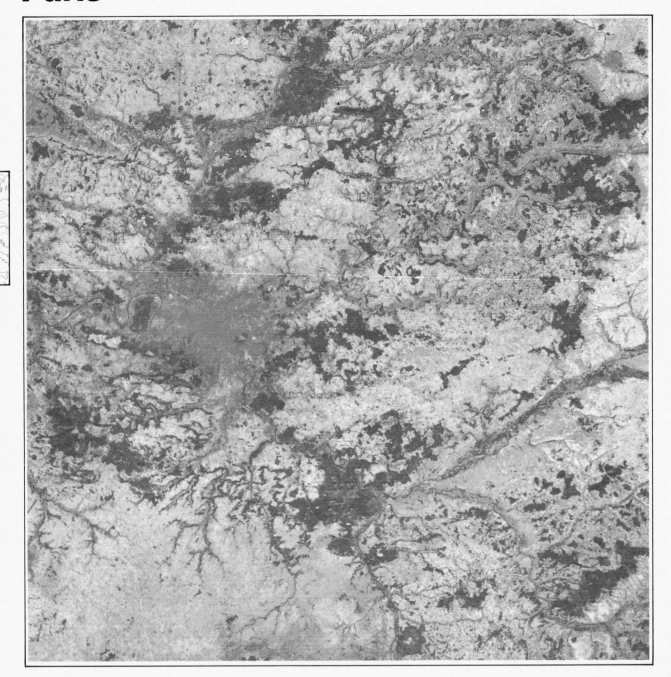

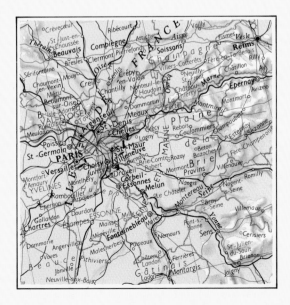

The city of Paris, astride the meandering River Seine, lies at the centre of a giant basin comprising several concentric belts of different rock strata, and containing most of Northern France. The resulting varied landscape is sprinkled with local names *(noms de pays)* that identify regions whose distinctive characters are readily apparent from this early spring scene. In Brie, the clay soils favour dairy farming, while Champagne's dry chalk country is given to cereals and vineyards and the super-fertile plain of Beauce is devoted to wheat and sugar-beet. Elsewhere, especially in Hurepoix, dark areas signify forest, which occupies poor sandy soils. *(Image taken in March)*

Lake Geneva

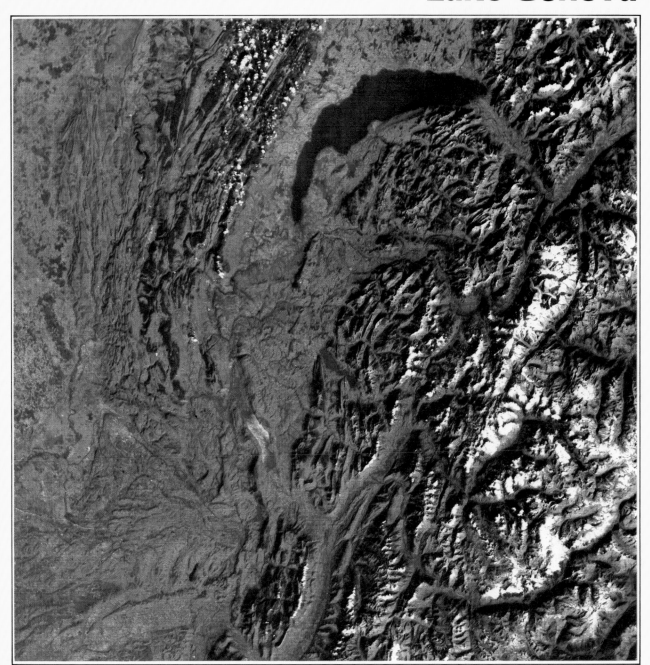

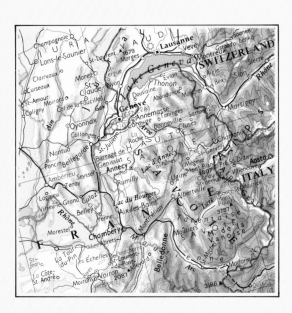

The Alps are the product of the same compressive forces which gave rise to the Himalayas in Asia. Rock strata buckled and overturned, while ice and water carved great valleys across the mountains. The result has been a landscape typified by this scene. Snow-capped summits like Mont Blanc stand highest, on account of their superior resistance to erosive powers. The valleys are fertile ribbons of agriculture reaching into the heart of the Alps, and serve as routes across them. Emerging from Lake Geneva, the Rhône divides the Alps from the Jura, gentler hills to the North, before opening out into lowlands. The region has a pink hue because it is Autumn and crops have been harvested. *(Image taken in October)*

The Po Valley, Italy

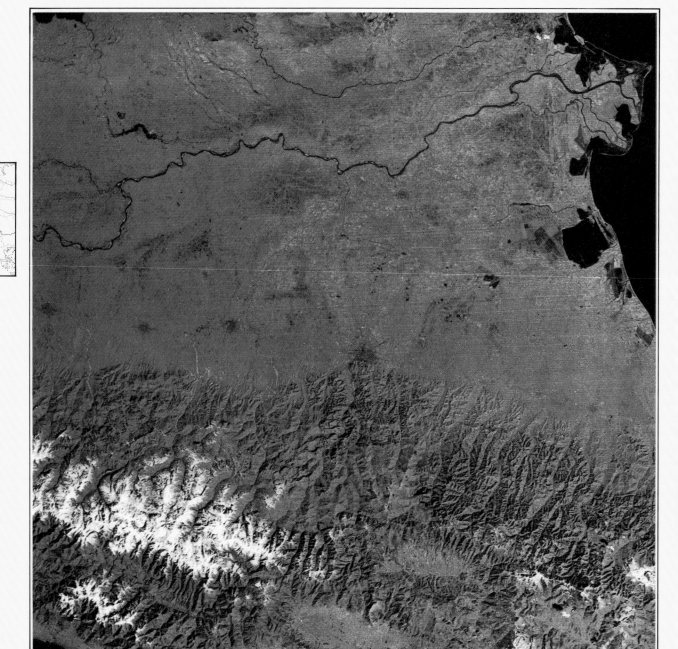

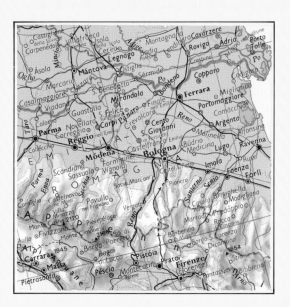

Winter in Northern Italy sees the higher summits of the Apennines capped by snow and the fields of the lower Po dark and sodden. Growing crops already show, however, in the Arno basin, the upper Plain and the drained lands near the coast. The Northern Plain is a very flat region, lying between mountain ranges to the north and south. Though watered by the Po and its tributaries, Italy's richest farming land has to be heavily irrigated in the hot and dry summer. The Plain is densely populated, many of the present-day cities being established in Roman times or earlier. Bologna, Modena, Parma and others strung out along the straight Via Emilia, grew up where it was met by roads leading down from Apennine passes. *(Image taken in February)*

The Danube

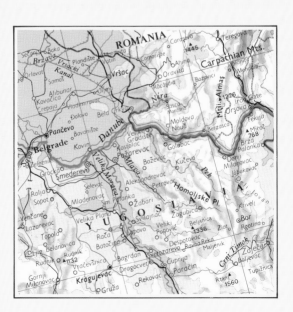

Dominating this view is the course of the River Danube, which winds across the Hungarian Plain, to breach the Carpathian Mountains as a fast-flowing torrent through the "Iron Gate" gorge, before crossing Romania and reaching the Black Sea. Below Belgrade, where it is met by the Sava, and, later, the Morava, the Danube separates two regions, whose differing characters are apparent from their image colouring. Formerly the floor of a huge ancient lake, the lush flat lowlands to the north now constitute Yugoslavia's richest agricultural land, given to a wide range of crops from wheat to market-gardening. The more rugged land on the river's right bank is mostly pasture land and dotted with many small industrial towns. *(Image taken in October)*

Athens

Only a narrow isthmus joins the Peloponnesus to mainland Greece, and this was breached by the construction of the Corinth Ship Canal in 1893. In this summer view, the peninsula is undergoing a long spell of uninterrupted hot and dry weather. It is a mountainous landscape, with little level ground and consists mainly of limestone, a rock highly pervious to rainwater. For a farmer, then, the Peloponnesus is largely unproductive, though orange and olive groves cluster around the southern bays, green vegetables occupy the plain of Argos, and grapes, dried for currants, line the shore of the Gulf of Corinth. Elsewhere, the lower scrub-covered mountain slopes are left to pasture for sheep and goats. *(Image taken in August)*

The Middle East

A land where several present-day international boundaries meet, this part of the Middle-East is laden with biblical and historical significance. Famous placenames such as Galilee, Nazareth, Beirut and Damascus can be located here. In more modern times, the region has witnessed military conflict along Israel's border and in Southern Lebanon. Geographically, it is also a frontier between rich Mediterranean farmland and the desert. To the west are the Israeli fruit growing *kibbutzim* of the Upper Jordan and the fertile croplands of the Beqaa valley. To the east, the desert takes over – cultivation is largely confined to oases near Damascus and bordering higher ground further south. *(Image taken in September)*

Samarkand

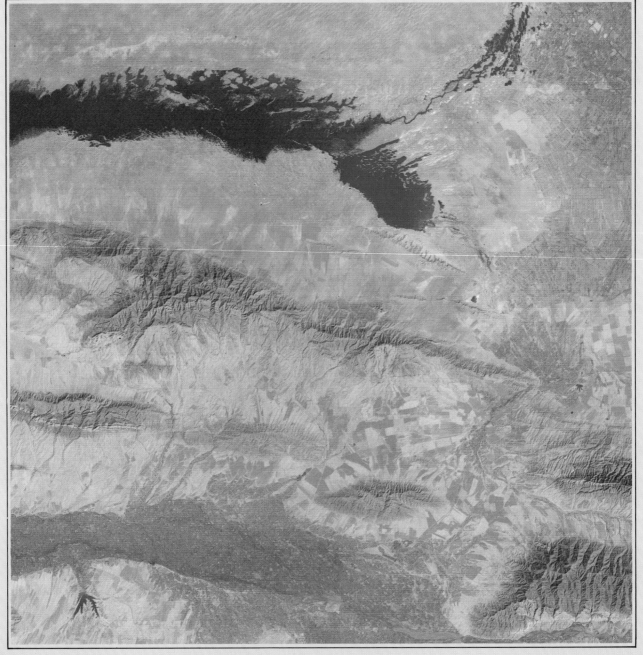

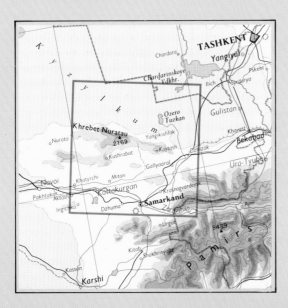

The ancient city of Samarkand, once Tamburlaine's capital, is visible amid the mountains and plains of this typical view of Central Asian Soviet Union. To the north is desert, the Kyzylkum, a name meaning "red sands". Running across the south are mountain chains, western arms of the great Pamirs. From here, rivers water the parched lands as they flow to meet inland lakes – such as Lake Tuzkan, seen here currently in flood – or, like the Zeravshan, to dissipate themselves in the sand. The bleak hues of the desert are thus relieved by lush valleys and oases with fields of cotton, rice, orchards, vineyards and melon plantations. *(Image taken in October)*

The Lower Volga

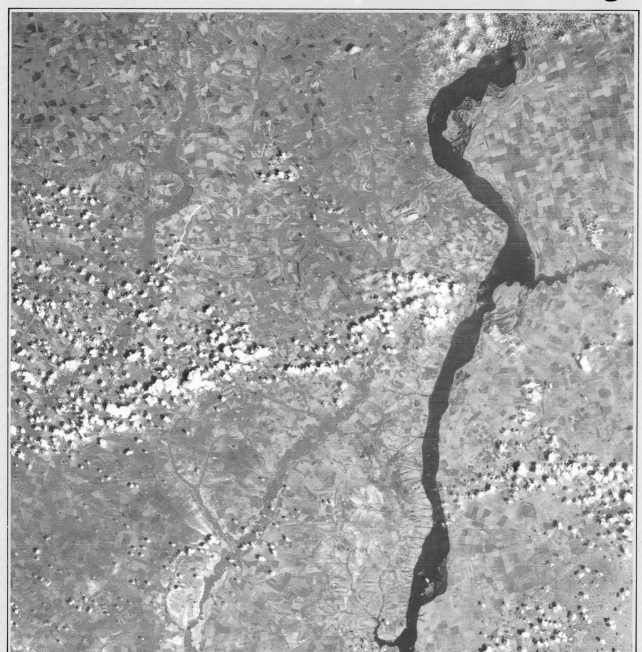

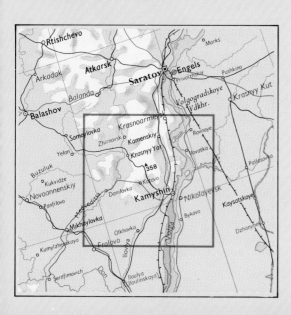

The Volga river, seen here as an elongated lake, is a natural frontier in more than one sense. Geographically, it traces a line where Atlantic climatic influences finally die out and the fertile prairies give way to semi-desert. Historically, it divides the Russian Empire into West and East, a meeting-place for Muscovite and Tatar cultures. In this scene, the contrast is enhanced by the presence of the Volga Heights to the west, where relief and woodland give variety to the mixed farmland. The eastern plains were formerly beneath the salt-waters of a larger Caspian Sea, but are now divided into the huge fields of State collective farms, benefitting from mechanization and irrigation. *(Image taken in July)*

The Himalayas

The Earth's crust is divided into giant "plates", many shifting independently, some actually thrusting into each other. One such area of collision is between India and the rest of Asia. The result has been a crumpling up of rocks on a gigantic scale, known to us as the Himalaya mountains. The range includes many peaks over 8000 m, among them the highest in the world, Mt. Everest, shown here. The image charts the descent from these snow-covered peaks, across the deeply-etched Lesser Himalayas and bamboo-forested Siwalik Hills, to the populous and intensively-farmed Ganges Plain of India, into which flow the gravel-laden streams from the mountains. *(Image taken in December)*

The Rann of Kutch

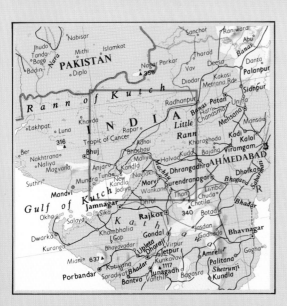

"Islands" of higher land in this view of Northwest India are welded together by vast expanses of mudflats and marshland known as the Rann of Kutch. There are, in fact, two "Ranns": the Little Rann, an extension of the low, muddy land and maze of channels and inlets at the head of the Gulf, which are occasionally inundated when rains are heavy, and the Great Rann, a vast saltmarsh stretching away to merge with the Thar Desert in the North. Cultivation is possible only on upland areas, particularly the ancient volcanic Kathiawar peninsula to the south, while other areas are elsewhere left to pasture land, scrub or forest. *(Image taken in January)*

The Ganges Delta

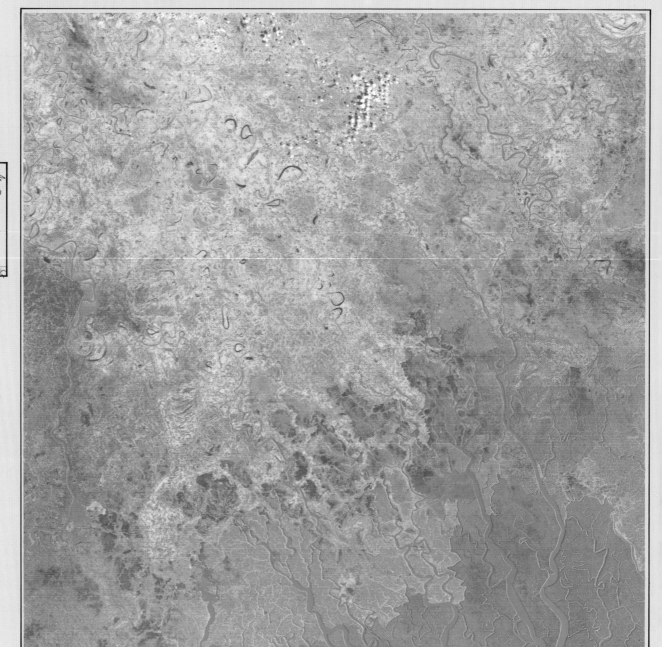

N

At the head of the Bay of Bengal, where the Ganges and hundreds of minor streams have built an immense delta, there is a land of contrasts. The central portion of the image, comprising the lighter "moribund" delta, strewn with oxbow lakes and abandoned channels, and the saline-forested Sundarbans of the "Mouths" is a region of little or no agricultural use. Eastwards into Bangladesh intensive cultivation on the new, fertile alluvial soils is possible, and millions of people live here, despite regular floods and the changing courses of rivers. The region to the west is also heavily populated, but this time packed into the teeming suburbs of Calcutta lining the banks of the River Hooghly. *(Image taken in November)*

The distinctive rectangular plan of its Inner City walls identifies the position of Peking, close to the mountains which border the great Eastern plain in the north. A level and fertile region, this plain suffers from a dry climate, though cereals are intensively cultivated in the hot summer growing season. Water for the capital comes from the Kuant'ing Reservoir, dammed from the waters of the Yunting River. This image is a winter scene, a time when cold winds sweep southeastwards from the Mongolian steppes over the mountains of Northern China and the Great Wall that meanders across them – but which is invisible here. *(Image taken in November)*

Canton and Hong Kong

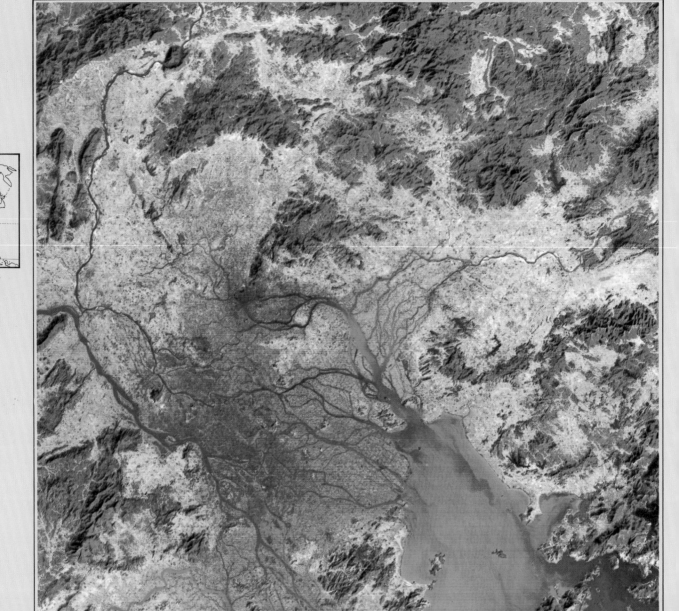

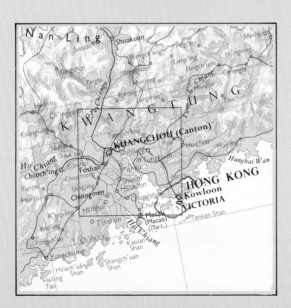

The Kwangtung plains are a meeting-place for rivers flowing down from the Nan Ling mountains. From here, they subdivide and reach the sea as a tangle of tiny channels. Just how much silt and gravel are brought down with them can be seen from the pale blue wash of the estuary – water usually comes out as dark blue or black in Landsat images. Floods have, in the past, spread these deposits across the lowlands, making them very fertile farming land, and still subject the area to frequent inundation. The image shows up waterlogged land on the north banks of the Hsi Chiang. Canton itself is situated where a spur of higher ground meets a navigable outlet to the sea. *(Image taken in December)*

Tokyo

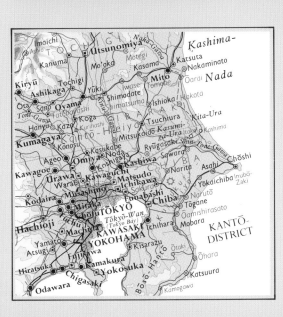

Tokyo's suburbs, strung out along the express-ways, reach like tentacles across the southern plains of the Kantō-Heiya. These fertile lowlands, a carpet of sediments washed down by mountain rivers, were once unproductive swamps, but are now drained to provide valuable farming land. The Tone river has built a classically symmetrical delta into the Pacific Ocean, and in so doing, has linked to the mainland the former island in the south now known as Boso-Hanto, and created Tokyo Bay. Besides serving as an excellent natural harbour, especially for the port of Yokohama, the Bay has paradoxically provided Tokyo with extra land, artificially reclaimed around its shores. *(Image taken in November)*

Canterbury Plains, New Zealand

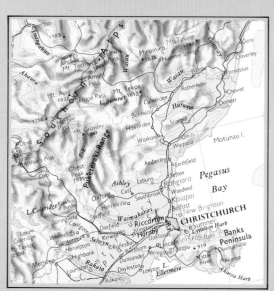

Swollen rivers rushing from the snow-capped Southern Alps carve entrenched courses in the wide alluvial plain which they themselves have built up over the ages. Sheep graze the fertile Canterbury plains and the tussock grass of the Downs rising behind them, although wheat and fodder crops, fruit and vegetables also thrive where the geometrically-laid irrigation channels offset the effects of a rather dry climate. Southeast of Christchurch are the twin volcanoes of the Banks peninsula, into which the sea has created two inlets by drowning deep glacial valleys. *(Image taken in August)*

Perth

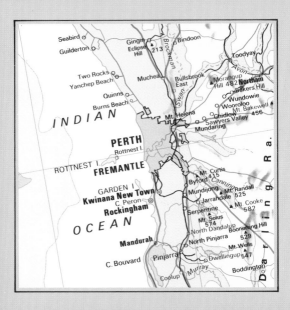

50km short of the coast, the vast ancient granite plateau of Western Australia drops several hundred metres to the coastal plain in a long fault scarp known as the Darling Range. Breaking through the forested uplands are the short perennial rivers with reservoirs built on them to supplement the more seasonal waters of the undulating plateau further inland, enabling extensive wheat and sheep farming to prosper in a favourable "Mediterranean" climate. On the coastal strip, fruit-orchards and vineyards can be seen clustered around Perth and the Swan valley, while the large fields to the north are dairy cattle pastures. *(Image taken in December)*

Sydney

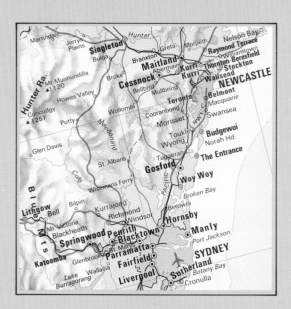

Sydney grew up on the banks of its excellent natural harbour, Port Jackson, which, like other inlets nearby, is the product of deep valley flooding by the sea. Its position on a rare section of the Eastern coastal strip which widens into a substantial plain – the Hunter valley further north is another – has permitted spacious expansion into the valuable farming lands of the Hawkesbury-Nepean lowlands. Rising further inland are the heavily-wrinkled Blue Mountains, an ancient plateau uplifted in geologically recent times into which many streams have cut steep, narrow gorges. *(Image taken in December)*

The Anti Atlas Mountains

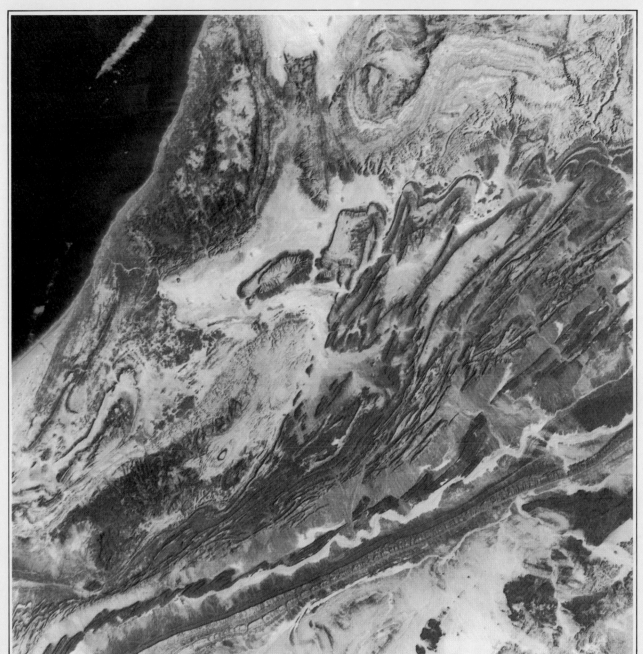

This view of the very edge of the Sahara Desert, where man's influence is confined to mere specks of farmland, captures a beautifully-patterned landscape showing off its geology. In the Anti-Atlas mountains, ancient domes encircled by younger rocks form the southwest guard to the Atlas chain stretching 2000km across Morocco and Algeria. To the south, the succession of ridges in the Djebel Bani are evidence of folded strata becoming more and more compressed as they approach the Oued Draa, the faulted edge of the great Saharan shield itself. *(Image taken in March)*

The Suez Canal

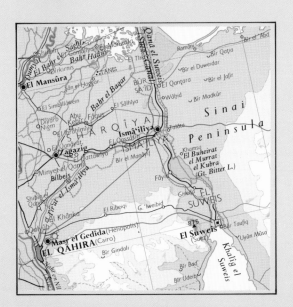

This picture illustrates supremely the impact of fresh water in arid lands. The empty desert, sandy and monotonous in Sinai, rugged and scored by dry valleys west of Suez, suddenly gives way to a region of intensive cultivation, home to millions of people. Responsible for this dramatic contrast is, quite simply, irrigation. Below Cairo, the Nile subdivides into two main branches, a number of smaller streams and hundreds of canals, enabling crops to be grown and the population to be fed. The "arm" of cultivation reaching out to Ismailiya demonstrates this effect in isolation. The larger cities can be picked out from the bright red of the delta – most conspicuously in the case of Cairo, capital of Egypt. *(Image taken in May)*

The Mangueni Plateau, Niger

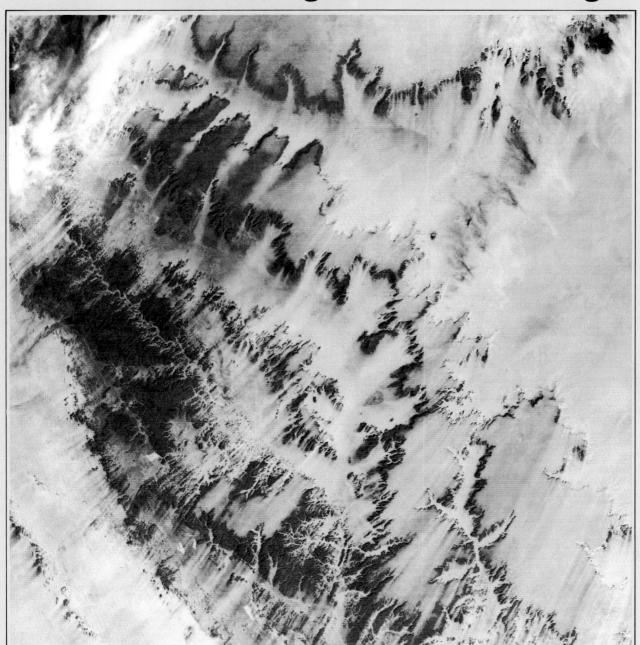

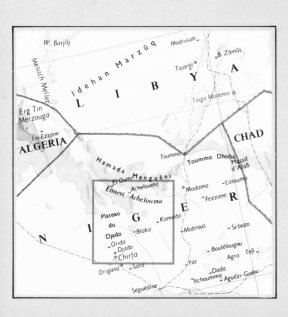

The Mangueni Plateau is a comparatively low "saddle" linking the Ahaggar and Tibesti highland ranges that arc around the southern fringes of the Marzuq sand sea. It is a bleak *hamada* landscape, where rocky platforms rise sharply from level ground, with canyons carved between them – eroded at some time by running water. The region is entirely desert now, but in the past, at the time of the Ice Age in Europe, the Sahara was watered by great rivers, whose valleys· became "fossilized" when aridity set in. The streaks in the sand, running across the image at right-angles to the lie of these valleys, give evidence of the strength and direction of northeasterly winds that blow across the desert almost every day. *(Image taken in October)*

Mount Kilimanjaro

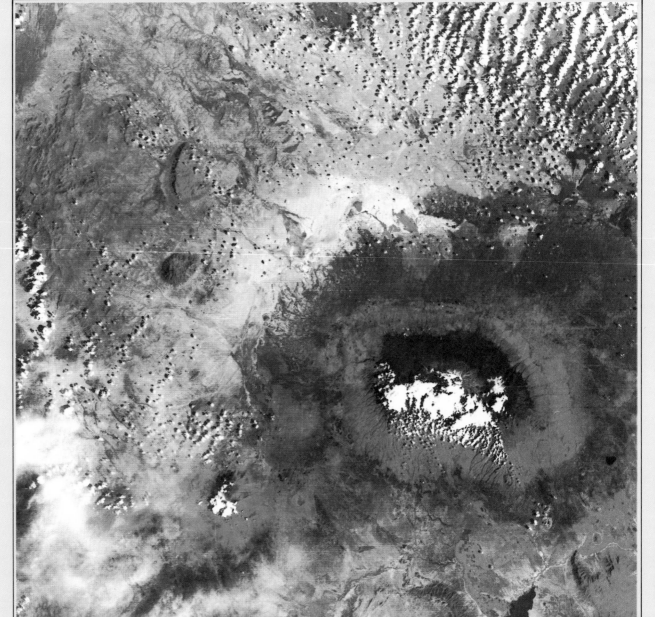

It is easy to see that the smears of red on the image correspond to points of high ground on the map. In East Africa, the type of vegetation is ruled by local climate, itself closely controlled by altitude. Here, the general principle – the higher you are, the wetter and cooler it is – takes on a visually stunning aspect, nowhere more so than on Kilimanjaro, the region's – and Africa's – highest mountain. Rising from the savannah and dry lakes of the Nyiri desert, this dormant volcano is encircled by a series of vegetation belts – cultivation, forest, heather – each matching the climate at their respective levels. Around the craters at the summit, just 350 km from the Equator, there are glaciers all year round. *(Image taken in January)*

The Zaire River

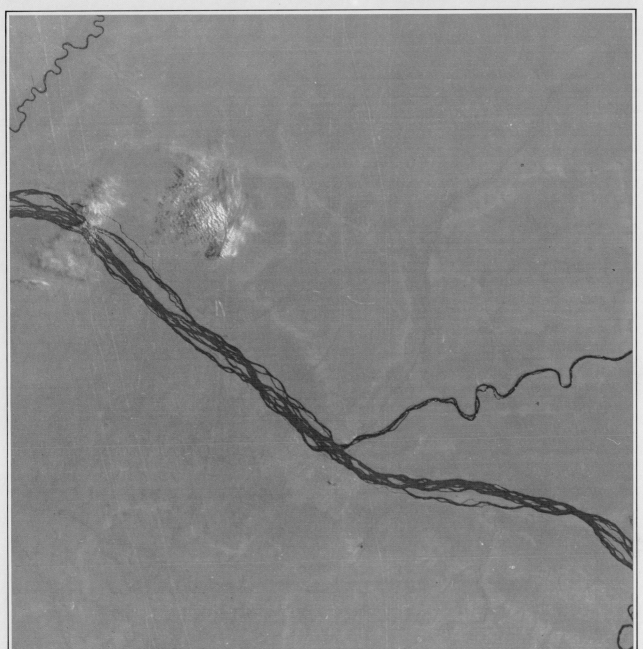

The tropical rain forest of Zaïre is, as the image emphatically demonstrates, monotonous, uniformly flat country, unbroken by sharp changes in relief. The constantly warm, humid and very wet climate sustains the unvaried dense forest cover comprising, however, a wide mix of tree species such as mahogany, ebony, teak and cedar. Across this landscape flows the Zaïre and its many tributaries, some only faintly visible here. With a gradient of only about 10cm per kilometre, the great river flows slowly in a wide, shallow channel, much braided to enable it to carry a heavy sediment load brought down from the mountains to the south and east. *(Image taken in March)*

Prince Edward Island

N

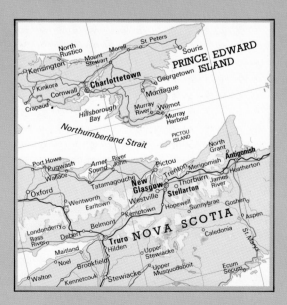

The Appalachian Range extends from the Southern United States as far north as the Gulf of St. Lawrence. Here, it divides, the central trough now flooded by the sea, with slightly higher land becoming islands such as Prince Edward Island. From January to March, its waters are sealed by pack-ice, but summers are long enough and soils sufficiently fertile for dairying and potato growing to take place. The southern arm of uplands forms most of Nova Scotia, a faulted, ice-scoured but even-surfaced plateau almost totally covered by evergreen forest. *(Image taken in January)*

Montreal

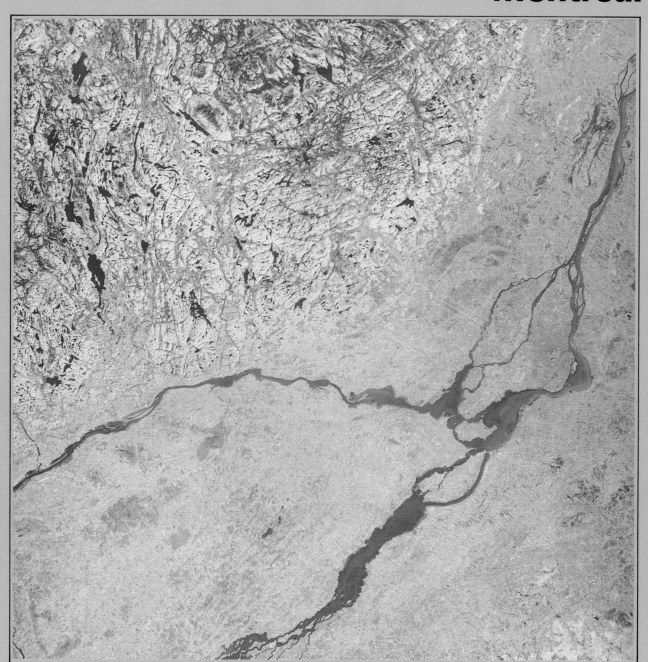

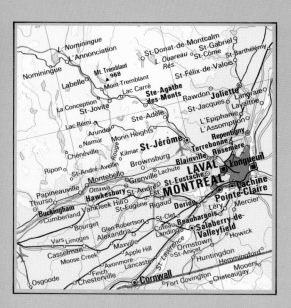

The much-scarred Laurentian Plateau occupies the north part of this scene, a vast shield of ancient rock formations, levelled by millions of years of erosion, finally shaped by Ice-Age glaciation, which scoured the surface and left behind thousands of tiny lakes. The deciduous trees can be distinguished here by their yellow "fall" colours from the red evergreens on higher ground. By contrast is the St. Lawrence plain, where sands and clays deposited by a former inland sea give rise to a productive region with a rich variety of crops. The city of Montreal grew from its command of the river-ways of Canada and routes south to the United States. *(Image taken in October)*

The Canadian Rockies

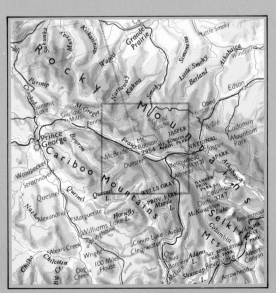

The Rocky Mountain Trench cuts across the Canadian Cordilleras pictured in this image – and for hundreds of miles northwest to the Yukon and southeast to Montana in the United States. This remarkably straight depression, occupied here by the Fraser river sharply divides the Rocky mountains from the Cariboo and Selkirk ranges, though, as the image illustrates, the landscape to either side is one of snow-capped summits and deep valleys with evidence of faulting and glacial erosion. From its linearity and geology, the Trench itself is obviously the product of faulting, but its exact origin is less clear. Could it have been carved by ice along a line of weakness, or was it simply dropped between long parallel cracks in the Earth's surface? *(Image taken in September)*

Cape Cod

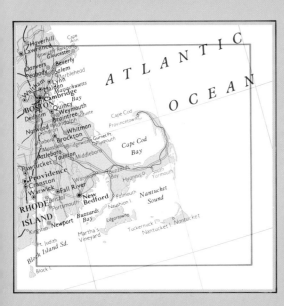

The remarkable outline of Cape Cod, poking out to sea like a scorpion's tail, is the work of two of nature's most potent agents: ice and sea. Ice-transported debris, or *moraine,* piled up where the Ice Age glaciers reached their southernmost extent, were left above the rising sea level as the islands and peninsulas around Nantucket Sound. By steadily removing sand alongshore, ocean waves have subsequently produced bars and spits, Cape Cod being the most spectacular of a number of examples shown in this image. The landscape provides for the nearby East Coast cities in several ways – holiday resorts, fishing harbours, and fertile land for garden produce. *(Image taken in July)*

Washington — Baltimore

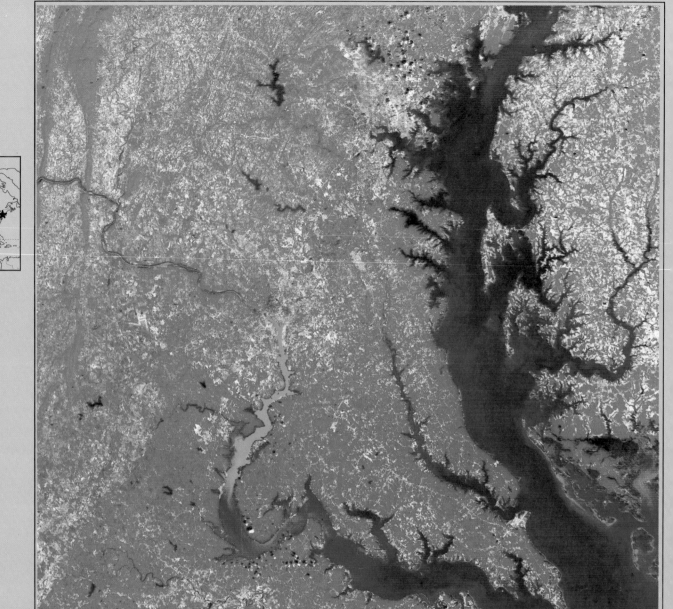

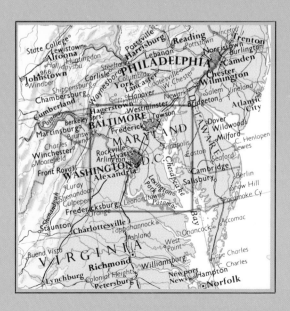

The cities of Washington and Baltimore may be thought of as forming the southern end of a virtually continuous urban agglomeration or *megalopolis* extending as far as Boston in the north. The use of intermediate land not yet swallowed up for urban use is typified here: orchards, vegetable gardens and dairying for city markets lie among stands of dense woodland. Washington's transitional position between the industrial North and agricultural South was considered an important factor when it was chosen as capital of the United States. Some of the city's landmarks are visible here: the Capitol and White House grounds, and the Mall which runs between them. *(Image taken in October)*

The Tennessee Valley

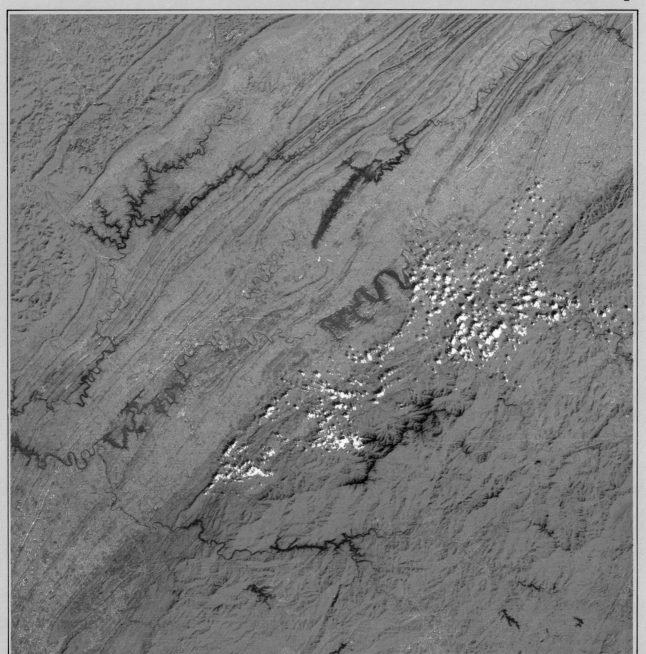

Three regions can be identified running northeast-southwest across this view of the Appalachian Mountains in Tennessee. The heavily-forested Great Smoky Mountains are the highest in Eastern United States, with Clingman's Dome rising above 2000m. Several rivers, many dammed to provide hydroelectric power, meander across the Appalachian Valley, a fertile agricultural corridor characterized by a succession of parallel limestone ridges cloaked in woodland. Separated from the valley by a faulted edge is the isolated Cumberland Plateau, a region of forested upland and limestone gorges, inhabited by poor mining communities. *(Image taken in October)*

Toronto — Buffalo

N

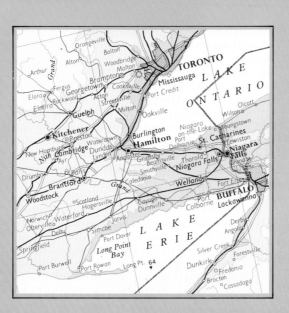

A quarter of a million years ago, a huge ice-cap covered much of North America. When it melted, water collected in huge depressions, becoming what we know as the Great Lakes. The pattern of rivers is now much changed since before the glaciation: the Niagara, between Lakes Erie and Ontario, makes a spectacular waterfall as it flows over the edge of a great limestone escarpment, the product of erosion by an ancient drainage system. Another legacy of the Ice Age has been a coating of fertile clays and sands spread over this region. In consequence, Canada's "Golden Horseshoe", bordering Lake Ontario from Toronto to the U.S. frontier, is rich crop and fruit-growing country, lately experiencing industrial and urban growth. *(Image taken in September)*

St. Louis, Missouri

St. Louis, standing at the meeting-place of major rivers and highways, could also be said to lie at the geographical crossroads of the United States. The Mississippi river is generally regarded as the border between the industrialized East and the open country of the West. Below St. Louis, the Mississippi valley opens out into the Gulf Plains of the Deep South. Most of the scene belongs, however, to the continent's agricultural heartland, the lowland prairies that stretch away to the north, beyond the Great Lakes into Canada. Here in Illinois, the corn, wheat and soyabean fields – now harvested – are laced with the deeper red of woods and meadows that follow the river courses and so display their intricate patterns on the landscape. *(Image taken in October)*

The Mississippi River

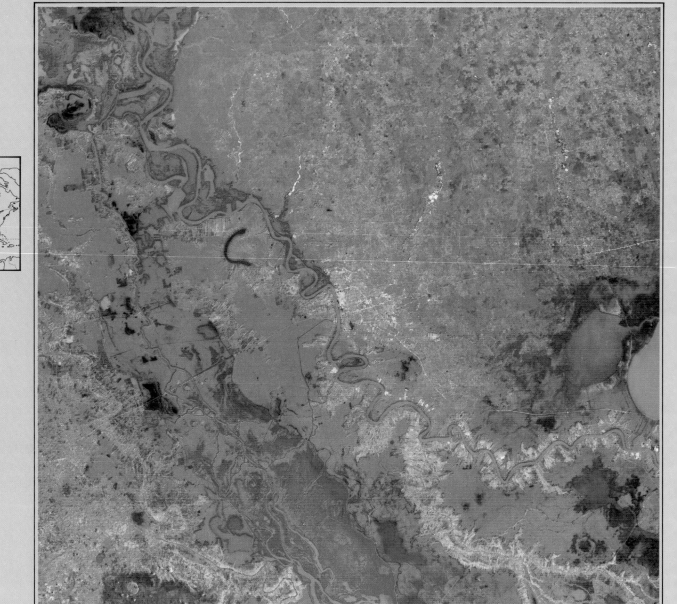

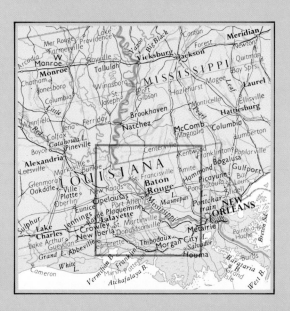

Meandering across the flat plains of Louisiana, the Mississippi is nearing the end of its journey to the Gulf of Mexico. Seen at high water during a spring flood, it is pale blue on the image with the great volume of sediment carried at that time. Especially to the west of the river, there is dense, swampy forest amid a jumble of smaller streams and lakes that represent older courses taken by the Mississippi to the sea. The farmland occupies the areas of higher land that envelop the river course in the southern part of the image. The distinctive field pattern, long strips of land perpendicular to the river-bank, was inherited from early French settlers. *(Image taken in May)*

Southern Florida

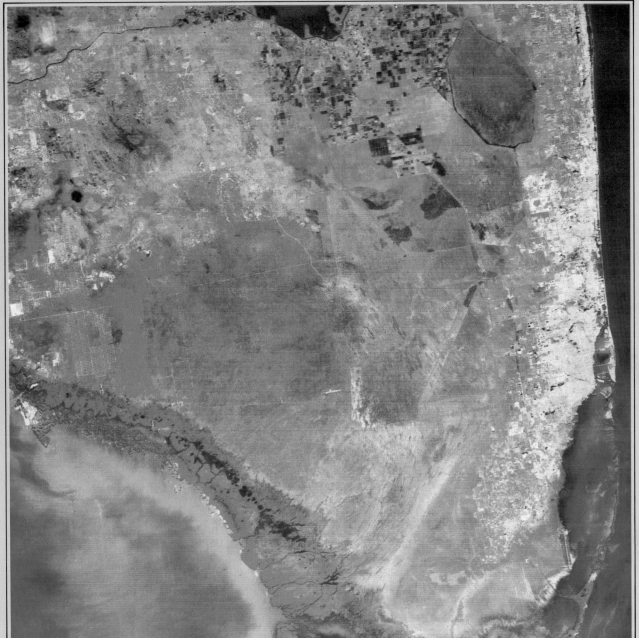

Southern Florida is a unique region of the United States. Almost entirely flat lowland, enjoying a tropical climate and covered by swamp and sand, it is also both a tourist boom area and rich farming country. Trapped behind the sand bars thrown up by Atlantic waves, the vast Everglades tall saw-grass swamp dominates this image – a grey mass, flecked with red marking the "tree-islands" of slightly higher rises. Man's shaping of the land-scape is betrayed by straight lines and rectangular patterns: the streets and blocks of the Eastern Gold Coast cities from Palm Beach to Miami, the orchards, gardens and sugar-cane fields around the southern shores of Lake Okeechobee. *(Image taken in March)*

The Grand Canyon

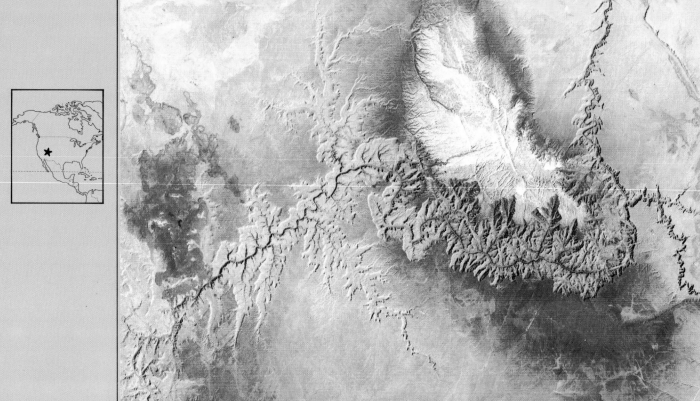

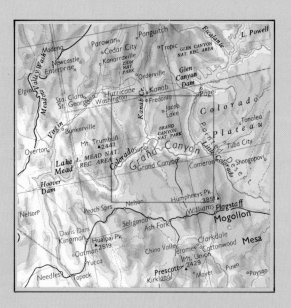

The Colorado River, maintaining its course by cutting deeply into the plateau that has been uplifted in geologically recent times, has sculpted one of the world's most spectacular natural features. 20 km by 1.6 km at its widest and deepest, the Grand Canyon has been hewn from rocks laid down successively in more or less horizontal, undisturbed layers. The resulting profile, weathered back through time, offers both an unparalleled insight into geological history – and breathtaking scenery that draws thousands of tourists every year to this largely semi-desert region. *(Image taken in May)*

The Canyon Lands of Utah

By the same process which created the Grand Canyon further downstream, the upper Colorado and its tributaries have found renewed energy from the uplifting of the Colorado Plateau to carve deep, if less impressive canyons for themselves. The region's climate is not too harsh – there is enough rainfall to support grasslands and dense pine forest on higher ground, masked by snow in this winter scene. It is the ruggedness and inaccessibility that has made farming and settlement difficult. Instead, other potential qualities have been exploited: plentiful supplies of fresh water are dammed in reservoirs, and the natural beauty of the canyon-lands draws tourists to the area every year. *(Image taken in February)*

Salton Sea, California

The Colorado River flows well to the East of this image, but its waters are responsible for bringing life to this eternally dry, sun-baked region. A trough between the arid Chocolate Mountains and the scrub-vegetated ranges to the west, its lowest depths reach 80m below sea-level. Here, water was channelled from the Colorado in the early 20th century and collected to form the Salton Sea. A modern irrigation system built from the All-American and Coachella canals that draw water from the Imperial Reservoir, sustains the level of the Sea, and the rich variety of fruit and grain crops filling the Imperial Valley to the south in a bright mosaic. Note how the character of land-use changes across the border at Mexicali. *(Image taken in July)*

San Francisco

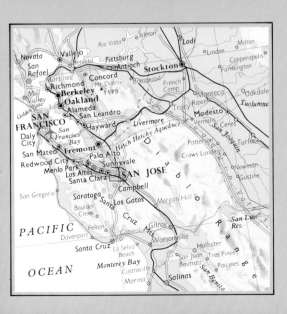

Faults, great fissures in the Earth's crust, run the length of America's west coast. Troughs, like San Francisco Bay and San Joaquin Valley, have been created where land has slumped between them. The former was drowned when the sea breached the Golden Gate, creating a magnificent deepwater harbour, around which San Francisco and the Bay Area cities grew up. The San Joaquin Valley, with its fertile soils and perfect Mediterranean climate, produces fruit, vegetables, wine, cotton and rice for sale in the rest of the world. Marking the edge of the redwood-forested Santa Cruz Mountains is the notorious San Andreas fault, responsible for earthquakes which destroyed San Francisco in 1906 and always threaten to do so again. *(Image taken in October)*

Mexico City

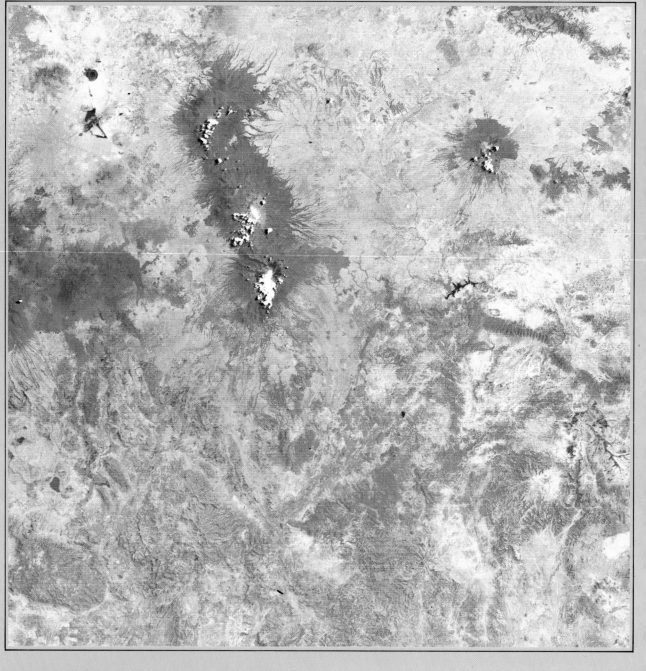

High above the Mesa Central soar the grand volcanoes, Popocatepetl, Iztacihuatl and La Malinche, snow-clad summits atop thickly-forested slopes. To this land of temperate climate and fertile volcanic soils, came the Indians, who farmed the land and founded cities where they settled. The great Aztec civilization originated at Tenochtitlán, by the shores of Lake Texcoco in the Valley of Mexico. Today, as in ancient times, maize and beans are the main crops of the plateau, and the old Aztec city, now called Mexico City, is one of the largest urban areas in the world, with a population of over 10 millions. *(Image taken in May)*

The Bolivian Altiplano

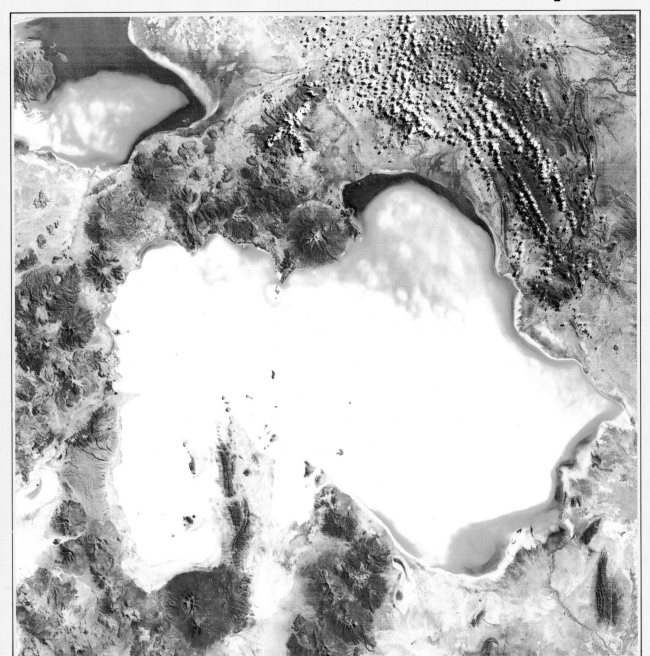

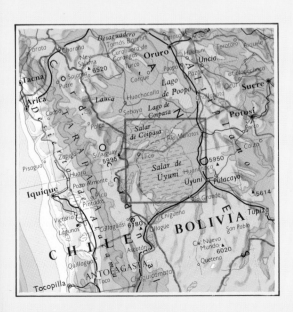

The Altiplano forms a comparatively level plateau at approximately 3000m between the higher peaks of the Andes Mountains, just north of where the Cordillera Occidental meets the Cordillera Oriental. In the centre of this image is the Salar de Uyuni, a vast salt flat fed by mountain streams. The western side of the salt flat is dominated by volcanic cones and lava flows. The environment is arid, remote and inhospitable, though not totally un-populated – and some cultivation is possible in river valleys protected from the harsh climate. (*Image taken in March*)

Southern Peru

From the Equator to Northern Chile, rivers flowing down the western slopes of the Andes cross a strip of lowland barely 50 km wide, before reaching the Pacific Ocean. This land is desert, one of the driest regions in the World. As the image shows, it is completely unvegetated, apart from the slithers of farmland hugging the streams. Inland, the Western Cordillera of the Andes rises abruptly to over 5000 m, its slopes appearing bright red from a cover of scrub and tussocky grass. Stretching away to the northeast is the rolling upland plateau known as the Altiplano. Between expanses of lighter-grey barren rock above the snowline, lie alpine grass and scrublands, grazed by herds of alpaca and llama. *(Image taken in April)*

Bahía Blanca, Argentina

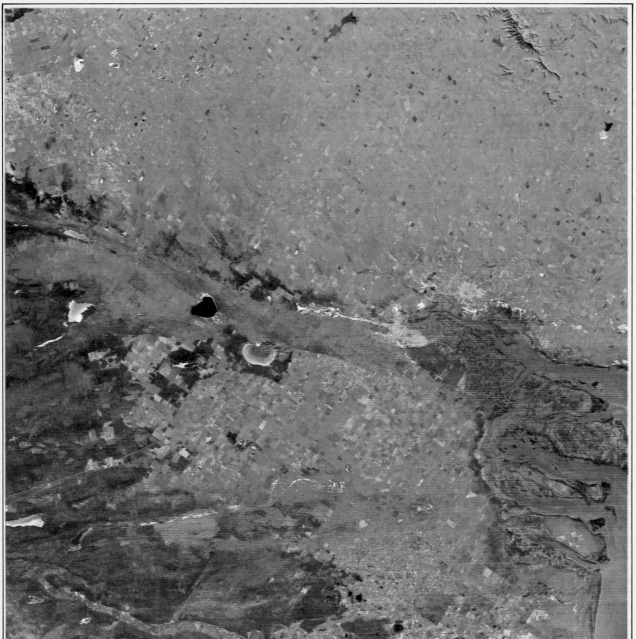

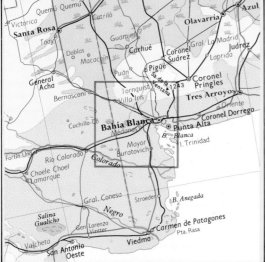

Travelling southwards, Bahía Blanca is the last important town of the fertile, highly-populated Pampas before the dry scrublands of remote Southern Argentina begin. This image captures the transition from one region to another. The north and east, undulating lowlands dotted by small lakes and depressions, is a patchwork of pinks, reds and browns – a reflection of the wide range of crops seen in the fields during their early growing season. To the south and west, there is not enough rainfall to allow cultivation. Watered only by rivers which cross it, the land is left to scrub or occasional livestock ranching where meagre grassland is found. *(Image taken in October)*

Lake Nihuil, Argentina

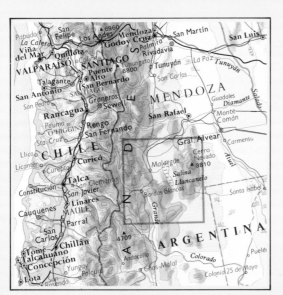

The region surrounding Llancanelo salt lake is a remote part of Argentina. Bleak lowland, broken by volcanic cones and set in the semi-arid rain-shadow of the Andes that tower to the west, it is for the most part uncultivated and uninhabited, largely left to scrub. Vines and fruit-trees grow in the few areas where water is available, close to the banks of the Rio Grande in the south of the image, and where water seeps from beneath a fan of sands and gravels laid down by the Rio Atuel emerging from the mountains. *(Image taken in March)*

GENERAL REFERENCE

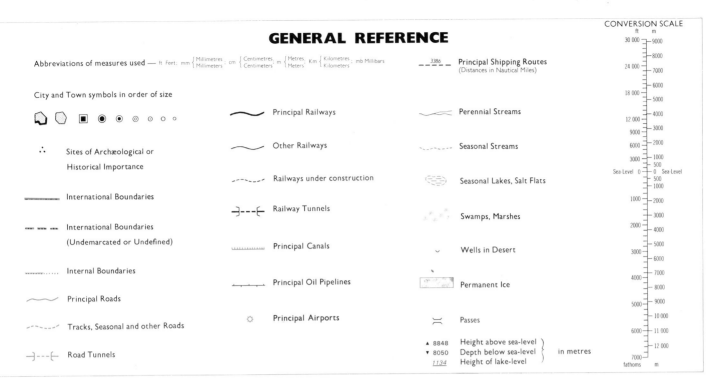

Abbreviations of measures used — ft Feet; mm { Millimetres / Millimeters } cm { Centimetres / Centimeters } m { Metres / Meters } Km { Kilometres / Kilometers } mb Millibars

City and Town symbols in order of size

⬡ ⬡ ▣ ● ● ◉ ○ ○ ○

Sites of Archæological or Historical Importance

International Boundaries

International Boundaries (Undemarcated or Undefined)

Internal Boundaries

Principal Roads

Tracks, Seasonal and other Roads

Road Tunnels

Principal Railways

Other Railways

Railways under construction

Railway Tunnels

Principal Canals

Principal Oil Pipelines

Principal Airports

Principal Shipping Routes (Distances in Nautical Miles)

Perennial Streams

Seasonal Streams

Seasonal Lakes, Salt Flats

Swamps, Marshes

Wells in Desert

Permanent Ice

Passes

▲ 8848 Height above sea-level
▼ 8050 Depth below sea-level ⎬ in metres
1134 Height of lake-level

CONVERSION SCALE

ft   m
30 000   9000
         8000
24 000   7000
         6000
18 000   5000
         4000
12 000   3000
9000
6000   2000
3000   1000
         500
Sea-Level 0   0 Sea-Level
         500
         1000
1000   2000
         3000
2000   4000
         5000
3000   6000
         7000
4000   8000
         9000
5000   10 000
         11 000
6000   12 000
7000
fathoms m

THE WORLD
Physical
1:150 000 000

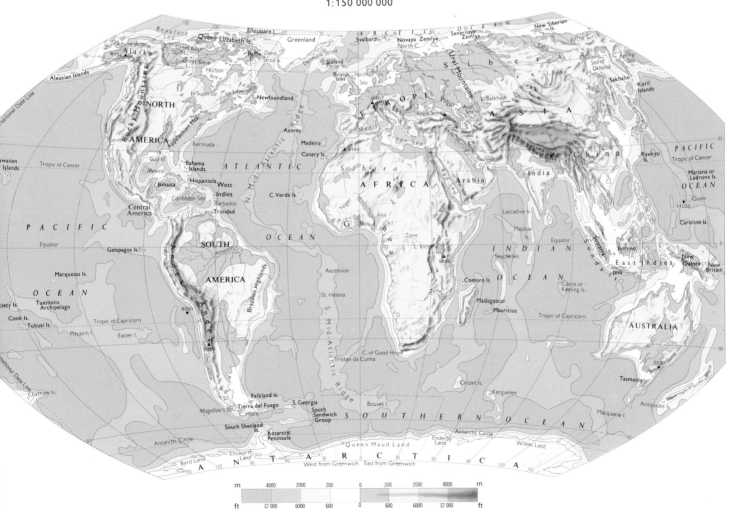

m   4000   2000   200   0   200   2000   4000   m
ft   12 000   6000   600   0   600   6000   12 000   ft

Projection: Hammer Equal Area

Projection: *Hammer Equal Area*

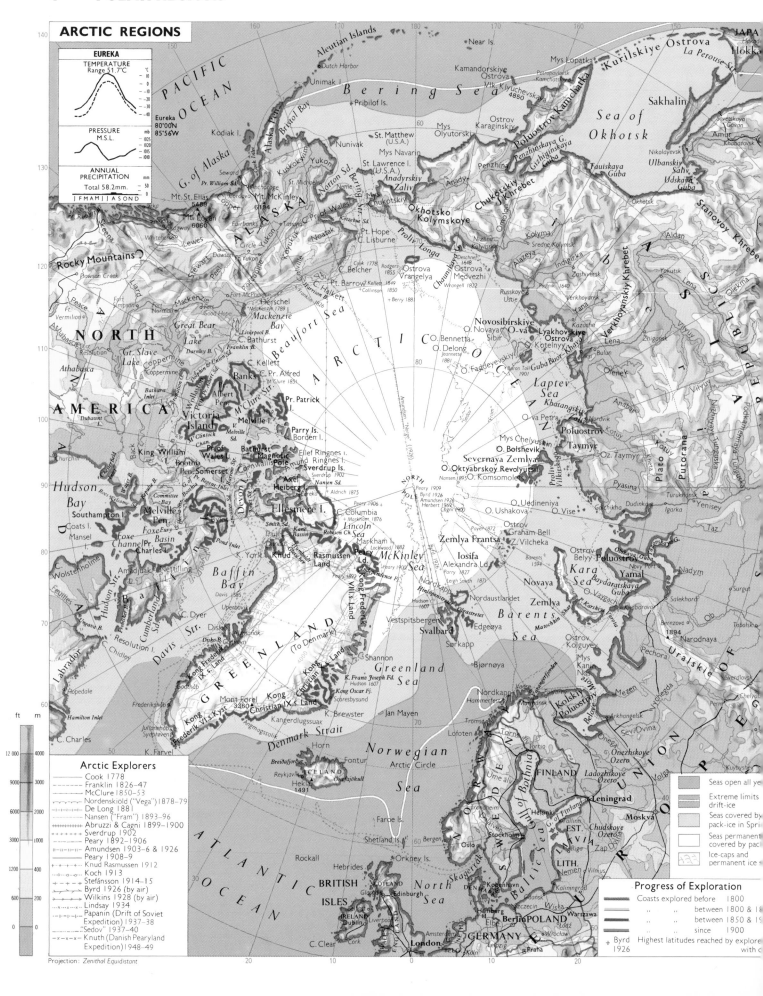

ARCTIC REGIONS

EUREKA
TEMPERATURE
Range 51.7°C

°C
10
0
-10
-20
-30
-40

Eureka
80°00'N
85°56'W

PRESSURE
M.S.L.

mb
1025
1020
1015
1010

ANNUAL
PRECIPITATION
Total 58.2mm.

50

0

J F M A M J J A S O N D

Arctic Explorers

Cook 1778
Franklin 1826–47
McClure 1850–53
Nordenskiöld ("Vega")1878–79
De Long 1881
Nansen ("Fram") 1893–96
Abruzzi & Cagni 1899–1900
Sverdrup 1902
Peary 1892–1906
Amundsen 1903–6 & 1926
Peary 1908–9
Knud Rasmussen 1912
Koch 1913
Stefánsson 1914–15
Byrd 1926 (by air)
Wilkins 1928 (by air)
Lindsay 1934
Papanin (Drift of Soviet
    Expedition) 1937–38
"Sedov" 1937–40
Knuth (Danish Pearyland
    Expedition)1948–49

Projection: Zenithal Equidistant

Seas open all ye
Extreme limits
drift-ice
Seas covered by
pack-ice in Spri
Seas permanent
covered by pac
Ice-caps and
permanent ice

Progress of Exploration

Coasts explored before   1800
    "   "   between 1800 & 18
    "   "   between 1850 & 19
    "   "   since   1900
+ Byrd Highest latitudes reached by explore
1926   with c

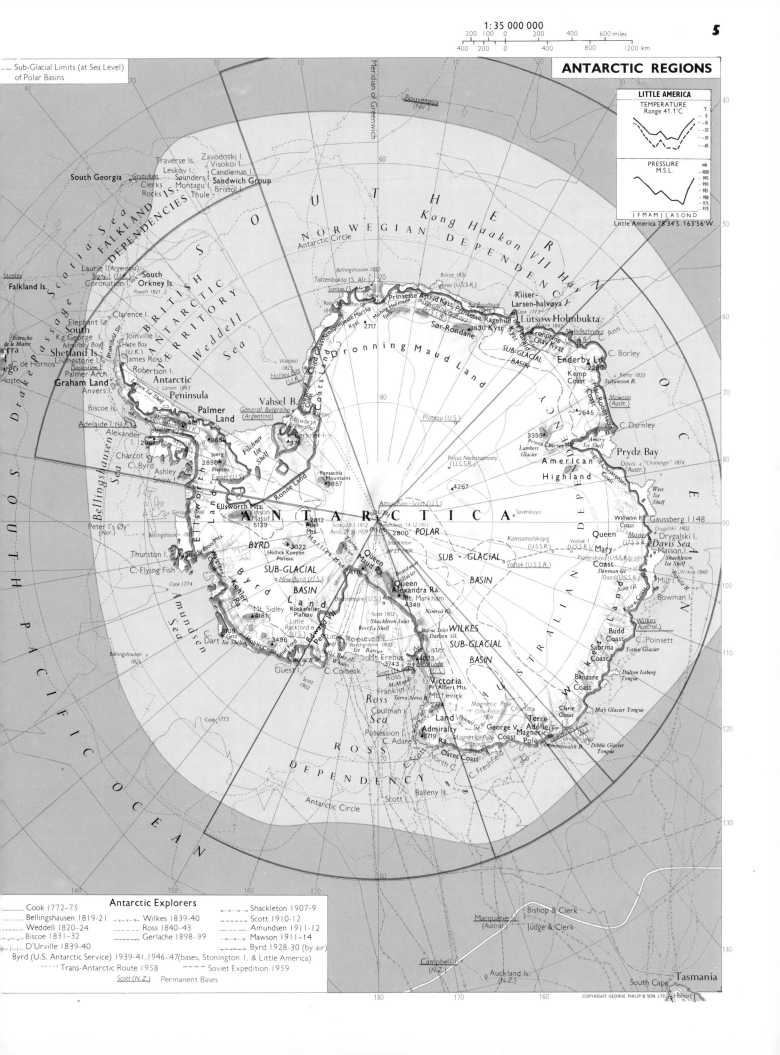

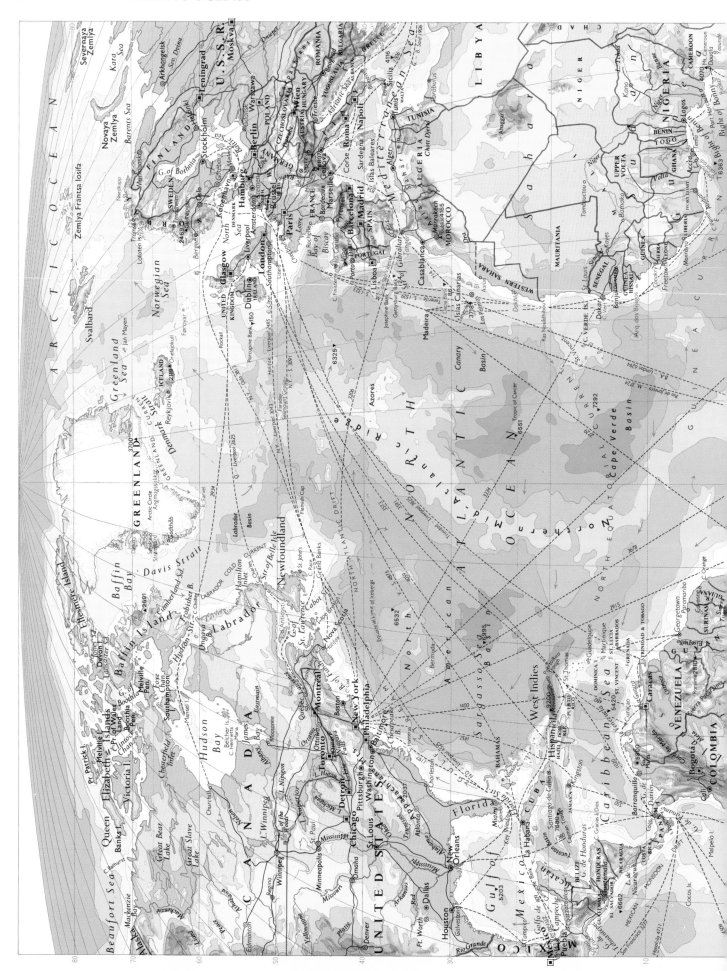

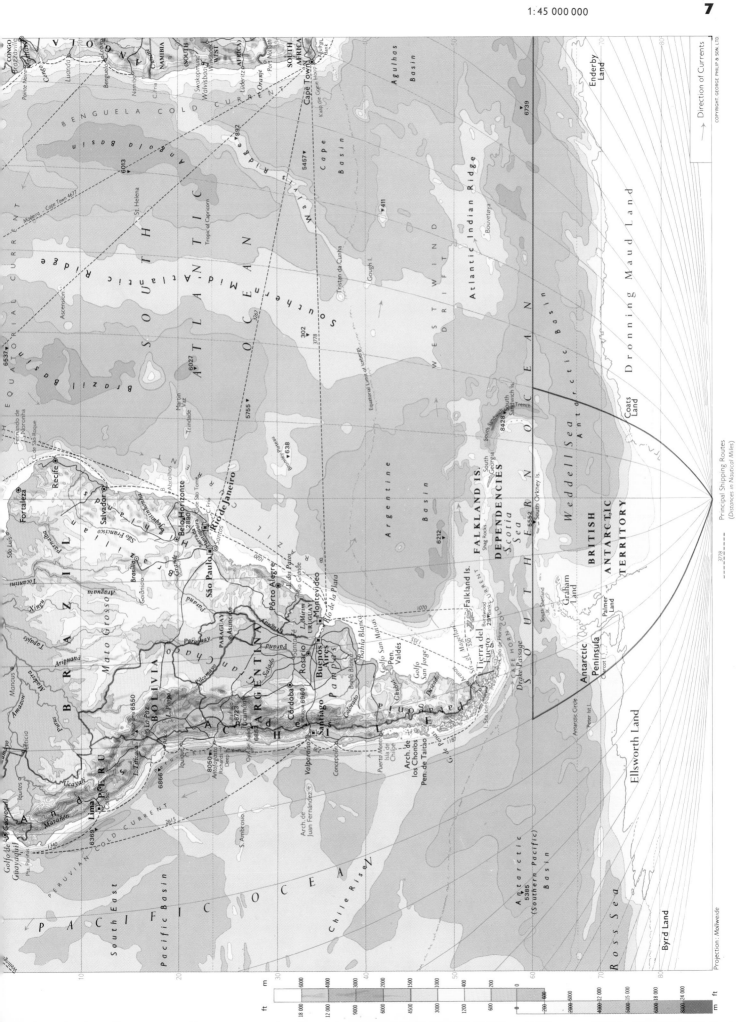

→ Direction of Currents

COPYRIGHT GEORGE PHILIP & SON, LTD.

Principal Shipping Routes
(Distances in Nautical Miles)

3778

Projection: Mollweide

ANGOLA

CONGO
(Brazzaville)

NAMIBIA
(SOUTH
WEST
AFRICA)

SOUTH
AFRICA

Cape Town

BENGUELA COLD CURRENT

Angola Basin

Walvis Ridge

Cape Basin

Agulhas Basin

Atlantic Indian Ridge

SOUTH ATLANTIC OCEAN

Mid-Atlantic Ridge

Brazil Basin

Southern

WEST WIND DRIFT

Dronning Maud Land

Enderby Land

Coats Land

Weddell Sea

BRITISH ANTARCTIC TERRITORY

Antarctic Peninsula

Ellsworth Land

Byrd Land

Ross Sea

SOUTHERN OCEAN

FALKLAND IS. DEPENDENCIES

South Georgia

Scotia Sea

South Sandwich Is.

South Orkney Is.

South Shetland Is.

Graham Land

Palmer Land

BRAZIL

Recife

Fortaleza

São Luis

Salvador

Belo Horizonte

Rio de Janeiro

São Paulo

Pôrto Alegre

Montevideo

URUGUAY

Buenos Aires

Rosario

Córdoba

ARGENTINA

PARAGUAY

Asunción

BOLIVIA

La Paz

PERU

Lima

Callao

Santiago

Valparaíso

Concepción

CHILE

Tierra del Fuego

Drake Passage

CAPE HORN

Falkland Is.

Argentine Basin

PERUVIAN COLD CURRENT

FALKLAND COLD CURRENT

PACIFIC OCEAN

South East Pacific Basin

Chile Rise

Antarctic (Southern Pacific) Basin

PACIFIC OCEAN

Antarctic Circle

Tropic of Capricorn

EQUATORIAL BASIN

EUROPEAN ORGANIZATIONS
1:40 000 000

	E.E.C. Members
	E.F.T.A. Member

All E.F.T.A. and associated states have Free Trade Agreements with the E.E.C.

	States with Association Agreement with E.E.C.
	Associate Member of E.F.T.A.
	States with Trading Agreement with E.E.C.
	Warsaw Pact Countries

The E.E.C. has Trading Agreements with certain countries in the Mediterranean, Pacific and Latin American areas.

Arctic Circle

NORWEGIAN SEA

Iceland
Reykjavik
Hekla 1491
Öræfajökull 2119
3734

Faroe Is.

Rockall
St. Kilda
Hebrides
Shetland Is.
Orkney Is.
Lindesne

British Isles
Ben Nevis 1343
Edinburgh
Belfast
Ireland
Dublin
Irish Sea
Snowdon 1085

NORTH SEA

C. Clear
St. George's Channel
Celtic Sea
Cardiff
Thames
London
Amsterdam
Frisian Is.
Netherlands
Lands End
Scilly Is.
English Channel
Channel Is.
Str. of Dover
Brussel
Ardennes
Eifel
Rhine
Taun

ATLANTIC OCEAN

Brittany
Paris
Seine
Loire
Saône
Massif Central
Mt. Dore 1888
Cévennes
Garonne
Gironde
4861
Bay of Biscay

Mt. Blanc 4807
Alps
Po

C. Finisterre
Cantabrian Mts.
Old Castile
Iberian
Douro
Maladetta 3404
Pyrenees
Ebro
G. of Lion
Rivi
Ligurian Sea

Flores
Terceira
Pico
Azores
São Miguel

Madrid
New Castile
Peninsula
Lisboa
C. da Roca
Tagus
Guadiana
Sierra Morena
C. St. Vincent

Corsica
Sardinia
Str. of Bon

6293

Madeira

Guadalquivir
Andalusia
Mulhacen 3478
Sa. Nevada
Str. of Gibraltar
C. Trafalgar
Gibraltar

Balearic Is.

MEDITE

Casablanca
Er Rif

Palma
Tenerife
Canary Is.
Gran Canaria
Fuerteventura

Toubkal 4165
Great
Atlas
Maritime Atlas
Alger
Tunis
Plateau of the Shotts
Saharan Atlas
Gu
Gab

Tropic of Cancer

Sahara

ft	m
12 000	4000
	30
6000	2000
3000	1000
1200	400
600	200
0	0
	25
200	600
2000	6000
4000	12 000

m ft

Projection: Bonne.

20   15   10   5   West from Greenwich   0   East from Greenwich   5   10

1:17 500 000

| 100 | | | 100 | 200 | 300 | 400 | 500 miles |

| 100 | 0 | 200 | 400 | 600 | 800 km |

Nordkapp Nordkinn

Lofoten

L. Inari

Lappland

Kebnekaise
2123

Scandinavia

Torne älv

Umeälv

Gulf of Bothnia

Indalsälven

Osto

Stockholm

Vänern

Mälaren

Vättern

København

Gotland

BALTIC SEA

Åland Is.

Helsinki

Finland

Gulf of Finland

Leningrad

Neva

L. Chudskoye

Dvina

Neman

Vistula

Warszawa

Oder

Berlino

North
European
Plain

Pripet

Pripet
Marshes

Kiyevo

Dnieper

Mts.
Prahaç

Sudetes

Moravia
Hts.

Bohemian Forest

Danube

Tatra
2655

Carpathians

Wien

Bakony Forest

Budapest

Plain of
Hungary

Drava

Sava

Dinaric Alps

Adriatic Sea

Gran Sasso
2914

Apennines

Dalmatia

Beograd

Morava

Drava

Tisza

Mureş

Transylvanian Alps

Bucureşti

Wallachia

Danube

Balkan

Sofiya

Rhodope

Balkan
Peninsula

Pindus

Dinaric Alps

Pesti

Calabria

Str. of
Otranto

Ionian
Sea

Ionian Is.

Morea

Athinai

3263

C. Spartivento

Sicily

Malta

Messina

5121

C. Matapan

Crete

MEDITERRANEAN SEA

Gulf of Sidra

White
Sea

Mezen

N. Dvina

Onega

L. Onega

Svir

Lake
Ladoga

Valdai
Hills

Volga

Central Russian Uplands

Moskva

Oka

Gorkiy

Rybinsk
Res.

Volga

Ukraine

Dnieper

Bug

Dniester

Prut

Odessa

Dnieper

Crimea

Sea of
Azov

Mouths
of the
Danube

Black Sea

2211

Strait of Kerch

Kuban

Istanbul

Bosporus

Sea of
Marmara

Dardanelles

Aegean Sea

Rhodes

Cyprus

Ankara

Kizil

L. Tuz

Anatolia

Erciyas
3770

Taurus Mts.

Halab

Bayrut

Tel Aviv-
Yafo

Dead
Sea

Levant

Nile Delta

Syrian

Desert

Kanin
Peninsula

Tundra

Pechora

Kola
Peninsula

Narodnaya
1894

Telpos Iz.
1617

Ural Mountains

West

Siberian

Plain

Ob

Irtysh

Tobol

Kama

Volga

Obshchi Syrt

Ural

Volga Heights

Tsimlyansk
Res.

Volga

Don

Caucasus

5633

Elbrus

Terek

Transcaucasia

Kura

Baku

Araks

Pontine Mts.

Ararat
5165

L. Van

Kura

Kurdistan

L. Urmia

Elburz Mts.

Tehran

Mesopotamia

Euphrates

Tigris

Baghdad

Persian
Gulf

Kirgiz

Steppe

Ust Urt
Plateau

Karagiye Depression
-132

Kara
Bogaz

Caspian Sea

-28

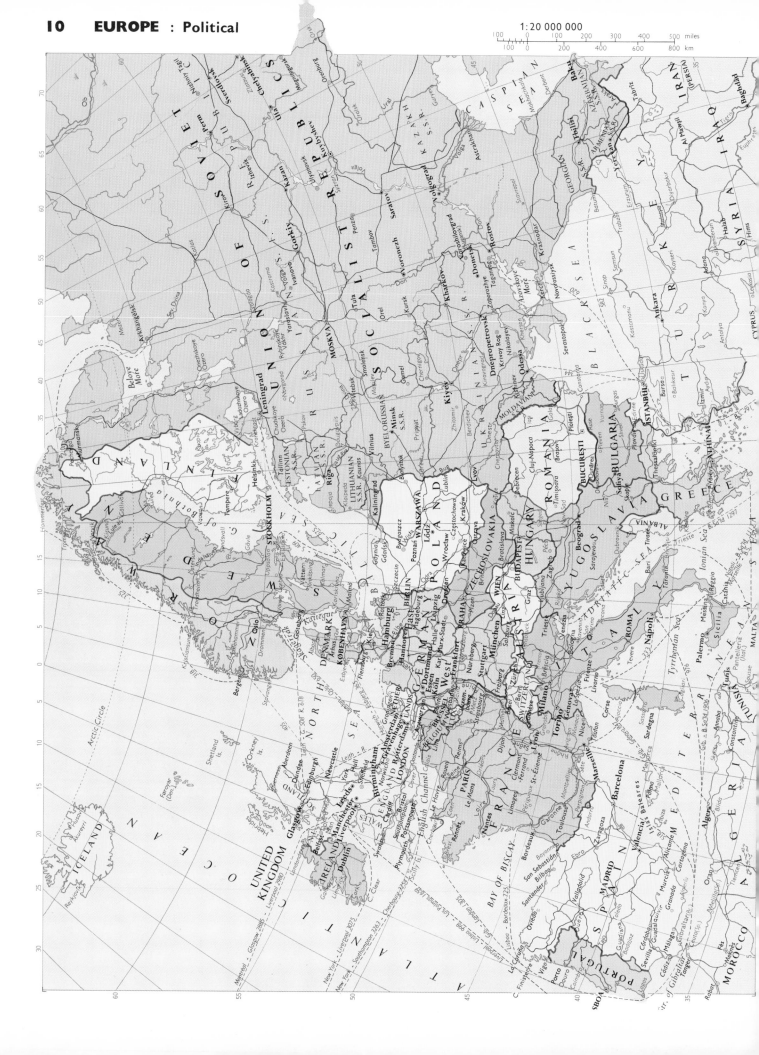

1:4 000 000

The DISTRICTS of Northern Ireland have been numbered and can be identified by reference to this table.

1	Londonderry	14	Craigavon
2	Limavady	15	Armagh
3	Coleraine	16	Newry & Mourne
4	Ballymoney	17	Banbridge
5	Moyle	18	Down
6	Larne	19	Lisburn
7	Ballymena	20	Antrim
8	Magherafelt	21	Newtownabbey
9	Cookstown	22	Carrickfergus
10	Strabane	23	North Down
11	Omagh	24	Ards
12	Fermanagh	25	Castlereagh
13	Dungannon	26	Belfast

1 Merseyside
2 Greater Manchester
3 West Yorkshire
4 South Yorkshire
5 West Glamorgan
6 Mid Glamorgan
7 South Glamorgan

Orkney Is.

Shetland Is.

Projection: Conical with two standard parallels

West from Greenwich   East from Greenwich
COPYRIGHT GEORGE PHILIP & SON. LTD.

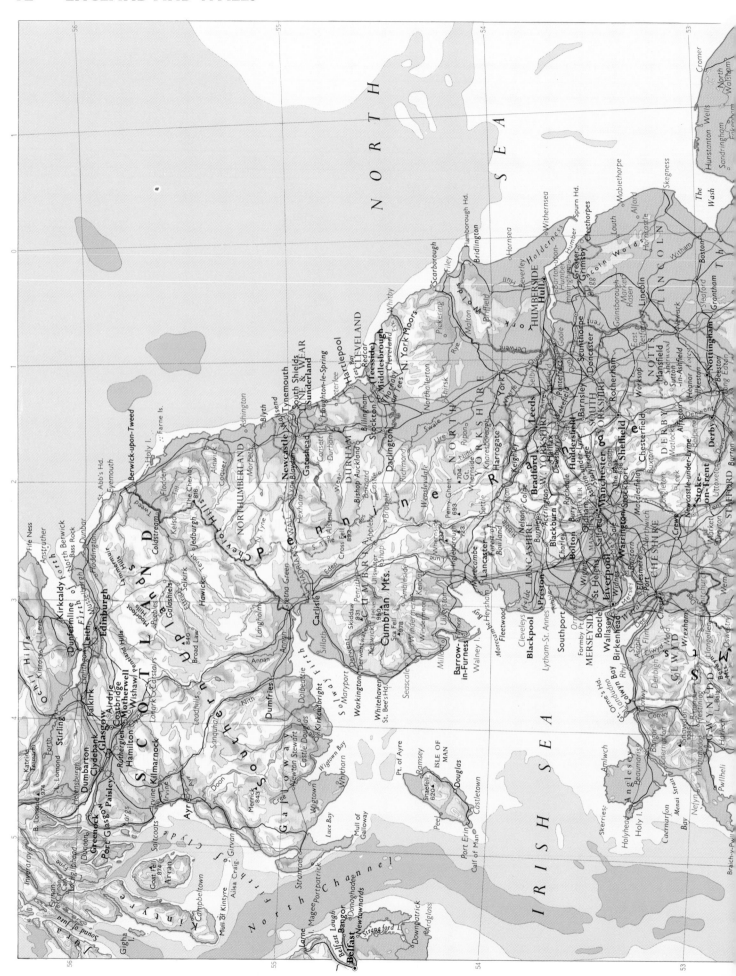

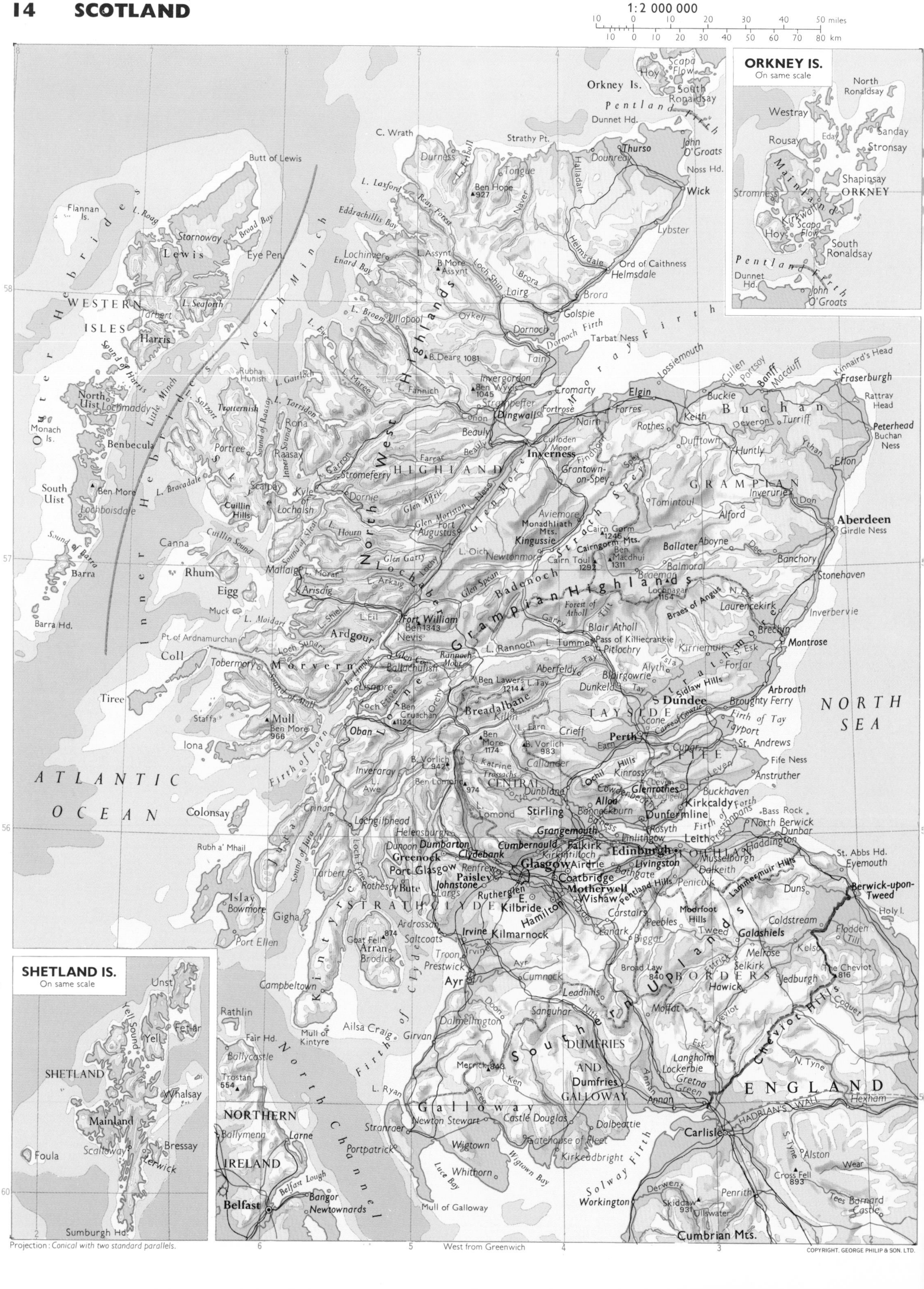

1:2 000 000

10   0   10   20   30   40   50 miles
10   0   10   20   30   40   50   60   70   80 km

ORKNEY IS.
On same scale

Orkney Is.
North Ronaldsay
Westray
Rousay   Eday   Sanday   Stronsay
Stromness   Mainland   ORKNEY
Shapinsay
Hoy   Kirkwall   Scapa Flow
South Ronaldsay
Dunnet Hd.   John O'Groats
Pentland Firth

SHETLAND IS.
On same scale

Unst
Yell   Fetlar
Yell Sound   Whalsay
SHETLAND
Mainland
Bressay
Foula   Scalloway   Lerwick
Sumburgh Hd.

Butt of Lewis
C. Wrath   Strathy Pt.
Durness   Tongue   Halladale   Thurso   John O'Groats
Reay Forest   Ben Hope 927   Naver   Dounreay   Wick
Flannan Is.   L. Roag   Stornoway   Broad Bay
Lewis   Eye Pen.   L. Laxford   Eddrachillis Bay   Helmsdale   Ord of Caithness   Lybster
WESTERN ISLES   Tarbert   L. Seaforth   Lochinver   Enard Bay   Assynt   B. More Assynt   Brora   Helmsdale
Harris   Sound of Harris   L. Ewe   Ullapool   Oykell   Brora   Golspie
North Uist   Lochmaddy   L. Maree   Fannich   B. Dearg 1081   Lairg   Dornoch   Dornoch Firth   Tarbat Ness
Monach Is.   Benbecula   Trotternish   Gairloch   HIGHLAND   Invergordon   Ben Wyvis 1045   Cromarty   Elgin   Buckie   Boddam   Cullen   Portsoy   Banff   Macduff   Fraserburgh
South Uist   Ben More   Raasay   Torridon   Strathpeffer   Dingwall   Nairn   Forres   Rothes   Keith   BUCHAN   Peterhead
Lochboisdale   Portree   Applecross   Stromeferry   Dornie   Beauly   INVERNESS   Culloden Moor   Findhorn   Dufftown   Huntly   Turriff   Deveron   Buchan Ness
Barra   Skye   Kyle of Lochalsh   Glen Affric   Glen Moriston   Fort Augustus   Culloden   GRAMPIAN   Inverurie   Elton
Barra Hd.   Cuillin Hills   L. Hourn   Glen Garry   L. Oich   Aviemore   Monadhliath Mts.   Cairn Gorm 1245   Tomintoul   Alford   Don   ABERDEEN
Canna   Cuillin Sound   Mallaig   L. Morar   Arisaig   Kingussie   Newtonmore   Cairn Toul   Ben Macdhui 1311   Ballater   Aboyne   Girdle Ness
Rhum   Eigg   L. Arkaig   Fort William   Ben Nevis 1343   Badenoch   Cairngorm Mts.   Lochnagar 1154   Balmoral   Braemar   Banchory   Stonehaven
Muck   Pt. of Ardnamurchan   Ardgour   GRAMPIAN HIGHLANDS   Blair Atholl   Forest of Atholl   Braes of Angus   Laurencekirk   Inverbervie
Coll   Tobermory   MORVERN   Ballachulish   Rannoch Moor   L. Rannoch   L. Tummel   Pitlochry   Pass of Killiecrankie   Kirriemuir   Brechin   Montrose
Tiree   Mull   Ben More 966   Glen Coe   Ben Lawers 1214   Aberfeldy   Tay   Blairgowrie   Alyth   Forfar   Arbroath   NORTH SEA
Staffa   Iona   Ben Cruachan 1124   BREADALBANE   Killin   Dunkeld   Sidlaw Hills   Broughty Ferry
Oban   Firth of Lorn   Ben More 1174   B. Vorlich 983   Crieff   Dundee   Firth of Tay   Tayport   St. Andrews   Fife Ness
ATLANTIC OCEAN   Inveraray   Awe   B. Vorlich 942   Ben Lomond 974   Callander   Earn   Perth   Cupar   FIFE   Anstruther
Colonsay   Lochgilphead   L. Katrine   CENTRAL   Dunblane   Kinross   Leven   Buckhaven   Bass Rock
Rubh a' Mhail   Crinan   Helensburgh   L. Lomond   Stirling   Alloa   Glenrothes   Kirkcaldy   North Berwick
Islay   Bowmore   Dunoon   Dumbarton   Cumbernauld   Falkirk   Grangemouth   Dunfermline   Rosyth   Leith   Dunbar
Port Ellen   Gigha   Greenock   Clydebank   Kirkintilloch   Bathgate   Linlithgow   Firth of Forth   Haddington   St. Abbs Hd.   Eyemouth
Jura   Tarbert   Port Glasgow   Renfrew   GLASGOW   Airdrie   Coatbridge   Livingston   EDINBURGH   LOTHIAN   Musselburgh   Dalkeith   Berwick-upon-Tweed
Sound of Jura   Rothesay   Bute   Paisley   Johnstone   Motherwell   Wishaw   Pentland Hills   Penicuik   Lammermuir Hills   Duns   Holy I.
Largs   Rutherglen   E. Kilbride   Hamilton   Carstairs   Peebles   Moorfoot Hills   Coldstream
Ardrossan   Goat Fell 874   Saltcoats   Irvine   Kilmarnock   Lanark   Biggar   Tweed   Galashiels   Kelso   Flodden
Campbeltown   Arran   Brodick   Troon   Prestwick   Cumnock   BORDERS   Melrose   Selkirk   Jedburgh   The Cheviot 816
Ailsa Craig   Ayr   Doon   Leadhills   Broad Law 840   Hawick   CHEVIOT HILLS
Mull of Kintyre   Girvan   Sanquhar   Moffat   Ettrick   Coquet
Rathlin   Fair Hd.   Dalmellington   Nith   SOUTHERN UPLANDS   Langholm   N. Tyne
Ballycastle   Merrick 843   DUMFRIES AND GALLOWAY   Lockerbie   Gretna Green   Hexham
Trostan 554   GALLOWAY   Ken   Dumfries   Annan   ENGLAND
NORTHERN   Newton Stewart   Castle Douglas   Dalbeattie   Esk   Carlisle   S. Tyne   Alston
Stranraer   Wigtown   Gatehouse of Fleet   Kirkcudbright   Solway Firth   HADRIAN'S WALL   Wear
Portpatrick   L. Ryan   Luce Bay   Wigtown Bay   Cross Fell 893
IRELAND   Whithorn   Workington   Derwent   Skiddaw 931   Penrith   Tees   Barnard Castle
Belfast   Belfast Lough   Bangor   Newtownards   Mull of Galloway   North Channel   Cumbrian Mts.   Ullswater

Projection: Conical with two standard parallels.

West from Greenwich

1 : 2 000 000

10   0   10   20   30   40   50 miles
10   0   10   20   30   40   50   60   70   80 km

Kintyre
Arran
Campbeltown
Mull of Kintyre
Ailsa Craig
NORTH CHANNEL
Fair Hd.
Rathlin I.
Giant's Causeway
Portrush
Malin Hd.
Carndonagh
Inishowen Pen.
Moville
Buncrana
Coleraine
Ballycastle
2
Ballymoney
554 Mt. Trostan
Stranraer
Portpatrick

Tory I.
Horn Hd.
Sheep Haven
Bloody Foreland
Gweedore
Errigal 752
Derryveagh Mts.
Letterkenny
DONEGAL
Aran I.
Londonderry
Limavady
Ballymena
Larne
Antrim
I. Magee
Carrickfergus
Bann
55

Gweebarra B.
Loughros More B.
Glenties
Bluestack 676
Finn
Lifford
Strabane
Sperrin Mts.
Sawel 683
Magherafelt
Belfast L.
Belfast
Bangor
Donaghadee
Newtownards
3   4
6
Rossan Pt.
Rathlin O Birne I.
Killybegs
Donegal
Ballyshannon
Omagh
ULSTER
NORTHERN IRELAND
Cookstown
Dungannon
L. Neagh
Lisburn
Ards Pen.
5
7

Donegal Bay
Bundoran
Erne
L. Erne
Irvinestown
Enniskillen
1
Blackwater
Portadown
Lurgan (Craigavon)
Armagh
Banbridge
Dromore
Slieve Donard 852
Dundrum
Newcastle
54

Broad Haven
Erris Hd.
Belmullet
Mullet Peninsula
Blacksod Bay
Sligo B.
Sligo
Ox Mts.
SLIGO
Collooney
L. Allen
LEITRIM
Arrow
Leitrim
Upper
L. Erne
Clones
Belturbet
Annalee
Cootehill
CAVAN
Cavan
Carrickmacross
Kingscourt
Monaghan
MONAGHAN
Castleblayney
Newry 577 St. Gullion
8
Warrenpoint
Mourne Mts.
Carlingford L.
Greenore
Dundalk
Dundalk Bay

Achill Hd.
Achill I.
Achill
Clare I.
Nephin 806
Conn
Killala
Killala B.
Ballina
Moy
Castlebar
MAYO
Clew Bay
Croagh Patrick 765
Westport
Claremorris
ROSCOMMON
Castlereagh
CONNACHT
Carrick-on-Shannon
Boyle
L. Key
Cavan
Oldcastle
Ceanannas Mor (Kells)
An Uaimh (Navan)
Drogheda
Balbriggan
LOUTH
Louth
Ardee
Blackwater

Inishbofin
Killary Harbour
Mweelrea 819
L. Mask
Ballinrobe
Robe
Roscommon
L. Ree
Longford
LONGFORD
Granard
L. Sheelin
L. Gowna
MEATH
Trim
Boyne
Athboy
Slyne Hd.
Twelve Pins
Clifden
Connemara
L. Corrib
Tuam
Suck
Athlone
WESTMEATH
Mullingar
Lambay I.
Swords

GALWAY
IRELAND
Ballinasloe
Clara
Maynooth
DUBLIN
Ireland's Eye
Howth Head
Aran Is.
Inishmore
Galway
Galway Bay
Clare
Athenry
Loughrea
Edenderry
Dublin (Baile Atha Cliath)
Dublin Bay
Dun Laoghaire
53

Kilkieran B.
Hags Hd.
Ennistymon
Liscannor Bay
Mal Bay
CLARE
Gort
Slieve Aughty
Portumna
L. Derg
Birr
S. Bloom
OFFALY
Tullamore
Daingean
Drochead Nua
Naas
Celbridge
LEINSTER
Portarlington
Mountmellick
Port Laoise
LAOIS
KILDARE
Kildare
Kippure 754
Poulaphouca Res.
Bray
WICKLOW
Wicklow
Wicklow Hd.

Miltown Malbay
Ennis
Kilkee
Loop Hd.
R. Shannon
Rineanna
Ardnacrusha 694
Killaloe
Ballina
Nenagh
Keeper
Roscrea
Templemore
Athy
Barrow
Carlow
CARLOW
Tullow
Muine Bheag
Lugnaquillia 923
Rathdrum
Avoca
Mizen Hd.
Arklow

Kilrush
Foynes
Rathkeale
Newcastle
Listowel
LIMERICK
Limerick
Golden Vale
Tipperary
Cashel
Thurles
TIPPERARY
Thurles
Kilkenny
KILKENNY
Callan
Slievenamon 722
Carrick-on-Suir
Clonmel
Enniscorthy
Mt. Leinster 796
WEXFORD
Goreyl
Cahore Pt.

Kerry Hd.
Brandon Bay
Tralee Bay
Brandon Mt. 953
Sl. Mish
Fenit
Tralee
Maine
MUNSTER
KERRY
Newcastle
Rath Luirc (Charleville)
Kanturk
Mallow
Newmarket
Mitchelstown
Gaitymore 920
Galty Mts.
Caher
Knockmealdown Mts.
Comeragh Mts.
Suir
WATERFORD
Clonmel
New Ross
Waterford
Wexford
Rosslare
Wexford Harbour
Greenore Pt.
Tuscar Rock
Carnsore Pt.
Saltee Is.

Dingle
Dingle Bay
Gt. Blasket I.
Dunmore Hd.
Valentia Harbour
Valentia I.
Skellig Rocks
Cahirciveen
Macgillycuddy's Reeks
Carrauntuohill 1040
Killarney
Lakes of Killarney
Kenmare
Killarney
Blackwater
Boggeragh Mts.
Macroom
Blarney
CORK
Cork
Lee
Youghal
Midleton
Youghal Harbour
Lismore
Dungarvan
Dungarvan Bay
Waterford Harbour
Hook Hd.
St. David's Hd.
52

Ballinskelligs B.
Kenmare River
Glengarriff
Caha Mts.
Bantry
Bandon
Passage West
Cobh
Crosshaven
Kinsale
Cork Harbour
Old Head of Kinsale

Crow Hd.
Bear I.
Bantry Bay
Dunmanus Bay
Mizen Hd.
Skull
Baltimore
Skibbereen
Clonakilty
Clonakilty Bay
Galley Hd.
Clear I.
C. Clear
Fastnet Rock

ATLANTIC OCEAN

IRISH SEA

St. George's Channel

ft	m
3000	1000
1200	400
600	200
300	100
0	0
100	300
200	600
m	ft

Projection : Conical with two standard parallels.

West from Greenwich

COPYRIGHT. GEORGE PHILIP & SON. LTD.

1:2 500 000

10   0   10   20   30   40   50 miles
10   0   10 20 30 40 50 60 70 80 km

NORTH SEA

ENGLAND

NETHERLANDS

BELGIUM

LUXEMBOURG

GERMANY

FRANCE

Major places (selected):

North Walsham, Caister, Great Yarmouth, Lowestoft, Beccles, Bungay, Southwold, Aldeburgh, Orford Ness, Dover, Calais, Gris Nez, Wissant, Boulogne-sur-Mer, Le Touquet-Paris-Plage, Berck, Abbeville, Amiens, Beauvais, Compiègne, Soissons, Reims, Épernay, Châlons-sur-Marne, PARIS, Versailles, St-Denis, Meaux, Melun, St-Dizier, Nancy, Metz, Strasbourg

Den Helder, Texel, Vlieland, Terschelling, Ameland, Schiermonnikoog, Leeuwarden, Harlingen, Franeker, Sneek, Groningen, Winschoten, Assen, Emmen, Hoogeveen, Meppel, Zwolle, Kampen, Lelystad, Enkhuizen, Hoorn, Edam, Alkmaar, Beverwijk, IJmuiden, Haarlem, Heemstede, Zandvoort, AMSTERDAM, Zaandam, Hilversum, Bussum, Amersfoort, Apeldoorn, Deventer, Almelo, Hengelo, Enschede, Osnabrück, Münster, Dortmund, Essen, Duisburg, Oberhausen, Mülheim, Bochum, Hagen, Wuppertal, Solingen, Remscheid, Düsseldorf, Mönchengladbach, Neuss, Krefeld, KÖLN (Cologne), Leverkusen, Bonn, Bad Godesberg, Aachen, Düren, Koblenz, Wiesbaden, Mainz

Leiden, Katwijk-aan-Zee, Wassenaar, Scheveningen, 's-GRAVENHAGE (The Hague), Voorburg, Delft, Hoek van Holland, ROTTERDAM, Schiedam, Vlaardingen, Dordrecht, Gouda, Utrecht, Zeist, Arnhem, Nijmegen, 's-Hertogenbosch, Tilburg, Breda, Roosendaal, Eindhoven, Helmond, Venlo, Roermond, Sittard, Heerlen, Maastricht, Kerkrade

Middelburg, Vlissingen (Flushing), Walcheren, Schouwen, Noord Beveland, Bergen-op-Zoom, Goeree, Zeebrugge, Knokke, Blankenberge, Oostende (Ostend), Nieuwpoort, Veurne, Brugge (Bruges), Gent (Gand), ANTWERPEN, Mechelen, Lier, Turnhout, Sint-Niklaas, Lokeren, Aalst, Dendermonde, BRUSSEL (Bruxelles), Leuven, Tienen, Hasselt, Genk, Tongeren, Liège, Herstal, Seraing, Verviers, Eupen, Malmédy, Namur, Charleroi, La Louvière, Mons, Nivelles, Wavre, Gembloux, Dinant, Marche-en-Famenne, Bastogne, Arlon, LUXEMBOURG, Esch, Diekirch, Echternach, Trier, Saarbrücken, Saarlouis, Völklingen

Roubaix, Tourcoing, Lille, Armentières, Béthune, Lens, Douai, Valenciennes, Cambrai, Arras, Maubeuge, Avesnes, St-Quentin, Laon, Charleville-Mézières, Sedan, Verdun, Thionville, Longwy

Projection: Conical with two standard parallels   East from Greenwich   COPYRIGHT. GEORGE PHILIP & SON. LTD

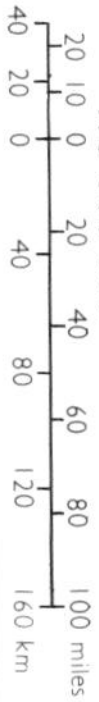

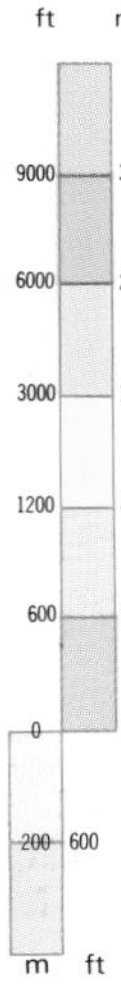

1:5 000 000

20 10 0 20 40 60 80 100 miles
40 20 0 40 80 120 160 km

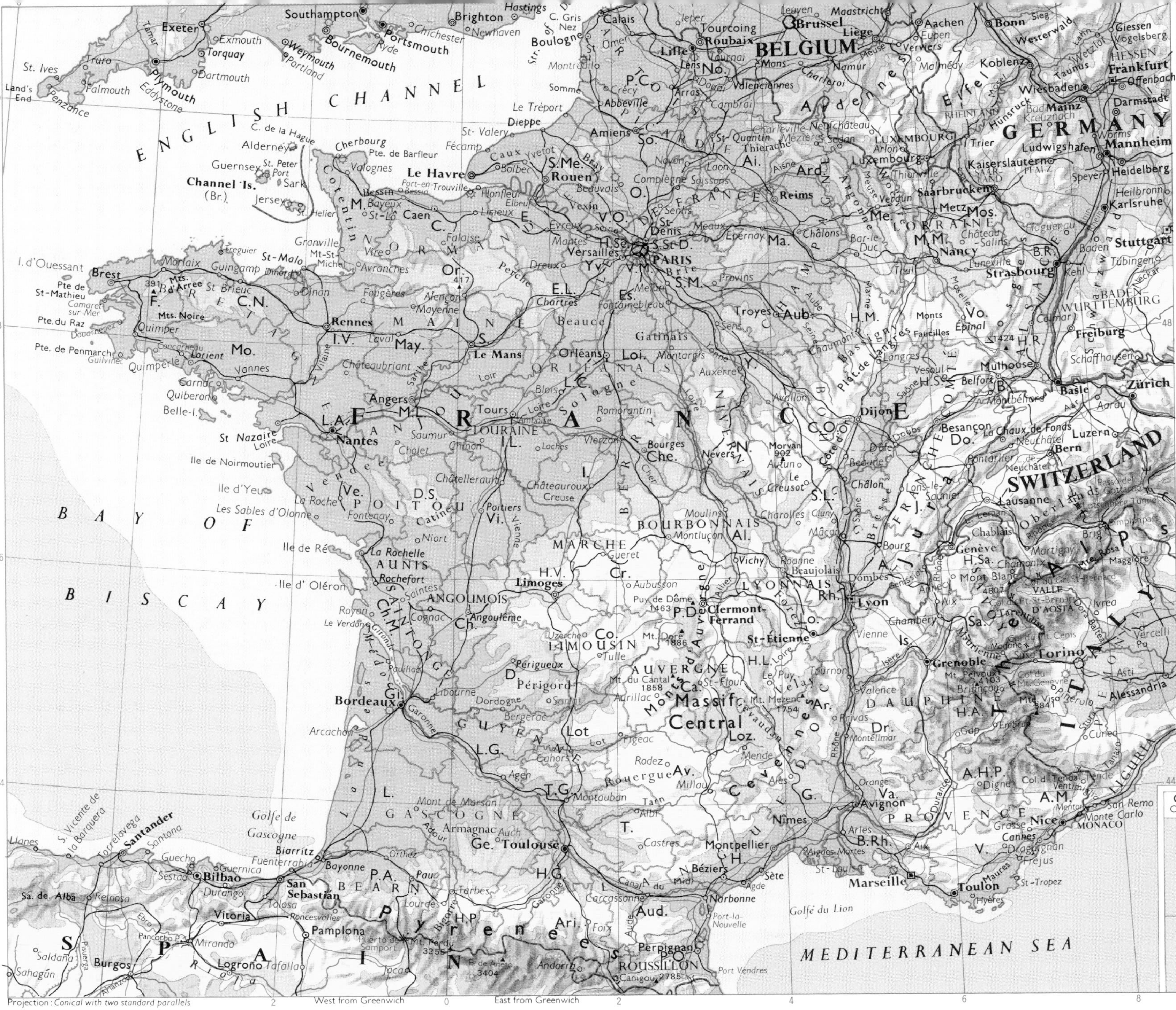

FRENCH DEPARTMENTS

Ai.	01	Ain
Al.	02	Aisne
A.M.		Allier
A.H.P.	04	Alpes-de-Haute-Provence
HA.	05	Hautes-Alpes
A.M.	06	Alpes-Maritimes
Ar.	07	Ardèche
Ar.	08	Ardennes
Ar.	09	Ariège
Aub.	10	Aube
Aud.	11	Aude
Av.	12	Aveyron
B.Rh.	13	Bouches-du-Rhône
C.	14	Calvados
Ch.M.	15	Charente-Maritime
Ch.	16	Charente
Cher	18	Cher
C.	19	Corrèze
a) Haute-Corse	20	b) Corse du Sud
C.O.	21	Côte-d'Or
C.N.	22	Côtes-du-Nord
Cr.	23	Creuse
Do.	24	Dordogne
Do.	25	Doubs
Dr.	26	Drôme
E.L.	27	Eure
E.L.	28	Eure-et-Loir
F.	29	Finistère
Ge.	30	Gard
H.G.	31	Haute-Garonne
Ge.	32	Gers
Gi.	33	Gironde
H.	34	Hérault
I.V.	35	Ille-et-Vilaine
In.	36	Indre
I.V.	37	Indre-et-Loire
Is.	38	Isère
Jura	39	Jura
L.	40	Landes
L.C.	41	Loir-et-Cher
Loi.	42	Loire
H.L.	43	Haute-Loire
L.A.	44	Loire-Atlantique
Loi.	45	Loiret
L.	46	Lot
L.G.	47	Lot-et-Garonne
Loz.	48	Lozère
M.L.	49	Maine-et-Loire
Ma.	50	Manche
Ma.	51	Marne
H.Ma.	52	Haute-Marne
Ma.	53	Mayenne
M.M.	54	Meurthe-et-Moselle
Me.	55	Meuse
Mo.	56	Morbihan
Mo.	57	Moselle
N.	58	Nièvre
N.	59	Nord
O.	60	Oise
Or.	61	Orne
P.C.	62	Pas-de-Calais
P.D.	63	Puy-de-Dôme
P.A.	64	Pyrénées-Atlantiques
H.P.	65	Hautes-Pyrénées
P.O.	66	Pyrénées-Orientales
B.R.	67	Bas-Rhin
H.R.	68	Haut-Rhin
Rh.	69	Rhône
H.Sa.	70	Haute-Saône
S.L.	71	Saône-et-Loire
Sa.	72	Sarthe
H.Sa.	73	Haute-Savoie
Sa.	74	Savoie
Pa.	75	Paris
S.M.	76	Seine-Maritime
S.M.	77	Seine-et-Marne
Yv.	78	Yvelines
D.S.	79	Deux-Sèvres
So.	80	Somme
T.	81	Tarn
T.G.	82	Tarn-et-Garonne
Va.	83	Var
Va.	84	Vaucluse
Ve.	85	Vendée
Vi.	86	Vienne
H.Vi.	87	Haute-Vienne
Vo.	88	Vosges
Yo.	89	Yonne
B.	90	Belfort
Es.	91	Essonne
H.Se.	92	Hauts-de-Seine
S.S.-D.	93	Seine-St-Denis
V.M.	94	Val-de-Marne
V.O.	95	Val-d'Oise

CORSICA
On same scale

Corse
Haute-Corse
Corse du Sud

COPYRIGHT GEORGE PHILIP & SON Ltd.

ENGLISH CHANNEL

BAY OF BISCAY

MEDITERRANEAN SEA

GERMANY

BELGIUM

SWITZERLAND

ITALY

SPAIN

FRANCE

Paris

Projection: Conical with two standard parallels

East from Greenwich
West from Greenwich

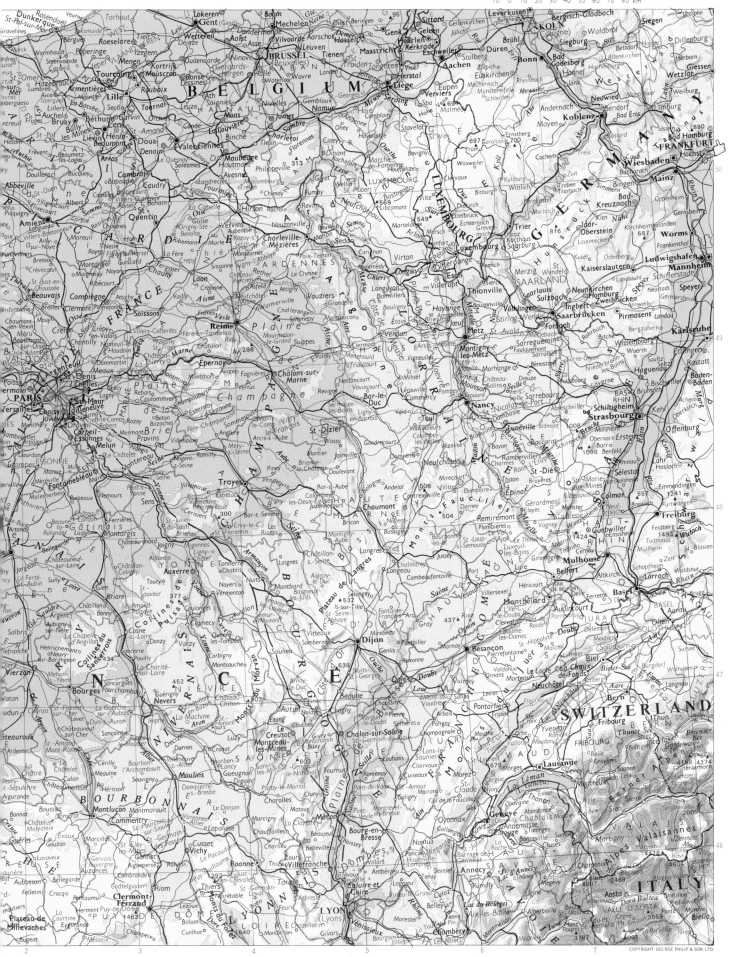

1:2 500 000
10 0 10 20 30 40 50 miles
10 0 10 20 30 40 50 60 70 80 km

BELGIUM

GERMANY

LUXEMBOURG

FRANCE

ARDENNES

CHAMPAGNE

LORRAINE

PARIS

BOURGOGNE

SWITZERLAND

ITALY

KÖLN
Bonn
Koblenz
FRANKFURT
Wiesbaden
Mainz
Mannheim
Ludwigshafen
Worms
Speyer
Karlsruhe
Strasbourg
Freiburg
Basel
Mulhouse
Belfort
Besançon
Dijon
Nancy
Metz
Saarbrücken
Luxembourg
Trier
Reims
Troyes
Lyon
Clermont-Ferrand
Bourges
Nevers
Moulins
Vichy
Mâcon
Chalon-sur-Saône
Lausanne
Lac Léman

COPYRIGHT GEORGE PHILIP & SON, LTD.

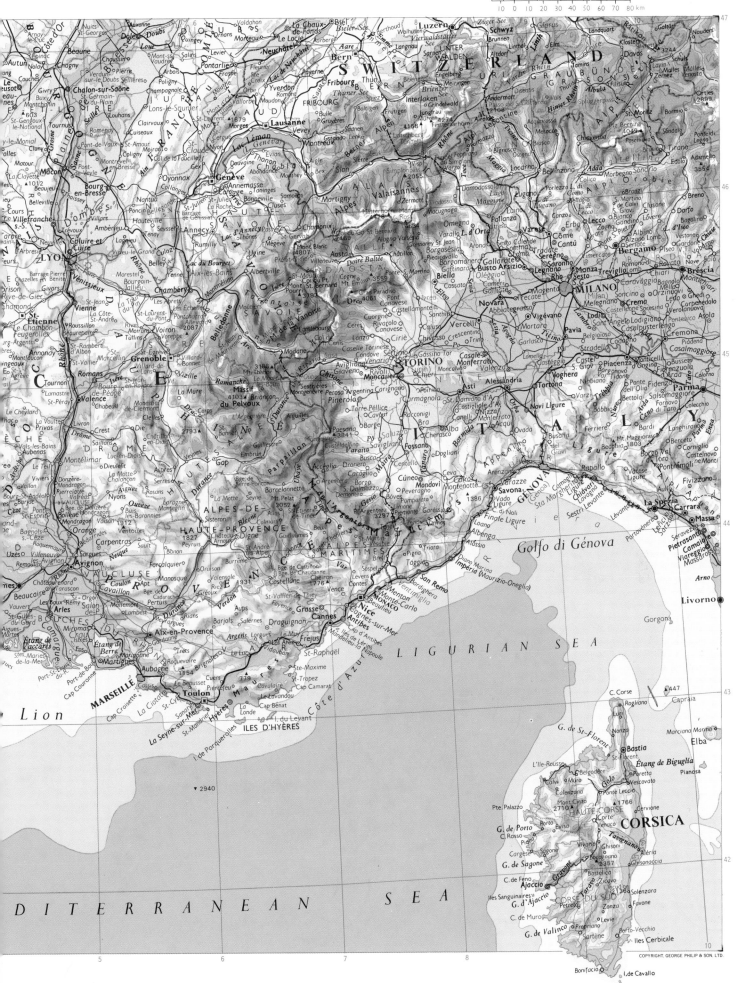

1 : 2 500 000

10   0   10   20   30   40   50 miles
0   10   20   30   40   50   60   70   80 km

SWITZERLAND

F R A N C E

I T A L Y

LYON

Genève

Lausanne

Bern

Luzern

MILANO

Torino

Grenoble

Valence

Gap

ALPES-DE-HAUTE-PROVENCE

PROVENCE

Bergamo

Brescia

Parma

Massa

Livorno

MARSEILLE

Toulon

Nice

MONACO

Monte-Carlo

Cannes

Antibes

San Remo

Imperia (Maurizio-Oneglia)

Golfo di Génova

GENOVA

La Spézia

ILES D'HYÈRES

Lion

L I G U R I A N   S E A

CORSICA

HAUTE-CORSE

CORSE DU SUD

Bastia

Ajaccio

Elba

Capraia

Gorgona

M E D I T E R R A N E A N   S E A

COPYRIGHT. GEORGE PHILIP & SON. LTD.

NORTH SEA

BALTIC

NETHERLANDS

BELGIUM

LUX.

FRANCE

WEST GERMANY

EAST GERMANY

CZECHOS

SWITZERLAND

AUSTRIA

ITALY

ADRIATIC SEA

Flensburg
SCHLESWIG
Kiel
HOLSTEIN
Lübeck
Rostock
Stralsund
Rügen
Szczecin (Stettin)
Hamburg
Schwerin
Bremen
Bremerhaven
Oldenburg
Wilhelmshaven
Groningen
Leeuwarden
Den Helder
Alkmaar
Haarlem
Amsterdam
's-Gravenhage (The Hague)
Leiden
Utrecht
Rotterdam
Dordrecht
Breda
Tilburg
Eindhoven
Antwerpen
Gent
Brugge
Oostende
Brussel (Bruxelles)
Lille
Roubaix
Tourcoing
Hannover
Braunschweig
BERLIN
Potsdam
Magdeburg
Halle
Leipzig
Dresden
Karl-Marx-Stadt (Chemnitz)
Zwickau
Erfurt
Jena
Gera
Plauen
Kassel
Köln (Cologne)
Bonn
Aachen
Liège
Namur
Düsseldorf
Essen
Dortmund
Duisburg
Wuppertal
Bochum
Mönchengladbach
NORDRHEIN WESTFALEN
Frankfurt
Offenbach
Mainz
Wiesbaden
Darmstadt
Mannheim
Heidelberg
Ludwigshafen
Worms
Luxemburg
Trier
Kaiserslautern
Saarbrücken
SAARLAND
PFALZ
Würzburg
Bamberg
Nürnberg
Fürth
Erlangen
Regensburg
Ingolstadt
Augsburg
München (Munich)
Stuttgart
Karlsruhe
Pforzheim
Heilbronn
Ulm
Freiburg
BADEN-WÜRTTEMBERG
BAYERN
Reims
Metz
Nancy
Strasbourg
Mulhouse
LORRAINE
Dijon
Besançon
Basel
Zürich
Bern
Genève
Lausanne
Luzern
Linz
Wien (Vienna)
Salzburg
Innsbruck
TIROL
STEIERMARK
KÄRNTEN
Graz
Klagenfurt
Praha (Prague)
Plzeň (Pilsen)
Brno
Milano (Milan)
Torino
Genova (Genoa)
Bologna
Venézia (Venice)
Ferrara
Modena
Parma
Padova (Padua)
Vicenza
Verona
Brescia
Bérgamo
Como
Trento
Bolzano
TRENTINO
LOMBARDIA
PIEMONTE
EMILIA
Ljubljana
Zagreb
Trieste
Rijeka

Mont Blanc 4807
Monte Rosa 4634

Projection: Conical with two standard parallels
East from Greenwich

1:5 000 000

50   0   50   100 miles

50   0   50   100   150 km

CENTRAL EUROPE POLITICAL

1:25 000 000

DENMARK

København

WEST GERMANY

EAST

POLAND

Warszawa

U.S.S.R.

BELGIUM

Berlin

's-Gravenhage

Bonn

Brussel

LUX.

Praha

CZECHOSLOVAKIA

FRANCE

Bern

SWITZ.

LIECHT.

Wien

AUSTRIA

HUNGARY

Budapest

ROMANIA

MONACO

ITALY

SAN MARINO

Beograd

Bucureşti

YUGOSLAVIA

BULGARIA

Sofiya

Roma

Place names (principal):

Zatoka Gdańska

Kaliningrad (Konigsberg)

Chernyakhovsk

Vilnius

LITHUANIAN S.S.R.

Zelenogradsk

Pregolya

Gusev

Alitus

Varena

R.S.F.S.R.

Gdynia

Sopot

Braniewo

Lyna

Kętrzyn

Gizycko

Suwałki

Augustów

Lida

Gdańsk (Danzig)

Elbląg

Malbork

Olsztyn

Grodno

Novogrudok

Starogard

Kwidzyń

Ostróda

Mosty

BYELORUSSIAN

Grudziądz

Iława

Pojezierze Mazurskie

Sokółka

Niemen

Volkovysk

Slonim

Chełmno

Wąbrzeźno

Mława

Ciechanów

Ostrów Mazowiecka

Brańsk

Hajnówka

Bereza

Toruń

Rypin

Lipno

Łomża

Ostrołęka

Białystok

Pułtusk

Czeremcha

Zhabinka

Włocławek

Wisła (Vistula)

Płock

Warszawa (Warsaw)

Mińsk Mazowiecki

Siedlce

Biała Podlaska

Brest

Pripyat

LAND

Kutno

Łowicz

Pruszków

Żyrardów

Otwock

Łuków

Międzyrzec Podlaska

Konin

Turek

Koło

Łęczyca

Grójec

Pilica

Włodawa

Dubrovitsa

Polesye

Sarny

Uzh

316

Desna

Kalisz

Zduńska Wola

Łódź

Radom

Kozienice

Puławy

Kovel

Styr

Goryn

Korosten

Ostrów Wielkopolski

Warta

Wieluń

Piotrków Trybunalski

Tomaszów Mazowiecki

Końskie

Lublin

Chełm

Zamość

Vladimir Volynskiy

Lutsk

Rovno

Korets

Novograd-Volynskiy

Radomyshl

Zhitomir

Kiyev

Borispol

Opole

Częstochowa

Radomsko

Kielce

Ostrowiec Świętokrzyski

Sandomierz

Kraśnik

Sokal

Dubno

Ostrog

Shepetovka

Starokonstantinov

Fastov

Belaya Tserkov

Tarnowskie Góry

Jędrzejów

Pińczów

Tarnobrzeg

390

Kamenka Bugskaya

Brody

Radekhov

Kremenets

Berdichev

Kazatin

Zabrze

Bytom

Zawiercie

Dąbrowa

Tarnowska

San

Przeworsk

Jarosław

Gorodok

Lvov

Zolochev

Ternopol

Khmelnitskiy

384

Vinnitsa

Gliwice

Chorzów

Sosnowiec

Katowice

Kraków

Wisła (Vistula)

Tarnów

Rzeszów

Przemyśl

471

Zolochev

U. S. S. R.

UKRAINIAN S.S.R.

Ostrava

Bielsko-Biała

Wieliczka

Nowy Sącz

Jasło

Sanok

Sambor

Dnestr

Drogobych

Borislav

Stryi

Buchach

Chortkov

Zhmerinka

Uman

Frýdek-Místek

Český Těšín

1725

Západné Beskydy

Tatry

Krosno

Dukelský Pr.

502

Turka

Ivano-Frankovsk

Zaleshchiki

Kamenets-Podolskiy

Bug

Pervomaisk

Jablunkovský Pr.

550

Žilina

Ružomberok

2655

Východné Beskydy

4380

Carpati

1881

Kolomyya

Snyatyn

Khotin

Mogilev-Podolskiy

Dnestr

VAKIA

SLOVAK S.S.R.

Nízke Tatry

Prešov

Košice

Uzhgorod

Nadvornaya

Yablonitse

931

Chernovtsy

Starozhinets

Yedintsy

Soroki

Kotovsk

Kremnica

Banská Bystrica

Zvolen

Slovenské Rudohorie

Sátoraljaújhely

Mukachevo

2061

Khust

Sighet

Storozhinets

Dorohoi

Beltsy

MOLDAVIAN

Nitra

N.

Zámky

Banská Štiavnica

Lučenec

Sajó

Hernad

Tokaj

Beregovo

Bodrog

Miskolc

Pietrosul

2305

Rădăuţi

Suceava

Botoşani

Iaşi

429

Kishinev

Bendery

Tiraspol

Komárno

Esztergom

Vác

Gyöngyös

Eger

Mezőkövesd

Nyíregyháza

Hajdúböszörmény

Satu Mare

Carei

Baia Mare

Someş

2102

Bistrita

Vatra-Dornei

Bistrita

Piatra Neamţ

Roman

Vaslui

Kagul

Belgorod Dnestrovskiy

Odessa

Győr

Tatabánya

Budapest

Újpest

Hatvan

Jászberény

Karcag

Szolnok

Debrecen

Del

Cluj-Napoca

Turda

Tîrgu Mureş

Praid

Odorheiul Secuiesc

Miercurea Ciuc

Bacău

Bîrlad

Tecuci

Székesfehérvár

Cegléd

Nagykőrös

Mezőtúr

Oradea

Salonta

Negru

Gyula Crişul

Mţii Bihor

1848

Aiud

Sighişoara

Sfîntu Gheorghe

Bretcu

Focşani

Galaţi

UNGARY

Dunaújváros

Kecskemét

Kiskunfélegyháza

Kiskőrös

Szentes

Hódmezővásárhely

Pul Alb

Abrud

Transilvania

Medias

Braşov

Rîmnicu Sărat

Brăila

467

Tulcea

Sulina

Kalocsa

Szekszárd

Kiskunhalas

Szeged

Makó

Arad

Alba-Iulia

Brad

Deva

Simeria

Hunedoara

Sibiu

Făgăraş

2535

Vf. Negoiu

Omul

2507

Cîmpina

Buzău

Râmnicu Sărat

Pécs

Bataszék

Baja

Subotica

Senta

Kikinda

Muresu

Lugoj

Carpaţii Meridionali

Turnu Roşu

350

Petroşani

2518

Prahova

Cîmpulung

Tîrgovişte

Ploieşti

Dunărea (Danube)

Cernavoda

Constanţa

Mohács

Sombor

Zrenjanin (Petrovgrad)

Bečej

Timişoara

Reşiţa

Peleaga

2509

Pîrîngul-Mare

Porta Orientalis

Tîrgu Jiu

Vîlcea

Piteşti

Argeş

Dîmboviţa

Bucureşti (Bucharest)

Ialomiţa

Călăraşi

Silistra

BLACK

Osijek

Novi Sad

Petrovaradin

Vršac

Bela Crkva

Mehadia

Valahia

Câlugăreni

Odžak

Brod

Sremska Mitrovica

Zemun

Pančevo

Orşova

Portile de Fier

Turnu-Severin

Iu

Slatina

Oltenita

SEA

Vinkovci

Bosna

Sava

Beograd (Belgrade)

Smederevo

Požarevac

Craiova

Vedea

Giurgiu

Ruse (Ruschuk)

Mangalia

Bijeljina

Drina

1346

Bor

Timok

Negotin

Vidin

Turnu Măgurele

Zimnicea

Olt Dunărea (Danube)

Corabia

GOSLAVIA

Han Pijesak

Zvornik

Užice

Valjevo

Morava

Zaječar

BULGARIA

Talbuhin

Sarajevo

Čačak

Kragujevac

COPYRIGHT, GEORGE PHILIP & SON, LTD.

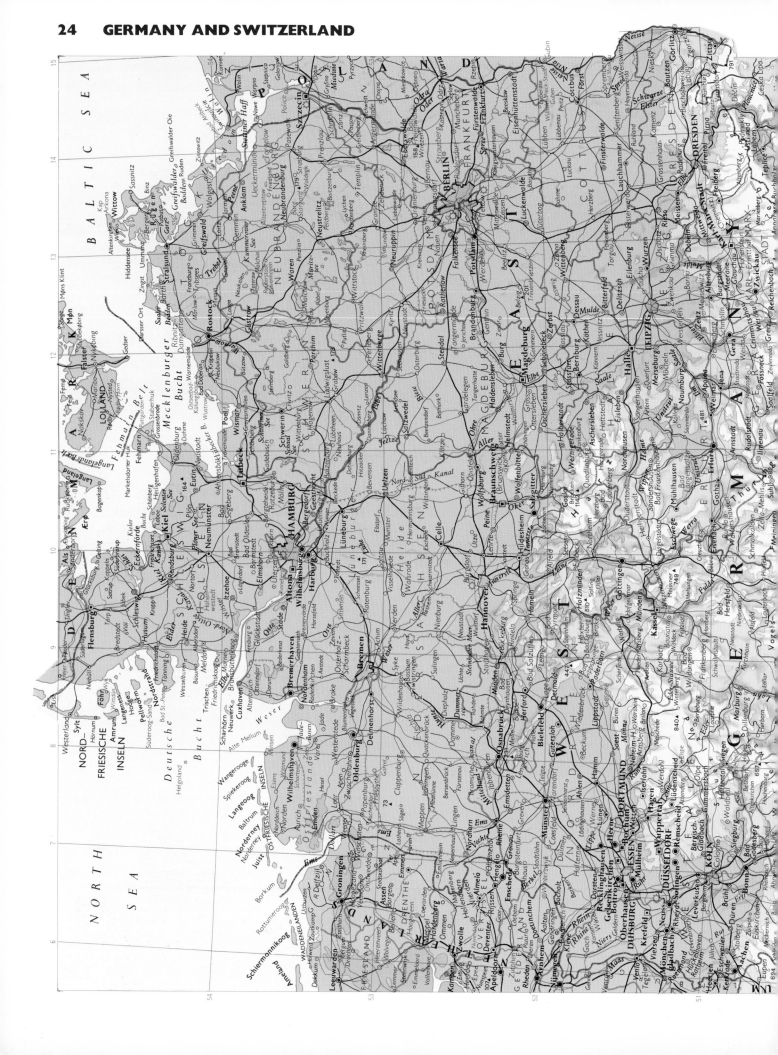

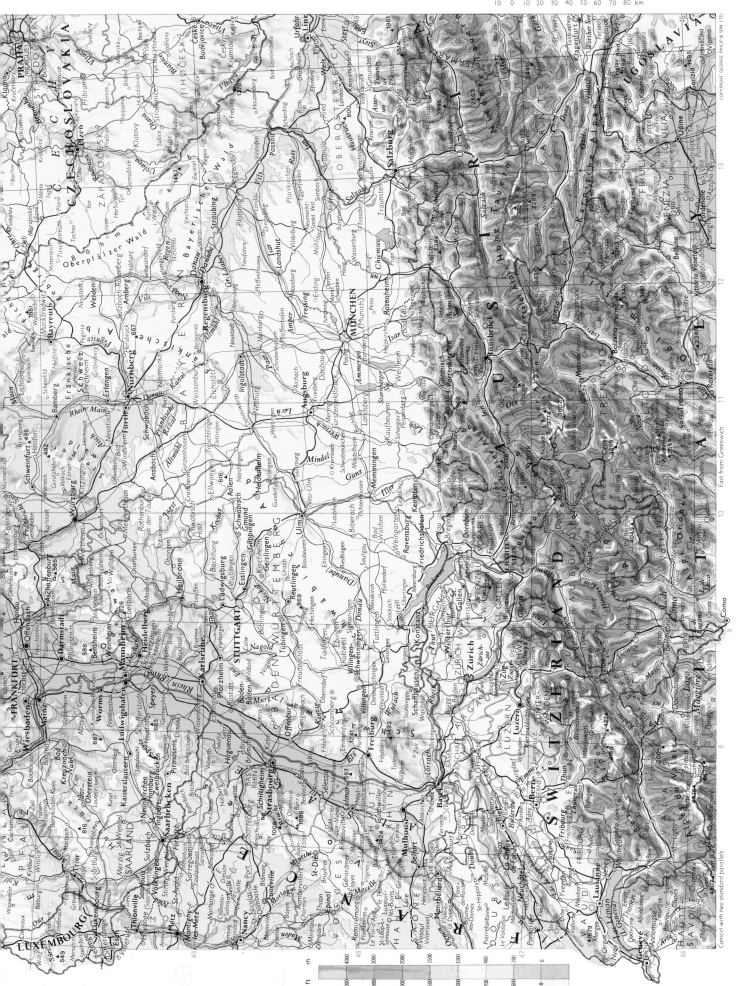

1:2 500 000

Projection: Conical with two standard parallels

1:5 000 000

50   0   50   100 miles

50   0   50   100   150 km

Projection: Conical with two standard parallels

East from Greenwich

West from Greenwich

1:2 500 000

MEDITERRANEAN SEA

MOROCCO

PORTUGAL

LISBOA (LISBON)

COPYRIGHT GEORGE PHILIP & SON, LTD.

Projection: Conical with two standard parallels

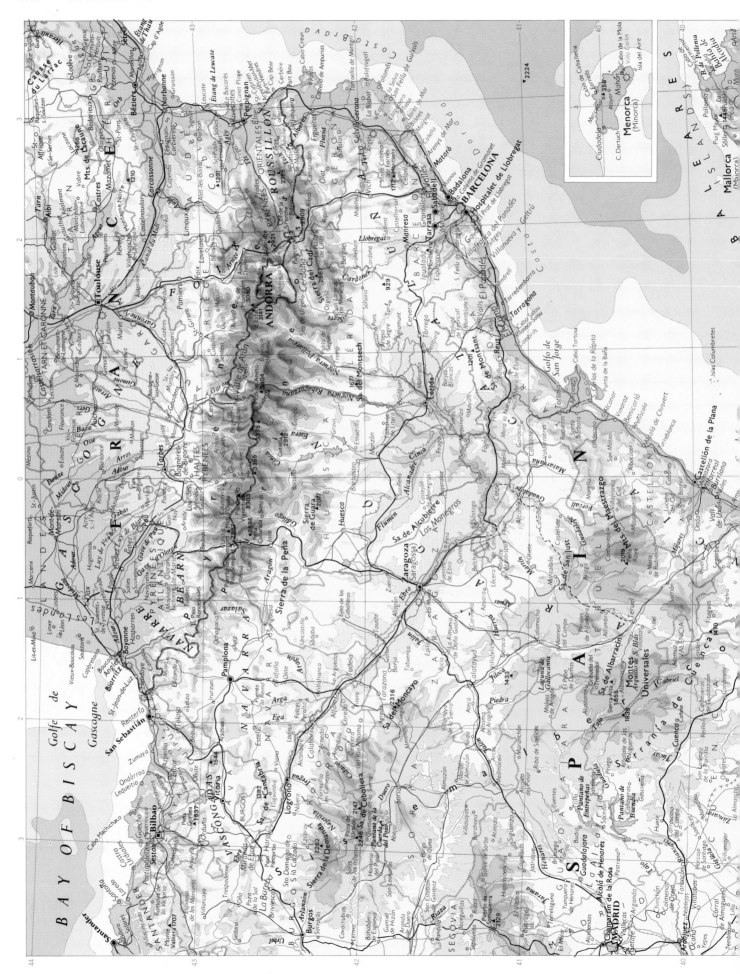

1:2 500 000

10   0   10   20   30   40   50 miles
10   0   10   20   30   40   50   60   70   80 km

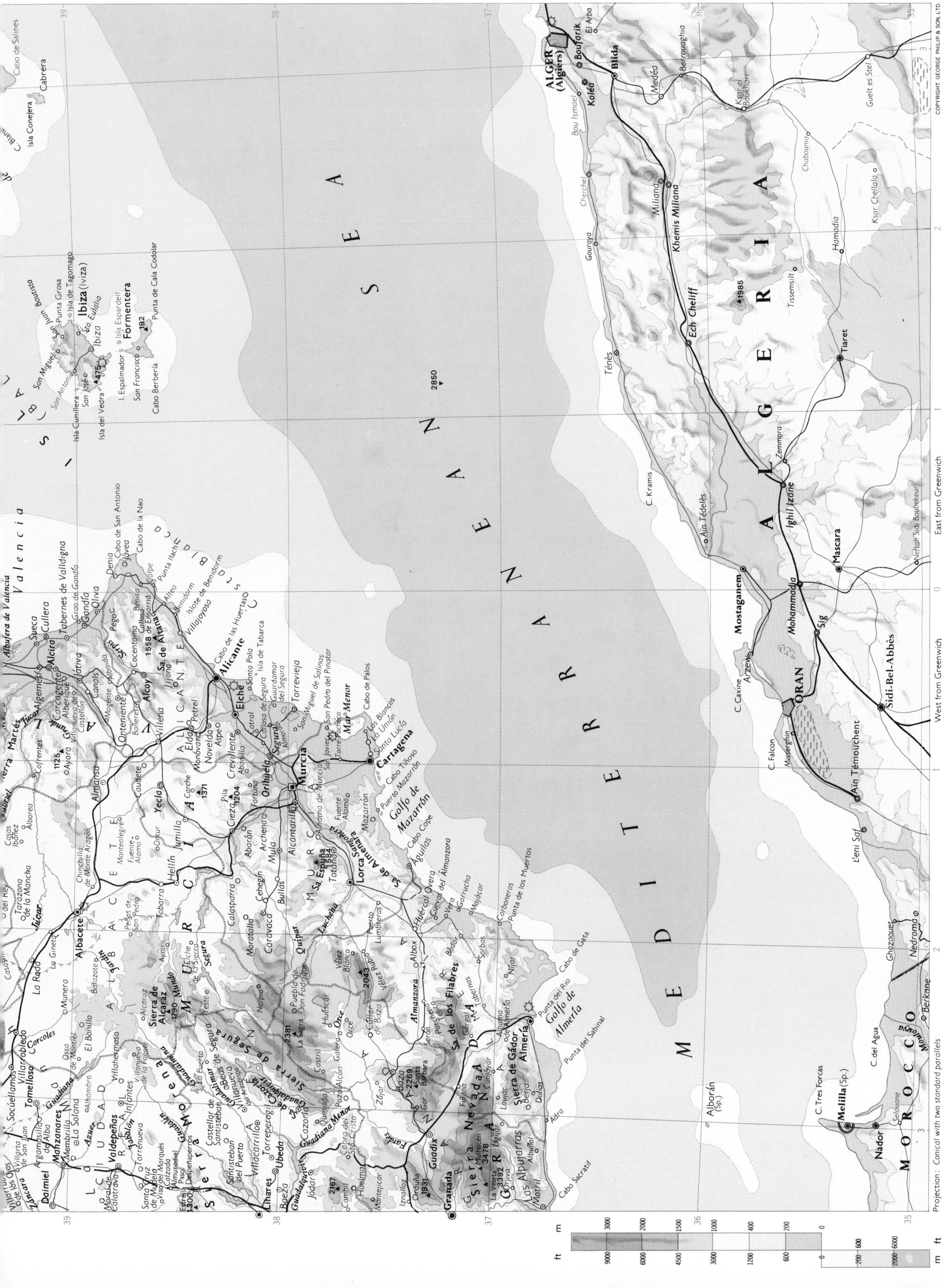

COPYRIGHT. GEORGE PHILIP & SON, LTD.

M E D I T E R R A N E A N   S E A

A L G E R I A

ALGER (Algiers)
Bou Farik
El Alba
Blida
Koléa
Médéa
Berrouaghia
Bou Ismael
Cherchell
Miliana
Khemis Miliana
Ksar el Boukhari
Chabounia
Ténès
Ech Cheliff
Gouraya
1985
Tissemsilt
Tiaret
Guelt es Stel
Ksar Chellala
Hamadia
C. K ramis
C. Kramis
Aïn Tédelès
Ighil Izane
Zemmora
Mascara
Mostaganem
Mohammadia
Sig
Sidi-Bel-Abbès
Arzew
C. Caxine
ORAN
C. Falcon
Misserghin
Sebkra
Aïn Témouchent
L'en Saf
Ghazaouet
Nedroma
C. del Agua
Berkane
Nador
Melilla (Sp.)
C. Tres Forcas
C. del Agua
Selouane

M O R O C C O

East from Greenwich
West from Greenwich

Projection: Conical with two standard parallels

B A L E A R I C   I S.

Cabo de Salines
Cabrera
Isla Conejera
San Miguel
Punta Grosa
Ibiza (Iviza)
San Antonio
San José
Ibiza
Sta. Eulalia
Isla Tagomago
Formentera
192
I. Espalmador
Isla Espardell
Punta de Cala Codolar
Isla del Vedra
Cabo Berbería
Punta de Cala Codolar

2850

Valencia
Albufera de Valencia
Cullera
Sueca
Alcira
Algemesí
Gandía
Grao de Gandía
Oliva
Pego
Denia
Cabo de San Antonio
Jávea
Javea
Cabo de la Nao
Benisa
Calpe
Altea
Benidorm
Punta Ifach
Villajoyosa
Cabo de las Huertas
ALICANTE
Santa Pola
Isla de Tabarca
Elche
Elx
Crevillente
Guardamar del Segura
Torrevieja
Cabo de Santa Pola
Mar Menor
Cabo de Palos
San Pedro del Pinatar
San Javier
Los Alcázares
Santa Lucía
La Unión
Cartagena
Cabo Tiñoso
Puerto Mazarrón
Golfo de Mazarrón
Cabo Cope
Águilas
Punta de los Muertos
Garrucha
Mojácar
Carboneras
Cabo de Gata
Golfo de Almería
Almería
Punta del Río
Punta del Sabinal
Roquetas de Mar
Adra
Motril

Alborán (Sp.)
Cabo Sacratif

Lorca
Puerto Lumbreras
Vélez Rubio
Vélez Blanco
Huércal-Overa
Albox
Cuevas del Almanzora
Sorbas
Níjar
Tabernes
Sierra de los Filabres
Sierra de Gádor
Sierra Nevada
Mulhacén 3478
Veleta
Granada
Guadix
Baza
Caniles
Serón
Orce
Sierra de Baza
Sierra de Cazorla

Murcia
Orihuela
Segura
Molina de Segura
Alcantarilla
Alhama de Murcia
Totana
Aledo
Sa. Espuña
Mula
Bullas
Cehegín
Caravaca
Moratalla
Calasparra
Archena
Abarán
Cieza
1204
Fortuna
Pila
Jumilla
Yecla
Villena
Sax
Elda
Petrel
Monóvar
Novelda
Aspe
Monforte del Cid
1371
Albacete
Hellín
Tobarra
Chinchilla de Monte-Aragón
Pozo Cañada
Almansa
Caudete
Montealegre
Ayora
Cofrentes
1125
La Roda
Madrigueras
Casas Ibáñez
Tarazona de la Mancha
Motilla del Palancar
Mota del Cuervo

Daimiel
Manzanares
Valdepeñas
Membrilla
La Solana
Socuéllamos
Tomelloso
Villarrobledo
Argamasilla de Alba
Alcázar de San Juan
Herencia
Villarrubia de los Ojos
Tomelloso
Guadiana
Santa Cruz de Mudela
Valdepeñas
Villanueva de los Infantes
El Bonillo
Munera
Lezuza
Ossa de Montiel
Villahermosa
El Ballestero
Alcaraz
Sierra de Alcaraz
Riópar
Sierra del Segura
Yeste
Segura de la Sierra
2381
Cazorla
Quesada
Úbeda
Baeza
Linares
Bailén
Jódar
Guadalquivir
Guadiana Menor

ft   m
9000   3000
6000   2000
4500   1500
3000   1000
1200   400
600   200
0   0
200   600
2000   6000
m   ft

1:10 000 000

50   0   50   100   150   200 miles
50   0   100   200   300 km

POLAND
Poznań
Płock
Wisła (Vistula)
Warszawa
Brest
Pinsk
Polesye
Chernigov
Desna
Sumy
Belgorod
Kharkov
Volgograd
Łódź
Wrocław
nica
Radom
Kielce
Lublin
Lutsko
Styr
Goryn
Pripyat
Pripyat
Nezhin
Konotop
U.   S.   S.   R.
Kursk
Kanamensk-Shakhtinskiy
Tsimlyanskoye Vdkhr.
Ostrava
Chorzów
Kraków
Tarnów
Przemyśl
Lvov
Vinnitsa
U.   S.   S.   R.
Kiyev
Zhitomir
Belaya Tserkov
Berdichev
Dnepr (Dnieper)
Pereyaslav Khmelnitskiy
Poltava
Slavyansk
Artemovsk
Voroshilovgrad
Kamensk-Shakhtinskiy
HOSLOVAKIA
Kamenets-Podol'skiy
Uman
Kremenchug
Pavlograd
Gorlovka
Makeyevka
Donets
Rostov
Slavkov
Jabłunkov
Žilina
Banská Stiavnica
Košice
Lvov
Chernovtsy
MOLDAVIAN
Beltsy
Kishinev
Bendery
Belgorod Dnestrovskiy
Ismail
Odessa
Kirovograd
Dnepropetrovsk
Krivoy Rog
Zaporozhye
Zhdanov (Mariupol)
Taganrog
Novocherkassk
Don
Manych
Bratislava
Miskolc
Debrecen
Nagybánya
Pietrosul 2305
Iaşi
Siret
Nikolayev
Kherson
Melitopol
Berdyansk
Yeisk
Oz. Manych Gudilo
Budapest
HUNGARY
Kecskemét
Oradea
Cluj-Napoca
Pietrosul 2102
Sea of Azov
Kerch
Krasnodar
Kuban
Maykop
Armavir
Tikhoretsk
Stavropol
Bulaton
Szeged
Hódmezővásárhely
Arad
ROMANIA
Braşov
Orasul Stalin
Galaţi
Belgorod Dnestrovskiy
Perekop
Krymskaya (Crimea)
Simferopol
Feodosiya
Novorossiysk
Tuapse
Pécs
Subotica
Timişoara
Mureş
Sibiu
Carpaţii Meridionali
2835
Brăila
Sulina
Yevpatoriya
Sevastopol
Balaklava
Yalta
Sukhumi
grab
Novi Sad
Petrovaradin
Sava
GO
Beograd
Craiova
Turnu-Severin
Dunărea (Danube)
Ploieşti
Bucureşti
Silistra
Constanţa
M. Tarkhankut
Karkinitskiy Zaliv
1545
BLACK   SEA
2211
Poti
Batumi
Rize
Banja Luka
Brod
Smederevo
Kragujevac
Morava
Niš
Pitesti
Turnu Severin
Tolbukhin
Ruse
Varna
Ince Burnu
Sinop
Samsun
Giresun
Tirebolu
Trabzon
BOSNA
Sarajevo
Durmitor 2522
Novi Pazar
Stara Planina
Pleven
Tŭrnovo
Shipchenski prokhod
Sliven
Burgas
Inebolu
Kastamonu
2366
Çorum
Amasya
Tokat
Sivas
Kuzey   Anadolu   Dağları
Erzincan
Firat
Mostar
Dubrovnik (Ragusa)
Cetinje
Kotor
CRNA GORA
Skopje
Vardar
Sofiya
Musala 2925
BULGARIA
Plovdiv
Maritsa
Rhodopi Planina
Edirne
Tekirdağ
Istanbul
Karadeniz Boğazı
Boğazı
Zonguldak
Ereğli
Bolu
Beypazarı
Ankara
Sivrihisar
Kızıl Irmak
Yozgat
Kırşehir
Kayseri
Erciyes Dağı 3770
Gürün
Keban
Malatya
argano
La Sila 1929
Barletta
Bari
Brindisi
Taranto
Golfo di Táranto
C. Sta. Maria di Leuca
ALBANIA
Durrës
Tiranë 2764
Bitola
Thessaloníki
Olimbos 2917
Alexandroúpolis
Eneż
Gelibolu
Gallipoli
Gökçeada
Çanakkale
Boğazı
Marmara Denizi
İznik Gölü
Bursa
Eskişehir
Kütahya
Afyon Karahisar
Bolvadin
Aksaray
Niğde
TURKEY
Tuz Gölü
Kırşehir
Maraş
Gaziantep
Osmaniye
Adana
İskenderun
İskenderun Körfezi
Mersin
Tarsus
Halab
Str. of Otranto
Kérkira
Kérkira
Nótia Pindhos
GREECE
Límnos
2033
Lésvos
Aegean
Sea
İzmir
Manisa
Turgutlu
Ödemiş
Aydın
Denizli
Muğla
Eğridir Gölü
Beyşehir Gölü
Konya
Karaman
Toros Dağları
Daği
Antakya
SYRIA
Hamah
Kefallinía
Vóveron
Nafpaktos
Ionian
Sea
Levkás
Vóriai Sporádhes
Évvoia
Khíos
Sámos
İkaria
Eğridir
Isparta
Burdur
Antalya
Antalya Körfezi
3086
Elmalı
Meğiste (Kastellórizon)
Al Lādhiqiyah
Bāniyās
Tarābulus
3083
Spartivento
Messina
Kefallinía
Zákinthos
Olympia
Pátrai
Piraievs
Athínai
Návplion
Kórinthos
Korinthiakós Kólpos
Thívai
Sfros
Ándros
Kikládhes
Náxos
Íos
Milos
Thíra
Dhodhekánisos
Ródhos
4486
CYPRUS
Morphou
1951
Nicosia
Famagusta
Larnaca
Limassol
Bayrūt (Beirut)
LEBANON
Şaydā
2814
Dimashq (Damascus)
'Ain Shaykh
4135
Spártí
Kalamáta
Pílos
Kíthira
Andikíthira
Khaniá
Ídhi Oros 2456
Iráklion
Kríti
Jabal ad Durūz
Akka
Hefa (Haifa)
ISRAEL
JORDAN
Jordan
Boşrā
N   E   A   N   S   E   A
3174
Cyrene
Darnah
Khalij Bómba
Tubruq
Tel Aviv-Yafo
Jerusalem
Dead Sea
Ammān
Ma'ān
Al Marj (Barce)
El 'Alamein
Matrûh
Khalîj el Salûm
Salûm
Rashîd
Baḥra el Burullus
Dumyât
Bur Sa'îd
El 'Arish
Petra
Banghāzī
Khalij Surt
Barqa
El Iskandarîya
El Mahalla el Kubra
Tanta
El Qantara
Ismā 'ilîya
Gebel el Tih
Sinai 2637
El Faiyûm
EGYPT
EL QÂHIRA
El Suweis
Khalîj el Suweis
Beni Suef
Nile
Khalîj al 'Aqaba
LIBYA

- - - - - Division between Greeks
and Turks in Cyprus;
Turks to the north.

12

SWITZERLAND

Brenner 1371

Passo del S. Gottardo 2108

Lyon

Genève

Merana Bressanone

Bolzano

TRENTINO-ALTO-ADIGE

Marmolada 3342

Villach

Klagenfurt

Bleiburg

Maribor

Nagyk

FRIULI VENEZIA GIULIA

Kobarid (Caporetto)

Karawanken 2863

Drave

Matterhorn Mte. Rosa 4478 4634

V. D'AOSTA

Bernina 4049

Ortles 3554

Adamello 3554

Belluno

Udine

Ljubljana

Celje

Sava

Drava Varaždin

Zagreb

HRV

Trento

Rovereto

Schio

Vittorio

Gorizia

Domodóssola

Locarno

Lago di Como

Bergamo

LOMBARDIA

Novara

Milano (Milan)

Brescia

Vicenza

VENETO

Verona

Treviso

Trieste

Istra

Rijeka (Fiume)

Kupa

Karlovac

Sisak

Torino (Turin)

PIEMONTE

Pavia

Cremona

Mantova (Mantua)

Pádova (Padua)

Venézia (Venice)

Golfo di Venézia

Koper

Rovinj

Pula (Pola)

Rt. Kamenjak

Kvarner

Cres

Krk

Senj

Banja Unać

BOSN

Grenoble

DAUPHINÉ

Chivasso

Casale

Vercelli

Po

Piacenza

Adige

Rovigo

Lošinj

Pag

Gospić

Kremen 1591

HER

Avignon

PROVENCE

Cuneo

Savona P. dei Giovi 472

Alessándria

Asti

Alba

Tánaro

Parma

Reggio

Módena

Ferrara

Comácchio

Ravenna

Dugi Otok

Zadar

Y

Marseille

Toulon

MONACO

Monte Carlo

Menton

Nice

San Remo

Impéria

Génova (Genoa)

La Spézia

Carrara

Lucca

Bologna

EMILIA ROMAGNA

Mte. Cimone 2165

Forlì

Cesena

Rimini

SAN MARINO

Pésaro

Fano

Senigállia

Ancona

Šibenik

Split

Brač

Hvar

MEDIT

MALTA
1:1 000 000

C. S. Dimitri

Gozo (Ghawdex)

Victoria (Rabat)

Comino (Kemmuna)

St. Pauls Bay

Mosta

Mdina

Rabat

Valletta

Luqa

Żurrieq

Marsaxlokk

Birżebbuġa

S.E. EUROPE
POLITICAL
1:25 000 000

SWITZ

LIECHT

AUSTRIA

Wien

Budapest

HUNGARY

U.S.S.R.

FRANCE

Bern

Venézia

Trieste

SAN MARINO

ITALY

ADRIATIC SEA

YUGOSLAVIA

Beograd

Bucureşti

ROMANIA

BULGARIA

Sofija

Corse (Fr.)

Roma

Napoli

Tiranë

ALBANIA

GREECE

Thessaloniki

AEGEAN SEA

TURKEY

Athínai

Sicilia

MALTA

Kríti

MEDITERRANEAN SEA

LIGURIAN SEA

CORSE (CORSICA) (Fr.)

Mt. Cinto 2710

Ajaccio

Bastia

Calvi

Aléria

Pto. Vecchio

Bonifacio

Bouches de Bonifacio

C. Corse

Capraia

Piombino

Elba

Portoferráio

Arno

Pisa

Livorno (Leghorn)

Volterra

Firenze (Florence)

Prato

Pistóia

Siena

Arezzo

TOSCANA

L. Trasimeno

Pso. di Porretta

San Benedetto

ADRIATIC SEA

Urbino

Loreto

Macerata

MARCHE

Civitanova

Áscoli Piceno

Teramo

Pescara

Ortona

Lanciano

Vasto

Térmoli

C. Corse

Orbetello

Mte. Argentário

Fiora

Viterbo

Civitavécchia

L. di Bracciano

Grosseto

Orvieto

Tévere

UMBRIA

Terni

Rieti

Gran Sasso 2914

Monti Vettore

Spoleto 2478

L. di Bolsena

Chiusi

Amiata 1738

ABRUZZI

L'Aquila

Chieti

Mte. Amaro 2795

ROMA (Rome)

Tívoli

Velletri

Frosinone

MOLISE

S. Severo

Campobasso

Monte Gargano

Monte S. Ángelo

G. di Manfredónia

Ostia

Ánzio

Latina

Sabáudia

Terracina

Fondi

Gaeta

Gariglíano

Fóggia

Cerignola

Barletta

Trani

Andria

Corato

Molfetta

B

Spinazzola

Ba

Putigna

CAMPAGNA

Isole Ponziane

Volturno

Ischia

Capri

Napoli (Naples)

Torre Annunziata

Vesúvio 1277

Nocera

Avellino

Benevento

Caserta

Aversa

Salerno

Sorrento

Castellammare

Sele

Éboli

Potenza

Matera

Agri

BASILICATA

Taran

TYRRHENIAN SEA

Ustica (It.)

Isole Eólie o Lípari

Strómboli

Salina

Lípari

Vulcano

C. Peloro

Palmi

CALABRIA

Reggio

C. Spartivento

Cariglíano

Cosenza

1929

Nicastro

Catanz

Pizzo

Sambiase

Squillace

Crotone

Milazzo

Messina

Sir. di Messina

Trápani

Erice

Castellammare

Palermo

Termini

Cefalù

Mistretta

Monti Nebrodi

Patti

Etna 3340

Giarre

Acireale

Catánia

Sciacca

Menfi

Selinunte

Castelvetrano

Marsala

Favignana

Isole Egadi

Alcamo

Segesta

SICILIA

Enna

Caltanissetta

Piazza Armerina

Caltagirone

Lentini

Augusta

Siracusa (Syracuse)

Adrano

Paterno

Gela

Licata

Agrigento

Favara

Canicattì

Vittória

Ragusa

Módica

Noto

C. Passero

Pantelleria (Ital.)

Lampedusa (Ital.)

Gozo

Comino

Valletta

Mdina

MALTA

1730

C. Bon

AFRICA

Projection: Conical with two standard parallels

ft m

12,000 4000

9000 3000

6000 2000

4500 1500

3000 1000

1200 400

600 200

0 0

200 600

m ft

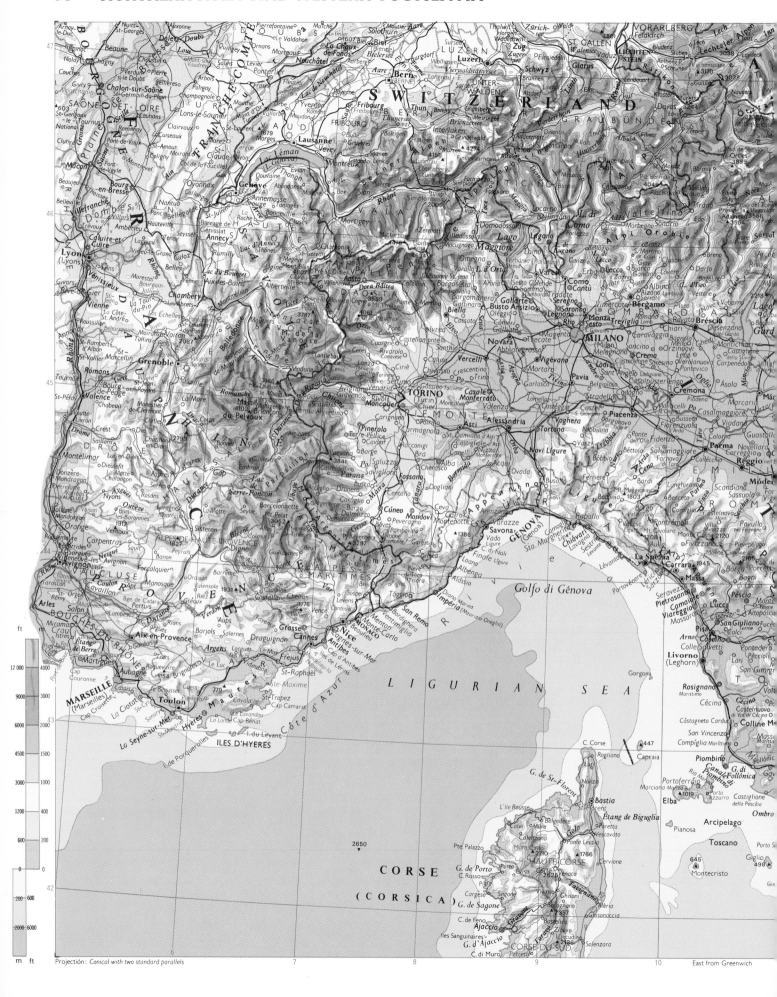

CORSE

CORSICA

CORSE-DU-SUD

Iles Sanguinaires
C. d'Ajaccio
C. di Muro
2136 Zonza
Petreto Bicchisano
Solenzara
Favone
G. de Valinco
Propriano
Porto-Vecchio
Sartène
Bonifacio
I. de Cavallo
Iles Cerbicales

Bouches de Bonifacio
Maddalena
Santa Teresa Gallura
La Maddalena
Caprera
Punta dello Scorno
Asinara
**Golfo dell'
Asinara**
Coghinas
Aggius
Témpio Pausania
Calangiánus
1362
M. Limbara
Pto. Cervo
Arzachena
Costa
Smeralda
Golfo Aranci
Olbia
G. di Ólbia
Tavolara
Porto Tórres
Sorso
Sennori
Oschiri
Tanaunella
C. dell'Argentiera
Sássari
Osilo
L. di Coghinas
Posada
Fertília
Ittiri
Ozieri
Buddusò
Siniscola
Alghero
Villanova
Monteleone
Bonorva
1259
Pattada
Bitti
C. Comino
Orune
Bosa
Macomer
Temo
Núoro
Dorgali
Oliena
Golfo di
Orosei
SARDEGNA
Ghilarza
L. del Tirso
Fonni
Baunei
C. di Monte Santu
Cábras
Oristano
Sórgono
Monti del
Gennargentu
1834
Arbatax
Lanusei
S A R D E G N A
M. Arci
812
Láconi
**Golfo di
Oristano**
Arborea
Terralba
Jerzu
Mandas
Nurri
SARDINIA
Gúspini
Arbus
Mogoro
Sanluri
Senorbì
C. Pécora
1236
Gonnosfanádiga
Villacidro
S. Vito
Villaputzu
Fluminimaggiore
M. Línas
Serramanna
Dolianova
Muravera
Iglésias
Guerri
Assémini
Sestu
Sinnai 1089
C. Ferrato
Portoscuso
Gonnesa
Síliqua
Selárgius
Carloforte
Carbonia
1116
Cágliari
Quartu Sant'Elena
C. Carbonara
San Pietro
Santadi
Serpentara
Sant'Antíoco
**Golfo di
Cágliari**
**Sant'
Antíoco**
Porto Botte
Pula
Teulada
G. di Palmas
C. Spartivento

T Y R R H E N I A N

S E A

▾3719

▾3589

Ustica

Vatican City
Fregene
Lido di Óstia
(Lido di Roma)
Prática
di Mare
Albano Laziale
Ánzio
Nettuno
Pontinia
Latina
Sabáudia
Monte Circeo 541
Terracina
**ROMA
(Rome)**
Tívoli
Palestrina
Valmontone
Cori
Cisterna di Latina
Aprília
Velletri
Anagni
Alatri
Véroli
Ferentino
Frosinone
Ceccano
Ceprano
Monte S.
Sonnino
Priverno
Fondi
1533
Gaeta
**Golfo di
Gaeta**
Mintúrno
Gariglian
Fórmia
Mondra
Vo
Zannone
Palmarola
Ísole
Ponziane
283
Ponza
Ventotene
Ísc

C. San Vito
Castellammare del Golfo
G. di Castellammare
Terrasini Favarotta
C. Gallo
Monreale
PALERMO
Bagheria
Levanzo
Trápani
Érice
1110
Cárini
Partínico
Misilmeri
Ísole Égadi
Alcamo
S. Giuseppe
Iato
Marettimo
Paceco
Favignana
Stagnone
Calatafimi
Salemi
Camporeale
Córleone
Marineo
1613
Belsito
Marsala
Gibellina
Prizzi
Lercara
Friddi
Partanna
Bisacquino
Castelvetrano
Sambuca
di Sicilia
S I C
Mazara
del Vallo
Menfi
Burgio
Mussomeli
Belice
Campobello di Mazara
Sciacca
Caltabellotta
Ribera
Platani
Racalmuto
Sicilian Channel
Cattólica Eraclea
Siculiana
Agrigento
Porto Empédocle
Naro
Palma di Montechiaro
Campobell
Pantelleria
Pantelleria 836
(It.)
1319
M E D I T E

Iles de la
Galite
Galite
C. Serrat
Bizerte
(Binzert)
C. Blanc
Cani
Plane
Zembra
Golfe de Tunis
C. Bon
El Kala
Tabarka
Menzel–Bourguiba
Mateur
Kelibia
Menzel-
Temime
ALGERIA
Medjerda
TUNIS
Halq el Oued
Bou Salem
Téboursouk
Béja
Soliman
Nabeul
T U N I S I A
Hammamet
Tébourbé
Tébourba
Zaghouan
Téborsoquk
Mellag
Medjerda

Projection: Conical with two standard parallels

East from Greenwich

ft m
9000 3000
6000 2000
4500 1500
3000 1000
1200 400
600 200
0
200 600
2000 6000
4000 12 000
m ft

1:2 500 000

ADRIATIC

SEA

IONIAN

SEA

MEDITERRANEAN SEA

Projection: Conical with two standard parallels

East from Greenwich

1:2 500 000

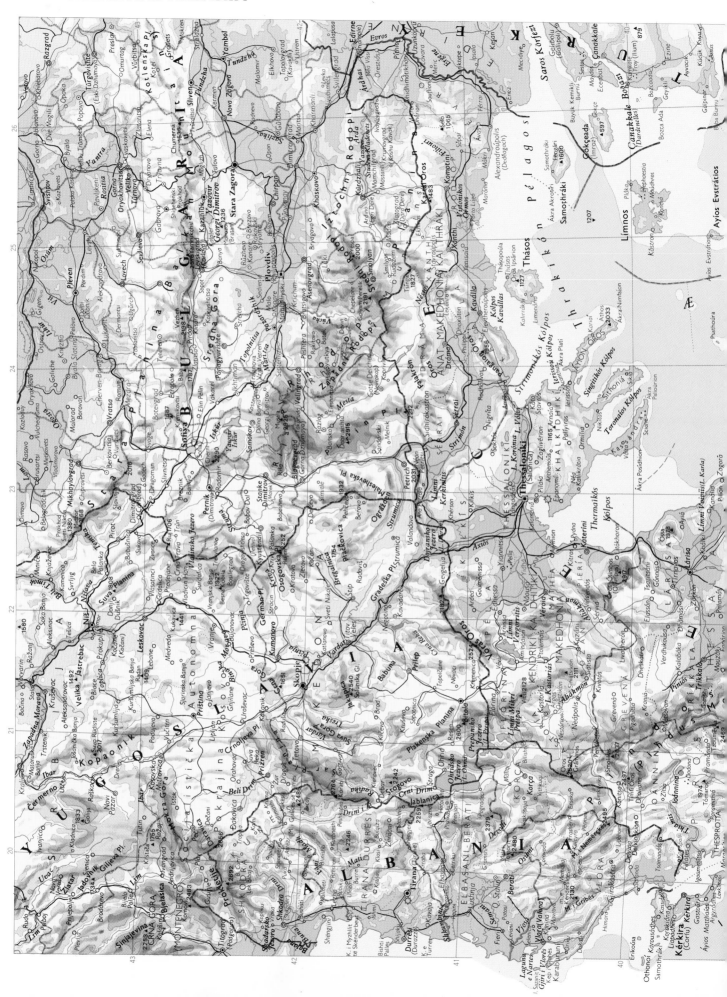

1:2 500 000

COPYRIGHT GEORGE PHILIP & SON LTD.

East from Greenwich

Projection: Conical with two standard parallels

Continuation Eastwards
on same scale

A E G E A N   S E A

I O N I A N   I S L A N D S

SEA OF CRETE
(Sea of Candia)

ARKHIPÉLAGOS
(CYCLADES)

KIKLÁDHES

Khíos (Chios)

Psará

Ikaría

Mikonos

Tinos

Ándros

Skíros

Skíros

Náxos

Páros

Íos

Thíra

Amorgós

Astipálaia

Sífnos

Sérifos

Kíthnos

Kéa

Mílos

ATHÍNAI
ATHENS

Piraeús

Pátrai

Korinthos

Kórinthos (Corinth)

Kalamata

Spárti (Sparta)

Trípolis

Návplion

PELOPÓNNISOS

ATTIKÍ

STEREÁ ELLÁS

AKHAÏA

DHÍTIKI ELLÁS

AITOLÍA

AKARNANÍA

ÍPIROS

ARKADÍA

LAKONÍA

MESSINÍA

ILÍA

ARGOLÍS

KORINTHÍA

BOIOTÍA

VIOTÍA

Taíyetos Óros

Párnon Óros

Iráklion (Candia)

C R E T E

KRÍTI

KHANÍA

Khaniá

Réthimnon

Ídhi Óros

Kólpos Mesará

Levkás (Santa Maura)

Kefallinía (Cephalonia)

Itháki (Ithaca)

Zákinthos (Zante)

Sámos

Kós

Ródhos (Rhodes)

Kárpathos

DHODEKÁNISOS
(DODECANESE)

Stenón Karpáthos

Stenón Kásos

Kérme Körfezi

Mántalya Körfezi

Kuşadasi Körfezi

Samsun Daği

Baba Daği

M U Ğ L A

A Y D I N

Astipálaia

Nísiros

Tílos

Sími

Saronikós Kólpos

Korinthiakós Kólpos

Argolikós Kólpos

Lakonikós Kólpos

Messiniakós Kólpos

Kiparissiakós Kólpos

Patraïkós Kólpos

Pátraïkós Kólpos

Kólpos Khaníon

Kólpos Soúdhas

Kólpos Kisámou

Kíthira (Cerigo)

Gávdhos

m   ft

3000 9000
2000 6000
1500 4500
1000 3000
600 1200
400 200
200 600
0   0
200 600
2000 6000
m   ft

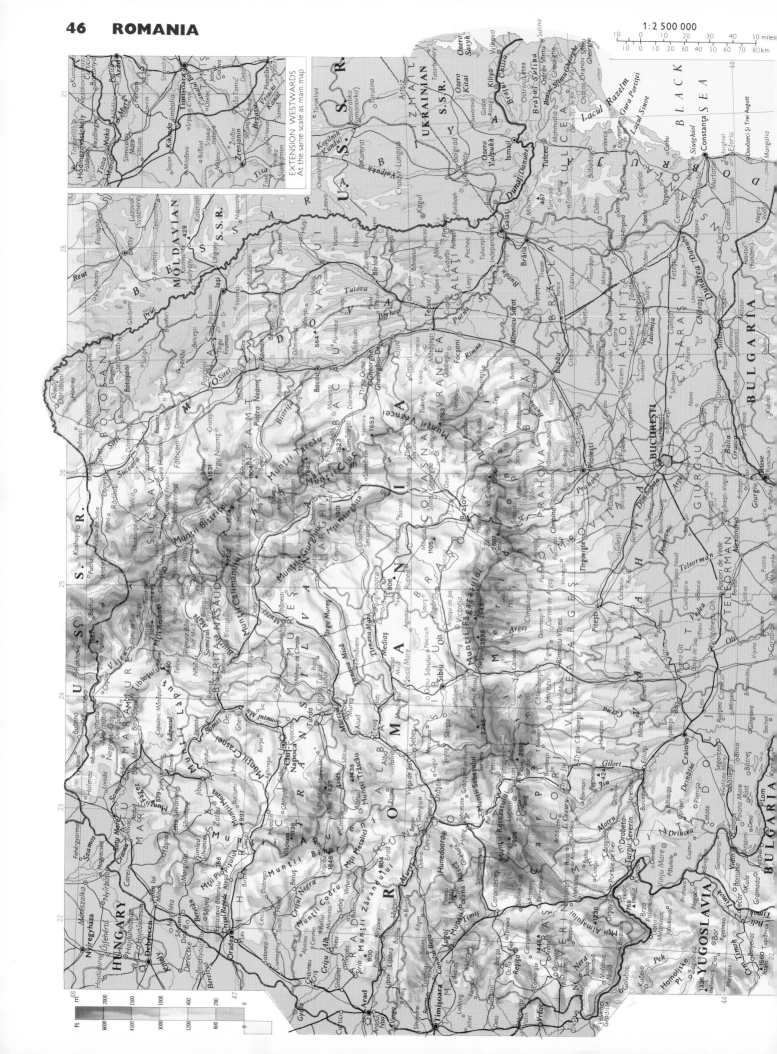

1:2 500 000

10 0 10 20 30 40 50 miles
10 0 10 20 30 40 50 60 70 80 km

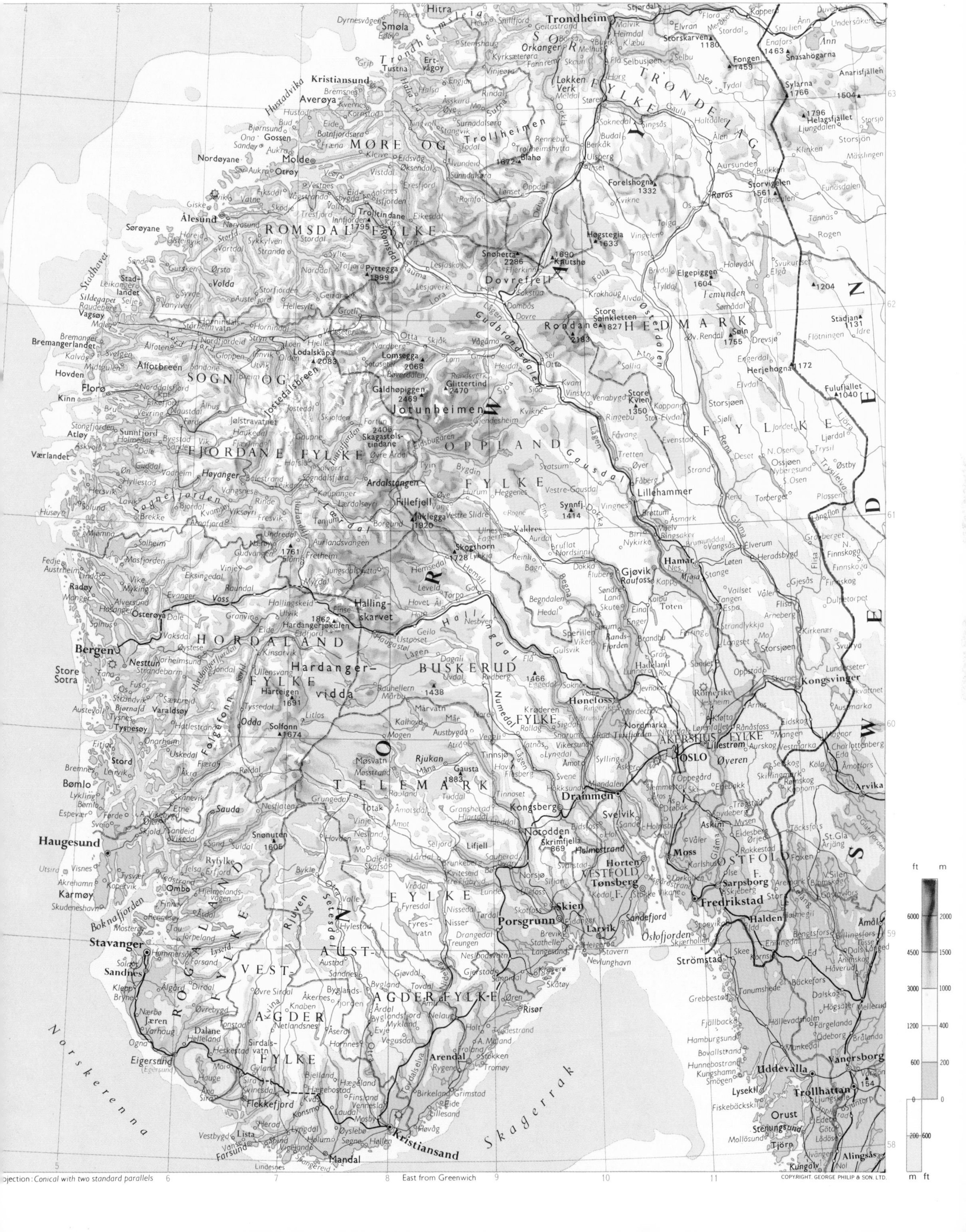

SOUTHERN NORWAY

Counties / Regions

SØR-TRØNDELAG FYLKE

MØRE OG ROMSDAL FYLKE

SOGN OG FJORDANE FYLKE

HEDMARK FYLKE

OPPLAND FYLKE

HORDALAND FYLKE

Hardanger-vidda

BUSKERUD FYLKE

TELEMARK FYLKE

ROGALAND FYLKE

VEST-AGDER FYLKE

AUST-AGDER FYLKE

VESTFOLD FYLKE

AKERSHUS FYLKE

ØSTFOLD F.

SVERIGE / SWEDEN

Jotunheimen

Dovrefjell

Trollheimen

Major cities and towns

Trondheim, Kristiansund, Ålesund, Molde, Bergen, Haugesund, Stavanger, Sandnes, Oslo, Drammen, Lillehammer, Hamar, Gjøvik, Kongsvinger, Lillestrøm, Moss, Sarpsborg, Fredrikstad, Halden, Skien, Porsgrunn, Larvik, Tønsberg, Horten, Sandefjord, Kristiansand, Mandal, Arendal, Flekkefjord, Eigersund, Røros, Notodden, Kongsberg, Hønefoss, Svelvik

Heights (metres)

Snøhetta 2286, Galdhøpiggen 2469, Glittertind 2470, Skagastølstindane 2405, Store Skagastølstind, Rondane 2183, Lodalskåpa 2083, Lomsegga 2068, Store Soknkletten 1827, Hardangerjøkulen 1862, Solfonn 1674, Gaustad 1883, Snønuten 1605, Høgstegia 1633, Synnfjell 1414, Skogshorn 1728, Pyttegga 1999, Trollindane 1672, Blåhø, Knutshø 1690, Elgpiggen 1604, Sylarna 1766, Helagsfjället 1796, Storvigelen 1561, Forelshogna 1332, Fongen 1459, Storsylen 1504, Sølen 1755, Herjehogna 1172, Fuluffjället 1040, Hallingskarvet

Water features

Norskerenna, Skagerrak, Oslofjorden, Sognefjorden, Hardangerfjord, Boknafjorden, Mjøsa, Femunden, Trondheimsfjorden

Projection: Conical with two standard parallels

East from Greenwich

COPYRIGHT. GEORGE PHILIP & SON LTD.

Elevation scale

ft	m
6000	2000
4500	1500
3000	1000
1200	400
600	200
0	0
600	200

1:2 500 000

10 0 10 20 30 40 50 miles
10 0 10 20 30 40 50 60 70 80 km

BALTIC SEA

Gotland
Visby

POLAND
Łeba
Słupsk
Ustka
Wieprz
Darłowo
Sławno

Bornholm
Rønne
Neksø
Svaneke
Gudhjem

Öland
Kalmar
Oskarshamn
Västervik

Norrköping
Linköping
Motala
Mjölby
Trollhättan
Göteborg
Borås
Mölndal
Alingsås
Varberg
Falkenberg
Halmstad
Helsingborg
Landskrona
Malmö
Lund
Trelleborg
Ystad
Kristianstad
Karlskrona
Karlshamn
Ronneby

JÖNKÖPINGS LÄN
Jönköping
Huskvarna
Nässjö
Värnamo
Ljungby
Växjö

KRONOBERGS LÄN
BLEKINGE LÄN
KRISTIANSTADS LÄN
MALMÖHUS LÄN
HALLANDS LÄN

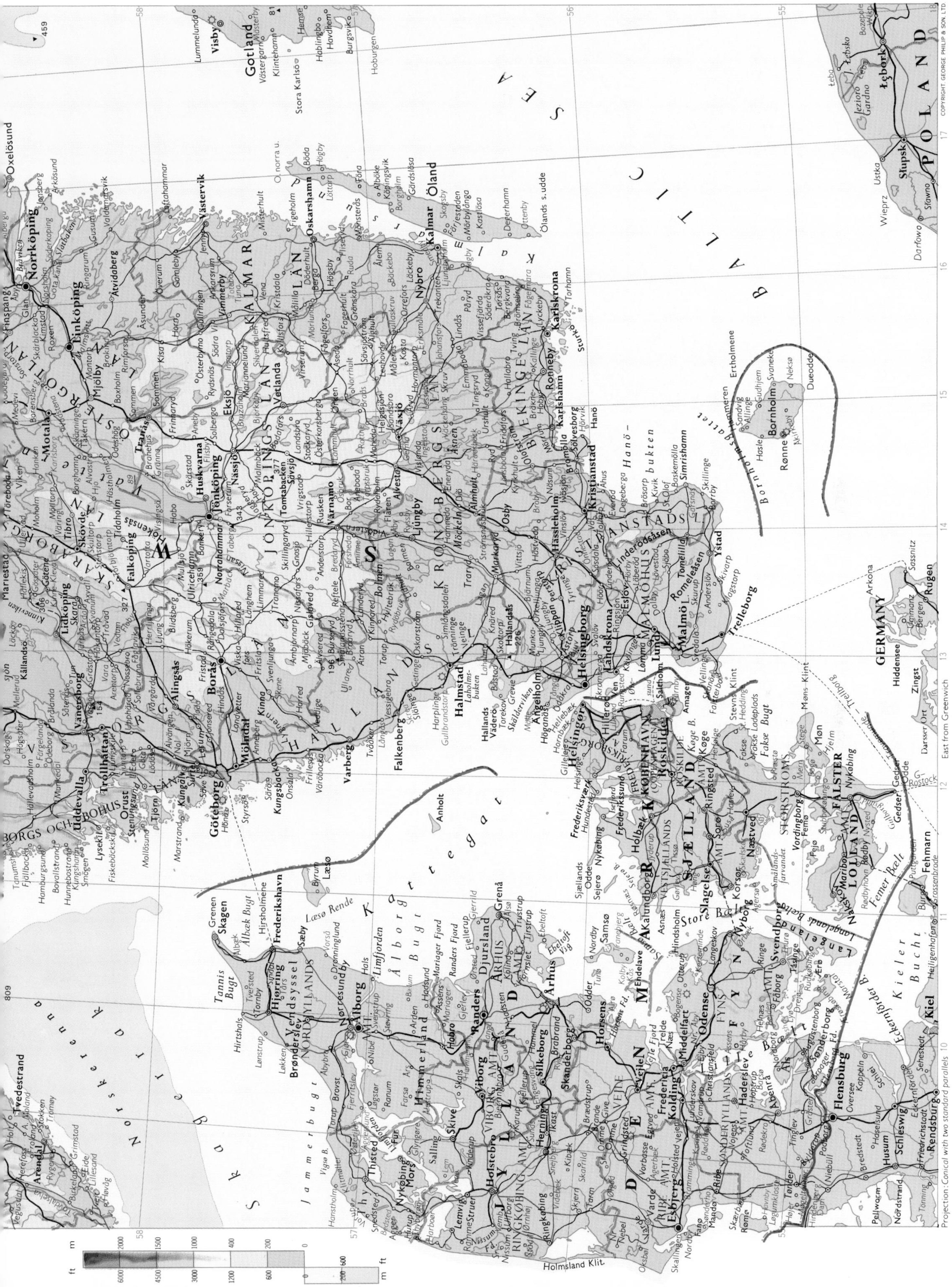

Kattegat
Skagerrak

GERMANY
Rügen
Hiddensee
Sassnitz
Rostock
Kiel
Flensburg
Rendsburg
Schleswig

DENMARK

JYLLAND
Skagen
Frederikshavn
Hjørring
Ålborg
NORDJYLLANDS AMT
Viborg
VIBORG AMT
Randers
Århus
ÅRHUS AMT
Silkeborg
Herning
RINGKØBING AMT
Esbjerg
RIBE AMT
Varde
Vejle
VEJLE AMT
Kolding
Fredericia
Horsens
Skanderborg
Haderslev
SØNDERJYLLANDS AMT
Åbenrå

FYN
 Odense
FYNS AMT
Svendborg
Middelfart
Nyborg
Faborg

SJÆLLAND
KØBENHAVN
København
Roskilde
ROSKILDE AMT
Køge
Holbæk
Kalundborg
Slagelse
Næstved
VESTSJÆLLANDS AMT
STORSTRØMS AMT
Vordingborg
Nykøbing

LOLLAND
Maribo
Nakskov
FALSTER
Gedser

Møn
Stevns Klint
Møns Klint

Storstrøms
Store Bælt
Lille Bælt
Femer Bælt

Projection: Conical with two standard parallels

East from Greenwich

ft m
6000 2000
4500 1500
3000 1000
1200 400
600 200
0 0
m ft

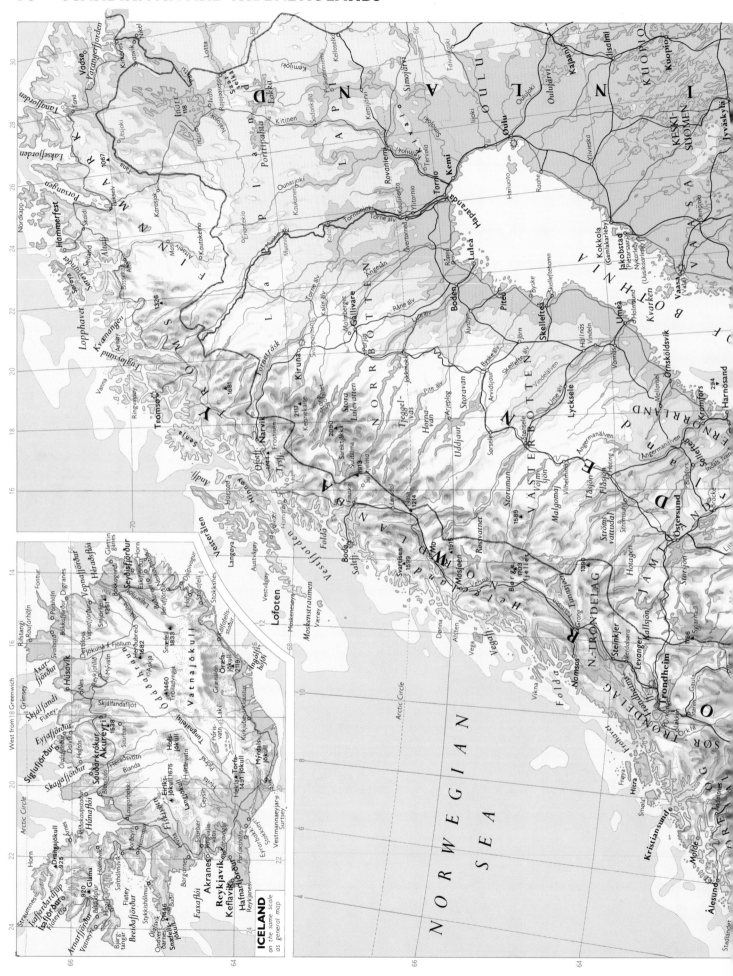

ICELAND
on the same scale
as general map

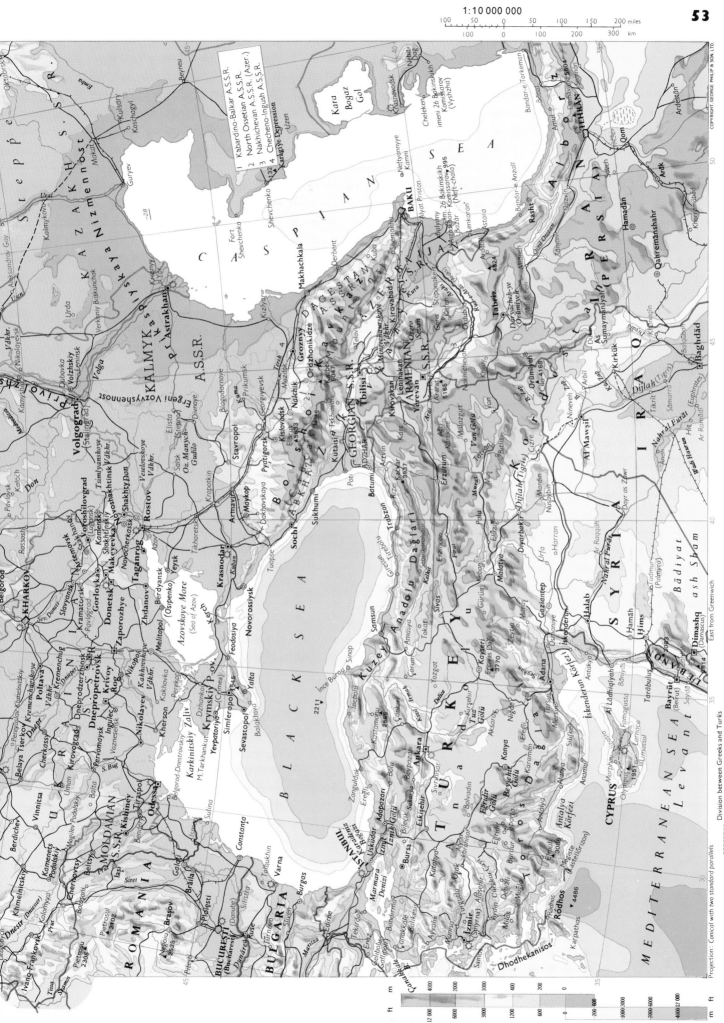

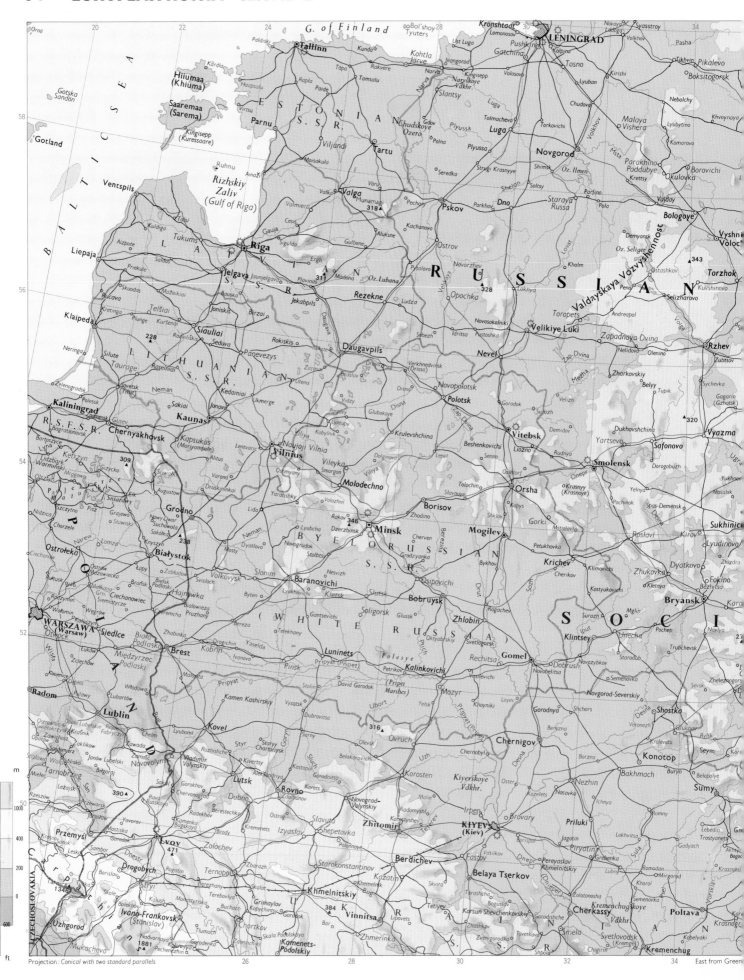

1 : 5 000 000

50   50   100 miles
50   0   50   100   150 km

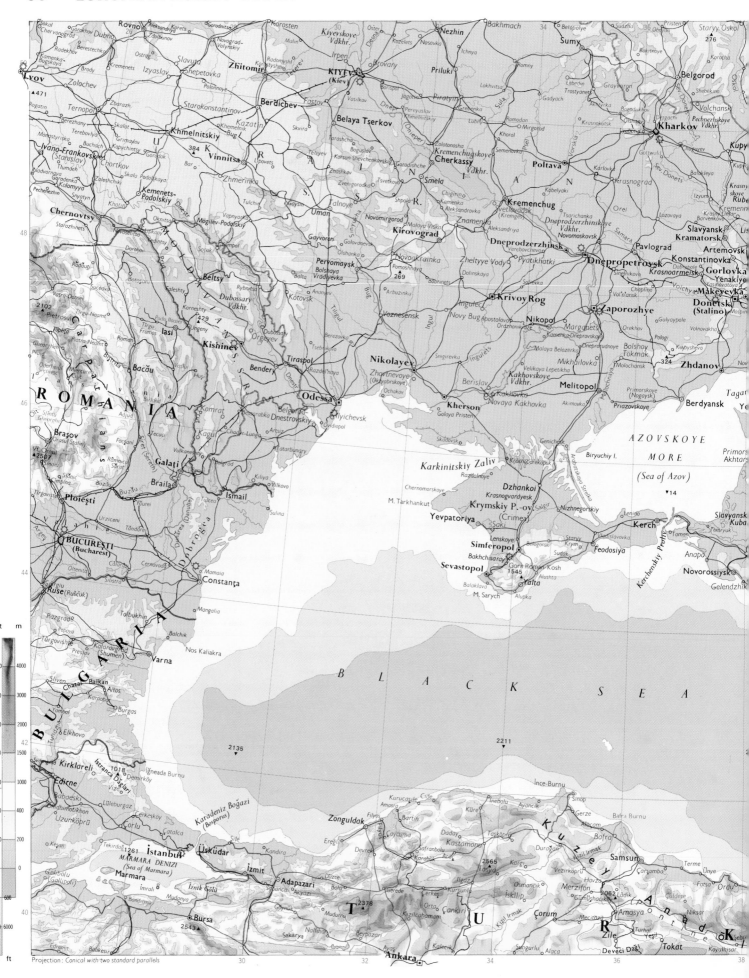

50 miles

50 0 50 100 150 km

50

48

46

44

42

Georgiu-Dezh
Yelan-Kolenovskiy
Bobrov
Khrenovoye
Talovaya
Povorino
Novokhopersk
Peski
Samoylovka
Krasnoarmeysk
Krasnyy Kut
Orlov Gay
Oz. Chalkar
Chalkar
Dzhambeyty
52

strogozhsk
Kameeka
Buturlinovka
239
Uryupinsk
Buzuluk
Kukvidze
Yelan
Zhirnovsk
Kamenka
Rovnoye
Novouzensk
Aleksandrov Gay
Mergenevskiy
Karsha

Pavlovsk
Kalach
Novoannenskiy
Novoanninskiy
Panfilovo
358
Vozyshennost
Volgogradskoye Vdkhr.
Ivatka
Pallasovka
Shungay
Urda
Kaztalovka
Mar-Ügen
Furmanovo
Ural
Buzartobe
Antonovka

Pavlovsk
Khoper
Serafimovich
Medveditsa
Ust Buzulukskaya
Mikhaylovka
Kamyshin
Nikolayevsk
Kaysatskoye
Verkhniy Baskunchak
Aleksandr Gay

Boguchar
Kantemirovka
Don
Veshenskaya
Kazanskaya
Kletskiy (Ilovlinskaya)
Ilovlya
Dubovka
Kapustin Yar
Eltan
Makhambet (Yamankhalinka)

tarobelsk
Melovoye
Chertkovo
Chir
Chir-Sovetskaya
Surovikino
Kolach na Donu
Krasnoslobodsk
Volzhskiy
Volga
Akhtubinsk (Petropavlovsk)
Vladimirovka
Topal
Zelënyy

onetsk
Millerovo
Kamensk-Shakhtinskiy
Lenin
Morozovsk
Belaya Kalitva
Volgograd (Stalingrad)
Krasnoarmeysk
K A Z A K H S.S.R.
Inderborskiy

Voroshilovgrad (Lugansk)
Glubokiy
ka
nunarsk
Krasnodon
Krasnyy Luch
Sverdlovsk
Krasnodonetskaya
Tsimlyanskoye Vdkhr.
Kotelnikovo
Chernyshkovskiy
Dbilnoye
Yenotayevka
Kopanovka
Novobogatinskoye
Guryev
-28

Rovenki
zhnoye
Gukovo
Krasny Sulin
Artemovsk
Ust-Donetskiy
Zimovniki
Zavetnoye
Bolshaya Martynovka
P r i k a s p i y s k a y a N i z m e n n o s t
28

oshakhtinsk
Shakhty
Konstantinovskiy
Volgodonsk
Dubovskoye
Krasnyy Yar
Ryushino
tveyi Kurgan
Tuzlov
Don

rog
Rostov
Batays k
Manych
Kuberle
K A L M Y K
A. S. S. R.
Astrakhan
Ramzy0
C A S P I A N

Azov
Katon
Zernograd
Veselovskoye Vdkhr.
Mechetinskaya
Remontnoye
Krasnoye
Kosika
Liman
Kultay

Yeya
Stara-minskaya
Kushchevskaya
Yegorlykskaya
Oz. Manych-Gudilo
Elista (Stepnoi)
Leninsk
Priyutnoye
Beloye Ozero
Kaspiyskiy
O. Kulaly
Mangyshlakskiy Zaliv
M. Tyub Karagan

Kanevskaya
Pavlovskaya
Belaya Glina
Krasnogvardeyskoye
Peschanokopskoye
Gigant
Divnoye
Kalaus
Kuma
Staryy Biryuzyak
Fort Shevchenko
P-ov. Mangyshlak

imashevsk
Tikhoretsk
Korenovsk
Kropotkin
Novoaleksandrovskaya
Izobil'nyy
Ipatovo
Svetlograd (Petrovskoye)
Arzgir
Beloye Ozero
Bryanskoye
O Tyuleniy
Shevchenko

Krasnodar
Armavir
Kuban
Stavropol
831
Blagodarnoye
Prikumsk
Vladimirovka
O Chechen
C
A
S
P
I
A
N
-28

Ust-Labinsk
Kurgannsk (Kurgannaya)
Nevinnomyssk
Zelenokumsk
Vorontsovo-Aleksandrevskoye)
S
800

adyzhensk
Maykop
Labinsk
Apsheronsk
Dakhovskaya
Urup
Kursavka
Mineralnyye Vody
Georgiyevsk
Aleksandriyskaya
Lopatin
E
A

Ilegorsk
B
o
l
s
h
o
y
Cherkessk
Pyatigorsk
Prokhladnyy
Mozdok
CHECHENO-
Kizlyar

Sochi
Matsesta
Krasnaya Polyana
Karachayevsk
Yessentuki
Kislovodsk
Nalchik
Nartkala
Malgobek
INGUSH
Groznyy
Gudermes
Sulak
Makhachkala

Adler
Gagra
Teberda
KABARDINO-
BALKAR A.S.S.R.
Elkhotovo
Baksan
A.S.S.R.
Kumtorkala
Kaspiysk

Gudata
Novyy Afon
A B K H A Z
A.S.S.R.
Elbrus 5633
Kodori
5203
Ordzhonikidze
Balta
Khasavyurt
Kizil Yurt
Buynaksk
Izberbash
Novokayakent

Sukhumi
Tkvarcheli
Tydubz
Dzhava
Tsogen
Kazbek 5047
Tebulos 4492
Agvali
Khunzakh
Akusha
Dogestanskiye Ogni

Ochamchire
Galn
Zugdidi
Rioni
G E O R G I A N
K
a
v
Tskhinvali (Staliniri)
Dusheti
Tyarata
Kakhib
Madzhalis
Derbent

Anaklia
Mikha-Tskhakaya
Kutaisi
Sachkhere
Tkibuli
Chiatura
Khashuri
Gori
Telavi
Kvareli
Lagodekhi
Kasumkent

Poti
S. S. R.
Samtredia
Zestafoni
Mtskheta
Kaspi
Gurdzhaani
D A G E S T A N A.S.S.R.
Akhti
Mikhaylovka

Kobuleti
Makharadze
Khulo
Borzhomi
Tbilisi
Signakhi
Alazan
Zakataly
Samur
Khachmas
Kuba
Divichi

Batumi
A D Z H A R
A.S.S.R.
Akhaltsikhe
Khrami
Manglisi
Shaumyani
Rustavi
Citeli-Ckaro
Mirzaani
Sheki (Nukha)
Bazar Dyuzi 4466
Baba dag 3629
Siazan

Hopa
Pazar
Akhalkalaki
Iori
Kura
Mingechaurskoye Vdkhr.
Kutkashen
Agdash
Shemakha
Mashtoga

Görele
Akçaabat
Artvin
Ardahan
3192
Alaverdi
Tauz
Mingechaur
Geokchay
Lyaki
Agsu
Surakhany
Artem

Trabzon
Rize
Kaçkar 3937
Ardanuç
Kisir
Çildir
Kirovakan
Kirovabad
Koshkana
Yevlakh
Shemakha
Sumgait
BAKU

rebolu
Gümüşhane
Çakirgöl 3063
D
a
E
g
l
a
r
i
Olt u
Aragats 4090
Ozero Sevan
Chanlar
Mir-Bashir
Barda
Kurdamir
Kazi Magamed
Alyata

Bayburt
Tortum
Narman
Sarikamis
Digor
A R M E N I A N
Echmiadzin
Yerevan
Kamo
Mir-Bashir
A Z E R B A I J A N S.S.R.
Terter
Agdzhabedi
Sobirabad
M. Byandovan

Gümüşhane
M
o
n
t
B
a
y
b
u
r
t
Şelim
Kağizman
S. S. R.
Mantuni
Aras
Agdam
Imishly
Kyurdamir

st from Greenwich
40
42
44
46
48
COPYRIGHT GEORGE PHILIP & SON LTD

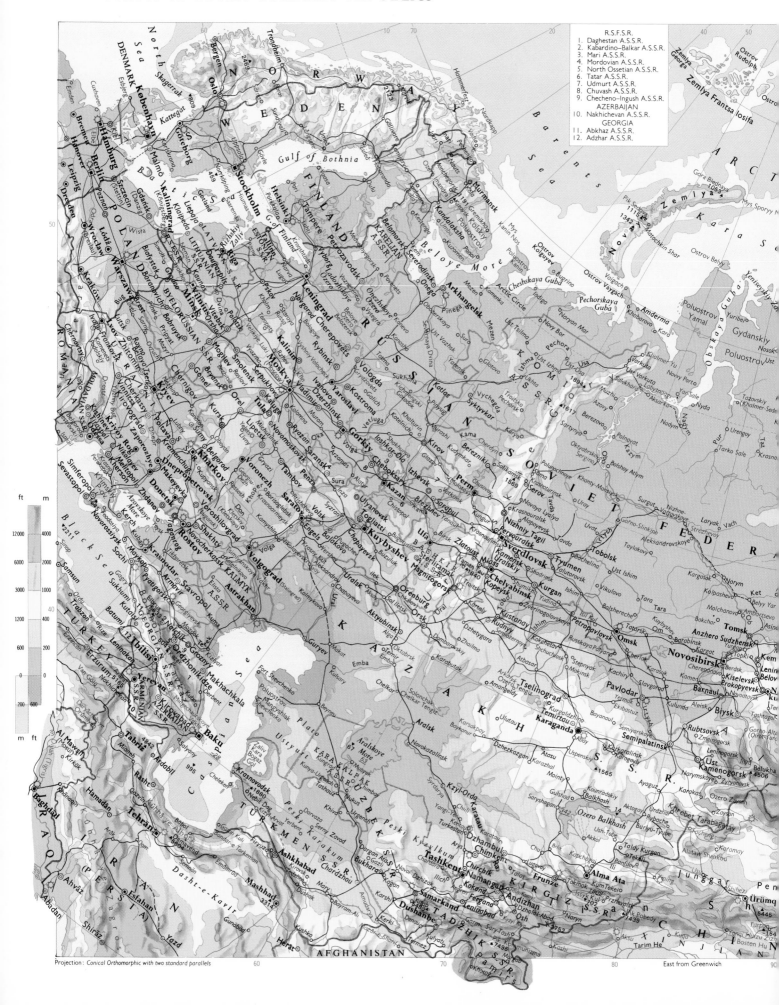

R.S.F.S.R.
1. Daghestan A.S.S.R.
2. Kabardino–Balkar A.S.S.R.
3. Mari A.S.S.R.
4. Mordovian A.S.S.R.
5. North Ossetian A.S.S.R.
6. Tatar A.S.S.R.
7. Udmurt A.S.S.R.
8. Chuvash A.S.S.R.
9. Checheno–Ingush A.S.S.R.
AZERBAIJAN
10. Nakhichevan A.S.S.R.
GEORGIA
11. Abkhaz A.S.S.R.
12. Adzhar A.S.S.R.

Projection: Conical Orthomorphic with two standard parallels   East from Greenwich

1:20 000 000

100   0   100   200   300   400   500 miles
100   0   200   400   600   800 km

OCEAN

Mys Dezhneva
(East C.)

St. Lawrence I.
(U.S.A.)

Severnaya
Zemlya

Laptev
Sea

East Siberian Sea

Ostrov Vrangelya

Chukotskoye
More

Bering
Sea

Poluostrov
Goryo Byrranga
Taymyr

Nordvik

Tiksi

Verkhoyansk

Khrebet Cherskogo

Okhotsko
Kolymskoye

Koryakskiy Khrebet

Petropavlovsk-
Kamchatskiy

Poluostrov
Kamchatka

Arctic Circle

YAKUT A.S.S.R

SOCIALIST REPUBLIC

Yakutsk

Vilyuysk

Sea of
Okhotsk

Sakhalin

Olekminsk

Kirensk

Bratsk

Nizhneudinsk

Komsomolsk

Khabarovsk

Sovetskaya Gavan

Yuzhno-Sakhalinsk

Krasnoyarsk

Cheremkhovo

Angarsk   Ulan Ude

Irkutsk

Chita

Blagoveshchensk

Birobidzhan

Hokkaidō

Sapporo

Hakodate

Ulaanbaatar
(Ulan Bator)

Qiqihar

Harbin

Ussuriysk

Vladivostok

Nakhodka

Sea of JAPAN

MONGOLIA

Changchun

Fushun

Shenyang

Anshan

Chǒngjin

North

Honshū

Niigata

GOBI

Saynshand

Dandong

Wǒnsan

Pyongyang

Seoul

South

Kanazawa

To-yama

Baotou

Zhangjiakou

Beijing

Lüda

Pusan

Sea of JAPAN

	Boundaries of U.S.S.R.
	Boundaries of S.S.R.
	Boundaries of A.S.S.R.

1:50 000 000

250   0   250   500   750   1000 miles

250   0   500   1000   1500   km

PACIFIC   OCEAN

Aleutian Is.

7822

Bering Sea

C. Dezhnev

Bering Str.

Kamchatka Peninsula

Klyuchevskaya Vol.
4850

Sredinny Ra.

Sea of Okhotsk

Sakhalin

Kurili Is.

Hokkaido

3776
Fuji San

Honshu

Japan

Sea of Japan

La Pérouse Str.

Korea Str.

Kyushu

Ryukyu Is.

Formosa

Guam

Bonin Is.

10 554

Tropic of Cancer

Cape Johnson
Deep
10 497

Philippine Is.

Luzon

Mindanao

Caroline Is.

11 000

New Guinea

Halmahera

Moluccas

Ceram

Banda Sea

Celebes Sea

Celebes

Molucca Strait

Makasar Strait

Borneo

Palawan

Kinabalu
4101

Sulu Sea

South China Sea

G. of Tonkin

Hainan

Si-kiang

Hong Kong (Red)

East China Sea

Great Plain of China

Hwang

Yellow Sea

Korea

Manchurian Plain

Great Khingan Mts.

Amur

Sungari

Stanovoy Ra.

Yablonovy Ra.

Verkhoyansk Range

Gydan Ra. (Kolyma)

Wrangel I.

New Siberian Is.

Kolyma

Indigirka

Aldan

Lena

Lower Tunguska

Olenek

Kotuy

Taimyr Peninsula

C. Chelyuskin

Severnaya Zemlya

ARCTIC   OCEAN

Lena

Central Siberian Plateau

Angara

Plateau of Mongolia

Sayan Mts.

Yenisei

Altai

Belukha
4506

Plateau

Tien Shan

Turfan Basin

Tarim

Lop Nor

Tokla Makan

Kunlun Shan

Koko Nor

Tsangpo

Plateau of Tibet

Everest
8882

Himalaya

Karakoram Ra.
8611

Pamirs

Hindu Kush

7495

Tarim Basin

L. Balkhash

Ili

Chu

Syr Darya

Amu Darya

Aral Sea

Turan Plain

Sulaiman Ra.

Thar Desert

Sutlej

Ganges

Yamuna

Brahmaputra

Irrawaddy

Salween

Mekong

Chao Phraya

G. of Thailand

Malay Peninsula

Str. of Malacca

Sumatra

Sunda Is.

Java

Bali

Lombok

Java Sea

East

Arafura Sea

Timor

Flores

Sunda Str.

Nicobar Is.

Andaman Is.

Bay of Bengal

Eastern Ghats

Godavari

Krishna

Deccan

Western Ghats

Narmada

Laccadive Is.

Maldive Is.

Gulf of Mannar

C. Comorin

Ceylon

Palk Strait

Equator

Chagos Arch.

INDIAN   OCEAN

Amirantes

Seychelles

Socotra

G. of Aden

Somali Peninsula

Ras Asir (C. Guardafui)

Red Sea

Arabian Sea

G. of Oman

Persian Gulf

Ar Rub' al Khali

Arabia

G. of Oman

Plateau of Iran

Elburz Mts.
5604

Great Salt Desert

Helmud

Hari Rud

Zagros Mts.

Tigris

Euphrates

Mesopotamia

Syrian Desert

Dead Sea

Sinai Pen.

Suez Canal

Nile

Libyan Desert

Red Sea

Taurus Mts.

Ararat
5165

Anatolia

Cyprus

Mediterranean Sea

Bosporus

Black Sea

Caucasus
Elbruz
5633

Caspian Sea

Ural

Ural Mountains

Ob
1640

Irtysh

Tobol

West Siberian Plain

Naronaya
1894

Ob

Narodnaya

Kara Sea

Novaya Zemlya

Barents Sea

Kolguyev

Kola Pen.

White Sea

N. Dvina

Finland

Baltic Sea

North European Plain

Central Russian Uplands

Don

Dnepr

Volga

Vistula

Oder

Elbe

Danube

Carpathians

Rhine

Adriatic Sea

North Sea

British Isles

Scandinavia

Iceland

Greenland

Arctic Circle

North Cape

Svalbard

Steppes

m   ft

6000   18 000
4000   12 000
2000   6000
1000   3000
400   1200
200   600
0   0

200   660
2000   6000
4000   12 000
6000   18 000
8000   24 000
m   ft

1:50 000 000

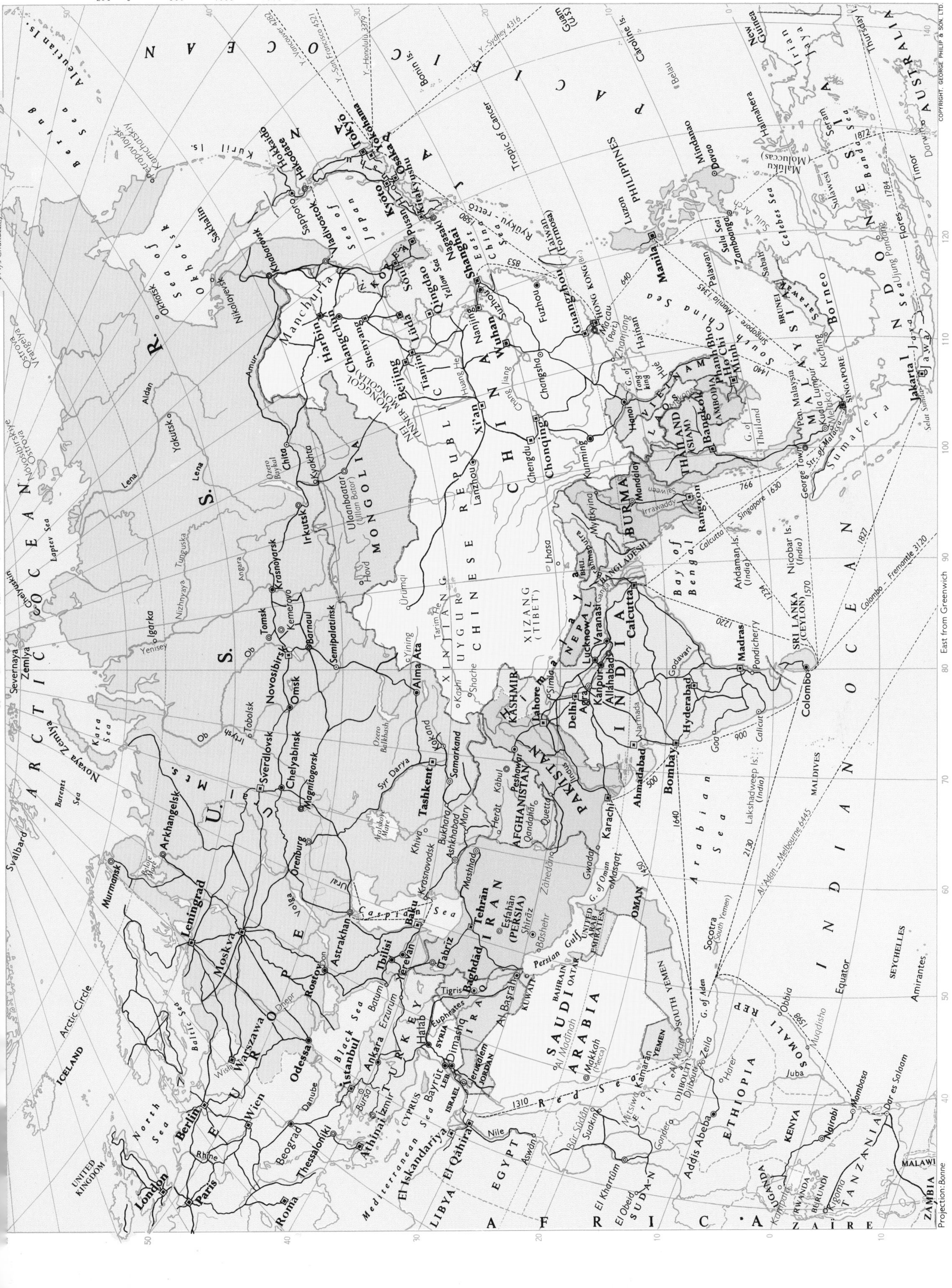

250 0 250 500 750 1000 miles

250 0 500 1000 1500 km

ARCTIC OCEAN

PACIFIC OCEAN

INDIAN OCEAN

Bering Sea

Aleutian Is.

Sea of Okhotsk

Kuril Is.

Sakhalin

Sea of Japan

JAPAN

Hokkaido

Tokyo Yokohama Osaka Kyoto Hakodate

HONSHU

Kyushu

Vladivostok

Khabarovsk

R. S. F. S. R.

U. S. S. R.

Manchuria

Harbin Changchun Shenyang

KOREA

Seoul Pusan

Beijing Tianjin

MONGOL (MONGOLIA)

INNER MONGOLIA

Ulanbaator (Ulan Bator)

Yellow Sea

Qingdao Jinan Nanjing Shanghai

East China Sea

CHINESE PEOPLE'S REPUBLIC

CHINA

Xi'an Lanzhou Wuhan

Chengdu Chongqing Changsha

Kunming Guangzhou Fuzhou

HONG KONG Macau Hainan

TAIWAN (FORMOSA)

PHILIPPINES

Luzon Manila Mindanao Davao

South China Sea

VIETNAM Hanoi Ho Chi Minh

LAOS CAMBODIA Phnom Penh

THAILAND (SIAM) Bangkok

BURMA Rangoon Mandalay

Irrawaddy

MALAYSIA Kuala Lumpur SINGAPORE

BRUNEI Borneo Sarawak Sabah

Celebes Sea Sulawesi

INDONESIA

Jakarta Sumatra Jawa Java Sea Borneo

Banda Sea Timor Moluccas

New Guinea Irian

AUSTRALIA

XIZANG (TIBET) Lhasa

UYGUR XINJIANG Urumqi Tarim He

Alma Ata Tashkent Samarkand Bukhara

KASHMIR Lahore Simla Delhi Agra

NEPAL BHUTAN

BANGLADESH Calcutta Dacca

INDIA

Lucknow Varanasi Kanpur Allahabad

Ahmadabad Bombay Hyderabad Madras

Bay of Bengal Andaman Is. Nicobar Is.

SRI LANKA (CEYLON) Colombo

MALDIVES Lakshadweep Is.

AFGHANISTAN Kabul Herat Qandahar

PAKISTAN Peshawar Quetta Karachi

IRAN (PERSIA) Tehran Esfahan Shiraz Mashhad Tabriz

Arabian Sea

OMAN Masqat UNITED ARAB EMIRATES QATAR BAHRAIN

SAUDI ARABIA Makkah (Mecca) Al Madinah

Persian Gulf KUWAIT Al Basrah

IRAQ Baghdad Euphrates Tigris

SYRIA Halab Dimashq LEBANON Bayrut

JORDAN ISRAEL Jerusalem

TURKEY Ankara Istanbul Izmir Erzurum Bursa

CYPRUS Mediterranean Sea

Black Sea Odessa Rostov

Moskva Leningrad Tbilisi Yerevan Baku

Caspian Sea Astrakhan Volga

EUROPE Warszawa Berlin Wien Beograd

London Paris Roma Athinai Thessaloniki

ICELAND UNITED KINGDOM

North Sea Baltic Sea Barents Sea Kara Sea

Novaya Zemlya Svalbard Murmansk Arkhangelsk

Sverdlovsk Chelyabinsk Magnitogorsk Omsk Novosibirsk

Tomsk Krasnoyarsk Irkutsk Chita Yakutsk

Lena Ob Yenisey Amur

YEMEN SOUTH YEMEN Aden G. of Aden Socotra

Red Sea EGYPT El Qahira El Iskandariya Nile

SUDAN El Khartum ETHIOPIA Addis Abeba

SOMALI REP. Muqdisho KENYA Nairobi Mombasa

TANZANIA Dar es Salaam UGANDA ZAIRE ZAMBIA MALAWI

AFRICA

Tropic of Cancer

East from Greenwich

Equator

Arctic Circle

COPYRIGHT GEORGE PHILIP & SON LTD.

Projection: Bonne

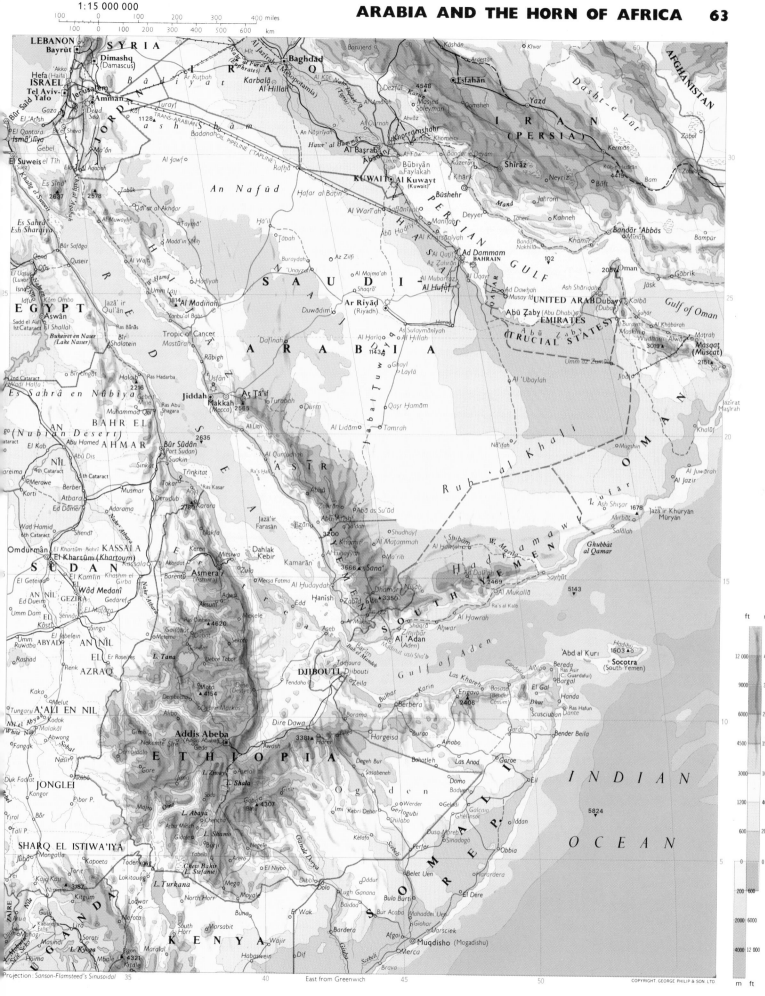

1:15 000 000

Projection: Sanson-Flamsteed's Sinusoidal

East from Greenwich

COPYRIGHT GEORGE PHILIP & SON LTD

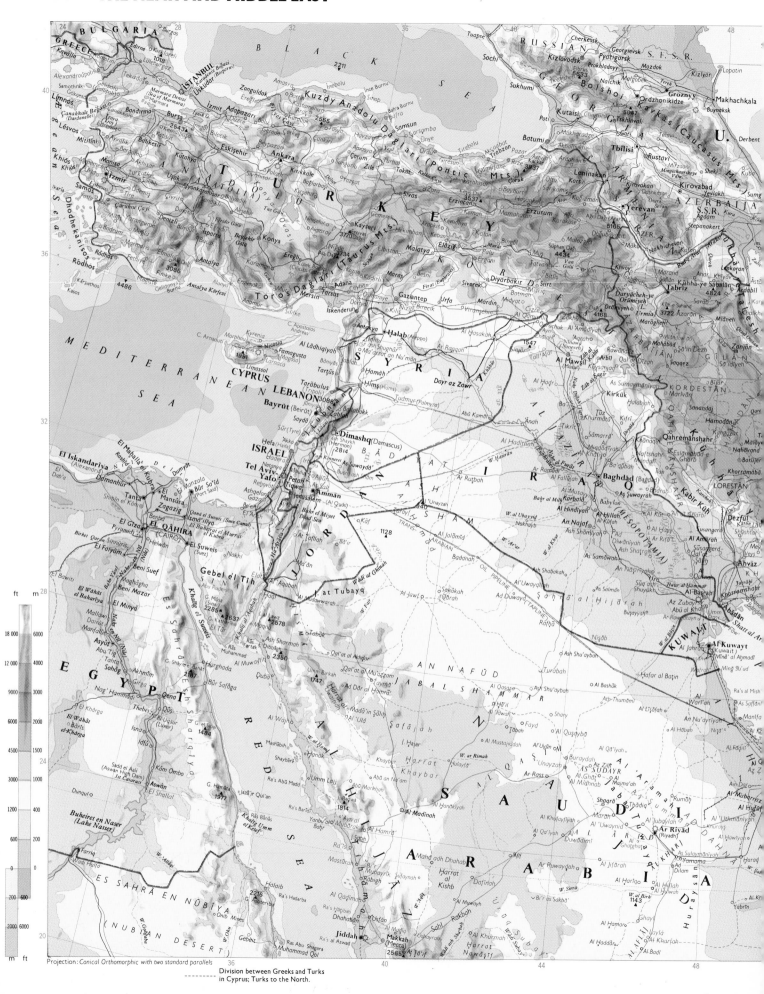

Division between Greeks and Turks
in Cyprus; Turks to the North.

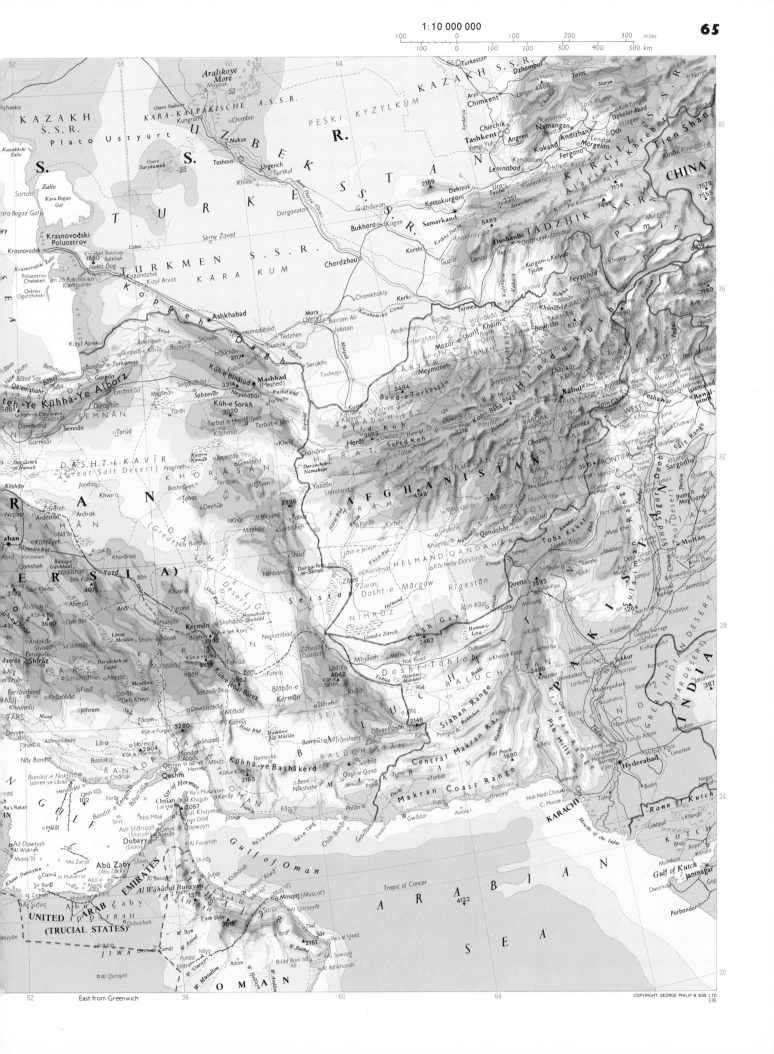

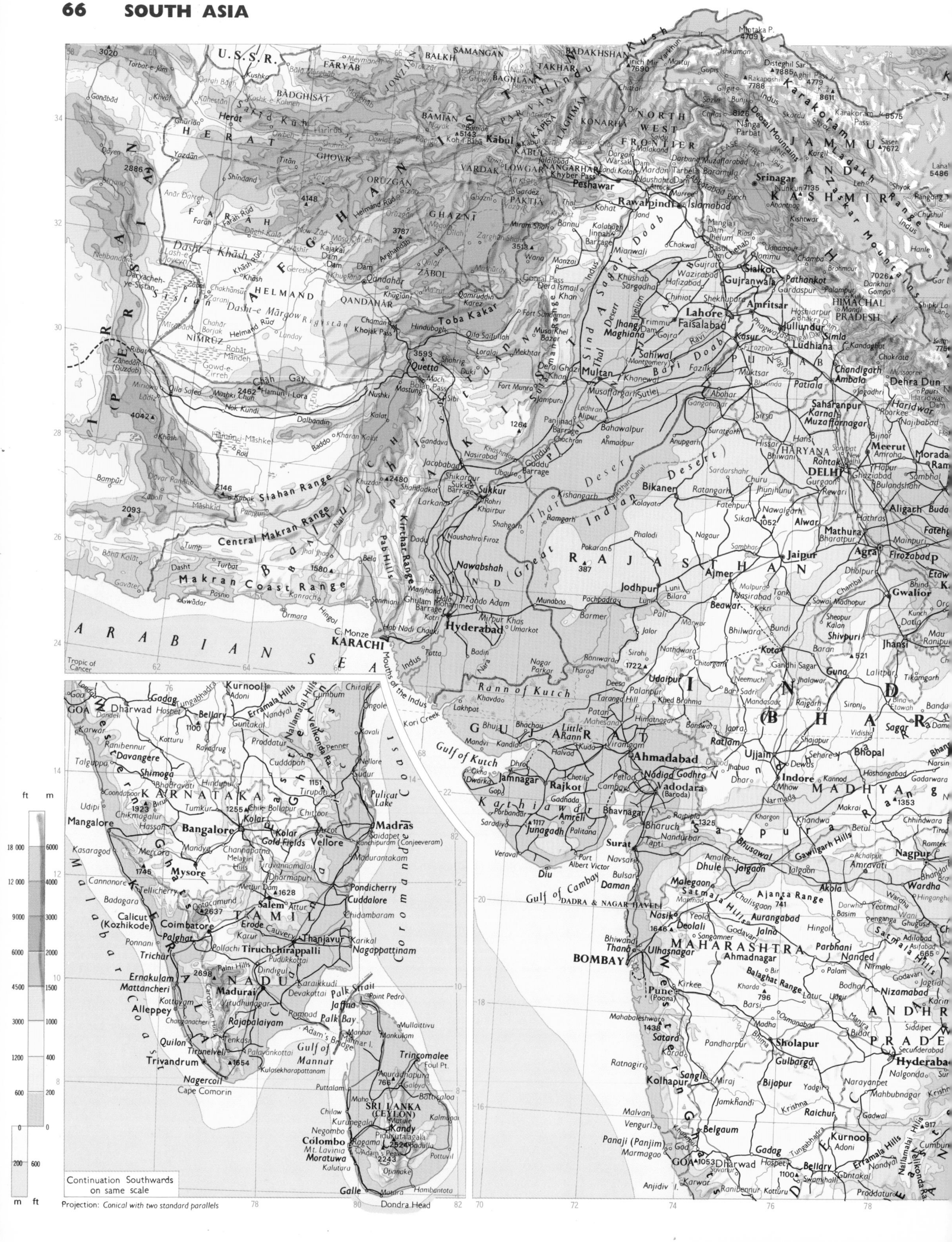

U.S.S.R.

AFGHANISTAN

HERAT · GHOWR · GHAZNI · HELMAND · NIMRUZ · ORŪZGĀN · QANDAHĀR · FARĀH · BADGHISĀT · FĀRYĀB · SAMANGAN · BALKH · JOWZJĀN · BAGHLĀN · TAKHAR · BADAKHSHAN · PARVĀN · KĀPISA · KONARHĀ · LAGHMAN · NANGARHĀR · PAKTIĀ · VARDAK · LOWGAR

Kabul · Kābul · Herāt · Qandahār · Quetta · Peshawar · Rawalpindi · Islamabad

NORTH WEST FRONTIER · JAMMU AND KASHMIR · Srinagar · HIMACHAL PRADESH

PAKISTAN

BALUCHISTAN · SIND · PUNJAB

Karachi · Hyderabad · Sukkur · Multan · Lahore · Amritsar · Faisalabad · Gujranwala · Sialkot

Makran Coast Range · Central Makran Range · Siahan Range · Kirthar Range · Pab Hills

ARABIAN SEA

Tropic of Cancer

Mouths of the Indus · Kori Creek

INDIA

RAJASTHAN · Thar (Great Indian) Desert · Jaipur · Jodhpur · Ajmer · Bikaner · Udaipur · Kota

HARYANA · DELHI · Meerut · Aligarh · Mathura · Agra · Gwalior · Jhansi

PUNJAB · Ludhiana · Chandigarh · Ambala · Dehra Dun · Haridwar · Saharanpur

GUJARAT · Ahmadabad · Rajkot · Jamnagar · Vadodara (Baroda) · Surat · Bhavnagar · Junagadh · Bharuch · Kathiawar · Little Rann · Rann of Kutch · Gulf of Kutch · Gulf of Cambay

MADHYA PRADESH · Indore · Bhopal · Ujjain · Ratlam · Nagpur · Satpura Range

MAHARASHTRA · Bombay · Pune (Poona) · Nasik · Aurangabad · Sholapur · Kolhapur · Satara · Ajanta Range · Ajanta Hills

ANDHRA PRADESH · Hyderabad · Secunderabad · Gulbarga · Bijapur

Daman · Diu · DADRA & NAGAR HAVELI

GOA · Panaji (Panjim) · Marmagao · Belgaum

Continuation (southern inset)

KARNATAKA · Bangalore · Mysore · Mangalore · Hubli · Dharwad · Bellary · Kurnool · Adoni · Bijapur

TAMIL NADU · Madras · Coimbatore · Madurai · Salem · Tiruchchirappalli · Vellore · Pondicherry · Cuddalore · Thanjavur · Tirunelveli · Trichur · Calicut (Kozhikode) · Trivandrum · Quilon · Nagercoil · Cape Comorin · Alleppey · Ernakulam · Mattancheri

Palghat · Palni Hills · Cardamom Hills · Nilgiri Hills

Gulf of Mannar · Palk Strait · Palk Bay · Adam's Bridge

Coromandel Coast · Malabar Coast

SRI LANKA (CEYLON) · Colombo · Moratuwa · Kandy · Jaffna · Trincomalee · Galle · Negombo · Anuradhapura · Dondra Head · Adam's Peak 2243 · Mt. Lavinia

Mannar I. · Point Pedro · Foul Pt.

Scale (left margin)

ft	m
18 000	6000
12 000	4000
9000	3000
6000	2000
4500	1500
3000	1000
1200	400
600	200
0	0
200	600

m · ft

Continuation Southwards on same scale

Projection: Conical with two standard parallels

1:10 000 000

50   0   50   100   150   200 miles
50   0   50   100   150   200   250   300 km

XINJIANG

UYGUR Shan Hoh Xil Shan

QINGHAI

C H I N E S E   R E P U B L I C

Bayan Har Shan

Ngoring Hu
Gyaring Hu
Maqên Gangri
Darlag

SICHUAN

XIZANG   Tanggula (Dangla) Shan

Tanggula Shankou

Siling Co

Nam Co

Nyainqêntanglha Shan

Lhasa

Xigazê   Gyangzê

Maquan He (Tsangpo)

Yarlung Zangbo Jiang (Brahmaputra)

ARUNACHAL PRADESH

NEPAL

Dhaulagiri 8221
Katmandu
Everest 8848
Kanchenjunga 8598

SIKKIM   BHUTAN

Darjeeling

Gorakhpur

Patna

Varanasi (Banaras) (Benares)

B I H A R

ASSAM

Gauhati
Shillong
MEGHALAYA
Cherrapunji

NAGALAND

MANIPUR
Imphal

Tura

WEST BENGAL

BANGLADESH

Dacca

TRIPURA
Agartala

MIZORAM

Comilla

Chittagong

CHIN

B U R M A

Jamshedpur
Haora   CALCUTTA
Kharagpur

Barisal

Mandalay

SHAN

Ranchi

O R I S S A

Cuttack
Bhubaneswar
Puri
Chilka Lake

Berhampur
Chatrapur

KAYAH

THAILAND (SIAM)

Chiengmai

Vishakhapatnam

B A Y   O F   B E N G A L

Rambre Kyun
Manaung Kyun

Rangoon

Gulf of Martaban

I N D I A N   O C E A N

Preparis North Channel
Pariparit Kyun (Burma)
Preparis South Channel
Koko Kyunzu (Burma)

Moscos
Maungmagan Is.
Islands
Lauingion Bok Is.

Tavoy

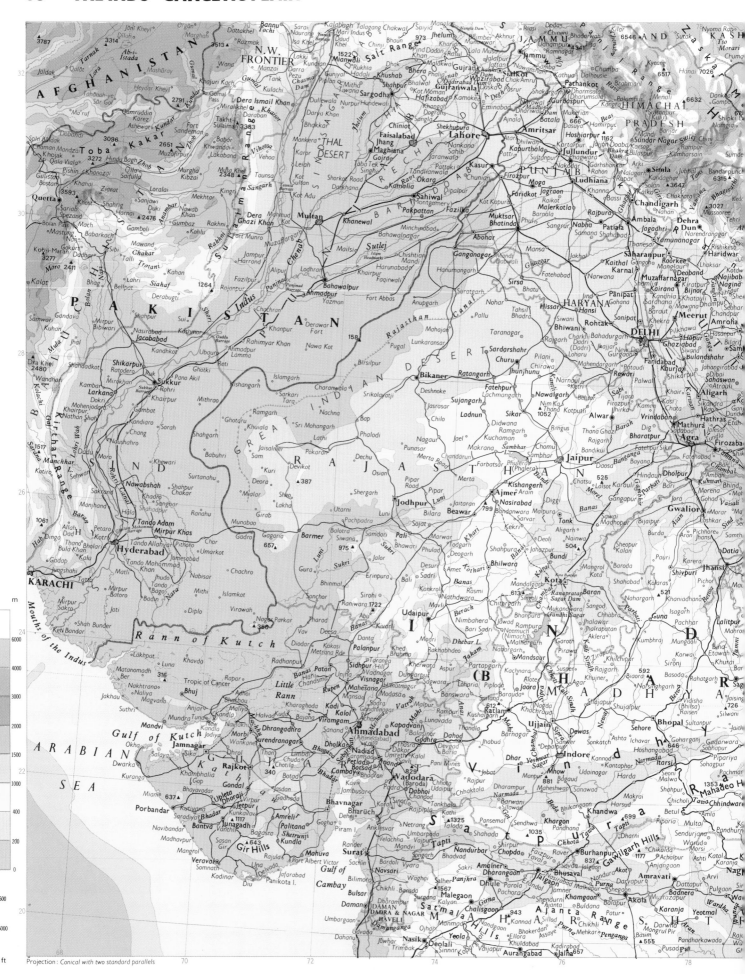

1:6 000 000

50   50   100   150 miles
50   0   50   100   150   200   250 km

S. ASIA: IRRIGATION
1:40 000 000
Irrigated Areas

CHINESE REPUBLIC

CHINESE REPUBLIC
TIBET

AFGHANISTAN   KASHMIR
Tarbela Dam   Mangla Dam
PAKISTAN   Jhelum   Bhakra Dam   NEPAL
Taunsa Barrage   Indus   Beas   Ganga   Gogra   BANGLA-   Brahmaputra
Guddu Barrage   Sutlej   Nangal Barrage   Triveni   DESH
Sukkur Barrage   Chenab   Yamuna   Canals   BURMA
Ghulam   Chambal   Ramganga   Ganga   Damodar   Barkal   Irrawaddy
Mohammad (Kotri)   Gandhi Sagar   Dehri   Rihand   Dam   Lake
Barrage   Rihand Dam   Damodar
Tropic of Cancer   Narmada   Dukwan   Mahanadi   Hirakud Dam
Kakrapar   Tapti
Khadakvasla   Bhima   Krishna   Rajahmundry
Lloyd Dam   Tungabhadra   Nagarjuna Sagar
INDIA   Tungabhadra Dam   Penner
Mettur   Cauvery
Dam
SRI LANKA

CHINESE REPUBLIC

G X I Z A N G

CHINESE REPUBLIC
T I B E T

CHINESE REPUBLIC

BAY OF BENGAL

Mouths of the Ganga
The Sandheads

CALCUTTA

BANGLADESH
DACCA

NEPAL

BHUTAN

SIKKIM

MEGHALAYA

TRIPURA

ASSAM

RAJSHAHI

O R I S S A

Mt Everest
8848

Kanchenjunga
8598

Lucknow

Allahabad

Varanasi (Banares, Benares)

Patna

Gaya

Ranchi

Jamshedpur

Jabalpur

Bilaspur

Raipur

Bhilai

Durg

Bhubaneswar

Cuttack

Puri

Chilka Lake

Kharagpur

Raurkela

Sambalpur

Hirakud Dam

Darjeeling

Gangtok

Katmandu

Lalitapur   Bhaktapur

Gorakhpur

Faizabad

Bahraich

Gonda

Darbhanga

Muzaffarpur

Bhagalpur

Munger

Bogra

Pabna

Kushtia

Khulna

Jessore

Barisal

Comilla

Agartala

Dhanbad

Asansol

Durgapur

Ranchi

Sunderbans

East from Greenwich

COPYRIGHT GEORGE PHILIP & SON LTD

1:6 000 000

50   0   50   100   150 miles
50   0   50   100   150   200   250 km

MADHYA PRADESH

MAHARASHTRA

Ajanta Range

Satmala Hills

Balaghat Range

BOMBAY

Thana
Kalyan
Nasik
Deolali
Ahmadnagar
Aurangabad
Jalna
Nanded

Pune (Poona)
Sholapur
Gulbarga
Kolhapur
Sangli
Miraj
Bijapur
Raichur
Secunderabad
HYDERABAD
Nizamabad
Karimnagar
Warangal

Belgaum
GOA
Panaji (Panjim)
Marmagao
Margao

KARNATAKA

Dharwad
Hospet
Bellary
Kurnool
Nellore
Gudur

Davangere
Chitradurga
Anantapur
Cuddapah
Tirupati

Mangalore
Udipi
Chikmagalur

BANGALORE
Mysore
Kolar Gold Fields
Vellore
MADRAS

Calicut
(Kozhikode)
Coimbatore
Salem
Pondicherry
Cuddalore

TAMIL NADU

Cochin
Ernakulam
Alleppey
Madurai
Tiruchchirappalli
(Trichinopoly)
Thanjavur (Tanjore)
Nagappattinam

Quilon
Trivandrum
Tuticorin
C. Comorin

ARABIAN SEA

BAY OF BENGAL

Coromandel Coast

Gulf of Mannar
(Manaar)

Vishakhapatnam

Vijayawada
(Bezwada)
Guntur
Machilipatnam (Bandar)

Rajahmundry
Kakinada (Cocanada)

SRI LANKA
(CEYLON)

SRI LANKA
On same scale

Palk Strait
Palk Bay
Jaffna
Jaffna Lagoon
Elephant Pass
Mannar I.
Trincomalee
Anuradhapura
Puttalam
Negombo
COLOMBO
Dehiwala
Moratuwa
Kandy
Galle
Matara
Dondra Head

Adam's Bridge
Palk Bay

ft   m
6000 2000
4500 1500
3000 1000
1200   400
600   200
0   0
200   600
2000 6000
4000 12 000
m   ft

Projection: Conical with two standard parallels

East from Greenwich

COPYRIGHT. GEORGE PHILIP & SON. LTD

1:10 000 000

50   0   50   100   150   200 miles
50   0   100   200   300 km

CHINA

INDIA

BANGLADESH

CHIN

BURMA

Mandalay
Maymyo
Meiktila
Minbu
Prome
Pegu
Bassein
Rangoon
Moulmein
Maulamyaing
Gulf of Martaban

KAYAH
Chiengmai
Lampang

THAILAND
(SIAM)

Nakhon Sawan
Phra Nakhon
Si Ayutthaya
Bangkok (Krung Thep)
Thonburi
Samut Prakan
Chon Buri

Nakhon Ratchasima
(Khorat)

Khorat

Phanom Dang Rek

LAOS

Luang Prabang
Vientiane

VIETNAM

Hanoi
Haiphong
Gulf of
Tongking

Hainan
Dao

Nanning

Da Nang (Tourane)
Hué

CAMBODIA

Tonlé Sap
Battambang
Phnom Penh

Phanh Bho
Ho Chi Minh (Saigon)

Andaman
Islands
North
Andaman
Middle
Andaman
South
Andaman

Preparis North Channel
Preparis South Channel
Koko Kyunzu (Burma)
Coco Channel

ANDAMAN
SEA

Moscos
Islands

Myeik Kyúnzu
(Mergui)

Archipelago)

Tavoy

Kho Khot Kra
Chumphon
(Isthmus of Kra)

G. of Thailand
(Siam)

Surat Thani
Nakhon Si Thammarat

Phuket

SOUTH CHINA SEA

George
Town
Butterworth
Pulau
Pinang
Ipoh

PENINSULAR
MALAYSIA

Kuala Lumpur
Kelang
Seremban
Melaka

Kuala Terengganu
Kuala Dungun

Kuantan

SUMATERA
INDONESIA

Johor Baharu
SINGAPORE

Kepulauan
Natuna Besar

INDONESIA

PENINSULAR MALAYSIA
AND SINGAPORE
1:6 000 000

50   0   50 miles
50   0   50 km

THAILAND
(SIAM)

PERLIS
Alor Setar
KEDAH
George Town
Butterworth
Bukit Mertajam
PINANG
Taiping
PERAK
Ipoh
Kampar
Telok
Anson

KELANTAN
Kota Baharu
Kuala Terengganu

TERENGGANU

PAHANG
Kuantan

SELANGOR
Kuala Lumpur
Petaling Jaya
Kelang
NEGERI
Seremban   SEMBILAN
MELAKA
Melaka
Bandar Maharani
(Muar)
Bandar Penggaram
(Batu Pahat)

JOHOR
Keluang

SUMATERA
INDONESIA

Johor Baharu
SINGAPORE
Straits of Singapore

Strait of Malacca

Projection : Conical with two standard parallels

East from Greenwich

COPYRIGHT GEORGE PHILIP & SON LTD

ft   m
9000   3000
6000   2000
4500   1500
3000   1000
1200   400
600   200
0   0
200   600
2000   6000
m   ft

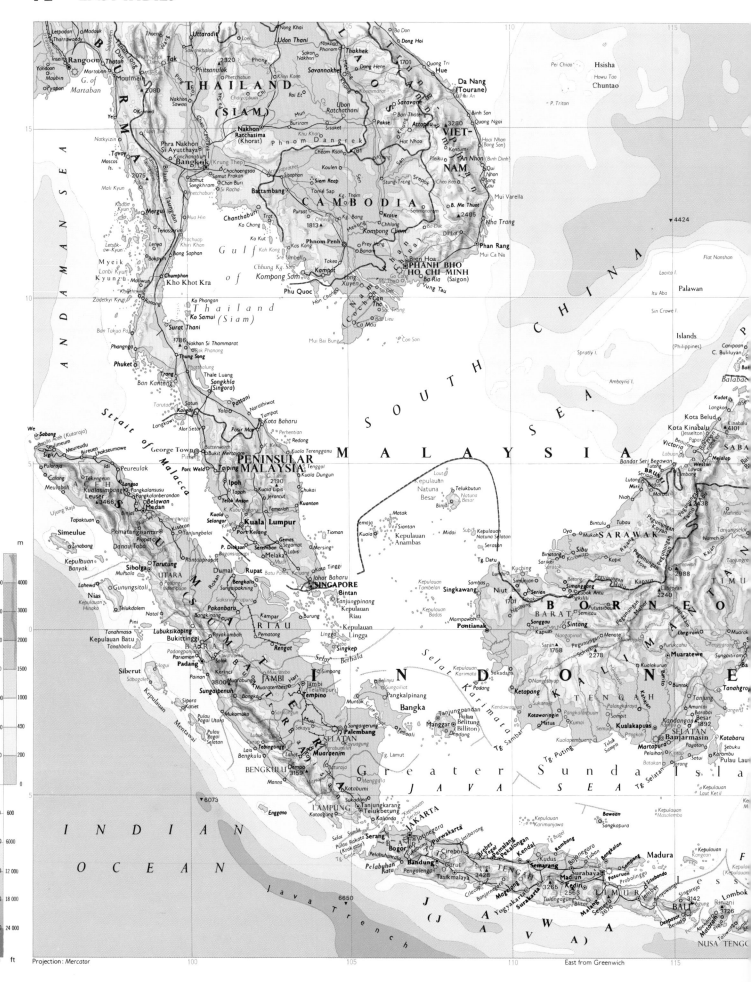

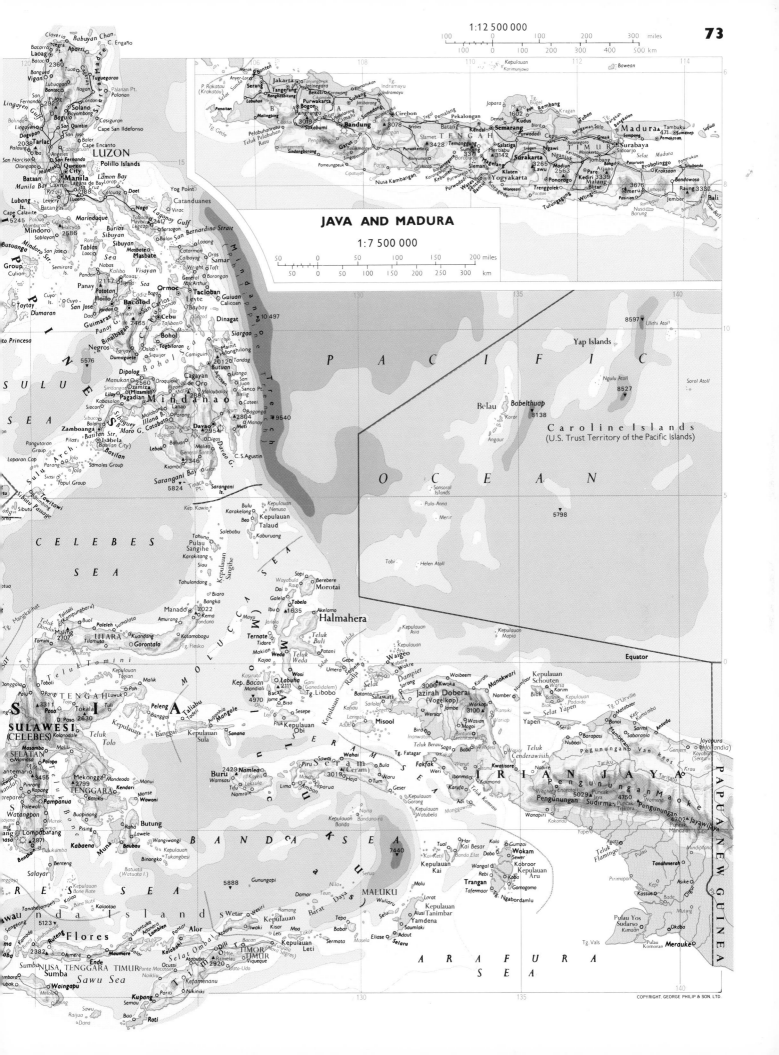

1:12 500 000

100   0   100   200   300 miles

100   0   100   200   300   400   500 km

JAVA AND MADURA

1:7 500 000

50   0   50   100   150   200 miles

50   0   50   100   150   200   250   300 km

LUZON

PHILIPPINE

SULU
SEA

CELEBES

SEA

Mindanao

SULAWESI
(CELEBES)

S U L A W E S I

TENGAH

SELATAN

TENGGARA

PACIFIC

OCEAN

Yap Islands

Caroline Islands
(U.S. Trust Territory of the Pacific Islands)

Belau   Babelthuap

Equator

Halmahera

MOLUCCA SEA

Ternate

MALUKU

SERAM SEA

Seram (Ceram)

Buru

BANDA   SEA

IRIAN JAYA

Pengunungan Maoke

Pegunungan
Sudirman

Pengunungan

Teluk
Cenderawisih

Jazirah Doberai
(Vogelkop)

Misool

Waigeo

PAPUA NEW GUINEA

Kepulauan
Kai

Kepulauan
Aru

Flores

NUSA TENGGARA TIMUR

TIMOR
TIMUR

A R A F U R A

S E A

Merauke

COPYRIGHT. GEORGE. PHILIP & SON. LTD.

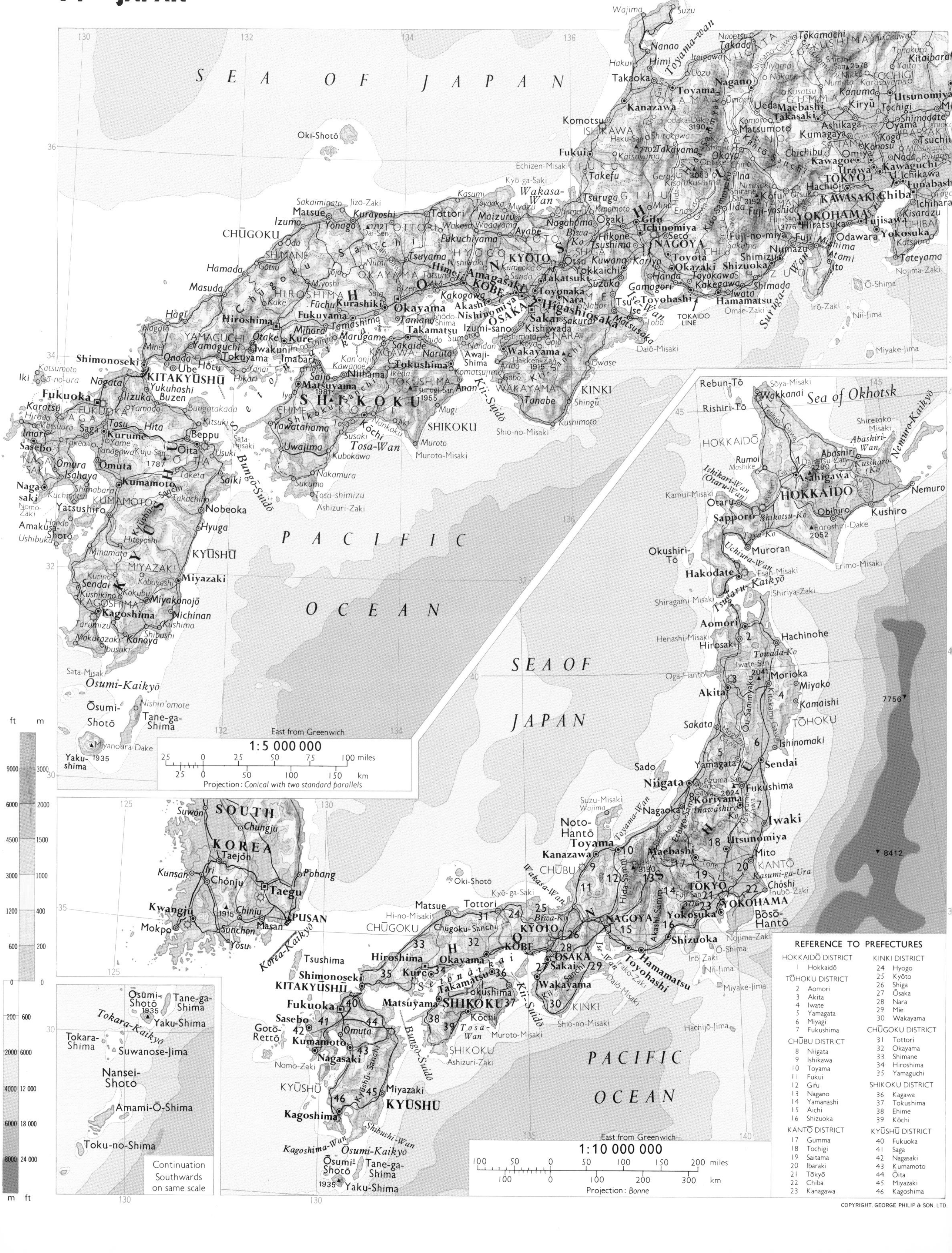

SEA OF JAPAN

PACIFIC OCEAN

SEA OF JAPAN

Sea of Okhotsk

CHŪGOKU
SHIKOKU
KYŪSHŪ
HOKKAIDŌ
TŌHOKU
KANTO
CHŪBU
KINKI

SOUTH KOREA

Major places:
Wajima, Suzu, Suzu-misaki, Nanao, Takada, Tōkamachi, Shirakawa, Kitaibara, Himi, Toyama-wan, NIIGATA, TOCHIGI, Takaoka, Nagano, Naoetsu, Nakano, Nikkō 2578, Kanazawa, Toyama, Uozu, Kusatsu, Maebashi, Ashikaga, Utsunomiya, Fukui, Komotsu, ISHIKAWA, Matsumoto, Takayama 3190, Kumagaya, Kiryū, Tochigi, Urawa, Echizen-Misaki, Katsuyama, GUMMA, Chichibu, Kōga, Kōnosu, Hachiōji, TOKYO, Ichikawa, Funabash, Takefu, Ontake 3063, Iida, Kōfu 3776, KAWASAKI, Chiba, Ichihara, Tsuruga, GIFU, Ichinomiya, NAGOYA, Toyota, YOKOHAMA, Fujisawa, Kisarazu, Tateyama

Matsue, Kurayoshi, Tottori, Maizuru, Ayabe, KYOTO, Hikone, Tsushima, Okazaki, Shizuoka, Hamamatsu, Hiroshima, Fukuyama, Okayama, KOBE, OSAKA, Himeji, Akashi, Nishinomiya, Sakai, Wakayama, Nara, Ise, Toyohashi

SHIKOKU, Matsuyama, Kōchi, Tokushima, Takamatsu, Uwajima, Tosa-Wan, Muroto, Kii-Suidō

KYŪSHŪ, Fukuoka, KITAKYŪSHŪ, Shimonoseki, Nagasaki, Kumamoto, Kagoshima, Miyazaki, Sasebo, Ōita, Beppu, Oita

HOKKAIDŌ, Sapporo, Asahigawa, Otaru, Hakodate, Kushiro, Nemuro, Muroran, Obihiro, Aomori, Hirosaki, Hachinohe, Akita, Morioka, Miyako, Kamaishi, Sendai, Yamagata, Niigata, Kōriyama, Fukushima, Iwaki, Sado

Ōsumi-Shotō, Tane-ga-Shima, Yaku-Shima, Tokara-Kaikyō, Tokara-Shima, Suwanose-Jima, Nansei-Shotō, Amami-Ō-Shima, Toku-no-Shima

Korea: Suwŏn, Chungju, Taejŏn, Kunsan, Chŏnju, Iri, Kwangju, Taegu, Chinju, Masan, PUSAN, Mokpo, Yŏsu, Sunchŏn, Tsushima

1:5 000 000
25 0 25 50 75 100 miles
25 0 50 100 150 km
Projection: Conical with two standard parallels
East from Greenwich

1:10 000 000
100 50 0 50 100 150 200 miles
100 0 100 200 300 km
Projection: Bonne
East from Greenwich

Continuation Southwards on same scale

ft	m
9000	3000
6000	2000
4500	1500
3000	1000
1200	400
600	200
0	0
600	200
6000	2000
12 000	4000
18 000	6000
24 000	8000
m	ft

REFERENCE TO PREFECTURES

HOKKAIDŌ DISTRICT		KINKI DISTRICT	
1	Hokkaidō	24	Hyogo
TŌHOKU DISTRICT		25	Kyōto
2	Aomori	26	Shiga
3	Akita	27	Ōsaka
4	Iwate	28	Nara
5	Yamagata	29	Mie
6	Miyagi	30	Wakayama
7	Fukushima	**CHŪGOKU DISTRICT**	
CHŪBU DISTRICT		31	Tottori
8	Niigata	32	Okayama
9	Ishikawa	33	Shimane
10	Toyama	34	Hiroshima
11	Fukui	35	Yamaguchi
12	Gifu	**SHIKOKU DISTRICT**	
13	Nagano	36	Kagawa
14	Yamanashi	37	Tokushima
15	Aichi	38	Ehime
16	Shizuoka	39	Kōchi
KANTO DISTRICT		**KYŪSHŪ DISTRICT**	
17	Gumma	40	Fukuoka
18	Tochigi	41	Saga
19	Saitama	42	Nagasaki
20	Ibaraki	43	Kumamoto
21	Tōkyō	44	Ōita
22	Chiba	45	Miyazaki
23	Kanagawa	46	Kagoshima

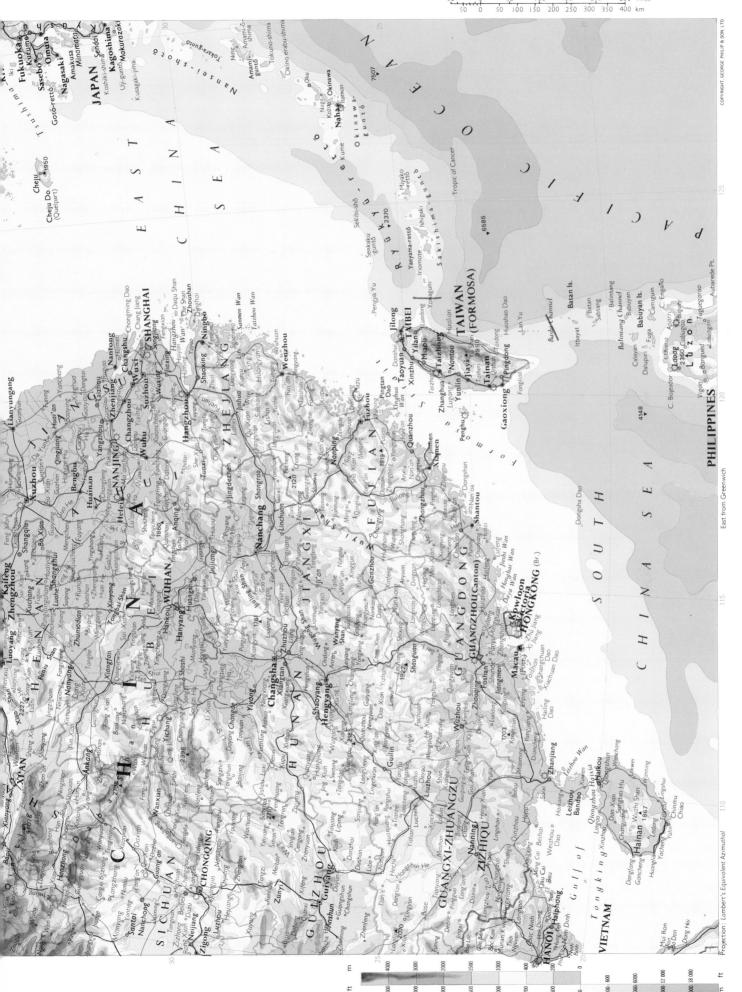

1:10 000 000

50   0   50   100   150   200   250   miles

50   0   50   100   150   200   250   300   350   400   km

PACIFIC OCEAN

EAST CHINA SEA

JAPAN

Fukuoka
Kurume
Omuta
Sasebo   Minamata
Nagasaki   Amakusa   Kagoshima   Makurazaki
Gotō-rettō

Tsushima

Iki

Koshiki-shima
Uji-guntō
Kusagaki-jima

Cheju
Cheju Do
(Quelpart)

Tokara-guntō
Nase

Amami-o-shima
Amami-guntō
Oku
Tokuno-shima

Okino erabu-shima

Nansei-shotō

Kume
Naha   Okinawa
Okinawa-guntō

7507

Nago

Kōzu

Miyako-rettō

Tropic of Cancer

Sekishi-shō   2370
Yoka-guni   Yaeyama-guntō
Iriomote   Ishigaki

Senkaku   Sakishima-guntō
guntō

6585

Batan Is.
Batan
Sabtang

Balintang

Babuyan Is.
Babuyan
Camiguin
Fuga
Dalupiri

RYUKYU   IS.

SOUTH CHINA SEA

CHINA

SHANGHAI

JIANGSU

Lianyungang
Xuzhou

HENAN

Kaifeng
Zhengzhou
Luoyang

XI'AN

SHAANXI

ANHUI

NANJING
HUBEI
WUHAN
Hankou
Hanyang

HUNAN

Changsha
Hengyang

GUIZHOU
Guiyang

CHONGQING

SICHUAN

GUANGXI-ZHUANGZU

Nanning

ZIZHIQU

VIETNAM

HANOI
Haiphong

Gulf of

Tongking

Hainan
Haikou

ZHEJIANG

Hangzhou
Ningbo
Wenzhou

JIANGXI

Nanchang

FUJIAN

Fuzhou

Quanzhou

Xiamen

GUANGDONG

GUANGZHOU
(Canton)

Macau
(Port.)

HONGKONG
(Br.)
Kowloon
Victoria

Shantou

Zhanjiang

Leizhou
Bandao

TAIWAN
(FORMOSA)

Jilong
TAIBEI
Taizhong
Tainan   3950
Gaoxiong

Penghu
Liedao

Dongsha Dao

Pratas

PHILIPPINES

Luzon

Aparri

C. Engaño

C. Bojeador

4148

Vigan

Bashi Channel

Balintang Channel

ft   m   m   ft

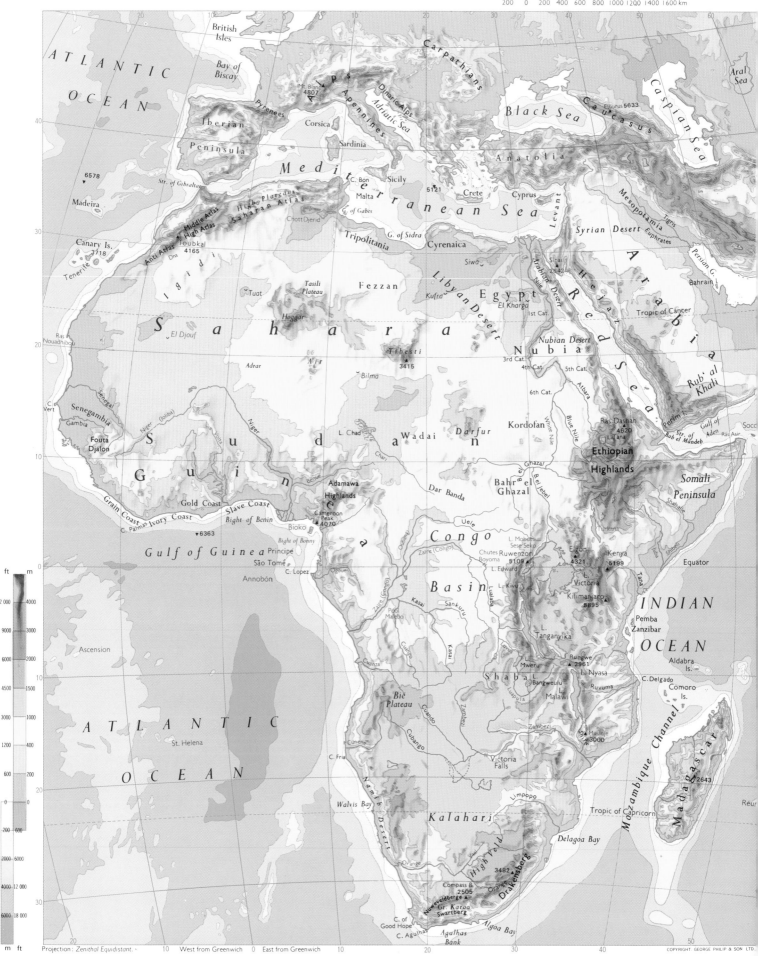

1 : 40 000 000

Projection: Zenithal Equidistant.

COPYRIGHT GEORGE PHILIP & SON LTD.

1:40 000 000

200 0 200 400 600 800 1000 miles
200 0 200 400 600 800 1000 1200 1400 1600 km

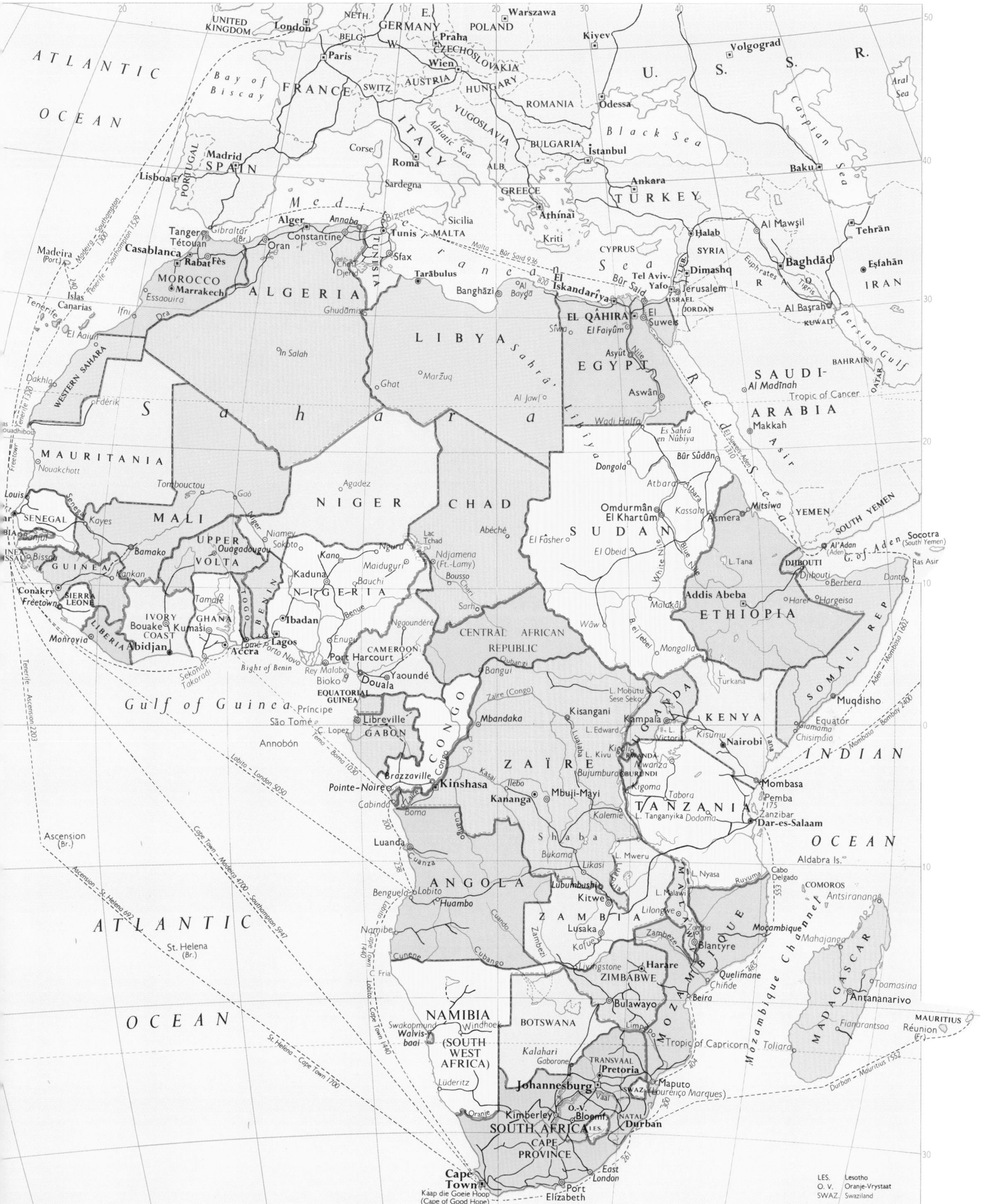

Projection: Zenithal Equidistant.

West from Greenwich   East from Greenwich

COPYRIGHT. GEORGE PHILIP & SON. LTD.

LES.   Lesotho
O.V.   Oranje-Vrystaat
SWAZ. Swaziland

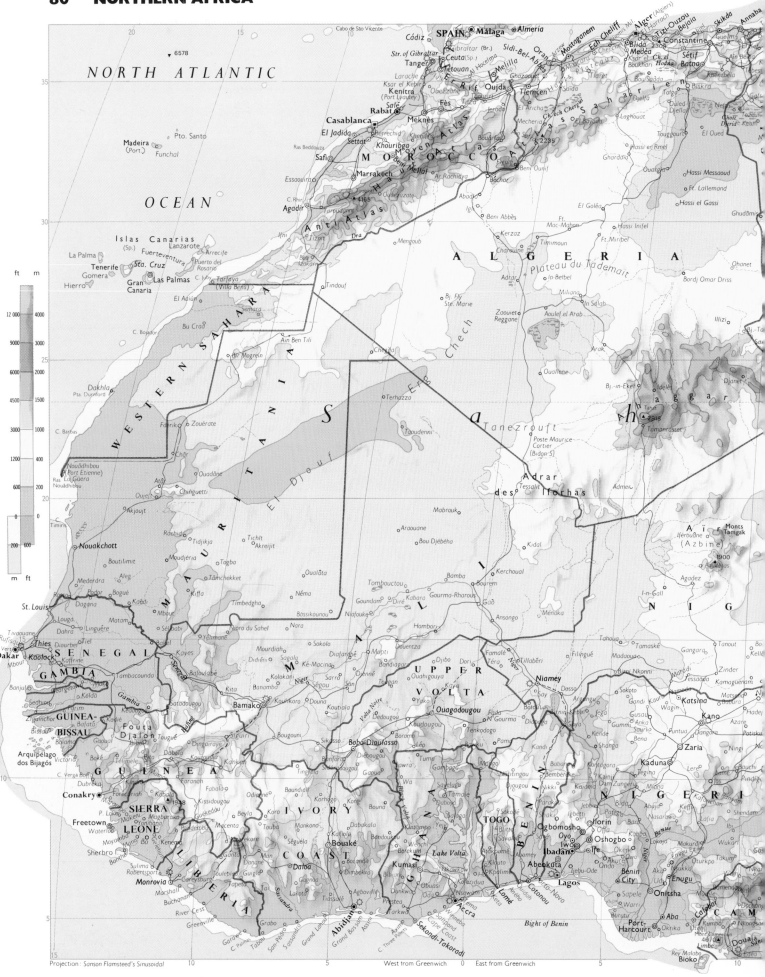

▲ 6578

NORTH ATLANTIC

OCEAN

Madeira
(Port.)
Pto. Santo
Funchal

Islas Canarias
(Sp.)
Lanzarote
Fuerteventura
La Palma
Arrecife
Tenerife
Sta. Cruz
Puerto del
Rosario
Gomera
Gran
Canaria
Las Palmas
Hierro

Cabo de São Vicente
Cádiz
SPAIN
Málaga
Almería
Gibraltar (Br.)
Str. of Gibraltar
Tanger
Ceuta (Sp.)
Melilla
Al Hoceima
Tétouan
Larache
Oued Zem
Kenitra
(Port Lyautey)
Salé
Rabat
Casablanca
El Jadida
Berrechid
Settat
Meknès
Fès
Taza
Khouribga
Safi
Essaouira
Marrakech
C. Rhir
Agadir
Ifni
C. Juby
Tarfaya
(Villa Bens)
El Aaiún
Semara
Bu Craâ
C. Bojador
Ain Ben Tili
Bir Mogrein
Zouérate
Fderik
Dakhla
Pta. Durnford
C. Barbas
Nouâdhibou
(Port Étienne)
Ras La Güera
Nouâdhibou
Akjoujt
Atâr
Chinguetti
Ouadâne
Oujeft
Timirist
Nouakchott
Boutilimit
Moudjéria
Togba
Mederdra
Aleg
Tâmchekket
Rachid
Tidjikja
Tichît
Akreijit
Kiffa
Néma
Oualâta
Bou Djébéha
Araouane
Timbedgha
Bossikounou
Niafouke
Tombouctou
Goundam
Diré
Kabara
Gourma-Rharous
Bamba
Gaô
Kerchoual

MOROCCO
Haut Atlas
Moyen Atlas
Anti Atlas
Taroudant
Ouarzazate
Beni Mellal
Ar Rachidya
Figuig
Beni Ounif
Béchar
Abadla
Ig
Beni Abbès
Adrar
Kerzaz
Timimoun
Charouine
Mengoub
Dra
Tiznit
Bou
Izakarn
WESTERN SAHARA
MAURITANIA
El Djouf
Chegga
Terhazza
Taoudenni
Er

SAHARA
Tanezrouft
Poste Maurice
Cortier
(Bidon 5)
Adrar
des Iforhas
Tessalit
Admer
Kidal
Mabrouk

ALGERIA
Plateau du Tademaït
Adrar
In-Belbel
Bj. Fly
Ste. Marie
Zaouiet
Reggane
Aoulef el Arab
Arak
Ouallene
Ft.
Mac-Mahon
Hassi Inifel
In Salah
Miliana
Bj.-in-Eker
Idelès
Tahat
2918
Tamanrasset
Djanet
Bj.-Tal
Illizi
El Goléa
Ghardaïa
Ouargla
Hassi Messaoud
Ft. Lallemand
Hassi el Gassi
Ghudâmis
Ghadâmès
Ohanet
Bordj Omar Driss

Ech Cheliff
Mostaganem
Oran
Mascara
Saïda
Mecheria
El Bayadh
Laghouat
Djelfa
Bou Saâda
Hodna
Ksar el
Boukhari
Médéa
Blida
Alger (Algiers)
Tizi-Ouzou
Bejaia
Sétif
Constantine
Guelma
Skikda
Annaba
Batna
Biskra
Touggourt
El Oued
Gabès
Chott
Djerid
El Golea

Tlemcen
Oujda
Jerada
El Aricha
Ain Sefra
Méchéria

HAGGAR
Aïr
Iférouâne
(Azbine)
Monts
Tamgak
Agadez
I-n-Gall
Anou Araren
In-Abangarit

St. Louis
Rufisque
C. Vert
Dakar
Kaolack
Thiès
Louga
Dahra
Tivaouane
Diourbel
Linguère
Matam
Podor
Bogué
Kaédi
Mbout
Sélibabi
Yélimané
Nioro du Sahel
Nara
Hombori
Douentza
Bandiagara
Mopti
Djenné
Ké-Macina
Ségou
Niono
Sokolo
Diafarabé
Sansanding
Goundam

SENEGAL
GAMBIA
Banjul
Ziguinchor
GUINEA-BISSAU
Bissau
Bolama
Arquipélago
dos Bijagós
Bafatá
Gabú
Koundara
Labé
Télimélé
Boké
Victoria
Dubréka
Conakry
SIERRA
LEONE
Freetown
Waterloo
Sherbro I.
Bonthe
Sulima

Kaffrine
Tambacounda
Kédougou
Bafoulabé
Kayes
Kita
Bamako
Koulikoro
Kati
Banamba
Kolokani
Ségou
Douentza

MALI
NIGER
Gao
Ansongo
Ménaka
Tahoua
Tamaské
Madaoua
Birni Nkonni
Dosso
Gaya
Niamey
Tillabéri
Téra
Filingué
Gangara
Tanout
Zinder
Maradi
Tessaoua
Katsina
Kano
Zaria
Kaduna

UPPER
VOLTA
Ouahigouya
Yako
Ouagadougou
Koudougou
Dédougou
Nouna
Tougan
Bobo-Dioulasso
Banfora
Gaoua
Tenkodogo
Fada N'Gourma
Diapaga
Kandi
BENIN
Natitingou
Djougou
Parakou
Nikki
Kandi
Gummi
Gusau
Sokoto
Gwandu
Argungu

GUINEA
Fouta
Djalon
Tougué
Dabola
Dinguiraye
Siguiri
Kankan
Kouroussa
Kissidougou
Faranah
Beyla
Kérouané
Macenta
N'Zérékoré
Guéckédou
Kabala
Makeni
Magburaka
Bo
Kenema
Pendembu
Koidu

IVORY
COAST
Odienné
Korhogo
Boundiali
Séguéla
Touba
Man
Danané
Daloa
Gagnoa
Divo
Dimbokro
Bouaké
Katiola
Dabakala
Bondoukou
Boundiali
Ferkéssédougou
Bouna
Agboville
Tiassalé
Grand Bassam
Abidjan
Sassandra
San Pédro
Tabou

LIBERIA
Monrovia
Marshall
Robertsport
Buchanan
River Cess
Greenville
Harper
Tapeta
Ganta
Gbarnga
Zwedru

GHANA
Tamale
Yendi
Salaga
Wa
Bolgatanga
Sunyani
Kumasi
Obuasi
Dunkwa
Prestea
Tarkwa
Sekondi-Takoradi
Cape Coast
Winneba
Accra
Ada
Ho
Lake Volta
Black Volta
Volta Noire
White Volta
Oti
Axim
Three Points

TOGO
Sokodé
Atakpamé
Blitta
Palimé
Lomé
Anécho

BENIN
Savalou
Abomey
Bohicon
Ouidah
Cotonou
Porto-Novo

NIGERIA
Ilorin
Offa
Ogbomosho
Oyo
Iwa
Oshogbo
Ede
Ife
Ijebu-Ode
Ibadan
Abeokuta
Lagos
Shagamu
Benin
City
Onitsha
Enugu
Aba
Port-
Harcourt
Owerri
Kaduna
Zaria
Kano
Gusau
Funtua
Jebba
Kontagora
Minna
Abuja
Bida
Lokoja
Makurdi
Lafia
Keffi

Bight of Benin
CAMEROON
Mt. Cameroon
4070
Limbe
Douala
Bioko
Rey Malabo
Kumba

Projection: Sanson Flamsteed's Sinusoidal

West from Greenwich | East from Greenwich

ft m
12 000 4000
9000 3000
6000 2000
4500 1500
3000 1000
1200 400
600 200
0 0
200 600
m ft

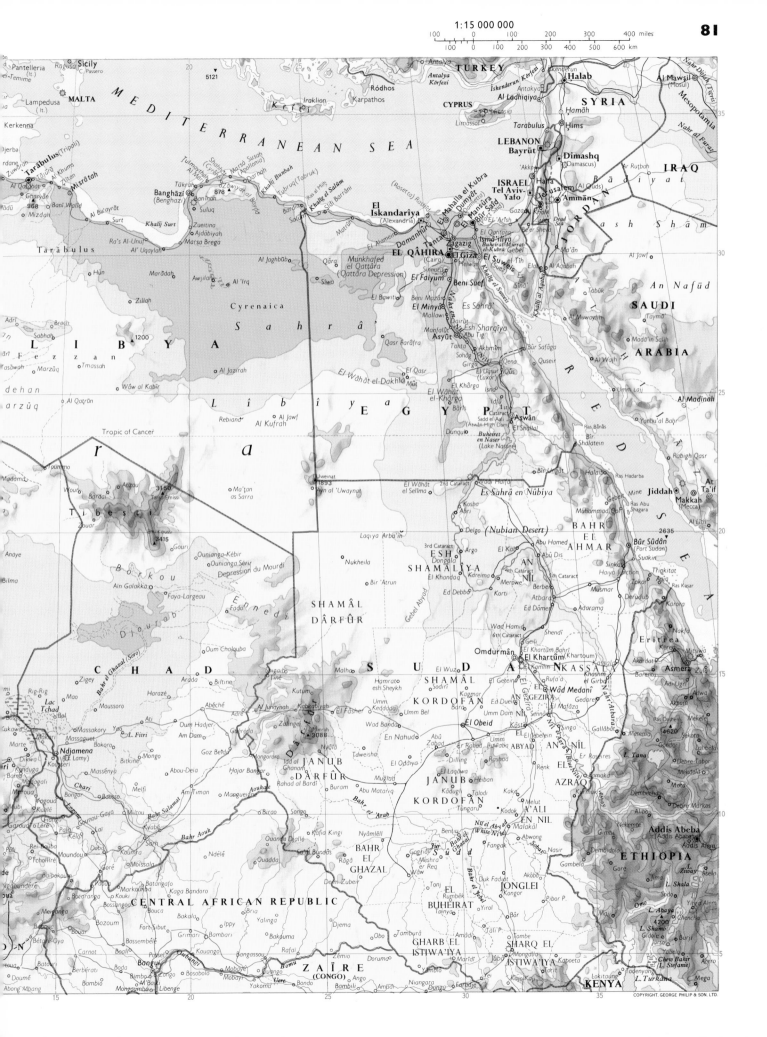

1:15 000 000

100   0   100   200   300   400 miles
100   0   100   200   300   400   500   600 km

MEDITERRANEAN SEA

TURKEY

Pantelleria (It.)
el-Temime
Lampedusa (It.)
MALTA
Kerkenna

Sicily
Ragusa
C. Passero

5121

Ródhos
Kríti
Iraklion
Karpathos

Antalya
Antalya Körfezi
İskenderun Körfezi
İskenderun
Halab
Al Mawşil (Mosul)

CYPRUS
Nicosia
Limassol
Al Ladhiqiya
Tarabulus
SYRIA
Hamāh
Hims
Dimashq (Damascus)
Ar Rutbah
IRAQ

Nahr Dijlah Tigris
Mesopotamia
Nahr al Furat

Tarābulus (Tripoli)
Al Khums
Misrātah
Zuwārah
Al Qabbah
Gharyān
968
Mizdah
Banī Walīd

Banghāzī (Benghazi)
878
Al Bu'ayrāt
Surt
Khalij Surt
Zueitina
Ajdābiyah
Marsa Brega
Ra's Al-Unūf
Al' Uqaylah

Tarābulus

LIBYA

Fezzan
Sabhah
Marzūq
Brach
Tmassah
Zillah
Hūn
Marādah
Awjilah
Al 'Iraq

Cyrenaica
Sahrâ'
Al Jaghbūb
Qāra
Munkhafed el Qattâra (Qattara Depression)
Siwa

El Iskandarîya (Alexandria)
Damanhûr
Tanta
Zagazig
EL QÂHIRA (Cairo)
EL GIZA
Helwân
El Faiyûm
Beni Suef

Rashid (Rosetta)
Mahalla el Kubra
El Mansûra
Bûr Sa'id
Dumyât
El Qantara
El 'Arîsh
Khân

ISRAEL
Tel Aviv-Yafo
Jerusalem (El Quds)
Ammān
Dead Sea
Be'er Sheva
Ma'ân

JORDAN

LEBANON
Bayrūt
Akko
Haifa

Al 'Aqabah
Tabūk
An Nafūd
SAUDI
ARABIA
Taymā'
Madâ'in Salih

Adrî
Sabhât
Tasāwah

dehan
arzûq

Al Qatrūn

Madama
Tummo

Tibesti
Zouar
Emi Koussi
3415

Bardaï
Aozou
3150
Tarso Emissi

Ennedi
Fada
Gouro
Ounianga-Kébir
Ounianga Sérir
Depression du Mourdi

Bodele
Djourab
Ain Galakka
Faya-Largeau

Bilma

Anaye

Tropic of Cancer
Rebiana
Al Jawf
Al Kufrah

Ma'tan as Sarra

1893
Uweinat
'Ayn al 'Uwaynat

Lîbîye
Sahrâ'

El Jazirah
Wāw al Kabīr

EGYPT

El Bawiti
El Wâhât el-Dakhla
El Qasr
Mût
El Qasr Farâfra

El Minya
Mallawi
Manfalût
Asyût
Sohâg
Girga
El Wâhât el-Khârga
El Khârga
Bâris

Es Sahrâ'
Esh Sharqîya
Abu Tig
Akhmîm
Qena
Isna
Idfu
Kôm Ombo
Aswân
(Aswan High Dam)
Sadd el Aali
El Shallâl
Dunqul

Es Sahrâ
en Nûbiya

Bûr Safâga
El Qusseir
El Uqsur (Luxor)
Qûs

Gebel
Ras Bânâs
Bîr Shalatein

Al Wâjh
Umm Lajj
Al Madinah

Yanbu' al Bahr

Rabigh Qasr

RED SEA

2nd Cataract
Wâdi Halfa
El Selîma
El Wâhât

Bîr Ungat
Halaïb
Ras Hadarba

Mine
Gebel Elba
Ras Abu Shagara

Jiddah
Makkah (Mecca)
At Ta'if
Al Lith

CHAD

Lac Tchad
Rig-Rig
Zigey
Mao
Bol

Ndjamena (El Lamy)
Kousseri
Massakory
Massaguet
Bokoro
Bitkine

SHAMÂL
DÂRFÛR

Nukheila

Bir 'Atrun

ESH
SHAMÂLIYA
Dongola
El Khandaq
Kareima
Merowe

3rd Cataract
Argo
Abu Hamed
Delgo
(Nubian Desert)
BAHR
EL AHMAR

Bûr Sûdân (Port Sudan)
Suakin

Laqiya Arba'in
Laqiya Arba'in

4th Cataract
5th Cataract
Muhammad Qol
Ras Abu Shagara

AN
NÎL
Berber
Atbara
Ed Dâmer
Adorama

Musmar
Haiya Junction
Trinkitat
Tokar
Derudub
Agig
Ras Kasar
Karora

2635

Sinkat

Wâd Hamid
6th Cataract
Shendi
Geili
Omdurmân
EL Khartûm Bahri
EL KHARTÛM
Khartoum

KASSALA
Kassala
El Girba

Eritrea
Akordat
Keren
Nakfa
Mitsiwa
Asmera

CENTRAL AFRICAN REPUBLIC

Biltine
Harazé
Tiné
Kutum
Kabkabiya
El Fasher
Malha
Umm Keddada

SHAMÂL
KORDOFAN

El Geteina
Wad Medanî
EL GEZIRA
El Mafâza
Gedaref

Sodiri
Hamrato esh Sheikh
Umm Bel
Wad Banda
En Nahud
Abû Zabad
Dilling
Rashad
Heiban

AN
NÎL
Rufa'a
Kâmlin
Sennâr
Singa
Ed Dueim
Umm Ruwaba
El Obeid

Barentu
Teseney
Gonder
L. Tana
4620
Debre Tabor

Kassab
Abéché
Adré
Am Dam
Goz Beïda
Biltine

DÂR
FÛR
Zalingei
Nyala
3088
Jebel Marra

JANUB
DÂRFÛR

Ghereda
Mongororo
Bîrkat
Ghanam

Rahad el Bardî
Buram
Abu Matariq
Mugläd

Umm Dam
ABYAD
El Odaiya
El Laqôwa
Kâdugli
Talodi
Kaka
Kodok

JANUB
KORDOFAN
Tungaru
N'ALI
EN NÎL
Malakâl

El Fûla
Renk

EL
AZRAQ
Er Roseires
Kurmuk

Er Rahad
Dembidolo
Nekemte

Addis Abeba
(Addis Ababa)
Addis Alem

ETHIOPIA

Moussoro
Massénya
Abou-Deia
Hajar Bangar
Am Timan
Aouk
Birao
Sorigo

Bahr
el Arab

Ed Da'ein
El Laqôwa

BAHR
EL
GHAZAL

Buram
Rafaï

Radôm
Derm Zubeir
Wâw
Meshra er Req
Gogriol
Tonj
El Rumbêk
EL BUHEIRAT
Toinya
Yirol
Bôr

JONGLEI
Kongor
Pibor P.

Ntl el Abyad (White Nile)
Bentiu
Fangak
Abwong
Nasir
Gambela

L. Ziway

Dembecha
Debre Markos

Mota

Nekemte
Gimbi

4200
L. Abaye
L. Shamo
Chencha
Burji

Garoua
Rei-Bouba
Tcholliré
Baïbokoum
Bozoum

Ippy
Bria
Yalinga
Bakouma
Djema
Obo
Tambura
Amâdi
Tombe
Kapoeta

GHARB EL
ISTIWA'IYA
SHARQ EL
ISTIWA'IYA

L. Stefanie
Chew Bahir

Chari
Bongor
Moundou
Doba
Goré
Moïssala
Batangafo
Markounda
Kouki
Bossangoa
Bossembélé
Bangui

Ndélé
Ouadda
Ouanga Djallé
Kafia Kingi
Nyâmléll
Raga

Yoye
Mega
L. Turkana

ZAÏRE
(CONGO)

Bangassou
Rafaï
Zémio
Djabal
Maridî
Jûbâ
Yei
Kajo Kaji

KENYA

COPYRIGHT. GEORGE PHILIP & SON. LTD.

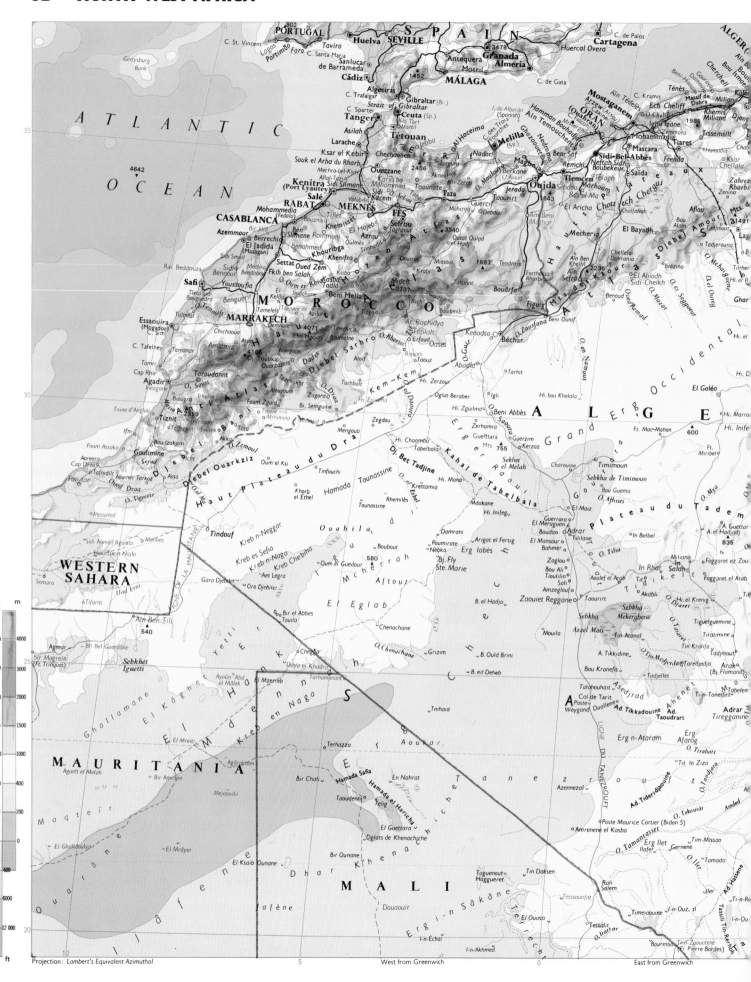

Projection: Lambert's Equivalent Azimuthal

West from Greenwich   East from Greenwich

1:8 000 000

50   0   50   100   150   200 miles

50   0   50   100   150   200   250   300 km

MEDITERRANEAN SEA

SICILY
Etna
3340
Marsala
CATANIA
Agrigento
Caltanissetta
Siracusa
Ragusa
C. Spartivento
C. Passero

Pantelleria
(Italian)

Linosa I.
Lampione I.
Lampedusa

Gozo
Valletta
MALTA

Menzel
Bourguiba
Bizerte (Binzert)
Annaba
Skikda
Jijel
Bejaia
El Kseur
El Kala
Tabarka
Mateur
Halq el Oued
TUNIS
Guelma
Souk Ahras
Béja
Jendouba
Zaghouan
Nabeul
Hammamet
G. de Hammamet
Kelibia
R. Mostefa
C. Bon
Menzel-Temime
Kairouan
Kalaa-Kebira
SOUSSE
Monastir
Moknine
El Mahdia
Djem
Rass Kaboudia
Djebiniana

CONSTANTINE
2004
Bordj bou
Arreridj
El Eulma
Sétif
Aïn M'lila
Batna
Biskra
Khenchela
2328
Tébessa
Thala
Sbeitla
Hadjeb El Aïoun
Sfax
Iles Kerkenna
1338
Fériana
Gafsa
Maharès
Kneiss Is.
1165
G. de Gabès
Djerba
Gabès
Djerba I.
El Kantara
Zarzis

CONSTANTINE
Batna
Chott el Hodna
Saâda
Ouled Djellal
Chott Melrhir
El Meghaïer
Touggourt
El Oued
Nefta
Tozeur
Chott el Fedjadj
Kebili
Hamma
Douz
Ksar Rhilane
Médenine
Ben Gardane
Zarzis
Bahiret el Bibane

Ouargla
Hassi Messaoud
B. Lahrache
B. Sif Fatima
Dehibat
Nālūt
Sināwan
Ghudāmis
Daraj
Tarābulus
(Tripoli)
Tājūrā
Al Khums
Zlītan
Misrātah
Khalij Surt
(Gulf of Sidra)

Banghāzī
(Benghazi)

Al Hammādah al Hamrā'

SABHAH
Sabhah (Sebha)

L I B Y A

Marzūq

Idehan Marzūq

Tropic of Cancer

Ténéré

Sarīr Tibasti

NIGER

CHAD

Tibesti
Emi Koussi
3415

COPYRIGHT GEORGE PHILIP & SON. LTD.

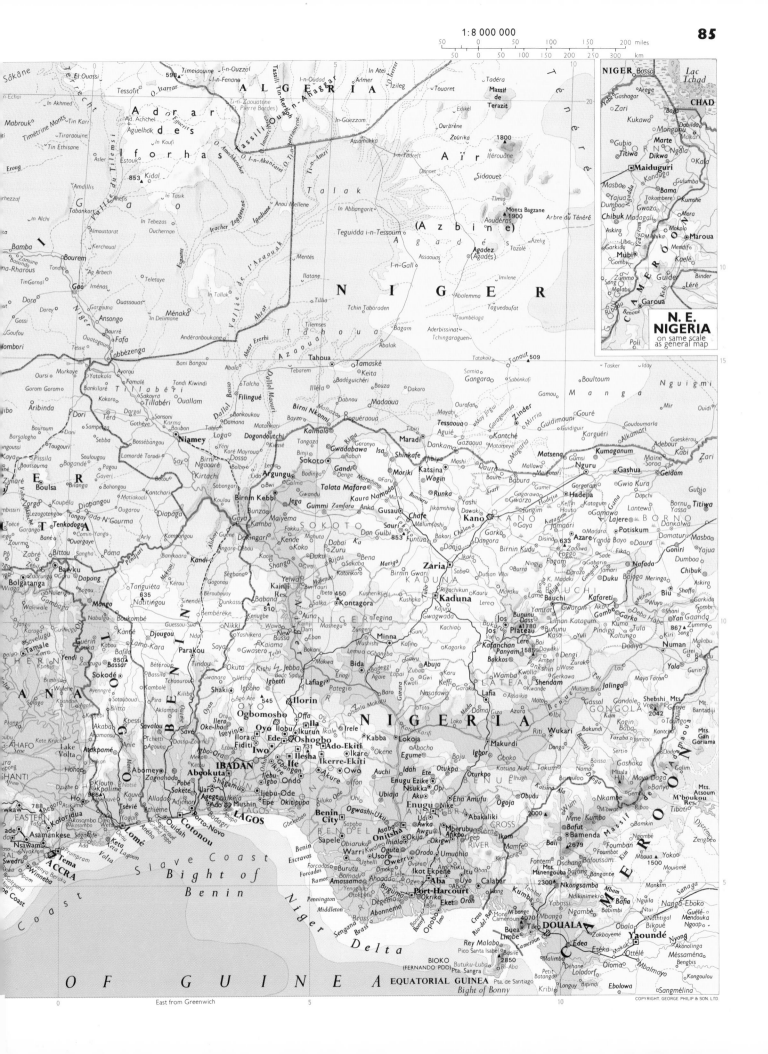

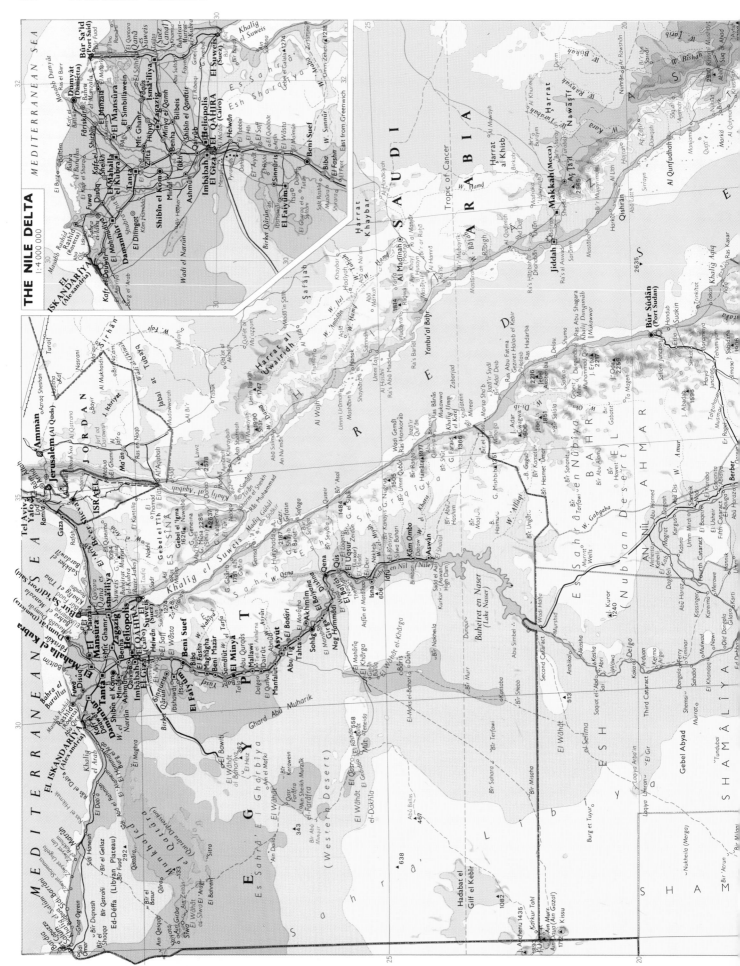

THE NILE DELTA
1:4 000 000

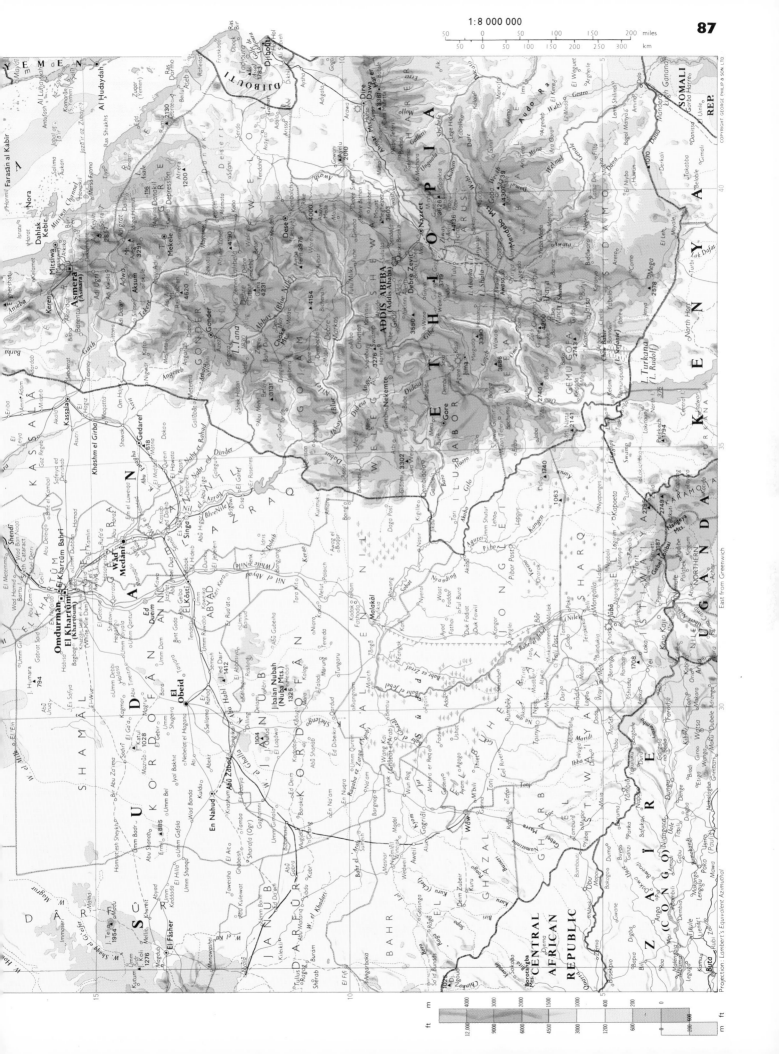

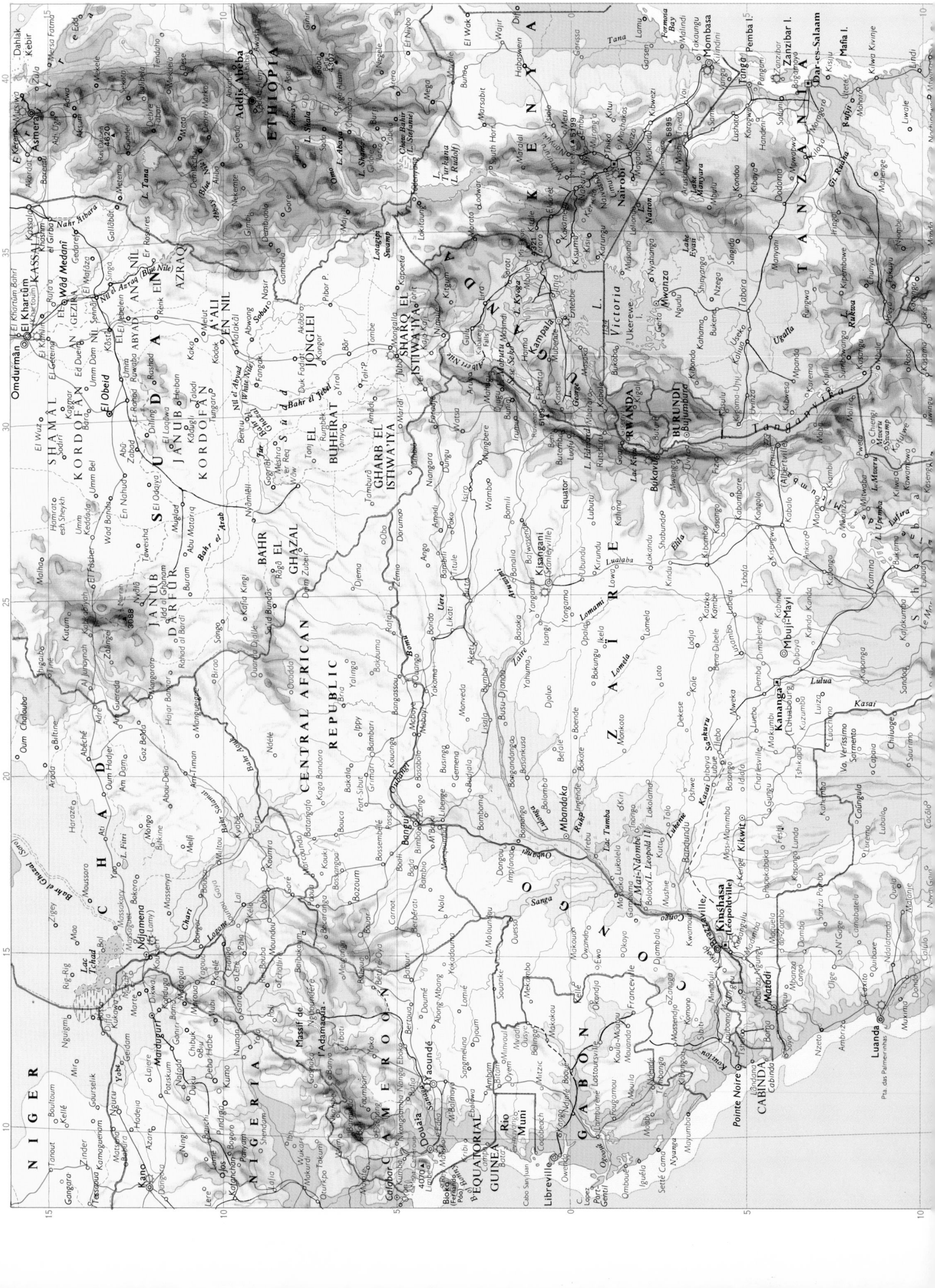

ETHIOPIA

KENYA

TANZANIA

SUDAN

CHAD

NIGER

NIGERIA

CAMEROON

CENTRAL AFRICAN REPUBLIC

EQUATORIAL GUINEA

GABON

CONGO

ZAIRE

UGANDA

RWANDA

BURUNDI

CABINDA

Rio Muni

SHAMAL KORDOFAN

JANUB KORDOFAN

SHAMAL DARFUR

JANUB DARFUR

BAHR EL GHAZAL

GHARB EL ISTIWA'IYA

SHARQ EL ISTIWA'IYA

AN NIL EL AZRAQ

AN NIL EL ABYAD

A'ALI EN NIL

BUHEIRAT

JONGLEI

Addis Abeba

Asmera

Omdurmān

El Khartūm

Nairobi

Kampala

Bujumbura

Kanânga

Mbuji-Mayi

Kinshasa (Léopoldville)

Brazzaville

Matâdi

Kisangani (Stanleyville)

Bangui

Ndjamena

Yaoundé

Douala

Libreville

Luanda

Lac Tchad

L. Victoria

L. Tana

Mombasa

Zanzibar I.

Pemba I.

Mafia I.

Dar-es-Salaam

Tanga

Congo

Kasai

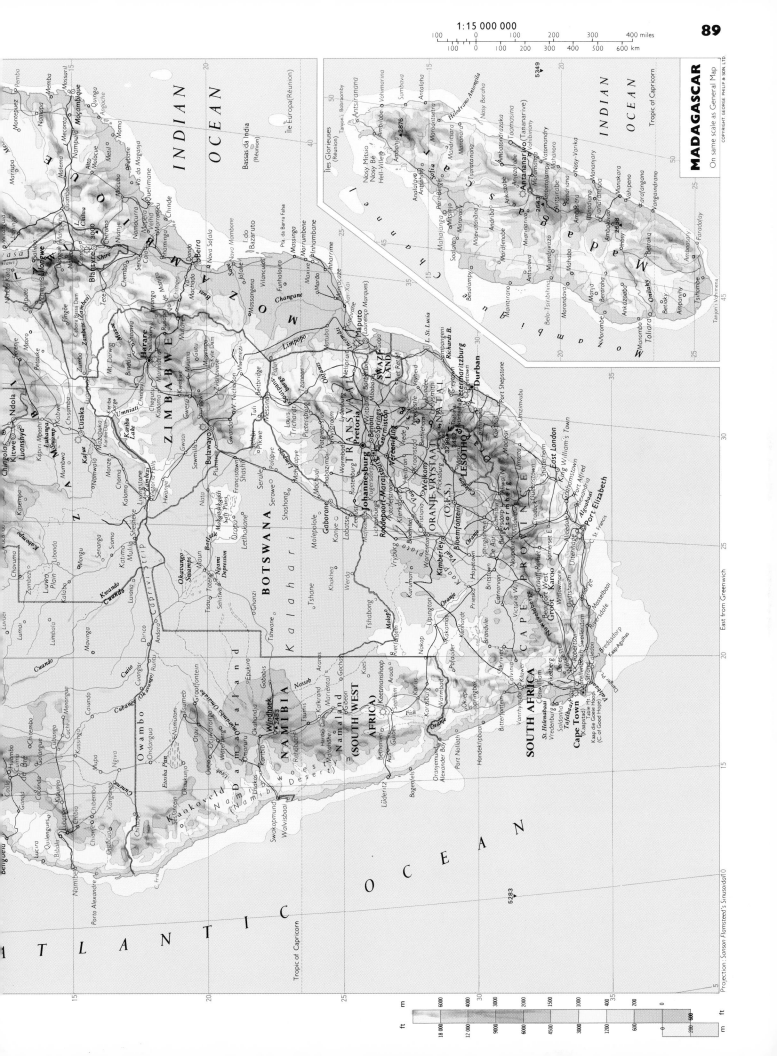

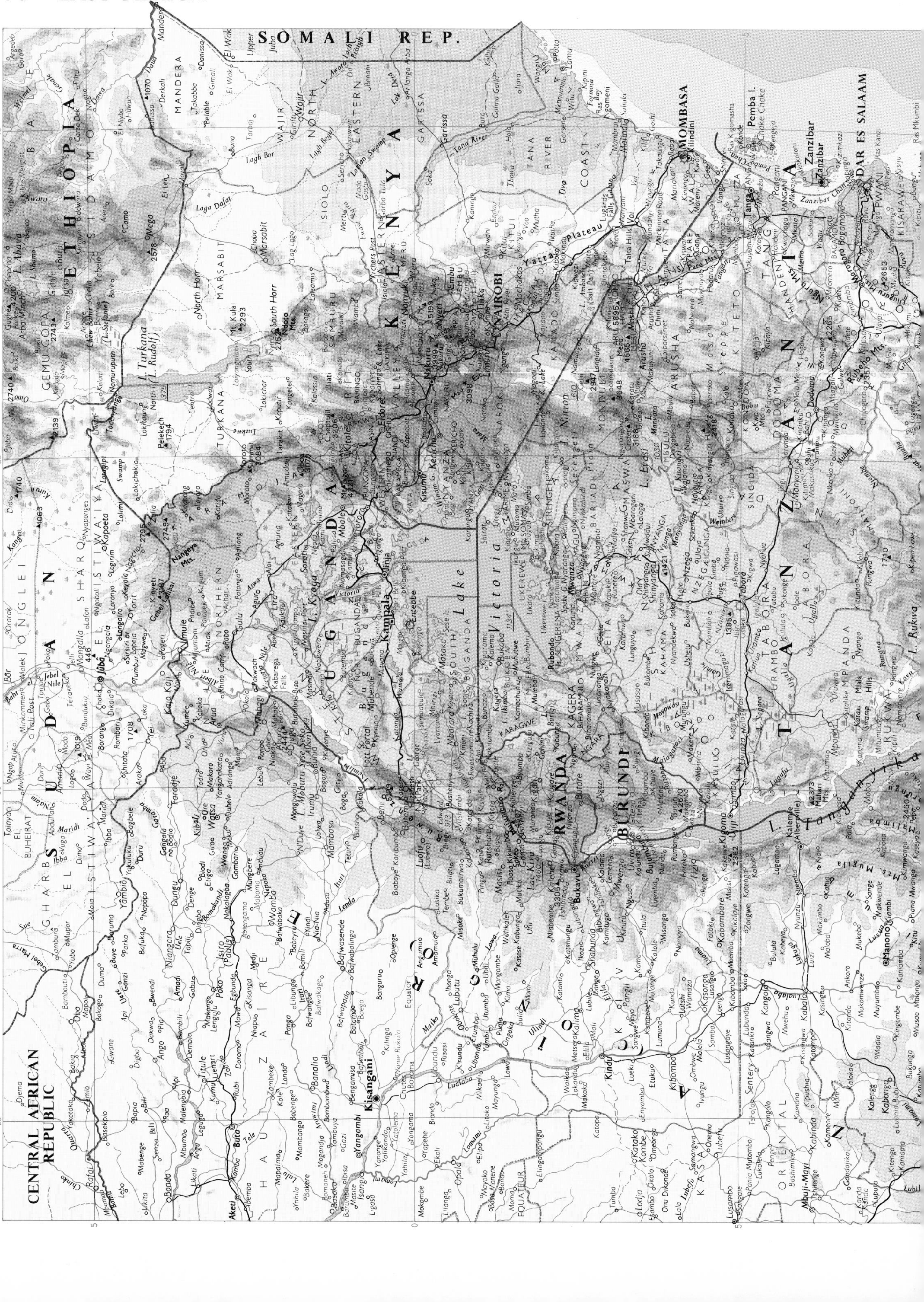

SOMALI REP.

ETHIOPIA

KENYA

UGANDA

TANZANIA

SUDAN

ZAIRE

RWANDA

BURUNDI

CENTRAL AFRICAN REPUBLIC

Lake Victoria

Nairobi

Kampala

Mombasa

DAR ES SALAAM

Zanzibar

Pemba I.

Kisangani

Dodoma

L. Turkana (L. Rudolf)

L. Tanganyika

L. Kyoga

L. Albert (L. Mobutu Sese Seko)

L. Edward

L. Kivu

Nakuru

Arusha

Tabora

Kigoma

Kitale

1:8 000 000

50 0 100 150 200 miles
50 0 100 200 300 km

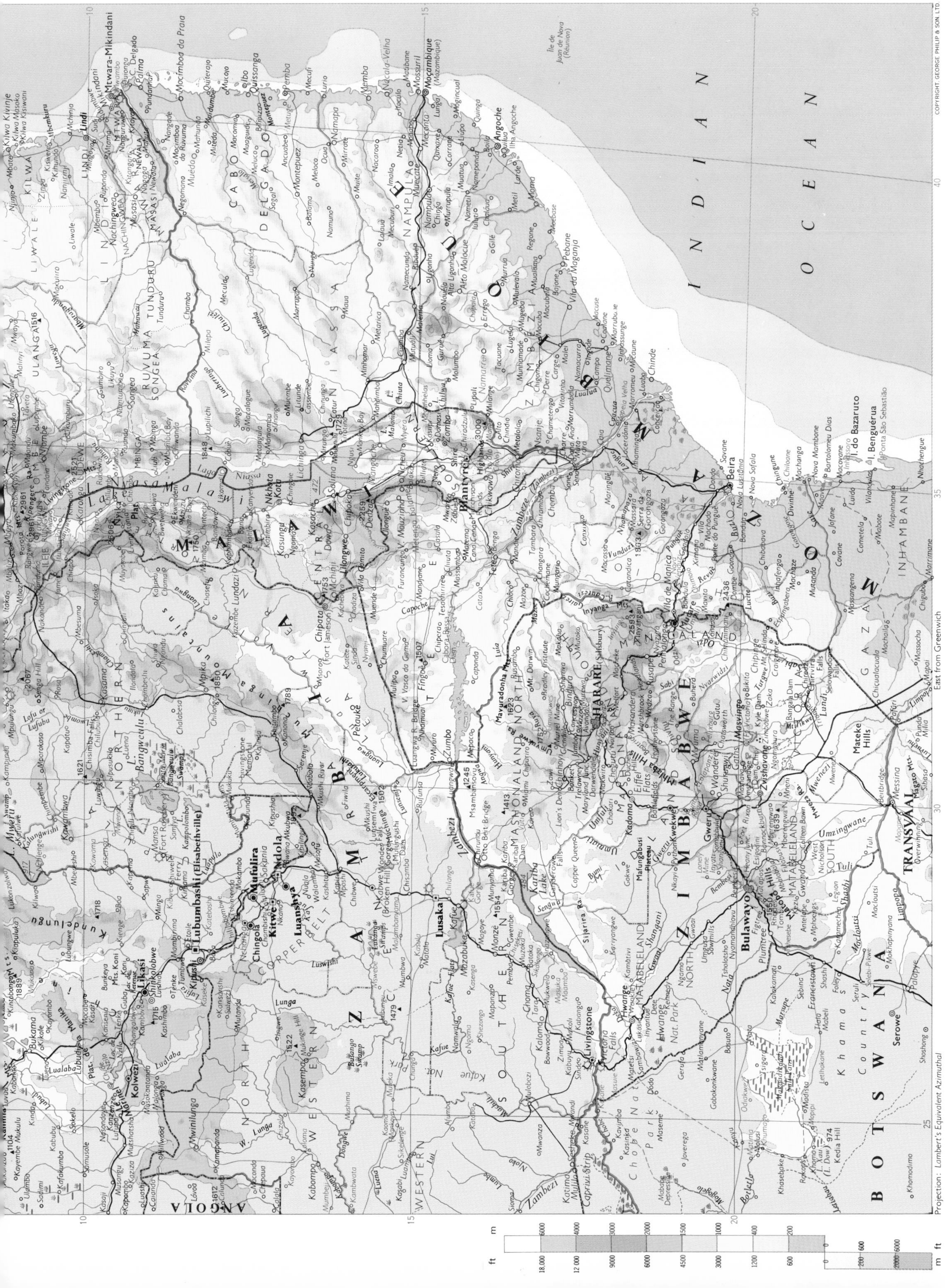

COPYRIGHT GEORGE PHILIP & SON LTD

I N D I A N   O C E A N

Projection: Lambert's Equivalent Azimuthal

East from Greenwich

A N G O L A

Z A M B I A

M A L A W I

MOZAMBIQUE

ZIMBABWE

BOTSWANA

TRANSVAAL

Lubumbashi (Elisabethville)

Kitwe • Ndola • Mufulira • Chingola • Luanshya

Lusaka

Livingstone

Harare (Salisbury)

Bulawayo

Gweru

Masvingo

Beira

Moçambique (Mozambique)

Lindi

Mtwara-Mikindani

Victoria Falls

Lake Kariba

Z a m b e z i

m   ft
6000   18 000
4000   12 000
3000   9000
2000   6000
1500   4500
1000   3000
 400   1200
 200   600
   0   0

m   ft
200 600
2000 6000

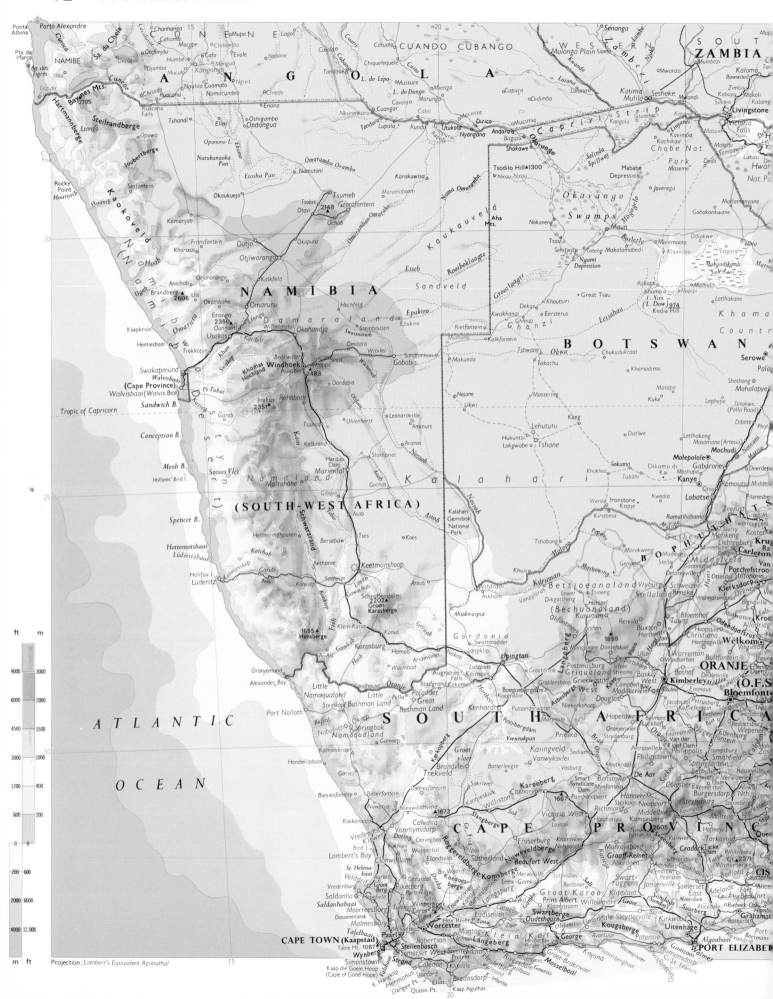

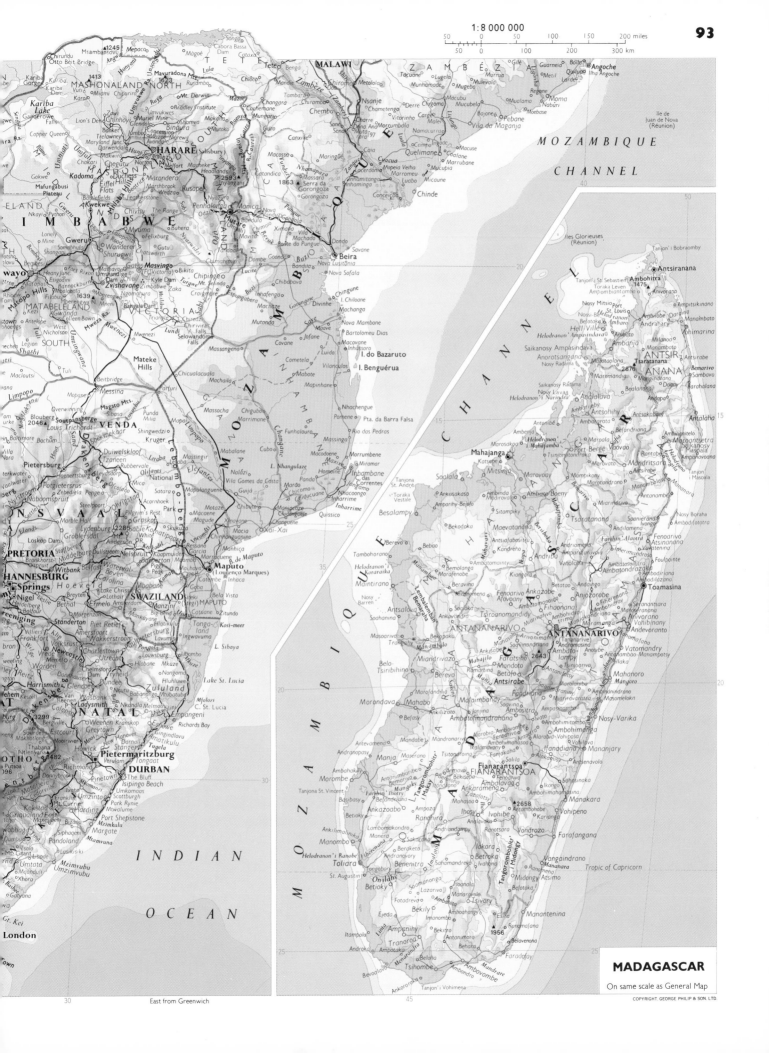

1:8 000 000

50   0   50   100   150   200 miles
50   0   100   200   300 km

MALAWI

MOZAMBIQUE

CHANNEL

MOZAMBIQUE

MASHONALAND NORTH

MASHONALAND SOUTH

HARARE (Salisbury)

ZIMBABWE

MATABELELAND

VICTORIA

MATABELELAND SOUTH

VENDA

TRANSVAAL

PRETORIA

JOHANNESBURG
Springs

SWAZILAND

MAPUTO

Maputo
(Lourenço Marques)

NATAL

DURBAN

Pietermaritzburg

INDIAN

OCEAN

London

MOZAMBIQUE CHANNEL

Iles Glorieuses
(Réunion)

Antsiranana

ANTSIRANANA

Mahajanga

MADAGASCAR

ANTANANARIVO

Antananarivo
(Tananarive)

Antsirabe

Toamasina

Fianarantsoa

MADAGASCAR

Toliara

Tropic of Capricorn

Faradofay

MADAGASCAR

On same scale as General Map

East from Greenwich

COPYRIGHT. GEORGE PHILIP & SON. LTD.

Leningrad
Moskva
Volga
Sverdlovsk
Omsk
Novosibirsk
Barnaul
EUROPE
U. S. S. R.
Tomsk
Irkutsk
Ozero
Baykal
Chita
Lena
Blagoveshchensk
Amur
Khabarovsk
Okhotsk
Sea of Okhotsk
Petropavlovsk
Kamchatka
Komandorskie Is. (U.S.S.R.)
Near Is.
7822
Aleutia
Aleutian Trench
Sakhalin
Gol Sakhalin
La Perouse Strait
Kuril Is.
Kuril Trench
Yokohama - Vancouver 4280
Emperor Seamount Chain
KURO SIWO
7168
Tashkent
Samarkand
Alma Ata
Karaganda
L. Balkhash
Semipalatinsk
Ulyasutay
Hovd
Ulaanbaatar
Ulan Ude
MONGOLIA
Manchuria
Harbin
Changchun
Shenyang
Antung
Vladivostok
Hakodate
Sendai
Sea of Japan
KOREA
Sōul S.
Pusan
JAPAN
Kyōto
Osaka
Nagoya
TOKYO
Yokohama
8412
Fujisan 3776
Afghanistan
Kabul
Srinagar
Lahore
PAKISTAN
Delhi
Agra
Kanpur
Varanasi
Ganges
Hyderabad
INDIA
Madras
Calcutta
Cuttack
Chittagong
BANGLA DESH
BURMA
Rangoon
Bay of Bengal
Andaman Is.
Mergui Arch.
Isthmus of Kra
Nicobar Is.
SRI LANKA
Colombo
1567
Kunlun Shan
XIZANG (TIBET)
Lhasa
Mt. Everest 8848
NEPAL
Brahmaputra
Irrawaddy
Mandalay
Chengtu
Kunming
THAILAND (SIAM)
Bangkok
CAMBODIA
Phnom Penh
Phanh Bho Ho Chi Minh (Saigon)
C. Camau
Gulf of Thailand
1078
George Town
PENINSULAR MALAYSIA
Kuala Lumpur
Melaka
SINGAPORE
1840
Urumqi
Lanzhou
Xi'an
CHINA
Chongqing
Wuhan
Nanjing
SHANGHAI
Hangzhou
Changsha
Fuzhou
Xiamen
Guangzhou
MACAU (Port.)
HONG KONG
Hanoi
Hainan
C. Engano
Manila
PHILIPPINES
Mindoro
Samar
Palawan
10,497
Mindanao Trench
South China Sea
Sulu Sea
Kinabalu
SABAH
4101
BRUNEI
SARAWAK
Natuna
Celebes Sea
Celebes
Borneo
Bangka
Palembang
Sumatra
Java Sea
Jakarta
Semarang
Surabaya
Bali
Flores Sea
Java
Sunda Strait
Christmas (Austral.)
Cocos (Keeling) Is. (Austral.)
Nias
INDONESIA
Beijing
Tianjin
Lūda
Jinan
Qingdao
Nagasaki
Kitakyūshū
Shikoku
Kyūshū
Ryukyu Is.
Yellow Sea
East China Sea
Wenzhou
Taibei
Taiwan (Formosa)
Chang Jiang
Huang He
South Honshū Ridge
KURO SIWO
1580
Japan Trench
10,554
Bonin Is.
Volcano Is.
6603
Marcus I.
Necker Ridge
Wake I. (U.S.)
Midway
PA
Northern Marianas
Guam (U.S.)
Mariana Trench
11,022
Yap
Belau
Fed. States of Micronesia
Truk
Ponape
Caroline Islands
U.S. TRUST TERR. OF THE PACIFIC ISLANDS
Bikini Atoll
Marshall Is.
Eniwetok Atoll
Micronesia
EQUATORIAL
Jaluit
Butaritari
Gilbert Is.
Banaba
NAURU
Melanesia
Moluccas
Halmahera
Dampier Strait
Ceram
Buru
Amboina
Banda Sea
Tanimbar I.
Aru Is.
7440
Irian Jaya
5029
New Guinea
PAPUA NEW GUINEA
Madang
Port Moresby
Bismarck Arch.
New Ireland
Rabaul
New Britain
9103
Admiralty Is.
SOLOMON ISLANDS
Honiara
Guadalcanal
9165
Sta. Cruz I.
TUVALU (Ellice Is.)
Funafuti
Ujung Pandang
Flores
Sumba
Timor
Arafura Sea
Torres Strait
Thursday I.
C. York
G. of Carpentaria
Arnhem
Darwin
Larrimah
Ashmore Is.
Wyndham
NORTHERN TERRITORY
Alice Springs
N.W. Cape
Onslow
Shark Bay
WESTERN AUSTRALIA
Geraldton
Perth
Fremantle
Geographe Bay
Albany
K. George Sd.
INDIAN OCEAN
Amsterdam I. (Fr.)
St. Paul I. (Fr.)
Crozet Is. (Fr.)
Kerguelen (Fr.)
Heard Is. (Aust.)
Timor
7450
Java Trench
Louisiade Arch.
Coral Sea Islands Territory
Cairns
Townsville
Mt. Isa
Longreach
Oodnadatta
L. Eyre
QUEENSLAND
Maryborough
Brisbane
Ipswich
AUSTRALIA
Kalgoorlie
SOUTH AUSTRALIA
Darling
NEW SOUTH WALES
Sydney
Newcastle
Wollongong
Adelaide
Murray
VICTORIA
Mt. Kosciusko 2230
Canberra
Ballarat
Geelong
Melbourne
Encounter Bay
Great Australian Bight
F. - A. 1353
Bass Strait
Launceston
TASMANIA
Hobart
Coral Sea Islands Territory
VANUATU
Vanua Levu
Vitu Levu
Suva
FIJI
Rotuma
Wallis & Futuna (Fr.)
Chesterfield Is.
New Caledonia (Fr.)
Noumea
7670
Loyalty Is.
Norfolk I. (Aust.)
Lord Howe I. (Aust.)
S - A 1274
Tasman Sea
Kermadec
10,047
Auckland
Hamilton
NEW ZEALAND
Cook Strait
Wellington
Nelson
Christchurch
Dunedin
Invercargill
Stewart
3764
Mt. Cook
Macquarie Is. (Austral.)
Campbell I. (N.Z.)
Auckland Is. (N.Z.)
Bounty Is.
Antipo

Great Divide
South East Indian Rise
Mid Oceanic Ridge
Indian Ocean Ridge
Indian-Antarctic Ridge
South
Colombo - Fremantle 3120
Cape Town - Fremantle 5615
Cape Town - Melbourne 5814
Cape Town - Hobart 5838
Al Adan - Melbourne 6445
1772
1140
1059
W 1293
1234 R
1244

ft   m
18 000   6000
12 000   4000
6000   2000
3000   1000
600   200
0   0
200   600
2000   6000
4000   12 000
6000   18 000
8000   24 000
m   ft

Projection: Mollweide's Homolographic
East from Greenwich

5615 Principal Shipping Routes
(Distances in Nautical Miles)

ALASKA
6050
Gulf of Alaska
I Bay
Juneau
Prince of Wales I.
Sitka
Kitimat
Queen Charlotte Is.
Prince Rupert

L. Athabaska
Churchill
Hudson Bay
Belcher Is.
Dawson Creek
Lynn Lake
Edmonton
Prince Albert
Saskatoon
Regina
L. Winnipeg
Winnipeg

GREENLAND
C. Farewell
Scheffervile
Hamilton Inlet
Labrador
Strait of Belle Isle

R O C K Y
C A N A D A
N O R T H   A M E R I C A

NORTH
Newfoundland
Anticosti
St. Lawrence
Québec
Pr. Edward I.
C. Race
C. Breton I.

Vancouver
Victoria
Vancouver I.
Seattle
Tacoma
Portland

Medicine Hat
Spokane
Helena
Butte
Boise
Bismarck
Missouri
Duluth
L. Superior
Sault Ste. Marie
Montréal
Ottawa
Toronto
Buffalo
L. Huron
Michigan
Milwaukee
CHICAGO
Detroit
Pittsburgh
L. Ontario
L. Erie
Boston
Saint John
Sable I.
C. Sable

NEW YORK
Philadelphia
Baltimore
Washington
Richmond
Norfolk

ATLANTIC

Mendocino Seascarp
C. Blanco
C. Mendocino
Sacramento
Oakland
San Francisco

Minneapolis
St. Paul
Cheyenne
Des Moines
Denver
Kansas City
St. Louis
Indianapolis
Cincinnati
Memphis
Atlanta
C. Hatteras

Los Angeles
San Diego

M o u n t a i n s
Salt Lake City
Colorado
Snake
UNITED STATES
Santa Fe
Oklahoma
Little Rock
Dallas
Austin
El Paso
Ciudad Juárez
Houston
San Antonio
New Orleans
Mobile
Jacksonville
Savannah
Florida
Tampa
Miami

OCEAN

Murray Seascarp
2091
6741
6418
CALIFORNIAN CURRENT

Guadalupe
6225
Pto. Eugenia

Sierra Madre
Gulf of California

Tropic of Cancer
C.S. Lucas

Clarion Fracture Zone

Hawaiian Is. (U.S.A.)
RIDGE
Honolulu
Oahu
Hawaii

Revilla Gigedo Is. (Mexico)
Aguascalientes
Guadalajara

Tampico
San Luis Potosí
MÉXICO
Puebla
Veracruz
Mérida
Yucatan Channel

La Habana
CUBA
BAHAMAS
West Indies
Hispaniola 9200
HAITI
DOM. REP.

Gulf of Mexico

Monterrey
Torreón
3277
Acapulco
5700

JAMAICA
Kingston
Santo Domingo
PUERTO RICO
St. Thomas (U.S.)
Virgin Is.
Leeward Is.

4711

I F I C

3666

Clipperton Fracture Zone
Clipperton I. (Fr.)

GUATEMALA
Guatemala
San Salvador
HONDURAS
Tegucigalpa
NICARAGUA
Managua
CENTRAL AMERICA
COSTA RICA
San José
PANAMA
Colón
Panamá Canal

Caribbean Sea
Barranquilla
Maracaibo
Curaçao (Ne.)
Windward Is.
TRINIDAD & TOBAGO
BARBADOS
Caracas
Orinoco
VENEZUELA
Guadeloupe (Fr.)
Martinique (Fr.)

CURRENT
Palmyra Is. (U.S.)
Teraina
Tabuaeran
Kirimati

Cocos I.
835
Medellín
Bogotá
Cali
COLOMBIA

E A N
Jarvis I. (U.S.)
Malden I.
Starbuck I.

Equator
Galápagos (Ecuador)
C.S. Francisco

Quito
ECUADOR
Guayaquil
Chimborazo 6267
Cuenca
Iquitos

Manaus
Amazon

BRAZIL

B A T I
Tongareva
Penrhyn
Manihiki
Suwarrow Is.

Vostok I.
Flint I.
Caroline I.

Marquesas Is.

C. Pariñas
Lobos I.
Chiclayo
Trujillo

SOUTH

Cook Islands (N.Z.)
1303
Society Is.
Windward Is.
Tahiti
FRENCH POLYNESIA

Leeward Is.
Tuamotu Archipelago

Tahiti - Panamá 4570
Auckland - Panamá 6510

East Pacific Ridge

Southeast Pacific Basin

6369
Callao
6550
Lima
Cuzco
L. Titicaca
Arequipa
Illampu & Ancohuma 6550
La Paz
Iquique

PERU
10
AMERICA

Austral
Rarotonga
Manuae

Seamount Chain
Tubuai Is. (Austral Is.)
Rapa Iti

Tuamotu Ridge
Pitcairn I. (U.K.)
Ducie I.

Tropic of Capricorn
Easter Is. (Chile)
Sala-y-Gomez (Chile)

San Félix (Chile)
San Ambrosio (Chile)

6866
Perú
Arica
8050
Antofagasta Trench
Chile
Salta
Tucumán
PARAGUAY
Asunción
Corrientes
Pto. Alegre

tern
Pacific - Antarctic Ridge
WEST WIND DRIFT

Chile Rise
Arch. de Juan Fernández (Chile)
Alejandro Selkirk
Robinson Crusoe

Aconcagua 6960
Valparaíso
Santiago
Córdoba
Rosario
Santa Fe
Paysandú
URUGUAY
Montevideo
Río de la Plata
La Plata
Buenos Aires

asin
Pacific - Antarctic Basin

Concepción
Neuquén
ARGENTINA
Mar del Plata

1355
1295

SOUTH ATLANTIC

G. of Penas
Chonos Arch.
Wellington Is.
Sta. Cruz
Punta Arenas
Str. of Magellan
Tierra del Fuego
C. Horn

CAPE HORN CURRENT
P.A. Valparaíso
1414
P.A. Buenos Aires - Montevideo

Patagonian
Argentine Basin
6212
Falkland Is. (U.K.)
Stanley
South Georgia

OCEAN

West from Greenwich
160 140 120 100 80 60 40 20
COPYRIGHT. GEORGE PHILIP & SON. LTD.

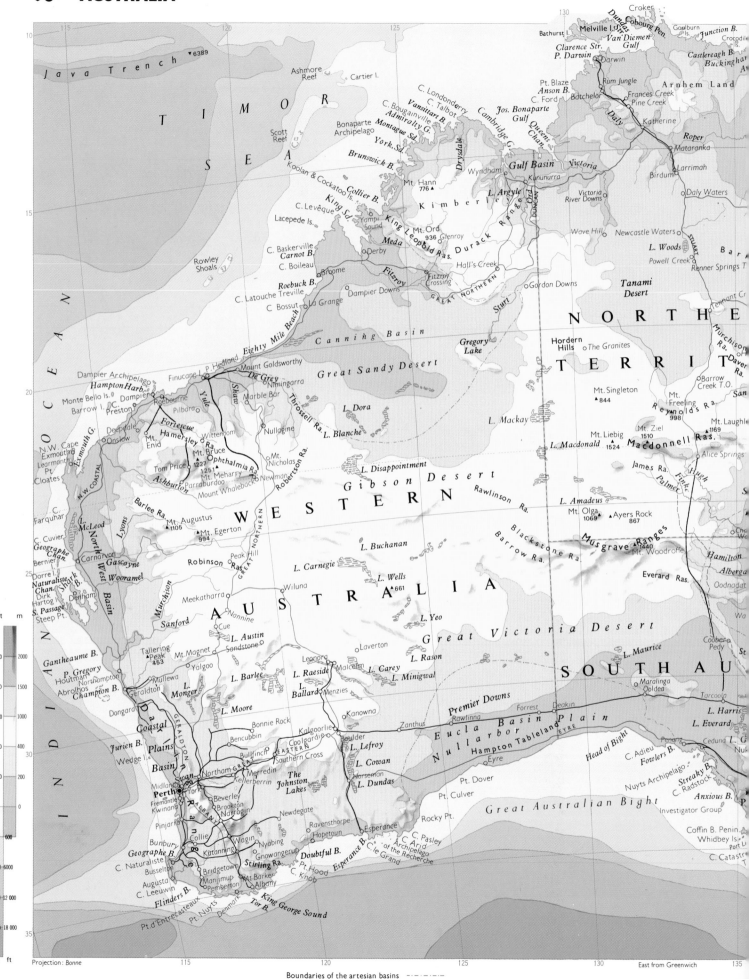

Java Trench ▼6389

T I M O R   S E A

Ashmore Reef
Cartier I.
Scott Reef
Rowley Shoals

C. Londonderry
C. Talbot
Vansittart B.
C. Bougainville
Admiralty G.
Montague Sd.
York Sd.
Brunswick B.
Koolan & Cockatoo Is.
Collier B.
King Sd.
C. Lévêque
Lacepede Is.
C. Baskerville
Carnot B.
C. Boileau
Broome
Roebuck B.
C. Latouche Treville
C. Bossut
La Grange

Croker
Cobourg Pen.
Dundas Str.
Melville I.
Van Diemen Gulf
Clarence Str.
P. Darwin
Darwin
Goulburn Is.
Junction B.
Crocodile
Bathurst I.
Castlereagh B.
Buckingham

Pt. Blaze
Anson B.
C. Ford
Batchelor
Rum Jungle
Frances Creek
Pine Creek
Arnhem Land
Katherine
Roper
Mataranka

Cambridge G.
Jos. Bonaparte Gulf
Queens Chan.
Wyndham
L. Argyle
Gulf Basin
Victoria
Kununurra
Birdum
Larrimah

Mt. Hann 776
K I M B E R L E Y
Glenroy
Meda
Derby
Fitzroy
Fitzroy Crossing
Hall's Creek

Mt. Ord 936
Durack Range
Victoria River Downs
Wave Hill
Newcastle Waters
L. Woods
Powell Creek
Renner Springs

Gordon Downs
Sturt

GREAT NORTHERN

Dampier Downs

Canning Basin

Eighty Mile Beach

Gregory Lake

Hordern Hills
The Granites

N O R T H E R
T E R R I T O R
Tanami Desert

Finucane
P. Hedland
Mount Goldsworthy
De Grey
Nimingarra
Marble Bar
Throssell Ra.

Great Sandy Desert

L. Dora
L. Blanche

Mt. Singleton 844

Barrow Creek T.O.

Mt. Freeling 998
Reynold's Ra.
San

Dampier Archipelago
Hampton Harb.
Monte Bello Is.
Barrow I.
Preston
C. Dampier
Roebourne
Pilbara
Yule
Shaw
Nullagine

L. Mackay

Mt. Liebig
L. Macdonald 1524
Mt. Ziel 1510
Macdonnell Ras.
Mt. Laughlen 1169

N.W. Cape
Exmouth G.
Learmonth
Pt. Cloates
Deepdale
Onslow
Mt. Enid
Fortescue
Hamersley Ra.
Wittenoom
Mt. Bruce
Ophthalmia Ra.
Tom Price 1227
Mt. Meharry 1251
Parraburdoo
Mount Whaleback
Newman
Mt. Nicholas
Robertson Ra.
Ashburton

L. Disappointment

G i b s o n   D e s e r t

Rawlinson Ra.

L. Macdonald 1524
James Ra.
Finke
Palmer
Hugh

Alice Springs

Mt. Olga 1069
Ayers Rock 867
Musgrave Ranges
Mt. Woodroffe 1440
Everard Ras.

C. Farquhar
L. McLeod
North West Basin
Barlee Ra.
Mt. Augustus 1105
Mt. Egerton 994
Peak Hill

W E S T E R N

Blackstone Ra.
Barrow Ra.

Everard Ras.
Oodnadat

C. Cuvier
Geographe Chan.
Bernier
Dorre I.
Naturaliste Chan.
Dirk Hartog I.
S. Passage
Steep Pt.
Denham
Shark B.
Wooramel
Gascoyne
Carnarvon
Lyons
Murchison

Robinson Ra.

L. Buchanan
L. Carnegie
L. Wells 661

A U S T R A L I A

Meekatharra
Sanford
Nannine
Cue
L. Austin
Sandstone
Wiluna

L. Yeo

G r e a t   V i c t o r i a   D e s e r t

Coober Pedy
L. Maurice

S O U T H   A U

Tallering Peak 453
Mt. Magnet
Yalgoo
Leonora
Laverton
L. Carey
L. Rason
Malcolm
Minigwal

Maralinga
Ooldea
Tarcoola

Gantheaume B.
P. Gregory
Houtman
Abrolhos
Northampton
Champion B.
Geraldton
Mullewa
Dongara
L. Barlee
L. Monger
L. Moore
Bonnie Rock

Raeside
Ballard
L. Raeside
Menzies
Kanowna
Kalgoorlie
Boulder
Coolgardie
Bullfinch
Southern Cross
Merredin
Kellerberrin
The Johnston Lakes
L. Lefroy
L. Cowan
L. Dundas
Norseman

Premier Downs
Forrest
Deakin
Rawlinna
Zanthus
Eucla Basin
Nullarbor Plain
Hampton Tableland
Eyre

L. Harris
L. Everard
Penong
Ceduna
Streaky B.
C. Radstock
Nuyts Archipelago
Anxious B.
Investigator Group

Coastal Plains Basin
Jurien B.
Wedge I.
Dandaragan
Midland
Swan
Perth
Fremantle
Kwinana
Northam
York
Beverley
Brookton
Narrogin
Pinjarra
Collie
Bunbury
Geographe B.
C. Naturaliste
Busselton
Augusta
C. Leeuwin
Flinders B.
Pt. d'Entrecasteaux

Newdegate
Ravensthorpe
Hopetoun
Nyabing
Gnowangerup
Doubtful B.
Esperance B.
Stirling Ra.
Mt. Barker
Albany
Bridgetown
Manjimup
Pemberton
Denmark
King George Sound

Rocky Pt.
Pt. Culver
Pt. Dover
C. Arid
C. Pasley
Archipelago of the Recherche
C. le Grand

Head of Bight
C. Adieu
Fowlers B.
Great Australian Bight

Coffin B. Penin.
Whidbey Is.
Port Li
C. Catast

I N D I A N   O C E A N

Projection: Bonne

Boundaries of the artesian basins – – – – – – –

East from Greenwich

ft m
6000 2000
4500 1500
3000 1000
1200 400
600 200
0 0
200 600
2000 6000
4000 12 000
6000 18 000
m ft

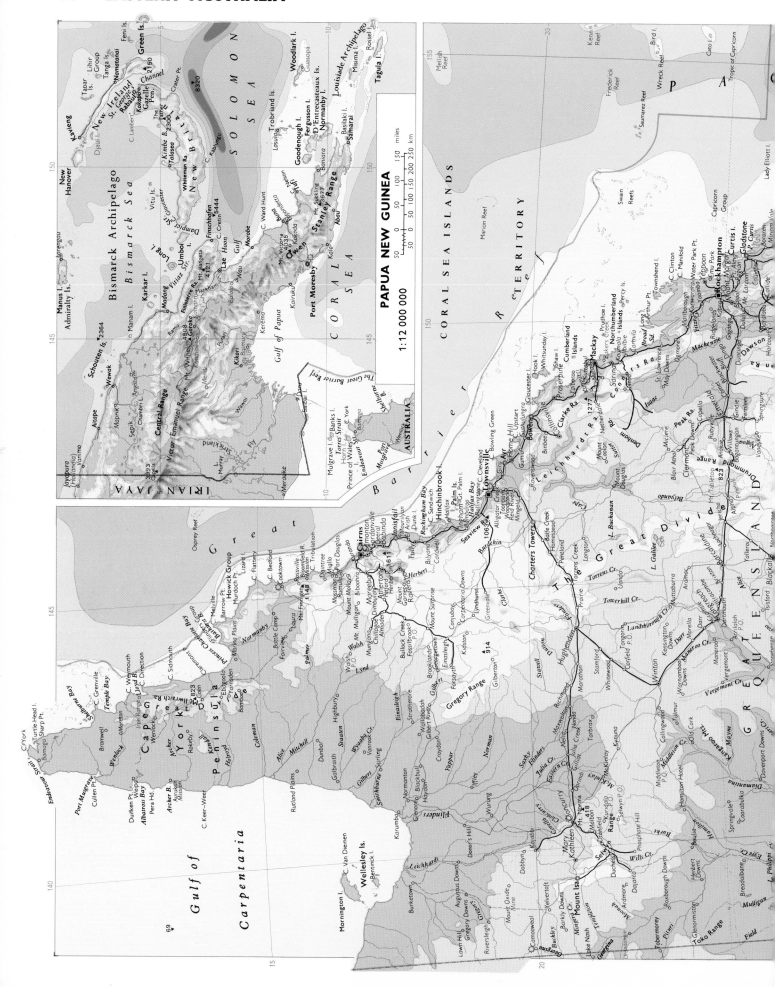

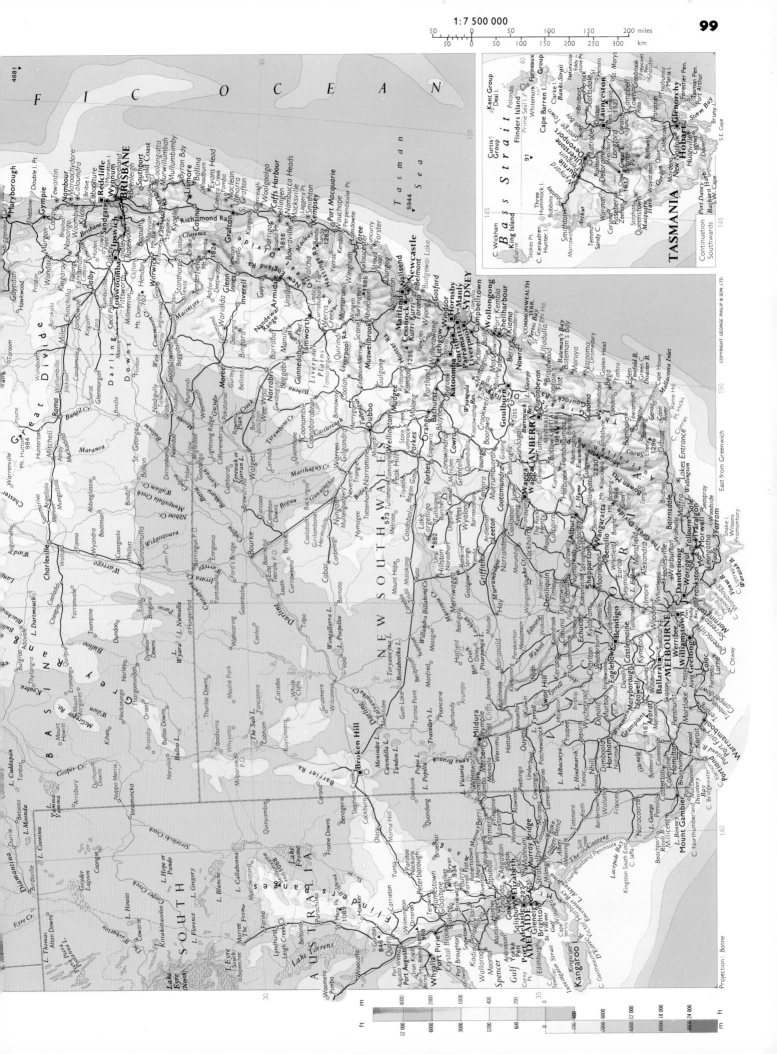

1 : 4 500 000

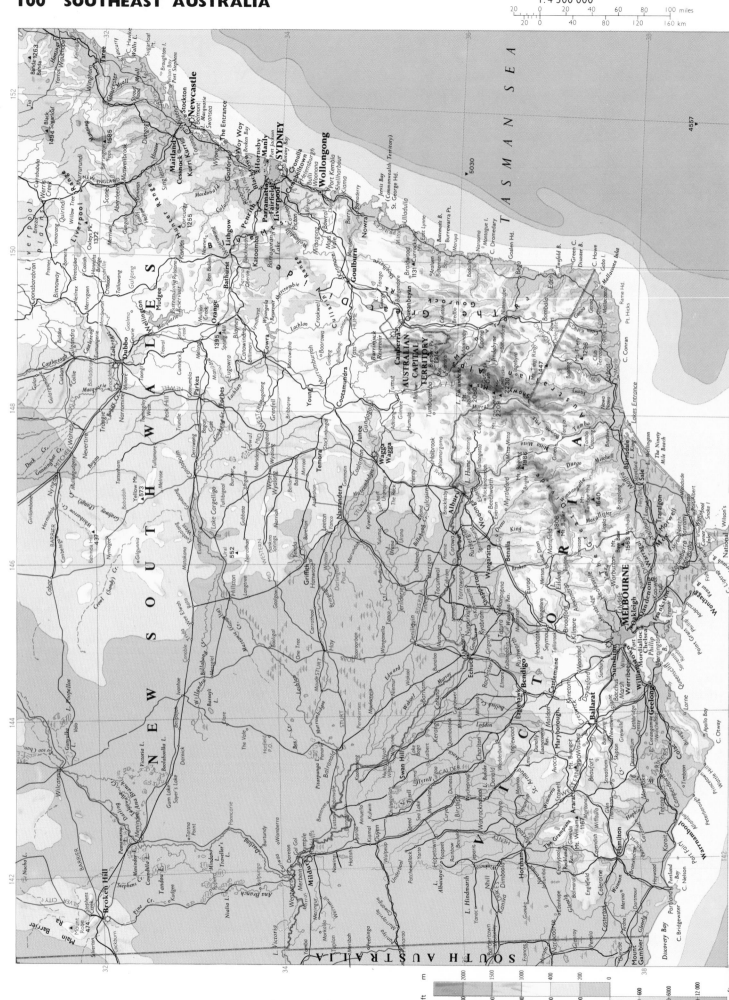

1:6 000 000

NEW ZEALAND & DEPENDENCIES
1:60 000 000

New Zealand Territory
Self-governing Territory

SAMOA ISLANDS
1:12 000 000

WESTERN SAMOA
Savaii · Apia
Upolu · American Samoa
Pago Pago · Manua Is.
Tutuila · Rose I.

FIJI AND TONGA ISLANDS
1:12 000 000

FIJI
Vanua Levu
Taveuni
Lautoka · Levuka
Nandi · Ovalau
Viti Levu
Suva · Koro Sea
Kandavu · Moala

TONGA
Tonga (Friendly) Is.
Vava'u
Tongatapu
Nuku'alofa

PACIFIC OCEAN
TASMAN SEA
SOUTHERN OCEAN

Three Kings Is.
C. Reinga
C. Maria van Diemen
North C.
Houhora
Kaitaia
Ahipara Bay
Reef Pt.
Opua · B. of Islands
C. Brett
Kaikohe
Hokianga Harb.
Whangaroa Bay
NORTHLAND
Dargaville
Whangarei
Bream Hd.
Bream Bay
Lit. Barrier I.
Gt. Barrier I.
Waipu
C. Rodney
Cuvier I.
Warkworth
Coromandel
Helensville
Hauraki Gulf
Whitianga
CENTRAL AUCKLAND
Takapuna
Devonport
AUCKLAND
Onehunga
Manukau
Thames
Waiuku
Mayor I.
Huntly
White I. · Runaway
Raglan
Tauranga Harb.
Bay of Plenty
Hamilton
Cambridge
Te Puke
Whakatane
Opotiki
SOUTH AUCKLAND
BAY OF PLENTY
Kawhia Harb.
Rotorua
Kawerau
Murupara
NORTH ISLAND
Te Kuiti
Taupo
EAST COAST
Gisborne
Poverty Bay
Waikaremoana
Mahia Peninsula
North Taranaki Bight
New Plymouth
Mt. Egmont
Stratford
Hawke Bay
Napier
Hastings
C. Kidnappers
Hawera
South Taranaki Bight
Wanganui
Palmerston N.
Feilding
Dannevirke
Waipukurau
C. Turnagain
C. Farewell
Golden Bay
D'Urville I.
French Pass
WELLINGTON
Masterton
Castle Pt.
Collingwood
Takaka
Tasman Bay
Picton
Nelson
Motueka
Blenheim
Cook Strait
TASMAN MTS.
Richmond
Wakefield
Seddon
Ward
Karamea Bight
Westport
Kaikoura
SPENSER MTS.
Hanmer Springs
Greymouth
Hokitika
Ross
SOUTH ISLAND
WESTLAND BIGHT
Canterbury Plains
Christchurch
Lyttelton
Banks Peninsula
Akaroa
SOUTHERN ALPS
Mt. Cook
Ashburton
Temuka
Timaru
St. Andrews
Waimate
Oamaru
Mt. Aspiring
Wanaka
Hawea
OTAGO
Queenstown
Cromwell
Alexandra
Roxburgh
Milford Sd.
Mt. Earnslaw
Te Anau
SOUTHLAND
Gore
Mataura
Invercargill
Bluff
Stewart I.
S.W. Cape
Dunedin
Mosgiel
Port Chalmers
Balclutha

WESTERN SAMOA
Tutuila (U.S.)
Savaii
Upolu
TONGA (Friendly Is.)
FIJI
Viti Levu
Vanua Levu
Fiji Is.
Lau or Eastern Group
Rotuma (Fiji)
Tokelau or Union Group
Rakahanga
Tongareva (Penrhyn) I.
Pukapuka (Danger)
Nassau
Suwarrow
Manihiki
Northern Group
Cook Is.
Niue
Palmerston Atoll
Aitutaki
Lower Group
Rarotonga
Mangaia
Tropic of Capricorn
PACIFIC OCEAN
Macauley
Raoul (Sunday) I.
Kermadec Is.
Curtis
Three Kings Is.
Auckland
NORTH I.
NEW ZEALAND
Cook Strait
Wellington
SOUTH I.
Christchurch
Tasman Sea
Dunedin
Chatham I.
Chatham Is.
Pitt I.
Bounty Is.
Stewart I.
Snares
Antipodes Is.
Campbell I.
Macquarie I. (Austr.)
SOUTHERN OCEAN

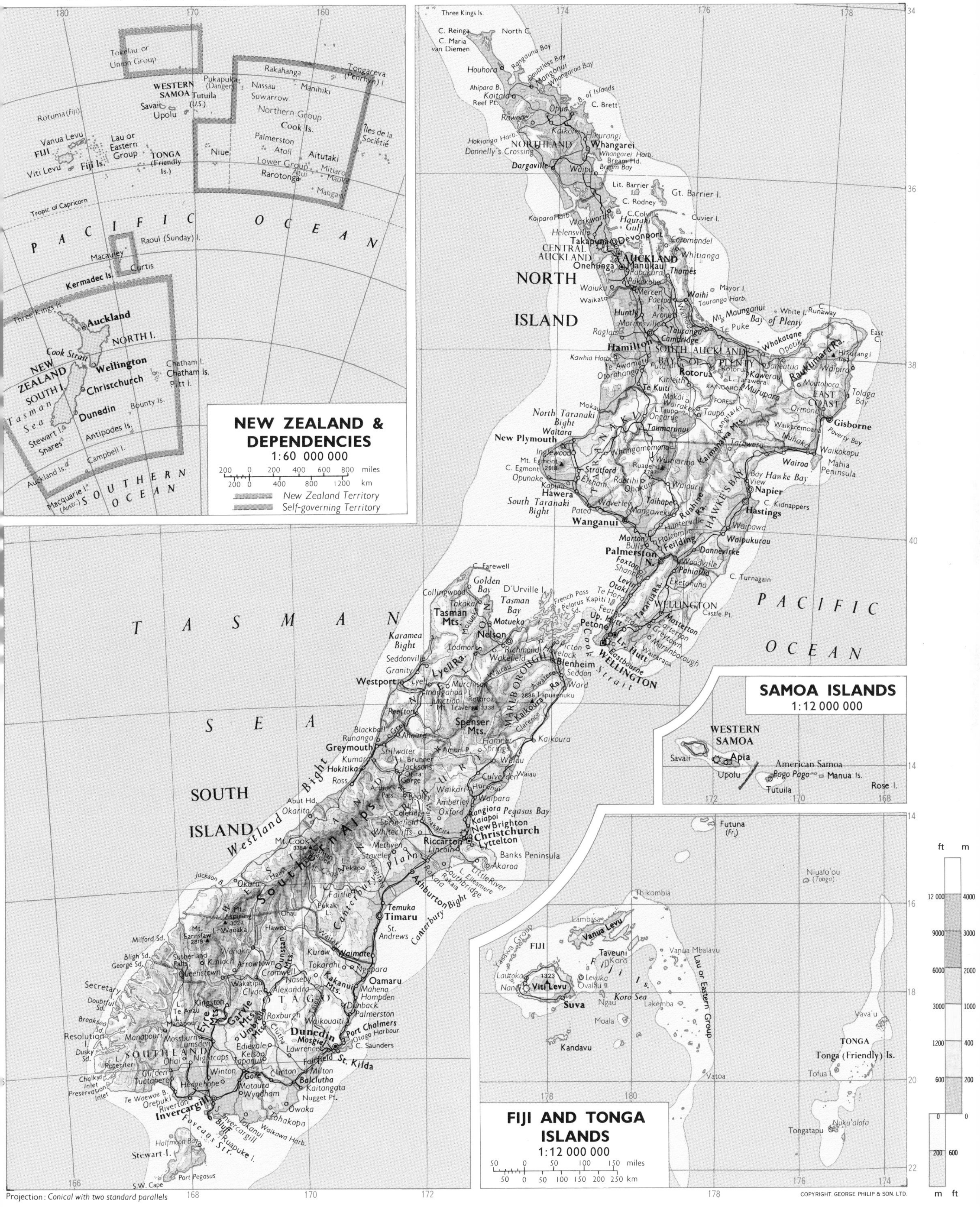

Projection: Conical with two standard parallels

COPYRIGHT. GEORGE PHILIP & SON. LTD.

ft	m
12 000	4000
9000	3000
6000	2000
3000	1000
1200	400
600	200
0	0
200	600

m ft

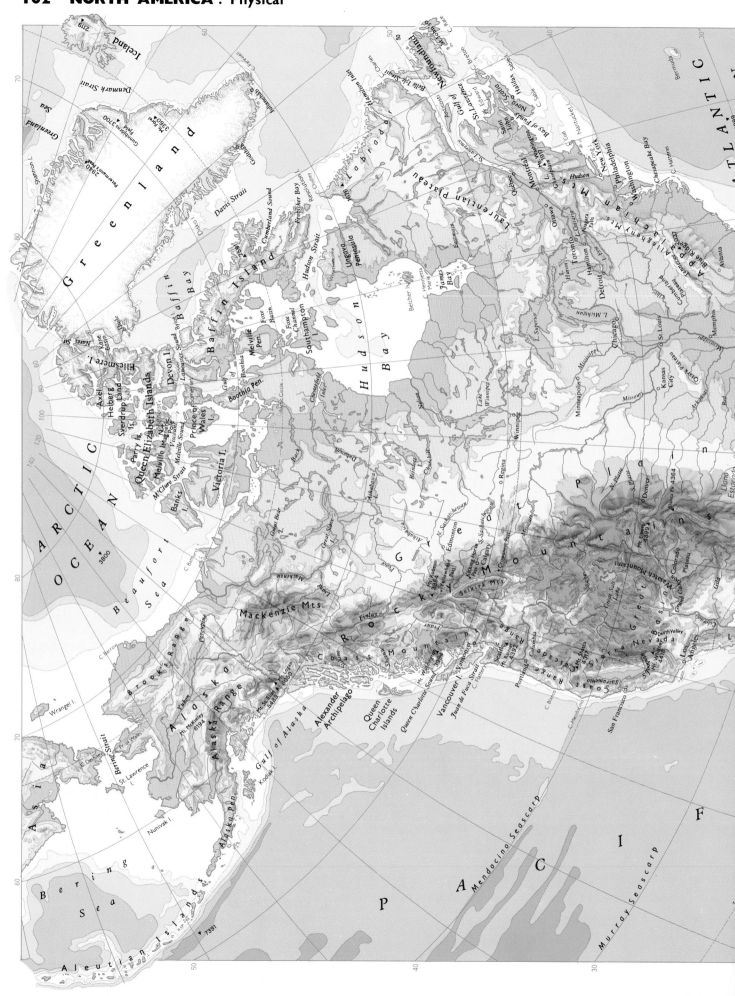

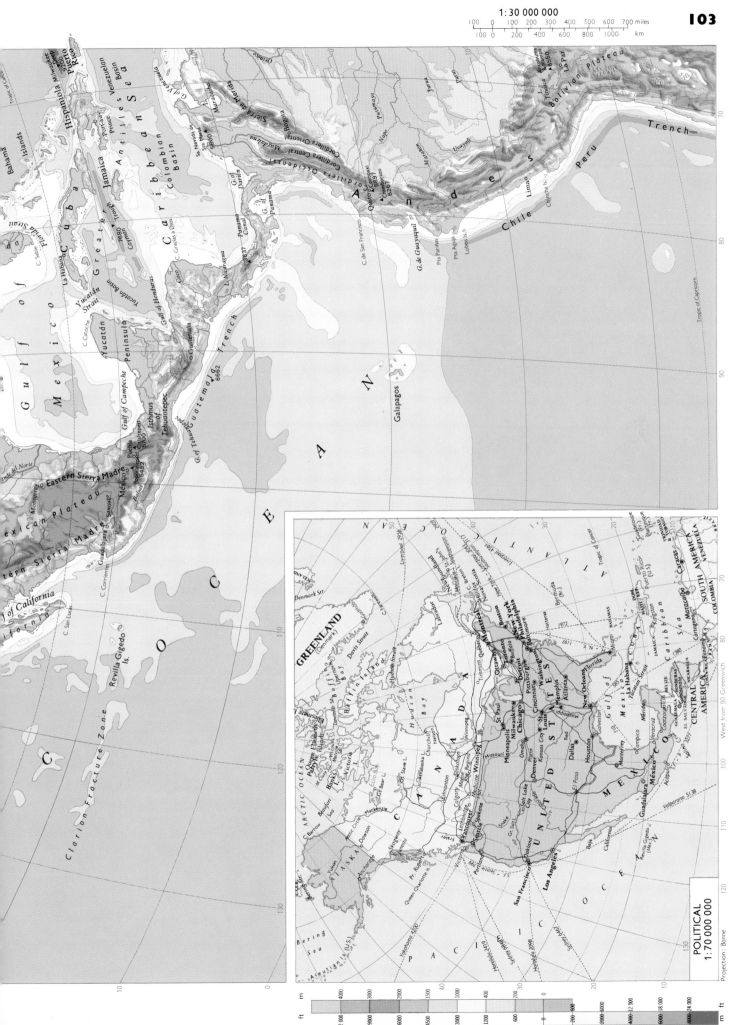

1:15 000 000

100 50 0 100 200 300 400 miles
100 0 100 200 300 400 500 600 km

GREENLAND

Angmagssalik

2850

Kong Frederik VI's Kyst

Sukkertoppen

Frederikshåb

Ivigtut

Kap Farvel

A T L A N T I C

Baffin Bay

Svartenhuk Halvø

Disko

Disko B.

Christianshåb

Sondre Stromfjord

Holsteinsborg

Gotthåb

on Island
ncaster Sound

2136

1890

Arctic Bay

Bylot I.

Pond Inlet

Pond Inlet

Milne Inlet

Scott I.

Clyde

C. Hewett

C. Dyer
Cape
Dyer

Home B.

Broughton Island

Padloping Island

Fury & Hecla Str.

Igloolik Island

Hall Lake

Melville Peninsula

Prince Charles I.

2591

Cumberland Peninsula

C. Mercy

Hoare B.

Pangnirtung

Cumberland Sd.

Davis Strait

V I C T O R I E S

Foxe Basin

Nettilling L.

B A F F I N

C. Dorchester

Foxe Penin.

Amadjuak L.

Frobisher Bay

Ross Welcome Sd.

Repulse Bay

Isthmus

Southampton

Coral Harbour

Bell Pen.

Mansel I.

Cape Dorset

Lake Harbour

Frobisher Bay

Resolution I.

Wager B.

Coats I.

T I N

Digges Is.

Saglouc (Sugluk)

Invujivik

H u d s o n   S t r a i t

C. Chidley

Koartac (Notre Dame de Koartac)

Maricourt (Wakeham)

Akpatok I.

u d s o n

Ottawa Isl.

257

Portland Promontory

Inoucdjouac (Port Harrison)

Arnaud (Bellin)

Payne (Bay)

Ungava Bay

Port Nouveau-Quebec George R.

1676

Hebron

Nutak

Bay

Sleeper Is.

King George Is.

King George Is.

Baker's Dozen Is.

P e n i n s u l a

Feuilles

Payne

Fort Chimo

George

Whale

Nain

N E W

Hopedale

Indian Harbour

Rigolet

Cartwright

L. Marine

Battle Har.

Belle Isle

D

Belcher Is.

C. Henrietta Maria

Pte. Louis-XIV

La Grande (Great Whale River)

Poste-de-la-Baleine

Grand Baleine

Kanaaupscow

La Grande

Kaniapiskau

Schefferville

Petitsikapau L.

COAST OF LABRADOR

Smallwood Reservoir

Churchill Falls

North West

Goose Bay

L. Melville

Indian Harbour

F

Winisk

Lac Bienville

Lobstick L.

Churchill

L

Natashquan

St.-Augustin Saguenay

A

James Bay

Akimiski I.

Nouveau Comptoir (Paint Hills)

Eastmain

L'Eau Claire

4128

Gagnon

Q U E B E C

Ashuanipi L.

Moisie

Romaine

Natashquan

I s l a n d

N E W F O U N D L A N D

Twillingate

Lewisporte

Gander

Bonavista

Carbonear

St. John's

Big out L.

Attawapiskat

Ft. George

Charlton I.

Eastmain

Fort Rupert (Rupert House)

Rupert R.

Mistassini L.

Chibougamau

Péribonca

Manicouagan L.

Sept Îles

Moisie

Port-Cartier

I. d'Anticosti

814

Grand Falls

Corner Brook

Buchans

Notre Dame B.

Grand L.

Deer Lake

Trinity B.

Placentia B.

Placentia

C. Race

Trepassey

R I O

Ft. Albany

Moosonee

Nottaway R.

Harricana

Senneterre

Lac Albanel

Dolbeau

L. St-Jean

Baie-Comeau

Betsiamites

Matane

Pén. de Gaspé

Gulf of St. Lawrence

Îs. de la Madeleine

Cabot Str.

 St.-PIERRE et MIQUELON (Fr.)

any

Albany R.

Joseph

Nakina

Kenogami

Missinaibi

Hearst

Cochrane

L. Abitibi

Taschereau

Rès. de Gouin

Roberval

Chicoutimi

1190

Tadoussac

Rimouski

Dalhousie

Campbellton

Bathurst

Chatham

Newcastle

C. North

Cheticamp

PR. EDWARD I.

Summerside Charlottetown

Cape Breton I.

Sydney

Glace Bay

Thunder Bay

Michipicoten

Langlac

Heron Bay

Oba

Franz

Timmins

Kirkland Lake

Noranda

Rouyn

Val d'Or

Haileybury

Cobalt

Témiscamingue

Rès. de Cabonga

La Tuque

Shawinigan

Trois-Rivières

Québec

Lévis

Thetford Mines

Woodstock

Edmundston

St.-Léonard

Amherst

Springhill

Windsor

Truro

N O V A

Dartmouth

Halifax

Bridgewater

Liverpool

pigeon

Nipigon

Mattagami

Kapuskasing

Haileybury

North Bay

Shawinigan

Joliette

Sorel

St.-Hyacinthe

Sherbrooke

M A I N E

Fredericton

Saint John

NEW BRUNSWICK

Moncton

Pictou

New Glasgow

Port Hawkesbury

Mulgrave

Sable I. (Nova Scotia)

6309

O C E A N

Thunder Bay

Copper Cliff

Sault Ste. Marie

Sudbury

North Channel

Pembroke

Hull

Ottawa

Cornwall

Granby

L. Champlain

1917

VERMONT

Augusta

Lewiston

Portland

C. Sable

Yarmouth

B. of Fundy

Keweenaw Bay

Marquette

Iron Mt.

Calumet

Keweenaw

Manistique

Cheboygan

Georgian Bay

Parry Sound

Owen Sound

Orillia

Barrie

Peterboro

Belleville

Kingston

Lachine

MONTRÉAL

Burlington

Concord

Manchester

NEW HAMPSHIRE

Lowell

MASS.

Boston

C. Cod

S

Antigo

Menominee

Green Bay

Appleton

Wausau

Traverse City

Cadillac

Ludington

Muskegon

Saginaw

Lake Huron

Owen Sound

Guelph

TORONTO

Oshawa

L. Ontario

Rochester

Syracuse

Utica

Albany

Springfield

Worcester

Providence

New Haven

Milwaukee

Racine

Kenosha

Manitowoc

Sheboygan

Appleton

WISCONSIN

L. Michigan

Grand Rapids

Kalamazoo

Kitchener

London

Brantford

Hamilton

Niagara Falls

Buffalo

NEW YORK

Rochester

Binghamton

Scranton

Waterbury

Bridgeport

CONN.

New York

CAGO

OIS

Gary

South Bend

INDIANA

Evanston

DETROIT

Toledo

OHIO

Windsor

Sarnia

Chatham

Lake Erie

Erie

Cleveland

Akron

Youngstown

Jamestown

Williamsport

PENNSYLVANIA

Reading

Allentown

Trenton

NEW YORK

Newark

Jersey City

NEW JERSEY

COPYRIGHT GEORGE PHILIP & SON, LTD.

80

70

60

60

50

40

80

70

40

30

30

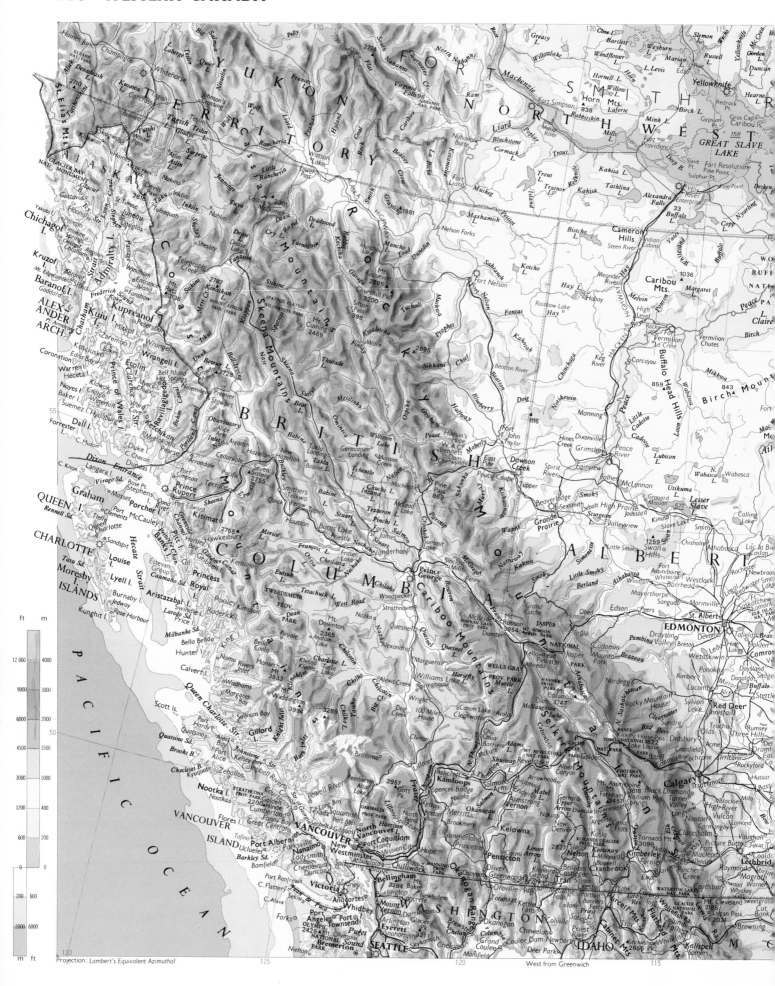

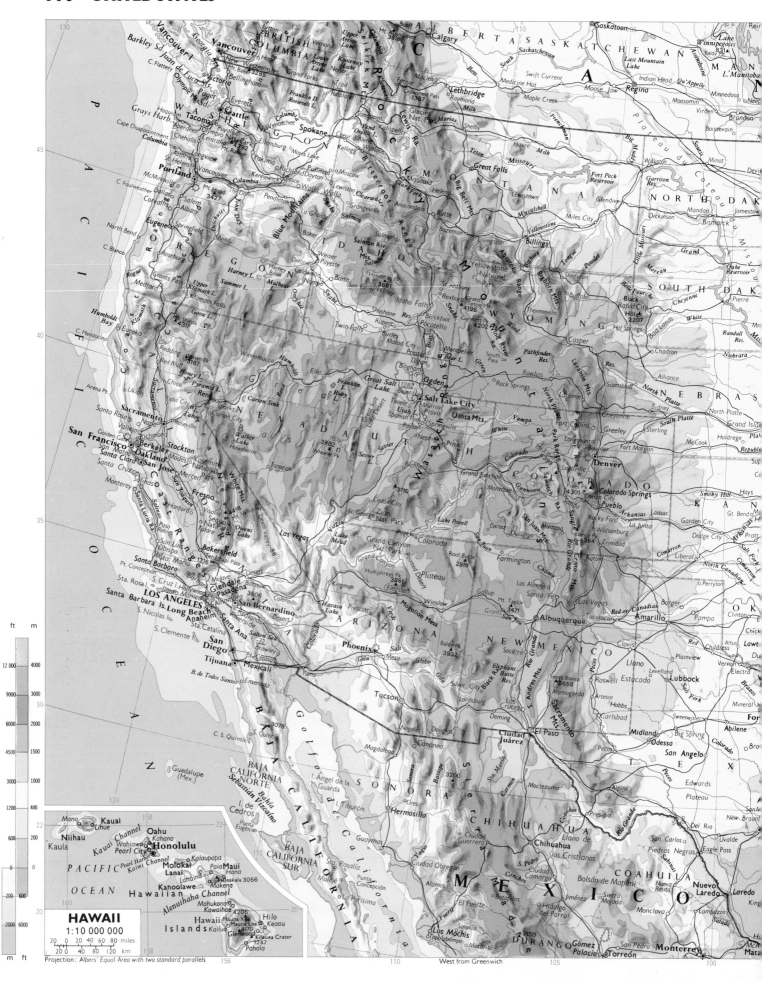

HAWAII
1:10 000 000

Projection: Albers' Equal Area with two standard parallels

1:12 000 000

50 0 50 100 150 200 250 300 miles
50 0 50 100 150 200 250 300 350 400 450 km

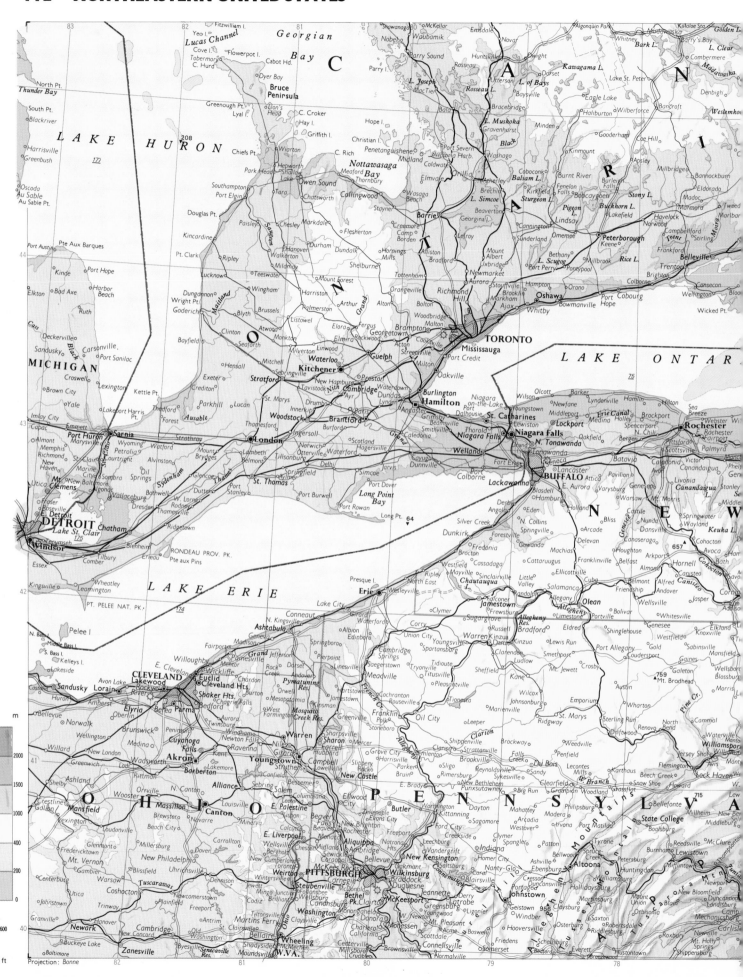

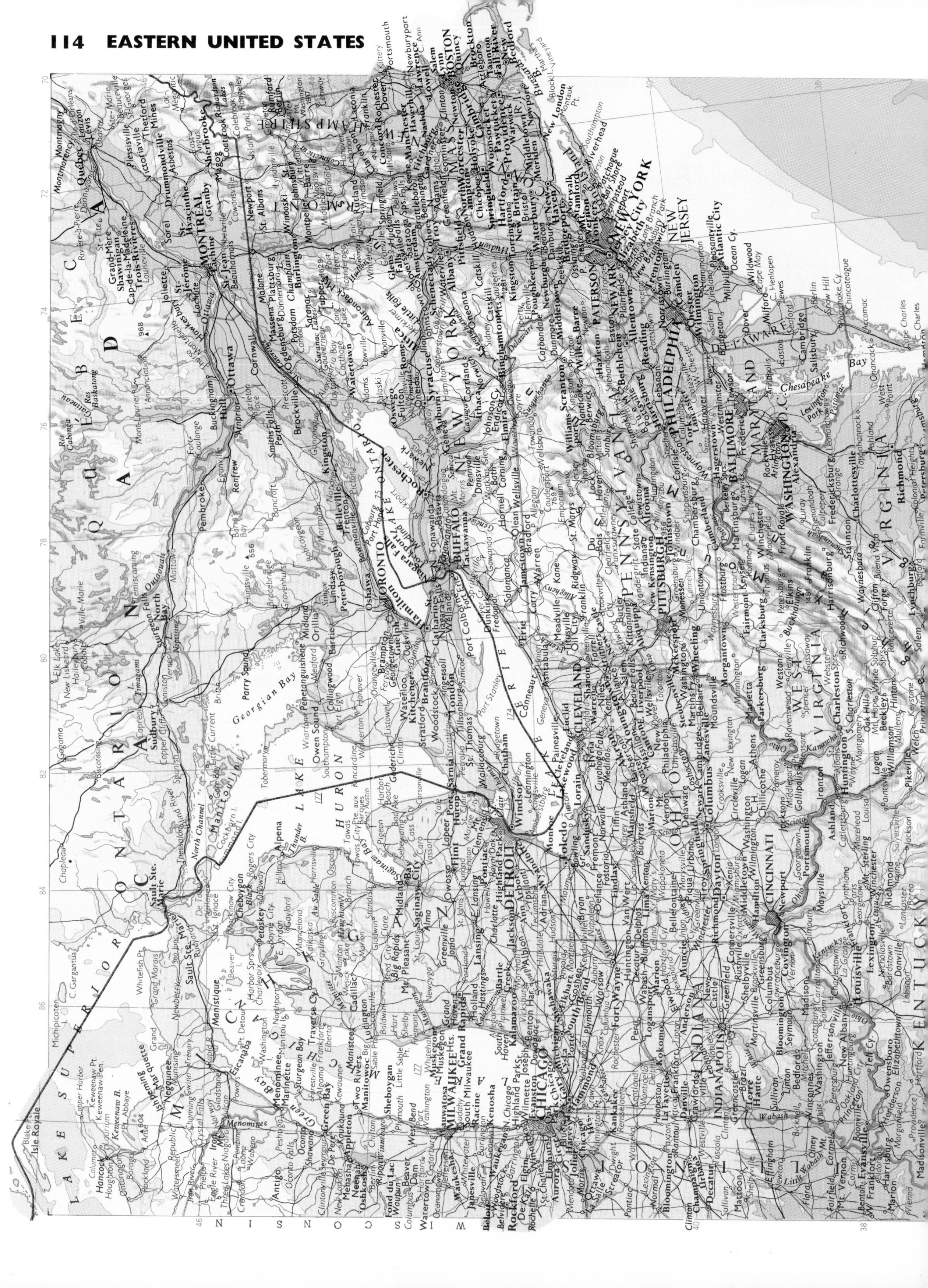
LAKE SUPERIOR
LAKE HURON
LAKE ERIE
LAKE ONTARIO
Georgian Bay
CHICAGO
MILWAUKEE
DETROIT
CLEVELAND
PITTSBURGH
BUFFALO
TORONTO
MONTREAL
Ottawa
Quebec
BOSTON
NEW YORK
PHILADELPHIA
BALTIMORE
WASHINGTON D.C.
CINCINNATI
INDIANAPOLIS
NEWARK
PATERSON

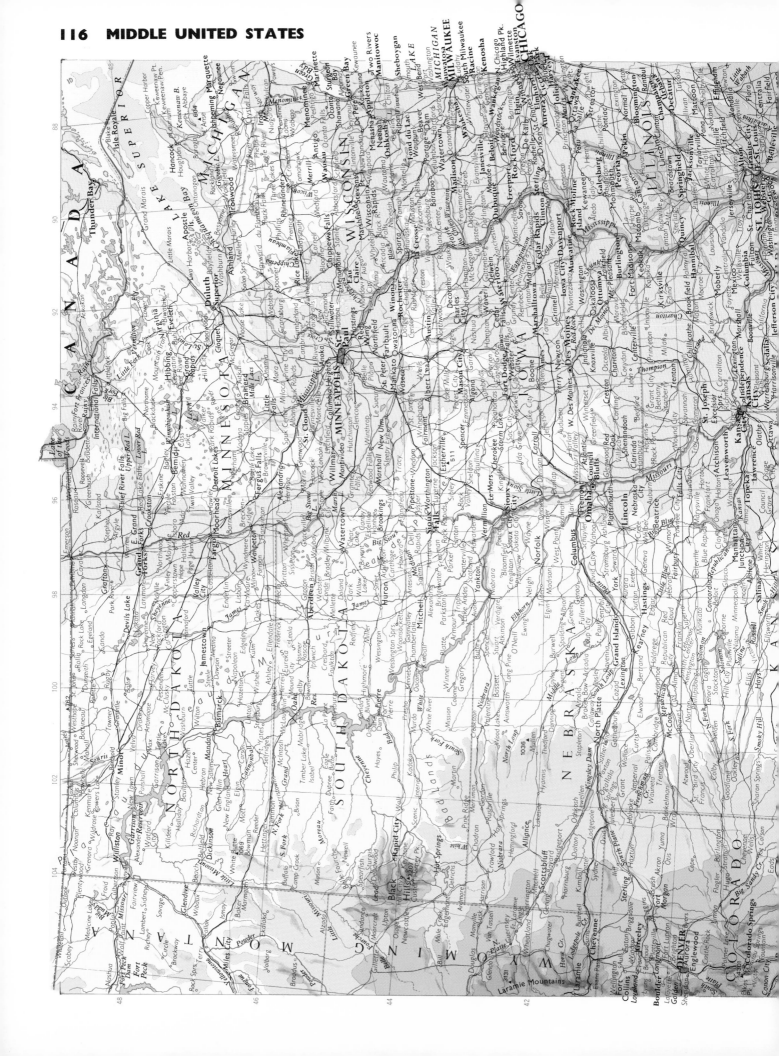

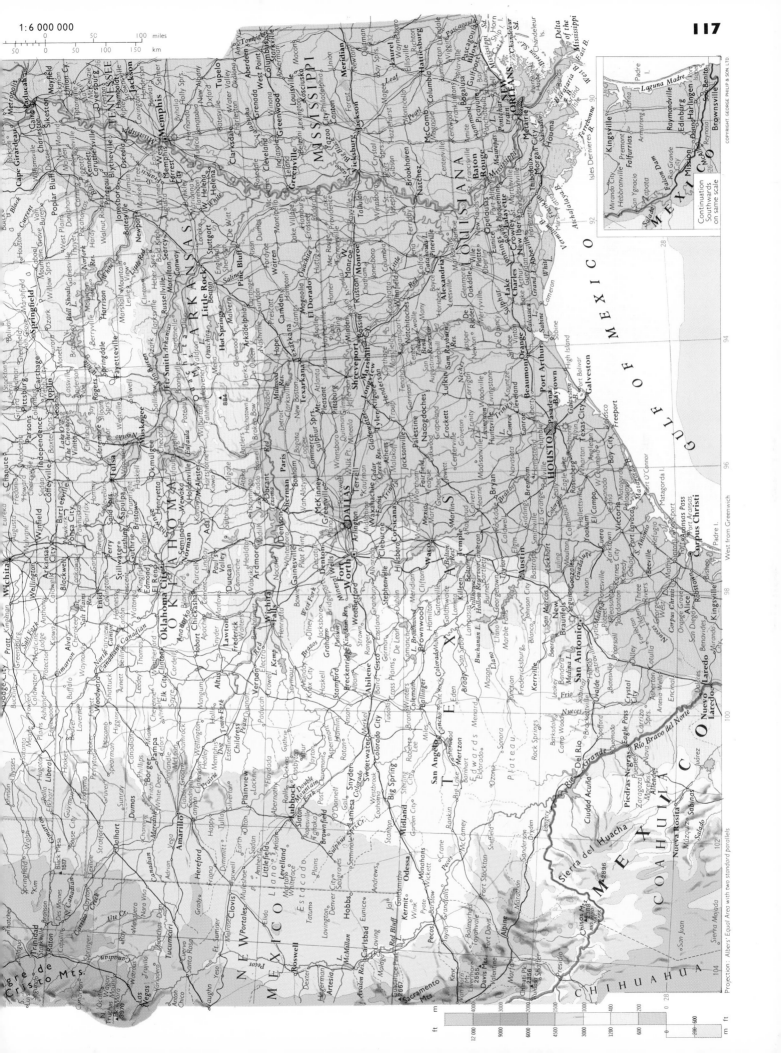

1:6 000 000

50　0　50　100 miles
50　0　50　100　150 km

1:12 000 000

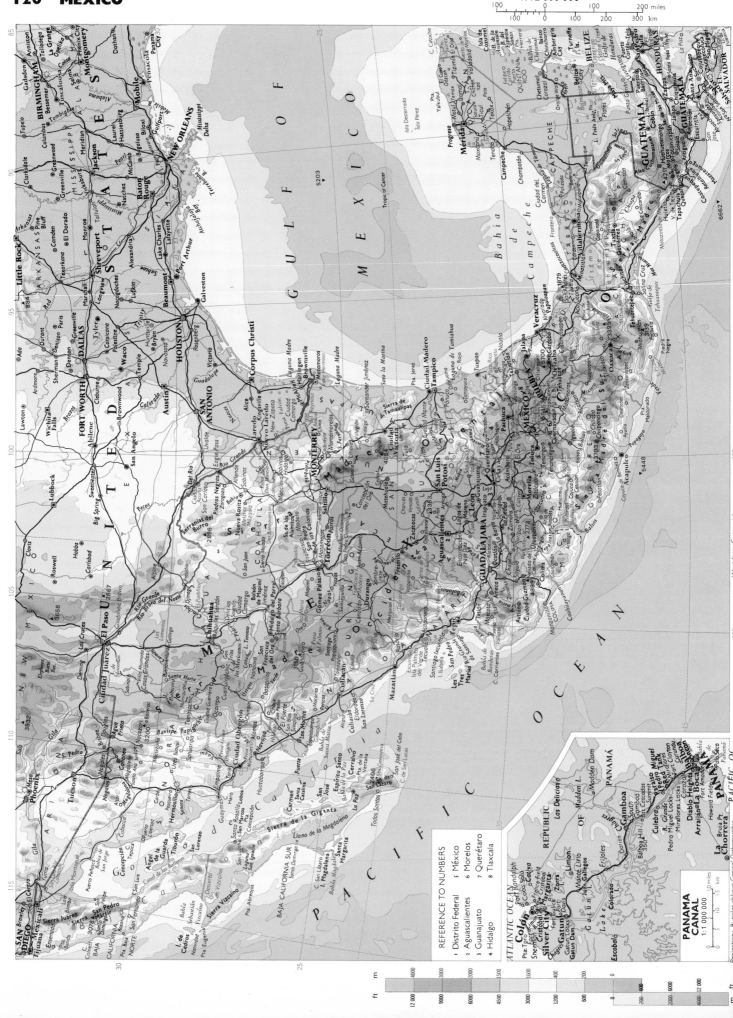

REFERENCE TO NUMBERS

1 Distrito Federal	5 México
2 Aguascalientes	6 Morelos
3 Guanajuato	7 Querétaro
4 Hidalgo	8 Tlaxcala

PANAMA CANAL
1:1 000 000

1:12 000 000

100   0   100   200 miles
100   0   100   200   300 km

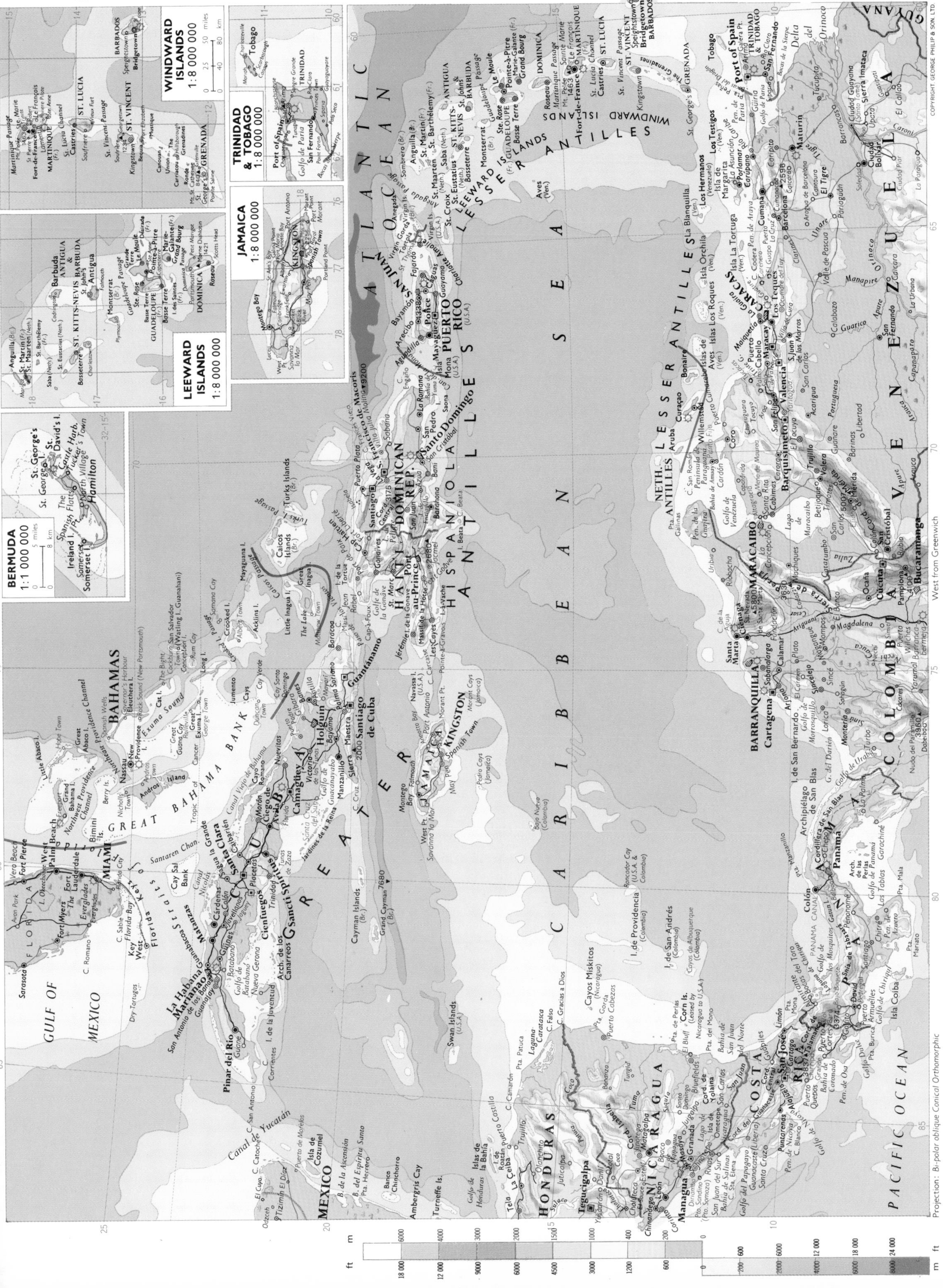

WINDWARD ISLANDS
1:8 000 000

TRINIDAD & TOBAGO
1:8 000 000

JAMAICA
1:8 000 000

BERMUDA
1:1 000 000

LEEWARD ISLANDS
1:8 000 000

ATLANTIC OCEAN

CARIBBEAN SEA

GULF OF MEXICO

PACIFIC OCEAN

BAHAMAS

GREAT BAHAMA BANK

CUBA

JAMAICA

HAITI

DOMINICAN REP.

HISPANIOLA

PUERTO RICO (U.S.A.)

GREATER ANTILLES

LESSER ANTILLES

LEEWARD ISLANDS

WINDWARD ISLANDS

NETH. ANTILLES

VENEZUELA

COLOMBIA

PANAMA

COSTA RICA

NICARAGUA

HONDURAS

MEXICO

FLORIDA

BARBADOS

La Habana
Santiago de Cuba
Kingston
Santo Domingo
Port-au-Prince
San Juan
Port of Spain
Caracas
Maracaibo
Barranquilla
Cartagena
Managua
Tegucigalpa
Panamá

Projection: Bi-polar oblique Conical Orthomorphic

West from Greenwich

COPYRIGHT GEORGE PHILIP & SON LTD.

1 : 30 000 000

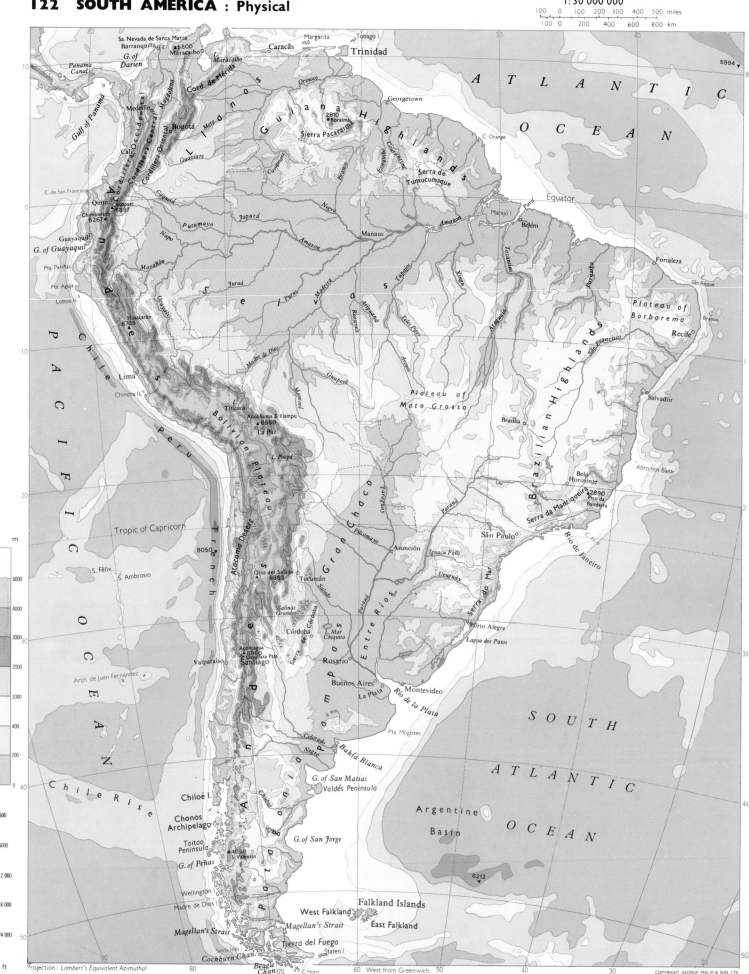

Projection: Lambert's Equivalent Azimuthal

COPYRIGHT. GEORGE PHILIP & SON. LTD.

1:30 000 000

100 0 100 200 300 400 500 miles
100 0 200 400 600 800 km

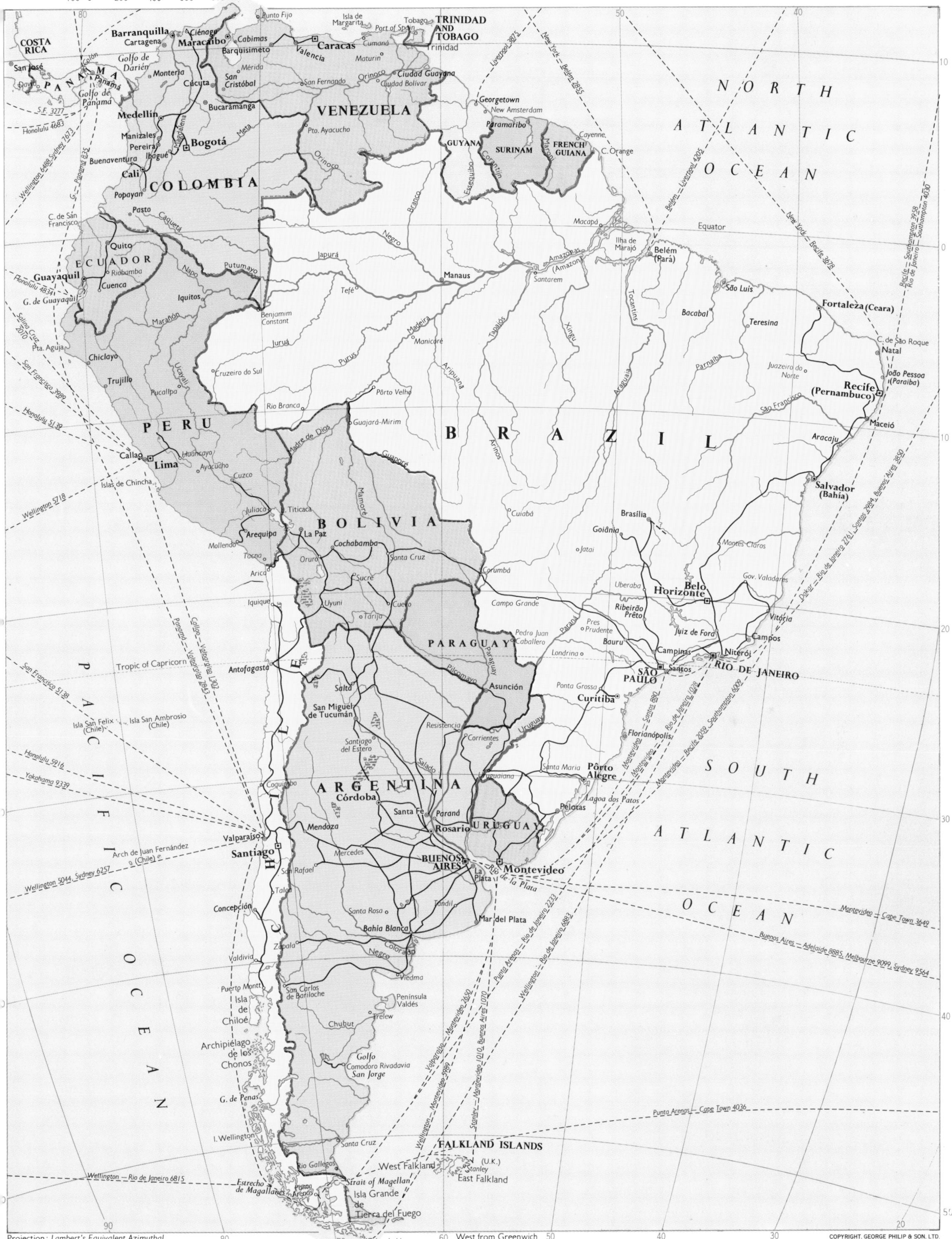

COSTA RICA
San José
David
Honolulu 7613
S.E. 3277
PANAMA
Panamá
Colón
Golfo de Panamá
Golfo de Darién

Barranquilla
Cartagena
Ciénaga
Maracaibo
Cabimas
Barquisimeto
Valencia
Caracas
Cumaná
Maturín
Port of Spain
Trinidad
TRINIDAD AND TOBAGO
Tobago
Punta Fijo
Isla de Margarita

Monteria
Mérida
San Fernando
Orinoco
Ciudad Guayana
Ciudad Bolívar
VENEZUELA
Cúcuta
San Cristóbal
Bucaramanga
Medellín
Manizales
Pereira
Ibagué
Buenaventura
Cali
Bogotá
Meta
Pto. Ayacucho
Georgetown
New Amsterdam
Paramaribo
Cayenne
C. Orange
GUYANA
SURINAM
FRENCH GUIANA

COLOMBIA
Popayán
Pasto
Caquetá
C. de San Francisco
Quito
Riobamba
ECUADOR
Guayaquil
Cuenca
G. de Guayaquil
Honolulu 48,341
Salina Cruz 2010
Pta. Aguja
Putumayo
Napo
Iquitos
Marañón
Benjamim Constant
Nørro
Japurá
Manaus
Santarém
Tefé
Macapá
Ilha de Marajó
Belém (Pará)
Equator

PERU
Chiclayo
Trujillo
Pucalpa
Cruzeiro do Sul
Ucayali
Juruá
Purus
Madeira
Aripuanã
Manicoré
Tocantins
São Luis
Teresina
Parnaíba
Fortaleza (Ceara)
C. de São Roque
Natal
João Pessoa (Paraíba)
Recife (Pernambuco)

Callao
Lima
Huancayo
Ayacucho
Cuzco
Madre de Dios
Guajará-Mirim
Rio Branca
Pôrto Velho
Guaporé
B R A Z I L
Xingu
Tapajós
Araguaia
Bacabal
Juazeiro do Norte
São Francisco
Maceió
Aracaju
Islas de Chinchа
Wellington 5718
Juliaca
Titicaca
Arequipa
La Paz
BOLIVIA
Cochabamba
Santa Cruz
Sucre
Oruro
Mamoré
Corumbá
Cuiabá
Brasília
Goiânia
Jataí
Montes Claros
Gov. Valadares
Salvador (Bahia)
Mallendo
Tacna
Arica
Iquique
Uyuni
Tarija
Cuevo
Campo Grande
Uberaba
Ribeirão Prêto
Belo Horizonte
Vitória
Antofagasta
PARAGUAY
Pilcomayo
Paraguay
Asunción
Pedro Juan Caballero
Pres. Prudente
Bauru
Londrina
Campinas
SÃO PAULO
Santos
Niterói
RIO DE JANEIRO
Campos
Juiz de Fora
Tropic of Capricorn
Salta
San Miguel de Tucumán
Resistencia
Corrientes
Paraná
Ponta Grossa
Curitiba
Florianópolis
Isla San Felix (Chile)
Isla San Ambrosio (Chile)
Honolulu 5916
Yokahama 9339
Santiago del Estero
Salado
Uruguay
Uruguaiana
Santa Maria
Pôrto Alegre
Lagoa dos Patos
Pelotas
ARGENTINA
Córdoba
Santa Fe
Rosario
URUGUAY
Coquimbo
Mendoza
Mercedes
Montevideo
Buenos Aires
La Plata
Rio de la Plata
Valparaíso
Santiago
San Rafael
Talca
Concepción
Santa Rosa
Tandil
Mar del Plata
Bahía Blanca
Arch. de Juan Fernández (Chile)
Wellington 5044   Sydney 6257
Zapala
Negro
Colorado
Valdivia
Viedma
Puerto Montt
San Carlos de Bariloche
Isla de Chiloé
Chubut
Trelew
Península Valdés
Archipiélago de los Chonos
Golfo Comodoro Rivadavia
San Jorge
G. de Penas
I. Wellington
Santa Cruz
Wellington – Rio de Janeiro 6815
Rio Gallegos
Estrecho de Magallanes
Strait of Magellan
Punta Arenas
Isla Grande de Tierra del Fuego
Cabo de Hornos (Cape Horn)
FALKLAND ISLANDS
West Falkland
Stanley
East Falkland
(U.K.)

NORTH ATLANTIC OCEAN
New York – Liverpool 3305
Liverpool 3973
Belém – Liverpool 4205
Recife – Southampton 3658
Rio de Janeiro – Southampton 4030
Recife – Southampton 3638
Rio de Janeiro – Buenos Aires 3590

SOUTH ATLANTIC OCEAN
Montevideo – Cape Town 3642
Buenos Aires – Adelaide 8885, Melbourne 9099, Sydney 9564
Punta Arenas – Cape Town 4036

PACIFIC OCEAN
San Francisco 5138
Callao – Valparaíso 1292
Valparaíso 2843
Panamá

Projection: Lambert's Equivalent Azimuthal
West from Greenwich
COPYRIGHT. GEORGE PHILIP & SON, LTD.

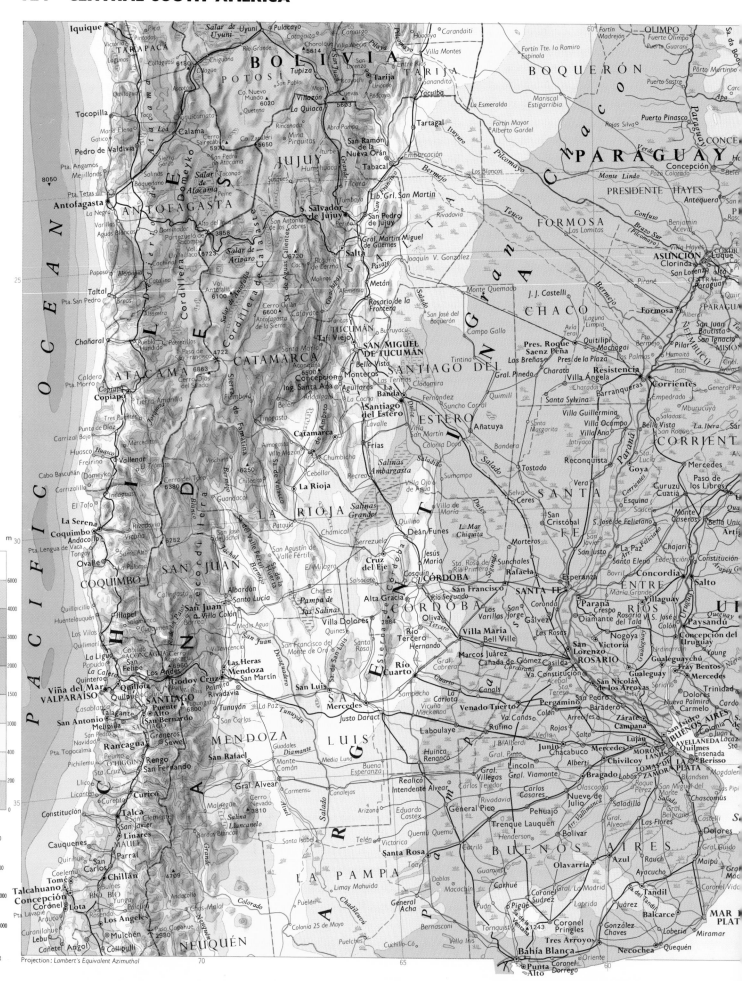

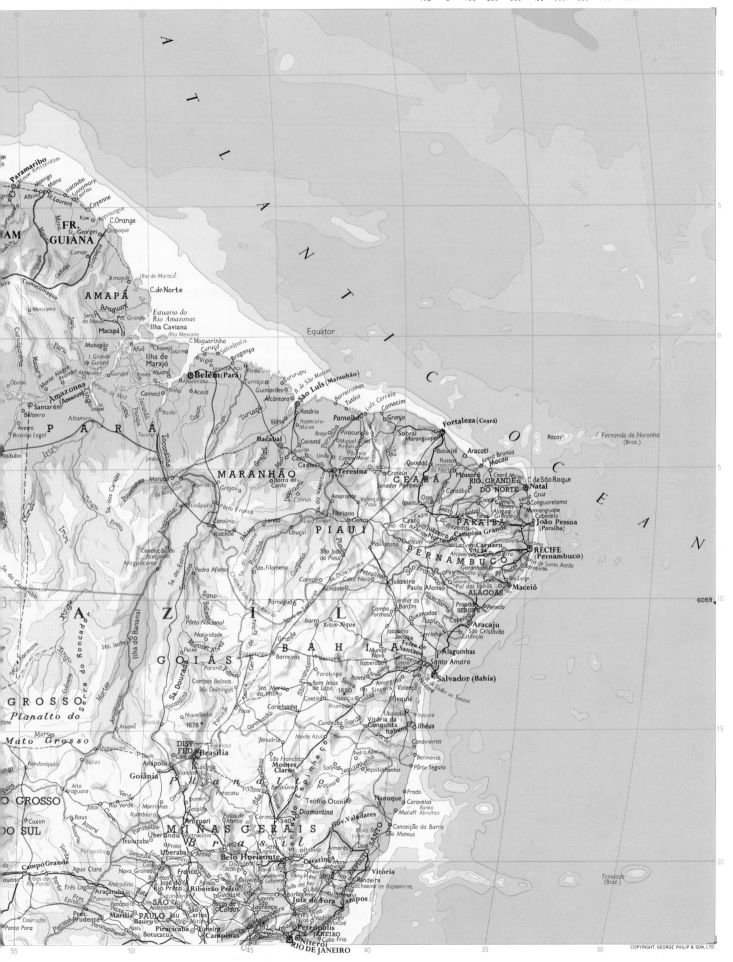

1:16 000 000

100   0   100   200   300   400   500 miles
100 0 100 200 300 400 500 600 700 800 km

A T L A N T I C

Paramaribo
Nieuw Amsterdam
Moengo   Mana
Albina   St. Laurent   Sinnamary   Kourou
Iracoubo   Cayenne
C. Orange
Approuague
FR.   St. Georges
GUIANA   Oiapoque
Camopi
Tumucumaque
Camopi

AM

Ilha de Maracá
A M A P Á
C. do Norte
Araguari
Serra   Rio Grande
do Navio
Macapá   Estuário do
Rio Amazonas
Ilha Caviana
Ilha Mexiana
Mazagão   C. Maguarinho   Equator

Merirumã
Afuá   Chaves   Sourea   Curuçá   Salinópolis
Jari   Ilha de   Vigia   Igarapé Açu   Bragança
Marajó   Breves   Muaná   Viseu
I. Grande   Pôrto
de Gurupá   Almeirim   Curralinho   Belém (Pará)   B. de São Marcos (Maranhão)
Óbidos   Prainha   Gurupá   Cametá   Acará   São Luís (Maranhão)   Alcântara
Monte Alegre   Breves   Turiaçu   Barreirinhas
Santarém   Altamira   Sousel   Baião   Guimarães
Belterra   Amazonas   Xingu   Tucuruí   Turiaçu   Tutóia   Luís Correia   Camocim
(Amazon)   Itapecuru-   Vigia
Avero   Brasília Legal   P A R Á   Jacundá   Mirim   Parnaíba   Granja   Fortaleza (Ceará)
Itaituba   Iriri   Tocantins   Viana   Brejo   Piracuruca   Sobral   Baturité
Maraba   Bacabal   Coroatá   Piripiri   Barras   Campo Maior   Maranguape   Aracati   Areia Branca
Rocas
Serra dos Carajás   Imperatriz   Codó   União   Ipu   Quixadá   Russas   Macau   Fernando de Noronha
M A R A N H Ã O   Caxias   Teresina   Oiticica   Crateús   Mossoró   Ceará Mirim   (Braz.)
Xingu   Grajaú   Barra do   Timon   Senador   Pompeu   Caicó   RIO GRANDE   Natal
Conceição do   Corda   Pompeu   Iguatu   Orós   Caraúbas   DO NORTE   C. de São Roque
Araguaia   Tocantinópolis   Pôrto Franco   Valença do Piauí   Nova
Araguacema   Carolina   Loreto   Amarante   Caicó   Currais   Cruz
Conceição do   Riachão   Floriano   Oeiras   Crato   Sousa   Canguaretama
Araguaia   Sta. Filomena   Uruçuí   Nova York   Juàzeiro do   Patos   Alagoa   Campina   Mamanguape
Araguacema   Pedro Afonso   P I A U I   São João   Chap. do Araripe   Norte   Sertânia   PARAÍBA   Cabedelo
B R A Z I L   do Piauí   Paulistana   Ouricuri   Serra   Caruaru   João Pessoa (Paraíba)
Sa. do Cachimbo   Natividade   Dois Irmãos   Arcoverde   PERNAMBUCO   RECIFE
Pôrto Nacional   Caracol   Casa Nova   Petrolina   Garanhuns   (Pernambuco)
Parnaguá   Remanso   Juàzeiro   Palmares   B. de Santo Antão
Xique-Xique   São   Petrolândia   Vitória   Palmares
Serra Formosa   Campo   Francisco   Pão de Açúcar   Maceió
G O I Á S   Ilha do Bananal   Barra   Formoso   Paulo Afonso   Gouveia   Largo
Senhor do   ALAGOAS   6059
Barreiras   Bonfim   Própria
Araguaia   Sta. Isabel   Queimadas   Capela   SERGIPE   Peneda
Campos Belos   Xique-Xique   Itapicuru   Aracaju
Tocantins   Sta. Maria   Jacobina   Serrinha   São Cristóvão
Sa. Dourada   da Vitória   B A H I A   Nova   Estância
Parãna   Barreiras   Feira de   Alagoinhas
Niquelândia   Bom Jesus   Serra   Santana   Santo Amaro
da Lapa   1850   Itaberaba   Cachoeira   Salvador (Bahia)
G R O S S O   Aruanã   Posse   Irecê   Ituaçu   Amargosa   Castro
Planalto do   Sta. Maria   Coité   Sincorá   Alves   B. de Todos os Santos
Carinhanha   Brumado   Valença
Mato   Grosso   Uruaçu   Condeúba   Jequié   Itacaré
1678   Januária   Monte Azul   Vitória da   Ubaitaba   Ilhéus
Rondonópolis   Baliza   Goiás   Formosa   Conquista   Itabuna
Januária   Canavieiras
DIST.   São   Pedra Azul   Belmonte
Goiás   Anápolis   FED.   Brasília   Francisco   Salinas   Jequitinhonha   Pôrto Seguro
Goiânia   Vianópolis   Iuiziânia   Montes   Jequitinhonha
DO   Alto   Claros   Araçuaí   Prado
GROSSO   Araguaia   Verde   Morrinhos   Comendador   Pirapora   Nanuque   Caravelas
Rio Verde   Itumbiara   Patos de   Diamantina   Teófilo Otoni   Mucuri   Banca
DO   Coxim   Baús   Minas   Corinto   Abrolhos
SUL   Jataí   Apore   Araguari   1340   Conceição da Barra
Uberlândia   Curvelo   Gov. Valadares   São Mateus
Campo Grande   Prata   Patrocínio   Araxá   Aimorés
Ribas do   Agua Clara   Uberaba   M I N A S   G E R A I S   Vitória
Rio Pardo   Nova Granada   Sacramento   Itabira   Bandeira
Três Lagoas   José   Franca   Belo Horizonte   Caratinga   Cachoeiro de Itapemirim
Andradina   Bonito   Ouro Prêto   Doce   Trindade
Pres.   Araçatuba   Rio Prêto   Ribeirão Prêto   Lavras   Barbacena   (Braz.)
Epitácio   Penápolis   São   Poços de   São Lourenço   Juiz de Fora   Campos
Dourados   Marília   PAULO   Jaú   Mogi-Mirim   Petrópolis   Cabo Frio
Bauru   Piracicaba   Campinas
Ponta Porã   Botucatu   Limeira   RIO DE JANEIRO
Niterói
RIO DE JANEIRO

O C E A N

6059
10

15

20

1:16 000 000

Projection: Sanson-Flamsteed's Sinusoidal

INDEX *

The number printed in bold type against each entry indicates the map page where the feature can be found. This is followed by its geographical coordinates. The first coordinate indicates latitude, i.e. distance north or south of the Equator. The second coordinate indicates longitude, i.e. distance east or west of the meridian of Greenwich in England (shown as 0° longitude). Both latitude and longitude are measured in degrees and minutes (with 60 minutes in a degree), and appear on the map as horizontal and vertical gridlines respectively. Thus the entry for Paris in France reads.

Paris, France   **19** 48 50 N 2 20 E

This entry indicates that Paris is on page 19, at latitude 48 degrees 50 minutes north (approximately five-sixths of the distance between horizontal gridlines 48 and 49, marked on either side of the page) and at longitude 2 degrees 20 minutes east (approximately one-third of the distance between vertical gridlines 2 and 3, marked at top and bottom of the page). Paris can be found where lines extended from these two points cross on the page. The geographical coordinates are sometimes only approximate but are close enough for the place to be located. Rivers have been indexed to their mouth or confluence.

An open square □ signifies that the name refers to an administrative subdivision of a country while a solid square ■ follows the name of a country. An arrow ⌒ follows the name of a river.

The alphabetical order of names composed of two or more words is governed primarily by the first word and then by the second. This rule applies even if the second word is a description or its abbreviation, R.,L.,I. for example. Names composed of a proper name (Gibraltar) and a description (Strait of) are positioned alphabetically by the proper name. If the same place name occurs twice or more times in the index and all are in the same country, each is followed by the name of the administrative subdivision in which it is located. The names are placed in the alphabetical order of the subdivisions. If the same place name occurs twice or more in the index and the places are in different countries they will be followed by their country names, the latter governing the alphabetical order. In a mixture of these situations the primary order is fixed by the alphabetical sequence of the countries and the secondary order by that of the country subdivisions.

Please refer to the table at the end of the index for the recent place name changes in India, Iran, Mozambique and Zimbabwe.

Abbreviations used in the index:

A. R.–Autonomous Region
A. S. S. R.–Autonomous Soviet Socialist Republic
Afghan.–Afghanistan
Afr.–Africa
Ala.–Alabama
Alas.–Alaska
Alg.–Algeria
Alta.–Alberta
Amer.–America
And. P.–Andhra Pradesh
Arch.–Archipelago
Argent.–Argentina
Ariz.–Arizona
Ark.–Arkansas
Atl. Oc. – Atlantic Ocean
Austral. – Australia
B. – Baie, Bahía, Bay, Bucht, Bugt
B.A. – Buenos Aires
B.C. – British Columbia
Bangla. – Bangladesh
Barr. – Barrage
Bay. – Bayern
Belg. – Belgium
Berks. – Berkshire
Bol. – Bolshoi
Boliv. – Bolivia
Bots. – Botswana
Br. – British
Bri. – Bridge
Bt. – Bight
Bucks. – Buckinghamshire
Bulg. – Bulgaria
C. – Cabo, Cap, Cape, Coast
C. Prov. – Cape Province
Calif. – California
Camb. – Cambodia
Cambs. – Cambridgeshire
Can. – Canada
Cent. – Central
Chan. – Channel
Co. – Country
Colomb. – Colombia
Colo. – Colorado
Conn. – Connecticut
Cord. – Cordillera
Cr. – Creek
Cumb. – Cumbria
Czech. – Czechoslovakia
D.C. – District of Columbia
Del. – Delaware
Dep. – Dependency
Derby. – Derbyshire
Des. – Desert
Dist. – District
Dj. – Djebel
Dumf. & Gall. – Dumfries and Galloway
E. – East
Eng. – England
Fed. – Federal, Federation
Fla. – Florida
For. – Forest
Fr. – France, French
Fs. – Falls
Ft. – Fort

G. – Golfe, Golfo, Gulf, Guba
Ga. – Georgia
Ger. – Germany
Glam. – Glamorgan
Glos. – Gloucestershire
Gr. – Grande, Great, Greater, Group
H.K. – Hong Kong
H.P. – Himachal Pradesh
Hants. – Hampshire
Harb. – Harbor, Harbour
Hd. – Head
Here. & Worcs. – Hereford and Worcester
Herts. – Hertfordshire
Hts. – Heights
Hung. – Hungary
I.o.M. – Isle of Man
I.(s). – Île, Ilha, Insel, Isla, Island, Isle
Id. – Idaho
Ill. – Illinois
Ind. – Indiana
Ind. Oc. – Indian Ocean
Indon. – Indonesia
J. – Jabal, Jabel, Jazira
Junc. – Junction
K. – Kap, Kapp
K. – Kuala
Kal. – Kalmyk A.S.S.R.
Kans. – Kansas
Kep. – Kepulauan
Ky. – Kentucky
L. – Lac, Lacul, Lago, Lagoa, Lake, Limni, Loch, Lough
La. – Lousiana
Lancs. – Lancashire
Leb. – Lebanon
Leics. – Leicestershire
Lim. – Limerick
Lincs. – Lincolnshire
Lit. – Little
Lr. – Lower
Mad. P. – Madhya Pradesh
Madag. – Madagascar
Malay. – Malaysia
Man. – Manitoba
Manch. – Manchester
Maran. – Maranhão
Mass. – Massachusetts
Md. – Maryland
Me. – Maine
Mend. – Mendoza
Mér. – Méridionale
Mich. – Michigan
Mid. – Middle
Minn. – Minnesota
Miss. – Mississippi
Mo. – Missouri
Mong. – Mongolia
Mont. – Montana
Moroc. – Morocco
Mozam. – Mozambique
Mt.(e). – Mont, Monte, Monti, Montaña, Mountain
Mys. – Mysore
N. – Nord, Norte, North, Northern, Nouveau

N.B. – New Brunswick
N.C. – North Carolina
N.D. – North Dakota
N.H. – New Hampshire
N.I. – North Island
N.J. – New Jersey
N. Mex. – New Mexico
N.S. – Nova Scotia
N.S.W. – New South Wales
N.T. – Northern Territory
N.W.T. – North West Territory
N.Y. – New York
N.Z. – New Zealand
Nat. – National
Nat.Park. – National Park
Nebr. – Nebraska
Neth. – Netherlands
Nev. – Nevada
Newf. – Newfoundland
Nic. – Nicaragua
Northants. – Northamptonshire
Northumb. – Northumberland
Notts. – Nottinghamshire
O. – Oued, ouadi
Occ. – Occidentale
O.F.S. – Orange Free State
Okla. – Oklahoma
Ont. – Ontario
Or. – Orientale
Oreg. – Oregon
Os. – Ostrov
Oxon. – Oxfordshire
Oz. – Ozero
P. – Pass, Passo, Pasul, Pulau
P.E.I. – Prince Edward Island
P.N.G. – Papua New Guinea
P.O. – Post Office
P. Rico.–Puerto Rico
Pa. – Pennsylvania
Pac. Oc. – Pacific Ocean
Pak. – Pakistan
Parag. – Paraguay
Pass. – Passage
Pen. – Peninsula, Peninsule
Phil. – Philippines
Pk. – Peak
Plat. – Plateau
P-ov. – Poluostrov
Port. – Portugal, Portuguese
Prom. – Promontory
Prov. – Province, Provincial
Pt. – Point
Pta. – Ponta, Punta
Pte. – Pointe
Qué. – Québec
Queens. – Queensland
R. – Rio, River
R.I. – Rhode Island
R.S.F.S.R. – Russian Soviet Federative Socialist Republic
Ra.(s). – Range(s)
Raj. – Rajasthan
Reg. – Region
Rep. – Republic
Res. – Reserve, Reservoir
Rhld. – Pfz. – Rheinland– Pfalz

S. – San, South
S. Afr. – South Africa
S. Austral. – South Australia
S.C. – South Carolina
S.D. – South Dakota
S.-Holst. – Schleswig-Holstein
S.I. – South Island
S. Leone–Sierra Leone
S.S.R. – Soviet Socialist Republic
Sa. – Serra, Sierra
Sard. – Sardinia
Sask. – Saskatchewan
Scot. – Scotland
Sd. – Sound
Sept. – Septentrionale
Sev. – Severnaja
Sib. – Siberia
Som. – Somerset
Span. – Spanish
Sprs. – Springs
St. – Saint
Sta. – Santa, Station
Staffs. – Staffordshire
Ste. – Sainte
Sto. – Santo
Str. – Strait, Stretto
Switz. – Switzerland
T.O. – Telegraph Office
Tas. – Tasmania
Tenn. – Tennessee
Terr. – Territory
Tex. – Texas
Tg. – Tanjung
Thai. – Thailand
Tipp. – Tipperary
Trans. – Transvaal
U.K. – United Kingdom
U.S.A. – United States of America
U.S.S.R. – Union of Soviet Socialist Republics
Ukr. – Ukraine
Ut.P. – Uttar Pradesh
Utd. – United
V. – Vorota
Va. – Virginia
Vdkhr. – Vodokhranilishche
Venez. – Venezuela
Vic. – Victoria
Viet. – Vietnam
Vol. – Volcano
Vt. – Vermont
W. – Wadi, West
W.A. – Western Australia
W. Isles–Western Isles
W. Va. – West Virginia
Wash. – Washington
Wilts. – Wiltshire
Wis. – Wisconsin
Wlkp. – Wielkopolski
Wyo. – Wyoming
Yorks. – Yorkshire
Yug. – Yugoslavia
Zap. – Zapadnaja
Zimb. – Zimbabwe

Aachen Ain el Mafki

A

Aachen	**24**	50 47N	6 4 E
Aâlâ en Nîl □	**87**	8 50N	29 55 E
Aalen	**25**	48 49N	10 6 E
Aalsmeer	**16**	52 17N	4 43 E
Aalst	**16**	50 56N	4 2 E
Aalten	**16**	51 56N	6 35 E
Aarau	**25**	47 23N	8 4 E
Aarberg	**25**	47 2N	7 16 E
Aare →	**25**	47 33N	8 14 E
Aargau □	**25**	47 26N	8 10 E
Aarschot	**16**	50 59N	4 49 E
Aba, Nigeria	**85**	5 10N	7 19 E
Aba, Zaïre	**90**	3 58N	30 17 E
Âbâ, Jazîrat	**87**	13 30N	32 31 E
Ābādān	**64**	30 22N	48 20 E
Abade, Ethiopia	**87**	9 22N	38 3 E
Abade, Iran	**65**	31 8N	52 40 E
Abadin	**30**	43 21N	7 29W
Abadla	**82**	31 2N	2 45W
Abaetetuba	**127**	1 40 S	48 50W
Abagnar Qi	**76**	43 52N	116 2 E
Abai	**125**	25 58 S	55 54W
Abak	**85**	4 58N	7 50 E
Abakaliki	**85**	6 22N	8 2 E
Abakan	**59**	53 40N	91 10 E
Abal Nam	**86**	25 20N	38 37 E
Abalemma	**85**	16 12N	7 50 E
Abanilla	**33**	38 12N	1 3W
Abano Terme	**39**	45 22N	11 46 E
Abarán	**33**	38 12N	1 23W
Abarqū	**65**	31 10N	53 20 E
'Abasān	**62**	31 19N	34 21 E
Abashiri	**74**	44 0N	144 15 E
Abashiri-Wan	**74**	44 0N	144 30 E
Abau	**98**	10 11 S	148 46 E
Abaújszántó	**27**	48 16N	21 12 E
Abay	**58**	49 38N	72 53 E
Abaya L.	**87**	6 30N	37 50 E
Abaza	**58**	52 39N	90 6 E
Abbadia San Salvatore	**39**	42 53N	11 40 E
Abbay (Nîl el Azraq) →	**87**	15 38N	32 31 E
Abbaye, Pt.	**114**	46 58N	88 4W
Abbé, L.	**87**	11 8N	41 47 E
Abbeville, France	**19**	50 6N	1 49 E
Abbeville, La., U.S.A.	**117**	30 0N	92 7W
Abbeville, S.C., U.S.A.	**115**	34 12N	82 21W
Abbiategrasso	**38**	45 23N	8 55 E
Abbieglassie	**99**	27 15 S	147 28 E
Abbotsford, B.C., Can.	**108**	49 5N	122 20W
Abbotsford, Qué., Can.	**113**	45 25N	72 53W
Abbotsford, U.S.A.	**116**	44 55N	90 20W
Abbottabad	**66**	34 10N	73 15 E
Abd al Kūrī	**63**	12 5N	52 20 E
Abéché	**81**	13 50N	20 35 E
Abejar	**32**	41 48N	2 47W
Abekr	**87**	12 45N	28 50 E
Abêlessa	**82**	22 58N	4 47 E
Abengourou	**84**	6 42N	3 27W
Åbenrå	**49**	55 3N	9 25 E
Abensberg	**25**	48 49N	11 51 E
Abeokuta	**85**	7 3N	3 19 E
Aber	**90**	2 12N	32 25 E
Aberaeron	**13**	52 15N	4 16W
Aberayron = Aberaeron	**13**	52 15N	4 16W
Abercorn	**99**	25 12 S	151 5 E
Abercorn = Mbala	**91**	8 46 S	31 17 E
Abercrombie →	**100**	33 54 S	149 8 E
Aberdare	**13**	51 43N	3 27W
Aberdare Ra.	**90**	0 15 S	36 50 E
Aberdeen, Austral.	**99**	32 9 S	150 56 E
Aberdeen, Can.	**109**	52 20N	106 8W
Aberdeen, S. Afr.	**92**	32 28 S	24 2 E
Aberdeen, U.K.	**14**	57 9N	2 6W
Aberdeen, Ala., U.S.A.	**115**	33 49N	88 33W
Aberdeen, Idaho, U.S.A.	**118**	42 57N	112 50W
Aberdeen, S.D., U.S.A.	**116**	45 30N	98 30W
Aberdeen, Wash., U.S.A.	**118**	47 0N	123 50W
Aberdovey	**13**	52 33N	4 3W
Aberfeldy	**14**	56 37N	3 50W
Abergaria-a-Velha	**30**	40 41N	8 32W
Abergavenny	**13**	51 49N	3 1W
Abernathy	**117**	33 49N	101 49W
Abert L.	**118**	42 40N	120 8W
Aberystwyth	**13**	52 25N	4 6W
Abha	**86**	18 0N	42 34 E
Abhayapuri	**69**	26 24N	90 38 E
Abidiya	**86**	18 18N	34 3 E
Abidjan	**84**	5 26N	3 58W
Abilene, Kans., U.S.A.	**116**	39 0N	97 16W
Abilene, Texas, U.S.A.	**117**	32 22N	99 40W
Abingdon, U.K.	**13**	51 40N	1 17W
Abingdon, Ill., U.S.A.	**116**	40 53N	90 23W
Abingdon, Va., U.S.A.	**115**	36 46N	81 56W
Abitau →	**109**	59 53N	109 3W
Abitau L.	**109**	60 27N	107 15W
Abitibi L.	**106**	48 40N	79 40W
Abiy Adi	**87**	13 39N	39 3 E
Abkhaz A.S.S.R. □	**57**	43 0N	41 0 E
Abkit	**59**	64 10N	157 10 E
Abnûb	**86**	27 18N	31 4 E
Åbo	**51**	60 28N	22 15 E
Abo, Massif d'	**83**	21 41N	16 8 E
Abocho	**85**	7 35N	6 56 E
Abohar	**68**	30 10N	74 10 E
Aboisso	**84**	5 30N	3 5W
Abomey	**85**	7 10N	2 5 E
Abondance	**21**	46 18N	6 42 E
Abong-Mbang	**88**	4 0N	13 8 E
Abonnema	**85**	4 41N	6 49 E
Abony	**27**	47 12N	20 3 E
Aboso	**84**	5 23N	1 57W
Abou-Deïa	**81**	11 20N	19 20 E
Aboyne	**14**	57 4N	2 48W
Abra Pampa	**124**	22 43 S	65 42W
Abrantes	**31**	39 24N	8 7W
Abraveses	**30**	40 41N	7 55W
Abreojos, Pta.	**120**	26 50N	113 40W
Abreschviller	**19**	48 39N	7 6 E
Abrets, Les	**21**	45 32N	5 35 E
Abri, Esh Shimâliya, Sudan	**86**	20 50N	30 27 E
Abri, Janub Kordofân, Sudan	**87**	11 40N	30 21 E
Abrud	**46**	46 19N	23 5 E
Abruzzi □	**39**	42 15N	14 0 E
Absaroka Ra.	**118**	44 40N	110 0W
Abū al Khaşīb	**64**	30 25N	48 0 E
Abū 'Alī	**64**	27 20N	49 27 E
Abu 'Arīsh	**63**	16 53N	42 48 E
Abû Ballas	**86**	24 26N	27 36 E
Abu Deleiq	**87**	15 57N	33 48 E
Abū Dhabī	**65**	24 28N	54 36 E
Abū Dīs	**62**	31 47N	35 16 E
Abû Dis	**86**	19 12N	33 38 E
Abû Dom	**87**	16 18N	32 25 E
Abû Gabra	**87**	11 2N	26 50 E
Abū Ghaush	**62**	31 48N	35 6 E
Abû Gubeiha	**87**	11 30N	31 15 E
Abu Habl, Khawr →	**87**	12 37N	31 0 E
Abu Hamed	**86**	19 32N	33 13 E
Abu Haraz	**87**	14 35N	33 30 E
Abû Haraz	**86**	19 8N	32 18 E
Abû Higar	**87**	12 50N	33 59 E
Abū Kamāl	**64**	34 30N	41 0 E
Abū Madd, Ra's	**64**	24 50N	37 7 E
Abū Markhah	**64**	25 4N	38 22 E
Abu Qir	**86**	31 18N	30 0 E
Abu Qireiya	**86**	24 5N	35 28 E
Abu Qurqâs	**86**	28 1N	30 44 E
Abû Rudies	**86**	29 0N	33 15 E
Abu Salama	**86**	27 10N	35 51 E
Abû Simbel	**86**	22 18N	31 40 E
Abu Tig	**86**	27 4N	31 15 E
Abu Tiga	**87**	12 47N	34 12 E
Abû Zabad	**87**	12 25N	29 10 E
Abū Zābī	**65**	24 28N	54 22 E
Abuja	**85**	9 16N	7 2 E
Abukuma-Gawa →	**74**	38 06N	140 52 E
Abunã	**126**	9 40 S	65 20W
Abunã →	**126**	9 41 S	65 20W
Aburo, Mt.	**90**	2 4N	30 53 E
Abut Hd.	**101**	43 7 S	170 15 E
Abwong	**87**	9 2N	32 14 E
Åby	**49**	58 40N	16 10 E
Aby, Lagune	**84**	5 15N	3 14W
Acámbaro	**120**	20 0N	100 40W
Acanthus	**44**	40 27N	23 47 E
Acaponeta	**120**	22 30N	105 20W
Acapulco	**120**	16 51N	99 56W
Acatlán	**120**	18 10N	98 3W
Acayucan	**120**	17 59N	94 58W
Accéglio	**38**	44 28N	6 59 E
Accomac	**114**	37 43N	75 40W
Accra	**85**	5 35N	0 6W
Accrington	**12**	53 46N	2 22W
Acebal	**124**	33 20 S	60 50W
Aceh □	**72**	4 15N	97 30 E
Acerenza	**41**	40 50N	15 58 E
Acerra	**41**	40 57N	14 22 E
Aceuchal	**31**	38 39N	6 30W
Achalpur	**68**	21 22N	77 32 E
Achenkirch	**26**	47 32N	11 45 E
Achensee	**26**	47 26N	11 45 E
Acher	**68**	23 10N	72 32 E
Achern	**25**	48 37N	8 5 E
Achill	**15**	53 56N	9 55W
Achill Hd.	**15**	53 59N	10 15W
Achill I.	**15**	53 58N	10 5W
Achill Sound	**15**	53 53N	9 55W
Achim	**24**	53 1N	9 2 E
Achinsk	**59**	56 20N	90 20 E
Achol	**87**	6 35N	31 32 E
Acireale	**41**	37 37N	15 9 E
Ackerman	**117**	33 20N	89 8W
Acklins I.	**121**	22 30N	74 0W
Acland, Mt.	**97**	24 50 S	148 20 E
Acme	**108**	51 33N	113 30W
Aconcagua □, Argent.	**124**	32 50 S	70 0W
Aconcagua □, Chile	**124**	32 15 S	70 30W
Aconcagua, Cerro	**124**	32 39 S	70 0W
Aconquija, Mt.	**124**	27 0 S	66 0W
Açores, Is. dos = Azores	**6**	38 44N	29 0W
Acquapendente	**39**	42 45N	11 50 E
Acquasanta	**39**	42 46N	13 24 E
Acquaviva delle Fonti	**41**	40 53N	16 50 E
Acqui	**38**	44 40N	8 28 E
Acre = 'Akko	**62**	32 55N	35 4 E
Acre □	**126**	9 1 S	71 0W
Acre →	**126**	8 45 S	67 22W
Acri	**41**	39 29N	16 23 E
Acs	**27**	47 42N	18 0 E
Actium	**44**	38 57N	20 45 E
Acton	**112**	43 38N	80 3W
Ad Dahnā	**64**	24 30N	48 10 E
Ad Dammām	**64**	26 20N	50 5 E
Ad Dār al Ḥamrā'	**64**	27 20N	37 45 E
Ad Dawhah	**65**	25 15N	51 35 E
Ad Dilam	**64**	23 55N	47 10 E
Ada, Ghana	**85**	5 44N	0 40 E
Ada, Minn., U.S.A.	**116**	47 20N	96 30W
Ada, Okla., U.S.A.	**117**	34 50N	96 45W
Ada, Yugo.	**42**	45 49N	20 9 E
Adaja →	**30**	41 32N	4 52W
Ådalslinden	**48**	63 27N	16 55 E
Adam	**65**	22 15N	57 28 E
Adamaoua, Massif de l'	**85**	7 20N	12 20 E
Adamawa Highlands = Adamaoua, Massif de l'	**85**	7 20N	12 20 E
Adamello, Mt.	**38**	46 10N	10 34 E
Adami Tulu	**87**	7 53N	38 41 E
Adaminaby	**99**	36 0 S	148 45 E
Adams, Mass., U.S.A.	**113**	42 38N	73 8W
Adams, N.Y., U.S.A.	**114**	43 50N	76 3W
Adams, Wis., U.S.A.	**116**	43 59N	89 50W
Adam's Bridge	**70**	9 15N	79 40 E
Adams Center	**113**	43 51N	76 1W
Adams L.	**108**	51 10N	119 40W
Adams, Mt.	**118**	46 10N	121 28W
Adam's Peak	**70**	6 48N	80 30 E
Adamuz	**31**	38 2N	4 32W
Adana	**64**	37 0N	35 16 E
Adanero	**30**	40 56N	4 36W
Adapazarı	**64**	40 48N	30 25 E
Adarama	**87**	17 10N	34 52 E
Adare, C.	**5**	71 0 S	171 0 E
Adaut	**73**	8 8 S	131 7 E
Adavale	**97**	25 52 S	144 32 E
Adda →	**38**	45 8N	9 53 E
Addis Ababa = Addis Abeba	**87**	9 2N	38 42 E
Addis Abeba	**87**	9 2N	38 42 E
Addis Alem	**87**	9 0N	38 17 E
Addison	**112**	42 9N	77 15W
Adebour	**85**	13 17N	11 50 E
Adel	**115**	31 10N	83 28W
Adelaide, Austral.	**97**	34 52 S	138 30 E
Adelaide, Madag.	**93**	32 42 S	26 20 E
Adelaide I.	**5**	67 15 S	68 30W
Adelaide Pen.	**104**	68 15N	97 30W
Adélie, Terre	**5**	68 0 S	140 0 E
Ademuz	**32**	40 5N	1 13W
Aden = Al 'Adan	**63**	12 45N	45 12 E
Aden, G. of	**63**	13 0N	50 0 E
Adendorp	**92**	32 25 S	24 30 E
Adgz	**82**	30 47N	6 30W
Adhoi	**68**	23 26N	70 32 E
Adi	**73**	4 15 S	133 30 E
Adi Daro	**87**	14 20N	38 14 E
Adi Keyih	**87**	14 51N	39 22 E
Adi Kwala	**87**	14 38N	38 48 E
Adi Ugri	**87**	14 58N	38 48 E
Adieu, C.	**96**	32 0 S	132 10 E
Adigala	**87**	10 24N	42 15 E
Adige →	**39**	45 9N	12 20 E
Adigrat	**87**	14 20N	39 26 E
Adilabad	**70**	19 33N	78 20 E
Adin	**118**	41 10N	121 0W
Adin Khel	**65**	32 45N	68 5 E
Adirampattinam	**70**	10 28N	79 20 E
Adirondack Mts.	**114**	44 0N	74 15W
Adjim	**83**	33 47N	10 50 E
Adjohon	**85**	6 41N	2 32 E
Adjud	**46**	46 7N	27 10 E
Adjumani	**90**	3 20N	31 50 E
Adlavik Is.	**107**	55 2N	57 45W
Adler	**57**	43 28N	39 52 E
Admer	**83**	20 21N	5 27 E
Admer, Erg d'	**83**	24 0N	9 5 E
Admiralty B.	**5**	62 0 S	59 0W
Admiralty G.	**96**	14 20 S	125 55 E
Admiralty I.	**104**	57 40N	134 35W
Admiralty Inlet	**118**	48 0N	122 40W
Admiralty Is.	**94**	2 0 S	147 0 E
Admiralty Ra.	**5**	72 0 S	164 0 E
Ado	**85**	6 36N	2 56 E
Ado Ekiti	**85**	7 38N	5 12 E
Adok	**87**	8 10N	30 20 E
Adola	**87**	11 14N	41 44 E
Adonara	**73**	8 15 S	123 5 E
Adoni	**70**	15 33N	77 18W
Adony	**27**	47 6N	18 52 E
Adour →	**20**	43 32N	1 32W
Adra, India	**69**	23 30N	86 42 E
Adra, Spain	**33**	36 43N	3 3W
Adrano	**41**	37 40N	14 49 E
Adrar	**82**	27 51N	0 11W
Adré	**81**	13 40N	22 20 E
Adrī	**83**	27 32N	13 2 E
Ádria	**39**	45 4N	12 3 E
Adrian, Mich., U.S.A.	**114**	41 55N	84 0W
Adrian, Tex., U.S.A.	**117**	35 19N	102 37W
Adriatic Sea	**34**	43 0N	16 0 E
Adua	**73**	1 45 S	129 50 E
Adur	**70**	9 8N	76 40 E
Adwa	**87**	14 15N	38 52 E
Adzhar A.S.S.R. □	**57**	42 0N	42 0 E
Adzopé	**84**	6 7N	3 49W
Ægean Sea	**35**	37 0N	25 0 E
Æolian Is. = Eólie	**41**	38 30N	14 50 E
Aerht'ai Shan	**75**	46 40N	92 45 E
Ærø	**49**	54 52N	10 25 E
Ærøskøbing	**49**	54 53N	10 24 E
Aëtós	**45**	37 15N	21 50 E
Afafi, Massif d'	**83**	22 11N	15 10 E
Afándou	**45**	36 18N	28 12 E
Afarag, Erg	**82**	23 50N	2 47 E
Affreville = Khemis Miliania	**82**	36 11N	2 14 E
Afghanistan ■	**65**	33 0N	65 0 E
Afgoi	**63**	2 7N	44 59 E
'Afif	**64**	23 53N	42 56 E
Afikpo	**85**	5 53N	7 54 E
Aflisses, O. →	**82**	28 40N	0 50 E
Aflou	**82**	34 7N	2 3 E
Afognak I.	**104**	58 10N	152 50W
Afragola	**41**	40 54N	14 15 E
Afrera	**87**	13 16N	41 5 E
Africa	**78**	10 0N	20 0 E
Afton	**113**	42 14N	75 31W
Aftout	**82**	26 50N	3 45W
Afuá	**127**	0 15 S	50 20W
Afula	**62**	32 37N	35 17 E
Afyonkarahisar	**64**	38 45N	30 33 E
Aga	**86**	30 55N	31 10 E
Agadès = Agadez	**85**	16 58N	7 59 E
Agadez	**85**	16 58N	7 59 E
Agadir	**82**	30 28N	9 35W
Agano →	**74**	37 57N	139 8 E
Agapa	**59**	71 27N	89 15 E
Agar	**68**	23 40N	76 2 E
Agaro	**87**	7 50N	36 38 E
Agartala	**67**	23 50N	91 23 E
Agăş	**46**	46 28N	26 15 E
Agassiz	**108**	49 14N	121 46W
Agats	**73**	5 33 S	138 0 E
Agattu I.	**104**	52 25N	172 30 E
Agbélouvé	**85**	6 35N	1 14 E
Agboville	**84**	5 55N	4 15W
Agdam	**57**	40 0N	46 58 E
Agdash	**57**	40 44N	47 22 E
Agde	**20**	43 19N	3 28 E
Agde, C. d'	**20**	43 16N	3 28 E
Agdzhabedi	**57**	40 5N	47 27 E
Agen	**20**	44 12N	0 38 E
Ager Tay	**83**	20 0N	17 41 E
Agersø	**49**	55 13N	11 12 E
Ageyevo	**55**	54 10N	36 27 E
Agger	**49**	56 47N	8 13 E
Ággius	**40**	40 56N	9 4 E
Aghil Mts.	**69**	36 0N	77 0 E
Aginskoye	**59**	51 6N	114 32 E
Agira	**41**	37 40N	14 30 E
Agly →	**20**	42 46N	3 3 E
Agnibilékrou	**84**	7 10N	3 11W
Agnita	**46**	45 59N	24 40 E
Agnone	**41**	41 49N	14 20 E
Agofie	**85**	8 27N	0 15 E
Agogna →	**38**	45 4N	8 52 E
Agogo	**87**	7 50N	28 45 E
Agon	**18**	49 2N	1 34W
Agön	**48**	61 34N	17 23 E
Ágordo	**39**	46 18N	12 2 E
Agout →	**20**	43 47N	1 41 E
Agra	**68**	27 17N	77 58 E
Agramunt	**32**	41 48N	1 6 E
Agreda	**32**	41 51N	1 55W
Agri →	**41**	40 13N	16 44 E
Ağri Daği	**64**	39 50N	44 15 E
Ağri Karakose	**64**	39 44N	43 3 E
Agrigento	**40**	37 19N	13 33 E
Agrinion	**45**	38 37N	21 27 E
Agrópoli	**41**	40 23N	14 59 E
Água Clara	**127**	20 25 S	52 45W
Agua Prieta	**120**	31 20N	109 32W
Aguadas	**126**	5 40N	75 38W
Aguadilla	**121**	18 27N	67 10W
Aguanish	**107**	50 14N	62 2W
Aguanus →	**107**	50 13N	62 5W
Aguapey →	**124**	29 7 S	56 36W
Aguaray Guazú →	**124**	24 47 S	57 19W
Aguarico →	**126**	0 59 S	75 11W
Aguas →	**32**	41 20N	0 30W
Aguas Blancas	**124**	24 15 S	69 55W
Aguas Calientes, Sierra de	**124**	25 26 S	66 40W
Aguascalientes	**120**	21 53N	102 12W
Aguascalientes □	**120**	22 0N	102 20W
Agudo	**31**	38 59N	4 52W
Águeda	**30**	40 34N	8 27W
Agueda →	**30**	41 2N	6 56W
Aguié	**85**	13 31N	7 46 E
Aguilafuente	**30**	41 13N	4 7W
Aguilar	**31**	37 31N	4 40W
Aguilar de Campóo	**30**	42 47N	4 15W
Aguilares	**124**	27 26 S	65 35W
Aguilas	**33**	37 23N	1 35W
Agulaa	**87**	13 40N	39 40 E
Agulhas, Kaap	**92**	34 52 S	20 0 E
Agung	**72**	8 20 S	115 28 E
'Agur	**62**	31 42N	34 55 E
Agur	**90**	2 28N	32 55 E
Agusan →	**73**	9 0N	125 30 E
Agvali	**57**	42 36N	46 8 E
Aha Mts.	**92**	19 45 S	21 0 E
Ahaggar	**83**	23 0N	6 30 E
Ahamansu	**85**	7 38N	0 35 E
Ahar	**64**	38 35N	47 0 E
Ahaus	**24**	52 4N	7 1 E
Ahelledjem	**83**	26 37N	6 58 E
Ahipara B.	**101**	35 5 S	173 5 E
Ahiri	**70**	19 30N	80 0 E
Ahlen	**24**	51 45N	7 52 E
Ahmadabad (Ahmedabad)	**68**	23 0N	72 40 E
Ahmadnagar (Ahmednagar)	**70**	19 7N	74 46 E
Ahmadpur	**68**	29 12N	71 10 E
Ahmar Mts.	**87**	9 20N	41 15 E
Ahoada	**85**	5 8N	6 36 E
Ahr →	**24**	50 33N	7 17 E
Ahrensbök	**24**	54 0N	10 34 E
Ahrweiler	**24**	50 31N	7 3 E
Aḩsā', Wāḩat al	**64**	25 50N	49 0 E
Ahuachapán	**120**	13 54N	89 52W
Åhus	**49**	55 56N	14 18 E
Ahvāz	**64**	31 20N	48 40 E
Ahvenanmaa = Åland	**51**	60 15N	20 0 E
Ahwar	**63**	13 30N	46 40 E
Ahzar	**85**	15 30N	3 20 E
Aichach	**25**	48 28N	11 9 E
Aichi □	**74**	35 0N	137 15 E
Aidone	**41**	37 26N	14 26 E
Aiello Cálabro	**41**	39 6N	16 12 E
Aigle	**25**	46 18N	6 58 E
Aigle, L'	**18**	48 46N	0 38 E
Aignay-le-Duc	**19**	47 40N	4 43 E
Aigre	**20**	45 54N	0 1 E
Aigua	**125**	34 13 S	54 46W
Aigueperse	**20**	46 3N	3 13 E
Aigues-Mortes	**21**	43 35N	4 12 E
Aigues-Mortes, G. d'	**21**	43 31N	4 3 E
Aiguilles	**21**	44 47N	6 51 E
Aiguillon	**20**	44 18N	0 21 E
Aiguillon, L'	**20**	46 20N	1 16W
Aigurande	**20**	46 27N	1 49 E
Aihui	**75**	50 10N	127 30 E
Aija	**126**	9 50 S	77 45W
Aijal	**67**	23 40N	92 44 E
Aiken	**115**	33 34N	81 50W
Aillant-sur-Tholon	**19**	47 52N	3 20 E
Aillik	**107**	55 11N	59 18W
Ailly-sur-Noye	**19**	49 45N	2 20 E
Ailsa Craig	**14**	55 15N	5 7W
'Ailūn	**62**	32 18N	35 47 E
Aim	**59**	59 0N	133 55 E
Aimere	**73**	8 45 S	121 3 E
Aimogasta	**124**	28 33 S	66 50W
Aimorés	**127**	19 30 S	41 4W
Ain □	**21**	46 5N	5 20 E
Ain →	**21**	45 45N	5 11 E
Ain Banaiyan	**65**	23 0N	51 0 E
Aïn Beïda	**83**	35 50N	7 29 E
Ain ben Khellil	**82**	33 15N	0 49W
Aïn Ben Tili	**82**	25 59N	9 27W
Aïn Beni Mathar	**82**	34 1N	2 0W
Aïn Benian	**82**	36 48N	2 55 E
Ain Dalla	**86**	27 20N	27 23 E
Ain Dar	**64**	25 55N	49 10 E
Ain el Mafki	**86**	27 30N	28 15 E

Aïn Galakka Alexandria

Aïn Galakka 81 18 10N 18 30 E
Ain Girba 86 29 20N 25 14 E
Aïn M'lila 83 36 2N 6 35 E
Ain Qeiqab 86 29 42N 24 55 E
Aïn-Sefra 82 32 47N 0 37W
Ain Sheikh Murzûk 86 26 47N 27 45 E
Ain Sukhna 86 29 32N 32 20 E
Aïn Tédelès 82 36 0N 0 21 E
Aïn-Témouchent 82 35 16N 1 8W
Aïn Touta 83 35 26N 5 54 E
Ain Zeitûn 86 29 10N 25 48 E
Aïn Zorah 82 34 37N 3 32W
Ainabo 63 9 0N 46 25 E
Ainaži 54 57 50N 24 24 E
Aínos Óros 45 38 10N 20 35 E
Ainsworth 116 42 33N 99 52W
Aïr 85 18 30N 8 0 E
Airaines 19 49 58N 1 55 E
Airdrie 14 55 53N 3 57W
Aire 19 50 37N 2 22 E
Aire →, France 19 49 18N 4 55 E
Aire →, U.K. 12 53 42N 0 55W
Aire, I. del 32 39 48N 4 16 E
Aire-sur-l'Adour 20 43 42N 0 15W
Airvault 18 46 50N 0 8W
Aisch → 25 49 46N 11 1 E
Aisne □ 19 49 42N 3 40 E
Aisne → 19 49 26N 2 50 E
Aitana, Sierra de 33 38 35N 0 24W
Aitape 98 3 11 S 142 22 E
Aitkin 116 46 32N 93 43W
Aitolía Kai Akarnanía □ 45 38 45N 21 18 E
Aitolikón 45 38 26N 21 21 E
Aiud 46 46 19N 23 44 E
Aix-en-Provence 21 43 32N 5 27 E
Aix-la-Chapelle = Aachen 24 50 47N 6 4 E
Aix-les-Bains 21 45 41N 5 53 E
Aix-sur-Vienne 20 45 48N 1 8 E
Aiyansh 108 55 17N 129 2W
Aíyina 45 37 45N 23 26 E
Aiyínion 44 40 28N 22 28 E
Aiyion 45 38 15N 22 5 E
Aizenay 18 46 44N 1 38W
Aizpute 54 56 43N 21 40 E
Ajaccio 21 41 55N 8 40 E
Ajaccio, G. d' 21 41 52N 8 40 E
Ajanta Ra. 70 20 28N 75 50 E
Ajax 112 43 50N 79 1W
Ajdâbiyah 83 30 54N 20 4 E
Ajdovščina 39 45 54N 13 54 E
Ajibar 87 10 35N 38 36 E
Ajka 27 47 4N 17 31 E
'Ajmān 65 25 25N 55 30 E
Ajmer 68 26 28N 74 37 E
Ajo 119 32 18N 112 54W
Ajok 87 9 15N 28 28 E
Ak Dağ 64 36 30N 30 0 E
Akaba 85 8 10N 1 2 E
Akabli 82 26 49N 1 31 E
Akaki Beseka 87 8 55N 38 45 E
Akala 87 15 39N 36 13 E
Akaroa 101 43 49 S 172 59 E
Akasha 86 21 10N 30 32 E
Akashi 74 34 45N 135 0 E
Akbou 83 36 31N 4 31 E
Akelamo 73 1 35N 129 40 E
Åkernes 47 58 45N 7 30 E
Akershus fylke □ 47 60 0N 11 10 E
Akeru → 70 17 25N 80 0 E
Aketi 88 2 38N 23 47 E
Akhaïa □ 45 38 5N 21 45 E
Akhalkalaki 57 41 27N 43 25 E
Akhaltsikhe 57 41 40N 43 0 E
Akharnaí 45 38 5N 23 44 E
Akhelóös → 45 38 36N 21 14 E
Akhendria 45 34 58N 25 16 E
Akhéron → 44 39 20N 20 29 E
Akhisar 64 38 56N 27 48 E
Akhladhókambos 45 37 31N 22 35 E
Akhmîm 86 26 31N 31 47 E
Akhtopol 43 42 6N 27 56 E
Akhtubinsk (Petropavlovskiy) 57 48 13N 46 7 E
Akhty 57 41 30N 47 45 E
Akhtyrka 54 50 25N 35 0 E
Akimiski I. 106 52 50N 81 30W
Akimovka 56 46 44N 35 0 E
Åkirkeby 49 55 4N 14 55 E
Akita 74 39 45N 140 7 E
Akita □ 74 39 40N 140 30 E
Akjoujt 84 19 45N 14 15W
Akka 82 29 22N 8 9W
'Akko 62 32 55N 35 4 E
Akkol 58 45 0N 75 39 E
Akköy 45 37 30N 27 18 E
Aklampa 85 8 15N 2 10 E
Aklavik 104 68 12N 135 0W
Akmonte 31 37 13N 6 38W
Aknoul 82 34 40N 3 55W
Ako 85 10 19N 10 48 E
Akobo → 87 7 48N 33 3 E
Akola 68 20 42N 77 2 E
Akonolinga 85 3 50N 12 18 E
Akordat 87 15 30N 37 40 E
Akosombo Dam 85 6 20N 0 5 E
Akot, India 68 21 10N 77 10 E
Akot, Sudan 87 6 31N 30 9 E
Akpatok I. 105 60 25N 68 8W
Akranes 50 64 19N 21 58W
Åkrehamn 47 59 15N 5 10 E
Akreijit 84 18 19N 9 11W
Akrítas Venétiko, Ákra 45 36 43N 21 54 E
Akron, Colo., U.S.A. 116 40 13N 103 15W
Akron, Ohio, U.S.A. 114 41 7N 81 31W
Akrotíri, Akra 44 40 26N 25 27 E
Aksai Chih 69 35 15N 79 55 E
Aksaray 64 38 25N 34 2 E
Aksarka 58 66 31N 67 50 E
Aksay 52 51 11N 53 0 E
Akşehir 64 38 18N 31 30 E
Aksenovo Zilovskoye 59 53 20N 117 40 E
Akstafa 57 41 7N 45 27 E
Aksu 75 41 5N 80 10 E
Aksum 87 14 5N 38 40 E
Aktogay 58 46 57N 79 40 E
Aktyubinsk 53 50 17N 57 10 E
Aku 85 6 40N 7 18 E
Akure 85 7 15N 5 5 E
Akureyri 50 65 40N 18 6W
Akusha 57 42 18N 47 30 E
Al Abyār 83 32 9N 20 29 E
Al 'Adan 63 12 45N 45 0 E
Al Amāda03yah 64 37 5N 43 30 E
Al Amārah 64 31 55N 47 15 E
Al 'Aqabah 62 29 31N 35 0 E
Al 'Aramah 64 25 30N 46 0 E
Al Ashkhara 65 21 50N 59 30 E
Al 'Ayzarīyah (Bethany) 62 31 47N 35 15 E
Al 'Azīzīyah 83 32 30N 13 1 E
Al Badī' 64 22 0N 46 35 E
Al Barkāt 83 24 56N 10 14 E
Al Başrah 64 30 30N 47 50 E
Al Bāzūrīyah 62 33 15N 35 16 E
Al Bīrah 62 31 55N 35 12 E
Al Bu'ayrāt 83 31 24N 15 44 E
Al Buqay'ah 62 32 15N 35 30 E
Al Dīwaniyah 64 32 0N 45 0 E
Al Fallūjah 64 33 20N 43 55 E
Al Fāw 64 30 0N 48 30 E
Al Fujayrah 65 25 7N 56 18 E
Al Ghaţghaţ 64 24 40N 46 15 E
Al Hābah 64 27 10N 47 0 E
Al Haddār 64 21 58N 45 57 E
Al Ḥadīthah 64 34 0N 41 13 E
Al Hāmad 64 31 30N 39 30 E
Al Ḥamar 64 22 23N 46 6 E
Al Hamādah al Ḥamrā' 83 29 30N 12 0 E
Al Hamrā 64 24 2N 38 55 E
Al Ḥarīq 64 23 29N 46 27 E
Al Harīr, W. → 62 32 44N 35 59 E
Al Harūj al Aswad 83 27 0N 17 10 E
Al Ḥasakah 64 36 35N 40 45 E
Al Ḥawīyah 64 24 40N 49 15 E
Al Ḥawrah 63 13 50N 47 35 E
Al Ḥawţah 63 16 5N 48 20 E
Al Ḥayy 64 32 5N 46 5 E
Al Ḥillah, Iraq 64 32 30N 44 25 E
Al Ḥillah, Si. Arab. 64 23 35N 46 50 E
Al Hindīyah 64 32 30N 44 10 E
Al Ḥişnn 62 32 29N 35 52 E
Al Hoceïma 82 35 8N 3 58W
Al Ḥudaydah 63 14 50N 43 0 E
Al Ḥufrah, Awbārī, Libya 83 25 32N 14 1 E
Al Ḥufrah, Misrātah, Libya 83 29 5N 18 3 E
Al Hūfuf 64 25 25N 49 45 E
Al Ḥulwah 64 23 24N 46 48 E
Al Husayyāt 83 30 24N 20 37 E
Al 'Idwah 64 27 15N 42 35 E
Al Irq 81 29 5N 21 35 E
Al Ittihad = Madīnat ash Sha'b 63 12 50N 45 0 E
Al Jāfūrah 64 25 0N 50 15 E
Al Jaghbūb 81 29 42N 24 38 E
Al Jahrah 64 29 25N 47 40 E
Al Jalāmīd 64 31 20N 39 45 E
Al Jawf, Libya 81 24 10N 23 24 E
Al Jawf, Si. Arab. 64 29 55N 39 40 E
Al Jazır 63 18 30N 56 31 E
Al Jazirah, Libya 81 26 10N 21 20 E
Al Jazirah, Si. Arab. 64 33 30N 44 0 E
Al Jubayl 64 27 0N 49 50 E
Al Jubaylah 64 24 55N 46 25 E
Al Junaynah 81 13 27N 22 45 E
Al Juwārah 63 19 0N 57 13 E
Al Khābūrah 65 23 57N 57 5 E
Al Khalīl = Hebron 62 31 32N 35 6 E
Al Khalūf 63 20 30N 58 13 E
Al Kharfah 64 22 0N 46 35 E
Al Kharj 64 24 0N 47 0 E
Al Khufayfīyah 64 24 50N 44 35 E
Al Khums 83 32 40N 14 17 E
Al Khums □ 83 31 20N 14 10 E
Al Khurmah 64 21 58N 42 3 E
Al Kufrah 81 24 17N 23 15 E
Al Kūt 64 32 30N 46 0 E
Al Kuwayt 64 29 30N 47 30 E
Al Lādhiqīyah 64 35 30N 35 45 E
Al Lidām 63 20 33N 44 45 E
Al Līth 86 20 9N 40 15 E
Al Lubban 62 32 9N 35 14 E
Al Luḥayyah 63 15 45N 42 40 E
Al Madīnah 64 24 35N 39 52 E
Al-Mafraq 62 32 17N 36 14 E
Al Majma'ah 64 25 57N 45 22 E
Al Manāmāh 65 26 10N 50 30 E
Al Marj 81 32 25N 20 30 E
Al Maşirah 63 20 25N 58 50 E
Al Matamma 63 16 10N 44 30 E
Al Mawşil 64 36 15N 43 5 E
Al Mazra 62 31 16N 35 31 E
Al Midhnab 64 25 50N 44 18 E
Al Miqdādīyah 64 34 0N 45 0 E
Al Mish'āb 64 28 12N 48 36 E
Al Mubarraz 64 25 30N 49 40 E
Al Muḥarraq 65 26 15N 50 40 E
Al Mukallā 63 14 33N 49 2 E
Al Mukhā 63 13 18N 43 15 E
Al Musayyib 64 32 40N 44 25 E
Al Mustajiddah 64 26 30N 41 50 E
Al Muwayliḥ 64 27 40N 35 30 E
Al Qaddāhīyah 83 31 15N 15 9 E
Al Qaḍīmah 64 22 20N 39 13 E
Al Qāmishli 64 37 10N 41 10 E
Al Qaryah ash Sharqīyah 83 30 28N 13 40 E
Al Qaşabát 83 32 39N 14 1 E
Al Qaţīf 64 26 35N 50 0 E
Al Qaţrūn 83 24 56N 15 3 E
Al Quaisūmah 64 28 10N 46 20 E
Al Quds 62 31 47N 35 10 E
Al Qunfidha 86 19 3N 41 4 E
Al Quraiyat 65 23 17N 58 53 E
Al Qurnah 64 31 1N 47 25 E
Al 'Ulá 64 26 35N 38 0 E
Al Uqaylah ash Sharqīgah 83 30 12N 19 10 E
Al Uqayr 64 25 40N 50 15 E
Al 'Uthmānīyahyah 64 25 5N 49 22 E
Al 'Uwaynid 64 24 50N 46 0 E
Al' 'Uwayqīlah ash Sharqīgah 64 30 30N 42 10 E
Al 'Uyūn 64 26 30N 43 50 E
Al Wajh 86 26 10N 36 30 E
Al Wakrah 65 25 10N 51 40 E
Al Wari'āh 64 27 51N 47 25 E
Al Wātīyah 83 32 28N 11 57 E
Al Yāmūn 62 32 29N 35 14 E
Ala 38 45 46N 11 0 E
Alabama □ 115 33 0N 87 0W
Alabama → 115 31 8N 87 57W
Alaçati 45 38 16N 26 23 E
Alaejos 30 41 18N 5 13W
Alagna Valsésia 38 45 51N 7 56 E
Alagoa Grande 127 7 3 S 35 35W
Alagoas □ 127 9 0 S 36 0W
Alagoinhas 127 12 7 S 38 20W
Alagón 32 41 46N 1 12W
Alagón → 31 39 44N 6 53W
Alajuela 121 10 2N 84 8W
Alakamisy 93 21 19 S 47 14 E
Alakurtti 52 67 0N 30 30 E
Alameda, Spain 31 37 12N 4 39W
Alameda, Idaho, U.S.A. 118 43 2N 112 30W
Alameda, N. Mex., U.S.A. 119 35 10N 106 43W
Alamitos, Sierra de los 120 37 21N 115 10W
Alamo 119 36 21N 115 10W
Alamogordo 119 32 59N 106 0W
Alamos 120 27 0N 109 0W
Alamosa 119 37 30N 106 0W
Åland 51 60 15N 20 0 E
Aland 70 17 36N 76 35 E
Alandroal 31 38 41N 7 24W
Alandur 70 13 0N 80 15 E
Alange, Presa de 31 38 45N 6 18W
Alanis 31 38 3N 5 43W
Alanya 64 36 38N 32 0 E
Alaotra, Farihin' 93 17 30 S 48 30 E
Alapayevsk 58 57 52N 61 42 E
Alar del Rey 30 42 38N 4 20W
Alaraz 30 40 45N 5 17W
Alaşehir 53 38 23N 28 30 E
Alaska □ 104 65 0N 150 0W
Alaska, G. of 104 58 0N 145 0W
Alaska Highway 108 60 0N 130 0W
Alaska Pen. 104 56 0N 160 0W
Alaska Range 104 62 50N 151 0W
Alássio 38 44 1N 8 10 E
Alataw Shankou 75 45 5N 81 57 E
Alatri 40 41 44N 13 21 E
Alatyr 55 54 45N 46 35 E
Alatyr → 55 54 52N 46 36 E
Alausi 126 2 0 S 78 50W
Álava □ 32 42 48N 2 28W
Alava, C. 118 48 10N 124 40W
Alaverdi 57 41 15N 44 37 E
Alawoona 99 34 45 S 140 30 E
Alayor 32 39 57N 4 8 E
Alazan → 57 41 5N 46 40 E
Alba 38 44 41N 8 1 E
Alba □ 46 46 10N 23 30 E
Alba de Tormes 30 40 50N 5 30W
Alba Iulia 46 46 8N 23 39 E
Albac 46 46 28N 23 1 E
Albacete 33 39 0N 1 50W
Albacete □ 33 38 50N 2 0W
Albacutya, L. 99 35 45 S 141 58 E
Ålbæk 49 57 36N 10 25 E
Ålbæk Bucht 49 57 35N 10 40 E
Albaida 33 38 51N 0 31W
Albalate de las Nogueras 32 40 22N 2 18W
Albalate del Arzobispo 32 41 6N 0 31W
Albania ■ 44 41 0N 20 0 E
Albano Laziale 40 41 44N 12 40 E
Albany, Austral. 96 35 1 S 117 58 E
Albany, Ga., U.S.A. 115 31 40N 84 10W
Albany, Minn., U.S.A. 116 45 37N 94 38W
Albany, N.Y., U.S.A. 114 42 35N 73 47W
Albany, Oreg., U.S.A. 118 44 41N 123 0W
Albany, Tex., U.S.A. 117 32 45N 99 20W
Albany → 106 52 17N 81 31W
Albardón 124 31 20 S 68 30W
Albarracín 32 40 25N 1 26W
Albarracín, Sierra de 32 40 30N 1 30W
Albatross B. 97 12 45 S 141 30 E
Albegna → 39 42 30N 11 11 E
Albemarle 115 35 27N 80 15W
Albemarle Sd. 115 36 0N 76 30W
Albenga 38 44 3N 8 12 E
Alberche → 30 39 58N 4 46W
Alberdi 124 26 14 S 58 20W
Alberes, Mts. 32 42 28N 2 56 E
Alberique 33 39 7N 0 31W
Albersdorf 24 54 8N 9 19 E
Albert 19 50 0N 2 38 E
Albert Canyon 108 51 8N 117 41W
Albert L. 99 35 30 S 139 10 E
Albert, L. = Mobutu Sese Seko, L. 90 1 30N 31 0 E
Albert Lea 116 43 32N 93 20W
Albert Nile → 90 3 36N 32 2 E
Alberta □ 108 54 40N 115 0W
Alberti 124 35 1 S 60 16W
Albertinia 92 34 11 S 21 34 E
Albertirsa 27 47 14N 19 37 E
Alberton 107 46 50N 64 0W
Albertville 21 45 40N 6 22 E
Albertville = Kalemie 90 5 55 S 29 9 E
Alberz, Reshteh-Ye Kūhhā-Ye 65 36 0N 52 0 E
Albi 20 43 56N 2 9 E
Albia 116 41 0N 92 50W
Albina 127 5 37N 54 15W
Albina, Ponta 92 15 52 S 11 44 E
Albino 38 45 47N 9 48 E
Albion, Idaho, U.S.A. 118 42 21N 113 37W
Albion, Mich., U.S.A. 114 42 15N 84 45W
Albion, Nebr., U.S.A. 116 41 47N 98 0W
Albion, Pa., U.S.A. 112 41 53N 80 21W
Albocácer 32 40 21N 0 1 E
Alböke 49 56 57N 16 47 E
Alborán 31 35 57N 3 0W
Alborea 33 39 17N 1 24W
Ålborg 49 57 2N 9 54 E
Ålborg B. 49 56 50N 10 35 E
Albox 33 37 23N 2 8W
Albreda 108 52 35N 119 10W
Albuera, La 31 38 45N 6 49W
Albufeira 31 37 5N 8 15W
Albula → 25 46 38N 9 30 E
Albuñol 33 36 48N 3 11W
Albuquerque 119 35 5N 106 47W
Albuquerque, Cayos de 121 12 10N 81 50W
Alburg 113 44 58N 73 19W
Alburno, Mte. 41 40 32N 15 15 E
Alburquerque 31 39 15N 6 59W
Albury 97 36 3 S 146 56 E
Alby 48 62 30N 15 28 E
Alcácer do Sal 31 38 22N 8 33W
Alcaçovas 31 38 23N 8 9W
Alcalá de Chisvert 32 40 19N 0 13 E
Alcalá de Guadaira 31 37 20N 5 50W
Alcalá de Henares 32 40 28N 3 22W
Alcalá de los Gazules 31 36 29N 5 43W
Alcalá la Real 31 37 27N 3 57W
Alcamo 40 37 59N 12 55 E
Alcanadre 32 42 24N 2 7W
Alcanadre → 32 41 43N 0 12W
Alcanar 32 40 33N 0 28 E
Alcanede 31 39 25N 8 49W
Alcanena 31 39 27N 8 40W
Alcañices 30 41 41N 6 21W
Alcaníz 32 41 2N 0 8W
Alcântara 127 2 20 S 44 30W
Alcántara 31 39 41N 6 57W
Alcantara L. 109 60 57N 108 9W
Alcantarilla 33 37 59N 1 12W
Alcaracejos 31 38 24N 4 58W
Alcaraz 33 38 40N 2 29W
Alcaraz, Sierra de 33 38 40N 2 20W
Alcarria, La 32 40 31N 2 45W
Alcaudete 31 37 35N 4 5W
Alcázar de San Juan 33 39 24N 3 12W
Alcira 33 39 9N 0 30W
Alcoa 115 35 50N 84 0W
Alcobaça 31 39 32N 9 0W
Alcobendas 32 40 32N 3 38W
Alcolea del Pinar 32 41 2N 2 28W
Alcora 32 40 5N 0 14W
Alcoutim 31 37 25N 7 28W
Alcova 118 42 37N 106 52W
Alcoy 33 38 43N 0 30W
Alcubierre, Sierra de 32 41 45N 0 22W
Alcublas 32 39 48N 0 43W
Alcudia 32 39 51N 3 7 E
Alcudia, B. de 32 39 47N 3 15 E
Alcudia, Sierra de la 31 38 34N 4 30W
Aldabra Is. 3 9 22 S 46 28 E
Aldan 59 58 40N 125 30 E
Aldan → 59 63 28N 129 35 E
Aldeburgh 13 52 9N 1 35 E
Aldeia Nova 31 37 55N 7 24W
Alder 118 45 27N 112 3W
Alderney 18 49 42N 2 12W
Aldershot 13 51 15N 0 43W
Aldersyde 108 50 40N 113 53W
Aledo 116 41 10N 90 50W
Alefa 87 11 55N 36 55 E
Aleg 84 17 3N 13 55W
Alegre 125 20 50 S 41 30W
Alegrete 125 29 40 S 56 0W
Aleisk 58 52 40N 83 0 E
Alejandro Selkirk, I. 95 33 50 S 80 15W
Aleksandriya, Ukraine S.S.R., U.S.S.R. 54 50 37N 26 19 E
Aleksandriya, Ukraine S.S.R., U.S.S.R. 56 48 42N 33 3 E
Aleksandriyskaya 57 43 59N 47 0 E
Aleksandrov 55 56 23N 38 44 E
Aleksandrovac, Srbija, Yugo. 42 44 28N 21 13 E
Aleksandrovac, Srbija, Yugo. 42 43 28N 21 3 E
Aleksandrovka 56 48 55N 32 20 E
Aleksandrovo 43 43 14N 24 51 E
Aleksandrovsk-Sakhaliniskiy 59 50 50N 142 20 E
Aleksandrovskiy Zavod 59 50 40N 117 50 E
Aleksandrovskoye 58 60 35N 77 50 E
Aleksandrów Kujawski 28 52 53N 18 43 E
Aleksandrów Łódźki 28 51 49N 19 17 E
Alekseyevka 55 50 43N 38 40 E
Aleksin 55 54 31N 37 9 E
Aleksinac 42 43 31N 21 42 E
Além Paraíba 125 21 52 S 42 41W
Alemania, Argent. 124 25 40 S 65 30W
Alemania, Chile 124 25 10 S 69 55W
Ålen 47 62 51N 11 17 E
Alençon 18 48 27N 0 4 E
Alenuihaha Chan. 110 20 25N 156 0W
Aleppo = Ḥalab 64 36 10N 37 15 E
Aléria 21 42 5N 9 26 E
Alert Bay 108 50 30N 126 55W
Alès 21 44 9N 4 5 E
Aleşd 46 47 3N 22 22 E
Alessándria 38 44 54N 8 37 E
Ålestrup 49 56 42N 9 29 E
Ålesund 47 62 28N 6 12 E
Alet-les-Bains 20 43 0N 2 14 E
Aleutian Is. 104 52 0N 175 0W
Aleutian Trench 94 48 0N 180 0
Alexander 116 47 51N 103 40W
Alexander Arch. 104 57 0N 135 0W
Alexander B. 92 28 36 S 16 33 E
Alexander City 115 32 58N 85 57W
Alexander I. 5 69 0 S 70 0W
Alexandra, Austral. 99 37 8 S 145 40 E
Alexandra, N.Z. 101 45 14 S 169 25 E
Alexandra Falls 108 60 29N 116 18W
Alexandria, B.C., Can. 108 52 35N 122 27W
Alexandria, Ont., Can. 106 45 19N 74 36W
Alexandria, Romania 46 43 57N 25 24 E
Alexandria, S. Afr. 92 33 38 S 26 28 E
Alexandria, Ind., U.S.A. 114 40 18N 85 40W
Alexandria, La., U.S.A. 117 31 20N 92 30W
Alexandria, Minn., U.S.A. 116 45 50N 95 20W
Alexandria, S.D., U.S.A. 116 43 40N 97 45W
Alexandria, Va., U.S.A. 114 38 47N 77 1W

Alexandria Amursk

Alexandria = El Iskandarîya **86** 31 0N 30 0 E
Alexandria Bay **114** 44 20N 75 52W
Alexandrina, L. **97** 35 25 S 139 10 E
Alexandroúpolis **44** 40 50N 25 54 E
Alexis → **107** 52 33N 56 8W
Alexis Creek **108** 52 10N 123 20W
Alfambra **32** 40 33N 1 5W
Alfândega da Fé **30** 41 20N 6 59W
Alfaro **32** 42 10N 1 50W
Alfatar **43** 43 59N 27 13 E
Alfeld **24** 52 0N 9 49 E
Alfenas **125** 21 20 S 46 10W
Alfiós → **45** 37 40N 21 33 E
Alfonsine **39** 44 30N 12 1 E
Alford **14** 57 13N 2 42W
Alfred, Me., U.S.A. **113** 43 28N 70 40W
Alfred, N.Y., U.S.A. **112** 42 15N 77 45W
Alfreton **12** 53 6N 1 22W
Alfta **48** 61 21N 16 4 E
Alga **58** 49 53N 57 20 E
Algaba, La **31** 37 27N 6 1W
Algar **31** 36 40N 5 39W
Ålgård **47** 58 46N 5 53 E
Algarinejo **31** 37 19N 4 9W
Algarve **31** 36 58N 8 20W
Algeciras **31** 36 9N 5 28W
Algemesí **33** 39 11N 0 27W
Alger **82** 36 42N 3 8 E
Algeria ■ **82** 35 10N 3 11 E
Alghero **40** 40 34N 8 20 E
Algiers = Alger **82** 36 42N 3 8 E
Algoabaai **92** 33 50 S 25 45 E
Algodonales **31** 36 54N 5 24W
Algodor → **30** 39 55N 3 53W
Algoma, Oreg., U.S.A. **118** 42 25N 121 54W
Algoma, Wis., U.S.A. **114** 44 35N 87 27W
Algona **116** 43 4N 94 14W
Algonac **112** 42 37N 82 32W
Alhama de Almería **33** 36 57N 2 34W
Alhama de Aragón **32** 41 18N 1 54W
Alhama de Granada **31** 37 0N 3 59W
Alhama de Murcia **33** 37 51N 1 25W
Alhambra, Spain **33** 38 54N 3 4W
Alhambra, U.S.A. **119** 34 2N 118 10W
Alhaurín el Grande **31** 36 39N 4 41W
Alhucemas = Al-Hoceïma **82** 35 8N 3 58W
'Alī al Gharbī **64** 32 30N 46 45 E
Ali Bayramly **57** 39 59N 48 52 E
Ali Sabieh **87** 11 10N 42 44 E
Ália **40** 37 47N 13 42 E
'Alīābād **65** 28 10N 57 35 E
Aliaga **32** 40 40N 0 42W
Aliákmon → **44** 40 30N 22 36 E
Alibag **70** 18 38N 72 56 E
Alibo **87** 9 52N 37 5 E
Alibunar **42** 45 5N 20 57 E
Alicante **33** 38 23N 0 30W
Alicante □ **33** 38 30N 0 37W
Alice, S. Afr. **92** 32 48 S 26 55 E
Alice, U.S.A. **117** 27 47N 98 1W
Alice →, Queens., Austral. **98** 24 2 S 144 50 E
Alice →, Queens., Austral. **98** 15 35 S 142 20 E
Alice Arm **108** 55 29N 129 31W
Alice, Punta dell' **41** 39 23N 17 10 E
Alice Springs **96** 23 40 S 133 50 E
Alicedale **92** 33 15 S 26 4 E
Aliceville **115** 33 9N 88 10W
Alick Cr. → **98** 20 55 S 142 20 E
Alicudi, I. **41** 38 33N 14 20 E
Alida **109** 49 25N 101 55W
Aligarh, Raj., India **68** 25 55N 76 15 E
Aligarh, Ut. P., India **68** 27 55N 78 10 E
Alīgūdarz **64** 33 25N 49 45 E
Alijó **30** 41 16N 7 27W
Alimena **41** 37 42N 14 4 E
Alimnia **45** 36 16N 27 43 E
Alingsås **49** 57 56N 12 31 E
Alipur **68** 29 25N 70 55 E
Alipur Duar **69** 26 30N 89 35 E
Aliquippa **114** 40 38N 80 18W
Aliste → **30** 41 34N 5 58W
Alitus **54** 54 24N 24 3 E
Alivérion **45** 38 24N 24 2 E
Aliwal North **92** 30 45 S 26 45 E
Alix **108** 52 24N 113 11W
Aljezur **31** 37 18N 8 49W
Aljustrel **31** 37 55N 8 10W
Alkamari **85** 13 27N 11 10 E
Alkmaar **16** 52 37N 4 45 E
All American Canal **119** 32 45N 115 0W
Allada **85** 6 41N 2 9 E
Allah Dad **68** 25 38N 67 34 E
Allahabad **69** 25 25N 81 58 E
Allakh-Yun **59** 60 50N 137 5 E
Allal Tazi **82** 34 30N 6 20W
Allan **109** 51 53N 106 4W
Allanche **20** 45 14N 2 57 E
Allanmyo **67** 19 30N 95 17 E
Allanridge **92** 27 45 S 26 40 E
Allanwater **106** 50 14N 90 10W
Allaqi, Wadi → **86** 23 7N 32 47 E
Allariz **30** 42 11N 7 50W
Allassac **20** 45 15N 1 29 E
Allegan **114** 42 32N 85 52W
Allegany **112** 42 6N 78 30W
Allegheny → **114** 40 27N 80 0W
Allegheny Mts. **114** 38 0N 80 0W
Allegheny Res. **112** 42 0N 78 55W
Allègre **20** 45 12N 3 41 E
Allen, Bog of **15** 53 15N 7 0W
Allen, L. **15** 54 12N 8 5W
Allenby (Hussein) Bridge **62** 31 53N 35 33 E
Allende **120** 28 20N 100 50W
Allentown **114** 40 36N 75 30W
Allentsteig **26** 48 41N 15 20 E
Alleppey **70** 9 30N 76 28 E
Aller → **24** 52 57N 9 10 E
Allevard **21** 45 24N 6 5 E
Alliance, Nebr., U.S.A. **116** 42 10N 102 50W
Alliance, Ohio, U.S.A. **114** 40 53N 81 7W
Allier □ **20** 46 25N 3 0 E
Allier → **19** 46 57N 3 4 E
Allingåbro **49** 56 28N 10 20 E
Allinge **49** 55 17N 14 50 E
Alliston **106** 44 9N 79 52W
Alloa **14** 56 7N 3 49W
Allos **21** 44 15N 6 38 E
Alma, Can. **107** 48 35N 71 40W
Alma, Ga., U.S.A. **115** 31 33N 82 28W
Alma, Kans., U.S.A. **116** 39 1N 96 22W
Alma, Mich., U.S.A. **114** 43 25N 84 40W
Alma, Nebr., U.S.A. **116** 40 10N 99 25W
Alma, Wis., U.S.A. **116** 44 19N 91 54W
'Almā ash Sha'b **62** 33 7N 35 9 E
Alma Ata **58** 43 15N 76 57 E
Almada **31** 38 40N 9 9W
Almaden **98** 17 22 S 144 40 E
Almadén **31** 38 49N 4 52W
Almagro **31** 38 50N 3 45W
Almanor, L. **118** 40 15N 121 11W
Almansa **33** 38 51N 1 5W
Almanza **30** 42 39N 5 3W
Almanzor, Pico de **30** 40 15N 5 18W
Almanzora → **33** 37 14N 1 46W
Almarcha, La **32** 39 41N 2 24W
Almaş, Mţii. **46** 44 49N 22 12 E
Almazán **32** 41 30N 2 30W
Almazora **32** 39 57N 0 3W
Almeirim, Brazil **127** 1 30 S 52 34W
Almeirim, Port. **31** 39 12N 8 37W
Almelo **16** 52 22N 6 42 E
Almenar **32** 41 43N 2 12W
Almenara **32** 39 46N 0 14W
Almenara, Sierra de **33** 37 34N 1 32W
Almendralejo **31** 38 41N 6 26W
Almería **33** 36 52N 2 27W
Almería □ **33** 37 20N 2 20W
Almería, G. de **33** 36 41N 2 28W
Almirante **14** 9 10N 82 30W
Almiropótamos **45** 38 16N 24 11 E
Almirós **45** 39 11N 22 45 E
Almodôvar **31** 37 31N 8 2W
Almodóvar del Campo **31** 38 43N 4 10W
Almogia **31** 36 50N 4 32W
Almonaster la Real **31** 37 52N 6 48W
Almont **112** 42 53N 83 2W
Almonte **113** 45 14N 76 12W
Almonte → **31** 39 41N 6 28W
Almora **69** 29 38N 79 40 E
Almoradi **33** 38 7N 0 46W
Almorox **30** 40 14N 4 24W
Almoustarat **85** 17 35N 0 8 E
Älmult **49** 56 33N 14 8 E
Almuñécar **31** 36 43N 3 41W
Almunia de Doña Godina, La **32** 41 29N 1 23W
Alnif **82** 31 10N 5 8W
Alnwick **12** 55 25N 1 42W
Aloi **90** 2 16N 33 10 E
Alonsa **109** 50 50N 99 0W
Alor **73** 8 15 S 124 30 E
Alor Setar **71** 6 7N 100 22 E
Alora **31** 36 49N 4 46W
Alosno **31** 37 33N 7 7W
Alougoum **82** 30 17N 6 56W
Alpedrinha **30** 40 6N 7 27W
Alpena **114** 45 6N 83 24W
Alpes-de-Haute-Provence □ **21** 44 8N 6 10 E
Alpes-Maritimes □ **21** 43 55N 7 10 E
Alpha **97** 23 39 S 146 37 E
Alpi Apuane **38** 44 7N 10 14 E
Alpi Lepontine **25** 46 22N 8 27 E
Alpi Orobie **38** 46 7N 10 0 E
Alpi Retiche **25** 46 30N 10 0 E
Alpiarça **31** 39 15N 8 35W
Alpine, Ariz., U.S.A. **119** 33 57N 109 4W
Alpine, Tex., U.S.A. **117** 30 25N 103 35W
Alps **22** 47 0N 8 0 E
Alpujarras, Las **33** 36 55N 3 20W
Alrø **49** 55 52N 10 5 E
Alsace **19** 48 15N 7 25 E
Alsask **109** 51 21N 109 59W
Alsásua **32** 42 54N 2 10W
Alsen **48** 63 23N 13 56 E
Alsfeld **24** 50 44N 9 19 E
Alsónémedi **27** 47 20N 19 15 E
Alsten **50** 65 58N 12 40 E
Alta **50** 69 57N 23 10 E
Alta Gracia **124** 31 40 S 64 30W
Alta Lake **108** 50 10N 123 0W
Alta, Sierra **32** 40 31N 1 30W
Altaelva → **50** 69 46N 23 45 E
Altafjorden **50** 70 5N 23 5 E
Altagracia **126** 10 45N 71 30W
Altai = Aerhatai Shan **75** 46 40N 92 45 E
Altamaha → **115** 31 19N 81 17W
Altamira, Brazil **127** 3 12 S 52 10W
Altamira, Chile **124** 25 47 S 69 51W
Altamira, Cuevas de **30** 43 20N 4 5W
Altamont **113** 42 43N 74 3W
Altamura **41** 40 50N 16 33 E
Altanbulag **75** 50 16N 106 30 E
Altar **120** 30 40N 111 50W
Altata **120** 24 30N 108 0W
Altavista **114** 37 9N 79 22W
Altay **75** 47 48N 88 10 E
Altdorf **25** 46 52N 8 36 E
Alte Mellum **24** 53 45N 8 6 E
Altea **33** 38 38N 0 2W
Altenberg **24** 50 46N 13 47 E
Altenbruch **24** 53 48N 8 44 E
Altenburg **24** 50 59N 12 28 E
Altenkirchen, Germ., E. **24** 54 38N 13 20 E
Altenkirchen, Germ., W. **24** 50 41N 7 38 E
Altenmarkt **26** 47 43N 14 39 E
Altenteptow **24** 53 42N 13 15 E
Alter do Chão **31** 39 12N 7 40W
Altkirch **19** 47 37N 7 15 E
Altmühl → **25** 48 54N 11 54 E
Alto Adige = Trentino-Alto Adige **38** 46 30N 11 0 E
Alto Araguaia **127** 17 15 S 53 20W
Alto Chindio **91** 16 19 S 35 25 E
Alto Cuchumatanes = Cuchumatanes, Sa. de los **120** 15 30N 91 10W
Alto del Inca **124** 24 10 S 68 10W
Alto Ligonha **91** 15 30 S 38 11 E
Alto Molocue **91** 15 50 S 37 35 E
Alto Paraná □ **125** 25 0 S 54 50W
Alton, Can. **112** 43 54N 80 5W
Alton, U.S.A. **116** 38 55N 90 5W
Alton Downs **99** 26 7 S 138 57 E
Altona, Austral. **100** 37 51 S 144 50 E
Altona, Ger. **24** 53 32N 9 56 E
Altoona **114** 40 32N 78 24W
Altopáscio **38** 43 50N 10 40 E
Altötting **25** 48 14N 12 41 E
Altstätten **25** 47 22N 9 33 E
Altun Shan **75** 38 30N 88 0 E
Alturas **118** 41 36N 120 37W
Altus **117** 34 30N 99 25W
Alucra **57** 40 22N 38 47 E
Aluksne **54** 57 24N 27 3 E
Alùla **63** 11 50N 50 45 E
Alupka **56** 44 23N 34 2 E
Alushta **56** 44 40N 34 25 E
Alusi **73** 7 35 S 131 40 E
Alustante **32** 40 36N 1 40W
Alva **117** 36 50N 98 50W
Alvaiázere **30** 39 49N 8 23W
Älvängen **49** 57 58N 12 8 E
Alvarado, Mexico **120** 18 40N 95 50W
Alvarado, U.S.A. **117** 32 25N 97 15W
Alvaro Obregón, Presa **120** 27 55N 109 52W
Alvdal **47** 62 6N 10 37 E
Alvear **124** 29 5 S 56 30W
Alverca **31** 38 56N 9 1W
Alvesta **49** 56 54N 14 35 E
Alvie **99** 38 14 S 143 30 E
Alvin **117** 29 23N 95 12W
Alvinston **113** 42 49N 81 52W
Alvito **31** 38 15N 8 0W
Älvros **48** 62 3N 14 38 E
Älvsborgs län □ **49** 58 30N 12 30 E
Älvsbyn **50** 65 40N 21 0 E
Alvsered **49** 57 14N 12 51 E
Alwar **68** 27 38N 76 34 E
Alwaye **70** 10 8N 76 24 E
Alxa Zuoqi **76** 38 50N 105 40 E
Alyangula **97** 13 55 S 136 30 E
Alyaskitovyy **59** 64 45N 141 30 E
Alyata **57** 39 58N 49 25 E
Alyth **14** 56 38N 3 15W
Alzada **116** 45 3N 104 22W
Alzano Lombardo **38** 45 44N 9 43 E
Alzey **25** 49 48N 8 4 E
Am Dam **81** 12 40N 20 35 E
Am Géréda **81** 12 53N 21 14 E
Am-Timan **81** 11 0N 20 10 E
Amadeus, L. **96** 24 54 S 131 0 E
Amâdi **87** 5 29N 30 25 E
Amadi **90** 3 40N 26 40 E
Amadjuak **105** 64 0N 72 39W
Amadjuak L. **105** 65 0N 71 8W
Amadora **31** 38 45N 9 13W
Amagasaki **74** 34 42N 135 20 E
Amager **49** 55 37N 12 35 E
Amakusa-Shotō **74** 32 15N 130 10 E
Åmål **48** 59 3N 12 42 E
Amalapuram **70** 16 35N 81 55 E
Amalfi **41** 40 39N 14 34 E
Amaliás **45** 37 47N 21 22 E
Amalner **68** 21 5N 75 5 E
Amambaí **125** 23 5 S 55 13W
Amambaí → **125** 23 22 S 53 56W
Amambay □ **125** 23 0 S 56 0W
Amambay, Cordillera de **125** 23 0 S 55 45W
Amándola **39** 42 59N 13 21 E
Amangeldy **58** 50 10N 65 10 E
Amantea **41** 39 8N 16 3 E
Amapá **127** 2 5N 50 50W
Amapá □ **127** 1 40N 52 0W
Amara **87** 10 25N 34 10 E
Amarante, Brazil **127** 6 14 S 42 50W
Amarante, Port. **30** 41 16N 8 5W
Amaranth **109** 50 36N 98 43W
Amaravati → **70** 11 0N 78 15 E
Amareleja **31** 38 12N 7 13W
Amargosa **127** 13 2 S 39 36W
Amarillo **117** 35 14N 101 46W
Amaro, Mt. **39** 42 5N 14 6 E
Amarpur **69** 25 5N 87 0 E
Amasra **64** 41 45N 32 30 E
Amassama **85** 5 1N 6 2 E
Amasya **64** 40 40N 35 50 E
Amatikulu **93** 29 3 S 31 33 E
Amatitlán **120** 14 29N 90 38W
Amatrice **39** 42 38N 13 16 E
Amazon = Amazonas → **127** 0 5 S 50 0W
Amazonas □ **126** 4 0 S 62 0W
Amazonas → **127** 0 5 S 50 0W
Ambad **70** 19 38N 75 50 E
Ambahakily **93** 21 36 S 43 41 E
Ambala **68** 30 23N 76 56 E
Ambalangoda **70** 6 15N 80 5 E
Ambalapuzha **70** 9 25N 76 25 E
Ambalavao **93** 21 50 S 46 56 E
Ambam **88** 2 20N 11 15 E
Ambanja **93** 13 40 S 48 27 E
Ambarchik **59** 69 40N 162 20 E
Ambarijeby **93** 14 56 S 47 41 E
Ambarnath **70** 19 12N 73 22 E
Ambaro, Helodranon' **93** 13 23 S 48 38 E
Ambartsevo **58** 57 30N 83 52 E
Ambasamudram **70** 8 43N 77 25 E
Ambato **126** 1 5 S 78 42W
Ambato Boeny **93** 16 28 S 46 43 E
Ambato, Sierra de **124** 28 25 S 66 10W
Ambatofinandrahana **93** 20 33 S 46 48 E
Ambatolampy **93** 19 20 S 47 35 E
Ambatondrazaka **93** 17 55 S 48 28 E
Ambatosoratra **93** 17 37 S 48 31 E
Ambenja **93** 15 17 S 46 58 E
Amberg **25** 49 25N 11 52 E
Ambergris Cay **120** 18 0N 88 0W
Ambérieu-en-Bugey **21** 45 57N 5 20 E
Amberley **101** 43 9 S 172 44 E
Ambert **20** 45 33N 3 44 E
Ambidédi **84** 14 35N 11 47W
Ambikapur **69** 23 15N 83 15 E
Ambikol **86** 21 20N 30 50 E
Ambinanindrano **93** 20 5 S 48 23 E
Ambjörnarp **49** 57 25N 13 17 E
Ambleside **12** 54 26N 2 58W
Ambo, Ethiopia **87** 12 20N 37 30 E
Ambo, Peru **126** 10 5 S 76 10W
Ambodifototra **93** 16 59 S 49 52 E
Ambodilazana **93** 18 6 S 49 10 E
Ambohimahasoa **93** 21 7 S 47 13 E
Ambohimanga **93** 20 52 S 47 36 E
Ambon **73** 3 35 S 128 20 E
Amboseli L. **90** 2 40 S 37 10 E
Ambositra **93** 20 31 S 47 25 E
Ambovombé **93** 25 11 S 46 5 E
Amboy **119** 34 33N 115 51W
Amboyna I. **72** 7 50N 112 50 E
Ambridge **112** 40 36N 80 15W
Ambriz **88** 7 48 S 13 8 E
Ambur **70** 12 48N 78 43 E
Amby **99** 26 30 S 148 11 E
Amchitka I. **104** 51 30N 179 0W
Amderma **58** 69 45N 61 30 E
Ameca **120** 20 30N 104 0W
Ameca → **120** 20 40N 105 15W
Amecameca **120** 19 7N 98 46W
Ameland **16** 53 27N 5 45 E
Amélia **39** 42 34N 12 25 E
Amélie-les-Bains-Palalda **20** 42 29N 2 41 E
Amen **59** 68 45N 180 0 E
Amendolaro **41** 39 58N 16 34 E
American Falls **118** 42 46N 112 56W
American Falls Res. **118** 43 0N 112 50W
American Highland **5** 73 0 S 75 0 E
American Samoa **101** 14 20 S 170 40W
Americana **125** 22 45 S 47 20W
Americus **115** 32 0N 84 10W
Amersfoort, Neth. **16** 52 9N 5 23 E
Amersfoort, S. Afr. **93** 26 59 S 29 53 E
Amery **109** 56 34N 94 3W
Amery Ice Shelf **5** 69 30 S 72 0 E
Ames **116** 42 0N 93 40W
Amesbury **113** 42 50N 70 52W
Amesdale **109** 50 2N 92 55W
Amfíklia **45** 38 38N 22 35 E
Amfilokhía **45** 38 52N 21 9 E
Amfípolis **44** 40 48N 23 52 E
Ámfissa **45** 38 32N 22 22 E
Amga **59** 60 50N 132 0 E
Amga → **59** 62 38N 134 32 E
Amgu **59** 45 45N 137 15 E
Amgun → **59** 52 56N 139 38 E
Amherst, Burma **67** 16 2N 97 20 E
Amherst, Can. **107** 45 48N 64 8W
Amherst, Mass., U.S.A. **113** 42 21N 72 30W
Amherst, Ohio, U.S.A. **112** 41 23N 82 15W
Amherst, Tex., U.S.A. **117** 34 0N 102 24W
Amherst I. **113** 44 8N 76 43W
Amherstburg **106** 42 6N 83 6W
Amiata, Mte. **39** 42 54N 11 40 E
Amiens **19** 49 54N 2 16 E
Amigdhalokefáli **45** 35 23N 23 30 E
Amindaion **44** 40 42N 21 42 E
Amirante Is. **3** 6 0 S 53 0 E
Amisk L. **109** 54 35N 102 15W
Amite **117** 30 47N 90 31W
Amizmiz **82** 31 12N 8 15W
Åmli **47** 58 45N 8 32 E
Amlwch **12** 53 24N 4 21W
Amm Adam **87** 16 20N 36 1 E
'Ammān **62** 31 57N 35 52 E
Ammanford **13** 51 48N 4 0W
Ammerån **48** 63 9N 16 13 E
Ammerån → **48** 63 9N 16 13 E
Ammersee **25** 48 0N 11 7 E
Ammi'ad **62** 32 55N 35 32 E
Amnéville **19** 49 16N 6 9 E
Amorebieta **32** 43 13N 2 44W
Amorgós **45** 36 50N 25 57 E
Amory **115** 33 59N 88 29W
Amos **106** 48 35N 78 5W
Åmot, Buskerud, Norway **47** 59 54N 9 54 E
Åmot, Telemark, Norway **47** 59 34N 8 0 E
Åmotsdal **47** 59 37N 8 26 E
Amour, Djebel **82** 33 42N 1 37 E
Amoy = Xiamen **76** 24 25N 118 4 E
Ampanihy **93** 24 40 S 44 45 E
Ampasindava, Helodranon' **93** 13 40 S 48 15 E
Ampasindava, Saikanosy **93** 13 42 S 47 55W
Amper **85** 9 25N 9 40 E
Amper → **25** 48 30N 11 57 E
Ampère **83** 35 44N 5 27 E
Ampezzo **39** 46 25N 12 48 E
Amposta **32** 40 43N 0 34 E
Ampotaka **93** 25 3 S 44 41 E
Ampoza **93** 22 20 S 44 44 E
Amqa **62** 32 59N 35 10 E
Amqui **107** 48 28N 67 27W
Amraoti **68** 20 55N 77 45 E
Amreli **68** 21 35N 71 17 E
Amrenene el Kasba **82** 22 10N 0 30 E
Amritsar **68** 31 35N 74 57 E
Amroha **68** 28 53N 78 30 E
Amrum **24** 54 37N 8 21 E
Amsel **83** 22 47N 5 29 E
Amsterdam, Neth. **16** 52 23N 4 54 E
Amsterdam, U.S.A. **114** 42 58N 74 10W
Amsterdam, I. **3** 37 30 S 77 30 E
Amstetten **26** 48 7N 14 51 E
Amudarya → **58** 43 40N 59 0 E
Amund Ringnes I. **4** 78 20N 96 25W
Amundsen Gulf **104** 71 0N 124 0W
Amundsen Sea **5** 72 0 S 115 0W
Amungen **48** 61 10N 15 40 E
Amuntai **72** 2 28 S 115 25 E
Amur → **59** 52 56N 141 10 E
Amurang **73** 1 5N 124 40 E
Amuri Pass **101** 42 31 S 172 11 E
Amurrio **32** 43 3N 3 0W
Amursk **59** 50 14N 136 54 E

Amurzet Arapkir

Amurzet 59 47 50N 131 5 E
Amusco 30 42 10N 4 28W
Amvrakikós Kólpos 45 39 0N 20 55 E
Amvrosiyevka 57 47 43N 38 30 E
Amzeglouf 82 26 50N 0 1 E
An Nafūd 64 28 15N 41 0 E
An Najaf 64 32 3N 44 15 E
An Nāqūrah 62 33 7N 35 8 E
An Nāşirīyah 64 31 0N 46 15 E
An Nawfaliyah 83 30 54N 17 58 E
An Nhon (Binh Dinh) 71 13 55N 109 7 E
An Nîl □ 86 19 30N 33 0 E
An Nîl el Abyad □ 87 14 0N 32 15 E
An Nîl el Azraq □ 87 12 30N 34 30 E
An Nu'ayrīyah 64 27 30N 48 30 E
An Uaimh 15 53 39N 6 40W
Ana-Sira 47 58 17N 6 25 E
Anabar → 59 73 8N 113 36 E
'Anabtā 62 32 19N 35 7 E
Anaconda 118 46 7N 113 0W
Anacortes 118 48 30N 122 40W
Anadarko 117 35 4N 98 15W
Anadia 30 40 26N 8 27W
Anadolu 64 38 0N 30 0 E
Anadyr 59 64 35N 177 20 E
Anadyr → 59 64 55N 176 5 E
Anadyrskiy Zaliv 59 64 0N 180 0 E
Anáfi 45 36 22N 25 48 E
Anafópoulo 45 36 17N 25 50 E
Anagni 40 41 44N 13 8 E
'Ānah 64 34 25N 42 0 E
Anahim Lake 108 52 28N 125 18W
Anáhuac 120 27 14N 100 9W
Anai Mudi, Mt. 70 10 12N 77 4 E
Anaimalai Hills 70 10 20N 76 40 E
Anakapalle 70 17 42N 83 06 E
Anakie 98 23 32 S 147 45 E
Anaklia 57 42 22N 41 35 E
Analalava 93 14 35 S 48 0 E
Anambar → 68 30 15N 68 50 E
Anambas, Kepulauan 72 3 20N 106 30 E
Anamoose 116 47 55N 100 20W
Anamosa 116 42 7N 91 30W
Anamur 64 36 8N 32 58 E
Anan 74 33 54N 134 40 E
Anand 68 22 32N 72 59 E
Anandpur 69 21 16N 86 13 E
Anánes 45 36 33N 24 9 E
Anantapur 70 14 39N 77 42 E
Anantnag 69 33 45N 75 10 E
Ananyev 56 47 44N 29 47 E
Anapa 56 44 55N 37 25 E
Anápolis 127 16 15 S 48 50W
Anār 65 30 55N 55 13 E
Anārak 65 33 25N 53 40 E
Anatolia = Anadolu 64 38 0N 30 0 E
Anatone 118 46 9N 117 4W
Añatuya 124 28 20 S 62 50W
Anaunethad L. 109 60 55N 104 25W
Anaye 81 19 15N 12 50 E
Ancenis 18 47 21N 1 10W
Anchorage 104 61 10N 149 50W
Anciāo 30 39 56N 8 27W
Ancohuma, Nevada 126 16 0 S 68 50W
Ancón 126 11 50 S 77 10W
Ancona 39 43 37N 13 30 E
Ancud 128 42 0 S 73 50W
Ancud, G. de 128 42 0 S 73 0W
Anda 76 46 24N 125 19 E
Andacollo, Argent. 124 37 10 S 70 42W
Andacollo, Chile 124 30 5 S 71 10W
Andalgalá 124 27 40 S 66 30W
Åndalsnes 47 62 35N 7 43 E
Andalucía 31 37 35N 5 0W
Andalusia 115 31 19N 86 30W
Andalusia = Andalucía 31 37 35N 5 0W
Andaman Is. 71 12 30N 92 30 E
Andaman Sea 72 13 0N 96 0 E
Andaman Str. 71 12 15N 92 20 E
Andara 92 18 2 S 21 9 E
Andelot 19 48 15N 5 18 E
Andelys, Les 18 49 15N 1 25 E
Andenne 16 50 30N 5 5 E
Andéranboukane 85 15 26N 3 2 E
Andermatt 25 46 38N 8 35 E
Andernach 24 50 24N 7 25 E
Andernos-les-Bains 20 44 44N 1 6W
Anderslöv 49 55 26N 13 19 E
Anderson, Calif., U.S.A. 118 40 30N 122 19W
Anderson, Ind., U.S.A. 114 40 5N 85 40W
Anderson, Mo., U.S.A. 117 36 43N 94 29W
Anderson, S.C., U.S.A. 115 34 32N 82 40W
Anderson → 104 69 42N 129 0W
Anderson, Mt. 93 25 5 S 30 42 E
Anderstorp 49 57 19N 13 39 E
Andes 126 5 40N 75 53W
Andes, Cord de los 126 20 0 S 68 0W
Andfjorden 50 69 10N 16 20 E
Andhra, L. 70 18 54N 73 32 E
Andhra Pradesh □ 70 16 0N 79 0 E
Andikíthira 45 35 52N 23 15 E
Andímilos 45 36 47N 24 12 E
Andíparos 45 37 0N 25 3 E
Andípaxoi 45 39 9N 20 13 E
Andipsara 45 38 30N 25 29 E
Andirrion 45 38 24N 21 46 E
Andizhan 58 41 10N 72 0 E
Andkhvoy 65 36 52N 65 8 E
Andol 70 17 51N 78 4 E
Andong 76 36 40N 128 43 E
Andorra ■ 32 42 30N 1 30 E
Andorra La Vella 32 42 31N 1 32 E
Andover, U.K. 13 51 13N 1 29W
Andover, N.Y., U.S.A. 112 42 11N 77 48W
Andover, Ohio, U.S.A. 112 41 35N 80 35W
Andrahary, Mt. 93 13 37 S 49 17 E
Andraitx 32 39 39N 2 25 E
Andramasina 93 19 11 S 47 35 E
Andranopasy 93 21 17 S 43 44 E
Andreanof Is. 104 52 0N 178 0W
Andreapol 54 56 40N 32 17 E
Andrespol 28 51 45N 19 34 E
Andrews, S.C., U.S.A. 115 33 29N 79 30W
Andrews, Tex., U.S.A. 117 32 18N 102 33W
Ándria 41 41 13N 16 17 E
Andriba 93 17 30 S 46 58 E
Andrijevica 42 42 45N 19 48 E
Andrítsaina 45 37 29N 21 52 E
Androka 93 24 58 S 44 2 E
Ándros 45 37 50N 24 57 E
Andros I. 121 24 30N 78 0W
Andros Town 121 24 43N 77 47W
Andrychów 27 49 51N 19 18 E
Andújar 31 38 3N 4 5W
Aneby 49 57 48N 14 49 E
Anegada I. 121 18 45N 64 20W
Anegada Passage 121 18 15N 63 45W
Anécho 85 6 12N 1 34 E
Anergane 82 31 4N 7 14W
Aneto, Pico de 32 42 37N 0 40 E
Ang Thong 71 14 35N 100 31 E
Angamos, Punta 124 23 1 S 70 32W
Ang'angxi 75 47 10N 123 48 E
Angara → 59 58 30N 97 0 E
Angarab 87 13 11N 37 7 E
Angarsk 59 52 30N 104 0 E
Angaston 99 34 30 S 139 8 E
Ånge 48 62 31N 15 35 E
Angel de la Guarda 120 29 30N 113 30W
Angeles 73 15 9N 120 33 E
Ängelholm 49 56 15N 12 58 E
Angellala 99 26 24 S 146 54 E
Angels Camp 119 38 8N 120 30W
Ängelsberg 48 59 58N 16 0 E
Anger → 87 9 37N 36 6 E
Angereb → 87 13 45N 36 40 E
Ångermanälven → 48 62 40N 18 0 E
Angermünde 24 53 1N 14 0 E
Angers, Can. 113 45 31N 75 29W
Angers, France 18 47 30N 0 35W
Angerville 19 48 19N 2 0 E
Ängesån → 50 66 50N 22 15 E
Anghiari 39 43 32N 12 3 E
Angikuni L. 109 62 0N 100 0W
Angkor 71 13 22N 103 50 E
Anglés 32 41 57N 2 38 E
Anglesey 12 53 17N 4 20W
Anglet 20 43 29N 1 31W
Angleton 117 29 12N 95 23W
Anglin → 20 46 42N 0 52 E
Anglure 19 48 35N 3 50 E
Angmagssalik 4 65 40N 37 20W
Ango 90 4 10N 26 5 E
Angoche 91 16 8 S 40 0 E
Angoche, I. 91 16 20 S 39 50 E
Angol 124 37 56 S 72 45W
Angola, Ind., U.S.A. 114 41 40N 85 0W
Angola, N.Y., U.S.A. 112 42 38N 79 2W
Angola ■ 89 12 0 S 18 0 E
Angoon 108 57 40N 134 40W
Angoram 98 4 4 S 144 4 E
Angoulême 20 45 39N 0 10 E
Angoumois 20 45 50N 0 25 E
Angra dos Reis 125 23 0 S 44 10W
Angren 58 41 1N 70 12 E
Angu 90 3 25N 24 28 E
Anguilla 121 18 14N 63 5W
Angus, Braes of 14 56 51N 3 10W
Anhanduí → 125 21 46 S 52 9W
Anholt 49 56 42N 11 33 E
Anhua 77 28 23N 111 12 E
Anhui □ 75 32 0N 117 0 E
Anhwei □ = Anhui □ 75 32 0N 117 0 E
Ánidhros 45 36 38N 25 43 E
Anie 85 7 42N 1 8 E
Animas 119 31 58N 108 58W
Ånimskog 49 58 53N 12 35 E
Anin 71 15 36N 97 50 E
Anina 42 45 6N 21 51 E
Anivorano 93 18 44 S 48 58 E
Anjangaon 68 21 10N 77 20 E
Anjar 68 23 6N 70 10 E
Anjidiv I. 70 14 40N 74 10 E
Anjou 18 47 20N 0 15W
Anjozorobe 93 18 22 S 47 52 E
Anju 76 39 36N 125 40 E
Anka 85 12 13N 5 58 E
Ankang 75 32 40N 109 1 E
Ankara 64 40 0N 32 54 E
Ankaramena 93 21 57 S 46 39 E
Ankazoabo 93 22 18 S 44 31 E
Ankazobe 93 18 20 S 47 10 E
Ankisabe 93 19 17 S 46 29 E
Anklam 24 53 48N 13 40 E
Anklesvar 68 21 38N 73 3 E
Ankober 87 9 35N 39 40 E
Ankoro 90 6 45 S 26 55 E
Anlu 77 31 15N 113 45 E
Ånn 48 63 19N 12 34 E
Ann Arbor 114 42 17N 83 45W
Ann C., Antarct. 5 66 30 S 50 30 E
Ann C., U.S.A. 114 42 39N 70 37W
Anna, U.S.A. 117 37 28N 89 10W
Anna, U.S.S.R. 55 51 28N 40 23 E
Annaba 83 36 50N 7 46 E
Annaberg-Buchholz 24 50 34N 12 58 E
Annalee → 15 54 3N 7 15W
Annam = Trung-Phan 71 16 30N 107 30 E
Annamitique, Chaîne 71 17 0N 106 0 E
Annan 14 55 0N 3 17W
Annan → 14 54 58N 3 18W
Annapolis 114 38 95N 76 30W
Annapolis Royal 107 44 44N 65 32W
Annapurna 69 28 34N 83 50 E
Anneberg 49 57 32N 12 6 E
Annecy 21 45 55N 6 8 E
Annecy, L. d' 21 45 52N 6 10 E
Annemasse 21 46 12N 6 16 E
Anning 75 24 55N 102 26 E
Anniston 115 33 45N 85 50W
Annobón 79 1 25 S 5 35 E
Annonay 21 45 15N 4 40 E
Annonciation, L' 106 46 25N 74 55W
Annot 21 43 58N 6 38 E
Annotto Bay 121 18 17N 77 3W
Annuello 99 34 53 S 142 55 E
Annville 113 40 18N 76 32W
Annweiler 25 49 12N 7 58 E
Áno Arkhánai 45 35 16N 25 11 E
Áno Porróia 44 41 17N 23 2 E
Áno Viánnos 45 35 2N 25 21 E
Anoka 116 45 10N 93 26W
Anorotsangana 93 13 56 S 47 55 E
Anqing 75 30 30N 117 3 E
Anren 77 26 43N 113 18 E
Ansāb 64 29 11N 44 43 E
Ansai 76 36 50N 109 20 E
Ansbach 25 49 17N 10 34 E
Anse au Loup, L' 107 51 32N 56 50W
Anse, L' 106 46 47N 88 28W
Anseba → 87 16 0N 38 30 E
Anshan 76 41 5N 122 58 E
Anshun 75 26 18N 105 57 E
Ansirabe 93 19 55 S 47 2 E
Ansley 116 41 19N 99 24W
Ansó 32 42 51N 0 48W
Anson 117 32 46N 99 54W
Anson B. 96 13 20 S 130 6 E
Ansongo 85 15 25N 0 35 E
Ansonia 113 41 21N 73 6W
Anstruther 14 56 14N 2 40W
Ansudu 73 2 11 S 139 22 E
Antabamba 126 14 40 S 73 0W
Antakya 64 36 14N 36 10 E
Antalaha 93 14 57 S 50 20 E
Antalya 64 36 52N 30 45 E
Antalya Körfezi 64 36 15N 31 30 E
Antananarivo 93 18 55 S 47 31 E
Antananarivo □ 93 19 0 S 47 0 E
Antanimbaribe 93 21 30 S 44 48 E
Antarctic Pen. 5 67 0 S 60 0W
Antarctica 5 90 0 S 0 0
Antelope 91 21 2 S 28 31 E
Antequera, Parag. 124 24 8 S 57 7W
Antequera, Spain 31 37 5N 4 33W
Antero Mt. 119 38 45N 106 15W
Anthemoús 44 40 31N 23 15 E
Anthony, Kans., U.S.A. 117 37 8N 98 2W
Anthony, N. Mex., U.S.A. 119 32 1N 106 37W
Anti Atlas, Mts. 82 30 0N 8 30W
Antibes 21 43 34N 7 6 E
Antibes, C. d' 21 43 31N 7 7 E
Anticosti, Î. d' 107 49 30N 63 0W
Antifer, C. d' 18 49 41N 0 10 E
Antigo 116 45 8N 89 5W
Antigonish 107 45 38N 61 58W
Antigua 120 14 34N 90 41W
Antigua & Barbuda ■ 121 17 0N 61 50W
Antilla 121 20 40N 75 50W
Antimony 119 38 7N 112 0W
Antioch 118 38 7N 121 45W
Antioche, Pertuis d' 20 46 6N 1 20W
Antioquia 126 6 40N 75 55W
Antipodes Is. 94 49 45 S 178 40 E
Antler 116 48 58N 101 18W
Antler → 109 49 8N 101 0W
Antlers 117 34 15N 95 35W
Antofagasta 124 23 50 S 70 30W
Antofagasta □ 124 24 0 S 69 0W
Antofagasta de la Sierra 124 26 5 S 67 20W
Antofalla 124 25 30 S 68 5W
Antofalla, Salar de 124 25 40 S 67 45W
Anton 117 33 49N 102 5W
Anton Chico 119 35 12N 105 5W
Antongila, Helodrano 93 15 30 S 49 50 E
Antonibé 93 15 7 S 47 24 E
Antonibé, Presqu'île d' 93 14 55 S 47 20 E
Antonina 125 25 26 S 48 42W
Antonito 119 37 4N 106 1W
Antonovo 57 49 25N 51 42 E
Antrain 18 48 28N 1 30W
Antrim 15 54 43N 6 13W
Antrim □ 15 54 55N 6 20W
Antrim, Mts. of 15 54 57N 6 8W
Antrodoco 39 42 25N 13 4 E
Antropovo 55 58 26N 42 51 E
Antsalova 93 18 40 S 44 37 E
Antsiranana 93 12 25 S 49 20 E
Antsohihy 93 14 50 S 47 59 E
Antwerp 113 44 12N 75 36W
Antwerp = Antwerpen 16 51 13N 4 25 E
Antwerpen 16 51 13N 4 25 E
Antwerpen □ 16 51 15N 4 40 E
Anupgarh 68 29 10N 73 10 E
Anuradhapura 70 8 22N 80 28 E
Anvers = Antwerpen 16 51 13N 4 25 E
Anvers I. 5 64 30 S 63 40W
Anvik 104 62 37N 160 20W
Anxi, Fujian, China 77 25 2N 118 12 E
Anxi, Gansu, China 75 40 30N 95 43 E
Anxious B. 96 33 24 S 134 45 E
Anyama 84 5 30N 4 3W
Anyang 76 36 5N 114 21 E
Anyer-Lor 73 6 6 S 105 56 E
Anyi, Jiangxi, China 77 28 49N 115 25 E
Anyi, Shanxi, China 77 35 2N 111 2 E
Anyuan 77 25 9N 115 21 E
'Anzah 62 32 22N 35 12 E
Anzhero-Sudzhensk 58 56 10N 86 0 E
Ánzio 40 41 28N 12 37 E
Aoiz 32 42 46N 1 22W
Aomori 74 40 45N 140 45 E
Aomori □ 74 40 45N 140 40 E
Aonla 68 28 16N 79 11 E
Aoreora 82 28 51N 10 53W
Aosta 38 45 43N 7 20 E
Aoudéras 85 17 45N 8 20 E
Aouinet Torkoz 82 28 31N 9 46W
Aoukar 82 23 50N 2 45W
Aouker 84 17 40N 10 0W
Aoulef el Arab 82 26 55N 1 2 E
Apa → 124 22 6 S 58 2W
Apache, Ariz., U.S.A. 119 31 46N 109 6W
Apache, Okla., U.S.A. 117 34 53N 98 22W
Apalachee B. 115 30 0N 84 0W
Apalachicola 115 29 40N 85 0W
Apapa 85 6 25N 3 25 E
Apaporis → 126 1 23 S 69 25W
Aparri 73 18 22N 121 38 E
Apateu 46 46 36N 21 47 E
Apatin 42 45 40N 19 0 E
Apàtity 52 67 34N 33 22 E
Apatzingán 120 19 0N 102 20W
Apeldoorn 16 52 13N 5 57 E
Apen 24 53 12N 7 47 E
Apenam 72 8 35 S 116 13 E
Apennines 9 44 20N 10 20 E
Apia 101 13 50 S 171 50W
Apiacás, Serra dos 126 9 50 S 57 0W
Apizaco 120 19 26N 98 9W
Aplao 126 16 0 S 72 40W
Apo, Mt. 73 6 53N 125 14 E
Apolda 24 51 1N 11 30 E
Apollo Bay 100 38 45 S 143 40 E
Apollonia 45 36 58N 24 43 E
Apollonia = Marsá Susah 81 32 52N 21 59 E
Apolo 126 14 30 S 68 30W
Apostle Is. 116 47 0N 90 30W
Apóstoles 125 28 0 S 56 0W
Apostolovo 56 47 39N 33 39 E
Apoteri 126 4 2N 58 32W
Appalachian Mts. 114 38 0N 80 0W
Appalachicola → 115 29 40N 85 0W
Appennini 41 41 0N 15 0 E
Appennino Ligure 38 44 30N 9 0 E
Appenzell-Ausser Rhoden □ 25 47 23N 9 23 E
Appenzell-Inner Rhoden □ 25 47 20N 9 25 E
Appiano 39 46 27N 11 17 E
Apple Hill 113 45 13N 74 46W
Appleby 12 54 35N 2 29W
Appleton 114 44 17N 88 25W
Approuague 127 4 20N 52 0W
Aprelevka, U.S.S.R. 55 55 33N 37 4 E
Aprelevka, U.S.S.R. 55 55 34N 37 4 E
Apricena 41 41 47N 15 25 E
Aprigliano 41 39 17N 16 19 E
Aprília 40 41 38N 12 38 E
Apsheronsk 57 44 28N 39 42 E
Apt 21 43 53N 5 24 E
Apucarana 125 23 55 S 51 33W
Apulia = Púglia 41 41 0N 16 30 E
Apure → 126 7 37N 66 25W
Apurimac → 126 12 17 S 73 56W
Apuseni, Munţii 46 46 30N 22 45 E
Aqabah = Al 'Aqabah 86 29 13N 35 0 E
'Aqabah, Khalīj al 64 28 15N 33 20 E
Āqcheh 65 37 0N 66 5 E
Aqīq 86 18 14N 38 12 E
Aqīq, Khalīg 86 18 20N 38 10 E
Aqrabā 62 32 9N 35 20 E
Aqrah 64 36 46N 43 45 E
Aquidauana 127 20 30 S 55 50W
Áquila, L' 39 42 21N 13 24 E
Aquiles Serdán 120 28 37N 105 54W
Ar Rachidiya 82 31 58N 4 20W
Ar Rafīd 62 32 57N 35 52 E
Ar Ramādī 64 33 25N 43 20 E
Ar Raml 83 26 45N 19 40 E
Ar Ramthā 62 32 34N 36 0 E
Ar Raqqah 64 36 0N 38 55 E
Ar Rass 64 25 50N 43 40 E
Ar Rifā'ī 64 31 50N 46 10 E
Ar Riyāḍ 64 24 41N 46 42 E
Ar Rummān 62 32 9N 35 48 E
Ar Ruţbah 64 33 0N 40 15 E
Ar Ruwayḍah 64 23 40N 44 40 E
Arab, Bahr el → 87 9 50N 29 0 E
Arab, Khalîg el 86 30 55N 29 0 E
Arab, Shatt al 64 30 0N 48 31 E
Arabatskaya Strelka 56 45 40N 35 0 E
Arabba 39 46 30N 11 51 E
Arabia 60 25 0N 45 0 E
Arabian Sea 60 16 0N 65 0 E
Arac 64 41 15N 33 21 E
Aracaju 127 10 55 S 37 4W
Aracataca 126 10 38N 74 9W
Aracati 127 4 30 S 37 44W
Araçatuba 125 21 10 S 50 30W
Aracena 31 37 53N 6 38W
Aracena, Sierra de 31 37 50N 6 50W
Araçuai 127 16 52 S 42 4W
'Arad 62 31 15N 35 12 E
Arad 42 46 10N 21 20 E
Arad □ 42 46 20N 22 0 E
Arada 81 15 0N 20 20 E
Aradu Nou 42 46 8N 21 20 E
Arafura Sea 73 9 0 S 135 0 E
Aragats 57 40 30N 44 15 E
Aragón 32 41 25N 1 0W
Aragón → 32 42 13N 1 44W
Aragona 40 37 24N 13 36 E
Araguacema 127 8 50 S 49 20W
Araguaia → 127 5 21 S 48 41W
Araguari 127 18 38 S 48 11W
Araguari → 127 1 15N 49 55W
Arak 82 25 20N 3 45 E
Arāk 64 34 0N 49 40 E
Arakan Coast 67 19 0N 94 0 E
Arakan Yoma 67 20 0N 94 40 E
Arákhova 45 38 28N 22 35 E
Araks = Aras, Rūd-e → 64 39 10N 47 10 E
Aral Sea = Aralskoye More 58 44 30N 60 0 E
Aralsk 58 46 50N 61 20 E
Aralskoye More 58 44 30N 60 0 E
Aramă, Mţii. de 46 47 10N 22 30 E
Aramac 97 22 58 S 145 14 E
Arambagh 69 22 53N 87 48 E
Aran I. 15 55 0N 8 30W
Aran Is. 15 53 5N 9 42W
Aranda de Duero 32 41 39N 3 42W
Aranđelovac 42 44 18N 20 27 E
Aranjuez 30 40 1N 3 40W
Aranos 92 24 9 S 19 7 E
Aransas Pass 117 27 55N 97 9W
Araouane 84 18 55N 3 30W
Arapahoe 116 40 22N 99 53W
Arapey Grande → 124 30 55 S 57 49W
Arapkir 64 39 5N 38 30 E

Arapongas

Aska

Arapongas **125** 23 29 S 51 28W
Araranguá **125** 29 0 S 49 30W
Araraquara **127** 21 50 S 48 0W
Ararás, Serra das **125** 25 0 S 53 10W
Ararat **97** 37 16 S 143 0 E
Ararat, Mt. = Ağri Daği **64** 39 50N 44 15 E
Araria **69** 26 9N 87 33 E
Araripe, Chapada do **127** 7 20 S 40 0W
Araruama, Lagoa de **125** 22 53 S 42 12W
Aras, Rūd-e → **64** 39 10N 47 10 E
Arauca **126** 7 0N 70 40W
Arauca → **126** 7 24N 66 35W
Arauco **124** 37 16 S 73 25W
Arauco □ **124** 37 40 S 73 25W
Arawa **87** 9 57N 41 58 E
Araxá **127** 19 35 S 46 55W
Araya, Pen. de **126** 10 40N 64 0W
Arba Minch **87** 6 0N 37 30 E
Arbatax **40** 39 57N 9 42 E
Arbaza **59** 52 40N 92 30 E
Arbīl **64** 36 15N 44 5 E
Arboga **48** 59 24N 15 52 E
Arbois **19** 46 55N 5 46 E
Arbore **87** 5 3N 36 50 E
Arborea **40** 39 46N 8 34 E
Arborfield **109** 53 6N 103 39W
Arborg **109** 50 54N 97 13W
Arbrå **48** 61 28N 16 22 E
Arbresie, L' **21** 45 50N 4 26 E
Arbroath **14** 56 34N 2 35W
Arbuckle **118** 39 3N 122 2W
Arbus **40** 39 30N 8 33 E
Arbuzinka **56** 47 0N 31 59 E
Arc **19** 47 28N 5 34 E
Arc → **21** 45 34N 6 12 E
Arcachon **20** 44 40N 1 10W
Arcachon, Bassin d' **20** 44 42N 1 10W
Arcade **112** 42 34N 78 25W
Arcadia, Fla., U.S.A. **115** 27 20N 81 50W
Arcadia, La., U.S.A. **117** 32 34N 92 53W
Arcadia, Nebr., U.S.A. **116** 41 29N 99 4W
Arcadia, Pa., U.S.A. **112** 40 46N 78 54W
Arcadia, Wis., U.S.A. **116** 44 13N 91 29W
Arcata **118** 40 55N 124 4W
Arcévia **39** 43 29N 12 58 E
Archangel = Arkhangelsk **52** 64 40N 41 0 E
Archar **42** 43 50N 22 54 E
Archbald **113** 41 30N 75 31W
Archena **33** 38 9N 1 16W
Archer → **97** 13 28 S 141 41 E
Archer B. **98** 13 20 S 141 30 E
Archers Post **90** 0 35N 37 35 E
Archidona **31** 37 6N 4 22W
Arci, Monte **40** 39 47N 8 44 E
Arcidosso **39** 42 51N 11 30 E
Arcila = Asilah **82** 35 29N 6 0W
Arcis-sur-Aube **19** 48 32N 4 10 E
Arco, Italy **38** 45 55N 10 54 E
Arco, U.S.A. **118** 43 45N 113 16W
Arcola **109** 49 40N 102 30W
Arcos **32** 41 12N 2 16W
Arcos de los Frontera **31** 36 45N 5 49W
Arcos de Valdevez **30** 41 55N 8 22W
Arcot **70** 12 53N 79 20 E
Arcoverde **127** 8 25 S 37 4W
Arcs, Les **21** 43 27N 6 29 E
Arctic Bay **105** 73 1N 85 7W
Arctic Ocean **4** 78 0N 160 0W
Arctic Red River **104** 67 15N 134 0W
Arda →, Bulg. **43** 41 40N 26 29 E
Arda →, Italy **38** 44 53N 9 52 E
Ardabīl **64** 38 15N 48 18 E
Ardahan **64** 41 7N 42 41 E
Ardakān **65** 30 20N 52 5 E
Årdal, Aust-Agder, Norway **47** 58 42N 7 48 E
Årdal, Rogaland, Norway **47** 59 9N 6 13 E
Ardales **31** 36 53N 4 51W
Årdalstangen **47** 61 14N 7 43 E
Ardatov **55** 54 51N 46 15 E
Ardea **44** 40 58N 22 3 E
Ardèche □ **21** 44 42N 4 16 E
Ardèche → **21** 44 16N 4 39 E
Ardee **15** 53 51N 6 32W
Arden **112** 44 43N 76 56W
Arden Stby. **49** 56 46N 9 52 E
Ardennes **16** 50 0N 5 10 E
Ardennes □ **19** 49 35N 4 40 E
Ardentes **19** 46 45N 1 50 E
Ardestān **65** 33 20N 52 25 E
Ardgour **14** 56 45N 5 25W
Árdhas → **44** 41 36N 26 25 E
Ardila → **31** 38 12N 7 28W
Ardino **43** 41 34N 25 9 E
Ardjuno **73** 7 49 S 112 34 E
Ardlethan **99** 34 22 S 146 53 E
Ardmore, Austral. **98** 21 39 S 139 11 E
Ardmore, Okla., U.S.A. **117** 34 10N 97 5W
Ardmore, Pa., U.S.A. **113** 39 58N 75 18W
Ardmore, S.D., U.S.A. **116** 43 0N 103 40W
Ardnacrusha **15** 52 43N 8 38W
Ardnamurchan, Pt. of **14** 56 44N 6 14W
Ardore Marina **41** 38 11N 16 10 E
Ardres **19** 50 50N 2 0 E
Ardrossan, Austral. **99** 34 26 S 137 53 E
Ardrossan, U.K. **14** 55 39N 4 50W
Ards □ **15** 54 35N 5 30W
Ards Pen. **15** 54 30N 5 25W
Ardud **46** 47 37N 22 52 E
Ardunac **57** 41 8N 42 5 E
Åre **48** 63 22N 13 15 E
Arecibo **121** 18 29N 66 42W
Areia Branca **127** 5 0 S 37 0W
Aremark **47** 59 15N 11 42 E
Arenas **30** 43 17N 4 50W
Arenas de San Pedro **30** 40 12N 5 5W
Arendal **47** 58 28N 8 46 E
Arendsee **24** 52 52N 11 27 E
Arenys de Mar **32** 41 35N 2 33 E
Arenzano **38** 44 24N 8 40 E
Areópolis **45** 36 40N 22 22 E
Arequipa **126** 16 20 S 71 30W
Arero **87** 4 41N 38 50 E
Arès **20** 44 47N 1 8W
Arévalo **30** 41 3N 4 43W
Arezzo **39** 43 28N 11 50 E
Arga → **32** 42 18N 1 47W
Argalastí **44** 39 13N 23 13 E
Argamasilla de Alba **33** 39 8N 3 5W
Arganda **32** 40 19N 3 26W
Arganil **30** 40 13N 8 3W
Argelès-Gazost **20** 43 0N 0 6W
Argelès-sur-Mer **20** 42 34N 3 1 E
Argens → **21** 43 24N 6 44 E
Argent-sur-Sauldre **19** 47 33N 2 25 E
Argenta, Can. **108** 50 20N 116 55W
Argenta, Italy **39** 44 37N 11 50 E
Argentan **18** 48 45N 0 1W
Argentário, Mte. **39** 42 23N 11 11 E
Argentat **20** 45 6N 1 56 E
Argentera **38** 44 23N 6 58 E
Argentera, Monte del **38** 44 12N 7 5 E
Argenteuil **19** 48 57N 2 14 E
Argentia **107** 47 18N 53 58W
Argentiera, C. dell' **40** 40 44N 8 8 E
Argentière, L' **21** 44 47N 6 33 E
Argentina ■ **128** 35 0 S 66 0W
Argentino, L. **128** 50 10 S 73 0W
Argenton-Château **18** 46 59N 0 27W
Argenton-sur-Creuse **20** 46 36N 1 30 E
Argeş □ **46** 45 0N 24 45 E
Argeş → **46** 44 30N 25 50 E
Arghandab → **66** 31 30N 64 15 E
Argo **86** 19 28N 30 30 E
Argolikós Kólpos **45** 37 20N 22 52 E
Argolís □ **45** 37 38N 22 50 E
Argonne **19** 49 0N 5 20 E
Árgos **45** 37 40N 22 43 E
Árgos Orestikón **44** 40 27N 21 26 E
Argostólion **45** 38 12N 20 33 E
Arguedas **32** 42 11N 1 36W
Arguello, Pt. **119** 34 34N 120 40W
Argun → **59** 53 20N 121 28 E
Argungu **85** 12 40N 4 31 E
Argyle **116** 48 23N 96 49W
Argyrádhes **44** 39 27N 19 58 E
Århus **49** 56 8N 10 11 E
Århus Amtskommune □ **49** 56 15N 10 15 E
Ariamsvlei **92** 28 9 S 19 51 E
Ariana **83** 36 52N 10 12 E
Ariano Irpino **41** 41 10N 15 4 E
Ariano nel Polèsine **39** 44 56N 12 5 E
Aribinda **85** 14 17N 0 52W
Arica, Chile **126** 18 32 S 70 20W
Arica, Colomb. **126** 2 0 S 71 50W
Arid, C. **96** 34 1 S 123 10 E
Aridh **64** 25 0N 46 0 E
Ariège □ **20** 42 56N 1 30 E
Ariège → **20** 43 30N 1 25 E
Arieş → **46** 46 24N 23 20 E
Arilje **42** 43 44N 20 7 E
Arima **121** 10 38N 61 17W
Arinos → **126** 10 25 S 58 20W
Ario de Rosales **120** 19 12N 102 0W
Aripuanã **126** 9 25 S 60 30W
Aripuanã → **126** 5 7 S 60 25W
Ariquemes **126** 9 55 S 63 6W
Arisaig **14** 56 55N 5 50W
Arîsh, W. el → **86** 31 9N 33 49 E
Arissa **87** 11 10N 41 35 E
Aristazabal I. **108** 52 40N 129 10W
Arivaca **119** 31 37N 111 25W
Arivonimamo **93** 19 1 S 47 11 E
Ariyalur **70** 11 8N 79 8 E
Ariza **74** 41 19N 2 3W
Arizaro, Salar de **124** 24 40 S 67 50W
Arizona **124** 35 45 S 65 25W
Arizona □ **119** 34 20N 111 30W
Arizpe **120** 30 20N 110 11W
Årjäng **48** 59 24N 12 8 E
Arjeplog **50** 66 3N 18 2 E
Arjona, Colomb. **126** 10 14N 75 22W
Arjona, Spain **31** 37 56N 4 4W
Arka **59** 60 15N 142 0 E
Arkadak **55** 51 58N 43 19 E
Arkadelphia **117** 34 5N 93 0W
Arkadhía □ **45** 37 30N 22 20 E
Arkaig, L. **14** 56 58N 5 10W
Arkalyk **58** 50 13N 66 50 E
Arkansas □ **117** 35 0N 92 30W
Arkansas → **117** 33 48N 91 4W
Arkansas City **117** 37 4N 97 3W
Árkathos → **44** 39 20N 21 4 E
Arkhángelos **45** 36 13N 28 7 E
Arkhangelsk **52** 64 40N 41 0 E
Arkhangelskoye **55** 51 32N 40 58 E
Arkiko **87** 15 33N 39 30 E
Arklow **15** 52 48N 6 10W
Árkoi **45** 37 24N 26 44 E
Arkona, Kap **24** 54 41N 13 26 E
Arkonam **70** 13 7N 79 43 E
Arkösund **49** 58 29N 16 56 E
Arkoúdhi **45** 38 33N 20 43 E
Arkticheskiy, Mys **59** 81 10N 95 0 E
Arkul **55** 57 17N 50 3 E
Arlanc **20** 45 25N 3 42 E
Arlanza → **30** 42 6N 4 9W
Arlanzón → **30** 42 3N 4 17W
Arlberg Pass **25** 47 9N 10 12 E
Arlee **118** 47 10N 114 4W
Arles **21** 43 41N 4 40 E
Arlington, S. Afr. **93** 28 1 S 27 53 E
Arlington, Oreg., U.S.A. **118** 45 48N 120 6W
Arlington, S.D., U.S.A. **116** 44 25N 97 4W
Arlington, Va., U.S.A. **114** 38 52N 77 5W
Arlington, Wash., U.S.A. **118** 48 11N 122 4W
Arlon **16** 49 42N 5 49 E
Arlöv **49** 55 38N 13 5 E
Arly **85** 11 35N 1 28 E
Armagh **15** 54 22N 6 40W
Armagh □ **15** 54 18N 6 37W
Armagnac **20** 43 44N 0 10 E
Armançon → **19** 47 59N 3 30 E
Armavir **57** 45 2N 41 7 E
Armenia **126** 4 35N 75 45W
Armenian S.S.R. □ **57** 40 0N 44 0 E
Armeniş **46** 45 13N 22 17 E
Armentières **19** 50 40N 2 50 E
Armidale **97** 30 30 S 151 40 E
Armour **116** 43 20N 98 25W
Armstrong, B.C., Can. **108** 50 25N 119 10W
Armstrong, Ont., Can. **106** 50 18N 89 4W
Armstrong, U.S.A. **117** 26 59N 97 48W
Armur **70** 18 48N 78 16 E
Arnaía **44** 40 30N 23 40 E
Arnaouti, C. **64** 35 0N 32 20 E
Arnarfjörður **50** 65 48N 23 40W
Arnaud → **105** 60 0N 70 0W
Arnay-le-Duc **19** 47 10N 4 27 E
Arnedillo **32** 42 13N 2 14W
Arnedo **32** 42 12N 2 5W
Årnes **50** 66 1N 21 31W
Årnes **47** 60 7N 11 28 E
Arnett **117** 36 9N 99 44W
Arnhem **16** 51 58N 5 55 E
Arnhem B. **96** 12 20 S 136 10 E
Arnhem, C. **97** 12 20 S 137 30 E
Arnhem Land **96** 13 10 S 134 30 E
Arni **70** 12 43N 79 19 E
Árnissa **44** 40 47N 21 49 E
Arno → **38** 43 41N 10 17 E
Arnold, Nebr., U.S.A. **116** 41 29N 100 10W
Arnold, Pa., U.S.A. **112** 40 36N 79 44W
Arnoldstein **26** 46 33N 13 43 E
Arnon → **19** 47 13N 2 1 E
Arnot **109** 55 56N 96 41W
Arnøy **50** 70 9N 20 40 E
Arnprior **106** 45 26N 76 21W
Arnsberg **24** 51 25N 8 2 E
Arnstadt **24** 50 50N 10 56 E
Aroab **92** 26 41 S 19 39 E
Aroánia Óri **45** 37 56N 22 12 E
Aroche **31** 37 56N 6 57W
Arolsen **24** 51 23N 9 1 E
Aron → **19** 46 50N 3 27 E
Arona **38** 45 45N 8 32 E
Arosa, Ria de → **30** 42 28N 8 57W
Arpajon, Cantal, France **20** 44 54N 2 28 E
Arpajon, Essonne, France **19** 48 37N 2 12 E
Arpino **40** 41 40N 13 35 E
Arrabury **99** 26 45 S 141 0 E
Arrah **69** 25 35N 84 32 E
Arraiján **120** 8 56N 79 36W
Arraiolos **31** 38 44N 7 59W
Arran **14** 55 34N 5 12W
Arrandale **108** 54 57N 130 0W
Arras **19** 50 17N 2 46 E
Arrats → **20** 44 6N 0 52 E
Arreau **20** 42 54N 0 22 E
Arrecife **80** 28 57N 13 37W
Arrecifes **124** 34 06 S 60 9W
Arrée, Mts. d' **18** 48 26N 3 55W
Arriaga **120** 21 55N 101 23W
Arrilalah P.O. **98** 23 43 S 143 54 E
Arromanches-les-Bains **18** 49 20N 0 38W
Arronches **31** 39 8N 7 16W
Arros, R **20** 43 40N 0 2W
Arrou **18** 48 6N 1 8 E
Arrow, L. **15** 54 3N 8 20W
Arrow Rock Res. **118** 43 45N 115 50W
Arrowhead **108** 50 40N 117 55W
Arrowtown **101** 44 57 S 168 50 E
Arroyo de la Luz **31** 39 30N 6 38W
Arroyo Grande **119** 35 9N 120 32W
Års **49** 56 48N 9 30 E
Ars **20** 46 13N 1 30W
Ars-sur-Moselle **19** 49 5N 6 4 E
Arsenault L. **109** 55 6N 108 32W
Arsiero **39** 45 49N 11 22 E
Arsikere **70** 13 15N 76 15 E
Arsk **55** 56 10N 49 50 E
Árta **45** 39 8N 21 2 E
Artá **32** 39 41N 3 21 E
Árta □ **44** 39 15N 21 5 E
Arteaga **120** 18 50N 102 20W
Arteijo **30** 43 19N 8 29W
Artem, Ostrov **57** 40 28N 50 20 E
Artemovsk, R.S.F.S.R., U.S.S.R. **59** 54 45N 93 35 E
Artemovsk, Ukraine S.S.R., U.S.S.R. **56** 48 35N 38 0 E
Artemovski **57** 47 45N 40 16 E
Artenay **19** 48 5N 1 50 E
Artern **24** 51 22N 11 18 E
Artesa de Segre **32** 41 54N 1 3 E
Artesia **117** 32 55N 104 25W
Artesia Wells **117** 28 17N 99 18W
Artesian **116** 44 2N 97 54W
Arthez-de-Béarn **20** 43 29N 0 38W
Arthington **84** 6 35N 10 45W
Arthur → **99** 41 2 S 144 40 E
Arthur Pt. **98** 22 7 S 150 3 E
Arthur's Pass **101** 42 54 S 171 35 E
Artigas **124** 30 20 S 56 30W
Artik **57** 40 38N 43 58 E
Artillery L. **109** 63 9N 107 52W
Artois **19** 50 20N 2 30 E
Artotina **45** 38 42N 22 2 E
Artsiz **56** 46 4N 29 26 E
Artvin **64** 41 14N 41 44 E
Aru, Kepulauan **73** 6 0 S 134 30 E
Aru Meru □ **90** 3 20 S 36 50 E
Arua **90** 3 1N 30 58 E
Aruanã **127** 14 54 S 51 10W
Aruba **121** 12 30N 70 0W
Arudy **20** 43 7N 0 28W
Arun → **69** 26 55N 87 10 E
Arunachal Pradesh □ **67** 28 0N 95 0 E
Aruppukottai **70** 9 31N 78 8 E
Arusha **90** 3 20 S 36 40 E
Arusha □ **90** 4 0 S 36 30 E
Arusha Chini **90** 3 32 S 37 20 E
Arusi □ **87** 7 45N 39 00 E
Aruvi → **70** 8 48N 79 53 E
Aruwimi → **90** 1 13N 23 36 E
Arvada **118** 44 43N 106 6W
Arvakalu **70** 8 20N 79 58 E
Arvayheer **75** 46 15N 102 48 E
Arve → **21** 46 11N 6 8 E
Arvi **68** 20 59N 78 16 E
Arvida **107** 48 25N 71 14W
Arvidsjaur **50** 65 35N 19 10 E
Arvika **48** 59 40N 12 36 E
Arxan **75** 47 11N 119 57 E
Arys **58** 42 26N 68 48 E
Arzachena **40** 41 5N 9 27 E
Arzamas **55** 55 27N 43 55 E
Arzew **82** 35 50N 0 23W
Arzgir **57** 45 18N 44 23 E
Arzignano **39** 45 30N 11 20 E
Aš **26** 50 13N 12 12 E
'As Saffānīyah **64** 28 5N 48 50 E
Aş Şāfī **62** 31 2N 35 28 E
As Salt **62** 32 2N 35 43 E
As Samāwah **64** 31 15N 45 15 E
As Samū' **62** 31 24N 35 4 E
As Sanamayn **62** 33 3N 36 10 E
As Sulaymānīyah **64** 24 9N 47 18 E
As Sulţan **83** 31 4N 17 8 E
As Sumaymānīyah **64** 35 35N 45 29 E
As Summān **64** 25 0N 47 0 E
As Suwaih **65** 22 10N 59 33 E
As Suwaydā' **64** 32 40N 36 30 E
Aş Şuwayrah **64** 32 55N 45 0 E
Asab **92** 25 30 S 18 0 E
Asaba **85** 6 12N 6 38 E
Asafo **84** 6 20N 2 40W
Asahigawa **74** 43 46N 142 22 E
Asale, L. **87** 14 0N 40 20 E
Asamankese **85** 5 50N 0 40W
Asansol **69** 23 40N 87 1 E
Åsarna **48** 62 39N 14 22 E
Asbe Teferi **87** 9 4N 40 49 E
Asbesberge **92** 29 0 S 23 0 E
Asbestos **107** 45 47N 71 58W
Asbury Park **114** 40 15N 74 1W
Ascensión, B. de la **120** 19 50N 87 20W
Ascension I. **7** 8 0 S 14 15W
Aschach **26** 48 22N 14 2 E
Aschaffenburg **25** 49 58N 9 8 E
Aschendorf **24** 53 2N 7 22 E
Aschersleben **24** 51 45N 11 28 E
Asciano **39** 43 14N 11 32 E
Áscoli Piceno **39** 42 51N 13 34 E
Áscoli Satriano **41** 41 11N 15 32 E
Ascope **126** 7 46 S 79 8W
Ascotán **124** 21 45 S 68 17W
Aseb **87** 13 0N 42 40 E
Åseda **49** 57 10N 15 20 E
Asedjrad **82** 24 51N 1 29 E
Asela **87** 8 0N 39 0 E
Asenovgrad **43** 42 1N 24 51 E
Aseral **47** 58 37N 7 25 E
Asfeld **19** 49 27N 4 5 E
Asfûn el Matâ'na **86** 25 26N 32 30 E
Åsgårdstrand **47** 59 22N 10 27 E
Ash Fork **119** 35 14N 112 32W
Ash Grove **117** 37 21N 93 36W
Ash Shām, Bādiyat **64** 32 0N 40 0 E
Ash Shāmiyah **64** 31 55N 44 35 E
Ash Shāriqah **65** 25 23N 55 26 E
Ash Shaţrah **64** 31 30N 46 10 E
Ash Shu'aybah **64** 27 53N 42 43 E
Ash Shu'bah **64** 28 54N 44 44 E
Ash Shūnah ash Shamālīyah **62** 32 37N 35 34 E
Asha **52** 55 0N 57 16 E
Ashaira **86** 21 40N 40 40 E
Ashanti □ **85** 7 30N 1 30W
Ashburn **115** 31 42N 83 40W
Ashburton **101** 43 53 S 171 48 E
Ashburton → **96** 21 40 S 114 56 E
Ashby-de-la-Zouch **12** 52 45N 1 29W
Ashcroft **108** 50 40N 121 20W
Ashdod **62** 31 49N 34 35 E
Ashdot Yaaqov **62** 32 39N 35 35 E
Asheboro **115** 35 43N 79 46W
Asherton **117** 28 25N 99 43W
Asheville **115** 35 39N 82 30W
Asheweig → **106** 54 17N 87 12W
Ashford, Austral. **99** 29 15 S 151 3 E
Ashford, U.K. **13** 51 8N 0 53 E
Ashford, U.S.A. **118** 46 45N 122 2W
Ashikaga **74** 36 28N 139 29 E
Ashizuri-Zaki **74** 32 44N 133 0 E
Ashkhabad **58** 38 0N 57 50 E
Ashland, Kans., U.S.A. **117** 37 13N 99 43W
Ashland, Ky., U.S.A. **114** 38 25N 82 40W
Ashland, Me., U.S.A. **107** 46 34N 68 26W
Ashland, Mont., U.S.A. **118** 45 41N 106 12W
Ashland, Nebr., U.S.A. **116** 41 5N 96 27W
Ashland, Ohio, U.S.A. **114** 40 52N 82 20W
Ashland, Oreg., U.S.A. **118** 42 10N 122 38W
Ashland, Pa., U.S.A. **113** 40 45N 76 22W
Ashland, Va., U.S.A. **114** 37 46N 77 30W
Ashland, Wis., U.S.A. **116** 46 40N 90 52W
Ashley, N.D., U.S.A. **116** 46 3N 99 23W
Ashley, Pa., U.S.A. **113** 41 12N 75 55W
Ashley Snow I. **5** 73 35 S 77 6W
Ashmont **108** 54 7N 111 35W
Ashmore Reef **96** 12 14 S 123 5 E
Ashmûn **86** 30 18N 30 55 E
Ashq'elon **62** 31 42N 34 35 E
Ashtabula **114** 41 52N 80 50W
Ashti **70** 18 50N 75 15 E
Ashton, S. Afr. **92** 33 50 S 20 5 E
Ashton, U.S.A. **118** 44 6N 111 30W
Ashton-under-Lyne **12** 53 30N 2 8W
Ashuanipi, L. **107** 52 45N 66 15W
Asia **60** 45 0N 75 0 E
Asia, Kepulauan **73** 1 0N 131 13 E
Asiago **39** 45 52N 11 30 E
Asifabad **70** 19 20N 79 24 E
Asike **73** 6 39 S 140 24 E
Asilah **82** 35 29N 6 0W
Asinara, G. dell' **40** 41 0N 8 30 E
Asinara I. **40** 41 5N 8 15 E
Asino **58** 57 0N 86 0 E
'Asīr □ **63** 18 40N 42 30 E
Asir, Ras **63** 11 55N 51 10 E
Aska **70** 19 2N 84 42 E

Asker Babana

Asker	**47**	59 50N	10 26 E
Askersund	**49**	58 53N	14 55 E
Askim	**47**	59 35N	11 10 E
Askja	**50**	65 3N	16 48W
Asl	**86**	29 33N	32 44 E
Asmār	**65**	35 10N	71 27 E
Asmera (Asmara)	**87**	15 19N	38 55 E
Asnæs	**49**	55 40N	11 0 E
Asni	**82**	31 17N	7 58W
Aso	**74**	33 0N	131 5 E
Asola	**38**	45 12N	10 25 E
Asoteriba, Jebel	**86**	21 51N	36 30 E
Asotin	**118**	46 20N	117 3W
Aspe	**33**	38 20N	0 40W
Aspen	**119**	39 12N	106 56W
Aspermont	**117**	33 11N	100 15W
Aspiring, Mt.	**101**	44 23 S	168 46 E
Aspres	**21**	44 32N	5 44 E
Aspromonte	**41**	38 10N	16 0 E
Aspur	**68**	23 58N	74 7 E
Asquith	**109**	52 8N	107 13W
Assa	**82**	28 35N	9 6W
Assâba	**84**	16 10N	11 45W
Assam □	**67**	26 0N	93 0 E
Assamakka	**85**	19 21N	5 38 E
Asse	**16**	50 24N	4 10 E
Assekrem	**83**	23 16N	5 49 E
Assémini	**40**	39 18N	9 0 E
Assen	**16**	53 0N	6 35 E
Assens, Fyn, Denmark	**49**	56 41N	10 3 E
Assens, Fyn, Denmark	**49**	55 16N	9 55 E
Assini	**84**	5 9N	3 17W
Assiniboia	**109**	49 40N	105 59W
Assiniboine →	**109**	49 53N	97 8W
Assis	**125**	22 40 S	50 20W
Assisi	**39**	43 4N	12 36 E
Ássos	**45**	38 22N	20 33 E
Assus	**44**	39 32N	26 22 E
Assynt, L.	**14**	58 25N	5 15W
Astaffort	**20**	44 4N	0 40 E
Astakidha	**45**	35 53N	26 50 E
Astara	**53**	38 30N	48 50 E
Asti	**38**	44 54N	8 11 E
Astipálaia	**45**	36 32N	26 22 E
Astorga	**30**	42 29N	6 8W
Astoria	**118**	46 16N	123 50W
Åstorp	**49**	56 6N	12 55 E
Astrakhan	**57**	46 25N	48 5 E
Astrakhan-Bazàr	**53**	39 14N	48 30 E
Astudillo	**30**	42 12N	4 22W
Asturias	**30**	43 15N	6 0W
Asunción	**124**	25 10 S	57 30W
Asunción, La	**126**	11 2N	63 53W
Asutri	**87**	15 25N	35 45 E
Aswa →	**90**	3 43N	31 55 E
Aswad, Ras al	**86**	21 20N	39 0 E
Aswân	**86**	24 4N	32 57 E
Aswân High Dam = Sadd el Aali	**86**	24 5N	32 54 E
Asyût	**86**	27 11N	31 4 E
Asyûti, Wadi →	**86**	27 11N	31 16 E
Aszód	**27**	47 39N	19 28 E
At Ţafilah	**64**	30 45N	35 30 E
At Ta'if	**86**	21 5N	40 27 E
Aţ Ţur	**62**	31 47N	35 14 E
Aţ Ţurrah	**62**	32 39N	35 59 E
Atacama □	**124**	27 30 S	70 0W
Atacama, Desierto de	**124**	24 0 S	69 20W
Atacama, Salar de	**124**	23 30N	68 20W
Atakor	**83**	23 27N	5 31 E
Atakpamé	**85**	7 31N	1 13 E
Atalándi	**45**	38 39N	22 58 E
Atalaya	**126**	10 45 S	73 50W
Atami	**74**	35 5N	139 4 E
Atapupu	**73**	9 0 S	124 51 E
Atâr	**80**	20 30N	13 5W
Atara	**59**	63 10N	129 10 E
Ataram, Erg n-	**82**	23 57N	2 0 E
Atarfe	**31**	37 13N	3 40W
Atascadero	**119**	35 32N	120 44W
Atasu	**58**	48 30N	71 0 E
Atauro	**73**	8 10 S	125 30 E
Atbara	**86**	17 42N	33 59 E
'Atbara →	**86**	17 40N	33 56 E
Atbasar	**58**	51 48N	68 20 E
Atchafalaya B.	**117**	29 30N	91 20W
Atchison	**116**	39 40N	95 10W
Atebubu	**85**	7 47N	1 0W
Ateca	**32**	41 20N	1 49W
Aterno →	**39**	42 11N	13 51 E
Atesine, Alpi	**38**	46 55N	11 30 E
Atessa	**39**	42 5N	14 27 E
Ath	**16**	50 38N	3 47 E
Ath Thāmāmi	**64**	27 45N	44 45 E
Athabasca	**108**	54 45N	113 20W
Athabasca →	**109**	58 40N	110 50W
Athabasca, L.	**109**	59 15N	109 15W
Athboy	**15**	53 37N	6 55W
Athenry	**15**	53 18N	8 45W
Athens, Can.	**113**	44 38N	75 57W
Athens, Ala., U.S.A.	**115**	34 49N	86 58W
Athens, Ga., U.S.A.	**115**	33 56N	83 24W
Athens, N.Y., U.S.A.	**113**	42 15N	73 48W
Athens, Ohio, U.S.A.	**114**	39 25N	82 6W
Athens, Pa., U.S.A.	**113**	41 57N	76 36W
Athens, Tenn., U.S.A.	**115**	35 45N	84 38W
Athens, Tex., U.S.A.	**117**	32 11N	95 48W
Athens = Athínai	**45**	37 58N	23 46 E
Atherley	**112**	44 37N	79 20W
Atherton	**97**	17 17 S	145 30 E
Athiéme	**85**	6 37N	1 40 E
Athínai	**45**	37 58N	23 46 E
Athlone	**15**	53 26N	7 57W
Athni	**70**	16 44N	75 6 E
Atholl, Forest of	**14**	56 51N	3 50W
Atholville	**107**	47 59N	66 43W
Áthos, Mt.	**44**	40 9N	24 22 E
Athy	**15**	53 0N	7 0W
Ati, Chad	**81**	13 13N	18 20 E
Ati, Sudan	**87**	13 5N	29 2 E
Atiak	**90**	3 12N	32 2 E
Atico	**126**	16 14 S	73 40W
Atienza	**32**	41 12N	2 52W
Atikokan	**106**	48 45N	91 37W
Atikonak L.	**107**	52 40N	64 32W
Atka	**59**	60 50N	151 48 E
Atkarsk	**55**	51 55N	45 2 E
Atkinson	**116**	42 35N	98 59W
Atlanta, Ga., U.S.A.	**115**	33 50N	84 24W
Atlanta, Tex., U.S.A.	**117**	33 7N	94 8W
Atlantic	**116**	41 25N	95 0W
Atlantic City	**114**	39 25N	74 25W
Atlantic Ocean	**6**	0 0	20 0W
Atlin	**104**	59 31N	133 41W
Atlin, L.	**108**	59 26N	133 45W
'Atlit	**62**	32 42N	34 56 E
Atløy	**47**	61 21N	4 58 E
Atmakur	**70**	14 37N	79 40 E
Atmore	**115**	31 2N	87 30W
Atna →	**47**	61 44N	10 49 E
Atoka	**117**	34 22N	96 10W
Átokos	**45**	38 28N	20 49 E
Atouguia	**31**	39 20N	9 20W
Atoyac →	**120**	16 30N	97 31W
Atrak →	**65**	37 50N	57 0 E
Ätran	**49**	57 7N	12 57 E
Atrauli	**68**	28 2N	78 20 E
Atri	**39**	42 35N	14 0 E
Atsbi	**87**	13 52N	39 50 E
Atsoum, Mts.	**85**	6 41N	12 57 E
Attalla	**115**	34 2N	86 5W
Attawapiskat	**106**	52 56N	82 24W
Attawapiskat →	**106**	52 57N	82 18W
Attawapiskat, L.	**106**	52 18N	87 54W
Attendorn	**24**	51 8N	7 54 E
Attersee	**26**	47 55N	13 32 E
Attica	**114**	40 20N	87 15W
Attichy	**19**	49 25N	3 3 E
Attigny	**19**	49 28N	4 35 E
Attikamagen L.	**107**	55 0N	66 30W
Attikí □	**45**	38 10N	23 40 E
'Attīl	**62**	32 23N	35 4 E
Attleboro	**114**	41 56N	71 18W
Attock	**66**	33 52N	72 20 E
Attopeu	**71**	14 48N	106 50 E
Attur	**70**	11 35N	78 30 E
Atuel →	**124**	36 17 S	66 50W
Åtvidaberg	**49**	58 12N	16 0 E
Atwater	**119**	37 21N	120 37W
Atwood, Can.	**112**	43 40N	81 1W
Atwood, U.S.A.	**116**	39 52N	101 3W
Au Sable →	**114**	44 25N	83 20W
Au Sable Pt.	**106**	46 40N	86 10W
Aubagne	**21**	43 17N	5 37 E
Aube □	**19**	48 15N	4 0 E
Aube →	**19**	48 34N	3 43 E
Aubenas	**21**	44 37N	4 24 E
Aubenton	**19**	49 50N	4 12 E
Aubigny-sur-Nère	**19**	47 30N	2 24 E
Aubin	**20**	44 33N	2 15 E
Aubrac, Mts. d'	**20**	44 38N	2 58 E
Auburn, Ala., U.S.A.	**115**	32 37N	85 30W
Auburn, Calif., U.S.A.	**118**	38 53N	121 4W
Auburn, Ind., U.S.A.	**114**	41 20N	85 0W
Auburn, N.Y., U.S.A.	**114**	42 57N	76 39W
Auburn, Nebr., U.S.A.	**116**	40 25N	95 50W
Auburn Range	**99**	25 15 S	150 30 E
Auburndale	**115**	28 5N	81 45W
Aubusson	**20**	45 57N	2 11 E
Auch	**20**	43 39N	0 36 E
Auchel	**19**	50 30N	2 29 E
Auchi	**85**	7 6N	6 13 E
Auckland	**101**	36 52 S	174 46 E
Auckland Is.	**94**	50 40 S	166 5 E
Aude □	**20**	43 8N	2 28 E
Aude →	**20**	43 13N	3 14 E
Auden	**106**	50 14N	87 53W
Auderville	**18**	49 43N	1 57W
Audierne	**18**	48 1N	4 34W
Audincourt	**19**	47 30N	6 50 E
Audo Ra.	**87**	6 20N	41 50 E
Audubon	**116**	41 43N	94 56W
Aue	**24**	50 34N	12 43 E
Auerbach	**24**	50 30N	12 25 E
Auffay	**18**	49 43N	1 07 E
Augathella	**97**	25 48 S	146 35 E
Augrabies Falls	**92**	28 35 S	20 20 E
Augsburg	**25**	48 22N	10 54 E
Augusta, Italy	**41**	37 14N	15 12 E
Augusta, Ark., U.S.A.	**117**	35 17N	91 25W
Augusta, Ga., U.S.A.	**115**	33 29N	81 59W
Augusta, Kans., U.S.A.	**117**	37 40N	97 0W
Augusta, Me., U.S.A.	**107**	44 20N	69 46W
Augusta, Mont., U.S.A.	**118**	47 30N	112 29W
Augusta, Wis., U.S.A.	**116**	44 41N	91 8W
Augustenborg	**49**	54 57N	9 53 E
Augusto Cardosa	**91**	12 40 S	34 50 E
Augustów	**28**	53 51N	23 00 E
Augustus Downs	**98**	18 35 S	139 55 E
Augustus, Mt.	**96**	24 20 S	116 50 E
Aukan	**87**	15 29N	40 50 E
Aulla	**38**	44 12N	10 0 E
Aulnay	**20**	46 2N	0 22W
Aulne →	**18**	48 17N	4 16W
Aulnoye	**19**	50 12N	3 50 E
Ault	**116**	40 40N	104 42W
Ault-Onival	**18**	50 5N	1 29 E
Aulus-les-Bains	**20**	42 49N	1 19 E
Aumale	**19**	49 46N	1 46 E
Aumont-Aubrac	**20**	44 43N	3 17 E
Auna	**85**	10 9N	4 42 E
Aundh	**70**	17 33N	74 23 E
Aunis	**20**	46 5N	0 50W
Auponhia	**73**	1 58 S	125 27 E
Aups	**21**	43 37N	6 15 E
Auraiya	**69**	26 28N	79 33 E
Aurangabad, Bihar, India	**69**	24 45N	84 18 E
Aurangabad, Maharashtra, India	**70**	19 50N	75 23 E
Auray	**18**	47 40N	3 0W
Aurès	**83**	35 8N	6 30 E
Aurich	**24**	53 28N	7 30 E
Aurillac	**20**	44 55N	2 26 E
Aurlandsvangen	**47**	60 55N	7 12 E
Auronza	**39**	46 33N	12 27 E
Aurora, Can.	**112**	44 0N	79 28W
Aurora, S. Afr.	**92**	32 40 S	18 29 E
Aurora, Colo., U.S.A.	**116**	39 44N	104 55W
Aurora, Ill., U.S.A.	**114**	41 42N	88 12W
Aurora, Mo., U.S.A.	**117**	36 58N	93 42W
Aurora, Nebr., U.S.A.	**116**	40 55N	98 0W
Aurora, Ohio, U.S.A.	**112**	41 21N	81 20W
Aurskog	**47**	59 55N	11 26 E
Aurukun Mission	**98**	13 20 S	141 45 E
Aus	**92**	26 35 S	16 12 E
Aust-Agder fylke □	**47**	58 55N	7 40 E
Austad	**47**	58 58N	7 37 E
Austerlitz = Slavkov	**27**	49 10N	16 52 E
Austevoll	**47**	60 5N	5 13 E
Austin, Minn., U.S.A.	**116**	43 37N	92 59W
Austin, Nev., U.S.A.	**118**	39 30N	117 1W
Austin, Pa., U.S.A.	**112**	41 40N	78 7W
Austin, Tex., U.S.A.	**117**	30 20N	97 45W
Austin, L.	**96**	27 40 S	118 0 E
Austral Downs	**97**	20 30 S	137 45 E
Austral Is. = Tubuai Is.	**95**	23 0 S	150 0W
Austral Seamount Chain	**95**	24 0 S	150 0W
Australia ■	**94**	23 0 S	135 0 E
Australian Alps	**97**	36 30 S	148 30 E
Australian Cap. Terr. □	**97**	35 30 S	149 0 E
Australian Dependency □	**5**	73 0 S	90 0 E
Austria ■	**26**	47 0N	14 0 E
Austvågøy	**50**	68 20N	14 40 E
Auterive	**20**	43 21N	1 29 E
Authie →	**19**	50 22N	1 38 E
Authon	**18**	48 12N	0 55 E
Autlán	**120**	19 40N	104 30W
Autun	**19**	46 58N	4 17 E
Auvergne	**20**	45 20N	3 15 E
Auvézère →	**20**	45 12N	0 50 E
Auxerre	**19**	47 48N	3 32 E
Auxi-le-Château	**19**	50 15N	2 8 E
Auxonne	**19**	47 10N	5 20 E
Auzances	**20**	46 2N	2 30 E
Auzat	**20**	45 27N	3 19 E
Avallon	**19**	47 30N	3 53 E
Avalon Pen.	**107**	47 30N	53 20W
Avalon Res.	**117**	32 30N	104 30W
Avanigadda	**70**	16 0N	80 56 E
Avaré	**125**	23 4 S	48 58W
Ávas	**44**	40 57N	25 56 E
Aveiro, Brazil	**127**	3 10 S	55 5W
Aveiro, Port.	**30**	40 37N	8 38W
Aveiro □	**30**	40 40N	8 35W
Āvej	**64**	35 40N	49 15 E
Avellaneda	**124**	34 50 S	58 10W
Avellino	**41**	40 54N	14 46 E
Averøya	**47**	63 0N	7 35 E
Aversa	**41**	40 58N	14 11 E
Avery	**118**	47 22N	115 56W
Aves, I. de	**121**	15 45N	63 55W
Aves, Is. de	**121**	12 0N	67 30W
Avesnes-sur-Helpe	**19**	50 8N	3 55 E
Avesta	**48**	60 9N	16 10 E
Aveyron □	**20**	44 22N	2 45 E
Aveyron →	**20**	44 7N	1 5 E
Avezzano	**39**	42 2N	13 24 E
Avgó	**45**	35 33N	25 37 E
Aviá Terai	**124**	26 45 S	60 50W
Aviano	**39**	46 3N	12 35 E
Avigliana	**38**	45 7N	7 13 E
Avigliano	**41**	40 44N	15 41 E
Avignon	**21**	43 57N	4 50 E
Ávila	**30**	40 39N	4 43W
Ávila □	**30**	40 30N	5 0W
Ávila, Sierra de	**30**	40 40N	5 0W
Avilés	**30**	43 35N	5 57W
Avionárion	**45**	38 31N	24 8 E
Avisio →	**39**	46 7N	11 5 E
Aviz	**31**	39 4N	7 53W
Avize	**19**	48 59N	4 0 E
Avoca, Austral.	**100**	37 5 S	143 26 E
Avoca, Ireland	**15**	52 52N	6 13W
Avoca, U.S.A.	**112**	42 24N	77 25W
Avoca →	**100**	35 40 S	143 43 E
Avola, Can.	**108**	51 45N	119 19W
Avola, Italy	**41**	36 56N	15 7 E
Avon, N.Y., U.S.A.	**112**	43 0N	77 42W
Avon, S.D., U.S.A.	**116**	43 0N	98 3W
Avon □	**13**	51 30N	2 40W
Avon →, Avon, U.K.	**13**	51 30N	2 43W
Avon →, Hants., U.K.	**13**	50 44N	1 45W
Avon →, Warwick, U.K.	**13**	52 0N	2 9W
Avon Downs	**97**	19 58 S	137 25 E
Avon, Îles	**97**	19 37 S	158 17 E
Avon Lake	**112**	41 28N	82 3W
Avondale	**91**	17 43 S	30 58 E
Avonlea	**109**	50 0N	105 0W
Avonmore	**113**	45 10N	74 58W
Avonmouth	**13**	51 30N	2 42W
Avramov	**43**	42 45N	26 38 E
Avranches	**18**	48 40N	1 20W
Avre →	**18**	48 47N	1 22 E
Avrig	**46**	45 43N	24 21 E
Avrillé	**20**	46 28N	1 28W
Avtovac	**42**	43 9N	18 35 E
Awag el Baqar	**87**	10 10N	33 10 E
'Awālī	**65**	26 0N	50 30 E
Awarja →	**70**	17 5N	76 15 E
'Awartā	**62**	32 10N	35 17 E
Awasa, L.	**87**	7 0N	38 30 E
Awash	**87**	9 1N	40 10 E
Awash →	**87**	11 45N	41 5 E
Awaso	**84**	6 15N	2 22W
Awatere →	**101**	41 37 S	174 10 E
Awbārī	**83**	26 46N	12 57 E
Awbārī □	**83**	26 35N	12 46 E
Awe, L.	**14**	56 15N	5 15W
Aweil	**87**	8 42N	27 20 E
Awgu	**85**	6 4N	7 24 E
Awjilah	**81**	29 8N	21 7 E
Ax-les-Thermes	**20**	42 44N	1 50 E
Axarfjörður	**50**	66 15N	16 45W
Axel Heiberg I.	**4**	80 0N	90 0W
Axim	**84**	4 51N	2 15W
Axintele	**46**	44 37N	26 47 E
Axiós →	**44**	40 57N	22 35 E
Axmarsbruk	**48**	61 3N	17 10 E
Axminster	**13**	50 47N	3 1W
Axstedt	**24**	53 26N	8 43 E
Axvall	**49**	58 23N	13 34 E
Ay	**19**	49 3N	4 0 E
Ayabaca	**126**	4 40 S	79 53W
Ayabe	**74**	35 20N	135 20 E
Ayacucho, Argent.	**124**	37 5 S	58 20W
Ayacucho, Peru	**126**	13 0 S	74 0W
Ayaguz	**58**	48 10N	80 0 E
Ayakudi	**70**	10 28N	77 56 E
Ayamonte	**31**	37 12N	7 24W
Ayan	**59**	56 30N	138 16 E
Ayancık	**56**	41 57N	34 18 E
Ayas	**56**	40 10N	32 14 E
Ayaviri	**126**	14 50 S	70 35W
Āybaq	**65**	36 15N	68 5 E
Ayenngré	**85**	8 40N	1 1 E
Ayeritam	**71**	5 24N	100 15 E
Ayer's Cliff	**113**	45 10N	72 3W
Ayers Rock	**96**	25 23 S	131 5 E
Aygues →	**21**	44 7N	4 43 E
Ayiá	**44**	39 43N	22 45 E
Ayia Ánna	**45**	38 52N	23 24 E
Ayia Marina	**45**	35 27N	26 53 E
Ayía Marína	**45**	37 11N	26 48 E
Ayía Paraskeví	**44**	39 14N	26 16 E
Ayia Rouméli	**45**	35 14N	23 58 E
Ayiássos	**45**	39 5N	26 23 E
Áyion Óros	**44**	40 25N	24 6 E
Áyios Andréas	**45**	37 21N	22 45 E
Áyios Evstrátios	**44**	39 34N	24 58 E
Áyios Evstrátios	**44**	39 30N	25 0 E
Áyios Ioannis, Ákra	**45**	35 20N	25 40 E
Áyios Kírikos	**45**	37 34N	26 17 E
Áyios Matthaios	**44**	39 30N	19 47 E
Áyios Mírono	**45**	35 15N	25 1 E
Áyios Nikólaos	**45**	35 11N	25 41 E
Áyios Pétros	**45**	38 38N	20 33 E
Áyios Yeóryios	**45**	37 28N	23 57 E
Aykathonisi	**45**	37 28N	27 0 E
Aykin	**52**	62 15N	49 56 E
Aylesbury	**13**	51 48N	0 49W
Aylmer	**112**	42 46N	80 59W
Aylmer L.	**104**	64 0N	110 8W
'Ayn al Mubārak	**64**	24 10N	38 10 E
'Ayn 'Arīk	**62**	31 54N	35 8 E
'Ayn Zaqqūt	**83**	29 0N	19 30 E
Ayn Zhālah	**64**	36 45N	42 35 E
Ayna	**33**	38 34N	2 3W
Ayolas	**124**	27 10 S	56 59W
Ayom	**87**	7 49N	28 23 E
Ayon, Ostrov	**59**	69 50N	169 0 E
Ayora	**33**	39 3N	1 3W
Ayr, Austral.	**97**	19 35 S	147 25 E
Ayr, U.K.	**14**	55 28N	4 37W
Ayr →	**14**	55 29N	4 40W
Ayre, Pt. of	**12**	54 27N	4 21W
Aysha	**87**	10 50N	42 23 E
Aytos	**43**	42 42N	27 16 E
Aytoska Planina	**43**	42 45N	27 30 E
Ayu, Kepulauan	**73**	0 35N	131 5 E
Ayutla	**120**	16 58N	99 17W
Ayvalık	**64**	39 20N	26 46 E
Az Ẓāhirīyah	**62**	31 25N	34 58 E
Az Ẓahrān	**64**	26 10N	50 7 E
Az Zarqā	**62**	32 5N	36 4 E
Az Zāwiyah	**83**	32 52N	12 56 E
Az-Zilfī	**64**	26 12N	44 52 E
Az Zubayr	**64**	30 20N	47 50 E
Azambuja	**31**	39 4N	8 51W
Azamgarh	**69**	26 5N	83 13 E
Azaouak, Vallée de l'	**85**	15 50N	3 20 E
Āzārbāijān □	**64**	37 0N	44 30 E
Azare	**85**	11 55N	10 10 E
Azay-le-Rideau	**18**	47 16N	0 30 E
Azazga	**83**	36 48N	4 22 E
Azbine = Aïr	**85**	18 0N	8 0 E
Azeffoun	**83**	36 51N	4 26 E
Azemmour	**82**	33 20N	9 20W
Azerbaijan S.S.R. □	**57**	40 20N	48 0 E
Azezo	**87**	12 28N	37 15 E
Azilal, Beni Mallal	**82**	32 0N	6 30W
Azimganj	**69**	24 14N	88 16 E
Aznalcóllar	**31**	37 32N	6 17W
Azogues	**126**	2 35 S	78 0W
Azor	**62**	32 2N	34 48 E
Azores	**6**	38 44N	29 0W
Azov	**57**	47 3N	39 25 E
Azov Sea = Azovskoye More	**56**	46 0N	36 30 E
Azovskoye More	**56**	46 0N	36 30 E
Azovy	**58**	64 55N	64 35 E
Azpeitia	**32**	43 12N	2 19W
Azrou	**82**	33 28N	5 19W
Aztec	**119**	36 54N	108 0W
Azúa de Compostela	**121**	18 25N	70 44W
Azuaga	**31**	38 16N	5 39W
Azuara	**32**	41 15N	0 53W
Azuer →	**31**	39 8N	3 36W
Azuero, Pen. de	**121**	7 30N	80 30W
Azul	**124**	36 42 S	59 43W
Azzaba	**83**	36 48N	7 6 E
Azzano Décimo	**39**	45 53N	12 46 E

B

Ba Don	**71**	17 45N	106 26 E
Ba Ngoi = Cam Lam	**71**	11 50N	109 10 E
Ba Xian	**76**	39 8N	116 22 E
Baa	**73**	10 50 S	123 0 E
Baamonde	**30**	43 7N	7 44W
Baarle Nassau	**16**	51 27N	4 56 E
Baarn	**16**	52 12N	5 17 E
Bāb el Māndeb	**63**	12 35N	43 25 E
Baba	**43**	42 44N	23 59 E
Baba Burnu	**44**	39 29N	26 2 E
Baba dag	**57**	41 0N	48 19W
Babadag	**46**	44 53N	28 44 E
Babaeski	**43**	41 26N	27 6 E
Babahoyo	**126**	1 40 S	79 30W
Babana	**85**	10 31N	3 46 E

Babar Bandula

Babar, Alg. 83 35 10N 7 6 E
Babar, Indon. 73 8 0S 129 30 E
Babar, Pak. 68 31 7N 69 32 E
Babarkach 68 29 45N 68 0 E
Babayevo 55 59 24N 35 55 E
Babb 118 48 56N 113 27W
Babenhausen 25 49 57N 8 56 E
Babia Gora 27 49 38N 19 38 E
Babile 87 9 16N 42 11 E
Babinda 98 17 20S 145 56 E
Babine 108 55 22N 126 37W
Babine → 108 55 45N 127 44W
Babine L. 108 54 48N 126 0W
Babo 73 2 30S 133 30 E
Babócsa 27 46 2N 17 21 E
Bābol 65 36 40N 52 50 E
Bābol Sar 65 36 45N 52 45 E
Baborówo Kietrz 27 50 7N 18 1 E
Baboua 88 5 49N 14 58 E
Babuna 42 41 30N 21 40 E
Babura 85 12 51N 8 59 E
Babušnica 42 43 7N 22 27 E
Babuyan Chan. 73 19 10N 122 0 E
Babylon, Iraq 64 32 40N 44 30 E
Babylon, U.S.A. 113 40 42N 73 20W
Bač 42 45 29N 19 17 E
Bac Kan 71 22 5N 105 50 E
Bac Ninh 71 21 13N 106 4 E
Bac Phan 71 22 0N 105 0 E
Bac Quang 71 22 30N 104 48 E
Bacabal 127 4 15S 44 45W
Bacan, Kepulauan 73 0 35S 127 30 E
Bacan, Pulau 73 0 50S 127 30 E
Bacarès, Le 20 42 47N 3 3 E
Bacarra 73 18 15N 120 37 E
Bacau 73 8 27S 126 27 E
Bacău 46 46 35N 26 55 E
Bacău □ 46 46 30N 26 45 E
Baccarat 19 48 28N 6 42 E
Bacchus Marsh 100 37 43S 144 27 E
Bacerac 120 30 18N 108 50W
Băceşti 46 46 50N 27 11 E
Bacharach 25 50 3N 7 46 E
Bachelina 58 57 45N 67 20 E
Bachuma 87 6 48N 35 53 E
Bačina 42 43 42N 21 23 E
Back → 104 65 10N 104 0W
Bačka Palanka 42 45 17N 19 27 E
Bačka Topola 42 45 49N 19 39 E
Bäckefors 49 58 48N 12 9 E
Bački Petrovac 42 45 29N 19 32 E
Backnang 25 48 57N 9 26 E
Backstairs Passage 97 35 40S 138 5 E
Bacolod 73 10 40N 122 57 E
Bacqueville 18 49 47N 1 0 E
Bacs-Kiskun □ 27 46 43N 19 30 E
Bácsalmás 27 46 8N 19 17 E
Bad → 116 44 22N 100 22W
Bad Aussee 26 47 43N 13 45 E
Bad Axe 106 43 48N 82 59W
Bad Bergzabern 25 49 6N 8 0 E
Bad Bramstedt 24 53 56N 9 53 E
Bad Doberan 24 54 6N 11 55 E
Bad Driburg 24 51 44N 9 0 E
Bad Ems 25 50 22N 7 44 E
Bad Frankenhausen 24 51 21N 11 3 E
Bad Freienwalde 24 52 47N 14 3 E
Bad Godesberg 24 50 41N 7 4 E
Bad Hersfeld 24 50 52N 9 42 E
Bad Hofgastein 26 47 17N 13 6 E
Bad Homburg 25 50 17N 8 33 E
Bad Honnef 24 50 39N 7 13 E
Bad Ischl 26 47 44N 13 38 E
Bad Kissingen 25 50 11N 10 5 E
Bad Kreuznach 25 49 47N 7 47 E
Bad Lands 116 43 40N 102 10W
Bad Langensalza 24 51 6N 10 40 E
Bad Lauterberg 24 51 38N 10 29 E
Bad Leonfelden 26 48 31N 14 18 E
Bad Lippspringe 24 51 47N 8 46 E
Bad Mergentheim 25 49 29N 9 47 E
Bad Münstereifel 24 50 33N 6 46 E
Bad Muskau 24 51 33N 14 43 E
Bad Nauheim 25 50 24N 8 45 E
Bad Oeynhausen 24 52 16N 8 45 E
Bad Oldesloe 24 53 48N 10 22 E
Bad Orb 25 50 16N 9 21 E
Bad Pyrmont 24 51 59N 9 15 E
Bad Reichenhall 25 47 44N 12 53 E
Bad St.-Peter 24 54 23N 8 32 E
Bad Salzuflen 24 52 8N 8 44 E
Bad Segeberg 24 53 58N 10 16 E
Bad Tölz 25 47 43N 11 34 E
Bad Waldsee 25 47 56N 9 46 E
Bad Wildungen 24 51 7N 9 10 E
Bad Wimpfen 25 49 12N 9 10 E
Bad Windsheim 25 49 29N 10 25 E
Badagara 70 11 35N 75 40 E
Badagri 85 6 25N 2 55 E
Badajoz 31 38 50N 6 59W
Badajoz □ 31 38 40N 6 30W
Badakhshan □ 65 36 30N 71 0 E
Badalona 32 41 26N 2 15 E
Badalzai 66 29 50N 65 35 E
Badampahar 69 22 10N 86 10 E
Badanah 64 30 58N 41 30 E
Badas 72 4 33N 114 25 E
Badas, Kepulauan 72 0 45N 107 5 E
Baddo → 66 28 0N 64 20 E
Bade 73 7 10S 139 35 E
Baden, Austria 27 48 1N 16 13 E
Baden, Can. 112 43 14N 80 40W
Baden, Switz. 25 47 28N 8 18 E
Baden-Baden 25 48 45N 8 15 E
Baden-Württemberg □ 25 48 40N 9 0 E
Badgastein 26 47 7N 13 9 E
Badger 107 49 0N 56 4W
Bādghīsāt □ 65 35 0N 63 0 E
Badia Polèsine 39 45 6N 11 30 E
Badin 68 24 38N 68 54 E
Badnera 68 20 48N 77 44 E
Badogo 84 11 2N 8 13W
Badong 77 31 1N 110 23 E
Badrinath 69 30 45N 79 30 E
Baduen 63 7 15N 47 40 E
Badulla 70 7 1N 81 7 E
Baena 31 37 37N 4 20W
Baeza 33 37 57N 3 25W
Bafa Gölü 45 37 30N 27 29 E
Bafang 85 5 9N 10 11 E
Bafatá 84 12 8N 14 40W
Baffin B. 4 72 0N 64 0W
Baffin I. 105 68 0N 75 0W
Bafia 88 4 40N 11 10 E
Bafilo 85 9 22N 1 22 E
Bafing → 84 13 49N 10 50W
Bafoulabé 84 13 50N 10 55W
Bafoussam 85 5 28N 10 25 E
Bafra 56 41 34N 35 54 E
Bafra, C. 56 41 44N 35 58 E
Bāft, Esfahān, Iran 65 31 40N 55 25 E
Bāft, Kermān, Iran 65 29 15N 56 38 E
Bafut 85 6 6N 10 2 E
Bafwasende 90 1 3N 27 5 E
Bagalkot 70 16 10N 75 40 E
Bagamoyo 90 6 28S 38 55 E
Bagamoyo □ 90 6 20S 38 30 E
Baganga 73 7 34N 126 33 E
Bagansiapiapi 72 2 12N 100 50 E
Bagasra 68 21 30N 71 0 E
Bagawi 87 12 20N 34 18 E
Bagdarin 59 54 26N 113 36 E
Bagé 125 31 20S 54 15W
Bagenalstown = Muine Bheag 15 52 42N 6 57W
Baggs 118 41 8N 107 46W
Baghdād 64 33 20N 44 30 E
Bagherhat 69 22 40N 89 47 E
Bagheria 40 38 5N 13 30 E
Bāghīn 65 30 12N 56 45 E
Baghlān 65 36 12N 69 0 E
Baghlān □ 65 36 0N 68 30 E
Bagley 116 47 30N 95 22W
Bagnacavallo 39 44 25N 11 58 E
Bagnara Cálabra 41 38 16N 15 49 E
Bagnères-de-Bigorre 20 43 5N 0 9 E
Bagnères-de-Luchon 20 42 47N 0 38 E
Bagni di Lucca 38 44 1N 10 37 E
Bagno di Romagna 39 43 50N 11 59 E
Bagnoles-de-l'Orne 18 48 32N 0 25W
Bagnoli di Sopra 39 45 13N 11 55 E
Bagnolo Mella 38 45 27N 10 14 E
Bagnols-les-Bains 20 44 30N 3 40 E
Bagnols-sur-Cèze 21 44 10N 4 36 E
Bagnorégio 39 42 38N 12 7 E
Bagolino 38 45 49N 10 28 E
Bagotville 107 48 22N 70 54W
Bagrdan 42 44 5N 21 11 E
Baguio 73 16 26N 120 34 E
Bahabón de Esgueva 32 41 52N 3 43W
Bahadurgarh 68 28 40N 76 57 E
Bahama, Canal Viejo de 121 22 10N 77 30W
Bahamas ■ 121 24 0N 75 0W
Baharîya, El Wâhât al 86 28 0N 28 50 E
Bahau 71 2 48N 102 26 E
Bahawalnagar 68 30 0N 73 15 E
Bahawalpur 68 29 24N 71 40 E
† Bahawalpur □ 68 29 5N 71 3 E
Baheri 69 28 45N 79 34 E
Bahi 90 5 58S 35 21 E
Bahi Swamp 90 6 10S 35 0 E
Bahia = Salvador 127 13 0S 38 30W
Bahia □ 127 12 0S 42 0W
Bahía Blanca 124 38 35S 62 13W
Bahía de Caráquez 126 0 40S 80 27W
Bahía, Islas de la 121 16 45N 86 15W
Bahía Laura 128 48 10S 66 30W
Bahía Negra 126 20 5S 58 5W
Bahir Dar 87 11 37N 37 10 E
Bahmer 82 27 32N 0 10W
Bahönye 27 46 25N 17 28 E
Bahr Aouk → 88 8 40N 19 0 E
Bahr el Ahmar □ 86 20 0N 35 0 E
Bahr el Ghazâl □ 87 7 0N 28 0 E
Bahr el Jebel → 87 7 30N 30 30 E
Bahr Salamat → 81 9 20N 18 0 E
Bahr Yûsef → 86 28 25N 30 35 E
Bahra el Burullus 86 31 28N 30 48 E
Bahraich 69 27 38N 81 37 E
Bahrain ■ 65 26 0N 50 35 E
Bai 84 13 35N 3 28W
Baia Mare 46 47 40N 23 35 E
Baia-Sprie 46 47 41N 23 43 E
Baïbokoum 81 7 46N 15 43 E
Baicheng 76 45 38N 122 42 E
Băicoi 46 45 3N 25 52 E
Baidoa 63 3 8N 43 30 E
Baie Comeau 107 49 12N 68 10W
Baie-St-Paul 107 47 28N 70 32W
Baie Trinité 107 49 25N 67 20W
Baie Verte 107 49 55N 56 12W
Baignes 20 45 23N 0 25W
Baigneux-les-Juifs 19 47 31N 4 39 E
Ba'ījī 64 35 0N 43 30 E
Baikal, L. = Baykal, Oz. 59 53 0N 108 0 E
Bailadila, Mt. 70 18 43N 81 15 E
Baile Atha Cliath = Dublin 15 53 20N 6 18W
Bailei 87 6 44N 40 18 E
Bailén 31 38 8N 3 48W
Băileşti 46 44 01N 23 20 E
Bailhongal 70 15 55N 74 53 E
Bailleul 19 50 44N 2 41 E
Bailundo 89 12 10S 15 50 E
Baimuru 98 7 35S 144 51 E
Bain-de-Bretagne 18 47 50N 1 40W
Bainbridge, Ga., U.S.A. 115 30 53N 84 34W
Bainbridge, N.Y., U.S.A. 113 42 17N 75 29W
Baing 73 10 14S 120 34 E
Bainville 116 48 8N 104 10W
Bā'ir 64 30 45N 36 55 E
Baird 117 32 25N 99 25W
Baird Mts. 104 67 10N 160 15W
Bairin Youqi 76 43 30N 118 35 E
Bairin Zuoqi 76 43 58N 119 15 E
Bairnsdale 97 37 48S 147 36 E
Baise → 20 44 17N 0 18 E
Baissa 85 7 14N 10 38 E
Baitadi 69 29 35N 80 25 E
Baiyin 76 36 45N 104 14 E
Baiyu Shan 76 37 15N 107 30 E
Baiyuda 86 17 35N 32 07 E
Baja 27 46 12N 18 59 E
Baja California 120 31 10N 115 12W
Baja, Pta. 120 29 50N 116 0W
Bajah, Wadi → 86 23 14N 39 20 E
Bajana 68 23 7N 71 49 E
Bajimba, Mt. 99 29 17S 152 6 E
Bajina Bašta 42 43 58N 19 35 E
Bajmok 42 45 57N 19 24 E
Bajo Nuevo 121 15 40N 78 50W
Bajoga 85 10 57N 11 20 E
Bajool 98 23 40S 150 35 E
Bak 27 46 43N 16 51 E
Bakala 88 6 15N 20 20 E
Bakar 39 45 18N 14 32 E
Bakchav 58 57 1N 82 5 E
Bakel 84 14 56N 12 20W
Baker, Calif., U.S.A. 119 35 16N 116 8W
Baker, Mont., U.S.A. 116 46 22N 104 12W
Baker, Nev., U.S.A. 118 38 59N 114 7W
Baker, Oreg., U.S.A. 118 44 50N 117 55W
Baker I. 94 0 10N 176 35W
Baker, L. 104 64 0N 96 0W
Baker Lake 104 64 20N 96 3W
Baker Mt. 118 48 50N 121 49W
Baker's Dozen Is. 106 56 45N 78 45W
Bakersfield, Calif., U.S.A. 119 35 25N 119 0W
Bakersfield, Vt., U.S.A. 113 44 46N 72 48W
Bakhchisaray 56 44 40N 33 45 E
Bakhmach 54 51 10N 32 45 E
Bakhtīārī □ 64 32 0N 49 0 E
Bakinskikh Komissarov, im 26 64 39 20N 49 15 E
Bakırköy 43 40 59N 28 53 E
Bakkafjörður 50 66 2N 14 48W
Bakkagerði 50 65 31N 13 49W
Bakony → 27 47 35N 17 54 E
Bakony Forest = Bakony Hegység 27 47 10N 17 30 E
Bakony Hegység 27 47 10N 17 30 E
Bakori 85 11 34N 7 25 E
Bakouma 88 5 40N 22 56 E
Bakov 26 50 27N 14 55 E
Baku 57 40 25N 49 45 E
Bala 112 45 1N 79 37W
Bal'ā 62 32 20N 35 6 E
Bala, L. = Tegid, L. 12 52 53N 3 38W
Balabac I. 72 8 0N 117 0 E
Balabac, Str. 72 7 53N 117 5 E
Balabakk 64 34 0N 36 10 E
Balabalangan, Kepulauan 72 2 20S 117 30 E
Bălăciţa 46 44 23N 23 8 E
Balaghat 69 21 49N 80 12 E
Balaghat Ra. 70 18 50N 76 30 E
Balaguer 32 41 50N 0 50 E
Balakhna 55 56 25N 43 32 E
Balaklava, Austral. 99 34 7S 138 22 E
Balaklava, U.S.S.R. 56 44 30N 33 30 E
Balakleya 56 49 28N 36 55 E
Balakovo 55 52 4N 47 55 E
Balanda 55 51 30N 44 40 E
Balangir 69 20 43N 83 35 E
Balapur 68 20 40N 76 45 E
Balashikha 55 55 49N 37 59 E
Balashov 55 51 30N 43 10 E
Balasinor 68 22 57N 73 23 E
Balasore 69 21 35N 87 3 E
Balassagyarmat 27 48 4N 19 15 E
Balât 86 25 36N 29 19 E
Balaton 27 46 50N 17 40 E
Balatonfüred 27 46 58N 17 54 E
Balatonszentgyörgy 27 46 41N 17 19 E
Balazote 33 38 54N 2 09W
Balboa 120 9 0N 79 30W
Balboa Hill 120 9 6N 79 44W
Balbriggan 15 53 35N 6 10W
Balcarce 124 38 0S 58 10W
Balcarres 109 50 50N 103 35W
Balchik 43 43 28N 28 11 E
Balclutha 101 46 15S 169 45 E
Bald Knob 117 35 20N 91 35W
Baldock L. 109 56 33N 97 57W
Baldwin, Fla., U.S.A. 115 30 15N 82 10W
Baldwin, Mich., U.S.A. 114 43 54N 85 53W
Baldwinsville 114 43 10N 76 19W
Bale 39 45 4N 13 46 E
Bale □ 87 6 20N 41 30 E
Baleares □ 32 39 30N 3 0 E
Baleares, Islas 32 39 30N 3 0 E
Balearic Is. = Baleares, Islas 32 39 30N 3 0 E
Băleni 46 45 48N 27 51 E
Baler 73 15 46N 121 34 E
Balfe's Creek 98 20 12S 145 55 E
Balfour 93 26 38S 28 35 E
Balfouriyya 62 32 38N 35 18 E
Bali, Camer. 85 5 54N 10 0 E
Bali, Indon. 72 8 20S 115 0 E
Bali □ 72 8 20S 115 0 E
Bali, Selat 73 8 30S 114 35 E
Baligród 27 49 20N 22 17 E
Balikesir 64 39 35N 27 58 E
Balikpapan 72 1 10S 116 55 E
Balimbing 73 5 10N 120 3 E
Baling 71 5 41N 100 55 E
Balipara 67 26 50N 92 45 E
Baliza 127 16 0S 52 20W
Balkan Mts. = Stara Planina 43 43 15N 23 0 E
Balkan Pen. 9 42 0N 22 0 E
Balkh 65 36 44N 66 47 E
Balkh □ 65 36 30N 67 0 E
Balkhash 58 46 50N 74 50 E
Balkhash, Ozero 58 46 0N 74 50 E
Ballachulish 14 56 40N 5 10W
Balladoran 100 31 52S 148 39 E
Ballarat 97 37 33S 143 50 E
Ballard, L. 96 29 20S 120 10 E
Ballarpur 70 19 50N 79 23 E
Ballater 14 57 2N 3 2W
Ballenas, Canal de las 120 29 10N 113 45W
Balleny Is. 5 66 30S 163 0 E
Ballia 69 25 46N 84 12 E
Ballina, Austral. 97 28 50S 153 31 E
Ballina, Mayo, Ireland 15 54 7N 9 10W
Ballina, Tipp., Ireland 15 52 49N 8 27W
Ballinasloe 15 53 20N 8 12W
Ballinger 117 31 45N 99 58W
Ballinrobe 15 53 36N 9 13W
Ballinskelligs B. 15 51 46N 10 11W
Ballon 18 48 10N 0 14 E
Ballycastle 15 55 12N 6 15W
Ballymena 15 54 53N 6 18W
Ballymena □ 15 54 53N 6 18W
Ballymoney 15 55 5N 6 30W
Ballymoney □ 15 55 5N 6 23W
Ballyshannon 15 54 30N 8 10W
Balmaceda 128 46 0S 71 50W
Balmazújváros 27 47 37N 21 21 E
Balmoral, Austral. 99 37 15S 141 48 E
Balmoral, U.K. 14 57 3N 3 13W
Balmorhea 117 31 2N 103 41W
Balonne → 97 28 47S 147 56 E
Balrampur 69 27 30N 82 20 E
Balranald 97 34 38S 143 33 E
Balş 46 44 22N 24 5 E
Balsas → 120 17 55N 102 10W
Bålsta 48 59 35N 17 30 E
Balston Spa 113 43 0N 73 52W
Balta, Romania 46 44 54N 22 38 E
Balta, U.S.A. 116 48 12N 100 7W
Balta, R.S.F.S.R., U.S.S.R. 57 42 58N 44 32 E
Balta, Ukraine S.S.R., U.S.S.R. 56 48 2N 29 45 E
Baltanás 30 41 56N 4 15W
Baltic Sea 51 56 0N 20 0 E
Baltîm 86 31 35N 31 10 E
Baltimore, Ireland 15 51 29N 9 22W
Baltimore, U.S.A. 114 39 18N 76 37W
Baltrum 24 53 43N 7 25 E
Baluchistan □ 65 27 30N 65 0 E
Balurghat 69 25 15N 88 44 E
Balygychan 59 63 56N 154 12 E
Bam 65 29 7N 58 14 E
Bama 85 11 33N 13 41 E
Bamako 84 12 34N 7 55W
Bamba 85 17 5N 1 24W
Bambari 88 5 40N 20 35 E
Bamberg, Ger. 25 49 54N 10 53 E
Bamberg, U.S.A. 115 33 19N 81 1W
Bambesi 87 9 45N 34 40 E
Bambey 84 14 42N 16 28W
Bambili 90 3 40N 26 0 E
Bamboo 98 14 34S 143 20 E
Bamenda 85 5 57N 10 11 E
Bamfield 108 48 45N 125 10W
Bāmīān □ 65 35 0N 67 0 E
Bamiancheng 76 43 15N 124 2 E
Bamkin 85 6 3N 11 27 E
Bampūr 65 27 15N 60 21 E
Ban Aranyaprathet 71 13 41N 102 30 E
Ban Ban 71 19 31N 103 30 E
Ban Bua Chum 71 15 11N 101 12 E
Ban Houei Sai 71 20 22N 100 32 E
Ban Khe Bo 71 19 10N 104 39 E
Ban Khun Yuam 71 18 49N 97 57 E
* Ban Me Thuot 71 12 40N 108 3 E
Ban Phai 71 16 4N 102 44 E
Ban Thateng 71 15 25N 106 27 E
Baña, Punta de la 32 40 33N 0 40 E
Banaba 94 0 45S 169 50 E
Banadar Daryay Oman □ 65 27 30N 56 0 E
Banalia 90 1 32N 25 5 E
Banam 71 11 20N 105 17 E
Banamba 84 13 29N 7 22W
Banana 98 24 28S 150 8 E
Bananal, I. do 127 11 30S 50 30W
Banaras = Varanasi 69 25 22N 83 8 E
Banas →, Gujarat, India 68 23 45N 71 25 E
Banas →, Madhya Pradesh, India 69 24 15N 81 30 E
Bânâs, Ras. 86 23 57N 35 50 E
Banbridge 15 54 21N 6 17W
Banbridge □ 15 54 21N 6 16W
Banbury 13 52 4N 1 21W
Banchory 14 57 3N 2 30W
Bancroft 106 45 3N 77 51W
Band 43 46 30N 24 25 E
Band-e Torkestān 65 35 30N 64 0 E
Banda 68 25 30N 80 26 E
Banda Aceh 72 5 35N 95 20 E
Banda Banda, Mt. 99 31 10S 152 28 E
Banda Elat 73 5 40S 133 5 E
Banda, Kepulauan 73 4 37S 129 50 E
Banda, La 124 27 45S 64 10W
Banda Sea 73 6 0S 130 0 E
Bandama → 84 6 32N 5 30W
Bandanaira 73 4 32S 129 54 E
Bandanwara 68 26 9N 74 38 E
Bandar = Machilipatnam 70 16 12N 81 12 E
Bandār 'Abbās 65 27 15N 56 15 E
Bandar-e Būshehr 65 28 55N 50 55 E
Bandar-e Chārak 65 26 45N 54 20 E
Bandar-e Deylam 64 30 5N 50 10 E
Bandar-e Lengeh 65 26 35N 54 58 E
Bandar-e Ma'shur 64 30 35N 49 10 E
Bandar-e Nakhīlū 65 26 58N 53 30 E
Bandar-e Rīg 65 29 30N 50 45 E
Bandar-e Shāh 65 37 0N 54 10 E
Bandar-e Shāhpūr 64 30 30N 49 5 E
Bandar-i-Pahlavī 64 37 30N 49 30 E
Bandar Seri Begawan 72 4 52N 115 0 E
Bandawe 91 11 58S 34 5 E
Bande 30 42 3N 7 58W
Bandeira, Pico da 125 20 26S 41 47W
Bandera, Argent. 124 28 55S 62 20W
Bandera, U.S.A. 117 29 45N 99 3W
Banderas, Bahía de 120 20 40N 105 30W
Bandia → 70 19 2N 80 28 E
Bandiagara 84 14 12N 3 29W
Bandırma 64 40 20N 28 0 E
Bandon 15 51 44N 8 45W
Bandon → 15 51 40N 8 41W
Bandula 91 19 0S 33 7 E

† *Now part of Punjab* □

* *Renamed Buon Me Thuot*

Bandundu Baume-les-Dames

Bandundu	88	3 15 S	17 22 E
Bandung	73	6 54 S	107 36 E
Băneasa	46	45 56N	27 55 E
Bañeres	33	38 44N	0 38W
Banes	121	21 0N	75 42W
Bañeza, La	30	42 17N	5 54W
Banff, Can.	108	51 10N	115 34W
Banff, U.K.	14	57 40N	2 32W
Banff Nat. Park	108	51 30N	116 15W
Banfora	84	10 40N	4 40W
Bang Hieng →	71	16 10N	105 10 E
Bang Lamung	71	13 3N	100 56 E
Bang Saphan	71	11 14N	99 28 E
Bangala Dam	91	21 7 S	31 25 E
Bangalore	70	12 59N	77 40 E
Bangante	85	5 8N	10 32 E
Bangaon	69	23 0N	88 47 E
Bangassou	88	4 55N	23 7 E
Bangeta, Mt.	98	6 21 S	147 3 E
Banggai	73	1 40 S	123 30 E
Banggi, P.	72	7 17N	117 12 E
Banghāzī	83	32 11N	20 3 E
Banghāzī □	83	32 7N	20 4 E
Bangil	73	7 36 S	112 50 E
Bangjang	87	11 23N	32 41 E
Bangka, Pulau, Sulawesi, Indon.	73	1 50N	125 5 E
Bangka, Pulau, Sumatera, Indon.	72	2 0 S	105 50 E
Bangka, Selat	72	2 30 S	105 30 E
Bangkalan	73	7 2 S	112 46 E
Bangkinang	72	0 18N	101 5 E
Bangko	72	2 5 S	102 9 E
Bangkok = Krung Thep	71	13 45N	100 35 E
Bangladesh ■	67	24 0N	90 0 E
Bangolo	84	7 1N	7 29W
Bangor, N. Ireland, U.K.	15	54 40N	5 40W
Bangor, Wales, U.K.	12	53 13N	4 9W
Bangor, Me., U.S.A.	107	44 48N	68 42W
Bangor, Pa., U.S.A.	113	40 51N	75 13W
Bangued	73	17 40N	120 37 E
Bangui	88	4 23N	18 35 E
Banguru	90	0 30N	27 10 E
Bangweulu, L.	91	11 0 S	30 0 E
Bangweulu Swamp	91	11 20 S	30 15 E
Bani	121	18 16N	70 22W
Bani →	84	14 30N	4 12W
Bani Bangou	85	15 3N	2 42 E
Bani, Djebel	82	29 16N	8 0W
Banī Na'īm	62	31 31N	35 10 E
Banī Suhaylah	62	31 21N	34 19 E
Bania	84	9 4N	3 6W
Baniara	98	9 44 S	149 54 E
Banīnah	83	32 0N	20 12 E
Bāniyās	64	35 10N	36 0 E
Banja Luka	42	44 49N	17 11 E
Banjar	73	7 24 S	108 30 E
Banjarmasin	72	3 20 S	114 35 E
Banjarnegara	73	7 24 S	109 42 E
Banjul	84	13 28N	16 40W
Bankeryd	49	57 53N	14 6 E
Banket	91	17 27 S	30 19 E
Bankilaré	85	14 35N	0 44 E
Bankipore	69	25 35N	85 10 E
Banks I., B.C., Can.	108	53 20N	130 0W
Banks I., N.W.T., Can.	4	73 15N	121 30W
Banks I., P.N.G.	97	10 10 S	142 15 E
Banks Pen.	101	43 45 S	173 15 E
Banks Str.	99	40 40 S	148 10 E
Bankura	69	23 11N	87 18 E
Bankya	42	42 43N	23 8 E
Bann →, Down, U.K.	15	54 30N	6 31W
Bann →, Londonderry, U.K.	15	55 10N	6 34W
Bannalec	18	47 57N	3 42W
Banning	119	33 58N	116 52W
Banningville = Bandundu	88	3 15 S	17 22 E
Bannockburn, Can.	112	44 39N	77 33W
Bannockburn, U.K.	14	56 5N	3 55W
Bannockburn, Zimb.	91	20 17 S	29 48 E
Bañolas	32	42 16N	2 44 E
Banon	21	44 2N	5 38 E
Baños de la Encina	31	38 10N	3 46W
Baños de Molgas	30	42 15N	7 40W
Bánovce	27	48 44N	18 16 E
Banská Bystrica	27	48 46N	19 14 E
Banská Štiavnica	27	48 25N	18 55 E
Bansko	43	41 52N	23 28 E
Banswara	68	23 32N	74 24 E
Banten	73	6 5 S	106 8 E
Bantry	15	51 40N	9 28W
Bantry, B.	15	51 35N	9 50W
Bantul	73	7 55 S	110 19 E
Bantva	68	21 29N	70 12 E
Bantval	70	12 55N	75 0 E
Banya	43	42 33N	24 50 E
Banyak, Kepulauan	72	2 10N	97 10 E
Banyo	85	6 52N	11 45 E
Banyuls	20	42 29N	3 8 E
Banyumas	73	7 32 S	109 18 E
Banyuwangi	73	8 13 S	114 21 E
Banzare Coast	5	68 0 S	125 0 E
Banzyville = Mobayi	88	4 15N	21 8 E
Baocheng	77	33 12N	106 56 E
Baode	76	39 1N	111 5 E
Baoding	76	38 50N	115 28 E
Baoji	77	34 20N	107 5 E
Baojing	77	28 45N	109 41 E
Baokang	77	31 54N	111 12 E
Baoshan	75	25 10N	99 5 E
Baotou	76	40 32N	110 2 E
Baoying	77	33 17N	119 20 E
Bap	68	27 23N	72 18 E
Bapatla	70	15 55N	80 30 E
Bapaume	19	50 7N	2 50 E
Bāqa el Gharbīyya	62	32 25N	35 2 E
Ba'qūbah	64	33 45N	44 50 E
Baquedano	124	23 20 S	69 52W
Bar, U.S.S.R.	56	49 4N	27 40 E
Bar, Yugo.	42	42 8N	19 8 E
Bar Harbor	107	44 15N	68 20W
Bar-le-Duc	19	48 47N	5 10 E
Bar-sur-Aube	19	48 14N	4 40 E
Bar-sur-Seine	19	48 7N	4 20 E
Barabai	72	2 32 S	115 34 E
Barabinsk	58	55 20N	78 20 E
Baraboo	116	43 28N	89 46W
Baracoa	121	20 20N	74 30W
Baradero	124	33 52 S	59 29W
Baraga	116	46 49N	88 29W
Barahona, Dom. Rep.	121	18 13N	71 7W
Barahona, Spain	32	41 17N	2 39W
Barail Range	67	25 15N	93 20 E
Baraka →	86	18 13N	37 35 E
Barakhola	67	25 0N	92 45 E
Barakot	69	21 33N	84 59 E
Barakula	99	26 30 S	150 33 E
Baralaba	98	24 13 S	149 50 E
Baralzon L.	109	60 0N	98 3W
Baramati	70	18 11N	74 33 E
Baramba	69	20 25N	85 23 E
Barameiya	86	18 32N	36 38 E
Baramula	69	34 15N	74 20 E
Baran	68	25 9N	76 40 E
Baranof I.	104	57 0N	135 10W
Baranovichi	54	53 10N	26 0 E
Baranów Sandomierski	28	50 29N	21 30 E
Baranya □	27	46 0N	18 15 E
Barão de Melgaço	126	11 50 S	60 45W
Baraolt	46	46 5N	25 34 E
Barapasi	73	2 15 S	137 5 E
Barasat	69	22 46N	88 31 E
Barat Daya, Kepulauan	73	7 30 S	128 0 E
Barataria B.	117	29 15N	89 45W
Baraut	68	29 13N	77 7 E
Barbacena	125	21 15 S	43 56W
Barbacoas	126	1 45N	78 0W
Barbados ■	121	13 0N	59 30W
Barban	39	45 5N	14 4 E
Barbastro	32	42 2N	0 5 E
Barbate	31	36 13N	5 56W
Barberino di Mugello	39	44 1N	11 15 E
Barberton, S. Afr.	93	25 42 S	31 2 E
Barberton, U.S.A.	114	41 0N	81 40W
Barbezieux	20	45 28N	0 9W
Barbigha	69	25 21N	85 47 E
Barbourville	115	36 57N	83 52W
Barbuda I.	121	17 30N	61 40W
Barca, La	120	20 20N	102 40W
Barcaldine	97	23 43 S	145 6 E
Barcarrota	31	38 31N	6 51W
Barcellona Pozzo di Gotto	41	38 8N	15 15 E
Barcelona, Spain	32	41 21N	2 10 E
Barcelona, Venez.	126	10 10N	64 40W
Barcelona □	32	41 30N	2 0 E
Barcelonette	21	44 23N	6 40 E
Barcelos	126	1 0 S	63 0W
Barcin	28	52 52N	17 55 E
Barcoo →	97	25 30 S	142 50 E
Barcs	27	45 58N	17 28 E
Barczewo	28	53 50N	20 42 E
Barda	57	40 25N	47 10 E
Bardai	83	21 25N	17 0 E
Bardas Blancas	124	35 49 S	69 45W
Bardejov	27	49 18N	21 15 E
Bardera	63	2 20N	42 27 E
Bardi	38	44 38N	9 43 E
Bardi, Ra's	64	24 17N	37 31 E
Bardia	81	31 45N	25 0 E
Bardo	28	50 31N	16 42 E
Bardoli	68	21 12N	73 5 E
Bardolino	38	45 33N	10 43 E
Bardsey I.	12	52 46N	4 47W
Bardstown	114	37 50N	85 29W
Bareilly	69	28 22N	79 27 E
Barentin	18	49 33N	0 58 E
Barenton	18	48 38N	0 50W
Barents Sea	4	73 0N	39 0 E
Barentu	87	15 2N	37 35 E
Barfleur	18	49 40N	1 17W
Barga, China	75	30 40N	81 20 E
Barga, Italy	38	44 5N	10 30 E
Bargal	63	11 25N	51 0 E
Bargara	98	24 50 S	152 25 E
Barge	38	44 43N	7 19 E
Barge, La	118	42 12N	110 4W
Bargnop	87	9 32N	28 25 E
Bargteheide	24	53 42N	10 13 E
Barguzin	59	53 37N	109 37 E
Barh	69	25 29N	85 46 E
Barhaj	69	26 18N	83 44 E
Barham	100	35 36 S	144 8 E
Barhi	69	24 15N	85 25 E
Bari, India	68	26 39N	77 39 E
Bari, Italy	41	41 6N	16 52 E
Bari Doab	68	30 20N	73 0 E
Bariadi □	90	2 45 S	34 40 E
Barīm	63	12 39N	43 25 E
Barinas	126	8 36N	70 15W
Baring C.	104	70 0N	117 30W
Baringo	90	0 47N	36 16 E
Baringo □	90	0 55N	36 0 E
Baringo, L.	90	0 47N	36 16 E
Baripada	69	21 57N	86 45 E
Bârîs	86	24 42N	30 31 E
Barisal	69	22 45N	90 20 E
Barisan, Bukit	72	3 30 S	102 15 E
Barito →	72	4 0 S	114 50 E
Barjac	21	44 20N	4 22 E
Barjols	21	43 34N	6 2 E
Barjūj, Wadi →	83	25 26N	12 12 E
Bark L.	112	45 27N	77 51W
Barka = Baraka →	87	18 13N	37 35 E
Barkah	65	23 40N	58 0 E
Barker	112	43 20N	78 35W
Barkley Sound	108	48 50N	125 10W
Barkly Downs	98	20 30 S	138 30 E
Barkly East	92	30 58 S	27 33 E
Barkly Tableland	97	17 50 S	136 40 E
Barkly West	92	28 5 S	24 31 E
Barkol, Wadi →	86	17 40N	32 0 E
Barksdale	117	29 47N	100 2W
Barlee, L.	96	29 15 S	119 30 E
Barlee Ra.	96	23 30 S	116 0 E
Barletta	41	41 20N	16 17 E
Barleur, Pointe de	18	49 42N	1 16W
Barlinek	28	53 0N	15 15 E
Barlow L.	109	62 00N	103 0W
Barmedman	99	34 9 S	147 21 E
Barmer	68	25 45N	71 20 E
Barmera	99	34 15 S	140 28 E
Barmouth	12	52 44N	4 3W
Barmstedt	24	53 47N	9 46 E
Barnagar	68	23 7N	75 19 E
Barnard Castle	12	54 33N	1 55W
Barnato	99	31 38 S	145 0 E
Barnaul	58	53 20N	83 40 E
Barne Inlet	5	80 15 S	160 0 E
Barnes	99	36 2 S	144 47 E
Barnesville	115	33 6N	84 9W
Barnet	13	51 37N	0 15W
Barneveld, Neth.	16	52 7N	5 36 E
Barneveld, U.S.A.	113	43 16N	75 14W
Barneville	18	49 23N	1 46W
Barney, Mt.	97	28 17 S	152 44 E
Barngo	99	25 3 S	147 20 E
Barnhart	117	31 10N	101 8W
Barnsley	12	53 33N	1 29W
Barnstaple	13	51 5N	4 3W
Barnsville	116	46 43N	96 28W
Baro	85	8 35N	6 18 E
Baro →	87	8 26N	33 13 E
Baroda	68	25 29N	76 35 E
Baroda = Vadodara	68	22 20N	73 10 E
Barpali	69	21 11N	83 35 E
Barqin	83	27 33N	13 34 E
Barques, Pte. aux	114	44 5N	82 55W
Barquinha	31	39 28N	8 25W
Barquísimeto	126	10 4N	69 19W
Barr	19	48 25N	7 28 E
Barra, Brazil	127	11 5 S	43 10W
Barra, U.K.	14	57 0N	7 30W
Barra do Corda	127	5 30 S	45 10W
Barra do Piraí	125	22 30 S	43 50W
Barra Falsa, Pta. da	93	22 58 S	35 37 E
Barra Hd.	14	56 47N	7 40W
Barra Mansa	125	22 35 S	44 12W
Barra, Sd. of	14	57 4N	7 25W
Barraba	99	30 21 S	150 35 E
Barrackpur	69	22 44N	88 30 E
Barrafranca	41	37 22N	14 10 E
Barranca, Lima, Peru	126	10 45 S	77 50W
Barranca, Loreto, Peru	126	4 50 S	76 50W
Barrancabermeja	126	7 0N	73 50W
Barrancas	126	8 55N	62 5W
Barrancos	31	38 10N	6 58W
Barranqueras	124	27 30 S	59 0W
Barranquilla	126	11 0N	74 50W
Barras	127	4 15 S	42 18W
Barraute	106	48 26N	77 38W
Barre	114	44 15N	72 30W
Barreal	124	31 33 S	69 28W
Barreiras	127	12 8 S	45 0W
Barreirinhas	127	2 30 S	42 50W
Barreiro	31	38 40N	9 6W
Barreiros	127	8 49 S	35 12W
Barrême	21	43 57N	6 23 E
Barren I.	71	12 17N	93 50 E
Barren, Nosy	93	18 25 S	43 40 E
Barretos	127	20 30 S	48 35W
Barrhead	108	54 10N	114 24W
Barrie	106	44 24N	79 40W
Barrier Ra.	97	31 0 S	141 30 E
Barrière	108	51 12N	120 7W
Barrington, Ill., U.S.A.	114	42 8N	88 5W
Barrington, R.I., U.S.A.	113	41 43N	71 20W
Barrington L.	109	56 55N	100 15W
Barrington Tops	97	32 6 S	151 28 E
Barrow	104	71 16N	156 50W
Barrow →	15	52 10N	6 57W
Barrow Creek T.O.	96	21 30 S	133 55 E
Barrow I.	96	20 45 S	115 20 E
Barrow-in-Furness	12	54 8N	3 15W
Barrow Pt.	98	14 20 S	144 40 E
Barrow Ra.	96	26 0 S	127 40 E
Barrow Str.	4	74 20N	95 0W
Barruecopardo	30	41 4N	6 40W
Barruelo	30	42 54N	4 17W
Barry	13	51 23N	3 19W
Barry's Bay	106	45 29N	77 41W
Barsalogho	85	13 25N	1 3W
Barsi	70	18 10N	75 50 E
Barsø	49	55 7N	9 33 E
Barstow, Calif., U.S.A.	119	34 58N	117 2W
Barstow, Tex., U.S.A.	117	31 28N	103 24W
Barth	24	54 20N	12 36 E
Bartica	126	6 25N	58 40W
Bartin	64	41 38N	32 21 E
Bartle Frere, Mt.	97	17 27 S	145 50 E
Bartlesville	117	36 50N	95 58W
Bartlett	117	30 46N	97 30W
Bartlett, L.	108	63 5N	118 20W
Bartolomeu Dias	91	21 10 S	35 8 E
Barton-upon-Humber	12	53 41N	0 27W
Bartoszyce	28	54 15N	20 55 E
Bartow	115	27 53N	81 49W
Barumba	90	1 3N	23 37 E
Baruth	24	52 3N	13 31 E
Barvenkovo	56	48 57N	37 0 E
Barwani	68	22 2N	74 57 E
Barycz →	28	51 42N	16 15 E
Barysh	55	53 39N	47 8 E
Bas-Rhin □	19	48 40N	7 30 E
Bašaid	42	45 38N	20 25 E
Bāsa'idū	65	26 35N	55 20 E
Basankusa	88	1 5N	19 50 E
Bascuñán, C.	124	28 52 S	71 35W
Basel (Basle)	25	47 35N	7 35 E
Basel-Stadt □	25	47 35N	7 35 E
Baselland □	25	47 26N	7 45 E
Basento →	41	40 21N	16 50 E
Bashkir A.S.S.R. □	52	54 0N	57 0 E
Basilaki I.	98	10 35 S	151 0 E
Basilan	73	6 35N	122 0 E
Basilan Str.	73	6 50N	122 0 E
Basildon	13	51 34N	0 29 E
Basilicata □	41	40 30N	16 0 E
Basim	70	20 3N	77 0 E
Basin	118	44 22N	108 2W
Basingstoke	13	51 15N	1 5W
Basirhat	69	22 40N	88 54 E
Baška	39	44 58N	14 45 E
Baskatong, Rés.	106	46 46N	75 50W
Baskerville C.	96	17 10 S	122 15 E
Basle = Basel	25	47 35N	7 35 E
Basmat	70	19 15N	77 12 E
Basoda	68	23 52N	77 54 E
Basoka	90	1 16N	23 40 E
Basongo	88	4 15 S	20 20 E
Basque Provinces = Vascongadas	32	42 50N	2 45W
Basra = Al Başrah	64	30 30N	47 50 E
Bass Rock	14	56 5N	2 40W
Bass Str.	97	39 15 S	146 30 E
Bassano	108	50 48N	112 20W
Bassano del Grappa	39	45 45N	11 45 E
Bassar	85	9 19N	0 57 E
Basse Santa-Su	84	13 13N	14 15W
Basse-Terre	121	16 0N	61 40W
Bassée, La	19	50 31N	2 49 E
Bassein	70	19 26N	72 48 E
Basseterre	121	17 17N	62 43W
Bassett, Nebr., U.S.A.	116	42 37N	99 30W
Bassett, Va., U.S.A.	115	36 48N	79 59W
Bassi	68	30 44N	76 21 E
Bassigny	19	48 0N	5 10 E
Bassikounou	84	15 55N	6 1W
Bassum	24	52 50N	8 42 E
Båstad	49	56 25N	12 51 E
Bastak	65	27 15N	54 25 E
Bastar	70	19 15N	81 40 E
Basti	69	26 52N	82 55 E
Bastia	21	42 40N	9 30 E
Bastia Umbra	39	43 4N	12 34 E
Bastide-Puylaurent, La	20	44 35N	3 55 E
Bastogne	16	50 1N	5 43 E
Bastrop	117	30 5N	97 22W
Basuto	92	19 50 S	26 25 E
Bat Yam	62	32 2N	34 44 E
Bata, Eq. Guin.	88	1 57N	9 50 E
Bata, Romania	46	46 1N	22 4 E
Bataan	73	14 40N	120 25 E
Batabanó	121	22 40N	82 20W
Batabanó, G. de	121	22 30N	82 30W
Batac	73	18 3N	120 34 E
Batagoy	59	67 38N	134 38 E
Batak	43	41 57N	24 12 E
Batakan	72	4 5 S	114 38 E
Batalha	31	39 40N	8 50W
Batama	90	0 58N	26 33 E
Batamay	59	63 30N	129 15 E
Batang, China	75	30 1N	99 0 E
Batang, Indon.	73	6 55 S	109 40 E
Batangafo	88	7 25N	18 20 E
Batangas	73	13 35N	121 10 E
Batanta	73	0 55 S	130 40 E
Batatais	125	20 54 S	47 37W
Batavia	114	43 0N	78 10W
Bataysk	57	47 3N	39 45 E
Batchelor	96	13 4 S	131 1 E
Bateman's B.	97	35 40 S	150 12 E
Batemans Bay	99	35 44 S	150 11 E
Batesburg	115	33 54N	81 32W
Batesville, Ark., U.S.A.	117	35 48N	91 40W
Batesville, Miss., U.S.A.	117	34 17N	89 58W
Batesville, Tex., U.S.A.	117	28 59N	99 38W
Bath, U.K.	13	51 22N	2 22W
Bath, Maine, U.S.A.	107	43 50N	69 49W
Bath, N.Y., U.S.A.	114	42 20N	77 17W
Bathgate	14	55 54N	3 38W
Bathurst, Austral.	97	33 25 S	149 31 E
Bathurst, Can.	107	47 37N	65 43W
Bathurst = Banjul	84	13 28N	16 40W
Bathurst B.	97	14 16 S	144 25 E
Bathurst, C.	104	70 34N	128 0W
Bathurst Harb.	99	43 15 S	146 10 E
Bathurst I., Austral.	96	11 30 S	130 10 E
Bathurst I., Can.	4	76 0N	100 30W
Bathurst In.	104	68 10N	108 50W
Bathurst Inlet	104	66 50N	108 1W
Batie	84	9 53N	2 53W
Batinah	65	24 0N	56 0 E
Batlow	99	35 31 S	148 9 E
Batman	64	37 55N	41 5 E
Batna	83	35 34N	6 15 E
Batočina	42	44 7N	21 5 E
Batoka	91	16 45 S	27 15 E
Baton Rouge	117	30 30N	91 5W
Batopilas	120	27 0N	107 45W
Batouri	88	4 30N	14 25 E
Battambang	71	13 7N	103 12 E
Batticaloa	70	7 43N	81 45 E
Battipáglia	41	40 38N	15 0 E
Battīr	62	31 44N	35 8 E
Battle, Can.	109	52 58N	110 52W
Battle, U.K.	13	50 55N	0 30 E
Battle →	109	52 43N	108 15W
Battle Camp	98	15 20 S	144 40 E
Battle Creek	114	42 20N	85 6W
Battle Harbour	107	52 16N	55 35W
Battle Lake	116	46 20N	95 43W
Battle Mountain	118	40 45N	117 0W
Battlefields	91	18 37 S	29 47 E
Battleford	109	52 45N	108 15W
Battonya	27	46 16N	21 3 E
Batu	87	6 55N	39 45 E
Batu Gajah	71	4 28N	101 3 E
Batu, Kepulauan	72	0 30 S	98 25 E
Batu Pahat	71	1 50N	102 56 E
Batuata	73	6 12 S	122 42 E
Batumi	57	41 30N	41 30 E
Baturaja	72	4 11 S	104 15 E
Baturité	127	4 28 S	38 45W
Bau	72	1 25N	110 9 E
Baubau	73	5 25 S	122 38 E
Bauchi	85	10 22N	9 48 E
Bauchi □	85	10 30N	10 0 E
Baud	18	47 52N	3 1W
Baudette	116	48 46N	94 35W
Baugé	18	47 31N	0 8W
Baule-Escoublac, La	18	47 18N	2 23W
Baume-les-Dames	19	47 22N	6 22 E

Baunatal Benavente

Baunatal 24 51 13N 9 25 E
Baunei 40 40 2N 9 41 E
Bauru 125 22 10S 49 0W
Baús 127 18 22S 52 47W
Bauska 54 56 24N 25 15 E
Bautzen 24 51 11N 14 25 E
Baux, Les 21 43 45N 4 51 E
Bavanište 42 44 49N 20 53 E
Bavaria = Bayern □ 25 49 7N 11 30 E
Båven 48 59 0N 16 56 E
Bavi Sadri 68 24 28N 74 30 E
Bavispe → 120 29 30N 109 11W
Baw Baw, Mt. 100 37 49S 146 19 E
Bawdwin 67 23 5N 97 20 E
Bawean 72 5 46S 112 35 E
Bawku 85 11 3N 0 19W
Bawlake 67 19 11N 97 21 E
Baxley 115 31 43N 82 23W
Baxter Springs 117 37 3N 94 45W
Bay Bulls 107 47 19N 52 50W
Bay City, Mich., U.S.A. 114 43 35N 83 51W
Bay City, Oreg., U.S.A. 118 45 45N 123 58W
Bay City, Tex., U.S.A. 117 28 59N 95 55W
Bay de Verde 107 48 5N 52 54W
Bay, Laguna de 73 14 20N 121 11 E
Bay Minette 115 30 54N 87 43W
Bay St. Louis 117 30 18N 89 22W
Bay Shore 114 40 44N 73 15W
Bay Springs 117 31 58N 89 18W
Bay View 101 39 25S 176 50 E
Baya 91 11 53S 27 25 E
Bayamo 121 20 20N 76 40W
Bayamón 121 18 24N 66 10W
Bayan 76 46 5N 127 24 E
Bayan Har Shan 75 34 0N 98 0 E
Bayan Hot = Alxa Zuoqi 76 38 50N 105 40 E
Bayan Obo 76 41 52N 109 59 E
Bayana 68 26 55N 77 18 E
Bayanaul 58 50 45N 75 45 E
Bayanhongor 75 46 8N 102 43 E
Bayard 116 41 48N 103 17W
Bayázeh 65 33 30N 54 40 E
Baybay 73 10 40N 124 55 E
Bayburt 64 40 15N 40 20 E
Bayerischer Wald 25 49 0N 13 0 E
Bayern □ 25 49 7N 11 30 E
Bayeux 18 49 17N 0 42W
Bayfield, Can. 112 43 34N 81 42W
Bayfield, U.S.A. 116 46 50N 90 48W
Baykal, Oz. 59 53 0N 108 0 E
Baykit 59 61 50N 95 50 E
Baykonur 58 47 48N 65 50 E
Baymak 52 52 36N 58 19 E
Baynes Mts. 92 17 15S 13 0 E
Bayombong 73 16 30N 121 10 E
Bayon 19 48 30N 6 20 E
Bayona 30 42 6N 8 52W
Bayonne, France 20 43 30N 1 28W
Bayonne, U.S.A. 113 40 41N 74 7W
Bayovar 126 5 50S 81 0W
Baypore → 70 11 10N 75 47 E
Bayram-Ali 58 37 37N 62 10 E
Bayreuth 25 49 56N 11 35 E
Bayrischzell 25 47 39N 12 1 E
Bayrūt 64 33 53N 35 31 E
Bayt Awlá 62 31 37N 35 2 E
Bayt Fajjār 62 31 38N 35 9 E
Bayt Fūrīk 62 32 11N 35 20 E
Bayt Ḩānūn 62 31 32N 34 32 E
Bayt Jālā 62 31 43N 35 11 E
Bayt Lahm 62 31 43N 35 12 E
Bayt Rīma 62 32 2N 35 6 E
Bayt Sāḩūr 62 31 42N 35 13 E
Bayt Ummar 62 31 38N 35 7 E
Bayt 'ūr al Taḩtā 62 31 54N 35 5 E
Baytin 62 31 56N 35 14 E
Baytown 117 29 42N 94 57W
Baytūniyā 62 31 54N 35 10 E
Bayzo 85 13 52N 4 35 E
Baza 33 37 30N 2 47W
Bazar Dyuzi 57 41 12N 47 50 E
Bazarny Karabulak 55 52 15N 46 20 E
Bazarnyy Syzgan 55 53 45N 46 40 E
Bazartobe 57 49 26N 51 45 E
Bazaruto, I. do 93 21 40S 35 28 E
Bazas 20 44 27N 0 13W
Bazhong 77 31 52N 106 46 E
Beach 116 46 57N 103 58W
Beach City 112 40 38N 81 35W
Beachport 99 37 29S 140 0 E
Beachy Head 13 50 44N 0 16 E
Beacon 114 41 32N 73 58W
Beaconia 109 50 25N 96 31W
Beaconsfield 97 41 11S 146 48 E
Beagle, Canal 128 55 0S 68 30W
Bealanana 93 14 33N 48 44 E
Beamsville 112 43 12N 79 28W
Béar, C. 20 42 31N 3 8 E
Bear I. 15 51 38N 9 50W
Bear L., B.C., Can. 108 56 10N 126 52W
Bear L., Man., Can. 109 55 8N 96 0W
Bear L., U.S.A. 118 42 0N 111 20W
Bearcreek 118 45 11N 109 6W
Beardmore 106 49 36N 87 57W
Beardmore Glacier 5 84 30S 170 0 E
Beardstown 116 40 0N 90 25W
Béarn 20 43 8N 0 36W
Bearpaw Mt. 118 48 15N 109 30W
Bearskin Lake 106 53 58N 91 2W
Beas de Segura 33 38 15N 2 53W
Beasain 32 43 3N 2 11W
Beata, C. 121 17 40N 71 30W
Beatrice, U.S.A. 116 40 20N 96 40W
Beatrice, Zimb. 91 18 15S 30 55 E
Beatrice, C. 97 14 20S 136 55 E
Beatton → 108 56 15N 120 45W
Beatton River 108 57 26N 121 20W
Beatty 119 36 58N 116 46W
Beaucaire 21 43 48N 4 39 E
Beauce, Plaine de la 19 48 10N 1 45 E
Beauceville 107 46 13N 70 46W
Beaudesert 99 27 59S 153 0 E
Beaufort, Austral. 100 37 25S 143 25 E
Beaufort, Malay. 72 5 30N 115 40 E
Beaufort, N.C., U.S.A. 115 34 45N 76 40W
Beaufort, S.C., U.S.A. 115 32 25N 80 40W
Beaufort Sea 4 72 0N 140 0W
Beaufort West 92 32 18S 22 36 E
Beaugency 19 47 47N 1 38 E
Beauharnois 106 45 20N 73 52W
Beaujeu 21 46 10N 4 35 E
Beaulieu 20 44 59N 1 50 E
Beaulieu → 108 62 3N 113 11W
Beauly 14 57 29N 4 27W
Beauly → 14 57 26N 4 28W
Beaumaris 12 53 16N 4 7W
Beaumetz-les-Loges 19 50 15N 2 40 E
Beaumont, Dordogne, France 20 44 45N 0 46 E
Beaumont, Sarthe, France 18 48 13N 0 8 E
Beaumont, U.S.A. 117 30 5N 94 8W
Beaumont-de-Lomagne 20 43 53N 0 59 E
Beaumont-le-Roger 18 49 4N 0 47 E
Beaumont-sur-Oise 19 49 9N 2 17 E
Beaune 19 47 2N 4 50 E
Beaune-la-Rolande 19 48 4N 2 25 E
Beaupréau 18 47 12N 1 00W
Beauséjour 109 50 5N 96 35W
Beausset, Le 21 43 10N 5 46 E
Beauvais 19 49 25N 2 8 E
Beauval 109 55 9N 107 37W
Beauvoir 18 46 55N 2 1W
Beauvoir-sur-Niort 20 46 12N 0 30W
Beaver, Alaska, U.S.A. 104 66 20N 147 30W
Beaver, Okla., U.S.A. 117 36 52N 100 31W
Beaver, Pa., U.S.A. 112 40 40N 80 18W
Beaver, Utah, U.S.A. 119 38 20N 112 45W
Beaver →, B.C., Can. 108 59 52N 124 20W
Beaver →, Sask., Can. 109 55 26N 107 45W
Beaver City 116 40 13N 99 50W
Beaver Dam 116 43 28N 88 50W
Beaver Falls 114 40 44N 80 20W
Beaver I. 106 45 40N 85 31W
Beaver, R 106 55 55N 87 48W
Beaverhill L., Alta., Can. 108 53 27N 112 32W
Beaverhill L., Man., Can. 109 54 5N 94 50W
Beaverhill L., N.W.T., Can. 109 63 2N 104 22W
Beaverlodge 108 55 11N 119 29W
Beavermouth 108 51 32N 117 23W
Beaverstone → 106 54 59N 89 25W
Beaverton 112 44 26N 79 9W
Beawar 68 26 3N 74 18 E
Bebedouro 125 21 0S 48 25W
Beboa 93 17 22S 44 33 E
Bebra 24 50 59N 9 48 E
Beccles 13 52 27N 1 33 E
Bečej 42 45 36N 20 3 E
Beceni 46 45 23N 26 48 E
Becerreá 30 42 51N 7 10W
Béchar 82 31 38N 2 18W
Bechyně 26 49 17N 14 29 E
Beckley 114 37 50N 81 8W
Beckum 24 51 46N 8 3 E
Bécon 18 47 30N 0 50W
Bečva → 27 49 31N 17 40 E
Bédar 33 37 11N 1 59W
Bédarieux 20 43 37N 3 10 E
Bédarrides 21 44 2N 4 54 E
Beddouza, Ras 82 32 33N 9 9W
Bedele 87 8 31N 36 23 E
Bederkesa 24 53 37N 8 50 E
Bedeso 87 9 58N 40 52 E
Bedford, Can. 106 45 7N 72 59W
Bedford, S. Afr. 92 32 40S 26 10 E
Bedford, U.K. 13 52 8N 0 29W
Bedford, Ind., U.S.A. 114 38 50N 86 30W
Bedford, Iowa, U.S.A. 116 40 40N 94 41W
Bedford, Ohio, U.S.A. 114 41 23N 81 32W
Bedford, Pa., U.S.A. 112 40 1N 78 30W
Bedford, Va., U.S.A. 114 37 25N 79 30W
Bedford □ 13 52 4N 0 28W
Bedford, C. 97 15 14S 145 21 E
Będków 28 51 36N 19 44 E
Bednja → 39 46 12N 16 25 E
Bednodemyanovsk 55 53 55N 43 15 E
Bedónia 38 44 28N 9 36 E
Bedourie 97 24 30S 139 30 E
Bedous 20 43 0N 0 36W
Będzin 28 50 19N 19 7 E
Beech Grove 114 39 40N 86 2W
Beechworth 99 36 22S 146 43 E
Beechy 109 50 53N 107 24W
Beelitz 24 52 14N 12 58 E
Beenleigh 99 27 43S 153 10 E
Be'er Sheva' 62 31 15N 34 48 E
Be'er Sheva' → 62 31 12N 34 40 E
Be'er Toviyya 62 31 44N 34 42 E
Be'eri 62 31 25N 34 30 E
Be'erotayim 62 32 19N 34 59 E
Beersheba = Be'er Sheva' 62 31 15N 34 48 E
Beeskow 24 52 9N 14 14 E
Beeston 12 52 55N 1 11W
Beetzendorf 24 52 42N 11 6 E
Beeville 117 28 27N 97 44W
Befale 88 0 25N 20 45 E
Befotaka 93 23 49S 47 0 E
Bega 97 36 41S 149 51 E
Bega, Canalul 42 45 37N 20 46 E
Bégard 18 48 38N 3 18W
* Begemdir & Simen □ 87 12 55N 37 30 E
Bègles 20 44 45N 0 35W
Begna → 47 60 41N 10 0 E
Begonte 30 43 10N 7 40W
Begu-Sarai 69 25 24N 86 9 E
Behbehān 64 30 30N 50 15 E
Behror 68 27 51N 76 20 E
Behshahr 65 36 45N 53 35 E
Bei Jiang → 75 23 2N 112 58 E
Bei'an 75 48 10N 126 20 E
Beibei 75 29 47N 106 22 E
Beihai 75 21 28N 109 6 E
Beijing 76 39 55N 116 20 E
Beijing □ 76 39 55N 116 20 E
Beilen 16 52 52N 6 27 E
Beilngries 25 49 1N 11 27 E
Beilpajah 99 32 54S 143 52 E
Beilul 87 13 2N 42 20 E
Beira 91 19 50S 34 52 E
Beirut = Bayrūt 64 33 53N 35 31 E
Beit Lāhiyah 62 31 32N 34 30 E
Beitaolaizhao 76 44 58N 125 58 E
Beitbridge 91 22 12S 30 0 E
Beiuş 46 46 40N 22 21 E
Beizhen 76 37 20N 118 2 E
Beja 31 38 2N 7 53W
Béja 83 36 43N 9 12 E
Beja □ 31 37 55N 7 55W
Bejaia 83 36 42N 5 2 E
Béjar 30 40 23N 5 46W
Bejestān 65 34 30N 58 5 E
Bekasi 73 6 20S 107 0 E
Békés 27 46 47N 21 9 E
Békés □ 27 46 45N 21 0 E
Békéscsaba 27 46 40N 21 5 E
Bekily 93 24 13S 45 19 E
Bekoji 87 7 40N 39 17 E
Bekok 71 2 20N 103 7 E
Bekwai 85 6 30N 1 34W
Bela, India 69 25 50N 82 0 E
Bela, Pak. 66 26 12N 66 20 E
Bela Crkva 42 44 55N 21 27 E
Bela Palanka 42 43 13N 22 17 E
Bela Vista, Brazil 124 22 12S 56 20W
Bela Vista, Mozam. 93 26 10S 32 44 E
Bélâbre 20 46 34N 1 8 E
Belalcázar 31 38 35N 5 10W
Belanovica 42 44 15N 20 23 E
Belavenona 93 24 50S 47 4 E
Belawan 72 3 33N 98 32 E
Belaya → 52 56 0N 54 32 E
Belaya Glina 57 46 5N 40 48 E
Belaya Kalitva 57 48 13N 40 50 E
Belaya Kholunitsa 55 58 41N 50 13 E
Belaya, Mt. 87 11 25N 36 8 E
Belaya Tserkov 54 49 45N 30 10 E
Belceşti 46 47 19N 27 7 E
Bełchatów 28 51 21N 19 22 E
Belcher, C. 4 71 0N 161 0W
Belcher Is. 106 56 15N 78 45W
Belchite 32 41 18N 0 43W
Belebey 52 54 7N 54 7 E
Belém (Pará) 127 1 20S 48 30W
Belén, Argent. 124 27 40S 67 5W
Belén, Parag. 124 23 30S 57 6W
Belen 119 34 40N 106 50W
Belene 43 43 39N 25 10 E
Bélesta 20 42 55N 1 56 E
Belet Uen 63 4 30N 45 5 E
Belev 55 53 50N 36 5 E
Belfast, S. Afr. 93 25 42S 30 2 E
Belfast, U.K. 15 54 35N 5 56W
Belfast, Maine, U.S.A. 107 44 30N 69 0W
Belfast, N.Y., U.S.A. 112 42 21N 78 9W
Belfast □ 15 54 35N 5 56W
Belfast, L. 15 54 40N 5 50W
Belfield 116 46 54N 103 11W
Belfort 19 47 38N 6 50 E
Belfort □ 19 47 38N 6 52 E
Belfry 118 45 10N 109 2W
Belgaum 70 15 55N 74 35 E
Belgioioso 38 45 9N 9 21 E
Belgium ■ 16 50 30N 5 0 E
Belgorod 56 50 35N 36 35 E
Belgorod-Dnestrovskiy 56 46 11N 30 23 E
Belgrade 118 45 50N 111 10W
Belgrade = Beograd 42 44 50N 20 37 E
Belhaven 115 35 34N 76 35W
Beli Drim → 42 42 6N 20 25 E
Beli Manastir 42 45 45N 18 36 E
Beli Timok → 42 43 53N 22 14 E
Belice → 40 37 35N 12 55 E
Belin 20 44 30N 0 47W
Belinga 88 1 10N 13 2 E
Belingwe 91 20 29S 29 57 E
Belingwe, N. 91 20 37S 29 55 E
Belinskiy (Chembar) 55 53 0N 43 25 E
Belinţ 42 45 48N 21 54 E
Belinyu 72 1 35S 105 50 E
Belitung, P. 72 3 10S 107 50 E
Beliu 46 46 30N 22 0 E
Belize ■ 120 17 0N 88 30W
Belize City 120 17 25N 88 0W
Beljanica 42 44 08N 21 43 E
Belkovskiy, Ostrov 59 75 32N 135 44 E
Bell → 106 49 48N 77 38W
Bell Bay 99 41 6S 146 53 E
Bell I. 107 50 46N 55 35W
Bell-Irving → 108 56 12N 129 5W
Bell Peninsula 105 63 50N 82 0W
Bell Ville 124 32 40S 62 40W
Bella Bella 108 52 10N 128 10W
Bella Coola 108 52 25N 126 40W
Bella Unión 124 30 15S 57 40W
Bella Vista, Corrientes, Argent. 124 28 33S 59 0W
Bella Vista, Tucuman, Argent. 124 27 10S 65 25W
Bellac 20 46 7N 1 3 E
Bellágio 38 45 59N 9 15 E
Bellaire 114 40 1N 80 46W
Bellary 70 15 10N 76 56 E
Bellata 99 29 53S 149 46 E
Belle Fourche 116 44 43N 103 52W
Belle Fourche → 116 44 25N 102 19W
Belle Glade 115 26 43N 80 38W
Belle-Île 18 47 20N 3 10W
Belle Isle 107 51 57N 55 25W
Belle-Isle-en-Terre 18 48 33N 3 23W
Belle Isle, Str. of 107 51 30N 56 30W
Belle, La 115 26 45N 81 22W
Belle Plaine, Iowa, U.S.A. 116 41 51N 92 18W
Belle Plaine, Minn., U.S.A. 116 44 35N 93 48W
Belle Yella 84 7 24N 10 0W
Belledonne 21 45 30N 6 10 E
Belledune 107 47 55N 65 50W
Bellefontaine 114 40 20N 83 45W
Bellefonte 114 40 56N 77 45W
Bellegarde, Ain, France 21 46 4N 5 49 E
Bellegarde, Creuse, France 20 45 59N 2 18 E
Bellegarde, Loiret, France 19 48 0N 2 26 E
Bellême 18 48 22N 0 34 E
Belleoram 107 47 31N 55 25W
Belleville, Can. 106 44 10N 77 23W
Belleville, Rhône, France 21 46 7N 4 45 E
Belleville, Vendée, France 18 46 48N 1 28W
Belleville, Ill., U.S.A. 116 38 30N 90 0W
Belleville, Kans., U.S.A. 116 39 51N 97 38W
Belleville, N.Y., U.S.A. 113 43 46N 76 10W
Bellevue, Can. 108 49 35N 114 22W
Bellevue, Idaho, U.S.A. 118 43 25N 114 23W
Bellevue, Ohio, U.S.A. 112 41 20N 82 48W
Bellevue, Pa., U.S.A. 112 40 29N 80 3W
Belley 21 45 46N 5 41 E
Bellin (Payne Bay) 105 60 0N 70 0W
Bellingen 99 30 25S 152 50 E
Bellingham 118 48 45N 122 27W
Bellingshausen Sea 5 66 0S 80 0W
Bellinzona 25 46 11N 9 1 E
Bellona Reefs 97 21 26S 159 0 E
Bellows Falls 114 43 10N 72 30W
Bellpat 68 29 0N 68 5 E
Bellpuig 32 41 37N 1 1 E
Belluno 39 46 8N 12 13 E
Bellville 117 29 58N 96 18W
Bellwood 112 40 36N 78 21W
Belmar 113 40 10N 74 2W
Bélmez 31 38 17N 5 17W
Belmont, Austral. 99 33 4S 151 42 E
Belmont, Can. 112 42 53N 81 5W
Belmont, U.S.A. 112 42 14N 78 3W
Belmonte, Brazil 127 16 0S 39 0W
Belmonte, Port. 30 40 21N 7 20W
Belmonte, Spain 32 39 34N 2 43W
Belmopan 120 17 18N 88 30W
Belmullet 15 54 13N 9 58W
Belo Horizonte 127 19 55S 43 56W
Belo-sur-Mer 93 20 42S 44 0 E
Belo-Tsiribihina 93 19 40S 44 30 E
Belogorsk, R.S.F.S.R., U.S.S.R. 59 51 0N 128 20 E
Belogorsk, Ukraine S.S.R., U.S.S.R. 56 45 3N 34 35 E
Belogradchik 42 43 53N 22 15 E
Belogradets 43 43 22N 27 18 E
Beloha 93 25 10S 45 3 E
Beloit, Kans., U.S.A. 116 39 32N 98 9W
Beloit, Wis., U.S.A. 116 42 35N 89 0W
Belokorovichi 54 51 7N 28 2 E
Belomorsk 52 64 35N 34 30 E
Belonia 67 23 15N 91 30 E
Belopolye 54 51 14N 34 20 E
Beloretsk 52 53 58N 58 24 E
Belovo 58 54 30N 86 0 E
Beloye More 52 66 30N 38 0 E
Beloye, Oz. 52 60 10N 37 35 E
Beloye Ozero 57 45 15N 46 50 E
Belozem 43 42 12N 25 2 E
Belozersk 55 60 0N 37 30 E
Belpasso 41 37 37N 15 0 E
Belsito 40 37 50N 13 47 E
Beltana 99 30 48S 138 25 E
Belterra 127 2 45S 55 0W
Beltinci 39 46 37N 16 20 E
Belton, S.C., U.S.A. 115 34 31N 82 39W
Belton, Tex., U.S.A. 117 31 4N 97 30W
Belton Res. 117 31 8N 97 32W
Beltsy 56 47 48N 28 0 E
Belturbet 15 54 6N 7 28W
Belukha 58 49 50N 86 50 E
Beluran 72 5 48N 117 35 E
Beluša 27 49 5N 18 27 E
Belušić 42 43 50N 21 10 E
Belvedere Marittimo 41 39 37N 15 52 E
Belvès 20 44 46N 1 0 E
Belvidere, Ill., U.S.A. 116 42 15N 88 55W
Belvidere, N.J., U.S.A. 113 40 48N 75 5W
Belvis de la Jara 31 39 45N 4 57W
Belyando → 97 21 38S 146 50 E
Belyy 54 55 48N 32 51 E
Belyy, Ostrov 58 73 30N 71 0 E
Belyy Yar 58 58 26N 84 39 E
Belzig 24 52 8N 12 36 E
Belzoni 117 33 12N 90 30W
Bełżyce 28 51 11N 22 17 E
Bemaraha, Lembalemban' i 93 18 40S 44 45 E
Bemarivo 93 21 45S 44 45 E
Bemarivo → 93 15 27S 47 40 E
Bemavo 93 21 33S 45 25 E
Bembéréke 85 10 11N 2 43 E
Bembesi 91 20 0S 28 58 E
Bembesi → 91 18 57S 27 47 E
Bembézar → 31 37 45N 5 13W
Bemidji 116 47 30N 94 50W
Ben 'Ammi 62 33 0N 35 7 E
Ben Cruachan 14 56 26N 5 8W
Ben Dearg 14 57 47N 4 58W
Ben Gardane 83 33 11N 11 11 E
Ben Hope 14 58 24N 4 36W
Ben Lawers 14 56 33N 4 13W
Ben Lomond, Austral. 97 41 38S 147 42 E
Ben Lomond, U.K. 14 56 12N 4 39W
Ben Macdhui 14 57 4N 3 40W
Ben Mhor 14 57 16N 7 21W
Ben More, Central, U.K. 14 56 23N 4 31W
Ben More, Strathclyde, U.K. 14 56 26N 6 2W
Ben More Assynt 14 58 7N 4 51W
Ben Nevis 14 56 48N 5 0W
Ben Slimane 82 33 38N 7 7W
Ben Vorlich 14 56 22N 4 15W
Ben Wyvis 14 57 40N 4 35W
Bena 85 11 20N 5 50 E
Bena Dibele 88 4 4S 22 50 E
Benagalbón 31 36 45N 4 15W
Benagerie 99 31 25S 140 22 E
Benahmed 82 33 4N 7 9W
Benalla 97 36 30S 146 0 E
Benambra, Mt. 100 36 31S 147 34 E
Benamejí 31 37 16N 4 33W
Benanee 99 34 31S 142 52 E
Benares = Varanasi 69 25 22N 83 8 E
Bénat, C. 21 43 5N 6 22 E
Benavente, Port. 31 38 59N 8 49W

* Renamed Gonder □

Benavente

Bilaspur

Benavente, Spain **30** 42 2N 5 43W
Benavides, Spain **30** 42 30N 5 54W
Benavides, U.S.A. **117** 27 35N 98 28W
Benbecula **14** 57 26N 7 21W
Bencubbin **96** 30 48S 117 52E
Bend **118** 44 2N 121 15W
Bendel □ **85** 6 0N 6 0E
Bender Beila **63** 9 30N 50 48E
Bendery **56** 46 50N 29 30E
Bendigo **97** 36 40S 144 15E
Bendorf **24** 50 26N 7 34E
Benē Beraq, Israel **62** 32 6N 34 51E
Benē Beraq, Israel **62** 32 6N 34 51E
Bénéna **84** 13 9N 4 17W
Benenitra **93** 23 27S 45 5E
Benešŏv **26** 49 46N 14 41E
Bénestroff **19** 48 54N 6 45E
Benet **20** 46 22N 0 35W
Benevento **41** 41 7N 14 45E
Benfeld **19** 48 22N 7 34E
Benga **91** 16 11S 33 40E
Bengal, Bay of **60** 15 0N 90 0E
Bengawan Solo → **73** 7 5S 112 35E
Bengbu **75** 32 58N 117 20E
Benghazi = Banghāzī **83** 32 11N 20 3E
Bengkalis **72** 1 30N 102 10E
Bengkulu **72** 3 50S 102 12E
Bengkulu □ **72** 3 48S 102 16E
Bengough **109** 49 25N 105 10W
Benguela **89** 12 37S 13 25E
Benguerir **82** 32 16N 7 56W
Benguérua, I. **93** 21 58S 35 28E
Benha **86** 30 26N 31 8E
Beni **90** 0 30N 29 27E
Beni → **126** 10 23S 65 24W
Beni Abbès **82** 30 5N 2 5W
Beni-Haoua **82** 36 30N 1 30E
Beni Mazâr **86** 28 32N 30 44E
Beni Mellal **82** 32 21N 6 21W
Beni Ounif **82** 32 0N 1 10W
Beni Saf **82** 35 17N 1 15W
Beni Suef **86** 29 5N 31 6E
Beniah L. **108** 63 23N 112 17W
Benicarló **32** 40 23N 0 23E
Benidorm **33** 38 33N 0 9W
Benidorm, Islote de **33** 38 31N 0 9W
Benin ■ **85** 10 0N 2 0E
Benin, Bight of **85** 5 0N 3 0E
Benin City **85** 6 20N 5 31E
Benisa **33** 38 43N 0 03E
Benjamin Aceval **124** 24 58S 57 34W
Benjamin Constant **126** 4 40S 70 15W
Benkelman **116** 40 7N 101 32W
Benkovac **39** 44 2N 15 37E
Benlidi **98** 24 35S 144 50E
Bennett **108** 59 56N 134 53W
Bennett, Ostrov **59** 76 21N 148 56E
Bennettsville **115** 34 38N 79 39W
Bennington **114** 42 52N 73 12W
Benoa **72** 8 50S 115 20E
Bénodet **18** 47 53N 4 7W
Benoni **93** 26 11S 28 18E
Benoud **82** 32 20N 0 16E
Bensheim **25** 49 40N 8 38E
Benson **119** 31 59N 110 19W
Bent **65** 26 20N 59 31E
Benteng **73** 6 10S 120 30E
Bentinck I. **97** 17 3S 139 35E
Bentiu **87** 9 10N 29 55E
Bento Gonçalves **125** 29 10S 51 31W
Benton, Ark., U.S.A. **117** 34 30N 92 35W
Benton, Ill., U.S.A. **116** 38 0N 88 55W
Benton Harbor **114** 42 10N 86 28W
Bentong **71** 3 31N 101 55E
Bentu Liben **87** 8 32N 38 21E
Benue □ **85** 7 30N 7 30E
Benue → **85** 7 48N 6 46E
Benxi **76** 41 20N 123 48E
Beo **73** 4 25N 126 50E
Beograd **42** 44 50N 20 37E
Beowawe **118** 40 35N 116 30W
Beppu **74** 33 15N 131 30E
Berati **44** 40 43N 19 59E
Berau, Teluk **73** 2 30S 132 30E
Berber **86** 18 0N 34 0E
Berbera **63** 10 30N 45 2E
Berbérati **88** 4 15N 15 40E
Berberia, C. del **33** 38 39N 1 24E
Berbice → **126** 6 20N 57 32W
Berceto **38** 44 30N 10 0E
Berchtesgaden **25** 47 37N 12 58E
Berck-sur-Mer **19** 50 25N 1 36E
Berdichev **56** 49 57N 28 30E
Berdsk **58** 54 47N 83 2E
Berdyansk **56** 46 45N 36 50E
Berea, Ky., U.S.A. **114** 37 35N 84 18W
Berea, Ohio, U.S.A. **112** 41 21N 81 50W
Berebere **73** 2 25N 128 45E
Bereda **63** 11 45N 51 0E
Berekum **84** 7 29N 2 34W
Berenice **86** 24 2N 35 25E
Berens → **109** 52 25N 97 2W
Berens I. **109** 52 18N 97 18W
Berens River **109** 52 25N 97 0W
Berestechko **54** 50 22N 25 5E
Bereşti **46** 46 6N 27 50E
Beretău → **46** 46 59N 21 7E
Berettyo → **27** 46 59N 21 7E
Berettyóújfalu **27** 47 13N 21 33E
Berevo, Majunga, Madag. **93** 17 14S 44 17E
Berevo, Tuléar, Madag. **93** 19 44S 44 58E
Bereza **54** 52 31N 24 51E
Berezhany **54** 49 26N 24 58E
Berezina → **54** 52 33N 30 14E
Berezna **55** 51 35N 31 46E
Berezniki **58** 59 24N 56 46E
Berezovka **56** 47 14N 30 55E
Berezovo **58** 64 0N 65 0E
Berg **47** 59 10N 11 18E
Berga, Spain **32** 42 6N 1 48E
Berga, Sweden **49** 57 14N 16 3E
Bergama **64** 39 8N 27 15E
Bérgamo **38** 45 42N 9 40E
Bergantiños **30** 43 20N 8 40W
Bergedorf **24** 53 28N 10 12E
Bergen, Ger. **24** 54 24N 13 26E
Bergen, Neth. **16** 52 40N 4 43E
Bergen, Norway **47** 60 23N 5 20E
Bergen, U.S.A. **112** 43 5N 77 56W
Bergen-op-Zoom **16** 51 30N 4 18E
Bergerac **20** 44 51N 0 30E
Bergheim **24** 50 57N 6 38E
Bergisch-Gladbach **24** 50 59N 7 9E
Bergkvara **49** 56 23N 16 5E
Bergsjö **48** 61 59N 17 3E
Bergues **19** 50 58N 2 24E
Bergum **16** 53 13N 5 59E
Bergvik **48** 61 16N 16 50E
Berhala, Selat **72** 1 0S 104 15E
Berhampore **69** 24 2N 88 27E
Berhampur **70** 19 15N 84 54E
Berheci → **46** 46 7N 27 19E
Bering Sea **94** 58 0N 167 0E
Bering Str. **104** 66 0N 170 0W
Beringen **16** 51 3N 5 14E
Beringovskiy **59** 63 3N 179 19E
Berislav **56** 46 50N 33 30E
Berisso **124** 34 56S 57 50W
Berja **33** 36 50N 2 56W
Berkane **82** 34 52N 2 20W
Berkeley **13** 51 41N 2 28W
Berkeley Springs **114** 39 38N 78 12W
Berkner I. **5** 79 30S 50 0W
Berkovitsa **43** 43 16N 23 8E
Berkshire □ **13** 51 30N 1 20W
Berland → **108** 54 0N 116 50W
Berlanga **31** 38 17N 5 50W
Berleburg **24** 51 3N 8 22E
Berlenga, Ilhas **31** 39 25N 9 30W
Berlin, Ger. **24** 52 32N 13 24E
Berlin, Md., U.S.A. **114** 38 19N 75 12W
Berlin, N.H., U.S.A. **114** 44 29N 71 10W
Berlin, Wis., U.S.A. **114** 43 58N 88 55W
Berlin, E. □ **24** 52 30N 13 30E
Berlin, W. □ **24** 52 30N 13 20E
Bermeja, Sierra **31** 36 30N 5 11W
Bermejo →, Formosa, Argent. **124** 26 51S 58 23W
Bermejo →, San Juan, Argent. **124** 32 30S 67 30W
Bermeo **32** 43 25N 2 47W
Bermillo de Sayago **30** 41 22N 6 8W
Bermuda ■ **121** 32 45N 65 0W
Bern (Berne) **25** 46 57N 7 28E
Bern (Berne) □ **25** 46 45N 7 40E
Bernado **119** 34 30N 106 53W
Bernalda **41** 40 24N 16 44E
Bernalillo **119** 35 17N 106 37W
Bernam → **71** 3 45N 101 5E
Bernardo de Irigoyen **125** 26 15S 53 40W
Bernasconi **124** 37 55S 63 44W
Bernau, Germ., E. **24** 52 40N 13 35E
Bernau, Germ., W. **25** 47 45N 12 20E
Bernay **18** 49 5N 0 35E
Bernburg **24** 51 40N 11 42E
Berndorf **26** 47 59N 16 1E
Berne = Bern **25** 46 57N 7 28E
Berneck **25** 51 3N 11 40E
Berner Alpen **25** 46 27N 7 35E
Bernese Oberland = Oberland **25** 46 27N 7 35E
Bernier I. **96** 24 50S 113 12E
Bernina, Piz **25** 46 20N 9 54E
Bernkastel-Kues **25** 49 55N 7 04E
Beror Hayil **62** 31 34N 34 38E
Béroubouay **85** 10 34N 2 46E
Beroun **26** 49 57N 14 5E
Berounka → **26** 50 0N 13 47E
Berovo **42** 41 38N 22 51E
Berrahal **83** 36 54N 7 33E
Berre, Étang de **21** 43 27N 5 5E
Berrechid **82** 33 18N 7 36W
Berri **99** 34 14S 140 35E
Berriane **82** 32 50N 3 46E
Berrigan **100** 35 38S 145 49E
Berrouaghia **82** 36 10N 2 53E
Berry, Austral. **99** 34 46S 150 43E
Berry, France **19** 47 0N 2 0E
Berry Is. **121** 25 40N 77 50W
Berryville **117** 36 23N 93 35W
Bersenbrück **24** 52 33N 7 56E
Berthold **116** 48 19N 101 45W
Berthoud **116** 40 21N 105 5W
Bertincourt **19** 50 5N 2 58E
Bertoua **88** 4 30N 13 45E
Bertrand **116** 40 35N 99 38W
Berufjörður **50** 64 48N 14 29W
Berwick **114** 41 4N 76 17W
Berwick-upon-Tweed **12** 55 47N 2 0W
Berwyn Mts. **12** 52 54N 3 26W
Berzasca **42** 44 39N 21 58E
Berzence **27** 46 12N 17 11E
Besalampy **93** 16 43S 44 29E
Besançon **19** 47 15N 6 0E
Besar **72** 2 40S 116 0E
Beserah **71** 3 50N 103 21E
Beshenkovichi **54** 55 2N 29 29E
Beška **42** 45 8N 20 6E
Beskydy **27** 49 35N 18 40E
Beslan **57** 43 15N 44 28E
Besna Kobila **42** 42 31N 22 10E
Besnard L. **109** 55 25N 106 0W
Besni **64** 37 41N 37 52E
Besor, N. → **62** 31 28N 34 22E
Beşparmak Daği **45** 37 32N 27 30E
Bessarabiya **46** 47 0N 28 10E
Bessarabka **56** 46 21N 28 58E
Bessèges **21** 44 18N 4 8E
Bessemer, Ala., U.S.A. **115** 33 25N 86 57W
Bessemer, Mich., U.S.A. **116** 46 27N 90 0W
Bessin **18** 49 21N 1 0W
Bessines-sur-Gartempe **20** 46 6N 1 22E
Bet Alfa **62** 32 31N 35 25E
Bet Dagan **62** 32 1N 34 49E
Bet Guvrin **62** 31 37N 34 54E
Bet Ha'Emeq **62** 32 58N 35 8E
Bet Hashitta **62** 32 31N 35 27E
Bet Qeshet **62** 32 41N 35 21E
Bet She'an **62** 32 30N 35 30E
Bet Shemesh **62** 31 44N 35 0E
Bet Tadjine, Djebel **82** 29 0N 3 30W
Bet Yosef **62** 32 34N 35 33E
Betafo **93** 19 50S 46 51E
Betanzos **30** 43 15N 8 12W
Bétaré Oya **88** 5 40N 14 5E
Bétera **32** 39 35N 0 28W
Bethal **93** 26 27S 29 28E
Bethanien **92** 26 31S 17 8E
Bethany, S. Afr. **92** 29 34S 25 59E
Bethany, U.S.A. **116** 40 18N 94 0W
Bethany = Al Ayzarīyah **62** 31 47N 35 15E
Bethel, Alaska, U.S.A. **104** 60 50N 161 50W
Bethel, Pa., U.S.A. **112** 40 20N 80 2W
Bethel, Vt., U.S.A. **113** 43 50N 72 37W
Bethlehem, S. Afr. **93** 28 14S 28 18E
Bethlehem, U.S.A. **114** 40 39N 75 24W
Bethlehem = Bayt Lahm **62** 31 43N 35 12E
Bethulie **92** 30 30S 25 59E
Béthune **19** 50 30N 2 38E
Béthune → **18** 49 53N 1 9E
Betioky **93** 23 48S 44 20E
Beton Bazoches **19** 48 42N 3 15E
Betong, Malay. **72** 1 24N 111 31E
Betong, Thai. **71** 5 45N 101 5E
Betoota **99** 25 45S 140 42E
Betroka **93** 23 16S 46 0E
Betsiamites **107** 48 56N 68 40W
Betsiamites → **107** 48 56N 68 38W
Betsiboka → **93** 16 3S 46 36E
Betsjoeanaland **92** 26 30S 22 30E
Bettiah **69** 26 48N 84 33E
Bèttola **38** 44 42N 9 32E
Betul **68** 21 58N 77 59E
Betzdorf **24** 50 47N 7 53E
Beuca **46** 44 14N 24 56E
Beuil **21** 44 6N 6 59E
Beulah **116** 47 18N 101 47W
Bevensen **24** 53 5N 10 34E
Beverley, Austral. **96** 32 9S 116 56E
Beverley, U.K. **12** 53 52N 0 26W
Beverly, Mass., U.S.A. **113** 42 32N 70 50W
Beverly, Wash., U.S.A. **118** 46 55N 119 59W
Beverly Hills **119** 34 4N 118 29W
Beverwijk **16** 52 28N 4 38E
Bex **25** 46 15N 7 0E
Beyin **84** 5 1N 2 41W
Beykoz **43** 41 8N 29 7E
Beyla **84** 8 30N 8 38W
Beynat **20** 45 8N 1 44E
Beyneu **58** 45 10N 55 3E
Beypazarı **64** 40 10N 31 56E
Beyşehir Gölü **64** 37 40N 31 45E
Bezdan **42** 45 50N 18 57E
Bezet **62** 33 4N 35 8E
Bezhetsk **55** 57 47N 36 39E
Bezhitsa **54** 53 19N 34 17E
Béziers **20** 43 20N 3 12E
Bezwada = Vijayawada **70** 16 31N 80 39E
Bhadra → **70** 14 0N 75 20E
Bhadrakh **69** 21 10N 86 30E
Bhadravati **70** 13 49N 75 40E
Bhagalpur **69** 25 10N 87 0E
Bhaisa **70** 19 10N 77 58E
Bhakkar **68** 31 40N 71 5E
Bhakra Dam **68** 31 30N 76 45E
Bhamo **67** 24 15N 97 15E
Bhamragarh **70** 19 30N 80 40E
Bhandara **69** 21 5N 79 42E
Bhanrer Ra. **68** 23 40N 79 45E
Bharatpur **68** 27 15N 77 30E
Bharuch **68** 21 47N 73 0E
Bhatghar L. **70** 18 10N 73 48E
Bhatiapara Ghat **69** 23 13N 89 42E
Bhatinda **68** 30 15N 74 57E
Bhatkal **70** 13 58N 74 35E
Bhatpara **69** 22 50N 88 25E
Bhattiprolu **70** 16 7N 80 45E
Bhaun **68** 32 55N 72 40E
Bhaunagar = Bhavnagar **68** 21 45N 72 10E
Bhavani **70** 11 27N 77 43E
Bhavani → **70** 11 0N 78 15E
Bhavnagar **68** 21 45N 72 10E
Bhawanipatna **70** 19 55N 80 10E
Bhera **68** 32 29N 72 57E
Bhilsa = Vidisha **68** 23 28N 77 53E
Bhilwara **68** 25 25N 74 38E
Bhima → **70** 16 25N 77 17E
Bhimavaram **70** 16 30N 81 30E
Bhind **68** 26 30N 78 46E
Bhir **70** 19 4N 75 46E
Bhiwandi **70** 19 20N 73 0E
Bhiwani **68** 28 50N 76 9E
Bhola **69** 22 45N 90 35E
Bhongir **70** 17 30N 78 56E
Bhopal **68** 23 20N 77 30E
Bhor **70** 18 12N 73 53E
Bhubaneswar **69** 20 15N 85 50E
Bhuj **68** 23 15N 69 49E
Bhumibol Dam **72** 17 15N 98 58E
Bhusaval **68** 21 3N 75 46E
Bhutan ■ **69** 27 25N 90 30E
Biafra, B. of = Bonny, Bight of **85** 3 30N 9 20E
Biak **73** 1 10S 136 6E
Biała **28** 50 24N 17 40E
Biała →, Białystok, Poland **28** 53 11N 23 4E
Biała →, Tarnów, Poland **27** 50 3N 20 55E
Biała Piska **28** 53 37N 22 5E
Biała Podlaska **28** 52 4N 23 6E
Biała Podlaska □ **28** 52 0N 23 0E
Biała Rawska **28** 51 48N 20 29E
Białobrzegi **28** 52 27N 21 3E
Białogard **28** 54 2N 15 58E
Białowieza **28** 52 41N 23 49E
Biały Bór **28** 53 53N 16 51E
Białystok **28** 53 10N 23 10E
Białystok □ **28** 53 9N 23 10E
Biancavilla **41** 37 39N 14 50E
Biaro **73** 2 5N 125 26E
Biarritz **20** 43 29N 1 33W
Biasca **25** 46 22N 8 58E
Biba **86** 28 55N 31 0E
Bibala **89** 14 44S 13 24E
Bibane, Bahiret el **83** 33 16N 11 13E
Bibbiena **39** 43 43N 11 50E
Bibby I. **109** 61 55N 93 0W
Biberach **25** 48 5N 9 49E
Bibey → **30** 42 24N 7 13W
Bibiani **84** 6 30N 2 8W
Bibile **70** 7 10N 81 25E
Biboohra **98** 16 56S 145 25E
Bibungwa **90** 2 40S 28 15E
Bic **107** 48 20N 68 41W
Bicaj **44** 42 0N 20 25E
Bicaz **46** 46 53N 26 5E
Biccari **41** 41 23N 15 12E
Biche, La → **108** 59 57N 123 50W
Bichena **87** 10 28N 38 10E
Bicknell, Ind., U.S.A. **114** 38 50N 87 20W
Bicknell, Utah, U.S.A. **119** 38 16N 111 35W
Bida **85** 9 3N 5 58E
Bidar **70** 17 55N 77 35E
Biddeford **107** 43 30N 70 28W
Biddiyā **62** 32 7N 35 4E
Biddū **62** 31 50N 35 8E
Biddwara **87** 5 11N 38 34E
Bideford **13** 51 1N 4 13W
Bidor **71** 4 6N 101 15E
Bié, Planalto de **89** 12 0S 16 0E
Bieber **118** 41 4N 121 6W
Biebrza → **28** 53 13N 22 25E
Biecz **27** 49 44N 21 15E
Biel (Bienne) **25** 47 8N 7 14E
Bielawa **28** 50 43N 16 37E
Bielé Karpaty **27** 49 5N 18 0E
Bielefeld **24** 52 2N 8 31E
Bielersee **25** 47 6N 7 5E
Biella **38** 45 33N 8 3E
Bielsk Podlaski **28** 52 47N 23 12E
Bielsko-Biała **27** 49 50N 19 2E
Bielsko-Biała □ **27** 49 45N 19 15E
Bien Hoa **71** 10 57N 106 49E
Bienfait **109** 49 10N 102 50W
Bienne = Biel **25** 47 8N 7 14E
Bienvenida **31** 38 18N 6 12W
Bienville, L. **106** 55 5N 72 40W
Biescas **32** 42 37N 0 20W
Biese → **24** 52 53N 11 46E
Biesiesfontein **92** 30 57S 17 58E
Bietigheim **25** 48 57N 9 8E
Biferno → **41** 41 59N 15 2E
Big → **107** 54 50N 58 55W
Big B. **107** 55 43N 60 35W
Big Beaver **109** 49 10N 105 10W
Big Belt Mts. **118** 46 50N 111 30W
Big Bend **93** 26 50S 32 2E
Big Bend Nat. Park **117** 29 15N 103 15W
Big Black → **117** 32 0N 91 5W
Big Blue → **116** 39 11N 96 40W
Big Cr. → **108** 51 42N 122 41W
Big Cypress Swamp **115** 26 12N 81 10W
Big Falls **116** 48 11N 93 48W
Big Fork → **116** 48 31N 93 43W
Big Horn **118** 46 11N 107 25W
Big Horn Mts. = Bighorn Mts. **118** 44 30N 107 30W
Big Lake **117** 31 12N 101 25W
Big Moose **113** 43 49N 74 58W
Big Muddy → **116** 48 8N 104 36W
Big Pine **119** 37 12N 118 17W
Big Piney **118** 42 32N 110 3W
Big Quill L. **109** 51 55N 104 50W
Big Rapids **114** 43 42N 85 27W
Big River **109** 53 50N 107 0W
Big Run **112** 40 57N 78 55W
Big Sable Pt. **114** 44 5N 86 30W
Big Sand L. **109** 57 45N 99 45W
Big Sandy **118** 48 12N 110 9W
Big Sandy Cr. → **116** 38 6N 102 29W
Big Sioux → **116** 42 30N 96 25W
Big Spring **117** 32 10N 101 25W
Big Springs **116** 41 4N 102 3W
Big Stone City **116** 45 20N 96 30W
Big Stone Gap **115** 36 52N 82 45W
Big Stone L. **116** 45 30N 96 35W
Big Trout L. **106** 53 40N 90 0W
Biganos **20** 44 39N 0 59W
Bigfork **118** 48 3N 114 2W
Biggar, Can. **109** 52 4N 108 0W
Biggar, U.K. **14** 55 38N 3 31W
Biggenden **99** 25 31S 152 4E
Bighorn → **118** 46 9N 107 28W
Bighorn Mts. **118** 44 30N 107 30W
Bignona **84** 12 52N 16 14W
Bigorre **20** 43 6N 0 5E
Bigstone L. **109** 53 42N 95 44W
Bigtimber **118** 45 53N 110 0W
Bigwa **90** 7 10S 39 10E
Bihać **39** 44 49N 15 57E
Bihar **69** 25 5N 85 40E
Bihar □ **69** 25 0N 86 0E
Biharamulo **90** 2 25S 31 25E
Biharamulo □ **90** 2 30S 31 20E
Biharkeresztes **27** 47 8N 21 44E
Bihor □ **46** 47 0N 22 10E
Bihor, Munţii **46** 46 29N 22 47E
Bijagós, Arquipélago dos **84** 11 15N 16 10W
Bijaipur **68** 26 2N 77 20E
Bijapur, Mad. P., India **70** 18 50N 80 50E
Bijapur, Mysore, India **70** 16 50N 75 55E
Bijār **64** 35 52N 47 35E
Bijeljina **42** 44 46N 19 17E
Bijelo Polje **42** 43 1N 19 45E
Bijie **77** 27 20N 105 16E
Bijnor **68** 29 27N 78 11E
Bikaner **68** 28 2N 73 18E
Bikapur **69** 26 30N 82 7E
Bikin **59** 46 50N 134 20E
Bikini Atoll **94** 12 0N 167 30E
Bikoué **85** 3 55N 11 50E
Bilād Banī Bū 'Ali **65** 22 0N 59 20E
Bilara **68** 26 14N 73 53E
Bilaspur, Mad. P., India **69** 22 2N 82 15E

Bilaspur Bogalusa

Bilaspur, Punjab, India 68 31 19N 76 50 E
Bilauk Taung dan 71 13 0N 99 0 E
Bilbao 32 43 16N 2 56W
Bilbeis 86 30 25N 31 34 E
Bilbor 46 47 6N 25 30 E
Bildudalur 50 65 41N 23 36W
Bileća 42 42 53N 18 27 E
Bilecik 64 40 5N 30 5 E
Biłgoraj 28 50 33N 22 42 E
Bilibino 59 68 3N 166 20 E
Bilibiza 91 12 30S 40 20 E
Bilir 59 65 40N 131 20 E
Bilishti 44 40 37N 21 2 E
Bill 116 43 18N 105 18W
Billabong Creek 100 35 5S 144 2 E
Billingham 12 54 36N 1 18W
Billings 118 45 43N 108 29W
Billingsfors 48 58 59N 12 15 E
Billiton Is = Belitung 72 3 10S 107 50 E
Billom 20 45 43N 3 20 E
Bilma 81 18 50N 13 30 E
Bilo Gora 42 45 53N 17 15 E
Biloela 97 24 24S 150 31 E
Biloxi 117 30 24N 88 53W
Bilpa Morea Claypan 99 25 0S 140 0 E
Biltine 81 14 40N 20 50 E
Bilyana 98 18 5S 145 50 E
Bilyarsk 55 54 58N 50 22 E
Bima 73 8 22S 118 49 E
Bimban 86 24 24N 32 54 E
Bimberi Peak 100 35 44S 148 51 E
Bimbila 85 8 54N 0 5 E
Bimbo 88 4 15N 18 33 E
Bimini Is. 121 25 42N 79 25W
Bin Xian 77 35 2N 108 4 E
Bina-Etawah 68 24 13N 78 14 E
Binalbagan 73 10 12N 122 50 E
Binalong 100 34 40S 148 39 E
Binalud, Kuh-e 65 36 30N 58 30 E
Binatang 72 2 10N 111 40 E
Binche 16 50 26N 4 10 E
Binda 99 27 52S 147 21 E
Bindle 99 27 40S 148 45 E
Bindura 91 17 18S 31 18 E
Bingara, N.S.W., Austral. 99 29 52S 150 36 E
Bingara, Queens., Austral. 99 28 10S 144 37 E
Bingen 25 49 57N 7 53 E
Bingerville 84 5 18N 3 49W
Bingham 107 45 5N 69 50W
Bingham Canyon 118 40 31N 112 10W
Binghamton 114 42 9N 75 54W
Bingöl 64 38 53N 40 29 E
Binh Dinh = An Nhon 71 13 55N 109 7 E
Binh Son 71 15 20N 108 40 E
Binjai 72 3 20N 98 30 E
Binnaway 99 31 28S 149 24 E
Binongko 73 5 55S 123 55 E
Binscarth 109 50 37N 101 17W
Bint Jubayl 62 33 8N 35 25 E
Bintan 72 1 0N 104 0 E
Bintulu 72 3 10N 113 0 E
Bintuni (Steenkool) 73 2 7S 133 32 E
Binyamina 62 32 32N 34 56 E
Binyang 77 23 12N 108 47 E
Binz 24 54 23N 13 37 E
Binzert = Bizerte 83 37 15N 9 50 E
Bio Bío □ 124 37 35S 72 0W
Biograd 39 43 56N 15 29 E
Biokovo 42 43 23N 17 0 E
Biougra 82 30 15N 9 14W
Biq'at Bet Netofa 62 32 49N 35 22 E
Bîr Abu Hashim 86 23 42N 34 6 E
Bîr Abu M'nqar 86 26 33N 27 33 E
Bîr Adal Deib 86 22 35N 36 10 E
Bi'r al Malfa 83 31 58N 15 18 E
Bir Aouine 83 32 25N 9 18 E
Bîr 'Asal 86 25 55N 34 20 E
Bir Autrun 81 18 15N 26 40 E
Bi'r Dhu'fān 83 31 59N 14 32 E
Bîr Diqnash 86 31 3N 25 23 E
Bir el Abbes 82 26 7N 6 9W
Bir el Ater 83 34 46N 8 3 E
Bîr el Basur 86 29 51N 25 49 E
Bîr el Gellaz 86 30 50N 26 40 E
Bîr el Shaqqa 86 30 54N 25 1 E
Bîr Fuad 86 30 35N 26 28 E
Bîr Haimur 86 22 45N 33 40 E
Bir Jdid 82 33 26N 8 0W
Bîr Kanayis 86 24 59N 33 15 E
Bîr Kerawein 86 27 10N 28 25 E
Bir Lahrache 83 32 1N 8 12 E
Bîr Maql 86 23 7N 33 40 E
Bîr Misaha 86 22 13N 27 59 E
Bir Mogrein 82 25 10N 11 25W
Bi'r Mubayrīk 64 23 22N 39 8 E
Bîr Murr 86 23 28N 30 10 E
Bi'r Nabālā 62 31 52N 35 12 E
Bîr Nakheila 86 24 1N 30 50 E
Bîr Qatrani 86 30 55N 26 10 E
Bîr Ranga 86 24 25N 35 15 E
Bir, Ras 87 12 0N 43 20 E
Bîr Sahara 86 22 54N 28 40 E
Bîr Seiyâla 86 26 10N 33 50 E
Bir Semguine 82 30 1N 5 39W
Bîr Shalatein 86 23 5N 35 25 E
Bîr Shebb 86 22 25N 29 40 E
Bîr Shût 86 23 50N 35 15 E
Bîr Terfawi 86 22 57N 28 55 E
Bîr Umm Qubûr 86 24 35N 34 2 E
Bîr Ungât 86 22 8N 33 48 E
Bîr Za'farâna 86 29 10N 32 40 E
Bîr Zāmūs 83 24 16N 15 6 E
Bi'r Zayt 62 31 59N 35 11 E
Bîr Zeidûn 86 25 45N 33 40 E
Bira 73 2 3S 132 2 E
Bîra 46 47 2N 27 3 E
Birak Sulaymān 62 31 42N 35 7 E
Biramféro 84 11 40N 9 10W
Birao 81 10 20N 22 47 E
Birawa 90 2 20S 28 48 E
Bîrca 46 43 59N 23 36 E
Birch Hills 109 52 59N 105 25W
Birch I. 109 52 26N 99 54W
Birch L., N.W.T., Can. 108 62 4N 116 33W
Birch L., Ont., Can. 106 51 23N 92 18W
Birch L., U.S.A. 106 47 48N 91 43W
Birch Mts. 108 57 30N 113 10W
Birch River 109 52 24N 101 6W
Birchip 99 35 56S 142 55 E
Birchiş 46 45 58N 22 9 E
Bird 109 56 30N 94 13W
Bird City 116 39 48N 101 33W
Bird I., Austral. 97 22 10S 155 28 E
Bird I., S. Afr. 92 32 3S 18 17 E
Bird I. = Aves, I. de 121 12 0N 67 30W
Birdlip 13 51 50N 2 7W
Birdsville 97 25 51S 139 20 E
Birdum 96 15 39S 133 13 E
Birecik 64 37 0N 38 0 E
Bireuen 72 5 14N 96 39 E
Birifo 84 13 30N 14 0W
Birigui 125 21 18S 50 16W
Birk 86 18 8N 41 30 E
Birka 86 22 11N 40 38 E
Birkenfeld 25 49 39N 7 11 E
Birkenhead 12 53 24N 3 1W
Birket Qârûn 86 29 30N 30 40 E
Birkfeld 26 47 21N 15 45 E
Birkhadem 82 36 43N 3 3 E
Bîrlad 46 46 15N 27 38 E
Birmingham, U.K. 13 52 30N 1 55W
Birmingham, U.S.A. 115 33 31N 86 50W
Birmitrapur 69 22 24N 84 46 E
Birni Ngaouré 85 13 5N 2 51 E
Birni Nkonni 85 13 55N 5 15 E
Birnin Gwari 85 11 0N 6 45 E
Birnin Kebbi 85 12 32N 4 12 E
Birnin Kudu 85 11 30N 9 29 E
Birobidzhan 59 48 50N 132 50 E
Birqin 62 32 27N 35 15 E
Birr 15 53 7N 7 55W
Birrie → 99 29 43S 146 37 E
Birsilpur 68 28 11N 72 15 E
Birsk 52 55 25N 55 30 E
Birtin 46 46 59N 22 31 E
Birtle 109 50 30N 101 5W
Biryuchiy 56 46 10N 35 0 E
Birzai 54 56 11N 24 45 E
Bîrzava 46 46 7N 21 59 E
Bisa 73 1 15S 127 28 E
Bisáccia 41 41 0N 15 20 E
Bisacquino 40 37 42N 13 13 E
Bisalpur 69 28 14N 79 48 E
Bisbal, La 32 41 58N 3 2 E
Bisbee 119 31 30N 110 0W
Biscarrosse, Étang de 20 44 21N 1 10W
Biscay, B. of 6 45 0N 2 0W
Biscayne B. 115 25 40N 80 12W
Biscéglie 41 41 14N 16 30 E
Bischofshofen 26 47 26N 13 14 E
Bischofswerda 24 51 8N 14 11 E
Bischwiller 19 48 41N 7 50 E
Biscoe Bay 5 77 0S 152 0W
Biscoe I. 5 66 0S 67 0W
Biscostasing 106 47 18N 82 9W
Biševo 39 42 57N 16 3 E
Bisha 87 15 30N 37 31 E
Bisha, Wadi → 86 21 24N 43 26 E
Bishop, Calif., U.S.A. 119 37 20N 118 26W
Bishop, Tex., U.S.A. 117 27 35N 97 49W
Bishop Auckland 12 54 40N 1 40W
Bishop's Falls 107 49 2N 55 30W
Bishop's Stortford 13 51 52N 0 11 E
Bisignano 41 39 30N 16 17 E
Bisina, L. 90 1 38N 33 56 E
Biskra 83 34 50N 5 44 E
Biskupiec 28 53 53N 20 58 E
Bislig 73 8 15N 126 27 E
Bismarck 116 46 49N 100 49W
Bismarck Arch. 94 2 30S 150 0 E
Bismarck Sea 98 4 10S 146 50 E
Bismark 24 52 39N 11 31 E
Biso 90 1 44N 31 26 E
Bison 116 45 34N 102 28W
Bispfors 50 63 1N 16 37 E
Bispgården 48 63 2N 16 40 E
Bissagos = Bijagós, Arquipélago dos 84 11 15N 16 10W
Bissau 84 11 45N 15 45W
Bissett 109 51 2N 95 41W
Bissikrima 84 10 50N 10 58W
Bistcho L. 108 59 45N 118 50W
Bistreţu 46 43 54N 23 23 E
Bistrica = Ilirska-Bistrica 39 45 34N 14 14 E
Bistriţa 46 47 9N 24 35 E
Bistriţa → 46 46 30N 26 57 E
Bistriţa Năsăud □ 46 47 15N 24 30 E
Bistriţei, Munţii 46 47 15N 25 40 E
Biswan 69 27 29N 81 2 E
Bisztynek 28 54 8N 20 53 E
Bitam 88 2 5N 11 25 E
Bitburg 25 49 58N 6 32 E
Bitche 19 49 2N 7 25 E
Bitkine 81 11 59N 18 13 E
Bitlis 64 38 20N 42 3 E
Bitola (Bitolj) 42 41 5N 21 10 E
Bitonto 41 41 7N 16 40 E
Bitter Creek 118 41 39N 108 36W
Bitter L. = Buheirat-Murrat-el-Kubra 86 30 15N 32 40 E
Bitterfeld 24 51 36N 12 20 E
Bitterfontein 92 31 0S 18 32 E
Bitterroot → 118 46 52N 114 6W
Bitterroot Range 118 46 0N 114 20W
Bitti 40 40 29N 9 20 E
Bittou 85 11 17N 0 18W
Biu 85 10 40N 12 3 E
Bivolari 46 47 31N 27 27 E
Bivolu 46 47 16N 25 58 E
Biwa-Ko 74 35 15N 136 10 E
Biwabik 116 47 33N 92 19W
Bixad 46 47 56N 23 28 E
Biyang 77 32 38N 113 21 E
Biysk 58 52 40N 85 0 E
Bizana 93 30 50S 29 52 E
Bizerte (Binzert) 83 37 15N 9 50 E
Bjargtangar 50 65 30N 24 30W
Bjelasica 42 42 50N 19 40 E
Bjelašnica 42 43 43N 18 9 E
Bjelovar 42 45 56N 16 49 E
Bjerringbro 49 56 23N 9 39 E
Björbo 48 60 27N 14 44 E
Björneborg 48 59 14N 14 16 E
Bjørnøya 4 74 30N 19 0 E
Bjuv 49 56 5N 12 55 E
Blace 42 43 18N 21 17 E
Blachownia 28 50 49N 18 56 E
Black →, Can. 112 44 42N 79 19W
Black →, Ark., U.S.A. 117 35 38N 91 19W
Black →, N.Y., U.S.A. 113 43 59N 76 4W
Black →, Wis., U.S.A. 116 43 52N 91 22W
Black Diamond 108 50 45N 114 14W
Black Forest = Schwarzwald 25 48 0N 8 0 E
Black Hills 116 44 0N 103 50W
Black I. 109 51 12N 96 30W
Black L., Can. 109 59 12N 105 15W
Black L., U.S.A. 114 45 28N 84 15W
Black Mesa, Mt. 117 36 57N 102 55W
Black Mt. = Mynydd Du 13 51 45N 3 45W
Black Mts. 13 51 52N 3 5W
Black Range 119 33 30N 107 55W
Black River 121 18 0N 77 50W
Black River Falls 116 44 23N 90 52W
Black Sea 9 43 30N 35 0 E
Black Sugarloaf, Mt. 100 31 18S 151 35 E
Black Volta → 84 8 41N 1 33W
Black Warrior → 115 32 32N 87 51W
Blackall 97 24 25S 145 45 E
Blackball 101 42 22S 171 26 E
Blackbull 98 17 55S 141 45 E
Blackburn 12 53 44N 2 30W
Blackduck 116 47 43N 94 32W
Blackfoot 118 43 13N 112 12W
Blackfoot → 118 46 52N 113 53W
Blackfoot River Res. 118 43 0N 111 35W
Blackie 108 50 36N 113 37W
Blackpool 12 53 48N 3 3W
Blackriver 112 44 46N 83 17W
Blacks Harbour 107 45 3N 66 49W
Blacksburg 114 37 17N 80 23W
Blacksod B. 15 54 6N 10 0W
Blackstone 114 37 6N 78 0W
Blackstone → 108 61 5N 122 55W
Blackstone Ra. 96 26 00S 129 00 E
Blackville 107 46 44N 65 50W
Blackwater 98 23 35S 148 53 E
Blackwater →, Ireland 15 51 55N 7 50W
Blackwater →, U.K. 15 54 31N 6 35W
Blackwater Cr. → 99 25 56S 144 30 E
Blackwell 117 36 55N 97 20W
Blaenau Ffestiniog 12 53 0N 3 57W
Blagaj 42 43 16N 17 55 E
Blagodarnoye 57 45 7N 43 37 E
Blagoevgrad (Gorna Dzhumayo) 42 42 2N 23 5 E
Blagoveshchensk 59 50 20N 127 30 E
Blain 18 47 29N 1 45W
Blaine 118 48 59N 122 43W
Blaine Lake 109 52 51N 106 52W
Blainville 19 48 33N 6 23 E
Blair 116 41 38N 96 10W
Blair Athol 97 22 42S 147 31 E
Blair Atholl 14 56 46N 3 50W
Blairgowrie 14 56 36N 3 20W
Blairmore 108 49 40N 114 25W
Blairsville 112 40 27N 79 15W
Blaj 46 46 10N 23 57 E
Blake Pt. 116 48 12N 88 27W
Blakely 115 31 22N 85 0W
Blâmont 19 48 35N 6 50 E
Blanc, C. 83 37 15N 9 56 E
Blanc, Le 20 46 37N 1 3 E
Blanc, Mont 21 45 48N 6 50 E
Blanca, Bahía 128 39 10S 61 30W
Blanca Peak 119 37 35N 105 29W
Blanchard 117 35 8N 97 40W
Blanche L., S. Austral., Austral. 97 29 15S 139 40 E
Blanche L., W. Austral., Austral. 96 22 25S 123 17 E
Blanco, S. Afr. 92 33 55S 22 23 E
Blanco, U.S.A. 117 30 7N 98 30W
Blanco → 124 30 20S 68 42W
Blanco, C., C. Rica 121 9 34N 85 8W
Blanco, C., Spain 33 39 21N 2 51 E
Blanco, C., U.S.A. 118 42 50N 124 40W
Blanda → 50 65 20N 19 40W
Blandford Forum 13 50 52N 2 10W
Blanding 119 37 35N 109 30W
Blanes 32 41 40N 2 48 E
Blanice → 26 49 10N 14 5 E
Blankenberge 16 51 20N 3 9 E
Blankenburg 24 51 46N 10 56 E
Blanquefort 20 44 55N 0 38W
Blanquillo 125 32 53S 55 37W
Blansko 27 49 22N 16 40 E
Blantyre 91 15 45S 35 0 E
Blarney 15 51 57N 8 35W
Błaski 28 51 38N 18 30 E
Blatná 26 49 25N 13 52 E
Blatnitsa 43 43 41N 28 32 E
Blato 39 42 56N 16 48 E
Blaubeuren 25 48 24N 9 47 E
Blaydon 12 54 56N 1 47W
Blaye 20 45 8N 0 40W
Blaye-les-Mines 20 44 1N 2 8 E
Blayney 99 33 32S 149 14 E
Blaze, Pt. 96 12 56S 130 11 E
Błażowa 27 49 53N 22 7 E
Bleckede 24 53 18N 10 43 E
Bled 39 46 27N 14 7 E
Blednaya, Gora 58 76 20N 65 0 E
Bleiburg 26 46 35N 14 49 E
Blejeşti 46 44 19N 25 27 E
Blekinge län □ 49 56 20N 15 20 E
Blenheim, Can. 112 42 20N 82 0W
Blenheim, N.Z. 101 41 38S 173 57 E
Bléone → 21 44 5N 6 0 E
Bletchley 13 51 59N 0 44W
Bleymard, Le 20 44 30N 3 42 E
Blida 82 36 30N 2 49 E
Blidet Amor 83 32 59N 5 58 E
Blidö 48 59 37N 18 53 E
Blidsberg 49 57 56N 13 30 E
Bligh Sound 101 44 47S 167 32 E
Blind River 106 46 10N 82 58W
Blinishti 44 41 52N 19 58 E
Blitar 73 8 5S 112 11 E
Blitta 85 8 23N 1 6 E
Block I. 114 41 11N 71 35W
Block Island Sd. 113 41 17N 71 35W
Bloemfontein 92 29 6S 26 14 E
Bloemhof 92 27 38S 25 32 E
Blois 18 47 35N 1 20 E
Blomskog 48 59 16N 12 2 E
Blönduós 50 65 40N 20 12W
Błonie 28 52 12N 20 37 E
Bloodvein → 109 51 47N 96 43W
Bloody Foreland 15 55 10N 8 18W
Bloomer 116 45 8N 91 30W
Bloomfield, Can. 112 43 59N 77 14W
Bloomfield, Iowa, U.S.A. 116 40 44N 92 26W
Bloomfield, N. Mexico, U.S.A. 119 36 46N 107 59W
Bloomfield, Nebr., U.S.A. 116 42 38N 97 40W
Bloomfield River Mission 98 15 56S 145 22 E
Bloomington, Ill., U.S.A. 116 40 27N 89 0W
Bloomington, Ind., U.S.A. 114 39 10N 86 30W
Bloomsburg 114 41 0N 76 30W
Blora 73 6 57S 111 25 E
Blossburg 112 41 40N 77 4W
Blouberg 93 23 8S 29 0 E
Blountstown 115 30 28N 85 5W
Bludenz 26 47 10N 9 50 E
Blue Island 114 41 40N 87 40W
Blue Lake 118 40 53N 124 0W
Blue Mesa Res. 119 38 30N 107 15W
Blue Mts., Austral. 97 33 40S 150 0 E
Blue Mts., Ore., U.S.A. 118 45 15N 119 0W
Blue Mts., Pa., U.S.A. 114 40 30N 76 30W
Blue Mud B. 97 13 30S 136 0 E
Blue Nile = An Nîl el Azraq □ 87 12 30N 34 30 E
Blue Nile = Nîl el Azraq → 87 15 38N 32 31 E
Blue Rapids 116 39 41N 96 39W
Blue Ridge Mts. 115 36 30N 80 15W
Blue Stack Mts. 15 54 46N 8 5W
Blueberry → 108 56 45N 120 49W
Bluefield 114 37 18N 81 14W
Bluefields 121 12 20N 83 50W
Bluff, Austral. 98 23 35S 149 4 E
Bluff, N.Z. 101 46 37S 168 20 E
Bluff, U.S.A. 119 37 17N 109 33W
Bluffton 114 40 43N 85 9W
Blumenau 125 27 0S 49 0W
Blumenthal 24 53 5N 8 20 E
Blunt 116 44 32N 100 0W
Bly 118 42 23N 121 0W
Blyberg 48 61 9N 14 11 E
Blyth, Can. 112 43 44N 81 26W
Blyth, U.K. 12 55 8N 1 32W
Blythe 119 33 40N 114 33W
Blytheswood 112 42 8N 82 37W
Bø 47 59 25N 9 3 E
Bo 84 7 55N 11 50W
Bo Duc 71 11 58N 106 50 E
Bo Hai 76 39 0N 120 0 E
Bo Xian 77 33 50N 115 45 E
Boa Vista 126 2 48N 60 30W
Boaco 121 12 29N 85 35W
Boal 30 43 25N 6 49W
Boatman 99 27 16S 146 55 E
Bobai 77 22 17N 109 59 E
Bobbili 70 18 35N 83 30 E
Bóbbio 38 44 47N 9 22 E
Bobcaygeon 106 44 33N 78 33W
Böblingen 25 48 41N 9 1 E
Bobo-Dioulasso 84 11 8N 4 13W
Boboc 43 45 13N 26 59 E
Bobolice 28 53 58N 16 37 E
Boboshevo 42 42 9N 23 0 E
Bobov Dol 42 42 20N 23 0 E
Bóbr → 28 52 4N 15 4 E
Bobraomby, Tanjon' i 93 12 40S 49 10 E
Bobrinets 56 48 4N 32 5 E
Bobrov 55 51 5N 40 2 E
Bobruysk 54 53 10N 29 15 E
Bôca do Acre 126 8 50S 67 27W
Boca, La 120 8 56N 79 30W
Boca Raton 115 26 21N 80 5W
Bocaiúva 127 17 7S 43 49W
Bocanda 84 7 5N 4 31W
Bocaranga 88 7 0N 15 35 E
Bocas del Toro 121 9 15N 82 20W
Boceguillas 32 41 20N 3 39W
Bochnia 27 49 58N 20 27 E
Bocholt 24 51 50N 6 35 E
Bochov 26 50 9N 13 3 E
Bochum 24 51 28N 7 12 E
Bockenem 24 52 1N 10 8 E
Boćki 28 52 39N 23 3 E
Bocşa Montană 42 45 21N 21 47 E
Boda 88 4 19N 17 26 E
Böda 49 57 15N 17 3 E
Bodafors 49 57 48N 14 23 E
Bodaybo 59 57 50N 114 0 E
Boden 50 65 50N 21 42 E
Bodensee 25 47 35N 9 25 E
Bodenteich 24 52 49N 10 41 E
Bodhan 70 18 40N 77 44 E
Bodinayakkanur 70 10 2N 77 10 E
Bodinga 85 12 58N 5 10 E
Bodmin 13 50 28N 4 44W
Bodmin Moor 13 50 33N 4 36W
Bodrog → 27 48 15N 21 35 E
Bodrum 64 37 5N 27 30 E
Bódva → 27 48 19N 20 45 E
Boegoebergdam 92 29 7S 22 9 E
Boën 21 45 44N 4 0 E
Boende 88 0 24S 21 12 E
Boerne 117 29 48N 98 41W
Boffa 84 10 16N 14 3W
Bogalusa 117 30 50N 89 55W

Bogan Brabant L.

Bogan → 97 29 59 S 146 17 E
Bogan Gate 99 33 7 S 147 49 E
Bogantungan 98 23 41 S 147 17 E
Bogata 117 33 26N 95 10W
Bogatić 42 44 51N 19 30 E
Bogenfels 92 27 25 S 15 25 E
Bogense 49 55 34N 10 5 E
Boggabilla 99 28 36 S 150 24 E
Boggabri 99 30 45 S 150 0 E
Boggeragh Mts. 15 52 2N 8 55W
Bognor Regis 13 50 47N 0 40W
Bogø 49 54 55N 12 2 E
Bogo 73 11 3N 124 0 E
Bogodukhov 54 50 9N 35 33 E
Bogong, Mt. 97 36 47 S 147 17 E
Bogor 73 6 36 S 106 48 E
Bogoroditsk 55 53 47N 38 8 E
Bogorodsk 55 56 4N 43 30 E
Bogorodskoye 59 52 22N 140 30 E
Bogoso 84 5 38N 2 3W
Bogota 126 4 34N 74 0W
Bogotol 58 56 15N 89 50 E
Bogra 69 24 51N 89 22 E
Boguchany 59 58 40N 97 30 E
Boguchar 57 49 55N 40 32 E
Bogué 84 16 45N 14 10W
Boguslav 56 49 47N 30 53 E
Boguszów 28 50 45N 16 12 E
Bohain 19 49 59N 3 28 E
Bohemia 26 50 0N 14 0 E
Bohemian Forest = Böhmerwald 25 49 30N 12 40 E
Bohena Cr. → 99 30 17 S 149 42 E
Bohinjska Bistrica 39 46 17N 14 1 E
Böhmerwald 25 49 30N 12 40 E
Böhmte 24 52 24N 8 20 E
Bohol 73 9 50N 124 10 E
Bohotleh 63 8 20N 46 25 E
Boi 85 9 35N 9 27 E
Boi, Pta. de 125 23 55 S 45 15W
Boiano 41 41 28N 14 29 E
Boileau, C. 96 17 40 S 122 7 E
Boinitsa 42 43 58N 22 32 E
Boise 118 43 43N 116 9W
Boise City 117 36 45N 102 30W
Boissevain 109 49 15N 100 5W
Boite → 39 46 5N 12 5 E
Boitzenburg 24 53 16N 13 36 E
Boizenburg 24 53 22N 10 42 E
Bojador C. 80 26 0N 14 30W
Bojana → 42 41 52N 19 22 E
Bojanowo 28 51 43N 16 42 E
Bojnūrd 65 37 30N 57 20 E
Bojonegoro 73 7 11 S 111 54 E
Boju 85 7 22N 7 55 E
Boka 42 45 22N 20 52 E
Boka Kotorska 42 42 23N 18 32 E
Bokala 84 8 31N 4 33W
Boké 84 10 56N 14 17W
Bokhara → 99 29 55 S 146 42 E
Bokkos 85 9 17N 9 1 E
Boknafjorden 47 59 14N 5 40 E
Bokoro 81 12 25N 17 14 E
Bokote 88 0 12 S 21 8 E
Bokpyin 71 11 18N 98 42 E
Boksitogorsk 54 59 32N 33 56 E
Bokungu 88 0 35 S 22 50 E
Bol, Chad 81 13 30N 15 0 E
Bol, Yugo. 39 43 18N 16 38 E
Bolama 84 11 30N 15 30W
Bolan Pass 66 29 50N 67 20 E
Bolaños → 120 21 14N 104 8W
Bolbec 18 49 30N 0 30 E
Boldeşti 46 45 3N 26 2 E
Bole, China 75 45 11N 81 37 E
Bole, Ethiopia 87 6 36N 37 20 E
Bolekhov 54 49 0N 24 0 E
Bolesławiec 28 51 17N 15 37 E
Bolgatanga 85 10 44N 0 53W
Bolgrad 56 45 40N 28 32 E
Boli, China 76 45 46N 130 31 E
Boli, Sudan 87 6 2N 28 48 E
Bolinao C. 73 16 23N 119 55 E
Bolívar, Argent. 124 36 15 S 60 53W
Bolívar, Colomb. 126 2 0N 77 0W
Bolivar, Mo., U.S.A. 117 37 38N 93 22W
Bolivar, Tenn., U.S.A. 117 35 14N 89 0W
Bolivia ■ 126 17 6 S 64 0W
Boljevac 42 43 51N 21 58 E
Bolkhov 55 53 25N 36 0 E
Bollène 21 44 18N 4 45 E
Bollnäs 48 61 21N 16 24 E
Bollon 99 28 2 S 147 29 E
Bollstabruk 48 63 1N 17 40 E
Bollullos 31 37 19N 6 32W
Bolmen 49 56 55N 13 40 E
Bolobo 88 2 6 S 16 20 E
Bologna 39 44 30N 11 20 E
Bologne 19 48 10N 5 8 E
Bologoye 54 57 55N 34 0 E
Bolomba 88 0 35N 19 0 E
Bolong 73 7 6N 122 16 E
Boloven, Cao Nguyen 71 15 10N 106 30 E
Bolpur 69 23 40N 87 45 E
Bolsena 39 42 40N 11 58 E
Bolsena, L. di 39 42 35N 11 55 E
Bolshaya Glushitsa 55 52 24N 50 29 E
Bolshaya Martynovka 57 47 12N 41 46 E
Bolshaya Vradiyevka 56 47 50N 30 40 E
Bolshereche 58 56 4N 74 45 E
Bolshevik, Ostrov 59 78 30N 102 0 E
Bolshezemelskaya Tundra 52 67 0N 56 0 E
Bolshoi Kavkas 57 42 50N 44 0 E
Bolshoy Anyuy → 59 68 30N 160 49 E
Bolshoy Atlym 58 62 25N 66 50 E
Bolshoy Begichev, Ostrov 59 74 20N 112 30 E
Bolshoy Lyakhovskiy, Ostrov 59 73 35N 142 0 E
Bolshoy Tokmak 56 47 16N 35 42 E
Bol'shoy Tyuters, Ostrov 54 59 51N 27 13 E
Bolsward 16 53 3N 5 32 E
Boltaña 32 42 28N 0 4 E
Boltigen 25 46 38N 7 24 E
Bolton, Can. 112 43 54N 79 45W
Bolton, U.K. 12 53 35N 2 26W
Bolu 64 40 45N 31 35 E
Bolvadin 64 38 45N 31 4 E
Bolzano (Bozen) 39 46 30N 11 20 E
Bom Despacho 127 19 43 S 45 15W
Bom Jesus da Lapa 127 13 15 S 43 25W
Boma 88 5 50 S 13 4 E
Bomaderry 99 34 52 S 150 37 E
Bombala 97 36 56 S 149 15 E
Bombarral 31 39 15N 9 9W
Bombay 70 18 55N 72 50 E
Bomboma 88 2 25N 18 55 E
Bombombwa 90 1 40N 25 40 E
Bomi Hills 84 7 1N 10 38W
Bomili 90 1 45N 27 5 E
Bomokandi → 90 3 39N 26 8 E
Bomongo 88 1 27N 18 21 E
Bomu → 88 4 40N 23 30 E
Bon C. 83 37 1N 11 2 E
Bonaire 121 12 10N 68 15W
Bonang 99 37 11 S 148 41 E
Bonanza 121 13 54N 84 35W
Bonaparte Archipelago 96 14 0 S 124 30 E
Boñar 30 42 52N 5 19W
Bonaventure 107 48 5N 65 32W
Bonavista 107 48 40N 53 5W
Bonavista, C. 107 48 42N 53 5W
Bondeno 39 44 53N 11 22 E
Bondo 88 3 55N 23 53 E
Bondoukou 84 8 2N 2 47W
Bondowoso 73 7 56 S 113 49 E
Bone Rate 73 7 25 S 121 5 E
Bone Rate, Kepulauan 73 6 30 S 121 10 E
Bone, Teluk 73 4 10 S 120 50 E
Bonefro 41 41 42N 14 55 E
Bo'ness 14 56 0N 3 38W
Bong Son = Hoai Nhon 71 14 28N 109 1 E
Bongandanga 88 1 24N 21 3 E
Bongor 81 10 35N 15 20 E
Bongouanou 84 6 42N 4 15W
Bonham 117 33 30N 96 10W
Bonifacio 21 41 24N 9 10 E
Bonifacio, Bouches de 40 41 12N 9 15 E
Bonin Is. 94 27 0N 142 0 E
Bonke 87 6 5N 37 16 E
Bonn 24 50 43N 7 6 E
Bonnat 20 46 20N 1 54 E
Bonne Terre 117 37 57N 90 33W
Bonners Ferry 118 48 38N 116 21W
Bonnétable 18 48 11N 0 25 E
Bonneuil-Matours 18 46 41N 0 34 E
Bonneval 18 48 11N 1 24 E
Bonneville 21 46 5N 6 24 E
Bonney, L. 99 37 50 S 140 20 E
Bonnie Rock 96 30 29 S 118 22 E
Bonny, France 19 47 34N 2 50 E
Bonny, Nigeria 85 4 25N 7 13 E
Bonny → 85 4 20N 7 10 E
Bonny, Bight of 88 3 30N 9 20 E
Bonnyville 109 54 20N 110 45W
Bonoi 73 1 45 S 137 41 E
Bonorva 40 40 25N 8 47 E
Bontang 72 0 10N 117 30 E
Bonthain 73 5 34 S 119 56 E
Bonthe 84 7 30N 12 33W
Bontoc 73 17 7N 120 58 E
Bonyeri 84 5 1N 2 46W
Bonyhád 27 46 18N 18 32 E
Booker 117 36 29N 100 30W
Boolaboolka, L. 99 32 38 S 143 10 E
Booligal 99 33 58 S 144 53 E
Boom 16 51 6N 4 20 E
Boonah 99 27 58 S 152 41 E
Boone, Iowa, U.S.A. 116 42 5N 93 53W
Boone, N.C., U.S.A. 115 36 14N 81 43W
Booneville, Ark., U.S.A. 117 35 10N 93 54W
Booneville, Miss., U.S.A. 115 34 39N 88 34W
Boonville, Ind., U.S.A. 114 38 3N 87 13W
Boonville, Mo., U.S.A. 116 38 57N 92 45W
Boonville, N.Y., U.S.A. 114 43 31N 75 20W
Boorindal 99 30 22 S 146 11 E
Boorowa 99 34 28 S 148 44 E
Boothia, Gulf of 105 71 0N 90 0W
Boothia Pen. 104 71 0N 94 0W
Bootle, Cumb., U.K. 12 54 17N 3 24W
Bootle, Merseyside, U.K. 12 53 28N 3 1W
Booué 88 0 5 S 11 55 E
Bopeechee 99 29 36 S 137 22 E
Bophuthatswana □ 92 26 0 S 26 0 E
Boppard 25 50 13N 7 36 E
Boquete 121 8 49N 82 27W
Bor 26 49 41N 12 45 E
Bôr 87 6 10N 31 40 E
Bor, Sweden 49 57 9N 14 10 E
Bor, Yugo. 42 44 8N 22 7 E
Borah, Mt. 118 44 19N 113 46W
Borama 63 9 55N 43 7 E
Borang 87 4 50N 30 59 E
Borås 49 57 43N 12 56 E
Borāzjān 65 29 22N 51 10 E
Borba, Brazil 126 4 12 S 59 34W
Borba, Port. 31 38 50N 7 26W
Borçka 57 41 25N 41 41 E
Bordeaux 20 44 50N 0 36W
Borden 107 46 18N 63 47W
Borden I. 4 78 30N 111 30W
Borders □ 14 55 35N 2 50W
Bordertown 97 36 19 S 140 45 E
Borðeyri 50 65 12N 21 6W
Bordighera 38 43 47N 7 40 E
Bordj bou Arreridj 83 36 4N 4 45 E
Bordj Bourguiba 83 32 12N 10 2 E
Bordj el Hobra 83 32 9N 4 51 E
Bordj Fly Ste. Marie 82 27 19N 2 32W
Bordj-in-Eker 83 24 9N 5 3 E
Bordj Menaiel 83 36 46N 3 43 E
Bordj Messouda 83 30 12N 9 25 E
Bordj Nili 83 33 28N 3 2 E
Bordj Omar Driss 83 28 10N 6 40 E
Bordj Zelfana 83 32 27N 4 15 E
Borek Wielkopolski 28 51 54N 17 11 E
Borensberg 49 58 34N 15 17 E
Borgarnes 50 64 32N 21 55W
Børgefjellet 50 65 20N 13 45 E
Borger, Neth. 16 52 54N 6 44 E
Borger, U.S.A. 117 35 40N 101 20W
Borghamn 49 58 23N 14 41 E
Borgholm 49 56 52N 16 39 E
Bórgia 41 38 50N 16 30 E
Borgo San Dalmazzo 38 44 19N 7 29 E
Borgo San Lorenzo 39 43 57N 11 21 E
Borgo Valsugano 39 46 3N 11 27 E
Borgomanero 38 45 41N 8 28 E
Borgonovo Val Tidone 38 45 1N 9 28 E
Borgorose 39 42 12N 13 14 E
Borgosésia 38 45 43N 8 17 E
Borgvattnet 48 63 26N 15 48 E
Borislav 54 49 18N 23 28 E
Borisoglebsk 55 51 27N 42 5 E
Borisoglebskiy 55 56 28N 43 59 E
Borisov 54 54 17N 28 28 E
Borispol 54 50 21N 30 59 E
Borja, Peru 126 4 20 S 77 40W
Borja, Spain 32 41 48N 1 34W
Borjas Blancas 32 41 31N 0 52 E
Borken 24 51 51N 6 52 E
Borkou 81 18 15N 18 50 E
Borkum 24 53 36N 6 42 E
Borlänge 48 60 29N 15 26 E
Borley, C. 5 66 15 S 52 30 E
Bormida → 38 44 23N 8 13 E
Bórmio 38 46 28N 10 22 E
Borna 24 51 8N 12 31 E
Borneo 72 1 0N 115 0 E
Bornholm 49 55 10N 15 0 E
Bornholmsgattet 49 55 15N 14 20 E
Borno □ 85 12 30N 12 30 E
Bornos 31 36 48N 5 42W
Bornu Yassa 85 12 14N 12 25 E
Borobudur 73 7 36 S 110 13 E
Borodino 54 55 31N 35 40 E
Borogontsy 59 62 42N 131 8 E
Boromo 84 11 45N 2 58W
Borongan 73 11 37N 125 26 E
Bororen 98 24 13 S 151 33 E
Borotangba Mts. 87 6 30N 25 0 E
Borovan 43 43 27N 23 45 E
Borovichi 54 58 25N 33 55 E
Borovsk 55 55 12N 36 24 E
Borrby 49 55 27N 14 10 E
Borriol 32 40 4N 0 4W
Borroloola 97 16 4 S 136 17 E
Borşa 46 47 41N 24 50 E
Borsod-Abaúj-Zemplén □ 27 48 20N 21 0 E
Bort-les-Orgues 20 45 24N 2 29 E
Borth 13 52 29N 4 3W
Borujerd 64 33 55N 48 50 E
Borzhomi 57 41 48N 43 28 E
Borzna 54 51 18N 32 26 E
Borzya 59 50 24N 116 31 E
Bosa 40 40 17N 8 32 E
Bosanska Brod 42 45 10N 18 0 E
Bosanska Dubica 39 45 10N 16 50 E
Bosanska Gradiška 42 45 10N 17 15 E
Bosanska Kostajnica 39 45 11N 16 33 E
Bosanska Krupa 39 44 53N 16 10 E
Bosanski Novi 39 45 2N 16 22 E
Bosanski Samac 42 45 3N 18 29 E
Bosansko Grahovo 39 44 12N 16 26 E
Bosansko Petrovac 39 44 35N 16 21 E
Bosaso 63 11 12N 49 18 E
Boscastle 13 50 42N 4 42W
Boscotrecase 41 40 46N 14 28 E
Bose 77 23 53N 106 35 E
Boshan 76 36 28N 117 49 E
Boshoek 92 25 30 S 27 9 E
Boshof 92 28 31 S 25 13 E
Boshrūyeh 65 33 50N 57 30 E
Bosilegrad 42 42 30N 22 27 E
Boskovice 27 49 29N 16 40 E
Bosna → 42 45 4N 18 29 E
Bosna i Hercegovina □ 42 44 0N 18 0 E
Bosnia = Bosna □ 42 44 0N 18 0 E
Bosnik 73 1 5 S 136 10 E
Bōsō-Hantō 74 35 20N 140 20 E
Bosobolo 88 4 15N 19 50 E
Bosporus = Karadeniz Boğazı 64 41 10N 29 10 E
Bossangoa 88 6 35N 17 30 E
Bossekop 50 69 57N 23 15 E
Bossembélé 81 5 25N 17 40 E
Bossier City 117 32 28N 93 48W
Bosso 85 13 43N 13 19 E
Bossut C. 96 18 42 S 121 35 E
Bosten Hu 75 41 55N 87 40 E
Boston, U.K. 12 52 59N 0 2W
Boston, U.S.A. 114 42 20N 71 0W
Boston Bar 108 49 52N 121 30W
Bosut → 42 45 20N 19 0 E
Boswell, Can. 108 49 28N 116 45W
Boswell, Okla., U.S.A. 117 34 1N 95 50W
Boswell, Pa., U.S.A. 112 40 9N 79 2W
Botad 68 22 15N 71 40 E
Botevgrad 43 42 55N 23 47 E
Bothaville 92 27 23 S 26 34 E
Bothnia, G. of 50 63 0N 20 0 E
Bothwell, Austral. 99 42 20 S 147 1 E
Bothwell, Can. 112 42 38N 81 52W
Boticas 30 41 41N 7 40W
Botletle → 92 20 10 S 23 15 E
Botoroaga 46 44 8N 25 32 E
Botoşani 46 47 42N 26 41 E
Botoşani □ 46 47 50N 26 50 E
Botro 84 7 51N 5 19W
Botswana ■ 92 22 0 S 24 0 E
Bottineau 116 48 49N 100 25W
Bottrop 24 51 34N 6 59 E
Botucatu 125 22 55 S 48 30W
Botwood 107 49 6N 55 23W
Bou Alam 82 33 50N 1 26 E
Bou Ali 82 27 11N 0 4W
Bou Djébéha 84 18 25N 2 45W
Bou Guema 82 28 49N 0 19 E
Bou Ismael 82 36 38N 2 42 E
Bou Izakarn 82 29 12N 9 46W
Bou Saâda 83 35 11N 4 9 E
Bou Salem 83 36 45N 9 2 E
Bouaké 84 7 40N 5 2W
Bouar 88 6 0N 15 40 E
Bouârfa 82 32 32N 1 58 E
Bouca 88 6 45N 18 25 E
Boucau 20 43 32N 1 29W
Bouches-du-Rhône □ 21 43 37N 5 2 E
Bouda 82 27 50N 0 27W
Boudenib 82 31 59N 3 31W
Boufarik 82 36 34N 2 58 E
Bougainville C. 96 13 57 S 126 4 E
Bougaroun, C. 83 37 6N 6 30 E
Bougie = Bejaia 83 36 42N 5 2 E
Bougouni 84 11 30N 7 20W
Bouillon 16 49 44N 5 3 E
Bouïra 83 36 20N 3 59 E
Boulder, Austral. 96 30 46 S 121 30 E
Boulder, Colo., U.S.A. 116 40 3N 105 10W
Boulder, Mont., U.S.A. 118 46 14N 112 4W
Boulder City 119 36 0N 114 50W
Boulder Dam = Hoover Dam 119 36 0N 114 45W
Bouli 84 15 17N 12 18W
Boulia 97 22 52 S 139 51 E
Bouligny 19 49 17N 5 45 E
Boulogne → 18 47 12N 1 47W
Boulogne-sur-Gesse 20 43 18N 0 38 E
Boulogne-sur-Mer 19 50 42N 1 36 E
Bouloire 18 47 58N 0 33 E
Boulsa 85 12 39N 0 34W
Boultoum 85 14 45N 10 25 E
Boumalne 82 31 25N 6 0W
Bouna 84 9 10N 3 0W
Boundiali 84 9 30N 6 20W
Bountiful 118 40 57N 111 58W
Bounty I. 94 48 0 S 178 30 E
Bourbon-Lancy 20 46 37N 3 45 E
Bourbon-l'Archambault 20 46 36N 3 4 E
Bourbonnais 20 46 28N 3 0 E
Bourbonne-les-Bains 19 47 59N 5 45 E
Bourem 85 17 0N 0 24W
Bourg 20 45 3N 0 34W
Bourg-Argental 21 45 18N 4 32 E
Bourg-de-Péage 21 45 2N 5 3 E
Bourg-en-Bresse 21 46 13N 5 12 E
Bourg-St.-Andéol 21 44 23N 4 39 E
Bourg-St.-Maurice 21 45 35N 6 46 E
Bourganeuf 20 45 57N 1 45 E
Bourges 19 47 9N 2 25 E
Bourget 113 45 26N 75 9W
Bourget, L. du 21 45 44N 5 52 E
Bourgneuf, B. de 18 47 3N 2 10W
Bourgneuf-en-Retz 18 47 2N 1 58W
Bourgneuf-la-Fôret, Le 18 48 10N 0 59W
Bourgogne 19 47 0N 4 30 E
Bourgoin-Jallieu 21 45 36N 5 17 E
Bourgueil 18 47 17N 0 10 E
Bourke 97 30 8 S 145 55 E
Bournemouth 13 50 43N 1 53W
Bourriot-Bergonce 20 44 7N 0 14W
Bouscat, Le 20 44 53N 0 32W
Boussac 20 46 22N 2 13 E
Boussens 20 43 12N 0 58 E
Bousso 81 10 34N 16 52 E
Boutilimit 84 17 45N 14 40W
Boutonne → 20 45 55N 0 43 E
Bouvet I. = Bouvetøya 7 54 26 S 3 24 E
Bouvetøya 7 54 26 S 3 24 E
Bouznika 82 33 46N 7 6W
Bouzonville 19 49 17N 6 32 E
Bova Marina 41 37 59N 15 56 E
Bovalino Marina 41 38 9N 16 10 E
Bovec 39 46 20N 13 33 E
Bovigny 16 50 12N 5 55 E
Bovill 118 46 58N 116 27W
Bovino 41 41 15N 15 20 E
Bow Island 108 49 50N 111 23W
Bowbells 116 48 47N 102 19W
Bowdle 116 45 30N 99 40W
Bowen 97 20 0 S 148 16 E
Bowen → 98 20 24 S 147 20 E
Bowen Mts. 99 37 0 S 148 0 E
Bowie, Ariz., U.S.A. 119 32 15N 109 30W
Bowie, Tex., U.S.A. 117 33 33N 97 50W
Bowland, Forest of 12 54 0N 2 30W
Bowling Green, Ky., U.S.A. 114 37 0N 86 25W
Bowling Green, Ohio, U.S.A. 114 41 22N 83 40W
Bowling Green, C. 97 19 19 S 147 25 E
Bowman 116 46 12N 103 21W
Bowman I. 5 65 0 S 104 0 E
Bowmans 99 34 10 S 138 17 E
Bowmanville 106 43 55N 78 41W
Bowmore 14 55 45N 6 18W
Bowral 97 34 26 S 150 27 E
Bowraville 99 30 37 S 152 52 E
Bowron → 108 54 3N 121 50W
Bowser L. 108 56 30N 129 30W
Bowsman 109 52 14N 101 12W
Bowwood 91 17 5 S 26 20 E
Boxelder Cr. → 118 47 20N 108 30W
Boxholm 49 58 12N 15 3 E
Boxtel 16 51 36N 5 20 E
Boyabat 56 41 28N 34 42 E
Boyce 117 31 25N 92 39W
Boyer → 108 58 27N 115 57W
Boyle 15 53 58N 8 19W
Boyne → 15 53 43N 6 15W
Boyne City 114 45 13N 85 1W
Boyni Qara 65 36 20N 67 0 E
Boynton Beach 115 26 31N 80 3W
Bozburun 45 36 43N 28 8 E
Bozcaada 44 39 49N 26 3 E
Bozeman 118 45 40N 111 0W
Bozen = Bolzano 39 46 30N 11 20 E
Bożepole Wielkopolski 28 54 33N 17 56 E
Boževac 42 44 32N 21 24 E
Bozouls 20 44 28N 2 43 E
Bozoum 88 6 25N 16 35 E
Bozovici 46 44 56N 22 1 E
Bra 38 44 41N 7 50 E
Brabant □ 16 50 46N 4 30 E
Brabant L. 109 55 58N 103 43W

Brabrand Buchares

Brabrand 49 56 9N 10 7 E
Brač 39 43 20N 16 40 E
Bracadale, L. 14 57 20N 6 30W
Bracciano 39 42 6N 12 10 E
Bracciano, L. di 39 42 8N 12 11 E
Bracebridge 106 45 2N 79 19W
Brach 83 27 31N 14 20 E
Bracieux 19 47 30N 1 30 E
Bräcke 48 62 45N 15 26 E
Brackettville 117 29 21N 100 20W
Bračk̇i Kanal 39 43 24N 16 40 E
Brad 46 46 10N 22 50 E
Brádano → 41 40 23N 16 51 E
Braddock 112 40 24N 79 51W
Bradenton 115 27 25N 82 35W
Bradford, Can. 112 44 7N 79 34W
Bradford, U.K. 12 53 47N 1 45W
Bradford, Pa., U.S.A. 114 41 58N 78 41W
Bradford, Vt., U.S.A. 113 43 59N 72 9W
Brădiceni 46 45 3N 23 4 E
Bradley, Ark., U.S.A. 117 33 7N 93 39W
Bradley, S.D., U.S.A. 116 45 10N 97 40W
Bradley Institute 91 17 7S 31 25 E
Bradore Bay 107 51 27N 57 18W
Bradshaw 97 15 21S 130 16 E
Brady 117 31 8N 99 25W
Brædstrup 49 55 58N 9 37 E
Braeside 113 45 28N 76 24W
Braga 30 41 35N 8 25W
Braga □ 30 41 30N 8 30W
Bragado 124 35 2S 60 27W
Bragança, Brazil 127 1 0S 47 2W
Bragança, Port. 30 41 48N 6 50W
Bragança □ 30 41 30N 6 45W
Bragança Paulista 125 22 55S 46 32W
Brahmanbaria 69 23 58N 91 15 E
Brahmani → 69 20 39N 86 46 E
Brahmaputra → 67 24 2N 90 59 E
Braich-y-pwll 12 52 47N 4 46W
Braidwood 99 35 27S 149 49 E
Brăila 46 45 19N 27 59 E
Brăila □ 46 45 5N 27 30 E
Brainerd 116 46 20N 94 10W
Braintree, U.K. 13 51 53N 0 34 E
Braintree, U.S.A. 113 42 11N 71 0W
Brak → 92 29 35S 22 55 E
Brake, Niedersachsen, Ger. 24 53 19N 8 30 E
Brake, Nordrhein, Ger. 24 51 43N 9 12 E
Bräkne-Hoby 49 56 14N 15 6 E
Brakwater 92 22 28S 17 3 E
Brålanda 49 58 34N 12 21 E
Bralorne 108 50 50N 123 45W
Bramberg 25 50 6N 10 40 E
Bramminge 49 55 28N 8 42 E
Brämön 48 62 14N 17 40 E
Brampton 106 43 45N 79 45W
Bramsche 24 52 25N 7 58 E
Bramwell 98 12 8S 142 37 E
Branco → 126 1 20S 61 50W
Brande 49 55 57N 9 8 E
Brandenburg 24 52 24N 12 33 E
Brandfort 92 28 40S 26 30 E
Brandon, Can. 109 49 50N 99 57W
Brandon, U.S.A. 113 43 48N 73 4W
Brandon B. 15 52 17N 10 8W
Brandon, Mt. 15 52 15N 10 15W
Brandsen 124 35 10S 58 15W
Brandval 47 60 19N 12 1 E
Brandvlei 92 30 25S 20 30 E
Brandýs 26 50 10N 14 40 E
Branford 113 41 15N 72 48W
Braniewo 28 54 25N 19 50 E
Bransfield Str. 5 63 0S 59 0W
Brańsk 28 52 44N 22 51 E
Branson, Colo., U.S.A. 117 37 4N 103 53W
Branson, Mo., U.S.A. 117 36 40N 93 18W
Brantford 106 43 10N 80 15W
Brantôme 20 45 22N 0 39 E
Branxholme 99 37 52S 141 49 E
Branzi 38 46 0N 9 46 E
Bras d'or, L. 107 45 50N 60 50W
Brasiléia 126 11 0S 68 45W
Brasília 127 15 47S 47 55 E
Braslav 54 55 38N 27 0 E
Braslovce 39 46 21N 15 3 E
Braşov 46 45 38N 25 35 E
Braşov □ 46 45 45N 25 15 E
Brass 85 4 35N 6 14 E
Brass → 85 4 15N 6 13 E
Brassac-les-Mines 20 45 24N 3 20 E
Brasschaat 16 51 19N 4 27 E
Brassey, Banjaran 72 5 0N 117 15 E
Brasstown Bald, Mt. 115 34 54N 83 45W
Bratislava 27 48 10N 17 7 E
Bratsigovo 43 42 1N 24 22 E
Bratsk 59 56 10N 101 30 E
Brattleboro 114 42 53N 72 37W
Braţul Chilia → 46 45 25N 29 20 E
Bratul Sfintu Gheorghe → 46 45 0N 29 20 E
Braţul Sulina → 46 45 10N 29 20 E
Bratunac 42 44 13N 19 21 E
Braunau 26 48 15N 13 3 E
Braunschweig 24 52 17N 10 28 E
Braunton 13 51 6N 4 9W
Brava 63 1 20N 44 8 E
Bråviken 48 58 38N 16 32 E
Bravo del Norte → 120 25 57N 97 9W
Brawley 119 32 58N 115 30W
Bray 15 53 12N 6 6W
Bray, Pays de 19 49 46N 1 26 E
Bray-sur-Seine 19 48 25N 3 14 E
Brazeau → 108 52 55N 115 14W
Brazil 114 39 32N 87 8W
Brazil ■ 127 10 0S 50 0W
Brazilian Highlands = Brasil, Planalto 122 18 0S 46 30W
Brazo Sur → 124 25 21S 57 42W
Brazos → 117 28 53N 95 23W
Brazzaville 88 4 9S 15 12 E
Brčko 42 44 54N 18 46 E
Brda → 28 53 8N 18 8 E
Breadalbane, Austral. 98 23 50S 139 35 E
Breadalbane, U.K. 14 56 30N 4 15W
Breaksea Sd. 101 45 35S 166 35 E
Bream Bay 101 35 56S 174 28 E
Bream Head 101 35 51S 174 36 E
Breas 124 25 29S 70 24W
Brebes 73 6 52S 109 3 E
Brechin, Can. 112 44 32N 79 10W
Brechin, U.K. 14 56 44N 2 40W
Breckenridge, Colo., U.S.A. 118 39 30N 106 2W
Breckenridge, Minn., U.S.A. 116 46 20N 96 36W
Breckenridge, Tex., U.S.A. 117 32 48N 98 55W
Břeclav 27 48 46N 16 53 E
Brecon 13 51 57N 3 23W
Brecon Beacons 13 51 53N 3 27W
Breda 16 51 35N 4 45 E
Bredaryd 49 57 10N 13 45 E
Bredasdorp 92 34 33S 20 2 E
Bredbo 99 35 58S 149 10 E
Bredstedt 24 54 37N 8 59 E
Bregalnica → 42 41 43N 22 9 E
Bregenz 26 47 30N 9 45 E
Bregovo 42 44 9N 22 39 E
Bréhal 18 48 53N 1 30W
Bréhat, I. de 18 48 51N 3 0W
Breiðafjörður 50 65 15N 23 15W
Breil 21 43 56N 7 31 E
Breisach 25 48 2N 7 37 E
Brejo 127 3 41S 42 47W
Brekke 47 61 1N 5 26 E
Breloux-la-Crèche 20 46 23N 0 19W
Bremangerlandet 47 61 51N 5 0 E
Bremen 24 53 4N 8 47 E
Bremen □ 24 53 6N 8 46 E
Bremerhaven 24 53 34N 8 35 E
Bremerton 118 47 30N 122 38W
Bremervörde 24 53 28N 9 10 E
Bremnes 47 59 47N 5 8 E
Bremsnes 47 63 6N 7 40 E
Brenes 31 37 32N 5 54W
Brenham 117 30 5N 96 27W
Brenner Pass 26 47 0N 11 30 E
Breno 38 45 57N 10 20 E
Brent, Can. 106 46 2N 78 29W
Brent, U.K. 13 51 33N 0 18W
Brenta → 39 45 11N 12 18 E
Brentwood 13 51 37N 0 19 E
Bréscia 38 45 33N 10 13 E
Breskens 16 51 23N 3 33 E
Breslau = Wrocław 28 51 5N 17 5 E
Bresle → 18 50 4N 1 22 E
Bresles 19 49 25N 2 13 E
Bressanone 39 46 43N 11 40 E
Bressay I. 14 60 10N 1 5W
Bresse, La 19 48 0N 6 53 E
Bresse, Plaine de 19 46 50N 5 10 E
Bressuire 18 46 51N 0 30W
Brest, France 18 48 24N 4 31W
Brest, U.S.S.R. 54 52 10N 23 40 E
Bretagne 18 48 0N 3 0W
Bretçu 46 46 7N 26 18 E
Breteuil, Eur, France 18 48 50N 0 53 E
Breteuil, Oise, France 19 49 38N 2 18 E
Breton 108 53 7N 114 28W
Breton, Pertuis 20 46 17N 1 25W
Breton Sd. 117 29 40N 89 12W
Brett, C. 101 35 10S 174 20 E
Bretten 25 49 2N 8 43 E
Brevard 115 35 19N 82 42W
Brevik 47 59 4N 9 42 E
Brewarrina 99 30 0S 146 51 E
Brewer 107 44 43N 68 50W
Brewster, N.Y., U.S.A. 113 41 23N 73 37W
Brewster, Wash., U.S.A. 118 48 10N 119 51W
Brewster, Kap 4 70 7N 22 0W
Brewton 115 31 9N 87 2W
Breyten 93 26 16S 30 0 E
Breytovo 55 58 18N 37 50 E
Brežice 39 45 54N 15 35 E
Brézina 82 33 4N 1 14 E
Březnice 26 49 32N 13 57 E
Breznik 42 42 44N 22 50 E
Brezno 27 48 50N 19 40 E
Brezovo 43 42 21N 25 5 E
Bria 88 6 30N 21 58 E
Briançon 21 44 54N 6 39 E
Briare 19 47 38N 2 45 E
Bribie I. 97 27 0S 152 58 E
Bricon 19 48 5N 5 0 E
Bricquebec 18 49 28N 1 38W
Bridgehampton 113 40 56N 72 19W
Bridgend 13 51 30N 3 35W
Bridgeport, Calif., U.S.A. 119 38 14N 119 15W
Bridgeport, Conn., U.S.A. 114 41 12N 73 12W
Bridgeport, Nebr., U.S.A. 116 41 42N 103 10W
Bridgeport, Tex., U.S.A. 117 33 15N 97 45W
Bridger 118 45 20N 108 58W
Bridgeton 114 39 29N 75 10W
Bridgetown, Austral. 96 33 58S 116 7 E
Bridgetown, Barbados 121 13 0N 59 30W
Bridgetown, Can. 107 44 55N 65 18W
Bridgewater, Can. 107 44 25N 64 31W
Bridgewater, Mass., U.S.A. 113 41 59N 70 56W
Bridgewater, S.D., U.S.A. 116 43 34N 97 29W
Bridgewater, C. 97 38 23S 141 23 E
Bridgnorth 13 52 33N 2 25W
Bridgton 113 44 5N 70 41W
Bridgwater 13 51 7N 3 0W
Bridlington 12 54 6N 0 11W
Bridport, Austral. 99 40 59S 147 23 E
Bridport, U.K. 13 50 43N 2 45W
Brie-Comte-Robert 19 48 40N 2 35 E
Brie, Plaine de la 19 48 35N 3 10 E
Briec 18 48 6N 4 0W
Brienne-le-Château 19 48 24N 4 30 E
Brienon 19 48 0N 3 35 E
Brienz 25 46 46N 8 2 E
Brienzersee 25 46 44N 7 53 E
Briey 19 49 14N 5 57 E
Brig 25 46 18N 7 59 E
Brigg 12 53 33N 0 30W
Briggsdale 116 40 40N 104 20W
Brigham City 118 41 30N 112 1W
Bright 99 36 42S 146 56 E
Brighton, Austral. 99 35 5S 138 30 E
Brighton, Can. 106 44 2N 77 44W
Brighton, U.K. 13 50 50N 0 9W
Brighton, U.S.A. 116 39 59N 104 50W
Brignogan-Plage 18 48 40N 4 20W
Brignoles 21 43 25N 6 5 E
Brihuega 32 40 45N 2 52W
Brikama 84 13 15N 16 45W
Brilliant, Can. 108 49 19N 117 38W
Brilliant, U.S.A. 112 40 15N 80 39W
Brilon 24 51 23N 8 32 E
Brindisi 41 40 39N 17 55 E
Brinje 39 45 0N 15 9 E
Brinkley 117 34 55N 91 15W
Brinkworth 99 33 42S 138 26 E
Brion, Î. 107 47 46N 61 26W
Brionne 18 49 11N 0 43 E
Brionski 39 44 55N 13 45 E
Brioude 20 45 18N 3 24 E
Briouze 18 48 42N 0 23W
Brisbane 97 27 25S 153 2 E
Brisbane → 99 27 24S 153 9 E
Brisighella 39 44 14N 11 46 E
Bristol, U.K. 13 51 26N 2 35W
Bristol, Conn., U.S.A. 114 41 44N 72 57W
Bristol, Pa., U.S.A. 113 40 6N 74 52W
Bristol, R.I., U.S.A. 113 41 40N 71 15W
Bristol, S.D., U.S.A. 116 45 25N 97 43W
Bristol, Tenn., U.S.A. 115 36 36N 82 11W
Bristol B. 104 58 0N 160 0W
Bristol Channel 13 51 18N 4 30W
Bristol I. 5 58 45S 28 0W
Bristol L. 119 34 23N 116 50W
Bristow 117 35 55N 96 28W
British Antarctic Territory □ 5 66 0S 45 0W
British Columbia □ 108 55 0N 125 15W
British Guiana = Guyana ■ 126 5 0N 59 0W
British Honduras = Belize ■ 120 17 0N 88 30W
British Isles 8 55 0N 4 0W
Brits 93 25 37S 27 48 E
Britstown 92 30 37S 23 30 E
Britt 106 45 46N 80 34W
Brittany = Bretagne 18 48 0N 3 0W
Britton 116 45 50N 97 47W
Brive-la-Gaillarde 20 45 10N 1 32 E
Briviesca 32 42 32N 3 19W
Brixton 98 23 32S 144 57 E
Brlik 58 44 0N 74 5 E
Brno 27 49 10N 16 35 E
Bro 48 59 31N 17 38 E
Broach = Bharuch 68 21 47N 73 0 E
Broad → 115 33 59N 82 39W
Broad B. 14 58 14N 6 16W
Broad Haven 15 54 20N 9 55W
Broad Law 14 55 30N 3 22W
Broad Sd. 97 22 0S 149 45 E
Broadford 100 37 14S 145 4 E
Broads, The 12 52 45N 1 30 E
Broadsound Ra. 97 22 50S 149 30 E
Broadus 116 45 28N 105 27W
Broadview 109 50 22N 102 35W
Broager 49 54 53N 9 40 E
Broaryd 49 57 7N 13 15 E
Brochet 109 57 53N 101 40W
Brochet, L. 109 58 36N 101 35W
Brock 109 51 26N 108 43W
Brocken 24 51 48N 10 40 E
Brockport 114 43 12N 77 56W
Brockton 113 42 8N 71 2W
Brockville 106 44 35N 75 41W
Brockway, Mont., U.S.A. 116 47 18N 105 46W
Brockway, Pa., U.S.A. 112 41 14N 78 48W
Brocton 112 42 25N 79 26W
Brod 42 41 35N 21 17 E
Brodarevo 42 43 14N 19 44 E
Brodeur Pen. 105 72 30N 88 10W
Brodick 14 55 34N 5 9W
Brodnica 28 53 15N 19 25 E
Brody 54 50 5N 25 10 E
Brogan 118 44 14N 117 32W
Broglie 18 49 0N 0 30 E
Brok 28 52 43N 21 52 E
Broken → 100 36 24S 145 24 E
Broken Bay 100 33 30S 151 15 E
Broken Bow, Nebr., U.S.A. 116 41 25N 99 35W
Broken Bow, Okla., U.S.A. 117 34 2N 94 43W
Broken Hill 97 31 58S 141 29 E
Broken Hill = Kabwe 91 14 27S 28 28 E
Brokind 49 58 13N 15 42 E
Bromfield 13 52 25N 2 45W
Bromley 13 51 20N 0 5 E
Bromölla 49 56 5N 14 28 E
Brønderslev 49 57 16N 9 57 E
Brong-Ahafo 84 7 50N 2 0W
Bronkhorstspruit 93 25 46S 28 45 E
Bronnitsy 55 55 27N 38 10 E
Bronte, Italy 41 37 48N 14 49 E
Bronte, U.S.A. 117 31 54N 100 18W
Bronte Park 99 42 8S 146 30 E
Brookfield 116 39 50N 93 4W
Brookhaven 117 31 40N 90 25W
Brookings, Oreg., U.S.A. 118 42 4N 124 10W
Brookings, S.D., U.S.A. 116 44 20N 96 45W
Brooklands 98 18 10S 144 0 E
Brooklin 112 43 55N 78 55W
Brookmere 108 49 52N 120 53W
Brooks 108 50 35N 111 55W
Brooks B. 108 50 15N 127 55W
Brooks L. 109 61 55N 106 35W
Brooks Ra. 104 68 40N 147 0W
Brooksville 115 28 32N 82 21W
Brookton 96 32 22S 117 1 E
Brookville 114 39 25N 85 0W
Brooloo 99 26 30S 152 43 E
Broom, L. 14 57 55N 5 15W
Broome 96 18 0S 122 15 E
Broons 18 48 20N 2 16W
Brora 14 58 0N 3 50W
Brora → 14 58 4N 3 52W
Brösarp 49 55 43N 14 6 E
Brosna → 15 53 8N 8 0W
Broşteni 46 47 14N 25 43
Brothers 118 43 56N 120 39
Brøttum 47 61 2N 10 34
Brou 18 48 13N 1 11
Brouage 20 45 52N 1 4
Broughton Island 105 67 33N 63 0
Broughty Ferry 14 56 29N 2 50
Broumov 27 50 35N 16 20
Brouwershaven 16 51 45N 3 55
Brovary 54 50 34N 30 48
Brovst 49 57 6N 9 31
Browerville 116 46 3N 94 50
Brown Willy 13 50 35N 4 34
Brownfield 117 33 10N 102 15
Browning 118 48 35N 113 0
Brownlee 109 50 43N 106 1
Brownsville, Oreg., U.S.A. 118 44 29N 123 0
Brownsville, Tenn., U.S.A. 117 35 35N 89 15
Brownsville, Tex., U.S.A. 117 25 56N 97 25
Brownwood 117 31 45N 99 0
Brownwood, L. 117 31 51N 98 35
Brozas 31 39 37N 6 47
Bru 47 61 32N 5 11
Bruas 71 4 31N 100 46
Bruay-en-Artois 19 50 29N 2 33
Bruce, Mt. 96 22 37S 118 8
Bruce Pen. 112 45 0N 81 30
Bruche → 19 48 34N 7 43
Bruchsal 25 49 9N 8 39
Bruck an der Leitha 27 48 1N 16 47
Bruck an der Mur 26 47 24N 15 16
Brückenau 25 50 17N 9 48
Brue → 13 51 10N 2 59
Bruges = Brugge 16 51 13N 3 13
Brugg 25 47 29N 8 11
Brugge 16 51 13N 3 13
Brühl 24 50 49N 6 51
Brûlé 108 53 15N 117 58W
Brûlon 18 47 58N 0 15W
Brumado 127 14 14S 41 40W
Brumath 19 48 43N 7 40 E
Brumunddal 47 60 53N 10 56 E
Brundidge 115 31 43N 85 45W
Bruneau 118 42 57N 115 55W
Bruneau → 118 42 57N 115 58W
Brunei = Bandar Seri Begawan 72 4 52N 115 0 E
Brunei ■ 72 4 50N 115 0 E
Brunflo 48 63 5N 14 50 E
Brunico 39 46 50N 11 55 E
Brunkeberg 47 59 26N 8 28 E
Brunna 48 59 52N 17 25 E
Brunnen 25 46 59N 8 37 E
Brunner 101 42 27S 171 20 E
Brunner, L. 101 42 37S 171 27 E
Brunnsvik 48 60 12N 15 8 E
Bruno 109 52 20N 105 30W
Brunsbüttelkoog 24 53 52N 9 13 E
Brunswick, Ga., U.S.A. 115 31 10N 81 30W
Brunswick, Md., U.S.A. 114 39 20N 77 38W
Brunswick, Me., U.S.A. 107 43 53N 69 50W
Brunswick, Mo., U.S.A. 116 39 26N 93 10W
Brunswick, Ohio, U.S.A. 112 41 15N 81 50W
Brunswick = Braunschweig 24 52 17N 10 28 E
Brunswick B. 96 15 15S 124 50 E
Brunswick, Pen. de 128 53 30S 71 30W
Bruntál 27 50 0N 17 27 E
Bruny I. 97 43 20S 147 15 E
Brusartsi 42 43 40N 23 5 E
Brush 116 40 17N 103 33W
Brushton 113 44 50N 74 62W
Brusio 25 46 14N 10 8 E
Brusque 125 27 5S 49 0W
Brussel 16 50 51N 4 21 E
Brussels, Can. 112 43 45N 81 25W
Brussels, Ont., Can. 112 43 44N 81 15W
Brussels = Bruxelles 16 50 51N 4 21 E
Bruthen 99 37 42S 147 50 E
Bruxelles 16 50 51N 4 21 E
Bruyères 19 48 10N 6 40 E
Brwinów 28 52 9N 20 40 E
Bryagovo 43 41 58N 25 8 E
Bryan, Ohio, U.S.A. 114 41 30N 84 30W
Bryan, Texas, U.S.A. 117 30 40N 96 27W
Bryan, Mt. 99 33 30S 139 0 E
Bryanka 57 48 32N 38 45 E
Bryansk 54 53 13N 34 25 E
Bryanskoye 57 44 20N 47 10 E
Bryant 116 44 35N 97 28W
Bryne 47 58 44N 5 38 E
Bryson City 115 35 28N 83 25W
Brza Palanka 42 44 28N 22 27 E
Brzava → 42 45 21N 20 45 E
Brzeg 28 50 52N 17 30 E
Brzeg Din 28 51 16N 16 41 E
Brześć Kujawski 28 52 36N 18 55 E
Brzesko 27 49 59N 20 34 E
Brzeszcze 27 49 59N 19 10 E
Brzeziny 28 51 49N 19 42 E
Brzozów 27 49 41N 22 3 E
Bû Athlah 83 30 9N 15 39 E
Bu Craa 80 26 45N 12 50W
Bua Yai 71 15 33N 102 26 E
Buabuq 86 31 29N 25 29 E
Buapinang 73 4 40S 121 30 E
Buayan 73 6 3N 125 6 E
Buba 84 11 40N 14 59W
Bubanza 90 3 6S 29 23 E
Bucak 64 37 28N 30 36 E
Bucaramanga 126 7 0N 73 0W
Bucchiánico 39 42 20N 14 10 E
Bucecea 46 47 47N 26 28 E
Buchach 54 49 5N 25 25 E
Buchan 14 57 32N 2 8W
Buchan Ness 14 57 29N 1 48W
Buchanan, Can. 109 51 40N 102 45W
Buchanan, Liberia 84 5 57N 10 2W
Buchanan, L., Queens., Austral. 98 21 35S 145 52 E
Buchanan, L., W. Australia, Austral. 96 25 33S 123 2 E
Buchanan, L., U.S.A. 117 30 50N 98 25W
Buchans 107 48 50N 56 52W
Bucharest = Bucureşti 46 44 27N 26 10 E

Buchholz Caeté

Buchholz 24 53 19N 9 51 E
Buchloe 25 48 3N 10 45 E
Bückeburg 24 52 16N 9 2 E
Buckeye 119 33 28N 112 40W
Buckhannon 114 39 2N 80 10W
Buckhaven 14 56 10N 3 2W
Buckie 14 57 40N 2 58W
Buckingham, Can. 106 45 37N 75 24W
Buckingham, U.K. 13 52 0N 0 59W
Buckingham □ 13 51 50N 0 55W
Buckingham B. 97 12 10 S 135 40 E
Buckingham Can. 70 14 0N 80 5 E
Buckinguy 99 31 3 S 147 30 E
Buckland Newton 13 50 45N 2 25W
Buckley 118 47 10N 122 2W
Bucklin 117 37 37N 99 40W
Bucquoy 19 50 9N 2 43 E
Buctouche 107 46 30N 64 45W
Bucureşti 46 44 27N 26 10 E
Bucyrus 114 40 48N 83 0W
Budafok 27 47 26N 19 2 E
Budalin 67 22 20N 95 10 E
Budapest 27 47 29N 19 5 E
Budaun 68 28 5N 79 10 E
Budd Coast 5 68 0 S 112 0 E
Buddusò 40 40 35N 9 18 E
Bude 13 50 49N 4 33W
Budeşti 46 44 13N 26 30 E
Budge Budge 69 22 30N 88 5 E
Búðareyri 50 65 2N 14 13W
Búðir 50 64 49N 23 23W
Budia 32 40 38N 2 46W
Budjala 88 2 50N 19 40 E
Budrio 39 44 31N 11 31 E
Budva 42 42 17N 18 50 E
Budzyń 28 52 54N 16 59 E
Buea 85 4 10N 9 9 E
Buena Vista, Colo., U.S.A. 119 38 56N 106 6W
Buena Vista, Va., U.S.A. 114 37 47N 79 23W
Buena Vista L. 119 35 15N 119 21W
Buenaventura, Colomb. 126 3 53N 77 4W
Buenaventura, Mexico 120 29 50N 107 30W
Buendía, Pantano de 32 40 25N 2 43W
Buenos Aires 124 34 30 S 58 20W
Buenos Aires □ 124 36 30 S 60 0W
Buenos Aires, Lago 128 46 35 S 72 30W
Buffalo, Mo., U.S.A. 117 37 40N 93 5W
Buffalo, N.Y., U.S.A. 114 42 55N 78 50W
Buffalo, Okla., U.S.A. 117 36 55N 99 42W
Buffalo, S.D., U.S.A. 116 45 39N 103 31W
Buffalo, Wyo., U.S.A. 118 44 25N 106 50W
Buffalo → 108 60 5N 115 5W
Buffalo Head Hills 108 57 25N 115 55W
Buffalo L. 108 52 27N 112 54W
Buffalo Narrows 109 55 51N 108 29W
Buffels → 92 29 36 S 17 15 E
Buford 115 34 5N 84 0W
Bug →, Poland 28 52 31N 21 5 E
Bug →, U.S.S.R. 56 46 59N 31 58 E
Buga 126 4 0N 76 15W
Buganda □ 90 0 0N 31 30 E
Buganga 90 0 3 S 32 0 E
Bugeat 20 45 36N 1 55 E
Bugel, Tanjung 72 6 26 S 111 3 E
Bugojno 42 44 2N 17 25 E
Bugsuk 72 8 15N 117 15 E
Bugt 76 48 47N 121 56 E
Bugue, Le 20 44 55N 0 56 E
Bugulma 52 54 33N 52 48 E
Buguma 85 4 42N 6 55 E
Buguruslan 52 53 39N 52 26 E
Buhăeşti 46 46 47N 27 32 E
Buheirat-Murrat-el-Kubra 86 30 15N 32 40 E
Buhl, Idaho, U.S.A. 118 42 35N 114 54W
Buhl, Minn., U.S.A. 116 47 30N 92 46W
Buhuşi 46 46 41N 26 45 E
Buick 117 37 38N 91 2W
Builth Wells 13 52 10N 3 26W
Buinsk 55 55 0N 48 18 E
Buir Nur 75 47 50N 117 42 E
Buis-les-Baronnies 21 44 17N 5 16 E
Buitrago 30 41 0N 3 38W
Bujalance 31 37 54N 4 23W
Buján 30 42 59N 8 36W
Bujanovac 42 42 28N 21 44 E
Bujaraloz 32 41 29N 0 10W
Buje 39 45 24N 13 39 E
Bujumbura (Usumbura) 90 3 16 S 29 18 E
Bük 27 47 22N 16 45 E
Buk 28 52 21N 16 30 E
Bukachacha 59 52 55N 116 50 E
Bukama 91 9 10 S 25 50 E
Bukavu 90 2 20 S 28 52 E
Bukene 90 4 15 S 32 48 E
Bukhara 58 39 48N 64 25 E
Bukima 90 1 50 S 33 25 E
Bukittinggi 72 0 20 S 100 20 E
Bukkapatnam 70 14 14N 77 46 E
Bukoba 90 1 20 S 31 49 E
Bukoba □ 90 1 30 S 32 0 E
Bukowno 27 50 17N 19 35 E
Bukuru 85 9 42N 8 48 E
Bukuya 90 0 40N 31 52 E
Bula, Guin.-Biss. 84 12 7N 15 43W
Bula, Indon. 73 3 6 S 130 30 E
Bulan 73 12 40N 123 52 E
Bulandshahr 68 28 28N 77 51 E
Bûlâq 86 25 10N 30 38 E
Bulawayo 91 20 7 S 28 32 E
Buldana 68 20 30N 76 18 E
Bulgan 75 48 45N 103 34 E
Bulgaria ■ 43 42 35N 25 30 E
Bulgroo 99 25 47 S 143 58 E
Bulhar 63 10 25N 44 30 E
Buli, Teluk 73 1 5N 128 25 E
Buliluyan, C. 72 8 20N 117 15 E
Bulki 87 6 11N 36 31 E
Bulkley → 108 55 15N 127 40W
Bull Shoals L. 117 36 40N 93 5W
Bullaque → 31 38 59N 4 17W
Bullas 33 38 2N 1 40W
Bulle 25 46 37N 7 3 E
Buller, Mt. 100 37 10 S 146 28 E
Bullfinch 96 30 58 S 119 3 E
Bulli 99 34 15 S 150 57 E
Bullock Creek 98 17 43 S 144 31 E
Bulloo → 97 28 43 S 142 30 E
Bulloo Downs 99 28 31 S 142 57 E
Bulloo L. 99 28 43 S 142 25 E
Bulls 101 40 10 S 175 24 E
Bully-les-Mines 19 50 27N 2 44 E
Bulnes 124 36 42 S 72 19W
Bulo Burti 63 3 50N 45 33 E
Bulolo 98 7 10 S 146 40 E
Bulqiza 44 41 30N 20 21 E
Bulsar 68 20 40N 72 58 E
Bultfontein 92 28 18 S 26 10 E
Bulu Karakelong 73 4 35N 126 50 E
Bulukumba 73 5 33 S 120 11 E
Bulun 59 70 37N 127 30 E
Bumba 88 2 13N 22 30 E
Bumbiri I. 90 1 40 S 31 55 E
Bumble Bee 119 34 8N 112 18W
Bumhpa Bum 67 26 51N 97 14 E
Bumi → 91 17 0 S 28 20 E
Buna, Kenya 90 2 58N 39 30 E
Buna, P.N.G. 98 8 42 S 148 27 E
Bunazi 90 1 3 S 31 23 E
Bunbah, Khalīj 81 32 20N 23 15 E
Bunbury 96 33 20 S 115 35 E
Buncrana 15 55 8N 7 28W
Bundaberg 97 24 54 S 152 22 E
Bünde 24 52 11N 8 33 E
Bundi 68 25 30N 75 35 E
Bundoran 15 54 24N 8 17W
Bundukia 87 5 14N 30 55 E
Bundure 100 35 10 S 146 1 E
Bungendore 100 35 14 S 149 30 E
Bungo-Suidō 74 33 0N 132 15 E
Bungoma 90 0 34N 34 34 E
Bungu 90 7 35 S 39 0 E
Bungun Shara 75 49 0N 104 0 E
Bunia 90 1 35N 30 20 E
Bunji 69 35 45N 74 40 E
Bunju 72 3 35N 117 50 E
Bunkerville 119 36 47N 114 6W
Bunkie 117 31 1N 92 12W
Bunnell 115 29 28N 81 12W
Buñol 33 39 25N 0 47W
Buntok 72 1 40 S 114 58 E
Bununu 85 9 51N 9 32 E
Bununu Dass 85 10 0N 9 31 E
Bunza 85 12 8N 4 0 E
Buol 73 1 15N 121 32 E
Buorkhaya, Mys 59 71 50N 132 40 E
Buqayq 64 26 0N 49 45 E
Buqei'a 62 32 58N 35 20 E
Bur Acaba 63 3 12N 44 20 E
Bûr Fuad 86 31 15N 32 20 E
Bûr Safâga 86 26 43N 33 57 E
Bûr Sa'îd 86 31 16N 32 18 E
Bûr Sûdân 86 19 32N 37 9 E
Bûr Taufiq 86 29 54N 32 32 E
Bura 90 1 4 S 39 58 E
Buraimī, Al Wāhāt al 65 24 10N 55 43 E
Burao 63 9 32N 45 32 E
Buras 117 29 20N 89 33W
Buraydah 64 26 20N 44 8 E
Burbank 119 34 9N 118 23W
Burcher 99 33 30 S 147 16 E
Burdekin → 98 19 38 S 147 25 E
Burdett 108 49 50N 111 32W
Burdur 64 37 45N 30 22 E
Burdwan 69 23 14N 87 39 E
Bure 87 10 40N 37 4 E
Bure → 12 52 38N 1 45 E
Bureba, La 32 42 36N 3 24W
Büren 24 51 33N 8 34 E
Bureya → 59 49 27N 129 30 E
Burford 112 43 7N 80 27W
Burg, Magdeburg, Ger. 24 52 16N 11 50 E
Burg, Schleswig-Holstein, Ger. 24 54 25N 11 10 E
Burg el Arab 86 30 54N 29 32 E
Burg et Tuyur 86 20 55N 27 56 E
Burgas 43 42 33N 27 29 E
Burgaski Zaliv 43 42 30N 27 39 E
Burgdorf, Ger. 24 52 27N 10 0 E
Burgdorf, Switz. 25 47 3N 7 37 E
Burgenland □ 27 47 20N 16 20 E
Burgeo 107 47 37N 57 38W
Burgersdorp 92 31 0 S 26 20 E
Burghausen 25 48 10N 12 50 E
Bùrgio 40 37 35N 13 18 E
Burglengenfeld 25 49 11N 12 2 E
Burgo de Osma 32 41 35N 3 4W
Burgohondo 30 40 26N 4 47W
Burgos 32 42 21N 3 41W
Burgos □ 32 42 21N 3 42W
Burgstädt 24 50 55N 12 49 E
Burgsteinfurt 24 52 9N 7 23 E
Burgsvik 49 57 3N 18 19 E
Burguillos del Cerro 31 38 23N 6 35W
Burgundy = Bourgogne 19 47 0N 4 30 E
Burhanpur 68 21 18N 76 14 E
Burhou 18 49 45N 2 15W
Buri Pen. 87 15 25N 39 55 E
Burias 73 12 55N 123 5 E
Burica, Pta. 121 8 3N 82 51W
Burigi, L. 90 2 2 S 31 22 E
Burin 107 47 1N 55 14W
Būrīn 62 32 11N 35 15 E
Buriram 71 15 0N 103 0 E
Burji 87 5 29N 37 51 E
Burkburnett 117 34 7N 98 35W
Burke 118 47 31N 115 56W
Burke → 98 23 12 S 139 33 E
Burketown 97 17 45 S 139 33 E
Burk's Falls 106 45 37N 79 24W
Burley 118 42 37N 113 55W
Burlington, Can. 112 43 18N 79 45W
Burlington, Colo., U.S.A. 116 39 21N 102 18W
Burlington, Iowa, U.S.A. 116 40 50N 91 5W
Burlington, Kans., U.S.A. 116 38 15N 95 47W
Burlington, N.C., U.S.A. 115 36 7N 79 27W
Burlington, N.J., U.S.A. 114 40 5N 74 50W
Burlington, Vt., U.S.A. 114 44 27N 73 14W
Burlington, Wash., U.S.A. 118 48 29N 122 19W
Burlington, Wis., U.S.A. 114 42 41N 88 18W
Burlyu-Tyube 58 46 30N 79 10 E
Burma ■ 67 21 0N 96 30 E
Burnaby I. 108 52 25N 131 19W
Burnet 117 30 45N 98 11W
Burnett → 97 24 45 S 152 23 E
Burney 118 40 56N 121 41W
Burnham 112 40 37N 77 34W
Burnie 97 41 4 S 145 56 E
Burnley 12 53 47N 2 15W
Burns, Oreg., U.S.A. 118 43 40N 119 4W
Burns, Wyo., U.S.A. 116 41 13N 104 18W
Burns Lake 108 54 20N 125 45W
Burnside → 104 66 51N 108 4W
Burnt River 112 44 41N 78 42W
Burntwood → 109 56 8N 96 34W
Burntwood L. 109 55 22N 100 26W
Burqā 62 32 18N 35 11 E
Burqān 64 29 0N 47 57 E
Burqin 75 47 43N 87 0 E
Burra 97 33 40 S 138 55 E
Burragorang, L. 100 33 52 S 150 37 E
Burreli 44 41 36N 20 1 E
Burrendong, L. 100 32 45 S 149 10 E
Burrewarra Pt. 100 35 50 S 150 15 E
Burriana 32 39 50N 0 4W
Burrinjuck Dam 100 35 0 S 148 34 E
Burrinjuck Res. 99 35 0 S 148 36 E
Burro, Serranías del 120 29 0N 102 0W
Burruyacú 124 26 30 S 64 40W
Burry Port 13 51 41N 4 17W
Bursa 64 40 15N 29 5 E
Burseryd 49 57 12N 13 17 E
Burstall 109 50 39N 109 54W
Burton L. 106 54 45N 78 20W
Burton-upon-Trent 12 52 48N 1 39W
Burtundy 99 33 45 S 142 15 E
Buru 73 3 30 S 126 30 E
Burullus, Bahra el 86 31 25N 31 0 E
Burundi ■ 90 3 15 S 30 0 E
Burung 72 0 24N 103 33 E
Bururi 90 3 57 S 29 37 E
Burutu 85 5 20N 5 29 E
Burwell 116 41 49N 99 8W
Bury 12 53 36N 2 19W
Bury St. Edmunds 13 52 15N 0 42 E
Buryat A.S.S.R. □ 59 53 0N 110 0 E
Buryn 54 51 13N 33 50 E
Burzenin 28 51 28N 18 47 E
Busalla 38 44 34N 8 58 E
Busango Swamp 91 14 15 S 25 45 E
Buşayyah 64 30 0N 46 10 E
Busca 38 44 31N 7 29 E
Bushati 44 41 58N 19 34 E
Bushell 109 59 31N 108 45W
Bushenyi 90 0 35 S 30 10 E
Bushnell, Ill., U.S.A. 116 40 32N 90 30W
Bushnell, Nebr., U.S.A. 116 41 18N 103 50W
Busia □ 90 0 25N 34 6 E
Busie 84 10 29N 2 22W
Businga 88 3 16N 20 59 E
Buskerud fylke □ 47 60 13N 9 0 E
Busko Zdrój 28 50 28N 20 42 E
Busoga □ 90 0 5N 33 30 E
Busovača 42 44 6N 17 53 E
Busra ash Shām 64 32 30N 36 25 E
Bussang 19 47 50N 6 50 E
Busselton 96 33 42 S 115 15 E
Busseto 38 44 59N 10 2 E
Bussum 16 52 16N 5 10 E
Bustard Hd. 97 24 0 S 151 48 E
Busto Arsizio 38 45 40N 8 50 E
Busto, C. 30 43 34N 6 28W
Busu-Djanoa 88 1 43N 21 23 E
Busuanga 73 12 10N 120 0 E
Büsum 24 54 7N 8 50 E
Buta 90 2 50N 24 53 E
Butare 90 2 31 S 29 52 E
Bute 14 55 48N 5 2W
Bute Inlet 108 50 40N 124 53W
Butemba 90 1 9N 31 37 E
Butembo 90 0 9N 29 18 E
Butera 41 37 10N 14 10 E
Butha Qi 76 48 0N 122 32 E
Butiaba 90 1 50N 31 20 E
Butler, Mo., U.S.A. 116 38 17N 94 18W
Butler, Pa., U.S.A. 114 40 52N 79 52W
Butom Odrzánski 28 51 44N 15 48 E
Butte, Mont., U.S.A. 118 46 0N 112 31W
Butte, Nebr., U.S.A. 116 42 56N 98 54W
Butterworth 71 5 24N 100 23 E
Button B. 109 58 45N 94 23W
Butuan 73 8 57N 125 33 E
Butuku-Luba 85 3 29N 8 33 E
Butung 73 5 0 S 122 45 E
Buturlinovka 55 50 50N 40 35 E
Butzbach 24 50 24N 8 40 E
Bützow 24 53 51N 11 59 E
Buxar 69 25 34N 83 58 E
Buxton, S. Afr. 92 27 38 S 24 42 E
Buxton, U.K. 12 53 16N 1 54W
Buxy 19 46 44N 4 40 E
Buy 55 58 28N 41 28 E
Buyaga 59 59 50N 127 0 E
Buynaksk 57 42 48N 47 7 E
Büyük Çekmece 43 41 2N 28 35 E
Büyük Kemikli Burun 44 40 20N 26 15 E
Buzançais 18 46 54N 1 25 E
Buzău 46 45 10N 26 50 E
Buzău □ 46 45 20N 26 30 E
Buzău → 46 45 10N 27 20 E
Buzău, Pasul 46 45 35N 26 12 E
Buzaymah 81 24 50N 22 2 E
Buzen 74 33 35N 131 5 E
Buzet 39 45 24N 13 58 E
Buzi → 91 19 50 S 34 43 E
Buziaş 42 45 38N 21 36 E
Buzuluk 52 52 48N 52 12 E
Buzuluk → 55 50 15N 42 7 E
Buzzards Bay 114 41 45N 70 38W
Bwana Mkubwe 91 13 8 S 28 38 E
Byala, Ruse, Bulg. 43 43 28N 25 44 E
Byala, Varna, Bulg. 43 42 53N 27 55 E
Byala Slatina 43 43 26N 23 55 E
Byandovan, Mys 57 39 45N 49 28 E
Bychawa 28 51 1N 22 36 E
Byczyna 28 51 7N 18 12 E
Bydgoszcz 28 53 10N 18 0 E
Bydgoszcz □ 28 53 16N 17 33 E
Byelorussian S.S.R. □ 54 53 30N 27 0 E
Byers 116 39 46N 104 13W
Byesville 112 39 56N 81 32W
Bygland 47 58 50N 7 48 E
Byglandsfjord 47 58 40N 7 50 E
Byglandsfjorden 47 58 44N 7 50 E
Byhalia 117 34 53N 89 41W
Bykhov 54 53 31N 30 14 E
Bykle 47 59 20N 7 22 E
Bykovo 57 49 50N 45 25 E
Bylas 119 33 11N 110 9W
Bylderup 49 54 57N 9 6 E
Bylot I. 105 73 13N 78 34W
Byrd, C. 5 69 38 S 76 7W
Byrd Land 5 79 30 S 125 0W
Byrd Sub-Glacial Basin 5 82 0 S 120 0W
Byrock 99 30 40 S 146 27 E
Byron, C. 97 28 38 S 153 40 E
Byrranga, Gory 59 75 0N 100 0 E
Byrum 49 57 16N 11 0 E
Byske 50 64 57N 21 11 E
Byske älv → 50 64 57N 21 13 E
Bystrzyca →, Lublin, Poland 28 51 21N 22 46 E
Bystrzyca →, Wrocław, Poland 28 51 12N 16 55 E
Bystrzyca Kłodzka 28 50 19N 16 39 E
Byten 54 52 50N 25 27 E
Bytom 28 50 25N 18 54 E
Bytów 28 54 10N 17 30 E
Byumba 90 1 35 S 30 4 E
Bzenec 27 48 58N 17 18 E
Bzura → 28 52 25N 20 15 E

C

Ca Mau 71 9 7N 105 8 E
Ca Mau, Mui = Bai Bung 71 8 35N 104 42 E
Caacupé 124 25 23 S 57 5W
Caála 89 12 46 S 15 30 E
Caamano Sd. 108 52 55N 129 25W
Caazapá 124 26 8 S 56 19W
Caazapá □ 125 26 10 S 56 0W
Caballeria, C. de 32 40 5N 4 5 E
Cabañaquinta 30 43 10N 5 38W
Cabanatuan 73 15 30N 120 58 E
Cabanes 32 40 9N 0 2 E
Cabano 107 47 40N 68 56W
Čabar 39 45 36N 14 39 E
Cabedelo 127 7 0 S 34 50W
Cabeza del Buey 31 38 44N 5 13W
Cabildo 124 32 30 S 71 5W
Cabimas 126 10 23N 71 25W
Cabinda 88 5 33 S 12 11 E
Cabinda □ 88 5 0 S 12 30 E
Cabinet Mts. 118 48 0N 115 30W
Cabo Blanco 128 47 15 S 65 47W
Cabo Frio 125 22 51 S 42 3W
Cabo Pantoja 126 1 0 S 75 10W
Cabonga, Réservoir 106 47 20N 76 40W
Cabool 117 37 10N 92 8W
Caboolture 99 27 5 S 152 58 E
Cabora Bassa Dam 91 15 20 S 32 50 E
Caborca (Heroica) 120 30 40N 112 10W
Cabot, Mt. 113 44 30N 71 25W
Cabot Strait 107 47 15N 59 40W
Cabra 31 37 30N 4 28W
Cabra del Santo Cristo 33 37 42N 3 16W
Cábras 40 39 57N 8 30 E
Cabrera, I. 33 39 8N 2 57 E
Cabrera, Sierra 30 42 12N 6 40W
Cabri 109 50 35N 108 25W
Cabriel → 33 39 14N 1 3W
Cacabelos 30 42 36N 6 44W
Čačak 42 43 54N 20 20 E
Cáceres, Brazil 126 16 5 S 57 40W
Cáceres, Spain 31 39 26N 6 23W
Cáceres □ 31 39 45N 6 0W
Cache Bay 106 46 22N 80 0W
Cachepo 31 37 20N 7 49W
Cachéu 84 12 14N 16 8W
Cachi 124 25 5 S 66 10W
Cachimbo, Serra do 127 9 30 S 55 0W
Cachoeira 127 12 30 S 39 0W
Cachoeira de Itapemirim 125 20 51 S 41 7W
Cachoeira do Sul 125 30 3 S 52 53W
Cachopo 31 37 20N 7 49W
Cacólo 88 10 9 S 19 21 E
Caconda 89 13 48 S 15 8 E
Cadarache, Barrage de 21 43 42N 5 47 E
Čadca 27 49 26N 18 45 E
Caddo 117 34 8N 96 18W
Cader Idris 12 52 43N 3 56W
Cadí, Sierra del 32 42 17N 1 42 E
Cadillac, Can. 106 48 14N 78 23W
Cadillac, France 20 44 38N 0 20W
Cadillac, U.S.A. 114 44 16N 85 25W
Cadiz 73 10 57N 123 15 E
Cádiz 31 36 30N 6 20W
Cadiz 112 40 13N 81 0W
Cádiz □ 31 36 36N 5 45W
Cádiz, G. de 31 36 40N 7 0W
Cadomin 108 53 2N 117 20W
Cadotte → 108 56 43N 117 10W
Cadours 20 43 44N 1 2 E
Caen 18 49 10N 0 22W
Caernarfon 12 53 8N 4 17W
Caernarfon B. 12 53 4N 4 40W
Caernarvon = Caernarfon 12 53 8N 4 17W
Caerphilly 13 51 34N 3 13W
Caesarea 62 32 30N 34 53 E
Caeté 127 19 55 S 43 40W

Carbonara, C. Cefalù

Carbonara, C. 40 39 8N 9 30 E
Carbondale, Colo, U.S.A. 118 39 30N 107 10W
Carbondale, Ill., U.S.A. 117 37 45N 89 10W
Carbondale, Pa., U.S.A. 114 41 37N 75 30W
Carbonear 107 47 42N 53 13W
Carboneras 33 37 0N 1 53W
Carboneras de Guadazaón 32 39 54N 1 50W
Carbonia 40 39 10N 8 30 E
Carcabuey 31 37 27N 4 17W
Carcagente 33 39 8N 0 28W
Carcajou 108 57 47N 117 6W
Carcans, Étang d' 20 45 6N 1 7W
Carcasse, C. 121 18 30N 74 28W
Carcassonne 20 43 13N 2 20 E
Carche 33 38 26N 1 9W
Carcross 104 60 13N 134 45W
Cardamom Hills 70 9 30N 77 15 E
Cárdenas, Cuba 121 23 0N 81 30W
Cárdenas, San Luis Potosí, Mexico 120 22 0N 99 41W
Cárdenas, Tabasco, Mexico 120 17 59N 93 21W
Cardenete 32 39 46N 1 41W
Cardiff 13 51 28N 3 11W
Cardigan 13 52 6N 4 41W
Cardigan B. 13 52 30N 4 30W
Cardinal 113 44 47N 75 23W
Cardona, Spain 32 41 56N 1 40 E
Cardona, Uruguay 124 33 53 S 57 18W
Cardoner → 32 41 41N 1 51 E
Cardross 109 49 50N 105 40W
Cardston 108 49 15N 113 20W
Cardwell 98 18 14 S 146 2 E
Careen L. 109 57 0N 108 11W
Carei 46 47 40N 22 29 E
Careme 73 6 55 S 108 27 E
Carentan 18 49 19N 1 15W
Carey, Idaho, U.S.A. 118 43 19N 113 58W
Carey, Ohio, U.S.A. 114 40 58N 83 22W
Carey, L. 96 29 0 S 122 15 E
Carey L. 109 62 12N 102 55W
Careysburg 84 6 34N 10 30W
Cargados Garajos 3 17 0 S 59 0 E
Cargèse 21 42 7N 8 35 E
Carhaix-Plouguer 18 48 18N 3 36W
Carhué 124 37 10 S 62 50W
Caribbean Sea 121 15 0N 75 0W
Cariboo Mts. 108 53 0N 121 0W
Caribou 107 46 55N 68 0W
Caribou →, Man., Can. 109 59 20N 94 44W
Caribou →, N.W.T., Can. 108 61 27N 125 45W
Caribou I. 106 47 22N 85 49W
Caribou Is. 108 61 55N 113 15W
Caribou L., Man., Can. 109 59 21N 96 10W
Caribou L., Ont., Can. 106 50 25N 89 5W
Caribou Mts. 108 59 12N 115 40W
Carignan 19 49 38N 5 10 E
Carignano 38 44 55N 7 40 E
Carinda 99 30 28 S 147 41 E
Cariñena 32 41 20N 1 13W
Carinhanha 127 14 15 S 44 46W
Carini 40 38 9N 13 10 E
Carinola 40 41 11N 13 58 E
Carinthia □ = Kärnten 26 46 52N 13 30 E
Caripito 126 10 8N 63 6W
Caritianas 126 9 20 S 63 6W
Carlbrod = Dimitrovgrad 42 43 0N 22 48 E
Carlentini 41 37 15N 15 2 E
Carleton Place 106 45 8N 76 9W
Carletonville 92 26 23 S 27 22 E
Carlin 118 40 44N 116 5W
Carlingford, L. 15 54 0N 6 5W
Carlinville 116 39 20N 89 55W
Carlisle, U.K. 12 54 54N 2 55W
Carlisle, U.S.A. 114 40 12N 77 10W
Carlitte, Pic 20 42 35N 1 55 E
Carloforte 40 39 10N 8 18 E
Carlos Casares 124 35 32 S 61 20W
Carlos Tejedor 124 35 25 S 62 25W
Carlota, La 124 33 30 S 63 20W
Carlow 15 52 50N 6 58W
Carlow □ 15 52 43N 6 50W
Carlsbad, Calif., U.S.A. 119 33 11N 117 25W
Carlsbad, N. Mex., U.S.A. 117 32 20N 104 14W
Carlyle, Can. 109 49 40N 102 20W
Carlyle, U.S.A. 116 38 38N 89 23W
Carmacks 104 62 5N 136 16W
Carmagnola 38 44 50N 7 42 E
Carman 109 49 30N 98 0W
Carmangay 108 50 10N 113 10W
Carmanville 107 49 23N 54 19W
Carmarthen 13 51 52N 4 20W
Carmarthen B. 13 51 40N 4 30W
Carmaux 20 44 3N 2 10 E
Carmel 113 41 25N 73 38W
Carmel-by-the-Sea 119 36 38N 121 55W
Carmel Mt. 62 32 45N 35 3 E
Carmelo 124 34 0 S 58 20W
Carmen, Colomb. 126 9 43N 75 8W
Carmen, Parag. 125 27 13 S 56 12W
Carmen de Patagones 128 40 50 S 63 0W
Carmen, I. 120 26 0N 111 20W
Cármenes 30 42 58N 5 34W
Carmensa 124 35 15 S 67 40W
Carmi 114 38 6N 88 10W
Carmila 98 21 55 S 149 24 E
Carmona 31 37 28N 5 42W
Carnarvon, Queens., Austral. 98 24 48 S 147 45 E
Carnarvon, W. Austral., Austral. 96 24 51 S 113 42 E
Carnarvon, S. Afr. 92 30 56 S 22 8 E
Carnarvon Ra. 99 25 15 S 148 30 E
Carnaxide 31 38 43N 9 14W
Carndonagh 15 55 15N 7 16W
Carnduff 109 49 10N 101 50W
Carnegie 112 40 24N 80 4W
Carnegie, L. 96 26 5 S 122 30 E
Carnic Alps = Karnische Alpen 26 46 36N 13 0 E
Carnot 88 4 59N 15 56 E
Carnot B. 96 17 20 S 121 30 E
Carnsore Pt. 15 52 10N 6 20W
Caro 114 43 29N 83 27W
Carol City 115 25 5N 80 16W
Carolina, Brazil 127 7 10 S 47 30W
Carolina, S. Afr. 93 26 5 S 30 6 E
Carolina, La 31 38 17N 3 38W
Caroline I. 95 9 15 S 150 3W
Caroline Is. 94 8 0N 150 0 E
Caron 109 50 30N 105 50W
Caroni → 126 8 21N 62 43W
Carovigno 41 40 42N 17 40 E
Carpathians 46 49 50N 21 0 E
Carpaţii Meridionali 46 45 30N 25 0 E
Carpenédolo 38 45 22N 10 25 E
Carpentaria Downs 98 18 44 S 144 20 E
Carpentaria, G. of 97 14 0 S 139 0 E
Carpentras 21 44 3N 5 2 E
Carpi 38 44 47N 10 52 E
Carpino 41 41 50N 15 51 E
Carpinteria 119 34 25N 119 31W
Carpio 30 41 13N 5 7W
Carrabelle 115 29 52N 84 40W
Carrara 38 44 5N 10 7 E
Carrascosa del Campo 32 40 2N 2 45W
Carrauntohill, Mt. 15 52 0N 9 49W
Carrick-on-Shannon 15 53 57N 8 7W
Carrick-on-Suir 15 52 22N 7 30W
Carrickfergus 15 54 43N 5 50W
Carrickfergus □ 15 54 43N 5 49W
Carrickmacross 15 54 0N 6 43W
Carrieton 99 32 25 S 138 31 E
Carrington 116 47 30N 99 7W
Carrión → 30 41 53N 4 32W
Carrión de los Condes 30 42 20N 4 37W
Carrizal Bajo 124 28 5 S 71 20W
Carrizalillo 124 29 5 S 71 30W
Carrizo Cr. 117 36 30N 103 40W
Carrizo Springs 117 28 28N 99 50W
Carrizozo 119 33 40N 105 57W
Carroll 116 42 2N 94 55W
Carrollton, Ga., U.S.A. 115 33 36N 85 5W
Carrollton, Ill., U.S.A. 116 39 20N 90 25W
Carrollton, Ky., U.S.A. 114 38 40N 85 10W
Carrollton, Mo., U.S.A. 116 39 19N 93 24W
Carrollton, Ohio, U.S.A. 112 40 31N 81 9W
Carron → 14 57 30N 5 30W
Carron, L. 14 57 22N 5 35W
Carrot → 109 53 50N 101 17W
Carrot River 109 53 17N 103 35W
Carrouges 18 48 34N 0 10W
Carruthers 109 52 52N 109 16W
Çarşamba 64 41 15N 36 45 E
Carse of Gowrie 14 56 30N 3 10W
Carsoli 39 42 7N 13 3 E
Carson 116 46 27N 101 29W
Carson City 118 39 12N 119 46W
Carson Sink 118 39 50N 118 40W
Carsonville 114 43 25N 82 39W
Carstairs 14 55 42N 3 41W
Cartagena, Colomb. 126 10 25N 75 33W
Cartagena, Spain 33 37 38N 0 59W
Cartago, Colomb. 126 4 45N 75 55W
Cartago, C. Rica 121 9 50N 85 52W
Cartaxo 31 39 10N 8 47W
Cartaya 31 37 16N 7 9W
Carteret 18 49 23N 1 47W
Cartersville 115 34 11N 84 48W
Carterton 101 41 2 S 175 31 E
Carthage, Ark., U.S.A. 117 34 4N 92 32W
Carthage, Ill., U.S.A. 116 40 25N 91 10W
Carthage, Mo., U.S.A. 117 37 10N 94 20W
Carthage, N.Y., U.S.A. 114 43 59N 75 37W
Carthage, S.D., U.S.A. 116 44 14N 97 38W
Carthage, Texas, U.S.A. 117 32 8N 94 20W
Cartier I. 96 12 31 S 123 29 E
Cartwright 107 53 41N 56 58W
Caruaru 127 8 15 S 35 55W
Carúpano 126 10 39N 63 15W
Caruthersville 117 36 10N 89 40W
Carvin 19 50 30N 2 57 E
Carvoeiro 126 1 30 S 61 59W
Carvoeiro, Cabo 31 39 21N 9 24W
Casa Branca 31 38 29N 8 12W
Casa Grande 119 32 53N 111 51W
Casa Nova 127 9 25 S 41 5W
Casablanca, Chile 124 33 20 S 71 25W
Casablanca, Moroc. 82 33 36N 7 36W
Casacalenda 41 41 45N 14 50 E
Casal di Principe 41 41 0N 14 8 E
Casalbordino 39 42 10N 14 34 E
Casale Monferrato 38 45 8N 8 28 E
Casalmaggiore 38 44 59N 10 25 E
Casalpusterlengo 38 45 10N 9 40 E
Casamance → 84 12 33N 16 46W
Casamássima 41 40 58N 16 55 E
Casarano 41 40 0N 18 10 E
Casares 31 36 27N 5 16W
Casas Grandes 120 30 22N 108 0W
Casas Ibañez 33 39 17N 1 30W
Casasimarro 33 39 22N 2 3W
Casatejada 30 39 54N 5 40W
Casavieja 30 40 17N 4 46W
Cascade, Idaho, U.S.A. 118 44 30N 116 2W
Cascade, Mont., U.S.A. 118 47 16N 111 46W
Cascade Locks 118 45 44N 121 54W
Cascade Ra. 102 47 0N 121 30W
Cascais 31 38 41N 9 25W
Cáscina 38 43 40N 10 32 E
Caselle Torinese 38 45 12N 7 39 E
Caserta 41 41 5N 14 20 E
Cashel 15 52 31N 7 53W
Cashmere 118 47 31N 120 30W
Casiguran 73 16 22N 122 7 E
Casilda 124 33 10 S 61 10W
Casimcea 46 44 45N 28 23 E
Casino 97 28 52 S 153 3 E
Casiquiare → 126 2 1N 67 7W
Caslan 108 54 38N 112 31W
Čáslav 26 49 54N 15 22 E
Casma 126 9 30 S 78 20W
Casola Valsenio 39 44 12N 11 40 E
Cásoli 39 42 7N 14 18 E
Caspe 32 41 14N 0 1W
Casper 118 42 52N 106 20W
Caspian Sea 53 43 0N 50 0 E
Casquets 18 49 46N 2 15W
Cass City 114 43 34N 83 24W
Cass Lake 116 47 23N 94 38W
Cassá de la Selva 32 41 53N 2 52 E
Cassano Iónio 41 39 47N 16 20 E
Cassel 19 50 48N 2 30 E
Casselman 113 45 19N 75 5W
Casselton 116 47 0N 97 15W
Cassiar 108 59 16N 129 40W
Cassiar Mts. 108 59 30N 130 30W
Cassino 40 41 30N 13 50 E
Cassis 21 43 14N 5 32 E
Cassville 117 36 45N 93 52W
Cástagneto Carducci 38 43 9N 10 36 E
Castéggio 38 45 1N 9 8 E
Castejón de Monegros 32 41 37N 0 15W
Castel di Sangro 39 41 47N 14 6 E
Castel San Giovanni 38 45 4N 9 25 E
Castel San Pietro 39 44 23N 11 30 E
Castelbuono 41 37 56N 14 4 E
Casteldelfino 38 44 35N 7 4 E
Castelfiorentino 38 43 36N 10 58 E
Castelfranco Emília 38 44 37N 11 2 E
Castelfranco Véneto 39 45 40N 11 56 E
Casteljaloux 20 44 19N 0 6 E
Castellabate 41 40 18N 14 55 E
Castellammare del Golfo 40 38 2N 12 53 E
Castellammare di Stábia 41 40 47N 14 29 E
Castellammare, G. di 40 38 5N 12 55 E
Castellamonte 38 45 23N 7 42 E
Castellana Grotte 41 40 53N 17 10 E
Castellane 21 43 50N 6 31 E
Castellaneta 41 40 40N 16 57 E
Castellar de Santisteban 33 38 16N 3 8W
Castelleone 38 45 19N 9 47 E
Castelli 124 36 7 S 57 47W
Castelló de Ampurias 32 42 15N 3 4 E
Castellón □ 32 40 15N 0 5W
Castellón de la Plana 32 39 58N 0 3W
Castellote 32 40 48N 0 15W
Castelltersol 32 41 45N 2 8 E
Castelmáuro 41 41 50N 14 40 E
Castelnau-de-Médoc 20 45 2N 0 48W
Castelnaudary 20 43 20N 1 58 E
Castelnovo ne' Monti 38 44 27N 10 26 E
Castelnuovo di Val di Cécina 38 43 12N 10 54 E
Castelo 125 20 33 S 41 14 E
Castelo Branco 30 39 50N 7 31W
Castelo Branco □ 30 39 52N 7 45W
Castelo de Paiva 30 41 2N 8 16W
Castelo de Vide 31 39 25N 7 27W
Castelsarrasin 20 44 2N 1 7 E
Casteltérmini 40 37 32N 13 38 E
Castelvetrano 40 37 40N 12 46 E
Casterton 99 37 30 S 141 30 E
Castets 20 43 52N 1 6W
Castiglione del Lago 39 43 7N 12 3 E
Castiglione della Pescáia 38 42 46N 10 53 E
Castiglione della Stiviere 38 45 23N 10 30 E
Castiglione Fiorentino 39 43 20N 11 55 E
Castilblanco 31 39 17N 5 5W
Castilla La Nueva 31 39 45N 3 20W
Castilla La Vieja 30 41 55N 4 0W
Castilla, Playa de 31 37 0N 6 33W
Castille = Castilla 30 40 0N 3 30W
Castillon, Barrage de 21 43 53N 6 33 E
Castillon-en-Couserans 20 42 56N 1 1 E
Castillon-la-Bataille 20 44 51N 0 2W
Castillonès 20 44 39N 0 37 E
Castillos 125 34 12 S 53 52W
Castle Dale 118 39 11N 111 1W
Castle Douglas 14 54 57N 3 57W
Castle Harbour 121 32 17N 64 44W
Castle Point 101 40 54 S 176 15 E
Castle Rock, Colo., U.S.A. 116 39 26N 104 50W
Castle Rock, Wash., U.S.A. 118 46 20N 122 58W
Castlebar 15 53 52N 9 17W
Castleblaney 15 54 7N 6 44W
Castlegar 108 49 20N 117 40W
Castlegate 118 39 45N 110 57W
Castlemaine 97 37 2 S 144 12 E
Castlereagh 15 53 47N 8 30W
Castlereagh □ 15 54 33N 5 53W
Castlereagh → 97 30 12 S 147 32 E
Castlereagh B. 96 12 10 S 135 10 E
Castletown 12 54 4N 4 40W
Castletown Bearhaven 15 51 40N 9 54W
Castlevale 98 24 30 S 146 48 E
Castor 108 52 15N 111 50W
Castres 20 43 37N 2 13 E
Castries 121 14 0N 60 50W
Castril 33 37 48N 2 46W
Castro, Brazil 125 24 45 S 50 0W
Castro, Chile 128 42 30 S 73 50W
Castro Alves 127 12 46 S 39 33W
Castro del Rio 31 37 41N 4 29W
Castro Marim 31 37 13N 7 26W
Castro Urdiales 32 43 23N 3 11W
Castro Verde 31 37 41N 8 4W
Castrojeriz 30 42 17N 4 9W
Castropol 30 43 32N 7 0W
Castroreale 41 38 5N 15 15 E
Castrovillari 41 39 49N 16 11 E
Castroville 117 29 20N 98 53W
Castuera 31 38 43N 5 37W
Casummit Lake 106 51 29N 92 22W
Cat I., Bahamas 121 24 30N 75 30W
Cat I., U.S.A. 117 30 15N 89 7W
Cat L. 106 51 40N 91 50W
Čata 27 47 58N 18 38 E
Catacáos 126 5 20 S 80 45W
Cataguases 125 21 23 S 42 39W
Catahoula L. 117 31 30N 92 5W
Catalão 127 18 10 S 47 57W
Catalina 107 48 31N 53 4W
Catalonia = Cataluña 32 41 40N 1 15 E
Cataluña 32 41 40N 1 15 E
Catamarca 124 28 30 S 65 50W
Catamarca □ 124 27 0 S 65 50W
Catanduanes 73 13 50N 124 20 E
Catanduva 125 21 5 S 48 58W
Catánia 41 37 31N 15 4 E
Catánia, G. di 41 37 25N 15 8 E
Catanzaro 41 38 54N 16 38 E
Catarman 73 12 28N 124 35 E
Catastrophe C. 96 34 59 S 136 0 E
Cateau, Le 19 50 6N 3 30 E
Cateel 73 7 47N 126 24 E
Cathcart 92 32 18 S 27 10 E
Cathlamet 118 46 12N 123 23W
Catio 84 11 17N 15 15W
Cativa 120 9 21N 79 49W
Catlettsburg 114 38 23N 82 38W
Cato I. 97 23 15 S 155 32 E
Catoche, C. 120 21 40N 87 8W
Catral 33 38 10N 0 47W
Catria, Mt. 39 43 28N 12 42 E
Catrimani 126 0 27N 61 41W
Catskill 114 42 14N 73 52W
Catskill Mts. 114 42 15N 74 15W
Cattaraugus 112 42 22N 78 52W
Cattólica 39 43 58N 12 43 E
Cattólica Eraclea 40 37 27N 13 24 E
Catuala 92 16 25 S 19 2 E
Catur 91 13 45 S 35 30 E
Cauca → 126 8 54N 74 28W
Caucaia 127 3 40 S 38 35W
Caucasus Mts. = Bolshoi Kavkas 57 42 50N 44 0 E
Caudebec-en-Caux 18 49 30N 0 42 E
Caudete 33 38 42N 1 2W
Caudry 19 50 7N 3 22 E
Caulnes 18 48 18N 2 10W
Caulónia 41 38 23N 16 25 E
Caúngula 88 8 26 S 18 38 E
Cauquenes 124 36 0 S 72 22W
Caura → 126 7 38N 64 53W
Cauresi → 91 17 8 S 33 0 E
Causapscal 107 48 19N 67 12W
Caussade 20 44 10N 1 33 E
Cauterets 20 42 52N 0 8W
Caux, Pays de 18 49 38N 0 35 E
Cava dei Tirreni 41 40 42N 14 42 E
Cávado → 30 41 32N 8 48W
Cavaillon 21 43 50N 5 2 E
Cavalaire-sur-Mer 21 43 10N 6 33 E
Cavalerie, La 20 44 0N 3 10 E
Cavalese 39 46 17N 11 29 E
Cavalier 116 48 50N 97 39W
Cavallo, Île de 21 41 22N 9 16 E
Cavally → 84 4 22N 7 32W
Cavan 15 54 0N 7 22W
Cavan □ 15 53 58N 7 10W
Cavárzere 39 45 8N 12 6 E
Cave City 114 37 13N 85 57W
Cavendish 99 37 31 S 142 2 E
Caviana, I. 127 0 10N 50 10W
Cavite 73 14 29N 120 55 E
Cavour 38 44 47N 7 22 E
Cavtat 42 42 35N 18 13 E
Cawndilla, L. 99 32 30 S 142 15 E
Cawnpore = Kanpur 69 26 28N 80 20 E
Caxias 127 4 55 S 43 20W
Caxias do Sul 125 29 10 S 51 10W
Caxine, C. 82 35 56N 0 27W
Caxito 88 8 30 S 13 30 E
Cay Sal Bank 121 23 45N 80 0W
Cayambe 126 0 3N 78 8W
Cayce 115 33 59N 81 10W
Cayenne 127 5 0N 52 18W
Cayes, Les 121 18 15N 73 46W
Cayeux-sur-Mer 19 50 10N 1 30 E
Caylus 20 44 15N 1 47 E
Cayman Is. 121 19 40N 80 30W
• Cayo 120 17 10N 89 0W
Cayo Romano 121 22 0N 78 0W
Cayuga, Can. 112 42 59N 79 50W
Cayuga, U.S.A. 113 42 54N 76 44W
Cayuga L. 114 42 45N 76 45W
Cazalla de la Sierra 31 37 56N 5 45W
Căzăneşti 46 44 36N 27 3 E
Cazaux et de Sanguinet, Étang de 20 44 29N 1 10W
Cazères 20 43 13N 1 5 E
Cazin 39 44 57N 15 57 E
Čazma 39 45 45N 16 39 E
Čazma → 39 45 35N 16 29 E
Cazombo 89 11 54 S 22 56 E
Cazorla 33 37 55N 3 2W
Cazorla, Sierra de 33 38 5N 2 55W
Cea → 30 42 0N 5 36W
Ceamurlia de Jos 43 44 43N 28 47 E
Ceanannus Mor 15 53 42N 6 53W
Ceará = Fortaleza 127 3 43 S 38 35W
Ceará □ 127 5 0 S 40 0W
Ceará Mirim 127 5 38 S 35 25W
Ceauru, L. 46 44 58N 23 11 E
Cebollar 124 29 10 S 66 35W
Cebollera, Sierra de 32 42 0N 2 30W
Cebreros 30 40 27N 4 28W
Cebu 73 10 18N 123 54 E
Ceccano 40 41 34N 13 18 E
Cece 27 46 46N 18 39 E
Cechi 84 6 15N 4 25W
Cecil Plains 99 27 30 S 151 11 E
Cécina 38 43 19N 10 33 E
Cécina → 38 43 19N 10 29 E
Ceclavin 30 39 50N 6 45W
Cedar → 116 41 17N 91 21W
Cedar City 119 37 41N 113 3W
Cedar Creek Res. 117 32 4N 96 5W
Cedar Falls 116 42 39N 92 29W
Cedar Key 115 29 9N 83 5W
Cedar L. 109 53 10N 100 0W
Cedar Rapids 116 42 0N 91 38W
Cedarburg 114 43 18N 87 55W
Cedartown 115 34 1N 85 15W
Cedarvale 108 55 1N 128 22W
Cedarville 118 41 37N 120 13W
Cedeira 30 43 39N 8 2W
Cedral 120 23 50N 100 42W
Cedrino → 40 40 23N 9 44 E
Cedro 127 6 34 S 39 3W
Cedros, I. de 120 28 10N 115 20W
Ceduna 96 32 7 S 133 46 E
Cedynia 28 52 53N 14 12 E
Cefalù 41 38 3N 14 1 E

Renamed N'gage

• Renamed San Ignacio

HIA

Cega Chelmsford

Cega → 30 41 33N 4 46W
Cegléd 27 47 11N 19 47 E
Céglie Messápico 41 40 39N 17 31 E
Cehegín 33 38 6N 1 48W
Cehu-Silvaniei 46 47 24N 23 9 E
Ceiba, La 121 15 40N 86 50W
Ceica 46 46 53N 22 10 E
Ceira → 30 40 13N 8 16W
Cekhira 83 34 20N 10 5 E
Celano 39 42 6N 13 30 E
Celanova 30 42 9N 7 58W
Celaya 120 20 31N 100 37W
Celbridge 15 53 20N 6 33W
Celebes = Sulawesi 73 2 0S 120 0 E
Celebes Sea 73 3 0N 123 0 E
Čelić 42 44 43N 18 47 E
Celina 114 40 32N 84 31W
Celje 39 46 16N 15 18 E
Celldömölk 27 47 16N 17 10 E
Celle 24 52 37N 10 4 E
Celorico da Beira 30 40 38N 7 24W
Cement 117 34 56N 98 8W
Cengong 77 27 13N 108 44 E
Cenis, Col du Mt. 21 45 15N 6 55 E
Ceno → 38 44 4N 10 5 E
Cenon 20 44 50N 0 33W
Centallo 38 44 30N 7 35 E
Center, N.D., U.S.A. 116 47 9N 101 17W
Center, Texas, U.S.A. 117 31 50N 94 10W
Centerfield 119 39 9N 111 56W
Centerville, Ala., U.S.A. 115 32 55N 87 7W
Centerville, Iowa, U.S.A. 116 40 45N 92 57W
Centerville, Miss., U.S.A. 117 31 10N 91 3W
Centerville, Pa., U.S.A. 112 40 3N 79 59W
Centerville, S.D., U.S.A. 116 43 10N 96 58W
Centerville, Tenn., U.S.A. 115 35 46N 87 29W
Centerville, Tex., U.S.A. 117 31 15N 95 56W
Cento 39 44 43N 11 16 E
Central 119 32 46N 108 9W
Central □, Kenya 90 0 30S 37 30 E
Central □, Malawi 91 13 30S 33 30 E
Central □, U.K. 14 56 10N 4 30W
Central □, Zambia 91 14 25S 28 50 E
Central African Republic ■ 88 7 0N 20 0 E
Central City, Ky., U.S.A. 114 37 20N 87 7W
Central City, Nebr., U.S.A. 116 41 8N 98 0W
Central, Cordillera, Colomb. 126 5 0N 75 0W
Central, Cordillera, C. Rica 121 10 10N 84 5W
Central I. 90 3 30N 36 0 E
Central Islip 113 40 49N 73 13W
Central Makran Range 65 26 30N 64 15 E
Central Patricia 106 51 30N 90 9W
Central Ra. 98 5 0S 143 0 E
Central Russian Uplands 9 54 0N 36 0 E
Central Siberian Plateau 59 65 0N 105 0 E
Centralia, Ill., U.S.A. 116 38 32N 89 5W
Centralia, Mo., U.S.A. 116 39 12N 92 6W
Centralia, Wash., U.S.A. 118 46 46N 122 59W
Centúripe 41 37 37N 14 41 E
Cephalonia = Kefallinía 45 38 15N 20 30 E
Cepin 42 45 32N 18 34 E
Ceprano 40 41 33N 13 30 E
Ceptura 46 45 1N 26 21 E
Cepu 73 7 12S 111 31 E
Ceram = Seram 73 3 10S 129 0 E
Ceram Sea = Seram Sea 73 2 30S 128 30 E
Cerbère 20 42 26N 3 10 E
Cerbicales, Îles 21 41 33N 9 22 E
Cerbu 46 44 46N 24 46 E
Cercal 31 37 48N 8 40W
Cercemaggiore 41 41 27N 14 43 E
Cerdaña 32 42 22N 1 35 E
Cerdedo 30 42 33N 8 23W
Cère → 20 44 55N 1 49 E
Cerea 39 45 12N 11 13 E
Ceres, Argent. 124 29 55S 61 55W
Ceres, Italy 38 45 19N 7 22 E
Ceres, S. Afr. 92 33 21S 19 18 E
Céret 20 42 30N 2 42 E
Cerignola 41 41 17N 15 53 E
Cerigo = Kíthira 45 36 15N 23 0 E
Cérilly 20 46 37N 2 50 E
Cerisiers 19 48 8N 3 30 E
Cerizay 18 46 50N 0 40W
Çerkeş 64 40 49N 32 52 E
Cerknica 39 45 48N 14 21 E
Cermerno 42 43 35N 20 25 E
Cerna 46 45 4N 28 17 E
Cerna → 46 44 45N 24 0 E
Cernavodă 46 44 22N 28 3 E
Cernay 19 47 44N 7 10 E
Cernik 42 45 17N 17 22 E
Cerralvo 120 24 20N 109 45 E
Cerreto Sannita 41 41 17N 14 34 E
Cerritos 120 22 27N 100 20W
Cerro 119 36 47N 105 36W
Certaldo 38 43 32N 11 2 E
Cervaro → 41 41 30N 15 52 E
Cervera 32 41 40N 1 16 E
Cervera de Pisuerga 30 42 51N 4 30W
Cervera del Río Alhama 32 42 2N 1 58W
Cérvia 39 44 15N 12 20 E
Cervignano del Friuli 39 45 49N 13 20 E
Cervinara 41 41 2N 14 36 E
Cervione 21 42 20N 9 29 E
Cervo 30 43 40N 7 24W
Cesaro 41 37 50N 14 38 E
Cesena 39 44 9N 12 14 E
Cesenático 39 44 12N 12 22 E
Cēsis 54 57 17N 25 28 E
Česká Lípa 26 50 45N 14 30 E
Česká Socialistická Republika □ 26 49 30N 14 40 E
Česká Třebová 27 49 54N 16 27 E
České Budějovice 26 48 55N 14 25 E
České Velenice 26 48 45N 15 1 E
Ceskomoravská Vrchovina 26 49 30N 15 40 E
Český Brod 26 50 4N 14 52 E
Český Krumlov 26 48 43N 14 21 E
Český Těšín 27 49 45N 18 39 E
Çeşme 45 38 20N 26 23 E
Cessnock 97 32 50S 151 21 E
Cestas 20 44 44N 0 41W
Cestos → 84 5 40N 9 10W
Cetate 46 44 7N 23 2 E
Cétin Grad 39 45 9N 15 45 E
Cetina → 39 43 26N 16 42 E
Cetinje 42 42 23N 18 59 E
Cetraro 41 39 30N 15 56 E
Ceuta 82 35 52N 5 18W
Ceva 38 44 23N 8 3 E
Cévennes 20 44 10N 3 50 E
Ceyhan 64 37 4N 35 47 E
Ceylon = Sri Lanka ■ 70 7 30N 80 50 E
Cèze → 21 44 13N 4 43 E
Cha Pa 71 22 20N 103 47 E
Chabeuil 21 44 54N 5 1 E
Chablais 21 46 20N 6 36 E
Chablis 19 47 47N 3 48 E
Chabounia 82 35 30N 2 38 E
Chacabuco 124 34 40S 60 27W
Chachapoyas 126 6 15S 77 50W
Chachro 68 25 5N 70 15 E
Chaco □ 124 26 30S 61 0W
Chad ■ 81 15 0N 17 15 E
Chad, L. = Tchad, L. 81 13 30N 14 30 E
Chadan 59 51 17N 91 35 E
Chadileuvú → 124 37 46S 66 0W
Chadiza 91 14 45S 32 27 E
Chadron 116 42 50N 103 0W
Chadyr-Lunga 56 46 3N 28 51 E
Chagda 59 58 45N 130 38 E
Chagny 19 46 57N 4 45 E
Chagoda 54 59 10N 35 15 E
Chagos Arch. 60 6 0S 72 0 E
Chágres → 120 9 10N 79 40W
Chāh Bahār 65 25 20N 60 40 E
Chāh Gay Hills 65 29 30N 64 0 E
Chaillé-les-Marais 20 46 25N 1 2W
Chaise-Dieu, La 20 45 20N 3 40 E
Chaize-le-Vicomte, La 18 46 40N 1 18W
Chaj Doab 68 32 15N 73 0 E
Chajari 124 30 42S 58 0W
Chake Chake 90 5 15S 39 45 E
Chakhansur 65 31 10N 62 0 E
Chakhansur □ 65 30 0N 62 0 E
Chakonipau, L. 107 56 18N 68 30W
Chakradharpur 69 22 45N 85 40 E
Chakwal 68 32 56N 72 53 E
Chala 126 15 48S 74 20W
Chalais 20 45 16N 0 3 E
Chalakudi 70 10 18N 76 20 E
Chalcis = Khalkis 45 38 27N 23 42 E
Chaleur B. 107 47 55N 65 30W
Chalhuanca 126 14 15S 73 15W
Chalindrey 19 47 48N 5 26 E
Chaling 77 26 58N 113 30 E
Chalisgaon 70 20 30N 75 10 E
Chalkar 57 50 35N 51 52 E
Chalkar Oz. 57 50 33N 51 45 E
Chalky Inlet 101 46 3S 166 31 E
Challans 18 46 50N 1 52W
Challapata 126 18 53S 66 50W
Challerange 19 49 18N 4 46 E
Challis 118 44 32N 114 25W
Chalna 69 22 36N 89 35 E
Chalon-sur-Saône 19 46 48N 4 50 E
Chalonnes 18 47 20N 0 45W
Châlons-sur-Marne 19 48 58N 4 20 E
Châlus 20 45 39N 0 58 E
Cham 25 49 12N 12 40 E
Chama 119 36 54N 106 35W
Chaman 66 30 58N 66 25 E
Chamarajnagar-Ramasamudram 70 11 52N 76 52 E
Chamartín de la Rosa 32 40 28N 3 40W
Chamba 68 32 35N 76 10 E
Chambal → 69 26 29N 79 15 E
Chamberlain 116 43 50N 99 21W
Chambers 119 35 13N 109 30W
Chambersburg 114 39 53N 77 41W
Chambéry 21 45 34N 5 55 E
Chambly 113 45 27N 73 17W
Chambois 18 48 48N 0 6 E
Chambon-Feugerolles, Le 21 45 24N 4 18 E
Chambord 107 48 25N 72 6W
Chambri L. 98 4 15S 143 10 E
Chamical 124 30 22S 66 27W
Chamonix 21 45 55N 6 51 E
Champa 69 22 2N 82 43 E
Champagne, Can. 108 60 49N 136 30W
Champagne, France 19 49 0N 4 40 E
Champagne, Plaine de 19 49 0N 4 30 E
Champagnole 19 46 45N 5 55 E
Champaign 114 40 8N 88 14W
Champaubert 19 48 50N 3 45 E
Champdeniers 20 46 29N 0 25W
Champeix 20 45 37N 3 8 E
Champion B. 96 28 44S 114 36 E
Champlain, Can. 106 46 27N 72 24W
Champlain, U.S.A. 114 44 59N 73 27W
Champlain, L. 114 44 30N 73 20W
Champotón 120 19 20N 90 50W
Chamusca 31 39 21N 8 29W
Chañaral 124 26 23S 70 40W
Chanasma 68 23 44N 72 5 E
Chandalar 104 67 30N 148 35W
Chandannagar 69 22 52N 88 24 E
Chandausi 68 28 27N 78 49 E
Chandeleur Is. 117 29 48N 88 51W
Chandeleur Sd. 117 29 58N 88 40W
Chandigarh 68 30 43N 76 47 E
Chandler, Can. 107 48 18N 64 46W
Chandler, Ariz., U.S.A. 119 33 20N 111 56W
Chandler, Okla., U.S.A. 117 35 43N 96 53W
Chandmani 75 45 22N 98 2 E
Chandpur, Bangla. 69 23 8N 90 45 E
Chandpur, India 68 29 8N 78 19 E
Chandrapur 70 19 57N 79 25 E
Chang 68 26 59N 68 30 E
Chang Jiang →, Jiangsu, China 75 31 48N 121 10 E
Chang Jiang →, Shanghai, China 75 31 35N 121 15 E
Changanacheri 70 9 25N 76 31 E
Changbai 76 41 25N 128 5 E
Changbai Shan 76 42 20N 129 0 E
Changchiak'ou = Zhangjiakou 76 40 48N 114 55 E
Ch'angchou = Changzhou 75 31 47N 119 58 E
Changchun 76 43 57N 125 17 E
Changde 75 29 4N 111 35 E
Changfeng 77 32 28N 117 10 E
Changhai = Shanghai 75 31 15N 121 26 E
Changjiang 75 19 20N 108 55 E
Changjin-chŏsuji 76 40 30N 127 15 E
Changle 77 25 59N 119 27 E
Changli 76 39 40N 119 13 E
Changning 77 26 28N 112 22 E
Changping 76 40 14N 116 12 E
Changsha 75 28 12N 113 0 E
Changshou 77 29 51N 107 8 E
Changshu 77 31 38N 120 43 E
Changshun 77 26 3N 106 25 E
Changtai 77 24 35N 117 42 E
Changting 75 25 50N 116 22 E
Changyang 77 30 30N 111 10 E
Changzhi 76 36 10N 113 6 E
Changzhou 75 31 47N 119 58 E
Chanhanga 92 16 0S 14 8 E
Chanlar 57 40 25N 46 10 E
Channapatna 70 12 40N 77 15 E
Channel Is., U.K. 18 49 30N 2 40W
Channel Is., U.S.A. 119 33 55N 119 26W
Channel-Port aux Basques 107 47 30N 59 9W
Channing, Mich., U.S.A. 114 46 9N 88 1W
Channing, Tex., U.S.A. 117 35 45N 102 20W
Chantada 30 42 36N 7 46W
Chanthaburi 71 12 38N 102 12 E
Chantilly 19 49 12N 2 29 E
Chantonnay 18 46 40N 1 3W
Chantrey Inlet 104 67 48N 96 20W
Chanute 117 37 45N 95 25W
Chanza → 31 37 32N 7 30W
Chao Hu 77 31 30N 117 30 E
Chao Phraya → 71 13 32N 100 36 E
Chao'an 75 23 42N 116 32 E
Chaoyang, Guangdong, China 75 23 17N 116 30 E
Chaoyang, Liaoning, China 76 41 35N 120 22 E
Chapala 91 15 50S 37 35 E
Chapala, Lago de 120 20 10N 103 20W
Chapayevo 57 50 25N 51 10 E
Chapayevsk 55 53 0N 49 40 E
Chapecó 125 27 14S 52 41W
Chapel Hill 115 35 53N 79 3W
Chapelle-d'Angillon, La 19 47 21N 2 25 E
Chapelle-Glain, La 18 47 38N 1 11W
Chapleau 106 47 50N 83 24W
Chaplin 109 50 28N 106 40W
Chaplino 56 48 8N 36 15 E
Chaplygin 55 53 15N 40 0 E
Chapra 69 25 48N 84 44 E
Châr 80 21 32N 12 45 E
Chara 59 56 54N 118 20 E
Charadai 124 27 35S 60 0W
Charagua 126 19 45S 63 10W
Charaña 126 17 30S 69 25W
Charata 124 27 13S 61 14W
Charcas 120 23 10N 101 20W
Charcoal L. 109 58 49N 102 22W
Charcot I. 5 70 0S 75 0W
Chard 13 50 52N 2 59W
Chardara 58 41 16N 67 59 E
Chardon 112 41 34N 81 17W
Chardzhou 58 39 6N 63 34 E
Charente 20 45 40N 0 5 E
Charente □ 20 45 50N 0 16 E
Charente → 20 45 57N 1 5W
Charente-Maritime □ 20 45 30N 0 35W
Charentsavan 57 40 35N 44 41 E
Chārīkār 65 35 0N 69 10 E
Charité, La 19 47 10N 3 0 E
Chariton → 116 39 19N 92 58W
Charkhari 69 25 24N 79 45 E
Charkhi Dadri 68 28 37N 76 17 E
Charleroi 16 50 24N 4 27 E
Charleroi 112 40 8N 79 54W
Charles, C. 114 37 10N 75 59W
Charles City 116 43 2N 92 41W
Charles L. 109 59 50N 110 33W
Charles Town 114 39 20N 77 50W
Charleston, Ill., U.S.A. 114 39 30N 88 10W
Charleston, Miss., U.S.A. 117 34 2N 90 3W
Charleston, Mo., U.S.A. 117 36 52N 89 20W
Charleston, S.C., U.S.A. 115 32 47N 79 56W
Charleston, W. Va., U.S.A. 114 38 24N 81 36W
Charleston Harb. 115 32 46N 79 55W
Charlestown, S. Afr. 93 27 26S 29 53 E
Charlestown, U.S.A. 114 38 29N 85 40W
Charlesville 88 5 27S 20 59 E
Charleville 97 26 24S 146 15 E
Charleville = Rath Luirc 15 52 21N 8 40W
Charleville-Mézières 19 49 44N 4 40 E
Charlevoix 114 45 19N 85 14W
Charlieu 21 46 10N 4 10 E
Charlotte, Mich., U.S.A. 114 42 36N 84 48W
Charlotte, N.C., U.S.A. 115 35 16N 80 46W
Charlotte Amalie 121 18 22N 64 56W
Charlotte Harbor 115 26 58N 82 4W
Charlotte Waters 96 25 56S 134 54 E
Charlottenberg 48 59 54N 12 17 E
Charlottesville 114 38 1N 78 30W
Charlottetown 107 46 14N 63 8W
Charlton, Austral. 99 36 16S 143 24 E
Charlton, U.S.A. 116 40 59N 93 20W
Charlton I. 106 52 0N 79 20W
Charmes 19 48 22N 6 17 E
Charny 107 46 43N 71 15W
Charolles 21 46 27N 4 16 E
Charost 19 47 0N 2 7 E
Charouine 82 29 0N 0 15W
Charre 91 17 13S 35 10 E
Charroux 20 46 9N 0 25 E
Charters Towers 97 20 5S 146 13 E
Chartre, La 18 47 42N 0 34 E
Chartres 18 48 29N 1 30 E
Chascomús 124 35 30S 58 0W
Chasefu 91 11 55S 33 8 E
Chasovnya-Uchurskaya 59 57 15N 132 50 E
Chasseneuil-sur-Bonnieure 20 45 52N 0 29 E
Chata 68 27 42N 77 30 E
Châtaigneraie, La 18 46 38N 0 45W
Chatal Balkan = Udvoy Balkan 43 42 50N 26 50 E
Château-Chinon 19 47 4N 3 56 E
Château-du-Loir 18 47 40N 0 25 E
Château-Gontier 18 47 50N 0 48W
Château-la-Vallière 18 47 30N 0 20 E
Château-Landon 19 48 8N 2 40 E
Château, Le 20 45 52N 1 12W
Château-Porcien 19 49 31N 4 13 E
Château-Renault 18 47 36N 0 56 E
Château-Salins 19 48 50N 6 30 E
Château-Thierry 19 49 3N 3 20 E
Châteaubourg 18 48 7N 1 25W
Châteaubriant 18 47 43N 1 23W
Châteaudun 18 48 3N 1 20 E
Châteaugiron 18 48 3N 1 30W
Châteauguay 113 45 23N 73 45W
Châteaulin 18 48 11N 4 8W
Châteaumeillant 20 46 35N 2 12 E
Châteauneuf 18 48 35N 1 15 E
Châteauneuf-du-Faou 18 48 11N 3 50W
Châteauneuf-sur-Charente 20 45 36N 0 3W
Châteauneuf-sur-Cher 19 46 52N 2 18 E
Châteauneuf-sur-Loire 19 47 52N 2 13 E
Châteaurenard 21 43 53N 4 51 E
Châteauroux 19 46 50N 1 40 E
Châteaux-Arnoux 21 44 6N 6 0 E
Châtelaillon-Plage 20 46 5N 1 5W
Châtelaudren 18 48 33N 2 59W
Châtelet, Le, Cher, France 20 46 40N 2 20 E
Châtelet, Le, Seine-et-Marne, France 19 48 30N 2 47 E
Châtelguyon 20 45 55N 3 4 E
Châtellerault 18 46 50N 0 30 E
Châtelus-Malvaleix 20 46 18N 2 1 E
Chatfield 116 43 15N 91 58W
Chatham, N.B., Can. 107 47 2N 65 28W
Chatham, Ont., Can. 106 42 24N 82 11W
Chatham, U.K. 13 51 22N 0 32 E
Chatham, La., U.S.A. 117 32 22N 92 26W
Chatham, N.Y., U.S.A. 113 42 21N 73 32W
Chatham Is. 94 44 0S 176 40W
Chatham Str. 108 57 0N 134 40W
Châtillon, Loiret, France 19 47 36N 2 44 E
Châtillon, Marne, France 19 49 5N 3 43 E
Chatillon 38 45 45N 7 40 E
Châtillon-Coligny 19 47 50N 2 51 E
Châtillon-en-Bazois 19 47 3N 3 39 E
Châtillon-en-Diois 21 44 41N 5 29 E
Châtillon-sur-Indre 18 46 59N 1 10 E
Châtillon-sur-Seine 19 47 50N 4 33 E
Châtillon-sur-Sèvre 18 46 56N 0 45W
Chatmohar 69 24 15N 89 15 E
Chatra 69 24 12N 84 56 E
Chatrapur 69 19 22N 85 2 E
Châtre, La 20 46 35N 1 59 E
Chats, L. des 113 45 30N 76 20W
Chatsworth, Can. 112 44 27N 80 54W
Chatsworth, Zimb. 91 19 38S 31 13 E
Chattahoochee 115 30 43N 84 51W
Chattanooga 115 35 2N 85 17W
Chaudanne, Barrage de 21 43 51N 6 32 E
Chaudes-Aigues 20 44 51N 3 1 E
Chauffailles 21 46 13N 4 20 E
Chauk 67 20 53N 94 49 E
Chaukan La 67 27 0N 97 15 E
Chaulnes 19 49 48N 2 47 E
Chaumont, France 19 48 7N 5 8 E
Chaumont, U.S.A. 113 44 4N 76 9W
Chaumont-en-Vexin 19 49 16N 1 53 E
Chaumont-sur-Loire 18 47 29N 1 11 E
Chaunay 20 46 13N 0 9 E
Chauny 19 49 37N 3 12 E
Chausey, Îs. 18 48 52N 1 49W
Chaussin 19 46 59N 5 22 E
Chautauqua 112 42 17N 79 30W
Chauvigny 18 46 34N 0 39 E
Chauvin 109 52 45N 110 10W
Chaux-de-Fonds, La 25 47 7N 6 50 E
Chaves, Brazil 127 0 15S 49 55W
Chaves, Port. 30 41 45N 7 32W
Chavuma 89 13 4S 22 40 E
Chaykovskiy 52 56 47N 54 9 E
Chazelles-sur-Lyon 21 45 39N 4 22 E
Chazy 113 44 52N 73 28W
Cheb (Eger) 26 50 9N 12 28 E
Cheboksary 55 56 8N 47 12 E
Cheboygan 114 45 38N 84 29W
Chebsara 55 59 10N 38 59 E
Chech, Erg 82 25 0N 2 15W
Chechaouen 82 35 9N 5 15W
Chechen, Os. 57 43 59N 47 40 E
Checheno-Ingush A.S.S.R. □ 57 43 30N 45 29 E
Chęciny 28 50 46N 20 28 E
Checleset B. 108 50 5N 127 35W
Checotah 117 35 31N 95 30W
Chedabucto B. 107 45 25N 61 8W
Cheduba I. 67 18 45N 93 40 E
Cheepie 99 26 33S 145 1 E
Chef-Boutonne 20 46 7N 0 4W
Chegdomyn 59 51 7N 133 1 E
Chegga 82 25 27N 5 40W
Chehalis 118 46 44N 122 59W
Cheiron 21 43 49N 6 58 E
Cheju Do 77 33 29N 126 34 E
Chekalin 55 54 10N 36 10 E
Chekiang = Zhejiang □ 75 29 0N 120 0 E
Chela, Sa. da 92 16 20S 13 20 E
Chelan 118 47 49N 120 0W
Chelan, L. 108 48 5N 120 30W
Cheleken 53 39 26N 53 7 E
Chelforó 128 39 0S 66 33W
Chéliff, O. → 82 36 0N 0 8 E
Chelkar 58 47 48N 59 39 E
Chelkar Tengiz, Solonchak 58 48 0N 62 30 E
Chellala Dahrania 82 33 2N 0 1 E
Chelles 19 48 52N 2 33 E
Chełm 28 51 8N 23 30 E
Chełm □ 28 51 15N 23 30 E
Chełmek 27 50 6N 19 16 E
Chełmno 28 53 20N 18 30 E
Chelmsford 13 51 44N 0 29 E

Chelmsford Dam

Cilician Gates P.

Chelmsford Dam 93 27 55 S 29 59 E
Chelmża 28 53 10N 18 39 E
Chelsea, Austral. 100 38 5 S 145 8 E
Chelsea, Can. 113 45 30N 75 47W
Chelsea, Okla., U.S.A. 117 36 35N 95 35W
Chelsea, Vt., U.S.A. 113 43 59N 72 27W
Cheltenham 13 51 55N 2 5W
Chelva 32 39 45N 1 0W
Chelyabinsk 58 55 10N 61 24 E
Chemainus 108 48 55N 123 42W
Chemillé 18 47 14N 0 45W
Chemnitz = Karl-Marx-Stadt 24 50 50N 12 55 E
Chemult 118 43 14N 121 47W
Chen, Gora 59 65 16N 141 50 E
Chen Xian 75 25 47N 113 1 E
Chenab → 68 30 23N 71 2 E
Chenachane, O. → 82 25 20N 3 20W
Chenango Forks 113 42 15N 75 51W
Chencha 87 6 15N 37 32 E
Chenchiang = Zhenjiang 75 32 12N 119 24 E
Cheney 118 47 29N 117 34W
Chengbu 77 26 18N 110 16 E
Chengcheng 77 35 8N 109 56 E
Chengde 76 40 59N 117 58 E
Chengdu 75 30 38N 104 2 E
Chenggu 77 33 10N 107 21 E
Chengjiang 75 24 39N 103 0 E
Ch'engtu = Chengdu 75 30 38N 104 2 E
Chengyang 76 36 18N 120 21 E
Chenxi 77 28 2N 110 12 E
Cheo Reo 71 13 25N 108 28 E
Cheom Ksan 71 14 13N 104 56 E
Chepelare 43 41 44N 24 40 E
Chepén 126 7 15 S 79 23W
Chepes 124 31 20 S 66 35W
Chepo 121 9 10N 79 6W
Cheptsa → 55 58 36N 50 4 E
Cheptulil, Mt. 90 1 25N 35 35 E
Chequamegon B. 116 46 40N 90 30W
Cher □ 19 47 10N 2 30 E
Cher → 18 47 21N 0 29 E
Cheran 69 25 45N 90 44 E
Cherasco 38 44 39N 7 50 E
Cheraw 115 34 42N 79 54W
Cherbourg 18 49 39N 1 40W
Cherchell 82 36 35N 2 12 E
Cherdakly 55 54 25N 48 50 E
Cherdyn 52 60 24N 56 29 E
Cheremkhovo 59 53 8N 103 1 E
Cherepanovo 58 54 15N 83 30 E
Cherepovets 55 59 5N 37 55 E
Chergui, Chott ech 82 34 21N 0 25 E
Cherikov 54 53 32N 31 20 E
Cherkassy 56 49 27N 32 4 E
Cherkessk 57 44 15N 42 5 E
Cherlak 58 54 15N 74 55 E
Chernaya Kholunitsa 55 58 51N 51 52 E
Cherni 43 42 35N 23 18 E
Chernigov 54 51 28N 31 20 E
Chernikovsk 52 54 48N 56 8 E
Chernobyl 54 51 13N 30 15 E
Chernogorsk 59 53 49N 91 18 E
Chernomorskoye 56 45 31N 32 40 E
Chernovskoye 55 58 48N 47 20 E
Chernovtsy 56 48 15N 25 52 E
Chernoye 59 70 30N 89 10 E
Chernyakhovsk 54 54 36N 21 48 E
Chernyshkovskiy 57 48 30N 42 13 E
Chernyshovskiy 59 63 0N 112 30 E
Cherokee, Iowa, U.S.A. 116 42 40N 95 30W
Cherokee, Okla., U.S.A. 117 36 45N 98 25W
Cherokees, L. O'The 117 36 50N 95 12W
Cherquenco 128 38 35 S 72 0W
Cherrapunji 67 25 17N 91 47 E
Cherry Creek 118 39 50N 114 58W
Cherryvale 117 37 20N 95 33W
Cherskiy 59 68 45N 161 18 E
Cherskogo Khrebet 59 65 0N 143 0 E
Chertkovo 57 49 25N 40 19 E
Cherven 54 53 45N 28 28 E
Cherven-Bryag 43 43 17N 24 7 E
Chervonograd 54 50 25N 24 10 E
Cherwell → 13 51 46N 1 18W
Chesapeake 114 36 43N 76 15W
Chesapeake Bay 114 38 0N 76 12W
Cheshire □ 12 53 14N 2 30W
Cheshskaya Guba 52 67 20N 47 0 E
Cheslatta L. 108 53 49N 125 20W
Chesley 112 44 17N 81 5W
Chesne, Le 19 49 30N 4 45 E
Cheste 33 39 30N 0 41W
Chester, U.K. 12 53 12N 2 53W
Chester, Calif., U.S.A. 118 40 22N 121 14W
Chester, Ill., U.S.A. 117 37 58N 89 50W
Chester, Mont., U.S.A. 118 48 31N 111 0W
Chester, N.Y., U.S.A. 113 41 22N 74 16W
Chester, Pa., U.S.A. 114 39 54N 75 20W
Chester, S.C., U.S.A. 115 34 44N 81 13W
Chesterfield 12 53 14N 1 26W
Chesterfield, Îles 94 19 52 S 158 15 E
Chesterfield In. 104 63 25N 90 45W
Chesterfield Inlet 104 63 30N 90 45W
Chesterton Range 99 25 30 S 147 27 E
Chesterville 113 45 6N 75 14W
Chesuncook L. 107 46 0N 69 10W
Chetaibi 83 37 1N 7 20 E
Chéticamp 107 46 37N 60 59W
Chetumal 120 18 30N 88 20W
Chetumal, Bahía de 120 18 40N 88 10W
Chetwynd 108 55 45N 121 36W
Chevanceaux 20 45 18N 0 14W
Cheviot Hills 12 55 20N 2 30W
Cheviot Ra. 99 25 20 S 143 45 E
Cheviot, The 12 55 29N 2 8W
Chew Bahir 87 4 40N 36 50 E
Chewelah 118 48 17N 117 43W
Cheyenne, Okla., U.S.A. 117 35 35N 99 40W
Cheyenne, Wyo., U.S.A. 116 41 9N 104 49W
Cheyenne → 116 44 40N 101 15W
Cheyenne Wells 116 38 51N 102 10W
Cheylard, Le 21 44 55N 4 25 E
Chhabra 68 24 40N 76 54 E
Chhatarpur 69 24 55N 79 35 E
Chhindwara 68 22 2N 78 59 E
Chhlong 71 12 15N 105 58 E
Chi → 71 15 11N 104 43 E
Chiamis 73 7 20 S 108 21 E
Chiamussu = Jiamusi 75 46 40N 130 26 E
Chiang Mai 71 18 47N 98 59 E
Chiange 89 15 35 S 13 40 E
Chiapa → 120 16 42N 93 0W
Chiapas □ 120 17 0N 92 45W
Chiaramonte Gulfi 41 37 1N 14 41 E
Chiaravalle 39 43 38N 13 17 E
Chiaravalle Centrale 41 38 41N 16 25 E
Chiari 38 45 31N 9 55 E
Chiatura 57 42 15N 43 17 E
Chiávari 38 44 20N 9 20 E
Chiavenna 38 46 18N 9 23 E
Chiba 74 35 30N 140 7 E
Chiba □ 74 35 30N 140 20 E
Chibabava 93 20 17 S 33 35 E
Chibatu 73 7 6 S 107 59 E
Chibemba, Angola 89 15 48 S 14 8 E
Chibemba, Angola 92 16 20 S 15 20 E
Chibia 89 15 10 S 13 42 E
Chibougamau 106 49 56N 74 24W
Chibougamau L. 106 49 50N 74 20W
Chibuk 85 10 52N 12 50 E
Chic-Chocs, Mts. 107 48 55N 66 0W
Chicacole = Srikakulam 70 18 14N 84 4 E
Chicago 114 41 53N 87 40W
Chicago Heights 114 41 29N 87 37W
Chichagof I. 108 58 0N 136 0W
Chichaoua 82 31 32N 8 44W
Chichén Itzá 120 20 40N 88 32W
Chichester 13 50 50N 0 47W
Chichibu 74 36 5N 139 10 E
Ch'ich'ihaerh = Qiqihar 75 47 26N 124 0 E
Chickasha 117 35 0N 98 0W
Chiclana de la Frontera 31 36 26N 6 9W
Chiclayo 126 6 42 S 79 50W
Chico 118 39 45N 121 54W
Chico →, Chubut, Argent. 118 44 0 S 67 0W
Chico →, Santa Cruz, Argent. 128 50 0 S 68 30W
Chicomo 93 24 31 S 34 6 E
Chicopee 114 42 6N 72 37W
Chicoutimi 107 48 28N 71 5W
Chidambaram 70 11 20N 79 45 E
Chidenguele 93 24 55 S 34 11 E
Chidley C. 105 60 23N 64 26W
Chiede 92 17 15 S 16 22 E
Chiefs Pt. 112 44 41N 81 18W
Chiemsee 25 47 53N 12 27 E
Chiengi 91 8 45 S 29 10 E
Chienti → 39 43 18N 13 45 E
Chieri 38 45 0N 7 50 E
Chiers → 19 49 39N 5 0 E
Chiese → 38 45 8N 10 25 E
Chieti 39 42 22N 14 10 E
Chifeng 76 42 18N 118 58 E
Chigirin 56 49 4N 32 38 E
Chignecto B. 107 45 30N 64 40W
Chiguana 124 21 0 S 67 58W
Chihli, G. of = Bo Hai 76 39 0N 120 0 E
Chihuahua 120 28 40N 106 3W
Chihuahua □ 120 28 40N 106 3W
Chiili 58 44 20N 66 15 E
Chik Bollapur 70 13 25N 77 45 E
Chikhli 68 20 20N 76 18 E
Chikmagalur 70 13 15N 75 45 E
Chikodi 70 16 26N 74 38 E
Chikwawa 91 16 2 S 34 50 E
Chilako → 108 53 53N 122 57W
Chilanga 91 15 33 S 28 16 E
Chilapa 120 17 40N 99 11W
Chilas 69 35 25N 74 5 E
Chilcotin → 108 51 44N 122 23W
Childers 97 25 15 S 152 17 E
Childress 117 34 30N 100 15W
Chile ■ 128 35 0 S 72 0W
Chile Rise 95 38 0 S 92 0W
Chilecito 124 29 10 S 67 30W
Chilete 126 7 10 S 78 50W
Chililabombwe 91 12 18 S 27 43 E
Chilin = Jilin 76 43 55N 126 30 E
Chilka L. 69 19 40N 85 25 E
Chilko → 108 52 0N 123 40W
Chilko, L. 108 51 20N 124 10W
Chillagoe 97 17 7 S 144 33 E
Chillán 124 36 40 S 72 10W
Chillicothe, Ill., U.S.A. 116 40 55N 89 32W
Chillicothe, Mo., U.S.A. 116 39 45N 93 30W
Chillicothe, Ohio, U.S.A. 114 39 20N 82 58W
Chilliwack 108 49 10N 121 54W
Chilo 68 27 25N 73 32 E
Chiloane, I. 93 20 40 S 34 55 E
Chiloé, I. de 128 42 30 S 73 50W
Chilpancingo 120 17 30N 99 30W
Chiltern Hills 13 51 44N 0 42W
Chilton 114 44 1N 88 12W
Chiluage 88 9 30 S 21 50 E
Chilubula 91 10 14 S 30 51 E
Chilumba 91 10 28 S 34 12 E
Chilwa, L. 91 15 15 S 35 40 E
Chimacum 118 48 1N 122 46W
Chimay 16 50 3N 4 20 E
Chimbay 58 42 57N 59 47 E
Chimborazo 126 1 29 S 78 55W
Chimbote 126 9 0 S 78 35W
Chimishliya 46 46 34N 28 44 E
Chimkent 58 42 18N 69 36 E
Chimoio 91 19 4 S 33 30 E
Chimpembe 91 9 31 S 29 33 E
Chin □ 67 22 0N 93 0 E
Chin Ling Shan = Qinling Shandi 77 33 50N 108 10 E
China 120 25 40N 99 20W
China ■ 75 30 0N 110 0 E
Chinan = Jinan 76 36 38N 117 1 E
Chinandega 121 12 35N 87 12W
Chinati Pk. 117 30 0N 104 25W
Chincha Alta 126 13 25 S 76 7W
Chinchilla 99 26 45 S 150 38 E
Chinchilla de Monte Aragón 33 38 53N 1 40W
Chinchón 32 40 9N 3 26W
Chinchorro, Banco 120 18 35N 87 20W
Chinchou = Jinzhou 76 41 5N 121 3 E
Chincoteague 114 37 58N 75 21W
Chinde 91 18 35 S 36 30 E
Chindwin → 67 21 26N 95 15 E
Chinga 91 15 13 S 38 35 E
Chingleput 70 12 42N 79 58 E
Chingola 91 12 31 S 27 53 E
Chingole 91 13 4 S 34 17 E
Ch'ingtao = Qingdao 76 36 5N 120 20 E
Chinguetti 80 20 25N 12 24W
Chingune 93 20 33 S 35 0 E
Chinhae 76 35 9N 128 47 E
Chinhanguanine 93 25 21 S 32 30 E
Chiniot 68 31 45N 73 0 E
Chinju 76 35 12N 128 2 E
Chinle 119 36 14N 109 38W
Chinnamanur 70 9 50N 77 24 E
Chinnampo 76 38 52N 125 10 E
Chinnur 70 18 57N 79 49 E
Chino Valley 119 34 54N 112 28W
Chinon 18 47 10N 0 15 E
Chinook, Can. 109 51 28N 110 59W
Chinook, U.S.A. 118 48 35N 109 19W
Chinsali 91 10 30 S 32 2 E
Chintamani 70 13 26N 78 3 E
Chióggia 39 45 13N 12 15 E
Chios = Khios 45 38 27N 26 9 E
* Chipai L. 106 52 56N 87 53W
Chipata 91 13 38 S 32 28 E
Chipatujah 73 7 45 S 108 0 E
Chipewyan L. 109 58 0N 98 27W
Chipinga 91 20 13 S 32 28 E
Chipiona 31 36 44N 6 26W
Chipley 115 30 45N 85 32W
Chiplun 70 17 31N 73 34 E
Chipman 107 46 6N 65 53W
Chipoka 91 13 57 S 34 28 E
Chippawa 112 43 5N 79 2W
Chippenham 13 51 27N 2 7W
Chippewa → 116 44 25N 92 10W
Chippewa Falls 116 44 55N 91 22W
Chiprovtsi 42 43 24N 22 52 E
Chiquián 126 10 10 S 77 0W
Chiquimula 120 14 51N 89 37W
Chiquinquira 126 5 37N 73 50W
Chir → 57 48 30N 43 0 E
Chirala 70 15 50N 80 26 E
Chiramba 91 16 55 S 34 39 E
Chirawa 68 28 14N 75 42 E
Chirayinkil 70 8 41N 76 49 E
Chirchik 58 41 29N 69 35 E
Chirfa 83 20 55N 12 22 E
Chiricahua Pk. 119 31 53N 109 14W
Chirikof I. 104 55 50N 155 40W
Chiriquí, Golfo de 121 8 0N 82 10W
Chiriquí, Lago de 121 9 10N 82 0W
† Chiriquí, Vol. de 121 8 55N 82 35W
Chirivira Falls 91 21 10 S 32 12 E
Chirnogi 46 44 7N 26 32 E
Chirpan 43 42 10N 25 19 E
Chirripó Grande, Cerro 121 9 29N 83 29W
Chisamba 91 14 55 S 28 20 E
Chisholm 108 54 55N 114 10W
Chishtian Mandi 68 29 50N 72 55 E
Chisimaio 79 0 22 S 42 32 E
Chisimba Falls 91 10 12 S 30 56 E
Chisineu Criş 42 46 32N 21 37 E
Chisone → 38 44 49N 7 25 E
Chisos Mts. 117 29 20N 103 15W
Chistopol 55 55 25N 50 38 E
Chita 59 52 0N 113 35 E
Chitapur 70 17 10N 77 5 E
Chitembo 89 13 30 S 16 50 E
Chitipa 91 9 41 S 33 19 E
Chitokoloki 89 13 50 S 23 13 E
Chitorgarh 68 24 52N 74 38 E
Chitrakot 70 19 10N 81 40 E
Chitral 66 35 50N 71 56 E
Chitravati → 70 14 45N 78 15 E
Chitré 121 7 59N 80 27W
Chittagong 67 22 19N 91 48 E
Chittagong □ 67 24 5N 91 0 E
Chittoor 70 13 15N 79 5 E
Chittur 70 10 40N 76 45 E
Chiusa 39 46 38N 11 34 E
Chiusi 39 43 1N 11 58 E
Chiva 33 39 27N 0 41W
Chivasso 38 45 10N 7 52 E
Chivilcoy 124 34 55 S 60 0W
Chiwanda 91 11 23 S 34 55 E
Chizela 91 13 10 S 25 0 E
Chkalov = Orenburg 52 52 0N 55 5 E
Chkolovsk 55 56 50N 43 10 E
Chlumec 26 50 9N 15 29 E
Chmielnik 28 50 37N 20 43 E
Choba 90 2 30N 38 5 E
Chobe National Park 92 18 0 S 25 0 E
Chocianów 28 51 27N 15 55 E
Chociwel 28 53 29N 15 21 E
Chodaków 28 52 16N 20 18 E
Chodavaram 70 17 50N 82 57 E
Chodecz 28 52 24N 19 2 E
Chodziez 28 52 58N 16 58 E
Choele Choel 128 39 11 S 65 40W
Choisy-le-Roi 19 48 45N 2 24 E
Choix 120 26 40N 108 23W
Chojna 28 52 58N 14 25 E
Chojnice 28 53 42N 17 32 E
Chojnów 28 51 18N 15 58 E
Choke Mts. 87 11 18N 37 15 E
Chokurdakh 59 70 38N 147 55 E
Cholet 18 47 4N 0 52W
Choluteca 121 13 20N 87 14W
Choma 91 16 48 S 26 59 E
Chomen Swamp 87 9 20N 37 10 E
Chomu 68 27 15N 75 40 E
Chomutov 26 50 28N 13 23 E
Chon Buri 71 13 21N 101 1 E
Chonan 76 36 48N 127 9 E

* Renamed Wapikopa, L.

† Renamed Barú, Vol.

Chone 126 0 40 S 80 0W
Chong'an 77 27 45N 118 0 E
Chongde 77 30 32N 120 26 E
Chongjin 76 41 47N 129 50 E
Chŏngju 76 39 40N 125 5 E
Chŏngju 76 36 39N 127 27 E
Chongli 76 40 58N 115 15 E
Chongqing 75 29 35N 106 25 E
Chongzuo 77 22 23N 107 20 E
Chŏnju 76 35 50N 127 4 E
Chonming Dao 77 31 40N 121 30 E
Chonos, Arch. de los 128 45 0 S 75 0W
Chopda 68 21 20N 75 15 E
Chopim → 125 25 35 S 53 5W
Chorley 12 53 39N 2 39W
Chorolque, Cerro 124 20 59 S 66 5W
Choroszcz 28 53 10N 22 59 E
Chorrera, La 120 8 50N 79 50W
Chortkov, U.S.S.R. 54 49 2N 25 46 E
Chortkov, U.S.S.R. 56 49 1N 25 42 E
Chŏrwŏn 76 38 15N 127 10 E
Chorzele 28 53 15N 20 55 E
Chorzów 28 50 18N 18 57 E
Chos-Malal 124 37 20 S 70 15W
Chosan 76 40 50N 125 47 E
Chōshi 74 35 45N 140 51 E
Choszczno 28 53 7N 15 25 E
Choteau 118 47 50N 112 10W
Chotila 68 22 23N 71 15 E
Chowchilla 119 37 11N 120 12W
Choybalsan 75 48 4N 114 30 E
Christchurch, N.Z. 101 43 33 S 172 47 E
Christchurch, U.K. 13 50 44N 1 33W
Christian I. 112 44 50N 80 12W
Christiana 92 27 52 S 25 8 E
Christiansfeld 49 55 21N 9 29 E
Christie B. 109 62 32N 111 10W
Christina → 109 56 40N 111 3W
Christmas I., Ind. Oc. 94 10 30 S 105 40 E
* Christmas I., Pac. Oc. 95 1 58N 157 27W
Chrudim 26 49 58N 15 43 E
Chrzanów 27 50 10N 19 21 E
Chtimba 91 10 35 S 34 13 E
Chu 58 43 36N 73 42 E
Chu → 71 19 53N 105 45 E
Chu Chua 108 51 22N 120 10W
Ch'uanchou = Quanzhou 75 24 55N 118 34 E
Chūbu □ 74 36 45N 137 30 E
Chubut → 128 43 20 S 65 5W
Chuchi L. 108 55 12N 124 30W
Chudovo 54 59 10N 31 41 E
Chudskoye, Oz. 54 58 13N 27 30 E
Chūgoku □ 74 35 0N 133 0 E
Chūgoku-Sanchi 74 35 0N 133 0 E
Chuguyev 56 49 55N 36 45 E
Chugwater 116 41 48N 104 47W
Chukai 71 4 13N 103 25 E
Chukhloma 55 58 45N 42 40 E
Chukotskiy Khrebet 59 68 0N 175 0 E
Chukotskoye More 59 68 0N 175 0W
Chula Vista 119 32 39N 117 8W
Chulman 59 56 52N 124 52 E
Chulucanas 126 5 8 S 80 10W
Chulym → 58 57 43N 83 51 E
Chumbicha 124 29 0 S 66 10W
Chumerna 43 42 45N 25 55 E
Chumikan 59 54 40N 135 10 E
Chumphon 71 10 35N 99 14 E
Chumuare 91 14 31 S 31 50 E
Chuna → 59 57 47N 94 37 E
Chun'an 77 29 35N 119 3 E
Chunchŏn 76 37 58N 127 44 E
Chunga 91 15 0 S 26 2 E
Chungking = Chongqing 75 29 35N 106 25 E
Chunian 68 30 57N 74 0 E
Chunya 91 8 30 S 33 27 E
Chunya □ 90 7 48 S 33 0 E
Chuquibamba 126 15 47 S 72 44W
Chuquicamata 124 22 15 S 69 0W
Chuquisaca □ 126 23 30 S 63 30W
Chur 25 46 52N 9 32 E
Churachandpur 67 24 20N 93 40 E
Churchill 109 58 47N 94 11W
Churchill →, Man., Can. 109 58 47N 94 12W
Churchill →, Newf., Can. 107 53 19N 60 10W
Churchill, C. 109 58 46N 93 12W
Churchill Falls 107 53 36N 64 19W
Churchill L. 109 55 55N 108 20W
Churchill Pk. 108 58 10N 125 10W
Churu 68 28 20N 74 50 E
Chushal 69 33 40N 78 40 E
Chusovoy 52 58 15N 57 40 E
Chuvash A.S.S.R. □ 55 55 30N 47 0 E
Ci Xian 76 36 20N 114 25 E
Ciacova 42 45 35N 21 10 E
Cianjur 73 6 51 S 107 7 E
Cibadok 73 6 53 S 106 47 E
Cibatu 73 7 8 S 107 59 E
Cicero 114 41 48N 87 48W
Cidacos → 32 42 21N 1 38W
Cide 56 41 53N 33 1 E
Ciechanów 28 52 52N 20 38 E
Ciechanów □ 28 53 0N 20 30 E
Ciechanowiec 28 52 40N 22 31 E
Ciechocinek 28 52 53N 18 45 E
Ciego de Avila 121 21 50N 78 50W
Ciénaga 126 11 1N 74 15W
Cienfuegos 121 22 10N 80 30W
Cieplice Śląskie Zdrój 28 50 50N 15 40 E
Cierp 20 42 55N 0 40 E
Cíes, Islas 30 42 12N 8 55W
Cieszanów 28 50 14N 23 8 E
Cieszyn 27 49 45N 18 35 E
Cieza 33 38 17N 1 23W
Cifuentes 32 40 47N 2 37W
Cijara, Pantano de 31 39 18N 4 52W
Cijulang 73 7 42 S 108 27 E
Cikajang 73 7 25 S 107 48 E
Cikampek 73 6 23 S 107 28 E
Cilacap 73 7 43 S 109 0 E
Çıldır 57 41 10N 43 20 E
Cilician Gates P. 64 37 20N 34 52 E

* Renamed Kirimati

Cîlnicu Columbus

Cîlnicu 46 44 54N 23 4 E
Cimahi 73 6 53 S 107 33 E
Cimarron, Kans., U.S.A. 117 37 50N 100 20W
Cimarron, N. Mex., U.S.A. 117 36 30N 104 52W
Cimarron → 117 36 10N 96 17W
Cimone, Mte. 38 44 10N 10 40 E
Cîmpic Turzii 46 46 34N 23 53 E
Cîmpina 46 45 10N 25 45 E
Cîmpulung, Argeş, Romania 46 45 17N 25 3 E
Cîmpulung, Moldovenesc, Romania 46 47 32N 25 30 E
Cîmpuri 43 46 0N 26 50 E
Cinca → 32 41 26N 0 21 E
Cincer 42 43 55N 17 5 E
Cincinnati 114 39 10N 84 26W
Cîndeşti 46 45 15N 26 42 E
Ciney 16 50 18N 5 5 E
Cingoli 39 43 23N 13 10 E
Cinigiano 39 42 53N 11 23 E
Cinto, Mt. 21 42 24N 8 54 E
Ciorani 46 44 45N 26 25 E
Ciotat, La 21 43 12N 5 36 E
Čiovo 39 43 30N 16 17 E
Circeo, Monte 40 41 14N 13 3 E
Circle, Alaska, U.S.A. 104 65 50N 144 10W
Circle, Montana, U.S.A. 116 47 26N 105 35W
Circleville, Ohio, U.S.A. 114 39 35N 82 57W
Circleville, Utah, U.S.A. 119 38 12N 112 24W
Cirebon 73 6 45 S 108 32 E
Cirencester 13 51 43N 1 59W
Cireşu 46 44 47N 22 31 E
Cirey-sur-Vezouze 19 48 35N 6 57 E
Ciriè 38 45 14N 7 35 E
Cirò 41 39 23N 17 3 E
Cisco 117 32 25N 99 0W
Cislău 46 45 14N 26 20 E
Cisna 27 49 12N 22 20 E
Cisnădie 46 45 42N 24 9 E
Cisterna di Latina 40 41 35N 12 50 E
Cisternino 41 40 45N 17 26 E
Citeli-Ckaro 57 41 33N 46 0 E
Citlaltépetl 120 19 0N 97 20W
Citrusdal 92 32 35 S 19 0 E
Città della Pieve 39 42 57N 12 0 E
Città di Castello 39 43 27N 12 14 E
Città Sant' Angelo 39 42 32N 14 5 E
Cittadella 39 45 39N 11 48 E
Cittaducale 39 42 24N 12 58 E
Cittanova 41 38 22N 16 5 E
Ciuc, Munţii 46 46 25N 26 5 E
Ciucaş 46 45 31N 25 56 E
Ciudad Acuña 120 29 20N 100 58W
Ciudad Altamirano 120 18 20N 100 40W
Ciudad Bolívar 126 8 5N 63 36W
Ciudad Camargo 120 27 41N 105 10W
Ciudad de Valles 120 22 0N 99 0W
Ciudad del Carmen 120 18 38N 91 50W
Ciudad Delicias = Delicias 120 28 10N 105 30W
Ciudad Guayana 126 8 0N 62 30W
Ciudad Guerrero 120 28 33N 107 28W
Ciudad Guzmán 120 19 40N 103 30W
Ciudad Juárez 120 31 40N 106 28W
Ciudad Madero 120 22 19N 97 50W
Ciudad Mante 120 22 50N 99 0W
Ciudad Obregón 120 27 28N 109 59W
Ciudad Real 31 38 59N 3 55W
Ciudad Real □ 31 38 50N 4 0W
Ciudad Rodrigo 30 40 35N 6 32W
Ciudad Trujillo = Sto. Domingo 121 18 30N 70 0W
Ciudad Victoria 120 23 41N 99 9W
Ciudadela 32 40 0N 3 50 E
Ciulniţa 46 44 26N 27 22 E
Cividale del Friuli 39 46 6N 13 25 E
Cività Castellana 39 42 18N 12 24 E
Civitanova Marche 39 43 18N 13 41 E
Civitavécchia 39 42 6N 11 46 E
Civitella del Tronto 39 42 48N 13 40 E
Civray 20 46 10N 0 17 E
Çivril 64 38 20N 29 43 E
Cixerri → 40 39 20N 8 40 E
Cizre 64 37 19N 42 10 E
Clacton-on-Sea 13 51 47N 1 10 E
Clain → 18 46 47N 0 33 E
Claire, L. 108 58 35N 112 5W
Clairemont 117 33 9N 100 44W
Clairton 112 40 18N 79 54W
Clairvaux-les-Lacs 21 46 35N 5 45 E
Claise → 18 46 56N 0 42 E
Clamecy 19 47 28N 3 30 E
Clanton 115 32 48N 86 36W
Clanwilliam 92 32 11 S 18 52 E
Clara 15 53 20N 7 38W
Clare, Austral. 99 33 50 S 138 37 E
Clare, U.S.A. 114 43 47N 84 45W
Clare □ 15 52 20N 9 0W
Clare → 15 53 22N 9 5W
Clare I. 15 53 48N 10 0W
Claremont 114 43 23N 72 20W
Claremont Pt. 98 14 1 S 143 41 E
Claremore 117 36 40N 95 37W
Claremorris 15 53 45N 9 0W
Clarence →, Austral. 97 29 25 S 153 22 E
Clarence →, N.Z. 101 42 10 S 173 56 E
Clarence I. 5 61 10 S 54 0W
Clarence, I. 128 54 0 S 72 0W
Clarence Str., Austral. 96 12 0 S 131 0 E
Clarence Str., U.S.A. 108 55 40N 132 10W
Clarendon, Ark., U.S.A. 117 34 41N 91 20W
Clarendon, Tex., U.S.A. 117 34 58N 100 54W
Clarenville 107 48 10N 54 1W
Claresholm 108 50 0N 113 33W
Clarie Coast 5 68 0 S 135 0 E
Clarinda 116 40 45N 95 0W
Clarion, Iowa, U.S.A. 116 42 41N 93 46W
Clarion, Pa., U.S.A. 112 41 12N 79 22W
Clarion → 112 41 9N 79 41W
Clarion Fracture Zone 95 20 0N 120 0W
Clark 116 44 55N 97 45W
Clark Fork 118 48 9N 116 9W
Clark Fork → 118 48 9N 116 15W
Clark Hill Res. 115 33 45N 82 20W
Clark, Pt. 112 44 4N 81 45W
Clarkdale 119 34 53N 112 3W
Clarke City 107 50 12N 66 38W
Clarke, I. 97 40 32 S 148 10 E
Clarke L. 109 54 24N 106 54W
Clarke Ra. 98 20 45 S 148 20 E
Clark's Fork → 118 45 39N 108 43W
Clark's Harbour 107 43 25N 65 38W
Clarks Summit 113 41 31N 75 44W
Clarksburg 114 39 18N 80 21W
Clarksdale 117 34 12N 90 33W
Clarkston 118 46 28N 117 2W
Clarksville, Ark., U.S.A. 117 35 29N 93 27W
Clarksville, Tenn., U.S.A. 115 36 32N 87 20W
Clarksville, Tex., U.S.A. 117 33 37N 94 59W
Clatskanie 118 46 9N 123 12W
Claude 117 35 8N 101 22W
Claveria 73 18 37N 121 4 E
Clay Center 116 39 27N 97 9W
Clayette, La 21 46 17N 4 19 E
Claypool 119 33 27N 110 55W
Claysville 112 40 5N 80 25W
Clayton, Idaho, U.S.A. 118 44 12N 114 31W
Clayton, N. Mex., U.S.A. 117 36 30N 103 10W
Cle Elum 118 47 15N 120 57W
Clear L. 118 39 5N 122 47W
Clear, C. 15 51 26N 9 30W
Clear I. 15 51 26N 9 30W
Clear Lake, S.D., U.S.A. 116 44 48N 96 41W
Clear Lake, Wash., U.S.A. 118 48 27N 122 15W
Clear Lake Res. 118 41 55N 121 10W
Clearfield, Pa., U.S.A. 114 41 0N 78 27W
Clearfield, Utah, U.S.A. 118 41 10N 112 0W
Clearmont 118 44 43N 106 29W
Clearwater, Can. 108 51 38N 120 2W
Clearwater, U.S.A. 115 27 58N 82 45W
Clearwater →, Alta., Can. 108 52 22N 114 57W
Clearwater →, Alta., Can. 109 56 44N 111 23W
Clearwater Cr. 108 61 36N 125 30W
Clearwater, Mts. 118 46 20N 115 30W
Clearwater Prov. Park 109 54 0N 101 0W
Cleburne 117 32 18N 97 25W
Clécy 18 48 55N 0 29W
Cleethorpes 12 53 33N 0 2W
Cleeve Cloud 13 51 56N 2 0W
Clelles 21 44 50N 5 38 E
Clerks Rocks 5 56 0 S 34 30W
Clermont, Austral. 97 22 49 S 147 39 E
Clermont, France 19 49 23N 2 24 E
Clermont-en-Argonne 19 49 5N 5 4 E
Clermont-Ferrand 20 45 46N 3 4 E
Clermont-l'Hérault 20 43 38N 3 26 E
Clerval 19 47 25N 6 30 E
Clervaux 16 50 4N 6 2 E
Cléry-Saint-André 19 47 50N 1 46 E
Cles 38 46 21N 11 4 E
Cleveland, Austral. 99 27 30 S 153 15 E
Cleveland, Miss., U.S.A. 117 33 43N 90 43W
Cleveland, Ohio, U.S.A. 114 41 28N 81 43W
Cleveland, Okla., U.S.A. 117 36 21N 96 33W
Cleveland, Tenn., U.S.A. 115 35 9N 84 52W
Cleveland, Tex., U.S.A. 117 30 18N 95 0W
Cleveland □ 12 54 35N 1 8 E
Cleveland, C. 97 19 11 S 147 1 E
Cleveland Heights 112 41 32N 81 30W
Clevelândia 125 26 24 S 52 23W
Clew B. 15 53 54N 9 50W
Clewiston 115 26 44N 80 50W
Clifden, Ireland 15 53 30N 10 2W
Clifden, N.Z. 101 46 1 S 167 42 E
Cliff 119 33 0N 108 36W
Clifton, Austral. 99 27 59 S 151 53 E
Clifton, Ariz., U.S.A. 119 33 8N 109 23W
Clifton, Tex., U.S.A. 117 31 46N 97 35W
Clifton Forge 114 37 49N 79 51W
Climax 109 49 10N 108 20W
Clinch → 115 36 0N 84 29W
Clingmans Dome 115 35 35N 83 30W
Clint 119 31 37N 106 11W
Clinton, B.C., Can. 108 51 6N 121 35W
Clinton, Ont., Can. 106 43 37N 81 32W
Clinton, N.Z. 101 46 12 S 169 23 E
Clinton, Ark., U.S.A. 117 35 37N 92 30W
Clinton, Ill., U.S.A. 116 40 8N 89 0W
Clinton, Ind., U.S.A. 114 39 40N 87 22W
Clinton, Iowa, U.S.A. 116 41 50N 90 12W
Clinton, Mass., U.S.A. 114 42 26N 71 40W
Clinton, Mo., U.S.A. 116 38 20N 93 46W
Clinton, N.C., U.S.A. 115 35 5N 78 15W
Clinton, Okla., U.S.A. 117 35 30N 99 0W
Clinton, S.C., U.S.A. 115 34 30N 81 54W
Clinton, Tenn., U.S.A. 115 36 6N 84 10W
Clinton C. 98 22 30 S 150 45 E
Clinton Colden L. 104 63 58N 107 27W
Clintonville 116 44 35N 88 46W
Clipperton Fracture Zone 95 19 0N 122 0W
Clipperton, I. 95 10 18N 109 13W
Clisson 18 47 5N 1 16W
Clive L. 108 63 13N 118 54W
Cloates, Pt. 96 22 43 S 113 40 E
Clocolan 93 28 55 S 27 34 E
Clodomira 124 27 35 S 64 14W
Clonakilty 15 51 37N 8 53W
Clonakilty B. 15 51 33N 8 50W
Cloncurry 97 20 40 S 140 28 E
Cloncurry → 98 18 37 S 140 40 E
Clones 15 54 10N 7 13W
Clonmel 15 52 22N 7 42W
Cloppenburg 24 52 50N 8 3 E
Cloquet 116 46 40N 92 30W
Clorinda 124 25 16 S 57 45W
Cloud Peak 118 44 23N 107 10W
Cloudcroft 119 33 0N 105 48W
Cloverdale 118 38 49N 123 0W
Clovis, Calif., U.S.A. 119 36 47N 119 45W
Clovis, N. Mex., U.S.A. 117 34 20N 103 10W
Cloyes 18 48 0N 1 14 E
Cluj-Napoca 46 46 47N 23 38 E
Cluj □ 46 46 45N 23 30 E
Clunes 99 37 20 S 143 45 E
Cluny 21 46 26N 4 38 E
Cluses 21 46 5N 6 35 E
Clusone 38 45 54N 9 58 E
Clutha → 101 46 20 S 169 49 E
Clwyd □ 12 53 5N 3 20W
Clwyd → 12 53 20N 3 30W
Clyde, Can. 105 70 30N 68 30W
Clyde, N.Z. 101 45 12 S 169 20 E
Clyde, U.S.A. 112 43 8N 76 52W
Clyde → 14 55 56N 4 29W
Clyde, Firth of 14 55 20N 5 0W
Clydebank 14 55 54N 4 25W
Clymer 112 42 3N 79 39W
Côa → 30 41 5N 7 6W
Coachella 119 33 44N 116 13W
Coahoma 117 32 17N 101 20W
Coahuayana → 120 18 41N 103 45W
Coahuila de Zaragoza □ 120 27 0N 103 0W
Coal → 108 59 39N 126 57W
Coalane 91 17 48 S 37 2 E
Coalcomán 120 18 40N 103 10W
Coaldale 108 49 45N 112 35W
Coalgate 117 34 35N 96 13W
Coalinga 119 36 10N 120 21W
Coalville, U.K. 12 52 43N 1 21W
Coalville, U.S.A. 118 40 58N 111 24W
Coari 126 4 8 S 63 7W
Coast □ 90 2 40 S 39 45 E
Coast Mts. 108 55 0N 129 0W
Coast Ranges 102 41 0N 123 0W
Coastal Plains Basin 96 30 10 S 115 30 E
Coatbridge 14 55 52N 4 2W
Coatepeque 120 14 46N 91 55W
Coatesville 114 39 59N 75 55W
Coaticook 107 45 10N 71 46W
Coats I. 105 62 30N 83 0W
Coats Land 5 77 0 S 25 0W
Coatzacoalcos 120 18 7N 94 25W
Cobadin 46 44 5N 28 13 E
Cobalt 106 47 25N 79 42W
Cobán 120 15 30N 90 21W
Cobar 97 31 27 S 145 48 E
Cóbh 15 51 50N 8 18W
Cobija 126 11 0 S 68 50W
Cobleskill 114 42 40N 74 30W
Coboconk 112 44 39N 78 48W
Cobourg 106 43 58N 78 10W
Cobourg Pen. 96 11 20 S 132 15 E
Cobram 99 35 54 S 145 40 E
Cobre 118 41 6N 114 25W
Coburg 25 50 15N 10 58 E
Coca 30 41 13N 4 32W
Cocanada = Kakinada 70 16 50N 82 11 E
Cocentaina 33 38 45N 0 27W
Cocha, La 124 27 50 S 65 40W
Cochabamba 126 17 26 S 66 10W
Cochem 25 50 8N 7 7 E
Cochemane 91 17 0 S 32 54 E
Cochin 70 9 59N 76 22 E
Cochin China = Nam-Phan 71 10 30N 106 0 E
Cochise 119 32 6N 109 58W
Cochran 115 32 25N 83 23W
Cochrane, Alta., Can. 108 51 11N 114 30W
Cochrane, Ont., Can. 106 49 0N 81 0W
Cochrane → 109 59 0N 103 40W
Cochrane, L. 128 47 10 S 72 0W
Cockatoo I. 96 16 6 S 123 37 E
Cockburn 99 32 5 S 141 0 E
Cockburn, Canal 128 54 30 S 72 0W
Cockburn I. 106 45 55N 83 22W
Coco → 121 15 0N 83 8W
Coco Chan. 71 13 50N 93 25 E
Coco Solo 120 9 22N 79 53W
Cocoa 115 28 22N 80 40W
Cocobeach 88 0 59N 9 34 E
Cocora 46 44 45N 27 3 E
Cocos I. 95 5 25N 87 55W
Cocos Is. 94 12 10 S 96 55 E
Cod, C. 111 42 8N 70 10W
Codajás 126 3 55 S 62 0W
Coderre 109 50 11N 106 31W
Codigoro 39 44 50N 12 5 E
Codó 127 4 30 S 43 55W
Codogno 38 45 10N 9 42 E
Codróipo 39 45 57N 13 0 E
Codru, Munţii 46 46 30N 22 15 E
Cody 118 44 35N 109 0W
Coe Hill 106 44 52N 77 50W
Coelemu 124 36 30 S 72 48W
Coen 97 13 52 S 143 12 E
Coesfeld 24 51 56N 7 10 E
Coeur d'Alene 118 47 45N 116 51W
Cœur d'Alene L. 118 47 32N 116 48W
Coevorden 16 52 40N 6 44 E
Coffeyville 117 37 0N 95 40W
Coffs Harbour 97 30 16 S 153 5 E
Cofrentes 33 39 13N 1 5W
Cogealac 46 44 36N 28 36 E
Coghinas → 40 40 55N 8 48 E
Coghinas, L. di 40 40 46N 9 3 E
Cognac 20 45 41N 0 20W
Cogne 38 45 37N 7 21 E
Cogolludo 32 40 59N 3 10W
Cohagen 118 47 2N 106 36W
Cohoes 114 42 47N 73 42W
Cohuna 99 35 45 S 144 15 E
Coiba, I. 121 7 30N 81 40W
Coig → 128 51 0 S 69 10W
Coihaique 128 45 30 S 71 45W
Coimbatore 70 11 2N 76 59 E
Coimbra, Brazil 126 19 55 S 57 48W
Coimbra, Port. 30 40 15N 8 27W
Coimbra □ 30 40 12N 8 25W
Coín 31 36 40N 4 48W
Cojimies 126 0 20N 80 0W
Cojocna 46 46 45N 23 50 E
Cojutepequé 120 13 41N 88 54W
Čoka 42 45 57N 20 12 E
Cokeville 118 42 4N 111 0W
Col di Tenda 38 44 7N 7 36 E
Colaba Pt. 70 18 54N 72 47 E
Colac 97 38 21 S 143 35 E
Colachel 70 8 10N 77 15 E
Colares 31 38 48N 9 30W
Colbeck, C. 5 77 6 S 157 48W
Colbinabbin 99 36 38 S 144 48 E
Colborne 112 44 0N 77 53W
Colby 116 39 27N 101 2W
Colchagua □ 124 34 30 S 71 0W
Colchester 13 51 54N 0 55 E
Coldstream 14 55 39N 2 14W
Coldwater, Can. 112 44 42N 79 40W
Coldwater, U.S.A. 117 37 18N 99 24W
Colebrook, Austral. 99 42 31 S 147 21 E
Colebrook, U.S.A. 114 44 54N 71 29W
Coleman, Can. 108 49 40N 114 30W
Coleman, U.S.A. 117 31 52N 99 30W
Coleman → 97 15 6 S 141 38 E
Colenso 93 28 44 S 29 50 E
Coleraine, Austral. 99 37 36 S 141 40 E
Coleraine, U.K. 15 55 8N 6 40 E
Coleraine □ 15 55 8N 6 40 E
Coleridge, L. 101 43 17 S 171 30 E
Coleroon → 70 11 25N 79 50 E
Colesberg 92 30 45 S 25 5 E
Colfax, La., U.S.A. 117 31 35N 92 39W
Colfax, Wash., U.S.A. 118 46 57N 117 28W
Colhué Huapi, L. 128 45 30 S 69 0W
Cólico 38 46 8N 9 22 E
Coligny 93 26 17 S 26 15 E
Colima 120 19 10N 103 40W
Colima □ 120 19 10N 103 40W
Colima, Nevado de 120 19 35N 103 45W
Colina 124 33 13 S 70 45W
Colina do Norte 84 12 28N 15 0W
Colinas 127 6 0 S 44 10W
Colinton 100 35 50 S 149 10 E
Coll 14 56 40N 6 35W
Collaguasi 124 21 5 S 68 45W
Collarada, Peña 32 42 43N 0 29W
Collarenebri 99 29 33 S 148 34 E
Collbran 119 39 16N 107 58W
Colle di Val d'Elsa 39 43 25N 11 7 E
Colle Salvetti 38 43 34N 10 27 E
Colle Sannita 41 41 22N 14 48 E
Collécchio 38 44 45N 10 10 E
Colleen Bawn 91 21 0 S 29 12 E
College Park 115 33 42N 84 27W
Collette 107 46 40N 65 30W
Collie 96 33 22 S 116 8 E
Collier B. 96 16 10 S 124 15 E
Colline Metallifere 38 43 10N 11 0 E
Collingwood, Austral. 98 22 20 S 142 31 E
Collingwood, Can. 106 44 29N 80 13W
Collingwood, N.Z. 101 40 41 S 172 40 E
Collins 106 50 17N 89 27W
Collinsville 97 20 30 S 147 56 E
Collipulli 124 37 55 S 72 30W
Collo 83 36 58N 6 37 E
Collonges 21 46 9N 5 52 E
Collooney 15 54 11N 8 28W
Colmar 19 48 5N 7 20 E
Colmars 21 44 11N 6 39 E
Colmenar 31 36 54N 4 20W
Colmenar de Oreja 32 40 6N 3 25W
Colmenar Viejo 30 40 39N 3 47W
Colne 12 53 51N 2 11W
Colo → 99 33 25 S 150 52 E
Cologna Véneta 39 45 19N 11 21 E
Cologne = Köln 24 50 56N 9 58 E
Colomb-Béchar = Béchar 82 31 38N 2 18W
Colombey-les-Belles 19 48 32N 5 54 E
Colombey-les-Deux-Églises 19 48 13N 4 50 E
Colômbia 127 20 10 S 48 40W
Colombia ■ 126 3 45N 73 0W
Colombo 70 6 56N 79 58 E
Colombus 119 31 54N 107 43W
Colome 116 43 20N 99 44W
Colón, Argent. 124 32 12 S 58 10W
Colón, Cuba 121 22 42N 80 54W
Colón, Panama 120 9 20N 79 54W
Colonella 39 42 52N 13 50 E
Colonia 124 34 25 S 57 50W
Colonia Dora 124 28 34 S 62 59W
Colonial Hts. 114 37 19N 77 25W
Colonne, C. delle 41 39 2N 17 11 E
Colonsay, Can. 109 51 59N 105 52W
Colonsay, U.K. 14 56 4N 6 12W
Colorado □ 110 37 40N 106 0W
Colorado →, Argent. 128 39 50 S 62 8W
Colorado →, Calif., U.S.A. 119 34 45N 114 40W
Colorado →, Tex., U.S.A. 117 28 36N 95 58W
Colorado City 117 32 25N 100 50W
Colorado Desert 110 34 20N 116 0W
Colorado, I. 120 9 12N 79 50W
Colorado Plateau 119 36 40N 110 30W
Colorado R. Aqueduct 119 34 17N 114 10W
Colorado Springs 116 38 55N 104 50W
Colorno 38 44 55N 10 21 E
Colton, N.Y., U.S.A. 113 44 34N 74 58W
Colton, Wash., U.S.A. 118 46 41N 117 6W
Columbia, La., U.S.A. 117 32 7N 92 5W
Columbia, Miss., U.S.A. 117 31 16N 89 50W
Columbia, Mo., U.S.A. 116 38 58N 92 20W
Columbia, Pa., U.S.A. 114 40 2N 76 30W
Columbia, S.C., U.S.A. 115 34 0N 81 0W
Columbia, Tenn., U.S.A. 115 35 40N 87 0W
Columbia → 118 46 15N 124 5W
Columbia Basin 118 47 30N 118 30W
Columbia, C. 4 83 0N 70 0W
Columbia City 114 41 8N 85 30W
Columbia, District of □ 114 38 55N 77 0W
Columbia Falls 118 48 25N 114 16W
Columbia Heights 116 45 5N 93 10W
Columbia, Mt. 108 52 8N 117 20W
Columbiana 112 40 53N 80 40W
Columbretes, Is. 32 39 50N 0 50 E
Columbus, Ga., U.S.A. 115 32 30N 84 58W
Columbus, Ind., U.S.A. 114 39 14N 85 55W
Columbus, Kans., U.S.A. 117 37 15N 94 30W
Columbus, Miss., U.S.A. 115 33 30N 88 26W
Columbus, Mont., U.S.A. 118 45 38N 109 14W
Columbus, N.D., U.S.A. 116 48 52N 102 48W
Columbus, Nebr., U.S.A. 116 41 30N 97 25W
Columbus, Ohio, U.S.A. 114 39 57N 83 1W
Columbus, Tex., U.S.A. 117 29 42N 96 33W
Columbus, Wis., U.S.A. 116 43 20N 89 2W

Colunga Cradock

Colunga 30 43 29N 5 16W
Colusa 118 39 15N 122 1W
Colville 118 48 33N 117 54W
Colville → 104 70 25N 151 0W
Colville, C. 101 36 29 S 175 21 E
Colwyn Bay 12 53 17N 3 44W
Coma 87 8 29N 36 53 E
Comácchio 39 44 41N 12 10 E
Comallo 128 41 0 S 70 5W
Comana 46 44 10N 26 10 E
Comanche, Okla., U.S.A. 117 34 27N 97 58W
Comanche, Tex., U.S.A. 117 31 55N 98 35W
Comănești 46 46 25N 26 26 E
Combahee → 115 32 30N 80 31W
Combeaufontaine 19 47 38N 5 54 E
Comber 112 42 14N 82 33W
Comblain-au-Pont 16 50 29N 5 35 E
Combles 19 50 0N 2 50 E
Combourg 18 48 25N 1 46W
Combronde 20 45 58N 3 5 E
Comeragh Mts. 15 52 17N 7 35W
Comet 98 23 36 S 148 38 E
Comilla 69 23 28N 91 10 E
Comino, C. 40 40 28N 9 47 E
Comino I. 36 36 0N 14 20 E
Cómiso 41 36 57N 14 35 E
Comitán 120 16 18N 92 9W
Commentry 20 46 20N 2 46 E
Commerce, Ga., U.S.A. 115 34 10N 83 25W
Commerce, Tex., U.S.A. 117 33 15N 95 50W
Commercy 19 48 46N 5 34 E
Committee B. 105 68 30N 86 30W
Commonwealth B. 5 67 0 S 144 0 E
Commoron Cr. → 99 28 22 S 150 8 E
Communism Pk. = Kommunisma, Pic 65 38 40N 72 0 E
Como 38 45 48N 9 5 E
Como, L. di 38 46 5N 9 17 E
Comodoro Rivadavia 128 45 50 S 67 40W
Comorin, C. 70 8 3N 77 40 E
Comoriște 42 45 10N 21 35 E
Comoro Is. 3 12 10 S 44 15 E
Comox 108 49 42N 124 55W
Compiègne 19 49 24N 2 50 E
Compíglia Maríttima 38 43 4N 10 37 E
Comporta 31 38 22N 8 46W
Comprida, I. 125 24 50 S 47 42W
Compton Downs 99 30 28 S 146 30 E
Côn Dao 71 8 45N 106 45 E
Conakry 84 9 29N 13 49W
Conara Junction 99 41 50 S 147 26 E
Concarneau 18 47 52N 3 56W
Conceição 91 18 47 S 36 7 E
Conceição da Barra 127 18 35 S 39 45W
Conceição do Araguaia 127 8 0 S 49 2W
Concepción, Argent. 124 27 20 S 65 35W
Concepción, Boliv. 126 16 15 S 62 8W
Concepción, Chile 124 36 50 S 73 0W
Concepción, Parag. 124 23 22 S 57 26W
Concepción □ 124 37 0 S 72 30W
Concepción → 120 30 32N 113 2W
Concepción del Oro 120 24 40N 101 30W
Concepción del Uruguay 124 32 35 S 58 20W
Concepción, L. 126 17 20 S 61 20W
Concepción, La = Ri-Aba 85 3 28N 8 40 E
Concepcion, Pt. 119 34 27N 120 27W
Concepción, Punta 120 26 55N 111 59W
Conception B. 92 23 55 S 14 22 E
Conception I. 121 23 52N 75 9W
Conception, Pt. 119 34 30N 120 34W
Concession 91 17 27 S 30 56 E
Conchas Dam 117 35 25N 104 10W
Conche 107 50 55N 55 58W
Conches 18 48 51N 2 43 E
Concho 119 34 32N 109 43W
Concho → 117 31 30N 99 45W
Conchos → 120 29 32N 104 25W
Concord, N.C., U.S.A. 115 35 28N 80 35W
Concord, N.H., U.S.A. 114 43 12N 71 30W
Concordia 124 31 20 S 58 2W
Concórdia 126 4 36 S 66 36W
Concordia 116 39 35N 97 40W
Concordia, La 120 16 8N 92 38W
Concots 20 44 26N 1 40 E
Concrete 118 48 35N 121 49W
Condamine → 97 27 7 S 149 48 E
Condat 20 45 21N 2 46 E
Condé 19 50 26N 3 34 E
Conde 116 45 13N 98 5W
Condé-sur-Noireau 18 48 51N 0 33W
Condeúba 127 14 52 S 42 0W
Condobolin 99 33 4 S 147 6 E
Condom 20 43 57N 0 22 E
Condon 118 45 15N 120 8W
Condove 38 45 8N 7 19 E
Conegliano 39 45 53N 12 18 E
Conejera, I. 33 39 11N 2 58 E
Conflans-en-Jarnisy 19 49 10N 5 52 E
Confolens 20 46 2N 0 40 E
Confuso → 124 25 9 S 57 34W
Congleton 12 53 10N 2 12W
Congo = Zaïre → 88 1 30N 28 0 E
Congo ■ 88 1 0 S 16 0 E
Congo Basin 78 0 10 S 24 30 E
Congonhas 125 20 30 S 43 52W
Congress 119 34 11N 112 56W
Conil 31 36 17N 6 10W
Coniston 106 46 29N 80 51W
Conjeevaram = Kanchipuram 70 12 52N 79 45 E
Conjuboy 98 18 35 S 144 35 E
Conklin 109 55 38N 111 5W
Conlea 99 30 7 S 144 35 E
Conn, L. 15 54 3N 9 15W
Connacht 15 53 23N 8 40W
Conneaut 114 41 55N 80 32W
Connecticut □ 114 41 40N 72 40W
Connecticut → 114 41 17N 72 21W
Connell 118 46 36N 118 51W
Connellsville 114 40 3N 79 32W
Connemara 15 53 29N 9 45W
Connemaugh → 112 40 38N 79 42W
Conner, La 118 48 22N 122 27W
Connerré 18 48 3N 0 30 E
Connersville 114 39 40N 85 10W
Connors Ra. 98 21 40 S 149 10 E
Conoble 99 32 55 S 144 33 E
Conon → 14 57 33N 4 28W
Cononaco → 126 1 32 S 75 35W
Cononbridge 14 57 32N 4 30W
Conquest 109 51 32N 107 14W
Conquet, Le 18 48 21N 4 46W
Conrad 118 48 11N 112 0W
Conran, C. 99 37 49 S 148 44 E
Conroe 117 30 15N 95 28W
Conselheiro Lafaiete 125 20 40 S 43 48W
Conshohocken 113 40 5N 75 18W
Consort 109 52 1N 110 46W
Constance = Konstanz 25 47 39N 9 10 E
Constance, L. = Bodensee 25 47 35N 9 25 E
Constanța 46 44 14N 28 38 E
Constanța □ 46 44 15N 28 15 E
Constantina 31 37 51N 5 40W
Constantine 83 36 25N 6 42 E
Constitución, Chile 124 35 20 S 72 30W
Constitución, Uruguay 124 42 0 S 57 50W
Consuegra 31 39 28N 3 36W
Consul 109 49 20N 109 30W
Contact 118 41 50N 114 56W
Contai 69 21 54N 87 46 E
Contamana 126 7 19 S 74 55W
Contarina 39 45 2N 12 13 E
Contas → 127 14 17 S 39 1W
Contes 21 43 49N 7 19 E
Contoocook 113 43 13N 71 45W
Contra Costa 93 25 9 S 33 30 E
Contres 18 47 24N 1 26 E
Contrexéville 19 48 6N 5 53 E
Conversano 41 40 57N 17 8 E
Conway, Ark., U.S.A. 117 35 5N 92 30W
Conway, N.H., U.S.A. 114 43 58N 71 8W
Conway, S.C., U.S.A. 115 33 49N 79 2W
Conway = Conwy 12 53 17N 3 50W
Conwy 12 53 17N 3 50W
Conwy → 12 53 18N 3 50W
Coober Pedy 96 29 1 S 134 43 E
Cooch Behar 69 26 22N 89 29 E
Cook 116 47 49N 92 39W
Cook, Bahía 128 55 10 S 70 0W
Cook Inlet 104 59 0N 151 0W
Cook Is. 95 17 0 S 160 0W
Cook, Mt. 101 43 36 S 170 9 E
Cook Strait 101 41 15 S 174 29 E
Cookeville 115 36 12N 85 30W
Cookhouse 92 32 44 S 25 47 E
Cookshire 113 45 25N 71 38W
Cookstown 15 54 40N 6 43W
Cookstown □ 15 54 40N 6 43W
Cooksville 112 43 36N 79 35W
Cooktown 97 15 30 S 145 16 E
Coolabah 99 31 1 S 146 43 E
Cooladdi 99 26 37 S 145 23 E
Coolah 99 31 48 S 149 41 E
Coolamon 99 34 46 S 147 8 E
Coolangatta 99 28 11 S 153 29 E
Coolgardie 96 30 55 S 121 8 E
Coolidge 119 33 1N 111 35W
Coolidge Dam 119 33 10N 110 30W
Cooma 97 36 12 S 149 8 E
Coonabarabran 99 31 14 S 149 18 E
Coonamble 97 30 56 S 148 27 E
Coondapoor 70 13 42N 74 40 E
Coongie 99 27 9 S 140 8 E
Coongoola 99 27 43 S 145 51 E
Cooninie, L. 99 26 4 S 139 59 E
Coonoor 70 11 21N 76 45 E
Cooper 117 33 20N 95 40W
Cooper → 115 33 0N 79 55W
Coopers Cr. → 97 28 29 S 137 46 E
Cooperstown, N.D., U.S.A. 116 47 30N 98 6W
Cooperstown, N.Y., U.S.A. 114 42 42N 74 57W
Coorabulka 98 23 41 S 140 20 E
Coorong, The 97 35 50 S 139 20 E
Cooroy 99 26 22 S 152 54 E
Coos Bay 118 43 26N 124 7W
Cootamundra 97 34 36 S 148 1 E
Cootehill 15 54 5N 7 5W
Cooyar 99 26 59 S 151 51 E
Cooyeana 98 24 29 S 138 45 E
Copahue Paso 124 37 49 S 71 8W
Copainalá 120 17 8N 93 11W
Cope 116 39 44N 102 50W
Cope, Cabo 33 37 26N 1 28W
Copenhagen = København 49 55 41N 12 34 E
Copertino 41 40 17N 18 2 E
Copiapó 124 27 30 S 70 20W
Copiapó → 124 27 19 S 70 56W
Copley 99 30 36 S 138 26 E
Copp L. 108 60 14N 114 40W
Copparo 39 44 52N 11 49 E
Copper Center 104 62 10N 145 25W
Copper Cliff 106 46 28N 81 4W
Copper Harbor 114 47 31N 87 55W
Copper Queen 91 17 29 S 29 18 E
Copperbelt □ 91 13 15 S 27 30 E
Coppermine 104 67 50N 115 5W
Coppermine → 104 67 49N 116 4W
Coquet → 12 55 18N 1 45W
Coquilhatville = Mbandaka 88 0 1N 18 18 E
Coquille 118 43 15N 124 12W
Coquimbo 124 30 0 S 71 20W
Coquimbo □ 124 31 0 S 71 0W
Corabia 46 43 48N 24 30 E
Coracora 126 15 5 S 73 45W
Coradi, Is. 41 40 27N 17 10 E
Coral Gables 115 25 45N 80 16W
Coral Harbour 105 64 8N 83 10W
Coral Sea 94 15 0 S 150 0 E
Coral Sea Islands Terr. 97 20 0 S 155 0 E
Corangamite, L. 100 38 0 S 143 30 E
Coraopolis 112 40 30N 80 10W
Corato 41 41 12N 16 22 E
Corbeil-Essonnes 19 48 36N 2 26 E
Corbie 19 49 54N 2 30 E
Corbières 20 42 55N 2 35 E
Corbigny 19 47 16N 3 40 E
Corbin 114 37 0N 84 3W
Corbones → 31 37 36N 5 39W
Corby 13 52 49N 0 31W
Corcoles → 33 39 40N 3 18W
Corcoran 119 36 6N 119 35W
Corcubión 30 42 56N 9 12W
Cordele 115 31 55N 83 49W
Cordell 117 35 18N 99 0W
Cordenons 39 45 59N 12 42 E
Cordes 20 44 5N 1 57 E
Córdoba, Argent. 124 31 20 S 64 10W
Córdoba, Mexico 120 18 50N 97 0W
Córdoba, Spain 31 37 50N 4 50W
Córdoba □, Argent. 124 31 22 S 64 15W
Córdoba □, Spain 31 38 5N 5 0W
Córdoba, Sierra de 124 31 10 S 64 25W
Cordon 73 16 42N 121 32 E
Cordova, Ala., U.S.A. 115 33 45N 87 12W
Cordova, Alaska, U.S.A. 104 60 36N 145 45W
Corella 32 42 7N 1 48W
Corella → 98 19 34 S 140 47 E
Corfield 98 21 40 S 143 21 E
Corfu = Kérkira 44 39 38N 19 50 E
Corgo 30 42 56N 7 25W
Cori 40 41 39N 12 53 E
Coria 30 40 0N 6 33W
Coricudgy, Mt. 100 32 51 S 150 24 E
Corigliano Cálabro 41 39 36N 16 31 E
Corinna 99 41 35 S 145 10 E
Corinth, Miss., U.S.A. 115 34 54N 88 30W
Corinth, N.Y., U.S.A. 113 43 15N 73 50W
Corinth = Kórinthos 45 38 19N 22 24 E
Corinth Canal 45 37 58N 23 0 E
Corinth, G. of = Korinthiakós 45 38 16N 22 30 E
Corinto, Brazil 127 18 20 S 44 30W
Corinto, Nic. 121 12 30N 87 10W
Corj □ 46 45 5N 23 25 E
Cork 15 51 54N 8 30W
Cork □ 15 51 50N 8 50W
Cork Harbour 15 51 46N 8 16W
Corlay 18 48 20N 3 5W
Corleone 40 37 48N 13 16 E
Corleto Perticara 41 40 23N 16 2 E
Çorlu 43 41 11N 27 49 E
Cormack L. 108 60 56N 121 37W
Cormòns 39 45 58N 13 29 E
Cormorant 109 54 14N 100 35W
Cormorant L. 109 54 15N 100 50W
Corn Is. = Maiz, Is. del 121 12 0N 83 0W
Cornélio Procópio 125 23 7 S 50 40W
Cornell 116 45 10N 91 8W
Corner Brook 107 48 57N 57 58W
Corner Inlet 97 38 45 S 146 20 E
Corniglio 38 44 29N 10 5 E
Corning, Ark., U.S.A. 117 36 27N 90 34W
Corning, Calif., U.S.A. 118 39 56N 122 9W
Corning, Iowa, U.S.A. 116 40 57N 94 40W
Corning, N.Y., U.S.A. 114 42 10N 77 3W
Corno, Monte 39 42 28N 13 34 E
Cornwall, Austral. 99 41 33 S 148 7 E
Cornwall, Can. 106 45 2N 74 44W
Cornwall □ 13 50 26N 4 40W
Cornwallis I. 4 75 8N 95 0W
Corny Pt. 99 34 55 S 137 0 E
Coro 126 11 25N 69 41W
Coroatá 127 4 8 S 44 0W
Corocoro 126 17 15 S 68 28W
Coroico 126 16 0 S 67 50W
Coromandel 101 36 45 S 175 31 E
Coromandel Coast 70 12 30N 81 0 E
Corona, Austral. 99 31 16 S 141 24 E
Corona, Calif., U.S.A. 119 33 49N 117 36W
Corona, N. Mex., U.S.A. 119 34 15N 105 32W
Coronada 119 32 45N 117 9W
Coronado, Bahía de 121 9 0N 83 40W
Coronation 108 52 5N 111 27W
Coronation Gulf 104 68 25N 110 0W
Coronation I., Antarct. 5 60 45 S 46 0W
Coronation I., U.S.A. 108 55 52N 134 20W
Coronda 124 31 58 S 60 56W
Coronel 124 37 0 S 73 10W
Coronel Bogado 124 27 11 S 56 18W
Coronel Dorrego 124 38 40 S 61 10W
Coronel Oviedo 124 25 24 S 56 30W
Coronel Pringles 124 38 0 S 61 30W
Coronel Suárez 124 37 30 S 61 52W
Coronel Vidal 124 37 28 S 57 45W
Çorovoda 44 40 31N 20 14 E
Corowa 99 35 58 S 146 21 E
Corozal, Belize 120 18 23N 88 23W
Corozal, Panama 120 8 59N 79 34W
Corps 21 44 50N 5 56 E
Corpus 125 27 10 S 55 30W
Corpus Christi 117 27 50N 97 28W
Corpus Christi L. 117 28 5N 97 54W
Corque 126 18 20 S 67 41W
Corral de Almaguer 32 39 45N 3 10W
Corréggio 38 44 46N 10 47 E
Correntes, C. das 93 24 6 S 35 34 E
Corrèze □ 20 45 20N 1 45 E
Correze → 20 45 10N 1 28 E
Corrib, L. 15 53 5N 9 10W
Corrientes 124 27 30 S 58 45W
Corrientes □ 124 28 0 S 57 0W
Corrientes →, Argent. 124 30 42 S 59 38W
Corrientes →, Peru 126 3 43 S 74 35W
Corrientes, C., Colomb. 126 5 30N 77 34W
Corrientes, C., Cuba 121 21 43N 84 30W
Corrientes, C., Mexico 120 20 25N 105 42W
Corrigan 117 31 0N 94 48W
Corry 114 41 55N 79 39W
Corse 21 42 0N 9 0 E
Corse, C. 21 43 1N 9 25 E
Corse-du-Sud □ 21 41 45N 9 0 E
Corsica = Corse 21 42 0N 9 0 E
Corsicana 117 32 5N 96 30W
Corté 21 42 19N 9 11 E
Corte do Pinto 31 37 42N 7 29W
Cortegana 31 37 52N 6 49W
Cortez 119 37 24N 108 35W
Cortina d'Ampezzo 39 46 32N 12 9 E
Cortland 114 42 35N 76 11W
Cortona 39 43 16N 12 0 E
Coruche 31 38 57N 8 30W
Çorum 64 40 30N 34 57 E
Corumbá 126 19 0 S 57 30W
Corumbá de Goiás 127 16 0 S 48 50W
Coruña, La 30 43 20N 8 25W
Coruña, La □ 30 43 10N 8 30W
Corund 46 46 30N 25 13 E
Corunna = La Coruña 30 43 20N 8 25W
Corvallis 118 44 36N 123 15W
Corvette, L. de la 106 53 25N 74 3W
Corydon 116 40 42N 93 22W
Cosalá 120 24 28N 106 40W
Cosamaloapan 120 18 23N 95 50W
Cosenza 41 39 17N 16 14 E
Coșereni 46 44 38N 26 35 E
Coshocton 114 40 17N 81 51W
Cosne-sur-Loire 19 47 24N 2 54 E
Cospeito 30 43 12N 7 34W
Cosquín 124 31 15 S 64 30W
Cossato 38 45 34N 8 10 E
Cossé-le-Vivien 18 47 57N 0 54W
Cosson → 19 47 30N 1 15 E
Costa Blanca 33 38 25N 0 10W
Costa Brava 32 41 30N 3 0 E
Costa del Sol 31 36 30N 4 30W
Costa Dorada 32 40 45N 1 15 E
Costa Rica ■ 121 10 0N 84 0W
Costa Smeralda 40 41 5N 9 35 E
Costigliole d'Asti 38 44 48N 8 11 E
Costilla 119 37 0N 105 30W
Coștiui 46 47 53N 24 2 E
Coswig 24 51 52N 12 31 E
Cotabato 73 7 14N 124 15 E
Cotagaita 124 20 45 S 65 40W
Côte d'Azur 21 43 25N 6 50 E
Côte d'Or 19 47 10N 4 50 E
Côte-d'Or □ 19 47 30N 4 50 E
Côte-St.-André, La 21 45 24N 5 15 E
Coteau des Prairies 116 44 30N 97 0W
Coteau du Missouri, Plat. du 116 47 0N 101 0W
Coteau Landing 113 45 15N 74 13W
Cotentin 18 49 30N 1 30W
Côtes de Meuse 19 49 15N 5 22 E
Côtes-du-Nord □ 18 48 25N 2 40W
Cotiella 32 42 31N 0 19 E
Cotina → 42 43 36N 18 50 E
Cotonou 85 6 20N 2 25 E
Cotopaxi, Vol. 126 0 40 S 78 30W
Cotronei 41 39 9N 16 45 E
Cotswold Hills 13 51 42N 2 10W
Cottage Grove 118 43 48N 123 2W
Cottbus 24 51 44N 14 20 E
Cottbus □ 24 51 43N 13 30 E
Cottonwood 119 34 48N 112 1W
Cotulla 117 28 26N 99 14W
Coubre, Pte. de la 20 45 42N 1 15W
Couches 19 46 53N 4 30 E
Couço 31 38 59N 8 17W
Coudersport 114 41 45N 77 40W
Couëron 18 47 13N 1 44W
Couesnon → 18 48 38N 1 32W
Couhe-Vérac 20 46 18N 0 12 E
Coulanges 19 47 30N 3 30 E
Coulee City 118 47 36N 119 18W
Coulman I. 5 73 35 S 170 0 E
Coulommiers 19 48 50N 3 3 E
Coulon → 21 43 51N 5 0 E
Coulonge → 106 45 52N 76 46W
Coulonges 20 46 28N 0 35W
Council, Alaska, U.S.A. 104 64 55N 163 45W
Council, Idaho, U.S.A. 118 44 44N 116 26W
Council Bluffs 116 41 20N 95 50W
Council Grove 116 38 41N 96 30W
Courantyne → 126 5 55N 57 5W
Courçon 20 46 15N 0 50W
Couronne, C. 21 43 19N 5 3 E
Cours 21 46 7N 4 19 E
Coursan 20 43 14N 3 4 E
Courseulles 18 49 20N 0 29W
Courtenay 108 49 45N 125 0W
Courtine, La 20 45 43N 2 16 E
Courtrai = Kortrijk 16 50 50N 3 17 E
Courtright 112 42 49N 82 28W
Courville 18 48 28N 1 15 E
Coushatta 117 32 0N 93 21W
Coutances 18 49 3N 1 28W
Couterne 18 48 30N 0 25W
Coutras 20 45 3N 0 8W
Coutts 108 49 0N 111 57W
Covarrubias 32 42 4N 3 31W
Covasna 46 45 50N 26 10 E
Covasna □ 46 45 50N 26 0 E
Coventry 13 52 25N 1 31W
Coventry L. 109 61 15N 106 15W
Covilhã 30 40 17N 7 31W
Covington, Ga., U.S.A. 115 33 36N 83 50W
Covington, Ky., U.S.A. 114 39 5N 84 30W
Covington, Okla., U.S.A. 117 36 21N 97 36W
Covington, Tenn., U.S.A. 117 35 34N 89 39W
Cowal, L. 97 33 40 S 147 25 E
Cowan 109 52 5N 100 45W
Cowan, L. 96 31 45 S 121 45 E
Cowan L. 109 54 0N 107 15W
Cowangie 99 35 12 S 141 26 E
Cowansville 113 45 14N 72 46W
Cowarie 99 27 45 S 138 15 E
Cowdenbeath 14 56 7N 3 20W
Cowes 13 50 45N 1 18W
Cowra 97 33 49 S 148 42 E
Coxim 127 18 30 S 54 55W
Cox's Bazar 67 21 26N 91 59 E
Cox's Cove 107 49 7N 58 5W
Coyuca de Benítez 120 17 1N 100 8W
Coyuca de Catalan 120 18 18N 100 41W
Cozad 116 40 55N 99 57W
Cozumel, Isla de 120 20 30N 86 40W
Craboon 99 32 3 S 149 30 E
Cracow 99 25 17 S 150 17 E
Cracow = Kraków 27 50 4N 19 57 E
Cradock 92 32 8 S 25 36 E

Craig Damba

Craig, Alaska, U.S.A. 108 55 30N 133 5W
Craig, Colo., U.S.A. 118 40 32N 107 33W
Craigavon = Lurgan 15 54 28N 6 20W
Craigmore 91 20 28 S 32 50 E
Crailsheim 25 49 7N 10 5 E
Craiova 46 44 21N 23 48 E
Cramsie 98 23 20 S 144 15 E
Cranberry Portage 109 54 35N 101 23W
Cranbrook, Austral. 99 42 0 S 148 5 E
Cranbrook, Can. 108 49 30N 115 46W
Crandon 116 45 32N 88 52W
Crane, Oregon, U.S.A. 118 43 21N 118 39W
Crane, Texas, U.S.A. 117 31 26N 102 27W
Cranston 113 41 47N 71 27W
Craon 18 47 50N 0 58W
Craonne 19 49 27N 3 46 E
Craponne 20 45 20N 3 51 E
Crasna 46 46 32N 27 51 E
Crasna → 46 47 44N 22 35 E
Crasnei, Munţii 46 47 0N 23 20 E
Crater, L. 118 42 55N 122 3W
Crater Pt. 98 5 25 S 152 9 E
Crateús 127 5 10 S 40 39W
Crati → 41 39 41N 16 30 E
Crato, Brazil 127 7 10 S 39 25W
Crato, Port. 31 39 16N 7 39W
Crau 21 43 32N 4 40 E
Crawford 116 42 40N 103 25W
Crawfordsville 114 40 2N 86 51W
Crawley 13 51 7N 0 10W
Crazy Mts. 118 46 14N 110 30W
Crean L. 109 54 5N 106 9W
Crécy-en-Brie 19 48 50N 2 53 E
Crécy-en-Ponthieu 19 50 15N 1 53 E
Crediton 112 43 17N 81 33W
Cree →, Can. 109 58 57N 105 47W
Cree →, U.K. 14 54 51N 4 24W
Cree L. 109 57 30N 106 30W
Creede 119 37 56N 106 59W
Creel 120 27 45N 107 38W
Creighton 116 42 30N 97 52W
Creil 19 49 15N 2 34 E
Crema 38 45 21N 9 40 E
Cremona 38 45 8N 10 2 E
Crepaja 42 45 1N 20 38 E
Crépy 19 49 37N 3 32 E
Crépy-en-Valois 19 49 14N 2 54 E
Cres 39 44 58N 14 25 E
Cresbard 116 45 13N 98 57W
Crescent, Okla., U.S.A. 117 35 58N 97 36W
Crescent, Oreg., U.S.A. 118 43 30N 121 37W
Crescent City 118 41 45N 124 12W
Crescentino 38 45 11N 8 7 E
Crespino 39 44 59N 11 51 E
Crespo 124 32 2 S 60 19W
Cressy 99 38 2 S 143 40 E
Crest 21 44 44N 5 2 E
Crested Butte 119 38 57N 107 0W
Crestline 112 40 46N 82 45W
Creston, Can. 108 49 10N 116 31W
Creston, Iowa, U.S.A. 116 41 0N 94 20W
Creston, Wash., U.S.A. 118 47 47N 118 36W
Creston, Wyo., U.S.A. 118 41 46N 107 50W
Crestview 115 30 45N 86 35W
Creswick 100 37 25 S 143 58 E
Crete 116 40 38N 96 58W
Crete = Kríti 45 35 15N 25 0 E
Crete, La 108 58 11N 116 24W
Crete, Sea of 45 36 0N 25 0 E
Cretin, C. 98 6 40 S 147 53 E
Creus, C. 32 42 20N 3 19 E
Creuse □ 20 46 0N 2 0 E
Creuse → 20 47 0N 0 34 E
Creusot, Le 19 46 50N 4 24 E
Creuzburg 24 51 3N 10 15 E
Crevalcore 39 44 41N 11 10 E
Crèvecœur-le-Grand 19 49 37N 2 5 E
Crevillente 33 38 12N 0 48W
Crewe 12 53 6N 2 28W
Crib Point 99 38 22 S 145 13 E
Criciúma 125 28 40 S 49 23W
Crieff 14 56 22N 3 50W
Crikvenica 39 45 11N 14 40 E
Crimea = Krymskaya 56 45 0N 34 0 E
Crimmitschau 24 50 48N 12 23 E
Crinan 14 56 6N 5 34W
Cristeşti 46 47 15N 26 33 E
Cristóbal 120 9 19N 79 54W
Crişul Alb → 42 46 42N 21 17 E
Crişul Negru → 46 46 38N 22 26 E
Crişul Repede → 46 46 55N 20 59 E
Crivitz 24 53 35N 11 39 E
Crna Gora 42 42 10N 21 30 E
Crna Gora □ 42 42 40N 19 20 E
Crna Reka → 42 41 33N 21 59 E
Crna Trava 42 42 49N 22 19 E
Crni Drim → 42 41 17N 20 40 E
Crni Timok → 42 43 53N 22 15 E
Crnoljeva Planina 42 42 20N 21 0 E
Črnomelj 39 45 33N 15 10 E
Croaghpatrick 15 53 46N 9 40W
Croatia = Hrvatska □ 39 45 20N 16 0 E
Crocker, Barisan 72 5 40N 116 30 E
Crocker I. 96 11 12 S 132 32 E
Crockett 117 31 20N 95 30W
Crocodile = Krokodil → 93 25 26 S 32 0 E
Crocodile Is. 96 12 3 S 134 58 E
Crocq 20 45 52N 2 21 E
Croisette, C. 21 43 13N 5 20 E
Croisic, Le 18 47 18N 2 30W
Croisic, Pte. du 18 47 19N 2 31W
Croix, La, L. 106 48 20N 92 15W
Cromarty, Can. 109 58 3N 94 9W
Cromarty, U.K. 14 57 40N 4 2W
Cromer 12 52 56N 1 18 E
Cromwell 101 45 3 S 169 14 E
Cronat 19 46 43N 3 40 E
Cronulla 100 34 3 S 151 8 E
Crooked →, Can. 108 54 50N 122 54W
Crooked →, U.S.A. 118 44 30N 121 16W
Crooked I. 121 22 50N 74 10W
Crookston, Minn., U.S.A. 116 47 50N 96 40W
Crookston, Nebr., U.S.A. 116 42 56N 100 45W
Crooksville 114 39 45N 82 8W
Crookwell 99 34 28 S 149 24 E
Crosby, Minn., U.S.A. 116 46 28N 93 57W
Crosby, N.D., U.S.A. 109 48 55N 103 18W
Crosby, Pa., U.S.A. 112 41 45N 78 23W
Crosbyton 117 33 37N 101 12W
Cross → 85 4 42N 8 21 E
Cross City 115 29 35N 83 5W
Cross Fell 12 54 44N 2 29W
Cross L. 109 54 45N 97 30W
Cross Plains 117 32 8N 99 7W
Cross River □ 85 6 0N 8 0 E
Cross Sound 104 58 20N 136 30W
Crosse, La, Kans., U.S.A. 116 38 33N 99 20W
Crosse, La, Wis., U.S.A. 116 43 48N 91 13W
Crossett 117 33 10N 91 57W
Crossfield 108 51 25N 114 0W
Crosshaven 15 51 48N 8 19W
Croton-on-Hudson 113 41 12N 73 55W
Crotone 41 39 5N 17 6 E
Crow → 108 59 41N 124 20W
Crow Agency 118 45 40N 107 30W
Crow Hd. 15 51 34N 10 9W
Crowell 117 33 59N 99 45W
Crowley 117 30 15N 92 20W
Crown Point 114 41 24N 87 23W
Crows Nest 99 27 16 S 152 4 E
Crowsnest Pass 108 49 40N 114 40W
Croydon, Austral. 97 18 13 S 142 14 E
Croydon, U.K. 13 51 18N 0 5W
Crozet Is. 3 46 27 S 52 0 E
Crozon 18 48 15N 4 30W
Cruz Alta 125 28 45 S 53 40W
Cruz, C. 121 19 50N 77 50W
Cruz del Eje 124 30 45 S 64 50W
Cruz, La 120 23 55N 106 54W
Cruzeiro 125 22 33 S 45 0W
Cruzeiro do Oeste 125 23 46 S 53 4W
Cruzeiro do Sul 126 7 35 S 72 35W
Cry L. 108 58 45N 129 0W
Crystal Brook 99 33 21 S 138 12 E
Crystal City, Mo., U.S.A. 116 38 15N 90 23W
Crystal City, Tex., U.S.A. 117 28 40N 99 50W
Crystal Falls 114 46 9N 88 11W
Crystal River 115 28 54N 82 35W
Crystal Springs 117 31 59N 90 25W
Csongrád 27 46 43N 20 12 E
Csongrád □ 27 46 32N 20 15 E
Csorna 27 47 38N 17 18 E
Csurgo 27 46 16N 17 9 E
Cu Lao Hon 71 10 54N 108 18 E
Cuácua → 91 17 54 S 37 0 E
Cuamato 92 17 2 S 15 7 E
Cuamba 91 14 45 S 36 22 E
Cuando → 89 14 0 S 19 30 E
Cuando Cubango □ 92 16 25 S 20 0 E
Cuangar 92 17 36 S 18 39 E
Cuarto → 124 33 25 S 63 2W
Cuba, Port. 31 38 10N 7 54W
Cuba, N. Mex., U.S.A. 119 36 0N 107 0W
Cuba, N.Y., U.S.A. 112 42 12N 78 18W
Cuba ■ 121 22 0N 79 0W
Cubango → 92 18 50 S 22 25 E
Cuchi 89 14 37 S 16 58 E
Cúcuta 126 7 54N 72 31W
Cudahy 114 42 54N 87 50W
Cudalbi 46 45 46N 27 41 E
Cuddalore 70 11 46N 79 45 E
Cuddapah 70 14 30N 78 47 E
Cuddapan, L. 99 25 45 S 141 26 E
Cudgewa 99 36 10 S 147 42 E
Cudillero 30 43 33N 6 9W
Cue 96 27 25 S 117 54 E
Cuéllar 30 41 23N 4 21W
Cuenca, Ecuador 126 2 50 S 79 9W
Cuenca, Spain 32 40 5N 2 10W
Cuenca □ 32 40 0N 2 0W
Cuenca, Serranía de 32 39 55N 1 50W
Cuerda del Pozo, Pantano de la 32 41 51N 2 44W
Cuernavaca 120 18 50N 99 20W
Cuero 117 29 5N 97 17W
Cuers 21 43 14N 6 5 E
Cuervo 117 35 5N 104 25W
Cuevas del Almanzora 33 37 18N 1 58W
Cuevo 126 20 15 S 63 30W
Cugir 46 45 48N 23 25 E
Cuiabá 127 15 30 S 56 0W
Cuiabá → 127 17 5 S 56 36W
Cuillin Hills 14 57 14N 6 15W
Cuillin Sd. 14 57 4N 6 20W
Cuiluan 76 47 51N 128 32 E
Cuima 89 13 25 S 15 45 E
Cuiseaux 21 46 30N 5 22 E
Cuito → 92 18 1 S 20 48 E
Cuitzeo, L. de 120 19 55N 101 5W
Cujmir 46 44 13N 22 57 E
Culan 20 46 34N 2 20 E
Culbertson 116 48 9N 104 30W
Culcairn 99 35 41 S 147 3 E
Culebra, Sierra de la 30 41 55N 6 20W
Culgoa → 99 29 56 S 146 20 E
Culiacán 120 24 50N 107 23W
Culion 73 11 54N 120 1 E
Cúllar de Baza 33 37 35N 2 34W
Cullarin Range 99 34 30 S 149 30 E
Cullen 14 57 45N 2 50W
Cullen Pt. 98 11 57 S 141 54 E
Cullera 33 39 9N 0 17W
Cullman 115 34 13N 86 50W
Culloden Moor 14 57 29N 4 7W
Culoz 21 45 47N 5 46 E
Culpeper 114 38 29N 77 59W
Culuene → 127 12 56 S 52 51W
Culver, Pt. 96 32 54 S 124 43 E
Culverden 101 42 47 S 172 49 E
Cumali 45 36 42N 27 28 E
Cumaná 126 10 30N 64 5W
Cumberland, B.C., Can. 108 49 40N 125 0W
Cumberland, Qué., Can. 113 45 30N 75 24W
Cumberland, Md., U.S.A. 114 39 40N 78 43W
Cumberland, Wis., U.S.A. 116 45 32N 92 3W
Cumberland → 115 36 15N 87 0W
Cumberland I. 115 30 52N 81 30W
Cumberland Is. 97 20 35 S 149 10 E
Cumberland L. 109 54 3N 102 18W
Cumberland Pen. 105 67 0N 64 0W
Cumberland Plat. 115 36 0N 84 30W
Cumberland Sd. 105 65 30N 66 0W
Cumborah 99 29 40 S 147 45 E
Cumbres Mayores 31 38 4N 6 39W
Cumbria □ 12 54 35N 2 55W
Cumbrian Mts. 12 54 30N 3 0W
Cumbum 70 15 40N 79 10 E
Cumnock, Austral. 99 32 59 S 148 46 E
Cumnock, U.K. 14 55 27N 4 18W
Cuncumén 124 31 53 S 70 38W
Cunene → 92 17 20 S 11 50 E
Cúneo 38 44 23N 7 31 E
Cunillera, I. 33 38 59N 1 13 E
Cunlhat 20 45 38N 3 32 E
Cunnamulla 97 28 2 S 145 38 E
Cuorgnè 38 45 23N 7 39 E
Cupar, Can. 109 50 57N 104 10W
Cupar, U.K. 14 56 20N 3 0W
Cupica, Golfo de 126 6 25N 77 30W
Ćuprija 42 43 57N 21 26 E
Curaçao 121 12 10N 69 0W
Curanilahue 124 37 29 S 73 28W
Curaray → 126 2 20 S 74 5W
Cure → 19 47 40N 3 41 E
Curepto 124 35 8 S 72 1W
Curiapo 126 8 33N 61 5W
Curicó 124 34 55 S 71 20W
Curicó □ 124 34 50 S 71 15W
Curitiba 125 25 20 S 49 10W
Currabubula 99 31 16 S 150 44 E
Currais Novos 127 6 13 S 36 30W
Curralinho 127 1 45 S 49 46W
Currant 118 38 51N 115 32W
Curraweena 99 30 47 S 145 54 E
Currawilla 99 25 10 S 141 20 E
Current → 117 37 15N 91 10W
Currie, Austral. 99 39 56 S 143 53 E
Currie, U.S.A. 118 40 16N 114 45W
Currie, Mt. 93 30 29 S 29 21 E
Currituck Sd. 115 36 20N 75 50W
Currockbilly Mt. 100 35 25 S 150 0 E
Curtea de Argeş 46 45 12N 24 42 E
Curtis, Spain 30 43 7N 8 4W
Curtis, U.S.A. 116 40 41N 100 32W
Curtis I. 97 23 35 S 151 10 E
Curuápanema → 127 2 25 S 55 2W
Curuçá 127 0 43 S 47 50W
Curuguaty 125 24 31 S 55 42W
Çürüksu Çayi → 53 37 27N 27 11 E
Curundu 120 8 59N 79 38W
Curup 72 4 26 S 102 13 E
Cururupu 127 1 50 S 44 50W
Curuzú Cuatiá 124 29 50 S 58 5W
Curvelo 127 18 45 S 44 27W
Cushing 117 35 59N 96 46W
Cushing, Mt. 108 57 35N 126 57W
Cusihuiriáchic 120 28 10N 106 50W
Cusna, Monte 38 44 13N 10 25 E
Cusset 20 46 8N 3 28 E
Custer 116 43 45N 103 38W
Cut Bank 118 48 40N 112 15W
Cuthbert 115 31 47N 84 47W
Cutro 41 39 1N 16 58 E
Cuttaburra → 99 29 43 S 144 22 E
Cuttack 69 20 25N 85 57 E
Cuvier, C. 96 23 14 S 113 22 E
Cuvier I. 101 36 27 S 175 50 E
Cuxhaven 24 53 51N 8 41 E
Cuyahoga Falls 114 41 8N 81 30W
Cuyo 73 10 50N 121 5 E
Cuzco, Boliv. 126 20 0 S 66 50W
Cuzco, Peru 126 13 32 S 72 0W
Čvrsnica 42 43 36N 17 35 E
Cwmbran 13 51 39N 3 0W
Cyangugu 90 2 29 S 28 54 E
Cybinka 28 52 12N 14 46 E
Cyclades = Kikladhes 45 37 20N 24 30 E
Cygnet 99 43 8 S 147 1 E
Cynthiana 114 38 23N 84 10W
Cypress Hills 109 49 40N 109 30W
Cyprus ■ 64 35 0N 33 0 E
Cyrenaica 81 27 0N 23 0 E
Cyrene = Shaḥḥāt 81 32 40N 21 35 E
Czaplinek 28 53 34N 16 14 E
Czar 109 52 27N 110 50W
Czarna →, Piotrkow Trybunalski, Poland 28 51 18N 19 55 E
Czarna →, Tarnobrzeg, Poland 28 50 3N 21 21 E
Czarna Woda 28 53 51N 18 6 E
Czarne 28 53 42N 16 58 E
Czarnków 28 52 55N 16 38 E
Czechoslovakia ■ 27 49 0N 17 0 E
Czechowice-Dziedzice 27 49 54N 18 59 E
Czeladz 28 50 16N 19 2 E
Czempiń 28 52 9N 16 33 E
Czeremcha 28 52 31N 23 21 E
Czersk 28 53 46N 17 58 E
Czerwieńsk 28 52 1N 15 13 E
Czerwionka 27 50 7N 18 37 E
Częstochowa 28 50 49N 19 7 E
Częstochowa □ 28 50 45N 19 0 E
Człopa 28 53 6N 16 6 E
Człuchów 28 53 41N 17 22 E
Czyzew 28 52 48N 22 19 E

D

Da → 71 21 15N 105 20 E
Da Hinggan Ling 75 48 0N 121 0 E
Da Lat 71 11 56N 108 25 E
Da Nang 71 16 4N 108 13 E
Da Qaidam 75 37 50N 95 15 E
Da Yunhe, Jiangsu, China 77 34 25N 120 5 E
Da Yunhe, Zhejiang, China 77 30 45N 120 35 E
Da'an 76 45 30N 124 7 E
Dab'a, Râs el 86 31 3N 28 31 E
Daba Shan 75 32 0N 109 0 E
Dabai 85 11 25N 5 15 E
Dabakala 84 8 15N 4 20W
Dabbūrīya 62 32 42N 35 22 E
Dabhoi 68 22 10N 73 20 E
Dąbie, Poland 28 53 27N 14 45 E
Dąbie, Poland 28 52 5N 18 50 E
Dabo 72 0 30 S 104 33 E
Dabola 84 10 50N 11 5W
Dabou 84 5 20N 4 23W
Daboya 85 9 30N 1 20W
Dąbrowa Górnicza 28 50 15N 19 10 E
Dąbrowa Tarnówska 27 50 10N 20 59 E
Dąbrówno 28 53 27N 20 2 E
Dabus → 87 10 48N 35 10 E
Dacato → 87 7 25N 42 40 E
Dacca 69 23 43N 90 26 E
Dacca □ 69 24 25N 90 25 E
Dachau 25 48 16N 11 27 E
Dadanawa 126 2 50N 59 30W
Daday 56 41 28N 33 27 E
Dade City 115 28 20N 82 12W
Dades, Oued → 82 30 58N 6 44W
Dadiya 85 9 35N 11 24 E
Dadra and Nagar Haveli □ 68 20 5N 73 0 E
Dadri = Charkhi Dadri 68 28 37N 76 17 E
Dadu 68 26 45N 67 45 E
Dăeni 46 44 51N 28 10 E
Daet 73 14 2N 122 55 E
Dafang 77 27 9N 105 39 E
Dagana 84 16 30N 15 35W
Dagash 86 19 19N 33 25 E
Dagestan A.S.S.R. □ 57 42 30N 47 0 E
Dagestanskiye Ogni 57 42 6N 48 12 E
Daghfeli 86 19 18N 32 40 E
Dagö = Hiiumaa 54 58 50N 22 45 E
Dagupan 73 16 3N 120 20 E
Dahab 86 28 30N 34 31 E
Dahlak Kebir 87 15 50N 40 10 E
Dahlenburg 24 53 11N 10 43 E
Dahlonega 115 34 35N 83 59W
Dahme, Germ., E. 24 51 51N 13 25 E
Dahme, Germ., W. 24 54 13N 11 5 E
Dahomey = Benin ■ 85 10 0N 2 0 E
Dahra 84 15 22N 15 30W
Dahra, Massif de 82 36 7N 1 21 E
Dai Shan 77 30 25N 122 10 E
Dai Xian 76 39 4N 112 58 E
Daimiel 33 39 5N 3 35W
Daingean 15 53 18N 7 15W
Daintree 98 16 20 S 145 20 E
Daiō-Misaki 74 34 15N 136 45 E
Dairût 86 27 34N 30 43 E
Daitari 69 21 10N 85 46 E
Dajarra 97 21 42 S 139 30 E
Dakar 84 14 34N 17 29W
Dakhla 80 23 50N 15 53W
Dakhla, El Wâhât el- 86 25 30N 28 50 E
Dakhovskaya 57 44 13N 40 13 E
Dakingari 85 11 37N 4 1 E
Dakor 68 22 45N 73 11 E
Dakoro 85 14 31N 6 46 E
Dakota City 116 42 27N 96 28W
Đakovica 42 42 22N 20 26 E
Đakovo 42 45 19N 18 24 E
Dalaba 84 10 42N 12 15W
Dalachi 76 36 48N 105 0 E
Dalai Nur 76 43 20N 116 45 E
Dalandzadgad 75 43 27N 104 30 E
Dalbandin 65 29 0N 64 23 E
Dalbeattie 14 54 55N 3 50W
Dalbosjön 49 58 40N 12 45 E
Dalby, Austral. 97 27 10 S 151 17 E
Dalby, Sweden 49 55 40N 13 22 E
Dale 47 61 22N 5 23 E
Dalen 47 59 26N 8 0 E
Dalga 86 27 39N 30 41 E
Dalhart 117 36 10N 102 30W
Dalhousie, Can. 107 48 5N 66 26W
Dalhousie, India 68 32 38N 76 0 E
Dali, Shaanxi, China 77 34 48N 109 58 E
Dali, Yunnan, China 75 25 40N 100 10 E
Daliang Shan 75 28 0N 102 45 E
Dalias 33 36 49N 2 52W
Dāliyat el Karmel 62 32 43N 35 2 E
Dalj 42 45 29N 18 59 E
Dalkeith 14 55 54N 3 5W
Dall I. 108 54 59N 133 25W
Dallarnil 99 25 19 S 152 2 E
Dallas, Oregon, U.S.A. 118 45 0N 123 15W
Dallas, Texas, U.S.A. 117 32 50N 96 50W
Dallol 87 14 14N 40 17 E
Dalmacija □ 42 43 20N 17 0 E
Dalmatia = Dalmacija □ 42 43 20N 17 0 E
Dalmellington 14 55 20N 4 25W
Dalnerechensk 59 45 50N 133 40 E
Daloa 84 7 0N 6 30W
Dalrymple, Mt. 97 21 1 S 148 39 E
Dalsjöfors 49 57 46N 13 5 E
Dalskog 49 58 44N 12 18 E
Dalton, Can. 106 48 11N 84 1W
Dalton, Ga., U.S.A. 115 34 47N 84 58W
Dalton, Mass., U.S.A. 113 42 28N 73 11W
Dalton, Nebr., U.S.A. 116 41 27N 103 0W
Dalton Iceberg Tongue 5 66 15 S 121 30 E
Daltonganj 69 24 0N 84 4 E
Dalvík 50 65 58N 18 32W
Daly → 96 13 35 S 130 19 E
Daly L. 109 56 32N 105 39W
Daly Waters 96 16 15 S 133 24 E
Dama, Wadi → 86 27 12N 35 50 E
Daman 68 20 25N 72 57 E
Daman □ 68 20 25N 72 58 E
Damanhûr 86 31 0N 30 30 E
Damar 73 7 7 S 128 40 E
Damaraland 92 21 0 S 17 0 E
Damascus = Dimashq 64 33 30N 36 18 E
Damaturu 85 11 45N 11 55 E
Damāvand 65 35 47N 52 0 E
Damāvand, Qolleh-ye 65 35 56N 52 10 E
Damba 88 6 44 S 15 20 E

Dāmghān — Dessye

Dāmghān	65	36 10N	54 17 E
Dāmienesti	46	46 44N	27 1 E
Damietta = Dumyât	86	31 24N	31 48 E
Daming	76	36 15N	115 6 E
Dāmīya	62	32 6N	35 34 E
Dammarie	19	48 20N	1 30 E
Dammartin	19	49 3N	2 41 E
Damme	24	52 32N	8 12 E
Damodar →	69	23 17N	87 35 E
Damoh	69	23 50N	79 28 E
Damous	82	36 31N	1 42 E
Dampier	96	20 41 S	116 42 E
Dampier Arch.	96	20 38 S	116 32 E
Dampier Downs	96	18 24 S	123 5 E
Dampier, Selat	73	0 40 S	131 0 E
Dampier Str.	98	5 50 S	148 0 E
Damville	18	48 51N	1 5 E
Damvillers	19	49 20N	5 21 E
Dan-Gulbi	85	11 40N	6 15 E
Dan Xian	77	19 31N	109 33 E
Dana	73	11 0 S	122 52 E
Dana, Lac	106	50 53N	77 20W
Danakil Depression	87	12 45N	41 0 E
Danao	73	10 31N	124 1 E
Danbury	114	41 23N	73 29W
Danby L.	119	34 17N	115 0W
Dandeldhura	69	29 20N	80 35 E
Dandenong	99	38 0 S	145 15 E
Dandong	76	40 10N	124 20 E
Danforth	107	45 39N	67 57W
• Danger Is.	95	10 53 S	165 49W
Danger Pt.	92	34 40 S	19 17 E
Dangla	87	11 18N	36 56 E
Dangora	85	11 30N	8 7 E
Dangshan	77	34 27N	116 22 E
Dangtu	77	31 32N	118 25 E
Dangyang	77	30 52N	111 44 E
Daniel	118	42 56N	110 2W
Daniel's Harbour	107	50 13N	57 35W
Danielskull	92	28 11 S	23 33 E
Danielson	113	41 50N	71 52W
Danilov	55	58 16N	40 13 E
Danilovgrad	42	42 38N	19 9 E
Danilovka	55	50 25N	44 12 E
Danissa	90	3 15N	40 58 E
Danja	85	11 21N	7 30 E
Dankalwa	85	11 52N	12 12 E
Dankama	85	13 20N	7 44 E
Dankov	55	53 20N	39 5 E
Danlí	121	14 4N	86 35W
Dannemora, Sweden	48	60 12N	17 51 E
Dannemora, U.S.A.	114	44 41N	73 44W
Dannenberg	24	53 7N	11 4 E
Dannevirke	101	40 12 S	176 8 E
Dannhauser	93	28 0 S	30 3 E
Danshui	77	25 12N	121 25 E
Dansville	114	42 32N	77 41W
Dantan	69	21 57N	87 20 E
Dante	63	10 25N	51 26 E
Danube →	43	45 20N	29 40 E
Danukandi	69	23 32N	90 43 E
Danvers	113	42 34N	70 55W
Danville, Ill., U.S.A.	114	40 10N	87 40W
Danville, Ky., U.S.A.	114	37 40N	84 45W
Danville, Va., U.S.A.	115	36 40N	79 20W
Danzhai	77	26 11N	107 48 E
Danzig = Gdańsk	28	54 22N	18 40 E
Dao	73	10 30N	121 57 E
Dão →	30	40 20N	8 11W
Dao Xian	77	25 36N	111 31 E
Daosa	68	26 52N	76 20 E
Daoud = Aïn Beïda	83	35 44N	7 22 E
Daoulas	18	48 22N	4 17W
Dapong	85	10 55N	0 16 E
Daqing Shan	76	40 40N	111 0 E
Daqu Shan	77	30 25N	122 20 E
Dar al Hamrā, Ad	64	27 22N	37 43 E
Dar es Salaam	90	6 50 S	39 12 E
Dar'ā	62	32 36N	36 7 E
Dārāb	65	28 50N	54 30 E
Darabani	46	48 10N	26 39 E
Daraj	83	30 10N	10 28 E
Daravica	42	42 32N	20 8 E
Daraw	86	24 22N	32 51 E
Darazo	85	11 1N	10 24 E
Darband	66	34 20N	72 50 E
Darbhanga	69	26 15N	85 55 E
Darby	118	46 2N	114 7W
Darda	42	45 40N	18 41 E
Dardanelle	117	35 12N	93 9W
Dardanelles = Canakkale Boğazi	44	40 0N	26 0 E
Darfo	38	45 52N	10 11 E
Dargai	66	34 25N	71 55 E
Dargan Ata	58	40 29N	62 10 E
Dargaville	101	35 57 S	173 52 E
Darhan Muminggan Lianheqi	76	41 40N	110 28 E
Dari	87	5 48N	30 26 E
Darien	120	9 7N	79 46W
Darién, G. del	126	9 0N	77 0W
Darjeeling	69	27 3N	88 18 E
Dark Cove	107	48 47N	54 13W
Darling →	97	34 4 S	141 54 E
Darling Downs	99	27 30 S	150 30 E
Darling Ra.	96	32 30 S	116 0 E
Darlington, U.K.	12	54 33N	1 33W
Darlington, S.C., U.S.A.	115	34 18N	79 50W
Darlington, Wis., U.S.A.	116	42 43N	90 7W
Darlington Point	100	34 37 S	146 1 E
Darłowo	28	54 25N	16 25 E
Dărmăneşti	46	46 21N	26 33 E
Darmstadt	25	49 51N	8 40 E
Darnah	81	32 40N	22 35 E
Darnall	93	29 23 S	31 18 E
Darnétal	18	49 25N	1 10 E
Darney	19	48 5N	6 0 E
Darnick	100	32 48 S	143 38 E
Darnley B.	104	69 30N	123 30W
Darnley, C.	5	68 0 S	69 0 E
Daroca	32	41 9N	1 25W
Darr	98	23 13 S	144 7 E
Darr →	98	23 39 S	143 50 E
Darrington	118	48 14N	121 37W
Darror →	63	10 30N	50 0 E
Darsana	69	23 35N	88 48 E
Darsi	70	15 46N	79 44 E
Darsser Ort	24	54 29N	12 31 E
Dart →	13	50 24N	3 36W
Dart, C.	5	73 6 S	126 20W
Dartmoor	13	50 36N	4 0W
Dartmouth, Austral.	98	23 31 S	144 44 E
Dartmouth, Can.	107	44 40N	63 30W
Dartmouth, U.K.	13	50 21N	3 35W
Dartmouth, L.	99	26 4 S	145 18 E
Dartuch, C.	32	39 55N	3 49 E
Daru	98	9 3 S	143 13 E
Daruvar	42	45 35N	17 14 E
Darvaza	58	40 11N	58 24 E
Darwha	68	20 15N	77 45 E
Darwin	96	12 25 S	130 51 E
Darwin Glacier	5	79 53 S	159 0 E
Daryacheh-ye-Sistan	65	31 0N	61 0 E
Daryapur	68	20 55N	77 20 E
Das	65	25 20N	53 30 E
Dashkesan	57	40 40N	46 0 E
Dasht →	65	25 10N	61 40 E
Dasht-e Kavīr	65	34 30N	55 0 E
Dasht-e Lūt	65	31 30N	58 0 E
Dasht-e Mārgow	65	30 40N	62 30 E
Daska	68	32 20N	74 20 E
Dassa-Zoume	85	7 46N	2 14 E
Dasseneiland	92	33 25 S	18 3 E
Datça	45	36 46N	27 40 E
Datia	68	25 39N	78 27 E
Datian	77	25 40N	117 50 E
Datong, Anhui, China	77	30 48N	117 44 E
Datong, Shanxi, China	76	40 6N	113 18 E
Dattapur	68	20 45N	78 15 E
Datu Piang	73	7 2N	124 30 E
Datu, Tanjung	72	2 5N	109 39 E
Daugava →	54	57 4N	24 3 E
Daugavpils	54	55 53N	26 32 E
Daulatabad	70	19 57N	75 15 E
Daun	25	50 10N	6 53 E
Dauphin	109	51 9N	100 5W
Dauphin I.	115	30 16N	88 10W
Dauphin L.	109	51 20N	99 45W
Dauphiné	21	45 15N	5 25 E
Dauqa	86	19 30N	41 0 E
Daura, Borno, Nigeria	85	11 31N	11 24 E
Daura, Kaduna, Nigeria	85	13 2N	8 21 E
Davangere	70	14 25N	75 55 E
Davao	73	7 0N	125 40 E
Davao, G. of	73	6 30N	125 48 E
Dāvar Panāh	65	27 25N	62 15 E
Davenport, Iowa, U.S.A.	116	41 30N	90 40W
Davenport, Wash., U.S.A.	118	47 40N	118 5W
Davenport Downs	98	24 8 S	141 7 E
Davenport Ra.	96	20 28 S	134 0 E
David	121	8 30N	82 30W
David City	116	41 18N	97 10W
David Gorodok	54	52 4N	27 8 E
Davidson	109	51 16N	105 59W
Davis, Antarct.	5	68 34 S	17 55 E
Davis, U.S.A.	118	38 33N	121 44W
Davis Dam	119	35 11N	114 35W
Davis Inlet	107	55 50N	60 59W
Davis Mts.	117	30 42N	104 15W
Davis Sea	5	66 0 S	92 0 E
Davis Str.	105	65 0N	58 0W
Davos	25	46 48N	9 49 E
Davy L.	109	58 53N	108 18W
Dawa →	87	4 11N	42 6 E
Dawaki, Bauchi, Nigeria	85	9 25N	9 33 E
Dawaki, Kano, Nigeria	85	12 5N	8 23 E
Dawes Ra.	98	24 40 S	150 40 E
Dawson, Can.	104	64 10N	139 30W
Dawson, Ga., U.S.A.	115	31 45N	84 28W
Dawson, N.D., U.S.A.	116	46 56N	99 45W
Dawson →	97	23 25 S	149 45 E
Dawson Creek	108	55 45N	120 15W
Dawson, I.	128	53 50 S	70 50W
Dawson Inlet	109	61 50N	93 25W
Dawson Range	98	24 30 S	149 48 E
Dax	20	43 44N	1 3W
Daxian	75	31 15N	107 23 E
Daxin	77	22 50N	107 11 E
Daxue Shan	75	30 30N	101 30 E
Daye	77	30 6N	114 58 E
Daylesford	100	37 21 S	144 9 E
Dayong	77	29 11N	110 30 E
Dayr Abū Sa'īd	62	32 30N	35 42 E
Dayr al-Ghuşūn	62	32 21N	35 4 E
Dayr az Zawr	64	35 20N	40 5 E
Dayr Dirwān	62	31 55N	35 15 E
Daysland	108	52 50N	112 20W
Dayton, Ohio, U.S.A.	114	39 45N	84 10W
Dayton, Pa., U.S.A.	112	40 54N	79 18W
Dayton, Tenn., U.S.A.	115	35 30N	85 1W
Dayton, Wash., U.S.A.	118	46 20N	118 10W
Daytona Beach	115	29 14N	81 0W
Dayu	77	25 24N	114 22 E
Dayville	118	44 33N	119 37W
Dazhu	77	30 41N	107 15 E
Dazu	77	29 40N	105 42 E
De Aar	92	30 39 S	24 0 E
De Funiak Springs	115	30 42N	86 10W
De Grey	96	20 12 S	119 12 E
De Land	115	29 1N	81 19W
De Leon	117	32 9N	98 35W
De Pere	114	44 28N	88 1W
De Queen	117	34 3N	94 24W
De Quincy	117	30 30N	93 27W
De Ridder	117	30 48N	93 15W
De Smet	116	44 25N	97 35W
De Soto	116	38 7N	90 33W
De Tour	114	45 59N	83 56W
De Witt	117	34 19N	91 20W
Dead Sea = Miyet, Bahr el	64	31 30N	35 30 E
Deadwood	116	44 23N	103 44W
Deadwood L.	108	59 10N	128 30W
Deakin	96	30 46 S	128 0 E
Deal	13	51 13N	1 25 E
Dealesville	92	28 41 S	25 44 E
Dean, Forest of	13	51 50N	2 35W
Deán Funes	124	30 20 S	64 20W
Dearborn	106	42 18N	83 15W
Dease →	108	59 56N	128 32W
Dease L.	108	58 40N	130 5W
Dease Lake	108	58 25N	130 6W
Death Valley	119	36 19N	116 52W
Death Valley Junc.	119	36 21N	116 30W
Death Valley Nat. Monument	119	36 30N	117 0W
Deauville	18	49 23N	0 2 E
Deba Habe	85	10 14N	11 20 E
Debaltsevo	56	48 22N	38 26 E
Debao	77	23 21N	106 46 E
Debar	42	41 31N	20 30 E
Debden	109	53 30N	106 50W
Debdou	82	33 59N	3 0W
Dębica	27	50 2N	21 25 E
Dęblin	28	51 34N	21 50 E
Debno	28	52 44N	14 41 E
Débo, L.	84	15 14N	4 15W
Debolt	108	55 12N	118 1W
Debrc	42	44 38N	19 53 E
Debre Birhan	87	9 41N	39 31 E
Debre Markos	87	10 20N	37 40 E
Debre May	87	11 20N	37 25 E
Debre Sina	87	9 51N	39 50 E
Debre Tabor	87	11 50N	38 26 E
Debre Zebit	87	11 48N	38 30 E
Debrecen	27	47 33N	21 42 E
Dečani	42	42 30N	20 10 E
Decatur, Ala., U.S.A.	115	34 35N	87 0W
Decatur, Ga., U.S.A.	115	33 47N	84 17W
Decatur, Ill., U.S.A.	116	39 50N	89 0W
Decatur, Ind., U.S.A.	114	40 50N	84 56W
Decatur, Texas, U.S.A.	117	33 15N	97 35W
Decazeville	20	44 34N	2 15 E
Deccan	70	18 0N	79 0 E
Deception I.	5	63 0 S	60 15W
Deception L.	109	56 33N	104 13W
Děčín	26	50 47N	14 12 E
Decize	19	46 50N	3 28 E
Deckerville	112	43 33N	82 46W
Decollatura	41	39 2N	16 21 E
Decorah	116	43 20N	91 50W
Deda	46	46 56N	24 50 E
Dedéagach = Alexandroúpolis	44	40 50N	25 54 E
Dedham	113	42 14N	71 10W
Dedilovo	55	53 59N	37 50 E
Dédougou	84	12 30N	3 25W
Deduru Oya	70	7 32N	79 50 E
Dedza	91	14 20 S	34 20 E
Dee →, Scot., U.K.	14	57 4N	2 7W
Dee →, Wales, U.K.	12	53 15N	3 7W
Deep B.	108	61 15N	116 35W
Deepdale	96	21 42 S	116 10 E
Deepwater	99	29 25 S	151 51 E
Deer →	109	58 23N	94 13W
Deer Lake, Newf., Can.	107	49 11N	57 27W
Deer Lake, Ontario, Can.	109	52 36N	94 20W
Deer Lodge	118	46 25N	112 40W
Deer Park	118	47 55N	117 21W
Deer River	116	47 21N	93 44W
Deeral	98	17 14 S	145 55 E
Deerdepoort	92	24 37 S	26 27 E
Deesa	68	24 18N	72 10 E
Deferiet	113	44 2N	75 41W
Defiance	114	41 20N	84 20W
Deganya	62	32 43N	35 34 E
Degebe →	31	38 13N	7 29W
Degeh Bur	63	8 11N	43 31 E
Degema	85	4 50N	6 48 E
Deggendorf	25	48 49N	12 59 E
Degloor	70	18 34N	77 33 E
Deh Bīd	65	30 39N	53 11 E
Deh Kheyr	65	28 45N	54 40 E
Dehibat	83	32 0N	10 47 E
Dehiwala	70	6 50N	79 51 E
Dehkareqan	64	37 43N	45 55 E
Dehra Dun	68	30 20N	78 4 E
Dehri	69	24 50N	84 15 E
Dehui	76	44 30N	125 40 E
Deinze	16	50 59N	3 32 E
Dej	46	47 10N	23 52 E
Deje	48	59 35N	13 29 E
Dekalb	116	41 55N	88 45W
Dekemhare	87	15 6N	39 0 E
Dekese	88	3 24 S	21 24 E
Del Norte	119	37 40N	106 27W
Del Rio	117	29 23N	100 50W
Delagua	117	37 21N	104 35W
Delai	86	17 21N	36 6 E
Delano	119	35 48N	119 13W
Delareyville	92	26 41 S	25 26 E
Delavan	116	42 40N	88 39W
Delaware	114	40 20N	83 0W
Delaware □	114	39 0N	75 40W
Delaware →	114	39 20N	75 25W
Delčevo	42	41 58N	22 46 E
Delegate	99	37 4 S	148 56 E
Delémont	25	47 22N	7 20 E
Delft	16	52 1N	4 22 E
Delft I.	70	9 30N	79 40 E
Delfzijl	16	53 20N	6 55 E
Delgado, C.	91	10 45 S	40 40 E
Delgo	86	20 6N	30 40 E
Delhi, Can.	112	42 51N	80 30W
Delhi, India	68	28 38N	77 17 E
Delhi, U.S.A.	113	42 17N	74 56W
Deli Jovan	42	44 13N	22 9 E
Delia	108	51 38N	112 23W
Delice →	64	39 45N	34 15 E
Delicias	120	28 10N	105 30W
Delitzsch	24	51 32N	12 22 E
Dell City	119	31 58N	105 19W
Dell Rapids	116	43 53N	96 44W
Delle	19	47 30N	7 2 E
Dellys	83	36 57N	3 57 E
Delmar	113	42 37N	73 47W
Delmenhorst	24	53 3N	8 37 E
Delmiro Gouveia	127	9 24 S	38 6W
Delnice	39	45 23N	14 50 E
Delong, Ostrova	59	76 40N	149 20 E
Deloraine, Austral.	99	41 30 S	146 40 E
Deloraine, Can.	109	49 15N	100 29W
Delorme, L.	107	54 31N	69 52W
Delphi, Greece	45	38 28N	22 30 E
Delphi, U.S.A.	114	40 37N	86 40W
Delphos	114	40 51N	84 17W
Delportshoop	92	28 22 S	24 20 E
Delray Beach	115	26 27N	80 4W
Delsbo	48	61 48N	16 32 E
Delta, Colo., U.S.A.	119	38 44N	108 5W
Delta, Utah, U.S.A.	118	39 21N	112 29W
Delungra	99	29 39 S	150 51 E
Delvina	44	39 59N	20 4 E
Delvinákion	44	39 57N	20 32 E
Demanda, Sierra de la	32	42 15N	3 0W
Demba	88	5 28 S	22 15 E
Dembecha	87	10 32N	37 30 E
Dembi	87	8 5N	36 25 E
Dembia	90	3 33N	25 48 E
Dembidolo	87	8 34N	34 50 E
Demer →	16	50 57N	4 42 E
Demetrias	44	39 22N	23 1 E
Demidov	54	55 16N	31 30 E
Deming	119	32 10N	107 50W
Demini →	126	0 46 S	62 56W
Demmin	24	53 54N	13 2 E
Demnate	82	31 44N	6 59W
Demonte	38	44 18N	7 18 E
Demopolis	115	32 30N	87 48W
Dempo, Mt.	72	4 2 S	103 15 E
Demyansk	54	57 40N	32 27 E
Den Burg	16	53 3N	4 47 E
Den Haag = 's Gravenhage	16	52 7N	4 17 E
Den Helder	16	52 57N	4 45 E
Den Oever	16	52 56N	5 2 E
Denain	19	50 20N	3 22 E
Denau	58	38 16N	67 54 E
Denbigh	12	53 12N	3 26W
Dendang	72	3 7 S	107 56 E
Dendermonde	16	51 2N	4 5 E
Deneba	87	9 47N	39 10 E
Deng Xian	77	32 34N	112 4 E
Denge	85	12 52N	5 21 E
Dengi	85	9 25N	9 55 E
Denham	96	25 56 S	113 31 E
Denham Ra.	97	21 55 S	147 46 E
Denia	33	38 49N	0 8 E
Deniliquin	97	35 30 S	144 58 E
Denison, Iowa, U.S.A.	116	42 0N	95 18W
Denison, Texas, U.S.A.	117	33 50N	96 40W
Denison Range	97	28 30 S	136 5 E
Denizli	64	37 42N	29 2 E
Denman Glacier	5	66 45 S	99 25 E
Denmark	96	34 59 S	117 25 E
Denmark ■	49	55 30N	9 0 E
Denmark Str.	6	66 0N	30 0W
Dennison	112	40 21N	81 21W
Denpasar	72	8 45 S	115 14 E
Denton, Mont., U.S.A.	118	47 25N	109 56W
Denton, Texas, U.S.A.	117	33 12N	97 10W
D'Entrecasteaux Is.	98	9 0 S	151 0 E
D'Entrecasteaux Pt.	96	34 50 S	115 57 E
Denu	85	6 4N	1 8 E
Denver	116	39 45N	105 0W
Denver City	117	32 58N	102 48W
Deoband	68	29 42N	77 43 E
Deobhog	70	19 53N	82 44 E
Deogarh	69	21 32N	84 45 E
Deoghar	69	24 30N	86 42 E
Deolali	70	19 58N	73 50 E
Deoli	68	25 50N	75 20 E
Deoria	69	26 31N	83 48 E
Deosai Mts.	69	35 40N	75 0 E
Depew	112	42 55N	78 43W
Deping	76	37 25N	116 58 E
Deposit	113	42 5N	75 23W
Deputatskiy	59	69 18N	139 54 E
Dêqên	75	28 34N	98 51 E
Deqing	77	23 8N	111 42 E
Dera Ghazi Khan	68	30 5N	70 43 E
Dera Ismail Khan	68	31 50N	70 50 E
* Dera Ismail Khan □	68	32 30N	70 0 E
Derbent	56	42 5N	48 4 E
Derby, Austral.	96	17 18 S	123 38 E
Derby, U.K.	12	52 55N	1 28W
Derby, Conn., U.S.A.	113	41 20N	73 5W
Derby, N.Y., U.S.A.	112	42 40N	78 59W
Derby □	12	52 55N	1 28W
Derecske	27	47 20N	21 33 E
Derg →	15	54 42N	7 26W
Derg, L.	15	53 0N	8 20W
Dergachi	55	50 9N	36 11 E
Dergaon	67	26 45N	94 0 E
Dermantsi	43	43 8N	24 17 E
Dernieres Isles	117	29 0N	90 45W
Derryveagh Mts.	15	55 0N	8 40W
Derudub	86	17 31N	36 7 E
Derval	18	47 40N	1 41W
Dervéni	45	38 8N	22 25 E
Derventa	42	44 59N	17 55 E
Derwent	109	53 41N	110 58W
Derwent →, Derby, U.K.	12	52 53N	1 17W
Derwent →, N. Yorks., U.K.	12	53 45N	0 57W
Derwentwater, L.	12	54 35N	3 9W
Des Moines, Iowa, U.S.A.	116	41 35N	93 37W
Des Moines, N. Mex., U.S.A.	117	36 50N	103 51W
Des Moines →	116	40 23N	91 25W
Desaguadero →, Argent.	124	34 30 S	66 46W
Desaguadero →, Boliv.	126	18 24 S	67 5W
Deschaillons	107	46 32N	72 7W
Descharme →	109	56 51N	109 13W
Deschutes →	118	45 30N	121 0W
Dese	87	11 5N	39 40 E
Desenzano del Gardo	38	45 28N	10 32 E
Desert Center	119	33 45N	115 27W
Deskenatlata L.	108	60 55N	112 3W
Desna →	54	50 33N	30 32 E
Desnătui →	46	44 15N	23 27 E
Desolación, I.	128	53 0 S	74 0W
Despeñaperros, Paso	33	38 24N	3 30W
Despotovac	42	44 6N	21 30 E
Dessau	24	51 49N	12 15 E
Dessye = Dese	87	11 5N	39 40 E

Renamed Pakapuka

* *Now part of North West Frontier □*

D'Estrees B. Donja Stubica

D'Estrees B. **99** 35 55 S 137 45 E
Desuri **68** 25 18N 73 35 E
Desvrès **19** 50 40N 1 48 E
Deta **42** 45 24N 21 13 E
Detinja → **42** 43 51N 19 45 E
Detmold **24** 51 55N 8 50 E
Detour Pt. **114** 45 37N 86 35W
Detroit, Mich., U.S.A. **106** 42 23N 83 5W
Detroit, Tex., U.S.A. **117** 33 40N 95 10W
Detroit Lakes **116** 46 50N 95 50W
Dett **91** 18 38 S 26 50 E
Deurne, Belg. **16** 51 12N 4 24 E
Deurne, Neth. **16** 51 27N 5 49 E
Deutsche Bucht **24** 54 10N 7 51 E
Deutschlandsberg **26** 46 49N 15 14 E
Deux-Sèvres □ **18** 46 35N 0 20W
Deva **46** 45 53N 22 55 E
Devakottai **70** 9 55N 78 45 E
Devaprayag **68** 30 13N 78 35 E
Dévaványa **27** 47 2N 20 59 E
Deveci Daği **56** 40 10N 36 0 E
Devecser **27** 47 6N 17 26 E
Deventer **16** 52 15N 6 10 E
Deveron → **14** 57 40N 2 31W
Devesel **46** 44 28N 22 41 E
Devgad Baria **68** 22 40N 73 55 E
Devgad, I. **70** 14 48N 74 5 E
Devils Lake **116** 48 5N 98 50W
Devils Paw **108** 58 47N 134 0W
Devil's Pt. **70** 9 26N 80 6 E
Devin **43** 41 44N 24 24 E
Devizes **13** 51 21N 2 0W
Devnya **43** 43 13N 27 33 E
Devolii → **44** 40 57N 20 15 E
Devon **108** 53 24N 113 44W
Devon I. **4** 75 10N 85 0W
Devonport, Austral. **97** 41 10 S 146 22 E
Devonport, N.Z. **101** 36 49 S 174 49 E
Devonport, U.K. **13** 50 23N 4 11W
Devonshire □ **13** 50 50N 3 40W
Dewas **68** 22 59N 76 3 E
Dewetsdorp **92** 29 33 S 26 39 E
Dewsbury **12** 53 42N 1 38W
Dexter, Mo., U.S.A. **117** 36 50N 90 0W
Dexter, N. Mex., U.S.A. **117** 33 15N 104 25W
Deyhūk **65** 33 15N 57 30 E
Deyyer **65** 27 55N 51 55 E
Dezadeash L. **108** 60 28N 136 58W
Dezfūl **64** 32 20N 48 30 E
Dezh Shāhpūr **64** 35 30N 46 25 E
Dezhneva, Mys **59** 66 5N 169 40W
Dezhou **76** 37 26N 116 18 E
Dháfni **45** 37 48N 22 1 E
Dhafra **65** 23 20N 54 0 E
Dhahaban **86** 21 58N 39 3 E
Dhahira **65** 23 40N 57 0 E
Dhahiriya = Aẓ Ẓāhirīyah **62** 31 25N 34 58 E
Dhahran = Aẓ Ẓahrān **64** 26 18N 50 10 E
Dhamar **63** 14 30N 44 20 E
Dhamási **44** 39 43N 22 11 E
Dhampur **68** 29 19N 78 33 E
Dhamtari **69** 20 42N 81 35 E
Dhanbad **69** 23 50N 86 30 E
Dhankuta **69** 26 55N 87 40 E
Dhanora **69** 20 20N 80 22 E
Dhar **68** 22 35N 75 26 E
Dharampur, Gujarat, India **70** 20 32N 73 17 E
Dharampur, Mad. P., India **68** 22 13N 75 18 E
Dharapuram **70** 10 45N 77 34 E
Dharmapuri **70** 12 10N 78 10 E
Dharmavaram **70** 14 29N 77 44 E
Dharmsala (Dharamsala) **68** 32 16N 76 23 E
Dhaulagiri **69** 28 39N 83 28 E
Dhebar, L. **68** 24 10N 74 0 E
Dhenkanal **69** 20 45N 85 35 E
Dhenoúsa **45** 37 8N 25 48 E
Dheskáti **44** 39 55N 21 49 E
Dhespotikó **45** 36 57N 24 58 E
Dhestina **45** 38 25N 22 31 E
Dhidhimótikhon **44** 41 22N 26 29 E
Dhíkti **45** 35 8N 25 22 E
Dhilianáta **45** 38 15N 20 34 E
Dhílos **45** 37 23N 25 15 E
Dhimitsána **45** 37 36N 22 3 E
Dhírfis **45** 38 40N 23 54 E
Dhodhekánisos **45** 36 35N 27 0 E
Dhokós **45** 37 20N 23 20 E
Dholiana **44** 39 54N 20 32 E
Dholka **68** 22 44N 72 29 E
Dholpur **68** 26 45N 77 59 E
Dhomokós **45** 39 10N 22 18 E
Dhond **70** 18 26N 74 40 E
Dhoraji **68** 21 45N 70 37 E
Dhoxáton **44** 41 9N 24 16 E
Dhragonisí **45** 37 27N 25 29 E
Dhrangadhra **68** 22 59N 71 31 E
Dhriopís **45** 37 25N 24 35 E
Dhrol **68** 22 33N 70 25 E
Dhubaibah **65** 23 25N 54 35 E
Dhubri **69** 26 2N 89 59 E
Dhula **63** 15 10N 47 30 E
Dhulia **68** 20 58N 74 50 E
Dhurm → **86** 20 18N 42 53 E
Di Linh, Cao Nguyen **71** 11 30N 108 0 E
Día **45** 35 26N 25 13 E
Diablo Heights **120** 8 58N 79 34W
Diafarabé **84** 14 9N 4 57W
Diala **84** 14 10N 10 0W
Dialakoro **84** 12 18N 7 54W
Diallassagou **84** 13 47N 3 41W
Diamante **124** 32 5 S 60 40W
Diamante → **124** 34 30 S 66 46W
Diamantina **127** 18 17 S 43 40W
Diamantina → **97** 26 45 S 139 10 E
Diamantino **127** 14 30 S 56 30W
Diamond Harbour **69** 22 11N 88 14 E
Diamond Mts. **118** 40 0N 115 58W
Diamondville **118** 41 51N 110 30W
Diancheng **77** 21 30N 111 4 E
Diano Marina **38** 43 55N 8 3 E
Dianra **84** 8 45N 6 14W
Diapaga **85** 12 5N 1 46 E
Diapangou **85** 12 5N 0 10 E
Diariguila **84** 10 35N 10 2W
Dibaya **88** 6 30 S 22 57 E
Dibaya-Lubue **88** 4 12 S 19 54 E
Dibbi **87** 4 10N 41 52 E
Dibble Glacier Tongue **5** 66 8 S 134 32 E
Dibete **92** 23 45 S 26 32 E
Dibrugarh **67** 27 29N 94 55 E
Dickinson **116** 46 50N 102 48W
Dickson **115** 36 5N 87 22W
Dickson City **113** 41 29N 75 40W
Dickson (Dikson) **58** 73 40N 80 5 E
Dicomano **39** 43 53N 11 30 E
Didesa, W. → **87** 10 2N 35 32 E
Didiéni **84** 13 53N 8 6W
Didsbury **108** 51 35N 114 10W
Didwana **68** 27 23N 17 36 E
Die **21** 44 47N 5 22 E
Diébougou **84** 11 0N 3 15W
Diefenbaker L. **109** 51 0N 106 55W
Diego Garcia **3** 7 50 S 72 50 E
Diekirch **16** 49 52N 6 10 E
Diélette **18** 49 33N 1 52W
Diéma **84** 14 32N 9 12W
Diémbéring **84** 12 29N 16 47W
Dien Bien **71** 21 20N 103 0 E
Diepholz **24** 52 37N 8 22 E
Dieppe **18** 49 54N 1 4 E
Dieren **16** 52 3N 6 6 E
Dierks **117** 34 9N 94 0W
Diest **16** 50 58N 5 4 E
Dieulefit **21** 44 32N 5 4 E
Dieuze **19** 48 49N 6 43 E
Differdange **16** 49 31N 5 54 E
Dig **68** 27 28N 77 20 E
Digba **90** 4 25N 25 48 E
Digby **107** 44 38N 65 50W
Digges **109** 58 40N 94 0W
Digges Is. **105** 62 40N 77 50W
Dighinala **67** 23 15N 92 5 E
Dighton **116** 38 30N 100 26W
Digne **21** 44 5N 6 12 E
Digoin **20** 46 29N 3 58 E
Digos **73** 6 45N 125 20 E
Digranes **50** 66 4N 14 44 E
Digras **70** 20 6N 77 45 E
Digul → **73** 7 7 S 138 42 E
Dihang → **67** 27 48N 95 30 E
Dijlah, Nahr → **64** 31 0N 47 25 E
Dijon **19** 47 20N 5 0 E
Dikala **87** 4 45N 31 28 E
Dikkil **87** 11 8N 42 20 E
Dikomu di Kai **92** 24 58 S 24 36 E
Diksmuide **16** 51 2N 2 52 E
Dikwa **85** 12 4N 13 30 E
Dila **87** 6 21N 38 22 E
Dili **73** 8 39 S 125 34 E
Dilizhan **57** 40 46N 44 57 E
Dilj **42** 45 29N 18 1 E
Dillenburg **24** 50 44N 8 17 E
Dilley **117** 28 40N 99 12W
Dilling **87** 12 3N 29 35 E
Dillingen **25** 48 32N 10 29 E
Dillon, Can. **109** 55 56N 108 35W
Dillon, Mont., U.S.A. **118** 45 9N 112 36W
Dillon, S.C., U.S.A. **115** 34 26N 79 20W
Dillon → **109** 55 56N 108 56W
Dilston **99** 41 22 S 147 10 E
Dimashq **64** 33 30N 36 18 E
Dimbokro **84** 6 45N 4 46W
Dimboola **99** 36 28 S 142 7 E
Dîmbovița □ **46** 45 0N 25 30 E
Dîmbovița → **46** 44 14N 26 13 E
Dimbovnic → **46** 44 28N 25 18 E
Dimbulah **98** 17 8 S 145 4 E
Dimitrovgrad, Bulg. **43** 42 5N 25 35 E
Dimitrovgrad, U.S.S.R. **55** 54 14N 49 39 E
Dimitrovgrad, Yugo. **42** 43 0N 22 48 E
Dimitrovo = Pernik **42** 42 35N 23 2 E
Dimmitt **117** 34 36N 102 16W
Dimo **87** 5 19N 29 10 E
Dimona **62** 31 2N 35 1 E
Dimovo **42** 43 43N 22 50 E
Dinagat **73** 10 10N 125 40 E
Dinajpur **69** 25 33N 88 43 E
Dinan **18** 48 28N 2 2W
Dinant **16** 50 16N 4 55 E
Dinapur **69** 25 38N 85 5 E
Dinar **64** 38 5N 30 15 E
Dinara Planina **39** 43 50N 16 35 E
Dinard **18** 48 38N 2 6W
Dinaric Alps = Dinara Planina **9** 43 50N 16 35 E
Dinder, Nahr ed → **87** 14 6N 33 40 E
Dindi → **70** 16 24N 78 15 E
Dindigul **70** 10 25N 78 0 E
Ding Xian **76** 38 30N 114 59 E
Dingbian **76** 37 35N 107 32 E
Dingelstädt **24** 51 19N 10 19 E
Dinghai **77** 30 1N 122 6 E
Dingle **15** 52 9N 10 17W
Dingle B. **15** 52 3N 10 20W
Dingmans Ferry **113** 41 13N 74 55W
Dingnan **77** 24 45N 115 0 E
Dingo **98** 23 38 S 149 19 E
Dingolfing **25** 48 38N 12 30 E
Dingtao **77** 35 5N 115 35 E
Dinguiraye **84** 11 18N 10 49W
Dingwall **14** 57 36N 4 26W
Dingxi **76** 35 30N 104 33 E
Dingxiang **76** 38 30N 112 58 E
Dinokwe (Palla Road) **92** 23 29 S 26 37 E
Dinosaur National Monument **118** 40 30N 108 58W
Dinuba **119** 36 31N 119 22W
Dio **49** 56 37N 14 15 E
Diósgyör **27** 48 7N 20 43 E
Diosig **46** 47 18N 22 2 E
Diourbel **84** 14 39N 16 12W
Diplo **68** 24 35N 69 35 E
Dipolog **73** 8 36N 123 20 E
Dipşa **46** 46 58N 24 27 E
Dir **66** 35 08N 71 59 E
Diré **84** 16 20N 3 25W
Dire Dawa **87** 9 35N 41 45 E
Direction, C. **97** 12 51 S 143 32 E
Diriamba **121** 11 51N 86 19W
Dirk Hartog I. **96** 25 50 S 113 5 E
Dirranbandi **97** 28 33 S 148 17 E
Disa **87** 12 5N 34 15 E
Disappointment, C. **118** 46 20N 124 0W
Disappointment L. **96** 23 20 S 122 40 E
Disaster B. **97** 37 15 S 150 0 E
Discovery B. **97** 38 10 S 140 40 E
Disentis **25** 46 42N 8 50 E
Dishna **86** 26 9N 32 32 E
Disina **85** 11 35N 9 50 E
Disko **4** 69 45N 53 30W
Disko Bugt **4** 69 10N 52 0W
Disna **54** 55 32N 28 11 E
Disna → **54** 55 34N 28 12 E
Distrito Federal □ **127** 15 45 S 47 45W
Disûq **86** 31 8N 30 35 E
Diu **68** 20 45N 70 58 E
Dives → **18** 49 18N 0 7W
Dives-sur-Mer **18** 49 18N 0 8W
Divi Pt. **70** 15 59N 81 9 E
Divichi **57** 41 15N 48 57 E
Divide **118** 45 48N 112 47W
Divinópolis **127** 20 10 S 44 54W
Divnoye **57** 45 55N 43 21 E
Divo **84** 5 48N 5 15W
Diwal Kol **66** 34 23N 67 52 E
Dixie **118** 45 37N 115 27W
Dixon, Ill., U.S.A. **116** 41 50N 89 30W
Dixon, Mont., U.S.A. **118** 47 19N 114 25W
Dixon, N. Mex., U.S.A. **119** 36 15N 105 57W
Dixon Entrance **108** 54 30N 132 0W
Dixonville **108** 56 32N 117 40W
Diyarbakir **64** 37 55N 40 18 E
Diz Chah **65** 35 30N 55 30 E
Djado **83** 21 4N 12 14 E
Djado, Plateau du **83** 21 29N 12 21 E
Djakarta = Jakarta **73** 6 9 S 106 49 E
Djamâa **83** 33 32N 5 59 E
Djamba **92** 16 45 S 13 58 E
Djambala **88** 2 32 S 14 30 E
Djanet **83** 24 35N 9 32 E
Djaul I. **98** 2 58 S 150 57 E
Djawa = Jawa **73** 7 0 S 110 0 E
Djebiniana **83** 35 1N 11 0 E
Djelfa **82** 34 40N 3 15 E
Djema **90** 6 3N 25 15 E
Djendel **82** 36 15N 2 25 E
Djeneïene **83** 31 45N 10 9 E
Djenné **84** 14 0N 4 30W
Djenoun, Garet el **83** 25 4N 5 31 E
Djerba **83** 33 52N 10 51 E
Djerba, Île de **83** 33 56N 11 0 E
Djerid, Chott **83** 33 42N 8 30 E
Djibo **85** 14 9N 1 35W
Djibouti **87** 11 30N 43 5 E
Djibouti ■ **63** 12 0N 43 0 E
Djolu **88** 0 35N 22 5 E
Djorong **72** 3 58 S 114 56 E
Djougou **85** 9 40N 1 45 E
Djoum **88** 2 41N 12 35 E
Djourab **81** 16 40N 18 50 E
Djugu **90** 1 55N 30 35 E
Djúpivogur **50** 64 39N 14 17W
Djursholm **48** 59 25N 18 6 E
Djursland **49** 56 27N 10 45 E
Dmitriev-Lgovskiy **54** 52 10N 35 0 E
Dmitriya Lapteva, Proliv **59** 73 0N 140 0 E
Dmitrov **55** 56 25N 37 32 E
Dmitrovsk-Orlovskiy **54** 52 29N 35 10 E
Dneiper = Dnepr → **56** 46 30N 32 18 E
Dnepr → **56** 46 30N 32 18 E
Dneprodzerzhinsk **56** 48 32N 34 37 E
Dneprodzerzhinskoye Vdkhr. **56** 49 0N 34 0 E
Dnepropetrovsk **56** 48 30N 35 0 E
Dneprorudnoye **56** 47 21N 34 58 E
Dnestr → **56** 46 18N 30 17 E
Dnestrovski = Belgorod **56** 50 35N 36 35 E
Dniester = Dnestr → **56** 46 18N 30 17 E
Dno **54** 57 50N 29 58 E
Doba **81** 8 40N 16 50 E
Dobbiaco **39** 46 44N 12 13 E
Dobbyn **97** 19 44 S 139 59 E
Dobczyce **27** 49 52N 20 25 E
Döbeln **24** 51 7N 13 10 E
Doberai, Jazirah **73** 1 25 S 133 0 E
Dobiegniew **28** 52 59N 15 45 E
Doblas **124** 37 5 S 64 0W
Dobo **73** 5 45 S 134 15 E
Doboj **42** 44 46N 18 6 E
Dobra, Konin, Poland **28** 51 55N 18 37 E
Dobra, Szczecin, Poland **28** 53 34N 15 20 E
Dobra, Dîmbovita, Romania **43** 44 52N 25 40 E
Dobra, Hunedoara, Romania **46** 45 54N 22 36 E
Dobre Miasto **28** 53 58N 20 26 E
Dobrinishta **43** 41 49N 23 34 E
Dobřiš **26** 49 46N 14 10 E
Dobrodzień **28** 50 45N 18 25 E
Dobropole **56** 48 25N 37 2 E
Dobruja **46** 44 30N 28 15 E
Dobrush **54** 52 28N 30 19 E
Dobrzyń nad Wisłą **28** 52 39N 19 22 E
Dobtong **87** 6 25N 31 40 E
Dodecanese = Dhodhekánisos **45** 36 35N 27 0 E
Dodge Center **116** 44 1N 92 50W
Dodge City **117** 37 42N 100 0W
Dodge L. **109** 59 50N 105 36W
Dodgeville **116** 42 55N 90 8W
Dodo **87** 5 10N 29 57 E
Dodola **87** 6 59N 39 11 E
Dodoma **90** 6 8 S 35 45 E
Dodoma □ **90** 6 0 S 36 0 E
Dodona **44** 39 40N 20 46 E
Dodsland **109** 51 50N 108 45W
Dodson **118** 48 23N 108 16W
Doetinchem **16** 51 59N 6 18 E
Doftana **46** 45 11N 25 45 E
Dog Creek **108** 51 35N 122 14W
Dog L., Man., Can. **109** 51 2N 98 31W
Dog L., Ont., Can. **106** 48 18N 89 30W
Doğanbey **45** 37 40N 27 10 E
Dogliani **38** 44 35N 7 55 E
Dogondoutchi **85** 13 38N 4 2 E
Dogran **68** 31 48N 73 35 E
Doguéraoua **85** 14 0N 5 31 E
Dohad **68** 22 50N 74 15 E
Dohazari **67** 22 10N 92 5 E
Doi **73** 2 14N 127 49 E
Doi Luang **71** 18 30N 101 0 E
Doig → **108** 56 25N 120 40W
Dois Irmãos, Sa. **127** 9 0 S 42 30W
Dojransko Jezero **42** 41 13N 22 44 E
Dokka **47** 60 49N 10 7 E
Dokka → **47** 61 7N 10 0 E
Dokkum **16** 53 20N 5 59 E
Dokri **68** 27 25N 68 7 E
Dol-de-Bretagne **18** 48 34N 1 47W
Doland **116** 44 55N 98 5W
Dolbeau **107** 48 53N 72 18W
Dole **19** 47 7N 5 31 E
Doleib, Wadi → **87** 12 10N 33 15 E
Dolgellau **12** 52 44N 3 53W
Dolgelley = Dolgellau **12** 52 44N 3 53W
Dolginovo **54** 54 39N 27 29 E
Dolianova **40** 39 23N 9 11 E
Dolinskaya **56** 48 6N 32 46 E
Dolj □ **46** 44 10N 23 30 E
Dollart **16** 53 20N 7 10 E
Dolna Banya **43** 42 18N 23 44 E
Dolni Dŭbnik **43** 43 24N 24 26 E
Dolo, Ethiopia **87** 4 11N 42 3 E
Dolo, Italy **39** 45 25N 12 4 E
Dolomites = Dolomiti **39** 46 30N 11 40 E
Dolomiti **39** 46 30N 11 40 E
Dolores, Argent. **124** 36 20 S 57 40W
Dolores, Uruguay **124** 33 34 S 58 15W
Dolores, Colo., U.S.A. **119** 37 30N 108 30W
Dolores, Tex., U.S.A. **117** 27 40N 99 38W
Dolores → **119** 38 49N 108 17W
Đolovo **42** 44 55N 20 52 E
Dolphin and Union Str. **104** 69 5N 114 45W
Dolphin C. **128** 51 10 S 59 0W
Dolsk **28** 51 59N 17 3 E
Dom Pedrito **125** 31 0 S 54 40W
Doma **85** 8 25N 8 18 E
Domasi **91** 15 15 S 35 22 E
Domazlice **26** 49 28N 13 0 E
Dombarovskiy **58** 50 46N 59 32 E
Dombasle **19** 48 38N 6 21 E
Dombes **21** 46 3N 5 0 E
Dombóvár **27** 46 21N 18 9 E
Dombrád **27** 48 13N 21 54 E
Domburg **16** 51 34N 3 30 E
Domel I. = Letsok-aw Kyun **71** 11 30N 98 25 E
Domérat **20** 46 21N 2 32 E
Domeyko **124** 29 0 S 71 0W
Domeyko, Cordillera **124** 24 30 S 69 0W
Domfront **18** 48 37N 0 40W
Dominador **124** 24 21 S 69 20W
Dominica ■ **121** 15 20N 61 20W
Dominican Rep. ■ **121** 19 0N 70 30W
Dömitz **24** 53 9N 11 13 E
Domme **20** 44 48N 1 12 E
Domo **63** 7 50N 47 10 E
Domodóssola **38** 46 6N 8 19 E
Dompaire **19** 48 14N 6 14 E
Dompierre-sur-Besbre **20** 46 31N 3 41 E
Dompim **84** 5 10N 2 5W
Domrémy **19** 48 26N 5 40 E
Domsjö **48** 63 16N 18 41 E
Domville, Mt. **99** 28 1 S 151 15 E
Domvraina **45** 38 15N 22 59 E
Domžale **39** 46 9N 14 35 E
Don →, India **70** 16 20N 76 15 E
Don →, Eng., U.K. **12** 53 41N 0 51W
Don →, Scot., U.K. **14** 57 14N 2 5W
Don →, U.S.S.R. **57** 47 4N 39 18 E
Don Benito **31** 38 53N 5 51W
Don Martín, Presa de **120** 27 30N 100 50W
Dona Ana **91** 17 25 S 35 5 E
Donaghadee **15** 54 38N 5 32W
Donald **99** 36 23 S 143 0 E
Donalda **108** 52 35N 112 34W
Donaldsonville **117** 30 2N 91 0W
Donalsonville **115** 31 3N 84 52W
Donau → **23** 48 10N 17 0 E
Donaueschingen **25** 47 57N 8 30 E
Donauwörth **25** 48 42N 10 47 E
Donawitz **26** 47 22N 15 4 E
Doncaster **12** 53 31N 1 9W
Dondo, Angola **88** 9 45 S 14 25 E
Dondo, Mozam. **91** 19 33 S 34 46 E
Dondo, Teluk **73** 0 29N 120 30 E
Dondra Head **70** 5 55N 80 40 E
Donegal **15** 54 39N 8 8W
Donegal □ **15** 54 53N 8 0W
Donegal B. **15** 54 30N 8 35W
Donets → **57** 47 33N 40 55 E
Donetsk **56** 48 0N 37 45 E
Donga **85** 7 45N 10 2 E
Dongara **96** 29 14 S 114 57 E
Dongargarh **69** 21 10N 80 40 E
Donges **18** 47 18N 2 4W
Dongfang **77** 18 50N 108 33 E
Donggala **73** 0 30 S 119 40 E
Donggou **76** 39 52N 124 10 E
Dongguan **77** 22 58N 113 44 E
Dongguang **76** 37 50N 116 30 E
Dongjingcheng **76** 44 0N 129 10 E
Donglan **77** 24 30N 107 21 E
Dongliu **77** 30 13N 116 55 E
Dongola **86** 19 9N 30 22 E
Dongou **88** 2 0N 18 5 E
Dongping **76** 35 55N 116 20 E
Dongshan **77** 23 43N 117 30 E
Dongsheng **76** 39 50N 110 0 E
Dongtai **77** 32 51N 120 21 E
Dongting Hu **75** 29 18N 112 45 E
Dongxing **75** 21 34N 108 0 E
Dongyang **77** 29 13N 120 15 E
Doniphan **117** 36 40N 90 50W
Donja Stubica **39** 45 59N 16 0 E

Donji Dušnik Dzhelinde

Donji Dušnik 42 43 12N 22 5 E
Donji Miholjac 42 45 45N 18 10 E
Donji Milanovac 42 44 28N 22 6 E
Donji Vakuf 42 44 8N 17 24 E
Donjon, Le 20 46 22N 3 48 E
Donna 50 66 6N 12 30 E
Donna 117 26 12N 98 2W
Donnaconna 107 46 41N 71 41W
Donnelly's Crossing 101 35 42 S 173 38 E
Donora 112 40 11N 79 50W
Donor's Hills 98 18 42 S 140 33 E
Donskoy 55 53 55N 38 15 E
Donya Lendava 39 46 35N 16 25 E
Donzère-Mondragon 21 44 28N 4 43 E
Donzère-Mondragon, Barrage de 21 44 13N 4 42 E
Donzy 19 47 20N 3 6 E
Doon → 14 55 26N 4 41W
Dor (Tantūra) 62 32 37N 34 55 E
Dora Báltea → 38 45 11N 8 5 E
Dora, L. 96 22 0 S 123 0 E
Dora Riparia → 38 45 5N 7 44 E
Dorada, La 126 5 30N 74 40W
Doran L. 109 61 13N 108 6W
Dorat, Le 20 46 14N 1 5 E
Dorchester 13 50 42N 2 28W
Dorchester, C. 105 65 27N 77 27W
Dordogne □ 20 45 5N 0 40 E
Dordogne → 20 45 2N 0 36W
Dordrecht, Neth. 16 51 48N 4 39 E
Dordrecht, S. Afr. 92 31 20 S 27 3 E
Dore → 20 45 50N 3 35 E
Doré L. 109 54 46N 107 17W
Doré Lake 109 54 38N 107 36W
Dore, Mt. 20 45 32N 2 50 E
Dorfen 25 48 16N 12 10 E
Dorgali 40 40 18N 9 35 E
Dori 85 14 3N 0 2W
Doring → 92 31 54 S 18 39 E
Dorion 106 45 23N 74 3W
Dormaa-Ahenkro 84 7 15N 2 52W
Dormo, Ras 87 13 14N 42 35 E
Dornberg 39 55 45N 13 50 E
Dornbirn 26 47 25N 9 45 E
Dornes 19 46 48N 3 18 E
Dornoch 14 57 52N 4 0W
Dornoch Firth 14 57 52N 4 0W
Doro 85 16 9N 0 51W
Dorog 27 47 42N 18 45 E
Dorogobuzh 54 54 50N 33 18 E
Dorohoi 46 47 56N 26 30 E
Döröö Nuur 75 48 0N 93 0 E
Dorre I. 96 25 13 S 113 12 E
Dorrigo 99 30 20 S 152 44 E
Dorris 118 41 59N 121 58W
Dorset, Can. 112 45 14N 78 54W
Dorset, U.S.A. 112 41 4N 80 40W
Dorset □ 13 50 48N 2 25W
Dorsten 24 51 40N 6 55 E
Dortmund 24 51 32N 7 28 E
Dörtyol 64 36 52N 36 12 E
Dorum 24 53 40N 8 33 E
Doruma 90 4 42N 27 33 E
Dos Bahías, C. 128 44 58 S 65 32W
Dos Cabezas 119 32 10N 109 37W
Dos Hermanas 31 37 16N 5 55W
Dosso 85 13 0N 3 13 E
Dothan 115 31 10N 85 25W
Douai 19 50 21N 3 4 E
Douala 88 4 0N 9 45 E
Douaouir 82 20 45N 3 0W
Douarnenez 18 48 6N 4 21W
Douăzeci Şi Trei August 46 43 55N 28 40 E
Double Island Pt. 99 25 56 S 153 11 E
Doubrava → 26 49 40N 15 30 E
Doubs □ 19 47 10N 6 20 E
Doubs → 19 46 53N 5 1 E
Doubtful B. 96 34 15 S 119 28 E
Doubtful Sd. 101 45 20 S 166 49 E
Doubtless B. 101 34 55 S 173 26 E
Doudeville 18 49 43N 0 47 E
Doué 18 47 11N 0 20W
Douentza 84 14 58N 2 48W
Douglas, S. Afr. 92 29 4 S 23 46 E
Douglas, U.K. 12 54 9N 4 29W
Douglas, Alaska, U.S.A. 108 58 23N 134 24W
Douglas, Ariz., U.S.A. 119 31 21N 109 30W
Douglas, Ga., U.S.A. 115 31 32N 82 52W
Douglas, Wyo., U.S.A. 116 42 45N 105 20W
Douglastown 107 48 46N 64 24W
Douglasville 115 33 46N 84 43W
Douirat 82 33 2N 4 11W
Doukáton, Ákra 45 38 34N 20 30 E
Doulevant 19 48 22N 4 53 E
Doullens 19 50 10N 2 20 E
Doumé 88 4 15N 13 25 E
Douna 84 13 13N 6 0W
Dounreay 14 58 34N 3 44W
Dourados 125 22 9 S 54 50W
Dourados → 125 21 58 S 54 18W
Dourdan 19 48 30N 2 0 E
Douro → 30 41 8N 8 40W
Douvaine 21 46 19N 6 16 E
Douz 83 33 25N 9 0 E
Douze → 20 43 54N 0 30W
Dove → 12 52 51N 1 36W
Dove Creek 119 37 46N 108 59W
Dover, Austral. 99 43 18 S 147 2 E
Dover, U.K. 13 51 7N 1 19 E
Dover, Del., U.S.A. 114 39 10N 75 31W
Dover, N.H., U.S.A. 114 43 12N 70 51W
Dover, N.J., U.S.A. 113 40 53N 74 34W
Dover, Ohio, U.S.A. 114 40 32N 81 30W
Dover-Foxcroft 107 45 14N 69 14W
Dover Plains 113 41 43N 73 35W
Dover, Pt. 96 32 32 S 125 32 E
Dover, Str. of 18 51 0N 1 30 E
Dovey → 13 52 32N 4 0W
Dovrefjell 47 62 15N 9 33 E
Dowa 91 13 38 S 33 58 E
Dowagiac 114 42 0N 86 8W
Dowlat Yār 65 34 30N 65 45 E
Dowlatabad 65 28 20N 56 40W
Down □ 15 54 20N 6 0W
Downey 118 42 29N 112 3W
Downham Market 13 52 36N 0 22 E
Downieville 118 39 34N 120 50W
Downpatrick 15 54 20N 5 43W
Downpatrick Hd. 15 54 20N 9 21W
Dowshī 65 35 35N 68 43 E
Doylestown 113 40 21N 75 10W
Draa, C. 82 28 47N 11 0W
Draa, Oued → 82 30 29N 6 1W
Drac → 21 45 13N 5 41 E
Drachten 16 53 7N 6 5 E
Drăgăneşti 46 44 9N 24 32 E
Drăgăneşti-Vlaşca 46 44 5N 25 33 E
Dragaš 42 42 5N 20 35 E
Drăgăsani 46 44 39N 24 17 E
Dragina 42 44 30N 19 25 E
Dragocvet 42 44 0N 21 15 E
Dragoman, Prokhod 42 43 0N 22 53 E
Dragonera, I. 32 39 35N 2 19 E
Dragovishtitsa (Perivol) 42 42 22N 22 39 E
Draguignan 21 43 30N 6 27 E
Drain 118 43 45N 123 17W
Drake, Austral. 99 28 55 S 152 25 E
Drake, U.S.A. 116 47 56N 100 21W
Drake Passage 5 58 0 S 68 0W
Drakensberg 93 31 0 S 28 0 E
Dráma 44 41 9N 24 10 E
Dráma □ 44 41 20N 24 0 E
Drammen 47 59 42N 10 12 E
Drangajökull 50 66 9N 22 15W
Drangedal 47 59 6N 9 3 E
Dranov, Ostrov 46 44 55N 29 30 E
Drau = Drava → 26 46 32N 14 58 E
Drava → 42 45 33N 18 55 E
Draveil 19 48 41N 2 25 E
Dravograd 39 46 36N 15 5 E
Drawa → 28 52 52N 15 59 E
Drawno 28 53 13N 15 46 E
Drawsko Pomorskie 28 53 35N 15 50 E
Drayton Valley 108 53 12N 114 58W
Dren 42 43 8N 20 44 E
Drenthe □ 16 52 52N 6 40 E
Dresden, Can. 112 42 35N 82 11W
Dresden, Ger. 24 51 2N 13 45 E
Dresden □ 24 51 12N 14 0 E
Dreux 18 48 44N 1 23 E
Drezdenko 28 52 50N 15 49 E
Driffield 12 54 0N 0 25W
Driftwood 112 41 22N 78 9W
Driggs 118 43 50N 111 8W
Drin i zi → 44 41 37N 20 28 E
Drina → 42 44 53N 19 21 E
Drincea → 46 44 20N 22 55 E
Drînceni 46 46 49N 28 10 E
Drini → 44 42 20N 20 0 E
Drinjača → 42 44 15N 19 8 E
Driva → 47 62 33N 9 38 E
Drivstua 47 62 26N 9 47 E
Drniš 39 43 51N 16 10 E
Drøbak 47 59 39N 10 39 E
Drobin 28 52 42N 19 58 E
Drogheda 15 53 45N 6 20W
Drogichin 54 52 15N 25 8 E
Drogobych 54 49 20N 23 30 E
Drohiczyn 28 52 24N 22 39 E
Droichead Nua 15 53 11N 6 50W
Droitwich 13 52 16N 2 10W
Drôme □ 21 44 38N 5 15 E
Drôme → 21 44 46N 4 46 E
Dromedary, C. 99 36 17 S 150 10 E
Dronero 38 44 29N 7 22 E
Dronfield 98 21 12 S 140 3 E
Dronne → 20 45 2N 0 9W
Dronning Maud Land 5 72 30 S 12 0 E
Dronninglund 49 57 10N 10 19 E
Dropt → 20 44 35N 0 6W
Drosendorf 26 48 52N 15 37 E
Drouzhba 43 43 15N 28 0 E
Drumbo 112 43 16N 80 35W
Drumheller 108 51 25N 112 40W
Drummond 118 46 40N 113 4W
Drummond I. 106 46 0N 83 40W
Drummond Ra. 97 23 45 S 147 10 E
Drummondville 106 45 55N 72 25W
Drumright 117 35 59N 96 38W
Druskininkai 54 54 3N 23 58 E
Drut → 54 53 3N 30 42 E
Druya 54 55 45N 27 28 E
Druzhina 59 68 14N 145 18 E
Drvar 39 44 21N 16 23 E
Drvenik 39 43 27N 16 3 E
Drwęca → 28 53 0N 18 42 E
Dry Tortugas 121 24 38N 82 55W
Dryanovo 43 42 59N 25 28 E
Dryden, Can. 109 49 47N 92 50W
Dryden, U.S.A. 117 30 3N 102 3W
Drygalski I. 5 66 0 S 92 0 E
Drysdale → 96 13 59 S 126 51 E
Drzewiczka → 28 51 36N 20 36 E
Dschang 85 5 32N 10 3 E
Du Bois 114 41 8N 78 46W
Du Quoin 116 38 0N 89 10W
Duanesburg 113 42 45N 74 11W
Duaringa 98 23 42 S 149 42 E
Dubā 64 27 10N 35 40 E
Dubai = Dubayy 65 25 18N 55 20 E
Dubawnt → 109 64 33N 100 6W
Dubawnt, L. 109 63 4N 101 42W
Dubayy 65 25 18N 55 20 E
Dubbo 97 32 11 S 148 35 E
Dubele 90 2 56N 29 35 E
Dubica 39 45 11N 16 48 E
Dublin, Ireland 15 53 20N 6 18W
Dublin, Ga., U.S.A. 115 32 30N 82 34W
Dublin, Tex., U.S.A. 117 32 0N 98 20W
Dublin □ 15 53 24N 6 20W
Dublin B. 15 53 18N 6 5W
Dubna, U.S.S.R. 55 54 8N 36 59 E
Dubna, U.S.S.R. 55 56 44N 37 10 E
Dubno 54 50 25N 25 45 E
Dubois 118 44 7N 112 9W
Dubossary 56 47 15N 29 10 E
Dubossasy Vdkhr. 56 47 30N 29 0 E
Dubovka 57 49 5N 44 50 E
Dubovskoye 57 47 28N 42 46 E
Dubrajpur 69 23 48N 87 25 E
Dubréka 84 9 46N 13 31W
Dubrovitsa 54 51 31N 26 35 E
Dubrovnik 42 42 39N 18 6 E
Dubrovskoye 59 58 55N 111 10 E
Dubuque 116 42 30N 90 41W
Duchang 77 29 18N 116 12 E
Duchesne 118 40 14N 110 22W
Duchess 97 21 20 S 139 50 E
Ducie I. 95 24 40 S 124 48W
Duck Lake 109 52 50N 106 16W
Duck Mt. Prov. Parks 109 51 45N 101 0W
Duderstadt 24 51 30N 10 15 E
Dudinka 59 69 30N 86 13 E
Dudley 13 52 30N 2 5W
Dudna → 70 19 17N 76 54 E
Dueñas 30 41 52N 4 33W
Dueodde 49 54 59N 15 4 E
Duero → 30 41 8N 8 40W
Duff Is. 94 9 53 S 167 8 E
Dufftown 14 57 26N 3 9W
Dugi 39 44 0N 15 0 E
Dugo Selo 39 45 51N 16 18 E
Duifken Pt. 97 12 33 S 141 38 E
Duisburg 24 51 27N 6 42 E
Duiwelskloof 93 23 42 S 30 10 E
Dukati 44 40 16N 19 32 E
Duke I. 108 54 50N 131 20W
Dukelsky průsmyk 27 49 25N 21 42 E
Dukhān 65 25 25N 50 50 E
Dukhovshchina 54 55 15N 32 27 E
Dukla 27 49 30N 21 35 E
Duku, Bauchi, Nigeria 85 10 43N 10 43 E
Duku, Sokoto, Nigeria 85 11 11N 4 55 E
Dulce → 124 30 32 S 62 33W
Dulce, Golfo 121 8 40N 83 20W
Dŭlgopol 43 43 3N 27 22 E
Dullewala 68 31 50N 71 25 E
Dülmen 24 51 49N 7 18 E
Dulovo 43 43 48N 27 9 E
Dululu 98 23 48 S 150 15 E
Duluth 116 46 48N 92 10W
Dum Dum 69 22 39N 88 33 E
Dum Duma 67 27 40N 95 40 E
Dum Hadjer 81 13 18N 19 41 E
Dumaguete 73 9 17N 123 15 E
Dumai 72 1 35N 101 28 E
Dumaran 73 10 33N 119 50 E
Dumaring 73 1 46N 118 10 E
Dumas, Ark., U.S.A. 117 33 52N 91 30W
Dumas, Tex., U.S.A. 117 35 50N 101 58W
Dumbarton 14 55 58N 4 35W
Dumbrăveni 46 46 14N 24 34 E
Dumfries 14 55 4N 3 37W
Dumfries & Galloway □ 14 55 0N 4 0W
Dumka 69 24 12N 87 15 E
Dümmersee 24 52 30N 8 21 E
Dumoine → 106 46 13N 77 51W
Dumoine L. 106 46 55N 77 55W
Dumraon 69 25 33N 84 8 E
Dumyât 86 31 24N 31 48 E
Dumyât, Masabb 86 31 28N 31 51 E
Dun Laoghaire 15 53 17N 6 9W
Dun-le-Palestel 20 46 18N 1 39 E
Dun-sur-Auron 19 46 53N 2 33 E
Duna → 27 45 51N 18 48 E
Dunaföldvár 27 46 50N 18 57 E
Dunaj → 27 48 5N 17 10 E
Dunajec → 27 50 15N 20 44 E
Dunajska Streda 27 48 0N 17 37 E
Dunapatai 27 46 39N 19 4 E
Dunărea → 46 45 30N 8 15 E
Dunaszekcsö 27 46 6N 18 45 E
Dunaújváros 27 47 0N 18 57 E
Dunav → 42 44 47N 21 20 E
Dunavtsi 42 43 57N 22 53 E
Dunback 101 45 23 S 170 36 E
Dunbar, Austral. 98 16 0 S 142 22 E
Dunbar, U.K. 14 56 0N 2 32W
Dunblane 14 56 10N 3 58W
Duncan, Can. 108 48 45N 123 40W
Duncan, Ariz., U.S.A. 119 32 46N 109 6W
Duncan, Okla., U.S.A. 117 34 25N 98 0W
Duncan L. 108 62 51N 113 58W
Duncan, L. 106 53 29N 77 58W
Duncan Pass. 71 11 0N 92 30 E
Duncan Town 121 22 15N 75 45W
Duncannon 112 40 23N 77 2W
Dundalk, Can. 112 44 10N 80 24W
Dundalk, Ireland 15 54 1N 6 25W
Dundalk Bay 15 53 55N 6 15W
Dundas 106 43 17N 79 59W
Dundas I. 108 54 30N 130 50W
Dundas, L. 96 32 35 S 121 50 E
Dundas Str. 96 11 15 S 131 35 E
Dundee, S. Afr. 93 28 11 S 30 15 E
Dundee, U.K. 14 56 29N 3 0W
Dundoo 99 27 40 S 144 37 E
Dundrum 15 54 17N 5 50W
Dundrum B. 15 54 12N 5 40W
Dundwara 68 27 48N 79 9 E
Dunedin, N.Z. 101 45 50 S 170 33 E
Dunedin, U.S.A. 115 28 1N 82 45W
Dunedin → 108 59 30N 124 5W
Dunfermline 14 56 5N 3 28W
Dungannon, Can. 112 43 51N 81 36W
Dungannon, U.K. 15 54 30N 6 47W
Dungannon □ 15 54 30N 6 55W
Dungarpur 68 23 52N 73 45 E
Dungarvan 15 52 6N 7 40W
Dungarvan Bay 15 52 5N 7 35W
Dungeness 13 50 54N 0 59 E
Dungo, L. do 92 17 15 S 19 0 E
Dungog 99 32 22 S 151 46 E
Dungu 90 3 40N 28 32 E
Dungunâb 86 21 10N 37 9 E
Dungunâb, Khalij 86 21 5N 37 12 E
Dunhinda Falls 70 7 5N 81 6 E
Dunhua 76 43 20N 128 14 E
Dunhuang 75 40 8N 94 36 E
Dunières 21 45 13N 4 20 E
Dunk I. 98 17 59 S 146 29 E
Dunkeld 14 56 34N 3 36W
Dunkerque 19 51 2N 2 20 E
Dunkery Beacon 13 51 15N 3 37W
Dunkirk 114 42 30N 79 18W
Dunkirk = Dunkerque 19 51 2N 2 20 E
Dunkuj 87 12 50N 32 49 E
Dunkwa, Central, Ghana 84 6 0N 1 47W
Dunkwa, Central, Ghana 85 5 30N 1 0W
Dunlap 116 41 50N 95 36W
Dunmanus B. 15 51 31N 9 50W
Dunmore 114 41 27N 75 38W
Dunmore Hd. 15 52 10N 10 35W
Dunn 115 35 18N 78 36W
Dunnellon 115 29 4N 82 28W
Dunnet Hd. 14 58 38N 3 22W
Dunning 116 41 52N 100 4W
Dunnville 112 42 54N 79 36W
Dunolly 99 36 51 S 143 44 E
Dunoon 14 55 57N 4 56W
Dunqul 86 23 26N 31 37 E
Duns 14 55 47N 2 20W
Dunseith 116 48 49N 100 2W
Dunsmuir 118 41 10N 122 18W
Dunstable 13 51 53N 0 31W
Dunstan Mts. 101 44 53 S 169 35 E
Dunster 108 53 8N 119 50W
Dunvegan L. 109 60 8N 107 10W
Duolun 76 42 12N 116 28 E
Dupree 116 45 4N 101 35W
Dupuyer 118 48 11N 112 31W
Duque de Caxias 125 22 45 S 43 19W
Duquesne 112 40 22N 79 55W
Dūrā 62 31 31N 35 1 E
Durack Range 96 16 50 S 127 40 E
Durance → 21 43 55N 4 45 E
Durand 114 42 54N 83 58W
Durango, Mexico 120 24 3N 104 39W
Durango, Spain 32 43 13N 2 40W
Durango, U.S.A. 119 37 16N 107 50W
Durango □ 120 25 0N 105 0W
Durant 117 34 0N 96 25W
Duratón → 30 41 37N 4 7W
Durazno 124 33 25 S 56 31W
Durazzo = Durrësi 44 41 19N 19 28 E
Durban, France 20 43 0N 2 49 E
Durban, S. Afr. 93 29 49 S 31 1 E
Dúrcal 31 37 0N 3 34W
Đurđevac 42 46 2N 17 3 E
Düren 24 50 48N 6 30 E
Durg 69 21 15N 81 22 E
Durgapur 69 23 30N 87 20 E
Durham, Can. 106 44 10N 80 49W
Durham, U.K. 12 54 47N 1 34W
Durham, U.S.A. 115 36 0N 78 55W
Durham □ 12 54 42N 1 45W
Durmitor 34 43 10N 19 0 E
Durness 14 58 34N 4 45W
Durrës 44 41 19N 19 28 E
Durrësi 44 41 19N 19 28 E
Durrie 99 25 40 S 140 15 E
Durtal 18 47 40N 0 18W
Duru 90 4 14N 28 50 E
D'Urville I. 101 40 50 S 173 55 E
D'Urville, Tanjung 73 1 28 S 137 54 E
Duryea 113 41 20N 75 45W
Dusa Mareb 63 5 30N 46 15 E
Dûsh 86 24 35N 30 41 E
Dushak 58 37 13N 60 1 E
Dushan 77 25 48N 107 30 E
Dushanbe 58 38 33N 68 48 E
Dusheti 57 42 10N 44 42 E
Dusky Sd. 101 45 47 S 166 30 E
Düsseldorf 24 51 15N 6 46 E
Duszniki-Zdrój 28 50 24N 16 24 E
Dutch Harbor 104 53 54N 166 35W
Dutlhe 92 23 58 S 23 46 E
Dutsan Wai 85 10 50N 8 10 E
Dutton 112 42 39N 81 30W
Dutton → 98 20 44 S 143 10 E
Duved 48 63 24N 12 55 E
Duvno 42 43 42N 17 13 E
Duwādimi 64 24 35N 44 15 E
Duyun 77 26 18N 107 29 E
Duzce 64 40 50N 31 10 E
Duzdab = Zāhedān 65 29 30N 60 50 E
Dve Mogili 43 43 35N 25 55 E
Dvina, Sev. 52 64 32N 40 30 E
Dvinsk = Daugavpils 54 55 53N 26 32 E
Dvinskaya Guba 52 65 0N 39 0 E
Dvor 39 45 4N 16 22 E
Dvorce 27 49 50N 17 34 E
Dvur Králové 26 50 27N 15 50 E
Dwarka 68 22 18N 69 8 E
Dwight, Can. 112 45 20N 79 1W
Dwight, U.S.A. 114 41 5N 88 25W
Dyakovskoya 55 60 5N 41 12 E
Dyatkovo 54 53 40N 34 27 E
Dyatlovo 54 53 28N 25 28 E
Dyer, C. 105 66 40N 61 0W
Dyer Plateau 5 70 45 S 65 30W
Dyersburg 117 36 2N 89 20W
Dyfed □ 13 52 0N 4 30W
Dyje → 27 48 37N 16 56 E
Dynevor Downs 99 28 10 S 144 20 E
Dynów 27 49 50N 22 11 E
Dysart 109 50 57N 104 2W
Dzamin Üüd 75 43 50N 111 58 E
Dzerzhinsk, Byelorussian S.S.R., U.S.S.R. 54 53 40N 27 1 E
Dzerzhinsk, R.S.F.S.R., U.S.S.R. 55 56 14N 43 30 E
Dzhalal-Abad 58 40 56N 73 0 E
Dzhalinda 59 53 26N 124 0 E
Dzhambeyty 57 50 15N 52 30 E
Dzhambul 58 42 54N 71 22 E
Dzhankoi 56 45 40N 34 20 E
Dzhanybek 57 49 25N 46 50 E
Dzhardzhan 59 68 10N 124 10 E
Dzhelinde 59 70 0N 114 20 E

Dzhetygara **Elbow**

Dzhetygara **58** 52 11N 61 12 E
Dzhezkazgan **58** 47 44N 67 40 E
Dzhikimde **59** 59 1N 121 47 E
Dzhizak **58** 40 6N 67 50 E
Dzhugdzur, Khrebet **59** 57 30N 138 0 E
Dzhungarskiye Vorota **58** 45 0N 82 0 E
Dzhvari **57** 42 42N 42 4 E
Działdowo **28** 53 15N 20 15 E
Działoszyce **28** 50 22N 20 20 E
Działoszyn **28** 51 6N 18 50 E
Dzierzgoń **28** 53 58N 19 20 E
Dzierzoniów **28** 50 45N 16 39 E
Dzioua **83** 33 14N 5 14 E
Dziwnów **28** 54 2N 14 45 E
Dzungarian Gate = Alataw Shankou **75** 45 5N 81 57 E
Dzuumod **75** 47 45N 106 58 E

E

Eabamet, L. **106** 51 30N 87 46W
Eads **116** 38 30N 102 46W
Eagle, Alaska, U.S.A. **104** 64 44N 141 7W
Eagle, Colo., U.S.A. **118** 39 39N 106 55W
Eagle → **107** 53 36N 57 26W
Eagle Butt **116** 45 1N 101 12W
Eagle Grove **116** 42 37N 93 53W
Eagle L., Calif., U.S.A. **118** 40 35N 120 50W
Eagle L., Me., U.S.A. **107** 46 23N 69 22W
Eagle Lake **117** 29 35N 96 21W
Eagle Nest **119** 36 33N 105 13W
Eagle Pass **117** 28 45N 100 35W
Eagle River **116** 45 55N 89 17W
Eaglehawk **99** 36 39 S 144 16 E
Ealing **13** 51 30N 0 19W
Earl Grey **109** 50 57N 104 43W
Earle **117** 35 18N 90 26W
Earlimart **119** 35 53N 119 16W
Earn → **14** 56 20N 3 19W
Earn, L. **14** 56 23N 4 14W
Earnslaw, Mt. **101** 44 32 S 168 27 E
Earth **117** 34 18N 102 30W
Easley **115** 34 52N 82 35W
East Angus **107** 45 30N 71 40W
East Aurora **112** 42 46N 78 38W
East B. **117** 29 2N 89 16W
East Bengal **67** 24 0N 90 0 E
East Beskids = Vychodné Beskydy **27** 49 30N 22 0 E
East Brady **112** 40 59N 79 36W
East C. **101** 37 42 S 178 35 E
East Chicago **114** 41 40N 87 30W
East China Sea **75** 30 5N 126 0 E
East Coulee **108** 51 23N 112 27W
East Falkland **128** 51 30 S 58 30W
East Grand Forks **116** 47 55N 97 5W
East Greenwich **113** 41 39N 71 27W
East Hartford **113** 41 45N 72 39W
East Helena **118** 46 37N 111 58W
East Indies **72** 0 0 120 0 E
East Jordan **114** 45 10N 85 7W
East Kilbride **14** 55 46N 4 10W
East Lansing **114** 42 44N 84 29W
East Liverpool **114** 40 39N 80 35W
East London **93** 33 0 S 27 55 E
East Orange **114** 40 46N 74 13W
East Pacific Ridge **95** 15 0 S 110 0W
East Pakistan = Bangladesh ■ **67** 24 0N 90 0 E
East Palestine **112** 40 50N 80 32W
East Pine **108** 55 48N 120 12W
East Pt. **107** 46 27N 61 58W
East Point **115** 33 40N 84 28W
East Providence **113** 41 48N 71 22W
East Retford **12** 53 19N 0 55W
East St. Louis **116** 38 37N 90 4W
East Schelde → = Oosterschelde **16** 51 38N 3 40 E
East Siberian Sea **59** 73 0N 160 0 E
East Stroudsburg **113** 41 1N 75 11W
East Sussex □ **13** 51 0N 0 20 E
East Tawas **114** 44 17N 83 31W
Eastbourne, N.Z. **101** 41 19 S 174 55 E
Eastbourne, U.K. **13** 50 46N 0 18 E
Eastend **109** 49 32N 108 50W
Easter I. **95** 27 8 S 109 23W
Easter Islands **95** 27 0 S 109 0W
Eastern □, Kenya **90** 0 0 S 38 30 E
Eastern □, Uganda **90** 1 50N 33 45 E
Eastern Cr. → **98** 20 40 S 141 35 E
Eastern Ghats **70** 14 0N 78 50 E
Eastern Province □ **84** 8 15N 11 0W
Easterville **109** 53 8N 99 49W
Easthampton **113** 42 15N 72 41W
Eastland **117** 32 26N 98 45W
Eastleigh **13** 50 58N 1 21W
Eastmain → **106** 52 27N 78 26W
Eastmain (East Main) **106** 52 10N 78 30W
Eastman, Can. **113** 45 18N 72 19W
Eastman, U.S.A. **115** 32 13N 83 20W
Easton, Md., U.S.A. **114** 38 47N 76 7W
Easton, Pa., U.S.A. **114** 40 41N 75 15W
Easton, Wash., U.S.A. **118** 47 14N 121 8W
Eastport **107** 44 57N 67 0W
Eaton **116** 40 35N 104 42W
Eatonia **109** 51 13N 109 25W
Eatonton **115** 33 22N 83 24W
Eatontown **113** 40 18N 74 7W
Eau Claire, S.C., U.S.A. **115** 34 5N 81 2W
Eau Claire, Wis., U.S.A. **116** 44 46N 91 30W
Eauze **20** 43 53N 0 7 E
Ebagoola **98** 14 15 S 143 12 E
Eban **85** 9 40N 4 50 E
Ebbw Vale **13** 51 47N 3 12W
Ebeggui **83** 26 2N 6 0 E
Ebensburg **112** 40 29N 78 43W
Ebensee **26** 47 48N 13 46 E
Eberbach **25** 49 27N 8 59 E
Eberswalde **24** 52 49N 13 50 E
Ebingen **25** 48 13N 9 1 E
Eboli **41** 40 39N 15 2 E
Ebolowa **88** 2 55N 11 10 E
Ebrach **25** 49 50N 10 30 E
Ébrié, Lagune **84** 5 12N 4 26W
Ebro → **32** 40 43N 0 54 E
Ebro, Pantano del **30** 43 0N 3 58W
Ebstorf **24** 53 2N 10 23 E
Eceabat **44** 40 11N 26 21 E
Écueillé **18** 47 10N 1 19 E
Echelles, Les **21** 45 27N 5 45 E
Echmiadzin **57** 40 12N 44 19 E
Echo Bay **106** 46 29N 84 4W
Echo Bay (Port Radium) **104** 66 05N 117 55W
Echoing → **109** 55 51N 92 5W
Echternach **16** 49 49N 6 25 E
Echuca **100** 36 10 S 144 20 E
Ecija **31** 37 30N 5 10W
Eckernförde **24** 54 26N 9 50 E
Écommoy **18** 47 50N 0 17 E
Écos **19** 49 9N 1 35 E
Écouché **18** 48 42N 0 10W
Ecuador ■ **126** 2 0 S 78 0W
Ed **49** 58 55N 11 55 E
Ed Dabbura **86** 17 40N 34 15 E
Ed Dâmer **86** 17 27N 34 0 E
Ed Debba **86** 18 0N 30 51 E
Ed-Déffa **86** 30 40N 26 30 E
Ed Deim **87** 10 10N 28 20 E
Ed Dueim **87** 14 0N 32 10 E
Edam, Can. **109** 53 11N 108 46W
Edam, Neth. **16** 52 31N 5 3 E
Edapally **70** 11 19N 78 3 E
Eday **14** 59 11N 2 47W
Edd **87** 14 0N 41 38 E
Eddrachillis B. **14** 58 16N 5 10W
Eddystone **13** 50 11N 4 16W
Eddystone Pt. **99** 40 59 S 148 20 E
Ede, Neth. **16** 52 4N 5 40 E
Ede, Nigeria **85** 7 45N 4 29 E
Édea **88** 3 51N 10 9 E
Edehon L. **109** 60 25N 97 15W
Edekel, Adrar **83** 23 56N 6 47 E
Eden, Austral. **99** 37 3 S 149 55 E
Eden, N.C., U.S.A. **115** 36 29N 79 53W
Eden, N.Y., U.S.A. **112** 42 39N 78 55W
Eden, Tex., U.S.A. **117** 31 16N 99 50W
Eden, Wyo., U.S.A. **118** 42 2N 109 27W
Eden → **12** 54 57N 3 2W
Eden L. **109** 56 38N 100 15W
Edenburg **92** 29 43 S 25 58 E
Edenderry **15** 53 21N 7 3W
Edenton **115** 36 5N 76 36W
Edenville **93** 27 37 S 27 34 E
Eder → **24** 51 15N 9 25 E
Ederstausee **24** 51 11N 9 0 E
Edgar **116** 40 25N 98 0W
Edgartown **113** 41 22N 70 28W
Edge Hill **13** 52 7N 1 28W
Edgefield **115** 33 50N 81 59W
Edgeley **116** 46 27N 98 41W
Edgemont **116** 43 15N 103 53W
Edgeøya **4** 77 45N 22 30 E
Edhessa **44** 40 48N 22 5 E
Edievale **101** 45 49 S 169 22 E
Edina, Liberia **84** 6 0N 10 10W
Edina, U.S.A. **116** 40 6N 92 10W
Edinburg **117** 26 22N 98 10W
Edinburgh **14** 55 57N 3 12W
Edirne **43** 41 40N 26 34 E
Edithburgh **99** 35 5 S 137 43 E
Edjeleh **83** 28 38N 9 50 E
Edmeston **113** 42 42N 75 15W
Edmond **117** 35 37N 97 30W
Edmonds **118** 47 47N 122 22W
Edmonton, Austral. **98** 17 2 S 145 46 E
Edmonton, Can. **108** 53 30N 113 30W
Edmund L. **109** 54 45N 93 17W
Edmundston **107** 47 23N 68 20W
Edna **117** 29 0N 96 40W
Edna Bay **108** 55 55N 133 40W
Edolo **38** 46 10N 10 21 E
Edremit **64** 39 34N 27 0 E
Edsbyn **48** 61 23N 15 49 E
Edsel Ford Ra. **5** 77 0 S 143 0W
Edsele **48** 63 25N 16 32 E
Edson **108** 53 35N 116 28W
Eduardo Castex **124** 35 50 S 64 18W
Edward → **99** 35 0 S 143 30 E
Edward I. **106** 48 22N 88 37W
Edward, L. **90** 0 25 S 29 40 E
Edward VII Pen. **5** 80 0 S 150 0W
Edwards Plat. **117** 30 30N 101 5W
Edwardsville **113** 41 15N 75 56W
Edzo **108** 62 49N 116 4W
Eekloo **16** 51 11N 3 33 E
Ef'e, Nahal **62** 31 9N 35 13 E
Eferding **26** 48 18N 14 1 E
Eferi **83** 24 30N 9 28 E
Effingham **114** 39 8N 88 30W
Eforie Sud **46** 44 1N 28 37 E
Ega → **32** 42 19N 1 55W
Égadi, Ísole **40** 37 55N 12 16 E
Eganville **106** 45 32N 77 5W
Egeland **116** 48 42N 99 6W
Egenolf L. **109** 59 3N 100 0W
Eger **27** 47 53N 20 27 E
Eger → **27** 47 38N 20 50 E
Egersund **47** 58 26N 6 1 E
Egerton, Mt. **96** 24 42 S 117 44 E
Egg L. **109** 55 5N 105 30W
Eggenburg **26** 48 38N 15 50 E
Eggenfelden **25** 48 24N 12 46 E
Égletons **20** 45 24N 2 3 E
Egmont, C. **101** 39 16 S 173 45 E
Egmont, Mt. **101** 39 17 S 174 5 E
Eğridir **64** 37 52N 30 51 E
Eğridir Gölü **64** 37 53N 30 50 E
Egtved **49** 55 38N 9 18 E
Égume **85** 7 30N 7 14 E
Éguzon **20** 46 27N 1 33 E
Egvekinot **59** 66 19N 179 50W
Egyek **27** 47 39N 20 52 E
Egypt ■ **86** 28 0N 31 0 E
Eha Amufu **85** 6 30N 7 46 E
Ehime □ **74** 33 30N 132 40 E
Ehingen **25** 48 16N 9 43 E
Ehrwald **26** 47 24N 10 56 E
Eibar **32** 43 11N 2 28W
Eichstatt **25** 48 53N 11 12 E
Eida **47** 60 32N 6 43 E
Eider → **24** 54 19N 8 58 E
Eidsvold **99** 25 25 S 151 12 E
Eifel **25** 50 10N 6 45 E
Eiffel Flats **91** 18 20 S 30 0 E
Eigg **14** 56 54N 6 10W
Eighty Mile Beach **96** 19 30 S 120 40 E
Eil **63** 8 0N 49 50 E
Eil, L. **14** 56 50N 5 15W
Eildon, L. **99** 37 10 S 146 0 E
Eileen L. **109** 62 16N 107 37W
Eilenburg **24** 51 28N 12 38 E
Ein el Luweiqa **87** 14 5N 33 50 E
Einasleigh **97** 18 32 S 144 5 E
Einasleigh → **98** 17 30 S 142 17 E
Einbeck **24** 51 48N 9 50 E
Eindhoven **16** 51 26N 5 30 E
Einsiedeln **25** 47 7N 8 46 E
Eiriksjökull **50** 64 46N 20 24W
Eirunepé **126** 6 35 S 69 53W
Eisenach **24** 50 58N 10 18 E
Eisenberg **24** 50 59N 11 50 E
Eisenerz **26** 47 32N 14 54 E
Eisenhüttenstadt **24** 52 9N 14 41 E
Eisenkappel **26** 46 29N 14 36 E
Eisenstadt **27** 47 51N 16 31 E
Eiserfeld **24** 50 50N 7 59 E
Eisfeld **24** 50 25N 10 54 E
Eisleben **24** 51 31N 11 31 E
Ejby **49** 55 25N 9 56 E
Eje, Sierra del **30** 42 24N 6 54W
Ejea de los Caballeros **32** 42 7N 1 9W
Ekalaka **116** 45 55N 104 30W
Eket **85** 4 38N 7 56 E
Eketahuna **101** 40 38 S 175 43 E
Ekhínos **44** 41 16N 25 1 E
Ekibastuz **58** 51 50N 75 10 E
Ekimchan **59** 53 0N 133 0W
Ekoli **90** 0 23 S 24 13 E
Eksjö **49** 57 40N 14 58W
Ekwan → **106** 53 12N 82 15W
Ekwan Pt. **106** 53 16N 82 7W
El Aaiún **80** 27 9N 13 12W
El Aat **62** 32 50N 35 45 E
El Abiodh-Sidi-Cheikh **82** 32 53N 0 31 E
El Aïoun **82** 34 33N 2 30W
El 'Aiyat **86** 29 36N 31 15 E
El Alamein **86** 30 48N 28 58 E
El 'Arag **86** 28 40N 26 20 E
El Arahal **31** 37 15N 5 33W
El Arba **82** 36 37N 3 12 E
El Aricha **82** 34 13N 1 10W
El Arïhã **62** 31 52N 35 27 E
El Arish **98** 17 35 S 146 1 E
El 'Arîsh **86** 31 8N 33 50 E
El Arrouch **83** 36 37N 6 53 E
• El Asnam **82** 36 10N 1 20 E
El Astillero **30** 43 24N 3 49W
El Badâri **86** 27 4N 31 25 E
El Bahrein **86** 28 30N 26 25 E
El Ballâs **86** 26 2N 32 43 E
El Balyana **86** 26 10N 32 3 E
El Baqeir **86** 18 40N 33 40 E
El Barco de Ávila **30** 40 21N 5 31W
El Barco de Valdeorras **30** 42 23N 7 0W
El Bauga **86** 18 18N 33 52 E
El Bawiti **86** 28 25N 28 45 E
El Bayadh **82** 33 40N 1 1 E
El Bierzo **30** 42 45N 6 30W
El Bluff **121** 11 59N 83 40W
El Bonillo **33** 38 57N 2 35W
El Cajon **119** 32 49N 117 0W
El Callao **126** 7 18N 61 50W
El Camp **32** 41 5N 1 10 E
El Campo **117** 29 10N 96 20W
El Castillo **31** 37 41N 6 19W
El Centro **119** 32 50N 115 40W
El Cerro, Boliv. **126** 17 30 S 61 40W
El Cerro, Spain **31** 37 45N 6 57W
El Coronil **31** 37 5N 5 38W
El Cuy **128** 39 55 S 68 25W
El Cuyo **120** 21 30N 87 40W
El Dab'a **86** 31 0N 28 27 E
El Deir **86** 25 25N 32 20 E
El Dere **63** 3 50N 47 8 E
El Dias **120** 20 40N 87 20W
El Dilingat **86** 30 50N 30 31 E
El Diviso **126** 1 22N 78 14W
El Djem **83** 35 18N 10 42 E
El Djouf **84** 20 0N 11 30 E
El Dorado, Ark., U.S.A. **117** 33 10N 92 40W
El Dorado, Kans., U.S.A. **117** 37 55N 96 56W
El Dorado, Venez. **126** 6 55N 61 37W
El Dorado Springs **117** 37 54N 93 59W
El Eglab **82** 26 20N 4 30W
El Escorial **30** 40 35N 4 7W
El Eulma **83** 36 9N 5 42 E
El Faiyûm **86** 29 19N 30 50 E
El Fâsher **87** 13 33N 25 26 E
El Fashn **86** 28 50N 30 54 E
El Ferrol **30** 43 29N 8 15W
El Fifi **87** 10 4N 25 0 E
El Fuerte **120** 26 30N 108 40W
El Gal **63** 10 58N 50 20 E
El Gebir **87** 13 40N 29 40 E
El Gedida **86** 25 40N 28 30 E
El Geteina **87** 14 50N 32 27 E
El Gezira □ **87** 15 0N 33 0 E
El Gîza **86** 30 0N 31 10 E
El Goléa **82** 30 30N 2 50 E
El Guettar **83** 34 5N 4 38 E
El Hadjira **83** 32 36N 5 30 E
El Hagiz **87** 15 15N 35 50 E
El Hajeb **82** 33 43N 5 13W
El Hammam **86** 30 52N 29 25 E
El Hank **82** 24 30N 7 0W
El Harrache **80** 36 45N 3 5 E
El Hawata **87** 13 25N 34 42 E
El Heiz **86** 27 50N 28 40 E
El 'Idisât **86** 25 30N 32 35 E
El Iskandarîya **86** 31 0N 30 0 E
El Istwâ'ya □ **87** 5 0N 30 0 E
El Jadida **80** 33 11N 8 17W
El Jebelein **81** 12 40N 32 55 E
El Kab **86** 19 27N 32 46 E
El Kala **83** 36 50N 8 30 E
El Kalâa **82** 32 4N 7 27W
El Kamlin **87** 15 3N 33 11 E
El Kantara, Alg. **83** 35 14N 5 45 E
El Kantara, Tunisia **83** 33 45N 10 58 E
El Karaba **86** 18 32N 33 41 E
El Kef **83** 36 12N 8 47 E
El Khandaq **86** 18 30N 30 30 E
El Khârga **86** 25 30N 30 33 E
El Khartûm **87** 15 31N 32 35 E
El Khartûm □ **87** 16 0N 33 0 E
El Khartûm Bahrî **87** 15 40N 32 31 E
El-Khroubs **83** 36 10N 6 55 E
El Khureiba **86** 28 3N 35 10 E
El Kseur **83** 36 46N 4 49 E
El Ksiba **82** 32 45N 6 1W
El Kuntilla **86** 30 1N 34 45 E
El Laqâwa **81** 11 25N 29 1 E
El Laqeita **86** 25 50N 33 15 E
El Leiya **87** 16 15N 35 28 E
El Mafâza **87** 13 38N 34 30 E
El Mahalla el Kubra **86** 31 0N 31 0 E
El Mahârîq **86** 25 35N 30 35 E
El Mahmûdîya **86** 31 10N 30 32 E
El Maiz **82** 28 19N 0 9W
El-Maks el-Bahari **86** 24 30N 30 40 E
El Manshâh **86** 26 26N 31 50 E
El Mansour **82** 27 47N 0 14W
El Mansûra **86** 31 0N 31 19 E
El Manzala **86** 31 10N 31 50 E
El Marâgha **86** 26 35N 31 10 E
El Masid **87** 15 15N 33 0 E
El Matariya **86** 31 15N 32 0 E
El Meghaier **83** 33 55N 5 58 E
El Meraguen **82** 28 0N 0 7W
El Metemma **87** 16 50N 33 10 E
El Milagro **124** 30 59 S 65 59W
El Milia **83** 36 51N 6 13 E
El Minyâ **86** 28 7N 30 33 E
El Molar **32** 40 42N 3 45W
El Mreyye **84** 18 0N 6 0W
El Obeid **87** 13 8N 30 10 E
El Odaiya **81** 12 8N 28 12 E
El Oro **120** 19 48N 100 8W
El Oro = Sta. María del Oro **120** 25 50N 105 20W
El Oued **83** 33 20N 6 58 E
El Palmito, Presa **120** 25 40N 105 30W
El Panadés **32** 41 10N 1 30 E
El Pardo **30** 40 31N 3 47W
El Paso **119** 31 50N 106 30W
El Pedernoso **33** 39 29N 2 45W
El Pedroso **31** 37 51N 5 45W
El Pobo de Dueñas **32** 40 46N 1 39W
El Portal **119** 37 44N 119 49W
El Prat de Llobregat **32** 41 18N 2 3 E
El Progreso **120** 15 26N 87 51W
El Provencío **33** 39 23N 2 35W
El Pueblito **120** 29 3N 105 4W
El Qâhira **86** 30 1N 31 14 E
El Qantara **86** 30 51N 32 20 E
El Qasr **86** 25 44N 28 42 E
El Quseima **86** 30 40N 34 15 E
El Qusîya **86** 27 29N 30 44 E
El Râshda **86** 25 36N 28 57 E
El Reno **117** 35 30N 98 0W
El Ribero **30** 42 30N 8 30W
El Rîdisiya **86** 24 56N 32 51 E
El Ronquillo **31** 37 44N 6 10W
El Rubio **31** 37 22N 5 0W
El Saff **86** 29 34N 31 16 E
El Salvador ■ **120** 13 50N 89 0W
El Sancejo **31** 37 4N 5 6W
El Sauce **121** 13 0N 86 40W
El Shallal **86** 24 0N 32 53 E
El Simbillawein **86** 30 48N 31 13 E
El Suweis **86** 29 58N 32 31 E
El Thamad **86** 29 40N 34 28 E
El Tigre **126** 8 44N 64 15W
El Tocuyo **126** 9 47N 69 48W
El Tofo **124** 29 22 S 71 18W
El Tránsito **124** 28 52 S 70 17W
El Tûr **86** 28 14N 33 36 E
El Turbio **128** 51 45 S 72 5W
El Uqsur **86** 25 41N 32 38 E
El Vado **32** 41 2N 3 18W
El Vallés **32** 41 35N 2 20 E
El Vigía **126** 8 38N 71 39W
El Wak **90** 2 49N 40 56 E
El Waqf **86** 25 45N 32 15 E
El Wâsta **86** 29 19N 31 12 E
El Weguet **87** 5 28N 42 17 E
El Wuz **81** 15 0N 30 7 E
Elafónisos **45** 36 29N 22 56 E
Elamanchili = Yellamanchilli **70** 17 26N 82 50 E
Elandsvlei **92** 32 19 S 19 31 E
Élassa **45** 35 18N 26 21 E
Elassón **44** 39 53N 22 12 E
Elat **62** 29 30N 34 56 E
Eláthia **45** 38 37N 22 46 E
Elâzığ **64** 38 37N 39 14 E
Elba, Italy **38** 42 48N 10 15 E
Elba, U.S.A. **115** 31 27N 86 4W
Elbasani **44** 41 9N 20 9 E
Elbasani-Berati □ **44** 40 58N 20 0 E
Elbe → **24** 53 50N 9 0 E
Elbert, Mt. **119** 39 5N 106 27W
Elberta **114** 44 35N 86 14W
Elberton **115** 34 7N 82 51W
Elbeuf **18** 49 17N 1 2 E
Elbidtan **64** 38 13N 37 12 E
Elbing = Elbląg **28** 54 10N 19 25 E
Elbląg **28** 54 10N 19 25 E
Elbląg □ **28** 54 15N 19 30 E
Elbow **109** 51 7N 106 35W

* *Renamed Ech Cheliff*

Estevan Group 108 53 3N 129 38W
Estherville 116 43 25N 94 50W
Estissac 19 48 16N 3 48 E
Eston 109 51 8N 108 40W
Estonian S.S.R. □ 54 58 30N 25 30 E
Estoril 31 38 42N 9 23W
Estouk 85 18 14N 1 2 E
Estrada, La 30 42 43N 8 27W
Estrêla, Serra da 30 40 10N 7 45W
Estrella 33 38 25N 3 35W
Estremoz 31 38 51N 7 39W
Estrondo, Serra do 127 7 20 S 48 0W
Esztergom 27 47 47N 18 44 E
Et Tîdra 84 19 45N 16 20W
Eṭ Ṭîra 62 32 14N 34 56 E
Étables-sur-Mer 18 48 38N 2 51W
Etah 68 27 35N 78 40 E
Étain 19 49 13N 5 38 E
Etamamu 107 50 18N 59 59W
Étampes 19 48 26N 2 10 E
Étang 19 46 52N 4 10 E
Etanga 92 17 55 S 13 00 E
Étaples 19 50 30N 1 39 E
Etawah 68 26 48N 79 6 E
Etawah → 115 34 20N 84 15W
Etawney L. 109 57 50N 96 50W
Eteh 85 7 2N 7 28 E
Ethel, Oued el → 82 28 31N 3 37W
Ethelbert 109 51 32N 100 25W
Ethiopia ■ 63 8 0N 40 0 E
Ethiopian Highlands 78 10 0N 37 0 E
Etive, L. 14 56 30N 5 12W
Etna, Mt. 41 37 45N 15 0 E
Etne 47 59 40N 5 56 E
Etoile 91 11 33 S 27 30 E
Etolin I. 108 56 5N 132 20W
Etosha Pan 92 18 40 S 16 30 E
Etowah 115 35 20N 84 30W
Étrépagny 18 49 18N 1 36 E
Étretat 18 49 42N 0 12 E
Étroits, Les 107 47 24N 68 54W
Etropole 43 42 50N 24 0 E
Ettlingen 25 48 58N 8 25 E
Ettrick Water 14 55 31N 2 55W
Etuku 90 3 42 S 25 45 E
Etzatlán 120 20 48N 104 5W
Eu 18 50 3N 1 26 E
Euabalong West 100 33 3 S 146 23 E
Euboea = Evvoia 45 38 40N 23 40 E
Eucla Basin 96 31 19 S 126 9 E
Euclid 114 41 32N 81 31W
Eucumbene, L. 99 36 2 S 148 40 E
Eudora 117 33 5N 91 17W
Eufaula, Ala., U.S.A. 115 31 55N 85 11W
Eufaula, Okla., U.S.A. 117 35 20N 95 33W
Eufaula, L. 117 35 15N 95 28W
Eugene 118 44 0N 123 8W
Eugenia, Punta 120 27 50N 115 5W
Eugowra 99 33 22 S 148 24 E
Eulo 99 28 10 S 145 3 E
Eunice, La., U.S.A. 117 30 35N 92 28W
Eunice, N. Mex., U.S.A. 117 32 30N 103 10W
Eupen 16 50 37N 6 3 E
Euphrates = Furāt, Nahr al → 64 31 0N 47 25 E
Eure □ 18 49 6N 1 0 E
Eure → 18 49 18N 1 12 E
Eure-et-Loir □ 18 48 22N 1 30 E
Eureka, Can. 4 80 0N 85 56W
Eureka, Calif., U.S.A. 118 40 50N 124 0W
Eureka, Kans., U.S.A. 117 37 50N 96 20W
Eureka, Mont., U.S.A. 118 48 53N 115 6W
Eureka, Nev., U.S.A. 118 39 32N 116 2W
Eureka, S.D., U.S.A. 116 45 49N 99 38W
Eureka, Utah, U.S.A. 118 40 0N 112 9W
Euroa 99 36 44 S 145 35 E
Europa, Picos de 30 43 10N 4 49W
Europa Pt. = Europa, Pta. de 31 36 3N 5 21W
Europa, Pta. de 31 36 3N 5 21W
Europe 8 50 0N 20 0 E
Europoort 16 51 57N 4 10 E
Euskirchen 24 50 40N 6 45 E
Eustis 115 28 54N 81 36W
Eutin 24 54 7N 10 38 E
Eutsuk L. 108 53 20N 126 45W
Eval 62 32 15N 35 15 E
Evale 92 16 33 S 15 44 E
Evanger 47 60 39N 6 7 E
Evans 116 40 25N 104 43W
Evans Head 99 29 7 S 153 27 E
Evans L. 106 50 50N 77 0W
Evans Mills 113 44 6N 75 48W
Evans Pass 116 41 0N 105 35W
Evanston, Ill., U.S.A. 114 42 0N 87 40W
Evanston, Wyo., U.S.A. 118 41 10N 111 0W
Evansville, Ind., U.S.A. 114 38 0N 87 35W
Evansville, Wis., U.S.A. 116 42 47N 89 18W
Évaux-les-Bains 20 46 12N 2 29 E
Eveleth 116 47 29N 92 46W
Even Yahuda 62 32 16N 34 53 E
Evensk 59 62 12N 159 30 E
Evenstad 47 61 25N 11 7 E
Everard, L. 96 31 30 S 135 0 E
Everard Ras. 96 27 5 S 132 28 E
Everest, Mt. 69 28 5N 86 58 E
Everett, Pa., U.S.A. 112 40 2N 78 24W
Everett, Wash., U.S.A. 118 48 0N 122 10W
Everglades, Fla., U.S.A. 115 26 0N 80 30W
Everglades, Fla., U.S.A. 115 25 52N 81 23W
Everglades Nat. Park. 115 25 27N 80 53W
Evergreen 115 31 28N 86 55W
Everson 118 48 57N 122 22W
Evesham 13 52 6N 1 57W
Evian-les-Bains 21 46 24N 6 35 E
Evinayong 88 1 26N 10 35 E
Évinos → 45 38 27N 21 40 E
Evisa 21 42 15N 8 48 E
Evje 47 58 36N 7 51 E
Évora 31 38 33N 7 57W
Évora □ 31 38 33N 7 50W
Évreux 18 49 0N 1 8 E
Evritania □ 45 39 5N 21 30 E
Évron 18 48 10N 0 24W
Évros □ 44 41 10N 26 0 E
Evrótas → 45 36 50N 22 40 E
Évvoia 45 38 30N 24 0 E
Évvoia □ 45 38 40N 23 40 E
Ewe, L. 14 57 49N 5 38W
Ewing 116 42 18N 98 22W
Ewo 88 0 48 S 14 45 E
Exaltación 126 13 10 S 65 20W
Excelsior Springs 116 39 20N 94 10W
Excideuil 20 45 20N 1 4 E
Exe → 13 50 38N 3 27W
Exeter, Can. 112 43 21N 81 29W
Exeter, U.K. 13 50 43N 3 31W
Exeter, Calif., U.S.A. 119 36 17N 119 9W
Exeter, N.H., U.S.A. 113 43 0N 70 58W
Exeter, Nebr., U.S.A. 116 40 43N 97 30W
Exmes 18 48 45N 0 10 E
Exmoor 13 51 10N 3 59W
Exmouth, Austral. 96 21 54 S 114 10 E
Exmouth, U.K. 13 50 37N 3 26W
Exmouth G. 96 22 15 S 114 15 E
Expedition Range 97 24 30 S 149 12 E
Extremadura 31 39 30N 6 5W
Exuma Sound 121 24 30N 76 20W
Eyasi, L. 90 3 30 S 35 0 E
Eyeberry L. 109 63 8N 104 43W
Eyemouth 14 55 53N 2 5W
Eygurande 20 45 40N 2 26 E
Eyjafjörður 50 66 15N 18 30W
Eymet 20 44 40N 0 25 E
Eymoutiers 20 45 40N 1 45 E
Eyrarbakki 50 63 52N 21 9W
Eyre 96 32 15 S 126 18 E
Eyre Cr. → 97 26 40 S 139 0 E
Eyre, L. 97 29 30 S 137 26 E
Eyre Mts. 101 45 25 S 168 25 E
Eyre (North), L. 97 28 30 S 137 20 E
Eyre Pen. 96 33 30 S 137 17 E
Eyre (South), L. 99 29 18 S 137 25 E
Eyzies, Les 20 44 56N 1 1 E
Ez Zeidab 86 17 25N 33 55 E
Ezcaray 32 42 19N 3 0W
Ezine 44 39 48N 26 12 E

F

Fabens 119 31 30N 106 8W
Fåborg 49 55 6N 10 15 E
Fabriano 39 43 20N 12 52 E
Făcăeni 46 44 32N 27 53 E
Facatativá 126 4 49N 74 22W
Fachi 80 18 6N 11 34 E
Facture 20 44 39N 0 58W
Fada 81 17 13N 21 34 E
Fada-n-Gourma 85 12 10N 0 30 E
Fadd 27 46 28N 18 49 E
Faddeyevskiy, Ostrov 59 76 0N 150 0 E
Fāḍilī 64 26 55N 49 10 E
Fadlab 86 17 42N 34 2 E
Faenza 39 44 17N 11 53 E
Fafa 85 15 22N 0 48 E
Fafe 30 41 27N 8 11W
Fagam 85 11 1N 10 1 E
Făgăras 46 45 48N 24 58 E
Făgăras, Munţii 46 45 40N 24 40 E
Fågelsjö 48 61 50N 14 35 E
Fagerhult 49 57 8N 15 40 E
Fagersta 48 60 1N 15 46 E
Făget 46 45 52N 22 10 E
Făget, Munţii 46 47 40N 23 10 E
Fagnano Castello 41 39 31N 16 4 E
Fagnano, L. 128 54 30 S 68 0W
Fagnières 19 48 58N 4 20 E
Fahraj 65 29 0N 59 0 E
Fahūd 65 22 18N 56 28 E
Fair Hd. 15 55 14N 6 10W
Fair Isle 11 59 30N 1 40W
Fairbank 119 31 44N 110 12W
Fairbanks 104 64 50N 147 50W
Fairbury 116 40 5N 97 5W
Fairfax 117 36 37N 96 45W
Fairfield, Austral. 100 33 53 S 150 57 E
Fairfield, Ala., U.S.A. 115 33 30N 87 0W
Fairfield, Calif., U.S.A. 118 38 14N 122 1W
Fairfield, Conn., U.S.A. 113 41 8N 73 16W
Fairfield, Idaho, U.S.A. 118 43 21N 114 46W
Fairfield, Ill., U.S.A. 114 38 20N 88 20W
Fairfield, Iowa, U.S.A. 116 41 0N 91 58W
Fairfield, Mont., U.S.A. 118 47 40N 112 0W
Fairfield, Texas, U.S.A. 117 31 40N 96 0W
Fairford 109 51 37N 98 38W
Fairhope 115 30 35N 87 50W
Fairlie 101 44 5 S 170 49 E
Fairmont, Minn., U.S.A. 116 43 37N 94 30W
Fairmont, W. Va., U.S.A. 114 39 29N 80 10W
Fairmont Hot Springs 108 50 20N 115 56W
Fairplay 119 39 9N 105 40W
Fairport, N.Y., U.S.A. 114 43 8N 77 29W
Fairport, Ohio, U.S.A. 112 41 45N 81 17W
Fairview, Austral. 98 15 31 S 144 17 E
Fairview, Can. 108 56 5N 118 25W
Fairview, N. Dak., U.S.A. 116 47 49N 104 7W
Fairview, Okla., U.S.A. 117 36 19N 98 30W
Fairview, Utah, U.S.A. 118 39 50N 111 0W
Fairweather, Mt. 104 58 55N 137 45W
Faith 116 45 2N 102 4W
Faizabad 69 26 45N 82 10 E
Faizpur 68 21 14N 75 49 E
Fajardo 121 18 20N 65 39W
Fakfak 73 3 0 S 132 15 E
Fakiya 43 42 10N 27 6 E
Fakobli 84 7 23N 7 23W
Fakse 49 55 15N 12 8 E
Fakse B. 49 55 11N 12 15 E
Fakse Ladeplads 49 55 11N 12 9 E
Faku 76 42 32N 123 21 E
Falaise 18 48 54N 0 12W
Falakrón Óros 44 41 15N 23 58 E
Falam 67 23 0N 93 45 E
Falces 32 42 24N 1 48W
Fălciu 46 46 17N 28 7 E
Falcon, C. 82 35 50N 0 50W
Falcon Dam 117 26 50N 99 20W
Falconara Marittima 39 43 37N 13 23 E
Falconer 112 42 7N 79 13W
Faléa 84 12 16N 11 17W
Falenki 55 58 22N 51 35 E
Faleshty 56 47 32N 27 44 E
Falfurrias 117 27 14N 98 8W
Falher 108 55 44N 117 15W
Falkenberg, Ger. 24 51 34N 13 13 E
Falkenberg, Sweden 49 56 54N 12 30 E
Falkensee 24 52 35N 13 6 E
Falkenstein 24 50 27N 12 24 E
Falkirk 14 56 0N 3 47W
Falkland Is. 128 51 30 S 59 0W
Falkland Is. Dependency □ 5 57 0 S 40 0W
Falkland Sd. 128 52 0 S 60 0W
Falkonéra 45 36 50N 23 52 E
Falköping 49 58 12N 13 33 E
Fall Brook 119 33 25N 117 12W
Fall River 114 41 45N 71 5W
Fall River Mills 118 41 1N 121 30W
Fallon, Mont., U.S.A. 116 46 52N 105 8W
Fallon, Nev., U.S.A. 118 39 31N 118 51W
Falls City, Nebr., U.S.A. 116 40 0N 95 40W
Falls City, Oreg., U.S.A. 118 44 54N 123 29W
Falls Creek 112 41 8N 78 49W
Falmouth, Jamaica 121 18 30N 77 40W
Falmouth, U.K. 13 50 9N 5 5W
Falmouth, U.S.A. 114 38 40N 84 20W
False Divi Pt. 70 15 43N 80 50 E
Falset 32 41 7N 0 50 E
Falso, C. 121 15 12N 83 21W
Falster 49 54 45N 11 55 E
Falsterbo 49 55 23N 12 50 E
Fălticeni 46 47 21N 26 20 E
Falun 48 60 37N 15 37 E
Famagusta 64 35 8N 33 55 E
Famatina, Sierra, de 124 27 30 S 68 0W
Family L. 109 51 54N 95 27W
Fan Xian 76 35 55N 115 38 E
Fana, Mali 84 13 0N 6 56W
Fana, Norway 47 60 16N 5 20 E
Fanárion 44 39 24N 21 47 E
Fandriana 93 20 14 S 47 21 E
Fang Xian 77 32 3N 110 40 E
Fangchang 77 31 5N 118 4 E
Fangcheng 77 33 18N 112 59 E
Fangliao 77 22 22N 120 38 E
Fangzheng 76 49 50N 128 48 E
Fani i Madh → 44 41 56N 20 16 E
Fanjiatun 76 43 40N 125 0 E
Fannich, L. 14 57 40N 5 0W
* Fanning I. 95 3 51N 159 22W
Fanny Bay 108 49 27N 124 48W
Fanø 49 55 25N 8 25 E
Fano 39 43 50N 13 0 E
Fanshaw 108 57 11N 133 30W
Fao (Al Fāw) 64 30 0N 48 30 E
Faqirwali 68 29 27N 73 0 E
Fara in Sabina 39 42 13N 12 44 E
Faradje 90 3 50N 29 45 E
Faradofay 93 25 2 S 47 0 E
Farafangana 93 22 49 S 47 50 E
Farâfra, El Wâhât el- 86 27 15N 28 20 E
Farāh 65 32 20N 62 7 E
Farāh □ 65 32 25N 62 10 E
Farahalana 93 14 26 S 50 10 E
Faraid, Gebel 86 23 33N 35 19 E
Faramana 84 11 56N 4 45W
Faranah 84 10 3N 10 45W
Farasān, Jazā'ir 63 16 45N 41 55 E
Faratsiho 93 19 24 S 46 57 E
Fardes → 33 37 35N 3 0W
Fareham 13 50 52N 1 11W
Farewell, C. 101 40 29 S 172 43 E
Farewell C. = Farvel, K. 4 59 48N 43 55W
Fargo 116 46 52N 96 40W
Fari'a → 62 32 12N 35 27 E
Faribault 116 44 15N 93 19W
Faridkot 68 30 44N 74 45 E
Faridpur 69 23 15N 89 55 E
Färila 48 61 48N 15 50 E
Farim 84 12 27N 15 9W
Farīmān 65 35 40N 59 49 E
Farina 99 30 3 S 138 15 E
Faringe 48 59 55N 18 7 E
Fâriskûr 86 31 20N 31 43 E
Farmakonisi 45 37 17N 27 8 E
Farmerville 117 32 48N 92 23W
Farmington, N. Mex., U.S.A. 119 36 45N 108 28W
Farmington, N.H., U.S.A. 113 43 25N 71 7W
Farmington, Utah, U.S.A. 118 41 0N 111 12W
Farmington → 113 41 51N 72 38W
Farmville 114 37 19N 78 22W
Farnborough 13 51 17N 0 46W
Farne Is. 12 55 38N 1 37W
Farnham 113 45 17N 72 59W
Faro, Brazil 127 2 10 S 56 39W
Faro, Port. 31 37 2N 7 55W
Faro □ 31 37 12N 8 10W
Faroe Is. 8 62 0N 7 0W
Farquhar, C. 96 23 50 S 113 36 E
Farrar → 14 57 30N 4 30W
Farrars, Cr. → 98 25 35 S 140 43 E
Farrāshband 65 28 57N 52 5 E
Farrell 114 41 13N 80 29W
Farrell Flat 99 33 48 S 138 48 E
Farrukhabad-cum-Fatehgarh 69 27 30N 79 32 E
Fars □ 65 29 30N 55 0 E
Fársala 44 39 17N 22 23 E
Farsø 49 56 46N 9 19 E
Farsund 47 58 5N 6 55 E
Fartak, Râs 64 28 5N 34 34 E
Fartura, Serra da 125 26 21 S 52 52W
Faru 85 12 48N 6 12 E
Farum 49 55 49N 12 21 E
Farvel, Kap 4 59 48N 43 55W
Farwell 117 34 25N 103 0W
Faryab □ 65 36 0N 65 0 E
Fasā 65 29 0N 53 39 E
Fasano 41 40 50N 17 20 E
Fashoda 87 9 50N 32 2 E
Fastnet Rock 15 51 22N 9 37W
Fastov 54 50 7N 29 57 E
Fatagar, Tanjung 73 2 46 S 131 57 E
Fatehgarh 69 27 25N 79 35 E
Fatehpur, Raj., India 68 28 0N 74 40 E
Fatehpur, Ut. P., India 69 25 56N 81 13 E
Fatesh 55 52 8N 35 57 E
Fatick 84 14 19N 16 27W
Fatima 107 47 24N 61 53W
Fátima 31 39 37N 8 39W
Fatoya 84 11 37N 9 10W
Faucille, Col de la 21 46 22N 6 2 E
Faucilles, Monts 19 48 5N 5 50 E
Faulkton 116 45 4N 99 8W
Faulquemont 19 49 3N 6 36 E
Fauquembergues 19 50 36N 2 5 E
Făurei 46 45 6N 27 19 E
Fauresmith 92 29 44 S 25 17 E
Fauske 50 67 17N 15 25 E
Fåvang 47 61 27N 10 11 E
Favara 40 37 19N 13 39 E
Favignana 40 37 56N 12 18 E
Favignana, I. 40 37 56N 12 18 E
Favone 21 41 47N 9 26 E
Favourable Lake 106 52 50N 93 39W
Fawn → 106 52 22N 88 20W
Faxaflói 50 64 29N 23 0W
Faya-Largeau 81 17 58N 19 6 E
Fayd 64 27 1N 42 52 E
Fayence 21 43 38N 6 42 E
Fayette, Ala., U.S.A. 115 33 40N 87 50W
Fayette, Mo., U.S.A. 116 39 10N 92 40W
Fayette, La 114 40 22N 86 52W
Fayetteville, Ark., U.S.A. 117 36 0N 94 5W
Fayetteville, N.C., U.S.A. 115 35 0N 78 58W
Fayetteville, Tenn., U.S.A. 115 35 8N 86 30W
Fayón 32 41 15N 0 20 E
Fazilka 68 30 27N 74 2 E
Fazilpur 68 29 18N 70 29 E
Fdérik 80 22 40N 12 45W
Feale → 15 52 26N 9 40W
Fear, C. 115 33 51N 78 0W
Feather → 118 38 47N 121 36W
Featherston 101 41 6 S 175 20 E
Featherstone 91 18 42 S 30 55 E
Fécamp 18 49 45N 0 22 E
Fedala = Mohammedia 82 33 44N 7 21W
Federación 124 31 0 S 57 55W
Fedjadj, Chott el 83 33 52N 9 14 E
Fedje 47 60 47N 4 43 E
Fehérgyarmat 27 48 0N 22 30 E
Fehmarn 24 54 26N 11 10 E
Fei Xian 77 35 18N 117 59 E
Feilding 101 40 13 S 175 35 E
Feira de Santana 127 12 15 S 38 57W
Fejér □ 27 47 9N 18 30 E
Fejø 49 54 55N 11 30 E
Fekete → 27 45 47N 18 15 E
Felanitx 33 39 28N 3 9 E
Feldbach 26 46 57N 15 52 E
Feldberg, Germ., E. 24 53 20N 13 26 E
Feldberg, Germ., W. 25 47 51N 7 58 E
Feldkirch 26 47 15N 9 37 E
Feldkirchen 26 46 44N 14 6 E
Felipe Carrillo Puerto 120 19 38N 88 3W
Felixstowe 13 51 58N 1 22 E
Felletin 20 45 53N 2 11 E
Feltre 39 46 1N 11 55 E
Femø 49 54 58N 11 53 E
Femunden 47 62 10N 11 53 E
Fen He → 76 35 36N 110 42 E
Fenelon Falls 112 44 32N 78 45W
Feneroa 87 13 5N 39 3 E
Feng Xian, Jiangsu, China 77 34 43N 116 35 E
Feng Xian, Shaanxi, China 77 33 54N 106 40 E
Fengári 44 40 25N 25 32 E
Fengcheng, Jiangxi, China 77 28 12N 115 48 E
Fengcheng, Liaoning, China 76 40 28N 124 5 E
Fengdu 77 29 55N 107 41 E
Fengfeng 76 36 28N 114 8 E
Fenghua 77 29 40N 121 25 E
Fenghuang 77 27 57N 109 29 E
Fengjie 75 31 5N 109 36 E
Fengkai 77 23 24N 111 30 E
Fengle 77 31 29N 112 29 E
Fengning 76 41 10N 116 33 E
Fengtai 76 39 50N 116 18 E
Fengxian 77 30 55N 121 26 E
Fengxiang 77 34 29N 107 25 E
Fengxin 77 28 41N 115 18 E
Fengyang 77 32 51N 117 29 E
Fengzhen 76 40 25N 113 2 E
Feni Is. 98 4 0 S 153 40 E
Fenit 15 52 17N 9 51W
Fennimore 116 42 58N 90 41W
Fenny 69 22 55N 91 32 E
Feno, C. de 21 41 58N 8 33 E
Fenoarivo Afovoany 93 18 26 S 46 34 E
Fenoarivo Atsinanana 93 17 22 S 49 25 E
Fens, The 12 52 45N 0 2 E
Fenton 114 42 47N 83 44W
Fenyang 76 37 18N 111 48 E
Feodosiya 56 45 2N 35 28 E
Fer, C. de 83 37 3N 7 10 E
Ferdow 65 33 58N 58 2 E
Fère-Champenoise 19 48 45N 4 0 E
Fère-en-Tardenois 19 49 10N 3 30 E
Fère, La 19 49 40N 3 20 E
Ferentino 40 41 42N 13 14 E
Ferfer 63 5 4N 45 9 E
Fergana 58 40 23N 71 19 E
Fergus 106 43 43N 80 24W
Fergus Falls 116 46 18N 96 7W
Fergusson I. 98 9 30 S 150 45 E
Fériana 83 34 59N 8 33 E
Feričanci 42 45 32N 18 0 E
Ferkane 83 34 37N 7 26 E
Ferkéssédougou 84 9 35N 5 6W
Ferlach 26 46 32N 14 18 E
Ferland 106 50 19N 88 27W

* *Renamed Tabuaeran*

Ferlo, Vallée du Fortuna

Ferlo, Vallée du 84 15 15N 14 15W
Fermanagh □ 15 54 21N 7 40W
Fermo 39 43 10N 13 42 E
Fermoselle 30 41 19N 6 27W
Fermoy 15 52 4N 8 18W
Fernán Nuñéz 31 37 40N 4 44W
Fernández 124 27 55 S 63 50W
Fernandina Beach 115 30 40N 81 30W
Fernando de Noronha 127 4 0 S 33 10W
Fernando Póo = Bioko 85 3 30N 8 40 E
Ferndale, Calif., U.S.A. 118 40 37N 124 12W
Ferndale, Wash., U.S.A. 118 48 51N 122 41W
Fernie 108 49 30N 115 5W
Fernlees 98 23 51 S 148 7 E
Fernley 118 39 36N 119 14W
Feroke 70 11 9N 75 46 E
Ferozepore 68 30 55N 74 40 E
Férrai 44 40 53N 26 10 E
Ferrandina 41 40 30N 16 28 E
Ferrara 39 44 50N 11 36 E
Ferrato, C. 40 39 18N 9 39 E
Ferreira do Alentejo 31 38 4N 8 6W
Ferreñafe 126 6 42 S 79 50W
Ferret, C. 20 44 38N 1 15W
Ferrette 19 47 30N 7 20 E
Ferriday 117 31 35N 91 33W
Ferrières 19 48 5N 2 48 E
Ferriete 38 44 40N 9 30 E
Ferron 119 39 3N 111 3W
Ferryland 107 47 2N 52 53W
Ferté-Bernard, La 18 48 10N 0 40 E
Ferté, La 19 48 57N 3 6 E
Ferté-Mace, La 18 48 35N 0 21W
Ferté-St.-Aubin, La 19 47 42N 1 57 E
Ferté-Vidame, La 18 48 37N 0 53 E
Fertile 116 47 31N 96 18W
Fertília 40 40 37N 8 13 E
Fertöszentmiklós 27 47 35N 16 53 E
Fès 82 34 0N 5 0W
Feshi 88 6 8 S 18 10 E
Fessenden 116 47 42N 99 38W
Feteşti 46 44 22N 27 51 E
Fethiye 64 36 36N 29 10 E
Fetlar 14 60 36N 0 52W
Feuilles → 105 58 47N 70 4W
Feurs 21 45 45N 4 13 E
Feyzābād 65 37 7N 70 33 E
Fezzan 81 27 0N 15 0 E
Ffestiniog 12 52 58N 3 56W
Fiambalá 124 27 45 S 67 37W
Fianarantsoa 93 21 26 S 47 5 E
Fianarantsoa □ 93 19 30 S 47 0 E
Fianga 81 9 55N 15 9 E
Fibiş 42 45 57N 21 26 E
Fichtelgebirge 25 50 10N 12 0 E
Ficksburg 93 28 51 S 27 53 E
Fidenza 38 44 51N 10 3 E
Field 106 46 31N 80 1W
Field → 98 23 48 S 138 0 E
Fieri 44 40 43N 19 33 E
Fife □ 14 56 13N 3 2W
Fife Ness 14 56 17N 2 35W
Fifth Cataract 86 18 22N 33 50 E
Figeac 20 44 37N 2 2 E
Figline Valdarno 39 43 37N 11 28 E
Figtree 91 20 22 S 28 20 E
Figueira Castelo Rodrigo 30 40 57N 6 58W
Figueira da Foz 30 40 7N 8 54W
Figueiró dos Vinhos 30 39 55N 8 16W
Figueras 32 42 18N 2 58 E
Figuig 82 32 5N 1 11W
Fihaonana 93 18 36 S 47 12 E
Fiherenana 93 18 29 S 48 24 E
Fiherenana → 93 23 19 S 43 37 E
Fiji ■ 101 17 20 S 179 0 E
Fika 85 11 15N 11 13 E
Filabres, Sierra de los 33 37 13N 2 20W
Filadélfia 41 38 47N 16 17 E
Fil'akovo 27 48 17N 19 50 E
Filchner Ice Shelf 5 78 0 S 60 0W
Filer 118 42 30N 114 35W
Filey 12 54 13N 0 18W
Filiaşi 46 44 32N 23 31 E
Filiátes 44 39 38N 20 16 E
Filiatrá 45 37 9N 21 35 E
Filicudi 41 38 35N 14 33 E
Filiourí → 44 41 15N 25 40 E
Filipów 28 54 11N 22 37 E
Filipstad 48 59 43N 14 9 E
Filisur 25 46 41N 9 40 E
Fillmore, Can. 109 49 50N 103 25W
Fillmore, Calif., U.S.A. 119 34 23N 118 58W
Fillmore, Utah, U.S.A. 119 38 58N 112 20W
Filottrano 39 43 28N 13 20 E
Filyos 56 41 34N 32 4 E
Filyos → 64 41 35N 32 10 E
Finale Lígure 38 44 10N 8 21 E
Finale nell' Emília 39 44 50N 11 18 E
Fiñana 33 37 10N 2 50W
Finch 113 45 11N 75 7W
Findhorn → 14 57 38N 3 38W
Findlay 114 41 0N 83 41W
Finger L. 109 53 33N 124 18W
Fingōe 91 15 12 S 31 50 E
Finike 64 36 21N 30 10 E
Finistère □ 18 48 20N 4 0W
Finisterre 30 42 54N 9 16W
Finisterre, C. 30 42 50N 9 19W
Finisterre Ra. 98 6 0 S 146 30 E
Finke → 96 27 0 S 136 10 E
Finland ■ 52 63 0N 27 0 E
Finland, G. of 52 60 0N 26 0 E
Finlay → 108 57 0N 125 10W
Finley, Austral. 99 35 38 S 145 35 E
Finley, U.S.A. 116 47 35N 97 50W
Finn → 15 54 50N 7 55W
Finnigan, Mt. 98 15 49 S 145 17 E
Finnmark fylke □ 50 69 30N 25 0 E
Finschhafen 98 6 33 S 147 50 E
Finse 47 60 36N 7 30 E
Finsteraarhorn 25 46 31N 8 10 E
Finsterwalde 24 51 37N 13 42 E
Finucane I. 96 20 19 S 118 30 E
Fiora → 39 42 20N 11 35 E
Fiorenzuola d'Arda 38 44 56N 9 54 E
Fīq 62 32 46N 35 41 E
Fire River 106 48 47N 83 21W
Firebag → 109 57 45N 111 21W
Firedrake L. 109 61 25N 104 30W
Firenze 39 43 47N 11 15 E
Firminy, Aveyron, France 20 44 32N 2 19 E
Firminy, Loire, France 21 45 23N 4 18 E
Firozabad 68 27 10N 78 25 E
Fīrūzābād 65 28 52N 52 35 E
Fīrūzkūh 65 35 50N 52 50 E
Firvale 108 52 27N 126 13W
Fish → 92 28 7 S 17 45 E
Fisher B. 109 51 35N 97 13W
Fishguard 13 51 59N 4 59W
Fishing L. 109 52 10N 95 24W
Fismes 19 49 20N 3 40 E
Fitchburg 114 42 35N 71 47W
Fitero 32 42 4N 1 52W
Fitjar 47 59 55N 5 17 E
Fitri, L. 81 12 50N 17 28 E
Fitz Roy 128 47 0 S 67 0W
Fitzgerald, Can. 108 59 51N 111 36W
Fitzgerald, U.S.A. 115 31 45N 83 16W
Fitzroy →, Queens., Austral. 98 23 32 S 150 52 E
Fitzroy →, W. Australia, Austral. 96 17 31 S 123 35 E
Fitzroy Crossing 96 18 9 S 125 38 E
Fitzwilliam I. 112 45 30N 81 45W
Fiume = Rijeka 39 45 20N 14 27 E
Fiumefreddo Brúzio 41 39 14N 16 4 E
Fivizzano 38 44 12N 10 11 E
Fizi 90 4 17 S 28 55 E
Fjæra 47 59 52N 6 22 E
Fjellerup 49 56 29N 10 34 E
Fjerritslev 49 57 5N 9 15 E
Fkih ben Salah 82 32 32N 6 45W
Flå, Buskerud, Norway 47 60 25N 9 28 E
Flå, Sør-Trøndelag, Norway 47 63 13N 10 18 E
Flagler 116 39 20N 103 4W
Flagstaff 119 35 10N 111 40W
Flaherty I. 106 56 15N 79 15W
Flambeau → 116 45 18N 91 15W
Flamborough Hd. 12 54 8N 0 4W
Flaming Gorge Dam 118 40 50N 109 46W
Flaming Gorge L. 118 41 15N 109 30W
Flamingo, Teluk 73 5 30 S 138 0 E
Flanders = Flandres 16 51 10N 3 15 E
Flandre Occidental □ 16 51 0N 3 0 E
Flandre Orientale □ 16 51 0N 4 0 E
Flandreau 116 44 5N 96 38W
Flandres, Plaines des 16 51 10N 3 15 E
Flannan Is. 11 58 9N 7 52W
Flåsjön 50 64 5N 15 40 E
Flat → 108 61 51N 128 0W
Flat River 117 37 50N 90 30W
Flatey, Barðastrandarsýsla, Iceland 50 66 10N 17 52W
Flatey, Suður-Þingeyjarsýsla, Iceland 50 65 22N 22 56W
Flathead L. 118 47 50N 114 0W
Flattery, C., Austral. 98 14 58 S 145 21 E
Flattery, C., U.S.A. 118 48 21N 124 43W
Flavy-le-Martel 19 49 43N 3 12 E
Flaxton 116 48 52N 102 24W
Flèche, La 18 47 42N 0 5W
Fleetwood 12 53 55N 3 1W
Flekkefjord 47 58 18N 6 39 E
Flemington 112 41 7N 77 28W
Flensborg Fjord 49 54 50N 9 40 E
Flensburg 24 54 46N 9 28 E
Flers 18 48 47N 0 33W
Flesherton 112 44 16N 80 33W
Flesko, Tanjung 73 0 29N 124 30 E
Fletton 13 52 34N 0 13W
Fleurance 20 43 52N 0 40 E
Fleurier 25 46 54N 6 35 E
Flin Flon 109 54 46N 101 53W
Flinders → 97 17 36 S 140 36 E
Flinders B. 96 34 19 S 115 19 E
Flinders Group 98 14 11 S 144 15 E
Flinders I. 97 40 0 S 148 0 E
Flinders Ranges 97 31 30 S 138 30 E
Flint, U.K. 12 53 15N 3 7W
Flint, U.S.A. 114 43 5N 83 40W
Flint → 115 30 52N 84 38W
Flint, I. 95 11 26 S 151 48W
Flinton 99 27 55 S 149 32 E
Fliseryd 49 57 6N 16 15 E
Flix 32 41 14N 0 32 E
Flixecourt 19 50 0N 2 5 E
Flodden 12 55 37N 2 8W
Floodwood 116 46 55N 92 55W
Flora, Norway 47 63 27N 11 22 E
Flora, U.S.A. 114 38 40N 88 30W
Florac 20 44 20N 3 37 E
Florala 115 31 0N 86 20W
Florence, Ala., U.S.A. 115 34 50N 87 40W
Florence, Ariz., U.S.A. 119 33 0N 111 25W
Florence, Colo., U.S.A. 116 38 26N 105 0W
Florence, Oreg., U.S.A. 118 44 0N 124 3W
Florence, S.C., U.S.A. 115 34 12N 79 44W
Florence = Firenze 39 43 47N 11 15 E
Florence, L. 99 28 53 S 138 9 E
Florennes 16 50 15N 4 35 E
Florensac 20 43 23N 3 28 E
Florenville 16 49 40N 5 19 E
Flores, Azores 8 39 13N 31 13W
Flores, Guat. 120 16 59N 89 50W
Flores, Indon. 73 8 35 S 121 0 E
Flores I. 108 49 20N 126 10W
Flores Sea 72 6 30 S 124 0 E
Floresville 117 29 10N 98 10W
Floriano 127 6 50 S 43 0W
Florianópolis 125 27 30 S 48 30W
Florida, Cuba 121 21 32N 78 14W
Florida, Uruguay 125 34 7 S 56 10W
Florida □ 115 28 30N 82 0W
Florida B. 121 25 0N 81 20W
Florida Keys 121 25 0N 80 40W
Florida, Straits of 121 25 0N 80 0W
Floridia 41 37 6N 15 9 E
Floridsdorf 27 48 14N 16 22 E
Flórina 44 40 48N 21 26 E
Flórina □ 44 40 45N 21 20 E
Florø 47 61 35N 5 1 E
Flower Sta. 113 45 10N 76 41W
Flower's Cove 107 51 14N 56 46W
Floydada 117 33 58N 101 18W
Fluk 73 1 42 S 127 44 E
Flumen → 32 41 43N 0 9W
Flumendosa → 40 39 26N 9 38 E
Fluminimaggiore 40 39 25N 8 30 E
Flushing = Vlissingen 16 51 26N 3 34 E
Fluviá → 32 42 12N 3 7 E
Fly → 94 8 25 S 143 0 E
Flying Fish, C. 5 72 6 S 102 29W
Foam Lake 109 51 40N 103 32W
Foča 42 43 31N 18 47 E
Focşani 46 45 41N 27 15 E
Fogang 77 23 52N 113 30 E
Foggaret el Arab 82 27 13N 2 49 E
Foggaret ez Zoua 82 27 20N 2 53 E
Fóggia 41 41 28N 15 31 E
Foggo 85 11 21N 9 57 E
Foglia → 39 43 55N 12 54 E
Fogo 107 49 43N 54 17W
Fogo I. 107 49 40N 54 5W
Fohnsdorf 26 47 12N 14 40 E
Föhr 24 54 40N 8 30 E
Foia 31 37 19N 8 37W
Foix 20 42 58N 1 38 E
Foix □ 20 43 0N 1 30 E
Fojnica 42 43 59N 17 51 E
Fokino 54 53 30N 34 22 E
Fokis □ 45 38 30N 22 15 E
Fokstua 47 62 7N 9 17 E
Folda, Nord-Trøndelag, Norway 50 64 41N 10 50 E
Folda, Nordland, Norway 50 67 38N 14 50 E
Földeák 27 46 19N 20 30 E
Folégandros 45 36 40N 24 55 E
Folette, La 115 36 23N 84 9W
Foleyet 106 48 15N 82 25W
Folgefonn 47 60 3N 6 23 E
Foligno 39 42 58N 12 40 E
Folkestone 13 51 5N 1 11 E
Folkston 115 30 55N 82 0W
Follett 117 36 30N 100 12W
Follónica 38 42 55N 10 45 E
Follónica, Golfo di 38 42 50N 10 40 E
Folsom 118 38 41N 121 7W
Fond-du-Lac 109 59 19N 107 12W
Fond du Lac 116 43 46N 88 26W
Fond-du-Lac → 109 59 17N 106 0W
Fonda 113 42 57N 74 23W
Fondi 40 41 21N 13 25 E
Fonfría 30 41 37N 6 9W
Fongen 47 63 11N 11 38 E
Fonni 40 40 5N 9 16 E
Fonsagrada 30 43 8N 7 4W
Fonseca, G. de 120 13 10N 87 40W
Fontaine-Française 19 47 32N 5 21 E
Fontainebleau 19 48 24N 2 40 E
Fontas → 108 58 14N 121 48W
Fonte Boa 126 2 33 S 66 0W
Fontem 85 5 32N 9 52 E
Fontenay-le-Comte 20 46 28N 0 48W
Fontur 50 66 23N 14 32W
Fonyód 27 46 44N 17 33 E
Foochow = Fuzhou 75 26 5N 119 16 E
Foping 77 33 41N 108 0 E
Foppiano 38 46 21N 8 24 E
Föra 49 57 1N 16 51 E
Forbach 19 49 10N 6 52 E
Forbes 97 33 22 S 148 0 E
Forbesganj 69 26 17N 87 18 E
Forcados 85 5 26N 5 26 E
Forcados → 85 5 25N 5 19 E
Forcall → 32 40 51N 0 16W
Forcalquier 21 43 58N 5 47 E
Forchheim 25 49 42N 11 4 E
Ford City 112 40 47N 79 31W
Førde 47 61 27N 5 53 E
Ford's Bridge 99 29 41 S 145 29 E
Fordyce 117 33 50N 92 20W
Forécariah 84 9 28N 13 10W
Forel, Mt. 4 66 52N 36 55W
Foremost 108 49 26N 111 34W
Forenza 41 40 50N 15 50 E
Forest, Can. 112 43 6N 82 0W
Forest, U.S.A. 117 32 21N 89 27W
Forest City, Iowa, U.S.A. 116 43 12N 93 39W
Forest City, N.C., U.S.A. 115 35 23N 81 50W
Forest City, Pa., U.S.A. 113 41 39N 75 29W
Forest Grove 118 45 31N 123 4W
Forestburg 108 52 35N 112 1W
Forestier Pen. 99 43 0 S 148 0 E
Forestville, Can. 107 48 48N 69 2W
Forestville, U.S.A. 114 44 41N 87 29W
Forez, Mts. du 20 45 40N 3 50 E
Forfar 14 56 40N 2 53W
Forges-les-Eaux 19 49 37N 1 30 E
Forks 118 47 56N 124 23W
Forli 39 44 14N 12 2 E
Forman 116 46 9N 97 43W
Formazza 38 46 23N 8 26 E
Formby Pt. 12 53 33N 3 7W
Formentera 33 38 43N 1 27 E
Formentor, C. de 32 39 58N 3 13 E
Fórmia 40 41 15N 13 34 E
Formigine 38 44 37N 10 51 E
Formiguères 20 42 37N 2 5 E
Formosa 124 26 15 S 58 10W
Formosa = Taiwan ■ 75 24 0N 121 0 E
Formosa □ 124 25 0 S 60 0W
Formosa Bay 90 2 40 S 40 20 E
Formosa, Serra 127 12 0 S 55 0W
Fornells 32 40 3N 4 7 E
Fornos de Algodres 30 40 38N 7 32W
Fornovo di Taro 38 44 42N 10 7 E
Forres 14 57 37N 3 38W
Forrest 99 38 33 S 143 47 E
Forrest City 117 35 0N 90 50W
Fors 48 60 14N 16 20 E
Forsa 48 61 44N 16 55 E
Forsand 47 58 54N 6 5 E
Forsayth 97 18 33 S 143 34 E
Forserum 49 57 42N 14 30 E
Forshaga 48 59 33N 13 29 E
Forskacka 48 60 39N 16 54 E
Forsmo 48 63 16N 17 11 E
Forst 24 51 43N 14 37 E
Forster 99 32 12 S 152 31 E
Forsyth, Ga., U.S.A. 115 33 4N 83 55W
Forsyth, Mont., U.S.A. 118 46 14N 106 37W
Fort Albany 106 52 15N 81 35W
Fort Amador 120 8 56N 79 32W
Fort Apache 119 33 50N 110 0W
Fort Assiniboine 108 54 20N 114 45W
Fort Augustus 14 57 9N 4 40W
Fort Beaufort 92 32 46 S 26 40 E
Fort Benton 118 47 50N 110 40W
Fort Bragg 118 39 28N 123 50W
Fort Bridger 118 41 22N 110 20W
Fort Chimo 105 58 6N 68 15W
Fort Chipewyan 109 58 42N 111 8W
Fort Clayton 120 9 0N 79 35W
Fort Collins 116 40 30N 105 4W
Fort-Coulonge 106 45 50N 76 45W
Fort Davis, Panama 120 9 17N 79 56W
Fort Davis, U.S.A. 117 30 38N 103 53W
Fort-de-France 121 14 36N 61 2W
Fort de Possel = Possel 88 5 5N 19 10 E
Fort Defiance 119 35 47N 109 4W
Fort Dodge 116 42 29N 94 10W
Fort Edward 113 43 16N 73 35W
Fort Frances 109 48 36N 93 24W
Fort Franklin 104 65 10N 123 30W
Fort Garland 119 37 28N 105 30W
Fort George 106 53 50N 79 0W
Fort Good-Hope 104 66 14N 128 40W
Fort Hancock 119 31 19N 105 56W
Fort Hertz (Putao) 67 27 28N 97 30 E
Fort Hope 106 51 30N 88 0W
Fort Huachuca 119 31 32N 110 30W
Fort Jameson = Chipata 91 13 38 S 32 28 E
Fort Kent 107 47 12N 68 30W
Fort Klamath 118 42 45N 122 0W
Fort Lallemand 83 31 13N 6 17 E
Fort-Lamy = Ndjamena 81 12 4N 15 8 E
Fort Laramie 116 42 15N 104 30W
Fort Lauderdale 115 26 10N 80 5W
Fort Liard 108 60 14N 123 30W
Fort Liberté 121 19 42N 71 51W
Fort Lupton 116 40 8N 104 48W
Fort Mackay 108 57 12N 111 41W
Fort McKenzie 107 57 20N 69 0W
Fort Macleod 108 49 45N 113 30W
Fort MacMahon 82 29 43N 1 45 E
Fort McMurray 108 56 44N 111 7W
Fort McPherson 104 67 30N 134 55W
Fort Madison 116 40 39N 91 20W
Fort Meade 115 27 45N 81 45W
Fort Miribel 82 29 25N 2 55 E
Fort Morgan 116 40 10N 103 50W
Fort Myers 115 26 39N 81 51W
Fort Nelson 108 58 50N 122 44W
Fort Nelson → 108 59 32N 124 0W
Fort Norman 104 64 57N 125 30W
Fort Payne 115 34 25N 85 44W
Fort Peck 118 48 1N 106 30W
Fort Peck Dam 118 48 0N 106 38W
Fort Peck L. 118 47 40N 107 0W
Fort Pierce 115 27 29N 80 19W
Fort Pierre 116 44 25N 100 25W
Fort Pierre Bordes = Ti-n-Zaouatene 82 20 0N 2 55 E
Fort Plain 113 42 56N 74 39W
Fort Portal 90 0 40N 30 20 E
Fort Providence 108 61 3N 117 40W
Fort Qu'Appelle 109 50 45N 103 50W
Fort Randolph 120 9 23N 79 53W
Fort Resolution 108 61 10N 113 40W
Fort Rixon 91 20 2S 29 17 E
Fort Roseberry = Mansa 91 11 10 S 28 50 E
Fort Rupert (Rupert House) 106 51 30N 78 40W
Fort Saint 83 30 19N 9 31 E
Fort St. James 108 54 30N 124 10W
Fort St. John 108 56 15N 120 50W
Fort Sandeman 68 31 20N 69 31 E
Fort Saskatchewan 108 53 40N 113 15W
Fort Scott 117 37 50N 94 40W
Fort Severn 106 56 0N 87 40W
Fort Sherman 120 9 22N 79 56W
Fort Shevchenko 57 43 40N 51 20 E
Fort-Sibut 88 5 46N 19 10 E
Fort Simpson 108 61 45N 121 15W
Fort Smith, Can. 108 60 0N 111 51W
Fort Smith, U.S.A. 117 35 25N 94 25W
Fort Stanton 119 33 33N 105 36W
Fort Stockton 117 30 54N 102 54W
Fort Sumner 117 34 24N 104 16W
Fort Thomas 119 33 2N 109 59W
Fort Trinquet = Bir Mogrein 80 25 10N 11 35W
Fort Valley 115 32 33N 83 52W
Fort Vermilion 108 58 24N 116 0W
• Fort Victoria 91 20 8 S 30 49 E
Fort Walton Beach 115 30 25N 86 40W
Fort Wayne 114 41 5N 85 10W
Fort William 14 56 48N 5 8W
Fort Worth 117 32 45N 97 25W
Fort Yates 116 46 8N 100 38W
Fort Yukon 104 66 35N 145 20W
Fortaleza 127 3 45 S 38 35W
Forteau 107 51 28N 56 58W
Fortescue → 96 21 20 S 116 5 E
Forth, Firth of 14 56 5N 2 55W
Forthassa Rharbia 82 32 52N 1 18W
Fortore → 39 41 55N 15 17 E
Fortrose 14 57 35N 4 10W
Fortuna, Spain 33 38 11N 1 7W
Fortuna, Cal., U.S.A. 118 40 38N 124 8W
Fortuna, N.D., U.S.A. 116 48 55N 103 48W

• *Renamed Masvingo*

Fortune B. Galley Hd.

Fortune B. 107 47 30N 55 22W
Forūr 65 26 20N 54 30 E
Fos 21 43 26N 4 56 E
Foshan 75 23 4N 113 5 E
Fossacesia 39 42 15N 14 30 E
Fossano 38 44 33N 7 40 E
Fossil 118 45 0N 120 9W
Fossilbrook P.O. 98 17 47 S 144 29 E
Fossombrone 39 43 41N 12 49 E
Fosston 116 47 33N 95 39W
Foster 113 45 17N 72 30W
Foster → 109 55 47N 105 49W
Fostoria 114 41 8N 83 25W
Fougamou 88 1 16 S 10 30 E
Fougères 18 48 21N 1 14W
Foul Pt. 70 8 35N 81 18 E
Foulness I. 13 51 36N 0 55 E
Foulness Pt. 13 51 36N 0 59 E
Foulpointe 93 17 41 S 49 31 E
Foum Assaka 82 29 8N 10 24W
Foum Zguid 82 30 2N 6 59W
Foumban 85 5 45N 10 50 E
Foundiougne 84 14 5N 16 32W
Fountain, Colo., U.S.A. 116 38 42N 104 40W
Fountain, Utah, U.S.A. 118 39 41N 111 37W
Fourchambault 19 47 0N 3 3 E
Fourchu 107 45 43N 60 17W
Fourmies 19 50 1N 4 2 E
Fournás 45 39 3N 21 52 E
Foúrnoi, Greece 45 37 36N 26 32 E
Foúrnoi, Greece 45 37 36N 26 28 E
Fours 19 46 50N 3 42 E
Fouta Djalon 84 11 20N 12 10W
Foux, Cap-à- 121 19 43N 73 27W
Foveaux Str. 101 46 42 S 168 10 E
Fowey 13 50 20N 4 39W
Fowler, Calif., U.S.A. 119 36 41N 119 41W
Fowler, Colo., U.S.A. 116 38 10N 104 0W
Fowler, Kans., U.S.A. 117 37 28N 100 7W
Fowlerton 117 28 26N 98 50W
Fownhope 13 52 0N 2 37W
Fox → 109 56 3N 93 18W
Fox Valley 109 50 30N 109 25W
Foxe Basin 105 68 30N 77 0W
Foxe Channel 105 66 0N 80 0W
Foxe Pen. 105 65 0N 76 0W
Foxen, L. 48 59 25N 11 55 E
Foxpark 118 41 4N 106 6W
Foxton 101 40 29 S 175 18 E
Foyle, Lough 15 55 6N 7 8W
Foynes 15 52 37N 9 5W
Foz 30 43 33N 7 20W
Fóz do Cunene 92 17 15 S 11 48 E
Foz do Gregório 126 6 47 S 70 44W
Foz do Iguaçu 125 25 30 S 54 30W
Frackville 113 40 46N 76 15W
Fraga 32 41 32N 0 21 E
Framingham 113 42 18N 71 26W
Frampol 28 50 41N 22 40 E
Franca 127 20 33 S 47 30W
Francavilla al Mare 39 42 25N 14 16 E
Francavilla Fontana 41 40 32N 17 35 E
France ■ 17 47 0N 3 0 E
Frances 99 36 41 S 140 55 E
Frances → 108 60 16N 129 10W
Frances L. 108 61 23N 129 30W
Franceville 88 1 40 S 13 32 E
Franche-Comté 19 46 30N 5 50 E
Francisco I. Madero, Coahuila, Mexico 120 25 48N 103 18W
Francisco I. Madero, Durango, Mexico 120 24 32N 104 22W
Francofonte 41 37 13N 14 50 E
François, Can. 107 47 35N 56 45W
François, Mart. 121 14 38N 60 57W
François L. 108 54 0N 125 30W
Franeker 16 53 12N 5 33 E
Frankado 87 12 30N 43 12 E
Frankenberg 24 51 3N 8 47 E
Frankenthal 25 49 32N 8 21 E
Frankenwald 25 50 18N 11 36 E
Frankfort, Madag. 93 27 17 S 28 30 E
Frankfort, Ind., U.S.A. 114 40 20N 86 33W
Frankfort, Kans., U.S.A. 116 39 42N 96 26W
Frankfort, Ky., U.S.A. 114 38 12N 84 52W
Frankfort, Mich., U.S.A. 114 44 38N 86 14W
Frankfurt □ 24 52 30N 14 0 E
Frankfurt am Main 25 50 7N 8 40 E
Frankfurt an der Oder 24 52 50N 14 31 E
Fränkische Alb 25 49 20N 11 30 E
Fränkische Rezal → 25 49 11N 11 1 E
Fränkische Saale → 25 50 30N 9 42 E
Fränkische Schweiz 25 49 45N 11 10 E
Franklin, Ky., U.S.A. 115 36 40N 86 30W
Franklin, La., U.S.A. 117 29 45N 91 30W
Franklin, Mass., U.S.A. 113 42 4N 71 23W
Franklin, N.H., U.S.A. 113 43 28N 71 39W
Franklin, N.J., U.S.A. 113 41 9N 74 38W
Franklin, Nebr., U.S.A. 116 40 9N 98 55W
Franklin, Pa., U.S.A. 114 41 22N 79 45W
Franklin, Tenn., U.S.A. 115 35 54N 86 53W
Franklin, Va., U.S.A. 115 36 40N 76 58W
Franklin, W. Va., U.S.A. 114 38 38N 79 21W
* Franklin □ 105 71 0N 99 0W
Franklin B. 104 69 45N 126 0W
Franklin D. Roosevelt L. 118 48 30N 118 16W
Franklin I. 5 76 10 S 168 30 E
Franklin, L. 118 40 20N 115 26W
Franklin Mts. 104 65 0N 125 0W
Franklin Str. 104 72 0N 96 0W
Franklinton 117 30 53N 90 10W
Franklinville 112 42 21N 78 28W
Franks Peak 118 43 50N 109 5W
Frankston 99 38 8 S 145 8 E
Fränsta 48 62 30N 16 11 E
Frantsa Josifa, Zemlya 58 82 0N 55 0 E
Franz 106 48 25N 84 30W
Franz Josef Land = Frantsa Josifa 58 79 0N 62 0 E
Franzburg 24 54 9N 12 52 E
Frascati 40 41 48N 12 41 E
Fraser →, B.C., Can. 108 49 7N 123 11W
Fraser →, Newf., Can. 107 56 39N 62 10W
Fraser I. 97 25 15 S 153 10 E
Fraser Lake 108 54 0N 124 50W
Fraserburg 92 31 55 S 21 30 E
Fraserburgh 14 57 41N 2 0W
Fraserdale 106 49 55N 81 37W
Frashëri 44 40 23N 20 26 E
Frasne 19 46 50N 6 10 E
Frauenfeld 25 47 34N 8 54 E
Fray Bentos 124 33 10 S 58 15W
Frechilla 30 42 8N 4 50W
Fredericia 49 55 34N 9 45 E
Frederick, Md., U.S.A. 114 39 25N 77 23W
Frederick, Okla., U.S.A. 117 34 22N 99 0W
Frederick, S.D., U.S.A. 116 45 55N 98 29W
Frederick Reef 97 20 58 S 154 23 E
Frederick Sd. 108 57 10N 134 0W
Fredericksburg, Tex., U.S.A. 117 30 17N 98 55W
Fredericksburg, Va., U.S.A. 114 38 16N 77 29W
Frederickstown 117 37 35N 90 15W
Fredericton 107 45 57N 66 40W
Fredericton Junc. 107 45 41N 66 40W
Frederikshavn 49 57 28N 10 31 E
Frederikssund 49 55 50N 12 3 E
Fredonia, Ariz., U.S.A. 119 36 59N 112 36W
Fredonia, Kans., U.S.A. 117 37 34N 95 50W
Fredonia, N.Y., U.S.A. 114 42 26N 79 20W
Fredrikstad 47 59 13N 10 57 E
Freehold 113 40 15N 74 18W
Freeland 113 41 3N 75 48W
Freeling, Mt. 96 22 35 S 133 06 E
Freels, C. 107 49 15N 53 30W
Freeman 116 43 25N 97 20W
Freeport, Bahamas 121 26 30N 78 47W
Freeport, Can. 107 44 15N 66 20W
Freeport, Ill., U.S.A. 116 42 18N 89 40W
Freeport, N.Y., U.S.A. 114 40 39N 73 35W
Freeport, Tex., U.S.A. 117 28 55N 95 22W
Freetown 84 8 30N 13 17W
Frégate, L. 106 53 15N 74 45W
Fregenal de la Sierra 31 38 10N 6 39W
Fregene 40 41 50N 12 12 E
Fregeneda, La 30 40 58N 6 54W
Fréhel, C. 18 48 40N 2 20W
Frei 47 63 4N 7 48 E
Freiberg 24 50 55N 13 20 E
Freibourg = Fribourg 25 46 49N 7 9 E
Freiburg, Baden, Ger. 25 48 0N 7 52 E
Freiburg, Niedersachsen, Ger. 24 53 49N 9 17 E
Freire 128 38 54 S 72 38W
Freirina 124 28 30 S 71 10W
Freising 25 48 24N 11 47 E
Freistadt 26 48 30N 14 30 E
Freital 24 51 0N 13 40 E
Fréjus 21 43 25N 6 44 E
Fremantle 96 32 7 S 115 47 E
Fremont, Mich., U.S.A. 114 43 29N 85 59W
Fremont, Nebr., U.S.A. 116 41 30N 96 30W
Fremont, Ohio, U.S.A. 114 41 20N 83 5W
Fremont → 119 38 15N 110 20W
Fremont, L. 118 43 0N 109 50W
French → 114 41 30N 80 2W
French Guiana ■ 127 4 0N 53 0W
French I. 100 38 20 S 145 22 E
French Terr. of Afars & Issas = Djibouti ■ 87 11 30N 42 15 E
Frenchglen 118 42 48N 119 0W
Frenchman → 118 48 24N 107 5W
Frenchman Butte 109 53 35N 109 38W
Frenchman Creek → 116 40 13N 100 50W
Frenda 82 35 2N 1 1 E
Fresco → 127 7 15 S 51 30W
Freshfield, C. 5 68 25 S 151 10 E
Fresnay 18 48 17N 0 1 E
Fresnillo 120 23 10N 103 0W
Fresno 119 36 47N 119 50W
Fresno Alhandiga 30 40 42N 5 37W
Fresno Res. 118 48 40N 110 0W
Freudenstadt 25 48 27N 8 25 E
Frévent 19 50 15N 2 17 E
Freycinet Pen. 97 42 10 S 148 25 E
Freyung 25 48 48N 13 33 E
Fria 84 10 27N 13 38W
Fria, C. 92 18 0 S 12 0 E
Frias 124 28 40 S 65 5W
Fribourg 25 46 49N 7 9 E
Fribourg □ 25 46 40N 7 0 E
Fridafors 49 56 25N 14 39 E
Friedberg, Bayern, Ger. 25 48 21N 10 59 E
Friedberg, Hessen, Ger. 25 50 21N 8 46 E
Friedland 24 53 40N 13 33 E
Friedrichshafen 25 47 39N 9 29 E
Friedrichskoog 24 54 1N 8 52 E
Friedrichsort 24 54 24N 10 11 E
Friedrichstadt 24 54 23N 9 6 E
Friendly (Tonga) Is. 101 22 0 S 173 0W
Friesach 26 46 57N 14 24 E
Friesack 24 52 43N 12 35 E
Friesland □ 16 53 5N 5 50 E
Friesoythe 24 53 1N 7 51 E
Frijoles 120 9 11N 79 48W
Frillesås 49 57 20N 12 12 E
Frinnaryd 49 57 55N 14 50 E
Frio → 117 28 30N 98 10W
Friona 117 34 40N 102 42W
Frisian Is. 24 53 30N 6 0 E
Fristad 49 57 50N 13 0 E
Fritch 117 35 40N 101 35W
Fritsla 49 57 33N 12 47 E
Fritzlar 24 51 8N 9 19 E
Friuli-Venezia Giulia □ 39 46 0N 13 0 E
Friville-Escarbotin 19 50 5N 1 33 E
Frobisher B. 105 62 30N 66 0W
Frobisher Bay 105 63 44N 68 31W
Frobisher L. 109 56 20N 108 15W
Frohavet 50 63 50N 9 35 E
Froid 116 48 20N 104 29W
Frolovo 57 49 45N 43 40 E
Fromberg 118 42 25N 108 58W
Frombork 28 54 21N 19 41 E
Frome 13 51 16N 2 17W
Frome, L. 97 30 45 S 139 45 E
Fromentine 18 46 53N 2 9W
Frómista 30 42 16N 4 25W
Front Range 118 40 0N 105 40W
Front Royal 114 38 55N 78 10W
Fronteira 31 39 3N 7 39W
Frontera 120 18 30N 92 40W
Frontignan 20 43 27N 3 45 E
Frosinone 40 41 38N 13 20 E
Frosolone 41 41 34N 14 27 E
Frostburg 114 39 43N 78 57W
Frostisen 50 68 14N 17 10 E
Frouard 19 48 47N 6 8 E
Fröví 48 59 28N 15 24 E
Frøya 47 63 43N 8 40 E
Fruges 19 50 30N 2 8 E
Frumoasa 46 46 28N 25 48 E
Frunze 58 42 54N 74 46 E
Fruška Gora 42 45 7N 19 30 E
Frutal 127 20 0 S 49 0W
Frutigen 25 46 35N 7 38 E
Frýdek-Místek 27 49 40N 18 20 E
Frýdlant, Severočeský, Czech. 26 50 56N 15 9 E
Frýdlant, Severomoravsky, Czech. 27 49 35N 18 20 E
Fryvaldov = Jeseník 27 50 0N 17 8 E
Fthiótis □ 45 38 50N 22 25 E
Fu Xian, Liaoning, China 76 39 38N 121 58 E
Fu Xian, Shaanxi, China 76 36 0N 109 20 E
Fucécchio 38 43 44N 10 51 E
Fucheng 76 37 50N 116 10 E
Fuchou = Fuzhou 75 26 5N 119 16 E
Fuchuan 77 24 50N 111 5 E
Fuchun Jiang → 77 30 5N 120 5 E
Fúcino, Conca del 39 42 1N 13 31 E
Fuding 77 27 20N 120 12 E
Fuencaliente 31 38 25N 4 18W
Fuengirola 31 36 32N 4 41W
Fuente Alamo 33 38 44N 1 24W
Fuente Álamo 33 37 42N 1 6W
Fuente de Cantos 31 38 15N 6 18W
Fuente de San Esteban, La 30 40 49N 6 15W
Fuente del Maestre 31 38 31N 6 28W
Fuente el Fresno 31 39 14N 3 46W
Fuente Ovejuna 31 38 15N 5 25W
Fuentes de Andalucía 31 37 28N 5 20W
Fuentes de Ebro 32 41 31N 0 38W
Fuentes de León 31 38 5N 6 32W
Fuentes de Oñoro 30 40 33N 6 52W
Fuentesaúco 30 41 15N 5 30W
Fuerte → 120 25 50N 109 25W
Fuerte Olimpo 124 21 0 S 57 51W
Fuerteventura 80 28 30N 14 0W
Fügët, Munţii 46 45 50N 22 9 E
Fugløysund 50 70 15N 20 20 E
Fugou 77 34 3N 114 25 E
Fuhai 75 47 2N 87 25 E
Fuji-no-miya 74 35 10N 138 40 E
Fuji-San 74 35 22N 138 44 E
Fujian □ 75 26 0N 118 0 E
Fujin 76 47 16N 132 1 E
Fujisawa 74 35 22N 139 29 E
Fukien = Fujian □ 75 26 0N 118 0 E
Fukuchiyama 74 35 19N 135 9 E
Fukui 74 36 0N 136 10 E
Fukui □ 74 36 0N 136 12 E
Fukuoka 74 33 39N 130 21 E
Fukuoka □ 74 33 30N 131 0 E
Fukushima 74 37 44N 140 28 E
Fukushima □ 74 37 30N 140 15 E
Fukuyama 74 34 35N 133 20 E
Fulda 24 50 32N 9 41 E
Fulda → 24 51 27N 9 40 E
Fuling 77 29 40N 107 20 E
Fullerton, Calif., U.S.A. 119 33 52N 117 58W
Fullerton, Nebr., U.S.A. 116 41 25N 98 0W
Fulton, Mo., U.S.A. 116 38 50N 91 55W
Fulton, N.Y., U.S.A. 114 43 20N 76 22W
Fulton, Tenn., U.S.A. 115 36 31N 88 53W
Fuluälven 48 61 18N 13 4 E
Fulufjället 48 61 32N 12 41 E
Fumay 19 50 0N 4 40 E
Fumel 20 44 30N 0 58 E
Funabashi 74 35 45N 140 0 E
Funafuti 94 8 30 S 179 0 E
Funchal 80 32 38N 16 54W
Fundación 126 10 31N 74 11W
Fundão 30 40 8N 7 30W
Fundy, B. of 107 45 0N 66 0W
Funing, Jiangsu, China 77 33 45N 119 50 E
Funing, Yunnan, China 77 23 35N 105 45 E
Funiu Shan 77 33 30N 112 20 E
Funsi 84 10 21N 1 54W
Funtua 85 11 30N 7 18 E
Fuping 76 38 48N 114 12 E
Fuqing 77 25 41N 119 21 E
Fur 49 56 50N 9 0 E
Furāt, Nahr al → 64 31 0N 47 25 E
Furmanov 55 57 10N 41 9 E
Furmanovo 57 49 42N 49 25 E
Furnas, Represa de 125 20 50 S 45 0W
Furneaux Group 97 40 10 S 147 50 E
Furness, Pen. 12 54 12N 3 10W
Fürstenau 24 52 32N 7 40 E
Fürstenberg 24 53 11N 13 9 E
Fürstenfeld 26 47 3N 16 3 E
Fürstenfeldbruck 25 48 10N 11 15 E
Fürstenwalde 24 52 20N 14 3 E
Fürth 25 49 29N 11 0 E
Furth im Wald 25 49 19N 12 51 E
Furtwangen 25 48 3N 8 14 E
Furudal 48 61 10N 15 11 E
Furusund 48 59 40N 18 55 E
Fury and Hecla Str. 105 69 56N 84 0W
Fusa 47 60 12N 5 37 E
Fusagasuga 126 4 21N 74 22W
Fuscaldo 41 39 25N 16 1 E
Fushan 76 37 30N 121 15 E
Fushë Arrëzi 44 42 4N 20 2 E
Fushun 76 41 50N 123 56 E
Fusong 76 42 20N 127 15 E
Füssen 25 47 35N 10 43 E
Fusui 77 22 40N 107 56 E
Futuna 94 14 25 S 178 20 E
Fuwa 86 31 12N 30 33 E
Fuxin 76 42 5N 121 48 E
Fuyang, Anhui, China 77 33 0N 115 48 E
Fuyang, Zhejiang, China 77 30 5N 119 57 E
Fuyu 76 45 12N 124 43 E
Fuyuan 75 48 20N 134 5 E
Füzesgyarmat 27 47 6N 21 14 E
Fuzhou, Fujian, China 75 26 5N 119 16 E
Fuzhou, Jiangxi, China 75 28 0N 116 25 E
Fylde 12 53 50N 2 58W
Fyn 49 55 20N 10 30 E
Fyne, L. 14 56 0N 5 20W
Fyns Amtskommune □ 49 55 15N 10 30 E
Fyresvatn 47 59 6N 8 10 E

G

Gaanda 85 10 10N 12 27 E
Gabarin 85 11 8N 10 27 E
Gabas → 20 43 46N 0 42W
Gabela 88 11 0 S 14 24 E
Gabès 83 33 53N 10 2 E
Gabès, Golfe de 83 34 0N 10 30 E
Gabgaba, W. 86 22 10N 33 5 E
Gabin 28 52 23N 19 41 E
Gabon ■ 88 0 10 S 10 0 E
Gaborone 92 24 45 S 25 57 E
Gabriels 113 44 26N 74 12W
Gabrovo 43 42 52N 25 19 E
Gacé 18 48 49N 0 20 E
Gach Sārān 65 30 15N 50 45 E
Gacko 42 43 10N 18 33 E
Gadag-Batgeri 70 15 30N 75 45 E
Gadamai 87 17 11N 36 10 E
Gadap 68 25 5N 67 28 E
Gadarwara 68 22 50N 78 50 E
Gadebusch 24 53 41N 11 6 E
Gadein 87 8 10N 28 45 E
Gadhada 68 22 0N 71 35 E
Gádor, Sierra de 33 36 57N 2 45W
Gadsden, Ala., U.S.A. 115 34 1N 86 0W
Gadsden, Ariz., U.S.A. 119 32 35N 114 47W
Gadwal 70 16 10N 77 50 E
Gadyach 54 50 21N 34 0 E
Găeşti 46 44 48N 25 19 E
Gaeta 40 41 12N 13 35 E
Gaeta, G. di 40 41 0N 13 25 E
Gaffney 115 35 3N 81 40W
Gafsa 83 32 24N 8 43 E
Gagarin (Gzhatsk) 54 55 38N 35 0 E
Gagetown 107 45 46N 66 10W
Gagino 55 55 15N 45 1 E
Gagliano del Capo 41 39 50N 18 23 E
Gagnef 48 60 36N 15 5 E
Gagnoa 84 6 56N 5 16W
Gagnon 107 51 50N 68 5W
Gagnon, L. 109 62 3N 110 27W
Gagra 57 43 20N 40 10 E
Gahini 90 1 50 S 30 30 E
Gahmar 69 25 27N 83 49 E
Gai Xian 76 40 22N 122 20 E
Gaibanda 69 25 20N 89 36 E
Gaïdhouronisi 45 34 53N 25 41 E
Gail 117 32 48N 101 25W
Gail → 26 46 36N 13 53 E
Gaillac 20 43 54N 1 54 E
Gaillon 18 49 10N 1 20 E
Gaines 112 41 46N 77 35W
Gainesville, Fla., U.S.A. 115 29 38N 82 20W
Gainesville, Ga., U.S.A. 115 34 17N 83 47W
Gainesville, Mo., U.S.A. 117 36 35N 92 26W
Gainesville, Tex., U.S.A. 117 33 40N 97 10W
Gainsborough 12 53 23N 0 46W
Gairdner L. 96 31 30 S 136 0 E
Gairloch, L. 14 57 43N 5 45W
Gaj 42 45 28N 17 3 E
Gal Oya Res. 70 7 5N 81 30 E
Galachipa 69 22 8N 90 26 E
Galán, Cerro 124 25 55 S 66 52W
Galana → 90 3 9 S 40 8 E
Galangue 89 13 42 S 16 9 E
Galanta 27 48 11N 17 45 E
Galápagos 95 0 0 89 0W
Galas → 71 4 55N 101 57 E
Galashiels 14 55 37N 2 50W
Galatás 45 37 30N 23 26 E
Galaţi 46 45 27N 28 2 E
Galaţi □ 46 45 45N 27 30 E
Galatina 41 40 10N 18 10 E
Galátone 41 40 8N 18 3 E
Galax 115 36 42N 80 57W
Galaxidhion 45 38 22N 22 23 E
Galbraith 98 16 25 S 141 30 E
Galcaio 63 6 30N 47 30 E
Galdhøpiggen 47 61 38N 8 18 E
Galela 73 1 50N 127 49 E
Galera 33 37 45N 2 33W
Galesburg 116 40 57N 90 23W
Galeton 112 41 43N 77 40W
Gali 57 42 37N 41 46 E
Galicea Mare 46 44 4N 23 19 E
Galich 55 58 23N 42 12 E
Galiche 43 43 34N 23 50 E
Galicia 30 42 43N 7 45W
Galilee = Hagalil 62 32 53N 35 18 E
Galilee, L. 98 22 20 S 145 50 E
Galion 112 40 43N 82 48W
Galite, Is. de la 83 37 30N 8 59 E
Galiuro Mts. 119 32 40N 110 30W
Gallabat 81 12 58N 36 11 E
Gallarate 38 45 40N 8 48 E
Gallardon 19 48 32N 1 47 E
Gallatin 115 36 24N 86 27W
Galle 70 6 5N 80 10 E
Gállego → 32 41 39N 0 51W
Gallegos → 128 51 35 S 69 0W
Galley Hd. 15 51 32N 8 56W

* *Now part of Central Arctic and Baffin* □

Galliate   Ghayl

Galliate 38 45 27N 8 44 E
Gallinas, Pta. 126 12 28N 71 40W
Gallipoli 41 40 8N 18 0 E
Gallipoli = Gelibolu 44 40 28N 26 43 E
Gallipolis 114 38 50N 82 10W
Gällivare 50 67 9N 20 40 E
Gallo, C. 40 38 13N 13 19 E
Gallocanta, Laguna de 32 40 58N 1 30W
Galloway 14 55 0N 4 25W
Galloway, Mull of 14 54 38N 4 50W
Gallup 119 35 30N 108 45W
Gallur 32 41 52N 1 19W
Gal'on 62 31 38N 34 51 E
Galong 99 34 37 S 148 34 E
Galtström 48 62 10N 17 30 E
Galtür 26 46 58N 10 11 E
Galty Mts. 15 52 22N 8 10W
Galtymore 15 52 22N 8 12W
Galva 116 41 10N 90 0W
Galve de Sorbe 32 41 13N 3 10W
Galveston 117 29 15N 94 48W
Galveston B. 117 29 30N 94 50W
Gálvez, Argent. 124 32 0 S 61 14W
Gálvez, Spain 31 39 42N 4 16W
Galway 15 53 16N 9 4W
Galway □ 15 53 16N 9 3W
Galway B. 15 53 10N 9 20W
Gamari, L. 87 11 32N 41 40 E
Gamawa 85 12 10N 10 31 E
Gambaga 85 10 30N 0 28W
Gambat 68 27 17N 68 26 E
Gambela 87 8 14N 34 38 E
Gambia ■ 84 13 25N 16 0W
Gambia → 84 13 28N 16 34W
Gamboa 120 9 8N 79 42W
Gamboli 68 29 53N 68 24 E
Gambos 89 14 37 S 14 40 E
Gamerco 119 35 33N 108 56W
Gammon → 109 51 24N 95 44W
Gammouda 83 35 3N 9 39 E
Gan 20 43 12N 0 27W
Gan Goriama, Mts. 85 7 44N 12 45 E
Gan Jiang → 75 29 15N 116 0 E
Gan Shemu'el 62 32 28N 34 56 E
Gan Yavne 62 31 48N 34 42 E
Ganado, Ariz., U.S.A. 119 35 46N 109 41W
Ganado, Tex., U.S.A. 117 29 4N 96 31W
Gananoque 106 44 20N 76 10W
Ganaveh 65 29 35N 50 35 E
Gancheng 77 18 51N 108 37 E
Gand = Gent 16 51 2N 3 42 E
Ganda 89 13 3 S 14 35 E
Gandak → 69 25 39N 85 13 E
Gandava 68 28 32N 67 32 E
Gander 107 48 58N 54 35W
Gander L. 107 48 58N 54 35W
Ganderowe Falls 91 17 20 S 29 10 E
Gandesa 32 41 3N 0 26 E
Gandhi Sagar 68 24 40N 75 40 E
Gandi 85 12 55N 5 49 E
Gandía 33 38 58N 0 9W
Gandino 38 45 50N 9 52 E
Gandole 85 8 28N 11 35 E
Ganedidalem = Gani 73 0 48 S 128 14 E
Ganetti 86 18 0N 31 10 E
Ganga → 69 23 20N 90 30 E
Ganga, Mouths of the 69 21 30N 90 0 E
Ganganagar 68 29 56N 73 56 E
Gangapur 68 26 32N 76 49 E
Gangara 85 14 35N 8 29 E
Gangavati 70 15 30N 76 36 E
Gangaw 67 22 5N 94 5 E
Gangdisê Shan 67 31 20N 81 0 E
Ganges 20 43 56N 3 42 E
Ganges = Ganga → 69 23 20N 90 30 E
Gangoh 68 29 46N 77 18 E
Gangtok 69 27 20N 88 37 E
Gani 73 0 48 S 128 14 E
Ganj 68 27 45N 78 57 E
Gannat 20 46 7N 3 11 E
Gannett Pk. 118 43 15N 109 38W
Gannvalley 116 44 3N 98 57W
Ganquan 76 36 20N 109 20 E
Gänserdorf 27 48 20N 16 43 E
Gansu □ 75 36 0N 104 0 E
Ganta (Gompa) 84 7 15N 8 59W
Gantheaume B. 96 27 40 S 114 10 E
Gantheaume, C. 99 36 4 S 137 32 E
Gantsevichi 54 52 49N 26 30 E
Ganyu 77 34 50N 119 8 E
Ganyushkino 57 46 35N 49 20 E
Ganzhou 75 25 51N 114 56 E
Gao □ 85 18 0N 1 0 E
Gao Bang 71 22 37N 106 18 E
Gao'an 77 28 26N 115 17 E
Gaomi 76 36 20N 119 42 E
Gaoping 76 35 45N 112 55 E
Gaoua 84 10 20N 3 8W
Gaoual 84 11 45N 13 25W
Gaoxiong 75 22 38N 120 18 E
Gaoyou 77 32 47N 119 26 E
Gaoyou Hu 77 32 45N 119 20 E
Gaoyuan 76 37 8N 117 58 E
Gap 21 44 33N 6 5 E
Gar 75 32 10N 79 58 E
Garachiné 121 8 0N 78 12W
Garanhuns 127 8 50 S 36 30W
Garawe 84 4 35N 8 0W
Garba Tula 90 0 30N 38 32 E
Garber 117 36 30N 97 36W
Garberville 118 40 11N 123 50W
Gard 63 9 30N 49 6 E
Gard □ 21 44 2N 4 10 E
Gard → 21 43 51N 4 37 E
Garda, L. di 38 45 40N 10 40 E
Gardala 81 5 40N 37 25 E
Gardanne 21 43 27N 5 27 E
Garde L. 109 62 50N 106 13W
Gardelegen 24 52 32N 11 21 E
Garden City, Kans., U.S.A. 117 38 0N 100 45W
Garden City, Tex., U.S.A. 117 31 52N 101 28W
Gardez 66 33 37N 69 9 E
Gardhíki 45 38 50N 21 55 E
Gardiner 118 45 3N 110 42W
Gardiners I. 113 41 4N 72 5W
Gardner 114 42 35N 72 0W
Gardner Canal 108 53 27N 128 8W
Gardnerville 118 38 59N 119 47W
Gardno, Jezioro 28 54 40N 17 7 E
Garešnica 42 45 36N 16 56 E
Garéssio 38 44 12N 8 1 E
Garfield 118 47 3N 117 8W
Gargaliánoi 45 37 4N 21 38 E
Gargano, Mte. 41 41 43N 15 43 E
Gargans, Mt. 20 45 37N 1 39 E
Gargouna 85 15 56N 0 13 E
Garhshankar 68 31 13N 76 11 E
Garibaldi Prov. Park 108 49 50N 122 40W
Garies 92 30 32 S 17 59 E
Garigliano → 40 41 13N 13 44 E
Garissa 90 0 25 S 39 40 E
Garissa □ 90 0 20 S 40 0 E
Garkida 85 10 27N 12 36 E
Garko 85 11 45N 8 53 E
Garland 118 41 47N 112 10W
Garlasco 38 45 11N 8 55 E
Garm 58 39 0N 70 20 E
Garmisch-Partenkirchen 25 47 30N 11 5 E
Garmsār 65 35 20N 52 25 E
Garner 116 43 4N 93 37W
Garnett 116 38 18N 95 12W
Garo Hills 69 25 30N 90 30 E
Garob 92 26 37 S 16 0 E
Garoe 63 8 25N 48 33 E
Garonne → 20 45 2N 0 36W
Garoua (Garwa) 85 9 19N 13 21 E
Garrel 24 52 58N 7 59 E
Garrigues 20 43 40N 3 30 E
Garrison, Mont., U.S.A. 118 46 30N 112 56W
Garrison, N.D., U.S.A. 116 47 39N 101 27W
Garrison, Tex., U.S.A. 117 31 50N 94 28W
Garrison Res. 116 47 30N 102 0W
Garrovillas 31 39 40N 6 33W
Garrucha 33 37 11N 1 49W
Garry → 14 56 47N 3 47W
Garry L. 104 65 58N 100 18W
Garsen 90 2 20 S 40 5 E
Garson → 109 56 20N 110 1W
Garson L. 109 56 19N 110 2W
Gartempe → 20 46 47N 0 49 E
Gartz 24 53 12N 14 23 E
Garu 85 10 55N 0 11W
Garut 73 7 14 S 107 53 E
Garvão 31 37 42N 8 21W
Garvie Mts. 101 45 30 S 168 50 E
Garwa 69 24 11N 83 47 E
Garwolin 28 51 55N 21 38 E
Gary 114 41 35N 87 20W
Garz 24 54 17N 13 21 E
Garzê 75 31 39N 99 58 E
Garzón 126 2 10N 75 40W
Gasan Kuli 58 37 40N 54 20 E
Gascogne 20 43 45N 0 20 E
Gascogne, G. de 32 44 0N 2 0W
Gascony = Gascogne 20 43 45N 0 20 E
Gascoyne → 96 24 52 S 113 37 E
Gascueña 32 40 18N 2 31W
Gash, Wadi → 87 16 48N 35 51 E
Gashaka 85 7 20N 11 29 E
Gashua 85 12 54N 11 0 E
Gaspé 107 48 52N 64 30W
Gaspé, C. 107 48 48N 64 7W
Gaspé, Pén. de 107 48 45N 65 40W
Gaspésie, Parc Prov. de la 107 48 55N 65 50W
Gassaway 114 38 42N 80 43W
Gássino Torinese 38 45 8N 7 50 E
Gassol 85 8 34N 10 25 E
Gastonia 115 35 17N 81 10W
Gastoúni 45 37 51N 21 15 E
Gastoúri 44 39 34N 19 54 E
Gastre 128 42 20 S 69 15W
Gata, C. de 33 36 41N 2 13W
Gata, Sierra de 30 40 20N 6 45W
Gataga → 108 58 35N 126 59W
Gătaia 42 45 26N 21 30 E
Gatchina 54 59 35N 30 9 E
Gateshead 12 54 57N 1 37W
Gatesville 117 31 29N 97 45W
Gaths 91 20 2 S 30 32 E
Gatico 124 22 29 S 70 20W
Gâtinais 19 48 5N 2 40 E
Gâtine, Hauteurs de 20 46 35N 0 45W
Gatineau 113 45 29N 75 39W
Gatineau → 106 45 27N 75 42W
Gatineau, Parc de la 106 45 40N 76 0W
* Gatooma 91 18 20 S 29 52 E
Gattinara 38 45 37N 8 22 E
Gatun 120 9 16N 79 55W
Gatun Dam 120 9 16N 79 55W
Gatun, L. 120 9 7N 79 56W
Gatun Locks 120 9 16N 79 55W
Gaucín 31 36 31N 5 19W
Gauer L. 109 57 0N 97 50W
Gauhati 67 26 10N 91 45 E
Gauja → 54 57 10N 24 16 E
Gaula → 47 63 21N 10 14 E
Gaussberg 5 66 45 S 89 0 E
Gausta 47 59 50N 8 37 E
Gavá 32 41 18N 2 0 E
Gavarnie 20 42 44N 0 3W
Gavāter 65 25 10N 61 31 E
Gavdhopoúla 45 34 56N 24 0 E
Gávdhos 45 34 50N 24 5 E
Gavião 31 39 28N 7 56W
Gävle 48 60 40N 17 9 E
Gävleborgs län □ 48 61 30N 16 15 E
Gavorrano 38 42 55N 10 49 E
Gavray 18 48 55N 1 20W
Gavrilov Yam 55 57 18N 39 49 E
Gávrion 45 37 54N 24 44 E
Gawachab 92 27 4 S 17 55 E
Gawilgarh Hills 68 21 15N 76 45 E
Gawler 97 34 30 S 138 42 E
Gawler Ranges 96 32 30 S 135 45 E
Gaxun Nur 75 42 22N 100 30 E
Gay 52 51 27N 58 27 E
Gaya, India 69 24 47N 85 4 E
Gaya, Niger 85 11 52N 3 28 E
Gaya, Nigeria 85 11 57N 9 0 E
Gaylord 114 45 1N 84 41W
Gayndah 97 25 35 S 151 32 E
Gaysin 56 48 57N 28 25 E
Gayvoron 56 48 22N 29 52 E
Gaza 62 31 30N 34 28 E
Gaza □ 93 23 10 S 32 45 E
Gaza Strip 62 31 29N 34 25 E
Gazaoua 85 13 32N 7 55 E
Gazelle Pen. 98 4 40 S 152 0 E
Gazi 90 1 3N 24 30 E
Gaziantep 64 37 6N 37 23 E
Gazli 58 40 14N 63 24 E
Gbarnga 84 7 19N 9 13W
Gbekebo 85 6 20N 4 56 E
Gboko 85 7 17N 9 4 E
Gbongan 85 7 28N 4 20 E
Gcuwa 93 32 20 S 28 11 E
Gdańsk 28 54 22N 18 40 E
Gdańsk □ 28 54 10N 18 30 E
Gdańska, Zatoka 28 54 30N 19 20 E
Gdov 54 58 48N 27 55 E
Gdynia 28 54 35N 18 33 E
Ge'a 62 31 38N 34 37 E
Gebe 73 0 5N 129 25 E
Gebeit Mine 86 21 3N 36 29 E
Gebel Mûsa 86 28 32N 33 59 E
Gecha 87 7 30N 35 18 E
Gedaref 87 14 2N 35 28 E
Gede, Tanjung 72 6 46 S 105 12 E
Gedera 62 31 49N 34 46 E
Gedo 87 9 2N 37 25 E
Gèdre 20 42 47N 0 2 E
Gedser 49 54 35N 11 55 E
Gedser Odde 49 54 30N 11 58 E
Geelong 97 38 10 S 144 22 E
Geestenseth 24 53 31N 8 51 E
Geesthacht 24 53 25N 10 20 E
Geidam 85 12 57N 11 57 E
Geikie → 109 57 45N 103 52W
Geili 87 16 1N 32 37 E
Geilo 47 60 32N 8 14 E
Geinica 27 48 51N 20 55 E
Geisingen 25 47 55N 8 37 E
Geislingen 25 48 37N 9 51 E
Geita 90 2 48 S 32 12 E
Geita □ 90 2 50 S 32 10 E
Gejiu 75 23 20N 103 10 E
Gel → 87 7 5N 29 10 E
Gel River 87 7 5N 29 10 E
Gela 41 37 6N 14 18 E
Gela, Golfo di 41 37 0N 14 8 E
Geladi 63 6 59N 46 30 E
Gelderland □ 16 52 5N 6 10 E
Geldermalsen 16 51 53N 5 17 E
Geldern 24 51 32N 6 18 E
Geldrop 16 51 25N 5 32 E
Geleen 16 50 57N 5 49 E
Gelehun 84 8 20N 11 40W
Gelendzhik 56 44 33N 38 10 E
Gelibolu 44 40 28N 26 43 E
Gelnhausen 25 50 12N 9 12 E
Gelsenkirchen 24 51 30N 7 5 E
Gelting 24 54 43N 9 53 E
Gemas 71 2 37N 102 36 E
Gembloux 16 50 34N 4 43 E
Gemena 88 3 13N 19 48 E
Gemerek 64 39 15N 36 10 E
Gemona del Friuli 39 46 16N 13 7 E
Gemsa 86 27 39N 33 35 E
Gemu-Gofa □ 87 5 40N 36 40 E
Gemünden 25 50 3N 9 43 E
Gen He → 76 50 16N 119 32 E
Genale 87 6 0N 39 30 E
Gençay 20 46 23N 0 23 E
Gendringen 16 51 52N 6 21 E
Geneina, Gebel 86 29 2N 33 55 E
General Acha 124 37 20 S 64 38W
General Alvear, Buenos Aires, Argent. 124 36 0 S 60 0W
General Alvear, Mendoza, Argent. 124 35 0 S 67 40W
General Artigas 124 26 52 S 56 16W
General Belgrano 124 36 35 S 58 47W
General Cabrera 124 32 53 S 63 52W
General Guido 124 36 40 S 57 50W
General Juan Madariaga 124 37 0 S 57 0W
General La Madrid 124 37 17 S 61 20W
General MacArthur 73 11 18N 125 28 E
General Martin Miguel de Güemes 124 24 35 S 65 0W
General Paz 124 27 45 S 57 36W
General Pico 124 35 45 S 63 50W
General Pinedo 124 27 15 S 61 20W
General Pinto 124 34 45 S 61 50W
General Santos 73 6 5N 125 14 E
General Toshevo 43 43 42N 28 6 E
General Trias 120 28 21N 106 22W
General Viamonte 124 35 1 S 61 3W
General Villegas 124 35 0 S 63 0W
Genesee, Idaho, U.S.A. 118 46 31N 116 59W
Genesee, Pa., U.S.A. 112 42 0N 77 54W
Genesee → 114 42 35N 78 0W
Geneseo, Ill., U.S.A. 116 41 25N 90 10W
Geneseo, Kans., U.S.A. 116 38 32N 98 8W
Geneseo, N.Y., U.S.A. 112 42 49N 77 49W
Geneva, Ala., U.S.A. 115 31 2N 85 52W
Geneva, N.Y., U.S.A. 114 42 53N 77 0W
Geneva, Nebr., U.S.A. 116 40 35N 97 35W
Geneva, Ohio, U.S.A. 114 41 49N 80 58W
Geneva = Genève 25 46 12N 6 9 E
Geneva, L. 114 42 38N 88 30W
Geneva, L. = Léman, Lac 25 46 26N 6 30 E
Genève 25 46 12N 6 9 E
Genève □ 25 46 10N 6 10 E
Gengenbach 25 48 25N 8 0 E
Genichesk 56 46 12N 34 50 E
Genil → 31 37 42N 5 19W
Génissiat, Barrage de 21 46 1N 5 48 E
Genjem 73 2 46 S 140 12 E
Genk 16 50 58N 5 32 E
Genlis 19 47 15N 5 12 E
Gennargentu, Mti. del 40 40 0N 9 10 E
Gennep 16 51 41N 5 59 E
Gennes 18 47 20N 0 17W
Genoa, Austral. 99 37 29 S 149 35 E
Genoa, N.Y., U.S.A. 113 42 40N 76 32W
Genoa, Nebr., U.S.A. 116 41 31N 97 44W
Genoa = Génova 38 44 24N 8 57 E
Génova 38 44 24N 8 56 E
Génova, Golfo di 38 44 0N 9 0 E
Gent 16 51 2N 3 42 E
Genthin 24 52 24N 12 10 E
Geographe B. 96 33 30 S 115 15 E
Geographe Chan. 96 24 30 S 113 0 E
Geokchay 57 40 42N 47 43 E
Georga, Zemlya 58 80 30N 49 0 E
George 92 33 58 S 22 29 E
George → 107 58 49N 66 10W
George, L., N.S.W., Austral. 99 35 10 S 149 25 E
George, L., S. Austral., Austral. 99 37 25 S 140 0 E
George, L., Uganda 90 0 5N 30 10 E
George, L., Fla., U.S.A. 115 29 15N 81 35W
George, L., N.Y., U.S.A. 113 43 30N 73 30W
George River = Port Nouveau 105 58 30N 65 50W
George Sound 101 44 52 S 167 25 E
George Town, Austral. 99 41 5 S 146 49 E
George Town, Bahamas 121 23 33N 75 47W
George Town, Malay. 71 5 25N 100 15 E
George V Coast 5 69 0 S 148 0 E
George VI Sound 5 71 0 S 68 0W
George West 117 28 18N 98 5W
Georgetown, Austral. 97 18 17 S 143 33 E
Georgetown, Ont., Can. 106 43 40N 79 56W
Georgetown, P.E.I., Can. 107 46 13N 62 24W
Georgetown, Gambia 84 13 30N 14 47W
Georgetown, Guyana 126 6 50N 58 12W
Georgetown, Colo., U.S.A. 118 39 46N 105 49W
Georgetown, Ky., U.S.A. 114 38 13N 84 33W
Georgetown, Ohio, U.S.A. 114 38 50N 83 50W
Georgetown, S.C., U.S.A. 115 33 22N 79 15W
Georgetown, Tex., U.S.A. 117 30 40N 97 45W
Georgi Dimitrov 43 42 15N 23 54 E
Georgi Dimitrov, Yazovir 43 42 37N 25 18 E
Georgia □ 115 32 0N 82 0W
Georgia, Str. of 108 49 25N 124 0W
Georgian B. 106 45 15N 81 0W
Georgian S.S.R. □ 57 42 0N 43 0 E
Georgievsk 57 44 12N 43 28 E
Georgina → 97 23 30 S 139 47 E
Georgiu-Dezh 55 51 3N 39 30 E
Gera 24 50 53N 12 11 E
Gera □ 24 50 45N 11 45 E
Geraardsbergen 16 50 45N 3 53 E
Geral de Goiás, Serra 127 12 0 S 46 0W
Geral, Serra 125 26 25 S 50 0W
Geraldine 118 47 36N 110 18W
Geraldton, Austral. 96 28 48 S 114 32 E
Geraldton, Can. 106 49 44N 86 59W
Gérardmer 19 48 3N 6 50 E
Gerede 56 40 45N 32 10 E
Gereshk 65 31 47N 64 35 E
Gérgal 33 37 7N 2 31W
Gerik 71 5 25N 101 0 E
Gering 116 41 51N 103 30W
Gerizim 62 32 13N 35 15 E
Gerlach 118 40 43N 119 27W
Gerlachovka 27 49 11N 20 7 E
Gerlogubi 63 6 53N 45 3 E
German Planina 42 42 20N 22 0 E
Germansen Landing 108 55 43N 124 40W
Germany, East ■ 24 52 0N 12 0 E
Germany, West ■ 24 52 0N 9 0 E
Germersheim 25 49 13N 8 20 E
Germiston 93 26 15 S 28 10 E
Gernsheim 25 49 44N 8 29 E
Gerolstein 25 50 12N 6 40 E
Gerolzhofen 25 49 54N 10 21 E
Gerona 32 41 58N 2 46 E
Gerona □ 32 42 11N 2 30 E
Gerrard 108 50 30N 117 17W
Gers □ 20 43 35N 0 38 E
Gers → 20 44 9N 0 39 E
Gersfeld 24 50 27N 9 57 E
Gersoppa Falls 70 14 12N 74 46 E
Gerufa 92 19 17 S 26 0 E
Geseke 24 51 38N 8 29 E
Geser 73 3 50 S 130 54 E
Gesso → 38 44 24N 7 33 E
Gestro, Wabi → 87 4 12N 42 2 E
Getafe 30 40 18N 3 44W
Gethsémani 107 50 13N 60 40W
Gettysburg, Pa., U.S.A. 114 39 47N 77 18W
Gettysburg, S.D., U.S.A. 116 45 3N 99 56W
Getz Ice Shelf 5 75 0 S 130 0W
Gévaudan 20 44 40N 3 40 E
Gevgelija 42 41 9N 22 30 E
Gévora → 31 38 53N 6 57W
Gex 21 46 21N 6 3 E
Geyikli 44 39 50N 26 12 E
Geyser 118 47 17N 110 30W
Geysir 50 64 19N 20 18W
Ghaghara → 69 25 45N 84 40 E
Ghalla, Wadi el → 87 10 25N 27 32 E
Ghana ■ 85 6 0N 1 0W
Ghansor 69 22 39N 80 1 E
Ghanzi 92 21 50 S 21 34 E
Ghanzi □ 92 21 50 S 21 45 E
Gharbîya, Es Sahrâ el 86 27 40N 26 30 E
Ghard Abû Muharik 86 26 50N 30 0 E
Ghardaïa 82 32 20N 3 37 E
Ghârib, G. 86 28 6N 32 54 E
Ghârib, Râs 86 28 6N 33 18 E
Gharyān 83 32 10N 13 0 E
Gharyān □ 83 30 35N 12 0 E
Ghat 83 24 59N 10 11 E
Ghatal 69 22 40N 87 46 E
Ghatampur 69 26 8N 80 13 E
Ghatprabha → 70 16 15N 75 20 E
Ghayl 64 21 40N 46 20 E

Renamed Kipungo

* Renamed Kadoma

Ghazal, Bahr el Gorki

Ghazal, Bahr el → 81 15 0N 17 0 E
Ghazâl, Bahr el → 87 9 31N 30 25 E
Ghazaouet 82 35 8N 1 50W
Ghaziabad 68 28 42N 77 26 E
Ghazipur 69 25 38N 83 35 E
Ghazni 66 33 30N 68 28 E
Ghaznī □ 65 33 0N 68 0 E
Ghedi 38 45 24N 10 16 E
Ghelari 46 45 38N 22 45 E
Ghèlinsor 63 6 28N 46 39 E
Ghent = Gand 16 51 2N 3 42 E
Gheorghe Gheorghiu-Dej 46 46 17N 26 47 E
Gheorgheni 46 46 43N 25 41 E
Ghergani 46 44 37N 25 37 E
Gherla 46 47 0N 23 57 E
Ghilarza 40 40 8N 8 50 E
Ghisonaccia 21 42 1N 9 26 E
Ghod → 70 18 30N 74 35 E
Ghot Ogrein 86 31 10N 25 20 E
Ghotaru 68 27 20N 70 1 E
Ghotki 68 28 5N 69 21 E
Ghowr □ 65 34 0N 64 20 E
Ghudāmis 83 30 11N 9 29 E
Ghugri 69 22 39N 80 41 E
Ghugus 70 19 58N 79 12 E
Ghulam Mohammad Barrage 68 25 30N 68 20 E
Ghūrīān 65 34 17N 61 25 E
Gia Nghia 71 12 0N 107 42 E
Gian 73 5 45N 125 20 E
Giannutri 38 42 16N 11 5 E
Giant Mts. = Krkonoše 26 50 50N 16 10 E
Giant's Causeway 15 55 15N 6 30W
Giarre 41 37 44N 15 10 E
Giaveno 38 45 3N 7 20 E
Gibara 121 21 9N 76 11W
Gibbon 116 40 49N 98 45W
Gibe → 87 7 20N 37 36 E
Gibellina 40 37 48N 13 0 E
Gibeon 92 25 7 S 17 45 E
Gibraléon 31 37 23N 6 58W
Gibraltar 31 36 7N 5 22W
Gibraltar, Str. of 31 35 55N 5 40W
Gibson Des. 96 24 0 S 126 0 E
Gibsons 108 49 24N 123 32W
Giddalur 70 15 20N 78 57 E
Giddings 117 30 11N 96 58W
Gidole 87 5 40N 37 25 E
Gien 19 47 40N 2 36 E
Giessen 24 50 34N 8 40 E
Gifatin, Geziret 86 27 10N 33 50 E
Gifhorn 24 52 29N 10 32 E
Gifu 74 35 30N 136 45 E
Gifu □ 74 35 40N 137 0 E
Gigant 57 46 28N 41 20 E
Giganta, Sa. de la 120 25 30N 111 30W
Gigen 43 43 40N 24 28 E
Gigha 14 55 42N 5 45W
Giglio 38 42 20N 10 52 E
Gignac 20 43 39N 3 32 E
Gigüela → 33 39 8N 3 44W
Gijón 30 43 32N 5 42W
Gil I. 108 53 12N 129 15W
Gila → 119 32 43N 114 33W
Gila Bend 119 33 0N 112 46W
Gila Bend Mts. 119 33 15N 113 0W
Gīlān □ 64 37 0N 48 0 E
Gilău 46 46 45N 23 23 E
Gilbert → 97 16 35 S 141 15 E
Gilbert Is. 94 1 0N 176 0 E
Gilbert Plains 109 51 9N 100 28W
Gilbert River 98 18 9 S 142 52 E
Gilberton 98 19 16 S 143 35 E
Gilf el Kebîr, Hadabat el 86 23 50N 25 50 E
Gilford I. 108 50 40N 126 30W
Gilgandra 97 31 43 S 148 39 E
Gilgil 90 0 30 S 36 20 E
Gilgit 69 35 50N 74 15 E
Giljeva Planina 42 43 9N 20 0 E
Gillam 109 56 20N 94 40W
Gilleleje 49 56 8N 12 19 E
Gillette 116 44 20N 105 30W
Gilliat 98 20 40 S 141 28 E
Gillingham 13 51 23N 0 34 E
Gilmer 117 32 44N 94 55W
Gilmore 99 35 20 S 148 12 E
Gilmour 106 44 48N 77 37W
Gilo → 87 8 10N 33 15 E
Gilort → 46 44 38N 23 32 E
Gilroy 119 37 1N 121 37W
Gimbi 87 9 3N 35 42 E
Gimigliano 41 38 58N 16 32 E
Gimli 109 50 40N 97 0W
Gimo 48 60 11N 18 12 E
Gimone → 20 44 0N 1 6 E
Gimont 20 43 38N 0 52 E
Gimzo 62 31 56N 34 56 E
Gin → 70 6 5N 80 7 E
Gin Gin 99 25 0 S 151 58 E
Ginâh 86 25 21N 30 30 E
Gindie 98 23 44 S 148 8 E
Gineta, La 33 39 8N 2 1W
Gingiova 46 43 54N 23 50 E
Ginir 87 7 6N 40 40 E
Ginosa 41 40 35N 16 45 E
Ginzo de Limia 30 42 3N 7 47W
Giohar 63 2 48N 45 30 E
Gióia del Colle 41 40 49N 16 55 E
Gióia, G. di 41 38 30N 15 50 E
Gióia Táuro 41 38 26N 15 53 E
Gioiosa Iónica 41 38 20N 16 19 E
Gióna, Óros 45 38 38N 22 14 E
Giong, Teluk 73 4 50N 118 20 E
Giovi, Passo dei 38 44 33N 8 57 E
Giovinazzo 41 41 10N 16 40 E
Gippsland 97 37 45 S 147 15 E
Gir Hills 68 21 0N 71 0 E
Girab 68 26 2N 70 38 E
Giraltovce 27 49 7N 21 32 E
Girard, Kans., U.S.A. 117 37 30N 94 50W
Girard, Ohio, U.S.A. 112 41 10N 80 42W
Girard, Pa., U.S.A. 112 42 1N 80 21W
Girardot 126 4 18N 74 48W
Girdle Ness 14 57 9N 2 2W
Giresun 64 40 55N 38 30 E
Girga 86 26 17N 31 55 E
Giridih 69 24 10N 86 21 E
Girifalco 41 38 49N 16 25 E
Girilambone 99 31 16 S 146 57 E
Giro 85 11 7N 4 42 E
Giromagny 19 47 44N 6 50 E
Gironde □ 20 44 45N 0 30W
Gironde → 20 45 32N 1 7W
Gironella 32 42 2N 1 53 E
Giru 98 19 30 S 147 5 E
Girvan 14 55 15N 4 50W
Gisborne 101 38 39 S 178 5 E
Gisenyi 90 1 41 S 29 15 E
Giske 47 62 30N 6 3 E
Gislaved 49 57 19N 13 32 E
Gisors 19 49 15N 1 47 E
Gitega (Kitega) 90 3 26 S 29 56 E
Giuba → 63 1 30N 42 35 E
Giugliano in Campania 41 40 55N 14 12 E
Giulianova 39 42 45N 13 58 E
Giurgeni 46 44 45N 27 48 E
Giurgiu 46 43 52N 25 57 E
Giv'at Brenner 62 31 52N 34 47 E
Giv'atayim 62 32 4N 34 49 E
Give 49 55 51N 9 13 E
Givet 19 50 8N 4 49 E
Givors 21 45 35N 4 45 E
Givry 19 46 41N 4 46 E
Giyon 87 8 33N 38 1 E
Giza = El Gîza 86 30 1N 31 11 E
Gizhiga 59 62 3N 160 30 E
Gizhiginskaya, Guba 59 61 0N 158 0 E
Giżycko 28 54 2N 21 48 E
Gizzeria 41 38 57N 16 10 E
Gjegjan 44 41 58N 20 3 E
Gjerstad 47 58 54N 9 0 E
Gjirokastra 44 40 7N 20 10 E
Gjoa Haven 104 68 20N 96 8W
Gjøl 49 57 4N 9 42 E
Gjøvik 47 60 47N 10 43 E
Glace Bay 107 46 11N 59 58W
Glacier B. 108 58 30N 136 10W
Glacier Nat. Park, Can. 108 51 15N 117 30W
Glacier Nat. Park, U.S.A. 118 48 35N 113 40W
Glacier Park 118 48 30N 113 18W
Glacier Peak Mt. 118 48 7N 121 7W
Gladewater 117 32 30N 94 58W
Gladstone, Austral. 99 33 15 S 138 22 E
Gladstone, Can. 109 50 13N 98 57W
Gladstone, U.S.A. 114 45 52N 87 1W
Gladwin 114 43 59N 84 29W
Gladys L. 108 59 50N 133 0W
Glafsfjorden 48 59 30N 12 37 E
Głagów Małapolski 27 50 10N 21 56 E
Gláma 50 65 48N 23 0W
Gláma → 47 59 12N 10 57 E
Glamoč 39 44 3N 16 51 E
Glan 49 58 37N 16 0 E
Glarus 25 47 3N 9 4 E
Glasco, Kans., U.S.A. 116 39 25N 97 50W
Glasco, N.Y., U.S.A. 113 42 3N 73 57W
Glasgow, U.K. 14 55 52N 4 14W
Glasgow, Ky., U.S.A. 114 37 2N 85 55W
Glasgow, Mont., U.S.A. 118 48 12N 106 35W
Glastonbury, U.K. 13 51 9N 2 42W
Glastonbury, U.S.A. 113 41 42N 72 27W
Glauchau 24 50 50N 12 33 E
Glazov 55 58 9N 52 40 E
Gleisdorf 26 47 6N 15 44 E
Gleiwitz = Gliwice 28 50 22N 18 41 E
Glen 113 44 7N 71 10W
Glen Affric 14 57 15N 5 0W
Glen Canyon Dam 119 37 0N 111 25W
Glen Canyon Nat. Recreation Area 119 37 30N 111 0W
Glen Coe 12 56 40N 5 0W
Glen Cove 113 40 51N 73 37W
Glen Garry 14 57 3N 5 7W
Glen Innes 97 29 44 S 151 44 E
Glen Lyon 113 41 10N 76 7W
Glen Mor 14 57 12N 4 37 E
Glen Moriston 14 57 10N 4 58W
Glen Orchy 14 56 27N 4 52W
Glen Spean 14 56 53N 4 40W
Glen Ullin 116 46 48N 101 46W
Glénans, Îles. de 18 47 42N 4 0W
Glenburnie 100 37 51 S 140 50 E
Glencoe, Can. 112 42 45N 81 43W
Glencoe, S. Afr. 93 28 11 S 30 11 E
Glencoe, U.S.A. 116 44 45N 94 10W
Glendale, Ariz., U.S.A. 119 33 40N 112 8W
Glendale, Calif., U.S.A. 119 34 7N 118 18W
Glendale, Oreg., U.S.A. 118 42 44N 123 29W
Glendale, Zimb. 91 17 22 S 31 5 E
Glendive 116 47 7N 104 40W
Glendo 116 42 30N 105 0W
Glenelg 99 34 58 S 138 31 E
Glenelg → 99 38 4 S 140 59 E
Glengarriff 15 51 45N 9 33W
Glengyle 98 24 48 S 139 37 E
Glenmora 117 31 1N 92 34W
Glenmorgan 99 27 14 S 149 42 E
Glenns Ferry 118 43 0N 115 15W
Glenorchy 99 42 49 S 147 18 E
Glenore 98 17 50 S 141 12 E
Glenormiston 98 22 55 S 138 50 E
Glenreagh 99 30 2 S 153 1 E
Glenrock 118 42 53N 105 55W
Glenrothes 14 56 12N 3 11W
Glens Falls 114 43 20N 73 40W
Glenties 15 54 48N 8 18W
Glenville 114 38 56N 80 50W
Glenwood, Alta., Can. 108 49 21N 113 31W
Glenwood, Newf., Can. 107 49 0N 54 58W
Glenwood, Ark., U.S.A. 117 34 20N 93 30W
Glenwood, Hawaii, U.S.A. 110 19 29N 155 10W
Glenwood, Iowa, U.S.A. 116 41 7N 95 41W
Glenwood, Minn., U.S.A. 116 45 38N 95 21W
Glenwood Sprs. 118 39 39N 107 21W
Glina 39 45 20N 16 6 E
Glinojeck 28 52 49N 20 21 E
Glittertind 47 61 40N 8 32 E
Gliwice 28 50 22N 18 41 E
Globe 119 33 25N 110 53W
Glodeanu Siliştea 46 44 50N 26 48 E
Glödnitz 26 46 53N 14 7 E
Glodyany 46 47 45N 27 31 E
Gloggnitz 26 47 41N 15 56 E
Głogów 28 51 37N 16 5 E
Głogowek 28 50 21N 17 53 E
Glorieuses, Îles 93 11 30 S 47 20 E
Glossop 12 53 27N 1 56W
Gloucester, Austral. 99 32 0 S 151 59 E
Gloucester, U.K. 13 51 52N 2 15W
Gloucester, U.S.A. 113 42 38N 70 39W
Gloucester, C. 98 5 26 S 148 21 E
Gloucester I. 98 20 0 S 148 30 E
Gloucestershire □ 13 51 44N 2 10W
Gloversville 114 43 5N 74 18W
Glovertown 107 48 40N 54 03W
Główno 28 51 59N 19 42 E
Głubczyce 27 50 13N 17 52 E
Glubokiy 57 48 35N 40 25 E
Glubokoye 54 55 10N 27 45 E
Glŭbovo 43 42 8N 25 55 E
Głuchołazy 28 50 19N 17 24 E
Glücksburg 24 54 48N 9 34 E
Glückstadt 24 53 46N 9 28 E
Glukhov 54 51 40N 33 58 E
Glussk 54 52 53N 28 41 E
Glyngøre 49 56 46N 8 52 E
Gmünd, Kärnten, Austria 26 46 54N 13 31 E
Gmünd, Niederösterreich, Austria 26 48 45N 15 0 E
Gmunden 26 47 55N 13 48 E
Gnarp 48 62 3N 17 16 E
Gnesta 48 59 3N 17 17 E
Gniew 28 53 50N 18 50 E
Gniewkowo 28 52 54N 18 25 E
Gniezno 28 52 30N 17 35 E
Gnjilane 42 42 28N 21 29 E
Gnoien 24 53 58N 12 41 E
Gnosjö 49 57 22N 13 43 E
Gnowangerup 96 33 58 S 117 59 E
Go Cong 71 10 22N 106 40 E
Goa 70 15 33N 73 59 E
Goa □ 70 15 33N 73 59 E
Goageb 92 26 49 S 17 15 E
Goalen Hd. 99 36 33 S 150 4 E
Goalpara 69 26 10N 90 40 E
Goalundo Ghat 69 23 50N 89 47 E
Goaso 84 6 48N 2 30W
Goat Fell 14 55 37N 5 11W
Goba 87 7 1N 39 59 E
Gobabis 92 22 30 S 19 0 E
Gobi 75 44 0N 111 0 E
Gobichettipalayam 70 11 31N 77 21 E
Gobo 87 5 40N 31 10 E
Goch 24 51 40N 6 9 E
Gochas 92 24 59 S 18 55 E
Godavari → 70 16 25N 82 18 E
Godavari Point 70 17 0N 82 20 E
Godbout 107 49 20N 67 38W
Godda 69 24 50N 87 13 E
Goddua 83 26 26N 14 19 E
Godech 42 43 1N 23 4 E
Godegård 49 58 43N 15 8 E
Goderich 106 43 45N 81 41W
Goderville 18 49 38N 0 22 E
Godhavn 4 69 15N 53 38W
Godhra 68 22 49N 73 40 E
Gödöllö 27 47 38N 19 25 E
Godoy Cruz 124 32 56 S 68 52W
Gods → 109 56 22N 92 51W
Gods L. 109 54 40N 94 15W
Godthåb 4 64 10N 51 35W
Godwin Austen (K2) 69 36 0N 77 0 E
Goeie Hoop, Kaap die 92 34 24 S 18 30 E
Goéland, L. au 106 49 50N 76 48W
Goeree 16 51 50N 4 0 E
Goes 16 51 30N 3 55 E
Gogama 106 47 35N 81 43W
Gogango 98 23 40 S 150 2 E
Gogebic, L. 116 46 20N 89 34W
Gogha 68 21 40N 72 20 E
Gogolin 28 50 30N 18 0 E
Gogra = Ghaghara → 67 26 0N 84 20 E
Gogriâl 87 8 30N 28 8 E
Goiânia 127 16 43 S 49 20W
Goiás 127 15 55 S 50 10W
Goiás □ 127 12 10 S 48 0W
Góis 30 40 10N 8 6W
Goisern 26 47 38N 13 38 E
Gojam □ 87 10 55N 36 30 E
Gojeb, Wabi → 87 7 12N 36 40 E
Gojra 68 31 10N 72 40 E
Gokak 70 16 11N 74 52 E
Gokarannath 69 27 57N 80 39 E
Gokarn 70 14 33N 74 17 E
Gökçeada 44 40 10N 25 50 E
Gokteik 67 22 26N 97 0 E
Gokurt 68 29 40N 67 26 E
Gola 69 28 3N 80 32 E
Golakganj 69 26 8N 89 52 E
Golaya Pristen 56 46 29N 32 32 E
Golchikha 4 71 45N 83 30 E
Golconda 118 40 58N 117 32W
Gold Beach 118 42 25N 124 25W
Gold Coast, Austral. 99 28 0 S 153 25 E
Gold Coast, W. Afr. 85 4 0N 1 40W
Gold Hill 118 42 28N 123 2W
Gold River 108 49 46N 126 3 E
Goldap 28 54 19N 22 18 E
Goldberg 24 53 34N 12 6 E
Golden, Can. 108 51 20N 117 59W
Golden, U.S.A. 116 39 42N 105 15W
Golden Bay 101 40 40 S 172 50 E
Golden Gate 118 37 54N 122 30W
Golden Hinde 108 49 40N 125 44W
Golden Lake 112 45 34N 77 21W
Golden Prairie 109 50 13N 109 37W
Golden Rock 70 10 45N 78 48 E
Golden Vale 15 52 33N 8 17W
Goldendale 118 45 53N 120 48W
Goldfield 119 37 45N 117 13W
Goldfields 109 59 28N 108 29W
Goldsand L. 109 57 2N 101 8W
Goldsboro 115 35 24N 77 59W
Goldsmith 117 32 0N 102 40W
Goldthwaite 117 31 25N 98 32W
Golegã 31 39 24N 8 29W
Golęniów 28 53 35N 14 50 E
Golfito 121 8 41N 83 5W
Golfo Aranci 40 41 0N 9 35 E
Goliad 117 28 40N 97 22W
Golija, Crna Gora, Yugo. 42 43 5N 18 45 E
Golija, Srbija, Yugo. 42 43 22N 20 15 E
Golina 28 52 15N 18 4 E
Göllersdorf 27 48 29N 16 7 E
Golo → 21 42 31N 9 32 E
Golovanevsk 56 48 25N 30 30 E
Golspie 14 57 58N 3 58W
Golub Dobrzyń 28 53 7N 19 2 E
Golubac 42 44 38N 21 38 E
Golyam Perelik 43 41 36N 24 33 E
Golyama Kamchiya → 43 43 10N 27 55 E
Goma, Rwanda 90 2 11 S 29 18 E
Goma, Zaïre 90 1 37 S 29 10 E
Gomare 92 19 25 S 22 8 E
Gomati → 69 25 32N 83 11 E
Gombari 90 2 45N 29 3 E
Gombe 85 10 19N 11 2 E
Gombe → 90 4 38 S 31 40 E
Gombi 85 10 12N 12 30 E
Gomel 54 52 28N 31 0 E
Gomera 80 28 7N 17 14W
Gómez Palacio 120 25 40N 104 0W
Gommern 24 52 5N 11 47 E
Gomogomo 73 6 39 S 134 43 E
Gomotartsi 42 44 6N 22 57 E
Gomphoi 44 39 31N 21 27 E
Gonābād 65 34 15N 58 45 E
Gonaïves 121 19 20N 72 42W
Gonâve, G. de la 121 19 29N 72 42W
Gonbab-e Kāvūs 65 37 20N 55 25 E
Gönc 27 48 28N 21 14 E
Gonda 69 27 9N 81 58 E
Gondal 68 21 58N 70 52 E
Gonder 87 12 39N 37 30 E
Gondia 69 21 23N 80 10 E
Gondola 91 19 10 S 33 37 E
Gondomar, Port. 30 41 10N 8 35W
Gondomar, Spain 30 42 7N 8 45W
Gondrecourt-le-Château 19 48 26N 5 30 E
Gonghe 75 36 18N 100 32 E
Gongola □ 85 8 0N 12 0 E
Gongola → 85 9 30N 12 4 E
Goniadz 28 53 30N 22 44 E
Goniri 85 11 30N 12 15 E
Gonnesa 40 39 17N 8 27 E
Gónnos 44 39 52N 22 29 E
Gonnosfanadiga 40 39 30N 8 39 E
Gonzales, Calif., U.S.A. 119 36 35N 121 30W
Gonzales, Tex., U.S.A. 117 29 30N 97 30W
González Chaves 124 38 02 S 60 05W
Good Hope, C. of = Goeie Hoop, K. die 92 34 24 S 18 30 E
Goodenough I. 98 9 20 S 150 15 E
Gooderham 106 44 54N 78 21W
Goodeve 109 51 4N 103 10W
Gooding 118 43 0N 114 44W
Goodland 116 39 22N 101 44W
Goodnight 117 35 4N 101 13W
Goodooga 99 29 3 S 147 28 E
Goodsoil 109 54 24N 109 13W
Goodsprings 119 35 51N 115 30W
Goole 12 53 42N 0 52W
Goolgowi 99 33 58 S 145 41 E
Goombalie 99 29 59 S 145 26 E
Goonda 91 19 48 S 33 57 E
Goondiwindi 97 28 30 S 150 21 E
Goor 16 52 13N 6 33 E
Gooray 99 28 25 S 150 2 E
Goose → 107 53 20N 60 35W
Goose Bay 107 53 15N 60 20W
Goose L. 118 42 0N 120 30W
Gooty 70 15 7N 77 41 E
Gopalganj, Bangla. 69 23 1N 89 50 E
Gopalganj, India 69 26 28N 84 30 E
Göppingen 25 48 42N 9 40 E
Gor 33 37 23N 2 58W
Góra, Leszno, Poland 28 51 40N 16 31 E
Góra, Płock, Poland 28 52 39N 20 6 E
Góra Kalwaria 28 51 59N 21 14 E
Gorakhpur 69 26 47N 83 23 E
Goražde 42 43 38N 18 58 E
Gorbatov 55 56 12N 43 2 E
Gorbea, Peña 32 43 1N 2 50W
Gorda, Punta 121 14 20N 83 10W
Gordon, Austral. 99 32 7 S 138 20 E
Gordon, U.S.A. 116 42 49N 102 12W
Gordon → 99 42 27 S 145 30 E
Gordon Downs 96 18 48 S 128 33 E
Gordon L., Alta., Can. 109 56 30N 110 25W
Gordon L., N.W.T., Can. 108 63 5N 113 11W
Gordonia 92 28 13 S 21 10 E
Gordonvale 98 17 5 S 145 50 E
Gore 99 28 17 S 151 30 E
Goré 81 7 59N 16 31 E
Gore, Ethiopia 87 8 12N 35 32 E
Gore, N.Z. 101 46 5 S 168 58 E
Gore Bay 106 45 57N 82 28W
Gorey 15 52 41N 6 18W
Gorgān 65 36 55N 54 30 E
Gorgona 38 43 27N 9 52 E
Gorgona, I. 126 3 0N 78 10W
Gorgora 87 12 15N 37 17 E
Gorham 113 44 23N 71 10W
Gori 57 42 0N 44 7 E
Gorinchem 16 51 50N 4 59 E
Goritsy 55 57 4N 36 43 E
Gorízia 39 45 56N 13 37 E
Górka 28 51 39N 16 58 E
Gorki 54 54 17N 30 59 E

Gorki Grindsted

Gorki = Gorkiy **55** 56 20N 44 0 E
Gorkiy **55** 56 20N 44 0 E
Gorkovskoye Vdkhr. **55** 57 2N 43 4 E
Gørlev **49** 55 30N 11 15 E
Gorlice **27** 49 35N 21 11 E
Görlitz **24** 51 10N 14 59 E
Gorlovka **56** 48 19N 38 5 E
Gorman **117** 32 15N 98 43W
Gorna Oryakhovitsa **43** 43 7N 25 40 E
Gornja Radgona **39** 46 40N 16 2 E
Gornja Tuzla **42** 44 35N 18 46 E
Gornji Grad **39** 46 20N 14 52 E
Gornji Milanovac **42** 44 00N 20 29 E
Gornji Vakuf **42** 43 57N 17 34 E
Gorno Ablanovo **43** 43 37N 25 43 E
Gorno-Altaysk **58** 51 50N 86 5 E
Gorno Slinkino **58** 60 5N 70 0 E
Gornyatski **52** 67 32N 64 3 E
Gornyy **55** 51 50N 48 30 E
Gorodenka **56** 48 41N 25 29 E
Gorodets **55** 56 38N 43 28 E
Gorodische **55** 53 13N 45 40 E
Gorodishche **56** 49 17N 31 27 E
Gorodnitsa **54** 50 46N 27 19 E
Gorodnya **54** 51 55N 31 33 E
Gorodok, Byelorussia, U.S.S.R. **54** 55 30N 30 3 E
Gorodok, Ukraine, U.S.S.R. **54** 49 46N 23 32 E
Goroka **98** 6 7 S 145 25 E
Gorokhov **54** 50 30N 24 45 E
Gorokhovets **55** 56 13N 42 39 E
Gorom Gorom **85** 14 26N 0 14W
Goromonzi **91** 17 52 S 31 22 E
Gorong, Kepulauan **73** 4 5 S 131 25 E
Gorongosa, Sa. da **91** 18 27 S 34 2 E
Gorongose → **93** 20 30 S 34 40 E
Gorontalo **73** 0 35N 123 5 E
Goronyo **85** 13 29N 5 39 E
Górowo Iławeckie **28** 54 17N 20 30 E
Gorron **18** 48 25N 0 50W
Gort **15** 53 4N 8 50W
Gorumahisani **69** 22 20N 86 24 E
Gorzkowice **28** 51 13N 19 36 E
Gorzno **28** 53 12N 19 38 E
Gorzów Śląski **28** 51 3N 18 22 E
Gorzów Wielkopolski **28** 52 43N 15 15 E
Gorzów Wielkopolski □ **28** 52 45N 15 30 E
Gosford **99** 33 23 S 151 18 E
Goshen, S. Afr. **92** 25 50 S 25 0 E
Goshen, Ind., U.S.A. **114** 41 36N 85 46W
Goshen, N.Y., U.S.A. **113** 41 23N 74 21W
Goslar **24** 51 55N 10 23 E
Gospič **39** 44 35N 15 23 E
Gosport **13** 50 48N 1 8W
Gostivar **42** 41 48N 20 57 E
Gostyń **28** 51 50N 17 3 E
Gostynin **28** 52 26N 19 29 E
Göta älv → **49** 57 42N 11 54 E
Göteborg **49** 57 43N 11 59 E
Götene **49** 58 32N 13 30 E
Gotha **24** 50 56N 10 42 E
Gothenburg **116** 40 58N 100 8W
Gotland **49** 57 30N 18 33 E
Gotō-Rettō **74** 32 55N 129 5 E
Gotse Delchev (Nevrokop) **43** 41 43N 23 46 E
Göttingen **24** 51 31N 9 55 E
Gottwaldov (Zlin) **27** 49 14N 17 40 E
Goubangzi **76** 41 20N 121 52 E
Gouda **16** 52 1N 4 42 E
Goudiry **84** 14 15N 12 45W
Gough I. **7** 40 10 S 9 45W
Gouin Rés. **106** 48 35N 74 40W
Gouitafla **84** 7 30N 5 53W
Goula Touila **82** 21 50N 1 57W
Goulburn **97** 34 44 S 149 44 E
Goulburn → **100** 36 6 S 144 55 E
Goulburn Is. **96** 11 40 S 133 20 E
Goulia **84** 10 1N 7 11W
Goulimine **82** 28 56N 10 0W
Goulmina **82** 31 41N 4 57W
Gouménissa **44** 40 56N 22 37 E
Gounou-Gaya **81** 9 38N 15 31 E
Goúra **45** 37 56N 22 20 E
Gourara **82** 29 0N 0 30 E
Gouraya **82** 36 31N 1 56 E
Gourdon **20** 44 44N 1 23 E
Gouré **85** 14 0N 10 10 E
Gouri **81** 19 36N 19 36 E
Gourits → **92** 34 21 S 21 52 E
Gourma Rharous **85** 16 55N 1 50W
Gournay-en-Bray **19** 49 29N 1 44 E
Gourock Ra. **99** 36 0 S 149 25 E
Goursi **84** 12 42N 2 37W
Gouverneur **113** 44 18N 75 30W
Gouzon **20** 46 12N 2 14 E
Govan **109** 51 20N 105 0W
Gove **97** 12 25 S 136 55 E
Governador Valadares **127** 18 15 S 41 57W
Gowan Ra. **98** 25 0 S 145 0 E
Gowanda **114** 42 29N 78 58W
Gowd-e Zirreh **65** 29 45N 62 0 E
Gower, The **13** 51 35N 4 10W
Gowna, L. **15** 53 52N 7 35W
Gowrie, Carse of **14** 56 30N 3 10W
Goya **124** 29 10 S 59 10W
Goyllarisquisga **126** 10 31 S 76 24W
Goz Beída **81** 12 10N 21 20 E
Goz Regeb **87** 16 3N 35 33 E
Gozdnica **28** 51 28N 15 4 E
Gozo (Ghawdex) **36** 36 0N 14 13 E
Graaff-Reinet **92** 32 13 S 24 32 E
Grabow **24** 53 17N 11 31 E
Grabów **28** 51 31N 18 7 E
Gračac **39** 44 18N 15 57 E
Gračanica **42** 44 43N 18 18 E
Graçay **19** 47 10N 1 50 E
Grace **118** 42 38N 111 46W
Graceville **116** 45 36N 96 23W
Gracias a Dios, C. **121** 15 0N 83 10W
Gradačac **42** 44 52N 18 26 E
Gradeška Planina **42** 41 30N 22 15 E
Gradets **43** 42 46N 26 30 E
Grado, Italy **39** 45 40N 13 20 E
Grado, Spain **30** 43 23N 6 4W
Gradule **99** 28 32 S 149 15 E
Grady **117** 34 52N 103 15W
Graeca, Lacul **46** 44 5N 26 10 E
Graénalon, L. **50** 64 10N 17 20W
Grafenau **25** 48 51N 13 24 E
Gräfenberg **25** 49 39N 11 15 E
Grafton, Austral. **97** 29 38 S 152 58 E
Grafton, U.S.A. **116** 48 30N 97 25W
Grafton, C. **97** 16 51 S 146 0 E
Gragnano **41** 40 42N 14 30 E
Graham, Can. **106** 49 20N 90 30W
Graham, N.C., U.S.A. **115** 36 5N 79 22W
Graham, Tex., U.S.A. **117** 33 7N 98 38W
Graham → **108** 56 31N 122 17W
Graham Bell, Os. **58** 80 5N 70 0 E
Graham I. **108** 53 40N 132 30W
Graham Land **5** 65 0 S 64 0W
Graham Mt. **119** 32 46N 109 58W
Grahamdale **109** 51 23N 98 30W
Grahamstown **92** 33 19 S 26 31 E
Grahovo **42** 42 40N 18 40 E
Graïba **83** 34 30N 10 13 E
Graie, Alpi **38** 45 30N 7 10 E
Grain Coast **84** 4 20N 10 0W
Grajaú **127** 5 50 S 46 4W
Grajaú → **127** 3 41 S 44 48W
Grajewo **28** 53 39N 22 30 E
Gral. Martin Miguel de Gäemes **124** 24 50 S 65 0W
Gramada **42** 43 49N 22 39 E
Gramat **20** 44 48N 1 43 E
Grammichele **41** 37 12N 14 37 E
Grámmos, Óros **44** 40 18N 20 47 E
Grampian □ **14** 57 0N 3 0W
Grampian Mts. **14** 56 50N 4 0W
Grampians, Mts. **99** 37 0 S 142 20 E
Gran Canaria **80** 27 55N 15 35W
Gran Chaco **124** 25 0 S 61 0W
Gran Paradiso **38** 45 33N 7 17 E
Gran Sasso d'Italia **39** 42 25N 13 30 E
Granada, Nic. **121** 11 58N 86 0W
Granada, Spain **33** 37 10N 3 35W
Granada, U.S.A. **117** 38 5N 102 20W
Granada □ **31** 37 18N 3 0W
Granard **15** 53 47N 7 30W
Granbury **117** 32 28N 97 48W
Granby **106** 45 25N 72 45W
Grand →, Mo., U.S.A. **116** 39 23N 93 6W
Grand →, Mo., U.S.A. **116** 39 23N 93 6W
Grand →, S.D., U.S.A. **116** 45 40N 100 32W
Grand Bahama **121** 26 40N 78 30W
Grand Bank **107** 47 6N 55 48W
Grand Bassam **84** 5 10N 3 49W
Grand Béréby **84** 4 38N 6 55W
Grand-Bourge **121** 15 53N 61 19W
Grand Canyon **119** 36 3N 112 9W
Grand Canyon National Park **119** 36 15N 112 20W
Grand Cayman **121** 19 20N 81 20W
Grand Cess **84** 4 40N 8 12W
Grand-Combe, La **21** 44 13N 4 2 E
Grand Coulee **118** 47 48N 119 1W
Grand Coulee Dam **118** 48 0N 118 50W
Grand Erg Occidental **82** 30 20N 1 0 E
Grand Erg Oriental **83** 30 0N 6 30 E
Grand Falls **107** 48 56N 55 40W
Grand Forks, Can. **108** 49 0N 118 30W
Grand Forks, U.S.A. **116** 48 0N 97 3W
Grand-Fougeray **18** 47 44N 1 43W
Grand Haven **114** 43 3N 86 13W
Grand I. **106** 46 30N 86 40W
Grand Island **116** 40 59N 98 25W
Grand Isle **117** 29 15N 89 58W
Grand Junction **119** 39 0N 108 30W
Grand L., N.B., Can. **107** 45 57N 66 7W
Grand L., Newf., Can. **107** 53 40N 60 30W
Grand L., Newf., Can. **107** 49 0N 57 30W
Grand L., U.S.A. **117** 29 55N 92 45W
Grand Lac Victoria **106** 47 35N 77 35W
Grand Lahou **84** 5 10N 5 0W
Grand Lake **118** 40 20N 105 54W
Grand-Lieu, Lac de **18** 47 6N 1 40W
Grand-Luce, Le **18** 47 52N 0 28 E
Grand Manan I. **107** 44 45N 66 52W
Grand Marais, Can. **116** 47 45N 90 25W
Grand Marais, U.S.A. **114** 46 39N 85 59W
Grand Mère **106** 46 36N 72 40W
Grand Popo **85** 6 15N 1 57 E
Grand Portage **106** 47 58N 89 41W
Grand-Pressigny, Le **18** 46 55N 0 48 E
Grand Rapids, Can. **109** 53 12N 99 19W
Grand Rapids, Mich., U.S.A. **114** 42 57N 86 40W
Grand Rapids, Minn., U.S.A. **116** 47 15N 93 29W
Grand St.-Bernard, Col. du **25** 45 53N 7 11 E
Grand Teton **118** 43 54N 111 50W
Grand Valley **118** 39 30N 108 2W
Grand View **109** 51 10N 100 42W
Grandas de Salime **30** 43 13N 6 53W
Grande →, Jujuy, Argent. **124** 24 20 S 65 2W
Grande →, Mendoza, Argent. **124** 36 52 S 69 45W
Grande →, Boliv. **126** 15 51 S 64 39W
Grande →, Bahia, Brazil **127** 11 30 S 44 30W
Grande →, Minas Gerais, Brazil **127** 20 6 S 51 4W
Grande →, Spain **33** 39 6N 0 48W
Grande →, U.S.A. **117** 25 57N 97 9W
Grande, B. **128** 50 30 S 68 20W
Grande Baie **107** 48 19N 70 52W
Grande Baleine → **106** 55 20N 77 50W
Grande Cache **108** 53 53N 119 8W
Grande, Coxilha **125** 28 18 S 51 30W
Grande de Santiago → **120** 21 20N 105 50W
Grande-Entrée **107** 47 30N 61 40W
Grande, La **118** 45 15N 118 0W
Grande-Motte, La **21** 43 23N 4 3 E
Grande Prairie **108** 55 10N 118 50W
Grande-Rivière **107** 48 26N 64 30W
Grande-Saulde → **19** 47 22N 1 55 E
Grande-Vallée **107** 49 14N 65 8W
Grandes-Bergeronnes **107** 48 16N 69 35W
Grandfalls **117** 31 21N 102 51W
Grandoe Mines **108** 56 29N 129 54W
Grândola **31** 38 12N 8 35W
Grandpré **19** 49 20N 4 50 E
Grandview **118** 46 13N 119 58W
Grandvilliers **19** 49 40N 1 57 E
Graneros **124** 34 5 S 70 45W
Grange, La, Ga., U.S.A. **115** 33 4N 85 0W
Grange, La, Ky., U.S.A. **114** 38 20N 85 20W
Grange, La, Tex., U.S.A. **117** 29 54N 96 52W
Grangemouth **14** 56 1N 3 43W
Granger, U.S.A. **118** 46 25N 120 5W
Granger, Wyo., U.S.A. **118** 41 35N 109 58W
Grängesberg **48** 60 6N 15 1 E
Grangeville **118** 45 57N 116 4W
Granite City **116** 38 45N 90 3W
Granite Falls **116** 44 45N 95 35W
Granite Pk. **118** 45 8N 109 52W
Granity **101** 41 39 S 171 51 E
Granja **127** 3 7 S 40 50W
Granja de Moreruela **30** 41 48N 5 44W
Granja de Torrehermosa **31** 38 19N 5 35W
Gränna **49** 58 1N 14 28 E
Granollers **32** 41 39N 2 18 E
Gransee **24** 53 0N 13 10 E
Grant **116** 40 53N 101 42W
Grant City **116** 40 30N 94 25W
Grant, Mt. **118** 38 34N 118 48W
Grant, Pt. **100** 38 32 S 145 6 E
Grant Range Mts. **119** 38 30N 115 30W
Grantham **12** 52 55N 0 39W
Grantown-on-Spey **14** 57 19N 3 36W
Grants **119** 35 14N 107 51W
Grants Pass **118** 42 30N 123 22W
Grantsburg **116** 45 46N 92 44W
Grantsville **118** 40 35N 112 32W
Granville, France **18** 48 50N 1 35W
Granville, N.D., U.S.A. **116** 48 18N 100 48W
Granville, N.Y., U.S.A. **114** 43 24N 73 16W
Granville L. **109** 56 18N 100 30W
Grao de Gandía **33** 39 0N 0 7W
Grapeland **117** 31 30N 95 31W
Gras, L. de **104** 64 30N 110 30W
Graskop **93** 24 56 S 30 49 E
Gräsö **48** 60 28N 18 35 E
Grass → **109** 56 3N 96 33W
Grass Range **118** 47 0N 109 0W
Grass River Prov. Park **109** 54 40N 100 50W
Grass Valley, Calif., U.S.A. **118** 39 18N 121 0W
Grass Valley, Oreg., U.S.A. **118** 45 22N 120 48W
Grassano **41** 40 38N 16 17 E
Grasse **21** 43 38N 6 56 E
Graubünden (Grisons) □ **25** 46 45N 9 30 E
Graulhet **20** 43 45N 1 58 E
Graus **32** 42 11N 0 20 E
Grave, Pte. de **20** 45 34N 1 4W
Gravelbourg **109** 49 50N 106 35W
Gravelines **19** 51 0N 2 10 E
's-Gravenhage **16** 52 7N 4 17 E
Gravenhurst **112** 44 52N 79 20W
Gravesend, Austral. **99** 29 35 S 150 20 E
Gravesend, U.K. **13** 51 25N 0 22 E
Gravina di Púglia **41** 40 48N 16 25 E
Gravois, Pointe-à- **121** 16 15N 73 56W
Gravone → **21** 41 58N 8 45 E
Gray **19** 47 27N 5 35 E
Grayling **114** 44 40N 84 42W
Grayling → **108** 59 21N 125 0W
Grays Harbor **118** 46 55N 124 8W
Grays L. **118** 43 8N 111 30W
Grayson **109** 50 45N 102 40W
Graz **26** 47 4N 15 27 E
Grazalema **31** 36 46N 5 23W
Grdelica **42** 42 55N 22 3 E
Greasy L. **108** 62 55N 122 12W
Great Abaco I. **121** 26 25N 77 10W
Great Australia Basin **97** 26 0 S 140 0 E
Great Australian Bight **96** 33 30 S 130 0 E
Great Bahama Bank **121** 23 15N 78 0W
Great Barrier I. **101** 36 11 S 175 25 E
Great Barrier Reef **97** 18 0 S 146 50 E
Great Barrington **113** 42 11N 73 22W
Great Basin **118** 40 0N 116 30W
Great Bear → **104** 65 0N 124 0W
Great Bear L. **104** 65 30N 120 0W
Great Bena **113** 41 57N 75 45W
Great Bend **116** 38 25N 98 55W
Great Blasket I. **15** 52 5N 10 30W
Great Britain **8** 54 0N 2 15W
Great Bushman Land **92** 29 20 S 19 20 E
Great Central **108** 49 20N 125 10W
Great Divide, The **100** 35 0 S 149 17 E
Great Dividing Ra. **97** 23 0 S 146 0 E
Great Exuma I. **121** 23 30N 75 50W
Great Falls, Can. **109** 50 27N 96 1W
Great Falls, U.S.A. **118** 47 27N 111 12W
Great Fish →, C. Prov., S. Afr. **92** 31 30 S 20 16 E
Great Fish →, C. Prov., S. Afr. **92** 33 28 S 27 5 E
Great Guana Cay **121** 24 0N 76 20W
Great Harbour Deep **107** 50 25N 56 32W
Great I. **109** 58 53N 96 35W
Great Inagua I. **121** 21 0N 73 20W
Great Indian Desert = Thar Desert **68** 28 0N 72 0 E
Great Lake **97** 41 50 S 146 40 E
Great Orme's Head **12** 53 20N 3 52W
Great Ouse → **12** 52 47N 0 22 E
Great Palm I. **98** 18 45 S 146 40 E
Great Plains **102** 47 0N 105 0W
Great Ruaha → **90** 7 56 S 37 52 E
Great Salt Lake **102** 41 0N 112 30W
Great Salt Lake Desert **118** 40 20N 113 50W
Great Salt Plains Res. **117** 36 40N 98 15W
Great Sandy Desert **96** 21 0 S 124 0 E
Great Scarcies → **84** 9 0N 13 0W
Great Slave L. **108** 61 23N 115 38W
Great Smoky Mt. Nat. Park **115** 35 39N 83 30W
Great Stour → **13** 51 15N 1 20 E
Great Victoria Des. **96** 29 30 S 126 30 E
Great Wall **76** 38 30N 109 30 E
Great Whernside **12** 54 9N 1 59W
Great Winterhoek **92** 33 07 S 19 10 E
Great Yarmouth **12** 52 40N 1 45 E
Greater Antilles **121** 17 40N 74 0W
Greater London □ **13** 51 30N 0 5W
Greater Manchester □ **12** 53 30N 2 15W
Greater Sunda Is. **72** 7 0 S 112 0 E
Grebbestad **49** 58 42N 11 15 E
Grebenka **54** 50 9N 32 22 E
Greco, Mte. **40** 41 48N 14 0 E
Gredos, Sierra de **30** 40 20N 5 0W
Greece ■ **44** 40 0N 23 0 E
Greeley, Colo., U.S.A. **116** 40 30N 104 40W
Greeley, Nebr., U.S.A. **116** 41 36N 98 32W
Green →, Ky., U.S.A. **114** 37 54N 87 30W
Green →, Utah, U.S.A. **119** 38 11N 109 53W
Green B. **114** 45 0N 87 30W
Green Bay **114** 44 30N 88 0W
Green C. **99** 37 13 S 150 1 E
Green Cove Springs **115** 29 59N 81 40W
Green Is. **98** 4 35 S 154 10 E
Green Island **101** 45 55 S 170 26 E
Green River **119** 38 59N 110 10W
Greenbush, Mich., U.S.A. **112** 44 35N 83 19W
Greenbush, Minn., U.S.A. **116** 48 46N 96 10W
Greencastle **114** 39 40N 86 48W
Greene **113** 42 20N 75 45W
Greenfield, Ind., U.S.A. **114** 39 47N 85 51W
Greenfield, Iowa, U.S.A. **116** 41 18N 94 28W
Greenfield, Mass., U.S.A. **114** 42 38N 72 38W
Greenfield, Miss., U.S.A. **117** 37 28N 93 50W
Greenfield Park **113** 45 29N 73 29W
Greenland □ **4** 66 0N 45 0W
Greenland Sea **4** 73 0N 10 0W
Greenock **14** 55 57N 4 46W
Greenore **15** 54 2N 6 8W
Greenore Pt. **15** 52 15N 6 20W
Greenport **113** 41 5N 72 23W
Greensboro, Ga., U.S.A. **115** 33 34N 83 12W
Greensboro, N.C., U.S.A. **115** 36 7N 79 46W
Greensburg, Ind., U.S.A. **114** 39 20N 85 30W
Greensburg, Kans., U.S.A. **117** 37 38N 99 20W
Greensburg, Pa., U.S.A. **114** 40 18N 79 31W
Greenville, Liberia **84** 5 1N 9 6W
Greenville, Ala., U.S.A. **115** 31 50N 86 37W
Greenville, Calif., U.S.A. **118** 40 8N 121 0W
Greenville, Ill., U.S.A. **116** 38 53N 89 22W
Greenville, Me., U.S.A. **107** 45 30N 69 32W
Greenville, Mich., U.S.A. **114** 43 12N 85 14W
Greenville, Miss., U.S.A. **117** 33 25N 91 0W
Greenville, N.C., U.S.A. **115** 35 37N 77 26W
Greenville, Ohio, U.S.A. **114** 40 5N 84 38W
Greenville, Pa., U.S.A. **114** 41 23N 80 22W
Greenville, S.C., U.S.A. **115** 34 54N 82 24W
Greenville, Tenn., U.S.A. **115** 36 13N 82 51W
Greenville, Tex., U.S.A. **117** 33 5N 96 5W
Greenwater Lake Prov. Park **109** 52 32N 103 30W
Greenwich, U.K. **13** 51 28N 0 0
Greenwich, Conn., U.S.A. **113** 41 1N 73 38W
Greenwich, N.Y., U.S.A. **113** 43 2N 73 36W
Greenwich, Ohio, U.S.A. **112** 41 1N 82 32W
Greenwood, Can. **108** 49 10N 118 40W
Greenwood, Miss., U.S.A. **117** 33 30N 90 4W
Greenwood, S.C., U.S.A. **115** 34 13N 82 13W
Gregory **116** 43 14N 99 20W
Gregory → **98** 17 53 S 139 17 E
Gregory Downs **98** 18 35 S 138 45 E
Gregory, L. **97** 28 55 S 139 0 E
Gregory Lake **96** 20 10 S 127 30 E
Gregory Ra. **97** 19 30 S 143 40 E
Greiffenberg **24** 53 6N 13 57 E
Greifswald **24** 54 6N 13 23 E
Greifswalder Bodden **24** 54 12N 13 35 E
Greifswalder Oie **24** 54 15N 13 55 E
Grein **26** 48 14N 14 51 E
Greiner Wald **26** 48 30N 15 0 E
Greiz **24** 50 39N 12 12 E
Gremikha **52** 67 50N 39 40 E
Grenå **49** 56 25N 10 53 E
Grenada **117** 33 45N 89 50W
Grenada ■ **121** 12 10N 61 40W
Grenade **20** 43 47N 1 17 E
Grenadines **121** 12 40N 61 20W
Grenen **49** 57 44N 10 40 E
Grenfell, Austral. **99** 33 52 S 148 8 E
Grenfell, Can. **109** 50 30N 102 56W
Grenoble **21** 45 12N 5 42 E
Grenora **116** 48 38N 103 54W
Grenville, C. **97** 12 0 S 143 13 E
Grenville Chan. **108** 53 40N 129 46W
Gréoux-les-Bains **21** 43 45N 5 52 E
Gresham **118** 45 30N 122 25W
Gresik **73** 7 13 S 112 38 E
Grëssoney St. Jean **38** 45 49N 7 47 E
Gretna Green **14** 55 0N 3 3W
Greven **24** 52 7N 7 36 E
Grevená **44** 40 4N 21 25 E
Grevená □ **44** 40 2N 21 25 E
Grevenbroich **24** 51 6N 6 32 E
Grevenmacher **16** 49 41N 6 26 E
Grevesmühlen **24** 53 51N 11 10 E
Grevie **49** 56 22N 12 46 E
Grey → **101** 42 27 S 171 12 E
Grey, C. **97** 13 0 S 136 35 E
Grey Range **97** 27 0 S 143 30 E
Grey Res. **107** 48 20N 56 30W
Greybull **118** 44 30N 108 3W
Greytown, N.Z. **101** 41 5 S 175 29 E
Greytown, S. Afr. **93** 29 1 S 30 36 E
Gribanovskiy **55** 51 28N 41 50 E
Gribbell I. **108** 53 23N 129 0W
Gridley **118** 39 27N 121 47W
Griekwastad **92** 28 49 S 23 15 E
Griffin **115** 33 17N 84 14W
Griffith **97** 34 18 S 146 2 E
Grillby **48** 59 38N 17 15 E
Grim, C. **97** 40 45 S 144 45 E
Grimari **88** 5 43N 20 6 E
Grimaylov **54** 49 20N 26 5 E
Grimma **24** 51 14N 12 44 E
Grimmen **24** 54 6N 13 2 E
Grimsby **112** 43 12N 79 34W
Grimsby,Greater **12** 53 35N 0 5W
Grimsey **50** 66 33N 18 0W
Grimshaw **108** 56 10N 117 40W
Grimstad **47** 58 22N 8 35 E
Grindelwald **25** 46 38N 8 2 E
Grindsted **49** 55 46N 8 55 E

Grindu Haifeng

Grindu **46** 44 44N 26 50 E
Grinnell **116** 41 45N 92 43W
Griñón **30** 40 13N 3 51W
Grintavec **39** 46 22N 14 32 E
Grip **47** 63 16N 7 37 E
Griqualand East **93** 30 30 S 29 0 E
Griqualand West **92** 28 40 S 23 30 E
Grisolles **20** 43 49N 1 19 E
Grisslehamn **48** 60 5N 18 49 E
Griz Nez, C. **19** 50 50N 1 35 E
Grmeč Planina **39** 44 43N 16 16 E
Groais I. **107** 50 55N 55 35W
Groblersdal **93** 25 15 S 29 25 E
Grobming **26** 47 27N 13 54 E
Grocka **42** 44 40N 20 42 E
Gródek **28** 53 6N 23 40 E
Grodkow **28** 50 43N 17 21 E
Grodno **54** 53 42N 23 52 E
Grodzisk Mázowiecki **28** 52 7N 20 37 E
Grodzisk Wielkopolski **28** 52 15N 16 22 E
Grodzyanka **54** 53 31N 28 42 E
Groesbeck **117** 31 32N 96 34W
Groix **18** 47 38N 3 29W
Groix, I. de **18** 47 38N 3 28W
Grójec **28** 51 50N 20 58 E
Gronau, Niedersachsen, Ger. **24** 52 5N 9 47 E
Gronau, Nordrhein-Westfalen, Ger. **24** 52 13N 7 2 E
Grong **50** 64 25N 12 8 E
Groningen **16** 53 15N 6 35 E
Groningen □ **16** 53 16N 6 40 E
Grönskåra **49** 57 5N 15 43 E
Groom **117** 35 12N 100 59W
Groot → **92** 33 45 S 24 36 E
Groot Berg → **92** 32 47 S 18 8 E
Groot-Brakrivier **92** 34 2 S 22 18 E
Groot Karoo **92** 32 35 S 23 0 E
Groote Eylandt **97** 14 0 S 136 40 E
Grootfontein **92** 19 31 S 18 6 E
Grootlaagte → **92** 20 55 S 21 27 E
Gros C. **108** 61 59N 113 32W
Grosa, P. **33** 39 6N 1 36 E
Grósio **38** 46 18N 10 17 E
Grosne → **21** 46 42N 4 56 E
Gross Glockner **26** 47 5N 12 40 E
Gross Ottersleben **24** 52 5N 11 33 E
Grossenbrode **24** 54 21N 11 4 E
Grossenhain **24** 51 17N 13 32 E
Grosseto **38** 42 45N 11 7 E
Grossgerungs **26** 48 34N 14 57 E
Groswater B. **107** 54 20N 57 40W
Groton, Conn., U.S.A. **113** 41 22N 72 12W
Groton, S.D., U.S.A. **116** 45 27N 98 6W
Grottáglie **41** 40 32N 17 25 E
Grottaminarda **41** 41 5N 15 4 E
Grottammare **39** 42 59N 13 52 E
Grouard Mission **108** 55 33N 116 9W
Grouin, Pointe du **18** 48 43N 1 51W
Groundhog → **106** 48 45N 82 58W
Grouse Creek **118** 41 44N 113 57W
Grove City **112** 41 10N 80 5W
Groveton, N.H., U.S.A. **114** 44 34N 71 30W
Groveton, Tex., U.S.A. **117** 31 5N 95 4W
Grožnjan **39** 45 22N 13 43 E
Groznyy **57** 43 20N 45 45 E
Grubišno Polje **42** 45 44N 17 12 E
Grudovo **43** 42 21N 27 10 E
Grudusk **28** 53 3N 20 38 E
Grudziądz **28** 53 30N 18 47 E
Gruissan **20** 43 8N 3 7 E
Grumo Áppula **41** 41 2N 16 43 E
Grums **48** 59 22N 13 5 E
Grünberg **24** 50 37N 8 55 E
Grundy Center **116** 42 22N 92 45W
Grungedal **47** 59 44N 7 43 E
Gruver **117** 36 19N 101 20W
Gruyères **25** 46 35N 7 4 E
Gruža **42** 43 54N 20 46 E
Gryazi **55** 52 30N 39 58 E
Gryazovets **55** 58 50N 40 10 E
Grybów **27** 49 36N 20 55 E
Grycksbo **48** 60 40N 15 29 E
Gryfice **28** 53 55N 15 13 E
Gryfino **28** 53 16N 14 29 E
Gryfow Sl. **28** 51 2N 15 24 E
Grythyttan **48** 59 41N 14 32 E
Grytviken **5** 53 50 S 37 10W
Gstaad **25** 46 28N 7 18 E
Guacanayabo, G. de **121** 20 40N 77 20W
Guachípas → **124** 25 40 S 65 30W
Guadajoz → **31** 37 50N 4 51W
Guadalajara, Mexico **120** 20 40N 103 20W
Guadalajara, Spain **32** 40 37N 3 12W
Guadalajara □ **32** 40 47N 3 0W
Guadalcanal, Solomon Is. **94** 9 32 S 160 12 E
Guadalcanal, Spain **31** 38 5N 5 52W
Guadalén → **31** 38 5N 3 32W
Guadales **124** 34 30 S 67 55W
Guadalete → **31** 36 35N 6 13W
Guadalhorce → **31** 36 41N 4 27W
Guadalimar → **33** 38 5N 3 28W
Guadalmena → **33** 38 19N 2 56W
Guadalmez → **31** 38 46N 5 4W
Guadalope → **32** 41 15N 0 3W
Guadalquivir → **31** 36 47N 6 22W
Guadalupe, Spain **31** 39 27N 5 17W
Guadalupe, U.S.A. **119** 34 59N 120 33W
Guadalupe → **117** 28 30N 96 53W
Guadalupe Bravos **120** 31 20N 106 10W
Guadalupe I. **95** 21 20N 118 50W
Guadalupe Pk. **119** 31 50N 105 30W
Guadalupe, Sierra de **31** 39 28N 5 30W
Guadarrama, Sierra de **30** 41 0N 4 0W
Guadeloupe **121** 16 20N 61 40W
Guadeloupe Passage **121** 16 50N 62 15W
Guadiamar → **31** 36 55N 6 24W
Guadiana → **31** 37 14N 7 22W
Guadiana Menor → **33** 37 56N 3 15W
Guadiaro → **31** 36 17N 5 17W
Guadiato → **31** 37 48N 5 5W
Guadiela → **32** 40 22N 2 49W
Guadix **33** 37 18N 3 11W
Guafo, Boca del **128** 43 35 S 74 0W
Guaíra **125** 24 5 S 54 10W
Guaira, La **126** 10 36N 66 56W
Guaitecas, Islas **128** 44 0 S 74 30W
Guajará-Mirim **126** 10 50 S 65 20W
Guajira, Pen. de la **126** 12 0N 72 0W
Gualdo Tadino **39** 43 14N 12 46 E
Gualeguay **124** 33 10 S 59 14W
Gualeguaychú **124** 33 3 S 59 31W
Guam **94** 13 27N 144 45 E
Guaminí **124** 37 1 S 62 28W
Guamúchil **120** 25 25N 108 3W
Guan Xian **75** 31 2N 103 38 E
Guanabacoa **121** 23 8N 82 18W
Guanacaste, Cordillera del **121** 10 40N 85 4W
Guanaceví **120** 25 40N 106 0W
Guanahani = San Salvador, I. **121** 24 0N 74 40W
Guanajay **121** 22 56N 82 42W
Guanajuato **120** 21 0N 101 20W
Guanajuato □ **120** 20 40N 101 20W
Guanare **126** 8 42N 69 12W
Guandacol **124** 29 30 S 68 40W
Guane **121** 22 10N 84 7W
Guang'an **77** 30 28N 106 35 E
Guangde **77** 30 54N 119 25 E
Guangdong □ **75** 23 0N 113 0 E
Guanghua **75** 32 22N 111 38 E
Guangshun **77** 26 8N 106 21 E
Guangxi Zhuangzu Zizhiqu □ **75** 24 0N 109 0 E
Guangyuan **77** 32 26N 105 51 E
Guangze **77** 27 30N 117 12 E
Guangzhou **75** 23 5N 113 10 E
Guanipa → **126** 9 56N 62 26W
Guantánamo **121** 20 10N 75 14W
Guantao **76** 36 42N 115 25 E
Guanyun **77** 34 20N 119 18 E
Guápiles **121** 10 10N 83 46W
Guaporé → **126** 11 55 S 65 4W
Guaqui **126** 16 41 S 68 54W
Guara, Sierra de **32** 42 19N 0 15W
Guarapari **125** 20 40 S 40 30W
Guarapuava **125** 25 20 S 51 30W
Guaratinguetá **125** 22 49 S 45 9W
Guaratuba **125** 25 53 S 48 38W
Guarda **30** 40 32N 7 20W
Guarda □ **30** 40 40N 7 20W
Guardafui, C. = Asir, Ras **63** 11 55N 51 16 E
Guardamar del Segura **33** 38 5N 0 39W
Guardavalle **41** 38 31N 16 30 E
Guardia, La **30** 41 56N 8 52W
Guardiagrele **39** 42 11N 14 11 E
Guardo **30** 42 47N 4 50W
Guareña **31** 38 51N 6 6W
Guareña → **30** 41 29N 5 23W
Guaria □ **124** 25 45 S 56 30W
Guarujá **125** 24 2 S 46 25W
Guarus **125** 21 44 S 41 20W
Guasdualito **126** 7 15N 70 44W
Guasipati **126** 7 28N 61 54W
Guastalla **38** 44 55N 10 40 E
Guatemala **120** 14 40N 90 22W
Guatemala ■ **120** 15 40N 90 30W
Guatire **126** 10 28N 66 32W
Guaviare → **126** 4 3N 67 44W
Guaxupé **125** 21 10 S 47 5W
Guayama **121** 17 59N 66 7W
Guayaquil **126** 2 15 S 79 52W
Guayaquil, G. de **126** 3 10 S 81 0W
Guaymas **120** 27 59N 110 54W
Guazhou **77** 32 17N 119 21 E
Guba **91** 10 38 S 26 27 E
Gûbâl **86** 27 30N 34 0 E
Gúbbio **39** 43 20N 12 34 E
Gubin **28** 51 57N 14 43 E
Gubio **85** 12 30N 12 42 E
Gubkin **55** 51 17N 37 32 E
Guča **42** 43 46N 20 15 E
Guchil **71** 5 35N 102 10 E
Gudalur **70** 11 30N 76 29 E
Gudata **57** 43 7N 40 10 E
Gudenå **49** 56 27N 9 40 E
Gudermes **57** 43 24N 46 5 E
Gudhjem **49** 55 12N 14 58 E
Gudiña, La **30** 42 4N 7 8W
Gudivada **70** 16 30N 81 3 E
Gudiyatam **70** 12 57N 78 55 E
Gudur **70** 14 12N 79 55 E
Guebwiller **19** 47 55N 7 12 E
Guecho **32** 43 21N 2 59W
Guékédou **84** 8 40N 10 5W
Guelma **83** 36 25N 7 29 E
Guelph **106** 43 35N 80 20W
Guelt es Stel **82** 35 12N 3 1 E
Guelttara **82** 29 23N 2 10W
Guemar **83** 33 30N 6 49 E
Guéméné-Penfao **18** 47 38N 1 50W
Guéméné-sur-Scorff **18** 48 4N 3 13W
Guéné **85** 11 44N 3 16 E
Guer **18** 47 54N 2 8W
Güera, La **80** 20 51N 17 0W
Guérande **18** 47 20N 2 26W
Guerche, La **18** 47 57N 1 16W
Guerche-sur-l'Aubois, La **19** 46 58N 2 56 E
Guercif **82** 34 14N 3 21W
Guéréda **81** 14 31N 22 5 E
Guéret **20** 46 11N 1 51 E
Guérigny **19** 47 6N 3 10 E
Guernica **32** 43 19N 2 40W
Guernsey, Chan. Is. **18** 49 30N 2 35W
Guernsey, U.S.A. **116** 42 19N 104 45W
Guerrara, Oasis, Alg. **83** 32 51N 4 22 E
Guerrara, Saoura, Alg. **82** 28 5N 0 8W
Guerrero □ **120** 17 30N 100 0W
Guerzim **82** 29 39N 1 40W
Guest I. **5** 76 18 S 148 0W
Gueugnon **21** 46 36N 4 4 E
Gueydan **117** 30 3N 92 30W
Guglionesi **41** 41 55N 14 54 E
Gui Jiang → **77** 23 30N 111 15 E
Gui Xian **77** 23 8N 109 35 E
Guia Lopes da Laguna **125** 21 26 S 56 7W
Guichi **77** 30 39N 117 27 E
Guider **85** 9 56N 13 57 E
Guidimouni **85** 13 42N 9 31 E
Guidong **77** 26 7N 113 57 E
Guiglo **84** 6 45N 7 30W
Guijo de Coria **30** 40 6N 6 28W
Guildford **13** 51 14N 0 34W
Guilford **107** 45 12N 69 25W
Guilin **75** 25 18N 110 15 E
Guillaumes **21** 44 5N 6 52 E
Guillestre **21** 44 39N 6 40 E
Guilvinec **18** 47 48N 4 17W
Guimarães, Braz. **127** 2 9 S 44 42W
Guimarães, Port. **30** 41 28N 8 24W
Guimaras **73** 10 35N 122 37 E
Guinea ■ **84** 10 20N 10 0W
Guinea-Bissau ■ **84** 12 0N 15 0W
Guinea, Gulf of **85** 3 0N 2 30 E
Güines **121** 22 50N 82 0W
Guingamp **18** 48 34N 3 10W
Guipavas **18** 48 26N 4 29W
Guiping **75** 23 21N 110 2 E
Guipúzcoa □ **32** 43 12N 2 15W
Guir, O. → **82** 31 29N 2 17W
Güiria **126** 10 32N 62 18W
Guiscard **19** 49 40N 3 0 E
Guise **19** 49 52N 3 35 E
Guitiriz **30** 43 11N 7 50W
Guiuan **73** 11 5N 125 55 E
Guixi **77** 28 16N 117 15 E
Guiyang, Guizhou, China **75** 26 32N 106 40 E
Guiyang, Hunan, China **77** 25 46N 112 42 E
Guizhou □ **75** 27 0N 107 0 E
Gujan-Mestras **20** 44 38N 1 4W
Gujarat □ **68** 23 20N 71 0 E
Gujranwala **68** 32 10N 74 12 E
Gujrat **68** 32 40N 74 2 E
Gukovo **57** 48 1N 39 58 E
Gulargambone **100** 31 20 S 148 30 E
Gulbarga **70** 17 20N 76 50 E
Gulbene **54** 57 8N 26 52 E
Guledgud **70** 16 3N 75 48 E
Gulf Basin **96** 15 20 S 129 0 E
Gulfport **117** 30 21N 89 3W
Gulgong **99** 32 20 S 149 49 E
Gulistan **68** 30 30N 66 35 E
Gull Lake **109** 50 10N 108 29W
Gullringen **49** 57 48N 15 44 E
Gulma **85** 12 40N 4 23 E
Gülpinar **44** 39 32N 26 10 E
Gulshad **58** 46 45N 74 25 E
Gulsvik **47** 60 24N 9 38 E
Gulu **90** 2 48N 32 17 E
Gulwe **90** 6 30 S 36 25 E
Gulyaypole **56** 47 45N 36 21 E
Gum Lake **99** 32 42 S 143 9 E
Gumal → **68** 31 40N 71 50 E
Gumbaz **68** 30 2N 69 0 E
Gumel **85** 12 39N 9 22 E
Gumiel de Hizán **32** 41 46N 3 41W
Gumlu **98** 19 53 S 147 41 E
Gumma □ **74** 36 30N 138 20 E
Gummersbach **24** 51 2N 7 32 E
Gummi **85** 12 4N 5 9 E
Gümüsane **64** 40 30N 39 30 E
Gümüşhaciköy **56** 40 50N 35 18 E
Gumzai **73** 5 28 S 134 42 E
Guna **68** 24 40N 77 19 E
Guna Mt. **87** 11 50N 37 40 E
Gundagai **99** 35 3 S 148 6 E
Gundelfingen **25** 48 33N 10 22 E
Gundih **73** 7 10 S 110 56 E
Gundlakamma → **70** 15 30N 80 15 E
Gungu **88** 5 43 S 19 20 E
Gunisao → **109** 53 56N 97 53W
Gunisao L. **109** 53 33N 96 15W
Gunnedah **97** 30 59 S 150 15 E
Gunning **100** 34 47 S 149 14 E
Gunnison, Colo., U.S.A. **119** 38 32N 106 56W
Gunnison, Utah, U.S.A. **118** 39 11N 111 48W
Gunnison → **119** 39 3N 108 30W
Guntakal **70** 15 11N 77 27 E
Guntersville **115** 34 18N 86 16W
Guntur **70** 16 23N 80 30 E
Gunung-Sitoli **72** 1 15N 97 30 E
Gunungapi **73** 6 45 S 126 30 E
Gunupur **70** 19 5N 83 50 E
Günz → **25** 48 27N 10 16 E
Gunza **88** 10 50 S 13 50 E
Günzburg **25** 48 27N 10 16 E
Gunzenhausen **25** 49 6N 10 45 E
Guo He → **77** 32 59N 117 10 E
Guoyang **77** 33 32N 116 12 E
Gupis **69** 36 15N 73 20 E
Gura **68** 25 12N 71 39 E
Gura Humorului **46** 47 35N 25 53 E
Gura-Teghii **46** 45 30N 26 25 E
Gurag **87** 8 20N 38 20 E
Gürchañ **64** 34 55N 49 25 E
Gurdaspur **68** 32 5N 75 31 E
Gurdon **117** 33 55N 93 10W
Gurdzhaani **57** 41 43N 45 52 E
Gurgaon **68** 28 27N 77 1 E
Gurghiu, Munţii **46** 46 41N 25 15 E
Gurk → **26** 46 35N 14 31 E
Gurkha **69** 28 5N 84 40 E
Gurley **99** 29 45 S 149 48 E
Gurun **71** 5 49N 100 27 E
Gurupá **127** 1 25 S 51 35W
Gurupá, I. Grande de **127** 1 25 S 51 45W
Gurupi → **127** 1 13 S 46 6W
Guryev **57** 47 5N 52 0 E
Gus-Khrustalnyy **55** 55 42N 40 44 E
Gusau **85** 12 12N 6 40 E
Gusev **54** 54 35N 22 10 E
Gushan **76** 39 50N 123 35 E
Gushi **77** 32 11N 115 41 E
Gushiago **85** 9 55N 0 15W
Gusinje **42** 42 35N 19 50 E
Gúspini **40** 39 32N 8 38 E
Gusselby **48** 59 38N 15 14 E
Güssing **27** 47 3N 16 20 E
Gustanj **39** 46 36N 14 49 E
Gustine **119** 37 14N 121 0 E
Güstrow **24** 53 47N 12 12 E
Gusum **49** 58 16N 16 30 E
Guta = Kalárovo **27** 47 54N 18 0 E
Gütersloh **24** 51 54N 8 25 E
Guthalongra **98** 19 52 S 147 50 E
Guthega Dam **100** 36 20 S 148 27 E
Guthrie **117** 35 55N 97 30W
Guttenberg **116** 42 46N 91 10W
Guyana ■ **126** 5 0N 59 0W
Guyang **76** 41 0N 110 5 E
Guyenne **20** 44 30N 0 40 E
Guymon **117** 36 45N 101 30W
Guyra **99** 30 15 S 151 40 E
Guyuan **76** 36 0N 106 20 E
Guzhen **77** 33 22N 117 18 E
Guzmán, Laguna de **120** 31 25N 107 25W
Gwa **67** 17 36N 94 34 E
Gwaai **91** 19 15 S 27 45 E
Gwabegar **99** 30 31 S 149 0 E
Gwadabawa **85** 13 28N 5 15 E
Gwâdar **66** 25 10N 62 18 E
Gwagwada **85** 10 15N 7 15 E
Gwalior **68** 26 12N 78 10 E
Gwanda **91** 20 55 S 29 0 E
Gwandu **85** 12 30N 4 41 E
Gwane **90** 4 45N 25 48 E
Gwaram **85** 10 15N 10 25 E
Gwarzo **85** 12 20N 8 55 E
Gwda → **28** 53 3N 16 44 E
Gweebarra B. **15** 54 52N 8 21W
Gweedore **15** 55 4N 8 15W
* Gwelo **91** 19 28 S 29 45 E
Gwent □ **13** 51 45N 2 55W
Gwi **85** 9 0N 7 10 E
Gwinn **114** 46 15N 87 29W
Gwio Kura **85** 12 40N 11 2 E
Gwol **84** 10 58N 1 59W
Gwoza **85** 11 5N 13 40 E
Gwydir → **97** 29 27 S 149 48 E
Gwynedd □ **12** 53 0N 4 0W
Gyaring Hu **75** 34 50N 97 40 E
Gydanskiy P-ov. **58** 70 0N 78 0 E
Gyland **47** 58 24N 6 45 E
Gympie **97** 26 11 S 152 38 E
Gyoda **74** 36 10N 139 30 E
Gyoma **27** 46 56N 20 50 E
Gyöngyös **27** 47 48N 20 0 E
Györ **27** 47 41N 17 40 E
Györ-Sopron □ **27** 47 40N 17 20 E
Gypsum Pt. **108** 61 53N 114 35W
Gypsumville **109** 51 45N 98 40W
Gyttorp **48** 59 31N 14 58 E
Gyula **27** 46 38N 21 17 E
Gzhatsk = Gagarin **54** 55 30N 35 0 E

H

Ha 'Arava **62** 30 50N 35 20 E
Haag **25** 48 11N 12 12 E
Haapamäki **50** 62 18N 24 28 E
Haapsalu **54** 58 56N 23 30 E
Haarlem **16** 52 23N 4 39 E
Haast → **101** 43 50 S 169 2 E
Hab Nadi Chauki **66** 25 0N 66 50 E
Habana, La **121** 23 8N 82 22W
Habaswein **90** 1 2N 39 30 E
Habay **108** 58 50N 118 44W
Habiganj **69** 24 24N 91 30 E
Hablingbo **49** 57 12N 18 16 E
Habo **49** 57 55N 14 6 E
Hachenburg **24** 50 40N 7 49 E
Hachijō-Jima **74** 33 5N 139 45 E
Hachinohe **74** 40 30N 141 29 E
Hachiōji **74** 35 40N 139 20 E
Hadali **68** 32 16N 72 11 E
Hadarba, Ras **86** 22 4N 36 51 E
Hadd, Ras al **65** 22 35N 59 50 E
Haddington **14** 55 57N 2 48W
Hadejia **85** 12 30N 10 5 E
Hadejia → **85** 12 50N 10 51 E
Haden **99** 27 13 S 151 54 E
Hadera **62** 32 27N 34 55 E
Hadera, N. → **62** 32 28N 34 52 E
Haderslev **49** 55 15N 9 30 E
Hadhra **86** 20 10N 41 5 E
Hadhramaut = Hadramawt **63** 15 30N 49 30 E
Hadibu **63** 12 35N 54 2 E
Hadjeb El Aïoun **83** 35 21N 9 32 E
Hadramawt **63** 15 30N 49 30 E
Hadrians Wall **12** 55 0N 2 30W
Hadsten **49** 56 19N 10 3 E
Hadsund **49** 56 44N 10 8 E
Haeju **76** 38 3N 125 45 E
Haerhpin = Harbin **76** 45 48N 126 40 E
Hafar al Batin **64** 28 25N 46 0 E
Hafizabad **68** 32 5N 73 40 E
Haflong **67** 25 10N 93 5 E
Hafnarfjörður **50** 64 4N 21 57W
Haft-Gel **64** 31 30N 49 32 E
Hafun, Ras **63** 10 29N 51 30 E
Hagalil **62** 32 53N 35 18 E
Hagari → **70** 15 40N 77 0 E
Hagen **24** 51 21N 7 29 E
Hagenow **24** 53 25N 11 10 E
Hagerman **117** 33 5N 104 22W
Hagerstown **114** 39 39N 77 46W
Hagetmau **20** 43 39N 0 37W
Hagfors **48** 60 3N 13 45 E
Häggenås **48** 63 24N 14 55 E
Hagi, Iceland **50** 65 28N 23 25W
Hagi, Japan **74** 34 30N 131 22 E
Hagolan **62** 33 0N 35 45 E
Hags Hd. **15** 52 57N 9 30W
Hague, C. de la **18** 49 44N 1 56W
Hague, The = s'-Gravenhage **16** 52 7N 4 17 E
Haguenau **19** 48 49N 7 47 E
Hai □ **90** 3 10 S 37 10 E
Haicheng **76** 40 50N 122 45 E
Haifeng **77** 22 58N 115 10 E

* *Renamed Gweru*

Haiger Håverud

Haiger 24 50 44N 8 12 E
Haikang 77 20 52N 110 8 E
Haikou 75 20 1N 110 16 E
Ḥā'il 64 27 28N 41 45 E
Hailar 75 49 10N 119 38 E
Hailar He → 76 49 30N 117 50 E
Hailey 118 43 30N 114 15W
Haileybury 106 47 30N 79 38W
Hailin 76 44 37N 129 30 E
Hailing Dao 77 21 35N 111 47 E
Hailong 76 42 32N 125 40 E
Hailun 75 47 28N 126 50 E
Hailuoto 50 65 3N 24 45 E
Haimen 77 31 52N 121 10 E
Hainan 77 19 0N 110 0 E
Hainan Dao 75 19 0N 109 30 E
Hainaut □ 16 50 30N 4 0 E
Hainburg 27 48 9N 16 56 E
Haines 118 44 51N 117 59W
Haines City 115 28 6N 81 35W
Haines Junction 108 60 45N 137 30W
Hainfeld 26 48 3N 15 48 E
Haining 77 30 28N 120 40 E
Haiphong 71 20 47N 106 41 E
Haiti ■ 121 19 0N 72 30W
Haiya Junction 86 18 20N 36 21 E
Haiyan 77 30 28N 120 58 E
Haiyang 76 36 47N 121 9 E
Haiyuan 76 36 35N 105 52 E
Haja 73 3 19 S 129 37 E
Hajar Bangar 81 10 40N 22 45 E
Hajar, Jabal 64 26 5N 39 10 E
Hajdú-Bihar □ 27 47 30N 21 30 E
Hajdúböszörmény 27 47 40N 21 30 E
Hajdúdurog 27 47 48N 21 30 E
Hajdúhadház 27 47 40N 21 40 E
Hajdúnánás 27 47 50N 21 26 E
Hajdúsámson 27 47 37N 21 42 E
Hajdúszobaszló 27 47 27N 21 22 E
Hajipur 69 25 45N 85 13 E
Hajówka 28 52 47N 23 35 E
Hajr 65 24 0N 56 34 E
Hakansson, Mts. 91 8 40 S 25 45 E
Håkantorp 49 58 18N 12 55 E
Hakken-Zan 74 34 10N 135 54 E
Hakodate 74 41 45N 140 44 E
Ḥalab = Aleppo 64 36 10N 37 15 E
Ḥalabjah 64 35 10N 45 58 E
Halaib 86 22 12N 36 30 E
Halbe 86 19 40N 42 15 E
Halberstadt 24 51 53N 11 2 E
Halcombe 101 40 8 S 175 30 E
Halcyon, Mt. 73 13 0N 121 30 E
Halden 47 59 9N 11 23 E
Haldensleben 24 52 17N 11 30 E
Haldia 67 22 5N 88 3 E
Haldwani-cum-Kathgodam 69 29 31N 79 30 E
Haleakala Crater 110 20 43N 156 12W
Haleyville 115 34 15N 87 40W
Half Assini 84 5 1N 2 50W
Halfway 118 44 56N 117 8W
Halfway → 108 56 12N 121 32W
Ḥalḥul 62 31 35N 35 7 E
Hali, Si. Arab. 86 18 40N 41 15 E
Hali, Yemen 63 18 30N 41 30 E
Haliburton 106 45 3N 78 30W
Halicarnassus 45 37 3N 27 30 E
Halifax, Austral. 98 18 32 S 146 22 E
Halifax, Can. 107 44 38N 63 35W
Halifax, U.K. 12 53 43N 1 51W
Halifax B. 97 18 50 S 147 0 E
Halifax I. 92 26 38 S 15 4 E
Halīl Rūd → 65 27 40N 58 30 E
Hall 26 47 17N 11 30 E
Hall Beach 105 68 46N 81 12W
Hallabro 49 56 22N 15 5 E
Hallands län □ 49 56 50N 12 50 E
Hallands Väderö 49 56 27N 12 34 E
Hallandsås 49 56 22N 13 0 E
Halle, Belg. 16 50 44N 4 13 E
Halle, Halle, Ger. 24 51 29N 12 0 E
Halle, Nordrhein-Westfalen, Ger. 24 52 4N 8 20 E
Halle □ 24 51 28N 11 58 E
Hällefors 48 59 47N 14 31 E
Hallefors 49 59 46N 14 30 E
Hallein 26 47 40N 13 5 E
Hällekis 49 58 38N 13 27 E
Hallett 99 33 25 S 138 55 E
Hallettsville 117 29 28N 96 57W
Hällevadsholm 49 58 35N 11 33 E
Halley Bay 5 75 31 S 26 36W
Hallia → 70 16 55N 79 20 E
Halliday 116 47 20N 102 25W
Halliday L. 109 61 21N 108 56W
Hallingskeid 47 60 40N 7 17 E
Hällnäs 50 64 19N 19 36 E
Hallock 109 48 47N 97 0W
Halls Creek 96 18 16 S 127 38 E
Hallsberg 48 59 5N 15 7 E
Hallstahammar 48 59 38N 16 15 E
Hallstatt 26 47 33N 13 38 E
Hallstavik 48 60 5N 18 37 E
Hallstead 113 41 56N 75 45W
Halmahera 73 0 40N 128 0 E
Halmeu 46 47 57N 23 2 E
Halmstad 49 56 41N 12 52 E
Halq el Oued 83 36 53N 10 18 E
Hals 49 56 59N 10 18 E
Halsa 47 63 3N 8 14 E
Halsafjorden 47 63 5N 8 10 E
Hälsingborg = Helsingborg 49 56 3N 12 42 E
Halstad 116 47 21N 96 50W
Haltdalen 47 62 56N 11 8 E
Haltern 24 51 44N 7 10 E
Halul 65 25 40N 52 40 E
Ham 19 49 45N 3 4 E
Hamab 92 28 7 S 19 16 E
Hamad 87 15 20N 33 32 E
Hamada 74 34 56N 132 4 E
Hamadān 64 34 52N 48 32 E
Hamadān □ 64 35 0N 49 0 E
Hamadia 82 35 28N 1 57 E
Hamāh 64 35 5N 36 40 E
Hamamatsu 74 34 45N 137 45 E
Hamar 47 60 48N 11 7 E
Hamarøy 50 68 5N 15 38 E
Hamâta, Gebel 86 24 17N 35 0 E
Hamber Prov. Park 108 52 20N 118 0W
Hamburg, Ger. 24 53 32N 9 59 E
Hamburg, Ark., U.S.A. 117 33 15N 91 47W
Hamburg, Iowa, U.S.A. 116 40 37N 95 38W
Hamburg, N.Y., U.S.A. 112 42 44N 78 50W
Hamburg, Pa., U.S.A. 113 40 33N 76 0W
Hamburg □ 24 53 30N 10 0 E
Hamden 113 41 21N 72 56W
Hamdh, W. → 86 24 55N 36 20 E
Hämeen lääni □ 51 61 24N 24 10 E
Hämeenlinna 50 61 0N 24 28 E
Hamélé 84 10 56N 2 45W
Hameln 24 52 7N 9 24 E
Hamer Koke 87 5 15N 36 45 E
Hamersley Ra. 96 22 0 S 117 45 E
Hamhung 76 39 54N 127 30 E
Hami 75 42 55N 93 25 E
Hamilton, Austral. 97 37 45 S 142 2 E
Hamilton, Berm. 121 32 15N 64 45W
Hamilton, Can. 106 43 15N 79 50W
Hamilton, N.Z. 101 37 47 S 175 19 E
Hamilton, U.K. 14 55 47N 4 2W
Hamilton, Mo., U.S.A. 116 39 45N 93 59W
Hamilton, Mont., U.S.A. 118 46 20N 114 6W
Hamilton, N.Y., U.S.A. 114 42 49N 75 31W
Hamilton, Ohio, U.S.A. 114 39 20N 84 35W
Hamilton, Tex., U.S.A. 117 31 40N 98 5W
Hamilton → 98 23 30 S 139 47 E
Hamilton Hotel 98 22 45 S 140 40 E
Hamilton Inlet 107 54 0N 57 30W
Hamiota 109 50 11N 100 38W
Hamlet 115 34 56N 79 40W
Hamley Bridge 99 34 17 S 138 35 E
Hamlin, N.Y., U.S.A. 112 43 17N 77 55W
Hamlin, Tex., U.S.A. 117 32 58N 100 8W
Hamm 24 51 40N 7 49 E
Hammam Bouhadjar 82 35 23N 0 58W
Hammamet 83 36 24N 10 38 E
Hammamet, G. de 83 36 10N 10 48 E
Hammarstrand 48 63 7N 16 20 E
Hammel 49 56 16N 9 52 E
Hammelburg 25 50 7N 9 54 E
Hammeren 49 55 18N 14 47 E
Hammerfest 50 70 39N 23 41 E
Hammond, Ind., U.S.A. 114 41 40N 87 30W
Hammond, La., U.S.A. 117 30 32N 90 30W
Hammonton 114 39 40N 74 47W
Hamneda 49 56 41N 13 51 E
Hamoyet, Jebel 86 17 33N 38 2 E
Hampden 101 45 18 S 170 50 E
Hampshire □ 13 51 3N 1 20W
Hampshire Downs 13 51 10N 1 10W
Hampton, Ark., U.S.A. 117 33 35N 92 29W
Hampton, Iowa, U.S.A. 116 42 42N 93 12W
Hampton, N.H., U.S.A. 113 42 56N 70 48W
Hampton, S.C., U.S.A. 115 32 52N 81 2W
Hampton, Va., U.S.A. 114 37 4N 76 18W
Hampton Harbour 96 20 30 S 116 30 E
Hampton Tableland 96 32 0 S 127 0 E
Hamrat esh Sheykh 87 14 38N 27 55 E
Han Jiang → 77 23 25N 116 40 E
Han Shui → 77 30 35N 114 18 E
Hana 110 20 45N 155 59W
Hanak 86 25 32N 37 0 E
Hanang 90 4 30 S 35 25 E
Hanau 25 50 8N 8 56 E
Hancheng 76 35 31N 110 25 E
Hancock, Mich., U.S.A. 116 47 10N 88 40W
Hancock, Minn., U.S.A. 116 45 26N 95 46W
Hancock, Pa., U.S.A. 113 41 57N 75 19W
Handa, Japan 74 34 53N 137 0 E
Handa, Somalia 63 10 37N 51 2 E
Handan 76 36 35N 114 28 E
Handen 48 59 12N 18 12 E
Handeni 90 5 25 S 38 2 E
Handeni □ 90 5 30 S 38 0 E
Handlová 27 48 45N 18 35 E
Handub 86 19 15N 37 16 E
Hanegev 62 30 50N 35 0 E
Haney 108 49 12N 122 40W
Hanford 119 36 23N 119 39W
Hangang → 76 37 50N 126 30 E
Hangayn Nuruu 75 47 30N 100 0 E
Hangchou = Hangzhou 75 30 18N 120 11 E
Hanggin Houqi 76 40 58N 107 4 E
Hangklip, K. 92 34 26 S 18 48 E
Hangö 51 59 50N 22 57 E
Hangu 76 39 18N 117 53 E
Hangzhou 75 30 18N 120 11 E
Hangzhou Wan 75 30 15N 120 45 E
Ḥanīsh J. 63 13 45N 42 46 E
Haniska 27 48 37N 21 15 E
Hanita 62 33 5N 35 10 E
Hankinson 116 46 9N 96 58W
Hanko 51 59 59N 22 57 E
Hankou 77 30 35N 114 30 E
Hanksville 119 38 19N 110 45W
Hanmer 101 42 32 S 172 50 E
Hann, Mt. 96 16 0 S 126 0 E
Hanna 108 51 40N 111 54W
Hannaford 116 47 23N 98 11W
Hannah 116 48 58N 98 42W
Hannah B. 106 51 40N 80 0W
Hannibal 116 39 42N 91 22W
Hannik 86 18 12N 32 20 E
Hannover 24 52 23N 9 43 E
Hanö 49 56 2N 14 50 E
Hanöbukten 49 55 35N 14 30 E
Hanoi 71 21 5N 105 55 E
Hanover, Can. 112 44 9N 81 2W
Hanover, S. Afr. 92 31 4 S 24 29 E
Hanover, N.H., U.S.A. 114 43 43N 72 17W
Hanover, Ohio, U.S.A. 112 40 5N 82 17W
Hanover, Pa., U.S.A. 114 39 46N 76 59W
Hanover = Hannover 24 52 23N 9 43 E
Hanover, I. 128 51 0 S 74 50W
Hansi 68 29 10N 75 57 E
Hansjö 48 61 10N 14 40 E
Hanson Range 96 27 0 S 136 30 E
Hanwood 100 34 22 S 146 2 E
Hanyang 77 30 35N 114 2 E
Hanyin 77 32 54N 108 28 E
Hanzhong 75 33 10N 107 1 E
Hanzhuang 77 34 33N 117 23 E
Haparanda 50 65 52N 24 8 E
Happy 117 34 47N 101 50W
Happy Camp 118 41 52N 123 22W
Happy Valley 107 53 15N 60 20W
Hapur 68 28 45N 77 45 E
Ḥaql 86 29 10N 35 0 E
Har 73 5 16 S 133 14 E
Har Hu 75 38 20N 97 38 E
Har Us Nuur 75 48 0N 92 0 E
Har Yehuda 62 31 35N 34 57 E
Ḥaraḍ 64 24 22N 49 0 E
Haraisan Plateau 64 23 0N 47 40 E
Haramsøya 47 62 39N 6 12 E
Harardera 63 4 33N 47 38 E
Harat 87 16 5N 39 26 E
Harazé, Chad 81 14 20N 19 12 E
Harazé, Chad 81 9 57N 20 48 E
Harbin 76 45 48N 126 40 E
Harboør 49 56 38N 8 10 E
Harbor Beach 114 43 50N 82 38W
Harbor Springs 114 45 28N 85 0W
Harbour Breton 107 47 29N 55 50W
Harbour Grace 107 47 40N 53 22W
Harburg 24 53 27N 9 58 E
Hårby 49 55 13N 10 7 E
Harcourt 98 24 17 S 149 55 E
Harda 68 22 27N 77 5 E
Hardangerfjorden 47 60 15N 6 0 E
Hardangerjøkulen 47 60 30N 7 0 E
Hardangervidda 47 60 20N 7 20 E
Hardap Dam 92 24 32 S 17 50 E
Hardenberg 16 52 34N 6 37 E
Harderwijk 16 52 21N 5 38 E
Hardin 118 45 44N 107 35W
Harding 93 30 35 S 29 55 E
Hardisty 108 52 40N 111 18W
Hardman 118 45 12N 119 40W
Hardoi 69 27 26N 80 6 E
Hardwar 68 29 58N 78 9 E
Hardwick 113 44 30N 72 20W
Hardy 117 36 20N 91 30W
Hardy, Pen. 128 55 30 S 68 20W
Hare B. 107 51 15N 55 45W
Hare Gilboa 62 32 31N 35 25 E
Hare Meron 62 32 59N 35 24 E
Haren 24 52 47N 7 18 E
Harer 87 9 20N 42 8 E
Harer □ 87 7 12N 42 0 E
Hareto 87 9 23N 37 6 E
Harfleur 18 49 30N 0 10 E
Hargeisa 63 9 30N 44 2 E
Harghita □ 46 46 30N 25 30 E
Harghita, Mţii 46 46 25N 25 35 E
Hargshamn 48 60 12N 18 30 E
Hari → 72 1 16 S 104 5 E
Haricha, Hamada el 82 22 40N 3 15W
Harihar 70 14 32N 75 44 E
Haringhata → 69 22 0N 89 58 E
Haripad 70 9 14N 76 28 E
Harīrūd 65 35 0N 61 0 E
Harīrūd → 65 34 20N 62 30 E
Harkat 86 20 25N 39 40 E
Harlan, Iowa, U.S.A. 116 41 37N 95 20W
Harlan, Tenn., U.S.A. 115 36 50N 83 20W
Harlech 12 52 52N 4 7W
Harlem 118 48 29N 108 47W
Harlingen, Neth. 16 53 11N 5 25 E
Harlingen, U.S.A. 117 26 20N 97 50W
Harlowton 118 46 30N 109 54W
Harmånger 48 61 55N 17 20 E
Harmil 87 16 30N 40 10 E
Harney Basin 118 43 30N 119 0W
Harney L. 118 43 0N 119 0W
Harney Pk. 116 43 52N 103 33W
Härnön 48 62 36N 18 0 E
Härnösand 48 62 38N 18 0 E
Haro 32 42 35N 2 55W
Haro, C. 120 27 50N 110 55W
Harp L. 107 55 5N 61 50W
Harpanahalli 70 14 47N 76 2 E
Harpe, La 116 40 30N 91 0W
Harper 84 4 25N 7 43W
Harplinge 49 56 45N 12 45 E
Harrand 68 29 28N 70 3 E
Ḥarrat al Kishb 64 22 30N 40 15 E
Ḥarrat al 'Uwairidh 64 26 50N 38 0 E
Harrat Khaibar 86 25 45N 40 0 E
Harrat Nawāṣīf 86 21 30N 42 0 E
Harriman 115 36 0N 84 35W
Harrington Harbour 107 50 31N 59 30W
Harris 14 57 50N 6 55W
Harris L. 96 31 10 S 135 10 E
Harris, Sd. of 14 57 44N 7 6W
Harrisburg, Ill., U.S.A. 117 37 42N 88 30W
Harrisburg, Nebr., U.S.A. 116 41 36N 103 46W
Harrisburg, Oreg., U.S.A. 118 44 16N 123 10W
Harrisburg, Pa., U.S.A. 114 40 18N 76 52W
Harrismith 93 28 15 S 29 8 E
Harrison, Ark., U.S.A. 117 36 10N 93 4W
Harrison, Idaho, U.S.A. 118 47 30N 116 51W
Harrison, Nebr., U.S.A. 116 42 42N 103 52W
Harrison B. 104 70 25N 151 30W
Harrison, C. 107 54 55N 57 55W
Harrison L. 108 49 33N 121 50W
Harrisonburg 114 38 28N 78 52W
Harrisonville 116 38 39N 94 21W
Harriston 106 43 57N 80 53W
Harrisville 106 44 40N 83 19W
Harrogate 12 53 59N 1 32W
Harrow, Can. 112 42 2N 82 55W
Harrow, U.K. 13 51 35N 0 15W
Harsefeld 24 53 26N 9 31 E
Harstad 50 68 48N 16 30 E
Hart 114 43 42N 86 21W
Hartbees → 92 28 45 S 20 32 E
Hartberg 26 47 17N 15 58 E
Hartford, Conn., U.S.A. 114 41 47N 72 41W
Hartford, Ky., U.S.A. 114 37 26N 86 50W
Hartford, S.D., U.S.A. 116 43 40N 96 58W
Hartford, Wis., U.S.A. 116 43 18N 88 25W
Hartford City 114 40 22N 85 20W
Hartland 107 46 20N 67 32W
Hartland Pt. 13 51 2N 4 32W
Hartlepool 12 54 42N 1 11W
Hartley 91 18 10 S 30 14 E
Hartley Bay 108 53 25N 129 15W
Hartmannberge 92 17 0 S 13 0 E
Hartney 109 49 30N 100 35W
Hartselle 115 34 25N 86 55W
Hartshorne 117 34 51N 95 30W
Hartsville 115 34 23N 80 2W
Hartwell 115 34 21N 82 52W
Harunabad 68 29 35N 73 8 E
Harur 70 12 3N 78 29 E
Harvey, Ill., U.S.A. 114 41 40N 87 40W
Harvey, N.D., U.S.A. 116 47 50N 99 58W
Harwich 13 51 56N 1 18 E
Haryana □ 68 29 0N 76 10 E
Harz 24 51 40N 10 40 E
Harzgerode 24 51 38N 11 8 E
Hasa 64 26 0N 49 0 E
Hasaheisa 87 14 44N 33 20 E
Hasani 86 25 0N 37 8 E
Hasanpur 68 28 43N 78 17 E
Haselünne 24 52 40N 7 30 E
Hasharon 62 32 12N 34 49 E
Hashefela 62 31 30N 34 43 E
Håsjö 48 63 1N 16 5 E
Haskell, Okla., U.S.A. 117 35 51N 95 40W
Haskell, Tex., U.S.A. 117 33 10N 99 45W
Haslach 25 48 16N 8 7 E
Hasle 49 55 11N 14 44 E
Haslev 49 55 18N 11 57 E
Hasparren 20 43 24N 1 18W
Hasselt 16 50 56N 5 21 E
Hassene, Ad. 82 21 0N 4 0 E
Hassfurt 25 50 2N 10 30 E
Hassi Berrekrem 83 33 45N 5 16 E
Hassi bou Khelala 82 30 17N 0 18W
Hassi Daoula 83 33 4N 5 38 E
Hassi Djafou 82 30 55N 3 35 E
Hassi el Abiod 82 31 47N 3 37 E
Hassi el Biod 83 28 30N 6 0 E
Hassi el Gassi 83 30 52N 6 5 E
Hassi el Hadjar 83 31 28N 4 45 E
Hassi er Rmel 82 32 56N 3 17 E
Hassi Imoulaye 83 29 54N 9 10 E
Hassi Inifel 82 29 50N 3 41 E
Hassi Marroket 82 30 10N 3 0 E
Hassi Messaoud 83 31 43N 6 8 E
Hassi Rhénami 83 31 50N 5 58 E
Hassi Tartrat 83 30 5N 6 28 E
Hassi Zerzour 82 30 51N 3 56W
Hastings, Can. 112 44 18N 77 57W
Hastings, N.Z. 101 39 39 S 176 52 E
Hastings, U.K. 13 50 51N 0 36 E
Hastings, Mich., U.S.A. 114 42 40N 85 20W
Hastings, Minn., U.S.A. 116 44 41N 92 51W
Hastings, Nebr., U.S.A. 116 40 34N 98 22W
Hastings Ra. 99 31 15 S 152 14 E
Hästveda 49 56 17N 13 55 E
Hat Nhao 71 14 46N 106 32 E
Hatch 119 32 45N 107 8W
Hatches Creek 96 20 56 S 135 12 E
Hatchet L. 109 58 36N 103 40W
Haţeg 46 45 36N 22 55 E
Haţeg, Mţii. 46 45 25N 23 0 E
Hatfield P.O. 99 33 54 S 143 49 E
Hatgal 75 50 26N 100 9 E
Hathras 68 27 36N 78 6 E
Hattah 99 34 48 S 142 17 E
Hatteras, C. 115 35 10N 75 30W
Hattiesburg 117 31 20N 89 20W
Hatvan 27 47 40N 19 45 E
Hau Bon = Cheo Reo 71 13 25N 108 28 E
Haug 47 60 23N 10 26 E
Haugastøl 47 60 30N 7 50 E
Haugesund 47 59 23N 5 13 E
Haultain → 109 55 51N 106 46W
Hauraki Gulf 101 36 35 S 175 5 E
Hauran 62 32 50N 36 15 E
Hausruck 26 48 6N 13 30 E
Haut Atlas 82 32 30N 5 0W
Haut-Rhin □ 19 48 0N 7 15 E
Haut Zaïre □ 90 2 20N 26 0 E
Hautah, Wahāt al 64 23 40N 47 0 E
Haute-Corse □ 21 42 30N 9 30 E
Haute-Garonne □ 20 43 28N 1 30 E
Haute-Loire □ 20 45 5N 3 50 E
Haute-Marne □ 19 48 10N 5 20 E
Haute-Saône □ 19 47 45N 6 10 E
Haute-Savoie □ 21 46 0N 6 20 E
Haute-Vienne □ 20 45 50N 1 10 E
Hauterive 107 49 10N 68 16W
Hautes-Alpes □ 21 44 42N 6 20 E
Hautes-Pyrénées □ 20 43 0N 0 10 E
Hauteville 21 45 58N 5 36 E
Hautmont 19 50 15N 3 55 E
Hauts-de-Seine □ 19 48 52N 2 15 E
Hauts Plateaux 82 34 14N 1 0 E
Hauzenberg 25 48 39N 13 38 E
Havana 116 40 19N 90 3W
Havana = La Habana 121 23 8N 82 22W
Havasu, L. 119 34 18N 114 28W
Havdhem 49 57 10N 18 20 E
Havelange 16 50 23N 5 15 E
Havelock, N.B., Can. 107 46 2N 65 24W
Havelock, Ont., Can. 106 44 26N 77 53W
Havelock, N.Z. 101 41 17 S 173 48 E
Havelock I. 71 11 55N 93 2 E
Haverfordwest 13 51 48N 4 59W
Haverhill 114 42 50N 71 2W
Haveri 70 14 53N 75 24 E
Havering 13 51 33N 0 20 E
Haverstraw 113 41 12N 73 58W
Håverud 49 58 50N 12 28 E

Havîrna Hogansville

Havîrna 46 48 4N 26 43 E
Havlíčkův Brod 26 49 36N 15 33 E
Havneby 49 55 5N 8 34 E
Havre 118 48 34N 109 40W
Havre -St.-Pierre 107 50 18N 63 33W
Havre-Aubert 107 47 12N 61 56W
Havre, Le 18 49 30N 0 5 E
Havza 64 41 0N 35 35 E
Haw → 115 35 36N 79 3W
Hawaii □ 110 20 30N 157 0W
Hawaii 110 20 0N 155 0W
Hawaiian Is. 110 20 30N 156 0W
Hawaiian Ridge 95 24 0N 165 0W
Hawarden, Can. 109 51 25N 106 36W
Hawarden, U.S.A. 116 43 2N 96 28W
Hawea Lake 101 44 28 S 169 19 E
Hawera 101 39 35 S 174 19 E
Hawick 14 55 25N 2 48W
Hawk Junction 106 48 5N 84 38W
Hawke B. 101 39 25 S 177 20 E
Hawke, C. 100 32 13 S 152 34 E
Hawker 97 31 59 S 138 22 E
Hawke's Bay □ 101 39 45 S 176 35 E
Hawkesbury 106 45 37N 74 37W
Hawkesbury → 97 33 30 S 151 10 E
Hawkesbury I. 108 53 37N 129 3W
Hawkinsville 115 32 17N 83 30W
Hawkwood 99 25 45 S 150 50 E
Hawley 116 46 58N 96 20W
Hawrān 62 32 45N 36 15 E
Hawthorne 118 38 31N 118 37W
Hawzen 87 13 58N 39 28 E
Haxtun 116 40 40N 102 39W
Hay, Austral. 97 34 30 S 144 51 E
Hay, U.K. 13 52 4N 3 9W
Hay →, Austral. 97 25 14 S 138 0 E
Hay →, Can. 108 60 50N 116 26W
Hay L. 108 58 50N 118 50W
Hay Lakes 108 53 12N 113 2W
Hay River 108 60 51N 115 44W
Hay Springs 116 42 40N 102 38W
Hayange 19 49 20N 6 2 E
Hayden, Ariz., U.S.A. 119 33 2N 110 48W
Hayden, Colo., U.S.A. 118 40 30N 107 22W
Haydon 98 18 0 S 141 30 E
Haye-Descartes, La 18 46 58N 0 42 E
Haye-du-Puits, La 18 49 17N 1 33W
Hayes 116 44 22N 101 1W
Hayes → 109 57 3N 92 12W
Haynesville 117 33 0N 93 7W
Hays, Can. 108 50 6N 111 48W
Hays, U.S.A. 116 38 55N 99 25W
Hayward 116 46 2N 91 30W
Hayward's Heath 13 51 0N 0 5W
Hazard 114 37 18N 83 10W
Hazaribagh 69 23 58N 85 26 E
Hazaribagh Road 69 24 12N 85 57 E
Hazebrouck 19 50 42N 2 31 E
Hazelton, Can. 108 55 20N 127 42W
Hazelton, U.S.A. 116 46 30N 100 15W
Hazen, N.D., U.S.A. 116 47 18N 101 38W
Hazen, Nev., U.S.A. 118 39 37N 119 2W
Hazlehurst, Ga., U.S.A. 115 31 50N 82 35W
Hazlehurst, Miss., U.S.A. 117 31 52N 90 24W
Hazleton 114 40 58N 76 0W
Hazor 62 33 2N 35 32 E
He Xian 77 24 27N 111 30 E
Head of Bight 96 31 30 S 131 25 E
Headlands 91 18 15 S 32 2 E
Healdsburg 118 38 33N 122 51W
Healdton 117 34 16N 97 31W
Healesville 99 37 35 S 145 30 E
Heanor 12 53 1N 1 20W
Heard I. 3 53 0 S 74 0 E
Hearne 117 30 54N 96 35W
Hearne B. 109 60 10N 99 10W
Hearne L. 108 62 20N 113 10W
Hearst 106 49 40N 83 41W
Heart → 116 46 40N 100 51W
Heart's Content 107 47 54N 53 27W
Heath Pt. 107 49 8N 61 40W
Heath Steele 107 47 17N 66 5W
Heavener 117 34 54N 94 36W
Hebbronville 117 27 20N 98 40W
Hebei □ 76 39 0N 116 0 E
Hebel 99 28 58 S 147 47 E
Heber Springs 117 35 29N 91 59W
Hebert 109 50 30N 107 10W
Hebgen, L. 118 44 50N 111 15W
Hebi 76 35 57N 114 7 E
Hebrides 14 57 30N 7 0W
Hebrides, Inner Is. 14 57 20N 6 40W
Hebrides, Outer Is. 14 57 30N 7 40W
Hebron, Can. 105 58 5N 62 30W
Hebron, N.D., U.S.A. 116 46 56N 102 2W
Hebron, Nebr., U.S.A. 116 40 15N 97 33W
Hebron = Al Khalil 62 31 32N 35 6 E
Heby 49 59 56N 16 53 E
Hecate Str. 108 53 10N 130 30W
Hechi 75 24 40N 108 2 E
Hechingen 25 48 20N 8 58 E
Hechuan 75 30 2N 106 12 E
Hecla 116 45 56N 98 8W
Hecla I. 109 51 10N 96 43W
Heddal 47 59 36N 9 9 E
Hédé 18 48 18N 1 49W
Hede 48 62 23N 13 30 E
Hedemora 48 60 18N 15 58 E
Hedley 117 34 53N 100 39W
Hedmark fylke □ 47 61 17N 11 40 E
Hedrum 47 59 7N 10 5 E
Heemstede 16 52 22N 4 37 E
Heerde 16 52 24N 6 2 E
Heerenveen 16 52 57N 5 55 E
Heerlen 16 50 55N 6 0 E
Hefa 62 32 46N 35 0 E
Hefei 75 31 52N 117 18 E
Hegang 75 47 20N 130 19 E
Hegyalja 27 48 25N 21 25 E
Heide 24 54 10N 9 7 E
Heidelberg, Ger. 25 49 23N 8 41 E
Heidelberg, C. Prov., S. Afr. 92 34 6 S 20 59 E
Heidelberg, Trans., S. Afr. 93 26 30 S 28 23 E
Heidenheim 25 48 40N 10 10 E
Heilbron 93 27 16 S 27 59 E
Heilbronn 25 49 8N 9 13 E
Heiligenblut 26 47 2N 12 51 E
Heiligenhafen 24 54 21N 10 58 E
Heiligenstadt 24 51 22N 10 9 E
Heilongjiang □ 75 48 0N 126 0 E
Heilunkiang = Heilongjiang □ 75 48 0N 126 0 E
Heim 47 63 26N 9 5 E
Heinola 51 61 13N 26 2 E
Heinze Is. 71 14 25N 97 45 E
Hejaz = Ḩijāz 64 26 0N 37 30 E
Hejian 76 38 25N 116 5 E
Hejiang 77 28 43N 105 46 E
Hekimhan 64 38 50N 38 0 E
Hekla 50 63 56N 19 35W
Hekou 75 22 30N 103 59 E
Hel 28 54 37N 18 47 E
Helagsfjället 48 62 54N 12 25 E
Helan Shan 76 39 0N 105 55 E
Helechosa 31 39 22N 4 53W
Helena, Ark., U.S.A. 117 34 30N 90 35W
Helena, Mont., U.S.A. 118 46 40N 112 0W
Helensburgh, Austral. 100 34 11 S 151 1 E
Helensburgh, U.K. 14 56 0N 4 44W
Helensville 101 36 41 S 174 29 E
Helez 62 31 36N 34 39 E
Helgasjön 49 57 0N 14 50 E
Helgeroa 47 59 0N 9 45 E
Helgoland 24 54 10N 7 51 E
Heligoland = Helgoland 24 54 10N 7 51 E
Heliopolis 86 30 6N 31 17 E
Hell-Ville 93 13 25 S 48 16 E
Hellebæk 49 56 4N 12 32 E
Helleland 47 58 33N 6 7 E
Hellendoorn 16 52 24N 6 27 E
Hellevoetsluis 16 51 50N 4 8 E
Hellin 33 38 31N 1 40W
Helmand □ 65 31 20N 64 0 E
Helmand → 66 31 12N 61 34 E
Helmand, Hamun 65 31 15N 61 15 E
Helme → 24 51 40N 11 20 E
Helmond 16 51 29N 5 41 E
Helmsdale 14 58 7N 3 40W
Helmstedt 24 52 16N 11 0 E
Helnæs 49 55 9N 10 0 E
Helper 118 39 44N 110 56W
Helsingborg 49 56 3N 12 42 E
Helsinge 49 56 2N 12 12 E
Helsingfors 51 60 15N 25 3 E
Helsingør 49 56 2N 12 35 E
Helsinki 51 60 15N 25 3 E
Helska, Mierzeja 28 54 45N 18 40 E
Helston 13 50 7N 5 17W
Helvellyn 12 54 31N 3 1W
Helwân 86 29 50N 31 20 E
Hemavati → 70 12 30N 76 20 E
Hemet 119 33 45N 116 59W
Hemingford 116 42 21N 103 4W
Hemphill 117 31 21N 93 49W
Hempstead 117 30 5N 96 5W
Hemse 49 57 15N 18 22 E
Hemsö 48 62 43N 18 5 E
Henan □ 75 34 0N 114 0 E
Henares → 32 40 24N 3 30W
Hendaye 20 43 23N 1 47W
Henderson, Argent. 124 36 18 S 61 43W
Henderson, Ky., U.S.A. 114 37 50N 87 38W
Henderson, N.C., U.S.A. 115 36 20N 78 25W
Henderson, Nev., U.S.A. 119 36 2N 115 0W
Henderson, Pa., U.S.A. 115 35 25N 88 40W
Henderson, Tex., U.S.A. 117 32 5N 94 49W
Hendersonville 115 35 21N 82 28W
Hendon 99 28 5 S 151 50 E
Hendorf 46 46 4N 24 55 E
Heng Xian 77 22 40N 109 17 E
Hengdaohezi 76 44 52N 129 0 E
Hengelo 16 52 3N 6 19 E
Hengshan, Hunan, China 77 27 16N 112 45 E
Hengshan, Shaanxi, China 76 37 58N 109 5 E
Hengshui 76 37 41N 115 40 E
Hengyang 75 26 52N 112 33 E
Hénin-Beaumont 19 50 25N 2 58 E
Henlopen, C. 114 38 48N 75 5W
Hennan, L. 48 62 3N 15 46 E
Hennebont 18 47 49N 3 19W
Hennenman 92 27 59 S 27 1 E
Hennessy 117 36 8N 97 53W
Hennigsdorf 24 52 38N 13 13 E
Henrichemont 19 47 20N 2 30 E
Henrietta 117 33 50N 98 15W
Henrietta Maria C. 106 55 9N 82 20W
Henrietta, Ostrov 59 77 6N 156 30 E
Henry 116 41 5N 89 20W
Henryetta 117 35 30N 96 0W
Hensall 112 43 26N 81 30W
Hentiyn Nuruu 75 48 30N 108 30 E
Henty 99 35 30 S 147 0 E
Henzada 67 17 38N 95 26 E
Hephaestia 44 39 55N 25 14 E
Heping 77 24 29N 115 0 E
Heppner 118 45 21N 119 34W
Hepu 77 21 40N 109 12 E
Hepworth 112 44 37N 81 9W
Herad 47 58 8N 6 47 E
Héraðsflói 50 65 42N 14 12W
Héraðsvötn → 50 65 45N 19 25W
Herāt 65 34 20N 62 7 E
Herāt □ 65 35 0N 62 0 E
Hérault □ 20 43 34N 3 15 E
Hérault → 20 43 17N 3 26 E
Herbault 18 47 36N 1 8 E
Herbert → 98 18 31 S 146 17 E
Herbert Downs 98 23 7 S 139 9 E
Herberton 98 17 20 S 145 25 E
Herbiers, Les 18 46 52N 1 0W
Herbignac 18 47 27N 2 18W
Herborn 24 50 40N 8 19 E
Herby 28 50 45N 18 50 E
Hercegnovi 42 42 30N 18 33 E
Herðubreið 50 65 11N 16 21W
Hereford, U.K. 13 52 4N 2 42W
Hereford, U.S.A. 117 34 50N 102 28W
Hereford and Worcester □ 13 52 10N 2 30W
Herefoss 47 58 32N 8 23 E
Herentals 16 51 12N 4 51 E
Herfølge 49 55 26N 12 9 E
Herford 24 52 7N 8 40 E
Héricourt 19 47 32N 6 45 E
Herington 116 38 43N 97 0W
Herisau 25 47 22N 9 17 E
Hérisson 20 46 32N 2 42 E
Herkimer 114 43 0N 74 59W
Herm 18 49 30N 2 28W
Hermagor 26 46 38N 13 23 E
Herman 116 45 51N 96 8W
Hermann 116 38 40N 91 25W
Hermannsburg 24 52 49N 10 6 E
Hermanus 92 34 27 S 19 12 E
Herment 20 45 45N 2 24 E
Hermidale 99 31 30 S 146 42 E
Hermiston 118 45 50N 119 16W
Hermitage 101 43 44 S 170 5 E
Hermite, I. 128 55 50 S 68 0W
Hermon, Mt. = Ash Shaykh, J. 64 33 20N 35 51 E
Hermosillo 120 29 10N 111 0W
Hernad → 27 47 56N 21 8 E
Hernandarias 125 25 20 S 54 40W
Hernando, Argent. 124 32 28 S 63 40W
Hernando, U.S.A. 117 34 50N 89 59W
Herne 24 51 33N 7 12 E
Herne Bay 13 51 22N 1 8 E
Herning 49 56 8N 8 58 E
Heroica Nogales = Nogales 120 31 20N 110 56W
Heron Bay 106 48 40N 86 25W
Herowābād 64 38 37N 48 32 E
Herreid 116 45 53N 100 5W
Herrera 31 37 26N 4 55W
Herrera de Alcántar 31 39 39N 7 25W
Herrera de Pisuerga 30 42 35N 4 20W
Herrera del Duque 31 39 10N 5 3W
Herrick 99 41 5 S 147 55 E
Herrin 117 37 50N 89 0W
Herrljunga 49 58 5N 13 1 E
Hersbruck 25 49 30N 11 25 E
Herstal 16 50 40N 5 38 E
Hersvik 47 61 10N 4 53 E
Hertford 13 51 47N 0 4W
Hertford □ 13 51 51N 0 5W
's-Hertogenbosch 16 51 42N 5 17 E
Hertzogville 92 28 9 S 25 30 E
Hervás 30 40 16N 5 52W
Hervey B. 97 25 0 S 152 52 E
• Hervey Is. 95 19 30 S 159 0W
Herzberg, Cottbus, Ger. 24 51 40N 13 13 E
Herzberg, Niedersachsen, Ger. 24 51 38N 10 20 E
Herzliyya 62 32 10N 34 50 E
Herzogenburg 26 48 17N 15 41 E
Hesdin 19 50 21N 2 0 E
Hesel 24 53 18N 7 36 E
Heskestad 47 58 28N 6 22 E
Hespeler 112 43 26N 80 19W
Hesse = Hessen 24 50 40N 9 20 E
Hessen □ 24 50 40N 9 20 E
Hettinger 116 46 0N 102 38W
Hettstedt 24 51 39N 11 30 E
Hève, C. de la 18 49 30N 0 5 E
Heves □ 27 47 50N 20 0 E
Hevron → 62 31 12N 34 42 E
Hewett, C. 105 70 16N 67 45W
Hex River 92 33 30 S 19 35 E
Hexham 12 54 58N 2 7W
Hexigten Qi 76 43 18N 117 30 E
Heyfield 100 37 59 S 146 47 E
Heysham 12 54 5N 2 53W
Heywood 99 38 8 S 141 37 E
Hi-no-Misaki 74 35 26N 132 38 E
Hialeah 115 25 49N 80 17W
Hiawatha, Kans., U.S.A. 116 39 55N 95 33W
Hiawatha, Utah, U.S.A. 118 39 29N 111 1W
Hibbing 116 47 30N 93 0W
Hickman 117 36 35N 89 8W
Hickory 115 35 46N 81 17W
Hicks Pt. 97 37 49 S 149 17 E
Hicksville 113 40 46N 73 30W
Hida 46 47 10N 23 19 E
Hida-Sammyaku 74 36 30N 137 40 E
Hidalgo 120 24 15N 99 26W
Hidalgo del Parral 120 26 58N 105 40W
Hidalgo, Presa M. 120 26 30N 108 35W
Hiddensee 24 54 30N 13 6 E
Hieflau 26 47 36N 14 46 E
Hiendelaencina 32 41 5N 3 0W
Hierro 80 27 44N 18 0 E
Higashiōsaka 74 34 40N 135 37 E
Higgins 117 36 9N 100 1W
High Atlas = Haut Atlas 82 32 30N 5 0W
High I. 107 56 40N 61 10W
High Island 117 29 32N 94 22W
High Level 108 58 31N 117 8W
High Point 115 35 57N 79 58W
High Prairie 108 55 30N 116 30W
High River 108 50 30N 113 50W
High Springs 115 29 50N 82 40W
High Tatra 27 49 30N 20 00 E
High Wycombe 13 51 37N 0 45W
Highbury 98 16 25 S 143 9 E
Highland □ 14 57 30N 5 0W
Highland Park 114 42 10N 87 50W
Highmore 116 44 35N 99 26W
Highrock L. 109 57 5N 105 32W
Higley 119 33 27N 111 46W
Hihya 86 30 40N 31 36 E
Hiiumaa 54 58 50N 22 45 E
Híjar 32 41 10N 0 27W
Ḩijārah, Şaḩrā' al 64 30 25N 44 30 E
Hiko 119 37 30N 115 13W
Hikone 74 35 15N 136 10 E
Hildburghhausen 25 50 24N 10 43 E
Hildesheim 24 52 9N 9 55 E
Hill City, Idaho, U.S.A. 118 43 20N 115 2W
Hill City, Kans., U.S.A. 116 39 25N 99 51W
Hill City, Minn., U.S.A. 116 46 57N 93 35W
Hill City, S.D., U.S.A. 116 43 58N 103 35W
Hill Island L. 109 60 30N 109 50W
Hillared 49 57 37N 13 10 E
Hillegom 16 52 18N 4 35 E
Hillerød 49 55 56N 12 19 E
Hillerstorp 49 57 20N 13 52 E
Hillingdon 13 51 33N 0 29W
Hillman 114 45 5N 83 52W
Hillmond 109 53 26N 109 41W
Hillsboro, Kans., U.S.A. 116 38 22N 97 10W
Hillsboro, N. Mex., U.S.A. 119 33 0N 107 35W
Hillsboro, N.D., U.S.A. 116 47 23N 97 9W
Hillsboro, N.H., U.S.A. 114 43 8N 71 56W
Hillsboro, Oreg., U.S.A: 118 45 31N 123 0W
Hillsboro, Tex., U.S.A. 117 32 0N 97 10W
Hillsdale, Mich., U.S.A. 114 41 55N 84 40W
Hillsdale, N.Y., U.S.A. 113 42 11N 73 30W
Hillsport 106 49 27N 85 34W
Hillston 97 33 30 S 145 31 E
Hilo 110 19 44N 155 5W
Hilonghilong 73 9 10N 125 45 E
Hilton 112 43 16N 77 48W
Hilversum 16 52 14N 5 10 E
Himachal Pradesh □ 68 31 30N 77 0 E
Himalaya 67 29 0N 84 0 E
Himara 44 40 8N 19 43 E
Himeji 74 34 50N 134 40 E
Himi 74 36 50N 137 0 E
Himmerland 49 56 45N 9 30 E
Ḩimş 64 34 40N 36 45 E
Hinako, Kepulauan 72 0 50N 97 20 E
Hinchinbrook I. 97 18 20 S 146 15 E
Hinckley, U.K. 13 52 33N 1 21W
Hinckley, U.S.A. 118 39 18N 112 41W
Hindås 49 57 42N 12 27 E
Hindaun 68 26 44N 77 5 E
Hindmarsh L. 99 36 5 S 141 55 E
Hindol 69 20 40N 85 10 E
Hindsholm 49 55 30N 10 40 E
Hindu Bagh 68 30 56N 67 50 E
Hindu Kush 65 36 0N 71 0 E
Hindupur 70 13 49N 77 32 E
Hines Creek 108 56 20N 118 40W
Hinganghat 68 20 30N 78 52 E
Hingham 118 48 34N 110 29W
Hingoli 70 19 41N 77 15 E
Hinlopenstretet 4 79 35N 18 40 E
Hinna 85 10 25N 11 35 E
Hinojosa del Duque 31 38 30N 5 9W
Hinsdale 118 48 26N 107 2W
Hinterrhein → 25 46 40N 9 25 E
Hinton, Can. 108 53 26N 117 34W
Hinton, U.S.A. 114 37 40N 80 51W
Hippolytushoef 16 52 54N 4 58 E
Hirakud 69 21 32N 83 51 E
Hirakud Dam 69 21 32N 83 45 E
Hiratsuka 74 35 19N 139 21 E
Hirhafok 83 23 49N 5 45 E
Hîrlău 46 47 23N 27 0 E
Hirosaki 74 40 34N 140 28 E
Hiroshima 74 34 24N 132 30 E
Hiroshima □ 74 34 50N 133 0 E
Hirsoholmene 49 57 30N 10 36 E
Hirson 19 49 55N 4 4 E
Hîrşova 46 44 40N 27 59 E
Hirtshals 49 57 36N 9 57 E
Ḩişn Dibā 65 25 45N 56 16 E
Hispaniola 121 19 0N 71 0W
Hissar 68 29 12N 75 45 E
Hita 74 33 20N 130 58 E
Hitachi 74 36 36N 140 39 E
Hitchin 13 51 57N 0 16W
Hitoyoshi 74 32 13N 130 45 E
Hitra 47 63 30N 8 45 E
Hitzacker 24 53 9N 11 1 E
Ḩiyyon, N. → 62 30 25N 35 10 E
Hjalmar L. 109 61 33N 109 25W
Hjälmare kanal 48 59 20N 15 59 E
Hjälmaren 48 59 18N 15 40 E
Hjartdal 47 59 37N 8 41 E
Hjerkinn 47 62 13N 9 33 E
Hjørring 49 57 29N 9 59 E
Hjorted 49 57 37N 16 19 E
Hjortkvarn 49 58 54N 15 26 E
Hlinsko 26 49 45N 15 54 E
Hlohovec 27 48 26N 17 49 E
Hńak 4 70 40N 52 10W
Ho 85 6 37N 0 27 E
Ho Chi Minh, Phanh Bho 71 10 58N 106 40 E
Hoa Binh 71 20 50N 105 20 E
Hoai Nhon (Bon Son) 71 14 28N 109 1 E
Hoare B. 105 65 17N 62 30W
Hobart, Austral. 97 42 50 S 147 21 E
Hobart, U.S.A. 117 35 0N 99 5W
Hobbs 117 32 40N 103 3W
Hobbs Coast 5 74 50 S 131 0W
Hoboken, Belg. 16 51 11N 4 21 E
Hoboken, U.S.A. 113 40 45N 74 4W
Hobro 49 56 39N 9 46 E
Hoburgen 49 56 55N 18 7 E
Hochatown 117 34 11N 94 39W
Hochschwab 26 47 35N 15 0 E
Höchst 25 50 6N 8 33 E
Höchstadt 25 49 42N 10 48 E
Hockenheim 25 49 18N 8 33 E
Hodgson 109 51 13N 97 36W
Hódmezövásárhely 27 46 28N 20 22 E
Hodna, Chott el 83 35 30N 5 0 E
Hodna, Monts du 83 35 52N 4 42 E
Hodonín 27 48 50N 17 10 E
Hoëdic 18 47 21N 2 52W
Hoek van Holland 16 52 0N 4 7 E
Hoëveld 93 26 30 S 30 0 E
Hof, Ger. 25 50 18N 11 55 E
Hof, Iceland 50 64 33N 14 40W
Höfðakaupstaður 50 65 50N 20 19W
Hofgeismar 24 51 29N 9 23 E
Hofors 48 60 31N 16 15 E
Hofsjökull 50 64 49N 18 48W
Hofsós 50 65 53N 19 26W
Hōfu 74 34 3N 131 34 E
Hogansville 115 33 14N 84 50W

• Renamed Manuae

Hogeland Hunterville

Hogeland 118 48 51N 108 40W
Hogenakai Falls 70 12 6N 77 50 E
Högfors 48 59 58N 15 3 E
Högsäter 49 58 38N 12 5 E
Högsby 49 57 10N 16 1 E
Högsjö 48 59 4N 15 44 E
Hoh Xil Shan 75 35 0N 89 0 E
Hohe Rhön 25 50 24N 9 58 E
Hohe Tauern 26 47 11N 12 40 E
Hohe Venn 16 50 30N 6 5 E
Hohenau 27 48 36N 16 55 E
Hohenems 26 47 22N 9 42 E
Hohenstein Ernstthal 24 50 48N 12 43 E
Hohenwald 115 35 35N 87 30W
Hohenwestedt 24 54 6N 9 30 E
Hohhot 76 40 52N 111 40 E
Hohoe 85 7 8N 0 32 E
Hoi An 71 15 30N 108 19 E
Hoi Xuan 71 20 25N 105 9 E
Hoisington 116 38 33N 98 50W
Højer 49 54 58N 8 42 E
Hok 49 57 31N 14 16 E
Hökensås 49 58 0N 14 5 E
Hökerum 49 57 51N 13 16 E
Hokianga Harbour 101 35 31 S 173 22 E
Hokitika 101 42 42 S 171 0 E
Hokkaidō □ 74 43 30N 143 0 E
Hokksund 47 59 44N 9 59 E
Hol-Hol 87 11 20N 42 50 E
Holbæk 49 55 43N 11 43 E
Holbrook, Austral. 99 35 42 S 147 18 E
Holbrook, U.S.A. 119 35 54N 110 10W
Holden, Can. 108 53 13N 112 11W
Holden, U.S.A. 118 39 0N 112 26W
Holdenville 117 35 5N 96 25W
Holderness 12 53 45N 0 5W
Holdfast 109 50 58N 105 25W
Holdrege 116 40 26N 99 22W
Hole 47 60 6N 10 12 E
Hole-Narsipur 70 12 48N 76 16 E
Holešov 27 49 20N 17 35 E
Holguín 121 20 50N 76 20W
Holíč 27 48 49N 17 10 E
Hollabrunn 26 48 34N 16 5 E
Hollams Bird I. 92 24 40 S 14 30 E
Holland 114 42 47N 86 7W
Hollandia = Jayapura 73 2 28 S 140 38 E
Höllen 47 58 6N 7 49 E
Hollfeld 25 49 56N 11 18 E
Hollick Kenyon Plateau 5 82 0 S 110 0W
Hollidaysburg 114 40 26N 78 25W
Hollis 117 34 45N 99 55W
Hollister, Calif., U.S.A. 119 36 51N 121 24W
Hollister, Idaho, U.S.A. 118 42 21N 114 40W
Holly 116 38 7N 102 7W
Holly Hill 115 29 15N 81 3W
Holly Springs 117 34 45N 89 25W
Hollywood, Calif., U.S.A. 110 34 7N 118 25W
Hollywood, Fla., U.S.A. 115 26 0N 80 9W
Holm 48 62 40N 16 40 E
Holman Island 104 70 42N 117 41W
Hólmavík 50 65 42N 21 40W
Holmedal 47 61 22N 5 11 E
Holmegil 48 59 10N 11 44 E
Holmestrand 47 59 31N 10 14 E
Holmsbu 47 59 32N 10 27 E
Holmsjön 48 62 26N 15 20 E
Holmsland Klit 49 56 0N 8 5 E
Holmsund 50 63 41N 20 20 E
Holod 46 46 49N 22 8 E
Holon 62 32 2N 34 47 E
Holroyd → 97 14 10 S 141 36 E
Holstebro 49 56 22N 8 37 E
Holsworthy 13 50 48N 4 21W
Holt 50 63 33N 19 48W
Holte 49 55 50N 12 29 E
Holton, Can. 107 54 31N 57 12W
Holton, U.S.A. 116 39 28N 95 44W
Holtville 119 32 50N 115 27W
Holum 47 58 6N 7 32 E
Holwerd 16 53 22N 5 54 E
Holy Cross 104 62 10N 159 52W
Holy I., England, U.K. 12 55 42N 1 48W
Holy I., Wales, U.K. 12 53 17N 4 37W
Holyhead 12 53 18N 4 38W
Holyoke, Colo., U.S.A. 116 40 39N 102 18W
Holyoke, Mass., U.S.A. 114 42 14N 72 37W
Holyrood 107 47 27N 53 8W
Holzkirchen 25 47 53N 11 42 E
Holzminden 24 51 49N 9 31 E
Homa Bay 90 0 36 S 34 30 E
• Homa Bay □ 90 0 50 S 34 30 E
Homalin 67 24 55N 95 0 E
Homberg 24 51 2N 9 20 E
Hombori 85 15 20N 1 38W
Homburg 25 49 19N 7 21 E
Home B. 105 68 40N 67 10W
Home Hill 97 19 43 S 147 25 E
Homedale 118 43 42N 116 59W
Homer, Alaska, U.S.A. 104 59 40N 151 35W
Homer, La., U.S.A. 117 32 50N 93 4W
Homestead, Austral. 98 20 20 S 145 40 E
Homestead, Fla., U.S.A. 115 25 29N 80 27W
Homestead, Oreg., U.S.A. 118 45 5N 116 57W
Hominy 117 36 26N 96 24W
Homnabad 70 17 45N 77 11 E
Homoine 93 23 55 S 35 8 E
Homoljske Planina 42 44 10N 21 45 E
Homorod 46 46 5N 25 15 E
Homs = Ḩimş 64 34 40N 36 45 E
Hon Chong 71 10 25N 104 30 E
Honan = Henan □ 75 34 0N 114 0 E
Honda 126 5 12N 74 45W
Hondeklipbaai 92 30 19 S 17 17 E
Hondo 117 29 22N 99 6W
Hondo → 120 18 25N 88 21W
Honduras ■ 121 14 40N 86 30W
Honduras, Golfo de 120 16 50N 87 0W
Honesdale 113 41 34N 75 17W
Honey L. 118 40 13N 120 14W
Honfleur 18 49 25N 0 13 E
Hong Kong ■ 75 22 11N 114 14 E
Hong'an 77 31 20N 114 40 E
Hongha → 71 22 0N 104 0 E
Honghai Wan 77 22 40N 115 0 E
Honghu 77 29 50N 113 30 E
Hongjiang 75 27 7N 109 59 E
Hongshui He → 75 23 48N 109 30 E
Hongtong 76 36 16N 111 40 E
Honguedo, Détroit d' 107 49 15N 64 0W
Hongze Hu 75 33 15N 118 35 E
Honiara 94 9 27 S 159 57 E
Honiton 13 50 48N 3 11W
Honkorâb, Ras 86 24 35N 35 10 E
Honolulu 110 21 19N 157 52W
Honshū 74 36 0N 138 0 E
Hontoria del Pinar 32 41 50N 3 10W
Hood Mt. 118 45 24N 121 41W
Hood, Pt. 96 34 23 S 119 34 E
Hood River 118 45 45N 121 31W
Hoodsport 118 47 24N 123 7W
Hooge 24 54 31N 8 36 E
Hoogeveen 16 52 44N 6 30 E
Hoogezand 16 53 11N 6 45 E
Hooghly → 69 21 56N 88 4 E
Hooghly-Chinsura 69 22 53N 88 27 E
Hook Hd. 15 52 8N 6 57W
Hook I. 98 20 4 S 149 0 E
Hook of Holland = Hoek van Holland 16 52 0N 4 7 E
Hooker 117 36 55N 101 10W
Hoopeston 114 40 30N 87 40W
Hoopstad 92 27 50 S 25 55 E
Hoorn 16 52 38N 5 4 E
Hoover Dam 119 36 0N 114 45W
Hooversville 112 40 8N 78 57W
Hop Bottom 113 41 41N 75 47W
Hopà 57 41 28N 41 30 E
Hope, Can. 108 49 25N 121 25 E
Hope, Ark., U.S.A. 117 33 40N 93 36W
Hope, N.D., U.S.A. 116 47 21N 97 42W
Hope Bay 5 65 0 S 55 0W
Hope, L. 99 28 24 S 139 18 E
Hope Pt. 104 68 20N 166 50W
Hope Town 121 26 35N 76 57W
Hopedale 107 55 28N 60 13W
Hopefield 92 33 3 S 18 22 E
Hopei = Hebei □ 76 39 0N 116 0 E
Hopelchén 120 19 46N 89 50W
Hopen 47 63 27N 8 2 E
Hopetoun, Vic., Austral. 99 35 42 S 142 22 E
Hopetoun, W. Australia, Austral. 100 33 57 S 120 7 E
Hopetown 92 29 34 S 24 3 E
Hopkins 116 40 31N 94 45W
Hopkins → 100 38 25 S 142 30 E
Hopkinsville 115 36 52N 87 26W
Hopland 118 39 0N 123 7W
Hoptrup 49 55 11N 9 28 E
Hoquiam 118 46 50N 123 55W
Horazdovice 26 49 19N 13 42 E
Horcajo de Santiago 32 39 50N 3 1W
Hordaland fylke □ 47 60 25N 6 15 E
Horden Hills 96 20 40 S 130 20 E
Horezu 46 45 6N 24 0 E
Horgen 25 47 15N 8 35 E
Horgoš 42 46 10N 20 0 E
Horice 26 50 21N 15 39 E
Horlick Mts. 5 84 0 S 102 0W
Hormoz 65 27 35N 55 0 E
Hormoz, Jaz. ye 65 27 8N 56 28 E
Hormuz Str. 65 26 30N 56 30 E
Horn, Austria 26 48 39N 15 40 E
Horn, Ísafjarðarsýsla, Iceland 50 66 28N 22 28W
Horn, Suður-Múlasýsla, Iceland 50 65 10N 13 31W
Horn → 108 61 30N 118 1W
Horn, Cape = Hornos, Cabo de 128 55 50 S 67 30W
Horn Head 15 55 13N 8 0W
Horn, I. 115 30 17N 88 40W
Horn Mts. 108 62 15N 119 15W
Hornachuelos 31 37 50N 5 14W
Hornavan 50 66 15N 17 30 E
Hornbæk 49 56 5N 12 26 E
Hornbeck 117 31 22N 93 20W
Hornbrook 118 41 58N 122 37W
Hornburg 24 52 2N 10 36 E
Horncastle 12 53 13N 0 8W
Horndal 48 60 18N 16 23 E
Hornell 114 42 23N 77 41W
Hornell L. 108 62 20N 119 25W
Hornepayne 106 49 14N 84 48W
Hornindal 47 61 58N 6 30 E
Hornnes 47 58 34N 7 45 E
Hornos, Cabo de 128 55 50 S 67 30W
Hornoy 19 49 50N 1 54 E
Hornsby 99 33 42 S 151 2 E
Hornsea 12 53 55N 0 10W
Hornslandet 48 61 35N 17 37 E
Hornslet 49 56 18N 10 19 E
Hörnum 24 54 44N 8 18 E
Horovice 26 49 48N 13 53 E
Horqin Youyi Qianqi 75 46 5N 122 3 E
Horqueta 124 23 15 S 56 55W
Horra, La 30 41 44N 3 53W
Horred 49 57 22N 12 28 E
Horse Cr. → 116 41 57N 103 58W
Horse Is. 107 50 15N 55 50W
Horsefly L. 108 52 25N 121 0W
Horsens 49 55 52N 9 51 E
Horsens Fjord 49 55 50N 10 0 E
Horseshoe Dam 119 33 45N 111 35W
Horsham, Austral. 97 36 44 S 142 13 E
Horsham, U.K. 13 51 4N 0 20W
Horšovský Týn 26 49 31N 12 58 E
Horten 47 59 25N 10 32 E
Hortobágy → 27 47 30N 21 6 E
Horton 116 39 42N 95 30W
Horton → 104 69 56N 126 52W
Hörvik 49 56 2N 14 45 E
Horwood, L. 106 48 5N 82 20W
Hosaina 87 7 30N 37 47 E
Hosdurga 70 13 49N 76 17 E
Hose, Pegunungan 72 2 5N 114 6 E
Hoshangabad 68 22 45N 77 45 E
Hoshiarpur 68 31 30N 75 58 E
Hosmer 116 45 36N 99 29W
Hospet 70 15 15N 76 20 E
Hospitalet de Llobregat 32 41 21N 2 6 E
Hospitalet, L' 20 42 36N 1 47 E
Hoste, I. 128 55 0 S 69 0W
Hostens 20 44 30N 0 40W
Hot 71 18 8N 98 29 E
Hot Creek Ra. 118 39 0N 116 0W
Hot Springs, Ari., U.S.A. 117 34 30N 93 0W
Hot Springs, S.D., U.S.A. 116 43 25N 103 30W
Hotagen 50 63 50N 14 30 E
Hotan 75 37 25N 79 55 E
Hotazel 92 27 17 S 23 00 E
Hotchkiss 119 38 47N 107 47W
Hoting 50 64 8N 16 15 E
Hotolishti 44 41 10N 20 25 E
Hottentotsbaai 92 26 8 S 14 59 E
Houat 18 47 24N 2 58W
Houck 119 35 15N 109 15W
Houdan 19 48 48N 1 35 E
Houffalize 16 50 8N 5 48 E
Houghton 116 47 9N 88 39W
Houghton L. 114 44 20N 84 40W
Houghton-le-Spring 12 54 51N 1 28W
Houhora 101 34 49 S 173 9 E
Houlton 107 46 5N 67 50W
Houma 117 29 35N 90 44W
Houndé 84 11 34N 3 31W
Hourtin 20 45 11N 1 4W
Hourtin, Étang d' 20 45 10N 1 6W
Houston, Can. 108 54 25N 126 39W
Houston, Mo., U.S.A. 117 37 20N 92 0W
Houston, Tex., U.S.A. 117 29 50N 95 20W
Houtman Abrolhos 96 28 43 S 113 48 E
Hov 49 55 55N 10 15 E
Hova 49 58 53N 14 14 E
Høvåg 47 58 10N 8 16 E
Hovd (Jargalant) 75 48 2N 91 37 E
Hovden 47 59 33N 7 22 E
Hove 13 50 50N 0 10W
Hovmantorp 49 56 47N 15 7 E
Hövsgöl Nuur 75 51 0N 100 30 E
Hovsta 48 59 22N 15 15 E
Howakil 87 15 10N 40 16 E
Howar, Wadi → 87 17 30N 27 8 E
Howard, Austral. 99 25 16 S 152 32 E
Howard, Kans., U.S.A. 117 37 30N 96 16W
Howard, Pa., U.S.A. 112 41 0N 77 40W
Howard, S.D., U.S.A. 116 44 2N 97 30W
Howard L. 109 62 15N 105 57W
Howe 118 43 48N 113 0W
Howe, C. 97 37 30 S 150 0 E
Howell 114 42 38N 83 56W
Howick, Can. 113 45 11N 73 51W
Howick, S. Afr. 93 29 28 S 30 14 E
Howick Group 98 14 20 S 145 30 E
Howitt, L. 99 27 40 S 138 40 E
Howley 107 49 12N 57 2W
Howrah 69 22 37N 88 20 E
Howth Hd. 15 53 21N 6 0W
Höxter 24 51 45N 9 26 E
Hoy I. 14 58 50N 3 15W
Hoya 24 52 47N 9 10 E
Hoyerswerda 24 51 26N 14 14 E
Hoyos 30 40 9N 6 45W
Hpungan Pass 67 27 30N 96 55 E
Hrádec Králové 26 50 15N 15 50 E
Hrádek 27 48 46N 16 16 E
Hranice 27 49 34N 17 45 E
Hron → 27 47 49N 18 45 E
Hrubieszów 28 50 49N 23 51 E
Hrubý Nizký Jeseník 27 50 7N 17 10 E
Hrvatska 39 45 20N 16 0 E
Hrvatska □ 42 45 20N 18 0 E
Hsenwi 67 23 22N 97 55 E
Hsiamen = Xiamen 75 24 25N 118 4 E
Hsian = Xi'an 77 34 15N 109 0 E
Hsinhailien = Lianyungang 77 34 40N 119 11 E
Hsüchou = Xuzhou 77 34 18N 117 18 E
Hua Hin 71 12 34N 99 58 E
Hua Xian, Henan, China 77 35 30N 114 30 E
Hua Xian, Shaanxi, China 77 34 30N 109 48 E
Huacheng 77 24 4N 115 37 E
Huacho 126 11 10 S 77 35W
Huachón 126 10 35 S 76 0W
Huachuan 76 46 50N 130 21 E
Huade 76 41 55N 113 59 E
Huadian 76 43 0N 126 40 E
Huai He → 75 33 0N 118 30 E
Huai'an 77 33 30N 119 10 E
Huaide 76 43 30N 124 40 E
Huainan 75 32 38N 116 58 E
Huaiyang 77 33 40N 114 52 E
Huaiyuan 77 24 31N 108 22 E
Huajianzi 76 41 23N 125 20 E
Huajuapan de Leon 120 17 50N 97 48W
Hualian 77 23 59N 121 37 E
Huallaga → 126 5 0 S 75 30W
Hualpai Pk. 119 35 8N 113 58W
Huambo 89 12 42 S 15 54 E
Huan Jiang → 76 34 28N 109 0 E
Huan Xian 76 36 33N 107 7 E
Huancabamba 126 5 10 S 79 15W
Huancane 126 15 10 S 69 44W
Huancapi 126 13 40 S 74 0W
Huancavelica 126 12 50 S 75 5W
Huancayo 126 12 5 S 75 12W
Huang He 75 37 55N 118 50 E
Huangchuan 77 32 15N 115 10 E
Huangliu 75 18 20N 108 50 E
Huanglong 76 35 30N 109 59 E
Huangshi 75 30 10N 115 3 E
Huangyan 77 28 38N 121 19 E
Huánuco 126 9 55 S 76 15W
Huaraz 126 9 30 S 77 32W
Huarmey 126 10 5 S 78 5W
Huascarán 126 9 8 S 77 36W
Huasco 124 28 30 S 71 15W
Huasco → 124 28 27 S 71 13W
Huatabampo 120 26 50N 109 50W
Huay Namota 120 21 56N 104 30W
Huayllay 126 11 03 S 76 21W
Hubbard 117 31 50N 96 50W
Hubbart Pt. 109 59 21N 94 41W
Hubei □ 75 31 0N 112 0 E
Hubli 70 15 22N 75 15 E
Hückelhoven-Ratheim 24 51 6N 6 13 E
Huczwa → 28 50 49N 23 58 E
Huddersfield 12 53 38N 1 49W
Hudi 86 17 43N 34 18 E
Hudiksvall 48 61 43N 17 10 E
Hudson, Can. 109 50 6N 92 09W
Hudson, Mass., U.S.A. 113 42 23N 71 35W
Hudson, Mich., U.S.A. 114 41 50N 84 20W
Hudson, N.Y., U.S.A. 114 42 15N 73 46W
Hudson, Wis., U.S.A. 116 44 57N 92 45W
Hudson, Wyo., U.S.A. 118 42 54N 108 37W
Hudson → 114 40 42N 74 2W
Hudson Bay, Can. 105 60 0N 86 0W
Hudson Bay, Sask., Can. 109 52 51N 102 23W
Hudson Falls 114 43 18N 73 34W
Hudson Hope 108 56 0N 121 54W
Hudson Mts. 5 74 32 S 99 20W
Hudson Str. 105 62 0N 70 0W
Hue 71 16 30N 107 35 E
Huebra → 30 41 2N 6 48W
Huedin 46 46 52N 23 2 E
Huelgoat 18 48 22N 3 46W
Huelma 33 37 39N 3 28W
Huelva 31 37 18N 6 57W
Huelva □ 31 37 40N 7 0W
Huelva → 31 37 27N 6 0W
Huentelauquén 124 31 38 S 71 33W
Huércal Overa 33 37 23N 1 57W
Huerta, Sa. de la 124 31 10 S 67 30W
Huertas, C. de las 33 38 21N 0 24W
Huerva → 32 41 39N 0 52W
Huesca 32 42 8N 0 25W
Huesca □ 32 42 20N 0 1 E
Huéscar 33 37 44N 2 35W
Huetamo 120 18 36N 100 54W
Huete 32 40 10N 2 43W
Hugh → 96 25 1 S 134 1 E
Hughenden 97 20 52 S 144 10 E
Hughes 104 66 0N 154 20W
Hugo 116 39 12N 103 27W
Hugoton 117 37 11N 101 22W
Hui Xian 76 35 27N 113 12 E
Hui'an 77 25 1N 118 43 E
Huichang 77 25 32N 115 45 E
Huichapán 120 20 24N 99 40W
Huihe 76 48 12N 119 17 E
Huila, Nevado del 126 3 0N 76 0W
Huilai 77 23 0N 116 18 E
Huimin 76 37 27N 117 28 E
Huinan 76 42 40N 126 2 E
Huinca Renancó 124 34 51 S 64 22W
Huining 76 35 38N 105 0 E
Huinong 76 39 5N 106 35 E
Huisne → 18 47 59N 0 11 E
Huize 75 26 24N 103 15 E
Huizhou 77 23 0N 114 23 E
Hukawng Valley 67 26 30N 96 30 E
Hukou 77 29 45N 116 21 E
Hukuntsi 92 23 58 S 21 45 E
Hula 87 6 33N 38 30 E
Hulan 75 46 1N 126 37 E
Ḩulayfā' 64 25 58N 40 45 E
Huld 75 45 5N 105 30 E
Hulda 62 31 50N 34 51 E
Hulin 76 45 48N 132 59 E
Hull, Can. 106 45 25N 75 44W
Hull, U.K. 12 53 45N 0 20W
Hull → 12 53 43N 0 25W
Hulst 16 51 17N 4 2 E
Hultsfred 49 57 30N 15 52 E
Hulun Nur 75 49 0N 117 30 E
Huma 76 51 43N 126 38 E
Huma He → 76 51 42N 126 42 E
Humahuaca 124 23 10 S 65 25W
Humaitá, Brazil 126 7 35 S 63 1W
Humaitá, Parag. 124 27 2 S 58 31W
Humansdorp 92 34 2 S 24 46 E
Humbe 92 16 40 S 14 55 E
Humber → 12 53 40N 0 10W
Humberside □ 12 53 50N 0 30W
Humble 117 29 59N 93 18W
Humboldt, Can. 109 52 15N 105 9W
Humboldt, Iowa, U.S.A. 116 42 42N 94 15W
Humboldt, Tenn., U.S.A. 117 35 50N 88 55W
Humboldt → 118 40 2N 118 31W
Humboldt Gletscher 4 79 30N 62 0W
Hume, L. 97 36 0 S 147 0 E
Humenné 27 48 55N 21 50 E
Humphreys Pk. 119 35 24N 111 38W
Humpolec 26 49 31N 15 20 E
Hūn 83 29 2N 16 0 E
Húnaflói 50 65 50N 20 50W
Hunan □ 75 27 30N 112 0 E
Hunchun 76 42 52N 130 28 E
Hundested 49 55 58N 11 52 E
Hundred Mile House 108 51 38N 121 18W
Hunedoara 46 45 40N 22 50 E
Hunedoara □ 46 45 50N 22 54 E
Hünfeld 24 50 40N 9 47 E
Hungary ■ 27 47 20N 19 20 E
Hungary, Plain of 9 47 0N 20 0 E
Hungerford 99 28 58 S 144 24 E
Hŭngnam 76 39 49N 127 45 E
Huni Valley 84 5 33N 1 56W
Hunsberge 92 27 45 S 17 12 E
Hunsrück 25 49 30N 7 0 E
Hunstanton 12 52 57N 0 30 E
Hunsur 70 12 16N 76 16 E
Hunte → 24 52 30N 8 19 E
Hunter, N.D., U.S.A. 116 47 12N 97 17W
Hunter, N.Y., U.S.A. 113 42 13N 74 13W
Hunter → 100 32 52 S 151 46 E
Hunter I., Austral. 97 40 30 S 144 45 E
Hunter I., Can. 108 51 55N 128 0W
Hunter Ra. 99 32 45 S 150 15 E
Hunters Road 91 19 9 S 29 49 E
Hunterton 99 26 12 S 148 30 E
Hunterville 101 39 56 S 175 35 E

• *Renamed South Nyanza*

Huntingburg   Inthanon, Doi

Huntingburg **114** 38 20N 86 58W
Huntingdon, Can. **106** 45 6N 74 10W
Huntingdon, U.K. **13** 52 20N 0 11W
Huntingdon, U.S.A. **114** 40 28N 78 1W
Huntington, Ind., U.S.A. **114** 40 52N 85 30W
Huntington, N.Y., U.S.A. **113** 40 52N 73 25W
Huntington, Oreg., U.S.A. **118** 44 22N 117 21W
Huntington, Ut., U.S.A. **118** 39 24N 111 1W
Huntington, W. Va., U.S.A. **114** 38 20N 82 30W
Huntington Beach **119** 33 40N 118 0W
Huntington Park **119** 33 58N 118 15W
Huntly, N.Z. **101** 37 34S 175 11 E
Huntly, U.K. **14** 57 27N 2 48W
Huntsville, Can. **106** 45 20N 79 14W
Huntsville, Ala., U.S.A. **115** 34 45N 86 35W
Huntsville, Tex., U.S.A. **117** 30 45N 95 35W
Hunyani → **91** 15 57S 30 39 E
Huo Xian **76** 36 36N 111 42 E
Huon, G. **98** 7 0S 147 30 E
Huonville **97** 43 0S 147 5 E
Huoqiu **77** 32 20N 116 12 E
Huoshao Dao **77** 22 40N 121 30 E
Hupeh □ = Hubei □ **75** 31 0N 112 0 E
Hurbanovo **27** 47 51N 18 11 E
Hure Qi **76** 42 45N 121 45 E
Hurezani **46** 44 49N 23 40 E
Hurghada **86** 27 15N 33 50 E
Hurley, N. Mex., U.S.A. **119** 32 45N 108 7W
Hurley, Wis., U.S.A. **116** 46 26N 90 10W
Huron, Ohio, U.S.A. **112** 41 22N 82 34W
Huron, S.D., U.S.A. **116** 44 22N 98 12W
Huron, L. **112** 45 0N 83 0W
Hurricane **119** 37 10N 113 12W
Hurso **87** 9 35N 41 33 E
Hurum, Buskerud, Norway **47** 59 36N 10 23 E
Hurum, Oppland, Norway **47** 61 9N 8 46 E
Hurunui → **101** 42 54S 173 18 E
Hurup **49** 56 46N 8 25 E
Húsavík **50** 66 3N 17 21W
Huşi **46** 46 41N 28 7 E
Huskvarna **49** 57 47N 14 15 E
Husøy **47** 61 3N 4 44 E
Hussar **108** 51 3N 112 41W
Hustopéce **27** 48 57N 16 43 E
Husum, Ger. **24** 54 27N 9 3 E
Husum, Sweden **48** 63 21N 19 12 E
Hutchinson, Kans., U.S.A. **117** 38 3N 97 59W
Hutchinson, Minn., U.S.A. **116** 44 50N 94 22W
Hutou **76** 45 58N 133 38 E
Huttenberg **26** 46 56N 14 33 E
Hüttental **24** 50 52N 8 1 E
Huttig **117** 33 5N 92 10W
Hutton, Mt. **99** 25 51S 148 20 E
Huwun **87** 4 23N 40 6 E
Ḩuwwārah **62** 32 9N 35 15 E
Huy **16** 50 31N 5 15 E
Hvaler **47** 59 4N 11 1 E
Hvammur **50** 65 13N 21 49W
Hvar **39** 43 11N 16 28 E
Hvarski Kanal **39** 43 15N 16 35 E
Hvitá **50** 64 40N 21 5W
Hvitá → **50** 64 0N 20 58W
Hvitárvatn **50** 64 37N 19 50W
Hvitsten **47** 59 35N 10 42 E
Hwang Ho = Huang He → **76** 37 50N 118 50 E
Hyannis **116** 42 0N 101 45W
Hyargas Nuur **75** 49 0N 93 0 E
Hyatts **114** 38 59N 76 55W
Hybo **48** 61 49N 16 15 E
Hyderabad, India **70** 17 22N 78 29 E
Hyderabad, Pak. **68** 25 23N 68 24 E
* Hyderabad □ **68** 25 3N 68 24 E
Hyères **21** 43 8N 6 9 E
Hyères, Îles d' **21** 43 0N 6 28 E
Hyesan **76** 41 20N 128 10 E
Hyland → **108** 59 52N 128 12W
Hylestad **47** 59 6N 7 29 E
Hyltebruk **49** 56 59N 13 15 E
Hyndman Pk. **118** 43 50N 114 10W
Hyōgo □ **74** 35 15N 135 0 E
Hyrum **118** 41 35N 111 56W
Hysham **118** 46 21N 107 11W
Hythe **13** 51 4N 1 5 E
Hyvinkää **51** 60 38N 24 50 E

I

I-n-Azaoua **83** 20 45N 7 31 E
I-n-Échaï **82** 20 10N 2 5W
I-n-Gall **85** 16 51N 7 1 E
I-n-Tabedog **82** 19 48N 1 11 E
Iabès, Erg **82** 27 30N 2 2W
Iaco → **126** 9 3S 68 34W
Iacobeni **46** 47 25N 25 20 E
Iakora **93** 23 6S 46 40 E
Ialomiţa □ **46** 44 30N 27 30 E
Ialomiţa → **46** 44 42N 27 51 E
Ianca **46** 45 6N 27 29 E
Iara **46** 46 31N 23 35 E
Iaşi **46** 47 20N 27 0 E
Iba **73** 15 22N 120 0 E
Ibadan **85** 7 22N 3 58 E
Ibagué **126** 4 20N 75 20W
Iballja **44** 42 12N 20 0 E
Ibăneşti **46** 46 45N 24 50 E
Ibar → **42** 43 43N 20 45 E
Ibaraki □ **74** 36 10N 140 10 E
Ibarra **126** 0 21N 78 7W
Ibba **87** 4 49N 29 2 E
Ibba, Bahr el **87** 5 30N 28 55 E
Ibbenbüren **24** 52 16N 7 41 E
Ibembo **90** 2 35N 23 35 E
Ibera, Laguna **124** 28 30S 57 9W
Iberian Peninsula **8** 40 0N 5 0W
Iberville **106** 45 19N 73 17W
Iberville, Lac d' **106** 55 55N 73 15W
Ibi **85** 8 15N 9 44 E
Ibiá **127** 19 30S 46 30W
Ibicuy **124** 33 55S 59 10W
Ibioapaba, Sa. da **127** 4 0S 41 30W
Ibiza **33** 38 54N 1 26 E
Íblei, Monti **41** 37 15N 14 45 E
Ibo **91** 12 22S 40 40 E
Ibonma **73** 3 29S 133 31 E
Ibotirama **127** 12 13S 43 12W
İbriktepe **44** 41 2N 26 33 E
Ibshawâi **86** 29 21N 30 40 E
Ibu **73** 1 35N 127 33 E
Iburg **24** 52 10N 8 3 E
Icá **126** 14 0S 75 48W
Iça → **126** 2 55S 67 58W
Içana **126** 0 21N 67 19W
Iceland ■ **50** 65 0N 19 0W
Icha **59** 55 30N 156 0 E
Ich'ang = Yichang **75** 30 40N 111 20 E
Ichchapuram **70** 19 10N 84 40 E
Ichihara **74** 35 28N 140 5 E
Ichihawa **74** 35 44N 139 55 E
Ichilo → **126** 15 57S 64 50W
Ichinomiya **74** 35 18N 136 48 E
Ichnya **54** 50 52N 32 24 E
Icht **82** 29 6N 8 54W
Icy Str. **108** 58 20N 135 30W
Ida Grove **116** 42 20N 95 25W
Idabel **117** 33 53N 94 50W
Idaga Hamus **87** 14 13N 39 48 E
Idah **85** 7 5N 6 40 E
Idaho □ **118** 44 10N 114 0W
Idaho City **118** 43 50N 115 52W
Idaho Falls **118** 43 30N 112 1W
Idaho Springs **118** 39 49N 105 30W
Idanha-a-Nova **30** 39 50N 7 15W
Idar-Oberstein **25** 49 43N 7 19 E
Idd el Ghanam **81** 11 30N 24 19 E
Iddan **63** 6 10N 48 55 E
Idehan **83** 27 10N 11 30 E
Idehan Marzūq **83** 24 50N 13 51 E
Idelès **83** 23 50N 5 53 E
Idfû **86** 25 0N 32 49 E
Ídhi Óros **45** 35 15N 24 45 E
Ídhra **45** 37 20N 23 28 E
Idi **72** 5 2N 97 37 E
Idi Amin Dada, L. = Edward, L. **90** 0 25S 29 40 E
Idiofa **88** 4 55S 19 42 E
Idkerberget **48** 60 22N 15 15 E
Idku, Bahra el **86** 31 18N 30 18 E
Idlip **64** 35 55N 36 38 E
Idna **62** 31 34N 34 58 E
Idrija **39** 46 0N 14 5 E
Idritsa **54** 56 25N 28 30 E
Idstein **25** 50 13N 8 17 E
Idutywa **93** 32 8S 28 18 E
Ieper **16** 50 51N 2 53 E
Ierápetra **45** 35 0N 25 44 E
Ierissós **44** 40 22N 23 52 E
Ierissóu Kólpos **44** 40 27N 23 57 E
Ierzu **40** 39 48N 9 32 E
Iesi **39** 43 32N 13 12 E
Ifach, Punta **33** 38 38N 0 5 E
Ifanadiana **93** 21 19S 47 39 E
Ife **85** 7 30N 4 31 E
Iférouâne **85** 19 5N 8 24 E
Iffley **98** 18 53S 141 12 E
Ifni **82** 29 29N 10 12W
Ifon **85** 6 58N 5 40 E
Iforas, Adrar des **85** 19 40N 1 40 E
Ifrane **82** 33 33N 5 7W
Iganga **90** 0 37N 33 28 E
Igarapava **127** 20 3S 47 47W
Igarapé Açu **127** 1 4S 47 33W
Igarka **59** 67 30N 86 33 E
Igatimi **125** 24 5S 55 40W
Igatpuri **70** 19 40N 73 35 E
Igbetti **85** 8 44N 4 8 E
Igbo-Ora **85** 7 29N 3 15 E
Igboho **85** 8 53N 3 50 E
Iggesund **48** 61 39N 17 10 E
Ighil Izane **82** 35 44N 0 31 E
Iglene **82** 22 57N 4 58 E
Iglésias **40** 39 19N 8 27 E
Igli **82** 30 25N 2 19W
Igloolik **105** 69 20N 81 49W
Igma **82** 29 9N 6 24W
Igma, Gebel el **86** 28 55N 34 0 E
Ignace **106** 49 30N 91 40W
Igoshevo **55** 59 25N 42 35 E
Igoumenítsa **44** 39 32N 20 18 E
Iguaçu → **125** 25 36S 54 36W
Iguaçu, Cat. del **125** 25 41S 54 26W
Iguala **120** 18 20N 99 40W
Igualada **32** 41 37N 1 37 E
Iguassu = Iguaçu **125** 25 41N 54 26W
Iguatu **127** 6 20S 39 18W
Iguéla **88** 2 0S 9 16 E
Igunga □ **90** 4 20S 33 45 E
Ihiala **85** 5 51N 6 55 E
Ihosy **93** 22 24S 46 8 E
Ihotry, L. **93** 21 56S 43 41 E
Ii **50** 65 19N 25 22 E
Iida **74** 35 35N 137 50 E
Iijoki → **50** 65 20N 25 20 E
Iisalmi **50** 63 32N 27 10 E
Iizuka **74** 33 38N 130 42 E
Ijebu-Igbo **85** 6 56N 4 1 E
Ijebu-Ode **85** 6 47N 3 58 E
IJmuiden **16** 52 28N 4 35 E
IJssel → **16** 52 35N 5 50 E
IJsselmeer **16** 52 45N 5 20 E
Ijuí → **125** 27 58S 55 20W
Ikale **85** 7 40N 5 37 E
Ikare **85** 7 32N 5 40 E
Ikaría **45** 37 35N 26 10 E
Ikast **49** 56 8N 9 10 E
Ikeja **85** 6 36N 3 23 E
Ikela **88** 1 6S 23 6 E
Ikerre-Ekiti **85** 7 25N 5 19 E
Ikhtiman **43** 42 27N 23 48 E
Iki **74** 33 45N 129 42 E
Ikimba L. **90** 1 30S 31 20 E
Ikire **85** 7 23N 4 15 E
Ikom **85** 6 0N 8 42 E
Ikopa → **93** 16 45S 46 40 E
Ikot Ekpene **85** 5 12N 7 40 E
Ikungu **90** 1 33S 33 42 E
Ikurun **85** 7 54N 4 40 E
Ila **85** 8 0N 4 39 E
Ilagan **73** 17 7N 121 53 E
Ilam **69** 26 58N 87 58 E
Ilanskiy **59** 56 14N 96 3 E
Ilaro **85** 6 53N 3 3 E
Iława **28** 53 36N 19 34 E
Ilayangudi **70** 9 34N 78 37 E
Ilbilbie **98** 21 45S 149 20 E
Île-à-la Crosse **109** 55 27N 107 53W
Île-à-la-Crosse, Lac **109** 55 40N 107 45W
Île-Bouchard, L' **18** 47 7N 0 26 E
Île-de-France **19** 49 0N 2 20 E
Île-sur-le-Doubs, L' **19** 47 26N 6 34 E
Ilebo **88** 4 17S 20 55 E
Ileje □ **91** 9 30S 33 25 E
Ilek **58** 51 32N 53 21 E
Ilek → **52** 51 30N 53 22 E
Ilero **85** 8 0N 3 20 E
Ilesha, Oyo, Nigeria **85** 7 37N 4 40 E
Ilesha, Oyo, Nigeria **85** 8 57N 3 28 E
Ilford **109** 56 4N 95 35W
Ilfov □ **46** 44 20N 26 0 E
Ilfracombe, Austral. **97** 23 30S 144 30 E
Ilfracombe, U.K. **13** 51 13N 4 8W
Ílhavo **30** 40 33N 8 43W
Ilhéus **127** 14 49S 39 2W
Ilia **46** 45 57N 22 40 E
Ilia □ **45** 37 45N 21 35 E
Ilich **58** 40 50N 68 27 E
Iliff **116** 40 50N 103 3W
Iligan **73** 8 12N 124 13 E
Iliki, L. **45** 38 24N 23 15 E
Iliodhrómia **44** 39 12N 23 50 E
Ilion **114** 43 0N 75 3W
Ilirska-Bistrica **39** 45 34N 14 14 E
Ilkal **70** 15 57N 76 8 E
Ilkeston **12** 52 59N 1 19W
Illana B. **73** 7 35N 123 45 E
Illapel **124** 32 0S 71 10W
'Illār **62** 32 23N 35 7 E
Ille **20** 42 40N 2 37 E
Ille-et-Vilaine □ **18** 48 10N 1 30W
Iller → **25** 48 23N 9 58 E
Illescas **30** 40 8N 3 51W
Illiers **18** 48 18N 1 15 E
Illimani **126** 16 30S 67 50W
Illinois □ **111** 40 15N 89 30W
Illinois → **111** 38 55N 90 28W
Illium = Troy **44** 39 57N 26 12 E
Illizi **83** 26 31N 8 32 E
Illora **31** 37 17N 3 53W
Ilm → **24** 51 7N 11 45 E
Ilmen, Oz. **54** 58 15N 31 10 E
Ilmenau **24** 50 41N 10 55 E
Ilo **126** 17 40S 71 20W
Ilobu **85** 7 45N 4 25 E
Iloilo **73** 10 45N 122 33 E
Ilok **42** 45 15N 19 20 E
Ilora **85** 7 45N 3 50 E
Ilorin **85** 8 30N 4 35 E
Iloulya **57** 49 15N 44 2 E
Ilovatka **55** 50 30N 45 50 E
Ilovlya → **57** 49 14N 43 54 E
Iłowa **28** 51 30N 15 10 E
Ilubabor □ **87** 7 25N 35 0 E
Ilukste **54** 55 55N 26 20 E
Ilva Mică **46** 47 17N 24 40 E
Ilwaki **73** 7 55S 126 30 E
Ilyichevsk **56** 46 10N 30 35 E
Iłża **28** 51 10N 21 15 E
Iłżanka → **28** 51 14N 21 48 E
Imabari **74** 34 4N 133 0 E
Imaloto → **93** 23 27S 45 13 E
Imandra, Oz. **52** 67 30N 33 0 E
Imari **74** 33 15N 129 52 E
Imasa **86** 18 0N 36 12 E
Imathía □ **44** 40 30N 22 15 E
Imbâbah **86** 30 5N 31 12 E
Imbler **118** 45 31N 118 0W
Imdahane **82** 32 8N 7 0W
imeni 26 Bakinskikh Komissarov (Neft-chala) **53** 39 19N 49 12 E
imeni 26 Bakinskikh Komissarov (Vyshzha) **53** 39 22N 54 10 E
Imeni Poliny Osipenko **59** 52 30N 136 29 E
Imeri, Serra **126** 0 50N 65 25W
Imerimandroso **93** 17 26S 48 35 E
Imi (Hinna) **87** 6 28N 42 10 E
Imishly **57** 39 49N 48 4 E
Imitek **82** 29 43N 8 10W
Imlay **118** 40 45N 118 9W
Imlay City **112** 43 0N 83 2W
Immenstadt **25** 47 34N 10 13 E
Immingham **12** 53 37N 0 12W
Immokalee **115** 26 25N 81 26W
Imo □ **85** 5 15N 7 20 E
Imola **39** 44 20N 11 42 E
Imotski **42** 43 27N 17 12 E
Imperatriz **127** 5 30S 47 29W
Impéria **38** 43 52N 8 0 E
Imperial, Can. **109** 51 21N 105 28W
Imperial, Calif., U.S.A. **119** 32 52N 115 34W
Imperial, Nebr., U.S.A. **116** 40 38N 101 39W
Imperial Dam **119** 32 50N 114 30W
Impfondo **88** 1 40N 18 0 E
Imphal **67** 24 48N 93 56 E
Imphy **19** 46 56N 3 15 E
İmroz = Gökçeada **44** 40 10N 25 50 E
Imst **26** 47 15N 10 44 E
Imuruan B. **73** 10 40N 119 10 E
In Belbel **82** 27 55N 1 12 E
In Delimane **85** 15 52N 1 31 E
In Rhar **82** 27 10N 1 59 E
In Salah **82** 27 10N 2 32 E
In Tallak **85** 16 19N 3 15 E
Ina **74** 35 50N 138 0 E
Ina-Bonchi **74** 35 45N 137 58 E
Inangahua Junc. **101** 41 52S 171 59 E
Inanwatan **73** 2 10S 132 14 E
Iñapari **126** 11 0S 69 40W
Inari **50** 68 54N 27 5 E
Inarijärvi **50** 69 0N 28 0 E
Inawashiro-Ko **74** 37 29N 140 6 E
Inca **32** 39 43N 2 54 E
Incaguasi **124** 29 12S 71 5W
İnce-Burnu **56** 42 7N 34 56 E
Inchon **76** 37 27N 126 40 E
Incio **30** 42 39N 7 21W
Incomáti → **93** 25 46S 32 43 E
Incudine, L' **21** 41 50N 9 12 E
Inda Silase **87** 14 10N 38 15 E
Indalsälven → **48** 62 36N 17 30 E
Indaw **67** 24 15N 96 5 E
Indbir **87** 8 7N 37 52 E
Independence, Calif., U.S.A. **119** 36 51N 118 14W
Independence, Iowa, U.S.A. **116** 42 27N 91 52W
Independence, Kans., U.S.A. **117** 37 10N 95 43W
Independence, Mo., U.S.A. **116** 39 3N 94 25W
Independence, Oreg., U.S.A. **118** 44 53N 123 12W
Independence Fjord **4** 82 10N 29 0W
Independence Mts. **118** 41 30N 116 2W
Independenţa **46** 45 25N 27 42 E
Inderborskiy **57** 48 30N 51 42 E
India ■ **3** 20 0N 78 0 E
Indian → **115** 27 59N 80 34W
Indian-Antarctic Ridge **94** 49 0S 120 0 E
Indian Cabins **108** 59 52N 117 40W
Indian Harbour **107** 54 27N 57 13W
Indian Head **109** 50 30N 103 41W
Indian Ocean **3** 5 0S 75 0 E
Indiana **114** 40 38N 79 9W
Indiana □ **114** 40 0N 86 0W
Indianapolis **114** 39 42N 86 10W
Indianola, Iowa, U.S.A. **116** 41 20N 93 32W
Indianola, Miss., U.S.A. **117** 33 27N 90 40W
Indiga **52** 67 50N 48 50 E
Indigirka → **59** 70 48N 148 54 E
Inđija **42** 45 6N 20 7 E
Indio **119** 33 46N 116 15W
Indonesia ■ **72** 5 0S 115 0 E
Indore **68** 22 42N 75 53 E
Indramayu **73** 6 21S 108 20 E
Indramayu, Tg. **73** 6 20S 108 20 E
Indravati → **70** 19 20N 80 20 E
Indre □ **19** 46 50N 1 39 E
Indre → **18** 47 16N 0 19 E
Indre-et-Loire □ **18** 47 12N 0 40 E
Indus → **68** 24 20N 67 47 E
Indus, Mouth of the **68** 24 00N 68 00 E
İnebolu **64** 41 55N 33 40 E
İnegöl **64** 40 5N 29 31 E
Ineu **42** 46 26N 21 51 E
Inezgane **82** 30 25N 9 29W
Infante, Kaap **92** 34 27S 20 51 E
Infantes **33** 38 43N 3 1W
Infiernillo, Presa del **120** 18 9N 102 0W
Infiesto **30** 43 21N 5 21W
Ingende **88** 0 12S 18 57 E
Ingenio Santa Ana **124** 27 25S 65 40W
Ingersoll **112** 43 4N 80 55W
Ingham **97** 18 43S 146 10 E
Ingleborough **12** 54 11N 2 23W
Inglewood, Queensland, Austral. **99** 28 25S 151 2 E
Inglewood, Vic., Austral. **99** 36 29S 143 53 E
Inglewood, N.Z. **101** 39 9S 174 14 E
Inglewood, U.S.A. **119** 33 58N 118 21W
Ingólfshöfði **50** 63 48N 16 39W
Ingolstadt **25** 48 45N 11 26 E
Ingomar **118** 46 35N 107 21W
Ingonish **107** 46 42N 60 18W
Ingore **84** 12 24N 15 48W
Ingrid Christensen Coast **5** 69 30S 76 00 E
Ingul → **56** 46 50N 32 15 E
Ingulec **56** 47 42N 33 14 E
Ingulets → **56** 46 41N 32 48 E
Inguri →, U.S.S.R. **57** 42 38N 41 35 E
Inguri →, U.S.S.R. **57** 42 15N 41 48 E
Inhaca, I. **93** 26 1S 32 57 E
Inhafenga **93** 20 36S 33 53 E
Inhambane **93** 23 54S 35 30 E
Inhambane □ **93** 22 30S 34 20 E
Inhaminga **91** 18 26S 35 0 E
Inharrime **93** 24 30S 35 0 E
Inharrime → **93** 24 30S 35 0 E
Iniesta **33** 39 27N 1 45W
Ining = Yining **75** 43 58N 81 10 E
Inirida → **126** 3 55N 67 52W
Inishbofin **15** 53 35N 10 12W
Inishmore **15** 53 8N 9 45W
Inishowen **15** 55 14N 7 15W
Injune **97** 25 53S 148 32 E
Inklin **108** 58 56N 133 5W
Inklin → **108** 58 50N 133 10W
Inkom **118** 42 51N 112 15W
Inle L. **67** 20 30N 96 58 E
Inn → **25** 48 35N 13 28 E
Innamincka **99** 27 44S 140 46 E
Inner Hebrides **14** 57 0N 6 30W
Inner Mongolia = Nei Monggol Zizhiqu □ **76** 42 0N 112 0 E
Inner Sound **14** 57 30N 5 55W
Innerkip **112** 43 13N 80 42W
Innerste → **24** 52 45N 9 40 E
Innetalling I. **106** 56 0N 79 0W
Innisfail, Austral. **97** 17 33S 146 5 E
Innisfail, Can. **108** 52 0N 113 57W
Innsbruck **26** 47 16N 11 23 E
Inny → **15** 53 30N 7 50W
Inongo **88** 1 55S 18 30 E
Inoucdjouac (Port Harrison) **105** 58 25N 78 15W
Inowrocław **28** 52 50N 18 12 E
Inquisivi **126** 16 50S 67 10W
Insein **67** 16 50N 96 5 E
Însurăţei **46** 44 50N 27 40 E
Inta **52** 66 5N 60 8 E
Intendente Alvear **124** 35 12S 63 32W
Interior **116** 43 46N 101 59W
Interlaken **25** 46 41N 7 50 E
International Falls **116** 48 36N 93 25W
Interview I. **71** 12 55N 92 42 E
Inthanon, Doi **71** 18 35N 98 29 E

* *Now part of Sind* □

Intiyaco Janikowo

Intiyaco 124 28 43 S 60 5W
Inútil, B. 128 53 30 S 70 15W
Inuvik 104 68 16N 133 40W
Inveraray 14 56 13N 5 5W
Inverbervie 14 56 50N 2 17W
Invercargill 101 46 24 S 168 24 E
Inverell 97 29 45 S 151 8 E
Invergordon 14 57 41N 4 10W
Invermere 108 50 30N 116 2W
Inverness, Can. 107 46 15N 61 19W
Inverness, U.K. 14 57 29N 4 12W
Inverness, U.S.A. 115 28 50N 82 20W
Inverurie 14 57 15N 2 21W
Investigator Group 96 34 45 S 134 20 E
Investigator Str. 97 35 30 S 137 0 E
Invona 112 40 46N 78 35W
Inya 58 50 28N 86 37 E
Inyanga 91 18 12 S 32 40 E
Inyangani 91 18 5 S 32 50 E
Inyantue 91 18 30 S 26 40 E
Inyazura 91 18 40 S 32 16 E
Inyo Range 119 37 0N 118 0W
Inyokern 119 35 38N 117 48W
Inza 55 53 55N 46 25 E
Inzhavino 55 52 22N 42 30 E
Ioánnina 44 39 42N 20 47 E
Ioánnina (Janinà) □ 44 39 39N 20 57 E
Iola 117 38 0N 95 20W
Ion Corvin 46 44 7N 27 50 E
Iona 14 56 20N 6 25W
Ione, Calif., U.S.A. 118 38 20N 120 56W
Ione, Wash., U.S.A. 118 48 44N 117 29W
Ionia 114 42 59N 85 7W
Ionian Is. = Iónioi Nísoi 45 38 40N 20 0 E
Ionian Sea 35 37 30N 17 30 E
Iónioi Nísoi 45 38 40N 20 0 E
Iori → 57 41 3N 46 17 E
Íos 45 36 41N 25 20 E
Iowa □ 116 42 18N 93 30W
Iowa City 116 41 40N 91 35W
Iowa Falls 116 42 30N 93 15W
Ipala 90 4 30 S 32 52 E
Ipameri 127 17 44 S 48 9W
Ipáti 45 38 52N 22 14 E
Ipatovo 57 45 45N 42 50 E
Ipel → 27 48 10N 19 35 E
Ipiales 126 0 50N 77 37W
Ipin = Yibin 75 28 45N 104 32 E
Ípiros □ 44 39 30N 20 30 E
Ipixuna 126 7 0 S 71 40W
Ipoh 71 4 35N 101 5 E
Ippy 88 6 5N 21 7 E
Ipsala 44 40 55N 26 23 E
Ipsárion Óros 44 40 40N 24 40 E
Ipswich, Austral. 97 27 35 S 152 40 E
Ipswich, U.K. 13 52 4N 1 9 E
Ipswich, Mass., U.S.A. 113 42 40N 70 50W
Ipswich, S.D., U.S.A. 116 45 28N 99 1W
Ipu 127 4 23 S 40 44W
Iput → 54 52 26N 31 2 E
Iquique 126 20 19 S 70 5W
Iquitos 126 3 45 S 73 10W
Iracoubo 127 5 30N 53 10W
Iráklia 45 36 50N 25 28 E
Iráklion 45 35 20N 25 12 E
Iráklion □ 45 35 10N 25 10 E
Irala 125 25 55 S 54 35W
Iramba □ 90 4 30 S 34 30 E
Iran ■ 65 33 0N 53 0 E
Iran, Pegunungan 72 2 20N 114 50 E
Iranamadu Tank 70 9 23N 80 29 E
Īrānshahr 65 27 15N 60 40 E
Irapuato 120 20 40N 101 30W
Iraq ■ 64 33 0N 44 0 E
Irarrar, O. → 82 20 0N 1 30 E
Irati 125 25 25 S 50 38W
Irbid 62 32 35N 35 48 E
Irebu 88 0 40 S 17 46 E
Iregua → 32 42 27N 2 24 E
Ireland ■ 15 53 0N 8 0W
Ireland I. 121 32 16N 64 50W
Ireland's Eye 15 53 25N 6 4W
Irele 85 7 40N 5 40 E
Iret 59 60 3N 154 20 E
Irgiz, Bol. 55 52 10N 49 10 E
Irhârharene 83 27 37N 7 30 E
Irharrhar, O. → 83 28 3N 6 15 E
Irherm 82 30 7N 8 18W
Irhil Mgoun 82 31 30N 6 28W
Irian Jaya □ 73 4 0 S 137 0 E
Irié 84 8 15N 9 10W
Iringa 90 7 48 S 35 43 E
Iringa □ 90 7 48 S 35 43 E
Irinjalakuda 70 10 21N 76 14 E
Iriri → 127 3 52 S 52 37W
Irish Sea 12 54 0N 5 0W
Irkineyeva 59 58 30N 96 49 E
Irkutsk 59 52 18N 104 20 E
Irma 109 52 55N 111 14W
Iroise, Mer d' 18 48 15N 4 45W
Iron Baron 99 32 58 S 137 11 E
Iron Gate = Portile de Fier 46 44 42N 22 30 E
Iron Knob 97 32 46 S 137 8 E
Iron Mountain 114 45 49N 88 4W
Iron River 116 46 6N 88 40W
Ironbridge 13 52 38N 2 29W
Ironstone Kopje 92 25 17 S 24 5 E
Ironton, Mo., U.S.A. 117 37 40N 90 40W
Ironton, Ohio, U.S.A. 114 38 35N 82 40W
Ironwood 116 46 30N 90 10W
Iroquois Falls 106 48 46N 80 41W
Irpen 54 50 30N 30 15 E
Irrara Cr. → 99 29 35 S 145 31 E
Irrawaddy □ 67 17 0N 95 0 E
Irrawaddy → 67 15 50N 95 6 E
Irsina 41 40 45N 16 15 E
Irtysh → 58 61 4N 68 52 E
Irumu 90 1 32N 29 53 E
Irún 32 43 20N 1 52W
Irurzun 32 42 55N 1 50W
Irvine, Can. 109 49 57N 110 16W
Irvine, U.K. 14 55 37N 4 40W
Irvine, U.S.A. 114 37 42N 83 58W
Irvinestown 15 54 28N 7 38W
Irymple 99 34 14 S 142 8 E
Is-sur-Tille 19 47 30N 5 10 E
Isa 85 13 14N 6 24 E
Isaac → 97 22 55 S 149 20 E
Isabel 116 45 27N 101 22W
Isabela, I. 120 21 51N 105 55W
Isabella, Cord. 121 13 30N 85 25W
Ísafjarðardjúp 50 66 10N 23 0W
Ísafjörður 50 66 5N 23 9W
Isagarh 68 24 48N 77 51 E
Isaka 90 3 56 S 32 59 E
Isangi 88 0 52N 24 10 E
Isar → 25 48 49N 12 58 E
Isarco → 39 46 57N 11 18 E
Ísari 45 37 22N 22 0 E
Isbergues 19 50 36N 2 24 E
Isbiceni 46 43 45N 24 40 E
Íschia 40 40 45N 13 51 E
Ise 74 34 25N 136 45 E
Ise-Wan 74 34 43N 136 43 E
Isefjord 49 55 53N 11 50 E
Iseo 38 45 40N 10 3 E
Iseo, L. d' 38 45 45N 10 3 E
Iseramagazi 90 4 37 S 32 10 E
Isère □ 21 45 15N 5 40 E
Isère → 21 44 59N 4 51 E
Iserlohn 24 51 22N 7 40 E
Isérnia 41 41 35N 14 12 E
Iseyin 85 8 0N 3 36 E
Ishikari-Wan (Otaru-Wan) 74 43 25N 141 1 E
Ishikawa □ 74 36 30N 136 30 E
Ishim 58 56 10N 69 30 E
Ishim → 58 57 45N 71 10 E
Ishinomaki 74 38 32N 141 20 E
Ishmi 44 41 33N 19 34 E
Ishpeming 114 46 30N 87 40W
Isigny-sur-Mer 18 49 19N 1 6W
Isil Kul 58 54 55N 71 16 E
Isiolo 90 0 24N 37 33 E
Isiolo □ 90 2 30N 37 30 E
Isipingo Beach 93 30 00 S 30 57 E
Isiro 90 2 53N 27 40 E
Isisford 98 24 15 S 144 21 E
İskenderun 64 36 32N 36 10 E
İskilip 56 40 50N 34 20 E
Iskůr → 43 43 45N 24 25 E
Iskůr, Yazovir 43 42 23N 23 30 E
Iskut → 108 56 45N 131 49W
Isla → 14 56 32N 3 20W
Isla Cristina 31 37 13N 7 17W
Islamabad 66 33 40N 73 10 E
Islamkot 68 24 42N 70 13 E
Islampur 70 17 2N 74 20 E
Island → 108 60 25N 121 12W
Island Falls, Can. 106 49 35N 81 20W
Island Falls, U.S.A. 107 46 0N 68 16W
Island L. 109 53 47N 94 25W
Island Pond 114 44 50N 71 50W
Islands, B. of, Can. 107 49 11N 58 15W
Islands, B. of, N.Z. 101 35 20 S 174 20 E
Islay 14 55 46N 6 10W
Isle → 20 44 55N 0 15W
Isle-Adam, L' 19 49 6N 2 14 E
Isle aux Morts 107 47 35N 59 0W
Isle-Jourdain, L', Gers, France 20 43 36N 1 5 E
Isle-Jourdain, L', Vienne, France 20 46 13N 0 31 E
Isle of Wight □ 13 50 40N 1 20W
Isle Royale 116 48 0N 88 50W
Isleta 119 34 58N 106 46W
Ismail 56 45 22N 28 46 E
Ismâ'ilîya 86 30 37N 32 18 E
Ismaning 25 48 14N 11 41 E
Ismay 116 46 33N 104 44W
Isna 86 25 17N 32 30 E
Isola del Gran Sasso d'Italia 39 42 30N 13 40 E
Ísola del Liri 40 41 39N 13 32 E
Ísola della Scala 38 45 16N 11 0 E
Ísola di Capo Rizzuto 41 38 56N 17 5 E
İsparta 64 37 47N 30 30 E
Isperikh 43 43 43N 26 50 E
Íspica 41 36 47N 14 53 E
İspir 57 40 40N 40 50 E
Israel ■ 62 32 0N 34 50 E
Issia 84 6 33N 6 33W
Issoire 20 45 32N 3 15 E
Issoudun 19 46 57N 2 0 E
Issyk-Kul, Ozero 58 42 25N 77 15 E
Ist 39 44 17N 14 47 E
İstanbul 64 41 0N 29 0 E
Istiaía 45 38 57N 23 9 E
Istok 42 42 45N 20 24 E
Istokpoga, L. 115 27 22N 81 14W
Istra, U.S.S.R. 55 55 55N 36 50 E
Istra, Yugo. 39 45 10N 14 0 E
Istranca Dağları 43 41 48N 27 30 E
Istres 21 43 31N 4 59 E
Istria = Istra 39 45 10N 14 0 E
Itá 124 25 29 S 57 21W
Itabaiana 127 7 18 S 35 19W
Itaberaba 127 12 32 S 40 18W
Itabira 127 19 37 S 43 13W
Itabirito 125 20 15 S 43 48W
Itabuna 127 14 48 S 39 16W
Itaituba 127 4 10 S 55 50W
Itajaí 125 27 50 S 48 39W
Itajubá 125 22 24 S 45 30W
Itaka 91 8 50 S 32 49 E
Italy ■ 36 42 0N 13 0 E
Itampolo 93 24 41 S 43 57 E
Itapecuru-Mirim 127 3 24 S 44 20W
Itaperuna 127 21 10 S 41 54W
Itapetininga 125 23 36 S 48 7W
Itapeva 125 23 59 S 48 59W
Itapicuru →, Bahia, Brazil 127 11 47 S 37 32W
Itapicuru →, Maranhão, Brazil 127 2 52 S 44 12W
Itapuá □ 125 26 40 S 55 40W
Itaquari 125 20 20 S 40 25W
Itaquatiara 126 2 58 S 58 30W
Itaquí 124 29 8 S 56 30W
Itararé 125 24 6 S 49 23W
Itarsi 68 22 36N 77 51 E
Itatí 124 27 16 S 58 15W
Itatuba 126 5 46 S 63 20W
Itchen → 13 50 57N 1 20W
Itéa 45 38 25N 22 25 E
Ithaca 114 42 25N 76 30W
Ithaca = Itháki 45 38 25N 20 43 E
Itháki 45 38 25N 20 40 E
Ito 74 34 58N 139 5 E
Itoman 77 26 7N 127 40 E
Iton → 18 49 9N 1 12 E
Itonamas → 126 12 28 S 64 24W
Itsa 86 29 15N 30 47 E
Íttiri 40 40 38N 8 32 E
Itu, Brazil 125 23 17 S 47 15W
Itu, Nigeria 85 5 10N 7 58 E
Ituaçu 127 13 50 S 41 18W
Ituiutaba 127 19 0 S 49 25W
Itumbiara 127 18 20 S 49 10W
Ituna 109 51 10N 103 24W
Itunge Port 91 9 40 S 33 55 E
Iturbe 124 23 0 S 65 25W
Ituri → 90 1 40N 27 1 E
Iturup, Ostrov 59 45 0N 148 0 E
Ituyuro → 124 22 40 S 63 50W
Itzehoe 24 53 56N 9 31 E
Ivaí → 125 23 18 S 53 42W
Ivalo 50 68 38N 27 35 E
Ivalojoki → 50 68 40N 27 40 E
Ivangorod 54 59 37N 28 40 E
Ivangrad 42 42 51N 19 52 E
Ivanhoe 97 32 56 S 144 20 E
Ivanhoe L. 109 60 25N 106 30W
Ivanić Grad 39 45 41N 16 25 E
Ivanjica 42 43 35N 20 12 E
Ivanjšcice 39 46 12N 16 13 E
Ivankoyskoye Vdkhr. 55 56 37N 36 32 E
Ivano-Frankovsk 56 48 56N 24 43 E
Ivano-Frankovsk (Stanislav) 54 48 40N 24 40 E
Ivanovo, Byelorussia, U.S.S.R. 54 52 7N 25 29 E
Ivanovo, R.S.F.S.R., U.S.S.R. 55 57 5N 41 0 E
Ivato 93 20 37 S 47 10 E
Ivaylovgrad 43 41 32N 26 8 E
Ivdel 52 60 42N 60 24 E
Ivinheima → 125 23 14 S 53 42W
Iviza = Ibiza 33 39 0N 1 30 E
Ivohibe 93 22 31 S 46 57 E
Ivory Coast ■ 84 7 30N 5 0W
Ivösjön 49 56 8N 14 25 E
Ivrea 38 45 30N 7 52 E
Ivugivik, (N.D. d'Ivugivic) 105 62 24N 77 55W
Iwahig 72 8 35N 117 32 E
Iwaki 74 37 3N 140 55 E
Iwakuni 74 34 15N 132 8 E
Iwata 74 34 42N 137 51 E
Iwate □ 74 39 30N 141 30 E
Iwate-San 74 39 51N 141 0 E
Iwo 85 7 39N 4 9 E
IwoniczZdrój 27 49 37N 21 47 E
Ixiamas 126 13 50 S 68 5W
Ixopo 93 30 11 S 30 5 E
Ixtepec 120 16 32N 95 10W
Ixtlán de Juárez 120 17 23N 96 28W
Ixtlán del Río 120 21 5N 104 21W
Izabel, L. de 120 15 30N 89 10W
Izamal 120 20 56N 89 1W
Izberbash 57 42 35N 47 52 E
Izbica 28 50 53N 23 10 E
Izbica Kujawska 28 52 25N 18 30 E
Izegem 16 50 55N 3 12 E
Izgrev 43 43 36N 26 58 E
Izhevsk 52 56 51N 53 14 E
İzmir (Smyrna) 53 38 25N 27 8 E
İzmit 64 40 45N 29 50 E
Iznajar 31 37 15N 4 19W
Iznalloz 33 37 24N 3 30W
Izobil'nyy 57 45 25N 41 44 E
Izola 39 45 32N 13 39 E
Izra 62 32 51N 36 15 E
Izra' 62 32 52N 36 5 E
Iztochni Rodopi 43 41 45N 25 30 E
Izumi-sano 74 34 23N 135 18 E
Izumo 74 35 20N 132 46 E
Izyaslav 54 50 5N 26 50 E
Izyum 56 49 12N 37 19 E

J

Jaba 87 6 20N 35 7 E
Jaba' 62 32 20N 35 13 E
Jabal el Awlîya 87 15 10N 32 31 E
Jabalón → 31 38 53N 4 5W
Jabalpur 69 23 9N 79 58 E
Jabālyah 62 31 32N 34 27 E
Jablah 64 35 20N 36 0 E
Jablanac 39 44 42N 14 56 E
Jablonec 26 50 43N 15 10 E
Jablonica 27 48 37N 17 26 E
Jabłonowo 28 53 23N 19 10 E
Jaboticabal 125 21 15 S 48 17W
Jabukovac 42 44 22N 22 21 E
Jaburu 126 5 30 S 64 0W
Jaca 32 42 35N 0 33W
Jacareí 125 23 20 S 46 0W
Jacarèzinho 125 23 5 S 50 0W
Jáchymov 26 50 22N 12 55 E
Jackman 107 45 35N 70 17W
Jacksboro 117 33 14N 98 15W
Jackson, Austral. 99 26 39 S 149 39 E
Jackson, Ala., U.S.A. 115 31 32N 87 53W
Jackson, Calif., U.S.A. 118 38 19N 120 47W
Jackson, Ky., U.S.A. 114 37 35N 83 22W
Jackson, Mich., U.S.A. 114 42 18N 84 25W
Jackson, Minn., U.S.A. 116 43 35N 95 0W
Jackson, Miss., U.S.A. 117 32 20N 90 10W
Jackson, Mo., U.S.A. 117 37 25N 89 42W
Jackson, Ohio, U.S.A. 114 39 0N 82 40W
Jackson, Tenn., U.S.A. 115 35 40N 88 50W
Jackson, Wyo., U.S.A. 118 43 30N 110 49W
Jackson Bay 101 43 58 S 168 42 E
Jackson, L. 118 43 55N 110 40W
Jacksons 101 42 46 S 171 32 E
Jacksonville, Ala., U.S.A. 115 33 49N 85 45W
Jacksonville, Fla., U.S.A. 115 30 15N 81 38W
Jacksonville, Ill., U.S.A. 116 39 42N 90 15W
Jacksonville, N.C., U.S.A. 115 34 50N 77 29W
Jacksonville, Oreg., U.S.A. 118 42 19N 122 56W
Jacksonville, Tex., U.S.A. 117 31 58N 95 19W
Jacksonville Beach 115 30 19N 81 26W
Jacmel 121 18 14N 72 32W
Jacob Lake 119 36 45N 112 12W
Jacobabad 68 28 20N 68 29 E
Jacobina 127 11 11 S 40 30W
Jacob's Well 62 32 13N 35 13 E
Jacques-Cartier, Mt. 107 48 57N 66 0W
Jacqueville 84 5 12N 4 25W
Jacuí → 125 30 2 S 51 15W
Jacundá → 127 1 57 S 50 26W
Jade 24 53 22N 8 14 E
Jadebusen 24 53 30N 8 15 E
Jadotville = Likasi 91 10 55 S 26 48 E
Jadovnik 42 43 20N 19 45 E
Jadów 28 52 28N 21 38 E
Jadraque 32 40 55N 2 55W
Jādū 83 32 0N 12 0 E
Jaén, Peru 126 5 25 S 78 40W
Jaén, Spain 31 37 44N 3 43W
Jaén □ 31 37 50N 3 30W
Jaerens Rev 47 58 45N 5 45 E
Jafène 82 20 35N 5 30W
Jaffa = Tel Aviv-Yafo 62 32 4N 34 48 E
Jaffa, C. 99 36 58 S 139 40 E
Jaffna 70 9 45N 80 2 E
Jagadhri 68 30 10N 77 20 E
Jagadishpur 69 25 30N 84 21 E
Jagdalpur 70 19 3N 82 0 E
Jagersfontein 92 29 44 S 25 27 E
Jagst → 25 49 14N 9 11 E
Jagtial 70 18 50N 79 0 E
Jaguariaíva 125 24 10 S 49 50W
Jaguaribe → 127 4 25 S 37 45W
Jagüey Grande 121 22 35N 81 7W
Jahangirabad 68 28 19N 78 4 E
Jahrom 65 28 30N 53 31 E
Jailolo 73 1 5N 127 30 E
Jailolo, Selat 73 0 5N 129 5 E
Jainti 69 26 45N 89 40 E
Jaipur 68 27 0N 75 50 E
Jajce 42 44 19N 17 17 E
Jajpur 69 20 53N 86 22 E
Jakarta 73 6 9 S 106 49 E
Jakobstad (Pietarsaari) 50 63 40N 22 43 E
Jakupica 42 41 45N 21 22 E
Jal 117 32 8N 103 8W
Jalai Nur 76 49 27N 117 42 E
Jalalabad, Afghan. 66 34 30N 70 29 E
Jalalabad, India 69 27 41N 79 42 E
Jalalpur Jattan 68 32 38N 74 11 E
Jalapa, Guat. 120 14 39N 89 59W
Jalapa, Mexico 120 19 30N 96 56W
Jalas, Jabal al 64 27 30N 36 30 E
Jalaun 69 26 8N 79 25 E
Jaleswar 69 26 38N 85 48 E
Jalgaon, Maharashtra, India 68 21 0N 75 42 E
Jalgaon, Maharashtra, India 68 21 2N 76 31 E
Jalingo 85 8 55N 11 25 E
Jalisco □ 120 20 0N 104 0W
Jallas → 30 42 54N 9 8W
Jalna 70 19 48N 75 38 E
Jalón → 32 41 47N 1 4W
Jalpa 120 21 38N 102 58W
Jalpaiguri 69 26 32N 88 46 E
Jalq 65 27 35N 62 46 E
Jaluit I. 94 6 0N 169 30 E
Jamaari 85 11 44N 9 53 E
Jamaica ■ 121 18 10N 77 30W
Jamalpur, Bangla. 69 24 52N 89 56 E
Jamalpur, India 69 25 18N 86 28 E
Jamalpurganj 69 23 2N 88 1 E
Jamanxim → 127 4 43 S 56 18W
Jambe 73 1 15 S 132 10 E
Jambi 72 1 38 S 103 30 E
Jambi □ 72 1 30 S 102 30 E
Jambusar 68 22 3N 72 51 E
James → 116 42 52N 97 18W
James B. 106 51 30N 80 0W
James Range 96 24 10 S 132 30 E
James Ross I. 5 63 58 S 57 50W
Jamestown, Austral. 97 33 10 S 138 32 E
Jamestown, S. Afr. 92 31 6 S 26 45 E
Jamestown, Ky., U.S.A. 114 37 0N 85 5W
Jamestown, N.D., U.S.A. 116 46 54N 98 42W
Jamestown, N.Y., U.S.A. 114 42 5N 79 18W
Jamestown, Pa., U.S.A. 112 41 32N 80 27W
Jamestown, Tenn., U.S.A. 115 36 25N 85 0W
Jamkhandi 70 16 30N 75 15 E
Jammā'īn 62 32 8N 35 12 E
Jammalamadugu 70 14 51N 78 25 E
Jammerbugt 49 57 15N 9 20 E
Jammu 68 32 43N 74 54 E
Jammu & Kashmir □ 66 34 25N 77 0 E
Jamnagar 68 22 30N 70 6 E
Jamner 68 20 45N 75 52 E
Jampur 68 29 39N 70 40 E
Jamrud Fort 66 33 59N 71 24 E
Jamshedpur 69 22 44N 86 12 E
Jamtara 69 23 59N 86 49 E
Jämtlands län □ 48 62 40N 13 50 E
Jan Kemp 92 27 55 S 24 51 E
Jan L. 109 54 56N 102 55W
Jan Mayen Is. 4 71 0N 9 0W
Jand 66 33 30N 72 6 E
Janda, Laguna de la 31 36 15N 5 45W
Jandaq 65 34 3N 54 22 E
Jandola 68 32 20N 70 9 E
Jandowae 99 26 45 S 151 7 E
Jándula → 31 38 3N 4 6W
Janesville 116 42 39N 89 1W
Janga 85 10 5N 1 0W
Jangaon 70 17 44N 79 5 E
Jangeru 72 2 20 S 116 29 E
Janikowo 28 52 45N 18 7 E

Janīn Jyväskylä

Janīn 62 32 28N 35 18 E
Janja 42 44 40N 19 17 E
Janjevo 42 42 35N 21 19 E
Janjina 42 42 58N 17 25 E
Jánoshalma 27 46 18N 19 21 E
Jánosháza 27 47 8N 17 12 E
Jánossomorja 27 47 47N 17 11 E
Janów 28 50 44N 19 27 E
Janów Lubelski 28 50 48N 22 23 E
Janów Podlaski 28 52 11N 23 11 E
Janowiec Wielkopolski 28 52 45N 17 30 E
Januária 127 15 25 S 44 25W
Janub Dârfûr □ 87 11 0N 25 0 E
Janub Kordofân □ 87 12 0N 30 0 E
Janville 19 48 10N 1 50 E
Janzé 18 47 55N 1 28W
Jaora 68 23 40N 75 10 E
Japan ■ 74 36 0N 136 0 E
Japan, Sea of 74 40 0N 135 0 E
Japan Trench 94 32 0N 142 0 E
Japara 73 6 30 S 110 40 E
Japen = Yapen 73 1 50 S 136 0 E
Japurá ~ 126 3 8 S 64 46W
Jaque 126 7 27N 78 8W
Jara, La 119 37 16N 106 0W
Jaraicejo 31 39 40N 5 49W
Jaraiz 30 40 4N 5 45W
Jarales 119 34 39N 106 51W
Jarama ~ 32 40 2N 3 39W
Jarandilla 30 40 8N 5 39W
Jaranwala 68 31 15N 73 26 E
Jarash 62 32 17N 35 54 E
Jarbidge 118 41 56N 115 27W
Jardim 124 21 28 S 56 2W
Jardín ~ 33 38 50N 2 10W
Jardines de la Reina, Is. 121 20 50N 78 50W
Jargalant (Kobdo) 75 48 2N 91 37 E
Jargeau 19 47 50N 2 1 E
Jarmen 24 53 56N 13 20 E
Jarnac 20 45 40N 0 11W
Jarny 19 49 9N 5 53 E
Jarocin 28 51 59N 17 29 E
Jaroměr 26 50 22N 15 52 E
Jarosław 27 50 2N 22 42 E
Järpås 49 58 23N 12 57 E
Järpen 48 63 21N 13 26 E
Jarso 87 5 15N 37 30 E
Jarvis 112 42 53N 80 6W
Jarvis I. 95 0 15 S 159 55W
Jarvornik 27 50 23N 17 2 E
Jarwa 69 27 38N 82 30 E
Jaša Tomić 42 45 26N 20 50 E
Jasien 28 51 46N 15 0 E
Jasin 71 2 20N 102 26 E
Jāsk 65 25 38N 57 45 E
Jasło 27 49 45N 21 30 E
Jasper, Alta., Can. 108 52 55N 118 5W
Jasper, Ont., Can. 113 44 52N 75 57W
Jasper, Ala., U.S.A. 115 33 48N 87 16W
Jasper, Fla., U.S.A. 115 30 31N 82 58W
Jasper, Minn., U.S.A. 116 43 52N 96 22W
Jasper, Tex., U.S.A. 117 30 59N 93 58W
Jasper Nat. Park 108 52 50N 118 8W
Jassy = Iaşi 46 47 10N 27 40 E
Jastrebarsko 39 45 41N 15 39 E
Jastrowie 28 53 26N 16 49 E
Jastrzębie Zdrój 27 49 57N 18 35 E
Jászapáti 27 47 32N 20 10 E
Jászárokszállás 27 47 39N 20 1 E
Jászberény 27 47 30N 19 55 E
Jászkiser 27 47 27N 20 20 E
Jászladány 27 47 23N 20 10 E
Jataí 127 17 58 S 51 48W
Jati 68 24 20N 68 19 E
Jatibarang 73 6 28 S 108 18 E
Jatinegara 73 6 13 S 106 52 E
Játiva 33 39 0N 0 32W
Jatobal 127 4 35 S 49 33W
Jatt 62 32 24N 35 2 E
Jaú 125 22 10 S 48 30W
Jauja 126 11 45 S 75 15W
Jaunjelgava 54 56 35N 25 0 E
Jaunpur 69 25 46N 82 44 E
Java = Jawa 73 7 0 S 110 0 E
Java Sea 72 4 35 S 107 15 E
Java Trench 94 10 0 S 110 0W
Javadi Hills 70 12 40N 78 40 E
Jávea 33 38 48N 0 10 E
Javhlant = Ulyasutay 75 47 56N 97 28 E
Javla 70 17 18N 75 9 E
Javron 18 48 25N 0 25W
Jawa 73 7 0 S 110 0 E
Jawor 28 51 4N 16 11 E
Jaworzno 27 50 13N 19 11 E
Jay 117 36 25N 94 46W
Jaya, Puncak 73 3 57 S 137 17 E
Jayapura 73 2 28 S 140 38 E
Jayawijaya, Pegunungan 73 5 0 S 139 0 E
Jayton 117 33 17N 100 35W
Jean 119 35 47N 115 20W
Jean Marie River 104 61 32N 120 38W
Jean Rabel 121 19 50N 73 5W
Jeanerette 117 29 52N 91 38W
Jeanette, Ostrov 59 76 43N 158 0 E
Jeannette 112 40 20N 79 36W
Jebba, Moroc. 82 35 11N 4 43W
Jebba, Nigeria 85 9 9N 4 48 E
Jebel, Bahr el ~ 81 15 38N 32 31 E
Jebel Qerri 87 16 16N 32 50 E
Jedburgh 14 55 28N 2 33W
Jedlicze 27 49 43N 21 40 E
Jedlnia-Letnisko 28 51 25N 21 19 E
Jędrzejów 28 50 35N 20 15 E
Jedwabne 28 53 17N 22 18 E
Jedway 108 52 17N 131 14W
Jeetze ~ 24 53 9N 11 6 E
Jefferson, Iowa, U.S.A. 116 42 3N 94 25W
Jefferson, Ohio, U.S.A. 112 41 40N 80 46W
Jefferson, Tex., U.S.A. 117 32 45N 94 23W
Jefferson, Wis., U.S.A. 116 43 0N 88 49W
Jefferson City, Mo., U.S.A. 116 38 34N 92 10W
Jefferson City, Tenn., U.S.A. 115 36 8N 83 30W
Jefferson, Mt., Nev., U.S.A. 118 38 51N 117 0W
Jefferson, Mt., Oreg., U.S.A. 118 44 45N 121 50W
Jeffersonville 114 38 20N 85 42W
Jega 85 12 15N 4 23 E
Jekabpils 54 56 29N 25 57 E
Jelenia Góra 28 50 50N 15 45 E
Jelenia Góra □ 28 51 0N 15 30 E
Jelgava 54 56 41N 23 49 E
Jelica 42 43 50N 20 17 E
Jelli 87 5 25N 31 45 E
Jellicoe 106 49 40N 87 30W
Jelšava 27 48 37N 20 15 E
Jemaja 72 3 5N 105 45 E
Jember 73 8 11 S 113 41 E
Jembongan 72 6 45N 117 20 E
Jemeppe 16 50 37N 5 30 E
Jemnice 26 49 1N 15 34 E
Jena, Ger. 24 50 56N 11 33 E
Jena, U.S.A. 117 31 41N 92 7W
Jenbach 26 47 24N 11 47 E
Jendouba 83 36 29N 8 47 E
Jenkins 114 37 13N 82 41W
Jennings 117 30 10N 92 45W
Jennings ~ 108 59 38N 132 5W
Jenny 49 57 47N 16 35 E
Jeparit 99 36 8 S 142 1 E
Jequié 127 13 51 S 40 5W
Jequitinhonha 127 16 30 S 41 0W
Jequitinhonha ~ 127 15 51 S 38 53W
Jerada 82 34 17N 2 10W
Jerantut 71 3 56N 102 22 E
Jérémie 121 18 40N 74 10W
Jerez de García Salinas 120 22 39N 103 0W
Jerez de la Frontera 31 36 41N 6 7W
Jerez de los Caballeros 31 38 20N 6 45W
Jerez, Punta 120 22 58N 97 40W
Jericho 98 23 38 S 146 6 E
Jericho = El Arīhā 62 31 52N 35 27 E
Jerichow 24 52 30N 12 2 E
Jerilderie 99 35 20 S 145 41 E
Jermyn 113 41 31N 75 31W
Jerome 119 34 50N 112 0W
Jerrobert 109 51 56N 109 8W
Jersey City 114 40 41N 74 8W
Jersey, I. 18 49 13N 2 7W
Jersey Shore 114 41 17N 77 18W
Jerseyville 116 39 5N 90 20W
Jerusalem 62 31 47N 35 10 E
Jervis B. 97 35 8 S 150 46 E
Jesenice 39 46 28N 14 3 E
Jeseník 27 50 0N 17 8 E
Jesenske 27 48 20N 20 10 E
Jesselton = Kota Kinabalu 72 6 0N 116 4 E
Jessnitz 24 51 42N 12 19 E
Jessore 69 23 10N 89 10 E
Jesup 115 31 36N 81 54W
Jesús María 124 30 59 S 64 5W
Jetmore 117 38 10N 99 57W
Jetpur 68 21 45N 70 10 E
Jevnaker 47 60 15N 10 26 E
Jewett, Ohio, U.S.A. 112 40 22N 81 2W
Jewett, Tex., U.S.A. 117 31 20N 96 8W
Jewett City 113 41 36N 72 0W
Jeypore 70 18 50N 82 38 E
Jeziorak, Jezioro 28 53 40N 19 35 E
Jeziorany 28 53 58N 20 46 E
Jeziorka ~ 28 51 59N 20 57 E
Jhajjar 68 28 37N 76 42 E
Jhal Jhao 66 26 20N 65 35 E
Jhalawar 68 24 40N 76 10 E
Jhang Maghiana 68 31 15N 72 22 E
Jhansi 68 25 30N 78 36 E
Jharia 69 23 45N 86 26 E
Jharsuguda 69 21 56N 84 5 E
Jhelum 68 33 0N 73 45 E
Jhelum ~ 68 31 20N 72 10 E
Jhunjhunu 68 28 10N 75 30 E
Ji Xian 76 36 7N 110 40 E
Jia Xian 76 38 12N 110 28 E
Jiamusi 75 46 40N 130 26 E
Ji'an 75 27 6N 114 59 E
Jianchuan 75 26 38N 99 55 E
Jiande 77 29 23N 119 15 E
Jiangbei 77 29 40N 106 34 E
Jiange 77 32 4N 105 32 E
Jiangjin 77 29 14N 106 14 E
Jiangling 75 30 25N 112 12 E
Jiangmen 75 22 32N 113 0 E
Jiangshan 77 28 40N 118 37 E
Jiangsu □ 75 33 0N 120 0 E
Jiangxi □ 75 27 30N 116 0 E
Jiangyin 77 31 54N 120 17 E
Jiangyong 77 25 20N 111 22 E
Jiangyou 77 31 44N 104 43 E
Jianning 77 26 50N 116 50 E
Jian'ou 75 27 3N 118 17 E
Jianshi 77 30 37N 109 38 E
Jianshui 75 23 36N 102 43 E
Jianyang 77 27 20N 118 5 E
Jiao Xian 76 36 18N 120 1 E
Jiaohe 76 38 2N 116 20 E
Jiaozhou Wan 76 36 5N 120 10 E
Jiaozuo 77 35 16N 113 12 E
Jiawang 77 34 28N 117 26 E
Jiaxing 75 30 49N 120 45 E
Jiayi 75 23 30N 120 24 E
Jibāl 63 22 10N 56 8 E
Jibiya 85 13 5N 7 12 E
Jibou 46 47 15N 23 17 E
Jibuti = Djibouti ■ 63 12 0N 43 0 E
Jičín 26 50 25N 15 28 E
Jiddah 64 21 29N 39 10 E
Jido 67 29 2N 94 58 E
Jifnā 62 31 58N 35 13 E
Jihlava 26 49 28N 15 35 E
Jihlava ~ 26 48 55N 16 36 E
Jihočeský □ 26 49 8N 14 35 E
Jihomoravský □ 27 49 5N 16 30 E
Jijel 83 36 52N 5 50 E
Jijiga 63 9 20N 42 50 E
Jijona 33 38 34N 0 30W
Jikamshi 85 12 12N 7 45 E
Jilin 76 43 44N 126 30 E
Jilin □ 76 44 0N 124 0 E
Jiloca ~ 32 41 21N 1 39W
Jilong 75 25 8N 121 42 E
Jílové 26 49 52N 14 29 E
Jima 87 7 40N 36 47 E
Jimbolia 42 45 47N 20 43 E
Jimena de la Frontera 31 36 27N 5 24W
Jiménez 120 27 10N 104 54W
Jimo 76 36 23N 120 30 E
Jin Xian 76 38 55N 121 42 E
Jinan 76 36 38N 117 1 E
Jincheng 76 35 29N 112 50 E
Jind 68 29 19N 76 22 E
Jindabyne 99 36 25 S 148 35 E
Jindabyne L. 100 36 20 S 148 38 E
Jindrichuv Hradeç 26 49 10N 15 2 E
Jing He ~ 77 34 27N 109 4 E
Jing Xian 77 26 33N 109 40 E
Jingchuan 76 35 20N 107 20 E
Jingdezhen 75 29 20N 117 11 E
Jinggu 75 23 35N 100 41 E
Jinghai 76 38 55N 116 55 E
Jingle 76 38 20N 111 55 E
Jingmen 77 31 0N 112 10 E
Jingning 76 35 30N 105 43 E
Jingshan 77 31 1N 113 7 E
Jingtai 76 37 10N 104 6 E
Jingxi 75 23 8N 106 27 E
Jingyu 76 42 25N 126 45 E
Jingyuan 76 36 30N 104 40 E
Jingziguan 77 33 15N 111 0 E
Jinhe 76 51 18N 121 32 E
Jinhua 75 29 8N 119 38 E
Jining, Nei Mongol Zizhiqu, China 76 41 5N 113 0 E
Jining, Shandong, China 77 35 22N 116 34 E
Jinja 90 0 25N 33 12 E
Jinjini 84 7 26N 3 42W
Jinmen Dao 77 24 25N 118 25 E
Jinnah Barrage 65 32 58N 71 33 E
Jinotega 121 13 6N 85 59W
Jinotepe 121 11 50N 86 10W
Jinshi 75 29 40N 111 50 E
Jinxiang 77 35 5N 116 22 E
Jinzhou 76 41 5N 121 3 E
Jiparaná (Machado) ~ 126 8 3 S 62 52W
Jipijapa 126 1 0 S 80 40W
Jiquilpan 120 19 57N 102 42W
Jishou 77 28 21N 109 43 E
Jisr al Ḥusayn (Allenby) Br. 62 31 53N 35 33 E
Jisr ash Shughūr 64 35 49N 36 18 E
Jitra 71 6 16N 100 25 E
Jiu ~ 46 44 40N 23 25 E
Jiudengkou 76 39 56N 106 40 E
Jiujiang 75 29 42N 115 58 E
Jiuling Shan 77 28 40N 114 40 E
Jiuquan 75 39 50N 98 20 E
Jixi 76 45 20N 130 50 E
Jizera ~ 26 50 10N 14 43 E
Jizl Wadi 86 25 30N 38 30 E
Joaçaba 125 27 5 S 51 31W
João Pessoa 127 7 10 S 34 52W
Joaquín V. González 124 25 10 S 64 0W
Jobourg, Nez de 18 49 41N 1 57W
Jódar 33 37 50N 3 21W
Jodhpur 68 26 23N 73 8 E
Joensuu 52 62 37N 29 49 E
Jœuf 19 49 12N 6 1 E
Joggins 107 45 42N 64 27W
Jogjakarta = Yogyakarta 73 7 49 S 110 22 E
Johannesburg 93 26 10 S 28 2 E
Johansfors 49 56 42N 15 32 E
John Day 118 44 25N 118 57W
John Day ~ 118 45 44N 120 39W
John H. Kerr Res. 115 36 20N 78 30W
John o' Groats 14 58 39N 3 3W
Johnson 117 37 35N 101 48W
Johnson City, N.Y., U.S.A. 114 42 7N 75 57W
Johnson City, Tenn., U.S.A. 115 36 18N 82 21W
Johnson City, Tex., U.S.A. 117 30 15N 98 24W
Johnsonburg 112 41 30N 78 40W
Johnson's Crossing 108 60 29N 133 18W
Johnston Falls = Mambilima Falls 91 10 31 S 28 45 E
Johnston I. 95 17 10N 169 8W
Johnstone Str. 108 50 28N 126 0W
Johnstown, N.Y., U.S.A. 114 43 1N 74 20W
Johnstown, Pa., U.S.A. 114 40 19N 78 53W
Johor □ 71 2 5N 103 20 E
Joigny 19 48 0N 3 20 E
Joinvile 125 26 15 S 48 55 E
Joinville 19 48 27N 5 10 E
Joinville I. 5 65 0 S 55 30W
Jokkmokk 50 66 35N 19 50 E
Jökulsá á Brú ~ 50 65 40N 14 16W
Jökulsá Fjöllum ~ 50 66 10N 16 30W
Joliet 114 41 30N 88 0W
Joliette 106 46 3N 73 24W
Jolo 73 6 0N 121 0 E
Jombang 73 7 33 S 112 14 E
Jome 73 1 16 S 127 30 E
Jomfruland 49 58 52N 9 36 E
Jönåker 49 58 44N 16 40 E
Jonava 54 55 8N 24 12 E
Jones Sound 4 76 0N 85 0W
Jonesboro, Ark., U.S.A. 117 35 50N 90 45W
Jonesboro, Ill., U.S.A. 117 37 26N 89 18W
Jonesboro, La., U.S.A. 117 32 15N 92 41W
Jonesport 107 44 32N 67 38W
Jonglei 87 6 25N 30 50 E
Joniskis 54 56 13N 23 35 E
Jönköping 49 57 45N 14 10 E
Jönköpings län □ 49 57 30N 14 30 E
Jonquière 107 48 27N 71 14W
Jonsberg 49 58 30N 16 48 E
Jonsered 49 57 45N 12 10 E
Jonzac 20 45 27N 0 28W
Joplin 117 37 0N 94 31W
Jordan, Phil. 73 10 41N 122 38 E
Jordan, U.S.A. 118 47 25N 106 58W
Jordan ■ 64 31 0N 36 0 E
Jordan ~ 62 31 48N 35 32 E
Jordan Valley 118 43 0N 117 2W
Jordanów 27 49 41N 19 49 E
Jorhat 67 26 45N 94 12 E
Jorm 65 36 50N 70 52 E
Jörn 50 65 4N 20 1 E
Jørpeland 47 59 3N 6 1 E
Jorquera ~ 124 28 3 S 69 58W
Jos 85 9 53N 8 51 E
Jošanička Banja 42 43 24N 20 47 E
José Batlle y Ordóñez 125 33 20 S 55 10W
Joseni 46 46 42N 25 29 E
Joseph 118 45 27N 117 13W
Joseph Bonaparte G. 96 14 35 S 128 50 E
Joseph City 119 35 0N 110 16W
Joseph, L., Newf., Can. 107 52 45N 65 18W
Joseph, L., Ont., Can. 112 45 10N 79 44W
Josselin 18 47 57N 2 33W
Jostedal 47 61 35N 7 15 E
Jotunheimen 47 61 35N 8 25 E
Jourdanton 117 28 54N 98 32W
Joussard 108 55 22N 115 50W
Jovellanos 121 22 40N 81 10W
Jowzjān □ 65 36 10N 66 0 E
Joyeuse 21 44 29N 4 16 E
Józefów 28 52 10N 21 11 E
Ju Xian 77 36 35N 118 20 E
Juan Aldama 120 24 20N 103 23W
Juan Bautista 119 36 55N 121 33W
Juan Bautista Alberdi 124 34 26 S 61 48W
Juan de Fuca Str. 118 48 15N 124 0W
Juan de Nova 93 17 3 S 43 45 E
Juan Fernández, Arch. de 95 33 50 S 80 0W
Juan José Castelli 124 25 27 S 60 57W
Juan L. Lacaze 124 34 26 S 57 25W
Juárez 124 37 40 S 59 43W
Juárez, Sierra de 120 32 0N 116 0W
Juàzeiro 127 9 30 S 40 30W
Juàzeiro do Norte 127 7 10 S 39 18W
Jubbulpore = Jabalpur 69 23 9N 79 58 E
Jübek 24 54 31N 9 24 E
Jubga 57 44 19N 38 48 E
Juby, C. 80 28 0N 12 59W
Júcar ~ 33 39 5N 0 10W
Juchitán 120 16 27N 95 5W
Judaea = Yehuda 62 31 35N 34 57 E
Judenburg 26 47 12N 14 38 E
Judith ~ 118 47 44N 109 38W
Judith Gap 118 46 40N 109 46W
Judith Pt. 113 41 20N 71 30W
Jugoslavia = Yugoslavia ■ 37 44 0N 20 0 E
Juigalpa 121 12 6N 85 26W
Juillac 20 45 20N 1 19 E
Juist 24 53 40N 7 0 E
Juiz de Fora 127 21 43 S 43 19W
Jujuy □ 124 23 20 S 65 40W
Julesberg 116 41 0N 102 20W
Juli 126 16 10 S 69 25W
Julia Cr. ~ 98 20 0 S 141 11 E
Julia Creek 97 20 39 S 141 44 E
Juliaca 126 15 25 S 70 10W
Julian 119 33 4N 116 38W
Julian Alps = Julijske Alpe 39 46 15N 14 1 E
Julianehåb 4 60 43N 46 0W
Jülich 24 50 55N 6 20 E
Julijske Alpe 39 46 15N 14 1 E
Jullundur 68 31 20N 75 40 E
Julu 76 37 15N 115 2 E
Jumbo 91 17 30 S 30 58 E
Jumentos Cays 121 23 0N 75 40 E
Jumet 16 50 27N 4 25 E
Jumilla 33 38 28N 1 19W
Jumla 69 29 15N 82 13 E
Jumna = Yamuna ~ 68 25 30N 81 53 E
Junagadh 68 21 30N 70 30 E
Junction, Tex., U.S.A. 117 30 29N 99 48W
Junction, Utah, U.S.A. 119 38 10N 112 15W
Junction B. 96 11 52 S 133 55 E
Junction City, Kans., U.S.A. 116 39 4N 96 55W
Junction City, Oreg., U.S.A. 118 44 14N 123 12W
Jundah 97 24 46 S 143 2 E
Jundiaí 125 24 30 S 47 0W
Juneau 104 58 20N 134 20W
Junee 97 34 53 S 147 35 E
Jungfrau 25 46 32N 7 58 E
Junggar Pendi 75 44 30N 86 0 E
Jungshahi 68 24 52N 67 44 E
Juniata ~ 112 40 30N 77 40W
Junín 124 34 33 S 60 57W
Junín de los Andes 128 39 45 S 71 0W
Jūniyah 64 33 59N 35 38 E
Junnar 70 19 12N 73 58 E
Junquera, La 32 42 25N 2 53 E
Junta, La 117 38 0N 103 30W
Juntura 118 43 44N 118 4W
Jupiter ~ 107 49 29N 63 37W
Jur, Nahr el ~ 87 8 45N 29 15 E
Jura, France 19 46 35N 6 5 E
Jura, U.K. 14 56 0N 5 50W
Jura □ 19 46 47N 5 45 E
Jura, Sd. of 14 55 57N 5 45W
Jura Suisse 25 47 10N 7 0 E
Jurado 126 7 7N 77 46W
Jurien B. 96 30 17 S 115 0 E
Jurilovca 46 44 46N 28 52 E
Juruá ~ 126 2 37 S 65 44W
Juruena ~ 126 7 20 S 58 3W
Juruti 127 2 9 S 56 4W
Jussey 19 47 50N 5 55 E
Justo Daract 124 33 52 S 65 12W
Jüterbog 24 52 0N 13 6 E
Juticalpa 121 14 40N 86 12W
Jutland = Jylland 8 56 25N 9 30 E
Juvigny-sous-Andaine 18 48 32N 0 30W
Juvisy 19 48 43N 2 23 E
Juwain 65 31 45N 61 30 E
Juzennecourt 19 48 10N 4 48 E
Jylland 8 56 25N 9 30 E
Jyväskylä 72 62 14N 25 50 E

K

K2 66 35 58N 76 32 E
Kaalasin 71 16 26N 103 30 E
Kaap die Goeie Hoop 92 34 24S 18 30 E
Kaap Plato 92 28 30S 24 0 E
Kaapkruis 92 21 43S 14 0 E
Kaapstad = Cape Town 92 33 55S 18 22 E
Kabaena 73 5 15S 122 0 E
Kabala 84 9 38N 11 37W
Kabale 90 1 15S 30 0 E
Kabalo 90 6 0S 27 0 E
Kabambare 90 4 41S 27 39 E
Kabango 91 8 35S 28 30 E
Kabanjahe 72 3 6N 98 30 E
Kabara 84 16 40N 2 50W
Kabardinka 56 44 40N 37 57 E
Kabardino-Balkar-A.S.S.R. □ 57 43 30N 43 30 E
Kabare 73 0 4S 130 58 E
Kabarega Falls 90 2 15N 31 30 E
Kabasalan 73 7 47N 122 44 E
Kabba 85 7 50N 6 3 E
Kabi 85 13 30N 12 35 E
Kabinakagami L. 106 48 54N 84 25W
Kabīr Kūh 64 33 0N 47 30 E
Kabīr, Zab al 64 36 0N 43 0 E
Kabkabīyah 81 13 50N 24 0 E
Kabna 86 19 6N 32 40 E
Kabompo 91 13 36S 24 14 E
Kabompo → 89 14 10S 23 11 E
Kabondo 91 8 58S 25 40 E
Kabongo 90 7 22S 25 33 E
Kabou 85 9 28N 0 55 E
Kaboudia, Rass 83 35 13N 11 10 E
Kabra 98 23 25S 150 25 E
Kabūd Gonbad 65 37 5N 59 45 E
Kabul 66 34 28N 69 11 E
Kabūl □ 65 34 30N 69 0 E
Kabul → 66 33 55N 72 14 E
Kabunga 90 1 38S 28 3 E
Kaburuang 73 3 50N 126 30 E
Kabushiya 87 16 54N 33 41 E
Kabwe 91 14 30S 28 29 E
Kačanik 42 42 13N 21 12 E
Kachanovo 54 57 25N 27 38 E
Kachebera 91 13 50S 32 50 E
Kachin □ 67 26 0N 97 30 E
Kachira, L. 90 0 40S 31 7 E
Kachiry 58 53 10N 75 50 E
Kachisi 87 9 40N 37 50 E
Kackar 57 40 45N 41 10 E
Kadan Kyun 72 12 30N 98 20 E
Kadarkút 27 46 13N 17 39 E
Kadayanallur 70 9 3N 77 22 E
Kade 85 6 7N 0 56W
Kadi 68 23 18N 72 23 E
Kadina 97 34 0S 137 43 E
Kadiri 70 14 12N 78 13 E
Kadirli 64 37 23N 36 5 E
Kadiyevka 57 48 35N 38 40 E
Kadoka 116 43 50N 101 31W
Kadom 55 54 37N 42 30 E
Kâdugli 81 11 0N 29 45 E
Kaduna 85 10 30N 7 21 E
Kaduna □ 85 11 0N 7 30 E
Kaédi 84 16 9N 13 28W
Kaelé 85 10 7N 14 27 E
Kaesŏng 76 37 58N 126 35 E
Kāf 64 31 25N 37 29 E
Kafakumba 88 9 38S 23 46 E
Kafan 53 39 18N 46 15 E
Kafanchan 85 9 40N 8 20 E
Kafareti 85 10 25N 11 12 E
Kaffrine 84 14 8N 15 36W
Kafia Kingi 81 9 20N 24 25 E
Kafinda 91 12 32S 30 20 E
Kafirévs, Ákra 45 38 9N 24 38 E
Kafr 'Ayn 62 32 3N 35 7 E
Kafr el Dauwâr 86 31 8N 30 8 E
Kafr el Sheikh 86 31 15N 30 50 E
Kafr Kammā 62 32 44N 35 26 E
Kafr Kannā 62 32 45N 35 20 E
Kafr Mālik 62 32 0N 35 18 E
Kafr Mandā 62 32 49N 35 15 E
Kafr Quaddūm 62 32 14N 35 7 E
Kafr Rā'ī 62 32 23N 35 9 E
Kafr Şīr 62 33 19N 35 23 E
Kafr Yāsīf 62 32 58N 35 10 E
Kafue 91 15 46S 28 9 E
Kafue Flats 91 15 40S 27 25 E
Kafulwe 91 9 0S 29 1 E
Kaga Bandoro 88 7 0N 19 10 E
Kagan 58 39 43N 64 33 E
Kagawa □ 74 34 15N 134 0 E
Kagera → 90 0 57S 31 47 E
Kağizman 64 40 5N 43 10 E
Kagoshima 74 31 35N 130 33 E
Kagoshima □ 74 31 30N 130 30 E
Kagoshima-Wan 74 31 25N 130 40 E
Kagul 56 45 50N 28 15 E
Kahajan → 72 3 40S 114 0 E
Kahama 90 4 8S 32 30 E
Kahama □ 90 3 50S 32 0 E
Kahe 90 3 30S 37 25 E
Kahemba 88 7 18S 18 55 E
Kahil, Djebel bou 83 34 26N 4 0 E
Kahniah → 108 58 15N 120 55W
Kahnūj 65 27 55N 57 40 E
Kahoka 116 40 25N 91 42W
Kahoolawe 110 20 33N 156 35W
Kai Besar 73 5 35S 133 0 E
Kai Kai 92 19 52S 21 15 E
Kai, Kepulauan 73 5 55S 132 45W
Kai-Ketjil 73 5 45S 132 40 E
Kaiama 85 9 36N 4 1 E
Kaiapoi 101 42 24S 172 40 E
Kaieteur Falls 126 5 1N 59 10W
Kaifeng 77 34 48N 114 21 E
Kaihua 77 29 12N 118 20 E
Kaiingveld 92 30 0S 22 0 E
Kaikohe 101 35 25S 173 49 E
Kaikoura 101 42 25S 173 43 E
Kaikoura Pen. 101 42 25S 173 43 E
Kaikoura Ra. 101 41 59S 173 41 E
Kailahun 84 8 18N 10 39W
Kaili 77 26 33N 107 59 E
Kailu 76 43 38N 121 18 E
Kailua 110 19 39N 156 0W
Kaimana 73 3 39S 133 45 E
Kaimanawa Mts. 101 39 15S 175 56 E
Kaimganj 69 27 33N 79 24 E
Kaimur Hill 69 24 30N 82 0 E
Kainantu 98 6 18S 145 52 E
Kaingaroa Forest 101 38 24S 176 30 E
Kainji Res. 85 10 1N 4 40 E
Kaipara Harbour 101 36 25S 174 14 E
Kaiping 77 22 23N 112 42 E
Kaipokok B. 107 54 54N 59 47W
Kairana 68 29 24N 77 15 E
Kaironi 73 0 47S 133 40 E
Kairouan 83 35 45N 10 5 E
Kairuku 98 8 51S 146 35 E
Kaiserslautern 25 49 30N 7 43 E
Kaitaia 101 35 8S 173 17 E
Kaitangata 101 46 17S 169 51 E
Kaithal 68 29 48N 76 26 E
Kaiwi Channel 110 21 13N 157 30W
Kaiyuan 76 42 28N 124 1 E
Kajaani 50 64 17N 27 46 E
Kajabbi 97 20 0S 140 1 E
Kajan → 72 2 55N 117 35 E
Kajang 71 2 59N 101 48 E
Kajiado 90 1 53S 36 48 E
Kajiado □ 90 2 0S 36 30 E
Kajo Kaji 87 3 58N 31 40 E
Kajoa 73 0 1N 127 28 E
Kaka 81 10 38N 32 10 E
Kakabeka Falls 106 48 24N 89 37W
Kakamega 90 0 20N 34 46 E
Kakamega □ 90 0 20N 34 46 E
Kakanj 42 44 9N 18 7 E
Kakanui Mts. 101 45 10S 170 30 E
Kakegawa 74 34 45N 138 1 E
Kakhib 57 42 28N 46 34 E
Kakhovka 56 46 40N 33 15 E
Kakhovskoye Vdkhr. 56 47 5N 34 16 E
Kakinada (Cocanada) 70 16 57N 82 11 E
Kakisa → 108 61 3N 118 10W
Kakisa L. 108 60 56N 117 43W
Kakwa → 108 54 37N 118 28W
Kala 85 12 2N 14 40 E
Kala Oya → 70 8 20N 79 45 E
Kalaa-Kebira 83 35 59N 10 32 E
Kalabagh 68 33 0N 71 28 E
Kalabahi 73 8 13S 124 31 E
Kalabáka 44 39 42N 21 39 E
Kalabo 89 14 58S 22 40 E
Kalach 55 50 22N 41 0 E
Kalach na Donu 57 48 43N 43 32 E
Kaladan → 67 20 20N 93 5 E
Kaladar 112 44 37N 77 5W
Kalahari 92 24 0S 21 30 E
Kalahari Gemsbok Nat. Park 92 25 30S 20 30 E
Kalahasti 70 13 45N 79 44 E
Kalakamati 93 20 40S 27 25 E
Kalakan 59 55 15N 116 45 E
Kalama, U.S.A. 118 46 0N 122 55W
Kalama, Zaïre 90 2 52S 28 35 E
Kalamariá 44 40 33N 22 55 E
Kalamata 45 37 3N 22 10 E
Kalamazoo 114 42 20N 85 35W
Kalamazoo → 114 42 40N 86 12W
Kalamb 70 18 3N 74 48 E
Kalambo Falls 91 8 37S 31 35 E
Kálamos, Greece 45 38 37N 20 55 E
Kálamos, Greece 45 38 17N 23 52 E
Kalamoti 45 38 15N 26 4 E
Kalan 64 39 7N 39 32 E
Kalao 73 7 21S 121 0 E
Kalaotoa 73 7 20S 121 50 E
Kälarne 48 62 59N 16 8 E
Kalárovo 27 47 54N 18 0 E
Kalasin 71 16 26N 103 30 E
Kalat 66 29 8N 66 31 E
* Kalat □ 68 27 30N 66 0 E
Kálathos (Calato) 45 36 9N 28 8 E
Kalaus → 57 45 40N 44 7 E
Kalávrita 45 38 3N 22 8 E
Kalecik 56 40 4N 33 26 E
Kalegauk Kyun 67 15 33N 97 35 E
Kalehe 90 2 6S 28 50 E
Kalema 90 1 12S 31 55 E
Kalemie 90 5 55S 29 9 E
Kalety 28 50 35N 18 52 E
Kalewa 67 23 10N 94 15 E
Kálfafellsstaður 50 64 11N 15 53W
Kalgan = Zhangjiakou 76 40 48N 114 55 E
Kalgoorlie 96 30 40S 121 22 E
Kaliakra, Nos 43 43 21N 28 30 E
Kalianda 72 5 50S 105 45 E
Kalibo 73 11 43N 122 22 E
Kaliganj Town 69 22 25N 89 8 E
Kalima 90 2 33S 26 32 E
Kalimantan Barat □ 72 0 0 110 30 E
Kalimantan Selatan □ 72 2 30S 115 30 E
Kalimantan Tengah □ 72 2 0S 113 30 E
Kalimantan Timur □ 72 1 30N 116 30 E
Kálimnos 45 37 0N 27 0 E
Kalimpong 69 27 4N 88 35 E
Kalinadi → 70 14 50N 74 7 E
Kalinin 55 56 55N 35 55 E
Kaliningrad 54 54 42N 20 32 E
Kalinkovichi 54 52 12N 29 20 E
Kalinovik 42 43 31N 18 29 E
Kalipetrovo (Stančevo) 43 44 5N 27 14 E
Kaliro 90 0 56N 33 30 E
Kalirrákhi 44 40 40N 24 35 E
Kalispell 118 48 10N 114 22W
Kalisz 28 51 45N 18 8 E
Kalisz □ 28 51 30N 18 0 E
Kalisz Pomorski 28 53 17N 15 55 E
Kaliua 90 5 5S 31 48 E
Kaliveli Tank 70 12 5N 79 50 E

* *Now part of Baluchistan* □

Kalix, → 50 65 50N 23 11 E
Kalka 68 30 46N 76 57 E
Kalkaska 106 44 44N 85 11W
Kalkfeld 92 20 57S 16 14 E
Kalkfontein 92 22 4S 20 57 E
Kalkrand 92 24 1S 17 35 E
Kallakurichi 70 11 44N 79 1 E
Kållandsö 49 58 40N 13 5 E
Kallia 62 31 46N 35 30 E
Kallidaikurichi 70 8 38N 77 31 E
Kallinge 49 56 15N 15 18 E
Kallithéa 45 37 55N 23 41 E
Kallmeti 44 41 51N 19 41 E
Kallonis, Kólpos 45 39 10N 26 10 E
Kallsjön 50 63 38N 13 0 E
Kalmalo 85 13 40N 5 20 E
Kalmar 49 56 40N 16 20 E
Kalmar län □ 49 57 25N 16 0 E
Kalmar sund 49 56 40N 16 25 E
Kalmyk A.S.S.R. □ 57 46 5N 46 1 E
Kalmykovo 57 49 0N 51 47 E
Kalna 69 23 13N 88 25 E
Kalo 98 10 1S 147 48 E
Kalocsa 27 46 32N 19 0 E
Kalofer 43 42 37N 24 59 E
Kaloko 90 6 47S 25 48 E
Kalol, Gujarat, India 68 23 15N 72 33 E
Kalol, Gujarat, India 68 22 37N 73 31 E
Kalolimnos 45 37 4N 27 8 E
Kalomo 91 17 0S 26 30 E
Kaloneron 45 37 20N 21 38 E
Kalpi 69 26 8N 79 47 E
Kalrayan Hills 70 11 45N 78 40 E
Kalsubai 70 19 35N 73 45 E
Kaltungo 85 9 48N 11 19 E
Kalu 68 25 5N 67 39 E
Kaluga 55 54 35N 36 10 E
Kalulushi 91 12 50S 28 3 E
Kalundborg 49 55 41N 11 5 E
Kalush 54 49 3N 24 23 E
Kałuszyn 28 52 13N 21 52 E
Kalutara 70 6 35N 80 0 E
Kalwaria 27 49 53N 19 41 E
Kalya 52 60 15N 59 59 E
Kalyan 68 20 30N 74 3 E
Kalyazin 55 57 15N 37 55 E
Kam Keut 71 18 20N 104 48 E
Kama 90 3 30S 27 5 E
Kama → 52 55 45N 52 0 E
Kamachumu 90 1 37S 31 37 E
Kamaishi 74 39 20N 142 0 E
Kamalia 68 30 44N 72 42 E
Kamandorskiye Ostrava 59 55 0N 167 0 E
Kamapanda 91 12 5S 24 0 E
Kamaran 63 15 21N 42 35 E
Kamativi 91 18 15S 27 27 E
Kamba 85 11 50N 3 45 E
Kambam 70 9 45N 77 16 E
Kambar 68 27 37N 68 1 E
Kambarka 52 56 15N 54 11 E
Kambia 84 9 3N 12 53W
Kambolé 91 8 47S 30 48 E
Kambove 91 10 51S 26 33 E
Kamchatka, P-ov. 59 57 0N 160 0 E
Kamen 58 53 50N 81 30 E
Kamen Kashirskiy 54 51 39N 24 56 E
Kamenica, Srbija, Yugo. 42 44 25N 19 40 E
Kamenica, Srbija, Yugo. 42 43 27N 22 27 E
Kamenice 26 49 18N 15 2 E
Kamenjak, Rt 39 44 47N 13 55 E
Kamenka, R.S.F.S.R., U.S.S.R. 52 65 58N 44 0 E
Kamenka, R.S.F.S.R., U.S.S.R. 55 50 47N 39 20 E
Kamenka, R.S.F.S.R., U.S.S.R. 55 53 10N 44 5 E
Kamenka, Ukraine S.S.R., U.S.S.R. 56 49 3N 32 6 E
Kamenka Bugskaya 54 50 8N 24 16 E
Kamenka Dneprovskaya 56 47 29N 34 14 E
Kameno 43 42 34N 27 18 E
Kamenolomini 57 47 40N 40 14 E
Kamensk-Shakhtinskiy 57 48 23N 40 20 E
Kamensk Uralskiy 58 56 25N 62 2 E
Kamenskiy, R.S.F.S.R., U.S.S.R. 55 50 48N 45 25 E
Kamenskiy, R.S.F.S.R., U.S.S.R. 57 49 20N 41 15 E
Kamenskoye 59 62 45N 165 30 E
Kamenyak 43 43 24N 26 57 E
Kamenz 24 51 17N 14 7 E
Kami 44 42 17N 20 18 E
Kamiah 118 46 12N 116 2W
Kamień Krajeński 28 53 32N 17 32 E
Kamień Pomorski 28 53 57N 14 43 E
Kamienna → 28 51 6N 21 47 E
Kamienna Góra 28 50 47N 16 2 E
Kamiensk 28 51 12N 19 29 E
Kamilukuak, L. 109 62 22N 101 40W
Kamina 91 8 45S 25 0 E
Kaminak L. 109 62 10N 95 0W
Kamituga 90 3 2S 28 10 E
Kamloops 108 50 40N 120 20W
Kamloops L. 108 50 45N 120 40W
Kamnik 39 46 14N 14 37 E
Kamo 57 40 21N 45 7 E
Kamoke 68 32 4N 74 4 E
Kamp → 26 48 23N 15 42 E
Kampala 90 0 20N 32 30 E
Kampar 71 4 18N 101 9 E
Kampar → 72 0 30N 103 8 E
Kampen 16 52 33N 5 53 E
Kampolombo, L. 91 11 37S 29 42 E
Kampot 71 10 36N 104 10 E
Kamptee 68 21 9N 79 19 E
Kampti 84 10 7N 3 25W
Kampuchea = Cambodia ■ 71 13 0N 105 0 E
Kampung → 73 5 44S 138 24 E
Kampungbaru = Tolitoli 73 1 5N 120 50 E
Kamrau, Teluk 73 3 30S 133 36 E
Kamsack 109 51 34N 101 54W
Kamskoye Ustye 55 55 10N 49 20 E
Kamskoye Vdkhr. 52 58 0N 56 0 E
Kamuchawie L. 109 56 18N 101 59W
Kamyshin 55 50 10N 45 24 E
Kamyzyak 57 46 4N 48 10 E
Kanaaupscow 106 54 2N 76 30W
Kanab 119 37 3N 112 29W
Kanab Creek 119 37 0N 112 40W
Kanagawa □ 74 35 20N 139 20 E
Kanairiktok → 107 55 2N 60 18W
Kanakapura 70 12 33N 77 28 E
Kanália 44 39 30N 22 53 E
Kananga 88 5 55S 22 18 E
Kanarraville 119 37 34N 113 12W
Kanash 55 55 30N 47 32 E
Kanastraíon, Ákra 44 39 57N 23 45 E
Kanawha → 114 38 50N 82 8W
Kanazawa 74 36 30N 136 38 E
Kanchanaburi 71 14 2N 99 31 E
Kanchenjunga 69 27 50N 88 10 E
Kanchipuram (Conjeeveram) 70 12 52N 79 45 E
Kańczuga 27 49 59N 22 25 E
Kanda Kanda 88 6 52S 23 48 E
Kandahar 65 31 32N 65 30 E
Kandalaksha 52 67 9N 32 30 E
Kandalakshkiy Zaliv 52 66 0N 35 0 E
Kandangan 72 2 50S 115 20 E
Kandanos 45 35 19N 23 44 E
Kandhila 45 37 46N 22 22 E
Kandhkot 68 28 16N 69 8 E
Kandhla 68 29 18N 77 19 E
Kandi, Benin 85 11 7N 2 55 E
Kandi, India 69 23 58N 88 5 E
Kandla 68 23 0N 70 10 E
Kandos 99 32 45S 149 58 E
Kandukur 70 15 12N 79 57 E
Kandy 70 7 18N 80 43 E
Kane 114 41 39N 78 53W
Kane Bassin 4 79 30N 68 0W
Kanevskaya 57 46 3N 39 3 E
Kanfanar 39 45 7N 13 50 E
Kangaba 84 11 56N 8 25W
Kangar 71 6 27N 100 12 E
Kangaroo I. 97 35 45S 137 0 E
Kangaroo Mts. 98 23 25S 142 0 E
Kangavar 64 34 40N 48 0 E
Kangean, Kepulauan 72 6 55S 115 23 E
Kangerdlugsuak 4 68 10N 32 20W
Kanggyee 76 41 0N 126 35 E
Kangnŭng 76 37 45N 128 54 E
Kango 88 0 11N 10 5 E
Kangto 67 27 50N 92 35 E
Kanhangad 70 12 21N 74 58 E
Kanheri 70 19 13N 72 50 E
Kani 84 8 29N 6 36W
Kaniama 90 7 30S 24 12 E
Kaniapiskau → 107 56 40N 69 30W
Kaniapiskau L. 107 54 10N 69 55W
Kanin Nos, Mys 52 68 45N 43 20 E
Kanin, P-ov. 52 68 0N 45 0 E
Kanina 44 40 23N 19 30 E
Kaniva 99 36 22S 141 18 E
Kanjiža 42 46 3N 20 4 E
Kankakee 114 41 6N 87 50W
Kankakee → 114 41 23N 88 16W
Kankan 84 10 23N 9 15W
Kanker 70 20 10N 81 40 E
Kankunskiy 59 57 37N 126 8 E
Kannapolis 115 35 32N 80 37W
Kannauj 69 27 3N 79 56 E
Kano 85 12 2N 8 30 E
Kano □ 85 11 45N 9 0 E
Kanoroba 84 9 7N 6 8W
Kanowit 72 2 14N 112 20 E
Kanowna 96 30 32S 121 31 E
Kanoya 74 31 25N 130 50 E
Kanpetlet 67 21 10N 93 59 E
Kanpur 69 26 28N 80 20 E
Kansas □ 116 38 40N 98 0W
Kansas → 116 39 7N 94 36W
Kansas City, Kans., U.S.A. 116 39 0N 94 40W
Kansas City, Mo., U.S.A. 116 39 3N 94 30W
Kansenia 91 10 20S 26 0 E
Kansk 59 56 20N 95 37 E
Kansu = Gansu □ 75 37 0N 103 0 E
Kantang 71 7 25N 99 31 E
Kantché 85 13 31N 8 30 E
Kanté 85 9 57N 1 3 E
Kantemirovka 57 49 43N 39 55 E
Kanturk 15 52 10N 8 55W
Kanuma 74 36 34N 139 42 E
Kanus 92 27 50S 18 39 E
Kanye 92 25 0S 25 28 E
Kanyu 92 20 7S 24 37 E
Kanzenze 91 10 30S 25 12 E
Kanzi, Ras 90 7 1S 39 33 E
Kaohsiung = Gaoxiong 75 22 38N 120 18 E
Kaokoveld 92 18 20S 13 37 E
Kaolack 84 14 5N 16 8W
Kapadvanj 68 23 5N 73 0 E
Kapanga 88 8 30S 22 40 E
Kapchagai 58 43 50N 77 10 E
Kapéllo, Ákra 45 36 9N 23 3 E
Kapema 91 10 45S 28 22 E
Kapfenberg 26 47 26N 15 18 E
Kapiri Mposhi 91 13 59S 28 43 E
Kapisa □ 65 35 0N 69 20 E
Kapiskau → 106 52 47N 81 55W
Kapit 72 2 0N 112 55 E
Kapiti I. 101 40 50S 174 56 E
Kaplice 26 48 42N 14 30 E
Kapoeta 87 4 50N 33 35 E
Kápolnásnyék 27 47 16N 18 41 E
Kapos → 27 46 44N 18 30 E
Kaposvár 27 46 25N 17 47 E
Kappeln 24 54 37N 9 56 E
Kapps 92 22 32S 17 18 E
Kaprije 39 43 42N 15 43 E
Kapsukas 54 54 33N 23 19 E
Kapuas → 72 0 25S 109 20 E
Kapuas Hulu, Pegunungan 72 1 30N 113 30 E
Kapulo 91 8 18S 29 15 E
Kapunda 99 34 20S 138 56 E
Kapurthala 68 31 23N 75 25 E
Kapuskasing 106 49 25N 82 30W
Kapuskasing → 106 49 49N 82 0W
Kapustin Yar 57 48 37N 45 40 E
Kaputir 90 2 5N 35 28 E

Kapuvár Kent

Kapuvár 27 47 36N 17 1 E
Kara, Turkey 45 36 58N 27 30 E
Kara, U.S.S.R. 58 69 10N 65 0 E
Kara Bogaz Gol, Zaliv 53 41 0N 53 30 E
Kara Burun 45 38 41N 26 28 E
Kara Kalpak A.S.S.R. □ 58 43 0N 60 0 E
Kara Sea 58 75 0N 70 0 E
Kara, Wadi 86 20 0N 41 25 E
Karabük 64 41 12N 32 37 E
Karaburuni 44 40 25N 19 20 E
Karabutak 58 49 59N 60 14 E
Karachala 57 39 45N 48 53 E
Karachayevsk 57 43 50N 42 0 E
Karachev 54 53 10N 35 5 E
Karachi 68 24 53N 67 0 E
Karachi □ 68 25 30N 67 0 E
Karád 27 46 41N 17 51 E
Karad 70 17 15N 74 10 E
Karadeniz Boğazı 64 41 10N 29 10 E
Karaga 85 9 58N 0 28W
Karaganda 58 49 50N 73 10 E
Karagayly 58 49 26N 76 0 E
Karaginskiy, Ostrov 59 58 45N 164 0 E
Karagiye Depression 53 43 27N 51 45 E
Karagwe □ 90 2 0 S 31 0 E
Karaikkudi 70 10 0N 78 45 E
Karaitivu I. 70 9 45N 79 52 E
Karaitivu, I. 70 8 22N 79 47 E
Karaj 65 35 48N 51 0 E
Karakas 58 48 20N 83 30 E
Karakitang 73 3 14N 125 28 E
Karakoram Pass 66 35 33N 77 50 E
Karakoram Ra. 66 35 30N 77 0 E
Karakum, Peski 58 39 30N 60 0 E
Karalon 59 57 5N 115 50 E
Karaman 64 37 14N 33 13 E
Karamay 75 45 30N 84 58 E
Karambu 72 3 53 S 116 6 E
Karamea Bight 101 41 22 S 171 40 E
Karamoja □ 90 3 0N 34 15 E
Karamsad 68 22 35N 72 50 E
Karanganjar 73 7 38 S 109 37 E
Karanja 68 20 29N 77 31 E
Karasburg 92 28 0 S 18 44 E
Karasino 58 66 50N 86 50 E
Karasjok 50 69 27N 25 30 E
Karasuk 58 53 44N 78 2 E
Karatau 58 43 10N 70 28 E
Karatau, Khrebet 58 43 30N 69 30 E
Karauli 68 26 30N 77 4 E
Karávi 45 36 49N 23 37 E
Karawanken 26 46 30N 14 40 E
Karazhal 58 48 2N 70 49 E
Karbalā 64 32 36N 44 3 E
Kårböle 48 61 59N 15 22 E
Karcag 27 47 19N 20 57 E
Karda 59 55 0N 103 16 E
Kardhámila 45 38 35N 26 5 E
Kardhitsa 44 39 23N 21 54 E
Kardhitsa □ 44 39 15N 21 50 E
Kärdla 54 58 50N 22 40 E
Kareeberge 92 30 50 S 22 0 E
Kareima 86 18 30N 31 49 E
Karelian A.S.S.R. □ 52 65 30N 32 30 E
Karen 71 12 49N 92 53 E
Kargānrūd 64 37 55N 49 0 E
Kargasok 58 59 3N 80 53 E
Kargat 58 55 10N 80 15 E
Kargı 56 41 11N 34 30 E
Kargil 69 34 32N 76 12 E
Kargopol 52 61 30N 38 58 E
Kargowa 28 52 5N 15 51 E
Karguéri 85 13 27N 10 30 E
Karia ba Mohammed 82 34 22N 5 12W
Kariaí 44 40 14N 24 19 E
Kariba 91 16 28 S 28 50 E
Kariba Gorge 91 16 30 S 28 50 E
Kariba Lake 91 16 40 S 28 25 E
Karibib 92 21 0 S 15 56 E
Karikal 70 10 59N 79 50 E
Karimata, Kepulauan 72 1 25 S 109 0 E
Karimata, Selat 72 2 0 S 108 40 E
Karimnagar 70 18 26N 79 10 E
Karimunjawa, Kepulauan 72 5 50 S 110 30 E
Karin 63 10 50N 45 52 E
Káristos 45 38 1N 24 29 E
Kariya 74 34 58N 137 1 E
Karkal 70 13 15N 74 56 E
Karkar I. 98 4 40 S 146 0 E
Karkaralinsk 58 49 26N 75 30 E
Karkinitskiy Zaliv 56 45 56N 33 0 E
Karkur 62 32 29N 34 57 E
Karkur Tohl 86 22 5N 25 5 E
Karl Libknekht 54 51 40N 35 35 E
Karl-Marx-Stadt 24 50 50N 12 55 E
Karl-Marx-Stadt □ 24 50 45N 13 0 E
Karla, L. = Voiviïs, L. 44 39 30N 22 45 E
Karlino 28 54 3N 15 53 E
Karlobag 39 44 32N 15 5 E
Karlovac 39 45 31N 15 36 E
Karlovka 56 49 29N 35 8 E
Karlovy Vary 26 50 13N 12 51 E
Karlsborg 49 58 33N 14 33 E
Karlshamn 49 56 10N 14 51 E
Karlskoga 48 59 22N 14 33 E
Karlskrona 49 56 10N 15 35 E
Karlsruhe 25 49 3N 8 23 E
Karlstad, Sweden 48 59 23N 13 30 E
Karlstad, U.S.A. 116 48 38N 96 30W
Karlstadt 25 49 57N 9 46 E
Karmøy 47 59 15N 5 15 E
Karnal 68 29 42N 77 2 E
Karnali → 69 29 0N 83 20 E
Karnaphuli Res. 67 22 40N 92 20 E
Karnataka □ 70 14 15N 76 0 E
Karnes City 117 28 53N 97 53W
Karnische Alpen 26 46 36N 13 0 E
Kärnten □ 26 46 52N 13 30 E
Karo 84 12 16N 3 18W
Karoi 91 16 48 S 29 45 E
Karonga 91 9 57 S 33 55 E
Karoonda 99 35 1 S 139 59 E
Káros 45 36 54N 25 40 E
Karousádhes 44 39 47N 19 45 E
Kárpathos 45 35 37N 27 10 E
Karpáthos, Stenón 45 36 0N 27 30 E
Karpinsk 52 59 45N 60 1 E
Karpogory 52 63 59N 44 27 E
Karrebæk 49 55 12N 11 39 E
Kars, Turkey 64 40 40N 43 5 E
Kars, U.S.S.R. 56 40 36N 43 5 E
Karsakpay 58 47 55N 66 40 E
Karsha 57 49 45N 51 35 E
Karshi 58 38 53N 65 48 E
Karst 39 45 35N 14 0 E
Karsun 55 54 14N 46 57 E
Kartál Óros 44 41 15N 25 13 E
Kartaly 58 53 3N 60 40 E
Kartapur 68 31 27N 75 32 E
Karthaus 112 41 8N 78 9W
Kartuzy 28 54 22N 18 10 E
Karufa 73 3 50 S 133 20 E
Karumba 98 17 31 S 140 50 E
Karumo 90 2 25 S 32 50 E
Karumwa 90 3 12 S 32 38 E
Karungu 90 0 50 S 34 10 E
Karup 49 56 19N 9 10 E
Karur 70 10 59N 78 2 E
Karviná 27 49 53N 18 25 E
Karwi 69 25 12N 80 57 E
Kas Kong 71 11 27N 102 12 E
Kasache 91 13 25 S 34 20 E
Kasai → 88 3 30 S 16 10 E
Kasai Oriental □ 90 5 0 S 24 30 E
Kasaji 91 10 25 S 23 27 E
Kasama 91 10 16 S 31 9 E
Kasane 92 17 34 S 24 50 E
Kasanga 91 8 30 S 31 10 E
Kasangulu 88 4 33 S 15 15 E
Kasaragod 70 12 30N 74 58 E
Kasba L. 109 60 20N 102 10W
Kasba Tadla 82 32 36N 6 17W
Kasempa 91 13 30 S 25 44 E
Kasenga 91 10 20 S 28 45 E
Kasese 90 0 13N 30 3 E
Kasewa 91 14 28 S 28 53 E
Kasganj 68 27 48N 78 42 E
Kashabowie 106 48 40N 90 26W
Kāshān 65 34 5N 51 30 E
Kashi 75 39 30N 76 2 E
Kashimbo 91 11 12 S 26 19 E
Kashin 55 57 20N 37 36 E
Kashipur, Orissa, India 70 19 16N 83 3 E
Kashipur, Ut. P., India 68 29 15N 79 0 E
Kashira 55 54 45N 38 10 E
Kāshmar 65 35 16N 58 26 E
Kashmir 69 34 0N 76 0 E
Kashmor 68 28 28N 69 32 E
Kashpirovka 55 53 0N 48 30 E
Kashun Noerh = Gaxun Nur 75 42 22N 100 30 E
Kasimov 55 54 55N 41 20 E
Kasinge 90 6 15 S 26 58 E
Kasiruta 73 0 25 S 127 12 E
Kaskaskia → 116 37 58N 89 57W
Kaskattama → 109 57 3N 90 4W
Kaskinen 50 62 22N 21 15 E
Kaskö 50 62 22N 21 15 E
Kaslo 108 49 55N 116 55W
Kasmere L. 109 59 34N 101 10W
Kasongo 90 4 30 S 26 33 E
Kasongo Lunda 88 6 35 S 16 49 E
Kásos 45 35 20N 26 55 E
Kasos, Stenón 45 35 30N 26 30 E
Kaspi 57 41 54N 44 17 E
Kaspichan 43 43 18N 27 11 E
Kaspiysk 57 42 52N 47 40 E
Kaspiyskiy 57 45 22N 47 23 E
Kassab ed Doleib 87 13 30N 33 35 E
Kassaba 86 22 40N 29 55 E
Kassala 87 16 0N 36 0 E
Kassalâ □ 87 15 20N 36 26 E
Kassándra 44 40 0N 23 30 E
Kassel 24 51 19N 9 32 E
Kassinga 89 15 5 S 16 4 E
Kassinger 86 18 46N 31 51 E
Kassue 73 6 58 S 139 21 E
Kastamonu 64 41 25N 33 43 E
Kastav 39 45 22N 14 20 E
Kastélli 45 35 29N 23 38 E
Kastéllion 45 35 12N 25 20 E
Kastellorizon = Megiste 35 36 8N 29 34 E
Kastellou, Ákra 45 35 30N 27 15 E
Kastlösa 49 56 26N 16 25 E
Kastóri 45 37 10N 22 17 E
Kastoria 44 40 30N 21 19 E
Kastoría □ 44 40 30N 21 15 E
Kastorías, L. 44 40 30N 21 20 E
Kastornoye 55 51 55N 38 2 E
Kastós 45 38 35N 20 55 E
Kástron 45 39 50N 25 2 E
Kastrosikiá 45 39 6N 20 36 E
Kasulu 90 4 37 S 30 5 E
Kasulu □ 90 4 37 S 30 5 E
Kasumkent 57 41 47N 48 15 E
Kasungu 91 13 0 S 33 29 E
Kasur 68 31 5N 74 25 E
Kata 59 58 46N 102 40 E
Kataba 91 16 5 S 25 10 E
Katako Kombe 90 3 25 S 24 20 E
Katákolon 45 37 38N 21 19 E
Katale 90 4 52 S 31 7 E
Katamatite 99 36 6 S 145 41 E
Katanda, Zaïre 90 0 55 S 29 21 E
Katanda, Zaïre 90 7 52 S 24 13 E
Katangi 69 21 56N 79 50 E
Katangli 59 51 42N 143 14 E
Katanning 96 33 40 S 117 33 E
Katastári 45 37 50N 20 45 E
Katavi Swamp 90 6 50 S 31 10 E
Kateríni 44 40 18N 22 37 E
Katha 67 24 10N 96 30 E
Katherîna, Gebel 86 28 30N 33 57 E
Katherine 96 14 27 S 132 20 E
Kathiawar 68 22 20N 71 0 E
Kati 84 12 41N 8 4W
Katiet 72 2 21 S 99 54 E
Katihar 69 25 34N 87 36 E
Katima Mulilo 92 17 28 S 24 13 E
Katimbira 91 12 40 S 34 0 E
Katiola 84 8 10N 5 10W
Katkopberg 92 30 0 S 20 0 E
Katlanovo 42 41 52N 21 40 E
Katmandu 69 27 45N 85 20 E
Kato Akhaïa 45 38 8N 21 33 E
Káto Stavros 44 40 39N 23 43 E
Katol 68 21 17N 78 38 E
Katompe 90 6 2 S 26 23 E
Katonga → 90 0 34N 31 50 E
Katoomba 97 33 41 S 150 19 E
Katowice 28 50 17N 19 5 E
Katowice □ 28 50 10N 19 0 E
Katrine, L. 14 56 15N 4 30W
Katrineholm 48 59 9N 16 12 E
Katsepe 93 15 45 S 46 15 E
Katsina Ala → 85 7 10N 9 20 E
Katsuura 74 35 10N 140 20 E
Kattawaz-Urgun □ 65 32 10N 68 20 E
Kattegatt 49 57 0N 11 20 E
Katumba 90 7 40 S 25 17 E
Katungu 90 2 55 S 40 3 E
Katwa 69 23 30N 88 5 E
Katwijk-aan-Zee 16 52 12N 4 24 E
Katy 28 51 2N 16 45 E
Kauai 110 22 0N 159 30W
Kauai Chan. 110 21 45N 158 50W
Kaub 25 50 5N 7 46 E
Kaufbeuren 25 47 50N 10 37 E
Kaufman 117 32 35N 96 20W
Kaukauna 114 44 20N 88 13W
Kaukauveld 92 20 0 S 20 15 E
Kaukonen 50 67 31N 24 53 E
Kauliranta 50 66 27N 23 41 E
Kaunas 54 54 54N 23 54 E
Kaura Namoda 85 12 37N 6 33 E
Kautokeino 50 69 0N 23 4 E
Kavacha 59 60 16N 169 51 E
Kavadarci 42 41 26N 22 3 E
Kavaja 44 41 11N 19 33 E
Kavali 70 14 55N 80 1 E
Kavála 44 40 57N 24 28 E
Kavála □ 44 41 5N 24 30 E
Kavála Kólpos 44 40 50N 24 25 E
Kavarna 43 43 26N 28 22 E
Kavieng 98 2 36 S 150 51 E
Kavkaz, Bolshoi 57 42 50N 44 0 E
Kavoúsi 45 35 7N 25 51 E
Kaw = Caux 127 4 30N 52 15W
Kawa 87 13 42N 32 34 E
Kawagama L. 112 45 18N 78 45W
Kawagoe 74 35 55N 139 29 E
Kawaguchi 74 35 52N 139 45 E
Kawaihae 110 20 3N 155 50W
Kawambwa 91 9 48 S 29 3 E
Kawardha 69 22 0N 81 17 E
Kawasaki 74 35 35N 139 42 E
Kawene 106 48 45N 91 15W
Kawerau 101 38 7 S 176 42 E
Kawhia Harbour 101 38 5 S 174 51 E
Kawio, Kepulauan 73 4 30N 125 30 E
Kawnro 67 22 48N 99 8 E
Kawthaung 71 10 5N 98 36 E
Kawthoolei □ = Kawthule 67 18 0N 97 30 E
Kawthule □ 67 18 0N 97 30 E
Kaya 85 13 4N 1 10W
Kayah □ 67 19 15N 97 15 E
Kayangulam 70 9 10N 76 33 E
Kaycee 118 43 45N 106 46W
Kayeli 73 3 20 S 127 10 E
Kayenta 119 36 46N 110 15W
Kayes 84 14 25N 11 30W
Kayima 84 8 54N 11 15W
Kayomba 91 13 11 S 24 2 E
Kayoro 85 11 0N 1 28W
Kayrunnera 99 30 40 S 142 30 E
Kaysatskoye 57 49 47N 46 49 E
Kayseri 64 38 45N 35 30 E
Kaysville 118 41 2N 111 58W
Kayuagung 72 3 24 S 104 50 E
Kazachinskoye 59 56 16N 107 36 E
Kazachye 59 70 52N 135 58 E
Kazakh S.S.R. □ 58 50 0N 70 0 E
Kazan 55 55 48N 49 3 E
Kazanlúk 43 42 38N 25 20 E
Kazanskaya 57 49 50N 41 10 E
Kazatin 56 49 45N 28 50 E
Kazbek 57 42 42N 44 30 E
Kāzerūn 65 29 38N 51 40 E
Kazi Magomed 57 40 3N 49 0 E
Kazimierz Dolny 28 51 19N 21 57 E
Kazimierza Wielka 28 50 15N 20 30 E
Kazincbarcika 27 48 17N 20 36 E
Kaztalovka 57 49 47N 48 43 E
Kazumba 88 6 25 S 22 5 E
Kazym → 58 63 54N 65 50 E
Kcynia 28 53 0N 17 30 E
Kè-Macina 84 13 58N 5 22W
Kéa 45 37 35N 24 22 E
Kea 45 37 30N 24 22 E
Keams Canyon 119 35 53N 110 9W
Kearney 116 40 45N 99 3W
Keban 64 38 50N 38 50 E
Kébi 84 9 18N 6 37W
Kebili 83 33 47N 9 0 E
Kebnekaise 50 67 53N 18 33 E
Kebri Dehar 63 6 45N 44 17 E
Kebumen 73 7 42 S 109 40 E
Kecel 27 46 31N 19 16 E
Kechika → 108 59 41N 127 12W
Kecskemét 27 46 57N 19 42 E
Kedada 87 5 25N 35 58 E
Kedah □ 71 5 50N 100 40 E
Kedainiai 54 55 15N 24 2 E
Kedgwick 107 47 40N 67 20W
Kedia Hill 92 21 28 S 24 37 E
Kediri 73 7 51 S 112 1 E
Kédougou 84 12 35N 12 10W
Kedzierzyn 28 50 20N 18 12 E
Keefers 108 50 0N 121 40W
Keeley L. 109 54 54N 108 8W
Keeling Is. = Cocos Is. 94 12 12 S 96 55 E
Keene 114 42 57N 72 17W
Keeper Hill 15 52 46N 8 17W
Keer-Weer, C. 97 14 0 S 141 32 E
Keeseville 113 44 29N 73 30W
Keetmanshoop 92 26 35 S 18 8 E
Keewatin 116 47 23N 93 0W
Keewatin □ 109 63 20N 95 0W
Keewatin → 109 56 29N 100 46W
Kefa □ 87 6 55N 36 30 E
Kefallinia 45 38 20N 20 30 E
Kefamenanu 73 9 28 S 124 29 E
Kefar 'Eqron 62 31 52N 34 49 E
Kefar Hasidim 62 32 47N 35 5 E
Kefar Nahum 62 32 54N 35 34 E
Kefar Sava 62 32 11N 34 54 E
Kefar Szold 62 33 11N 35 39 E
Kefar Vitkin 62 32 22N 34 53 E
Kefar Yehezqel 62 32 34N 35 22 E
Kefar Yona 62 32 20N 34 54 E
Kefar Zekharya 62 31 43N 34 57 E
Kefar Zetim 62 32 48N 35 27 E
Keffi 85 8 55N 7 43 E
Keflavík 50 64 2N 22 35W
Keg River 108 57 54N 117 55W
Kegahka 107 50 9N 61 18W
Kegalla 70 7 15N 80 21 E
Kehl 25 48 34N 7 50 E
Keighley 12 53 52N 1 54W
Keimoes 92 28 41 S 21 0 E
Keita 85 14 46N 5 56 E
Keith, Austral. 99 36 6 S 140 20 E
Keith, U.K. 14 57 33N 2 58W
Keith Arm 104 64 20N 122 15W
Kekri 68 26 0N 75 10 E
Kël 59 69 30N 124 10 E
Kelamet 87 16 0N 38 30 E
Kelan 76 38 43N 111 31 E
Kelang 71 3 2N 101 26 E
Kelani Ganga → 70 6 58N 79 50 E
Kelantan □ 71 5 10N 102 0 E
Kelantan → 71 6 13N 102 14 E
Këlcyra 44 40 22N 20 12 E
Kelheim 25 48 58N 11 57 E
Kelibia 83 36 50N 11 3 E
Kellé 88 0 8 S 14 38 E
Keller 118 48 2N 118 44W
Kellerberrin 96 31 36 S 117 38 E
Kellett C. 4 72 0N 126 0W
Kelleys I. 112 41 35N 82 42W
Kellogg 118 47 30N 116 5W
Kelloselkä 50 66 56N 28 53 E
Kells = Ceanannus Mor 15 53 42N 6 53W
Kélo 81 9 10N 15 45 E
Kelowna 108 49 50N 119 25W
Kelsey Bay 108 50 25N 126 0W
Kelso, N.Z. 101 45 54 S 169 15 E
Kelso, U.K. 14 55 36N 2 27W
Kelso, U.S.A. 118 46 10N 122 57W
Keluang 71 2 3N 103 18 E
Kelvington 109 52 10N 103 30W
Kem 52 65 0N 34 38 E
Kem → 52 64 57N 34 41 E
Kem-Kem 82 30 40N 4 30W
Kema 73 1 22N 125 8 E
Kemah 64 39 32N 39 5 E
Kemano 108 53 35N 128 0W
Kembolcha 87 11 2N 39 42 E
Kemenets-Podolskiy 56 48 40N 26 40 E
Kemerovo 58 55 20N 86 5 E
Kemi 50 65 44N 24 34 E
Kemi älv = Kemijoki → 50 65 47N 24 32 E
Kemijärvi 50 66 43N 27 22 E
Kemijoki → 50 65 47N 24 32 E
Kemmerer 118 41 52N 110 30W
Kemp Coast 5 69 0S 55 0 E
Kemp L. 117 33 45N 99 15W
Kempsey 97 31 1 S 152 50 E
Kempt, L. 106 47 25N 74 22W
Kempten 25 47 42N 10 18 E
Kemptville 106 45 0N 75 38W
Kenadsa 82 31 48N 2 26W
Kendal, Indon. 72 6 56 S 110 14 E
Kendal, U.K. 12 54 19N 2 44W
Kendall 99 31 35 S 152 44 E
Kendall → 98 14 4 S 141 35 E
Kendallville 114 41 25N 85 15W
Kendari 73 3 50 S 122 30 E
Kendawangan 72 2 32 S 110 17 E
Kende 85 11 30N 4 12 E
Kendervicës, m. e. 44 40 15N 19 52 E
Kendrapara 69 20 35N 86 30 E
Kendrick 118 46 43N 116 41W
Kenedy 117 28 49N 97 51W
Kenema 84 7 50N 11 14W
Keng Tung 67 21 0N 99 30 E
Kenge 88 4 50 S 17 4 E
Kengeja 90 5 26 S 39 45 E
Kenhardt 92 29 19 S 21 12 E
Kénitra (Port Lyautey) 82 34 15N 6 40W
Kenmare, Ireland 15 51 52N 9 35W
Kenmare, U.S.A. 116 48 40N 102 4W
Kenmare → 15 51 40N 10 0W
Kenmore 100 34 44 S 149 45 E
Kenn Reef 97 21 12 S 155 46 E
Kennebec 116 43 56N 99 54W
Kennedy 91 18 52 S 27 10 E
Kennedy Taungdeik 67 23 15N 93 45 E
Kennet → 13 51 24N 0 58W
Kennett 117 36 7N 90 0W
Kennewick 118 46 11N 119 2W
Kénogami 107 48 25N 71 15W
Kenogami → 106 51 6N 84 28W
Kenora 109 49 47N 94 29W
Kenosha 114 42 33N 87 48W
Kensington, Can. 107 46 28N 63 34W
Kensington, U.S.A. 116 39 48N 99 2W
Kensington Downs 98 22 31 S 144 19 E
Kent, Ohio, U.S.A. 114 41 8N 81 20W

Kent Kiparissía

Kent, Oreg., U.S.A. **118** 45 11N 120 45W
Kent, Tex., U.S.A. **117** 31 5N 104 12W
Kent □ **13** 51 12N 0 40 E
Kent Group **99** 39 30S 147 20 E
Kent Pen. **104** 68 30N 107 0W
Kentau **58** 43 32N 68 36 E
Kentland **114** 40 45N 87 25W
Kenton **114** 40 40N 83 35W
Kentucky □ **114** 37 20N 85 0W
Kentucky → **114** 38 41N 85 11W
Kentucky Dam **114** 37 2N 88 15W
Kentucky L. **115** 36 25N 88 0W
Kentville **107** 45 6N 64 29W
Kentwood **117** 31 0N 90 30W
Kenya ■ **90** 1 0N 38 0 E
Kenya, Mt. **90** 0 10S 37 18 E
Keokuk **116** 40 25N 91 24W
Kep-i-Gjuhës **44** 40 28N 19 15 E
Kepi **73** 6 32S 139 19 E
Kepice **28** 54 16N 16 51 E
Kępno **28** 51 18N 17 58 E
Keppel B. **97** 23 21S 150 55 E
Kepsut **64** 39 40N 28 9 E
Kerala □ **70** 11 0N 76 15 E
Kerang **97** 35 40S 143 55 E
Keratéa **45** 37 48N 23 58 E
Keraudren, C. **99** 19 58S 119 45 E
Keray **65** 26 15N 57 30 E
Kerch **56** 45 20N 36 20 E
Kerchenskiy Proliv **56** 45 10N 36 30 E
Kerchoual **85** 17 12N 0 20 E
Kerem Maharal **62** 32 39N 34 59 E
Kerema **98** 7 58S 145 50 E
Keren **87** 15 45N 38 28 E
Kerewan **84** 13 29N 16 10W
Kerguelen **3** 48 15S 69 10 E
Keri **45** 37 40N 20 49 E
Keri Kera **87** 12 21N 32 42 E
Kericho **90** 0 22S 35 15 E
Kericho □ **90** 0 30S 35 15 E
Kerinci **72** 1 40S 101 15 E
Kerkenna, Iles **83** 34 48N 11 11 E
Kerki **58** 37 50N 65 12 E
Kerkinítis, Límni **44** 41 12N 23 10 E
Kérkira **44** 39 38N 19 50 E
Kerkrade **16** 50 53N 6 4 E
Kerma **86** 19 33N 30 32 E
Kermadec Is. **94** 30 0S 178 15W
Kermadec Trench **94** 30 30S 176 0W
Kermān **65** 30 15N 57 1 E
Kermān □ **65** 30 0N 57 0 E
Kermānshāh **64** 34 23N 47 0 E
Kermānshāhān □ **64** 34 0N 46 30 E
Kerme Körfezi **45** 36 55N 27 50 E
Kermen **43** 42 30N 26 16 E
Kermit **117** 31 56N 103 3W
Kern → **119** 35 16N 119 18W
Kerrobert **109** 52 0N 109 11W
Kerrville **117** 30 1N 99 8W
Kerry □ **15** 52 7N 9 35W
Kerry Hd. **15** 52 26N 9 56W
Kersa **87** 9 28N 41 48 E
Kerteminde **49** 55 28N 10 39 E
Kertosono **73** 7 38S 112 9 E
Kerulen → **75** 48 48N 117 0 E
Kerzaz **82** 29 29N 1 37W
Kesagami → **106** 51 40N 79 45W
Kesagami L. **106** 50 23N 80 15W
Keşan **44** 40 49N 26 38 E
Keski-Suomen lääni □ **50** 62 0N 25 30 E
Kestell **93** 28 17S 28 42 E
Kestenga **52** 66 0N 31 50 E
Keswick **12** 54 35N 3 9W
Keszthely **27** 46 50N 17 15 E
Ket → **58** 58 55N 81 32 E
Keta **85** 5 49N 1 0 E
Ketapang **72** 1 55S 110 0 E
Ketchikan **104** 55 25N 131 40W
Ketchum **118** 43 41N 114 27W
Kete Krachi **85** 7 46N 0 1W
Ketef, Khalîg Umm el **86** 23 40N 35 35 E
Keti Bandar **68** 24 8N 67 27 E
Ketri **68** 28 1N 75 50 E
Kętrzyn **28** 54 7N 21 22 E
Kettering **13** 52 24N 0 44W
Kettle → **109** 56 40N 89 34W
Kettle Falls **118** 48 41N 118 2W
Kety **27** 49 51N 19 16 E
Kevin **118** 48 45N 111 58W
Kewanee **116** 41 18N 89 55W
Kewaunee **114** 44 27N 87 30W
Keweenaw B. **114** 46 56N 88 23W
Keweenaw Pen. **114** 47 30N 88 0W
Keweenaw Pt. **114** 47 26N 87 40W
Key Harbour **106** 45 50N 80 45W
Key West **121** 24 33N 82 0W
Keyport **113** 40 26N 74 12W
Keyser **114** 39 26N 79 0W
Keystone, S.D., U.S.A. **116** 43 54N 103 27W
Keystone, W. Va., U.S.A. **114** 37 30N 81 30W
Kezhma **59** 58 59N 101 9 E
Kežmarok **27** 49 10N 20 28 E
Khabarovo **58** 69 30N 60 30 E
Khabarovsk **59** 48 30N 135 5 E
Khābūr → **64** 35 0N 40 30 E
Khachmas **57** 41 31N 48 42 E
Khachraud **68** 23 25N 75 20 E
Khadari, W. el → **87** 10 29N 27 15 E
Khadro **68** 26 11N 68 50 E
Khadyzhensk **57** 44 26N 39 32 E
Khagaria **69** 25 30N 86 32 E
Khaibar **86** 25 49N 39 16 E
Khaipur, Bahawalpur, Pak. **68** 29 34N 72 17 E
Khaipur, Hyderabad, Pak. **68** 27 32N 68 49 E
Khair **68** 27 57N 77 46 E
Khairabad **69** 27 33N 80 47 E
Khairagarh Raj **69** 21 27N 81 2 E
* Khairpur □ **68** 27 20N 69 8 E
Khakhea **92** 24 48S 23 22 E
Khalfallah **82** 34 20N 0 16 E
Khalij-e-Fars □ **65** 28 20N 51 45 E
Khalilabad **69** 26 48N 83 5 E
Khálki **44** 39 36N 22 30 E
Khalkidhikí □ **44** 40 25N 23 20 E
Khalkís **45** 38 27N 23 42 E
Khalmer-Sede = Tazovskiy **58** 67 30N 78 30 E
Khalmer Yu **58** 67 58N 65 1 E
Khalturin **55** 58 40N 48 50 E
Khamaria **69** 23 10N 80 52 E
Khamas Country **92** 21 45S 26 30 E
Khambhalia **68** 22 14N 69 41 E
Khamgaon **68** 20 42N 76 37 E
Khamilonísion **45** 35 50N 26 15 E
Khamir **63** 16 0N 44 0 E
Khammam **70** 17 11N 80 6 E
Khān Yūnis **62** 31 21N 34 18 E
Khānābād **65** 36 45N 69 5 E
Khānaqīn **64** 34 23N 45 25 E
Khandrá **45** 35 3N 26 8 E
Khandwa **68** 21 49N 76 22 E
Khandyga **59** 62 42N 135 35 E
Khanewal **68** 30 20N 71 55 E
• Khanh Hung **71** 9 37N 105 50 E
Khaniá **45** 35 30N 24 4 E
Khaniá □ **45** 35 30N 24 0 E
Khanion Kólpos **45** 35 33N 23 55 E
Khanka, Oz. **59** 45 0N 132 30 E
Khanna **68** 30 42N 76 16 E
Khanpur **68** 28 42N 70 35 E
Khanty-Mansiysk **58** 61 0N 69 0 E
Khapcheranga **59** 49 42N 112 24 E
Kharagpur **69** 22 20N 87 25 E
Kharaij **86** 21 25N 41 0 E
Kharan Kalat **66** 28 34N 65 21 E
Kharānaq **65** 32 20N 54 45 E
Kharda **70** 18 40N 75 34 E
Khârga, El Wâhât el **86** 25 10N 30 35 E
Khargon **68** 21 45N 75 40 E
Kharit, Wadi el → **86** 24 26N 33 3 E
Khārk, Jazireh **64** 29 15N 50 28 E
Kharkov **56** 49 58N 36 20 E
Kharmanli **43** 41 55N 25 55 E
Kharovsk **55** 59 56N 40 13 E
Kharsāniya **64** 27 10N 49 10 E
Khartoum = El Khartûm **87** 15 31N 32 35 E
Khasab **65** 26 14N 56 15 E
Khasavyurt **57** 43 16N 46 40 E
Khasebake **92** 20 42S 24 29 E
Khāsh **65** 28 15N 61 15 E
Khashm el Girba **87** 14 59N 35 58 E
Khashuri **57** 41 58N 43 35 E
Khasi Hills **69** 25 30N 91 30 E
Khaskovo **43** 41 56N 25 30 E
Khatanga **59** 72 0N 102 20 E
Khatanga → **59** 72 55N 106 0 E
Khatangskiy, Saliv **4** 66 0N 112 0 E
Khatauli **68** 29 17N 77 43 E
Khatyrka **59** 62 3N 175 15 E
Khavār □ **64** 37 20N 47 0 E
Khaybar, Harrat **64** 25 45N 40 0 E
Khazzân Jabal el Awliyâ **87** 15 24N 32 20 E
Khed, Maharashtra, India **70** 17 43N 73 27 E
Khed, Maharashtra, India **70** 18 51N 73 56 E
Khekra **68** 28 52N 77 20 E
Khemelnik **56** 49 33N 27 58 E
Khemis Miliana **82** 36 11N 2 14 E
Khemissèt **82** 33 50N 6 1W
Khemmarat **71** 16 10N 105 15 E
Khenchela **83** 35 28N 7 11 E
Khenifra **82** 32 58N 5 46W
Kherrata **83** 36 27N 5 13 E
Khérson **44** 41 5N 22 47 E
Kherson **56** 46 35N 32 35 E
Khersónisos Akrotíri **45** 35 30N 24 10 E
Kheta → **59** 71 54N 102 6 E
Khiliomódhion **45** 37 48N 22 51 E
Khilok **59** 51 30N 110 45 E
Khimki **55** 55 50N 37 20 E
Khíos **45** 38 27N 26 9 E
Khisar-Momina Banya **43** 42 30N 24 44 E
Khiuma = Hiiumaa **54** 58 50N 22 45 E
Khiva **58** 41 30N 60 18 E
Khīyāv **64** 38 30N 47 45 E
Khlebarovo **43** 43 37N 26 15 E
Khlong → **71** 15 30N 98 50 E
Khmelnitskiy **56** 49 23N 27 0 E
Khmer Rep. = Cambodia ■ **71** 12 15N 105 0 E
Khojak P. **65** 30 55N 66 30 E
Khokholskiy **55** 51 35N 38 40 E
Kholm, Afghan. **65** 36 45N 67 40 E
Kholm, U.S.S.R. **54** 57 10N 31 15 E
Kholmsk **59** 47 40N 142 5 E
Khomas Hochland **92** 22 40S 16 0 E
Khomeyn **64** 33 40N 50 7 E
Khomo **92** 21 7S 24 35 E
Khon Kaen **71** 16 30N 102 47 E
Khong **71** 14 5N 105 56 E
Khong → **71** 15 0N 106 50 E
Khonu **59** 66 30N 143 12 E
Khoper → **55** 49 30N 42 20 E
Khor el 'Atash **87** 13 20N 34 15 E
Khóra **45** 37 3N 21 42 E
Khóra Sfakion **45** 35 15N 24 9 E
Khorāsān □ **65** 34 0N 58 0 E
Khorat = Nakhon Ratchasima **71** 14 59N 102 12 E
Khorat, Cao Nguyen **71** 15 30N 102 50 E
Khorb el Ethel **82** 28 30N 6 17W
Khorixas **92** 20 16S 14 59 E
Khorog **58** 37 30N 71 36 E
Khorol **56** 49 48N 33 15 E
Khorramābād **64** 33 30N 48 25 E
Khorramshahr **64** 30 29N 48 15 E
Khotin **56** 48 31N 26 27 E
Khouribga **82** 32 58N 6 57W
Khowai **67** 24 5N 91 40 E
Khoyniki **54** 51 54N 29 55 E
Khrami → **57** 41 30N 45 0 E
Khrenovoye **55** 51 4N 40 16 E
Khristianá **45** 36 14N 25 13 E
Khtapodhiá **45** 37 24N 25 34 E
Khu Khan **71** 14 42N 104 12 E
Khulna **69** 22 45N 89 34 E
Khulo **57** 41 33N 42 19 E
Khumago **92** 20 26S 24 32 E
Khunzakh **57** 42 35N 46 42 E
Khūr **65** 32 55N 58 18 E
Khurai **68** 24 3N 78 23 E
Khurayş **64** 24 55N 48 5 E
Khurja **68** 28 15N 77 58 E
Khūryān Mūryān, Jazā 'ir **63** 17 30N 55 58 E
Khushab **68** 32 20N 72 20 E
Khuzdar **66** 27 52N 66 30 E
Khūzetān □ **64** 31 0N 50 0 E
Khvalynsk **55** 52 30N 48 2 E
Khvatovka **55** 52 24N 46 32 E
Khvor **65** 33 45N 55 0 E
Khvormūj **65** 28 40N 51 30 E
Khvoy **64** 38 35N 45 0 E
Khvoynaya **54** 58 58N 34 28 E
Khyber Pass **66** 34 10N 71 8 E
Kiabukwa **91** 8 40S 24 48 E
Kiadho → **70** 19 37N 77 40 E
Kiama **99** 34 40S 150 50 E
Kiamba **73** 6 2N 124 46 E
Kiambi **90** 7 15S 28 0 E
Kiambu **90** 1 8S 36 50 E
Kiangsi = Jiangxi □ **75** 27 30N 116 0 E
Kiangsu = Jiangsu □ **75** 33 0N 120 0 E
Kiáton **45** 38 2N 22 43 E
Kibæk **49** 56 2N 8 51 E
Kibanga Port **90** 0 10N 32 58 E
Kibangou **88** 3 26S 12 22 E
Kibara **90** 2 8S 33 30 E
Kibare, Mts. **90** 8 25S 27 10 E
Kibombo **90** 3 57S 25 53 E
Kibondo **90** 3 35S 30 45 E
Kibondo □ **90** 4 0S 30 55 E
Kibumbu **90** 3 32S 29 45 E
Kibungu **90** 2 10S 30 32 E
Kibuye, Burundi **90** 3 39S 29 59 E
Kibuye, Rwanda **90** 2 3S 29 21 E
Kibwesa **90** 6 30S 29 58 E
Kibwezi **90** 2 27S 37 57 E
Kičevo **42** 41 34N 20 59 E
Kichiga **59** 59 50N 163 5 E
Kicking Horse Pass **108** 51 28N 116 16W
Kidal **85** 18 26N 1 22 E
Kidderminster **13** 52 24N 2 13W
Kidete **90** 6 25S 37 17 E
Kidira **84** 14 28N 12 13W
Kidnappers, C. **101** 39 38S 177 5 E
Kidston **98** 18 52S 144 8 E
Kidugallo **90** 6 49S 38 15 E
Kiel **24** 54 16N 10 8 E
Kiel Kanal = Nord-Ostee-Kanal **24** 54 15N 9 40 E
Kielce **28** 50 52N 20 42 E
Kielce □ **28** 50 40N 20 40 E
Kieler Bucht **24** 54 30N 10 30 E
Kienge **91** 10 30S 27 30 E
Kiessé **85** 13 29N 4 1 E
Kiev = Kiyev **54** 50 30N 30 28 E
Kifār 'Aşyūn **62** 31 39N 35 7 E
Kiffa **84** 16 37N 11 24W
Kifisiá **45** 38 4N 23 49 E
Kifissós → **45** 38 35N 23 20 E
Kifrī **64** 34 45N 45 0 E
Kigali **90** 1 59S 30 4 E
Kigarama **90** 1 1S 31 50 E
Kigoma □ **90** 5 0S 30 0 E
Kigoma-Ujiji **90** 4 55S 29 36 E
Kigomasha, Ras **90** 4 58S 38 58 E
Kihee **99** 27 23S 142 37 E
Kii-Suidō **74** 33 40N 135 0 E
Kikinda **42** 45 50N 20 30 E
Kikládhes **45** 37 20N 24 30 E
Kikládhes □ **45** 37 0N 25 0 E
Kikori **98** 7 25S 144 15 E
Kikori → **98** 7 38S 144 20 E
Kikwit **88** 5 5S 18 45 E
Kilafors **48** 61 14N 16 36 E
Kilakarai **70** 9 12N 78 47 E
Kilalki **45** 36 15N 27 35 E
Kilauea Crater **110** 19 24N 155 17W
Kilcoy **99** 26 59S 152 30 E
Kildare **15** 53 10N 6 50W
Kildare □ **15** 53 10N 6 50W
Kilgore **117** 32 22N 94 55W
Kilifi **90** 3 40S 39 48 E
Kilifi □ **90** 3 30S 39 40 E
Kilimanjaro **90** 3 7S 37 20 E
Kilimanjaro □ **90** 4 0S 38 0 E
Kilindini **90** 4 4S 39 40 E
Kilis **64** 36 50N 37 10 E
Kiliya **56** 45 28N 29 16 E
Kilju **76** 40 57N 129 25 E
Kilkee **15** 52 41N 9 40W
Kilkenny **15** 52 40N 7 17W
Kilkenny □ **15** 52 35N 7 15W
Kilkieran B. **15** 53 18N 9 45W
Kilkís **44** 40 58N 22 57 E
Kilkís □ **44** 41 5N 22 50 E
Killala **15** 54 13N 9 12W
Killala B. **15** 54 20N 9 12W
Killaloe **15** 52 48N 8 28W
Killaloe Sta. **112** 45 33N 77 25W
Killam **108** 52 47N 111 51W
Killarney, Can. **106** 45 55N 81 30W
Killarney, Ireland **15** 52 2N 9 30W
Killarney, Lakes of **15** 52 0N 9 30W
Killary Harbour **15** 53 38N 9 52W
Killdeer, Can. **109** 49 6N 106 22W
Killdeer, U.S.A. **116** 47 26N 102 48W
Killeen **117** 31 7N 97 45W
Killiecrankie, Pass of **14** 56 44N 3 46W
Killin **14** 56 28N 4 20W
Killíni, Ilia, Greece **45** 37 55N 21 8 E
Killíni, Korinthía, Greece **45** 37 54N 22 25 E
Killybegs **15** 54 38N 8 26W
Kilmarnock **14** 55 36N 4 30W
Kilmez **55** 56 58N 50 55 E
Kilmez → **55** 56 58N 50 28 E
Kilmore **99** 37 25S 144 53 E
Kilondo **91** 9 45S 34 20 E
Kilosa **90** 6 48S 37 0 E
Kilosa □ **90** 6 48S 37 0 E
Kilrush **15** 52 39N 9 30W
Kilsmo **48** 59 6N 15 35 E
Kilwa □ **91** 9 0S 39 0 E
Kilwa Kisiwani **91** 8 58S 39 32 E
Kilwa Kivinje **91** 8 45S 39 25 E
Kilwa Masoko **91** 8 55S 39 30 E
Kim **117** 37 18N 103 20W
Kimaam **73** 7 58S 138 53 E
Kimamba **90** 6 45S 37 10 E
Kimba **97** 33 8S 136 23 E
Kimball, Nebr., U.S.A. **116** 41 17N 103 40W
Kimball, S.D., U.S.A. **116** 43 47N 98 57W
Kimbe **98** 5 33S 150 11 E
Kimbe B. **98** 5 15S 150 30 E
Kimberley, Austral. **96** 16 20S 127 0 E
Kimberley, Can. **108** 49 40N 115 59W
Kimberley, S. Afr. **92** 28 43S 24 46 E
Kimberly **118** 42 33N 114 25W
Kimchaek **76** 40 40N 129 10 E
Kimchŏn **76** 36 11N 128 4 E
Kimi **45** 38 38N 24 6 E
Kimolos **45** 36 48N 24 37 E
Kimovsk **55** 54 0N 38 29 E
Kimparana **84** 12 48N 5 0W
Kimry **55** 56 55N 37 15 E
Kimsquit **108** 52 45N 126 57W
Kimstad **49** 58 35N 15 58 E
Kinabalu **72** 6 0N 116 0 E
Kínaros **45** 36 59N 26 15 E
Kinaskan L. **108** 57 38N 130 8W
Kincaid **109** 49 40N 107 0W
Kincardine **106** 44 10N 81 40W
Kinda **91** 9 18S 25 4 E
Kindersley **109** 51 30N 109 10W
Kindia **84** 10 0N 12 52W
Kindu **90** 2 55S 25 50 E
Kinel **55** 53 15N 50 40 E
Kineshma **55** 57 30N 42 5 E
Kinesi **90** 1 25S 33 50 E
King City **119** 36 11N 121 8W
King Cr. → **98** 24 35S 139 30 E
King Frederick VI Land = Kong Frederik VI.s. Kyst **4** 63 0N 43 0W
King George B. **128** 51 30S 60 30W
King George I. **5** 60 0S 60 0W
King George Is. **105** 57 20N 80 30W
King George Sd. **96** 35 5S 118 0 E
King I., Austral. **97** 39 50S 144 0 E
King I., Can. **108** 52 10N 127 40W
King I. = Kadah Kyun **71** 12 30N 98 20 E
King Leopold Ranges **96** 17 30S 125 45 E
King, Mt. **99** 25 10S 147 30 E
King Sd. **96** 16 50S 123 20 E
King William I. **104** 69 10N 97 25W
King William's Town **92** 32 51S 27 22 E
Kingaroy **97** 26 32S 151 51 E
Kingfisher **117** 35 50N 97 55W
Kingisepp **54** 59 25N 28 40 E
Kingisepp (Kuressaare) **54** 58 15N 22 30 E
Kingman, Ariz., U.S.A. **119** 35 12N 114 2W
Kingman, Kans., U.S.A. **117** 37 41N 98 9W
Kings → **119** 36 10N 119 50W
Kings Canyon National Park **119** 37 0N 118 35W
King's Lynn **12** 52 45N 0 25 E
Kings Mountain **115** 35 13N 81 20W
King's Peak **118** 40 46N 110 27W
Kingsbridge **13** 50 17N 3 46W
Kingsburg **119** 36 35N 119 36W
Kingscote **99** 35 40S 137 38 E
Kingscourt **15** 53 55N 6 48W
Kingsley **116** 42 37N 95 58W
Kingsley Dam **116** 41 20N 101 40W
Kingsport **115** 36 33N 82 36W
Kingston, Can. **106** 44 14N 76 30W
Kingston, Jamaica **121** 18 0N 76 50W
Kingston, N.Z. **101** 45 20S 168 43 E
Kingston, N.Y., U.S.A. **114** 41 55N 74 0W
Kingston, Pa., U.S.A. **114** 41 19N 75 58W
Kingston, R.I., U.S.A. **113** 41 29N 71 30W
Kingston South East **97** 36 51S 139 55 E
Kingston-upon-Thames **13** 51 23N 0 20W
Kingstown **121** 13 10N 61 10W
Kingstree **115** 33 40N 79 48W
Kingsville, Can. **106** 42 2N 82 45W
Kingsville, U.S.A. **117** 27 30N 97 53W
Kingussie **14** 57 5N 4 2W
Kinistino **109** 52 57N 105 2W
Kinkala **88** 4 18S 14 49 E
Kinleith **101** 38 20S 175 56 E
Kinmount **112** 44 48N 78 45W
Kinn **47** 61 34N 4 45 E
Kinna **49** 57 32N 12 42 E
Kinnaird **108** 49 17N 117 39W
Kinnairds Hd. **14** 57 40N 2 0W
Kinnared **49** 57 2N 13 7 E
Kinneret **62** 32 44N 35 34 E
Kinneret, Yam **62** 32 45N 35 35 E
Kinoje → **106** 52 8N 81 25W
Kinoni **90** 0 41S 30 28 E
Kinross **14** 56 13N 3 25W
Kinsale **15** 51 42N 8 31W
Kinsale, Old Hd. of **15** 51 37N 8 32W
Kinsarvik **47** 60 22N 6 43 E
Kinshasa **88** 4 20S 15 15 E
Kinsley **117** 37 57N 99 30W
Kinston **115** 35 18N 77 35W
Kintampo **85** 8 5N 1 41W
Kintap **72** 3 51S 115 13 E
Kintyre **14** 55 30N 5 35W
Kintyre, Mull of **14** 55 17N 5 55W
Kinushseo → **106** 55 15N 83 45W
Kinuso **108** 55 20N 115 25W
Kinyangiri **90** 4 25S 34 37 E
Kinzig → **25** 48 37N 7 49 E
Kinzua **112** 41 52N 78 58W
Kinzua Dam **112** 41 53N 79 0W
Kióni **45** 38 27N 20 41 E
Kiosk **106** 46 6N 78 53W
Kiowa, Kans., U.S.A. **117** 37 3N 98 30W
Kiowa, Okla., U.S.A. **117** 34 45N 95 50W
Kipahigan L. **109** 55 20N 101 55W
Kipanga **90** 6 15S 35 20 E
Kiparissía **45** 37 15N 21 40 E

Now part of Sind □

• Renamed Soc Trang

Kiparissiakós Kólpos Kopliku

Kiparissiakós Kólpos 45 37 25N 21 25 E
Kipembawe 90 7 38S 33 27 E
Kipengere Ra. 91 9 12S 34 15 E
Kipili 90 7 28S 30 32 E
Kipini 90 2 30S 40 32 E
Kipling 109 50 6N 102 38W
Kippure 15 53 11N 6 23W
Kipushi 91 11 48S 27 12 E
Kirandul 70 18 33N 81 10 E
Kiratpur 68 29 32N 78 12 E
Kirchhain 24 50 49N 8 54 E
Kirchheim 25 48 38N 9 20 E
Kirchheim-Bolanden 25 49 40N 8 0 E
Kirchschlag 27 47 30N 16 19 E
Kirensk 59 57 50N 107 55 E
Kirgiz S.S.R. □ 58 42 0N 75 0 E
Kirgiziya Steppe 53 50 0N 55 0 E
Kiri 88 1 29S 19 0 E
Kiribati ■ 94 1 0N 176 0 E
Kiriburu 69 22 0N 85 0 E
Kırıkkale 64 39 51N 33 32 E
Kirillov 55 59 51N 38 14 E
Kirin = Jilin 76 43 55N 126 30 E
Kirin = Jilin □ 76 44 0N 126 0 E
Kirindi → 70 6 15N 81 20 E
Kirishi 54 59 28N 31 59 E
Kirkcaldy 14 56 7N 3 10W
Kirkcudbright 14 54 50N 4 3W
Kirkee 70 18 34N 73 56 E
Kirkenær 47 60 27N 12 3 E
Kirkenes 50 69 40N 30 5 E
Kirkintilloch 14 55 57N 4 10W
Kirkjubæjarklaustur 50 63 47N 18 4W
Kirkland 119 34 29N 112 46W
Kirkland Lake 106 48 9N 80 2W
Kırklareli 43 41 44N 27 15 E
Kirksville 116 40 8N 92 35W
Kirkūk 64 35 30N 44 21 E
Kirkwall 14 58 59N 2 59W
Kirkwood 92 33 22S 25 15 E
Kirlampudi 70 17 12N 82 12 E
Kirn 25 49 46N 7 29 E
Kirov, R.S.F.S.R., U.S.S.R. 54 54 3N 34 20 E
Kirov, R.S.F.S.R., U.S.S.R. 58 58 35N 49 40 E
Kirovabad 57 40 45N 46 20 E
Kirovakan 57 40 48N 44 30 E
Kirovo-Chepetsk 55 58 28N 50 0 E
Kirovograd 56 48 35N 32 20 E
Kirovsk, R.S.F.S.R., U.S.S.R. 52 67 48N 33 50 E
Kirovsk, Turkmen S.S.R., U.S.S.R. 58 37 42N 60 23 E
Kirovsk, Ukraine S.S.R., U.S.S.R. 57 48 35N 38 30 E
Kirovski 57 45 51N 48 11 E
Kirovskiy 59 54 27N 155 42 E
Kirriemuir, Can. 109 51 56N 110 20W
Kirriemuir, U.K. 14 56 41N 3 0W
Kirsanov 55 52 35N 42 40 E
Kırşehir 64 39 14N 34 5 E
Kirstonia 92 25 30S 23 45 E
Kirtachi 85 12 52N 2 30 E
Kirteh 65 32 15N 63 0 E
Kirthar Range 68 27 0N 67 0 E
Kiruna 50 67 52N 20 15 E
Kirundu 90 0 50S 25 35 E
Kirya 55 55 5N 46 45 E
Kiryū 74 36 24N 139 20 E
Kisa 49 58 0N 15 39 E
Kisaga 90 4 30S 34 23 E
Kisámou, Kólpos 45 35 30N 23 38 E
Kisanga 90 2 30N 26 35 E
Kisangani 90 0 35N 25 15 E
Kisar 73 8 5S 127 10 E
Kisaran 72 3 0N 99 37 E
Kisarawe 90 6 53S 39 0 E
Kisarawe □ 90 7 3S 39 0 E
Kisarazu 74 35 23N 139 55 E
Kisbér 27 47 30N 18 0 E
Kiselevsk 58 54 5N 86 39 E
Kishanganj 69 26 3N 88 14 E
Kishangarh 68 27 50N 70 30 E
Kishi 85 9 1N 3 52 E
Kishinev 56 47 0N 28 50 E
Kishiwada 74 34 28N 135 22 E
Kishon 62 32 49N 35 2 E
Kishorganj 69 24 26N 90 40 E
Kishtwar 69 33 20N 75 48 E
Kisii 90 0 40S 34 45 E
Kisii □ 90 0 40S 34 45 E
Kisiju 90 7 23S 39 19 E
Kısır, Dağ 57 41 0N 43 5 E
Kisizi 90 1 0S 29 58 E
Kiska I. 104 52 0N 177 30 E
Kiskatinaw → 108 56 8N 120 10W
Kiskittogisu L. 109 54 13N 98 20W
Kiskomárom = Zalakomár 27 46 33N 17 10 E
Kiskörös 27 46 37N 19 20 E
Kiskundorozsma 27 46 16N 20 5 E
Kiskunfélegyháza 27 46 42N 19 53 E
Kiskunhalas 27 46 28N 19 37 E
Kiskunmajsa 27 46 30N 19 48 E
Kislovodsk 57 43 50N 42 45 E
Kiso-Sammyaku 74 35 45N 137 45 E
Kisoro 90 1 17S 29 48 E
Kispest 27 47 27N 19 9 E
Kissidougou 84 9 5N 10 0W
Kissimmee 115 28 18N 81 22W
Kissimmee → 115 27 20N 80 55W
Kississing L. 109 55 10N 101 20W
Kistanje 39 43 58N 15 55 E
Kisterenye 27 48 3N 19 50 E
Kisújszállás 27 47 12N 20 50 E
Kisumu 90 0 3S 34 45 E
Kisvárda 27 48 14N 22 4 E
Kiswani 90 4 5S 37 57 E
Kiswere 90 9 27S 39 30 E
Kit Carson 116 38 48N 102 45W
Kita 84 13 5N 9 25W
Kitab 58 39 7N 66 52 E
Kitaibaraki 74 36 50N 140 45 E
Kitakami-Gawa → 74 38 25N 141 19 E
Kitakyūshū 74 33 50N 130 50 E
Kitale 90 1 0N 35 0 E
Kitangiri, L. 90 4 5S 34 20 E
Kitaya 91 10 38S 40 8 E
Kitchener 106 43 27N 80 29W
Kitega = Citega 90 3 30S 29 58 E
Kitengo 90 7 26S 24 8 E
Kiteto □ 90 5 0S 37 0 E
Kitgum 90 3 17N 32 52 E
Kíthira 45 36 9N 23 0 E
Kíthnos 45 37 26N 24 27 E
Kitimat 108 54 3N 128 38W
Kitinen → 50 67 34N 26 40 E
Kitiyab 87 17 13N 33 35 E
Kitros 44 40 22N 22 34 E
Kittakittaooloo, L. 99 28 3S 138 14 E
Kittanning 114 40 49N 79 30W
Kittatinny Mts. 113 41 0N 75 0W
Kittery 114 43 7N 70 42W
Kitui 90 1 17S 38 0 E
Kitui □ 90 1 30S 38 25 E
Kitwe 91 12 54S 28 13 E
Kitzbühel 26 47 27N 12 24 E
Kitzingen 25 49 44N 10 9 E
Kivalo 50 66 18N 26 0 E
Kivarli 68 24 33N 72 46 E
Kivotós 44 40 13N 21 26 E
Kivu □ 90 3 10S 27 0 E
Kivu, L. 90 1 48S 29 0 E
Kiyev 54 50 30N 30 28 E
Kiyevskoye Vdkhr. 54 51 0N 30 0 E
Kizel 52 59 3N 57 40 E
Kiziguru 90 1 46S 30 23 E
Kızıl Irmak → 56 39 15N 36 0 E
Kizil Yurt 57 43 13N 46 54 E
Kızılcahamam 56 40 30N 32 30 E
Kizimkazi 90 6 28S 39 30 E
Kizlyar 57 43 51N 46 40 E
Kizyl-Arvat 58 38 58N 56 15 E
Kjellerup 49 56 17N 9 25 E
Kladanj 42 44 14N 18 42 E
Kladnica 42 43 23N 20 2 E
Kladno 26 50 10N 14 7 E
Kladovo 42 44 36N 22 33 E
Klagenfurt 26 46 38N 14 20 E
Klagshamn 49 55 32N 12 53 E
Klagstorp 49 55 22N 13 23 E
Klaipeda 54 55 43N 21 10 E
Klamath → 118 41 40N 124 4W
Klamath Falls 118 42 20N 121 50W
Klamath Mts. 118 41 20N 123 0W
Klanjec 39 46 3N 15 45 E
Klappan → 108 58 0N 129 43W
Klaten 73 7 43S 110 36 E
Klatovy 26 49 23N 13 18 E
Klawak 108 55 35N 133 0W
Klawer 92 31 44S 18 36 E
Kłecko 28 52 38N 17 25 E
Kleczew 28 52 22N 18 9 E
Kleena Kleene 108 52 0N 124 59W
Klein 118 46 26N 108 31W
Klein-Karas 92 27 33S 18 7 E
Klein Karoo 92 33 45S 21 30 E
Klekovača 39 44 25N 16 32 E
Klemtu 108 52 35N 128 55W
Klenovec, Czech. 27 48 36N 19 54 E
Klenovec, Yugo. 42 41 32N 20 49 E
Klerksdorp 92 26 51S 26 38 E
Kleszczele 28 52 35N 23 19 E
Kletnya 54 53 23N 33 12 E
Kletsk 54 53 5N 26 45 E
Kletskiy 57 49 20N 43 0 E
Kleve 24 51 46N 6 10 E
Klickitat 118 45 50N 121 10W
Klimovichi 54 53 36N 32 0 E
Klin 55 56 20N 36 48 E
Klinaklini → 108 51 21N 125 40W
Klintsey 54 52 50N 32 10 E
Klipplaat 92 33 0S 24 22 E
Klisura 43 42 40N 24 28 E
Klitmøller 49 57 3N 8 30 E
Kljajićevo 42 45 45N 19 17 E
Ključ 39 44 32N 16 48 E
Kłobuck 28 50 55N 18 55 E
Kłodawa 28 52 15N 18 55 E
Kłodzko 28 50 28N 16 38 E
Klondike 104 64 0N 139 26W
Klosi 44 41 28N 20 10 E
Klosterneuburg 27 48 18N 16 19 E
Klosters 25 46 52N 9 52 E
Klötze 24 52 38N 11 9 E
Klouto 85 6 57N 0 44 E
Kluane L. 104 61 15N 138 40W
Kluczbork 28 50 58N 18 12 E
Klyuchevskaya, Guba 59 55 50N 160 30 E
Knaresborough 12 54 1N 1 29W
Knee L., Man., Can. 109 55 3N 94 45W
Knee L., Sask., Can. 109 55 51N 107 0W
Kneïss, I. 83 34 22N 10 18 E
Knezha 43 43 30N 24 5 E
Knić 42 43 53N 20 45 E
Knight Inlet 108 50 45N 125 40W
Knighton 13 52 21N 3 2W
Knight's Landing 118 38 50N 121 43W
Knin 39 44 1N 16 17 E
Knittelfeld 26 47 13N 14 51 E
Knjaževac 42 43 35N 22 18 E
Knob, C. 96 34 32S 119 16 E
Knockmealdown Mts. 15 52 16N 8 0W
Knokke 16 51 20N 3 17 E
Knossos 45 35 16N 25 10 E
Knox 114 41 18N 86 36W
Knox, C. 108 54 11N 133 5W
Knox City 117 33 26N 99 49W
Knox Coast 5 66 30S 108 0 E
Knoxville, Iowa, U.S.A. 116 41 20N 93 5W
Knoxville, Tenn., U.S.A. 115 35 58N 83 57W
Knurów 27 50 13N 18 38 E
Knutshø 47 62 18N 9 41 E
Knysna 92 34 2S 23 2 E
Knyszyn 28 53 20N 22 56 E
Ko Chang 71 12 0N 102 20 E
Ko Kut 71 11 40N 102 32 E
Ko Phra Thong 71 9 6N 98 15 E
Ko Tao 71 10 6N 99 48 E
Koartac (Notre Dame de Koartac) 105 60 55N 69 40W
Koba, Aru, Indon. 73 6 37S 134 37 E
Koba, Bangka, Indon. 72 2 26S 106 14 E
Kobarid 39 46 15N 13 30 E
Kobayashi 74 31 56N 130 59 E
Kobdo = Hovd 75 48 2N 91 37 E
Kōbe 74 34 45N 135 10 E
Kobelyaki 56 49 11N 34 9 E
København 49 55 41N 12 34 E
Koblenz 25 50 21N 7 36 E
Kobo 87 12 2N 39 56 E
Kobrin 54 52 15N 24 22 E
Kobroor, Kepulauan 73 6 10S 134 30 E
Kobuleti 57 41 55N 41 45 E
Kobylin 28 51 43N 17 12 E
Kobyłka 28 52 21N 21 10 E
Kobylkino 55 54 8N 43 56 E
Kobylnik 54 54 58N 26 39 E
Kočane 42 43 12N 21 52 E
Kočani 42 41 55N 22 25 E
Koçarlı 45 37 45N 27 43 E
Koceljevo 42 44 28N 19 50 E
Kočevje 39 45 39N 14 50 E
Kochas 69 25 15N 83 56 E
Kocher → 25 49 14N 9 12 E
Kocheya 59 52 32N 120 42 E
Kōchi 74 33 30N 133 35 E
Kōchi □ 74 33 40N 133 30 E
Kochiu = Gejiu 75 23 20N 103 10 E
Kock 28 51 38N 22 27 E
Koddiyar Bay 70 8 33N 81 15 E
Kodiak 104 57 30N 152 45W
Kodiak I. 104 57 30N 152 45W
Kodiang 71 6 21N 100 18 E
Kodinar 68 20 46N 70 46 E
Kodori → 57 42 47N 41 10 E
Koes 92 26 0S 19 15 E
Kofiau 73 1 11S 129 50 E
Köflach 26 47 4N 15 5 E
Koforidua 85 6 3N 0 17W
Kōfu 74 35 40N 138 30 E
Kogaluk → 107 56 12N 61 44W
Kogin Baba 85 7 55N 11 35 E
Koh-i-Bābā 65 34 30N 67 0 E
Kohat 66 33 40N 71 29 E
Kohima 67 25 35N 94 10 E
Kohler Ra. 5 77 0S 110 0W
Kohtla Järve 54 59 20N 27 20 E
Kojetin 27 49 21N 17 20 E
Koka 86 20 5N 30 35 E
Kokand 58 40 30N 70 57 E
Kokanee Glacier Prov. Park 108 49 47N 117 10W
Kokas 73 2 42S 132 26 E
Kokava 27 48 35N 19 50 E
Kokchetav 58 53 20N 69 25 E
Kokemäenjoki → 51 61 32N 21 44 E
Kokhma 55 56 55N 41 18 E
Kokkola (Gamlakarleby) 50 63 50N 23 8 E
Koko 85 11 28N 4 29 E
Koko Kyunzu 71 14 10N 93 25 E
Kokoda 98 8 54S 147 47 E
Kokolopozo 84 5 8N 6 5W
Kokomo 114 40 30N 86 6W
Kokonau 73 4 43S 136 26 E
Kokopo 98 4 22S 152 19 E
Kokoro 85 14 12N 0 55 E
Koksoak → 105 58 30N 68 10W
Kokstad 93 30 32S 29 29 E
Kokuora 59 71 35N 144 50 E
Kola, Indon. 73 5 35S 134 30 E
Kola, U.S.S.R. 52 68 45N 33 8 E
Kola Pen. = Kolskiy P-ov. 52 67 30N 38 0 E
Kolahun 84 8 15N 10 4W
Kolaka 73 4 3S 121 46 E
Kolar 70 13 12N 78 15 E
Kolar Gold Fields 70 12 58N 78 16 E
Kolari 50 67 20N 23 48 E
Kolarovgrad 43 43 18N 26 55 E
Kolašin 42 42 50N 19 31 E
Kolby Kås 49 55 48N 10 32 E
Kolchugino 55 56 17N 39 22 E
Kolda 84 12 55N 14 57W
Kolding 49 55 30N 9 29 E
Kole 88 3 16S 22 42 E
Koléa 82 36 38N 2 46 E
* Kolepom, Pulau 73 8 0S 138 30 E
Kolguyev, Ostrov 52 69 20N 48 30 E
Kolhapur 70 16 43N 74 15 E
Kolia 84 9 46N 6 28W
Kolín 26 50 2N 15 9 E
Kolind 49 56 21N 10 34 E
Kölleda 24 51 11N 11 14 E
Kollegal 70 12 9N 77 9 E
Kolleru L. 70 16 40N 81 10 E
Kolmanskop 92 26 45S 15 14 E
Köln 24 50 56N 6 58 E
Kolno 28 53 25N 21 56 E
Koło 28 52 14N 18 40 E
Kołobrzeg 28 54 10N 15 35 E
Kologriv 55 58 48N 44 25 E
Kolokani 84 13 35N 7 45W
Kolomna 55 55 8N 38 45 E
Kolomyya 56 48 31N 25 2 E
Kolondiéba 84 11 5N 6 54W
Kolonodale 73 2 3S 121 25 E
Kolosib 67 24 15N 92 45 E
Kolpashevo 58 58 20N 83 5 E
Kolpino 54 59 44N 30 39 E
Kolpny 55 52 12N 37 10 E
Kolskiy Poluostrov 52 67 30N 38 0 E
Kolskiy Zaliv 52 69 23N 34 0 E
Kolubara → 42 44 35N 20 15 E
Kolumna 28 51 36N 19 14 E
Koluszki 28 51 45N 19 46 E
Kolwezi 91 10 40S 25 25 E
Kolyberovo 55 55 15N 38 40 E
Kolyma → 59 69 30N 161 0 E
Kolymskoye, Okhotsko 59 63 0N 157 0 E
Kôm Ombo 86 24 25N 32 52 E
Komárno 27 47 49N 18 5 E
Komárom 27 47 43N 18 7 E
Komárom □ 27 47 35N 18 20 E
Komarovo 54 58 38N 33 40 E
Komatipoort 93 25 25S 31 55 E
Kombissiri 85 12 4N 1 20W
Kombori 84 13 26N 3 56W
Kombóti 45 39 6N 21 5 E
Komen 39 45 49N 13 45 E
Komenda 85 5 4N 1 28W
Komi A.S.S.R. □ 52 64 0N 55 0 E
Komiža 39 43 3N 16 11 E
Komló 27 46 15N 18 16 E
Kommamur Canal 70 16 0N 80 25 E
Kommunarsk 57 48 30N 38 45 E
Kommunizma, Pik 58 39 0N 72 2 E
Komnes 47 59 30N 9 55 E
Komodo 73 8 37S 119 20 E
Komoé 84 5 12N 3 44W
Komono 88 3 10S 13 20 E
Komoran, Pulau 73 8 18S 138 45 E
Komotini 44 41 9N 25 26 E
Komovi 42 42 41N 19 39 E
Kompong Cham 71 12 0N 105 30 E
Kompong Chhnang 71 12 20N 104 35 E
Kompong Speu 71 11 26N 104 32 E
Kompong Thom 71 12 35N 104 51 E
Komrat 56 46 18N 28 40 E
Komsberge 92 32 40S 20 45 E
Komsomolets, Ostrov 59 80 30N 95 0 E
Komsomolsk, R.S.F.S.R., U.S.S.R. 55 57 2N 40 20 E
Komsomolsk, R.S.F.S.R., U.S.S.R. 59 50 30N 137 0 E
Komsomolskaya 5 66 33S 93 1 E
Komsomolskiy 55 53 30N 49 30 E
Konakovo 55 56 52N 36 45 E
Konarhá □ 65 35 30N 71 3 E
Konawa 117 34 59N 96 46W
Kondagaon 70 19 35N 81 35 E
Kondakovo 59 69 36N 152 0 E
Konde 90 4 57S 39 45 E
Kondiá 44 39 49N 25 10 E
Kondoa 90 4 55S 35 50 E
Kondoa □ 90 5 0S 36 0 E
Kondopaga 52 62 12N 34 17 E
Kondratyevo 59 57 22N 98 15 E
Konduga 85 11 35N 13 26 E
Konevo 52 62 8N 39 20 E
Kong 84 8 54N 4 36W
Kong Christian IX.s Land 4 68 0N 36 0W
Kong Christian X.s Land 4 74 0N 29 0W
Kong Franz Joseph Fd. 4 73 20N 24 30W
Kong Frederik IX.s Land 4 67 0N 52 0W
Kong Frederik VI.s Kyst 4 63 0N 43 0W
Kong Frederik VIII.s Land 4 78 30N 26 0W
Kong, Koh 71 11 20N 103 0 E
Kong Oscar Fjord 4 72 20N 24 0W
Konga 49 56 30N 15 6 E
Kongeå 49 55 24N 9 39 E
Kongju 76 36 30N 127 0 E
Konglu 67 27 13N 97 57 E
Kongolo, Kasai Or., Zaïre 90 5 26S 24 49 E
Kongolo, Shaba, Zaïre 90 5 22S 27 0 E
Kongor 81 7 1N 31 27 E
Kongoussi 85 13 19N 1 32W
Kongsberg 47 59 39N 9 39 E
Kongsvinger 47 60 12N 12 2 E
Kongwa 90 6 11S 36 26 E
Koni 91 10 40S 27 11 E
Koni, Mts. 91 10 36S 27 10 E
Koniecpol 28 50 46N 19 40 E
Königsberg = Kaliningrad 54 54 42N 20 32 E
Königshofen 25 50 18N 10 29 E
Königslutter 24 52 14N 10 50 E
Königswusterhausen 24 52 19N 13 38 E
Konin 28 52 12N 18 15 E
Konin □ 28 52 15N 18 30 E
Konispoli 44 39 42N 20 10 E
Kónitsa 44 40 5N 20 48 E
Konjic 42 43 42N 17 58 E
Konjice 39 46 20N 15 28 E
Konkouré → 84 9 50N 13 42W
Könnern 24 51 40N 11 45 E
Konnur 70 16 14N 74 49 E
Kono 84 8 30N 11 5W
Konongo 85 6 40N 1 15W
Konosha 52 61 0N 40 5 E
Konotop 54 51 12N 33 7 E
Konqi He → 75 40 45N 90 10 E
Końskie 28 51 15N 20 23 E
Konsmo 47 58 16N 7 23 E
Konstantinovka 56 48 32N 37 39 E
Konstantinovski 57 47 33N 41 10 E
Konstantynów Łódźki 28 51 45N 19 20 E
Konstanz 25 47 39N 9 10 E
Kontagora 85 10 23N 5 27 E
Kontum 71 14 24N 108 0 E
Konya 64 37 52N 32 35 E
Konya Ovasi 64 38 30N 33 0 E
Konz 25 49 41N 6 36 E
Konza 90 1 45S 37 7 E
Koo-wee-rup 100 38 13S 145 28 E
Koolan I. 96 16 0S 123 45 E
Kooloonong 99 34 48S 143 10 E
Koondrook 99 35 33S 144 8 E
Koorawatha 99 34 2S 148 33 E
Kooskia 118 46 9N 115 59W
Koostatak 109 51 26N 97 26W
Kootenai → 118 49 15N 117 39W
Kootenay L. 108 49 45N 116 50W
Kootenay Nat. Park 108 51 0N 116 0W
Kopanovka 57 47 28N 46 50 E
Kopaonik Planina 42 43 10N 21 50 E
Kopargaon 70 19 51N 74 28 E
Kópavogur 50 64 6N 21 55W
Koper 39 45 31N 13 44 E
Kopervik 47 59 17N 5 17 E
Kopeysk 58 55 7N 61 37 E
Köping 48 59 31N 16 3 E
Kopiste 39 42 48N 16 42 E
Kopliku 44 42 15N 19 25 E

* *Renamed Yos Sudarso, P.*

Köpmanholmen Kulen Vakuf

Köpmanholmen 48 63 10N 18 35 E
Koppal 70 15 23N 76 5 E
Koppang 47 61 34N 11 3 E
Kopparbergs län □ 48 61 20N 14 15 E
Koppeh Dāgh 65 38 0N 58 0 E
Kopperå 47 63 24N 11 50 E
Koppom 48 59 43N 12 10 E
Koprivlen 43 41 36N 23 53 E
Koprivnica 39 46 12N 16 45 E
Koprivshtitsa 43 42 40N 24 19 E
Kopychintsy 54 49 7N 25 58 E
Kopys 54 54 20N 30 17 E
Korab 42 41 44N 20 40 E
Korakiána 44 39 42N 19 45 E
Koraput 70 18 50N 82 40 E
Korba 69 22 20N 82 45 E
Korbach 24 51 17N 8 50 E
Korça 44 40 37N 20 50 E
Korça □ 44 40 40N 20 50 E
Korčula 39 42 57N 17 8 E
Korčulanski Kanal 39 43 3N 16 40 E
Kordestan 64 35 30N 42 0 E
Kordestān □ 64 36 0N 47 0 E
Korea Bay 76 39 0N 124 0 E
Koregaon 70 17 40N 74 10 E
Korenevo 54 51 27N 34 55 E
Korenovsk 57 45 30N 39 22 E
Korets 54 50 40N 27 5 E
Korgus 86 19 16N 33 29 E
Korhogo 84 9 29N 5 28W
Koribundu 84 7 41N 11 46W
Korim 73 0 58 S 136 10 E
Korinthía □ 45 37 50N 22 35 E
Korinthiakós Kólpos 45 38 16N 22 30 E
Kórinthos 45 37 56N 22 55 E
Korioumé 84 16 35N 3 0W
Kōriyama 74 37 24N 140 23 E
Körmend 27 47 5N 16 35 E
Kornat 39 43 50N 15 20 E
Korneshty 56 47 21N 28 1 E
Korneuburg 27 48 20N 16 20 E
Kornsjø 47 58 57N 11 39 E
Kornstad 47 62 59N 7 27 E
Koro, Fiji 101 17 19 S 179 23 E
Koro, Ivory C. 84 8 32N 7 30W
Koro, Mali 84 14 1N 2 58W
Koro Sea 101 17 30 S 179 45W
Korocha 55 50 55N 37 30 E
Korogwe 90 5 5 S 38 25 E
Korogwe □ 90 5 0 S 38 20 E
Koroit 99 38 18 S 142 24 E
Koróni 45 36 48N 21 57 E
Korónia, Limni 44 40 47N 23 37 E
Koronís 45 37 12N 25 35 E
Koronowo 28 53 19N 17 55 E
Koror 73 7 20N 134 28 E
Körös → 27 46 43N 20 12 E
Kőröstarcsa 27 46 53N 21 3 E
Korosten 54 50 57N 28 25 E
Korotoyak 55 51 1N 39 2 E
Korraraika, Helodranon' i 93 17 45 S 43 57 E
Korsakov 59 46 36N 142 42 E
Korshunovo 59 58 37N 110 10 E
Korsun Shevchenkovskiy 56 49 26N 31 16 E
Korsze 28 54 11N 21 9 E
Korti 86 18 6N 31 33 E
Kortrijk 16 50 50N 3 17 E
Korwai 68 24 7N 78 5 E
Koryakskiy Khrebet 59 61 0N 171 0 E
Kos 45 36 50N 27 15 E
Kosa 87 7 50N 36 50 E
Kosaya Gora 55 54 10N 37 30 E
Koschagyl 53 46 40N 54 0 E
Kościan 28 52 5N 16 40 E
Kościerzyna 28 54 8N 17 59 E
Kosciusko 117 33 3N 89 34W
Kosciusko I. 108 56 0N 133 40W
Kosciusko, Mt. 97 36 27 S 148 16 E
Kösély → 27 47 25N 21 5 E
Kosgi 70 16 58N 77 43 E
Kosha 86 20 50N 30 30 E
K'oshih = Kashi 75 39 30N 76 2 E
Koshk-e Kohneh 65 34 55N 62 30 E
Kosi 68 27 48N 77 29 E
Kosi-meer 93 27 0 S 32 50 E
Košice 27 48 42N 21 15 E
Kosjerić 42 44 0N 19 55 E
Koslan 52 63 28N 48 52 E
Kosŏng 76 38 40N 128 22 E
Kosovo, Pokrajina 42 42 40N 21 5 E
Kosovo, Soc. Aut. Pokrajina □ 42 42 30N 21 0 E
Kosovska-Mitrovica 42 42 54N 20 52 E
Kostajnica 39 45 17N 16 30 E
Kostamuksa 52 62 34N 32 44 E
Kostanjevica 39 45 51N 15 27 E
Kostelec 27 50 14N 16 35 E
Kostenets 43 42 15N 23 52 E
Koster 92 25 52 S 26 54 E
Kôstî 87 13 8N 32 43 E
Kostolac 42 44 37N 21 15 E
Kostopol 54 50 51N 26 22 E
Kostroma 55 57 50N 40 58 E
Kostromskoye Vdkhr. 55 57 52N 40 49 E
Kostrzyn, Poland 28 52 24N 17 14 E
Kostrzyn, Poland 28 52 35N 14 39 E
Kostyukovichi 54 53 20N 32 4 E
Koszalin 28 53 50N 16 8 E
Koszalin □ 28 53 40N 16 10 E
Köszeg 27 47 23N 16 33 E
Kot Adu 68 30 30N 71 0 E
Kot Moman 68 32 13N 73 0 E
Kota 68 25 14N 75 49 E
Kota Baharu 71 6 7N 102 14 E
Kota Belud 72 6 21N 116 26 E
Kota Kinabalu 72 6 0N 116 4 E
Kota Tinggi 71 1 44N 103 53 E
Kotaagung 72 5 38 S 104 29 E
Kotabaru 72 3 20 S 116 20 E
Kotabumi 72 4 49 S 104 54 E
Kotagede 73 7 54 S 110 26 E
Kotamobagu 73 0 57N 124 31 E
Kotaneelee → 108 60 11N 123 42W
Kotawaringin 72 2 28 S 111 27 E
Kotcho L. 108 59 7N 121 12W
Kotel 43 42 52N 26 26 E
Kotelnich 55 58 20N 48 10 E
Kotelnikovo 57 47 38N 43 8 E
Kotelnyy, Ostrov 59 75 10N 139 0 E
Kothagudam 70 17 30N 80 40 E
Kothapet 70 19 21N 79 28 E
Köthen 24 51 44N 11 59 E
Kothi 69 24 45N 80 40 E
Kotiro 68 26 17N 67 13 E
Kotka 51 60 28N 26 58 E
Kotlas 52 61 15N 47 0 E
Kotlenska Planina 43 42 56N 26 30 E
Kotli 66 33 30N 73 55 E
Kotonkoro 85 11 3N 5 58 E
Kotor 42 42 25N 18 47 E
Kotor Varoš 42 44 38N 17 22 E
Kotoriba 39 46 23N 16 48 E
Kotovo 55 50 22N 44 45 E
Kotovsk 56 47 45N 29 35 E
Kotputli 68 27 43N 76 12 E
Kotri 68 25 22N 68 22 E
Kotri → 70 19 15N 80 35 E
Kótronas 45 36 38N 22 29 E
Kötschach-Mauthen 26 46 41N 13 1 E
Kottayam 70 9 35N 76 33 E
Kottur 70 10 34N 76 56 E
Kotuy → 59 71 54N 102 6 E
Kotzebue 104 66 50N 162 40W
Kouango 88 5 0N 20 10 E
Koudougou 84 12 10N 2 20W
Koufonisi 45 34 56N 26 8 E
Koufonísia 45 36 57N 25 35 E
Kougaberge 92 33 48 S 23 50 E
Kouibli 84 7 15N 7 14W
Kouilou → 88 4 10 S 12 5 E
Kouki 88 7 22N 17 3 E
Koula Moutou 88 1 15 S 12 25 E
Koulen 71 13 50N 104 40 E
Koulikoro 84 12 40N 7 50W
Koumala 98 21 38 S 149 15 E
Koumankou 84 11 58N 6 6W
Koumbia, Guin. 84 11 48N 13 29W
Koumbia, Upp. Vol. 84 11 10N 3 50W
Koumboum 84 10 25N 13 0W
Koumpenntoum 84 13 59N 14 34W
Koumra 81 8 50N 17 35 E
Koundara 84 12 29N 13 18W
Kounradskiy 58 46 59N 75 0 E
Kountze 117 30 20N 94 22W
Koupéla 85 12 11N 0 21W
Kourizo, Passe de 83 22 28N 15 27 E
Kouroussa 84 10 45N 9 45W
Koussané 84 13 53N 11 14W
Kousseri 81 12 0N 14 55 E
Koutiala 84 12 25N 5 23W
Kouto 84 9 53N 6 25W
Kouvé 85 6 25N 1 25 E
Kovačica 42 45 5N 20 38 E
Kovdor 52 67 34N 30 24 E
Kovel 54 51 10N 24 20 E
Kovilpatti 70 9 10N 77 50 E
Kovin 42 44 44N 20 59 E
Kovrov 55 56 25N 41 25 E
Kovur, Andhra Pradesh, India 70 17 3N 81 39 E
Kovur, Andhra Pradesh, India 70 14 30N 80 1 E
Kowal 28 52 32N 19 7 E
Kowalewo Pomorskie 28 53 10N 18 52 E
Kowkash 106 50 20N 87 12W
Kowloon 75 22 20N 114 15 E
Koyabuti 73 2 36 S 140 37 E
Koyan, Pegunungan 72 3 15N 114 30 E
Koyuk 104 64 55N 161 20W
Koyukuk → 104 64 56N 157 30W
Koyulhisar 56 40 20N 37 52 E
Koza 77 26 19N 127 46 E
Kozan 64 37 35N 35 50 E
Kozáni 44 40 19N 21 47 E
Kozáni □ 44 40 18N 21 45 E
Kozara 39 45 0N 17 0 E
Kozarac 39 44 58N 16 48 E
Kozelsk 54 54 2N 35 48 E
Kozhikode = Calicut 70 11 15N 75 43 E
Kozhva 52 65 10N 57 0 E
Koziegłowy 28 50 37N 19 8 E
Kozienice 28 51 35N 21 34 E
Kozje 39 46 5N 15 35 E
Kozle 28 50 20N 18 8 E
Kozloduy 43 43 45N 23 42 E
Kozlovets 43 43 30N 25 20 E
Koźmin 28 51 48N 17 27 E
Kozmodemyansk 55 56 20N 46 36 E
Kozuchów 28 51 45N 15 31 E
Kpabia 85 9 10N 0 20W
Kpalimé 85 6 57N 0 44 E
Kpandae 85 8 30N 0 2W
Kpessi 85 8 4N 1 16 E
Kra Buri 71 10 22N 98 46 E
Kra, Isthmus of = Kra, Kho Khot 71 10 15N 99 30 E
Kra, Kho Khot 71 10 15N 99 30 E
Kragan 73 6 43 S 111 38 E
Kragerø 47 58 52N 9 25 E
Kragujevac 42 44 2N 20 56 E
Krajenka 28 53 18N 16 59 E
Krakatau = Rakata, Pulau 72 6 10 S 105 20 E
Kraków 27 50 4N 19 57 E
Kraków □ 27 50 0N 20 0 E
Kraksaan 73 7 43 S 113 23 E
Kråkstad 47 59 39N 10 55 E
Králiky 27 50 6N 16 45 E
Kraljevo 42 43 44N 20 41 E
Kralovice 26 49 59N 13 29 E
Královský Chlmec 27 48 27N 22 0 E
Kralupy 26 50 13N 14 20 E
Kramatorsk 56 48 50N 37 30 E
Kramer 119 35 0N 117 38W
Kramfors 48 62 55N 17 48 E
Kramis, C. 82 36 26N 0 45 E
Krångede 48 63 9N 16 10 E
Kraniá 44 39 53N 21 18 E
Kranídhion 45 37 20N 23 10 E
Kranj 39 46 16N 14 22 E
Kranjska Gora 39 46 29N 13 48 E
Krapina 39 46 10N 15 52 E
Krapina → 39 45 50N 15 50 E
Krapivna 55 53 58N 37 10 E
Krapkowice 28 50 29N 17 56 E
Krasavino 52 60 58N 46 29 E
Kraskino 59 42 44N 130 48 E
Kraslice 26 50 19N 12 31 E
Krasnaya Gorbatka 55 55 52N 41 45 E
Krasnaya Polyana 57 43 40N 40 13 E
Kraśnik 28 50 55N 22 5 E
Kraśnik Fabryczny 28 50 58N 22 11 E
Krasnoarmeisk 56 48 18N 37 11 E
Krasnoarmeysk, R.S.F.S.R., U.S.S.R. 55 51 0N 45 42 E
Krasnoarmeysk, R.S.F.S.R., U.S.S.R. 57 48 30N 44 25 E
Krasnodar 57 45 5N 39 0 E
Krasnodon 57 48 17N 39 44 E
Krasnodonetskaya 57 48 5N 40 50 E
Krasnogorskiy 55 56 10N 48 28 E
Krasnograd 56 49 27N 35 27 E
Krasnogvardeyskoye 57 45 52N 41 33 E
Krasnogvardyesk 56 45 32N 34 16 E
Krasnokamsk 52 58 4N 55 48 E
Krasnokutsk 54 50 10N 34 50 E
Krasnoperekopsk 56 46 0N 33 54 E
Krasnoselkupsk 58 65 20N 82 10 E
Krasnoslobodsk, R.S.F.S.R., U.S.S.R. 55 54 25N 43 45 E
Krasnoslobodsk, R.S.F.S.R., U.S.S.R. 57 48 42N 44 33 E
Krasnoturinsk 58 59 46N 60 12 E
Krasnoufimsk 52 56 57N 57 46 E
Krasnouralsk 52 58 21N 60 3 E
Krasnovishersk 52 60 23N 57 3 E
Krasnovodsk 53 40 0N 52 52 E
Krasnoyarsk 59 56 8N 93 0 E
Krasnoye, Kalmyk A.S.S.R., U.S.S.R. 57 46 16N 45 0 E
Krasnoye, R.S.F.S.R., U.S.S.R. 55 59 15N 47 40 E
Krasnoye = Krasnyy 54 54 25N 31 30 E
Krasnozavodsk 55 56 27N 38 25 E
Krasny Liman 56 48 58N 37 50 E
Krasny Sulin 57 47 52N 40 8 E
Krasnystaw 28 50 57N 23 5 E
Krasnyy 54 54 25N 31 30 E
Krasnyy Kholm 55 58 10N 37 10 E
Krasnyy Kut 55 50 50N 47 0 E
Krasnyy Luch 57 48 13N 39 0 E
Krasnyy Profintern 55 57 45N 40 27 E
Krasnyy Yar, Kalmyk A.S.S.R., U.S.S.R. 57 46 43N 48 23 E
Krasnyy Yar, R.S.F.S.R., U.S.S.R. 55 53 30N 50 22 E
Krasnyy Yar, R.S.F.S.R., U.S.S.R. 55 50 42N 44 45 E
Krasnyye Baki 55 57 8N 45 10 E
Krasnyyoskolskoye Vdkhr. 56 49 30N 37 30 E
Kraszna → 27 48 0N 22 20 E
Kratie 71 12 32N 106 10 E
Kratovo 42 42 6N 22 10 E
Krau 73 3 19 S 140 5 E
Kravanh, Chuor Phnum 71 12 0N 103 32 E
Krawang 73 6 19N 107 18 E
Krefeld 24 51 20N 6 32 E
Krémaston, Límni 45 38 52N 21 30 E
Kremenchug 56 49 5N 33 25 E
Kremenchugskoye Vdkhr. 56 49 20N 32 30 E
Kremenets 56 50 8N 25 43 E
Kremenica 42 40 55N 21 25 E
Kremennaya 56 49 1N 38 10 E
Kremges = Svetlovodsk 56 49 5N 33 15 E
Kremikovtsi 43 42 46N 23 28 E
Kremmen 24 52 45N 13 1 E
Kremmling 118 40 10N 106 30W
Kremnica 27 48 45N 18 50 E
Krems 26 48 25N 15 36 E
Kremsmünster 26 48 3N 14 8 E
Kretinga 54 55 53N 21 15 E
Krettamia 82 28 47N 3 27W
Krettsy 54 58 15N 32 30 E
Kreuzberg 25 50 22N 9 58 E
Kribi 88 2 57N 9 56 E
Krichem 43 42 8N 24 28 E
Krichev 54 53 45N 31 50 E
Krim 39 45 53N 14 30 E
Krionéri 45 38 20N 21 35 E
Krishna → 70 15 57N 80 59 E
Krishnagiri 70 12 32N 78 16 E
Krishnanagar 69 23 24N 88 33 E
Krishnaraja Sagara 70 12 20N 76 30 E
Kristiansand 47 58 9N 8 1 E
Kristianstad 49 56 2N 14 9 E
Kristiansund 47 63 7N 7 45 E
Kristiinankaupunki 50 62 16N 21 21 E
Kristinehamn 48 59 18N 14 13 E
Kristinestad 50 62 16N 21 21 E
Kriti 45 35 15N 25 0 E
Kritsá 45 35 10N 25 41 E
Kriva → 42 42 5N 21 47 E
Kriva Palanka 42 42 11N 22 19 E
Krivaja → 42 44 27N 18 9 E
Krivelj 42 44 8N 22 5 E
Krivoy Rog 56 47 51N 33 20 E
Križevci 39 46 3N 16 32 E
Krk 39 45 8N 14 40 E
Krka → 39 45 50N 15 30 E
Krkonoše 26 50 50N 15 35 E
Krnov 27 50 5N 17 40 E
Krobia 28 51 47N 16 59 E
Kročehlavy 26 50 8N 14 9 E
Krøderen 47 60 9N 9 49 E
Krokawo 28 54 47N 18 9 E
Krokeaí 45 36 53N 22 32 E
Krokom 48 63 20N 14 30 E
Krolevets 54 51 35N 33 20 E
Kroměříz 27 49 18N 17 21 E
Krompachy 27 48 54N 20 52 E
Kromy 54 52 40N 35 48 E
Kronach 25 50 14N 11 19 E
Kronobergs län □ 49 56 45N 14 30 E
Kronprins Olav Kyst 5 69 0 S 42 0 E
Kronprinsesse Märtha Kyst 5 73 30 S 10 0 E
Kronshtadt 54 60 5N 29 45 E
Kroonstad 92 27 43 S 27 19 E
Kröpelin 24 54 4N 11 48 E
Kropotkin, R.S.F.S.R., U.S.S.R. 57 45 28N 40 28 E
Kropotkin, R.S.F.S.R., U.S.S.R. 59 59 0N 115 30 E
Kropp 24 54 24N 9 32 E
Krościenko 27 49 29N 20 25 E
Krośniewice 28 52 15N 19 11 E
Krosno 27 49 42N 21 46 E
Krosno □ 27 49 35N 22 0 E
Krosno Odrzańskie 28 52 3N 15 7 E
Krotoszyn 28 51 42N 17 23 E
Krraba 44 41 13N 20 0 E
Krško 39 45 57N 15 30 E
Krstača 42 42 57N 20 8 E
Kruger Nat. Park 93 24 0 S 31 40 E
Krugersdorp 93 26 5 S 27 46 E
Kruis, Kaap 92 21 55 S 13 57 E
Kruja 44 41 32N 19 46 E
Krulevshchina 54 55 5N 27 45 E
Kruma 44 42 14N 20 28 E
Krumbach 25 48 15N 10 22 E
Krumovgrad 43 41 29N 25 38 E
Krung Thep 71 13 45N 100 35 E
Krupanj 42 44 25N 19 22 E
Krupina 27 48 22N 19 5 E
Krupinica → 27 48 15N 18 52 E
Kruševac 42 43 35N 21 28 E
Kruševo 42 41 23N 21 19 E
Kruszwica 28 52 40N 18 20 E
Kruzof I. 108 57 10N 135 40W
Krylbo 48 60 7N 16 15 E
Krymsk Abinsk 56 44 50N 38 0 E
Krymskiy P-ov. 56 45 0N 34 0 E
Krynica 27 49 25N 20 57 E
Krynica Morska 28 54 23N 19 28 E
Krynki 28 53 17N 23 43 E
Krzepice 28 50 58N 18 50 E
Krzeszów 28 50 24N 22 21 E
Krzeszowice 27 50 8N 19 37 E
Krzna → 28 51 59N 22 47 E
Krzywiń 28 51 58N 16 50 E
Krzyz 28 52 52N 16 0 E
Ksabi 82 32 51N 4 13W
Ksar Chellala 82 35 13N 2 19 E
Ksar el Boukhari 82 35 51N 2 52 E
Ksar el Kebir 82 35 0N 6 0W
Ksar es Souk = Ar Rachidiya 82 31 58N 4 20W
Ksar Rhilane 83 33 0N 9 39 E
Ksiba, El 82 32 46N 6 0W
Ksour, Mts. des 82 32 45N 0 30W
Kstovo 55 56 12N 44 13 E
Kuala 72 2 55N 105 47 E
Kuala Kangsar 71 4 46N 100 56 E
Kuala Kerai 71 5 30N 102 12 E
Kuala Kubu Baharu 71 3 34N 101 39 E
Kuala Lipis 71 4 10N 102 3 E
Kuala Lumpur 71 3 9N 101 41 E
Kuala Sedili Besar 71 1 55N 104 5 E
Kuala Terengganu 72 5 20N 103 8 E
Kualakapuas 72 2 55 S 114 20 E
Kualakurun 72 1 10 S 113 50 E
Kualapembuang 72 3 14 S 112 38 E
Kualasimpang 72 4 17N 98 3 E
Kuandang 73 0 56N 123 1 E
Kuandian 76 40 45N 124 45 E
Kuangchou = Guangzhou 75 23 5N 113 10 E
Kuantan 71 3 49N 103 20 E
Kuba 57 41 21N 48 32 E
Kubak 66 27 10N 63 10 E
Kuban → 56 45 20N 37 30 E
Kubenskoye, Oz. 55 59 40N 39 25 E
Kuberle 57 47 0N 42 20 E
Kubrat 43 43 49N 26 31 E
Kučevo 42 44 30N 21 40 E
Kuchaman 68 27 13N 74 47 E
Kuchenspitze 26 47 7N 10 12 E
Kuching 72 1 33N 110 25 E
Kuçove = Qytet Stalin 44 40 47N 19 57 E
Kücük Kuyu 44 39 35N 26 27 E
Kudalier → 70 18 35N 79 48 E
Kudat 72 6 55N 116 55 E
Kudremukh, Mt. 70 13 15N 75 20 E
Kudus 73 6 48 S 110 51 E
Kudymkar 58 59 1N 54 39 E
Kueiyang = Guiyang 75 26 32N 106 40 E
Kufrinjah 62 32 20N 35 41 E
Kufstein 26 47 35N 12 11 E
Kugong I. 106 56 18N 79 50W
Kūh-e 'Alijūq 65 31 30N 51 41 E
Kūh-e Dīnār 65 30 40N 51 0 E
Kūh-e-Hazārān 65 29 35N 57 20 E
Kūh-e-Jebāl Bārez 65 29 0N 58 0 E
Kūh-e Sorkh 65 35 30N 58 45 E
Kūh-e Taftān 65 28 40N 61 0 E
Kūhak 65 27 12N 63 10 E
Kūhhā-ye-Bashākerd 65 26 45N 59 0 E
Kūhhā-ye Sabalān 64 38 15N 47 45 E
Kuhnsdorf 26 46 37N 14 38 E
Kūhpāyeh 65 32 44N 52 20 E
Kuile He → 76 49 32N 124 42 E
Kuito 89 12 22 S 16 55 E
Kukavica 42 42 48N 21 57 E
Kukawa 85 12 58N 13 27 E
Kukësi 44 42 5N 20 20 E
Kukësi □ 44 42 25N 20 15 E
Kukmor 55 56 11N 50 54 E
Kukvidze 55 50 40N 43 15 E
Kula, Bulg. 42 43 52N 22 36 E
Kula, Yugo. 42 45 37N 19 32 E
Kulai 71 1 44N 103 35 E
Kulal, Mt. 90 2 42N 36 57 E
Kulaly, O. 57 45 0N 50 0 E
Kulasekharapattanam 70 8 20N 78 0 E
Kuldiga 54 56 58N 21 59 E
Kuldja = Yining 75 43 58N 81 10 E
Kuldu 87 12 50N 28 30 E
Kulebaki 55 55 22N 42 25 E
Kulen Vakuf 39 44 35N 16 2 E

Kuli

Lampang

Kuli 57 42 2N 47 12 E
Küllük 45 37 12N 27 36 E
Kulm 116 46 22N 98 58W
Kulmbach 25 50 6N 11 27 E
Kulsary 58 46 59N 54 1 E
Kultay 57 45 5N 51 40 E
Kulti 69 23 43N 86 50 E
Kulunda 58 52 35N 78 57 E
Kulwin 99 35 0S 142 42 E
Kulyab 58 37 55N 69 50 E
Kum Tekei 58 43 10N 79 30 E
Kuma ⤳ 57 44 55N 47 0 E
Kumaganum 85 13 8N 10 38 E
Kumagaya 74 36 9N 139 22 E
Kumai 72 2 44S 111 43 E
Kumamba, Kepulauan 73 1 36S 138 45 E
Kumamoto 74 32 45N 130 45 E
Kumamoto □ 74 32 55N 130 55 E
Kumanovo 42 42 9N 21 42 E
Kumara 101 42 37S 171 12 E
Kumasi 84 6 41N 1 38W
Kumba 88 4 36N 9 24 E
Kumbakonam 70 10 58N 79 25 E
Kumbarilla 99 27 15S 150 55 E
Kumbo 85 6 15N 10 36 E
Kumbukkan Oya ⤳ 70 6 35N 81 40 E
Kumeny 55 58 10N 49 47 E
Kumertau 52 52 46N 55 47 E
Kumi 90 1 30N 33 58 E
Kumkale 44 40 0N 26 13 E
Kumla 48 59 8N 15 10 E
Kummerower See 24 53 47N 12 52 E
Kumo 85 10 1N 11 12 E
Kumon Bum 67 26 30N 97 15 E
Kumta 70 14 29N 74 25 E
Kumtorkala 57 43 2N 46 50 E
Kumylzhenskaya 57 49 51N 42 38 E
Kunágota 27 46 26N 21 3 E
Kunama 99 35 35S 148 4 E
Kunashir, Ostrov 59 44 0N 146 0 E
Kunch 68 26 0N 79 10 E
Kunda 54 59 30N 26 34 E
Kundiawa 98 6 2S 145 1 E
Kundla 68 21 21N 71 25 E
Kungala 99 29 58S 153 7 E
Kungälv 49 57 53N 11 59 E
Kunghit I. 108 52 6N 131 3W
Kungrad 58 43 6N 58 54 E
Kungsbacka 49 57 30N 12 5 E
Kungur 52 57 25N 56 57 E
Kungurri 98 21 3S 148 46 E
Kunhegyes 27 47 22N 20 36 E
Kuningan 73 6 59S 108 29 E
Kunlong 67 23 20N 98 50 E
Kunlun Shan 75 36 0N 85 0 E
Kunmadaras 27 47 28N 20 45 E
Kunming 75 25 1N 102 41 E
Kunnamkulam 70 10 38N 76 7 E
Kunsan 76 35 59N 126 45 E
Kunshan 77 31 22N 120 58 E
Kunszentmárton 27 46 50N 20 20 E
Kununurra 96 15 40S 128 50 E
Kunwarara 98 22 55S 150 9 E
Kunya-Urgenoh 58 42 19N 59 10 E
Künzelsau 25 49 17N 9 41 E
Kuopio 50 62 53N 27 35 E
Kuopion lääni □ 50 63 25N 27 10 E
Kupa ⤳ 39 45 28N 16 24 E
Kupang 73 10 19S 123 39 E
Kupres 42 44 1N 17 15 E
Kupyansk 56 49 52N 37 35 E
Kupyansk-Uzlovoi 56 49 45N 37 34 E
Kuqa 75 41 35N 82 30 E
Kura ⤳ 57 39 50N 49 20 E
Kuranda 98 16 48S 145 35 E
Kurashiki 74 34 40N 133 50 E
Kurayoshi 74 35 26N 133 50 E
Kurduvadi 70 18 8N 75 29 E
Kŭrdzhali 43 41 38N 25 21 E
Kure 74 34 14N 132 32 E
Kuressaare = Kingisepp 54 58 15N 22 15 E
Kurgaldzhino 58 50 35N 70 20 E
Kurgan 58 55 26N 65 18 E
Kurganinsk 57 44 54N 40 34 E
Kurgannaya = Kurganinsk 57 44 54N 40 34 E
Kuria Maria I. = Khūryān Mūryān, Jazā 'ir 63 17 30N 55 58 E
Kurichchi 70 11 36N 77 35 E
Kuridala P.O 98 21 16S 140 29 E
Kuril Is. = Kurilskiye Os. 59 45 0N 150 0 E
Kuril Trench 94 44 0N 153 0 E
Kurilsk 59 45 14N 147 53 E
Kurilskiye Ostrova 59 45 0N 150 0 E
Kuring Kuru 92 17 42S 18 32 E
Kurkur 86 23 50N 32 0 E
Kurkūrah 83 31 30N 20 1 E
Kurla 70 19 5N 72 52 E
Kurlovskiy 55 55 25N 40 40 E
Kurmuk 87 10 33N 34 21 E
Kurnool 70 15 45N 78 0 E
Kurovskoye 55 55 35N 38 55 E
Kurow 101 44 44S 170 29 E
Kurów 28 51 23N 22 12 E
Kurrajong 99 33 33S 150 42 E
Kurri Kurri 99 32 50S 151 28 E
Kursavka 57 44 29N 42 32 E
Kuršenai 54 56 1N 23 3 E
Kurseong 69 26 56N 88 18 E
Kursk 55 51 42N 36 11 E
Kuršumlija 42 43 9N 21 19 E
Kuršumlijska Banja 42 43 3N 21 11 E
Kuru (Chel), Bahr el 87 8 10N 26 50 E
Kuruktag 75 41 0N 89 0 E
Kuruman 92 27 28S 23 28 E
Kurume 74 33 15N 130 30 E
Kurunegala 70 7 30N 80 23 E
Kurya 59 61 15N 108 10 E
Kuşada Körfezı 45 37 56N 27 0 E
Kuşadası 45 37 52N 27 15 E
Kusawa L. 108 60 20N 136 13W
Kusel 25 49 31N 7 25 E
Kushchevskaya 57 46 33N 39 35 E
Kushiro 74 43 0N 144 25 E
Kushiro ⤳ 74 42 59N 144 23 E
Kushka 58 35 20N 62 18 E
Kushtia 69 23 55N 89 5 E
Kushum ⤳ 57 49 0N 50 20 E
Kushva 52 58 18N 59 45 E
Kuskokwim ⤳ 104 60 17N 162 27W
Kuskokwim Bay 104 59 50N 162 56W
Kussharo-Ko 74 43 38N 144 21 E
Kustanay 58 53 10N 63 35 E
Kütahya 64 39 30N 30 2 E
Kutaisi 57 42 19N 42 40 E
Kutaraja = Banda Aceh 72 5 35N 95 20 E
Kutch, G. of 68 22 50N 69 15 E
Kutch, Rann of 68 24 0N 70 0 E
Kutina 39 45 29N 16 48 E
Kutiyana 68 21 36N 70 2 E
Kutjevo 42 45 23N 17 55 E
Kutkashen 57 40 58N 47 47 E
Kutná Hora 26 49 57N 15 16 E
Kutno 28 52 15N 19 23 E
Kuttabul 98 21 5S 148 48 E
Kutu 88 2 40S 18 11 E
Kutum 87 14 10N 24 40 E
Kúty 27 48 40N 17 3 E
Kuvshinovo 54 57 2N 34 11 E
Kuwait = Al Kuwayt 64 29 30N 47 30 E
Kuwait ■ 64 29 30N 47 30 E
Kuwana 74 35 0N 136 43 E
Kuybyshev 58 55 27N 78 19 E
Kuybyshev 58 53 8N 50 6 E
Kuybyshevskoye Vdkhr. 55 55 2N 49 30 E
Küysanjaq 64 36 5N 44 38 E
Kuyto, Oz. 52 64 40N 31 0 E
Kuyumba 59 60 58N 96 59 E
Kuzey Anadolu Dağlari 64 41 30N 35 0 E
Kuzhithura 70 8 18N 77 11 E
Kuzmin 42 45 2N 19 25 E
Kuznetsk 55 53 12N 46 40 E
Kuzomen 52 66 22N 36 50 E
Kvænangen 50 70 5N 21 15 E
Kvam 47 61 40N 9 42 E
Kvamsøy 47 61 7N 6 28 E
Kvareli 57 41 27N 45 47 E
Kvarner 39 44 50N 14 10 E
Kvarnerič 39 44 43N 14 37 E
Kvernes 47 63 1N 7 44 E
Kvillsfors 49 57 24N 15 29 E
Kvine ⤳ 47 58 17N 6 56 E
Kvinesdal 47 58 19N 6 57 E
Kviteseid 47 59 24N 8 29 E
Kwabhaga 93 30 51S 29 0 E
Kwadacha ⤳ 108 57 28N 125 38W
Kwakhanai 92 21 39S 21 16 E
Kwakoegron 127 5 12N 55 25W
Kwale, Kenya 90 4 15S 39 31 E
Kwale, Nigeria 85 5 46N 6 26 E
Kwale □ 90 4 15S 39 10 E
Kwamouth 88 3 9S 16 12 E
Kwando ⤳ 92 18 27S 23 32 E
Kwangsi-Chuang = Guangxi Zhuangzu □ 75 24 0N 109 0 E
Kwangtung = Guangdong □ 75 23 0N 113 0 E
Kwara □ 85 8 0N 5 0 E
Kwataboahegan ⤳ 106 51 9N 80 50W
Kwatisore 73 3 18S 134 50 E
Kweichow = Guizhou □ 75 27 0N 107 0 E
Kwidzyn 28 53 44N 18 55 E
Kwiguk 104 63 45N 164 35W
Kwimba □ 90 3 0S 33 0 E
Kwinana 96 32 15S 115 47 E
Kwisa ⤳ 28 51 34N 15 24 E
Kwoka 73 0 31S 132 27 E
Kyabé 81 9 30N 19 0 E
Kyabra Cr. ⤳ 99 25 36S 142 55 E
Kyabram 99 36 19S 145 4 E
Kyaikto 71 17 20N 97 3 E
Kyakhta 59 50 30N 106 25 E
Kyangin 67 18 20N 95 20 E
Kyaukpadaung 67 20 52N 95 8 E
Kyaukpyu 67 19 28N 93 30 E
Kyaukse 67 21 36N 96 10 E
Kyenjojo 90 0 40N 30 37 E
Kyle Dam 91 20 15S 31 0 E
Kyle of Lochalsh 14 57 17N 5 43W
Kyll ⤳ 25 49 48N 6 42 E
Kyllburg 25 50 2N 6 35 E
Kyneton 99 37 10S 144 29 E
Kynuna 98 21 37S 141 55 E
Kyō-ga-Saki 74 35 45N 135 15 E
Kyoga, L. 90 1 35N 33 0 E
Kyogle 99 28 40S 153 0 E
Kyongju 76 35 51N 129 14 E
Kyongpyaw 67 17 12N 95 10 E
Kyōto 74 35 0N 135 45 E
Kyōto □ 74 35 15N 135 45 E
Kyren 59 51 45N 101 45 E
Kyrenia 64 35 20N 33 20 E
Kyritz 24 52 57N 12 25 E
Kystatyam 59 67 20N 123 10 E
Kytal Ktakh 59 65 30N 123 40 E
Kyulyunken 59 64 10N 137 5 E
Kyunhla 67 23 25N 95 15 E
Kyuquot 108 50 3N 127 25W
Kyurdamir 57 40 25N 48 3 E
Kyūshū 74 33 0N 131 0 E
Kyūshū-Sanchi 74 32 35N 131 17 E
Kyustendil 42 42 16N 22 41 E
Kyusyur 59 70 39N 127 15 E
Kywong 99 34 58S 146 44 E
Kyzyl 59 51 50N 94 30 E
Kyzyl-Kiya 58 40 16N 72 8 E
Kyzylkum, Peski 58 42 30N 65 0 E
Kzyl-Orda 58 44 48N 65 28 E

L

Laa 27 48 43N 16 23 E
Laaber ⤳ 25 49 0N 12 3 E
Laage 24 53 55N 12 21 E
Laasphe 24 50 56N 8 23 E
Laba ⤳ 57 45 11N 39 42 E
Labastide 20 43 28N 2 39 E
Labastide-Murat 20 44 39N 1 33 E
Labbézenga 85 15 2N 0 48 E
Labdah = Leptis Magna 83 32 40N 14 12 E
Labé 84 11 24N 12 16W
Labe = Elbe ⤳ 26 50 50N 14 12 E
Laberec ⤳ 27 48 37N 21 58 E
Laberge, L. 108 61 11N 135 12W
Labin 39 45 5N 14 8 E
Labinsk 57 44 40N 40 48 E
Labis 71 2 22N 103 2 E
Labiszyn 28 52 57N 17 54 E
Laboe 24 54 25N 10 13 E
Labouheyre 20 44 13N 0 55W
Laboulaye 124 34 10S 63 30W
Labra, Peña 30 43 3N 4 26W
Labrador City 107 52 57N 66 55W
Labrador, Coast of □ 105 53 20N 61 0W
Lábrea 126 7 15S 64 51W
Labrède 20 44 41N 0 32W
Labuan 72 5 21N 115 13 E
Labuha 73 0 30S 127 30 E
Labuhan 73 6 26S 105 50 E
Labuhanbajo 73 8 28S 120 1 E
Labuk, Telok 72 6 10N 117 50 E
Labytnangi 58 66 39N 66 21 E
Łabźenica 28 53 18N 17 15 E
Lac Allard 107 50 33N 63 24W
Lac Bouchette 107 48 16N 72 11W
Lac du Flambeau 116 46 1N 89 51W
Lac Édouard 106 47 40N 72 16W
Lac la Biche 108 54 45N 111 58W
Lac la Martre 104 63 8N 117 16W
Lac-Mégantic 107 45 35N 70 53W
Lac Seul 109 50 28N 92 0W
Lacanau, Étang de 20 44 58N 1 7W
Lacanau-Médoc 20 44 59N 1 5W
Lacantúm ⤳ 120 16 36N 90 40W
Lacara ⤳ 31 38 55N 6 25W
Lacaune 20 43 43N 2 40 E
Lacaune, Mts. de 20 43 43N 2 50 E
Laccadive Is. = Lakshadweep Is. 60 10 0N 72 30 E
Lacepede B. 99 36 40S 139 40 E
Lacepede Is. 96 16 55S 122 0 E
Lacerdónia 91 18 3S 35 35 E
Lachine 106 45 30N 73 40W
Lachlan ⤳ 97 34 22S 143 55 E
Lachmangarh 68 27 50N 75 4 E
Lachute 106 45 39N 74 21W
Lackawanna 114 42 49N 78 50W
Lacolle 113 45 5N 73 22W
Lacombe 108 52 30N 113 44W
Lacona 113 43 37N 76 5W
Láconi 40 39 54N 9 4 E
Laconia 114 43 32N 71 30W
Lacq 20 43 25N 0 35W
Lacrosse 118 46 51N 117 58W
Ladakh Ra. 69 34 0N 78 0 E
Lądekzdrój 28 50 21N 16 53 E
Ládhon ⤳ 45 37 40N 21 50 E
Ladik 56 40 57N 35 58 E
Ladismith 92 33 28S 21 15 E
Lādīz 65 28 55N 61 15 E
Ladnun 68 27 38N 74 25 E
Ladoga, L. = Ladozhskoye Oz. 52 61 15N 30 30 E
Ladon 19 48 0N 2 30 E
Ladozhskoye Ozero 52 61 15N 30 30 E
Lady Grey 92 30 43S 27 13 E
Ladybrand 92 29 9S 27 29 E
Ladysmith, Can. 108 49 0N 123 49W
Ladysmith, S. Afr. 93 28 32S 29 46 E
Ladysmith, U.S.A. 116 45 27N 91 4W
Lae 94 6 40S 147 2 E
Læsø 49 57 15N 10 53 E
Læsø Rende 49 57 20N 10 45 E
Lafayette, Colo., U.S.A. 116 40 0N 105 2W
Lafayette, Ga., U.S.A. 115 34 44N 85 15W
Lafayette, La., U.S.A. 117 30 18N 92 0W
Lafayette, Tenn., U.S.A. 115 36 35N 86 0W
Laferte ⤳ 108 61 53N 117 44W
Lafia 85 8 30N 8 34 E
Lafiagi 85 8 52N 5 20 E
Lafleche 109 49 45N 106 40W
Lafon 87 5 5N 32 29 E
Laforsen 48 61 56N 15 3 E
Lagan ⤳, Sweden 49 56 56N 13 58 E
Lagan ⤳, U.K. 15 54 35N 5 55W
Lagarfljót ⤳ 50 65 40N 14 18W
Lage, Ger. 24 52 0N 8 47 E
Lage, Spain 30 43 13N 9 0W
Lågen ⤳, Oppland, Norway 47 61 8N 10 25 E
Lågen ⤳, Vestfold, Norway 47 59 3N 10 5 E
Lägerdorf 24 53 53N 9 35 E
Laggers Pt. 99 30 52S 153 4 E
Laghán □ 65 34 20N 70 0 E
Laghouat 82 33 50N 2 59 E
Lagnieu 21 45 55N 5 20 E
Lagny 19 48 52N 2 40 E
Lago 41 39 9N 16 8 E
Lagôa 31 37 8N 8 27W
Lagoaça 30 41 11N 6 44W
Lagodekhi 57 41 50N 46 22 E
Lagónegro 41 40 8N 15 45 E
Lagonoy Gulf 73 13 50N 123 50 E
Lagos, Nigeria 85 6 25N 3 27 E
Lagos, Port. 31 37 5N 8 41W
Lagos de Moreno 120 21 21N 101 55W
Lagrange 96 18 45S 121 43 E
Laguardia 32 42 33N 2 35W
Laguépie 20 44 8N 1 57 E
Laguna, Brazil 125 28 30S 48 50W
Laguna, U.S.A. 119 35 3N 107 28W
Laguna Beach 119 33 31N 117 52W
Laguna Dam 119 32 55N 114 30W
Laguna de la Janda 31 36 15N 5 45W
Laguna Limpia 124 26 32S 59 45W
Laguna Madre 120 27 0N 97 20W
Lagunas, Chile 124 21 0S 69 45W
Lagunas, Peru 126 5 10S 75 35W
Laha 76 48 12N 124 35 E
Lahad Datu 73 5 0N 118 20 E
Laharpur 69 27 43N 80 56 E
Lahat 72 3 45S 103 30 E
Lahewa 72 1 22N 97 12 E
Lahijan 64 37 10N 50 6 E
Lahn ⤳ 25 50 52N 8 35 E
Laholm 49 56 30N 13 2 E
Laholmsbukten 49 56 30N 12 45 E
Lahontan Res. 118 39 28N 118 58W
Lahore 68 31 32N 74 22 E
Lahore □ 68 31 55N 74 5 E
* Lahr 25 48 20N 7 52 E
Lahti 51 60 58N 25 40 E
Laï 81 9 25N 16 18 E
Lai Chau 71 22 5N 103 3 E
Laibin 75 23 42N 109 14 E
Laidley 99 27 39S 152 20 E
Laifeng 77 29 27N 109 20 E
Laignes 19 47 50N 4 20 E
Laikipia □ 90 0 30N 36 30 E
Laingsburg 92 33 9S 20 52 E
Lairg 14 58 1N 4 24W
Lais 72 3 35S 102 0 E
Laiyang 76 36 59N 120 45 E
Laizhou Wan 76 37 30N 119 30 E
Laja ⤳ 120 20 55N 100 46W
Lajere 85 11 58N 11 25 E
Lajes 125 27 48S 50 20W
Lajkovac 42 44 27N 20 14 E
Lajosmizse 27 47 3N 19 32 E
Lakaband 68 31 2N 69 15 E
Lakar 73 8 15S 128 17 E
Lake Andes 116 43 10N 98 32W
Lake Anse 114 46 42N 88 25W
Lake Arthur 117 30 8N 92 40W
Lake Cargelligo 97 33 15S 146 22 E
Lake Charles 117 30 15N 93 10W
Lake City, Colo, U.S.A. 119 38 3N 107 27W
Lake City, Fla., U.S.A. 115 30 10N 82 40W
Lake City, Iowa, U.S.A. 116 42 12N 94 42W
Lake City, Mich., U.S.A. 114 44 20N 85 10W
Lake City, Minn., U.S.A. 116 44 28N 92 21W
Lake City, Pa., U.S.A. 112 42 2N 80 20W
Lake City, S.C., U.S.A. 115 33 51N 79 44W
Lake George 113 43 25N 73 43W
Lake Harbour 105 62 50N 69 50W
Lake Havasu City 119 34 25N 114 29W
Lake Lenore 109 52 24N 104 59W
Lake Louise 108 51 30N 116 10W
Lake Mead Nat. Rec. Area 119 36 0N 114 30W
Lake Mills 116 43 23N 93 33W
Lake Nash 98 20 57S 138 0 E
Lake Providence 117 32 49N 91 12W
Lake River 106 54 30N 82 31W
Lake Superior Prov. Park 106 47 45N 84 45W
Lake Village 117 33 20N 91 19W
Lake Wales 115 27 55N 81 32W
Lake Worth 115 26 36N 80 3W
Lakefield 106 44 25N 78 16W
Lakeland 115 28 0N 82 0W
Lakemba 101 18 13S 178 47W
Lakes Entrance 99 37 50S 148 0 E
Lakeside, Ariz., U.S.A. 119 34 12N 109 59W
Lakeside, Nebr., U.S.A. 116 42 5N 102 24W
Lakeview 118 42 15N 120 22W
Lakewood, N.J., U.S.A. 114 40 5N 74 13W
Lakewood, Ohio, U.S.A. 114 41 28N 81 50W
Lakhaniá 45 35 58N 27 54 E
Lákhi 45 35 24N 23 57 E
Lakhpat 68 23 48N 68 47 E
Laki 50 64 4N 18 14W
Lakin 117 37 58N 101 18W
Lakitusaki ⤳ 106 54 21N 82 25W
Lakonía □ 45 36 55N 22 30 E
Lakonikós Kólpos 45 36 40N 22 40 E
Lakota, Ivory C. 84 5 50N 5 30W
Lakota, U.S.A. 116 48 0N 98 22W
Laksefjorden 50 70 45N 26 50 E
Lakselv 50 70 2N 24 56 E
Lakshmi Kantapur 69 22 5N 88 20 E
Lala Ghat 67 24 30N 92 40 E
Lala Musa 68 32 40N 73 57 E
Lalago 90 3 28S 33 58 E
Lalapanzi 91 19 20S 30 15 E
Lalganj 69 25 52N 85 13 E
Lalibela 87 12 2N 39 2 E
Lalin 76 45 12N 127 0 E
Lalín 30 42 40N 8 5W
Lalinde 20 44 50N 0 44 E
Lalitpur 68 24 42N 78 28 E
Lama Kara 85 9 30N 1 15 E
Lamaing 67 15 25N 97 53 E
Lamar, Colo., U.S.A. 116 38 9N 102 35W
Lamar, Mo., U.S.A. 117 37 30N 94 20W
Lamas 126 6 28S 76 31W
Lamastre 21 44 59N 4 35 E
Lambach 26 48 6N 13 51 E
Lamballe 18 48 29N 2 31W
Lambaréné 88 0 41S 10 12 E
Lambasa 101 16 30S 179 10 E
Lambay I. 15 53 30N 6 0W
Lambert 116 47 44N 104 39W
Lambert Glacier 5 71 0S 70 0 E
Lambesc 21 43 39N 5 16 E
Lambi Kyun (Sullivan I.) 71 10 50N 98 20 E
Lámbia 45 37 52N 21 53 E
Lambro ⤳ 38 45 8N 9 32 E
Lame 85 45 35N 106 40W
Lame Deer 118 45 45N 106 40W
Lamego 30 41 5N 7 52W
Lamèque 107 47 45N 64 38W
Lameroo 99 35 19S 140 33 E
Lamesa 117 32 45N 101 57W
Lamía 45 38 55N 22 26 E
† Lamitan 73 6 40N 122 10 E
Lammermuir Hills 14 55 50N 2 40W
Lamoille 118 40 47N 115 31W
Lamon Bay 73 14 30N 122 20 E
Lamont 108 53 46N 112 50W
Lampa 126 15 22S 70 22W
Lampang, Thai. 71 18 18N 99 31 E
Lampang, Thai. 71 18 16N 99 32 E

* *Now part of Punjab* □

† *Renamed Isabela*

Lampasas Lenora

Lampasas 117 31 5N 98 10W
Lampaul 18 48 28N 5 7W
Lampazos de Naranjo 120 27 2N 100 32W
Lampedusa 36 35 36N 12 40 E
Lampeter 13 52 6N 4 6W
Lampione 83 35 33N 12 20 E
Lampman 109 49 25N 102 50W
Lamprechtshausen 26 48 0N 12 58 E
Lamprey 109 58 33N 94 8W
Lampung □ 72 5 30 S 104 30 E
Lamu 90 2 16 S 40 55 E
Lamu □ 90 2 0 S 40 45 E
Lamut, Tg. 72 3 50 S 105 58 E
Lamy 119 35 30N 105 58W
Lan Xian 76 38 15N 111 35 E
Lan Yu 77 22 5N 121 35 E
Lanai I. 110 20 50N 156 55W
Lanak La 69 34 27N 79 32 E
Lanak'o Shank'ou = Lanak La 69 34 27N 79 32 E
Lanao, L. 73 7 52N 124 15 E
Lanark, Can. 113 45 1N 76 22W
Lanark, U.K. 14 55 40N 3 48W
Lancashire □ 12 53 40N 2 30W
Lancaster, Can. 113 45 10N 74 30W
Lancaster, U.K. 12 54 3N 2 48W
Lancaster, Calif., U.S.A. 119 34 47N 118 8W
Lancaster, Ky., U.S.A. 114 37 40N 84 40W
Lancaster, N.H., U.S.A. 114 44 27N 71 33W
Lancaster, N.Y., U.S.A. 112 42 53N 78 43W
Lancaster, Pa., U.S.A. 114 40 4N 76 19W
Lancaster, S.C., U.S.A. 115 34 45N 80 47W
Lancaster, Wis., U.S.A. 116 42 48N 90 43W
Lancaster Sd. 4 74 13N 84 0W
Lancer 109 50 48N 108 53W
Lanchow = Lanzhou 76 36 1N 103 52 E
Lanciano 39 42 15N 14 22 E
Łancut 27 50 10N 22 13 E
Lándana 88 5 11 S 12 5 E
Landau, Bayern, Ger. 25 48 41N 12 41 E
Landau, Rhld-Pfz., Ger. 25 49 12N 8 7 E
Landeck 26 47 9N 10 34 E
Landen 16 50 45N 5 5 E
Lander 118 42 50N 108 49W
Landerneau 18 48 28N 4 17W
Landeryd 49 57 7N 13 15 E
Landes □ 20 43 57N 0 48W
Landes, Les 20 44 20N 1 0W
Landete 32 39 56N 1 25W
Landi Kotal 66 34 7N 71 6 E
Landivisiau 18 48 31N 4 6W
Landquart 25 46 58N 9 32 E
Landrecies 19 50 7N 3 40 E
Land's End 13 50 4N 5 43W
Landsberg 25 48 3N 10 52 E
Landsborough Cr. → 98 22 28 S 144 35 E
Landsbro 49 57 24N 14 56 E
Landshut 25 48 31N 12 10 E
Landskrona 49 55 53N 12 50 E
Landstuhl 25 49 25N 7 34 E
Landvetter 49 57 41N 12 17 E
Lanesboro 113 41 57N 75 34W
Lanett 115 33 0N 85 15W
Lang Bay 108 49 45N 124 21W
Lang Shan 76 41 0N 106 30 E
Lang Son 71 21 52N 106 42 E
La'nga Co 67 30 45N 81 15 E
Lángadhás 44 40 46N 23 2 E
Langádhia 45 37 43N 22 1 E
Långan → 48 63 19N 14 44 E
Langara I. 108 54 14N 133 1W
Langdon 116 48 47N 98 24W
Langeac 20 45 7N 3 29 E
Langeais 18 47 20N 0 24 E
Langeb Baraka → 86 17 28N 36 50 E
Langeberge, C. Prov., S. Afr. 92 33 55 S 21 40 E
Langeberge, C. Prov., S. Afr. 92 28 15 S 22 33 E
Langeland 49 54 56N 10 48 E
Langen 25 49 59N 8 40 E
Langenburg 109 50 51N 101 43W
Langeness 24 54 34N 8 35 E
Langenlois 26 48 29N 15 40 E
Langeoog 24 53 44N 7 33 E
Langeskov 49 55 22N 10 35 E
Langesund 47 59 0N 9 45 E
Länghem 49 57 36N 13 14 E
Langhirano 38 44 39N 10 16 E
Langholm 14 55 9N 2 59W
Langjökull 50 64 39N 20 12W
Langkawi, P. 71 6 25N 99 45 E
Langkon 72 6 30N 116 40 E
Langlade 107 46 50N 56 20W
Langlois 118 42 54N 124 26W
Langnau 25 46 56N 7 47 E
Langogne 20 44 43N 3 50 E
Langon 20 44 33N 0 16W
Langøya 50 68 45N 14 50 E
Langpran, Gunong 72 1 0N 114 23 E
Langres 19 47 52N 5 20 E
Langres, Plateau de 19 47 45N 5 3 E
Langsa 72 4 30N 97 57 E
Långsele 48 63 12N 17 4 E
Långshyttan 48 60 27N 16 2 E
Langtry 117 29 50N 101 33W
Languedoc 20 43 58N 4 0 E
Langxiangzhen 76 39 43N 116 8 E
Langzhong 75 31 38N 105 58 E
Lanigan 109 51 51N 105 2W
Lankao 77 34 48N 114 50 E
Lannemezan 20 43 8N 0 23 E
Lannilis 18 48 35N 4 32W
Lannion 18 48 46N 3 29W
Lanouaille 20 45 24N 1 9 E
Lansdale 113 40 14N 75 18W
Lansdowne, Austral. 99 31 48 S 152 30 E
Lansdowne, Can. 113 44 24N 76 1W
Lansdowne House 106 52 14N 87 53W
Lansford 113 40 48N 75 55W
Lansing 114 42 47N 84 40W
Lanslebourg 21 45 17N 6 52 E
Lant, Pulau 72 4 10 S 116 0 E
Lanus 124 34 44 S 58 27W
Lanusei 40 39 53N 9 31 E
Lanxi 77 29 13N 119 28 E
Lanzarote 80 29 0N 13 40W
Lanzhou 76 36 1N 103 52 E
Lanzo Torinese 38 45 16N 7 29 E
Lao → 41 39 45N 15 45 E
Lao Cai 71 22 30N 103 57 E
Laoag 73 18 7N 120 34 E
Laoang 73 12 32N 125 8 E
Laoha He → 76 43 25N 120 35 E
Laois □ 15 53 0N 7 20W
Laon 19 49 33N 3 35 E
Laona 114 45 32N 88 41W
Laos ■ 71 17 45N 105 0 E
Lapa 125 25 46 S 49 44W
Lapalisse 20 46 15N 3 38 E
Laparan Cap 73 6 0N 120 0 E
Lapeer 114 43 3N 83 20W
Lapi □ 50 67 0N 27 0 E
Lapland = Lappland 50 68 7N 24 0 E
Laporte 113 41 27N 76 30W
Lapovo 42 44 10N 21 2 E
Lappland 50 68 7N 24 0 E
Laprairie 113 45 20N 73 30W
Laprida 124 37 34 S 60 45W
Laptev Sea 59 76 0N 125 0 E
Lapuş, Munţii 46 47 20N 23 50 E
Lapush 118 47 56N 124 33W
Lăpusul → 46 47 25N 23 40 E
Łapy 28 52 59N 22 52 E
Lār 65 27 40N 54 14 E
Larabanga 84 9 16N 1 56W
Laracha 30 43 15N 8 35W
Larache 82 35 10N 6 5W
Laragne-Monteglin 21 44 18N 5 49 E
Laramie 116 41 20N 105 38W
Laramie Mts. 116 42 0N 105 30W
Laranjeiras do Sul 125 25 23 S 52 23W
Larantuka 73 8 21 S 122 55 E
Larap 73 14 18N 122 39 E
Larat 73 7 0 S 132 0 E
Lårdal 47 59 25N 8 10 E
Larde 91 16 28 S 39 43 E
Larder Lake 106 48 5N 79 40W
Lárdhos, Ákra 45 36 4N 28 10 E
Laredo, Spain 32 43 26N 3 28W
Laredo, U.S.A. 117 27 34N 99 29W
Laredo Sd. 108 52 30N 128 53W
Largentière 21 44 34N 4 18 E
Largs 14 55 48N 4 51W
Lari 38 43 34N 10 35 E
Lariang 73 1 26 S 119 17 E
Larimore 116 47 55N 97 35W
Larino 41 41 48N 14 54 E
Lárisa 44 39 49N 22 28 E
Lárisa □ 44 39 39N 22 24 E
Larkana 68 27 32N 68 18 E
Larkollen 47 59 20N 10 41 E
Larnaca 64 35 0N 33 35 E
Larne 15 54 52N 5 50W
Larned 116 38 15N 99 10W
Larrimah 96 15 35 S 133 12 E
Larsen Ice Shelf 5 67 0 S 62 0W
Larvik 47 59 4N 10 0 E
Laryak 58 61 15N 80 0 E
Larzac, Causse du 20 44 0N 3 17 E
Las Animas 117 38 8N 103 18W
Las Anod 63 8 26N 47 19 E
Las Blancos 33 37 38N 0 49W
Las Brenãs 124 27 5 S 61 7W
Las Cabezas de San Juan 31 37 0N 5 58W
Las Cascadas 120 9 5N 79 41W
Las Cruces 119 32 18N 106 50W
Las Flores 124 36 10 S 59 7W
Las Heras 124 32 51 S 68 49W
Las Khoreh 63 11 10N 48 20 E
Las Lajas 128 38 30 S 70 25W
Las Lomitas 124 24 43 S 60 35W
Las Marismas 31 37 5N 6 20W
Las Navas de la Concepción 31 37 56N 5 30W
Las Navas de Tolosa 31 38 18N 3 38W
Las Palmas, Argent. 124 27 8 S 58 45W
Las Palmas, Canary Is. 80 28 7N 15 26W
Las Palmas □ 80 28 10N 15 28W
Las Piedras 125 34 44 S 56 14W
Las Pipinas 124 35 30 S 57 19W
Las Plumas 128 43 40 S 67 15W
Las Rosas 124 32 30 S 61 35W
Las Tablas 121 7 49N 80 14W
Las Termas 124 27 29 S 64 52W
Las Varillas 124 31 50 S 62 50W
Las Vegas, N. Mex., U.S.A. 119 35 35N 105 10W
Las Vegas, Nev., U.S.A. 119 36 10N 115 5W
Lascano 125 33 35 S 54 12W
Lascaux 20 45 5N 1 10 E
Lashburn 109 53 10N 109 40W
Lashio 67 22 56N 97 45 E
Lashkar 68 26 10N 78 10 E
Łasin 28 53 30N 19 2 E
Lasíthi □ 45 35 5N 25 50 E
Lask 28 51 34N 19 8 E
Łaskarzew 28 51 48N 21 36 E
Laško 39 46 10N 15 16 E
Lassay 18 48 27N 0 30W
Lassen Pk. 118 40 29N 121 31W
Last Mountain L. 109 51 5N 105 14W
Lastoursville 88 0 55 S 12 38 E
Lastovo 39 42 46N 16 55 E
Lastovski Kanal 39 42 50N 17 0 E
Latacunga 126 0 50 S 78 35W
Latakia = Al Lādhiqīyah 64 35 30N 35 45 E
Latchford 106 47 20N 79 50W
Laterza 41 40 38N 16 47 E
Lathen 24 52 51N 7 21 E
Latiano 41 40 33N 17 43 E
Latina 40 41 26N 12 53 E
Latisana 39 45 47N 13 1 E
Latium = Lazio 39 42 10N 12 30 E
Latorica → 27 48 28N 21 50 E
Latouche Treville, C. 96 18 27 S 121 49 E
Latrobe 112 40 19N 79 21W
Latrônico 41 40 5N 16 0 E
Latrun 62 31 50N 34 58 E
Latur 70 18 25N 76 40 E
Latvian S.S.R. □ 54 56 50N 24 0 E
Lau (Eastern) Group 101 17 0 S 178 30W
Lauchhammer 24 51 35N 13 48 E
Laudal 47 58 15N 7 30 E
Lauenburg 24 53 23N 10 33 E
Lauffen 25 49 4N 9 9 E
Laugarbakki 50 65 20N 20 55W
Laujar 33 37 0N 2 54W
Launceston, Austral. 97 41 24 S 147 8 E
Launceston, U.K. 13 50 38N 4 21W
Laune → 15 52 5N 9 40W
Launglon Bok 71 13 50N 97 54 E
Laupheim 25 48 13N 9 53 E
Laura 97 15 32 S 144 32 E
Laureana di Borrello 41 38 28N 16 5 E
Laurel, Miss., U.S.A. 117 31 41N 89 9W
Laurel, Mont., U.S.A. 118 45 46N 108 49W
Laurencekirk 14 56 50N 2 30W
Laurens 115 34 32N 82 2W
Laurentian Plat. 107 52 0N 70 0W
Laurentides, Parc Prov. des 107 47 45N 71 15W
Lauria 41 40 3N 15 50 E
Laurie I. 5 60 44 S 44 37W
Laurie L. 109 56 35N 101 57W
Laurinburg 115 34 50N 79 25W
Laurium 114 47 14N 88 26W
Lausanne 25 46 32N 6 38 E
Laut, Kepulauan 72 4 45N 108 0 E
Laut Ketil, Kepulauan 72 4 45 S 115 40 E
Lauterbach 24 50 39N 9 23 E
Lauterecken 25 49 38N 7 35 E
Lautoka 101 17 37 S 177 27 E
Lauzon 107 46 48N 71 10W
Lava Hot Springs 118 42 38N 112 1W
Lavadores 30 42 14N 8 41W
Lavagna 38 44 18N 9 22 E
Laval 18 48 4N 0 48W
Lavalle 124 28 15 S 65 15W
Lavandou, Le 21 43 8N 6 22 E
Lávara 44 41 19N 26 22 E
Lavardac 20 44 12N 0 20 E
Lavaur 20 43 30N 1 49 E
Lavaveix 20 46 5N 2 8 E
Lavelanet 20 42 57N 1 51 E
Lavello 41 41 4N 15 47 E
Laverendrye Prov. Park 106 46 15N 17 15W
Laverne 117 36 43N 99 58W
Laverton 96 28 44 S 122 29 E
Lavi 62 32 47N 35 25 E
Lavik 47 61 6N 5 25 E
Lávkos 45 39 9N 23 14 E
Lavos 30 40 6N 8 49W
Lavras 125 21 20 S 45 0W
Lavre 31 38 46N 8 22W
Lavrentiya 59 65 35N 171 0W
Lávrion 45 37 40N 24 4 E
Lavumisa 93 27 20 S 31 55 E
Lawas 72 4 55N 115 25 E
Lawele 73 5 16 S 123 3 E
Lawn Hill 98 18 36 S 138 33 E
Lawng Pit 67 25 30N 97 25 E
Lawra 84 10 39N 2 51W
Lawrence, Kans., U.S.A. 116 39 0N 95 10W
Lawrence, Mass., U.S.A. 114 42 40N 71 9W
Lawrenceburg, Ind., U.S.A. 114 39 5N 84 50W
Lawrenceburg, Tenn., U.S.A. 115 35 12N 87 19W
Lawrenceville 115 33 55N 83 59W
Lawton 117 34 33N 98 25W
Lawu 73 7 40 S 111 13 E
Laxford, L. 14 58 25N 5 10W
Laxmeshwar 70 15 9N 75 28 E
Laylá 64 22 10N 46 40 E
Layon → 18 47 20N 0 45W
Laysan I. 95 25 30N 167 0W
Laytonville 118 39 44N 123 29W
Lazarevac 42 44 23N 20 17 E
Lazio □ 39 42 10N 12 30 E
Łazy 28 50 27N 19 24 E
Lea → 13 51 30N 0 10W
Lead 116 44 20N 103 40W
Leader 109 50 50N 109 30W
Leadhills 14 55 25N 3 47W
Leadville 119 39 17N 106 23W
Leaf → 117 31 0N 88 45W
Leakey 117 29 45N 99 45W
Leamington, Can. 106 42 3N 82 36W
Leamington, U.K. 13 52 18N 1 32W
Leamington, U.S.A. 118 39 37N 112 17W
Leandro Norte Alem 125 27 34 S 55 15W
Learmonth 96 22 13 S 114 10 E
Leask 109 53 5N 106 45W
Leavenworth, Mo., U.S.A. 116 39 25N 95 0W
Leavenworth, Wash., U.S.A. 118 47 44N 120 37W
Łeba 28 54 45N 17 32 E
Łeba → 28 54 46N 17 33 E
Lebak 73 6 32N 124 5 E
Lebane 42 42 56N 21 44 E
Lebanon, Ind., U.S.A. 114 40 3N 86 28W
Lebanon, Kans., U.S.A. 116 39 50N 98 35W
Lebanon, Ky., U.S.A. 114 37 35N 85 15W
Lebanon, Mo., U.S.A. 117 37 40N 92 40W
Lebanon, Oreg., U.S.A. 118 44 31N 122 57W
Lebanon, Pa., U.S.A. 114 40 20N 76 28W
Lebanon, Tenn., U.S.A. 115 36 15N 86 20W
Lebanon ■ 64 34 0N 36 0 E
Lebec 119 34 50N 118 59W
Lebedin 54 50 35N 34 30 E
Lebedyan 55 53 0N 39 10 E
Lebombo-berge 93 24 30 S 32 0 E
Lębork 28 54 33N 17 46 E
Lebrija 31 36 53N 6 5W
Łebsko, Jezioro 28 54 40N 17 25 E
Lebu 124 37 40 S 73 47W
Lecce 41 40 20N 18 10 E
Lecco 38 45 50N 9 27 E
Lecco, L. di. 38 45 51N 9 22 E
Lécera 32 41 13N 0 43W
Lech 26 47 13N 10 9 E
Lech → 25 48 44N 10 56 E
Lechang 77 25 10N 113 20 E
Lechtaler Alpen 26 47 15N 10 30 E
Lectoure 20 43 56N 0 38 E
Łeczna 28 51 18N 22 53 E
Łeczyca 28 52 5N 19 15 E
Ledbury 13 52 3N 2 25W
Ledeč 26 49 41N 15 18 E
Ledesma 30 41 6N 5 59W
Ledong 77 18 41N 109 5 E
Leduc 108 53 15N 113 30W
Ledyczek 28 53 33N 16 59 E
Lee, Mass., U.S.A. 113 42 17N 73 18W
Lee, Nev., U.S.A. 118 40 35N 115 36W
Lee → 15 51 50N 8 30W
Leech L. 116 47 9N 94 23W
Leedey 117 35 53N 99 24W
Leeds, U.K. 12 53 48N 1 34W
Leeds, U.S.A. 115 33 32N 86 30W
Leek 12 53 7N 2 2W
Leer 24 53 13N 7 29 E
Leesburg 115 28 47N 81 52W
Leesville 117 31 12N 93 15W
Leeton 97 34 33 S 146 23 E
Leetonia 112 40 53N 80 45W
Leeuwarden 16 53 15N 5 48 E
Leeuwin, C. 96 34 20 S 115 9 E
Leeward Is., Atl. Oc. 121 16 30N 63 30W
Leeward Is., Pac. Oc. 95 16 0 S 147 0W
Lefors 117 35 30N 100 50W
Lefroy, L. 96 31 21 S 121 40 E
Łeg → 28 50 42N 21 50 E
Legal 108 53 55N 113 35W
Legazpi 73 13 10N 123 45 E
Leghorn = Livorno 38 43 32N 10 18 E
Legion 91 21 25 S 28 30 E
Legionowo 28 52 25N 20 50 E
Legnago 39 45 10N 11 19 E
Legnano 38 45 35N 8 55 E
Legnica 28 51 12N 16 10 E
Legnica □ 28 51 30N 16 0 E
Legrad 39 46 17N 16 51 E
Legume 99 28 20 S 152 19 E
Leh 69 34 9N 77 35 E
Lehi 118 40 20N 111 51W
Lehighton 113 40 50N 75 44W
Lehliu 46 44 29N 26 20 E
Lehrte 24 52 22N 9 58 E
Lehututu 92 23 54 S 21 55 E
Leiah 68 30 58N 70 58 E
Leibnitz 26 46 47N 15 34 E
Leicester 13 52 39N 1 9W
Leicester □ 13 52 40N 1 10W
Leichhardt → 97 17 35 S 139 48 E
Leichhardt Ra. 98 20 46 S 147 40 E
Leiden 16 52 9N 4 30 E
Leie → 16 51 2N 3 45 E
Leigh Creek 97 30 28 S 138 24 E
Leikanger 47 61 10N 6 52 E
Leine → 24 52 20N 9 50 E
Leinster □ 15 53 0N 7 10W
Leinster, Mt. 15 52 38N 6 47W
Leipzig 24 51 20N 12 23 E
Leipzig □ 24 51 20N 12 30 E
Leiria 31 39 46N 8 53W
Leiria □ 31 39 46N 8 53W
Leith 14 55 59N 3 10W
Leith Hill 13 51 10N 0 23W
Leitha → 27 48 0N 16 35 E
Leitrim 15 54 0N 8 5W
Leitrim □ 15 54 8N 8 0W
Leiyang 77 26 27N 112 45 E
Leiza 32 43 5N 1 55W
Leizhou Bandao 77 21 0N 110 0 E
Leizhou Wan 77 20 50N 110 20 E
Lek → 16 52 0N 6 0 E
Lekáni 44 41 10N 24 35 E
Lekhainá 45 37 57N 21 16 E
Leksula 73 3 46 S 126 31 E
Leland 117 33 25N 90 52W
Leland Lakes 109 60 0N 110 59W
Leleque 128 42 28 S 71 0W
Lelystad 16 52 30N 5 25 E
Lema 85 12 58N 4 13 E
Léman, Lac 25 46 26N 6 30 E
Lemera 90 3 0 S 28 55 E
Lemery 73 13 51N 120 56 E
Lemgo 24 52 2N 8 52 E
Lemhi Ra. 118 44 30N 113 30W
Lemmer 16 52 51N 5 43 E
Lemmon 116 45 59N 102 10W
Lemoore 119 36 23N 119 46W
Lempdes 20 45 22N 3 17 E
Lemvig 49 56 33N 8 20 E
Lena → 59 72 52N 126 40 E
Lenartovce 27 48 18N 20 19 E
Lencloître 18 46 50N 0 20 E
Lendinara 39 45 4N 11 37 E
Lengau de Vaca, Pta. 124 30 14 S 71 38W
Lengerich 24 52 12N 7 50 E
Lenggong 71 5 6N 100 58 E
Lenggries 25 47 41N 11 34 E
Lengyeltóti 27 46 40N 17 40 E
Lenhovda 49 57 0N 15 16 E
Lenin 57 48 20N 40 56 E
Leninabad 58 40 17N 69 37 E
Leninakan 57 40 47N 43 50 E
Leningrad 54 59 55N 30 20 E
Lenino 56 45 17N 35 46 E
Leninogorsk 58 50 20N 83 30 E
Leninsk, R.S.F.S.R., U.S.S.R. 57 48 40N 45 15 E
Leninsk, R.S.F.S.R., U.S.S.R. 57 46 10N 43 46 E
Leninsk-Kuznetskiy 58 54 44N 86 10 E
Leninskaya Sloboda 55 56 7N 44 29 E
Leninskoye, R.S.F.S.R., U.S.S.R. 55 58 23N 47 3 E
Leninskoye, R.S.F.S.R., U.S.S.R. 59 47 56N 132 38 E
Lenk 25 46 27N 7 28 E
Lenkoran 53 39 45N 48 50 E
Lenmalu 73 1 45 S 130 15 E
Lenne → 24 51 25N 7 30 E
Lennoxville 113 45 22N 71 51W
Leno 38 45 24N 10 14 E
Lenoir 115 35 55N 81 36W
Lenoir City 115 35 40N 84 20W
Lenora 116 39 39N 100 1W

Lenore L. Liteni

Lenore L. 109 52 30N 104 59W
Lenox 113 42 20N 73 18W
Lens 19 50 26N 2 50 E
Lensk (Mukhtuya) 59 60 48N 114 55 E
Lenskoye 56 45 3N 34 1 E
Lenti 27 46 37N 16 33 E
Lentini 41 37 18N 15 0 E
Lentvaric 54 54 39N 25 3 E
Lenzen 24 53 6N 11 26 E
Léo 84 11 3N 2 2W
Leoben 26 47 22N 15 5 E
Leola 116 45 47N 98 58W
Leominster, U.K. 13 52 15N 2 43W
Leominster, U.S.A. 114 42 32N 71 45W
Léon 20 43 53N 1 18W
León, Mexico 120 21 7N 101 30W
León, Nic. 121 12 20N 86 51W
León, Spain 30 42 38N 5 34W
Leon 116 40 40N 93 40W
León □ 30 42 40N 5 55W
León, Montañas de 30 42 30N 6 18W
Leonardtown 114 38 19N 76 39W
Leonforte 41 37 39N 14 22 E
Leongatha 99 38 30S 145 58 E
Leonídhion 45 37 9N 22 52 E
Leonora 96 28 49S 121 19 E
Léopold II, Lac = Mai-Ndombe 88 2 0S 18 20 E
Leopoldina 125 21 28S 42 40W
Leopoldsburg 16 51 7N 5 13 E
Léopoldville = Kinshasa 88 4 20S 15 15 E
Leoti 116 38 31N 101 19W
Leoville 109 53 39N 107 33W
Lépa, L. do 92 17 0S 19 0 E
Lepe 31 37 15N 7 12W
Lepel 54 54 50N 28 40 E
Lepikha 59 64 45N 125 55 E
Leping 77 28 47N 117 7 E
Lepontino, Alpi 38 46 22N 8 27 E
Lepsény 27 47 0N 18 15 E
Leptis Magna 83 32 40N 14 12 E
Lequeitio 32 43 20N 2 32W
Lercara Friddi 40 37 42N 13 36 E
Léré 81 9 39N 14 13 E
Lere 85 9 43N 9 18 E
Leribe 93 28 51S 28 3 E
Lérici 38 44 4N 9 58 E
Lérida 32 41 37N 0 39 E
Lérida □ 32 42 6N 1 0 E
Lérins, Is. de 21 43 31N 7 3 E
Lerma 30 42 0N 3 47W
Léros 45 37 10N 26 50 E
Lérouville 19 48 50N 5 30 E
Lerwick 14 60 10N 1 10W
Les 46 46 58N 21 50 E
Lesbos, I. = Lésvos 45 39 10N 26 20 E
Leshukonskoye 52 64 54N 45 46 E
Lésina, L. di 39 41 53N 15 25 E
Lesja 47 62 7N 8 51 E
Lesjaverk 47 62 12N 8 34 E
Lesko 27 49 30N 22 23 E
Leskov I. 5 56 0S 28 0W
Leskovac 42 43 0N 21 58 E
Leskoviku 44 40 10N 20 34 E
Leslie 117 35 50N 92 35W
Lesna 28 51 0N 15 15 E
Lesneven 18 48 35N 4 20W
Lešnica 42 44 39N 19 20 E
Lesnoye 54 58 15N 35 18 E
Lesotho ■ 93 29 40S 28 0 E
Lesozavodsk 59 45 30N 133 29 E
Lesparre-Médoc 20 45 18N 0 57W
Lessay 18 49 14N 1 30W
Lesse → 16 50 15N 4 54 E
Lesser Antilles 121 15 0N 61 0W
Lesser Slave L. 108 55 30N 115 25W
Lessines 16 50 42N 3 50 E
Lestock 109 51 19N 103 59W
Lésvos 45 39 10N 26 20 E
Leszno 28 51 50N 16 30 E
Leszno □ 28 51 45N 16 30 E
Letchworth 13 51 58N 0 13W
Letea, Ostrov 46 45 18N 29 20 E
Lethbridge 108 49 45N 112 45W
Leti 73 8 10S 127 40 E
Leti, Kepulauan 73 8 10S 128 0 E
Letiahau → 92 21 16S 24 0 E
Leticia 126 4 9S 70 0W
Leting 76 39 23N 118 55 E
Letlhakeng 92 24 0S 24 59 E
Letpadan 67 17 45N 95 45 E
Letpan 67 19 28N 94 10 E
Letsôk-aw Kyun (Domel I.) 71 11 30N 98 25 E
Letterkenny 15 54 57N 7 42W
Leu 46 44 10N 24 0 E
Leucate 20 42 56N 3 3 E
Leucate, Étang de 20 42 50N 3 0 E
Leuk 25 46 19N 7 37 E
Leuser, G. 72 3 46N 97 12 E
Leutkirch 25 47 49N 10 1 E
Leuven (Louvain) 16 50 52N 4 42 E
Leuze, Hainaut, Belg. 16 50 36N 3 37 E
Leuze, Namur, Belg. 16 50 33N 4 54 E
Lev Tolstoy 55 53 13N 39 29 E
Levádhia 45 38 27N 22 54 E
Levan 118 39 37N 111 52W
Levanger 47 63 45N 11 19 E
Levani 44 40 40N 19 28 E
Levant, I. du 21 43 3N 6 28 E
Lévanto 38 44 10N 9 37 E
Levanzo 40 38 0N 12 19 E
Levelland 117 33 38N 102 23W
Leven 14 56 12N 3 0W
Leven, L. 14 56 12N 3 22W
Leven, Toraka 93 12 30S 47 45 E
Levens 21 43 50N 7 12 E
Leveque C. 96 16 20S 123 0 E
Leverano 41 40 16N 18 0 E
Leverkusen 24 51 2N 6 59 E
Levet 19 46 56N 2 22 E
Levice 27 48 13N 18 35 E
Levick, Mt. 5 75 0S 164 0 E
Levico 39 46 0N 11 18 E
Levie 21 41 40N 9 7 E
Levier 19 46 58N 6 8 E
Levin 101 40 37S 175 18 E
Lévis 107 46 48N 71 9W
Levis, L. 108 62 37N 117 58W
Levítha 45 37 0N 26 28 E
Levittown, N.Y., U.S.A. 113 40 41N 73 31W
Levittown, Pa., U.S.A. 113 40 10N 74 51W
Levka 43 41 52N 26 15 E
Lévka 45 35 18N 24 3 E
Levkás 45 38 40N 20 43 E
Levkímmi 44 39 25N 20 3 E
Levkôsia = Nicosia 64 35 10N 33 25 E
Levoča 27 49 2N 20 35 E
Levroux 19 47 0N 1 38 E
Levski 43 43 21N 25 10 E
Levskigrad 43 42 38N 24 47 E
Lewellen 116 41 22N 102 5W
Lewes, U.K. 13 50 53N 0 2 E
Lewes, U.S.A. 114 38 45N 75 8W
Lewin Brzeski 28 50 45N 17 37 E
Lewis 14 58 10N 6 40W
Lewis, Butt of 14 58 30N 6 12W
Lewis Ra. 118 48 0N 113 15W
Lewisburg, Pa., U.S.A. 112 40 57N 76 57W
Lewisburg, Tenn., U.S.A. 115 35 29N 86 46W
Lewisporte 107 49 15N 55 3W
Lewiston, Idaho, U.S.A. 118 46 25N 117 0W
Lewiston, Utah, U.S.A. 118 41 58N 111 56W
Lewistown, Mont., U.S.A. 118 47 0N 109 25W
Lewistown, Pa., U.S.A. 114 40 37N 77 33W
Lexington, Ill., U.S.A. 116 40 37N 88 47W
Lexington, Ky., U.S.A. 114 38 6N 84 30W
Lexington, Miss., U.S.A. 117 33 8N 90 2W
Lexington, Mo., U.S.A. 116 39 7N 93 55W
Lexington, N.C., U.S.A. 115 35 50N 80 13W
Lexington, Nebr., U.S.A. 116 40 48N 99 45W
Lexington, Ohio, U.S.A. 112 40 39N 82 35W
Lexington, Oreg., U.S.A. 118 45 29N 119 46W
Lexington, Tenn., U.S.A. 115 35 38N 88 25W
Lexington Park 114 38 16N 76 27W
Leyre → 20 44 39N 1 1W
Leyte 73 11 0N 125 0 E
Lezajsk 28 50 16N 22 25 E
Lezay 20 46 17N 0 0 E
Lezha 44 41 47N 19 42 E
Lézignan-Corbières 20 43 13N 2 43 E
Lezoux 20 45 49N 3 21 E
Lgov 54 51 42N 35 16 E
Lhasa 75 29 25N 90 58 E
Lhazê 75 29 5N 87 38 E
Lhokseumawe 72 5 10N 97 10 E
Lhuntsi Dzong 67 27 39N 91 10 E
Li Shui → 77 29 24N 112 1 E
Li Xian, Gansu, China 77 34 10N 105 5 E
Li Xian, Hunan, China 77 29 36N 111 42 E
Liádhoi 45 36 50N 26 11 E
Lianga 73 8 38N 126 6 E
Liangdang 77 33 56N 106 18 E
Lianhua 77 27 3N 113 54 E
Lianjiang 77 26 12N 119 27 E
Lianping 77 24 26N 114 30 E
Lianshanguan 76 40 53N 123 43 E
Lianyungang 77 34 40N 119 11 E
Liao He → 76 41 0N 121 50 E
Liaocheng 76 36 28N 115 58 E
Liaodong Bandao 76 40 0N 122 30 E
Liaodong Wan 76 40 20N 121 10 E
Liaoning □ 76 42 0N 122 0 E
Liaoyang 76 41 15N 122 58 E
Liaoyuan 76 42 58N 125 2 E
Liaozhong 76 41 23N 122 50 E
Liapádhes 44 39 42N 19 40 E
Liard → 108 61 51N 121 18W
Libau = Liepaja 54 56 30N 21 0 E
Libby 118 48 20N 115 33W
Libenge 88 3 40N 18 55 E
Liberal, Kans., U.S.A. 117 37 4N 101 0W
Liberal, Mo., U.S.A. 117 37 35N 94 30W
Liberec 26 50 47N 15 7 E
Liberia 121 10 40N 85 30W
Liberia ■ 84 6 30N 9 30W
Liberty, Mo., U.S.A. 116 39 15N 94 24W
Liberty, Tex., U.S.A. 117 30 5N 94 50W
Libiaz 27 50 7N 19 21 E
Libo 77 25 22N 107 53 E
Libobo, Tanjung 73 0 54S 128 28 E
Libohava 44 40 3N 20 10 E
Libonda 89 14 28S 23 12 E
Libourne 20 44 55N 0 14W
Libramont 16 49 55N 5 23 E
Librazhdi 44 41 12N 20 22 E
Libreville 88 0 25N 9 26 E
Libya ■ 81 27 0N 17 0 E
Libyan Plateau = Ed-Déffa 86 30 40N 26 30 E
Licantén 124 35 55S 72 0W
Licata 40 37 6N 13 55 E
Lichfield 12 52 40N 1 50W
Lichinga 91 13 13S 35 11 E
Lichtenburg 92 26 8S 26 8 E
Lichtenfels 25 50 7N 11 4 E
Lichuan 77 30 18N 108 57 E
Licosa, Punta 41 40 15N 14 53 E
Lida, U.S.A. 119 37 30N 117 30W
Lida, U.S.S.R. 54 53 53N 25 15 E
Lidhult 49 56 50N 13 27 E
Lidingö 48 59 22N 18 8 E
Lidköping 49 58 31N 13 14 E
Lido, Italy 39 45 25N 12 23 E
Lido, Niger 85 12 54N 3 44 E
Lido di Ostia 40 41 44N 12 14 E
Lidzbark 28 53 15N 19 49 E
Lidzbark Warminski 28 54 7N 20 34 E
Liebenwalde 24 52 51N 13 23 E
Lieberose 24 51 59N 14 18 E
Liebling 42 45 36N 21 20 E
Liechtenstein ■ 25 47 8N 9 35 E
Liège 16 50 38N 5 35 E
Liège □ 16 50 32N 5 35 E
Liegnitz = Legnica 28 51 12N 16 10 E
Lienart 90 3 3N 25 31 E
Lienyünchiangshih =
Lianyungang 77 34 40N 119 11 E
Lienz 26 46 50N 12 46 E
Liepaja 54 56 30N 21 0 E
Lier 16 51 7N 4 34 E
Lieşta 46 45 38N 27 34 E
Liévin 19 50 24N 2 47 E
Lièvre → 106 45 31N 75 26W
Liezen 26 47 34N 14 15 E
Liffey → 15 53 21N 6 20W
Lifford 15 54 50N 7 30W
Liffré 18 48 12N 1 30W
Lifjell 47 59 27N 8 45 E
Lightning Ridge 99 29 22S 148 0 E
Lignano 39 45 42N 13 8 E
Ligny-en-Barrois 19 48 36N 5 20 E
Ligny-le-Châtel 19 47 54N 3 45 E
Ligoúrion 45 37 37N 23 2 E
Ligua, La 124 32 30S 71 16W
Ligueil 18 47 2N 0 49 E
Liguria □ 38 44 30N 9 0 E
Ligurian Sea 38 43 20N 9 0 E
Lihir Group 98 3 0S 152 35 E
Lihou Reefs and Cays 97 17 25S 151 40 E
Lihue 110 21 59N 159 24W
Lijiang 75 26 55N 100 20 E
Likasi 91 10 55S 26 48 E
Likati 88 3 20N 24 0 E
Likhoslavl 54 57 12N 35 30 E
Likhovski 57 48 10N 40 10 E
Likoma I. 91 12 3S 34 45 E
Likumburu 91 9 43S 35 8 E
Liling 77 27 42N 113 29 E
Lille 19 50 38N 3 3 E
Lille Bælt 49 55 20N 9 45 E
Lillebonne 18 49 30N 0 32 E
Lillehammer 47 61 8N 10 30 E
Lillers 19 50 35N 2 28 E
Lillesand 47 58 15N 8 23 E
Lilleshall 13 52 45N 2 22W
Lillestrøm 47 59 58N 11 5 E
Lillo 32 39 45N 3 20W
Lillooet → 108 49 15N 121 57W
Lilongwe 91 14 0S 33 48 E
Liloy 73 8 4N 122 39 E
Lim → 42 43 0N 19 40 E
Lima, Indon. 73 3 37S 128 4 E
Lima, Peru 126 12 0S 77 0W
Lima, Sweden 48 60 55N 13 20 E
Lima, Mont., U.S.A. 118 44 41N 112 38W
Lima, Ohio, U.S.A. 114 40 42N 84 5W
Lima → 30 41 41N 8 50W
Limages 113 45 20N 75 16W
Liman 57 45 45N 47 12 E
Limanowa 27 49 42N 20 22 E
Limassol 64 34 42N 33 1 E
Limavady 15 55 3N 6 58W
Limavady □ 15 55 0N 6 55W
Limay → 128 39 0S 68 0W
Limay Mahuida 124 37 10S 66 45W
Limbang 72 4 42N 115 6 E
Limbara, Monti 40 40 50N 9 10 E
Limbdi 68 22 34N 71 51 E
Limbri 99 31 3S 151 5 E
Limburg 25 50 22N 8 4 E
Limburg □, Belg. 16 51 2N 5 25 E
Limburg □, Neth. 16 51 20N 5 55 E
Limedsforsen 48 60 52N 13 25 E
Limeira 125 22 35S 47 28W
Limenária 44 40 38N 24 32 E
Limerick 15 52 40N 8 38W
Limerick □ 15 52 30N 8 50W
Limestone 112 42 2N 78 39W
Limestone → 109 56 31N 94 7W
Limfjorden 49 56 55N 9 0 E
Limia → 30 41 41N 8 50W
Limmared 49 57 34N 13 20 E
Limmen Bight 96 14 40S 135 35 E
Límni 45 38 43N 23 18 E
Límnos 44 39 50N 25 5 E
Limoeiro do Norte 127 5 5S 38 0W
Limoges 20 45 50N 1 15 E
Limón 121 10 0N 83 2W
Limon, Panama 120 9 17N 79 45W
Limon, U.S.A. 116 39 18N 103 38W
Limon B. 120 9 22N 79 56W
Limone Piemonte 38 44 12N 7 32 E
Limousin 20 46 0N 1 0 E
Limousin, Plateaux du 20 46 0N 1 0 E
Limoux 20 43 4N 2 12 E
Limpopo → 93 25 15S 33 30 E
Limuru 90 1 2S 36 35 E
Linares, Chile 124 35 50S 71 40W
Linares, Mexico 120 24 50N 99 40W
Linares, Spain 33 38 10N 3 40W
Linares □ 124 36 0S 71 0W
Linas Mte. 40 39 25N 8 38 E
Lincheng 76 37 25N 114 30 E
Linchuan 75 27 57N 116 15 E
Lincoln, Argent. 124 34 55S 61 30W
Lincoln, N.Z. 101 43 38S 172 30 E
Lincoln, U.K. 12 53 14N 0 32W
Lincoln, Ill., U.S.A. 116 40 10N 89 20W
Lincoln, Kans., U.S.A. 116 39 6N 98 9W
Lincoln, Maine, U.S.A. 107 45 27N 68 29W
Lincoln, N. Mex., U.S.A. 119 33 30N 105 26W
Lincoln, N.H., U.S.A. 113 44 3N 71 40W
Lincoln, Nebr., U.S.A. 116 40 50N 96 42W
Lincoln □ 12 53 14N 0 32W
Lincoln Sea 4 84 0N 55 0W
Lincoln Wolds 12 53 20N 0 5W
Lincolnton 115 35 30N 81 15W
Lind 118 47 0N 118 33W
Lindås, Norway 47 60 44N 5 9 E
Lindås, Sweden 49 56 38N 15 35 E
Lindau 25 47 33N 9 41 E
Linden, Guyana 126 6 0N 58 10W
Linden, U.S.A. 117 33 0N 94 20W
Linderöd 49 55 56N 13 47 E
Linderödsåsen 49 55 53N 13 53 E
Lindesberg 48 59 36N 15 15 E
Lindesnes 47 57 58N 7 3 E
Lindi 91 9 58S 39 38 E
Lindi □ 91 9 40S 38 30 E
Lindi → 90 0 33N 25 5 E
Lindian 76 47 11N 124 52 E
Lindoso 30 41 52N 8 11W
Lindow 24 52 58N 12 58 E
Lindsay, Can. 106 44 22N 78 43W
Lindsay, Calif., U.S.A. 119 36 14N 119 6W
Lindsay, Okla., U.S.A. 117 34 51N 97 37W
Lindsborg 116 38 35N 97 40W
Línea de la Concepción, La 31 36 15N 5 23W
Linfen 76 36 3N 111 30 E
Ling Xian 76 37 22N 116 30 E
Lingao 77 19 56N 109 42 E
Lingayen 73 16 1N 120 14 E
Lingayen G. 73 16 10N 120 15 E
Lingchuan 77 25 26N 110 21 E
Lingen 24 52 32N 7 21 E
Lingga 72 0 12S 104 37 E
Lingga, Kepulauan 72 0 10S 104 30 E
Linghed 48 60 48N 15 55 E
Lingle 116 42 10N 104 18W
Lingling 77 26 17N 111 37 E
Lingshan 77 22 25N 109 18 E
Lingshi 76 36 48N 111 48 E
Lingshui 77 18 27N 110 0 E
Lingtai 77 35 0N 107 40 E
Linguéré 84 15 25N 15 5W
Lingyuan 76 41 10N 119 15 E
Lingyun 75 25 2N 106 35 E
Linh Cam 71 18 31N 105 31 E
Linhai 75 28 50N 121 8 E
Linhe 76 40 48N 107 20 E
Linjiang 76 41 50N 127 0 E
Linköping 49 58 28N 15 36 E
Linkou 76 45 15N 130 18 E
Linlithgow 14 55 58N 3 38W
Linn, Mt. 118 40 0N 123 0W
Linnhe, L. 14 56 36N 5 25W
Linosa, I. 83 35 51N 12 50 E
Linqing 76 36 50N 115 42 E
Lins 125 21 40S 49 44W
Lintao 76 35 18N 103 52 E
Linth → 25 47 7N 9 7W
Linthal 25 46 54N 9 0 E
Lintlaw 109 52 4N 103 14W
Linton, Can. 107 47 15N 72 16W
Linton, Ind., U.S.A. 114 39 0N 87 10W
Linton, N. Dak., U.S.A. 116 46 21N 100 12W
Linville 99 26 50S 152 11 E
Linwood 112 43 35N 80 43W
Linwu 77 25 19N 112 31 E
Linxe 20 43 56N 1 13W
Linxi 76 43 36N 118 2 E
Linxia 75 35 36N 103 10 E
Linyanti → 92 17 50S 25 5 E
Linyi 77 35 5N 118 21 E
Linz, Austria 26 48 18N 14 18 E
Linz, Ger. 24 50 33N 7 18 E
Lion-d'Angers, Le 18 47 37N 0 43W
Lion, G. du 20 43 0N 4 0 E
Lioni 41 40 52N 15 10 E
Lion's Den 91 17 15S 30 5 E
Lion's Head 106 44 58N 81 15W
Liozno 54 55 0N 30 50 E
Lipali 91 15 50S 35 50 E
Lipari 41 38 26N 14 58 E
Lipari, Is. 41 38 30N 14 50 E
Lipetsk 55 52 37N 39 35 E
Lipiany 28 53 2N 14 58 E
Liping 77 26 15N 109 7 E
Lipkany 56 48 14N 26 48 E
Lipljan 42 42 31N 21 7 E
Lipnik 27 49 32N 17 36 E
Lipno 28 52 49N 19 15 E
Lipova 42 46 8N 21 42 E
Lipovets 56 49 12N 29 1 E
Lippe → 24 51 39N 6 38 E
Lippstadt 24 51 40N 8 19 E
Lipscomb 117 36 16N 100 16W
Lipsko 28 51 9N 21 40 E
Lipsói 45 37 19N 26 50 E
Liptovsky Svaty Milkulaš 27 49 6N 19 35 E
Liptrap C. 99 38 50S 145 55 E
Lira 90 2 17N 32 57 E
Liri → 40 41 25N 13 52 E
Liria 32 39 37N 0 35W
Lisala 88 2 12N 21 38 E
Lisboa 31 38 42N 9 10W
Lisboa □ 31 39 0N 9 12W
Lisbon, N. Dak., U.S.A. 116 46 30N 97 46W
Lisbon, N.H., U.S.A. 113 44 13N 71 52W
Lisbon, Ohio, U.S.A. 112 40 45N 80 42W
Lisbon = Lisboa 31 38 42N 9 10W
Lisburn 15 54 30N 6 9W
Lisburne, C. 104 68 50N 166 0W
Liscannor, B. 15 52 57N 9 24W
Liscia → 40 41 11N 9 9 E
Lishi 76 37 31N 111 8 E
Lishui 75 28 28N 119 54 E
Lisianski I. 94 26 2N 174 0W
Lisichansk 56 48 55N 38 30 E
Lisieux 18 49 10N 0 12 E
Lisle-sur-Tarn 20 43 52N 1 49 E
Lismore, Austral. 97 28 44S 153 21 E
Lismore, Ireland 15 52 8N 7 58W
Lisse 16 52 16N 4 33 E
List 24 55 1N 8 26 E
Lista 47 58 7N 6 39 E
Lister, Mt. 5 78 0S 162 0 E
Liston 99 28 39S 152 6 E
Listowel, Can. 106 43 44N 80 58W
Listowel, Ireland 15 52 27N 9 30W
Lit-et-Mixe 20 44 2N 1 15W
Litang, China 77 23 12N 109 8 E
Litang, Malay. 73 5 27N 118 31 E
Litani →, Leb. 62 33 20N 35 14 E
Litani →, Surinam 62 3 40N 54 0W
Litchfield, Conn., U.S.A. 113 41 44N 73 12W
Litchfield, Ill., U.S.A. 116 39 10N 89 40W
Litchfield, Minn., U.S.A. 116 45 5N 94 31W
Liteni 46 47 32N 26 32 E

Lithgow — Low Rocky Pt.

Lithgow **97** 33 25S 150 8E
Líthinon, Ákra **45** 34 55N 24 44E
Lithuanian S.S.R. □ **54** 55 30N 24 0E
Litija **39** 46 3N 14 50E
Litókhoron **44** 40 8N 22 34E
Litoměřice **26** 50 33N 14 10E
Litomysl **27** 49 52N 16 20E
Litschau **26** 48 58N 15 4E
Little Abaco I. **121** 26 50N 77 30W
Little America **5** 79 0S 160 0W
Little Andaman I. **71** 10 40N 92 15E
Little Barrier I. **101** 36 12S 175 8E
Little Belt Mts. **118** 46 50N 111 0W
Little Blue → **116** 39 41N 96 40W
Little Bushman Land **92** 29 10S 18 10E
Little Cadotte → **108** 56 41N 117 6W
Little Churchill → **109** 57 30N 95 22W
Little Colorado → **119** 36 11N 111 48W
Little Current **106** 45 55N 82 0W
Little Current → **106** 50 57N 84 36W
Little Falls, Minn., U.S.A. **116** 45 58N 94 19W
Little Falls, N.Y., U.S.A. **114** 43 3N 74 50W
Little Fork → **116** 48 31N 93 35W
Little Grand Rapids **109** 52 0N 95 29W
Little Humboldt → **118** 41 0N 117 43W
Little Inagua I. **121** 21 40N 73 50W
Little Lake **119** 35 58N 117 58W
Little Marais **116** 47 24N 91 8W
Little Minch **14** 57 35N 6 45W
Little Missouri → **116** 47 30N 102 25W
Little Namaqualand **92** 29 0S 17 9E
Little Ouse → **13** 52 25N 0 50E
Little Rann of Kutch **68** 23 25N 71 25E
Little Red → **117** 35 11N 91 27W
Little River **101** 43 45S 172 49E
Little Rock **117** 34 41N 92 10W
Little Ruaha → **90** 7 57S 37 53E
Little Sable Pt. **114** 43 40N 86 32W
Little Sioux → **116** 41 49N 96 4W
Little Smoky → **108** 54 44N 117 11W
Little Snake → **118** 40 27N 108 26W
Little Valley **112** 42 15N 78 48W
Little Wabash → **114** 37 54N 88 5W
Littlefield **117** 33 57N 102 17W
Littlefork **116** 48 24N 93 35W
Littlehampton **13** 50 48N 0 32W
Littleton **114** 44 19N 71 47W
Liuba **77** 33 38N 106 55E
Liucheng **77** 24 38N 109 14E
Liukang Tenggaja **73** 6 45S 118 50E
Liuli **91** 11 3S 34 38E
Liuwa Plain **89** 14 20S 22 30E
Liuyang **77** 28 10N 113 37E
Liuzhou **75** 24 22N 109 22E
Livada **46** 47 52N 23 5E
Livadherón **44** 40 2N 21 57E
Livarot **18** 49 0N 0 9E
Live Oak **115** 30 17N 83 0W
Livermore, Mt. **117** 30 45N 104 8W
Liverpool, Austral. **97** 33 54S 150 58E
Liverpool, Can. **107** 44 5N 64 41W
Liverpool, U.K. **12** 53 25N 3 0W
Liverpool Plains **97** 31 15S 150 15E
Liverpool Ra. **97** 31 50S 150 30E
Livingston, Guat. **120** 15 50N 88 50W
Livingston, U.S.A. **118** 45 40N 110 40W
Livingstone, U.S.A. **117** 30 44N 94 54W
Livingstone, Zambia **91** 17 46S 25 52E
Livingstone I. **5** 63 0S 60 15W
Livingstone Memorial **91** 12 20S 30 18E
Livingstone Mts. **91** 9 40S 34 20E
Livingstonia **91** 10 38S 34 5E
Livno **42** 43 50N 17 0E
Livny **55** 52 30N 37 30E
Livorno **38** 43 32N 10 18E
Livramento **125** 30 55S 55 30W
Livron-sur-Drôme **21** 44 46N 4 51E
Liwale **91** 9 48S 37 58E
Liwale □ **91** 9 0S 38 0E
Liwiec → **28** 52 36N 21 34E
Lixoúrion **45** 38 14N 20 24E
Lizard I. **98** 14 42S 145 30E
Lizard Pt. **13** 49 57N 5 11W
Lizzano **41** 40 23N 17 25E
Ljig **42** 44 13N 20 18E
Ljubija **39** 44 55N 16 35E
Ljubinje **42** 42 58N 18 5E
Ljubljana **39** 46 4N 14 33E
Ljubno **39** 46 25N 14 46E
Ljubovija **42** 44 11N 19 22E
Ljubuški **42** 43 12N 17 34E
Ljung **49** 58 1N 13 3E
Ljungan → **48** 62 18N 17 23E
Ljungaverk **48** 62 30N 16 5E
Ljungby **49** 56 49N 13 55E
Ljusdal **48** 61 46N 16 3E
Ljusnan → **48** 61 12N 17 8E
Ljusne **48** 61 13N 17 7E
Ljutomer **39** 46 31N 16 11E
Llagostera **32** 41 50N 2 54E
Llancanelo, Salina **124** 35 40S 69 8W
Llandeilo **13** 51 53N 4 0W
Llandovery **13** 51 59N 3 49W
Llandrindod Wells **13** 52 15N 3 23W
Llandudno **12** 53 19N 3 51W
Llanelli **13** 51 41N 4 11W
Llanes **30** 43 25N 4 50W
Llangollen **12** 52 58N 3 10W
Llanidloes **13** 52 28N 3 31W
Llano **117** 30 45N 98 41W
Llano → **117** 30 50N 98 25W
Llano Estacado **117** 34 0N 103 0W
Llanos **126** 5 0N 71 35W
Llera **120** 23 19N 99 1W
Llerena **31** 38 17N 6 0W
Llico **124** 34 46S 72 5W
Llobregat → **32** 41 19N 2 9E
Lloret de Mar **32** 41 41N 2 53E
Lloyd B. **98** 12 45S 143 27E
Lloyd L. **109** 57 22N 108 57W
Lloydminster **109** 53 17N 110 0W
Lluchmayor **33** 39 29N 2 53E
Llullaillaco, volcán **124** 24 43S 68 30W
Loa **119** 38 18N 111 40W
Loa → **124** 21 26S 70 41W
Loano **38** 44 8N 8 14E
Lobatse **92** 25 12S 25 40E
Löbau **24** 51 5N 14 42E
Lobenstein **24** 50 25N 11 39E
Lobería **124** 38 10S 58 40W
Łobez **28** 53 38N 15 39E
Lobito **89** 12 18S 13 35E
Lobón, Canal de **31** 38 50N 6 55W
Lobos **124** 35 10S 59 0W
Lobos, I. **120** 27 15N 110 30W
Lobos, Is. **122** 6 57S 80 45W
Lobstick L. **107** 54 0N 65 0W
Loc Binh **71** 21 46N 106 54E
Loc Ninh **71** 11 50N 106 34E
Locarno **25** 46 10N 8 47E
Lochaber **14** 56 55N 5 0W
Lochcarron **14** 57 25N 5 30W
Loche, La **109** 56 29N 109 26W
Lochem **16** 52 9N 6 26E
Loches **18** 47 7N 1 0E
Lochgelly **14** 56 7N 3 18W
Lochgilphead **14** 56 2N 5 37W
Lochinver **14** 58 9N 5 15W
Lochnagar, Austral. **98** 23 33S 145 38E
Lochnagar, U.K. **14** 56 57N 3 14W
Łochów **28** 52 33N 21 42E
Lochy → **14** 56 52N 5 3W
Lock **99** 33 34S 135 46E
Lock Haven **114** 41 7N 77 31W
Lockeport **107** 43 47N 65 4W
Lockerbie **14** 55 7N 3 21W
Lockhart, Austral. **99** 35 14S 146 40E
Lockhart, U.S.A. **117** 29 55N 97 40W
Lockney **117** 34 7N 101 27W
Lockport **114** 43 12N 78 42W
Locle, Le **25** 47 3N 6 44E
Locminé **18** 47 54N 2 51W
Locri **41** 38 14N 16 14E
Locronan **18** 48 7N 4 15W
Loctudy **18** 47 50N 4 12W
Lod **62** 31 57N 34 54E
Lodalskåpa **47** 61 47N 7 13E
Loddon → **100** 35 31S 143 51E
Lodeinoye Pole **52** 60 44N 33 33E
Lodève **20** 43 44N 3 19E
Lodge Grass **118** 45 21N 107 20W
Lodgepole **116** 41 12N 102 40W
Lodgepole Cr. → **116** 41 20N 104 30W
Lodhran **68** 29 32N 71 30E
Lodi, Italy **38** 45 19N 9 30E
Lodi, U.S.A. **118** 38 12N 121 16W
Lodja **90** 3 30S 23 23E
Lodosa **32** 42 25N 2 4W
Lödöse **49** 58 2N 12 9E
Lodwar **90** 3 10N 35 40E
Łódź **28** 51 45N 19 27E
Łódź □ **28** 51 45N 19 27E
Loengo **90** 4 48S 26 30E
Lofer **26** 47 35N 12 41E
Lofoten **50** 68 30N 15 0E
Lofsdalen **48** 62 10N 13 20E
Lofsen → **48** 62 7N 13 57E
Loftahammar **49** 57 54N 16 41E
Logan, Kans., U.S.A. **116** 39 40N 99 35W
Logan, Ohio, U.S.A. **114** 39 25N 82 22W
Logan, Utah, U.S.A. **118** 41 45N 111 50W
Logan, W. Va., U.S.A. **114** 37 51N 81 59W
Logan, Mt. **104** 60 31N 140 22W
Logan Pass **108** 48 41N 113 44W
Logansport, Ind., U.S.A. **114** 40 45N 86 21W
Logansport, La., U.S.A. **117** 31 58N 93 58W
Logar □ **65** 34 0N 69 0E
Logo **87** 5 20N 30 18E
Logroño **32** 42 28N 2 27W
* Logroño □ **32** 42 28N 2 27W
Logrosán **31** 39 20N 5 32W
Løgstør **49** 56 58N 9 14E
Lohardaga **69** 23 27N 84 45E
Lohja **51** 60 12N 24 5E
Lohr **25** 50 0N 9 35E
Loi-kaw **67** 19 40N 97 17E
Loimaa **51** 60 50N 23 5E
Loir → **18** 47 33N 0 32W
Loir-et-Cher □ **18** 47 40N 1 20E
Loire □ **21** 45 40N 4 5E
Loire → **18** 47 16N 2 10W
Loire-Atlantique □ **18** 47 25N 1 40W
Loiret □ **19** 47 58N 2 10E
Loitz **24** 53 58N 13 8E
Loja, Ecuador **126** 3 59S 79 16W
Loja, Spain **31** 37 10N 4 10W
Loji **73** 1 38S 127 28E
Loka **87** 4 13N 31 0E
Lokandu **90** 2 30S 25 45E
Løken **47** 59 48N 11 29E
Lokeren **16** 51 6N 3 59E
Lokhvitsa **54** 50 25N 33 18E
Lokichokio **90** 4 19N 34 13E
Lokitaung **90** 4 12N 35 48E
Lokka **50** 67 49N 27 45E
Løkken **49** 57 22N 9 41E
Løkkenverk **47** 63 8N 9 45E
Loknya **54** 56 49N 30 4E
Lokoja **85** 7 47N 6 45E
Lokolama **88** 2 35S 19 50E
Lokwei **77** 19 5N 110 31E
Lol → **87** 9 13N 26 30E
Lola **84** 7 52N 8 29W
Lolibai, Gebel **87** 3 50N 33 0E
Lolimi **87** 4 35N 34 0E
Loliondo **90** 2 2S 35 39E
Lolland **49** 54 45N 11 30E
Lollar **24** 50 39N 8 43E
Lolo **118** 46 50N 114 8W
Lolodorf **85** 3 16N 10 49E
Lom **43** 43 48N 23 12E
Lom → **42** 43 45N 23 15E
Loma **118** 47 59N 110 29W
Lomami → **90** 0 46N 24 16E
Lomas de Zamóra **124** 34 45S 58 25W
Lombard **118** 46 7N 111 28W
Lombardia □ **38** 45 35N 9 45E
Lombardy = Lombardia **38** 45 35N 9 45E
Lombez **20** 43 29N 0 55E
Lomblen **73** 8 30S 123 32E
Lombok **72** 8 45S 116 30E
Lomé **85** 6 9N 1 20E
Lomela **88** 2 19S 23 15E
Lomela → **88** 1 30S 22 50E
Lomello **38** 45 5N 8 46E
Lometa **117** 31 15N 98 25W
Lomié **88** 3 13N 13 38E
Lomma **49** 55 43N 13 6E
Lomond **108** 50 24N 112 36W
Lomond, L. **14** 56 8N 4 38W
Lomonosov **54** 59 57N 29 53E
Lompobatang **73** 5 24S 119 56E
Lompoc **119** 34 41N 120 32W
Lomsegga **47** 61 49N 8 21E
Łomza **28** 53 10N 22 2E
Łomza □ **28** 53 0N 22 30E
Lonavla **70** 18 46N 73 29E
Loncoche **128** 39 20S 72 50W
Londa **70** 15 30N 74 30E
Londe, La **21** 43 8N 6 14E
Londiani **90** 0 10S 35 33E
Londinières **18** 49 50N 1 25E
London, Can. **106** 42 59N 81 15W
London, U.K. **13** 51 30N 0 5W
London, Ky., U.S.A. **114** 37 11N 84 5W
London, Ohio, U.S.A. **114** 39 54N 83 28W
London, Greater □ **13** 51 30N 0 5W
Londonderry **15** 55 0N 7 20W
Londonderry □ **15** 55 0N 7 20W
Londonderry, C. **96** 13 45S 126 55E
Londonderry, I. **128** 55 0S 71 0W
Londrina **125** 23 18S 51 10W
Lone Pine **119** 36 35N 118 2W
Long Beach, Calif., U.S.A. **119** 33 46N 118 12W
Long Beach, N.Y., U.S.A. **113** 40 35N 73 40W
Long Beach, Wash., U.S.A. **118** 46 20N 124 1W
Long Branch **114** 40 19N 74 0W
Long Creek **118** 44 43N 119 6W
Long Eaton **12** 52 54N 1 16W
Long I., Austral. **98** 22 8S 149 53E
Long I., Bahamas **121** 23 20N 75 10W
Long I., P.N.G. **98** 5 20S 147 5E
Long I., U.S.A. **114** 40 50N 73 20W
Long I. Sd. **113** 41 10N 73 0W
Long L. **106** 49 30N 86 50W
Long Lake **113** 43 57N 74 25W
Long Pine **116** 42 33N 99 41W
Long Pt., Newf., Can. **107** 48 47N 58 46W
Long Pt., Ont., Can. **112** 42 35N 80 2W
Long Point B. **112** 42 40N 80 10W
Long Range Mts. **107** 49 30N 57 30W
Long Str. **4** 70 0N 175 0E
Long Xian **77** 34 55N 106 55E
Long Xuyen **71** 10 19N 105 28E
Longá **45** 36 53N 21 55E
Long'an **77** 23 10N 107 40E
Longarone **39** 46 15N 12 18E
Longchuan **77** 24 5N 115 17E
Longde **76** 35 30N 106 20E
Longeau **19** 47 47N 5 20E
Longford, Austral. **99** 41 32S 147 3E
Longford, Ireland **15** 53 43N 7 50W
Longford □ **15** 53 42N 7 45W
Longhua **76** 41 18N 117 45E
Longido **90** 2 43S 36 42E
Longiram **72** 0 5S 115 45E
Longjiang **76** 47 20N 123 12E
Longkou **76** 37 40N 120 18E
Longlac **106** 49 45N 86 25W
Longlin **77** 24 47N 105 20E
Longmen **77** 23 40N 114 18E
Longmont **116** 40 10N 105 4W
Longnan **77** 24 55N 114 47E
Longnawan **72** 1 51N 114 55E
Longobucco **41** 39 27N 16 37E
Longone → **81** 10 0N 15 40E
Longquan **77** 28 7N 119 10E
Longreach **97** 23 28S 144 14E
Longs Peak **118** 40 20N 105 37W
Longshan **77** 29 29N 109 25E
Longsheng **77** 25 48N 110 0E
Longton **98** 20 58S 145 55E
Longtown **13** 51 58N 2 59W
Longué **18** 47 22N 0 8W
Longueau **19** 49 52N 2 21E
Longueuil **113** 45 32N 73 28W
Longuyon **19** 49 27N 5 35E
Longview, Can. **108** 50 32N 114 10W
Longview, Tex., U.S.A. **117** 32 30N 94 45W
Longview, Wash., U.S.A. **118** 46 9N 122 58W
Longwy **19** 49 30N 5 45E
Longxi **76** 34 53N 104 40E
Longzhou **77** 22 22N 106 50E
Lonigo **39** 45 23N 11 22E
Löningen **24** 52 43N 7 44E
Lonja → **39** 45 30N 16 40E
Lonoke **117** 34 48N 91 57W
Lons-le-Saunier **19** 46 40N 5 31E
Lønstrup **49** 57 29N 9 47E
Looc **73** 12 20N 112 5E
Lookout, C., Can. **106** 55 18N 83 56W
Lookout, C., U.S.A. **115** 34 30N 76 30W
Loolmalasin **90** 3 0S 35 53E
Loon →, Alta., Can. **108** 57 8N 115 3W
Loon →, Man., Can. **109** 55 53N 101 59W
Loon Lake **109** 54 2N 109 10W
Loop Hd. **15** 52 34N 9 55W
Lop Nor = Lop Nur **75** 40 20N 90 10E
Lop Nur **75** 40 20N 90 10E
Lopare **42** 44 39N 18 46E
Lopatin **57** 43 50N 47 35E
Lopatina, G. **59** 50 47N 143 10E
Lopaye **87** 6 37N 33 40E
Lopera **31** 37 56N 4 14W
Lopez, C. **88** 0 47S 8 40E
Lopphavet **50** 70 27N 21 15E
Lora →, Afghan. **65** 32 0N 67 15E
Lora →, Norway **47** 62 8N 8 42E
Lora del Río **31** 37 39N 5 33W
Lora, Hamun-i- **66** 29 38N 64 58E
Lora, La **30** 42 45N 4 0W
Lorain **114** 41 28N 82 55W
Loralai **68** 30 20N 68 41E
Lorca **33** 37 41N 1 42W
Lord Howe I. **94** 31 33S 159 6E
Lord Howe Ridge **94** 30 0S 162 30E
Lordsburg **119** 32 22N 108 45W
Lorengau **98** 2 1S 147 15E
Loreto, Brazil **127** 7 5S 45 10W
Loreto, Italy **39** 43 26N 13 36E
Loreto Aprutina **39** 42 24N 13 59E
Lorgues **21** 43 28N 6 22E
Lorient **18** 47 45N 3 23W
Loristān □ **64** 33 20N 47 0E
Lorn **14** 56 26N 5 10W
Lorn, Firth of **14** 56 20N 5 40W
Lorne **99** 38 33S 143 59E
Lörrach **25** 47 36N 7 38E
Lorraine **19** 49 0N 6 0E
Lorrainville **106** 47 21N 79 23W
Los Alamos **119** 35 57N 106 17W
Los Andes **124** 32 50S 70 40W
Los Angeles, Chile **124** 37 28S 72 23W
Los Angeles, U.S.A. **119** 34 0N 118 10W
Los Angeles Aqueduct **119** 35 25N 118 0W
Los Banos **119** 37 8N 120 56W
Los Barrios **31** 36 11N 5 30W
Los Blancos **124** 23 40S 62 30W
Los Gatos **119** 37 15N 121 59W
Los Hermanos **126** 11 45N 84 25W
Los, Îles de **84** 9 30N 13 50W
Los Lamentos **120** 30 36N 105 50W
Los Lunas **119** 34 48N 106 47W
Los Mochis **120** 25 45N 109 5W
Los Monegros **32** 41 29N 0 13W
Los Olivos **119** 34 40N 120 7W
Los Palacios y Villafranca **31** 37 10N 5 55W
Los Roques **126** 11 50N 66 45W
Los Santos de Maimona **31** 38 27N 6 22W
Los Testigos **126** 11 23N 63 6W
Los Vilos **124** 32 10S 71 30W
Los Yébenes **31** 39 36N 3 55W
Loshkalakh **59** 62 45N 147 20E
Łosice **28** 52 13N 22 43E
Lošinj **39** 44 30N 14 30E
Lossiemouth **14** 57 43N 3 17W
Losuia **98** 8 30S 151 4E
Lot □ **20** 44 39N 1 40E
Lot → **20** 44 18N 0 20E
Lot-et-Garonne □ **20** 44 22N 0 30E
Lota **124** 37 5S 73 10W
Løten **47** 60 51N 11 21E
Lothian □ **14** 55 50N 3 0W
Lothiers **19** 46 42N 1 33E
Lotschbergtunnel **25** 46 26N 7 43E
Lottefors **48** 61 25N 16 24E
Loubomo **88** 4 9S 12 47E
Loudéac **18** 48 11N 2 47W
Loudon **115** 35 35N 84 22W
Loudonville **112** 40 40N 82 15W
Loudun **18** 47 0N 0 5E
Loué **18** 47 59N 0 9W
Loue → **19** 47 1N 5 27E
Louga **84** 15 45N 16 5W
Loughborough **12** 52 46N 1 11W
Loughrea **15** 53 11N 8 33W
Loughros More B. **15** 54 48N 8 30W
Louhans **21** 46 38N 5 12E
Louis Trichardt **93** 23 0S 29 43E
Louis XIV, Pte. **106** 54 37N 79 45W
Louisa **114** 38 5N 82 40W
Louisbourg **107** 45 55N 60 0W
Louise I. **108** 52 55N 131 50W
Louiseville **106** 46 20N 72 56W
Louisiade Arch. **94** 11 10S 153 0E
Louisiana **116** 39 25N 91 0W
Louisiana □ **117** 30 50N 92 0W
Louisville, Ky., U.S.A. **114** 38 15N 85 45W
Louisville, Miss., U.S.A. **117** 33 7N 89 3W
Loulay **20** 46 3N 0 30W
Loulé **31** 37 9N 8 0W
Lount L. **109** 50 10N 94 20W
Louny **26** 50 20N 13 48E
Loup City **116** 41 19N 98 57W
Loupe, La **18** 48 29N 1 1E
Lourdes **20** 43 6N 0 3W
Lourdes-du-Blanc-Sablon **107** 51 24N 57 12W
Lourenço-Marques = Maputo **93** 25 58S 32 32E
Loures **31** 38 50N 9 9W
Lourinhã **31** 39 14N 9 17W
Louroux-Béconnais, Le **18** 47 30N 0 55W
Lousã **30** 40 7N 8 14W
Louth, Austral. **99** 30 30S 145 8E
Louth, Ireland **15** 53 47N 6 33W
Louth, U.K. **12** 53 23N 0 0W
Louth □ **15** 53 55N 6 30W
Loutrá Aidhipsoú **45** 38 54N 23 2E
Loutráki **45** 38 0N 22 57E
Louvière, La **16** 50 27N 4 10E
Louviers **18** 49 12N 1 10E
Lovat → **54** 58 14N 30 28E
Lovćen **42** 42 23N 18 51E
Love **109** 53 29N 104 10W
Lovech **43** 43 8N 24 42E
Loveland **116** 40 27N 105 4W
Lovell **118** 44 51N 108 20W
Lovelock **118** 40 17N 118 25W
Lóvere **38** 45 50N 10 4E
Loviisa **51** 60 28N 26 12E
Loving **117** 32 17N 104 4W
Lovington **117** 33 0N 103 20W
Lovios **30** 41 55N 8 4W
Lovisa **51** 60 28N 26 12E
Lovosice **26** 50 30N 14 2E
Lovran **39** 45 18N 14 15E
Lovrin **42** 45 58N 20 48E
Lövstabukten **48** 60 35N 17 45E
Low Rocky Pt. **97** 42 59S 145 29E

* *Renamed La Rioja* □

Lowa McLure

Lowa 90 1 25 S 25 47 E
Lowa → 90 1 24 S 25 51 E
Lowell 114 42 38N 71 19W
Lower Arrow L. 108 49 40N 118 5W
Lower Austria = Niederösterreich □ 26 48 25N 15 40 E
Lower Hutt 101 41 10 S 174 55 E
Lower L. 118 41 17N 120 3W
Lower Lake 118 38 56N 122 36W
Lower Neguac 107 47 20N 65 10W
Lower Post 108 59 58N 128 30W
Lower Red L. 116 47 58N 95 0W
Lower Saxony = Niedersachsen □ 24 52 45N 9 0 E
Lowestoft 13 52 29N 1 44 E
Łowicz 28 52 6N 19 55 E
Lowville 114 43 48N 75 30W
Loxton 97 34 28 S 140 31 E
Loyalty Is. = Loyauté, Is. 94 21 0 S 167 30 E
Loyang = Luoyang 77 34 40N 112 26 E
Loyev, U.S.S.R. 54 51 55N 30 40 E
Loyev, U.S.S.R. 54 51 56N 30 46 E
Loyoro 90 3 22N 34 14 E
Lož 39 45 43N 30 14 E
Lozère □ 20 44 35N 3 30 E
Loznica 42 44 32N 19 14 E
Lozovaya 56 49 0N 36 20 E
Luachimo 88 7 23 S 20 48 E
Luacono 88 11 15 S 21 37 E
Lualaba → 90 0 26N 25 20 E
Luampa 91 15 4 S 24 20 E
Lu'an 77 31 45N 116 29 E
Luan Chau 71 21 38N 103 24 E
Luan Xian 76 39 40N 118 40 E
Luanda 88 8 50 S 13 15 E
Luang Prabang 71 19 52N 102 10 E
Luangwa Valley 91 13 30 S 31 30 E
Luanping 76 40 53N 117 23 E
Luanshya 91 13 3 S 28 28 E
Luapula □ 91 11 0 S 29 0 E
Luapula → 91 9 26 S 28 33 E
Luarca 30 43 32N 6 32W
Luashi 91 10 50 S 23 36 E
Luau 88 10 40 S 22 10 E
Lubaczów 28 50 10N 23 8 E
Lubalo 88 9 10 S 19 15 E
Lubań 28 51 5N 15 15 E
Lubana, Ozero 54 56 45N 27 0 E
Lubang Is. 73 13 50N 120 12 E
Lubartów 28 51 28N 22 42 E
Lubawa 28 53 30N 19 48 E
Lübben 24 51 56N 13 54 E
Lübbenau 24 51 49N 13 59 E
Lubbock 117 33 40N 101 53W
Lübeck 24 53 52N 10 41 E
Lübecker Bucht 24 54 3N 11 0 E
Lubefu 90 4 47 S 24 27 E
Lubefu → 90 4 10 S 23 0 E
Lubero = Luofu 90 0 1 S 29 15 E
Lubicon L. 108 56 23N 115 56W
Lubień Kujawski 28 52 23N 19 9 E
Lubin 28 51 24N 16 11 E
Lublin 28 51 12N 22 38 E
Lublin □ 28 51 5N 22 30 E
Lubliniec 28 50 43N 18 45 E
Lubny 54 50 3N 32 58 E
Lubok Antu 72 1 3N 111 50 E
Lubon 28 52 21N 16 51 E
Lubongola 90 2 35 S 27 50 E
Lubotin 27 49 17N 20 53 E
Lubran 64 34 0N 36 0 E
Lubraniec 28 52 33N 18 50 E
Lubsko 28 51 45N 14 57 E
Lübtheen 24 53 18N 11 4 E
Lubuagan 73 17 21N 121 10 E
Lubudi → 91 9 0 S 25 35 E
Lubuklinggau 72 3 15 S 102 55 E
Lubuksikaping 72 0 10N 100 15 E
Lubumbashi 91 11 40 S 27 28 E
Lubunda 90 5 12 S 26 41 E
Lubungu 91 14 35 S 26 24 E
Lubutu 90 0 45 S 26 30 E
Luc-en-Diois 21 44 36N 5 28 E
Luc, Le 21 43 23N 6 21 E
Lucan 112 43 11N 81 24W
Lucca 38 43 50N 10 30 E
Luce Bay 14 54 45N 4 48W
Lucea 121 18 25N 78 10W
Lucedale 115 30 55N 88 34W
Lucena, Phil. 73 13 56N 121 37 E
Lucena, Spain 31 37 27N 4 31W
Lucena del Cid 32 40 9N 0 17W
Lučenec 27 48 18N 19 42 E
Lucera 41 41 30N 15 20 E
Lucerne = Luzern 25 47 3N 8 18 E
Luchena → 33 37 44N 1 50W
Lucheringo → 91 11 43 S 36 17 E
Lüchow 24 52 58N 11 8 E
Lucira 89 14 0 S 12 35 E
Luckau 24 51 50N 13 43 E
Luckenwalde 24 52 5N 13 11 E
Lucknow 69 26 50N 81 0 E
Luçon 20 46 28N 1 10W
Lüda 76 38 50N 121 40 E
Luda Kamchiya → 43 43 3N 27 29 E
Ludbreg 39 46 15N 16 38 E
Lüdenscheid 24 51 13N 7 37 E
Lüderitz 92 26 41 S 15 8 E
Ludewe □ 91 10 0 S 34 50 E
Ludhiana 68 30 57N 75 56 E
Lüdinghausen 24 51 46N 7 28 E
Ludington 114 43 58N 86 27W
Ludlow, U.K. 13 52 23N 2 42W
Ludlow, Calif., U.S.A. 119 34 43N 116 10W
Ludlow, Vt., U.S.A. 113 43 25N 72 40W
Ludus 46 46 29N 24 5 E
Ludvika 48 60 8N 15 14 E
Ludwigsburg 25 48 53N 9 11 E
Ludwigshafen 25 49 27N 8 27 E
Ludwigslust 24 53 19N 11 28 E
Ludza 54 56 32N 27 43 E
Luebo 88 5 21 S 21 23 E
Lueki 90 3 20 S 25 48 E
Luena, Zaïre 91 9 28 S 25 43 E
Luena, Zambia 91 10 40 S 30 25 E
Lüeyang 77 33 22N 106 10 E
Lufeng 77 22 57N 115 38 E
Lufkin 117 31 25N 94 40W
Lufupa 91 10 37 S 24 56 E
Luga 54 58 40N 29 55 E
Luga → 54 59 40N 28 18 E
Lugang 77 24 4N 120 23 E
Lugano 25 46 0N 8 57 E
Lugano, L. di 25 46 0N 9 0 E
Lugansk = Voroshilovgrad 57 48 35N 39 20 E
Lugard's Falls 90 3 6 S 38 41 E
Lugela 91 16 25 S 36 43 E
Lugenda → 91 11 25 S 38 33 E
Lugh Ganana 63 3 48N 42 34 E
Lugnaquilla 15 52 58N 6 28W
Lugnvik 48 62 56N 17 55 E
Lugo, Italy 39 44 25N 11 53 E
Lugo, Spain 30 43 2N 7 35W
Lugo □ 30 43 0N 7 30W
Lugoj 42 45 42N 21 57 E
Lugones 30 43 26N 5 50W
Lugovoy 58 42 54N 72 45 E
Luhe → 24 53 18N 10 11 E
Luiana 92 17 25 S 22 59 E
Luino 38 46 0N 8 42 E
Luís Correia 127 3 0 S 41 35W
Luitpold Coast 5 78 30 S 32 0W
Luize 88 7 40 S 22 30 E
Luizi 90 6 0 S 27 25 E
Luján 124 34 45 S 59 5W
Lukanga Swamps 91 14 30 S 27 40 E
Lukenie → 88 3 0 S 18 50 E
Lukhisaral 69 25 11N 86 5 E
Lŭki 43 41 50N 24 43 E
Lukolela, Equateur, Zaïre 88 1 10 S 17 12 E
Lukolela, Kasai Or., Zaïre 90 5 23 S 24 32 E
Lukosi 91 18 30 S 26 30 E
Lukovit 43 43 13N 24 11 E
Łuków 28 51 55N 22 23 E
Lukoyanov 55 55 2N 44 29 E
Lule älv → 50 65 35N 22 10 E
Luleå 50 65 35N 22 10 E
Lüleburgaz 43 41 23N 27 22 E
Luling 117 29 45N 97 40W
Lulong 76 39 53N 118 51 E
Lulonga → 88 1 0N 19 0 E
Lulua → 88 6 30 S 22 50 E
Luluabourg = Kananga 88 5 55 S 22 26 E
Lumai 89 13 13 S 21 25 E
Lumajang 73 8 8 S 113 16 E
Lumbala 89 14 18 S 21 18 E
Lumberton, Miss., U.S.A. 117 31 4N 89 28W
Lumberton, N. Mex., U.S.A. 119 36 58N 106 57W
Lumberton, N.C., U.S.A. 115 34 37N 78 59W
Lumbres 19 50 40N 2 5 E
Lumbwa 90 0 12 S 35 28 E
Lumby 108 50 10N 118 50W
Lumsden 101 45 44 S 168 27 E
Lumut 71 4 13N 100 37 E
Lunavada 68 23 8N 73 37 E
Lunca 46 47 22N 25 1 E
Lund, Sweden 49 55 44N 13 12 E
Lund, U.S.A. 118 38 53N 115 0W
Lundazi 91 12 20 S 33 7 E
Lunde 47 59 17N 9 5 E
Lunderskov 49 55 29N 9 19 E
Lundi → 91 21 43 S 32 34 E
Lundu 72 1 40N 109 50 E
Lundy 13 51 10N 4 41W
Lune → 12 54 0N 2 51W
Lüneburg 24 53 15N 10 23 E
Lüneburg Heath = Lüneburger Heide 24 53 0N 10 0 E
Lüneburger Heide 24 53 0N 10 0 E
Lunel 21 43 39N 4 9 E
Lünen 24 51 36N 7 31 E
Lunenburg 107 44 22N 64 18W
Lunéville 19 48 36N 6 30 E
Lunga → 91 14 34 S 26 25 E
Lungi Airport 84 8 40N 13 17W
Lungleh 67 22 55N 92 45 E
Luni 68 26 0N 73 6 E
Luni → 68 24 41N 71 14 E
Luninets 54 52 15N 26 50 E
Luning 118 38 30N 118 10W
Lunino 55 53 35N 45 6 E
Lunner 47 60 19N 10 35 E
Lunsemfwa → 91 14 54 S 30 12 E
Lunsemfwa Falls 91 14 30 S 29 6 E
Luo He → 77 34 35N 110 20 E
Luobei 76 47 35N 130 50 E
Luocheng 77 24 48N 108 53 E
Luochuan 76 35 45N 109 26 E
Luoding 77 22 45N 111 40 E
Luodong 77 24 41N 121 46 E
Luofu 90 0 10 S 29 15 E
Luoning 77 34 35N 111 40 E
Luoyang 77 34 40N 112 26 E
Luoyuan 77 26 28N 119 30 E
Luozi 88 4 54 S 14 0 E
Lupeni 46 45 21N 23 13 E
Łupków 27 49 15N 22 4 E
Luque, Parag. 124 25 19 S 57 25W
Luque, Spain 31 37 35N 4 16W
Luray 114 38 39N 78 26W
Lure 19 47 40N 6 30 E
Luremo 88 8 30 S 17 50 E
Lurgan 15 54 28N 6 20W
Lusaka 91 15 28 S 28 16 E
Lusambo 90 4 58 S 23 28 E
Lusangaye 90 4 54 S 26 0 E
Luseland 109 52 5N 109 24W
Lushan 77 33 45N 112 55 E
Lushih 77 34 3N 111 3 E
Lushnja 44 40 55N 19 41 E
Lushoto 90 4 47 S 38 20 E
Lushoto □ 90 4 45 S 38 20 E
Lüshun 76 38 45N 121 15 E
Lusignan 20 46 26N 0 8 E
Lusigny-sur-Barse 19 48 16N 4 15 E
Lusk 116 42 47N 104 27W
Lussac-les-Châteaux 20 46 24N 0 43 E
Luta = Lüda 76 38 50N 121 40 E
Luton 13 51 53N 0 24W
Lutong 72 4 30N 114 0 E
Lutsk 54 50 50N 25 15 E
Lützow Holmbukta 5 69 10 S 37 30 E
Luverne 116 43 35N 96 12W
Luvua 91 8 48 S 25 17 E
Luwegu → 91 8 31 S 37 23 E
Luwuk 73 0 56 S 122 47 E
Luxembourg 16 49 37N 6 9 E
Luxembourg ■ 16 50 0N 6 0 E
Luxembourg □ 16 49 58N 5 30 E
Luxeuil-les-Bains 19 47 49N 6 24 E
Luxi 77 28 20N 110 7 E
Luxor = El Uqsur 86 25 41N 32 38 E
Luy → 20 43 39N 1 9W
Luy-de-Béarn → 20 43 39N 0 48W
Luy-de-France → 20 43 39N 0 48W
Luz-St-Sauveur 20 42 53N 0 1 E
Luza 52 60 39N 47 10 E
Luzern 25 47 3N 8 18 E
Luzern □ 25 47 2N 7 55 E
Luzhai 77 24 29N 109 42 E
Luzhou 75 28 52N 105 20 E
Luziânia 127 16 20 S 48 0W
Luzon 73 16 0N 121 0 E
Luzy 19 46 47N 3 58 E
Luzzi 41 39 28N 16 17 E
Lvov 54 49 50N 24 0 E
Lwówek 28 52 28N 16 10 E
Lwówek Śląski 28 51 7N 15 38 E
Lyakhovichi 54 53 2N 26 32 E
Lyakhovskiye, Ostrova 59 73 40N 141 0 E
Lyaki 57 40 34N 47 22 E
Lyallpur = Faisalabad 68 31 30N 73 5 E
Lyaskovets 43 43 6N 25 44 E
Lychen 24 53 13N 13 20 E
Lyckeby 49 56 12N 15 37 E
Lycksele 50 64 38N 18 40 E
Lycosura 45 37 20N 22 3 E
Lydda = Lod 62 31 57N 34 54 E
Lydenburg 93 25 10 S 30 29 E
Lyell 101 41 48 S 172 4 E
Lyell I. 108 52 40N 131 35W
Lyell Range 101 41 38 S 172 20 E
Lygnern 49 57 30N 12 15 E
Lykling 47 59 42N 5 12 E
Lyman 118 41 24N 110 15W
Lyme Regis 13 50 44N 2 57W
Lymington 13 50 46N 1 32W
Łyńa → 28 54 37N 21 14 E
Lynchburg 114 37 23N 79 10W
Lynd → 98 16 28 S 143 18 E
Lynd Ra. 99 25 30 S 149 20 E
Lynden, Can. 112 43 14N 80 9W
Lynden, U.S.A. 118 48 56N 122 32W
Lyndhurst 99 30 15 S 138 18 E
Lyndonville, N.Y., U.S.A. 112 43 19N 78 25W
Lyndonville, Vt., U.S.A. 113 44 32N 72 1W
Lyngdal, Aust-Agder, Norway 47 58 8N 7 7 E
Lyngdal, Buskerud, Norway 47 59 54N 9 32 E
Lynn 114 42 28N 70 57W
Lynn Canal 108 58 50N 135 20W
Lynn Lake 109 56 51N 101 3W
Lynton 13 51 14N 3 50W
Lyntupy 54 55 4N 26 23 E
Lynx L. 109 62 25N 106 15W
Lyø 49 55 3N 10 9 E
Lyon 21 45 46N 4 50 E
Lyonnais 21 45 45N 4 15 E
Lyons, Colo., U.S.A. 116 40 17N 105 15W
Lyons, Ga., U.S.A. 115 32 10N 82 15W
Lyons, Kans., U.S.A. 116 38 24N 98 13W
Lyons, N.Y., U.S.A. 114 43 3N 77 0W
Lyons = Lyon 21 45 46N 4 50 E
Lyrestad 49 58 48N 14 4 E
Lys → 19 50 39N 2 24 E
Lysá 26 50 11N 14 51 E
Lysekil 49 58 17N 11 26 E
Lyskovo 55 56 0N 45 3 E
Lysva 52 58 07N 57 49 E
Lysvik 48 60 1N 13 9 E
Lytle 117 29 14N 98 46W
Lyttelton 101 43 35 S 172 44 E
Lytton 108 50 13N 121 31W
Lyuban 54 59 16N 31 18 E
Lyubcha 54 53 46N 26 1 E
Lyubertsy 55 55 39N 37 50 E
Lyubim 55 58 20N 40 39 E
Lyubimets 43 41 50N 26 5 E
Lyuboml, U.S.S.R. 54 51 10N 24 2 E
Lyuboml, U.S.S.R. 54 51 11N 24 4 E
Lyubotin 56 50 0N 36 0 E
Lyubytino 54 58 50N 33 16 E
Lyudinovo 54 53 52N 34 28 E

M

Mā'ad 62 32 37N 35 36 E
Ma'alah 64 26 31N 47 20 E
Maamba 92 17 17 S 26 28 E
Ma'ânn 64 30 12N 35 44 E
Ma'anshan 77 31 44N 118 29 E
Ma'arrat un Nu'man 64 35 38N 36 40 E
Maas → 16 51 45N 4 32 E
Maaseik 16 51 6N 5 45 E
Maassluis 16 51 56N 4 16 E
Maastricht 16 50 50N 5 40 E
Maave 93 21 4 S 34 47 E
Mabel L. 108 50 35N 118 43W
Mabenge 90 4 15N 24 12 E
Mablethorpe 12 53 21N 0 14 E
Maboma 90 2 30N 28 10 E
Mabrouk 85 19 29N 1 15W
Mabton 118 46 15N 120 12W
Mac Nutt 109 51 5N 101 36W
Mac Tier 112 45 9N 79 46W
Macachín 124 37 10 S 63 43W
Macaé 125 22 20 S 41 43W
McAlester 117 34 57N 95 46W
McAllen 117 26 12N 98 15W
Macallister → 100 38 2 S 146 59 E
Macamic 106 48 45N 79 0W
Macão 31 39 35N 7 59W
Macao = Macau ■ 75 22 16N 113 35 E
Macapá 127 0 5N 51 4W
McArthur → 97 15 54 S 136 40 E
McArthur River 97 16 27 S 136 7 E
Macau 127 5 0 S 36 40W
Macau ■ 75 22 16N 113 35 E
McBride 108 53 20N 120 19W
McCall 118 44 55N 116 6W
McCamey 117 31 8N 102 15W
McCammon 118 42 41N 112 11W
McCauley I. 108 53 40N 130 15W
Macclesfield 12 53 16N 2 9W
McClintock 109 57 50N 94 10W
McCloud 118 41 14N 122 5W
McClure 112 40 42N 77 20W
McClure Str. 4 75 0N 119 0W
McClusky 116 47 30N 100 31W
McComb 117 31 13N 90 30W
McCook 116 40 15N 100 35W
McCusker → 109 55 32N 108 39W
McDame 108 59 44N 128 59W
McDermitt 118 42 0N 117 45W
Macdonald → 100 33 22 S 151 0 E
McDonald Is. 3 54 0 S 73 0 E
Macdonald L. 96 23 30 S 129 0 E
Macdonnell Ranges 96 23 40 S 133 0 E
Macdougall L. 104 66 0N 98 27W
MacDowell L. 106 52 15N 92 45W
Macduff 14 57 40N 2 30W
Maceda 30 42 16N 7 39W
* Macedo de Cavaleiros 88 11 25 S 16 45 E
Macedonia = Makedhonia 44 40 39N 22 0 E
Macedonia = Makedonija 42 41 53N 21 40 E
Maceió 127 9 40 S 35 41W
Maceira 31 39 41N 8 55W
Macenta 84 8 35N 9 32W
Macerata 39 43 19N 13 28 E
McFarlane → 109 59 12N 107 58W
Macfarlane, L. 97 32 0 S 136 40 E
McGehee 117 33 40N 91 25W
McGill 118 39 27N 114 50W
Macgillycuddy's Reeks 15 52 2N 9 45W
MacGregor 109 49 57N 98 48W
McGregor, Iowa, U.S.A. 116 42 58N 91 15W
McGregor, Minn., U.S.A. 116 46 37N 93 17W
McGregor → 108 55 10N 122 0W
McGregor Ra. 99 27 0 S 142 45 E
Mach 66 29 50N 67 20 E
Machado = Jiparana → 126 8 3 S 62 52W
Machagai 124 26 56 S 60 2W
Machakos 90 1 30 S 37 15 E
Machakos □ 90 1 30 S 37 15 E
Machala 126 3 20 S 79 57W
Machanga 93 20 59 S 35 0 E
Machattie, L. 97 24 50 S 139 48 E
Machava 93 25 54 S 32 28 E
Machece 91 19 15 S 35 32 E
Machecoul 18 47 0N 1 49W
Macheng 77 31 12N 115 2 E
Machevna 59 61 20N 172 20 E
Machezo 31 39 21N 4 20W
Machias 107 44 40N 67 28W
Machichaco, Cabo 32 43 28N 2 47W
Machichi → 109 57 3N 92 6W
Machilipatnam 70 16 12N 81 8 E
Machine, La 19 46 54N 3 27 E
Machiques 126 10 4N 72 34W
Machupicchu 126 13 8 S 72 30W
Machynlleth 13 52 36N 3 51W
** Macias Nguema Biyoga 85 3 30N 8 40 E
Maciejowice 28 51 36N 21 26 E
McIlwraith Ra. 97 13 50 S 143 20 E
Măcin 46 45 16N 28 8 E
Macina 84 14 50N 5 0W
McIntosh 116 45 57N 101 20W
McIntosh L. 109 55 45N 105 0W
Macintyre → 97 28 37 S 150 47 E
Macizo Galaico 30 42 30N 7 30W
Mackay, Austral. 97 21 8 S 149 11 E
Mackay, U.S.A. 118 43 58N 113 37W
Mackay → 108 57 10N 111 38W
Mackay, L. 96 22 30 S 129 0 E
McKees Rock 112 40 27N 80 3W
McKeesport 114 40 21N 79 50W
Mackenzie 108 55 20N 123 05W
McKenzie 115 36 10N 88 31W
† Mackenzie □ 104 61 30N 115 0W
Mackenzie →, Austral. 97 23 38 S 149 46 E
Mackenzie →, Can. 104 69 10N 134 20W
McKenzie → 118 44 2N 123 6W
Mackenzie City = Linden 126 6 0N 58 10W
Mackenzie Highway 108 58 0N 117 15W
Mackenzie Mts. 104 64 0N 130 0W
Mackinaw City 114 45 47N 84 44W
McKinlay 98 21 16 S 141 18 E
McKinlay → 98 20 50 S 141 28 E
McKinley, Mt. 104 63 2N 151 0W
McKinley Sea 4 84 0N 10 0W
McKinney 117 33 10N 96 40W
Mackinnon Road 90 3 40 S 39 1 E
McKittrick 119 35 18N 119 39W
Macksville 99 30 40 S 152 56 E
McLaughlin 116 45 50N 100 50W
Maclean 97 29 26 S 153 16 E
McLean 117 35 15N 100 35W
McLeansboro 116 38 5N 88 30W
Maclear 93 31 2 S 28 23 E
Macleay → 97 30 56 S 153 0 E
McLennan 108 55 42N 116 50W
McLeod, B. 109 62 53N 110 0W
McLeod L. 96 24 9 S 113 47 E
MacLeod Lake 108 54 58N 123 0W
M'Clintock Chan. 104 72 0N 102 0W
McLoughlin, Mt. 118 42 10N 122 19W
McLure 108 51 2N 120 13W

* *Renamed Andulo*
** *Renamed Bioko*
† *Now part of Fort Smith and Inuvik* □

McMechen Mamahatun

McMechen **112** 39 57N 80 44W
McMillan L. **117** 32 40N 104 20W
McMinnville, Oreg., U.S.A. **118** 45 16N 123 11W
McMinnville, Tenn., U.S.A. **115** 35 43N 85 45W
McMorran **109** 51 19N 108 42W
McMurdo Sd. **5** 77 0S 170 0E
McMurray = Fort McMurray **108** 56 45N 111 27W
McNary **119** 34 4N 109 53W
McNaughton L. **108** 52 0N 118 10W
Macodoene **93** 23 32S 35 5E
Macomb **116** 40 25N 90 40W
Macomer **40** 40 16N 8 48E
Mâcon **21** 46 19N 4 50E
Macon, Ga., U.S.A. **115** 32 50N 83 37W
Macon, Miss., U.S.A. **115** 33 7N 88 31W
Macon, Mo., U.S.A. **116** 39 40N 92 26W
Macondo **89** 12 37S 23 46E
Macossa **91** 17 55S 33 56E
Macoun L. **109** 56 32N 103 40W
Macovane **93** 21 30S 35 0E
McPherson **116** 38 25N 97 40W
Macpherson Ra. **99** 28 15S 153 15E
Macquarie → **97** 30 5S 147 30E
Macquarie Harbour **97** 42 15S 145 23E
Macquarie Is. **94** 54 36S 158 55E
Macquarie, L. **100** 33 4S 151 36E
MacRobertson Coast **5** 68 30S 63 0E
Macroom **15** 51 54N 8 57W
Macubela **91** 16 53S 37 49E
Macugnaga **38** 45 57N 7 58E
Macuiza **91** 18 7S 34 29E
Macuse **91** 17 45S 37 10E
Macuspana **120** 17 46N 92 36W
Macusse **92** 17 48S 20 23E
Mácuzari, Presa **120** 27 10N 109 10W
McVille **116** 47 46N 98 11W
Madā 'in Salih **86** 26 51N 37 58E
Madagali **85** 10 56N 13 33E
Madagascar ■ **93** 20 0S 47 0E
Madā'in Sālih **64** 26 46N 37 57E
Madama **83** 22 0N 13 40E
Madame I. **107** 45 30N 60 58W
Madan **43** 41 30N 24 57E
Madanapalle **70** 13 33N 78 28E
Madang **94** 5 12S 145 49E
Madaoua **85** 14 5N 6 27E
Madara **85** 11 45N 10 35E
Madaripur **69** 23 19N 90 15E
Madauk **67** 17 56N 96 52E
Madawaska **112** 45 30N 77 55W
Madawaska → **106** 45 27N 76 21W
Madaya **67** 22 12N 96 10E
Madbar **87** 6 17N 30 45E
Maddalena **40** 41 15N 9 23E
Maddalena, La **40** 41 13N 9 25E
Maddaloni **41** 41 4N 14 23E
Madden Dam **120** 9 13N 79 37W
Madden Lake **120** 9 20N 79 37W
Madeira **80** 32 50N 17 0W
Madeira → **126** 3 22S 58 45W
Madeleine, Îs. de la **107** 47 30N 61 40W
Madera **119** 37 0N 120 1W
Madha **70** 18 0N 75 30E
Madhubani **69** 26 21N 86 7E
Madhya Pradesh □ **68** 21 50N 81 0E
Madill **117** 34 5N 96 49W
Madimba **88** 5 0S 15 0E
Madīnat ash Sha'b **63** 12 50N 45 0E
Madingou **88** 4 10S 13 33E
Madirovalo **93** 16 26S 46 32E
Madison, Fla., U.S.A. **115** 30 29N 83 39W
Madison, Ind., U.S.A. **114** 38 42N 85 20W
Madison, Nebr., U.S.A. **116** 41 53N 97 25W
Madison, Ohio, U.S.A. **112** 41 45N 81 4W
Madison, S.D., U.S.A. **116** 44 0N 97 8W
Madison, Wis., U.S.A. **116** 43 5N 89 25W
Madison → **118** 45 56N 111 30W
Madison Junc. **118** 44 42N 110 56W
Madisonville, Ky., U.S.A. **114** 37 20N 87 30W
Madisonville, Tex., U.S.A. **117** 30 57N 95 55W
Madista **92** 21 15S 25 6E
Madiun **73** 7 38S 111 32E
Madley **13** 52 3N 2 51W
Madol **87** 9 3N 27 45E
Madon → **19** 48 36N 6 6E
Madona **54** 56 53N 26 5E
Madonie, Le **40** 37 50N 13 50E
Madras, India **70** 13 8N 80 19E
Madras, U.S.A. **118** 44 40N 121 10W
Madras = Tamil Nadu □ **70** 11 0N 77 0E
Madre de Dios → **126** 10 59S 66 8W
Madre de Dios, I. **128** 50 20S 75 10W
Madre del Sur, Sierra **120** 17 30N 100 0W
Madre, Laguna, Mexico **120** 25 0N 97 30W
Madre, Laguna, U.S.A. **117** 25 0N 97 40W
Madre Occidental, Sierra **120** 27 0N 107 0W
Madre Oriental, Sierra **120** 25 0N 100 0W
Madre, Sierra, Mexico **120** 16 0N 93 0W
Madre, Sierra, Phil. **73** 17 0N 122 0E
Madri **68** 24 16N 73 32E
Madrid **30** 40 25N 3 45W
Madrid □ **30** 40 30N 3 45W
Madridejos **31** 39 28N 3 33W
Madrigal de las Altas Torres **30** 41 5N 5 0W
Madrona, Sierra **31** 38 27N 4 16W
Madroñera **31** 39 26N 5 42W
Madu **87** 14 37N 26 4E
Madura, Selat **73** 7 30S 113 20E
Madurai **70** 9 55N 78 10E
Madurantakam **70** 12 30N 79 50E
Madzhalis **57** 42 9N 47 47E
Mae Hong Son **71** 19 16N 98 1E
Mae Sot **71** 16 43N 98 34E
Maebashi **74** 36 24N 139 4E
Maella **32** 41 8N 0 7E
Măeruş **46** 45 53N 25 31E
Maesteg **13** 51 36N 3 40W
Maestra, Sierra **121** 20 15N 77 0W
Maestrazgo, Mts. del **32** 40 30N 0 25W
Maevatanana **93** 16 56S 46 49E
Ma'fan **83** 25 56N 14 29E
Mafeking, Can. **109** 52 40N 101 10W
* Mafeking, S. Afr. **92** 25 50S 25 38E
Maféré **84** 5 30N 3 2W
Mafeteng **92** 29 51S 27 15E
Maffra **99** 37 53S 146 58E
Mafia **90** 7 45S 39 50E
Mafra, Brazil **125** 26 10S 50 0W
Mafra, Port. **31** 38 55N 9 20W
Mafungabusi Plateau **91** 18 30S 29 8E
Magadan **59** 59 38N 150 50E
Magadi **90** 1 54S 36 19E
Magadi, L. **90** 1 54S 36 19E
Magaliesburg **93** 26 1S 27 32E
Magallanes, Estrecho de **128** 52 30S 75 0W
Magangué **126** 9 14N 74 45W
Magaria **85** 13 4N 9 5E
Magburaka **84** 8 47N 12 0W
Magdalena, Argent. **124** 35 5S 57 30W
Magdalena, Boliv. **126** 13 13S 63 57W
Magdalena, Malay. **72** 4 25N 117 55E
Magdalena, Mexico **120** 30 50N 112 0W
Magdalena, U.S.A. **119** 34 10N 107 20W
Magdalena →, Colomb. **126** 11 6N 74 51W
Magdalena →, Mexico **120** 30 40N 112 25W
Magdalena, B. **120** 24 30N 112 10W
Magdalena, I. **120** 24 40N 112 15W
Magdalena, Llano de la **120** 25 0N 111 30W
Magdeburg **24** 52 8N 11 36E
Magdeburg □ **24** 52 20N 11 30E
Magdi'el **62** 32 10N 34 54E
Magdub **87** 13 42N 25 5E
Magee **117** 31 53N 89 45W
Magee, I. **15** 54 48N 5 44W
Magelang **73** 7 29S 110 13E
Magellan's Str. = Magallanes, Est. de **128** 52 30S 75 0W
Magenta **38** 45 28N 8 53E
Maggia → **25** 46 18N 8 36E
Maggiorasca, Mte. **38** 44 33N 9 29E
Maggiore, L. **38** 46 0N 8 35E
Maghama **84** 15 32N 12 57W
Maghār **62** 32 54N 35 24E
Magherafelt **15** 54 44N 6 37W
Maghnia **82** 34 50N 1 43W
Magione **39** 43 10N 12 12E
Maglaj **42** 44 33N 18 7E
Magliano in Toscana **39** 42 36N 11 18E
Máglie **41** 40 8N 18 17E
Magnac-Laval **20** 46 13N 1 11E
Magnetic Pole, 1976 (North) **4** 76 12N 100 12W
Magnetic Pole, 1976 (South) **5** 68 48S 139 30E
Magnisía □ **44** 39 15N 22 45E
Magnitogorsk **52** 53 27N 59 4E
Magnolia, Ark., U.S.A. **117** 33 18N 93 12W
Magnolia, Miss., U.S.A. **117** 31 8N 90 28W
Magnor **47** 59 56N 12 15E
Magny-en-Vexin **19** 49 9N 1 47E
Magog **107** 45 18N 72 9W
Magoro **90** 1 45N 34 12E
Magosa = Famagusta **64** 35 8N 33 55E
Magoye **91** 16 1S 27 30E
Magpie L. **107** 51 0N 64 41W
Magrath **108** 49 25N 112 50W
Magro → **33** 39 11N 0 25W
Magrur, Wadi → **87** 16 5N 26 30E
Magu □ **90** 2 31S 33 28E
Maguarinho, C. **127** 0 15S 48 30W
Maguse L. **109** 61 40N 95 10W
Maguse Pt. **109** 61 20N 93 50W
Magwe **67** 20 10N 95 0E
Mahābād **64** 36 50N 45 45E
Mahabaleshwar **70** 17 58N 73 43E
Mahabharat Lekh **69** 28 30N 82 0E
Mahabo **93** 20 23S 44 40E
Mahad **70** 18 6N 73 29E
Mahadeo Hills **68** 22 20N 78 30E
Mahadeopur **70** 18 48N 80 0E
Mahagi **90** 2 20N 31 0E
Mahajamba → **93** 15 33S 47 8E
Mahajamba, Helodranon' i **93** 15 24S 47 5E
Mahajan **68** 28 48N 73 56E
Mahajanga □ **93** 17 0S 47 0E
Mahajilo → **93** 19 42S 45 22E
Mahakam → **72** 0 35S 117 17E
Mahalapye **92** 23 1S 26 51E
Maḥallāt **65** 33 55N 50 30E
Mahanadi → **69** 20 20N 86 25E
Mahanoro **93** 19 54S 48 48E
Mahanoy City **113** 40 48N 76 10W
Maharashtra □ **70** 20 30N 75 30E
Maharès **83** 34 32N 10 29E
Mahari Mts. **90** 6 20S 30 0E
Mahasolo **93** 19 7S 46 22E
Mahaweli → Ganga **70** 8 30N 81 15E
Mahboobabad **70** 17 42N 80 2E
Mahbubnagar **70** 16 45N 77 59E
Mahdia **83** 35 28N 11 0E
Mahé **70** 11 42N 75 34E
Mahendra Giri **70** 8 20N 77 30E
Mahenge **91** 8 45S 36 41E
Maheno **101** 45 10S 170 50E
Mahia Pen. **101** 39 9S 177 55E
Mahirija **82** 34 0N 3 16W
Mahmiya **87** 17 12N 33 43E
Mahmud Kot **68** 30 16N 71 0E
Mahmudia **46** 45 5N 29 5E
Mahnomen **116** 47 22N 95 57W
Mahoba **69** 25 15N 79 55E
Mahón **32** 39 53N 4 16E
Mahone Bay **107** 44 39N 64 20W
Mahuta **85** 11 32N 4 58E
Mai-Ndombe, L. **88** 2 0S 18 20E
Maîche **19** 47 16N 6 48E
Maicurú → **127** 2 14S 54 17W
Máida **41** 38 51N 16 21E
Maidenhead **13** 51 31N 0 42W
Maidi **87** 16 20N 42 45E
Maidstone, Can. **109** 53 5N 109 20W
Maidstone, U.K. **13** 51 16N 0 31E
Maiduguri **85** 12 0N 13 20E
Maignelay **19** 49 32N 2 30E
Maigudo **87** 7 30N 37 8E
Maijdi **69** 22 48N 91 10E
Maikala Ra. **69** 22 0N 81 0E
Mailly-le-Camp **19** 48 41N 4 12E
Mailsi **68** 29 48N 72 15E
Main →, Ger. **25** 50 0N 8 18E
Main →, U.K. **15** 54 49N 6 20W
Main Centre **109** 50 35N 107 21W
Mainburg **25** 48 37N 11 49E
Maine **18** 48 0N 0 0E
Maine □ **107** 45 20N 69 0W
Maine → **15** 52 10N 9 40W
Maine-et-Loire □ **18** 47 31N 0 30W
Maïne-Soroa **85** 13 13N 12 2E
Maingkwan **67** 26 15N 96 37E
Mainit, L. **73** 9 31N 125 30E
Mainland, Orkney, U.K. **14** 59 0N 3 10W
Mainland, Shetland, U.K. **14** 60 15N 1 22W
Mainpuri **68** 27 18N 79 4E
Maintenon **19** 48 35N 1 35E
Maintirano **93** 18 3S 44 1E
Mainz **25** 50 0N 8 17E
Maipú **124** 36 52S 57 50W
Maiquetía **126** 10 36N 66 57W
Maira → **38** 44 49N 7 38E
Mairabari **67** 26 30N 92 22E
Maisi, Pta. de **121** 20 10N 74 10W
Maisse **19** 48 24N 2 21E
Maitland, N.S.W., Austral. **97** 32 33S 151 36E
Maitland, S. Australia, Austral. **99** 34 23S 137 40E
Maitland → **112** 43 45N 81 33W
Maiyema **85** 12 5N 4 25E
Maizuru **74** 35 25N 135 22E
Majalengka **73** 6 55S 108 14E
Majd el Kurūm **62** 32 56N 35 15E
Majene **73** 3 38S 118 57E
Majevica Planina **42** 44 45N 18 50E
Maji **87** 6 12N 35 30E
Major **109** 51 52N 109 37W
Majorca, I. = Mallorca **32** 39 30N 3 0E
Maka **84** 13 40N 14 10W
Makak **85** 3 36N 11 0E
Makale **73** 3 6S 119 51E
Makamba **90** 4 8S 29 49E
Makari **88** 12 35N 14 28E
Makarikari = Makgadikgadi Salt Pans **92** 20 40S 25 45E
Makarovo **59** 57 40N 107 45E
Makarska **42** 43 20N 17 2E
Makaryev **55** 57 52N 43 50E
Makasar = Ujung Pandang **73** 5 10S 119 20E
Makasar, Selat **73** 1 0S 118 20E
Makat **58** 47 39N 53 19E
Makedhonía □ **44** 40 39N 22 0E
Makedonija □ **42** 41 53N 21 40E
Makena **110** 20 39N 156 27W
Makeni **84** 8 55N 12 5W
Makeyevka **56** 48 0N 38 0E
Makgadikgadi Salt Pans **92** 20 40S 25 45E
Makhachkala **57** 43 0N 47 30E
Makhambet, U.S.S.R. **57** 47 43N 51 40E
Makhambet, U.S.S.R. **57** 47 40N 51 35E
Makharadze **57** 41 55N 42 2E
Makian **73** 0 20N 127 20E
** Makin **94** 3 30N 174 0E
Makindu **90** 2 18S 37 50E
Makinsk **58** 52 37N 70 26E
Makkah **86** 21 30N 39 54E
Makkovik **107** 55 10N 59 10W
† Maklakovo **59** 58 16N 92 29E
Makó **27** 46 14N 20 33E
Makokou **88** 0 40N 12 50E
Makongo **90** 3 25N 26 17E
Makoro **90** 3 10N 29 59E
Makoua **88** 0 5S 15 50E
Maków Mazowiecki **28** 52 52N 21 6E
Maków Podhal **27** 49 43N 19 45E
Makrá **45** 36 15N 25 54E
Makran **65** 26 13N 61 30E
Makran Coast Range **66** 25 40N 64 0E
Makrana **68** 27 2N 74 46E
Mákri **44** 40 52N 25 40E
Maksimkin Yar **58** 58 42N 86 50E
Maktar **83** 35 48N 9 12E
Mākū **64** 39 15N 44 31E
Makumbi **88** 5 50S 20 43E
Makunda **92** 22 30S 20 7E
Makurazaki **74** 31 15N 130 20E
Makurdi **85** 7 43N 8 35E
Makwassie **92** 27 17S 26 0E
Mal B. **15** 52 50N 9 30W
Mal i Gjalicës së Lumës **44** 42 2N 20 25E
Mal i Gribës **44** 40 17N 19 45E
Mal i Nemërçkës **44** 40 15N 20 15E
Mal i Tomorit **44** 40 42N 20 11E
Mala Kapela **39** 44 45N 15 30E
Mala, Pta. **121** 7 28N 80 2W
Malabang **73** 7 36N 124 3E
Malabar Coast **70** 11 0N 75 0E
Malacca, Str. of **71** 3 0N 101 0E
Malacky **27** 48 27N 17 0E
Malad City **118** 42 10N 112 20E
Málaga **31** 36 43N 4 23W
Malaga **117** 32 12N 104 2W
Málaga □ **31** 36 38N 4 58W
Malagarasi **90** 5 5S 30 50E
Malagarasi → **90** 5 12S 29 47E
Malagón **31** 39 11N 3 52W
Malagón → **31** 37 35N 7 29W
Malaimbandy **93** 20 20S 45 36E
Malakâl **87** 9 33N 31 40E
Malakand **66** 34 40N 71 55E
Malakoff **117** 32 10N 95 55W
Malamyzh **59** 50 0N 136 50E
Malang **73** 7 59S 112 45E
Malanje **88** 9 36S 16 17E
Mälaren **48** 59 30N 17 10E
Malargüe **124** 35 32S 69 30W
Malartic **106** 48 9N 78 9W
Malatya **64** 38 25N 38 20E
Malawi ■ **91** 13 0S 34 0E
Malawi, L. **91** 12 30S 34 30E
Malay Pen. **71** 7 25N 100 0E
* Malaya □ **71** 4 0N 102 0E
Malaya Belozërka **56** 47 12N 34 56E
Malaya Vishera **54** 58 55N 32 25E
Malaya Viska **56** 48 39N 31 36E
Malaybalay **73** 8 5N 125 7E
Malāyer **64** 34 19N 48 51E
Malaysia ■ **72** 5 0N 110 0E
Malazgirt **64** 39 10N 42 33E
Malbaie, La **107** 47 40N 70 10W
Malbon **98** 21 5S 140 17E
Malbork **28** 54 3N 19 1E
Malcésine **38** 45 46N 10 48E
Malchin **24** 53 43N 12 44E
Malchow **24** 53 29N 12 25E
Malcolm **96** 28 51S 121 25E
Malczyce **28** 51 14N 16 29E
Maldegem **16** 51 14N 3 26E
Malden, Mass., U.S.A. **113** 42 26N 71 5W
Malden, Mo., U.S.A. **117** 36 35N 90 0W
Malden I. **95** 4 3S 155 1W
Maldives ■ **60** 7 0N 73 0E
Maldonado **125** 35 0S 55 0W
Maldonado, Punta **120** 16 19N 98 35W
Malé **38** 46 20N 10 55E
Malé Karpaty **27** 48 30N 17 20E
Maléa, Ákra **45** 36 28N 23 7E
Malegaon **68** 20 30N 74 38E
Malei **91** 17 12S 36 58E
Malela **90** 4 22S 26 8E
Mälerås **49** 56 54N 15 34E
Malerkotla **68** 30 32N 75 58E
Máles **45** 35 6N 25 35E
Malesherbes **19** 48 15N 2 24E
Maleshevska Planina **42** 41 38N 23 7E
Malestroit **18** 47 49N 2 25W
Malfa **41** 38 35N 14 50E
Malgobek **57** 43 30N 44 34E
Malgomaj **50** 64 40N 16 30E
Malgrat **32** 41 39N 2 46E
Malha **81** 15 8N 25 10E
Malheur → **118** 44 3N 116 59W
Malheur L. **118** 43 19N 118 42W
Mali **84** 12 10N 12 20W
Mali ■ **85** 15 0N 2 0W
Mali → **67** 25 40N 97 40E
Mali Kanal **42** 45 36N 19 24E
Mali Kyun **71** 13 0N 98 20E
Malih → **62** 32 20N 35 34E
Malik **73** 0 39S 123 16E
Malili **73** 2 42S 121 6E
Malimba, Mts. **90** 7 30S 29 30E
Malin **54** 50 46N 29 3E
Malin Hd. **15** 55 18N 7 24W
Malinau **72** 3 35N 116 40E
Malindi **90** 3 12S 40 5E
Maling **73** 1 0N 121 0E
Malingping **73** 6 45S 106 2E
Malinyi **91** 8 56S 36 0E
Maliqi **44** 40 45N 20 48E
Malita **73** 6 19N 125 39E
Maljenik **42** 43 59N 21 55E
Malkapur, Maharashtra, India **68** 20 53N 73 58E
Malkapur, Maharashtra, India **70** 16 57N 73 58E
Małkinia Górna **28** 52 42N 22 5E
Malko Tŭrnovo **43** 41 59N 27 31E
Mallacoota **100** 37 40S 149 40E
Mallacoota Inlet **97** 37 34S 149 40E
Mallaig **14** 57 0N 5 50W
Mallawan **69** 27 4N 80 12E
Mallawi **86** 27 44N 30 44E
Mallemort **21** 43 44N 5 11E
Málles Venosta **38** 46 42N 10 32E
Mállia **45** 35 17N 25 27E
Mallorca **32** 39 30N 3 0E
Mallorytown **113** 44 29N 75 53W
Mallow **15** 52 8N 8 40W
Malmbäck **49** 57 34N 14 28E
Malmberget **50** 67 11N 20 40E
Malmédy **16** 50 25N 6 2E
Malmesbury **92** 33 28S 18 41E
Malmö **49** 55 36N 12 59E
Malmöhus län □ **49** 55 45N 13 30E
Malmslätt **49** 58 27N 15 33E
Malmyzh **55** 56 35N 50 41E
Malnaş **46** 46 2N 25 49E
Malo Konare **43** 42 12N 24 24E
Maloarkhangelsk **55** 52 28N 36 30E
Malolos **73** 14 50N 120 49E
Malombe L. **91** 14 40S 35 15E
Malomir **43** 42 16N 26 30E
Malone **114** 44 50N 74 19W
Malorad **43** 43 28N 23 41E
Malorita **54** 51 50N 24 3E
Maloyaroslovets **55** 55 2N 36 20E
Malozemelskaya Tundra **52** 67 0N 50 0E
Malpartida **31** 39 26N 6 30W
Malpelo **126** 4 3N 81 35W
Malpica **30** 43 19N 8 50W
Malprabha → **70** 16 20N 76 5E
Malta, Idaho, U.S.A. **118** 42 15N 113 30W
Malta, Mont., U.S.A. **118** 48 20N 107 55W
Malta ■ **36** 35 50N 14 30E
Malta Channel **40** 36 40N 14 0E
Malton, Can. **112** 43 42N 79 38W
Malton, U.K. **12** 54 9N 0 48W
Maluku **73** 1 0S 127 0E
Maluku □ **73** 3 0S 128 0E
Maluku, Kepulauan **73** 3 0S 128 0E
Malumfashi **85** 11 48N 7 39E
Malung **48** 60 42N 13 44E
Malvalli **70** 12 28N 77 8E
Malvan **70** 16 2N 73 30E
Malvern, U.K. **13** 52 7N 2 19W
Malvern, U.S.A. **117** 34 22N 92 50W
Malvern Hills **13** 52 0N 2 19W
Malvérnia **93** 22 6S 31 42E
Malvik **47** 63 25N 10 40E
Malvinas, Is. = Falkland Is. **128** 51 30S 59 0W
Malya **90** 3 5S 33 38E
Malyy Lyakhovskiy, Ostrov **59** 74 7N 140 36E
Mama **59** 58 18N 112 54E
Mamadysh **55** 55 44N 51 23E
Mamahatun **64** 39 50N 40 23E

* Renamed Mafikeng

* Renamed Peninsular Malaysia

† Renamed Lesosibirsk

** Renamed Butaritari

Mamaia Market Harborough

Mamaia 46 44 18N 28 37 E
Mamanguape 127 6 50 S 35 4W
Mamasa 73 2 55 S 119 20 E
Mambasa 90 1 22N 29 3 E
Mamberamo → 73 2 0 S 137 50 E
Mambilima 91 10 31 S 28 45 E
Mambirima 91 11 25 S 27 33 E
Mambo 90 4 52 S 38 22 E
Mambrui 90 3 5 S 40 5 E
Mamburao 73 13 13N 120 39 E
Mameigwess L. 106 52 35N 87 50W
Mamers 18 48 21N 0 22 E
Mamfe 85 5 50N 9 15 E
Mámmola 41 38 23N 16 13 E
Mammoth 119 32 46N 110 43W
Mamoré → 126 10 23 S 65 53W
Mamou 84 10 15N 12 0W
Mampatá 84 11 54N 14 53W
Mampawah 72 0 30N 109 5 E
Mampong 85 7 6N 1 26W
Mamry, Jezioro 28 54 5N 21 50 E
Mamuju 73 2 41 S 118 50 E
Man 84 7 30N 7 40W
Man → 70 17 31N 75 32 E
Man, I. of 12 54 15N 4 30W
Man Na 67 23 27N 97 19 E
Mana 127 5 45N 53 55W
Mâna → 47 59 55N 8 50 E
Manaar, Gulf of 70 8 30N 79 0 E
Manacapuru 126 3 16 S 60 37W
Manacor 32 39 34N 3 13 E
Manado 73 1 29N 124 51 E
Managua 121 12 6N 86 20W
Managua, L. 121 12 20N 86 30W
Manakara 93 22 8 S 48 1 E
Manam I. 98 4 5 S 145 0 E
Manamāh, Al 65 26 11N 50 35 E
Manambao → 93 17 35 S 44 0 E
Manambato 93 13 43 S 49 7 E
Manambolo → 93 19 18 S 44 22 E
Manambolosy 93 16 2 S 49 40 E
Mananara 93 16 10 S 49 46 E
Mananara → 93 23 21 S 47 42 E
Mananjary 93 21 13 S 48 20 E
Manantenina 93 24 17 S 47 19 E
Manaos = Manaus 126 3 0 S 60 0W
Manapouri 101 45 34 S 167 39 E
Manapouri, L. 101 45 32 S 167 32 E
Manar → 70 18 50N 77 20 E
Manas 75 44 17N 85 56 E
Manasir 65 24 30N 51 10 E
Manaslu, Mt. 69 28 33N 84 33 E
Manasquan 113 40 7N 74 3W
Manassa 119 37 12N 105 58W
Manaung 67 18 45N 93 40 E
Manaus 126 3 0 S 60 0W
Manawan L. 109 55 24N 103 14W
Manay 73 7 17N 126 33 E
Mancelona 114 44 54N 85 5W
Mancha, La 33 39 10N 2 54W
Mancha Real 31 37 48N 3 39W
Manche □ 18 49 10N 1 20W
Manchegorsk 52 67 40N 32 40 E
Manchester, U.K. 12 53 30N 2 15W
Manchester, Conn., U.S.A. 114 41 47N 72 30W
Manchester, Ga., U.S.A. 115 32 53N 84 32W
Manchester, Iowa, U.S.A. 116 42 28N 91 27W
Manchester, Ky., U.S.A. 114 37 9N 83 45W
Manchester, N.H., U.S.A. 114 42 58N 71 29W
Manchester, N.Y., U.S.A. 112 42 56N 77 16W
Manchester, Vt., U.S.A. 113 43 10N 73 5W
Manchester L. 109 61 28N 107 29W
Manciano 39 42 35N 11 30 E
Mancifa 87 6 53N 41 50 E
Mand → 65 28 20N 52 30 E
Manda, Chunya, Tanz. 90 6 51 S 32 29 E
Manda, Ludewe, Tanz. 91 10 30 S 34 40 E
Mandaguari 125 23 32 S 51 42W
Mandal 47 58 2N 7 25 E
Mandalay 67 22 0N 96 4 E
Mandale = Mandalay 67 22 0N 96 4 E
Mandalī 64 33 43N 45 28 E
Mandalya Körfezi 45 37 15N 27 20 E
Mandan 116 46 50N 101 0W
Mandapeta 70 16 47N 81 56 E
Mandar, Teluk 73 3 35 S 119 15 E
Mandas 40 39 40N 9 8 E
Mandasaur 68 24 3N 75 8 E
Mandasor = Mandasaur 68 24 3N 75 8 E
Mandawai (Katingan) → 72 3 30 S 113 0 E
Mandelieu-la-Napoule 21 43 34N 6 57 E
Mandera 90 3 55N 41 53 E
Mandera □ 90 3 30N 41 0 E
Mandi 68 31 39N 76 58 E
Mandioli 73 0 40 S 127 20 E
Mandla 69 22 39N 80 30 E
Mandø 49 55 18N 8 33 E
Mandoto 93 19 34 S 46 17 E
Mandoúdhion 45 38 48N 23 29 E
Mandráki 45 36 36N 27 11 E
Mandrare → 93 25 10 S 46 30 E
Mandritsara 93 15 50 S 48 49 E
Mandúria 41 40 25N 17 38 E
Mandvi 68 22 51N 69 22 E
Mandya 70 12 30N 77 0 E
Mandzai 68 30 55N 67 6 E
Mané 85 12 59N 1 21W
Manenguoba, Mts. 85 5 0N 9 50 E
Maner → 70 18 30N 79 40 E
Maneroo 98 23 22 S 143 53 E
Maneroo Cr. → 98 23 21 S 143 53 E
Manfalût 86 27 20N 30 52 E
Manfred 99 33 19 S 143 45 E
Manfredónia 41 41 40N 15 55 E
Manfredónia, G. di 41 41 30N 16 10 E
Manga, Niger 85 15 0N 14 0 E
Manga, Upp. Vol. 85 11 40N 1 4W
Mangaia 101 21 55 S 157 55W
Mangalagiri 70 16 26N 80 36 E
Mangalia 46 43 50N 28 35 E
Mangalore 70 12 55N 74 47 E
Manganeses 30 41 45N 5 43W
Mangaon 70 18 15N 73 20 E
Manger 47 60 38N 5 3 E
Manggar 72 2 50 S 108 10 E
Manggawitu 73 4 8 S 133 32 E
Mangkalihat, Tanjung 73 1 2N 118 59 E
Manglaur 68 29 44N 77 49 E
Mangnai 75 37 52N 91 43 E
Mango 85 10 20N 0 30 E
Mangoky → 93 21 29 S 43 41 E
Mangole 73 1 50 S 125 55 E
Mangombe 90 1 20 S 26 48 E
Mangonui 101 35 1 S 173 32 E
Mangualde 30 40 38N 7 48W
Mangueigne 81 10 30N 21 15 E
Mangueira, Lagoa da 125 33 0 S 52 50W
Manguéni, Hamada 83 22 35N 12 40 E
Mangum 117 34 50N 99 30W
Mangyshlak P-ov. 57 44 30N 52 30 E
Mangyshlakskiy Zaliv 57 44 40N 50 50 E
Manhattan, Kans., U.S.A. 116 39 10N 96 40W
Manhattan, Nev., U.S.A. 119 38 31N 117 3W
Manhiça 93 25 23 S 32 49 E
Manhuaçu 127 20 15 S 42 2W
Mania → 93 19 42 S 45 22 E
Maniago 39 46 11N 12 40 E
Manica e Sofala □ 93 19 10 S 33 45 E
Manicaland □ 91 19 0 S 32 30 E
Manicoré 126 5 48 S 61 16W
Manicouagan → 107 49 30N 68 30W
Manicouagan L. 107 51 25N 68 15W
Manīfah 64 27 44N 49 0 E
Manigotagan 109 51 6N 96 18W
Manigotagan L. 109 50 52N 95 37W
Manihiki 95 10 24 S 161 1W
Manika, Plat. de la 91 10 0 S 25 5 E
Manila, Phil. 73 14 40N 121 3 E
Manila, U.S.A. 118 41 0N 109 44W
Manila B. 73 14 0N 120 0 E
Manilla 99 30 45 S 150 43 E
Manimpé 84 14 11N 5 28W
Manipur □ 67 25 0N 94 0 E
Manipur → 67 23 45N 94 20 E
Manisa 64 38 38N 27 30 E
Manistee 114 44 15N 86 20W
Manistee → 114 44 15N 86 21W
Manistique 114 45 59N 86 18W
Manito L. 109 52 43N 109 43W
Manitoba □ 109 55 30N 97 0W
Manitoba, L. 109 51 0N 98 45W
Manitou 109 49 15N 98 32W
Manitou I. 106 47 22N 87 30W
Manitou Is. 114 45 8N 86 0W
Manitou L., Ont., Can. 109 49 15N 93 0W
Manitou L., Qué., Can. 107 50 55N 65 17W
Manitou Springs 116 38 52N 104 55W
Manitoulin I. 106 45 40N 82 30W
Manitowaning 106 45 46N 81 49W
Manitowoc 114 44 8N 87 40W
Manizales 126 5 5N 75 32W
Manja 93 21 26 S 44 20 E
Manjakandriana 93 18 55 S 47 47 E
Manjeri 70 11 7N 76 11 E
Manjhand 68 25 50N 68 10 E
Manjil 64 36 46N 49 30 E
Manjimup 96 34 15 S 116 6 E
Manjra → 70 18 49N 77 52 E
Mankato, Kans., U.S.A. 116 39 49N 98 11W
Mankato, Minn., U.S.A. 116 44 8N 93 59W
Mankayana 93 26 38 S 31 6 E
Mankono 84 8 1N 6 10W
Mankota 109 49 25N 107 5W
Manlleu 32 42 2N 2 17 E
Manly 99 33 48 S 151 17 E
Manmad 70 20 18N 74 28 E
Manna 72 4 25 S 102 55 E
Mannahill 99 32 25 S 140 0 E
Mannar 70 9 1N 79 54 E
Mannar, G. of 70 8 30N 79 0 E
Mannar I. 70 9 5N 79 45 E
Mannargudi 70 10 45N 79 51 E
Mannheim 25 49 28N 8 29 E
Manning, Can. 108 56 53N 117 39W
Manning, U.S.A. 115 33 40N 80 9W
Manning → 100 31 52 S 152 43 E
Manning Prov. Park 108 49 5N 120 45W
Mannington 114 39 35N 80 25W
Mannu → 40 39 15N 9 32 E
Mannu, C. 40 40 2N 8 24 E
Mannum 99 34 50 S 139 20 E
Mano 84 8 3N 12 2W
Manokwari 73 0 54 S 134 0 E
Manolás 45 38 4N 21 21 E
Manombo 93 22 57 S 43 28 E
Manono 90 7 15 S 27 25 E
Manosque 21 43 49N 5 47 E
Manouane L. 107 50 45N 70 45W
Manresa 32 41 48N 1 50 E
Mans, Le 18 48 0N 0 10 E
Mansa, Gujarat, India 68 23 27N 72 45 E
Mansa, Punjab, India 68 30 0N 75 27 E
Mansa, Zambia 91 11 13 S 28 55 E
Mansel I. 105 62 0N 80 0W
Mansfield, Austral. 100 37 4 S 146 6 E
Mansfield, U.K. 12 53 8N 1 12W
Mansfield, La., U.S.A. 117 32 2N 93 40W
Mansfield, Mass., U.S.A. 113 42 2N 71 12W
Mansfield, Ohio, U.S.A. 114 40 45N 82 30W
Mansfield, Pa., U.S.A. 112 41 48N 77 4W
Mansfield, Wash., U.S.A. 118 47 51N 119 44W
Mansilla de las Mulas 30 42 30N 5 25W
Mansle 20 45 52N 0 9 E
Mansoa 84 12 0N 15 20W
Manson Creek 108 55 37N 124 32W
Mansoura 83 36 1N 4 31 E
Manta 126 1 0 S 80 40W
Mantalingajan, Mt. 72 8 55N 117 45 E
Mantare 90 2 42 S 33 13 E
Manteca 119 37 50N 121 12W
Manteo 115 35 55N 75 41W
Mantes-la-Jolie 19 49 0N 1 41 E
Manthani 70 18 40N 79 35 E
Manthelan 18 47 9N 0 47 E
Manti 118 39 23N 111 32W
Mantiqueira, Serra da 125 22 0 S 44 0W
Manton 114 44 23N 85 25W
Mantorp 49 58 21N 15 20 E
Mántova 38 45 20N 10 42 E
Mänttä 50 62 0N 24 40 E
Mantua = Mántova 38 45 20N 10 42 E
Manturovo 55 58 30N 44 30 E
Manu 126 12 10 S 70 51W
Manua Is. 101 14 13 S 169 35W
Manuel Alves → 127 11 19 S 48 28W
Manui 73 3 35 S 123 5 E
Manukan 73 8 14N 123 3 E
Manus I. 98 2 0 S 147 0 E
Manvi 70 15 57N 76 59 E
Manville 116 42 48N 104 36W
Manwath 70 19 19N 76 32 E
Many 117 31 36N 93 28W
Manyane 92 23 21 S 21 42 E
Manyara, L. 90 3 40 S 35 50 E
Manych → 57 47 15N 40 0 E
Manych-Gudilo, Oz. 57 46 24N 42 38 E
Manyonga → 90 4 10 S 34 15 E
Manyoni 90 5 45 S 34 55 E
Manyoni □ 90 6 30 S 34 30 E
Manzai 68 32 12N 70 15 E
Manzala, Bahra el 86 31 10N 31 56 E
Manzanares 33 39 0N 3 22W
Manzaneda, Cabeza de 30 42 12N 7 15W
Manzanillo, Cuba 121 20 20N 77 31W
Manzanillo, Mexico 120 19 0N 104 20W
Manzanillo, Pta. 121 9 30N 79 40W
Manzano Mts. 119 34 30N 106 45W
Manzhouli 75 49 35N 117 25 E
Manzini 93 26 30 S 31 25 E
Mao 81 14 4N 15 19 E
Maoke, Pegunungan 73 3 40 S 137 30 E
Maoming 75 21 50N 110 54 E
Mapam Yumco 75 30 45N 81 28 E
Mapia, Kepulauan 73 0 50N 134 20 E
Mapimí 120 25 50N 103 50W
Mapimí, Bolsón de 120 27 30N 104 15W
Mapinga 90 6 40 S 39 12 E
Mapinhane 93 22 20 S 35 0 E
Maple Creek 109 49 55N 109 29W
Mapleton 118 44 4N 123 58W
Maplewood 116 38 33N 90 18W
Maprik 98 3 44 S 143 3 E
Mapuca 70 15 36N 73 46 E
Mapuera → 126 1 5 S 57 2W
Maputo 93 25 58 S 32 32 E
Maputo, B. de 93 25 50 S 32 45 E
Maqnā 64 28 25N 34 50 E
Maquela do Zombo 88 6 0 S 15 15 E
Maquinchao 128 41 15 S 68 50W
Maquoketa 116 42 4N 90 40W
Mår → 47 59 59N 8 46 E
Mar Chiquita, L. 124 30 40 S 62 50W
Mar del Plata 124 38 0 S 57 30W
Mar Menor, L. 33 37 40N 0 45W
Mar, Serra do 125 25 30 S 49 0W
Mara 90 1 30 S 34 32 E
Mara □ 90 1 45 S 34 20 E
Maraã 126 1 52 S 65 25W
Marabá 127 5 20 S 49 5W
Maracá, I. de 127 2 10N 50 30W
Maracaibo 126 10 40N 71 37W
Maracaibo, Lago de 126 9 40N 71 30W
Maracaju 125 21 38 S 55 9W
Maracay 126 10 15N 67 28W
Marādah 83 29 15N 19 15 E
Maradi 85 13 29N 8 10 E
Maradun 85 12 35N 6 18 E
Marāgheh 64 37 30N 46 12 E
Marāh 64 25 0N 45 35 E
Marajó, Ilha de 127 1 0 S 49 30W
Maralal 90 1 0N 36 38 E
Maralinga 96 30 13 S 131 32 E
Marama 99 35 10 S 140 10 E
Marampa 84 8 45N 12 28W
Maramureş □ 46 47 45N 24 0 E
Marana 119 32 30N 111 9W
Maranchón 32 41 6N 2 15W
Marand 64 38 30N 45 45 E
Marandellas 91 18 5 S 31 42 E
Maranguape 127 3 55 S 38 50W
Maranhão = São Luis 127 2 39 S 44 15W
Maranhão □ 127 5 0 S 46 0W
Marano, L. di 39 45 42N 13 13 E
Maranoa → 97 27 50 S 148 37 E
Marañón → 126 4 30 S 73 35W
Maraş 64 37 37N 36 53 E
Mărăşeşti 46 45 52N 27 14 E
Maratea 41 39 59N 15 43 E
Marateca 31 38 34N 8 40W
Marathókambos 45 37 43N 26 42 E
Marathon, Austral. 98 20 51 S 143 32 E
Marathon, Can. 106 48 44N 86 23W
Marathón 45 38 11N 23 58 E
Marathon, N.Y., U.S.A. 113 42 25N 76 3W
Marathon, Tex., U.S.A. 117 30 15N 103 15W
Maratua 73 2 10N 118 35 E
Marbella 31 36 30N 4 57W
Marble Bar 96 21 9 S 119 44 E
Marble Falls 117 30 30N 98 15W
Marblehead 113 42 29N 70 51W
Marburg 24 50 49N 8 36 E
Marby 48 63 7N 14 18 E
Marcal → 27 47 41N 17 32 E
Marcali 27 46 35N 17 25 E
Marcaria 38 45 7N 10 34 E
March 13 52 33N 0 5 E
Marchand = Rommani 82 33 20N 6 40W
Marché 20 46 0N 1 20 E
Marche □ 39 43 22N 13 10 E
Marche-en-Famenne 16 50 14N 5 19 E
Marchena 31 37 18N 5 23W
Marches = Marche 39 43 22N 13 10 E
Marciana Marina 38 42 44N 10 12 E
Marcianise 41 41 3N 14 16 E
Marcigny 21 46 17N 4 2 E
Marcillac-Vallon 20 44 29N 2 27 E
Marcillat 20 46 12N 2 38 E
Marck 19 50 57N 1 57 E
Marckolsheim 19 48 10N 7 30 E
Marcos Juárez 124 32 42 S 62 5W
Marcus 94 24 0N 153 45 E
Marcus Necker Ridge 94 20 0N 175 0 E
Marcy Mt. 113 44 7N 73 55W
Mardin 64 37 20N 40 43 E
Maree L. 14 57 40N 5 30W
Mareeba 97 16 59 S 145 28 E
Marek 73 4 41 S 120 24 E
Marek = Stanke Dimitrov 42 42 17N 23 9 E
Maremma 38 42 45N 11 15 E
Maréna 84 14 0N 7 20W
Marenberg 39 46 38N 15 13 E
Marengo 116 41 42N 92 5W
Marennes 20 45 49N 1 7W
Marenyi 90 4 22 S 39 8 E
Marerano 93 21 23 S 44 52 E
Marèttimo 40 37 58N 12 5 E
Mareuil-sur-Lay 20 46 32N 1 14W
Marfa 117 30 15N 104 0W
Marganets 56 47 40N 34 40 E
Margao 70 15 12N 73 58 E
Margaret Bay 108 51 20N 126 35W
Margaret L. 108 58 56N 115 25W
Margarita 120 9 20N 79 55W
Margarita, Isla de 126 11 0N 64 0W
Margarítion 44 39 22N 20 26 E
Margate, S. Afr. 93 30 50 S 30 20 E
Margate, U.K. 13 51 23N 1 24 E
Margeride, Mts. de la 20 44 43N 3 38 E
Margherita di Savoia 41 41 25N 16 5 E
Marghita 46 47 22N 22 22 E
Margonin 28 52 58N 17 5 E
Marguerite 108 52 30N 122 25W
Marhoum 82 34 27N 0 11W
Mari, A.S.S.R. □ 55 56 30N 48 0 E
María Elena 124 22 18 S 69 40W
María Grande 124 31 45 S 59 55W
Maria I. 96 14 52 S 135 45 E
Maria van Diemen, C. 101 34 29 S 172 40 E
Mariager 49 56 40N 10 0 E
Mariager Fjord 49 56 42N 10 19 E
Mariakani 90 3 50 S 39 27 E
Marian L. 108 63 0N 116 15W
Mariana Is. 94 17 0N 145 0 E
Mariana Trench 94 13 0N 145 0 E
Marianao 121 23 8N 82 24W
Marianna, Ark., U.S.A. 117 34 48N 90 48W
Marianna, Fla., U.S.A. 115 30 45N 85 15W
Mariannelund 49 57 37N 15 35 E
Mariánské Lázně 26 49 48N 12 41 E
Marias → 118 47 56N 110 30W
Mariato, Punta 121 7 12N 80 52W
Mariazell 26 47 47N 15 19 E
Ma'rib 63 15 25N 45 30 E
Maribo 49 54 48N 11 30 E
Maribor 39 46 36N 15 40 E
Marico → 92 23 35 S 26 57 E
Maricopa, Ariz., U.S.A. 119 33 5N 112 2W
Maricopa, Calif., U.S.A. 119 35 7N 119 27W
Maridi 87 4 55N 29 25 E
Maridi, Wadi → 87 6 15N 29 21 E
Marie-Galante 121 15 56N 61 16W
Mariecourt 105 61 30N 72 0W
Mariefred 48 59 15N 17 12 E
Mariehamn 51 60 5N 19 55 E
Marienberg, Ger. 24 50 40N 13 10 E
Marienberg, Neth. 16 52 30N 6 35 E
Marienbourg 16 50 6N 4 31 E
Mariental 92 24 36 S 18 0 E
Marienville 112 41 27N 79 8W
Mariestad 49 58 43N 13 50 E
Marietta, Ga., U.S.A. 115 34 0N 84 30W
Marietta, Ohio, U.S.A. 114 39 27N 81 27W
Marieville 113 45 26N 73 10W
Marignane 21 43 25N 5 13 E
Mariinsk 58 56 10N 87 20 E
Mariinskiy Posad 55 56 10N 47 45 E
Marília 125 22 13 S 50 0W
Marin 30 42 23N 8 42W
Marina di Cirò 41 39 22N 17 8 E
Mariña, La 30 43 30N 7 40W
Marina Plains 98 14 37 S 143 57 E
Marinduque 73 13 25N 122 0 E
Marine City 114 42 45N 82 29W
Marinel, Le 91 10 25 S 25 17 E
Marineo 40 37 57N 13 23 E
Marinette, Ariz., U.S.A. 119 33 41N 112 16W
Marinette, Wis., U.S.A. 114 45 4N 87 40W
Maringá 125 23 26 S 52 2W
Marinha Grande 31 39 45N 8 56W
Marion, Ala., U.S.A. 115 32 33N 87 20W
Marion, Ill., U.S.A. 117 37 45N 88 55W
Marion, Ind., U.S.A. 114 40 35N 85 40W
Marion, Iowa, U.S.A. 116 42 2N 91 36W
Marion, Kans., U.S.A. 116 38 25N 97 2W
Marion, Mich., U.S.A. 114 44 7N 85 8W
Marion, N.C., U.S.A. 115 35 42N 82 0W
Marion, Ohio, U.S.A. 114 40 38N 83 8W
Marion, S.C., U.S.A. 115 34 11N 79 22W
Marion, Va., U.S.A. 115 36 51N 81 29W
Marion, L. 115 33 30N 80 15W
Marion Reef 97 19 10 S 152 17 E
Mariposa 119 37 31N 119 59W
Mariscal Estigarribia 124 22 3 S 60 40W
Maritime Alps = Alpes Maritimes 38 44 10N 7 10 E
Maritsa 43 42 1N 25 50 E
Maritsá 45 36 22N 28 10 E
Maritsa → 43 42 15N 24 0 E
Mariyampole = Kapsukas 54 54 33N 23 19 E
Marka 86 18 14N 41 19 E
Markapur 70 15 44N 79 19 E
Markaryd 49 56 28N 13 35 E
Markdale 112 44 19N 80 39W
Marked Tree 117 35 35N 90 24W
Markelsdorfer Huk 24 54 33N 11 0 E
Marken 16 52 26N 5 12 E
Market Drayton 12 52 55N 2 30W
Market Harborough 13 52 29N 0 55W

Markham Mbulu

Markham 112 43 52N 79 16W
Markham → 98 6 41S 147 2E
Markham I. 4 84 0N 0 45W
Markham L. 109 62 30N 102 35W
Markham Mt. 5 83 0S 164 0E
Marki 28 52 20N 21 2E
Markoupoulon 45 37 53N 23 57E
Markovac 42 44 14N 21 7E
Markovo 59 64 40N 169 40E
Markoye 85 14 39N 0 2E
Marks 55 51 45N 46 50E
Marksville 117 31 10N 92 2W
Markt Schwaben 25 48 14N 11 49E
Marktredwitz 25 50 1N 12 2E
Marlboro 113 42 19N 71 33W
Marlborough 98 22 46S 149 52E
Marlborough □ 101 41 45S 173 33E
Marlborough Downs 13 51 25N 1 55W
Marle 19 49 43N 3 47E
Marlin 117 31 25N 96 50W
Marlow, Ger. 24 54 8N 12 34E
Marlow, U.S.A. 117 34 40N 97 58W
Marmagao 70 15 25N 73 56E
Marmande 20 44 30N 0 10E
Marmara 56 40 35N 27 38E
Marmara Denizi 64 40 45N 28 15E
Marmara, Sea of = Marmara Denizi 64 40 45N 28 15E
Marmaris 64 36 50N 28 14E
Marmarth 116 46 21N 103 52W
Marmion L. 106 48 55N 91 20W
Marmolada, Mte. 39 46 25N 11 55E
Marmolejo 31 38 3N 4 13W
Marmora 106 44 28N 77 41W
Marnay 19 47 20N 5 48E
Marne 24 53 57N 9 1E
Marne □ 19 49 0N 4 10E
Marne → 19 8 23N 18 36E
Marnoo 100 36 40S 142 54E
Marnueli 57 41 30N 44 48E
Maroala 93 15 23S 47 59E
Maroantsetra 93 15 26S 49 44E
Maromandia 93 14 13S 48 5E
Maroni → 127 4 0N 52 0W
Marónia 44 40 53N 25 24E
Maroochydore 99 26 29S 153 5E
Maroona 99 37 27S 142 54E
Maros → 27 46 15N 20 13E
Marosakoa 93 15 26S 46 38E
Marostica 39 45 44N 11 40E
Maroua 85 10 40N 14 20E
Marovoay 93 16 6S 46 39E
Marquard 92 28 40S 27 28E
Marqueira 31 38 41N 9 9W
Marquesas Is. 95 9 30S 140 0W
Marquette 114 46 30N 87 21W
Marquise 19 50 50N 1 40E
Marra, Gebel 87 7 20N 27 35E
Marradi 39 44 5N 11 37E
Marrakech 82 31 9N 8 0W
Marrawah 99 40 55S 144 42E
Marree 97 29 39S 138 1E
Marrimane 93 22 58S 33 34E
Marronne → 20 45 4N 1 56E
Marroquí, Punta 31 36 0N 5 37W
Marrowie Creek 99 33 23S 145 40E
Marrubane 91 18 0S 37 0E
Marrupa 91 13 8S 37 30E
Mars, Le 116 43 0N 96 0W
Marsa Brega 83 30 24N 19 37E
Marsá Susah 81 32 52N 21 59E
Marsabit 90 2 18N 38 0E
Marsabit □ 90 2 45N 37 45E
Marsala 40 37 48N 12 25E
Marsaxlokk (Medport) 36 35 47N 14 32E
Marsciano 39 42 54N 12 20E
Marsden 99 33 47S 147 32E
Marseillan 20 43 23N 3 31E
Marseille 21 43 18N 5 23E
Marseilles = Marseille 21 43 18N 5 23E
Marsh I. 117 29 35N 91 50W
Marsh L. 116 45 5N 96 0W
Marshall, Liberia 84 6 8N 10 22W
Marshall, Ark., U.S.A. 117 35 58N 92 40W
Marshall, Mich., U.S.A. 114 42 17N 84 59W
Marshall, Minn., U.S.A. 116 44 25N 95 45W
Marshall, Mo., U.S.A. 116 39 8N 93 15W
Marshall, Tex., U.S.A. 117 32 29N 94 20W
Marshall Is. 94 9 0N 171 0E
Marshalltown 116 42 5N 92 56W
Marshfield, Mo., U.S.A. 117 37 20N 92 58W
Marshfield, Wis., U.S.A. 116 44 42N 90 10W
Mársico Nuovo 41 40 26N 15 43E
Märsta 48 59 37N 17 52E
Marstal 49 54 51N 10 30E
Marstrand 49 57 53N 11 35E
Mart 117 31 34N 96 51W
Marta → 39 42 14N 11 42E
Martaban 67 16 30N 97 35E
Martaban, G. of 67 16 5N 96 30E
Martagne 18 46 59N 0 57W
Martano 41 40 14N 18 18E
Martapura, Kalimantan, Indon. 72 3 22S 114 47E
Martapura, Sumatera, Indon. 72 4 19S 104 22E
Marte 85 12 23N 13 46E
Martel 20 44 57N 1 37E
Martelange 16 49 49N 5 43E
Martés, Sierra 33 39 20N 1 0W
Marthaguy Creek → 99 30 16S 147 35E
Martha's Vineyard 114 41 25N 70 35W
Martigné-Ferchaud 18 47 50N 1 20W
Martigny 25 46 6N 7 3E
Martigues 21 43 24N 5 4E
Martil 82 35 36N 5 15W
Martin, Czech. 27 49 6N 18 48E
Martin, S.D., U.S.A. 116 43 11N 101 45W
Martin, Tenn., U.S.A. 117 36 23N 88 51W
Martín → 32 41 18N 0 19W
Martin, L. 115 32 45N 85 50W
Martina Franca 41 40 42N 17 20E
Martinborough 101 41 14S 175 29E
Martinique 121 14 40N 61 0W
Martinique Passage 121 15 15N 61 0W
Martínon 45 38 35N 23 15E
Martinópolis 125 22 11S 51 12W
Martins Ferry 113 40 5N 80 46W
Martinsberg 26 48 22N 15 9E
Martinsburg, Pa., U.S.A. 112 40 18N 78 21W
Martinsburg, W. Va., U.S.A. 114 39 30N 77 57W
Martinsville, Ind., U.S.A. 114 39 29N 86 23W
Martinsville, Va., U.S.A. 115 36 41N 79 52W
Marton 101 40 4S 175 23E
Martorell 32 41 28N 1 56E
Martos 31 37 44N 3 58W
Martuni 57 40 9N 45 10E
Maru 85 12 22N 6 22E
Marudi 72 4 10N 114 19E
Ma'ruf 65 31 30N 67 6E
Marugame 74 34 15N 133 40E
Marúggio 41 40 20N 17 33E
Marulan 99 34 43S 150 3E
Marunga 92 17 28S 20 2E
Marungu, Mts. 90 7 30S 30 0E
Mårvatn 47 60 8N 8 14E
Marvejols 20 44 33N 3 19E
Marwar 68 25 43N 73 45E
Mary 58 37 40N 61 50E
Mary Frances L. 109 63 19N 106 13W
Mary Kathleen 97 20 44S 139 48E
Maryborough, Queens., Austral. 97 25 31S 152 37E
Maryborough, Vic., Austral. 97 37 0S 143 44E
Maryfield 109 49 50N 101 35W
Maryland □ 114 39 10N 76 40W
Maryland Jc. 91 17 45S 30 31E
Maryport 12 54 43N 3 30W
Mary's Harbour 107 52 18N 55 51W
Marystown 107 47 10N 55 10W
Marysvale 119 38 25N 112 17W
Marysville, Can. 108 49 35N 116 0W
Marysville, Calif., U.S.A. 118 39 14N 121 40W
Marysville, Kans., U.S.A. 116 39 50N 96 49W
Marysville, Mich., U.S.A. 112 42 55N 82 29W
Marysville, Ohio, U.S.A. 114 40 15N 83 20W
Maryvale 99 28 4S 152 12E
Maryville 115 35 50N 84 0W
Marzūq 83 25 53N 13 57E
Masada = Mesada 62 31 20N 35 19E
Masahunga 90 2 6S 33 18E
Masai Steppe 90 4 30S 36 30E
Masaka 90 0 21S 31 45E
Masalembo, Kepulauan 72 5 35S 114 30E
Masalima, Kepulauan 72 5 4S 117 5E
Masamba 73 2 30S 120 15E
Masan 76 35 11N 128 32E
Masanasa 33 39 25N 0 25W
Masandam, Ras 65 26 30N 56 30E
Masasi 91 10 45S 38 52E
Masasi □ 91 10 45S 38 50E
Masaya 121 12 0N 86 7W
Masba 85 10 35N 13 1E
Masbate 73 12 21N 123 36E
Mascara 82 35 26N 0 6E
Mascota 120 20 30N 104 50W
Masela 73 8 9S 129 51E
Maseru 92 29 18S 27 30E
Mashaba 91 20 2S 30 29E
Mashābih 64 25 35N 36 30E
Mashan 77 23 40N 108 11E
Mashhad 65 36 20N 59 35E
Mashi 85 13 0N 7 54E
Mashike 74 43 31N 141 30E
Mashkel, Hamun-i- 66 28 30N 63 0E
Mashki Chah 66 29 5N 62 30E
Mashtaga 57 40 35N 50 0E
Masi 50 69 26N 23 40E
Masi Manimba 88 4 40S 17 54E
Masindi 90 1 40N 31 43E
Masindi Port 90 1 43N 32 2E
Masisea 126 8 35S 74 22W
Masisi 90 1 23S 28 49E
Masjed Soleyman 64 31 55N 49 18E
Mask, L. 15 53 36N 9 24W
Maski 70 15 56N 76 46E
Maslen Nos 43 42 18N 27 48E
Maslinica 39 43 24N 16 13E
Masnou 32 41 28N 2 20E
Masoala, Tanjon' i 93 15 59S 50 13E
Masoarivo 93 19 3S 44 19E
Masohi 73 3 2S 128 15E
Masomeloka 93 20 17S 48 37E
Mason, S.D., U.S.A. 116 45 12N 103 27W
Mason, Tex., U.S.A. 117 30 45N 99 15W
Mason City, Iowa, U.S.A. 116 43 9N 93 12W
Mason City, Wash., U.S.A. 118 48 0N 119 0W
Masqat 65 23 37N 58 36E
Massa 38 44 2N 10 7E
Massa Maríttima 38 43 3N 10 52E
Massa, O. → 82 30 2N 9 40W
Massachusetts □ 114 42 25N 72 0W
Massachusetts B. 113 42 30N 70 0W
Massada 62 33 41N 35 36E
Massafra 41 40 35N 17 8E
Massaguet 81 12 28N 15 26E
Massakory 81 13 0N 15 49E
Massangena 93 21 34S 33 0E
Massarosa 38 43 53N 10 17E
Massat 20 42 53N 1 21E
Massawa = Mitsiwa 87 15 35N 39 25E
Massena 114 44 52N 74 55W
Massénya 81 11 21N 16 9E
Masset 108 54 2N 132 10W
Massiac 20 45 15N 3 11E
Massif Central 20 45 30N 2 21E
Massillon 114 40 47N 81 30W
Massinga 93 23 46S 35 22E
Masson 113 45 32N 75 25W
Masson I. 5 66 10S 93 20E
Mastaba 86 20 52N 39 30E
Mastanli = Momchilgrad 43 41 33N 25 23E
Masterton 101 40 56S 175 39E
Mástikho, Ákra 45 38 10N 26 2E
Mastuj 69 36 20N 72 36E
Mastung 66 29 50N 66 56E
Mastura 86 23 7N 38 52E
Masuda 74 34 40N 131 51E
Maswa □ 90 3 30S 34 0E
Matabeleland North □ 91 19 0S 28 0E
Matabeleland South □ 91 21 0S 29 0E
Mataboor 73 1 41S 138 3E
Matachel → 31 38 50N 6 17W
Matachewan 106 47 56N 80 39W
Matad 75 47 11N 115 27E
Matadi 88 5 52S 13 31E
Matagalpa 121 13 0N 85 58W
Matagami 106 49 45N 77 34W
Matagami, L. 106 49 50N 77 40W
Matagorda 117 28 43N 96 0W
Matagorda B. 117 28 30N 96 15W
Matagorda I. 117 28 10N 96 40W
Matak, P. 72 3 18N 106 16E
Matakana 99 32 59S 145 54E
Matale 70 7 30N 80 37E
Matam 84 15 34N 13 17W
Matameye 85 13 26N 8 28E
Matamoros, Coahuila, Mexico 120 25 33N 103 15W
Matamoros, Puebla, Mexico 120 18 2N 98 17W
Matamoros, Tamaulipas, Mexico 120 25 50N 97 30W
Ma'ṭan as Sarra 81 21 45N 22 0E
Matandu → 91 8 45S 34 19E
Matane 107 48 50N 67 33W
Matankari 85 13 46N 4 1E
Matanuska 104 61 39N 149 19W
Matanzas 121 23 0N 81 40W
Matapan, C. = Taínaron, Akra 45 36 22N 22 27E
Matapédia 107 48 0N 66 59W
Matara 70 5 58N 80 30E
Mataram 72 8 41S 116 10E
Matarani 126 77 0S 72 10W
Mataranka 96 14 55S 133 4E
Mataró 32 41 32N 2 29E
Matarraña → 32 41 14N 0 22E
Mataruška Banja 42 43 40N 20 45E
Matatiele 93 30 20S 28 49E
Mataura 101 46 11S 168 51E
Matehuala 120 23 40N 100 40W
Mateke Hills 91 21 48S 31 0E
Matélica 39 43 15N 13 0E
Matera 41 40 40N 16 37E
Mátészalka 27 47 58N 22 20E
Matetsi 91 18 12S 26 0E
Mateur 83 37 0N 9 40E
Matfors 48 62 21N 17 2E
Matha 20 45 52N 0 20W
Matheson Island 109 51 45N 96 56W
Mathis 117 28 4N 97 48W
Mathura 68 27 30N 77 40E
Mati 73 6 55N 126 15E
Mati → 44 41 40N 20 0E
Matías Romero 120 16 53N 95 2W
Matibane 91 14 49S 40 45E
Matima 92 20 15S 24 26E
Matlock 12 53 8N 1 32W
Matmata 83 33 37N 9 59E
Matna 87 13 49N 35 10E
Mato Grosso □ 127 14 0S 55 0W
Mato Grosso, Planalto do 127 15 0S 59 57W
Matochkin Shar 58 73 10N 56 40E
Matopo Hills 91 20 36S 28 20E
Matopos 91 20 20S 28 29E
Matosinhos 30 41 11N 8 42W
Matour 21 46 19N 4 29E
Matrah 65 23 37N 58 30E
Matrûh 86 31 19N 27 9E
Matsena 85 13 5N 10 5E
Matsesta 57 43 34N 39 51E
Matsue 74 35 25N 133 10E
Matsumoto 74 36 15N 138 0E
Matsuyama 74 33 45N 132 45E
Mattagami → 106 50 43N 81 29W
Mattancheri 70 9 50N 76 15E
Mattawa 106 46 20N 78 45W
Mattawamkeag 107 45 30N 68 21W
Matterhorn 25 45 58N 7 39E
Mattersburg 27 47 44N 16 24E
Matthew Town 121 20 57N 73 40W
Matthew's Ridge 126 7 37N 60 10W
Mattice 106 49 40N 83 20W
Mattituck 113 40 58N 72 32W
Mattmar 48 63 18N 13 45E
Matua 72 2 58S 110 46E
Matuba 93 24 28S 32 49E
Matucana 126 11 55S 76 25W
Matun 66 33 22N 69 58E
Maturín 126 9 45N 63 11W
Matveyev Kurgan 57 47 35N 38 47E
Mau-é-ele 93 24 18S 34 2E
Mau Escarpment 90 0 40S 36 0E
Mau Ranipur 68 25 16N 79 8E
Maubeuge 19 50 17N 3 57E
Maubourguet 20 43 29N 0 1E
Maude 99 34 29S 144 18E
Maudheim 5 71 5S 11 0W
Maudin Sun 67 16 0N 94 30E
Maués 126 3 20S 57 45W
Maui 110 20 45N 156 20E
Mauke 101 20 09S 157 20W
Maule □ 124 36 5S 72 30W
Mauléon-Licharre 20 43 14N 0 54W
Maumee 114 41 35N 83 40W
Maumee → 114 41 42N 83 28W
Maumere 73 8 38S 122 13E
Maun 92 20 0S 23 26E
Mauna Kea 110 19 50N 155 28W
Mauna Loa 110 21 8N 157 10W
Maunath Bhanjan 69 25 56N 83 33E
Maungmagan Kyunzu 71 14 0N 97 48E
Maupin 118 45 12N 121 9W
Maure-de-Bretagne 18 47 53N 2 0W
Maurepas L. 117 30 18N 90 35W
Maures 21 43 15N 6 15E
Mauriac 20 45 13N 2 19E
Maurice L. 96 29 30S 131 0E
Mauritania ■ 80 20 50N 10 0W
Mauritius ■ 3 20 0S 57 0E
Mauron 18 48 9N 2 18W
Maurs 20 44 43N 2 12E
Mauston 116 43 48N 90 5W
Mauterndorf 26 47 9N 13 40E
Mauvezin 20 43 44N 0 53E
Mauzé-sur-le-Mignon 20 46 12N 0 41W
Mavelikara 70 9 14N 76 32E
Mavinga 89 15 50S 20 21E
Mavli 68 24 45N 73 55E
Mavqi'im 62 31 38N 34 32E
Mavrova 44 40 26N 19 32E
Mavuradonha Mts. 91 16 30S 31 30E
Mawa 90 2 45N 26 40E
Mawana 68 29 6N 77 58E
Mawand 68 29 33N 68 38E
Mawk Mai 67 20 14N 97 37E
Mawson Base 5 67 30S 62 53E
Max 116 47 50N 101 20W
Maxcanú 120 20 40N 92 0W
Maxhamish L. 108 59 50N 123 17W
Maxixe 93 23 54S 35 17E
Maxville 113 45 17N 74 51W
Maxwelton 98 20 43S 142 41E
May Downs 98 22 38S 148 55E
May Glacier Tongue 5 66 08S 130 35E
May Pen 121 17 58N 77 15W
Maya 32 43 12N 1 29W
Maya → 59 54 31N 134 41E
Maya Mts. 120 16 30N 89 0W
Mayaguana 121 22 30N 72 44W
Mayagüez 121 18 12N 67 9W
Mayahi 85 13 58N 7 40E
Mayals 32 41 22N 0 30E
Mayarí 121 20 40N 75 41W
Mayavaram = Mayuram 70 11 3N 79 42E
Maybell 118 40 30N 108 4W
Maychew 87 12 50N 39 31E
Maydena 99 42 45S 146 30E
Maydos 44 40 13N 26 20E
Mayen 25 50 18N 7 10E
Mayenne 18 48 20N 0 38W
Mayenne □ 18 48 10N 0 40W
Mayenne → 18 47 30N 0 32W
Mayer 119 34 28N 112 17W
Mayerthorpe 108 53 57N 115 8W
Mayfield 115 36 45N 88 40W
Mayhill 119 32 58N 105 30W
Maykop 57 44 35N 40 25E
Maymyo 71 22 2N 96 28E
Maynooth 15 53 22N 6 38W
Mayo 104 63 38N 135 57W
Mayo □ 15 53 47N 9 7W
Mayo → 120 26 45N 109 47W
Mayo L. 104 63 45N 135 0W
Mayon, Mt. 73 13 15N 123 42E
Mayor I. 101 37 16S 176 17E
Mayorga 30 42 10N 5 16W
Mayskiy 57 43 47N 44 2E
Mayson L. 109 57 55N 107 10W
Maysville 114 38 39N 83 46W
Maythalūn 62 32 21N 35 16E
Mayu 73 1 30N 126 30E
Mayuram 70 11 3N 79 42E
Mayville, N.D., U.S.A. 116 47 30N 97 23W
Mayville, N.Y., U.S.A. 112 42 14N 79 31W
Mayya 59 61 44N 130 18E
Mazabuka 91 15 52S 27 44E
Mazagán = El Jadida 82 33 11N 8 17W
Mazagão 127 0 7S 51 16W
Mazamet 20 43 30N 2 20E
Mazán 126 3 30S 73 0W
Mazan Deran □ 65 36 30N 52 0E
Mazar-e Sharif 65 36 41N 67 0E
Mazar, O. → 82 31 50N 1 36E
Mazara del Vallo 40 37 40N 12 34E
Mazarredo 128 47 10S 66 50W
Mazarrón 33 37 38N 1 19W
Mazarrón, Golfo de 33 37 27N 1 19W
Mazaruni → 126 6 25N 58 35W
Mazatenango 120 14 35N 91 30W
Mazatlán 120 23 10N 106 30W
Mažeikiai 54 56 20N 22 20E
Māzhān 65 32 30N 59 0E
Mazīnān 65 36 19N 56 56E
Mazoe, Mozam. 91 16 42S 33 7E
Mazoe, Zimb. 91 17 28S 30 58E
Mazrûb 87 14 0N 29 20E
Mazu Dao 77 26 10N 119 55E
Mazurian Lakes = Mazurski, Pojezierze 28 53 50N 21 0E
Mazurski, Pojezierze 28 53 50N 21 0E
Mazzarino 41 37 19N 14 12E
Mbaba 84 14 59N 16 44W
Mbabane 93 26 18S 31 6E
Mbagne 84 16 6N 14 47W
M'bahiakro 84 7 33N 4 19W
Mbaïki 88 3 53N 18 1E
Mbala 91 8 46S 31 24E
Mbale 90 1 8N 34 12E
Mbalmayo 88 3 33N 11 33E
Mbamba Bay 91 11 13S 34 49E
Mbandaka 88 0 1N 18 18E
Mbanga 85 4 30N 9 33E
Mbanza Congo 88 6 18S 14 16E
Mbanza Ngungu 88 5 12S 14 53E
Mbarara 90 0 35S 30 40E
Mbatto 84 6 28N 4 22W
Mbenkuru → 91 9 25S 39 50E
Mberubu 85 6 10N 7 38E
Mbesuma 91 10 0S 32 2E
Mbeya 91 8 54S 33 29E
Mbeya □ 90 8 15S 33 30E
Mbinga 91 10 50S 35 0E
Mbinga □ 91 10 50S 35 0E
Mbini = Rio Muni □ 88 1 30N 10 0E
Mboki 87 5 19N 25 58E
Mboro 84 15 9N 16 54W
Mboune 84 14 42N 13 34W
Mbour 84 14 22N 16 54W
Mbout 84 16 1N 12 38W
Mbozi □ 91 9 0S 32 50E
Mbuji-Mayi 90 6 9S 23 40E
Mbulu 90 3 45S 35 30E
Mbulu □ 90 3 52S 35 33E

Mburucuyá Miarinarivo

Mburucuyá	124	28 1S	58 14W
Mcherrah	82	27 0N	4 30W
Mchinja	91	9 44S	39 45 E
Mchinji	91	13 47S	32 58 E
Mdennah	82	24 37N	6 0W
Mdina	36	35 51N	14 25 E
Mead, L.	119	36 1N	114 44W
Meade	117	37 18N	100 25W
Meadow Lake	109	54 10N	108 26W
Meadow Lake Prov. Park	109	54 27N	109 0W
Meadow Valley Wash →	119	36 39N	114 35W
Meadville	114	41 39N	80 9W
Meaford	106	44 36N	80 35W
Mealhada	30	40 22N	8 27W
Mealy Mts.	107	53 10N	58 0W
Meander River	108	59 2N	117 42W
Meares, C.	118	45 37N	124 0W
Mearim →	127	3 4S	44 35W
Meath □	15	53 32N	6 40W
Meath Park	109	53 27N	105 22W
Meaulne	20	46 36N	2 36 E
Meaux	19	48 58N	2 50 E
Mecanhelas	91	15 12S	35 54 E
Mecca	119	33 37N	116 3W
Mecca = Makkah	86	21 30N	39 54 E
Mechanicsburg	112	40 12N	77 0W
Mechanicville	113	42 54N	73 41W
Mechara	87	8 36N	40 20 E
Mechelen	16	51 2N	4 29 E
Mecheria	82	33 35N	0 18W
Mechernich	24	50 35N	6 39 E
Mechetinskaya	57	46 45N	40 32 E
Mechra Benâbbou	82	32 39N	7 48W
Mecidiye	44	40 38N	26 32 E
Mecitözü	56	40 32N	35 17 E
Meconta	91	14 59S	39 50 E
Meda	30	40 57N	7 18W
Meda →	96	17 20S	123 50 E
Medak	70	18 1N	78 15 E
Medan	72	3 40N	98 38 E
Medanosa, Pta.	128	48 8S	66 0W
Medawachchiya	70	8 30N	80 30 E
Medéa	82	36 12N	2 50 E
Mededa	42	43 44N	19 15 E
Medellín	126	6 15N	75 35W
Medemblik	16	52 46N	5 8 E
Médenine	83	33 21N	10 30 E
Mederdra	84	17 0N	15 38W
Medford, Oreg., U.S.A.	118	42 20N	122 52W
Medford, Wis., U.S.A.	116	45 9N	90 21W
Medgidia	46	44 15N	28 19 E
Medi	87	5 4N	30 42 E
Media Agua	124	31 58S	68 25W
Media Luna	124	34 45S	66 44W
Mediaş	46	46 9N	24 22 E
Medical Lake	118	47 35N	117 42W
Medicina	39	44 29N	11 38 E
Medicine Bow	118	41 56N	106 11W
Medicine Bow Pk.	118	41 21N	106 19W
Medicine Bow Ra.	118	41 10N	106 25W
Medicine Hat	109	50 0N	110 45W
Medicine Lake	116	48 30N	104 30W
Medicine Lodge	117	37 20N	98 37W
Medina, N.D., U.S.A.	116	46 57N	99 20W
Medina, N.Y., U.S.A.	114	43 15N	78 27W
Medina, Ohio, U.S.A.	114	41 9N	81 50W
Medina = Al Madīnah	64	24 35N	39 35 E
Medina →	117	29 10N	98 20W
Medina de Rioseco	30	41 53N	5 3W
Medina del Campo	30	41 18N	4 55W
Medina L.	117	29 35N	98 58W
Medina-Sidonia	31	36 28N	5 57W
Medinaceli	32	41 12N	2 30W
Mediterranean Sea	34	35 0N	15 0 E
Medjerda, O. →	83	37 7N	10 13 E
Medley	109	54 25N	110 16W
Médoc	20	45 10N	0 56W
Medstead	109	53 19N	108 5W
Medulin	39	44 49N	13 55 E
Medveda	42	42 50N	21 32 E
Medveditsa →, R.S.F.S.R., U.S.S.R.	55	49 35N	42 41 E
Medveditsa →, R.S.F.S.R., U.S.S.R.	55	57 5N	37 30 E
Medvedok	55	57 20N	50 1 E
Medvezhi, Ostrava	59	71 0N	161 0 E
Medvezhyegorsk	52	63 0N	34 25 E
Medway →	13	51 28N	0 45 E
Medyn	55	54 58N	35 52 E
Medzev	27	48 43N	20 55 E
Medzilaborce	27	49 17N	21 52 E
Meekatharra	96	26 32S	118 29 E
Meeker	118	40 1N	107 58W
Meerane	24	50 51N	12 30 E
Meersburg	25	47 42N	9 16 E
Meerut	68	29 1N	77 42 E
Meeteetse	118	44 10N	108 56W
Mega	87	3 57N	38 19 E
Megálo Khorío	45	36 27N	27 24 E
Megálo Petalí	45	38 0N	24 15 E
Megalópolis	45	37 25N	22 7 E
Meganisi	45	38 39N	20 48 E
Mégara	45	37 58N	23 22 E
Megarine	83	33 14N	6 2 E
Megdhova →	45	39 10N	21 45 E
Mégève	21	45 51N	6 37 E
Meghezez, Mt.	87	9 18N	39 26 E
Meghna →	69	22 50N	90 50 E
Megiddo	62	32 36N	35 11 E
Mégiscane, L.	106	48 35N	75 55W
Megiste	35	36 8N	29 34 E
Mehadia	46	44 56N	22 23 E
Mehaïguene, O. →	82	32 15N	2 59 E
Meharry, Mt.	96	22 59S	118 35 E
Mehedinţi □	46	44 40N	22 45 E
Meheisa	86	19 38N	32 57 E
Mehndawal	69	26 58N	83 5 E
Mehsana	68	23 39N	72 26 E
Mehun-sur-Yèvre	19	47 10N	2 13 E
Mei Jiang →	77	24 25N	116 35 E
Mei Xian	75	24 16N	116 6 E
Meiganga	88	6 30N	14 25 E
Meiktila	67	20 53N	95 54 E
Meiningen	24	50 32N	10 25 E
Me'ir Shefeya	62	32 35N	34 58 E
Meira, Sierra de	30	43 15N	7 15W
Meiringen	25	46 43N	8 12 E
Meissen	24	51 10N	13 29 E
Meissner	24	51 13N	9 51 E
Meitan	77	27 45N	107 29 E
Méjean, Causse	20	44 15N	3 30 E
Mejillones	124	23 10S	70 30W
Mékambo	88	1 2N	13 50 E
Mekdela	87	11 24N	39 10 E
Mekele	87	13 33N	39 30 E
Meklong = Samut Songkhram	71	13 24N	100 1 E
Meknès	82	33 57N	5 33W
Meko	85	7 27N	2 52 E
Mekong →	71	9 30N	106 15 E
Mekongga	73	3 39S	121 15 E
Melagiri Hills	70	12 20N	77 30 E
Melah, Sebkhet el	82	29 20N	1 30W
Melaka	71	2 15N	102 15 E
Melaka □	71	2 20N	102 15 E
Melalap	72	5 10N	116 5 E
Mélambes	45	35 8N	24 40 E
Melanesia	94	4 0S	155 0 E
Melapalaiyam	70	8 39N	77 44 E
Melbourne, Austral.	97	37 50S	145 0 E
Melbourne, U.S.A.	115	28 4N	80 35W
Melchor Múzquiz	120	27 50N	101 30W
Melchor Ocampo (San Pedro Ocampo)	120	24 52N	101 40W
Méldola	39	44 7N	12 3 E
Meldorf	24	54 5N	9 5 E
Mêle-sur-Sarthe, Le	18	48 31N	0 22 E
Melegnano	38	45 21N	9 20 E
Melenci	42	45 32N	20 20 E
Melenki	55	55 20N	41 37 E
Mélèzes →	105	57 30N	71 0W
Melfi, Chad	81	11 0N	17 59 E
Melfi, Italy	41	41 0N	15 33 E
Melfort, Can.	109	52 50N	104 37W
Melfort, Zimb.	91	18 0S	31 25 E
Melgaço	30	42 7N	8 15W
Melgar de Fernamental	30	42 27N	4 17W
Melhus	47	63 17N	10 18 E
Meligalá	45	37 15N	21 59 E
Melilla	82	35 21N	2 57W
Melilot	62	31 22N	34 37 E
Melipilla	124	33 42S	71 15W
Mélissa Óros	45	37 32N	26 4 E
Melita	109	49 15N	101 0W
Mélito di Porto Salvo	41	37 55N	15 47 E
Melitopol	56	46 50N	35 22 E
Melk	26	48 13N	15 20 E
Mellan-Fryken	48	59 45N	13 10 E
Mellansel	50	63 25N	18 17 E
Melle, France	20	46 14N	0 10W
Melle, Ger.	24	52 12N	8 20 E
Mellégue, O. →	83	36 32N	8 51 E
Mellen	116	46 19N	90 36W
Mellerud	49	58 41N	12 28 E
Mellette	116	45 11N	98 29W
Mellid	30	42 55N	8 1W
Mellish Reef	97	17 25S	155 50 E
Mellit	87	14 7N	25 34 E
Mellrichstadt	25	50 26N	10 19 E
Melnik	43	41 30N	23 25 E
Mělník	26	50 22N	14 23 E
Melo	125	32 20S	54 10W
Melolo	73	9 53S	120 40 E
Melovoye	57	49 25N	40 5 E
Melrhir, Chott	83	34 25N	6 24 E
Melrose, Austral.	99	32 42S	146 57 E
Melrose, U.K.	14	53 35N	2 44W
Melrose, U.S.A.	117	34 27N	103 33W
Melstone	118	46 36N	107 50W
Melsungen	24	51 8N	9 34 E
Melton Mowbray	12	52 46N	0 52W
Melun	19	48 32N	2 39 E
Melur	70	10 2N	78 23 E
Melut	87	10 30N	32 13 E
Melville	109	50 55N	102 50W
Melville B.	97	12 0S	136 45 E
Melville, C.	97	14 11S	144 30 E
Melville I., Austral.	96	11 30S	131 0 E
Melville I., Can.	4	75 30N	112 0W
Melville, L.	107	53 30N	60 0W
Melville Pen.	105	68 0N	84 0W
Melvin →	108	59 11N	117 31W
Mélykút	27	46 11N	19 25 E
Memaliaj	44	40 25N	19 58 E
Memba	91	14 11S	40 30 E
Memboro	73	9 30S	119 30 E
Membrilla	33	38 59N	3 21W
Memel	93	27 38S	29 36 E
Memel = Klaipeda	54	55 43N	21 10 E
Memmingen	25	47 59N	10 12 E
Memphis, Tenn., U.S.A.	117	35 7N	90 0W
Memphis, Tex., U.S.A.	117	34 45N	100 30W
Mena	117	34 40N	94 15W
Mena →	87	5 40N	40 50 E
Menai Strait	12	53 14N	4 10W
Ménaka	85	15 59N	2 18 E
Menam = Chao Phraya →	71	13 32N	100 36 E
Menarandra →	93	25 17S	44 30 E
Menard	117	30 57N	99 48W
Menasha	114	44 13N	88 27W
Menate	72	0 12S	113 3 E
Mendawai →	72	3 17S	113 21 E
Mende	20	44 31N	3 30 E
Mendebo Mts.	87	7 0N	39 22 E
Menderes →	64	37 25N	28 45 E
Mendi, Ethiopia	87	9 47N	35 4 E
Mendi, P.N.G.	98	6 11S	143 39 E
Mendip Hills	13	51 17N	2 40W
Mendocino	118	39 26N	123 50W
Mendocino Seascarp	95	41 0N	140 0W
Mendota, Calif., U.S.A.	119	36 46N	120 24W
Mendota, Ill., U.S.A.	116	41 35N	89 5W
Mendoza	124	32 50S	68 52W
Mendoza □	124	33 0S	69 0W
Mene Grande	126	9 49N	70 56W
Menemen	64	38 34N	27 3 E
Menen	16	50 47N	3 7 E
Menfi	40	37 36N	12 57 E
Mengcheng	77	33 18N	116 31 E
Mengeš	39	46 24N	14 35 E
Menggala	72	4 30S	105 15 E
Mengíbar	31	37 58N	3 48W
Mengoub	82	29 49N	5 26W
Mengshan	77	24 14N	110 55 E
Mengzi	75	23 20N	103 22 E
Menihek L.	107	54 0N	67 0W
Menin = Menen	16	50 47N	3 7 E
Menindee	97	32 20S	142 25 E
Menindee, L.	99	32 20S	142 25 E
Meningie	99	35 35S	139 0 E
Menominee	114	45 9N	87 39W
Menominee →	114	45 5N	87 36W
Menomonie	116	44 50N	91 54W
Menongue	89	14 48S	17 52 E
Menorca	32	40 0N	4 0 E
Mentawai, Kepulauan	72	2 0S	99 0 E
Menton	21	43 50N	7 29 E
Mentor	112	41 40N	81 21W
Menzel-Bourguiba	83	39 9N	9 49 E
Menzel Chaker	83	35 0N	10 26 E
Menzel-Temime	83	36 46N	11 0 E
Menzelinsk	52	55 53N	53 1 E
Menzies	96	29 40S	120 58 E
Me'ona (Tarshiha)	62	33 1N	35 15 E
Mepaco	91	15 57S	30 48 E
Meppel	16	52 42N	6 12 E
Meppen	24	52 41N	7 20 E
Mequinenza	32	41 22N	0 17 E
Mer Rouge	117	32 47N	91 48W
Merabéllou, Kólpos	45	35 10N	25 50 E
Merak	73	5 56S	106 0 E
Meran = Merano	39	46 40N	11 10 E
Merano	39	46 40N	11 10 E
Merate	38	45 42N	9 23 E
Merauke	73	8 29S	140 24 E
Merbabu	73	7 30S	110 40 E
Merbein	99	34 10S	142 2 E
Merca	63	1 48N	44 50 E
Mercadal	32	39 59N	4 5 E
Mercara	70	12 30N	75 45 E
Mercato Saraceno	39	43 57N	12 11 E
Merced	119	37 18N	120 30W
Mercedes, Buenos Aires, Argent.	124	34 40S	59 30W
Mercedes, Corrientes, Argent.	124	29 10S	58 5W
Mercedes, San Luis, Argent.	124	33 40S	65 21W
Mercedes, Uruguay	124	33 12S	58 0W
Merceditas	124	28 20S	70 35W
Mercer, N.Z.	101	37 16S	175 5 E
Mercer, U.S.A.	112	41 14N	80 13W
Mercy C.	105	65 0N	63 30W
Merdrignac	18	48 11N	2 27W
Meredith C.	128	52 15S	60 40W
Meredith, L.	117	35 30N	101 35W
Merei	46	45 7N	26 43 E
Méréville	19	48 20N	2 5 E
Mergenevsky	57	49 59N	51 15 E
Mergui Arch. = Myeik Kyunzu	71	11 30N	97 30 E
Mérida, Mexico	120	20 9N	89 40W
Mérida, Spain	31	38 55N	6 25W
Mérida, Venez.	126	8 24N	71 8W
Meriden	114	41 33N	72 47W
Meridian, Idaho, U.S.A.	118	43 41N	116 25W
Meridian, Miss., U.S.A.	115	32 20N	88 42W
Meridian, Tex., U.S.A.	117	31 55N	97 37W
Mering	25	48 15N	11 0 E
Meringur	100	34 20S	141 19 E
Meriruma	127	1 15N	54 50W
Merkel	117	32 30N	100 0W
Merksem	16	51 16N	4 25 E
Merlebach	19	49 5N	6 52 E
Merlerault, Le	18	48 41N	0 16 E
Mern	49	55 3N	12 3 E
Merowe	86	18 29N	31 46 E
Merredin	96	31 28S	118 18 E
Merrick	14	55 8N	4 30W
Merrickville	113	44 55N	75 50W
Merrill, Oregon, U.S.A.	118	42 2N	121 37W
Merrill, Wis., U.S.A.	116	45 11N	89 41W
Merriman	116	42 55N	101 42W
Merritt	108	50 10N	120 45W
Merriwa	99	32 6S	150 22 E
Merriwagga	99	33 47S	145 43 E
Merry I.	106	55 29N	77 31W
Merrygoen	99	31 51S	149 12 E
Merryville	117	30 47N	93 31W
Mersa Fatma	87	14 57N	40 17 E
Mersch	16	49 44N	6 7 E
Merseburg	24	51 20N	12 0 E
Mersey →	12	53 20N	2 56W
Merseyside □	12	53 25N	2 55W
Mersin	64	36 51N	34 36 E
Mersing	71	2 25N	103 50 E
Merta	68	26 39N	74 4 E
Merthyr Tydfil	13	51 45N	3 23W
Mértola	31	37 40N	7 40 E
Mertzon	117	31 17N	100 48W
Méru	19	49 13N	2 8 E
Meru, Kenya	90	0 3N	37 40 E
Meru, Tanz.	90	3 15S	36 46 E
Meru □	90	0 3N	37 46 E
Merville	19	50 38N	2 38 E
Méry-sur-Seine	19	48 31N	3 54 E
Merzifon	56	40 53N	35 32 E
Merzig	25	49 26N	6 37 E
Merzouga, Erg Tin	83	24 0N	11 4 E
Mesa	119	33 20N	111 56W
Mesa, La, Calif., U.S.A.	119	32 48N	117 5W
Mesa, La, N. Mex., U.S.A.	119	32 6N	106 48W
Mesach Mellet	83	24 30N	11 30 E
Mesada	62	31 20N	35 19 E
Mesagne	41	40 34N	17 48 E
Mesaras, Kólpos	45	35 6N	24 47 E
Meschede	24	51 20N	8 17 E
Mesfinto	87	13 20N	37 22 E
Mesgouez, L.	106	51 20N	75 0W
Meshchovsk	54	54 22N	35 17 E
Meshed = Mashhad	65	36 20N	59 35 E
Meshoppen	113	41 36N	76 3W
Meshra er Req	81	8 25N	29 18 E
Mesick	114	44 24N	85 42W
Mesilinka →	108	56 6N	124 30W
Mesilla	119	32 20N	106 50W
Meslay-du-Maine	18	47 58N	0 33W
Mesocco	25	46 23N	9 12 E
Mesolóngion	45	38 21N	21 28 E
Mesopotamia = Al Jazirah	64	33 30N	44 0 E
Mesoraca	41	39 5N	16 47 E
Mésou Volímais	45	37 53N	20 35 E
Mess Cr. →	108	57 55N	131 14W
Messac	18	47 49N	1 50W
Messad	82	34 8N	3 30 E
Messalo →	91	12 25S	39 15 E
Méssaména	85	3 48N	12 49 E
Messeix	20	45 37N	2 33 E
Messeue	45	37 12N	21 58 E
Messina, Italy	41	38 10N	15 32 E
Messina, S. Afr.	93	22 20S	30 0 E
Messina, Str. di	41	38 5N	15 35 E
Messíni	45	37 4N	22 1 E
Messínia □	45	37 10N	22 0 E
Messiniakós, Kólpos	45	36 45N	22 5 E
Messkirch	25	47 59N	9 7 E
Mesta →	43	41 30N	24 0 E
Mestà, Ákra	45	38 16N	25 53 E
Mestanza	31	38 35N	4 4W
Město Teplá	26	49 59N	12 52 E
Mestre	39	45 30N	12 13 E
Městys Zelezná Ruda	26	49 8N	13 15 E
Meta →	126	6 12N	67 28W
Metairie	117	29 59N	90 9W
Metalici, Munţii	42	46 15N	22 50 E
Metaline Falls	118	48 52N	117 22W
Metán	124	25 30S	65 0W
Metauro →	39	43 50N	13 3 E
Metema	87	12 56N	36 13 E
Metengobalame	91	14 49S	34 30 E
Méthana	45	37 35N	23 23 E
Methóni	45	36 49N	21 42 E
Methven	101	43 38S	171 40 E
Methy L.	109	56 28N	109 30W
Metkovets	43	43 37N	23 10 E
Metković	42	43 6N	17 39 E
Metlakatla	108	55 10N	131 33W
Metlaoui	83	34 24N	8 24 E
Metlika	39	45 40N	15 20 E
Metropolis	117	37 10N	88 47W
Métsovon	44	39 48N	21 12 E
Mettuppalaiyam	70	11 18N	76 59 E
Mettur	70	11 48N	77 47 E
Mettur Dam	70	11 45N	77 45 E
Metulla	62	33 17N	35 34 E
Metz	19	49 8N	6 10 E
Meulaboh	72	4 11N	96 3 E
Meulan	19	49 0N	1 52 E
Meung-sur-Loire	19	47 50N	1 40 E
Meureudu	72	5 19N	96 10 E
Meurthe →	19	48 47N	6 9 E
Meurthe-et-Moselle □	19	48 52N	6 0 E
Meuse □	19	49 8N	5 25 E
Meuse →	16	50 45N	5 41 E
Meuselwitz	24	51 3N	12 18 E
Mexborough	12	53 29N	1 18W
Mexia	117	31 38N	96 32W
Mexiana, I.	127	0 0	49 30W
Mexicali	120	32 40N	115 30W
México	120	19 20N	99 10W
Mexico, Me., U.S.A.	113	44 35N	70 30W
Mexico, Mo., U.S.A.	116	39 10N	91 55W
Mexico ■	120	20 0N	100 0W
México □	120	19 20N	99 10W
Mexico, G. of	120	25 0N	90 0W
Meyenburg	24	53 19N	12 15 E
Meymac	20	45 32N	2 10 E
Meymaneh	65	35 53N	64 38 E
Meyrargues	21	43 38N	5 32 E
Meyrueis	20	44 12N	3 27 E
Meyssac	20	45 3N	1 40 E
Mezdra	43	43 12N	23 42 E
Mèze	20	43 27N	3 36 E
Mezen	52	65 50N	44 20 E
Mézenc	21	44 55N	4 11 E
Mezeş, Munţii	46	47 5N	23 5 E
Mezha →	54	55 50N	31 45 E
Mézidon	18	49 5N	0 1W
Mézilhac	21	44 49N	4 21 E
Mézin	20	44 4N	0 16 E
Mezöberény	27	46 49N	21 3 E
Mezöfalva	27	46 55N	18 49 E
Mezöhegyes	27	46 19N	20 49 E
Mezökövácsháza	27	46 25N	20 57 E
Mezökövesd	27	47 49N	20 35 E
Mézos	20	44 5N	1 10W
Mezötúr	27	47 0N	20 41 E
Mezquital	120	23 29N	104 23W
Mezzolombardo	38	46 13N	11 5 E
Mgeta	91	8 22S	36 6 E
Mglin	54	53 2N	32 50 E
Mhlaba Hills	91	18 30S	30 30 E
Mhow	68	22 33N	75 50 E
Miahuatlán	120	16 21N	96 36W
Miajadas	31	39 9N	5 54W
Mialar	68	26 15N	70 20 E
Miallo	98	16 28S	145 22 E
Miami, Ariz., U.S.A.	119	33 25N	110 54W
Miami, Fla., U.S.A.	115	25 45N	80 15W
Miami, Tex., U.S.A.	117	35 44N	100 38W
Miami →	114	39 20N	84 40W
Miami Beach	115	25 49N	80 6W
Miamisburg	114	39 40N	84 11W
Mian Xian	77	33 10N	106 32 E
Mianchi	77	34 48N	111 48 E
Mīāndow āb	64	37 0N	46 5 E
Miandrivazo	93	19 31S	45 29 E
Mīāneh	64	37 30N	47 40 E
Mianwali	68	32 38N	71 28 E
Mianyang, Hubei, China	77	30 25N	113 25 E
Mianyang, Sichuan, China	77	31 22N	104 47 E
Miaoli	75	24 37N	120 49 E
Miarinarivo	93	18 57S	46 55 E

Miass Mobutu Sese Seko, L.

Miass	52	54 59N	60 6 E
Miasteczko Kraj	28	53 7N	17 1 E
Miastko	28	54 0N	16 58 E
Micăsasa	46	46 7N	24 7 E
Michalovce	27	48 47N	21 58 E
Michelstadt	25	49 40N	9 0 E
Michigan □	111	44 40N	85 40W
Michigan City	114	41 42N	86 56W
Michigan, L.	114	44 0N	87 0W
Michipicoten	106	47 55N	84 55W
Michipicoten I.	106	47 40N	85 40W
Michoacan □	120	19 0N	102 0W
Michurin	43	42 9N	27 51 E
Michurinsk	55	52 58N	40 27 E
Miclere	98	22 34 S	147 32 E
Mico, Pta.	121	12 0N	83 30W
Micronesia	94	11 0N	160 0 E
Mid Glamorgan □	13	51 40N	3 25W
Mid-Indian Ridge	94	40 0 S	75 0 E
Mid-Oceanic Ridge	94	42 0 S	90 0 E
Midai, P.	72	3 0N	107 47 E
Midale	109	49 25N	103 20W
Midas	118	41 14N	116 48W
Middagsfjället	48	63 27N	12 19 E
Middelburg, Neth.	16	51 30N	3 36 E
Middelburg, C. Prov., S. Afr.	92	31 30 S	25 0 E
Middelburg, Trans., S. Afr.	93	25 49 S	29 28 E
Middelfart	49	55 30N	9 43 E
Middle Alkali L.	118	41 30N	120 3W
Middle Andaman I.	71	12 30N	92 30 E
Middle Loup →	116	41 17N	98 23W
Middleboro	113	41 56N	70 52W
Middleburg, N.Y., U.S.A.	113	42 36N	74 19W
Middleburg, Pa., U.S.A.	112	40 46N	77 5W
Middlebury	113	44 0N	73 9W
Middleport	114	39 0N	82 5W
Middlesboro	115	36 36N	83 43W
Middlesbrough	12	54 35N	1 14W
Middlesex	113	40 36N	74 30W
Middleton	107	44 57N	65 4W
Middleton Cr. →	98	22 35 S	141 51 E
Middleton P.O.	98	22 22 S	141 32 E
Middletown, Conn., U.S.A.	114	41 37N	72 40W
Middletown, N.Y., U.S.A.	114	41 28N	74 28W
Middletown, Ohio, U.S.A.	114	39 29N	84 25W
Middletown, Pa., U.S.A.	113	40 12N	76 44W
Midelt	82	32 46N	4 44W
Midi, Canal du	20	43 45N	1 21 E
Midi d'Ossau	32	42 50N	0 25W
Midland, Austral.	96	31 54 S	115 59 E
Midland, Can.	106	44 45N	79 50W
Midland, Mich., U.S.A.	114	43 37N	84 17W
Midland, Pa., U.S.A.	112	40 39N	80 27W
Midland, Tex., U.S.A.	117	32 0N	102 3W
Midlands □	91	19 40 S	29 0 E
Midleton	15	51 52N	8 12W
Midlothian	117	32 30N	97 0W
Midnapore	69	22 25N	87 21 E
Midongy Atsimo	93	23 35 S	47 1 E
Midongy, Tangorombohitr' i	93	23 30 S	47 0 E
Midour →	20	43 54N	0 30W
Midouze →	20	43 48N	0 51W
Midvale	118	40 39N	111 58W
Midway Is.	94	28 13N	177 22W
Midwest	118	43 27N	106 19W
Midyat	64	37 25N	41 23 E
Midzur	42	43 24N	22 40 E
Mie □	74	34 30N	136 10 E
Miechów	28	50 21N	20 5 E
Miedwie, Jezioro	28	53 17N	14 54 E
Międzybód	28	51 25N	17 34 E
Międzychód	28	52 35N	15 53 E
Międzylesie	28	50 8N	16 40 E
Międzyrzec Podlaski	28	51 58N	22 45 E
Międzyrzecz	28	52 26N	15 35 E
Międzyzdroje	28	53 56N	14 26 E
Miejska	28	51 39N	16 58 E
Miélan	20	43 27N	0 19 E
Mielec	28	50 15N	21 25 E
Mienga	92	17 12 S	19 48 E
Miercurea Ciuc	46	46 21N	25 48 E
Mieres	30	43 18N	5 48W
Mieroszów	28	50 40N	16 11 E
Mieso	87	9 15N	40 43 E
Mieszkowice	28	52 47N	14 30 E
Migdāl	62	32 51N	35 30 E
Migdal Afeq	62	32 5N	34 58 E
Migennes	19	47 58N	3 31 E
Migliarino	39	44 45N	11 56 E
Miguel Alemán, Presa	120	18 15N	96 40W
Miguel Alves	127	4 11 S	42 55W
Mihara	74	34 24N	133 5 E
Mijares →	32	39 55N	0 1W
Mijas	31	36 36N	4 40W
Mikese	90	6 48 S	37 55 E
Mikha-Tskhakaya	57	42 15N	42 7 E
Mikhailovka	56	47 36N	35 16 E
Mikhaylov	55	54 14N	39 0 E
Mikhaylovgrad	43	43 27N	23 16 E
Mikhaylovka, Azerbaijan, U.S.S.R.	57	41 31N	48 52 E
Mikhaylovka, R.S.F.S.R., U.S.S.R.	55	50 3N	43 5 E
Mikhnevo	55	55 4N	37 59 E
Mikínai	45	37 43N	22 46 E
Mikindani	91	10 15 S	40 2 E
Mikkeli	51	61 43N	27 15 E
Mikkeli □	50	62 0N	28 0 E
Mikkwa →	108	58 25N	114 46W
Mikniya	87	17 0N	33 45 E
Mikołajki	28	53 49N	21 37 E
Mikołów	27	50 10N	18 50 E
Míkonos	45	37 30N	25 25 E
Mikrí Préspa, Límni	44	40 47N	21 3 E
Mikrón Dhérion	44	41 19N	26 6 E
Mikstat	28	51 32N	17 59 E
Mikulov	27	48 48N	16 39 E
Mikumi	90	7 26 S	37 0 E
Mikun	52	62 20N	50 0 E
Mikura-Jima	74	33 52N	139 36 E
Milaca	116	45 45N	93 40W
Milagro	126	2 11 S	79 36W
Milan, Mo., U.S.A.	116	40 10N	93 5W
Milan, Tenn., U.S.A.	115	35 55N	88 45W
Milan = Milano	38	45 28N	9 10 E
Milange	91	16 3 S	35 45 E
Milano	38	45 28N	9 10 E
Milâs	64	37 20N	27 50 E
Milazzo	41	38 13N	15 13 E
Milbank	116	45 17N	96 38W
Milden	109	51 29N	107 32W
Mildmay	112	44 3N	81 7W
Mildura	97	34 13 S	142 9 E
Miléai	44	39 20N	23 9 E
Miles, Austral.	97	26 40 S	150 9 E
Miles, U.S.A.	117	31 39N	100 11W
Miles City	116	46 24N	105 50W
Milestone	109	49 59N	104 31W
Mileto	41	38 37N	16 3 E
Miletto, Mte.	41	41 26N	14 23 E
Miletus	45	37 20N	27 33 E
Milevsko	26	49 27N	14 21 E
Milford, Conn., U.S.A.	113	41 13N	73 4W
Milford, Del., U.S.A.	114	38 52N	75 27W
Milford, Mass., U.S.A.	113	42 8N	71 30W
Milford, Pa., U.S.A.	113	41 20N	74 47W
Milford, Utah, U.S.A.	119	38 20N	113 0W
Milford Haven	13	51 43N	5 2W
Milford Haven, B.	13	51 40N	5 10W
Milford Sd.	101	44 41 S	167 47 E
Milḩ, Baḩr al	64	32 40N	43 35 E
Milḩ, Ras al	81	31 54N	25 6 E
Miliana, Aïn Salah, Alg.	82	27 20N	2 32 E
Miliana, Médéa, Alg.	82	36 20N	2 15 E
Milicz	28	51 31N	17 19 E
Militello in Val di Catánia	41	37 16N	14 46 E
Milk →	118	48 5N	106 15W
Milk River	108	49 10N	112 5W
Milk, Wadi el →	86	17 55N	30 20 E
Mill City	118	44 45N	122 28W
Mill I.	5	66 0 S	101 30 E
Millau	20	44 8N	3 4 E
Millbridge	112	44 41N	77 36W
Millbrook	112	44 10N	78 29W
Mille	115	33 7N	83 15W
Mille Lacs, L.	116	46 10N	93 30W
Mille Lacs, L. des	106	48 45N	90 35W
Millen	115	32 50N	81 57W
Miller	116	44 35N	98 59W
Millerovo	57	48 57N	40 28 E
Millersburg, Ohio, U.S.A.	112	40 32N	81 52W
Millersburg, Pa., U.S.A.	112	40 32N	76 58W
Millerton	113	41 57N	73 32W
Millevaches, Plateau de	20	45 45N	2 0 E
Millicent	97	37 34 S	140 21 E
Millinocket	107	45 45N	68 45W
Millmerran	99	27 53 S	151 16 E
Mills L.	108	61 30N	118 20W
Millsboro	112	40 0N	80 0W
Milltown Malbay	15	52 51N	9 25W
Millville	114	39 22N	75 0W
Millwood Res.	117	33 45N	94 0W
Milly	19	48 24N	2 28 E
Milna	39	43 20N	16 28 E
Milne Inlet	105	72 30N	80 0W
Milnor	116	46 19N	97 29W
Milo	108	50 34N	112 53W
Mílos	45	36 44N	24 25 E
Miloševo	42	45 42N	20 20 E
Miłosław	28	52 12N	17 32 E
Milparinka P.O.	99	29 46 S	141 57 E
Miltenberg	25	49 41N	9 13 E
Milton, Can.	112	43 33N	79 53W
Milton, N.Z.	101	46 7 S	169 59 E
Milton, U.K.	14	57 18N	4 32W
Milton, Fla., U.S.A.	115	30 38N	87 0W
Milton, Pa., U.S.A.	114	41 0N	76 53W
Milton-Freewater	118	45 57N	118 24W
Milton Keynes	13	52 3N	0 42W
Miltou	81	10 14N	17 26 E
Milverton	112	43 34N	80 55W
Milwaukee	114	43 9N	87 58W
Milwaukie	118	45 27N	122 39W
Mim	84	6 57N	2 33W
Mimizan	20	44 12N	1 13W
Mimon	26	50 38N	14 43 E
Min Jiang →, Fujian, China	75	26 0N	119 35 E
Min Jiang →, Sichuan, China	75	28 45N	104 40 E
Min Xian	77	34 25N	104 0 E
Mina	119	38 21N	118 9W
Mina Pirquitas	124	22 40 S	66 30W
Mīnā Su'ud	64	28 45N	48 28 E
Mīnā'al Aḩmadī	64	29 5N	48 10 E
Mīnāb	65	27 10N	57 1 E
Minago →	109	54 33N	98 59W
Minaki	109	49 59N	94 40W
Minamata	74	32 10N	130 30 E
Minas	125	34 20 S	55 10W
Minas Basin	107	45 20N	64 12W
Minas de Rio Tinto	31	37 42N	6 35W
Minas de San Quintín	31	38 49N	4 23W
Minas Gerais □	127	18 50 S	46 0W
Minas, Sierra de las	120	15 9N	89 31W
Minatitlán	120	17 58N	94 35W
Minbu	67	20 10N	94 52 E
Mincio →	38	45 4N	10 59 E
Mindanao	73	8 0N	125 0 E
* Mindanao Sea	73	9 0N	124 0 E
Mindanao Trench	73	8 0N	128 0 E
Mindel →	25	48 31N	10 23 E
Mindelheim	25	48 4N	10 30 E
Minden, Can.	112	44 55N	78 43W
Minden, Ger.	24	52 18N	8 45 E
Minden, U.S.A.	117	32 40N	93 20W
Mindiptana	73	5 55 S	140 22 E
Mindona, L.	100	33 6 S	142 6 E
Mindoro	73	13 0N	121 0 E
Mindoro Strait	73	12 30N	120 30 E
Mindouli	88	4 12 S	14 28 E
Minehead	13	51 12N	3 29W
Mineoia	117	32 40N	95 30W
Mineral Wells	117	32 50N	98 5W
Mineralnyye Vody	57	44 2N	43 8 E
Minersville, Pa., U.S.A.	113	40 11N	76 17W
Minersville, Utah, U.S.A.	119	38 14N	112 58W
Minerva	112	40 43N	81 8W
Minervino Murge	41	41 6N	16 4 E
Minetto	113	43 24N	76 28W
Mingan	107	50 20N	64 0W
Mingechaur	57	40 45N	47 0 E
Mingechaurskoye Vdkhr.	57	40 56N	47 20 E
Mingela	98	19 52 S	146 38 E
Mingera Cr. →	98	20 38 S	138 10 E
Minggang	77	32 24N	114 3 E
Mingin	67	22 50N	94 30 E
Minglanilla	32	39 34N	1 38W
Mingorria	30	40 45N	4 40W
Mingxi	77	26 18N	117 12 E
Minićevo	42	43 42N	22 18 E
Minidoka	118	42 47N	113 34W
Minigwal L.	96	29 31 S	123 14 E
Minipi, L.	107	52 25N	60 45W
Mink L.	108	61 54N	117 40W
Minna	85	9 37N	6 30 E
Minneapolis, Kans., U.S.A.	116	39 11N	97 40W
Minneapolis, Minn., U.S.A.	116	44 58N	93 20W
Minnedosa	109	50 14N	99 50W
Minnesota □	116	46 40N	94 0W
Minnesund	47	60 23N	11 14 E
Minnitaki L.	106	49 57N	92 10W
Miño →	30	41 52N	8 40W
Minoa	45	35 6N	25 45 E
Minorca = Menorca	32	40 0N	4 0 E
Minore	99	32 14 S	148 27 E
Minot	116	48 10N	101 15W
Minqing	77	26 15N	118 50 E
Minquiers, Les	18	48 58N	2 8W
Minsen	24	53 43N	7 58 E
Minsk	54	53 52N	27 30 E
Mińsk Mazowiecki	28	52 10N	21 33 E
Mintaka Pass	69	37 0N	74 58 E
Minto	104	64 55N	149 20W
Minton	109	49 10N	104 35W
Minturn	118	39 35N	106 25W
Minturno	40	41 15N	13 43 E
Minûf	86	30 26N	30 52 E
Minusinsk	59	53 50N	91 20 E
Minutang	67	28 15N	96 30 E
Minvoul	88	2 9N	12 8 E
Minya el Qamh	86	30 31N	31 21 E
Mionica	42	44 14N	20 6 E
Mir	85	14 5N	11 59 E
Mir-Bashir	57	40 20N	46 58 E
Mira, Italy	39	45 26N	12 9 E
Mira, Port.	30	40 26N	8 44W
Mira →	31	37 43N	8 47W
Mirabella Eclano	41	41 3N	14 59 E
Miraflores Locks	120	8 59N	79 36W
Miraj	70	16 50N	74 45 E
Miram	98	21 15 S	148 55 E
Miramar, Argent.	124	38 15 S	57 50W
Miramar, Mozam.	93	23 50 S	35 35 E
Miramas	21	43 33N	4 59 E
Mirambeau	20	45 23N	0 35W
Miramichi B.	107	47 15N	65 0W
Miramont-de-Guyenne	20	44 37N	0 21 E
Miranda	127	20 10 S	56 15W
Miranda de Ebro	32	42 41N	2 57W
Miranda do Corvo	30	40 6N	8 20W
Miranda do Douro	30	41 30N	6 16W
Mirande	20	43 31N	0 25 E
Mirandela	30	41 32N	7 10W
Mirando City	117	27 28N	98 59W
Mirandola	38	44 53N	11 2 E
Mirandópolis	125	21 9 S	51 6W
Mirango	91	13 32 S	34 58 E
Mirano	39	45 29N	12 6 E
Mirassol	125	20 46 S	49 28W
Mirbāţ	63	17 0N	54 45 E
Mirear	86	23 15N	35 41 E
Mirebeau, Côte-d'or, France	19	47 25N	5 20 E
Mirebeau, Vienne, France	18	46 49N	0 10 E
Mirecourt	19	48 20N	6 10 E
Mirgorod	54	49 58N	33 37 E
Miri	72	4 18N	114 0 E
Miriam Vale	98	24 20 S	151 33 E
Mirim, Lagoa	125	32 45 S	52 50W
Mirnyy, Antarct.	5	66 33 S	93 1 E
Mirnyy, U.S.S.R.	59	62 33N	113 53 E
Miroč	42	44 32N	22 16 E
Mirond L.	109	55 6N	102 47W
Mirosławiec	28	53 20N	16 5 E
Mirpur Bibiwari	68	28 33N	67 44 E
Mirpur Khas	68	25 30N	69 0 E
Mirpur Sakro	68	24 33N	67 41 E
Mirria	85	13 43N	9 7 E
Mirror	108	52 30N	113 7W
Mîrşani	46	44 1N	23 59 E
Mirsk	28	50 58N	15 23 E
Miryang	76	35 31N	128 44 E
Mirzaani	57	41 24N	46 5 E
Mirzapur-cum-Vindhyachal	69	25 10N	82 34 E
Miscou I.	107	47 57N	64 31W
Mish'āb, Ra'as al	64	28 15N	48 43 E
Mishan	75	45 37N	131 48 E
Mishawaka	114	41 40N	86 8W
Mishbih, Gebel	86	22 38N	34 44 E
Mishima	74	35 10N	138 52 E
Mishmar Ayyalon	62	31 52N	34 57 E
Mishmar Ha' Emeq	62	32 37N	35 7 E
Mishmar Ha Negev	62	31 22N	34 48 E
Mishmar Ha Yarden	62	33 0N	35 36 E
Misilmeri	40	38 2N	13 25 E
Misima I.	98	10 40 S	152 45 E
Misiones □, Argent.	125	27 0 S	55 0W
Misiones □, Parag.	124	27 0 S	56 0W
Miskīn	65	23 44N	56 52 E
Miskitos, Cayos	121	14 26N	82 50W
Miskolc	27	48 7N	20 50 E
Misoke	90	0 42 S	28 2 E
Misool	73	1 52 S	130 10 E
Misrātah	83	32 24N	15 3 E
Misrātah □	83	29 0N	16 0 E
Misriç	64	37 55N	41 40 E
Missanabie	106	48 20N	84 6W
Missinaibi →	106	50 43N	81 29W
Missinaibi L.	106	48 23N	83 40W
Mission, S.D., U.S.A.	116	43 21N	100 36W
Mission, Tex., U.S.A.	117	26 15N	98 20W
Mission City	108	49 10N	122 15W
Missisa L.	106	52 20N	85 7W
Mississagi →	106	46 15N	83 9W
Mississippi →	117	29 0N	89 15W
Mississippi, Delta of the	117	29 15N	90 30W
Mississippi L.	113	45 5N	76 10W
Mississippi □	117	33 25N	89 0W
Missoula	118	46 52N	114 0W
Missouri □	116	38 25N	92 30W
Missouri →	116	38 50N	90 8W
Missouri Valley	116	41 33N	95 53W
Mistake B.	109	62 8N	93 0W
Mistassini →	107	48 42N	72 20W
Mistassini L.	106	51 0N	73 30W
Mistastin L.	107	55 57N	63 20W
Mistatim	109	52 52N	103 22W
Mistelbach	27	48 34N	16 34 E
Misterbianco	41	37 32N	15 0 E
Mistretta	41	37 56N	14 20 E
Misty L.	109	58 53N	101 40W
Mît Ghamr	86	30 42N	31 12 E
Mitatib	87	15 59N	36 12 E
Mitchell, Austral.	97	26 29 S	147 58 E
Mitchell, Can.	112	43 28N	81 12W
Mitchell, Ind., U.S.A.	114	38 42N	86 25W
Mitchell, Nebr., U.S.A.	116	41 58N	103 45W
Mitchell, Oreg., U.S.A.	118	44 31N	120 8W
Mitchell, S.D., U.S.A.	116	43 40N	98 0W
Mitchell →	97	15 12 S	141 35 E
Mitchell, Mt.	115	35 40N	82 20W
Mitchelstown	15	52 16N	8 18W
Mitha Tiwana	68	32 13N	72 6 E
Míthimna	44	39 20N	26 12 E
Mitiaro, I.	101	19 49 S	157 43W
Mitilíni	45	39 6N	26 35 E
Mitilinoí	45	37 42N	26 56 E
Mitla	120	16 55N	96 24W
Mito	74	36 20N	140 30 E
Mitsinjo	93	16 1 S	45 52 E
Mitsiwa	87	15 35N	39 25 E
Mitsiwa Channel	87	15 30N	40 0 E
Mitta Mitta →	100	36 14 S	147 10 E
Mittagong	99	34 28 S	150 29 E
Mittelland Kanal	24	52 23N	7 45 E
Mittenwalde	24	52 16N	13 33 E
Mitterteich	25	49 57N	12 15 E
Mittweida	24	50 59N	13 0 E
Mitú	126	1 8N	70 3W
Mitumba	90	7 8 S	31 2 E
Mitumba, Chaîne des	90	6 0 S	29 0 E
Mitwaba	91	8 2 S	27 17 E
Mityana	90	0 23N	32 2 E
Mitzic	88	0 45N	11 40 E
Mixteco →	120	18 11N	98 30W
Miyagi □	74	38 15N	140 45 E
Miyâh, W. el →	86	25 0N	33 23 E
Miyake-Jima	74	34 0N	139 30 E
Miyako	74	39 40N	141 59 E
Miyakonojō	74	31 40N	131 5 E
Miyazaki	74	31 56N	131 30 E
Miyazaki □	74	32 30N	131 30 E
Miyazu	74	35 35N	135 10 E
Miyet, Bahr el	64	31 30N	35 30 E
Miyun	76	40 28N	116 50 E
Mizal	64	23 59N	45 11 E
Mizamis = Ozamiz	73	8 15N	123 50 E
Mizdah	83	31 30N	13 0 E
Mizen Hd., Cork, Ireland	15	51 27N	9 50W
Mizen Hd., Wicklow, Ireland	15	52 52N	6 4W
Mizhi	76	37 47N	110 12 E
Mizil	46	44 59N	26 29 E
Mizoram □	67	23 30N	92 40 E
Mizpe Ramon	62	30 34N	34 49 E
Mjöbäck	49	57 28N	12 53 E
Mjölby	49	58 20N	15 10 E
Mjømna	47	60 55N	4 55 E
Mjörn	49	57 55N	12 25 E
Mjøsa	47	60 48N	11 0 E
Mkata	90	5 45 S	38 20 E
Mkokotoni	90	5 55 S	39 15 E
Mkomazi	90	4 40 S	38 7 E
Mkulwe	91	8 37 S	32 20 E
Mkumbi, Ras	90	7 38 S	39 55 E
Mkushi	91	14 25 S	29 15 E
Mkushi River	91	13 32 S	29 45 E
Mkuze →	93	27 45 S	32 30 E
Mladá Boleslav	26	50 27N	14 53 E
Mladenovac	42	44 28N	20 44 E
Mlala Hills	90	6 50 S	31 40 E
Mlange	91	16 2 S	35 33 E
Mlava →	42	44 45N	21 13 E
Mława	28	53 9N	20 25 E
Mlinište	39	44 15N	16 50 E
Mljet	42	42 43N	17 30 E
Mljetski Kanal	42	42 48N	17 35 E
Młynąry	28	54 12N	19 46 E
Młynary	28	54 12N	19 43 E
Mme	85	6 18N	10 14 E
Mo	47	59 28N	7 50 E
Mo i Rana	50	66 15N	14 7 E
Moa	73	8 0 S	128 0 E
Moa →	84	6 59N	11 36 E
Moab	119	38 40N	109 35W
Moabi	88	2 24 S	10 59 E
Moala	101	18 36 S	179 53 E
Moalie Park	99	29 42 S	143 3 E
Moaña	30	42 18N	8 43W
Moapa	119	36 45N	114 37W
Moba	90	7 0 S	29 48 E
Mobaye	88	4 25N	21 5 E
Mobayi	88	4 15N	21 8 E
Moberley	116	39 25N	92 25W
Moberly →	108	56 12N	120 55W
Mobile	115	30 41N	88 3W
Mobile B.	115	30 30N	88 0W
Mobile, Pt.	115	30 15N	88 0W
Mobridge	116	45 31N	100 28W
Mobutu Sese Seko, L.	90	1 30N	31 0 E

* *Renamed Bohol Sea*

Mocabe Kasari Moosup

Mocabe Kasari 91 9 58S 26 12E
Moçambique 91 15 3S 40 42E
Moçambique □ 91 14 45S 38 30E
* Moçâmedes 89 15 7S 12 11E
* Moçâmedes □ 92 16 35S 12 30E
Mochudi 92 24 27S 26 7E
Mocimboa da Praia 91 11 25S 40 20E
Mociu 46 46 40N 24 3E
Möckeln 49 56 40N 14 15E
Moclips 118 47 14N 124 10W
Mocoa 126 1 7N 76 35W
Mococa 125 21 28S 47 0W
Mocorito 120 25 30N 107 53W
Moctezuma 120 29 50N 109 0W
Moctezuma → 120 21 59N 98 34W
Mocuba 91 16 54S 36 57E
Modalen 47 60 49N 5 48E
Modane 21 45 12N 6 40E
Modasa 68 23 30N 73 21E
Modder → 92 29 2S 24 37E
Modderrivier 92 29 2S 24 38E
Módena 38 44 39N 10 55E
Modena 119 37 55N 113 56W
Modesto 119 37 43N 121 0W
Módica 41 36 52N 14 45E
Modigliana 39 44 9N 11 48E
Modlin 28 52 24N 20 41E
Mödling 27 48 5N 16 17E
Modo 87 5 31N 30 33E
Modra 27 48 19N 17 20E
Modriča 42 44 57N 18 17E
Moe 97 38 12S 146 19E
Moebase 91 17 3S 38 41E
Moei → 71 17 25N 98 10E
Moëlan-sur-Mer 18 47 49N 3 38W
Moengo 127 5 45N 54 20W
Moffat 14 55 20N 3 27W
Moga 68 30 48N 75 8E
Mogadishu = Muqdisho 63 2 2N 45 25E
Mogador = Essaouira 82 31 32N 9 48W
Mogadouro 30 41 22N 6 47W
Mogami → 74 38 45N 140 0E
Mogaung 67 25 20N 97 0E
Møgeltønder 49 54 57N 8 48E
Mogente 33 38 52N 0 45W
Mogho 87 4 54N 40 16E
Mogi das Cruzes 125 23 31S 46 11W
Mogi-Guaçu → 125 20 53S 48 10W
Mogi-Mirim 125 22 29S 47 0W
Mogielnica 28 51 42N 20 41E
Mogilev 54 53 55N 30 18E
Mogilev-Podolskiy 56 48 20N 27 40E
Mogilno 28 52 39N 17 55E
Mogincual 91 15 35S 40 25E
Mogliano Véneto 39 45 33N 12 15E
Mogocha 59 53 40N 119 50E
Mogoi 73 1 55S 133 10E
Mogok 67 23 0N 96 40E
Mogollon 119 33 25N 108 48W
Mogollon Mesa 119 35 0N 111 0W
Moguer 31 37 15N 6 52W
Mohács 27 45 58N 18 41E
Mohall 116 48 46N 101 30W
Moḩammadābād 65 37 52N 59 5E
Mohammadia 82 35 33N 0 3E
Mohammedia 82 33 44N 7 21W
Mohawk 119 32 45N 113 50W
Mohawk → 113 42 47N 73 42W
Mohe 76 53 28N 122 17E
Moheda 49 57 1N 14 35E
Möhne → 24 51 29N 7 57E
Moholm 49 58 37N 14 5E
Mohon 19 49 45N 4 44E
Mohoro 90 8 6S 39 8E
Moia 87 5 3N 28 2E
Moidart, L. 14 56 47N 5 40W
Moinabad 70 17 44N 77 16E
Moineşti 46 46 28N 26 31E
Mointy 58 47 10N 73 18E
Moirans 21 45 20N 5 33E
Moirans-en-Montagne 21 46 26N 5 43E
Moires 45 35 4N 24 56E
Moisakula 54 58 3N 25 12E
Moisie 107 50 12N 66 1W
Moisie → 107 50 14N 66 5W
Moissac 20 44 7N 1 5E
Moïssala 81 8 21N 17 46E
Moita 31 38 38N 8 58W
Mojácar 33 37 6N 1 55W
Mojados 30 41 26N 4 40W
Mojave 119 35 8N 118 8W
Mojave Desert 119 35 0N 116 30W
Mojo, Boliv. 124 21 48S 65 33W
Mojo, Ethiopia 87 8 35N 39 5E
Mojo, Indon. 72 8 10S 117 40E
Mojokerto 73 7 29S 112 25E
Mokai 101 38 32S 175 56E
Mokambo 91 12 25S 28 20E
Mokameh 69 25 24N 85 55E
Mokhós 45 35 16N 25 27E
Mokhotlong 93 29 22S 29 2E
Moknine 83 35 35N 10 58E
Mokokchung 67 26 15N 94 30E
Mokra Gora 42 42 50N 20 30E
Mokronog 39 45 57N 15 9E
Moksha → 55 54 45N 41 53E
Mokshan 55 53 25N 44 35E
Mol 16 51 11N 5 5E
Mola, C. de la 32 39 40N 4 20E
Mola di Bari 41 41 3N 17 5E
Moláoi 45 36 49N 22 56E
Molat 39 44 15N 14 50E
Molchanovo 58 57 40N 83 50E
Mold 12 53 10N 3 10W
Moldava nad Bodvou 27 48 38N 21 0E
Moldavia = Moldova 46 46 30N 27 0E
Moldavian S.S.R. □ 56 47 0N 28 0E
Molde 47 62 45N 7 9E
Moldova 46 46 30N 27 0E
Moldova Nouă 42 44 45N 21 41E
Moldoveanu 43 45 36N 24 45E
Molepolole 92 24 28S 25 28E
Molfetta 41 41 12N 16 35E
Molina de Aragón 32 40 46N 1 52W
Moline 116 41 30N 90 30W
Molinella 39 44 38N 11 40E
Molinos 124 25 28S 66 15W
Moliro 90 8 12S 30 30E
Molise □ 39 41 45N 14 30E
Moliterno 41 40 14N 15 50E
Mollahat 69 22 56N 89 48E
Mölle 49 56 17N 12 31E
Molledo 30 43 8N 4 6W
Mollendo 126 17 0S 72 0W
Mollerusa 32 41 37N 0 54E
Mollina 31 37 8N 4 38W
Mölln 24 53 37N 10 41E
Mölltorp 49 58 30N 14 26E
Mölndal 49 57 40N 12 3E
Molochansk 56 47 15N 35 35E
Molochnaya → 56 47 0N 35 30E
Molodechno 54 54 20N 26 50E
Molokai 110 21 8N 157 0W
Moloma → 55 58 20N 48 15E
Molong 99 33 5S 148 54E
Molopo → 92 28 30S 20 13E
Mólos 45 38 47N 22 37E
Moloundou 88 2 8N 15 15E
Molsheim 19 48 33N 7 29E
Molson L. 109 54 22N 96 40W
Molteno 92 31 22S 26 22E
Molu 73 6 45S 131 40E
Molucca Sea 73 4 0S 124 0E
Moluccas = Maluku 73 1 0S 127 0E
Molusi 92 20 21S 24 29E
Moma, Mozam. 91 16 47S 39 4E
Moma, Zaïre 90 1 35S 23 52E
Momanga 92 18 7S 21 41E
Mombasa 90 4 2S 39 43E
Mombuey 30 42 3N 6 20W
Momchilgrad 43 41 33N 25 23E
Momi 90 1 42S 27 0E
Mompós 126 9 14N 74 26W
Møn 49 54 57N 12 15E
Mon → 67 20 25N 94 30E
Mona, Canal de la 121 18 30N 67 45W
Mona, I. 121 18 5N 67 54W
Mona, Pta. 121 9 37N 82 36W
Mona, Punta 31 36 43N 3 45W
Monach Is. 14 57 32N 7 40W
Monaco ■ 21 43 46N 7 23E
Monadhliath Mts. 14 57 10N 4 4W
Monaghan 15 54 15N 6 58W
Monaghan □ 15 54 10N 7 0W
Monahans 117 31 35N 102 50W
Monapo 91 14 56S 40 19E
Monarch Mt. 108 51 55N 125 57W
Monastier-sur-Gazeille, Le 20 44 57N 3 59E
Monastir 83 35 50N 10 49E
Monastyriska 54 49 8N 25 14E
Moncada 32 39 30N 0 24W
Moncalieri 38 45 0N 7 40E
Moncalvo 38 45 3N 8 15E
Moncão 30 42 4N 8 27W
Moncarapacho 31 37 5N 7 46W
Moncayo, Sierra del 32 41 48N 1 50W
Mönchengladbach 24 51 12N 6 23E
Monchique 31 37 19N 8 38W
Monclova 120 26 50N 101 30W
Moncontour 18 48 22N 2 38W
Moncoutant 18 46 43N 0 35W
Moncton 107 46 7N 64 51W
Mondego → 30 40 9N 8 52W
Mondego, Cabo 30 40 11N 8 54W
Mondeodo 73 3 34S 122 9E
Mondolfo 39 43 45N 13 8E
Mondoñedo 30 43 25N 7 23W
Mondovì 38 44 23N 7 49E
Mondovi 116 44 37N 91 40W
Mondragon 21 44 13N 4 44E
Mondragone 40 41 8N 13 52E
Monduli □ 90 3 0S 36 0E
Monemvasia 45 36 41N 23 3E
Monessen 114 40 9N 79 50W
Monesterio 31 38 6N 6 15W
Monestier-de-Clermont 21 44 55N 5 38E
Monêtier-les-Bains, Le 21 44 58N 6 30E
Monett 117 36 55N 93 56W
Monfalcone 39 45 49N 13 32E
Monflanquin 20 44 32N 0 47E
Monforte 31 39 6N 7 25W
Monforte de Lemos 30 42 31N 7 33W
Mong Cai 71 21 27N 107 54E
Mong Hsu 67 21 54N 98 30E
Mong Kung 67 21 35N 97 35E
Mong Lang 71 21 29N 97 52E
Mong Nai 67 20 32N 97 46E
Mong Pawk 67 22 4N 99 16E
Mong Ton 67 20 17N 98 45E
Mong Wa 67 21 26N 100 27E
Mong Yai 67 22 21N 98 3E
Mongalla 87 5 8N 31 42E
Mongers, L. 96 29 25S 117 5E
Monghyr 69 25 23N 86 30E
Mongla 69 22 8N 89 35E
Mongo 81 12 14N 18 43E
Mongolia ■ 75 47 0N 103 0E
Mongonu 85 12 40N 13 32E
Mongororo 81 12 3N 22 26E
Mongu 89 15 16S 23 12E
Môngua 92 16 43S 15 20E
Monistrol 20 45 57N 3 38E
Monistrol-St-Loire 21 45 17N 4 11E
Monkey Bay 91 14 7S 35 1E
Mońki 28 53 23N 22 48E
Monkira 98 24 46S 140 30E
Monkoto 88 1 38S 20 35E
Monmouth, U.K. 13 51 48N 2 43W
Monmouth, U.S.A. 116 40 50N 90 40W
Mono, L. 119 38 0N 119 9W
Monongahela 112 40 12N 79 56W
Monópoli 41 40 57N 17 18E
Monor 27 47 21N 19 27E
Monóvar 33 38 28N 0 53W
Monqoumba 88 3 33N 18 40E
Monreal del Campo 32 40 47N 1 20W
Monreale 40 38 6N 13 16E
Monroe, Ga., U.S.A. 115 33 47N 83 43W
Monroe, La., U.S.A. 117 32 32N 92 4W
Monroe, Mich., U.S.A. 114 41 55N 83 26W
Monroe, N.C., U.S.A. 115 35 2N 80 37W
Monroe, N.Y., U.S.A. 113 41 19N 74 11W
Monroe, Utah, U.S.A. 119 38 45N 112 5W
Monroe, Wis., U.S.A. 116 42 38N 89 40W
Monroe City 116 39 40N 91 40W
Monroeville 115 31 33N 87 15W
Monrovia, Liberia 84 6 18N 10 47W
Monrovia, U.S.A. 119 34 7N 118 1W
Mons 16 50 27N 3 58E
Monsaraz 31 38 28N 7 22W
Monse 73 4 0S 123 10E
Monségur 20 44 38N 0 4E
Monsélice 39 45 16N 11 46E
Mont-de-Marsan 20 43 54N 0 31W
Mont d'Or, Tunnel 19 46 45N 6 18E
Mont-Dore, Le 20 45 35N 2 50E
Mont-Joli 107 48 37N 68 10W
Mont Laurier 106 46 35N 75 30W
Mont-sous-Vaudrey 19 46 58N 5 36E
Mont-St-Michel, Le 18 48 40N 1 30W
Mont Tremblant Prov. Park 106 46 30N 74 30W
Montabaur 24 50 26N 7 49E
Montagnac 20 43 29N 3 28E
Montagnana 39 45 13N 11 29E
Montagu 92 33 45S 20 8E
Montagu I. 5 58 25S 26 20W
Montague, Can. 107 46 10N 62 39W
Montague, Calif., U.S.A. 118 41 47N 122 30W
Montague, Mass., U.S.A. 113 42 31N 72 33W
Montague, I. 120 31 40N 114 56W
Montague I. 104 60 0N 147 0W
Montague Sd. 96 14 28S 125 20E
Montaigu 18 46 59N 1 18W
Montalbán 32 40 50N 0 45W
Montalbano di Elicona 41 38 1N 15 0E
Montalbano Iónico 41 40 17N 16 33E
Montalbo 32 39 53N 2 42W
Montalcino 39 43 4N 11 30E
Montalegre 30 41 49N 7 47W
Montalto di Castro 39 42 20N 11 36E
Montalto Uffugo 41 39 25N 16 9E
Montamarta 30 41 39N 5 49W
Montaña 126 6 0S 73 0W
Montana □ 110 47 0N 110 0W
Montánchez 31 39 15N 6 8W
Montargis 19 48 0N 2 43E
Montauban 20 44 0N 1 21E
Montauk 114 41 3N 71 57W
Montauk Pt. 113 41 4N 71 52W
Montbard 19 47 38N 4 20E
Montbéliard 19 47 31N 6 48E
Montblanch 32 41 23N 1 4E
Montbrison 21 45 36N 4 3E
Montcalm, Pic de 20 42 40N 1 25E
Montceau-les-Mines 19 46 40N 4 23E
Montchanin 38 46 47N 4 30E
Montclair 113 40 53N 74 13W
Montcornet 19 49 40N 4 0E
Montcuq 20 44 21N 1 13E
Montdidier 19 49 38N 2 35E
Monte Alegre 127 2 0S 54 0W
Monte Azul 127 15 9S 42 53W
Monte Bello Is. 96 20 30S 115 45E
Monte-Carlo 21 43 46N 7 23E
Monte Caseros 124 30 10S 57 50W
Monte Comán 124 34 40S 67 53W
Monte Lindo → 124 23 56S 57 12W
Monte Quemado 124 25 53S 62 41W
Monte Redondo 30 39 53N 8 50W
Monte San Giovanni 40 41 39N 13 33E
Monte San Savino 39 43 20N 11 42E
Monte Sant' Ángelo 41 41 42N 15 59E
Monte Santu, C. di 40 40 5N 9 42E
Monte Vista 119 37 40N 106 8W
Monteagudo 125 27 14S 54 8W
Montealegre 33 38 48N 1 17W
Montebello 106 45 40N 74 55W
Montebelluna 39 45 47N 12 3E
Montebourg 18 49 30N 1 20W
Montecastrilli 39 42 40N 12 30E
Montecatini Terme 38 43 55N 10 48E
Montecristi 126 1 0S 80 40W
Montecristo 38 42 20N 10 20E
Montefalco 39 42 53N 12 38E
Montefiascone 39 42 31N 12 2E
Montefrío 31 37 20N 4 0W
Montego Bay 121 18 30N 78 0W
Montegranaro 39 43 13N 13 38E
Montehanin 19 46 46N 4 44E
Montejicar 33 37 33N 3 30W
Montélimar 21 44 33N 4 45E
Montella 41 40 50N 15 0E
Montellano 31 36 59N 5 36W
Montello 116 43 49N 89 21W
Montelupo Fiorentino 38 43 44N 11 2E
Montemor-o-Novo 31 38 40N 8 12W
Montemor-o-Velho 30 40 11N 8 40W
Montemorelos 120 25 11N 99 42W
Montendre 20 45 16N 0 26W
Montenegro 125 29 39S 51 29W
Montenegro = Crna Gora □ 42 42 40N 19 20E
Montenero di Bisaccia 39 42 0N 14 47E
Montepuez 91 13 8S 38 59E
Montepuez → 91 12 32S 40 27E
Montepulciano 39 43 5N 11 46E
Montereale 39 42 31N 13 13E
Montereau 19 48 22N 2 57E
Monterey 119 36 35N 121 57W
Montería 126 8 46N 75 53W
Monteros 124 27 11S 65 30W
Monterotondo 39 42 3N 12 36E
Monterrey 120 25 40N 100 30W
Montes Claros 127 16 30S 43 50W
Montesano 118 47 0N 123 39W
Montesárchio 41 41 5N 14 37E
Montescaglioso 41 40 34N 16 40E
Montesilvano 39 42 30N 14 8E
Montevarchi 39 43 30N 11 32E
Montevideo 125 34 50S 56 11W
Montezuma 116 41 32N 92 35W
Montfaucon, Haute-Loire, France 21 45 11N 4 20E
Montfaucon, Meuse, France 19 49 16N 5 8E
Montfort-l'Amaury 19 48 47N 1 49E
Montfort-sur-Meu 18 48 8N 1 58W
Montgenèvre 21 44 56N 6 42E
Montgomery, U.K. 13 52 34N 3 9W
Montgomery, Ala., U.S.A. 115 32 20N 86 20W
Montgomery, W. Va., U.S.A. 114 38 9N 81 21W
Montgomery = Sahiwal 68 30 45N 73 8E
Montguyon 20 45 12N 0 12W
Monthey 25 46 15N 6 56E
Monticelli d'Ongina 38 45 3N 9 56E
Monticello, Ark., U.S.A. 117 33 40N 91 48W
Monticello, Fla., U.S.A. 115 30 35N 83 50W
Monticello, Ind., U.S.A. 114 40 40N 86 45W
Monticello, Iowa, U.S.A. 116 42 18N 91 12W
Monticello, Ky., U.S.A. 115 36 52N 84 50W
Monticello, Minn., U.S.A. 116 45 17N 93 52W
Monticello, Miss., U.S.A. 117 31 35N 90 8W
Monticello, N.Y., U.S.A. 113 41 37N 74 42W
Monticello, Utah, U.S.A. 119 37 55N 109 27W
Montichiari 38 45 28N 10 29E
Montier 19 48 30N 4 45E
Montignac 20 45 4N 1 10E
Montigny-les-Metz 19 49 7N 6 10E
Montigny-sur-Aube 19 47 57N 4 45E
Montijo 31 38 52N 6 39W
Montijo, Presa de 31 38 55N 6 26W
Montilla 31 37 36N 4 40W
Montivideo 116 44 55N 95 40W
Montlhéry 19 48 39N 2 15E
Montluçon 20 46 22N 2 36E
Montmagny 107 46 58N 70 34W
Montmarault 20 46 19N 2 57E
Montmartre 109 50 14N 103 27W
Montmédy 19 49 30N 5 20E
Montmélian 21 45 30N 6 4E
Montmirail 19 48 51N 3 30E
Montmoreau-St-Cybard 20 45 23N 0 8E
Montmorency 107 46 53N 71 11W
Montmorillon 20 46 26N 0 50E
Montmort 19 48 55N 3 49E
Monto 97 24 52S 151 6E
Montoire 18 47 45N 0 52E
Montório al Vomano 39 42 35N 13 38E
Montoro 31 38 1N 4 27W
Montour Falls 112 42 20N 76 51W
Montpelier, Idaho, U.S.A. 118 42 15N 111 20W
Montpelier, Ohio, U.S.A. 114 41 34N 84 40W
Montpelier, Vt., U.S.A. 114 44 15N 72 38W
Montpellier 20 43 37N 3 52E
Montpezat-de-Quercy 20 44 15N 1 30E
Montpon 20 45 2N 0 11E
Montréal, Can. 106 45 31N 73 34W
Montréal, France 20 43 13N 2 8E
Montreal L. 109 54 20N 105 45W
Montreal Lake 109 54 3N 105 46W
Montredon-Labessonnié 20 43 45N 2 18E
Montréjeau 20 43 6N 0 35E
Montrésor 18 47 10N 1 10E
Montreuil 19 50 27N 1 45E
Montreuil-Bellay 18 47 8N 0 9W
Montreux 25 46 26N 6 55E
Montrevault 18 47 17N 1 2W
Montrevel-en-Bresse 21 46 21N 5 8E
Montrichard 18 47 20N 1 10E
Montrose, U.K. 14 56 43N 2 28W
Montrose, Col., U.S.A. 119 38 30N 107 52W
Montrose, Pa., U.S.A. 113 41 50N 75 55W
Monts, Pte des 107 49 20N 67 12W
Monts-sur-Guesnes 18 46 55N 0 13E
Montsalvy 20 44 41N 2 30E
Montsant, Sierra de 32 41 17N 1 0E
Montsauche 19 47 13N 4 0E
Montsech, Sierra del 32 42 0N 0 45E
Montseny 32 41 55N 2 25W
Montserrat, Spain 32 41 36N 1 49E
Montserrat, W. Indies 121 16 40N 62 10W
Montuenga 30 41 3N 4 38W
Montuiri 32 39 34N 2 59E
Monveda 88 2 52N 21 30E
Monywa 67 22 7N 95 11E
Monza 38 45 35N 9 15E
Monze 91 16 17S 27 29E
Monze, C. 66 24 47N 66 37E
Monzón 32 41 52N 0 10E
Moolawatana 99 29 55S 139 45E
Moonah → 98 22 3S 138 33E
Moonbeam 106 49 20N 82 10W
Moonie 99 27 46S 150 20E
Moonie → 97 29 19S 148 43E
Moonta 99 34 6S 137 32E
Mooraberree 98 25 13S 140 54E
Moorcroft 116 44 17N 104 58W
Moore, L. 96 29 50S 117 35E
Moorefield 114 39 5N 78 59W
Moores Res. 113 44 45N 71 50W
Mooresville 115 35 36N 80 45W
Moorfoot Hills 14 55 44N 3 8W
Moorhead 116 46 51N 96 44W
Mooroopna 99 36 25S 145 22E
Moorreesburg 92 33 6S 18 38E
Moosburg 25 48 28N 11 57E
Moose → 106 51 20N 80 25W
Moose Factory 106 51 16N 80 32W
Moose I. 109 51 42N 97 10W
Moose Jaw 109 50 24N 105 30W
Moose Jaw Cr. → 109 50 34N 105 18W
Moose Lake, Can. 109 53 43N 100 20W
Moose Lake, U.S.A. 116 46 27N 92 48W
Moose Mountain Cr. → 109 49 13N 102 12W
Moose Mountain Prov. Park 109 49 48N 102 25W
Moose River 106 50 48N 81 17W
Moosehead L. 107 45 34N 69 40W
Moosomin 109 50 9N 101 40W
Moosonee 106 51 17N 80 39W
Moosup 113 41 44N 71 52W

* *Renamed Namibe*

Mopipi Mullsjö

Mopipi 92 21 6S 24 55 E
Mopoi 90 5 6N 26 54 E
Mopti 84 14 30N 4 0W
Moqatta 87 14 38N 35 50 E
Moquegua 126 17 15S 70 46W
Mór 27 47 25N 18 12 E
Móra 31 38 55N 8 10W
Mora, Sweden 48 61 2N 14 38 E
Mora, Minn., U.S.A. 116 45 52N 93 19W
Mora, N. Mex., U.S.A. 119 35 58N 105 21W
Mora de Ebro 32 41 6N 0 38 E
Mora de Rubielos 32 40 15N 0 45W
Mora la Nueva 32 41 7N 0 39 E
Morača → 42 42 20N 19 9 E
Moradabad 68 28 50N 78 50 E
Morafenobe 93 17 50S 44 53 E
Morąg 28 53 55N 19 56 E
Moral de Calatrava 33 38 51N 3 33W
Moraleja 30 40 6N 6 43W
Moran, Kans., U.S.A. 117 37 53N 94 35W
Moran, Wyo., U.S.A. 118 43 53N 110 37W
Morano Cálabro 41 39 51N 16 8 E
Morant Cays 121 17 22N 76 0W
Morant Pt. 121 17 55N 76 12W
Morar L. 14 56 57N 5 40W
Moratalla 33 38 14N 1 49W
Moratuwa 70 6 45N 79 55 E
Morava → 27 48 10N 16 59 E
Moravia 116 40 50N 92 50W
Moravian Hts. = Ceskemoravská V. 26 49 30N 15 40 E
Moravica → 42 43 52N 20 8 E
Moravice → 27 49 50N 17 43 E
Moravita 42 45 17N 21 14 E
Moravská Třebová 27 49 45N 16 40 E
Moravské Budějovice 26 49 4N 15 49 E
Morawhanna 126 8 30N 59 40W
Moray Firth 14 57 50N 3 30W
Morbach 25 49 48N 7 7 E
Morbegno 38 46 8N 9 34 E
Morbihan □ 18 47 55N 2 50W
Morcenx 20 44 0N 0 55W
Mordelles 18 48 5N 1 52W
Morden 109 49 15N 98 10W
Mordialloc 100 38 1S 145 6 E
Mordovian A.S.S.R. □ 55 54 20N 44 30 E
Mordovo 55 52 6N 40 50 E
Mordy 28 52 13N 22 31 E
Møre og Romsdal fylke □ 47 62 30N 8 0 E
Morea 9 37 45N 22 10 E
Moreau → 116 45 15N 100 43W
Morecambe 12 54 5N 2 52W
Morecambe B. 12 54 7N 3 0W
Moree 97 29 28S 149 54 E
Morehead 114 38 12N 83 22W
Morehead City 115 34 46N 76 44W
Morelia 120 19 40N 101 11W
Morella, Austral. 98 23 0S 143 52 E
Morella, Spain 32 40 35N 0 5W
Morelos □ 120 18 40N 99 10W
Morena, Sierra 31 38 20N 4 0W
Morenci 119 33 7N 109 20W
Moreni 46 44 59N 25 36 E
Moresby I. 108 52 30N 131 40W
Morestel 21 45 40N 5 28 E
Moret 19 48 22N 2 58 E
Moreton 98 12 22S 142 30 E
Moreton B. 97 27 10S 153 10 E
Moreton I. 97 27 10S 153 25 E
Moreuil 19 49 46N 2 30 E
Morez 21 46 31N 6 2 E
Morgan, Austral. 99 34 0S 139 35 E
Morgan, U.S.A. 118 41 3N 111 44W
Morgan City 117 29 40N 91 15W
Morganfield 114 37 40N 87 55W
Morganton 115 35 46N 81 48W
Morgantown 114 39 39N 79 58W
Morganville 99 25 10S 151 50 E
Morgat 18 48 15N 4 32W
Morgenzon 93 26 45S 29 36 E
Morges 25 46 31N 6 29 E
Morhange 19 48 55N 6 38 E
Mori 38 45 51N 10 59 E
Moriarty 119 35 3N 106 2W
Morice L. 108 53 50N 127 40W
Moriki 85 12 52N 6 30 E
Morinville 108 53 49N 113 41W
Morioka 74 39 45N 141 8 E
Morkalla 99 34 23S 141 10 E
Morlaàs 20 43 21N 0 18W
Morlaix 18 48 36N 3 52W
Mormanno 41 39 53N 15 59 E
Mormant 19 48 37N 2 52 E
Mornington 99 38 15S 145 5 E
Mornington I. 97 16 30S 139 30 E
Mornington, I. 128 49 50S 75 30W
Mórnos → 45 38 30N 22 0 E
Moro 87 10 50N 30 9 E
Moro G. 73 6 30N 123 0 E
Morobe 98 7 49S 147 38 E
Morocco ■ 82 32 0N 5 50W
Morococha 126 11 40S 76 5W
Morogoro 90 6 50S 37 40 E
Morogoro □ 90 8 0S 37 0 E
Moroleón 120 20 8N 101 32W
Morombe 93 21 45S 43 22 E
Moron 124 34 39S 58 37W
Morón 121 22 8N 78 39W
Mörön → 75 47 14N 110 37 E
Morón de Almazán 32 41 29N 2 27W
Morón de la Frontera 31 37 6N 5 28W
Morondava 93 20 17S 44 17 E
Morondo 84 8 57N 6 47W
Moronou 84 6 16N 4 59W
Morotai 73 2 10N 128 30 E
Moroto 90 2 28N 34 42 E
Moroto Summit 90 2 30N 34 43 E
Morozov (Bratan) 43 42 30N 25 10 E
Morozovsk 57 48 25N 41 50 E
Morpeth 12 55 11N 1 41W
Morphou 64 35 12N 32 59 E
Morrilton 117 35 10N 92 45W
Morrinhos 127 17 45S 49 10W
Morrinsville 101 37 40S 175 32 E
Morris, Can. 109 49 25N 97 22W
Morris, Ill., U.S.A. 114 41 20N 88 20W
Morris, Minn., U.S.A. 116 45 33N 95 56W
Morrisburg 106 44 55N 75 7W
Morrison 116 41 47N 90 0W
Morristown, Ariz., U.S.A. 119 33 54N 112 35W
Morristown, N.J., U.S.A. 113 40 48N 74 30W
Morristown, S.D., U.S.A. 116 45 57N 101 44W
Morristown, Tenn., U.S.A. 115 36 18N 83 20W
Morro Bay 119 35 27N 120 54W
Morro, Pta. 124 27 6S 71 0W
Morrosquillo, Golfo de 121 9 35N 75 40W
Mörrum 49 56 12N 14 45 E
Mors 49 56 50N 8 45 E
Morshansk 55 53 28N 41 50 E
Mörsil 48 63 19N 13 40 E
Mortagne 20 45 28N 0 49W
Mortagne → 19 48 33N 6 27 E
Mortagne-au-Perche 18 48 31N 0 33 E
Mortain 18 48 40N 0 57W
Mortara 38 45 15N 8 43 E
Morteau 19 47 3N 6 35 E
Morteros 124 30 50S 62 0W
Mortes, R. das → 127 11 45S 50 44W
Mortlake 99 38 5S 142 50 E
Morton, Tex., U.S.A. 117 33 39N 102 49W
Morton, Wash., U.S.A. 118 46 33N 122 17W
Morundah 99 34 57S 146 19 E
Moruya 99 35 58S 150 3 E
Morvan, Mts. du 19 47 5N 4 0 E
Morven 99 26 22S 147 5 E
Morvern 14 56 38N 5 44W
Morvi 68 22 50N 70 42 E
Morwell 97 38 10S 146 22 E
Moryn 28 52 51N 14 22 E
Morzhovets, Ostrov 52 66 44N 42 35 E
Mosalsk 54 54 30N 34 55 E
Mosbach 25 49 21N 9 9 E
Moščenice 39 45 17N 14 16 E
Mosciano Sant' Ángelo 39 42 42N 13 52 E
Moscos Is. 72 14 0N 97 30 E
Moscow 118 46 45N 116 59W
Moscow = Moskva 55 55 45N 37 35 E
Mosel → 16 50 22N 7 36 E
Moselle = Mosel → 16 50 22N 7 36 E
Moselle □ 19 48 59N 6 33 E
Moses Lake 118 47 9N 119 17W
Mosgiel 101 45 53S 170 21 E
Moshi 90 3 22S 37 18 E
Moshi □ 90 3 22S 37 18 E
Moshupa 92 24 46S 25 29 E
Mośina 28 52 15N 16 50 E
Mosjøen 50 65 51N 13 12 E
Moskenesøya 50 67 58N 13 0 E
Moskenstraumen 50 67 47N 12 45 E
Moskva 55 55 45N 37 35 E
Moskva → 55 55 5N 38 51 E
Moslavačka Gora 39 45 40N 16 37 E
Mosomane (Artesia) 92 24 2S 26 19 E
Mosonmagyaróvár 27 47 52N 17 18 E
Mošorin 42 45 19N 20 4 E
Mospino 56 47 52N 38 0 E
Mosquera 126 2 35N 78 24W
Mosquero 117 35 48N 103 57W
Mosqueruela 32 40 21N 0 27W
Mosquitos, Golfo de los 121 9 15N 81 10W
Moss 47 59 27N 10 40 E
Moss Vale 99 34 32S 150 25 E
Mossaka 88 1 15S 16 45 E
Mossbank 109 49 56N 105 56W
Mossburn 101 45 41S 168 15 E
Mosselbaai 92 34 11S 22 8 E
Mossendjo 88 2 55S 12 42 E
Mossgiel 99 33 15S 144 5 E
Mossman 97 16 21S 145 15 E
Mossoró 127 5 10S 37 15W
Møsstrand 47 59 51N 8 4 E
Mossuril 91 14 58S 40 42 E
Mossy → 109 54 5N 102 58W
Most 26 50 31N 13 38 E
Mostaganem 82 35 54N 0 5 E
Mostar 42 43 22N 17 50 E
Mostardas 125 31 2S 50 51W
Mostefa, Rass 83 36 55N 11 3 E
Mosterøy 47 59 5N 5 37 E
Mostiska 54 49 48N 23 4 E
Mosty 54 53 27N 24 38 E
Mosul = Al Mawşil 64 36 20N 43 5 E
Mosvatn 47 59 52N 8 5 E
Mota del Cuervo 32 39 30N 2 52W
Mota del Marqués 30 41 38N 5 11W
Motagua → 120 15 44N 88 14W
Motala 49 58 32N 15 1 E
Mothe-Achard, La 18 46 37N 1 40W
Motherwell 14 55 48N 4 0W
Motihari 69 26 30N 84 55 E
Motilla del Palancar 32 39 34N 1 55W
Motnik 39 46 14N 14 54 E
Motovun 39 45 20N 13 50 E
Motozintla de Mendoza 120 15 21N 92 14W
Motril 33 36 31N 3 37W
Motru → 46 44 44N 22 59 E
Mott 116 46 25N 102 29W
Motte-Chalançon, La 21 44 30N 5 21 E
Motte, La 21 44 20N 6 3 E
Móttola 41 40 38N 17 0 E
Motueka 101 41 7S 173 1 E
Motul 120 21 0N 89 20W
Mouanda 88 1 28S 13 7 E
Mouchalagane → 107 50 56N 68 41W
Moucontant 18 46 43N 0 36W
Moúdhros 44 39 50N 25 18 E
Moudjeria 84 17 50N 12 28W
Moudon 25 46 40N 6 49 E
Mouila 88 1 50S 11 0 E
Moulamein 99 35 3S 144 1 E
Moule 121 16 20N 61 22W
Moulins 20 46 35N 3 19 E
Moulmein 67 16 30N 97 40 E
Moulouya, O. → 82 35 5N 2 25W
Moulton 117 29 35N 97 8W
Moultrie 115 31 11N 83 47W
Moultrie, L. 115 33 25N 80 10W
Mound City, Mo., U.S.A. 116 40 2N 95 25W
Mound City, S.D., U.S.A. 116 45 46N 100 3W
Moúnda, Akra 45 38 5N 20 45 E
Moundou 81 8 40N 16 10 E
Moundsville 114 39 53N 80 43W
Mount Airy 115 36 31N 80 37W
Mount Albert 112 44 8N 79 19W
Mount Angel 118 45 4N 122 46W
Mount Barker, S.A., Austral. 99 35 5S 138 52 E
Mount Barker, W.A., Austral. 96 34 38S 117 40 E
Mount Carmel, Ill., U.S.A. 114 38 20N 87 48W
Mount Carmel, Pa., U.S.A. 114 40 46N 76 25W
Mount Clemens 106 42 35N 82 50W
Mount Coolon 98 21 25S 147 25 E
Mount Darwin 91 16 45S 31 33 E
Mount Desert I. 107 44 15N 68 25W
Mount Dora 115 28 49N 81 32W
Mount Douglas 98 21 35S 146 50 E
Mount Edgecumbe 108 57 8N 135 22W
Mount Enid 96 21 42S 116 26 E
Mount Forest 106 43 59N 80 43W
Mount Gambier 97 37 50S 140 46 E
Mount Garnet 98 17 37S 145 6 E
Mount Hope 114 37 52N 81 9W
Mount Horeb 116 43 0N 89 42W
Mount Howitt 99 26 31S 142 16 E
Mount Isa 97 20 42S 139 26 E
Mount Larcom 98 23 48S 150 59 E
Mount Lofty Ra. 97 34 35S 139 5 E
Mount McKinley Nat. Park 104 64 0N 150 0W
Mount Magnet 96 28 2S 117 47 E
Mount Margaret 99 26 54S 143 21 E
Mount Maunganui 101 37 40S 176 14 E
Mount Morgan 97 23 40S 150 25 E
Mount Morris 114 42 43N 77 50W
Mount Mulligan 98 16 45S 144 47 E
Mount Nicholas 96 22 54S 120 27 E
Mount Oxide Mine 98 19 30S 139 29 E
Mount Pearl 107 47 31N 52 47W
Mount Perry 99 25 13S 151 42 E
Mount Pleasant, Iowa, U.S.A. 116 41 0N 91 35W
Mount Pleasant, Mich., U.S.A. 114 43 35N 84 47W
Mount Pleasant, Pa., U.S.A. 112 40 9N 79 31W
Mount Pleasant, S.C., U.S.A. 115 32 45N 79 48W
Mount Pleasant, Tenn., U.S.A. 115 35 31N 87 11W
Mount Pleasant, Tex., U.S.A. 117 33 5N 95 0W
Mount Pleasant, Ut., U.S.A. 118 39 40N 111 29W
Mount Pocono 113 41 8N 75 21W
Mount Rainier Nat. Park. 118 46 50N 121 43W
Mount Revelstoke Nat. Park 108 51 5N 118 30W
Mount Robson 108 52 56N 119 15W
Mount Robson Prov. Park 108 53 0N 119 0W
Mount Shasta 118 41 20N 122 18W
Mount Sterling, Ill., U.S.A. 116 40 0N 90 40W
Mount Sterling, Ky., U.S.A. 114 38 0N 84 0W
Mount Surprise 98 18 10S 144 17 E
Mount Union 112 40 22N 77 51W
Mount Vernon, Ind., U.S.A. 116 38 17N 88 57W
Mount Vernon, N.Y., U.S.A. 114 40 57N 73 49W
Mount Vernon, Ohio, U.S.A. 114 40 20N 82 30W
Mount Vernon, Wash., U.S.A. 108 48 25N 122 20W
Mount Whaleback 96 23 18S 119 44 E
Mountain City, Nev., U.S.A. 118 41 54N 116 0W
Mountain City, Tenn., U.S.A. 115 36 30N 81 50W
Mountain Grove 117 37 5N 92 20W
Mountain Home, Ark., U.S.A. 117 36 20N 92 25W
Mountain Home, Idaho, U.S.A. 118 43 11N 115 45W
Mountain Iron 116 47 30N 92 37W
Mountain Park. 108 52 50N 117 15W
Mountain View, Ark., U.S.A. 117 35 52N 92 10W
Mountain View, Calif., U.S.A. 119 37 26N 122 5W
Mountainair 119 34 35N 106 15W
Mountmellick 15 53 7N 7 20W
Moura, Austral. 98 24 35S 149 58 E
Moura, Brazil 126 1 32S 61 38W
Moura, Port. 31 38 7N 7 30W
Mourão 31 38 22N 7 22W
Mourdi Depression 81 18 10N 23 0 E
Mourdiah 84 14 35N 7 25W
Moure, La 116 46 27N 98 17W
Mourenx 20 43 23N 0 36W
Mouri 85 5 6N 1 14W
Mourilyan 98 17 35S 146 3 E
Mourmelon-le-Grand 19 49 8N 4 22 E
Mourne → 15 54 45N 7 39W
Mourne Mts. 15 54 10N 6 0W
Mouscron 16 50 45N 3 12 E
Moussoro 81 13 41N 16 35 E
Mouthe 19 46 44N 6 12 E
Moutier 25 47 16N 7 21 E
Moûtiers 21 45 29N 6 31 E
Moutong 73 0 28N 121 13 E
Mouy 19 49 18N 2 20 E
Mouzáki 44 39 25N 21 37 E
Moville 15 55 11N 7 3W
Moy → 15 54 5N 8 50W
Moyale, Ethiopia 87 3 34N 39 4 E
Moyale, Kenya 90 3 30N 39 0 E
Moyamba 84 8 4N 12 30W
Moyen Atlas 80 32 0N 5 0W
Moyle □ 15 55 10N 6 15W
Moyobamba 126 6 0S 77 0W
Moyyero → 59 68 44N 103 42 E
Mozambique = Moçambique 91 15 3S 40 42 E
Mozambique ■ 91 19 0S 35 0 E
Mozambique Chan. 93 20 0S 39 0 E
Mozdok 57 43 45N 44 48 E
Mozhaysk 55 55 30N 36 2 E
Mozhga 55 56 26N 52 15 E
Mozirje 39 46 22N 14 58 E
Mozyr 54 52 0N 29 15 E
Mpanda 90 6 23S 31 1 E
Mpanda □ 90 6 23S 31 40 E
Mpésoba 84 12 31N 5 39W
Mpika 91 11 51S 31 25 E
Mpulungu 91 8 51S 31 5 E
Mpwapwa 90 6 23S 36 30 E
Mpwapwa □ 90 6 30S 36 20 E
Mrągowo 28 53 52N 21 18 E
Mramor 42 43 20N 21 45 E
Mrimina 82 29 50N 7 9W
Mrkonjić Grad 42 44 26N 17 4 E
Mrkopalj 39 45 21N 14 52 E
Mrocza 28 53 16N 17 35 E
Msab, Oued en → 83 32 25N 5 20 E
Msaken 83 35 49N 10 33 E
Msambansovu 91 15 50S 30 3 E
M'sila 83 35 46N 4 30 E
Msta → 54 58 25N 31 20 E
Mstislavl 54 54 0N 31 50 E
Mszana Dolna 27 49 41N 20 5 E
Mszczonów 28 51 58N 20 33 E
Mtama 91 10 17S 39 21 E
Mtilikwe → 91 21 9S 31 30 E
Mtsensk 55 53 25N 36 30 E
Mtskheta 57 41 52N 44 45 E
Mtwara-Mikindani 91 10 20S 40 20 E
Mu Us Shamo 76 39 0N 109 0 E
Muaná 127 1 25S 49 15W
Muang Chiang Rai 71 19 52N 99 50 E
Muang Lamphun 71 18 40N 99 2 E
Muang Phichit 71 16 29N 100 21 E
Muar 71 2 3N 102 34 E
Muar → 71 2 15N 102 48 E
Muarabungo 72 1 28S 102 52 E
Muaradjuloi 72 0 12S 114 3 E
Muaraenim 72 3 40S 103 50 E
Muarakaman 72 0 2S 116 45 E
Muaratebo 72 1 30S 102 26 E
Muaratembesi 72 1 42S 103 8 E
Muaratewe 72 0 58S 114 52 E
Mubarakpur 69 26 6N 83 18 E
Mubende 90 0 33N 31 22 E
Mubi 85 10 18N 13 16 E
Mücheln 24 51 18N 11 49 E
Muchinga Mts. 91 11 30S 31 30 E
Muchkapskiy 55 51 52N 42 28 E
Muck 14 56 50N 6 15W
Muckadilla 99 26 35S 148 23 E
Mucuri 127 18 0S 39 36W
Mucusso 92 18 1S 21 25 E
Mudanjiang 76 44 38N 129 30 E
Mudanya 56 40 25N 28 50 E
Muddy → 119 38 0N 110 22W
Mudgee 97 32 32S 149 31 E
Mudjatik → 109 56 1N 107 36W
Muecate 91 14 55S 39 40 E
Muêda 91 11 36S 39 28 E
Muela, La 32 41 36N 1 7W
Muerto, Mar 120 16 10N 94 10W
Muertos, Punta de los 33 36 57N 1 54W
Mufindi □ 91 8 30S 35 20 E
Mufulira 91 12 32S 28 15 E
Mufumbiro Range 90 1 25S 29 30 E
Mugardos 30 43 27N 8 15W
Muge 31 39 3N 8 40W
Muge → 31 39 8N 8 44W
Múggia 39 45 36N 13 47 E
Mugia 30 43 3N 9 10W
Mugila, Mts. 90 7 0S 28 50 E
Muğla 64 37 15N 28 22 E
Müglizh 43 42 37N 25 32 E
Mugshin 63 19 35N 54 40 E
Mugu 69 29 45N 82 30 E
Muhammad Qol 86 20 53N 37 9 E
Muhammad Râs 86 27 42N 34 13 E
Muhammadabad 69 26 4N 83 25 E
Muharraqa = Sa'ad 62 31 28N 34 33 E
Muhesi → 90 7 0S 35 20 E
Muheza □ 90 5 0S 39 0 E
Mühldorf 25 48 14N 12 33 E
Mühlhausen 24 51 12N 10 29 E
Mühlig Hofmann fjella 5 72 30S 5 0 E
Muhutwe 90 1 35S 31 45 E
Mui Bai Bung 71 8 35N 104 42 E
Mui Ron 71 18 7N 106 27 E
Muikamachi 74 37 15N 138 50 E
Muine Bheag 15 52 42N 6 57W
Muiños 30 41 58N 7 59W
Mukachevo 54 48 27N 22 45 E
Mukah 72 2 55N 112 5 E
Mukawwa, Geziret 86 23 55N 35 53 E
Mukden = Shenyang 76 41 48N 123 27 E
Mukhtolovo 55 55 29N 43 15 E
Mukishi 91 8 30S 24 44 E
Mukomuko 72 2 30S 101 10 E
Mukomwenze 90 6 49S 27 15 E
Muktsar 68 30 30N 74 30 E
Mukur 66 32 50N 67 42 E
Mukutawa → 109 53 10N 97 24W
Mukwela 91 17 0S 26 40 E
Mula 33 38 3N 1 33W
Mula → 70 18 34N 74 21 E
Mulange 90 3 40S 27 10 E
• Mulatas, Arch. de las 121 9 50N 78 31W
Mulchén 124 37 45S 72 20W
Mulde → 24 51 10N 12 48 E
Mule Creek 116 43 19N 104 8W
Muleba 90 1 50S 31 37 E
Muleba □ 90 2 0S 31 30 E
Muleshoe 117 34 17N 102 42W
Mulgrave 107 45 38N 61 31W
Mulgrave I. 98 10 5S 142 10 E
Mulhacén 33 37 4N 3 20W
Mülheim 24 51 26N 6 53 E
Mulhouse 19 47 40N 7 20 E
Muling He → 76 45 53N 133 30 E
Mull 14 56 27N 6 0W
Mullaittvu 70 9 15N 80 49 E
Mullen 116 42 5N 101 0W
Mullengudgery 99 31 43S 147 23 E
Mullens 114 37 34N 81 22W
Muller, Pegunungan 72 0 30N 113 30 E
Mullet Pen. 15 54 10N 10 2W
Mullewa 96 28 29S 115 30 E
Müllheim 25 47 48N 7 37 E
Mulligan → 98 26 40S 139 0 E
Mullin 117 31 33N 98 38W
Mullingar 15 53 31N 7 20W
Mullins 115 34 12N 79 15W
Mullsjö 49 57 56N 13 55 E

• Renamed San Blas, Arch. de

Mullumbimby Nanjeko

Mullumbimby **99** 28 30 S 153 30 E
Mulobezi **91** 16 45 S 25 7 E
Mulshi L. **70** 18 30N 73 48 E
Multai **68** 21 50N 78 21 E
Multan **68** 30 15N 71 36 E
* Multan □ **68** 30 29N 72 29 E
Multrå **48** 63 10N 17 24 E
Mulumbe, Mts. **91** 8 40 S 27 30 E
Mulungushi Dam **91** 14 48 S 28 48 E
Mulvane **117** 37 30N 97 15W
Mulwad **86** 18 45N 30 39 E
Mulwala **100** 35 59 S 146 0 E
Mumra **57** 45 45N 47 41 E
Mun → **71** 15 17N 103 0 E
Muna **73** 5 0 S 122 30 E
Munamagi **54** 57 43N 27 4 E
Münchberg **25** 50 11N 11 48 E
Muncheberg **24** 52 30N 14 9 E
München **25** 48 8N 11 33 E
Munchen-Gladbach = Mönchengladbach **24** 51 12N 6 23 E
Muncho Lake **108** 59 0N 125 50W
Muncie **114** 40 10N 85 20W
Mundakayam **70** 9 30N 76 50 E
Mundala, Puncak **73** 4 30 S 141 0 E
Mundare **108** 53 35N 112 20W
Munday **117** 33 26N 99 39W
Münden **24** 51 25N 9 42 E
Mundo → **33** 38 30N 2 15W
Mundo Novo **127** 11 50 S 40 29W
Mundra **68** 22 54N 69 48 E
Munera **33** 39 2N 2 29W
Muneru → **70** 16 45N 80 3 E
Mungallala **99** 26 28 S 147 34 E
Mungallala Cr. → **99** 28 53 S 147 5 E
Mungana **98** 17 8 S 144 27 E
Mungaoli **68** 24 24N 78 7 E
Mungari **91** 17 12 S 33 30 E
Mungbere **90** 2 36N 28 28 E
Mungindi **97** 28 58 S 149 1 E
Munhango **89** 12 10 S 18 38 E
Munich = München **25** 48 8N 11 33 E
Munising **114** 46 25N 86 39W
Munjiye **86** 18 47N 41 20 E
Munka-Ljungby **49** 56 16N 12 58 E
Munkedal **49** 58 28N 11 40 E
Munkfors **48** 59 50N 13 30 E
Munku-Sardyk **59** 51 45N 100 20 E
Münnerstadt **25** 50 15N 10 11 E
Muñoz Gamero, Pen. **128** 52 30 S 73 5 E
Munroe L. **109** 59 13N 98 35W
Munster, France **19** 48 2N 7 8 E
Munster, Ger. **24** 52 59N 10 5 E
Münster **24** 51 58N 7 37 E
Munster □ **15** 52 20N 8 40W
Muntele Mare **46** 46 30N 23 12 E
Muntok **72** 2 5 S 105 10 E
Munyak **58** 43 30N 59 15 E
Munyama **91** 16 5 S 28 31 E
Muon Pak Beng **71** 19 51N 101 4 E
Muonio **50** 67 57N 23 40 E
Mupa **89** 16 5 S 15 50 E
Muping **76** 37 22N 121 36 E
Muqaddam, Wadi → **86** 18 4N 31 30 E
Muqdisho **63** 2 2N 45 25 E
Mur → **26** 46 18N 16 53 E
Mur-de-Bretagne **18** 48 12N 3 0W
Mura → **39** 46 18N 16 53 E
Murallón, Cuerro **128** 49 48 S 73 30W
Muranda **90** 1 52 S 29 20 E
Murang'a **90** 0 45 S 37 9 E
Murashi **55** 59 30N 49 0 E
Murat **20** 45 7N 2 53 E
Murau **26** 47 6N 14 10 E
Muravera **40** 39 25N 9 35 E
Murça **30** 41 24N 7 28W
Murchison → **96** 27 45 S 114 0 E
Murchison Falls = Kabarega Falls **90** 2 15N 31 38 E
Murchison Ra. **96** 20 0 S 134 10 E
Murchison Rapids **91** 15 55 S 34 35 E
Murcia **33** 38 20N 1 10W
Murcia □ **33** 37 50N 1 30W
Murdo **116** 43 56N 100 43W
Murdoch Pt. **98** 14 37 S 144 55 E
Mure, La **21** 44 55N 5 48 E
Mureş □ **46** 46 45N 24 40 E
Mureş (Mureşul) → **46** 46 15N 20 13 E
Muret **20** 43 30N 1 20 E
Murfatlar **46** 44 10N 28 26 E
Murfreesboro **115** 35 50N 86 21W
Murg → **25** 48 55N 8 10 E
Murgab **58** 38 10N 74 2 E
Murgeni **46** 46 12N 28 1 E
Murgon **97** 26 15 S 151 54 E
Muriaé **125** 21 8 S 42 23W
Murias de Paredes **30** 42 52N 6 11W
Muriel Mine **91** 17 14 S 30 40 E
Müritz see **24** 53 25N 12 40 E
Murka **90** 3 27 S 38 0 E
Murmansk **52** 68 57N 33 10 E
Murnau **25** 47 40N 11 11 E
Muro, France **21** 42 34N 8 54 E
Muro, Spain **32** 39 44N 3 3 E
Muro, C. de **21** 41 44N 8 37 E
Muro Lucano **41** 40 45N 15 30 E
Murom **55** 55 35N 42 3 E
Muroran **74** 42 25N 141 0 E
Muros **30** 42 45N 9 5W
Muros y de Noya, Ría de **30** 42 45N 9 0W
Muroto-Misaki **74** 33 15N 134 10 E
Murowana Goślina **28** 52 35N 17 0 E
Murphy **118** 43 11N 116 33W
Murphysboro **117** 37 50N 89 20W
Murrat **86** 18 51N 29 33 E
Murray, Ky., U.S.A. **115** 36 40N 88 20W
Murray, Utah, U.S.A. **118** 40 41N 111 58W
Murray →, Austral. **97** 35 20 S 139 22 E
Murray →, Can. **108** 56 11N 120 45W
Murray Bridge **97** 35 6 S 139 14 E
Murray Harbour **107** 46 0N 62 28W
Murray, L., P.N.G. **98** 7 0 S 141 35 E
Murray, L., U.S.A. **115** 34 8N 81 30W
Murray Seascarp **95** 30 0N 135 0W
Murraysburg **92** 31 58 S 23 47 E
Murrayville **100** 35 16 S 141 11 E
Murree **66** 33 56N 73 28 E
Murrumbidgee → **97** 34 43 S 143 12 E
Murrumburrah **99** 34 32 S 148 22 E
Murrurundi **99** 31 42 S 150 51 E
Mursala **72** 1 41N 98 28 E
Murshid **86** 21 40N 31 10 E
Murshidabad **69** 24 11N 88 19 E
Murska Sobota **39** 46 39N 16 12 E
Murtazapur **68** 20 40N 77 25 E
Murtle L. **108** 52 8N 119 38W
Murtoa **99** 36 35 S 142 28 E
Murtosa **30** 40 44N 8 40W
Murungu **90** 4 12 S 31 10 E
Murwara **69** 23 46N 80 28 E
Murwillumbah **97** 28 18 S 153 27 E
Muryo **73** 6 36 S 110 53 E
Mürz → **26** 47 30N 15 25 E
Mürzzuschlag **26** 47 36N 15 41 E
Muş **64** 38 45N 41 30 E
Musa Khel Bazar **68** 30 59N 69 52 E
Mūsá Qal'eh **65** 32 20N 64 50 E
Musairik, Wadi → **86** 19 30N 43 10 E
Musala **43** 42 13N 23 37 E
Musan, Kor., N. **76** 42 12N 129 12 E
Musan, Kor., N. **76** 42 12N 129 12 E
Musangu **91** 10 28 S 23 55 E
Musasa **90** 3 25 S 31 30 E
Musay'id **65** 25 0N 51 33 E
Muscat = Masqat **65** 23 37N 58 36 E
Muscat & Oman = Oman ■ **63** 23 0N 58 0 E
Muscatine **116** 41 25N 91 5W
Musel **30** 43 34N 5 42W
Musgrave Ras. **96** 26 0 S 132 0 E
Mushie **88** 2 56 S 16 55 E
Mushin **85** 6 32N 3 21 E
Musi →, India **70** 16 41N 79 40 E
Musi →, Indon. **72** 2 20 S 104 56 E
Muskeg → **108** 60 20N 123 20W
Muskegon **114** 43 15N 86 17W
Muskegon → **114** 43 25N 86 0W
Muskegon Hts. **114** 43 12N 86 17W
Muskogee **117** 35 50N 95 25W
Muskwa → **108** 58 47N 122 48W
Musmar **86** 18 13N 35 40 E
Musofu **91** 13 30 S 29 0 E
Musoma **90** 1 30 S 33 48 E
Musoma □ **90** 1 50 S 34 30 E
Musquaro, L. **107** 50 38N 61 5W
Musquodoboit Harbour **107** 44 50N 63 9W
Musselburgh **14** 55 57N 3 3W
Musselshell → **118** 47 21N 107 58W
Mussidan **20** 45 2N 0 22 E
Mussomeli **40** 37 35N 13 43 E
Mussooree **68** 30 27N 78 6 E
Mussuco **92** 17 2 S 19 3 E
Mustang **69** 29 10N 83 55 E
Musters, L. **128** 45 20 S 69 25W
Muswellbrook **97** 32 16 S 150 56 E
Muszyna **27** 49 22N 20 55 E
Mût **86** 25 28N 28 58 E
Mut **64** 36 40N 33 28 E
Mutanda, Mozam. **93** 21 0 S 33 34 E
Mutanda, Zambia **91** 12 24 S 26 13 E
Mutaray **59** 60 56N 101 0 E
Muting **73** 7 23 S 140 20 E
Mutshatsha **91** 10 35 S 24 20 E
Muttaburra **97** 22 38 S 144 29 E
Mutuáli **91** 14 55 S 37 0 E
Muvatupusha **70** 9 53N 76 35 E
Muxima **88** 9 33 S 13 58 E
Muy, Le **21** 43 28N 6 34 E
Muya **59** 56 27N 115 50 E
Muyinga **90** 3 14 S 30 33 E
Muzaffarabad **69** 34 25N 73 30 E
Muzaffargarh **68** 30 5N 71 14 E
Muzaffarnagar **68** 29 26N 77 40 E
Muzaffarpur **69** 26 7N 85 23 E
Muzhi **58** 65 25N 64 40 E
Muzillac **18** 47 35N 2 30W
Muzon C. **108** 54 40N 132 40W
Muztag **75** 36 20N 87 28 E
Mvôlô **87** 6 2N 29 53 E
Mwadui **90** 3 26 S 33 32 E
Mwambo **91** 10 30 S 40 22 E
Mwandi **91** 17 30 S 24 51 E
Mwanza, Tanz. **90** 2 30 S 32 58 E
Mwanza, Zaïre **90** 7 55 S 26 43 E
Mwanza, Zambia **91** 16 58 S 24 28 E
Mwanza □ **90** 2 0 S 33 0 E
Mwaya **91** 9 32 S 33 55 E
Mweelrea **15** 53 37N 9 48W
Mweka **88** 4 50 S 21 34 E
Mwenga **90** 3 1 S 28 28 E
Mweru, L. **91** 9 0 S 28 40 E
Mweza Range **91** 21 0 S 30 0 E
Mwilambwe **90** 8 7 S 25 0 E
Mwimbi **91** 8 38 S 31 39 E
Mwinilunga **91** 11 43 S 24 25 E
My Tho **71** 10 29N 106 23 E
Mya, O. → **83** 30 46N 4 54 E
Myall → **100** 32 30 S 152 15 E
Myanaung **67** 18 18N 95 22 E
Myaungmya **67** 16 30N 94 40 E
Mycenae = Mikínai **45** 37 43N 22 46 E
Myeik Kyunzu **71** 11 30N 97 30 E
Myerstown **113** 40 22N 76 18W
Myitkyina **67** 25 24N 97 26 E
Myjava **27** 48 41N 17 37 E
Mymensingh **69** 24 45N 90 24 E
Myndus **45** 37 3N 27 14 E
Mynydd ddu **13** 51 45N 3 45W
Myrdal **47** 60 43N 7 10 E
Mýrdalsjökull **50** 63 40N 19 6W
Myrtle Beach **115** 33 43N 78 50W
Myrtle Creek **118** 43 0N 123 9W
Myrtle Point **118** 43 0N 124 4W
Myrtleford **100** 36 34 S 146 44 E
Mysen **47** 59 33N 11 20 E
Myslenice **27** 49 51N 19 57 E
Myślibórz **28** 52 55N 14 50 E
Mysłowice **27** 50 15N 19 12 E
Mysore **70** 12 17N 76 41 E
Mysore □ = Karnataka **70** 13 15N 77 0 E
Mystic **113** 41 21N 71 58W
Mystishchi **55** 55 50N 37 50 E
Myszków **28** 50 45N 19 22 E
Myszyniec **28** 53 23N 21 21 E
Myton **118** 40 10N 110 2W
Mývatn **50** 65 36N 17 0W
Mze → **26** 49 46N 13 24 E
Mzimba **91** 11 55 S 33 39 E
Mzimvubu → **93** 31 38 S 29 33 E
Mzuzu **91** 11 30 S 33 55 E

N

N' Dioum **84** 16 31N 14 39W
Naab → **25** 49 1N 12 2 E
Na'am **87** 9 42N 28 27 E
Na'an **62** 31 53N 34 52 E
Naantali **51** 60 29N 22 2 E
Naas **15** 53 12N 6 40W
Nababiep **92** 29 36 S 17 46 E
Nabadwip **69** 23 34N 88 20 E
Nabas **73** 11 47N 122 6 E
Nabburg **25** 49 27N 12 11 E
* Nabereznyje Celny **58** 55 42N 52 19 E
Nabeul **83** 36 30N 10 44 E
Nabha **68** 30 26N 76 14 E
Nabire **73** 3 15 S 135 26 E
Nabisar **68** 25 8N 69 40 E
Nabisipi → **107** 50 14N 62 13W
Nabiswera **90** 1 27N 32 15 E
Nablus = Nābulus **62** 32 14N 35 15 E
Naboomspruit **93** 24 32 S 28 40 E
Nābulus **62** 32 14N 35 15 E
Nacala-Velha **91** 14 32 S 40 34 E
Nacaroa **91** 14 22 S 39 56 E
Naches **118** 46 48N 120 42W
Nachingwea **91** 10 23 S 38 49 E
Nachingwea □ **91** 10 30 S 38 30 E
Nachna **68** 27 34N 71 41 E
Náchod **27** 50 25N 16 8 E
Nacka **48** 59 17N 18 12 E
Nackara **99** 32 48 S 139 12 E
Naco **119** 31 24N 109 58W
Nacogdoches **117** 31 33N 94 39W
Nacozari **120** 30 24N 109 39W
Nadi **86** 18 40N 33 41 E
Nadiad **68** 22 41N 72 56 E
Nădlac **42** 46 10N 20 50 E
Nador **82** 35 14N 2 58W
Nadūshan **65** 32 2N 53 35 E
Nadvoitsy **52** 63 52N 34 14 E
Nadvornaya **56** 48 37N 24 30 E
Nadym **58** 65 35N 72 42 E
Nadym → **58** 66 12N 72 0 E
Nærbø **47** 58 40N 5 39 E
Næstved **49** 55 13N 11 44 E
Nafada **85** 11 8N 11 20 E
Naft-e Shāh **64** 34 0N 45 30 E
Nafūd ad Dahy **64** 22 0N 45 0 E
Nafūsah, Jabal **83** 32 12N 12 30 E
Nag Hammâdi **86** 26 2N 32 18 E
Naga **73** 13 38N 123 15 E
Naga, Kreb en **82** 24 12N 6 0W
Nagagami → **106** 49 40N 84 40W
Nagaland □ **67** 26 0N 94 30 E
Nagano **74** 36 40N 138 10 E
Nagano □ **74** 36 15N 138 0 E
Nagaoka **74** 37 27N 138 50 E
Nagappattinam **70** 10 46N 79 51 E
Nagar Parkar **68** 24 28N 70 46 E
Nagari Hills **70** 13 3N 79 45 E
Nagarjuna Sagar **70** 16 35N 79 17 E
Nagasaki **74** 32 47N 129 50 E
Nagasaki □ **74** 32 50N 129 40 E
Nagaur **68** 27 15N 73 45 E
Nagbhil **70** 20 34N 79 55 E
Nagercoil **70** 8 12N 77 26 E
Nagina **68** 29 30N 78 30 E
Nagīneh **65** 34 20N 57 15 E
Nago **77** 26 36N 128 0 E
Nagold **25** 34 14N 57 2 E
Nagold → **25** 48 52N 8 42 E
Nagoorin **98** 24 17 S 151 15 E
Nagornyy **59** 55 58N 124 57 E
Nagorsk **55** 59 18N 50 48 E
Nagoya **74** 35 10N 136 50 E
Nagpur **68** 21 8N 79 10 E
Nagyatád **27** 46 14N 17 22 E
Nagyecsed **27** 47 53N 22 24 E
Nagykanizsa **27** 46 28N 17 0 E
Nagykörös **27** 47 5N 19 48 E
Nagyléta **27** 47 23N 21 55 E
Naha **77** 26 13N 127 42 E
Nahalal **62** 32 41N 35 12 E
Nahanni Butte **108** 61 2N 123 31W
Nahanni Nat. Park **108** 61 15N 125 0W
Nahariyya **62** 33 1N 35 5 E
Nahāvand **64** 34 10N 48 22 E
Nahe → **25** 49 58N 7 57 E
Nahf **62** 32 56N 35 18 E
Nahîya, Wadi → **86** 28 55N 31 0 E
Nahlin **108** 58 55N 131 38W
Nahud **86** 18 12N 41 40 E
Naicam **109** 52 30N 104 30W
Nā'ifah **63** 19 59N 50 46 E
Naila **25** 50 19N 11 43 E
Nain **107** 56 34N 61 40W
Nā'īn **65** 32 54N 53 0 E
Naini Tal **69** 29 30N 79 30 E
Naintré **18** 46 46N 0 29 E
Naipu **46** 44 12N 25 47 E
Naira **73** 4 28 S 130 0 E
Nairn **14** 57 35N 3 54W
Nairobi **90** 1 17 S 36 48 E
Naivasha **90** 0 40 S 36 30 E
Naivasha L. **90** 0 48 S 36 20 E
Najac **20** 44 14N 1 58 E
Najafābād **65** 32 40N 51 15 E
Najd **64** 26 30N 42 0 E
Nájera **32** 42 26N 2 48W
Najerilla → **32** 42 32N 2 48W
Najibabad **68** 29 40N 78 20 E
Najin **76** 42 12N 130 15 E
Nakalagba **90** 2 50N 27 58 E
Nakamura **74** 33 0N 133 0 E
Nakfa **87** 16 40N 38 32 E
Nakhichevan A.S.S.R. □ **53** 39 14N 45 30 E
Nakhl **86** 29 55N 33 43 E
Nakhodka **59** 42 53N 132 54 E
Nakhon Phanom **71** 17 23N 104 43 E
Nakhon Ratchasima (Khorat) **71** 14 59N 102 12 E
Nakhon Sawan **71** 15 35N 100 10 E
Nakhon Si Thammarat **71** 8 29N 100 0 E
Nakina, B.C., Can. **108** 59 12N 132 52W
Nakina, Ont., Can. **106** 50 10N 86 40W
Nakło nad Notecią **28** 53 9N 17 38 E
Nakodar **68** 31 8N 75 31 E
Nakskov **49** 54 50N 11 8 E
Näkten **48** 62 48N 14 38 E
Naktong → **76** 35 7N 128 57 E
Nakuru **90** 0 15 S 36 4 E
Nakuru □ **90** 0 15 S 35 5 E
Nakuru, L. **90** 0 23 S 36 5 E
Nakusp **108** 50 20N 117 45W
Nal → **66** 25 20N 65 30 E
Nalchik **57** 43 30N 43 33 E
Nälden **48** 63 21N 14 14 E
Näldsjön **48** 63 25N 14 15 E
Nalerigu **85** 10 35N 0 25W
Nalgonda **70** 17 6N 79 15 E
Nalhati **69** 24 17N 87 52 E
Nallamalai Hills **70** 15 30N 78 50 E
Nalón → **30** 43 32N 6 4W
Nālūt **83** 31 54N 11 0 E
Nam Co **75** 30 30N 90 45 E
Nam Dinh **71** 20 25N 106 5 E
Nam-Phan **72** 10 30N 106 0 E
Nam Phong **71** 16 42N 102 52 E
Nam Tha **71** 20 58N 101 30 E
Nama unde **92** 17 18 S 15 50 E
Namak, Daryācheh-ye **65** 34 30N 52 0 E
Namak, Kavir-e **65** 34 30N 57 30 E
Namakkal **70** 11 13N 78 13 E
Namaland **92** 24 30 S 17 0 E
Namangan **58** 41 0N 71 40 E
Namapa **91** 13 43 S 39 50 E
Namaqualand **92** 30 0 S 18 0 E
Namasagali **90** 1 2N 33 0 E
Namatanai **98** 3 40 S 152 29 E
Namber **73** 1 2 S 134 49 E
Nambour **97** 26 32 S 152 58 E
Nambucca Heads **99** 30 37 S 153 0 E
Namche Bazar **69** 27 51N 86 47 E
Namecunda **91** 14 54 S 37 37 E
Nameh **72** 2 34N 116 21 E
Nameponda **91** 15 50 S 39 50 E
Náměšt' nad Oslavou **27** 49 12N 16 10 E
Námestovo **27** 49 24N 19 25 E
Nametil **91** 15 40 S 39 21 E
Namew L. **109** 54 14N 101 56W
Namib Desert = Namib Woestyn **92** 22 30 S 15 0 E
Namib-Woestyn **92** 22 30 S 15 0 E
Namibia ■ **92** 22 0 S 18 9 E
Namlea **73** 3 18 S 127 5 E
Namoi → **99** 30 12 S 149 30 E
Namous, O. en → **82** 31 0N 0 15W
Nampa **118** 43 34N 116 34W
Nampula **91** 15 6N 39 15 E
Namrole **73** 3 46 S 126 46 E
Namse Shankou **67** 30 0N 82 25 E
Namsen → **50** 64 27N 11 42 E
Namsos **50** 64 29N 11 30 E
Namtay **59** 62 43N 129 37 E
Namtu **67** 23 5N 97 28 E
Namtumbo **91** 10 30 S 36 4 E
Namu **108** 51 52N 127 50W
Namucha Shank'ou **69** 30 0N 82 28 E
Namur **16** 50 27N 4 52 E
Namur □ **16** 50 17N 5 0 E
Namutoni **92** 18 49 S 16 55 E
Namwala **91** 15 44 S 26 30 E
Namysłów **28** 51 6N 17 42 E
Nan **71** 18 52N 100 42 E
Nana **46** 44 17N 26 34 E
Nanaimo **108** 49 10N 124 0W
Nanam **76** 41 44N 129 40 E
Nanan **77** 24 59N 118 21 E
Nanango **97** 26 40 S 152 0 E
Nan'ao **77** 23 28N 117 5 E
Nanao **74** 37 0N 137 0 E
Nanbu **77** 31 18N 106 3 E
Nanchang **75** 28 42N 115 55 E
Nancheng **77** 27 33N 116 35 E
Nanching = Nanjing **75** 32 2N 118 47 E
Nanchong **75** 30 43N 106 2 E
Nanchuan **77** 29 9N 107 6 E
Nancy **19** 48 42N 6 12 E
Nanda Devi **69** 30 23N 79 59 E
Nandan **77** 24 58N 107 29 E
Nander **70** 19 10N 77 20 E
Nandewar Ra. **99** 30 15 S 150 35 E
Nandi **101** 17 42 S 177 20 E
Nandi □ **90** 0 15N 35 0 E
Nandikotkur **70** 15 52N 78 18 E
Nandura **68** 20 52N 76 25 E
Nandurbar **68** 21 20N 74 15 E
Nandyal **70** 15 30N 78 30 E
Nanga-Eboko **88** 4 41N 12 22 E
Nanga Parbat **69** 35 10N 74 35 E
Nangade **91** 11 5 S 39 36 E
Nangapinoh **72** 0 20 S 111 44 E
Nangarhár □ **65** 34 20N 70 0 E
Nangatayap **72** 1 32 S 110 34 E
Nangeya Mts. **90** 3 30N 33 30 E
Nangis **19** 48 33N 3 0 E
Nanjangud **70** 12 6N 76 43 E
Nanjeko **91** 15 31 S 23 30 E

* *Now part of Punjab* □

* *Renamed Brezhnev*

Nanjiang Nevis

Nanjiang 77 32 28N 106 51 E
Nanjing 75 32 2N 118 47 E
Nanjirinji 91 9 41S 39 5 E
Nankana Sahib 68 31 27N 73 38 E
Nankang 77 25 40N 114 45 E
Nanking = Nanjing 75 32 2N 118 47 E
Nannine 96 26 51S 118 18 E
Nanning 75 22 48N 108 20 E
Nanpara 69 27 52N 81 33 E
Nanpi 76 38 2N 116 45 E
Nanping 75 26 38N 118 10 E
Nanripe 91 13 52S 38 52 E
Nansei-Shotō 74 26 0N 128 0 E
Nansen Sd. 4 81 0N 91 0W
Nansio 90 2 3S 33 4 E
Nant 20 44 1N 3 18 E
Nantes 18 47 12N 1 33W
Nanteuil-le-Haudouin 19 49 9N 2 48 E
Nantiat 20 46 1N 1 11 E
Nanticoke 114 41 12N 76 1W
Nanton 108 50 21N 113 46W
Nantong 77 32 1N 120 52 E
Nantua 21 46 10N 5 35 E
Nantucket I. 102 41 16N 70 3W
Nanuque 127 17 50S 40 21W
Nanxiong 77 25 6N 114 15 E
Nanyang 75 33 11N 112 30 E
Nanyuan 76 39 44N 116 22 E
Nanyuki 90 0 2N 37 4 E
Nanzhang 77 31 45N 111 50 E
Náo, C. de la 33 38 44N 0 14 E
Naococane L. 107 52 50N 70 45W
Naoetsu 74 37 12N 138 10 E
Naogaon 69 24 52N 88 52 E
Naoli He → 76 47 18N 134 9 E
Náousa 44 40 42N 22 9 E
Napa 118 38 18N 122 17W
Napanee 106 44 15N 77 0W
Napanoch 113 41 44N 74 22W
Napier 101 39 30S 176 56 E
Naples 115 26 10N 81 45W
Naples = Nápoli 41 40 50N 14 17 E
Napo → 126 3 20S 72 40W
Napoleon, N. Dak., U.S.A. 116 46 32N 99 49W
Napoleon, Ohio, U.S.A. 114 41 24N 84 7W
Nápoli 41 40 50N 14 17 E
Nápoli, G. di 41 40 40N 14 10 E
Napopo 90 4 15N 28 0 E
Nappa Merrie 99 27 36S 141 7 E
Naqâda 86 25 53N 32 42 E
Nara, Japan 74 34 40N 135 49 E
Nara, Mali 84 15 10N 7 20W
Nara □ 74 34 30N 136 0 E
Nara, Canal 68 24 30N 69 20 E
Nara Visa 117 35 39N 103 10W
Naracoorte 97 36 58S 140 45 E
Naradhan 99 33 34S 146 17 E
Narasapur 70 16 26N 81 40 E
Narasaropet 70 16 14N 80 4 E
Narathiwat 71 6 30N 101 48 E
Narayanganj 69 23 40N 90 33 E
Narayanpet 70 16 45N 77 30 E
Narbonne 20 43 11N 3 0 E
Narcea → 30 43 33N 6 44W
Nardò 41 40 10N 18 0 E
Narew 28 52 55N 23 31 E
Narew → 28 52 26N 20 41 E
Nari → 68 29 40N 68 0 E
Narindra, Helodranon' i 93 14 55S 47 30 E
Narmada → 68 21 38N 72 36 E
Narnaul 68 28 5N 76 11 E
Narni 39 42 30N 12 30 E
Naro, Ghana 84 10 22N 2 27W
Naro, Italy 40 37 18N 13 48 E
Naro Fominsk 55 55 23N 36 43 E
Narodnaya, G. 52 65 5N 60 0 E
Narok 90 1 55S 33 52 E
Narok □ 90 1 20S 36 30 E
Narón 30 43 32N 8 9W
Narooma 99 36 14S 150 4 E
Narowal 68 32 6N 74 52 E
Narrabri 97 30 19S 149 46 E
Narran → 99 28 37S 148 12 E
Narrandera 97 34 42S 146 31 E
Narraway → 108 55 44N 119 55W
Narrogin 96 32 58S 117 14 E
Narromine 97 32 12S 148 12 E
Narsampet 70 17 57N 79 58 E
Narsimhapur 68 22 54N 79 14 E
Nartkala 57 43 33N 43 51 E
Narva 54 59 23N 28 12 E
Narva → 54 59 27N 28 2 E
Narvik 50 68 28N 17 26 E
Narvskoye Vdkhr. 54 59 18N 28 14 E
Narwana 68 29 39N 76 6 E
Naryan-Mar 52 68 0N 53 0 E
Naryilco 99 28 37S 141 53 E
Narym 58 59 0N 81 30 E
Narymskoye 58 49 10N 84 15 E
Naryn 58 41 26N 75 58 E
Nasa 50 66 29N 15 23 E
Nasarawa 85 8 32N 7 41 E
Năsăud 46 47 19N 24 29 E
Naseby 101 45 1S 170 10 E
Naser, Buheirat en 86 23 0N 32 30 E
Nashua, Iowa, U.S.A. 116 42 55N 92 34W
Nashua, Mont., U.S.A. 118 48 10N 106 25W
Nashua, N.H., U.S.A. 114 42 50N 71 25W
Nashville, Ark., U.S.A. 117 33 56N 93 50W
Nashville, Ga., U.S.A. 115 31 3N 83 15W
Nashville, Tenn., U.S.A. 115 36 12N 86 46W
Našice 42 45 32N 18 4 E
Nasielsk 28 52 35N 20 50 E
Nasik 70 19 58N 73 50 E
Nasirabad 68 26 15N 74 45 E
Naskaupi → 107 53 47N 60 51W
Naso 41 38 8N 14 46 E
Nass → 108 55 0N 129 40W
Nassau, Bahamas 121 25 0N 77 20W
Nassau, U.S.A. 113 42 30N 73 34W
Nassau, Bahía 128 55 20S 68 0W
Nasser City = Kôm Ombo 86 24 25N 32 52 E
Nasser, L. = Naser, Buheiret en 86 23 0N 32 30 E
Nassian 84 8 28N 3 28W
Nässjö 49 57 39N 14 42 E
Nastopoka Is. 106 57 0N 77 0W
Näsum 49 56 10N 14 29 E
Näsviken 48 61 46N 16 52 E
Nat Kyizin 71 14 57N 97 59 E
Nata 92 20 12S 26 12 E
Natagaima 126 3 37N 75 6W
Natal, Brazil 127 5 47S 35 13W
Natal, Can. 108 49 43N 114 51W
Natal, Indon. 72 0 35N 99 7 E
Natal □ 93 28 30S 30 30 E
Natalinci 42 44 15N 20 49 E
Naṭanz 65 33 30N 51 55 E
Natashquan 107 50 14N 61 46W
Natashquan → 107 50 7N 61 50W
Natchez 117 31 35N 91 25W
Natchitoches 117 31 47N 93 4W
Nathalia 99 36 1S 145 13 E
Nathdwara 68 24 55N 73 50 E
Natick 113 42 16N 71 19W
Natih 65 22 25N 56 30 E
Natimuk 99 36 42S 142 0 E
Nation → 108 55 30N 123 32W
National City 119 32 39N 117 7W
Natitingou 85 10 20N 1 26 E
Natividad, I. 120 27 50N 115 10W
Natoma 116 39 14N 99 0W
Natron, L. 90 2 20S 36 0 E
Natrona 112 40 39N 79 43W
Natrûn, W. el. → 86 30 25N 30 13 E
Natuna Besar, Kepulauan 72 4 0N 108 15 E
Natuna Selatan, Kepulauan 72 2 45N 109 0 E
Natural Bridge 113 44 5N 75 30W
Naturaliste, C. 96 33 32S 115 0 E
Naturaliste C. 99 40 50S 148 15 E
Naturaliste Channel 96 25 20S 113 0 E
Naubinway 106 46 7N 85 27W
Naucelle 20 44 13N 2 20 E
Nauders 26 46 54N 10 30 E
Nauen 24 52 36N 12 52 E
Naugatuck 113 41 28N 73 4W
Naujoji Vilnia 54 54 48N 25 27 E
Naumburg 24 51 10N 11 48 E
Nauru 94 1 0S 166 0 E
Nauru Is. 94 0 32S 166 55 E
Nauta 126 4 31S 73 35W
Nautla 120 20 20N 96 50W
Nava del Rey 30 41 22N 5 6W
Navacerrada, Puerto de 30 40 47N 4 0W
Navahermosa 31 39 41N 4 28W
Navajo Res. 119 36 55N 107 30W
Navalcarnero 30 40 17N 4 5W
Navalmoral de la Mata 30 39 52N 5 33W
Navalvillar de Pela 31 39 9N 5 24W
Navan = An Uaimh 15 53 39N 6 40W
Navare 20 43 20N 1 20W
Navarino, I. 128 55 0S 67 40W
Navarra □ 32 42 40N 1 40W
Navarre, France 20 43 15N 1 20W
Navarre, U.S.A. 112 40 43N 81 31W
Navarrenx 20 43 20N 0 45W
Navas del Marqués, Las 30 40 36N 4 20W
Navasota 117 30 20N 96 5W
Navassa 121 18 30N 75 0W
Nave 38 45 35N 10 17 E
Naver → 14 58 34N 4 15W
Navia 30 43 35N 6 42W
Navia → 30 43 15N 6 50W
Navia de Suarna 30 42 58N 6 59W
Navidad 124 33 57S 71 50W
Navlya 54 52 53N 34 30 E
Navoi 58 40 9N 65 22 E
Navojoa 120 27 0N 109 30W
Navolok 52 62 33N 39 57 E
Návpaktos 45 38 23N 21 50 E
Návplion 45 37 33N 22 50 E
Navrongo 85 10 51N 1 3W
Navsari 68 20 57N 72 59 E
Nawa Kot 68 28 21N 71 24 E
Nawabganj, Bangla. 69 24 35N 88 14 E
Nawabganj, India 69 26 56N 81 14 E
Nawabganj, Bareilly 69 28 32N 79 40 E
Nawabshah 68 26 15N 68 25 E
Nawada 69 24 50N 85 33 E
Nawakot 69 27 55N 85 10 E
Nawalgarh 68 27 50N 75 15 E
Nawapara 69 20 46N 82 33 E
Nawāsīf, Harrat 64 21 20N 42 10 E
Nawi 86 18 32N 30 50 E
Náxos 45 37 8N 25 25 E
Nay 20 43 10N 0 18W
Nây Band 65 27 20N 52 40 E
Nayakhan 59 61 56N 159 0 E
Nayarit □ 120 22 0N 105 0W
Nayé 84 14 28N 12 12W
Nazaré 31 39 36N 9 4W
Nazas 120 25 10N 104 6W
Nazas → 120 25 35N 103 25W
Naze, The 13 51 53N 1 19 E
Nazerat 62 32 42N 35 17 E
Nazir Hat 67 22 35N 91 49 E
Nazko 108 53 1N 123 37W
Nazko → 108 53 7N 123 34W
Nazret 87 8 32N 39 22 E
Nchanga 91 12 30S 27 49 E
Ncheu 91 14 50S 34 47 E
Ndala 90 4 45S 33 15 E
Ndalatando 88 9 12S 14 48 E
Ndali 85 9 50N 2 46 E
Ndareda 90 4 12S 35 30 E
Ndélé 81 8 25N 20 36 E
Ndendé 88 2 22S 11 23 E
Ndjamena 81 12 10N 14 59 E
Ndjolé 88 0 10S 10 45 E
Ndola 91 13 0S 28 34 E
Ndoto Mts. 90 2 0N 37 0 E
Nduguti 90 4 18S 34 41 E
Nea → 47 63 15N 11 0 E
Néa Epidhavros 45 37 40N 23 7 E
Néa Flippiás 44 39 12N 20 53 E
Néa Kallikrátia 44 40 21N 23 1 E
Néa Víssi 44 41 34N 26 33 E
Neagh, Lough 15 54 35N 6 25W
Neah Bay 118 48 25N 124 40W
Neamţ □ 46 47 0N 26 20 E
Neápolis, Kozan, Greece 44 40 20N 21 24 E
Neápolis, Lakonia, Greece 45 36 27N 23 8 E
Near Is. 104 53 0N 172 0 E
Neath 13 51 39N 3 49W
Nebbou 85 11 9N 1 51W
Nebine Cr. → 99 29 27S 146 56 E
Nebit Dag 58 39 30N 54 22 E
Nebolchy, U.S.S.R. 54 59 12N 32 58 E
Nebolchy, U.S.S.R. 54 59 8N 33 18 E
Nebraska □ 116 41 30N 100 0W
Nebraska City 116 40 40N 95 52W
Nèbrodi, Monti 40 37 55N 14 50 E
Necedah 116 44 2N 90 7W
Nechako → 108 53 30N 122 44W
Neches → 117 29 55N 93 52W
Neckar → 25 49 31N 8 26 E
Necochea 124 38 30S 58 50W
Nedelišće 39 46 23N 16 22 E
Nédha → 45 37 25N 21 45 E
Nedroma 82 35 1N 1 45W
Nedstrand 47 59 21N 5 49 E
Needles 119 34 50N 114 35W
Needles, The 13 50 39N 1 35W
Ñeembucú □ 124 27 0S 58 0W
Neemuch (Nimach) 68 24 30N 74 56 E
Neenah 114 44 10N 88 30W
Neepawa 109 50 15N 99 30W
Nefta 83 33 53N 7 50 E
Neftah Sidi Boubekeur 82 35 1N 0 4 E
Neftegorsk 57 44 25N 39 45 E
Neftyannyye Kamni 53 40 20N 50 55 E
Negapatam = Nagappattinam 70 10 46N 79 50 E
Negaunee 114 46 30N 87 36W
Negba 62 31 40N 34 41 E
Negele 87 5 20N 39 36 E
Negeri Sembilan □ 71 2 50N 102 10 E
Negev = Hanegev 62 30 50N 35 0 E
Negoiu 46 45 35N 24 32 E
Negombo 70 7 12N 79 50 E
Negotin 42 44 16N 22 37 E
Negotino 42 41 29N 22 9 E
Negra, La 124 23 46S 70 18W
Negra, Peña 30 42 11N 6 30W
Negra Pt. 73 18 40N 120 50 E
Negreira 30 42 54N 8 45W
Negreşti 46 46 50N 27 30 E
Négrine 83 34 30N 7 30 E
Negro →, Argent. 128 41 2S 62 47W
Negro →, Brazil 126 3 0S 60 0W
Negro →, Uruguay 125 33 24S 58 22W
Negros 73 10 0N 123 0 E
Negru Vodă 46 43 47N 28 21 E
Nehbandān 65 31 35N 60 5 E
Neheim-Hüsten 24 51 27N 7 58 E
Nehoiaşu 46 45 24N 26 20 E
Nei Monggol Zizhiqu □ 76 42 0N 112 0 E
Neidpath 109 50 12N 107 20W
Neihart 118 47 0N 110 44W
Neijiang 75 29 35N 104 55 E
Neilton 118 17 24N 123 52W
Neira de Jusá 30 42 53N 7 14W
Neisse → 24 52 4N 14 46 E
Neiva 126 2 56N 75 18W
Neixiang 77 33 10N 111 52 E
Nejanilini L. 109 59 33N 97 48W
Nejo 87 9 30N 35 28 E
Nekemte 87 9 4N 36 30 E
Nêkheb 86 25 10N 32 48 E
Neksø 49 55 4N 15 8 E
Nelas 30 40 32N 7 52W
Nelaug 47 58 39N 8 40 E
Nelia 98 20 39S 142 12 E
Nelidovo 54 56 13N 32 49 E
Neligh 116 42 11N 98 2W
Nelkan 59 57 40N 136 4 E
Nellikuppam 70 11 46N 79 43 E
Nellore 70 14 27N 79 59 E
Nelma 59 47 39N 139 0 E
Nelson, Austral. 100 38 3S 141 2 E
Nelson, Can. 108 49 30N 117 20W
Nelson, N.Z. 101 41 18S 173 16 E
Nelson, U.K. 12 53 50N 2 14W
Nelson, Ariz., U.S.A. 119 35 35N 113 16W
Nelson, Nev., U.S.A. 119 35 46N 114 48W
Nelson □ 101 42 11S 172 15 E
Nelson → 109 54 33N 98 2W
Nelson, C., Austral. 99 38 26S 141 32 E
Nelson, C., P.N.G. 98 9 0S 149 20 E
Nelson, Estrecho 128 51 30S 75 0W
Nelson Forks 108 59 30N 124 0W
Nelson House 109 55 47N 98 51W
Nelson L. 109 55 48N 100 7W
Nelspruit 93 25 29S 30 59 E
Néma 84 16 40N 7 15W
Neman (Nemunas) → 54 55 25N 21 10 E
Neméa 45 37 49N 22 40 E
Nemeiben L. 109 55 20N 105 20W
Nemira 46 46 17N 26 19 E
Nemours 19 48 16N 2 40 E
Nemunas = Neman → 54 55 25N 21 10 E
Nemuro 74 43 20N 145 35 E
Nemuro-Kaikyō 74 43 30N 145 30 E
Nemuy 59 55 40N 136 9 E
Nen Jiang → 76 45 28N 124 30 E
Nenagh 15 52 52N 8 11W
Nenana 104 64 30N 149 20W
Nene → 12 52 38N 0 13 E
Nenjiang 75 49 10N 125 10 E
Neno 91 15 25S 34 40 E
Nenusa, Kepulauan 73 4 45N 127 1 E
Neodesha 117 37 30N 95 37W
Néon Petritsi 44 41 16N 23 15 E
Neosho 117 36 56N 94 28W
Neosho → 117 35 59N 95 10W
Nepal ■ 69 28 0N 84 30 E
Nepalganj 69 28 5N 81 40 E
Nephi 118 39 43N 111 52W
Nephin 15 54 1N 9 21W
Nepomuk 26 49 29N 13 35 E
Neptune City 113 40 13N 74 4W
Néra → 42 44 48N 21 25 E
Nérac 20 44 8N 0 21 E
Nerchinsk 59 52 0N 116 39 E
Nerchinskiy Zavod 59 51 20N 119 40 E
Nereju 46 45 43N 26 43 E
Nerekhta 55 57 26N 40 38 E
Néret L. 107 54 45N 70 44W
Neretva → 42 43 1N 17 27 E
Neretvanski Kanal 42 43 7N 17 10 E
Neringa 54 55 30N 21 5 E
Nerja 31 36 43N 3 55W
Nerl → 55 56 11N 40 34 E
Nerokoúrou 45 35 29N 24 3 E
Nerpio 33 38 11N 2 16W
Nerva 31 37 42N 6 30W
Nes 50 65 53N 17 24W
Nes Ziyyona 62 31 56N 34 48W
Nesbyen 47 60 34N 9 35 E
Nesebŭr 43 42 41N 27 46 E
Nesflaten 47 59 38N 6 48 E
Neskaupstaður 50 65 9N 13 42W
Nesland 47 59 31N 7 59 E
Neslandsvatn 47 58 57N 9 10 E
Nesle 19 49 45N 2 53 E
Nesodden 47 59 48N 10 40 E
Nesque → 21 43 59N 4 59 E
Ness, Loch 14 57 15N 4 30W
Nestórion Óros 44 40 24N 21 5 E
Néstos → 44 41 20N 24 35 E
Nesttun 47 60 19N 5 21 E
Nesvizh 54 53 14N 26 38 E
Netanya 62 32 20N 34 51 E
Nète → 16 51 7N 4 14 E
Nether Stowey 13 51 0N 3 10W
Netherbury 13 50 46N 2 45W
Netherdale 97 21 10S 148 33 E
Netherlands ■ 16 52 0N 5 30 E
Netherlands Antilles □ 121 12 30N 68 0W
Netherlands Guiana = Surinam ■ 127 4 0N 56 0W
Neto → 41 39 13N 17 8 E
Netrakona 69 24 53N 90 47 E
Nettancourt 19 48 51N 4 57 E
Nettilling L. 105 66 30N 71 0W
Nettuno 40 41 29N 12 40 E
Netzahualcoyotl, Presa 120 17 10N 93 30W
Neu-Isenburg 25 50 3N 8 42 E
Neu-Ulm 25 48 23N 10 2 E
Neubrandenburg 24 53 33N 13 17 E
Neubrandenburg □ 24 53 30N 13 20 E
Neubukow 24 54 1N 11 40 E
Neuburg 25 48 43N 11 11 E
Neuchâtel 25 47 0N 6 55 E
Neuchâtel □ 25 47 0N 6 55 E
Neuchâtel, Lac de 25 46 53N 6 50 E
Neudau 26 47 11N 16 6 E
Neuenhaus 24 52 30N 6 55 E
Neuf-Brisach 19 48 0N 7 30 E
Neufahrn 25 48 44N 12 11 E
Neufchâteau, Belg. 16 49 50N 5 25 E
Neufchâteau, France 19 48 21N 5 40 E
Neufchâtel 19 49 43N 1 30 E
Neufchâtel-sur-Aisne 19 49 26N 4 0 E
Neuhaus 24 53 16N 10 54 E
Neuillé-Pont-Pierre 18 47 33N 0 33 E
Neuilly-St-Front 19 49 10N 3 15 E
Neukalen 24 53 49N 12 48 E
Neumarkt 25 49 16N 11 28 E
Neumarkt-Sankt Veit 25 48 22N 12 30 E
Neumünster 24 54 4N 9 58 E
Neung-sur-Beuvron 19 47 30N 1 50 E
Neunkirchen, Austria 26 47 43N 16 4 E
Neunkirchen, Ger. 25 49 23N 7 12 E
Neuquén 128 38 55S 68 0 E
Neuquén □ 124 38 0S 69 50W
Neuruppin 24 52 56N 12 48 E
Neuse → 115 35 5N 76 30W
Neusiedl 27 47 57N 16 50 E
Neusiedler See 27 47 50N 16 47 E
Neuss 24 51 12N 6 39 E
Neussargues-Moissac 20 45 9N 3 1 E
Neustadt, Baden-W., Ger. 25 47 54N 8 13 E
Neustadt, Bayern, Ger. 25 50 23N 11 0 E
Neustadt, Bayern, Ger. 25 49 42N 12 10 E
Neustadt, Bayern, Ger. 25 48 48N 11 47 E
Neustadt, Bayern, Ger. 25 49 34N 10 37 E
Neustadt, Gera, Ger. 24 50 45N 11 43 E
Neustadt, Hessen, Ger. 24 50 51N 9 9 E
Neustadt, Niedersachsen, Ger. 24 52 30N 9 30 E
Neustadt, Potsdam, Ger. 24 52 50N 12 27 E
Neustadt, Rhld-Pfz., Ger. 25 49 21N 8 10 E
Neustadt, Schleswig-Holstein, Ger. 24 54 6N 10 49 E
Neustrelitz 24 53 22N 13 4 E
Neuvic 20 45 23N 2 16 E
Neuville, Rhône, France 21 45 52N 4 51 E
Neuville, Vienne, France 18 46 41N 0 15 E
Neuville-aux-Bois 19 48 4N 2 3 E
Neuvy-le-Roi 18 47 36N 0 36 E
Neuvy-St-Sépulchure 20 46 35N 1 48 E
Neuvy-sur-Barangeon 19 47 20N 2 15 E
Neuwerk 24 53 55N 8 30 E
Neuwied 24 50 26N 7 29 E
Neva → 52 59 50N 30 30 E
Nevada 117 37 51N 94 22W
Nevada □ 118 39 20N 117 0W
Nevada City 118 39 20N 121 0W
Nevada de Sta. Marta, Sa. 126 10 55N 73 50W
Nevada, Sierra, Spain 33 37 3N 3 15W
Nevada, Sierra, U.S.A. 118 39 0N 120 30W
Nevado, Cerro 124 35 30S 68 32W
Nevanka 59 56 31N 98 55 E
Nevasa 70 19 34N 75 0 E
Nevel 54 56 0N 29 55 E
Nevers 19 47 0N 3 9 E
Nevertire 99 31 50S 147 44 E
Nevesinje 42 43 14N 18 6 E
Neville 109 49 58N 107 39W
Nevinnomyssk 57 44 40N 42 0 E
Nevis 121 17 0N 62 30W

Nevlunghavn **Nootka I.**

Place	Page	Lat.	Long.
Nevlunghavn	**47**	55 58N	9 52 E
Nevrokop = Gotse Delchev	**43**	41 33N	23 46 E
Nevşehir	**64**	38 33N	34 40 E
Nevyansk	**52**	57 30N	60 13 E
New Albany, Ind., U.S.A.	**114**	38 20N	85 50W
New Albany, Miss., U.S.A.	**117**	34 30N	89 0W
New Albany, Pa., U.S.A.	**113**	41 35N	76 28W
New Amsterdam	**126**	6 15N	57 36W
New Bedford	**114**	41 40N	70 52W
New Bern	**115**	35 8N	77 3W
New Bethlehem	**112**	41 0N	79 22W
New Bloomfield	**112**	40 24N	77 12W
New Boston	**117**	33 27N	94 21W
New Braunfels	**117**	29 43N	98 9W
New Brighton, N.Z.	**101**	43 29 S	172 43 E
New Brighton, U.S.A.	**112**	40 42N	80 19W
New Britain, P.N.G.	**94**	5 50 S	150 20 E
New Britain, U.S.A.	**114**	41 41N	72 47W
New Brunswick	**114**	40 30N	74 28W
New Brunswick □	**107**	46 50N	66 30W
New Bussa	**85**	9 53N	4 31 E
New Byrd	**5**	80 0 S	120 0W
New Caledonia = Nouvelle-Calédonie	**94**	21 0 S	165 0 E
New Castile = Castilla La Neuva	**31**	39 45N	3 20W
New Castle, Ind., U.S.A.	**114**	39 55N	85 23W
New Castle, Pa., U.S.A.	**114**	41 0N	80 20W
New City	**113**	41 8N	74 0W
New Cristóbal	**120**	9 22N	79 40W
New Cumberland	**112**	40 30N	80 36W
New Delhi	**68**	28 37N	77 13 E
New Denver	**108**	50 0N	117 25W
New England	**116**	46 36N	102 47W
New England Ra.	**97**	30 20 S	151 45 E
New Forest	**13**	50 53N	1 40W
New Glasgow	**107**	45 35N	62 36W
New Guinea	**94**	4 0 S	136 0 E
New Hamburg	**112**	43 23N	80 42W
New Hampshire □	**114**	43 40N	71 40W
New Hampton	**116**	43 2N	92 20W
New Hanover, P.N.G.	**98**	2 30 S	150 10 E
New Hanover, S. Afr.	**93**	29 22 S	30 31 E
New Haven, Conn., U.S.A.	**114**	41 20N	72 54W
New Haven, Mich., U.S.A.	**112**	42 44N	82 46W
New Hazelton	**108**	55 20N	127 30W
* New Hebrides	**94**	15 0 S	168 0 E
New Iberia	**117**	30 2N	91 54W
New Ireland	**94**	3 20 S	151 50 E
New Jersey □	**114**	40 30N	74 10W
New Kensington	**114**	40 36N	79 43W
New Lexington	**114**	39 40N	82 15W
New Liskeard	**106**	47 31N	79 41W
New London, Conn., U.S.A.	**114**	41 23N	72 8W
New London, Minn., U.S.A.	**116**	45 17N	94 55W
New London, Ohio, U.S.A.	**112**	41 4N	82 25W
New London, Wis., U.S.A.	**116**	44 23N	88 43W
New Madrid	**117**	36 40N	89 30W
New Meadows	**118**	45 0N	116 32W
New Mexico □	**110**	34 30N	106 0W
New Milford, Conn., U.S.A.	**113**	41 35N	73 25W
New Milford, Pa., U.S.A.	**113**	41 50N	75 45W
New Norfolk	**97**	42 46 S	147 2 E
New Orleans	**117**	30 0N	90 5W
New Philadelphia	**114**	40 29N	81 25W
New Plymouth, N.Z.	**101**	39 4 S	174 5 E
New Plymouth, U.S.A.	**118**	43 58N	116 49W
New Providence	**121**	25 25N	78 35W
New Radnor	**13**	52 15N	3 10W
New Richmond	**116**	45 6N	92 34W
New Roads	**117**	30 43N	91 30W
New Rochelle	**113**	40 55N	73 46W
New Rockford	**116**	47 44N	99 7W
New Ross	**15**	52 24N	6 58W
New Salem	**116**	46 51N	101 25W
New Siberian Is. = Novosibirskiye Os.	**59**	75 0N	142 0 E
New Smyrna Beach	**115**	29 0N	80 50W
New South Wales □	**97**	33 0 S	146 0 E
New Town	**116**	47 59N	102 30W
New Ulm	**116**	44 15N	94 30W
New Waterford	**107**	46 13N	60 4W
New Westminster	**108**	49 13N	122 55W
New York □	**114**	42 40N	76 0W
New York City	**114**	40 45N	74 0W
New Zealand ■	**94**	40 0 S	176 0 E
Newala	**91**	10 58 S	39 18 E
Newala □	**91**	10 46 S	39 20 E
Newark, Del., U.S.A.	**114**	39 42N	75 45W
Newark, N.J., U.S.A.	**114**	40 41N	74 12W
Newark, N.Y., U.S.A.	**114**	43 2N	77 10W
Newark, Ohio, U.S.A.	**114**	40 5N	82 24W
Newark-on-Trent	**12**	53 6N	0 48W
Newaygo	**114**	43 25N	85 48W
Newberg	**118**	45 22N	123 0W
Newberry, Mich., U.S.A.	**114**	46 20N	85 32W
Newberry, S.C., U.S.A.	**115**	34 17N	81 37W
Newbrook	**108**	54 24N	112 57W
Newburgh	**114**	41 30N	74 1W
Newbury, U.K.	**13**	51 24N	1 19W
Newbury, U.S.A.	**113**	44 7N	72 6W
Newburyport	**114**	42 48N	70 50W
Newcastle, Austral.	**97**	33 0 S	151 46 E
Newcastle, Can.	**107**	47 1N	65 38W
Newcastle, S. Afr.	**93**	27 45 S	29 58 E
Newcastle, U.K.	**15**	54 13N	5 54W
Newcastle, U.S.A.	**116**	43 50N	104 12W
Newcastle Emlyn	**13**	52 2N	4 29W
Newcastle Ra.	**97**	15 45 S	130 15 E
Newcastle-under-Lyme	**12**	53 2N	2 15W
Newcastle-upon-Tyne	**12**	54 59N	1 37W
Newcastle Waters	**96**	17 30 S	133 28 E
Newdegate	**96**	33 6 S	119 0 E
Newe Etan	**62**	32 30N	35 32 E
Newe Sha'anan	**62**	32 47N	34 59 E
Newe Zohar	**62**	31 9N	35 21 E
Newell	**116**	44 48N	103 25W
Newenham, C.	**104**	58 40N	162 15W
Newfoundland	**107**	48 30N	56 0W
Newfoundland □	**107**	53 0N	58 0W
Newhalem	**108**	48 41N	121 16W
Newham	**13**	51 31N	0 2 E
Newhaven	**13**	50 47N	0 4 E
Newkirk	**117**	36 52N	97 3W
Newman, Mt.	**96**	23 20 S	119 34 E
Newmarket, Can.	**112**	44 3N	79 28W
Newmarket, Ireland	**15**	52 13N	9 0W
Newmarket, U.K.	**13**	52 15N	0 23 E
Newmarket, U.S.A.	**113**	43 4N	70 57W
Newnan	**115**	33 22N	84 48W
Newnes	**99**	33 9 S	150 16 E
Newport, Gwent, U.K.	**13**	51 35N	3 0W
Newport, I. of W., U.K.	**13**	50 42N	1 18W
Newport, Salop, U.K.	**13**	52 47N	2 22W
Newport, Ark., U.S.A.	**117**	35 38N	91 15W
Newport, Ky., U.S.A.	**114**	39 5N	84 23W
Newport, N.H., U.S.A.	**114**	43 23N	72 8W
Newport, Oreg., U.S.A.	**118**	44 41N	124 2W
Newport, Pa., U.S.A.	**112**	40 28N	77 8W
Newport, R.I., U.S.A.	**114**	41 13N	71 19W
Newport, Tenn., U.S.A.	**115**	35 59N	83 12W
Newport, Vt., U.S.A.	**114**	44 57N	72 17W
Newport, Wash., U.S.A.	**118**	48 11N	117 2W
Newport Beach	**119**	33 40N	117 58W
Newport News	**114**	37 2N	76 30W
Newquay	**13**	50 24N	5 6W
Newry	**15**	54 10N	6 20W
Newry & Mourne □	**15**	54 10N	6 15W
Newton, Iowa, U.S.A.	**116**	41 40N	93 3W
Newton, Mass., U.S.A.	**114**	42 21N	71 10W
Newton, Miss., U.S.A.	**117**	32 19N	89 10W
Newton, N.C., U.S.A.	**115**	35 42N	81 10W
Newton, N.J., U.S.A.	**114**	41 3N	74 46W
Newton, Texas, U.S.A.	**117**	30 54N	93 42W
Newton Abbot	**13**	50 32N	3 37W
Newton Boyd	**99**	29 45 S	152 16 E
Newton Stewart	**14**	54 57N	4 30W
Newtonmore	**14**	57 4N	4 7W
Newtown	**13**	52 31N	3 19W
Newtownabbey	**15**	54 40N	5 55W
Newtownabbey □	**15**	54 45N	6 0W
Newtownards	**15**	54 37N	5 40W
Newville	**112**	40 10N	77 24W
Nexon	**20**	45 41N	1 11 E
Neya	**55**	58 21N	43 49 E
Neyrīz	**65**	29 15N	54 19 E
Neyshābūr	**65**	36 10N	58 50 E
Neyyattinkara	**70**	8 26N	77 5 E
Nezhin	**54**	51 5N	31 55 E
Nezperce	**118**	46 13N	116 15W
Ngabang	**72**	0 23N	109 55 E
Ngabordamlu, Tanjung	**73**	6 56 S	134 11 E
Ngambé	**85**	5 48N	11 29 E
Ngami Depression	**92**	20 30 S	22 46 E
Ngamo	**91**	19 3 S	27 32 E
Nganglong Kangri	**67**	33 0N	81 0 E
Nganjuk	**73**	7 32 S	111 55 E
Ngaoundéré	**88**	7 15N	13 35 E
Ngapara	**101**	44 57 S	170 46 E
Ngara	**90**	2 29 S	30 40 E
Ngara □	**90**	2 29 S	30 40 E
Ngau	**101**	18 2 S	179 18 E
Ngawi	**73**	7 24 S	111 26 E
Ngha Lo	**71**	21 33N	104 28 E
Ngiva	**92**	16 48 S	15 50 E
Ngoma	**91**	13 8 S	33 45 E
Ngomahura	**91**	20 26 S	30 43 E
Ngomba	**91**	8 20 S	32 53 E
Ngop	**87**	6 17N	30 9 E
Ngoring Hu	**75**	34 55N	97 5 E
Ngorkou	**84**	15 40N	3 41W
Ngorongoro	**90**	3 11 S	35 32 E
Ngozi	**90**	2 54 S	29 50 E
Ngudu	**90**	2 58 S	33 25 E
Nguigmi	**81**	14 20N	13 20 E
Ngunga	**90**	3 37 S	33 37 E
Ngunza	**88**	11 10 S	13 48 E
Nguru	**85**	12 56N	10 29 E
Nguru Mts.	**90**	6 0 S	37 30 E
Nha Trang	**71**	12 16N	109 10 E
Nhacoongo	**93**	24 18 S	35 14 E
Nhangutazi, L.	**93**	24 0 S	34 30 E
Nhill	**99**	36 18 S	141 40 E
Nia-nia	**90**	1 30N	27 40 E
Niafounké	**84**	16 0N	4 5W
Niagara	**114**	45 45N	88 0W
Niagara Falls, Can.	**106**	43 7N	79 5W
Niagara Falls, U.S.A.	**114**	43 5N	79 0W
Niagara-on-the-Lake	**112**	43 15N	79 4W
Niah	**72**	3 58N	113 46 E
Nialia, L.	**100**	33 20 S	141 42 E
Niamey	**85**	13 27N	2 6 E
Nianforando	**84**	9 37N	10 36W
Nianfors	**48**	61 36N	16 46 E
Niangara	**90**	3 42N	27 50 E
Nianzishan	**76**	47 31N	122 53 E
Nias	**72**	1 0N	97 30 E
Niassa □	**91**	13 30 S	36 0 E
Nibbiano	**38**	44 54N	9 20 E
Nibe	**49**	56 59N	9 38 E
Nibong Tebal	**71**	5 10N	100 29 E
Nicaragua ■	**121**	11 40N	85 30W
Nicaragua, Lago de	**121**	12 0N	85 30W
Nicastro	**41**	39 0N	16 18 E
Nice	**21**	43 42N	7 14 E
Niceville	**115**	30 30N	86 30W
Nichinan	**74**	31 38N	131 23 E
Nicholás, Canal	**121**	23 30N	80 5W
Nicholasville	**114**	37 54N	84 31W
Nichols	**113**	42 1N	76 22W
Nicholson	**113**	41 37N	75 47W
Nicobar Is.	**60**	9 0N	93 0 E
Nicola	**108**	50 12N	120 40W
Nicolet	**106**	46 17N	72 35W
Nicolls Town	**121**	25 8N	78 0W
Nicopolis	**45**	39 2N	20 37 E
Nicosia, Cyprus	**64**	35 10N	33 25 E
Nicosia, Italy	**41**	37 45N	14 22 E
Nicótera	**41**	38 33N	15 57 E
Nicoya, G. de	**121**	10 0N	85 0W
Nicoya, Pen. de	**121**	9 45N	85 40W
Nidd →	**12**	54 1N	1 32W
Nidda	**24**	50 24N	9 2 E
Nidda →	**25**	50 6N	8 34 E
Nidzica	**28**	53 25N	20 28 E
Niebüll	**24**	54 47N	8 49 E
Nied →	**19**	49 23N	6 40 E
Niederaula	**24**	50 48N	9 37 E
Niederbronn	**19**	48 57N	7 39 E
Niedere Tauern	**26**	47 20N	14 0 E
Niedermarsberg	**24**	51 28N	8 52 E
Niederösterreich □	**26**	48 25N	15 40 E
Niedersachsen □	**24**	52 45N	9 0 E
Niellé	**84**	10 5N	5 38W
Niemba	**90**	5 58 S	28 24 E
Niemcza	**28**	50 42N	16 47 E
Niemodlin	**28**	50 38N	17 38 E
Niemur	**100**	35 17 S	144 9 E
Nienburg	**24**	52 38N	9 15 E
Niepołomice	**27**	50 3N	20 13 E
Niers →	**24**	51 45N	5 58 E
Niesky	**24**	51 18N	14 48 E
Nieszawa	**28**	52 52N	18 50 E
Nieuw Amsterdam	**127**	5 53N	55 5W
Nieuw Nickerie	**127**	6 0N	56 59W
Nieuwpoort	**16**	51 8N	2 45 E
Nieves	**30**	42 7N	8 26W
Nièvre □	**19**	47 10N	3 40 E
Niğde	**64**	38 0N	34 40 E
Nigel	**93**	26 27 S	28 25 E
Niger ■	**85**	13 30N	10 0 E
Niger □	**85**	10 0N	5 0 E
Niger →	**85**	5 33N	6 33 E
Nigeria ■	**85**	8 30N	8 0 E
Nightcaps	**101**	45 57 S	168 2 E
Nigríta	**44**	40 56N	23 29 E
Nihtaur	**69**	29 20N	78 23 E
Nii-Jima	**74**	34 20N	139 15 E
Niigata	**74**	37 58N	139 0 E
Niigata □	**74**	37 15N	138 45 E
Niihama	**74**	33 55N	133 16 E
Niihau	**110**	21 55N	160 10W
Nijar	**33**	36 53N	2 15W
Nijkerk	**16**	52 13N	5 30 E
Nijmegen	**16**	51 50N	5 52 E
Nijverdal	**16**	52 22N	6 28 E
Nike	**85**	6 26N	7 29 E
Nikel	**50**	69 24N	30 12 E
Nikiniki	**73**	9 49 S	124 30 E
Nikitas	**44**	40 13N	23 34 E
Nikki	**85**	9 58N	3 12 E
Nikkō	**74**	36 45N	139 35 E
Nikolayev	**56**	46 58N	32 0 E
Nikolayevsk	**55**	50 0N	45 35 E
Nikolayevsk-na-Amur	**59**	53 8N	140 44 E
Nikolsk	**55**	59 30N	45 28 E
Nikolskoye	**59**	55 12N	166 0 E
Nikopol, Bulg.	**43**	43 43N	24 54 E
Nikopol, U.S.S.R.	**56**	47 35N	34 25 E
Niksar	**56**	40 31N	37 2 E
Nīkshahr	**65**	26 15N	60 10 E
Nikšić	**42**	42 50N	18 57 E
Nîl el Abyad →	**87**	15 38N	32 31 E
Nîl el Azraq →	**87**	15 38N	32 31 E
Nîl, Nahr en →	**86**	30 10N	31 6 E
Niland	**119**	33 16N	115 30W
Nile = Nîl, Nahr en →	**86**	30 10N	31 6 E
Nile □	**90**	2 0N	31 30 E
Nile Delta	**86**	31 40N	31 0 E
Niles	**114**	41 8N	80 40W
Nilgiri Hills	**70**	11 30N	76 30 E
Nimach = Neemuch	**68**	24 30N	74 56 E
Nimbahera	**68**	24 37N	74 45 E
Nîmes	**21**	43 50N	4 23 E
Nimfaíon, Ákra-	**44**	40 5N	24 20 E
Nimingarra	**96**	20 31 S	119 55 E
Nimmitabel	**99**	36 29 S	149 15 E
Nimneryskiy	**59**	57 50N	125 10 E
Nimrod Glacier	**5**	82 27 S	161 0 E
Nimule	**87**	3 32N	32 3 E
Nin	**39**	44 16N	15 12 E
Nindigully	**99**	28 21 S	148 50 E
Ninemile	**108**	56 0N	130 7W
Ninety Mile Beach, The	**97**	38 15 S	147 24 E
Nineveh = Nīnawá	**64**	36 25N	43 10 E
Ning'an	**76**	44 22N	129 20 E
Ningbo	**75**	29 51N	121 28 E
Ningde	**75**	26 38N	119 23 E
Ningdu	**77**	26 25N	115 59 E
Ningjin	**76**	37 35N	114 57 E
Ningming	**77**	22 8N	107 4 E
Ningpo = Ningbo	**75**	29 51N	121 28 E
Ningqiang	**77**	32 47N	106 15 E
Ningshan	**77**	33 21N	108 21 E
Ningsia Hui A.R. = Ningxia Huizu Zizhiqu □	**76**	38 0N	106 0 E
Ningwu	**76**	39 0N	112 18 E
Ningxia Huizu Zizhiqu □	**76**	38 0N	106 0 E
Ningxiang	**77**	28 15N	112 30 E
Ningyuan	**77**	25 37N	111 57 E
Ninh Binh	**71**	20 15N	105 55 E
Ninove	**16**	50 51N	4 2 E
Nioaque	**125**	21 5 S	55 50W
Niobrara	**116**	42 48N	97 59W
Niobrara →	**116**	42 45N	98 0W
Niono	**84**	14 15N	6 0W
Nioro du Rip	**84**	13 40N	15 50W
Nioro du Sahel	**84**	15 15N	9 30W
Niort	**20**	46 19N	0 29W
Nipani	**70**	16 20N	74 25 E
Nipawin	**109**	53 20N	104 0W
Nipawin Prov. Park	**109**	54 0N	104 37W
Nipigon	**106**	49 0N	88 17W
Nipigon, L.	**106**	49 50N	88 30W
Nipin →	**109**	55 46N	108 35W
Nipishish L.	**107**	54 12N	60 45W
Nipissing L.	**106**	46 20N	80 0W
Nipomo	**119**	35 4N	120 29W
Niquelândia	**127**	14 33 S	48 23W
Nira →	**70**	17 58N	75 8 E
Nirmal	**70**	19 3N	78 20 E
Nirmali	**69**	26 20N	86 35 E
Niš	**42**	43 19N	21 58 E
Nisa	**31**	39 30N	7 41W
Nişāb	**63**	14 25N	46 29 E
Nišava →	**42**	43 20N	21 46 E
Niscemi	**41**	37 8N	14 21 E
Nishinomiya	**74**	34 45N	135 20 E
Nísiros	**45**	36 35N	27 12 E
Niskibi →	**106**	56 29N	88 9W
Nisko	**28**	50 35N	22 7 E
Nisporeny	**46**	47 4N	28 10 E
Nissafors	**49**	57 25N	13 37 E
Nissan →	**49**	56 40N	12 51 E
Nissedal	**47**	59 10N	8 30 E
Nisser	**47**	59 7N	8 28 E
Nissum Fjord	**49**	56 20N	8 11 E
Nisutlin →	**108**	60 14N	132 34W
Nitjā'	**64**	27 15N	48 35 E
Nitchequon	**107**	53 10N	70 58W
Niterói	**125**	22 52 S	43 0W
Nith →	**14**	55 20N	3 5W
Nitra	**27**	48 19N	18 4 E
Nitra →	**27**	47 46N	18 10 E
Nittedal	**47**	60 1N	10 57 E
Nittendau	**25**	49 12N	12 16 E
Niuafo'ou	**101**	15 30 S	175 58W
Niue I. (Savage I.)	**95**	19 2 S	169 54W
Niut	**72**	0 55N	110 6 E
Nivelles	**16**	50 35N	4 20 E
Nivernais	**19**	47 0N	3 40 E
Nixon, Nev., U.S.A.	**118**	39 54N	119 22W
Nixon, Tex., U.S.A.	**117**	29 17N	97 45W
Nizam Sagar	**70**	18 10N	77 58 E
Nizamabad	**70**	18 45N	78 7 E
Nizamghat	**67**	28 20N	95 45 E
Nizhne Kolymsk	**59**	68 34N	160 55 E
Nizhne-Vartovskoye	**58**	60 56N	76 38 E
Nizhneangarsk	**59**	55 47N	109 30 E
Nizhnegorskiy	**56**	45 27N	34 38 E
Nizhneudinsk	**59**	54 54N	99 3 E
Nizhneyansk	**59**	71 26N	136 4 E
Nizhniy Lomov	**55**	53 34N	43 38 E
Nizhniy Novgorod = Gorkiy	**55**	56 20N	44 0 E
Nizhniy Tagil	**52**	57 55N	59 57 E
Nizhnyaya Tunguska →	**59**	64 20N	93 0 E
Nizip	**64**	37 5N	37 50 E
Nízké Tatry	**27**	48 55N	20 0 E
Nizza Monferrato	**38**	44 46N	8 22 E
Njakwa	**91**	11 1 S	33 56 E
Njanji	**91**	14 25 S	31 46 E
Njinjo	**91**	8 48 S	38 54 E
Njombe	**91**	9 20 S	34 50 E
Njombe □	**91**	9 20 S	34 49 E
Njombe →	**90**	6 56 S	35 6 E
Nkambe	**85**	6 35N	10 40 E
Nkana	**91**	12 50 S	28 8 E
Nkawkaw	**85**	6 36N	0 49W
Nkhota Kota	**91**	12 56 S	34 15 E
Nkongsamba	**88**	4 55N	9 55 E
Nkwanta	**84**	6 10N	2 10W
Noatak	**104**	67 32N	162 59W
Nobel	**112**	45 25N	80 6W
Nobeoka	**74**	32 36N	131 41 E
Noblejas	**32**	39 58N	3 26W
Noblesville	**114**	40 1N	85 59W
Noce →	**38**	46 9N	11 4 E
Nocera Inferiore	**41**	40 45N	14 37 E
Nocera Terinese	**41**	39 2N	16 9 E
Nocera Umbra	**39**	43 8N	12 47 E
Noci	**41**	40 47N	17 7 E
Nockatunga	**99**	27 42 S	142 42 E
Nocona	**117**	33 48N	97 45W
Nocrich	**46**	45 55N	24 26 E
Noel	**117**	36 36N	94 29W
Nogales, Mexico	**120**	31 20N	110 56W
Nogales, U.S.A.	**119**	31 33N	110 56W
Nogat →	**28**	54 17N	19 17 E
Nōgata	**74**	33 48N	130 44 E
Nogent-en-Bassigny	**19**	48 0N	5 20 E
Nogent-le-Rotrou	**18**	48 20N	0 50 E
Nogent-sur-Seine	**19**	48 30N	3 30 E
Noginsk, Moskva, U.S.S.R.	**55**	55 50N	38 25 E
Noginsk, Sib., U.S.S.R.	**59**	64 30N	90 50 E
Nogoa →	**97**	23 40 S	147 55 E
Nogoyá	**124**	32 24 S	59 48W
Nógrád □	**27**	48 0N	19 30 E
Nogueira de Ramuin	**30**	42 21N	7 43W
Noguera Pallaresa →	**32**	42 15N	1 0 E
Noguera Ribagorzana →	**32**	41 40N	0 43 E
Nohar	**68**	29 11N	74 49 E
Noi →	**71**	14 50N	100 15 E
Noire, Mt.	**18**	48 11N	3 40W
Noirétable	**20**	45 48N	3 46 E
Noirmoutier	**18**	47 0N	2 15W
Noirmoutier, Î. de	**18**	46 58N	2 10W
Nojane	**92**	23 15 S	20 14 E
Nok Kundi	**66**	28 50N	62 45 E
Nokaneng	**92**	19 40 S	22 17 E
Nokhtuysk	**59**	60 0N	117 45 E
Nokomis	**109**	51 35N	105 0W
Nokomis L.	**109**	57 0N	103 0W
Nol	**49**	57 56N	12 5 E
Nola, C. Afr. Rep.	**88**	3 35N	16 4 E
Nola, Italy	**41**	40 54N	14 29 E
Nolay	**19**	46 58N	4 35 E
Noli, C. di	**38**	44 12N	8 26 E
Nolinsk	**55**	57 28N	49 57 E
Noma Omuramba →	**92**	18 52 S	20 53 E
Noman L.	**109**	62 15N	108 55W
Nome	**104**	64 30N	165 24W
Nonacho L.	**109**	61 42N	109 40W
Nonancourt	**18**	48 47N	1 11 E
Nonant-le-Pin	**18**	48 42N	0 12 E
Nonda	**98**	20 40 S	142 28 E
Nong Khae	**71**	14 29N	100 53 E
Nong Khai	**71**	17 50N	102 46 E
Nong'an	**76**	44 25N	125 5 E
Nonoava	**120**	27 28N	106 44W
Nontron	**20**	45 31N	0 40 E
Noonan	**116**	48 51N	102 59W
Noondoo	**99**	28 35 S	148 30 E
Noord Brabant □	**16**	51 40N	5 0 E
Noord Holland □	**16**	52 30N	4 45 E
Noordbeveland	**16**	51 35N	3 50 E
Noordoostpolder	**16**	52 45N	5 45 E
Noordwijk aan Zee	**16**	52 14N	4 26 E
Nootka	**108**	49 38N	126 38W
Nootka I.	**108**	49 32N	126 42W

* *Renamed Vanuatu* ■

Nóqui Nyköping

Name	Page	Lat.	Long.
Nóqui	88	5 55S	13 30 E
Nora, Ethiopia	87	16 6N	40 4 E
Nora, Sweden	48	59 32N	15 2 E
Noranda	106	48 20N	79 0W
Norberg	48	60 4N	15 56 E
Nórcia	39	42 50N	13 5 E
Nord □	19	50 15N	3 30 E
Nord-Ostee Kanal	24	54 15N	9 40 E
Nord-Süd Kanal	24	53 0N	10 32 E
Nord-Trøndelag fylke □	50	64 20N	12 0 E
Nordagutu	47	59 25N	9 20 E
Nordaustlandet	4	79 14N	23 0 E
Nordborg	49	55 5N	9 50 E
Nordby, Arhus, Denmark	49	55 58N	10 32 E
Nordby, Ribe, Denmark	49	55 27N	8 24 E
Norddal	47	62 15N	7 14 E
Norddalsfjord	47	61 39N	5 23 E
Norddeich	24	53 37N	7 10 E
Nordegg	108	52 29N	116 5W
Norden	24	53 35N	7 12 E
Nordenham	24	53 29N	8 28 E
Norderhov	47	60 7N	10 17 E
Norderney	24	53 42N	7 15 E
Nordfjord	47	61 55N	5 30 E
Nordfriesische Inseln	24	54 40N	8 20 E
Nordhausen	24	51 29N	10 47 E
Nordhorn	24	52 27N	7 4 E
Nordjyllands Amtskommune □	49	57 0N	10 0 E
Nordkapp, Norway	50	71 10N	25 44 E
Nordkapp, Svalb.	4	80 31N	20 0 E
Nordkinn	9	71 8N	27 40 E
Nordland fylke □	50	65 40N	13 0 E
Nördlingen	25	48 50N	10 30 E
Nordrhein-Westfalen □	24	51 45N	7 30 E
Nordstrand	24	54 27N	8 50 E
Nordvik	59	74 2N	111 32 E
Nore	47	60 10N	9 0 E
Nore →	15	52 40N	7 20W
Norefjell	47	60 16N	9 29 E
Norembega	106	48 59N	80 43W
Noresund	47	60 11N	9 37 E
Norfolk, Nebr., U.S.A.	116	42 3N	97 25W
Norfolk, Va., U.S.A.	114	36 40N	76 15W
Norfolk □	12	52 39N	1 0 E
Norfolk Broads	12	52 30N	1 15 E
Norfolk I.	94	28 58S	168 3 E
Norfork Res.	117	36 13N	92 15W
Norilsk	59	69 20N	88 6 E
Norley	99	27 45S	143 48 E
Norma, Mt.	98	20 55S	140 42 E
Normal	116	40 30N	89 0W
Norman	117	35 12N	97 30W
Norman →	97	17 28S	140 49 E
Norman Wells	104	65 17N	126 51W
Normanby →	97	14 23S	144 10 E
Normanby I.	98	10 55S	151 5 E
Normandie	18	48 45N	0 10 E
Normandie, Collines de	18	48 55N	0 45W
Normandin	106	48 49N	72 31W
Normandy = Normandie	18	48 45N	0 10 E
Normanton	97	17 40S	141 10 E
Norquay	109	51 53N	102 5W
Norquinco	128	41 51S	70 55W
Norrahammar	49	57 43N	14 7 E
Norrbotten □	50	66 30N	22 30 E
Norrby	50	64 55N	18 15 E
Nørre Åby	49	55 27N	9 52 E
Nørre Nebel	49	55 47N	8 17 E
Nørresundby	49	57 5N	9 52 E
Norris	118	45 40N	111 40W
Norristown	114	40 9N	75 21W
Norrköping	49	58 37N	16 11 E
Norrland □	50	66 50N	18 0 E
Norrtälje	48	59 46N	18 42 E
Norsholm	49	58 31N	15 59 E
Norsk	59	52 30N	130 0 E
North Adams	114	42 42N	73 6W
North America	102	40 0N	100 0W
North Andaman I.	71	13 15N	92 40 E
North Atlantic Ocean	6	30 0N	50 0W
North Battleford	109	52 50N	108 17W
North Bay	106	46 20N	79 30W
North Belcher Is.	106	56 50N	79 50W
North Bend, Can.	108	49 50N	121 27W
North Bend, Oreg., U.S.A.	118	43 28N	124 14W
North Bend, Pa., U.S.A.	112	41 20N	77 42W
North Berwick, U.K.	14	56 4N	2 44W
North Berwick, U.S.A.	113	43 18N	70 43W
North Buganda □	90	1 0N	32 0 E
North Canadian →	117	35 17N	95 31W
North C., Antarct.	5	71 0S	166 0 E
North C., Can.	107	47 2N	60 20W
North C., N.Z.	101	34 23S	173 4 E
North Caribou L.	106	52 50N	90 40W
North Carolina □	115	35 30N	80 0W
North Channel, Br. Is.	14	55 0N	5 30W
North Channel, Can.	106	46 0N	83 0W
North Chicago	114	42 19N	87 50W
North Dakota □	116	47 30N	100 0W
North Down □	15	54 40N	5 45W
North Downs	13	51 17N	0 30 E
North East	112	42 17N	79 50W
North East Frontier Agency = Arunachal Pradesh □	67	28 0N	95 0 E
North East Providence Chan.	121	26 0N	76 0W
North Eastern □	90	1 30N	40 0 E
North Esk →	14	56 44N	2 25W
North European Plain	9	55 0N	20 0 E
North Foreland	13	51 22N	1 28 E
North Frisian Is. = Nordfr'sche Inseln	24	54 50N	8 20 E
North Henik L.	109	61 45N	97 40W
North Horr	90	3 20N	37 8 E
North I., Kenya	90	4 5N	36 5 E
North I., N.Z.	101	38 0S	175 0 E
North Kingsville	112	41 53N	80 42W
North Knife →	109	58 53N	94 45W
North Koel →	69	24 45N	83 50 E
North Korea ■	76	40 0N	127 0 E
North Lakhimpur	67	27 14N	94 7 E
North Las Vegas	119	36 15N	115 6W
North Loup →	116	41 17N	98 23W
North Mashonaland □	91	16 30S	30 0 E
North Minch	14	58 5N	5 55W
North Nahanni →	108	62 15N	123 20W
North Ossetian A.S.S.R. □	57	43 30N	44 30 E
North Palisade	119	37 6N	118 32W
North Platte	116	41 10N	100 50W
North Platte →	116	41 15N	100 45W
North Pt.	107	47 5N	64 0W
North Pole	4	90 0N	0 0 E
North Portal	109	49 0N	102 33W
North Powder	118	45 2N	117 59W
North Ronaldsay	14	59 20N	2 30W
North Sea	8	56 0N	4 0 E
North Sentinel I.	71	11 35N	92 15 E
North Sporades = Voríai Sporádhes	45	39 15N	23 30 E
North Stradbroke I.	97	27 35S	153 28 E
North Sydney	107	46 12N	60 15W
North Thompson →	108	50 40N	120 20W
North Tonawanda	114	43 5N	78 50W
North Troy	113	44 59N	72 24W
North Truchas Pk.	119	36 0N	105 30W
North Twin I.	106	53 20N	80 0W
North Tyne →	12	54 59N	2 7W
North Uist	14	57 40N	7 15W
North Vancouver	108	49 25N	123 3W
North Vernon	114	39 0N	85 35W
North Village	121	32 15N	64 45W
North Wabiskaw L.	108	56 0N	113 55W
North Walsham	12	52 49N	1 22 E
North West Basin	96	25 45S	115 0 E
North West C.	96	21 45S	114 9 E
North West Christmas I. Ridge	95	6 30N	165 0W
North West Highlands	14	57 35N	5 2W
North West Providence Channel	121	26 0N	78 0W
North West River	107	53 30N	60 10W
North Western □	91	13 30S	25 30 E
North York Moors	12	54 25N	0 50W
North Yorkshire □	12	54 15N	1 25W
Northallerton	12	54 20N	1 26W
Northam	96	31 35S	116 42 E
Northampton, Austral.	96	28 27S	114 33 E
Northampton, U.K.	13	52 14N	0 54W
Northampton, Mass., U.S.A.	114	42 22N	72 31W
Northampton, Pa., U.S.A.	113	40 38N	75 24W
Northampton □	13	52 16N	0 55W
Northampton Downs	98	24 35S	145 48 E
Northbridge	113	42 12N	71 40W
Northeim	24	51 42N	10 0 E
Northern □, Malawi	91	11 0S	34 0 E
Northern □, Uganda	90	3 5N	32 30 E
Northern □, Zambia	91	10 30S	31 0 E
Northern Circars	70	17 30N	82 30 E
Northern Group	101	10 00S	160 00W
Northern Indian L.	109	57 20N	97 20W
Northern Ireland □	15	54 45N	7 0W
Northern Light, L.	106	48 15N	90 39W
Northern Province □	84	9 15N	11 30W
Northern Territory □	96	16 0S	133 0 E
Northfield	116	44 30N	93 10W
Northome	116	47 53N	94 15W
Northport, Ala., U.S.A.	115	33 15N	87 35W
Northport, Mich., U.S.A.	114	45 8N	85 39W
Northport, Wash., U.S.A.	118	48 55N	117 48W
Northumberland □	12	55 12N	2 0W
Northumberland, C.	97	38 5S	140 40 E
Northumberland Is.	98	21 30S	149 50 E
Northumberland Str.	107	46 20N	64 0W
Northwest Territories □	104	65 0N	100 0W
Northwich	12	53 16N	2 30W
Northwood, Iowa, U.S.A.	116	43 27N	93 0W
Northwood, N.D., U.S.A.	116	47 44N	97 30W
Norton, U.S.A.	116	39 50N	99 53W
Norton, Zimb.	91	17 52S	30 40 E
Norton Sd.	104	64 0N	164 0W
Nortorf	24	54 14N	9 47 E
Norwalk, Conn., U.S.A.	114	41 9N	73 25W
Norwalk, Ohio, U.S.A.	114	41 13N	82 38W
Norway	114	45 46N	87 57W
Norway House	109	53 59N	97 50W
Norwegian Dependency	5	66 0S	15 0 E
Norwegian Sea	6	66 0N	1 0 E
Norwich, Can.	112	42 59N	80 36W
Norwich, U.K.	12	52 38N	1 17 E
Norwich, Conn., U.S.A.	113	41 33N	72 5W
Norwich, N.Y., U.S.A.	114	42 32N	75 30W
Norwood, Can.	112	44 23N	77 59W
Norwood, U.S.A.	113	42 10N	71 10W
Nosok	58	70 10N	82 20 E
Nosovka	54	50 50N	31 37 E
Noşratābād	65	29 55N	60 0 E
Noss Hd.	14	58 29N	3 4W
Nossebro	49	58 12N	12 43 E
Nossob →	92	26 55S	20 37 E
Nosy Boraha	93	16 50S	49 55 E
Nosy Varika	93	20 35S	48 32 E
Noteć →	28	52 44N	15 26 E
Notigi Dam	109	56 40N	99 10W
Notikewin →	108	57 2N	117 38W
Notios Evvoïkos Kólpos	45	38 20N	24 0 E
Noto	41	36 52N	15 4 E
Noto, G. di	41	36 50N	15 10 E
Noto-Hanto	74	37 0N	137 0 E
Notodden	47	59 35N	9 17 E
Notre-Dame	107	46 18N	64 46W
Notre Dame B.	107	49 45N	55 30W
Notre Dame de Koartac	105	60 55N	69 40W
Notsé	85	7 0N	1 17 E
Nottaway →	106	51 22N	78 55W
Nøtterøy	47	59 14N	10 24 E
Nottingham	12	52 57N	1 10W
Nottingham □	12	53 10N	1 0W
Nottoway →	114	36 33N	76 55W
Notwani →	92	23 35S	26 58 E
Nouâdhibou	80	20 54N	17 0W
Nouâdhibou, Ras	80	20 50N	17 0W
Nouakchott	84	18 9N	15 58W
Nouméa	94	22 17S	166 30 E
Noupoort	92	31 10S	24 57 E
Nouveau Comptoir (Paint Hills)	106	53 0N	78 49W
Nouvelle Calédonie	94	21 0S	165 0 E
Nouzonville	19	49 48N	4 44 E
Nová Baňa	27	48 28N	18 39 E
Nová Bystřice	26	49 2N	15 8 E
† Nova Chaves	88	10 31S	21 15 E
Nova Cruz	127	6 28S	35 25W
Nova Esperança	125	23 8S	52 24W
Nova Friburgo	125	22 16S	42 30W
Nova Gaia	88	10 10S	17 35 E
Nova Gradiška	42	45 17N	17 28 E
Nova Iguaçu	125	22 45S	43 28W
Nova Iorque	127	7 0S	44 5W
Nova Lamego	84	12 19N	14 11W
Nova Lima	125	19 59S	43 51W
Nova Lisboa = Huambo	89	12 42S	15 44 E
Nova Lusitânia	91	19 50S	34 34 E
Nova Mambone	93	21 0S	35 3 E
Nova Mesto	39	45 47N	15 12 E
Nova Paka	26	50 29N	15 30 E
Nova Scotia □	107	45 10N	63 0W
Nova Sofala	93	20 7S	34 42 E
Nova Varoš	42	43 29N	19 48 E
Nova Venécia	127	18 45S	40 24W
Nova Zagora	43	42 32N	25 59 E
Novaci, Romania	46	45 10N	23 42 E
Novaci, Yugo.	42	41 5N	21 29 E
Noval Iorque	127	6 48S	44 0W
Novaleksandrovskaya	57	45 29N	41 17 E
Novannenskiy	55	50 32N	42 39 E
Novara	38	45 27N	8 36 E
Novaya Kakhovka	56	46 42N	33 27 E
Novaya Ladoga	52	60 7N	32 16 E
Novaya Lyalya	58	59 10N	60 35 E
Novaya Sibir, O.	59	75 10N	150 0 E
Novaya Zemlya	58	75 0N	56 0 E
Nové Město	27	48 45N	17 50 E
Nové Zámky	27	48 0N	18 8 E
Novelda	33	38 24N	0 45W
Novellara	38	44 50N	10 43 E
Noventa Vicentina	39	45 18N	11 30 E
Novgorod	54	58 30N	31 25 E
Novgorod-Severskiy	54	52 2N	33 10 E
Novi Bečej	42	45 36N	20 10 E
Novi Grad	39	45 19N	13 33 E
Novi Kneževa	42	46 4N	20 8 E
• Novi Krichim	43	42 8N	24 31 E
Novi Ligure	38	44 45N	8 47 E
Novi Pazar, Bulg.	43	43 25N	27 15 E
Novi Pazar, Yugo.	42	43 12N	20 28 E
Novi Sad	42	45 18N	19 52 E
Novi Vinodolski	39	45 10N	14 48 E
Novigrad	39	44 10N	15 32 E
Nôvo Hamburgo	125	29 37S	51 7W
Novo-Zavidovskiy	55	56 32N	36 29 E
Novoakrainka	56	48 25N	31 30 E
Novoaltaysk	58	53 30N	84 0 E
Novoazovsk	56	47 15N	38 4 E
Novobelitsa	54	52 27N	31 2 E
Novobogatinskoye	57	47 20N	51 11 E
Novocherkassk	57	47 27N	40 5 E
Novodevichye	55	53 37N	48 50 E
Novograd-Volynskiy	54	50 34N	27 35 E
Novogrudok	54	53 40N	25 50 E
Novokayakent	57	42 30N	47 52 E
Novokazalinsk	58	45 48N	62 6 E
Novokhopersk	55	51 5N	41 39 E
Novokuybyshevsk	55	53 7N	49 58 E
Novokuznetsk	58	53 45N	87 10 E
Novomirgorod	56	48 45N	31 33 E
Novomoskovsk, R.S.F.S.R., U.S.S.R.	55	54 5N	38 15 E
Novomoskovsk, Ukraine, U.S.S.R.	56	48 33N	35 17 E
Novopolotsk	54	55 32N	28 37 E
Novorossiysk	56	44 43N	37 46 E
Novorybnoye	59	72 50N	105 50 E
Novorzhev	54	57 3N	29 25 E
Novoselitsa	56	48 14N	26 15 E
Novoshakhtinsk	57	47 46N	39 58 E
Novosibirsk	58	55 0N	83 5 E
Novosibirskiye Ostrava	59	75 0N	142 0 E
Novosil	55	52 58N	36 58 E
Novosokolniki	54	56 33N	30 5 E
Novotroitsk	52	51 10N	58 15 E
Novotulskiy	55	54 10N	37 43 E
Novouzensk	55	50 32N	48 17 E
Novovolynsk	54	50 45N	24 4 E
Novovyatsk	55	58 29N	49 44 E
Novozybkov	54	52 30N	32 0 E
Novska	42	45 19N	17 0 E
Novvy Port	58	67 40N	72 30 E
Novy Bug	56	47 34N	32 29 E
Nový Bydzov	26	50 14N	15 29 E
Novy Dwór Mazowiecki	28	52 26N	20 44 E
Nový Jičín	27	49 30N	18 0 E
Novyy Afon	57	43 7N	40 50 E
Novyy Oskol	55	50 44N	37 55 E
Now Shahr	65	36 40N	51 30 E
Nowa Deba	28	50 26N	21 41 E
Nowa Huta	27	50 5N	20 30 E
Nowa Ruda	28	50 35N	16 30 E
Nowa Skalmierzyce	28	51 43N	18 0 E
Nowa Sól	28	51 48N	15 44 E
Nowe	28	53 41N	18 44 E
Nowe Miasteczko	28	51 42N	15 42 E
Nowe Miasto	28	51 38N	20 34 E
Nowe Miasto Lubawskie	28	53 27N	19 33 E
Nowe Warpno	28	53 42N	14 18 E
Nowgong	67	26 20N	92 50 E
Nowingi	100	34 33S	142 15 E
Nowogard	28	53 41N	15 10 E
Nowogród	28	53 14N	21 53 E
Nowra	97	34 53S	150 35 E
Nowy Dwór, Białystok, Poland	28	53 40N	23 30 E
Nowy Dwór, Gdansk, Poland	28	54 13N	19 7 E
Nowy Korczyn	28	50 19N	20 48 E
Nowy Sącz	27	49 40N	20 41 E
Nowy Sącz □	27	49 30N	20 30 E
Nowy Staw	28	54 13N	19 2 E
Nowy Tomyśl	28	52 19N	16 10 E
Noxen	113	41 25N	76 4W
Noxon	118	48 0N	115 43W
Noya	30	42 48N	8 53W
Noyant	18	47 30N	0 6 E
Noyers	19	47 40N	4 0 E
Noyes I.	108	55 30N	133 40W
Noyon	19	49 34N	3 0 E
Nozay	18	47 34N	1 38W
Nsa, O. en →	83	32 28N	5 24 E
Nsanje	91	16 55S	35 12 E
Nsawam	85	5 50N	0 24W
Nsomba	91	10 45S	29 51 E
Nsukka	85	6 51N	7 29 E
Nuanetsi →	91	22 40S	31 50 E
Nuba Mts. = Nubah, Jibalan	87	12 0N	31 0 E
Nubah, Jibalan	87	12 0N	31 0 E
Nûbîya, Es Sahrâ En	86	21 30N	33 30 E
Ñuble □	124	37 0S	72 0W
Nuboai	73	2 10S	136 30 E
Nueces →	117	27 50N	97 30W
Nueima →	62	31 54N	35 25 E
Nueltin L.	109	60 30N	99 30W
Nueva Gerona	121	21 53N	82 49W
Nueva Imperial	128	38 45S	72 58W
Nueva Palmira	124	33 52S	58 20W
Nueva Rosita	120	28 0N	101 11W
Nueva San Salvador	120	13 40N	89 18W
Nuéve de Julio	124	35 30S	61 0W
Nuevitas	121	21 30N	77 20W
Nuevo, Golfo	128	43 0S	64 30W
Nuevo Laredo	120	27 30N	99 30W
Nuevo León □	120	25 0N	100 0W
Nugget Pt.	101	46 27S	169 50 E
Nugrus, Gebel	86	24 47N	34 35 E
Nuhaka	101	39 3S	177 45 E
Nuits	19	47 44N	4 12 E
Nuits-St-Georges	19	47 10N	4 56 E
Nukheila (Merga)	86	19 1N	26 21 E
Nuku'alofa	101	21 10S	174 0W
Nukus	58	42 20N	59 7 E
Nulato	104	64 40N	158 10W
Nules	32	39 51N	0 9W
Nullagine	96	21 53S	120 6 E
Nullarbor Plain	96	30 45S	129 0 E
Numalla, L.	99	28 43S	144 20 E
Numan	85	9 29N	12 3 E
Numata	74	36 45N	139 4 E
Numatinna →	87	7 38N	27 20 E
Numazu	74	35 7N	138 51 E
Numfoor	73	1 0S	134 50 E
Numurkah	99	36 5S	145 26 E
Nunaksaluk I.	107	55 49N	60 20W
Nuneaton	13	52 32N	1 29W
Nungo	91	13 23S	37 43 E
Nungwe	90	2 48S	32 2 E
Nunivak	104	60 0N	166 0W
Nunkun	69	33 57N	76 2 E
Nunspeet	16	52 21N	5 45 E
Nuomin He →	76	46 45N	126 55 E
Nuoro	40	40 20N	9 20 E
Nuqayy, Jabal	83	23 11N	19 30 E
Nure →	38	45 3N	9 49 E
Nuremburg = Nürnberg	25	49 26N	11 5 E
Nuriootpa	99	34 27S	139 0 E
Nurlat	55	54 29N	50 45 E
Nürnberg	25	49 26N	11 5 E
Nurran, L. = Terewah, L.	99	29 52S	147 35 E
Nurri	40	39 43N	9 13 E
Nurzec →	28	52 37N	22 25 E
Nusa Barung	73	8 22S	113 20 E
Nusa Kambangan	73	7 47S	109 0 E
Nusa Tenggara Barat □	72	8 50S	117 30 E
Nusa Tenggara Timur □	73	9 30S	122 0 E
Nushki	66	29 35N	66 0 E
Nutak	105	57 28N	61 59W
Nuwakot	69	28 10N	83 55 E
Nuwara Eliya	70	6 58N	80 48 E
Nuweiba'	86	28 58N	34 40 E
Nuweveldberge	92	32 10S	21 45 E
Nuyts Arch.	96	32 35S	133 20 E
Nuyts, Pt.	96	35 4S	116 38 E
Nuzvid	70	16 47N	80 53 E
Nxau-Nxau	92	18 57S	21 4 E
Nyaake (Webo)	84	4 52N	7 37W
Nyabing	96	33 30S	118 7 E
Nyack	113	41 5N	73 57W
Nyadal	48	62 48N	17 59 E
Nyah West	100	35 16S	143 21 E
Nyahanga	90	2 20S	33 37 E
Nyahua	90	5 25S	33 23 E
Nyahururu	90	0 2N	36 27 E
Nyainqentanglha Shan	75	30 0N	90 0 E
Nyakanazi	90	3 2S	31 10 E
Nyakrom	85	5 40N	0 50W
Nyâlâ	87	12 2N	24 58 E
Nyamandhlovu	91	19 55S	28 16 E
Nyambiti	90	2 48S	33 27 E
Nyamwaga	90	1 27S	34 33 E
Nyandekwa	90	3 57S	32 32 E
Nyanding →,	87	8 40N	32 41 E
Nyandoma	52	61 40N	40 12 E
Nyangana	92	18 0S	20 40 E
Nyanguge	90	2 30S	33 12 E
Nyankpala	85	9 21N	0 58W
Nyanza, Burundi	90	4 21S	29 36 E
Nyanza, Rwanda	90	2 20S	29 42 E
Nyanza □	90	0 10S	34 15 E
Nyarling →	108	60 41N	113 23W
Nyasa, L. = Malawi, L.	91	12 0S	34 30 E
Nyazepetrovsk	52	56 3N	59 36 E
Nyazwidzi →	91	20 0S	31 17 E
Nyborg	49	55 18N	10 47 E
Nybro	49	56 44N	15 55 E
Nyda	58	66 40N	72 58 E
Nyeri	90	0 23S	36 56 E
Nyerol	87	8 41N	32 1 E
Nyhem	48	62 54N	15 37 E
Nyiel	87	6 9N	31 13 E
Nyinahin	84	6 43N	2 3W
Nyirbátor	27	47 49N	22 9 E
Nyíregyháza	27	47 58N	21 47 E
Nykarleby	50	63 22N	22 31 E
Nykøbing, Sjælland, Denmark	49	55 55N	11 40 E
Nykøbing, Storstrøm, Denmark	49	54 56N	11 52 E
Nykøbing, Viborg, Denmark	49	56 48N	8 51 E
Nyköping	49	58 45N	17 0 E

• *Renamed Stamboliyski*

† *Renamed Muconda*

Nykroppa Onehunga

Nykroppa 48 59 37N 14 18 E
Nykvarn 48 59 11N 17 25 E
Nyland 48 63 1N 17 45 E
Nylstroom 93 24 42 S 28 22 E
Nymagee 99 32 7 S 146 20 E
Nymburk 26 50 10N 15 1 E
Nynäshamn 48 58 54N 17 57 E
Nyngan 99 31 30 S 147 8 E
Nyon 25 46 23N 6 14 E
Nyong → 85 3 17N 9 54 E
Nyons 21 44 22N 5 10 E
Nyord 49 55 4N 12 13 E
Nyou 85 12 42N 2 1W
Nysa 28 50 30N 17 22 E
Nysa →, Poland/Poland 28 52 4N 14 46 E
Nysa →, Poland 28 50 49N 17 40 E
Nyssa 118 43 56N 117 2W
Nysted 49 54 40N 11 44 E
Nyunzu 90 5 57 S 27 58 E
Nyurba 59 63 17N 118 28 E
Nzega 90 4 10 S 33 12 E
Nzega □ 90 4 10 S 33 10 E
N'Zérékoré 84 7 49N 8 48W
Nzeto 88 7 10 S 12 52 E
Nzilo, Chutes de 91 10 18 S 25 27 E
Nzubuka 90 4 45 S 32 50 E

O

Oacoma 116 43 50N 99 26W
Oahe 116 44 33N 100 29W
Oahe Dam 116 44 28N 100 25W
Oahe Res. 116 45 30N 100 25W
Oahu 110 21 30N 158 0W
Oak Creek 118 40 15N 106 59W
Oak Harb. 118 48 20N 122 38W
Oak Hill 114 38 0N 81 7W
Oak Park 114 41 55N 87 45W
Oak Ridge 115 36 1N 84 12W
Oakbank 99 33 4 S 140 33 E
Oakdale, Calif., U.S.A. 119 46 14N 98 4W
Oakdale, La., U.S.A. 117 30 50N 92 38W
Oakengates 12 52 42N 2 29W
Oakes 116 46 14N 98 4W
Oakesdale 118 47 11N 117 15W
Oakey 99 27 25 S 151 43 E
Oakham 12 52 40N 0 43W
Oakland, Calif., U.S.A. 119 37 50N 122 18W
Oakland, Oreg., U.S.A. 118 43 23N 123 18W
Oakland City 114 38 20N 87 20W
Oakleigh 100 37 54 S 145 6 E
Oakley, Id., U.S.A. 118 42 14N 113 55W
Oakley, Kans., U.S.A. 116 39 8N 100 51W
Oakridge 118 43 47N 122 31W
Oakwood 117 31 35N 94 45W
Oamaru 101 45 5 S 170 59 E
Oates Coast 5 69 0 S 160 0 E
Oatman 119 35 1N 114 19W
Oaxaca 120 17 2N 96 40W
Oaxaca □ 120 17 0N 97 0W
Ob → 58 66 45N 69 30 E
Oba 106 49 4N 84 7W
Obala 85 4 9N 11 32 E
Oban, N.Z. 101 46 55 S 168 10 E
Oban, U.K. 14 56 25N 5 30W
Obbia 63 5 25N 48 30 E
Obed 108 53 30N 117 10W
Obera 125 27 21 S 55 2W
Oberammergau 25 47 35N 11 3 E
Oberdrauburg 26 46 44N 12 58 E
Oberengadin 25 46 35N 9 55 E
Oberhausen 24 51 28N 6 50 E
Oberkirch 25 48 31N 8 5 E
Oberlin, Kans., U.S.A. 116 39 52N 100 31W
Oberlin, La., U.S.A. 117 30 42N 92 42W
Oberlin, Ohio, U.S.A. 112 41 15N 82 10W
Obernai 19 48 28N 7 30 E
Oberndorf 25 48 17N 8 35 E
Oberon 99 33 45 S 149 52 E
Oberösterreich □ 26 48 10N 14 0 E
Oberpfälzer Wald 25 49 30N 12 25 E
Oberstdorf 25 47 25N 10 16 E
Obi, Kepulauan 73 1 23 S 127 45 E
Obiaruku 85 5 51N 6 9 E
Óbidos, Brazil 127 1 50 S 55 30W
Óbidos, Port. 31 39 19N 9 10W
Obihiro 74 42 56N 143 12 E
Obilatu 73 1 25 S 127 20 E
Obilnoye 57 47 32N 44 30 E
Obing 25 48 0N 12 25 E
Obisfelde 24 52 27N 10 57 E
Objat 20 45 16N 1 24 E
Obluchye 59 49 1N 131 4 E
Obninsk 55 55 8N 36 37 E
Obo, C. Afr. Rep. 90 5 20N 26 32 E
Obo, Ethiopia 87 3 46N 38 52 E
Oboa, Mt. 90 1 45N 34 45 E
Obock 87 12 0N 43 20 E
Oborniki 28 52 39N 16 50 E
Oborniki Śląskie 28 51 17N 16 53 E
Oboyan 55 51 13N 36 37 E
Obrenovac 42 44 40N 20 11 E
Obrovac 39 44 11N 15 41 E
Observatory Inlet 108 55 10N 129 54W
Obshchi Syrt 9 52 0N 53 0 E
Obskaya Guba 58 69 0N 73 0 E
Obuasi 85 6 17N 1 40W
Obubra 85 6 8N 8 20 E
Obzor 43 42 50N 27 52 E
Ocala 115 29 11N 82 5W
Ocampo 120 28 9N 108 24W
Ocaña 32 39 55N 3 30W
Ocanomowoc 116 43 7N 88 30W
Ocate 117 36 12N 104 59W
Occidental, Cordillera 126 5 0N 76 0W
Ocean City 114 39 18N 74 34W
Ocean, I. = Banaba 94 0 52 S 169 35 E
Ocean Park 118 46 30N 124 2W
Oceanlake 118 45 0N 124 0W
Oceanport 113 40 20N 74 3W
Oceanside 119 33 13N 117 26W
Ochagavia 32 42 55N 1 5W
Ochamchire 57 42 46N 41 32 E
Ochil Hills 14 56 14N 3 40W
Ochre River 109 51 4N 99 47W
Ochsenfurt 25 49 38N 10 3 E
Ochsenhausen 25 48 4N 9 57 E
Ocilla 115 31 35N 83 12W
Ockelbo 48 60 54N 16 45 E
Ocmulgee → 115 31 58N 82 32W
Ocna Mureş 46 46 23N 23 55 E
Ocna Sibiului 46 45 52N 24 2 E
Ocnele Mari 46 45 8N 24 18 E
Oconee → 115 31 58N 82 32W
Oconto 114 44 52N 87 53W
Oconto Falls 114 44 52N 88 10W
Ocotal 121 13 41N 86 31W
Ocotlán 120 20 21N 102 42W
Ocreza → 31 39 32N 7 50W
Ócsa 27 47 17N 19 15 E
Octave 119 34 10N 112 43W
Octeville 18 49 38N 1 40W
Ocumare del Tuy 126 10 7N 66 46W
Ocussi 73 9 20 S 124 23 E
Oda 85 5 50N 0 51W
Oda, Jebel 86 20 21N 36 39 E
Ódáðahraun 50 65 5N 17 0W
Ödåkra 49 56 7N 12 45 E
Odawara 74 35 20N 139 6 E
Odda 47 60 3N 6 35 E
Odder 49 55 58N 10 10 E
Oddur 63 4 11N 43 52 E
Ödeborg 49 58 32N 11 58 E
Odei → 109 56 6N 96 54W
Odemira 31 37 35N 8 40W
Ödemiş 64 38 15N 28 0 E
Odendaalsrus 92 27 48 S 26 45 E
Odense 49 55 22N 10 23 E
Odenwald 25 49 40N 9 0 E
Oder → 24 53 33N 14 38 E
Oderzo 39 45 47N 12 29 E
Odessa, Can. 113 44 17N 76 43W
Odessa, Tex., U.S.A. 117 31 51N 102 23W
Odessa, Wash., U.S.A. 118 47 19N 118 35W
Odessa, U.S.S.R. 56 46 30N 30 45 E
Odiakwe 92 20 12 S 25 17 E
Odiel → 31 37 10N 6 55W
Odienné 84 9 30N 7 34W
Odobeşti 46 45 43N 27 4 E
Odolanów 28 51 34N 17 40 E
O'Donnell 117 33 0N 101 48W
Odorheiul Secuiesc 46 46 21N 25 21 E
Odoyevo 55 53 56N 36 42 E
Odra →, Poland 28 53 33N 14 38 E
Odra →, Spain 30 42 14N 4 17W
Odžaci 42 45 30N 19 17 E
Odžak 42 45 3N 18 18 E
Oeiras, Brazil 127 7 0 S 42 8W
Oeiras, Port. 31 38 41N 9 18W
Oelrichs 116 43 11N 103 14W
Oelsnitz 24 50 24N 12 11 E
Oelwein 116 42 41N 91 55W
Ofanto → 41 41 22N 16 13 E
Offa 85 8 13N 4 42 E
Offaly □ 15 53 15N 7 30W
Offenbach 25 50 6N 8 46 E
Offenburg 25 48 29N 7 56 E
Offerdal 48 63 28N 14 0 E
Offida 39 42 56N 13 40 E
Offranville 18 49 52N 1 0 E
Ofidhousa 45 36 33N 26 8 E
Ofotfjorden 50 68 27N 16 40 E
Oga-Hantō 74 39 58N 139 47 E
Ogahalla 106 50 6N 85 51W
Ōgaki 74 35 21N 136 37 E
Ogallala 116 41 12N 101 40W
Ogbomosho 85 8 1N 4 11 E
Ogden, Iowa, U.S.A. 116 42 3N 94 0W
Ogden, Utah, U.S.A. 118 41 13N 112 1W
Ogdensburg 114 44 40N 75 27W
Ogeechee → 115 31 51N 81 6W
Oglio → 38 45 2N 10 39 E
Ogmore 98 22 37 S 149 35 E
Ogna 47 58 31N 5 48 E
Ognon → 19 47 16N 5 28 E
Ogoja 85 6 38N 8 39 E
Ogoki → 106 51 38N 85 57W
Ogoki L. 106 50 50N 87 10W
Ogoki Res. 106 50 45N 88 15W
Ogooué → 88 1 0 S 10 0 E
Ogosta → 43 43 48N 23 55 E
Ogowe = Ogooué → 88 1 0 S 10 0 E
Ograźden 42 41 30N 22 50 E
Ogrein 86 17 55N 34 50 E
Ogulin 39 45 16N 15 16 E
Ogun □ 85 7 0N 3 0 E
Oguta 85 5 44N 6 44 E
Ogwashi-Uku 85 6 15N 6 30 E
Ogwe 85 5 0N 7 14 E
Ohai 101 44 55 S 168 0 E
Ohakune 101 39 24 S 175 24 E
Ohau, L. 101 44 15 S 169 53 E
Ohey 16 50 26N 5 8 E
O'Higgins □ 124 34 15 S 70 45W
Ohio □ 114 40 20N 14 10 E
Ohio → 114 38 0N 86 0W
Ohre →, Czech. 26 50 30N 14 10 E
Ohre →, Ger. 24 52 18N 11 47 E
Ohrid 42 41 8N 20 52 E
Ohridsko, Jezero 42 41 8N 20 52 E
Ohrigstad 93 24 19 S 30 36 E
Öhringen 25 49 11N 9 31 E
Oil City 114 41 26N 79 40W
Oinousa 45 38 33N 26 14 E
Oise □ 19 49 28N 2 30 E
Oise → 19 49 0N 2 4 E
Ōita 74 33 14N 131 36 E
Ōita □ 74 33 15N 131 30 E
Oiticica 127 5 3 S 41 5W
Ojai 119 34 28N 119 16W
Ojinaga 120 29 34N 104 25W
Ojos del Salado, Cerro 124 27 0 S 68 40W
Oka → 55 56 20N 43 59 E
Okaba 73 8 6 S 139 42 E
Okahandja 92 22 0 S 16 59 E
Okahukura 94 38 48 S 175 14 E
Okanagan L. 108 50 0N 119 30W
Okandja 88 0 35 S 13 45 E
Okanogan 118 48 6N 119 43W
Okanogan → 118 48 6N 119 43W
Okány 27 46 52N 21 21 E
Okaputa 92 20 5 S 17 0 E
Okara 68 30 50N 73 31 E
Okarito 101 43 15 S 170 9 E
Okavango Swamps 92 18 45 S 22 45 E
Okaya 74 36 0N 138 10 E
Okayama 74 34 40N 133 54 E
Okayama □ 74 35 0N 133 50 E
Okazaki 74 34 57N 137 10 E
Oke-Iho 85 8 1N 3 18 E
Okeechobee 115 27 16N 80 46W
Okeechobee L. 115 27 0N 80 50W
Okefenokee Swamp 115 30 50N 82 15W
Okehampton 13 50 44N 4 1W
Okene 85 7 32N 6 11 E
Oker → 24 52 30N 10 22 E
Okha 59 53 40N 143 0 E
Ókhi Óros 45 38 5N 24 25 E
Okhotsk 59 59 20N 143 10 E
Okhotsk, Sea of 59 55 0N 145 0 E
Okhotskiy Perevoz 59 61 52N 135 35 E
Okhotsko Kolymskoye 59 63 0N 157 0 E
Oki-Shotō 74 36 5N 133 15 E
Okiep 92 29 39 S 17 53 E
Okigwi 85 5 52N 7 20 E
Okija 85 5 54N 6 55 E
Okinawa □ 77 26 40N 128 0 E
Okitipupa 85 6 31N 4 50 E
Oklahoma □ 117 35 20N 97 30W
Oklahoma City 117 35 25N 97 30W
Okmulgee 117 35 38N 96 0W
Oknitsa 56 48 25N 27 30 E
Okolo 90 2 37N 31 8 E
Okolona 117 34 0N 88 45W
Okondeka 92 21 38 S 15 37 E
Okonek 28 53 32N 16 51 E
Okrika 85 4 40N 7 10 E
Oktabrsk 58 49 28N 57 25 E
Oktyabrsk 55 53 11N 48 40 E
Oktyabrskiy, Byelorussia, U.S.S.R. 54 52 38N 28 53 E
Oktyabrskiy, R.S.F.S.R., U.S.S.R. 52 54 28N 53 28 E
Oktyabrskoy Revolyutsii, Os. 59 79 30N 97 0 E
Oktyabrskoye 58 62 28N 66 3 E
Oktyabrskoye = Zhovtnevoye 56 47 54N 32 2 E
Okulovka 54 58 25N 33 19 E
Okuru 101 43 55 S 168 55 E
Okushiri-Tō 74 42 15N 139 30 E
Okuta 85 9 14N 3 12 E
Okwa → 92 22 30 S 23 0 E
Ola 117 35 2N 93 10W
Ólafsfjörður 50 66 4N 18 39W
Ólafsvík 50 64 53N 23 43W
Olancha 119 36 15N 118 1W
Olanchito 121 15 30N 86 30W
Öland 49 56 45N 16 38 E
Olargues 20 43 34N 2 53 E
Olary 99 32 18 S 140 19 E
Olascoaga 124 35 15 S 60 39W
Olathe 116 38 50N 94 50W
Olavarría 124 36 55 S 60 20W
Oława 28 50 57N 17 20 E
Ólbia 40 40 55N 9 30 E
Ólbia, G. di 40 40 55N 9 35 E
Old Bahama Chan. = Bahama, Canal Viejo de 121 22 10N 77 30W
Old Castile = Castilla la Vieja □ 30 41 55N 4 0W
Old Castle 15 53 46N 7 10W
Old Cork 98 22 57 S 141 52 E
Old Crow 104 67 30N 140 5 E
Old Dongola 86 18 11N 30 44 E
Old Forge, N.Y., U.S.A. 113 43 43N 74 58W
Old Forge, Pa., U.S.A. 113 41 20N 75 46W
Old Fort → 109 58 36N 110 24W
Old Shinyanga 90 3 33 S 33 27 E
Old Speckle, Mt. 113 44 35N 70 57W
Old Town 107 45 0N 68 41W
Old Wives L. 109 50 5N 106 0W
Oldbury 13 51 38N 2 30W
Oldeani 90 3 22 S 35 35 E
Oldenburg, Niedersachsen, Ger. 24 53 10N 8 10 E
Oldenburg, Schleswig-Holstein, Ger. 24 54 16N 10 53 E
Oldenzaal 16 52 19N 6 53 E
Oldham 12 53 33N 2 8W
Oldman → 108 49 57N 111 42W
Olds 108 51 50N 114 10W
Olean 114 42 8N 78 25W
Olecko 28 54 2N 22 31 E
Oléggio 38 45 36N 8 38 E
Oleiros 30 39 56N 7 56W
Olekma → 59 60 22N 120 42 E
Olekminsk 59 60 25N 120 30 E
Olenegorsk 52 68 9N 33 18 E
Olenek 59 68 28N 112 18 E
Olenek → 59 73 0N 120 10 E
Olenino 54 56 15N 33 30 E
Oléron, Île d' 20 45 55N 1 15W
Oleśnica 28 51 13N 17 22 E
Olesno 28 50 51N 18 26 E
Olevsk 54 51 12N 27 39 E
Olga 59 43 50N 135 14 E
Olga, L. 106 49 47N 77 15W
Olga, Mt. 96 25 20 S 130 50 E
Olgastretet 4 78 35N 25 0 E
Ølgod 49 55 49N 8 36 E
Olhão 31 37 3N 7 48W
Olib 39 44 23N 14 44 E
Olib, I. 39 44 23N 14 44 E
Oliena 40 40 18N 9 22 E
Oliete 32 41 1N 0 41W
Olifants → 93 24 5 S 31 20 E
Olifantshoek 92 27 57 S 22 42 E
Ólimbos 45 35 44N 27 11 E
Ólimbos, Óros 44 40 6N 22 23 E
Olímpia 125 20 44 S 48 54W
Olimpo □ 124 20 30 S 58 45W
Olite 32 42 29N 1 40W
Oliva, Argent. 124 32 0 S 63 38W
Oliva, Spain 33 38 58N 0 9W
Oliva de la Frontera 31 38 17N 6 54W
Oliva, Punta del 30 43 37N 5 28W
Olivares 32 39 46N 2 20W
Oliveira 127 20 39 S 44 50W
Oliveira de Azemeis 30 40 49N 8 29W
Olivença 91 11 47 S 35 13 E
Olivenza 31 38 41N 7 9W
Oliver 108 49 13N 119 37W
Oliver L. 109 56 56N 103 22W
Olkhovka 57 49 48N 44 32 E
Olkusz 28 50 18N 19 33 E
Ollagüe 124 21 15 S 68 10W
Olmedo 30 41 20N 4 43W
Olney, Ill., U.S.A. 114 38 40N 88 0W
Olney, Tex., U.S.A. 117 33 25N 98 45W
Olofström 49 56 17N 14 32 E
Oloma 85 3 29N 11 19 E
Olomane → 107 50 14N 60 37W
Olomouc 27 49 38N 17 12 E
Olonets 52 61 10N 33 0 E
Olongapo 73 14 50N 120 18 E
Oloron, Gave d' 20 43 33N 1 5W
Oloron-Ste-Marie 20 43 11N 0 38W
Olot 32 42 11N 2 30 E
Olovo 42 44 8N 18 35 E
Olovyannaya 59 50 58N 115 35 E
Oloy → 59 66 29N 159 29 E
Olpe 24 51 2N 7 50 E
Olshanka 56 48 16N 30 58 E
Olshany 56 50 3N 35 53 E
Olsztyn 28 53 48N 20 29 E
Olsztyn □ 28 54 0N 21 0 E
Olsztynek 28 53 34N 20 19 E
Olt □ 46 44 20N 24 30 E
Olt → 46 43 50N 24 40 E
Olten 25 47 21N 7 53 E
Olteniţa 46 44 7N 26 42 E
Olton 117 34 16N 102 7W
Oltu 64 40 35N 41 58 E
Olvega 32 41 47N 2 0W
Olvera 31 36 55N 5 18W
Olympia, Greece 45 37 39N 21 39 E
Olympia, U.S.A. 118 47 0N 122 58W
Olympic Mts. 118 47 50N 123 45W
Olympic Nat. Park 118 47 48N 123 30W
Olympus, Mt. 118 47 52N 123 40W
Olympus, Mt. = Ólimbos, Óros 44 40 6N 22 23 E
Olyphant 113 41 27N 75 36W
Om → 58 54 59N 73 22 E
Om Hajer 87 14 20N 36 41 E
Ōmachi 74 36 30N 137 50 E
Omagh 15 54 36N 7 20W
Omagh □ 15 54 35N 7 15W
Omaha 116 41 15N 96 0W
Omak 118 48 24N 119 31W
Oman ■ 63 23 0N 58 0 E
Oman, G. of 65 24 30N 58 30 E
Omaruru 92 21 26 S 16 0 E
Omaruru → 92 22 7 S 14 15 E
Omate 126 16 45 S 71 0W
Ombai, Selat 73 8 30 S 124 50 E
Ombo 47 59 18N 6 0 E
Omboué 88 1 35 S 9 15 E
Ombrone → 38 42 39N 11 0 E
Omchi 83 21 22N 17 53 E
Omdurmân 87 15 40N 32 28 E
Omegna 38 45 52N 8 23 E
Omeonga 90 3 40 S 24 22 E
Ometepe, Isla de 121 11 32N 85 35W
Ometepec 120 16 39N 98 23W
Omez 62 32 22N 35 0 E
Omineca → 108 56 3N 124 16W
Omiš 39 43 28N 16 40 E
Omisalj 39 45 13N 14 32 E
Omitara 92 22 16 S 18 2 E
Ōmiya 74 35 54N 139 38 E
Omme Å → 49 55 56N 8 32 E
Ommen 16 52 31N 6 26 E
Omo → 81 6 25N 36 10 E
Omolon → 59 68 42N 158 36 E
Omsk 58 55 0N 73 12 E
Omsukchan 59 62 32N 155 48 E
Omul, Vf. 46 45 27N 25 29 E
Omulew → 28 53 5N 21 33 E
Ōmura 74 32 56N 130 0 E
Omurtag 43 43 8N 26 26 E
Ōmuta 74 33 0N 130 26 E
Omutninsk 55 58 45N 52 4 E
Oña 32 42 43N 3 25W
Onaga 116 39 32N 96 12W
Onalaska 116 43 53N 91 14W
Onamia 116 46 4N 93 38W
Onancock 114 37 42N 75 49W
Onang 73 3 2 S 118 49 E
Onaping L. 106 47 3N 81 30W
Onarheim 47 59 57N 5 35 E
Oñate 32 43 3N 2 25W
Onavas 120 28 28N 109 30W
Onawa 116 42 2N 96 2W
Onaway 114 45 21N 84 11W
Oncesti 46 43 56N 25 52 E
Oncócua 92 16 30 S 13 25 E
Onda 32 39 55N 0 17W
Ondangua 92 17 57 S 16 4 E
Ondárroa 32 43 19N 2 25W
Ondava → 27 48 27N 21 48 E
Ondo 85 7 4N 4 47 E
Ondo □ 85 7 0N 5 0 E
Öndörhaan 75 47 19N 110 39 E
Öndverðarnes 50 64 52N 24 0W
Onega 52 64 0N 38 10 E
Onega → 52 63 58N 37 55 E
Onega, G. of = Onezhskaya G. 52 64 30N 37 0 E
Onega, L. = Onezhskoye Oz. 52 62 0N 35 30 E
Onehunga 101 36 55 S 174 48 E

Oneida Ouesso

Oneida 114 43 5N 75 40W
Oneida L. 114 43 12N 76 0W
O'Neill 116 42 30N 98 38W
Onekotan, Ostrov 59 49 25N 154 45 E
Onema 90 4 35 S 24 30 E
Oneonta, Ala., U.S.A. 115 33 58N 86 29W
Oneonta, N.Y., U.S.A. 114 42 26N 75 5W
Onezhskaya Guba 52 64 30N 37 0 E
Onezhskoye Ozero 52 62 0N 35 30 E
Ongarue 101 38 42 S 175 19 E
Ongniud Qi 76 43 0N 118 38 E
Ongoka 90 1 20 S 26 0 E
Ongole 70 15 33N 80 2 E
Onguren 59 53 38N 107 36 E
Oni 57 42 33N 43 26 E
Onida 116 44 42N 100 5W
Onilahy → 93 23 34 S 43 45 E
Onitsha 85 6 6N 6 42 E
Onoda 74 34 2N 131 25 E
Ons, Islas d' 30 42 23N 8 55W
Onsala 49 57 26N 12 0 E
Onslow 96 21 40 S 115 12 E
Onslow B. 115 34 20N 77 20W
Onstwedde 16 53 2N 7 4 E
Ontake-San 74 35 53N 137 29 E
Ontaneda 30 43 12N 3 57W
Ontario, Calif., U.S.A. 119 34 2N 117 40W
Ontario, Oreg., U.S.A. 118 44 1N 117 1W
Ontario □ 106 52 0N 88 10W
Ontario, L. 106 43 40N 78 0W
Onteniente 33 38 50N 0 35W
Ontonagon 116 46 52N 89 19W
Ontur 33 38 38N 1 29W
Oodnadatta 96 27 33 S 135 30 E
Ooldea 96 30 27 S 131 50 E
Oona River 108 53 57N 130 16W
Oorindi 98 20 40 S 141 1 E
Oost-Vlaanderen □ 16 51 5N 3 50 E
Oostende 16 51 15N 2 50 E
Oosterhout 16 51 39N 4 47 E
Oosterschelde 16 51 33N 4 0 E
Ootacamund 70 11 30N 76 44 E
Ootsa L. 108 53 50N 126 2W
Ootsi 92 25 2 S 25 45 E
Opaka 43 43 28N 26 10 E
Opala, U.S.S.R. 59 51 58N 156 30 E
Opala, Zaïre 88 0 40 S 24 20 E
Opalenica 28 52 18N 16 24 E
Opan 43 42 13N 25 41 E
Opanake 70 6 35N 80 40 E
Opasatika 106 49 30N 82 50W
Opasquia 109 53 16N 93 34W
Opatija 39 45 21N 14 17 E
Opatów 28 50 50N 21 27 E
Opava 27 49 57N 17 58 E
Opelousas 117 30 35N 92 7W
Opémisca L. 106 50 0N 75 0W
Opheim 118 48 52N 106 30W
Ophir 104 63 10N 156 40W
Ophthalmia Ra. 96 23 15 S 119 30 E
Opi 85 6 36N 7 28 E
Opinaca → 106 52 15N 78 2W
Opinaca L. 106 52 39N 76 20W
Opiskotish, L. 107 53 10N 67 50W
Opobo 85 4 35N 7 34 E
Opochka 54 56 42N 28 45 E
Opoczno 28 51 22N 20 18 E
Opole 28 50 42N 17 58 E
Opole □ 28 50 40N 17 56 E
Oporto = Porto 30 41 8N 8 40W
Opotiki 101 38 1 S 177 19 E
Opp 115 31 19N 86 13W
Oppegård 47 59 48N 10 48 E
Oppenheim 25 49 50N 8 22 E
Óppido Mamertina 41 38 16N 15 59 E
Oppland fylke □ 47 61 15N 9 40 E
Oppstad 47 60 17N 11 40 E
Oprtalj 39 45 23N 13 50 E
Opua 101 35 19 S 174 9 E
Opunake 101 39 26 S 173 52 E
Opuzen 42 43 1N 17 34 E
Or Yehuda 62 32 2N 34 50 E
Ora, Israel 62 30 55N 35 1 E
Ora, Italy 39 46 20N 11 19 E
Oracle 119 32 36N 110 46W
Oradea 46 47 2N 21 58 E
Öræfajökull 50 64 2N 16 39W
Orahovac 42 42 24N 20 40 E
Orahovica 42 45 35N 17 52 E
Orai 69 25 58N 79 30 E
Oraison 21 43 55N 5 55 E
Oran, Alg. 82 35 45N 0 39W
Oran, Argent. 124 23 10 S 64 20W
Orange, Austral. 97 33 15 S 149 7 E
Orange, France 21 44 8N 4 47 E
Orange, Mass., U.S.A. 113 42 35N 72 15W
Orange, Tex., U.S.A. 117 30 10N 93 50W
Orange, Va., U.S.A. 114 38 17N 78 5W
Orange, C. 127 4 20N 51 30W
Orange Free State = Oranje Vrystaat □ 92 28 30 S 27 0 E
Orange Grove 117 27 57N 97 57W
Orange Walk 120 18 6N 88 33W
Orangeburg 115 33 35N 80 53W
Orangeville 106 43 55N 80 5W
Oranienburg 24 52 45N 13 15 E
Oranje → 92 28 41 S 16 28 E
Oranje Vrystaat □ 92 28 30 S 27 0 E
Oranjemund 92 28 38 S 16 29 E
Or'Aquiva 62 32 30N 34 54 E
Oras 73 12 9N 125 28 E
Orašje 42 45 1N 18 42 E
Orăştie 46 45 50N 23 10 E
Oraşul Stalin = Braşov 46 45 38N 25 35 E
Orava → 27 49 24N 19 20 E
Oravita 42 45 2N 21 43 E
Orb → 20 43 17N 3 17 E
Orba → 38 44 53N 8 37 E
Ørbæk 49 55 17N 10 39 E
Orbe 25 46 43N 6 32 E
Orbec 18 49 1N 0 23 E
Orbetello 39 42 26N 11 11 E
Órbigo → 30 42 5N 5 42W
Orbost 97 37 40 S 148 29 E
Örbyhus 48 60 15N 17 43 E
Orce 33 37 44N 2 28W
Orce → 33 37 44N 2 28W
Orchies 19 50 28N 3 14 E
Orchila, Isla 126 11 48N 66 10W
Orco → 38 45 10N 7 52 E
Ord → 96 15 33 S 138 15 E
Ord, Mt. 96 17 20 S 125 34 E
Ordenes 30 43 5N 8 29W
Orderville 119 37 18N 112 43W
Ordos = Mu Us Shamo 76 39 0N 109 0 E
Ordu 64 40 55N 37 53 E
Orduña, Álava, Spain 32 42 58N 2 58 E
Orduña, Granada, Spain 33 37 20N 3 30W
Ordway 116 38 15N 103 42W
Ordzhonikidze, R.S.F.S.R., U.S.S.R. 57 43 0N 44 43 E
Ordzhonikidze, Ukraine S.S.R., U.S.S.R. 56 47 39N 34 3 E
Ore, Sweden 48 61 8N 15 10 E
Ore, Zaïre 90 3 17N 29 30 E
Ore Mts. = Erzgebirge 24 50 25N 13 0 E
Orebić 42 43 0N 17 11 E
Örebro 48 59 20N 15 18 E
Örebro län □ 48 59 27N 15 0 E
Oregon 116 42 1N 89 20W
Oregon □ 118 44 0N 121 0W
Oregon City 118 45 21N 122 35W
Öregrund 48 60 21N 18 30 E
Öregrundsgrepen 48 60 25N 18 15 E
Orekhov 56 47 30N 35 48 E
Orekhovo-Zuyevo 55 55 50N 38 55 E
Orel 55 52 57N 36 3 E
Orel → 56 48 30N 34 54 E
Orellana, Canal de 31 39 2N 6 0W
Orellana la Vieja 31 39 1N 5 32W
Orellana, Pantano de 31 39 5N 5 10W
Orem 118 40 20N 111 45W
Oren 45 37 3N 27 57 E
Orenburg 52 51 45N 55 6 E
Orense 30 42 19N 7 55W
Orense □ 30 42 15N 7 51W
Orepuki 101 46 19 S 167 46 E
Orestiás 44 41 30N 26 33 E
Øresund 49 55 45N 12 45 E
Orford Ness 13 52 6N 1 31 E
Orgañá 32 42 13N 1 20 E
Orgaz 31 39 39N 3 53W
Orgeyev 56 47 24N 28 50 E
Orgon 21 43 47N 5 3 E
Orgūn 65 32 55N 69 12 E
Orhon Gol → 75 49 30N 106 0 E
Ória 41 40 30N 17 38 E
Orient 99 28 7 S 142 50 E
Oriental, Cordillera 126 6 0N 73 0W
Oriente 124 38 44 S 60 37W
Origny-Ste-Benoîte 19 49 50N 3 30 E
Orihuela 33 38 7N 0 55W
Orihuela del Tremedal 32 40 33N 1 39W
Oriku 44 40 20N 19 30 E
Orinoco → 126 9 15N 61 30W
Orissa □ 69 20 0N 84 0 E
Oristano 40 39 54N 8 35 E
Oristano, Golfo di 40 39 50N 8 22 E
Orizaba 120 18 50N 97 10W
Orizare 43 42 44N 27 39 E
Ørje 47 59 29N 11 39 E
Orjen 42 42 35N 18 34 E
Orjiva 33 36 53N 3 24W
Orkanger 47 63 18N 9 52 E
Orkelljunga 49 56 17N 13 17 E
Örkény 27 47 9N 19 26 E
Orkla → 47 63 18N 9 51 E
Orkney 92 26 58 S 26 40 E
Orkney □ 14 59 0N 3 0W
Orkney Is. 14 59 0N 3 0W
Orla 28 52 42N 23 20 E
Orland 118 39 46N 122 12W
Orlando 115 28 30N 81 25W
Orlando, C. d' 41 38 10N 14 43 E
Orléanais 19 48 0N 2 0 E
Orléans 19 47 54N 1 52 E
Orleans 113 44 49N 72 10W
Orléans, Î. d' 107 46 54N 70 58W
Orlice → 26 50 5N 16 10 E
Orlické Hory 27 50 15N 16 30 E
Orlik 59 52 30N 99 55 E
Orlov 27 49 17N 20 51 E
Orlov Gay 55 50 56N 48 19 E
Orlovat 42 45 14N 20 33 E
Ormara 66 25 16N 64 33 E
Ormea 38 44 9N 7 54 E
Ormília 44 40 16N 23 39 E
Ormoc 73 11 0N 124 37 E
Ormond, N.Z. 101 38 33 S 177 56 E
Ormond, U.S.A. 115 29 13N 81 5W
Ormož 39 46 25N 16 10 E
Ormstown 113 45 8N 74 0W
Ornans 19 47 7N 6 10 E
Orne □ 18 48 40N 0 5 E
Orne → 18 49 18N 0 15W
Orneta 28 54 8N 20 9 E
Ørnhøj 49 56 13N 8 34 E
Ornö 48 59 4N 18 24 E
Örnsköldsvik 48 63 17N 18 40 E
Oro → 120 25 35N 105 2W
Orocué 126 4 48N 71 20W
Orodo 85 5 34N 7 4 E
Orogrande 119 32 20N 106 4W
Orol 30 43 34N 7 39W
Oromocto 107 45 54N 66 29W
Oron 85 4 48N 8 14 E
Orono 112 43 59N 78 37W
Oropesa 30 39 57N 5 10W
Oroqen Zizhiqi 76 50 34N 123 43 E
Oroquieta 73 8 32N 123 44 E
Orós 127 6 15 S 38 55W
Orosei, G. di 40 40 15N 9 40 E
Orosháza 27 46 32N 20 42 E
Orotukan 59 62 16N 151 42 E
Oroville, Calif., U.S.A. 118 39 31N 121 30W
Oroville, Wash., U.S.A. 118 48 58N 119 30W
Orrefors 49 56 50N 15 45 E
Orroroo 99 32 43 S 138 38 E
Orrville 112 40 50N 81 46W
Orsa 48 61 7N 14 37 E
Orsara di Púglia 41 41 17N 15 16 E
Orsasjön 48 61 7N 14 37 E
Orsha 54 54 30N 30 25 E
Orsk 52 51 12N 58 34 E
Ørslev 49 55 3N 11 56 E
Orsogna 39 42 13N 14 17 E
Orşova 46 44 41N 22 25 E
Ørsted 49 56 30N 10 20 E
Orta, L. d' 38 45 48N 8 21 E
Orta Nova 41 41 20N 15 40 E
Orte 39 42 28N 12 23 E
Ortegal, C. 30 43 43N 7 52W
Orthez 20 43 29N 0 48W
Ortigueira 30 43 40N 7 50W
Ortles 38 46 31N 10 33 E
Ortón → 126 10 50 S 67 0W
Ortona 39 42 21N 14 24 E
Orune 40 40 25N 9 20 E
Oruro 126 18 0 S 67 9W
Orust 49 58 10N 11 40 E
Orūzgān □ 65 33 30N 66 0 E
Orvault 18 47 17N 1 38W
Orvieto 39 42 43N 12 8 E
Orwell 112 41 32N 80 52W
Orwell → 13 52 2N 1 12 E
Oryakhovo 43 43 40N 23 57 E
Orzinuovi 38 45 24N 9 55 E
Orzyc → 28 52 46N 21 14 E
Orzysz 28 53 50N 21 58 E
Os 47 60 9N 5 30 E
Osa 52 57 17N 55 26 E
Osa → 28 53 33N 18 46 E
Osa, Pen. de 121 8 0N 84 0W
Osage, Iowa, U.S.A. 116 43 15N 92 50W
Osage, Wyo., U.S.A. 116 43 59N 104 25W
Osage → 116 38 35N 91 57W
Osage City 116 38 43N 95 51W
Ōsaka 74 34 40N 135 30 E
Ōsaka □ 74 34 30N 135 30 E
Osawatomie 116 38 30N 94 55W
Osborne 116 39 30N 98 45W
Osby 49 56 23N 13 59 E
Osceola, Ark., U.S.A. 117 35 40N 90 0W
Osceola, Iowa, U.S.A. 116 41 0N 93 20W
Oschatz 24 51 17N 13 8 E
Oschersleben 24 52 2N 11 13 E
Öschiri 40 40 43N 9 7 E
Oscoda 114 44 26N 83 20W
Oscoda-Au-Sable 112 44 26N 83 20W
Osečina 42 44 23N 19 34 E
Ösel = Saaremaa 54 58 30N 22 30W
Osëry 55 54 52N 38 28 E
Osh 58 40 37N 72 49 E
Oshawa 106 43 50N 78 50W
ŌShima 74 34 44N 139 24 E
Oshkosh, Nebr., U.S.A. 116 41 27N 102 20W
Oshkosh, Wis., U.S.A. 116 44 3N 88 35W
Oshmyany 54 54 26N 25 52 E
Oshogbo 85 7 48N 4 37 E
Oshwe 88 3 25 S 19 28 E
Osica de Jos 46 44 14N 24 20 E
Osieczna 28 51 55N 16 40 E
Osijek 42 45 34N 18 41 E
Ósilo 40 40 45N 8 41 E
Osimo 39 43 28N 13 30 E
Osintorf 54 54 40N 30 39 E
Osipenko = Berdyansk 56 46 45N 36 50 E
Osipovichi 54 53 19N 28 33 E
Oskaloosa 116 41 18N 92 40W
Oskarshamn 49 57 15N 16 27 E
Oskélanéo 106 48 5N 75 15W
Oskol → 55 49 6N 37 25 E
Oslo 47 59 55N 10 45 E
Oslob 73 9 31N 123 26 E
Oslofjorden 47 59 20N 10 35 E
Osmanabad 70 18 5N 76 10 E
Osmancık 56 40 45N 34 47 E
Osmaniye 64 37 5N 36 10 E
Ösmo 48 58 58N 17 55 E
Osnabrück 24 52 16N 8 2 E
Ośno Lubuskie 28 52 28N 14 51 E
Osobláha 27 50 17N 17 44 E
Osogovska Planina 42 42 10N 22 30 E
Osor 38 44 42N 14 24 E
Osorio 125 29 53 S 50 17W
Osorno, Chile 128 40 25 S 73 0W
Osorno, Spain 30 42 24N 4 22W
Osoyoos 108 49 0N 119 30W
Ospika → 108 56 20N 124 0W
Osprey Reef 97 13 52 S 146 36 E
Oss 16 51 46N 5 32 E
Ossa de Montiel 33 38 58N 2 45W
Ossa, Mt. 97 41 52 S 146 3 E
Óssa, Oros 44 39 47N 22 42 E
Ossabaw I. 115 31 45N 81 8W
Osse → 20 44 7N 0 17 E
Ossining 114 41 9N 73 50W
Ossipee 113 43 41N 71 9W
Ossokmanuan L. 107 53 25N 65 0W
Ossora 59 59 20N 163 13 E
Ostashkov 54 57 4N 33 2 E
Oste → 24 53 30N 9 12 E
Ostend = Oostende 16 51 15N 2 50 E
Oster 54 50 57N 30 53 E
Osterburg 24 52 47N 11 44 E
Osterburken 25 49 26N 9 25 E
Österbybruk 48 60 13N 17 55 E
Österbymo 49 57 49N 15 15 E
Östergötlands län □ 49 58 35N 15 45 E
Osterholz-Scharmbeck 24 53 14N 8 48 E
Østerild 49 57 2N 8 51 E
Österkorsberga 49 57 18N 15 6 E
Osterøya 47 60 32N 5 30 E
Östersund 48 63 10N 14 38 E
Østfold fylke □ 47 59 25N 11 25 E
Ostfreisland 24 53 20N 7 30 E
Ostfriesische Inseln 24 53 45N 7 15 E
Óstia, Lido di (Lido di Roma) 40 41 43N 12 17 E
Ostiglía 39 45 4N 11 9 E
Ostra 39 43 40N 13 5 E
Ostrava 27 49 51N 18 18 E
Ostróda 28 53 42N 19 58 E
Ostrog 54 50 20N 26 30 E
Ostrogozhsk 55 50 55N 39 7 E
Ostrogróg Sźamotuły 28 52 37N 16 33 E
Ostrołeka 28 53 4N 21 32 E
Ostrołeka □ 28 53 0N 21 30 E
Ostrov, Bulg. 43 43 40N 24 9 E
Ostrov, Romania 46 44 6N 27 24 E
Ostrov, U.S.S.R. 54 57 25N 28 20 E
Ostrów Lubelski 28 51 29N 22 51 E
Ostrów Mazowiecka 28 52 50N 21 51 E
Ostrów Wielkopolski 28 51 36N 17 44 E
Ostrowiec-Świętokrzyski 28 50 55N 21 22 E
Ostrozac 42 43 43N 17 49 E
Ostrzeszów 28 51 25N 17 52 E
Ostseebad-Külungsborn 24 54 10N 11 40 E
Ostuni 41 40 44N 17 34 E
Osum → 43 43 40N 24 50 E
Osumi → 44 40 40N 20 10 E
Ōsumi-Kaikyō 74 30 55N 131 0 E
Osuna 31 37 14N 5 8W
Oswego 114 43 29N 76 30W
Oswestry 12 52 52N 3 3W
Oświecim 27 50 2N 19 11 E
Otago □ 101 44 44 S 169 10 E
Otago Harb. 101 45 47 S 170 42 E
Ōtake 74 34 12N 132 13 E
Otaki 101 40 45 S 175 10 E
Otaru 74 43 10N 141 0 E
Otava → 26 49 26N 14 12 E
Otavalo 126 0 13N 78 20W
Otavi 92 19 40 S 17 24 E
Otchinjau 92 16 30 S 13 56 E
Otelec 42 45 36N 20 50 E
Otero de Rey 30 43 6N 7 36W
Othello 118 46 53N 119 8W
Othonoí 44 39 52N 19 22 E
Óthris, Óros 45 39 4N 22 42 E
Otira Gorge 101 42 53 S 171 33 E
Otis 116 40 12N 102 58W
Otjiwarongo 92 20 30 S 16 33 E
Otmuchów 28 50 28N 17 10 E
Otočac 39 44 53N 15 12 E
Otorohanga 101 38 12 S 175 14 E
Otoskwin → 106 52 13N 88 6W
Otosquen 109 53 17N 102 1W
Otra → 47 58 8N 8 1 E
Otranto 41 40 9N 18 28 E
Otranto, C. d' 41 40 7N 18 30 E
Otranto, Str. of 41 40 15N 18 40 E
Ōtsu 74 35 0N 135 50 E
Otta 47 61 46N 9 32 E
Otta → 47 61 46N 9 31 E
Ottapalam 70 10 46N 76 23 E
Ottawa, Can. 106 45 27N 75 42W
Ottawa, Ill., U.S.A. 116 41 20N 88 55W
Ottawa, Kans., U.S.A. 116 38 40N 95 6W
Ottawa = Outaouais → 106 45 27N 74 8W
Ottawa Is. 105 59 35N 80 10W
Ottélé 85 3 38N 11 19 E
Ottenby 49 56 15N 16 24 E
Otter L. 109 55 35N 104 39W
Otter Rapids, Ont., Can. 106 50 11N 81 39W
Otter Rapids, Sask., Can. 109 55 38N 104 44W
Otterberg 25 49 30N 7 46 E
Otterndorf 24 53 47N 8 52 E
Ottersheim 26 48 21N 14 12 E
Otterup 49 55 30N 10 22 E
Otterville 112 42 55N 80 36W
Otto Beit Bridge 91 15 59 S 28 56 E
Ottosdal 92 26 46 S 25 59 E
Ottoshoop 92 25 45 S 25 58 E
Ottsjö 48 63 13N 13 2 E
Ottumwa 116 41 0N 92 25W
Otu 85 8 14N 3 22 E
Otukpa (Al Owuho) 85 7 9N 7 41 E
Oturkpo 85 7 16N 8 8 E
Otway, Bahía 128 53 30 S 74 0W
Otway, C. 97 38 52 S 143 30 E
Otwock 28 52 5N 21 20 E
Ötz 26 47 13N 10 53 E
Ötz → 26 47 14N 10 50 E
Ötztaler Alpen 26 46 45N 11 0 E
Ou → 71 20 4N 102 13 E
Ou-Sammyaku 74 39 20N 140 35 E
Ouachita → 117 31 38N 91 49W
Ouachita, L. 117 34 40N 93 25W
Ouachita Mts. 117 34 50N 94 30W
Ouadâne 80 20 50N 11 40W
Ouadda 81 8 15N 22 20 E
Ouagadougou 85 12 25N 1 30W
Ouahigouya 84 13 31N 2 25W
Ouahila 82 27 50N 5 0W
Ouahran = Oran 82 35 49N 0 39W
Oualâta 84 17 20N 6 55W
Ouallene 82 24 41N 1 11 E
Ouanda Djallé 81 8 55N 22 53 E
Ouango 88 4 19N 22 30 E
Ouargla 83 31 59N 5 16 E
Ouarkziz, Djebel 82 28 50N 8 0W
Ouarzazate 82 30 55N 6 50W
Ouatagouna 85 15 11N 0 43 E
Oubangi → 88 1 0N 17 50 E
Oubarakai, O. → 83 27 20N 9 0 E
Ouche → 19 47 6N 5 16 E
Ouddorp 16 51 50N 3 57 E
Oude Rijn → 16 52 12N 4 24 E
Oudenaarde 16 50 50N 3 37 E
Oudon 18 47 22N 1 19W
Oudon → 18 47 38N 1 18 E
Oudtshoorn 92 33 35 S 22 14 E
Oued Zem 82 32 52N 6 34W
Ouellé 84 7 26N 4 1W
Ouenza 83 35 57N 8 4 E
Ouessa 84 11 4N 2 47W
Ouessant, Île d' 18 48 28N 5 6W
Ouesso 88 1 37N 16 5 E

Ouest, Pte. Papua New Guinea

Ouest, Pte. 107 49 52N 64 40W
Ouezzane 82 34 51N 5 35W
Ouidah 85 6 25N 2 0 E
Ouistreham 18 49 17N 0 18W
Oujda 82 34 41N 1 55W
Oujeft 80 20 2N 13 0W
Ould Yenjé 84 15 38N 12 16W
Ouled Djellal 83 34 28N 5 2 E
Ouled Naïl, Mts. des 82 34 30N 3 30 E
Oulmès 82 33 17N 6 0W
Oulu 50 65 1N 25 29 E
Oulu □ 50 65 10N 27 20 E
Oulujärvi 50 64 25N 27 15 E
Oulujoki → 50 65 1N 25 30 E
Oulx 38 45 2N 6 49 E
Oum Chalouba 81 15 48N 20 46 E
Oum-el-Bouaghi 83 35 55N 7 6 E
Oum el Ksi 82 29 4N 6 59W
Oum-er-Rbia, O. → 82 33 19N 8 21W
Oumè 84 6 21N 5 27W
Ounane, Dj. 83 25 4N 7 19 E
Ounguati 92 21 54S 15 46 E
Ounianga-Kébir 81 19 4N 20 29 E
Ounianga Sérir 81 18 54N 19 51 E
Our → 16 49 55N 6 5 E
Ouray 119 38 3N 107 40W
Ourcq → 19 49 1N 3 1 E
Oureg, Oued el → 82 32 34N 2 10 E
Ouricuri 127 7 53S 40 5W
Ourinhos 125 23 0S 49 54W
Ourique 31 37 38N 8 16W
Ouro Fino 125 22 16S 46 25W
Ouro Prêto 125 20 20S 43 30W
Ouro Sogui 84 15 36N 13 19W
Oursi 85 14 41N 0 27W
Ourthe → 16 50 29N 5 35 E
Ouse 99 42 38S 146 42 E
Ouse →, Sussex, U.K. 13 50 43N 0 3 E
Ouse →, Yorks., U.K. 12 54 3N 0 7 E
Oust 20 42 52N 1 13 E
Oust → 18 47 35N 2 6W
Outaouais → 106 45 27N 74 8W
Outardes → 107 49 24N 69 30W
Outat Oulad el Haj 82 33 22N 3 42W
Outer Hebrides 14 57 30N 7 40W
Outer I. 107 51 10N 58 35W
Outes 30 42 52N 8 55W
Outjo 92 20 5S 16 7 E
Outlook, Can. 109 51 30N 107 0W
Outlook, U.S.A. 116 48 53N 104 46W
Outreau 19 50 40N 1 36 E
Ouvèze → 21 43 59N 4 51 E
Ouyen 97 35 1S 142 22 E
Ouzouer-le-Marché 18 47 54N 1 32 E
Ovada 38 44 39N 8 40 E
Ovalau 101 17 40S 178 48 E
Ovalle 124 30 33S 71 18W
Ovar 30 40 51N 8 40W
Ovens → 100 36 2S 146 12 E
Over Flakkee 16 51 45N 4 5 E
Overijssel □ 16 52 25N 6 35 E
Overpelt 16 51 12N 5 20 E
Overton 119 36 32N 114 31W
Övertorneå 50 66 23N 23 38 E
Overum 49 58 0N 16 20 E
Ovid 116 41 0N 102 17W
Ovidiopol 56 46 15N 30 30 E
Oviedo 30 43 25N 5 50W
Oviedo □ 30 43 20N 6 0W
Oviken 48 63 0N 14 23 E
Oviksfjällen 48 63 0N 13 49 E
Ovoro 85 5 26N 7 16 E
Övre Sirdal 47 58 48N 6 43 E
Ovruch 54 51 25N 28 45 E
Owaka 101 46 27S 169 40 E
Owambo 92 17 20S 16 30 E
Owase 74 34 7N 136 12 E
Owatonna 116 44 3N 93 10W
Owbeh 65 34 28N 63 10 E
Owego 114 42 6N 76 17W
Owen Falls 90 0 30N 33 5 E
Owen Sound 106 44 35N 80 55W
Owen Stanley Range 98 8 30S 147 0 E
Owendo 88 0 17N 9 30 E
Owens L. 119 36 20N 118 0W
Owensboro 114 37 40N 87 5W
Owensville 116 38 20N 91 30W
Owerri 85 5 29N 7 0 E
Owl → 109 57 51N 92 44W
Owo 85 7 10N 5 39 E
Owosso 114 43 0N 84 10W
Owyhee 118 42 0N 116 3W
Owyhee → 118 43 46N 117 2W
Owyhee Res. 118 43 40N 117 16W
Ox Mts. 15 54 6N 9 0W
Oxberg 48 61 7N 14 11 E
Oxelösund 49 58 43N 17 15 E
Oxford, N.Z. 101 43 18S 172 11 E
Oxford, U.K. 13 51 45N 1 15W
Oxford, Miss., U.S.A. 117 34 22N 89 30W
Oxford, N.C., U.S.A. 115 36 19N 78 36W
Oxford, Ohio, U.S.A. 114 39 30N 84 40W
Oxford □ 13 51 45N 1 15W
Oxford L. 109 54 51N 95 37W
Oxía 45 38 16N 21 5 E
Oxílithos 45 38 35N 24 7 E
Oxley 99 34 11S 144 6 E
Oxnard 119 34 10N 119 14W
Oya 72 2 55N 111 55 E
Oyem 88 1 34N 11 31 E
Oyen 109 51 22N 110 28W
Öyeren 47 59 50N 11 15 E
Oykel → 14 57 55N 4 26W
Oymyakon 59 63 25N 142 44 E
Oyo 85 7 46N 3 56 E
Oyo □ 85 8 0N 3 30 E
Oyonnax 21 46 16N 5 40 E
Oyster B. 113 40 52N 73 32W
Øystese 47 60 22N 6 9 E
Ozamis (Mizamis) 73 8 15N 123 50 E
Ozark, Ala., U.S.A. 115 31 29N 85 39W
Ozark, Ark., U.S.A. 117 35 30N 93 50W
Ozark, Mo., U.S.A. 117 37 0N 93 15W
Ozark Plateau 117 37 20N 91 40W
Ozarks, L. of 116 38 10N 92 40W
Ózd 27 48 14N 20 15 E
Ozieri 40 40 35N 9 0 E
Ozimek 28 50 41N 18 11 E
Ozona 117 30 43N 101 11W
Ozorków 28 51 57N 19 16 E
Ozren 42 43 55N 18 29 E
Ozuluama 120 21 40N 97 50W
Ozun 46 45 47N 25 50 E

P

Pa 84 11 33N 3 19W
Pa-an 67 16 51N 97 40 E
Pa Sak → 71 15 30N 101 0 E
Paar → 25 48 13N 10 59 E
Paarl 92 33 45S 18 56 E
Paatsi → 50 68 55N 29 0 E
Paauilo 110 20 3N 155 22W
Pab Hills 66 26 30N 66 45 E
Pabianice 28 51 40N 19 20 E
Pabna 69 24 1N 89 18 E
Pabo 90 3 1N 32 10 E
Pacaja → 127 1 56S 50 50W
Pacaraima, Sierra 126 4 0N 62 30W
Pacasmayo 126 7 20S 79 35W
Pacaudière, La 20 46 11N 3 52 E
Paceco 40 37 59N 12 32 E
Pachhar 68 24 40N 77 42 E
Pachino 41 36 43N 15 4 E
Pachora 68 20 38N 75 29 E
Pachuca 120 20 10N 98 40W
Pacific 108 54 48N 128 28W
Pacific-Antarctic Basin 95 46 0S 95 0W
Pacific-Antarctic Ridge 95 43 0S 115 0W
Pacific Grove 119 36 38N 121 58W
Pacific Ocean 94 10 0N 140 0W
Pacitan 73 8 12S 111 7 E
Pacofi 108 53 0N 132 30W
Pacov 26 49 27N 15 0 E
Pacsa 27 46 44N 17 2 E
Paczków 28 50 28N 17 0 E
Padaido, Kepulauan 73 1 5S 138 0 E
Padalarang 73 7 50S 107 30 E
Padang 72 1 0S 100 20 E
Padangpanjang 72 0 40S 100 20 E
Padangsidempuan 72 1 30N 99 15 E
Padborg 49 54 49N 9 21 E
Paddockwood 109 53 30N 105 30W
Paderborn 24 51 42N 8 44 E
Padeşul 46 45 40N 22 22 E
Padina 46 44 50N 27 8 E
Padloping Island 105 67 0N 62 50W
Padmanabhapuram 70 8 16N 77 17 E
Pádova 39 45 24N 11 52 E
Padra 68 22 15N 73 7 E
Padrauna 69 26 54N 83 59 E
Padre I. 117 27 0N 97 20W
Padrón 30 42 41N 8 39W
Padstow 12 50 33N 4 57W
Padua = Pádova 39 45 24N 11 52 E
Paducah, Ky., U.S.A. 114 37 0N 88 40W
Paducah, Tex., U.S.A. 117 34 3N 100 16W
Padul 31 37 1N 3 38W
Padula 41 40 20N 15 40 E
Padwa 70 18 27N 82 47 E
Paeroa 101 37 23S 175 41 E
Paesana 38 44 40N 7 18 E
Pag 39 44 30N 14 50 E
Paga 85 11 1N 1 8W
Pagadian 73 7 55N 123 30 E
Pagai Selatan 72 3 0S 100 15W
Pagai Utara 72 2 35S 100 0 E
Pagalu = Annobón 79 1 25S 5 36 E
Pagastikós Kólpos 44 39 15N 23 0 E
Pagatan 72 3 33S 115 59 E
Page, Ariz., U.S.A. 119 36 57N 111 27W
Page, N.D., U.S.A. 116 47 11N 97 37W
Paglieta 39 42 10N 14 30 E
Pagny-sur-Moselle 19 48 59N 6 2 E
Pago Pago 101 14 16S 170 43W
Pagosa Springs 119 37 16N 107 4W
Pagwa River 106 50 2N 85 14W
Pahala 110 19 12N 155 25W
Pahang □ 71 3 40N 102 20 E
Pahang → 71 3 30N 103 9 E
Pahiatua 101 40 27S 175 50 E
Pahokee 115 26 50N 80 40W
Pahrump 119 36 15N 116 0W
Paia 110 20 54N 156 22W
Paide 54 58 57N 25 31 E
Paignton 13 50 26N 3 33W
Päijänne, L. 51 61 30N 25 30 E
Pailin 71 12 46N 102 36 E
Paimbœuf 18 47 17N 2 0W
Paimpol 18 48 48N 3 4W
Painan 72 1 21S 100 34 E
Painesville 114 41 42N 81 18W
Paint I. 109 55 28N 97 57W
Paint Rock 117 31 30N 99 56W
Painted Desert 119 36 0N 111 30W
Paintsville 114 37 50N 82 50W
Paisley, Can. 112 44 18N 81 16W
Paisley, U.K. 14 55 51N 4 27W
Paisley, U.S.A. 118 42 43N 120 40W
Paita 126 5 11S 81 9W
Paiva → 30 41 4N 8 16W
Pajares 30 43 1N 5 46W
Pajares, Puerto de 30 43 0N 5 46W
Pajeczno 28 51 10N 19 0 E
Pak Lay 71 18 15N 101 27 E
Pakala 70 13 29N 79 8 E
Pakanbaru 72 0 30N 101 15 E
Pakaraima Mts. 126 6 0N 60 0W
Pakistan ■ 66 30 0N 70 0 E
Pakistan, East = Bangladesh ■ 67 24 0N 90 0 E
Pakokku 67 21 20N 95 0 E
Pakosc 28 52 48N 18 6 E
Pakpattan 68 30 25N 73 27 E
Pakrac 42 45 27N 17 12 E
Paks 27 46 38N 18 55 E
Pakse 71 15 5N 105 52 E
Paktīā □ 65 33 0N 69 15 E
Pakwach 90 2 28N 31 27 E
Pala, Chad 81 9 25N 15 5 E
Pala, Zaïre 90 6 45S 29 30 E
Palabek 90 3 22N 32 33 E
Palacios 117 28 44N 96 12W
Palafrugell 32 41 55N 3 10 E
Palagiano 41 40 35N 17 0 E
Palagonía 41 37 20N 14 43 E
Palagruža 39 42 24N 16 15 E
Palaiokastron 45 35 12N 26 18 E
Palaiokhóra 45 35 16N 23 39 E
Pálairos 45 38 45N 20 51 E
Palais, Le 18 47 20N 3 10W
Palakol 70 16 31N 81 46 E
Palam 70 19 0N 77 0 E
Palamás 44 39 26N 22 4 E
Palamós 32 41 50N 3 10 E
Palampur 68 32 10N 76 30 E
Palana, Austral. 99 39 45S 147 55 E
Palana, U.S.S.R. 59 59 10N 159 59 E
Palanan 73 17 8N 122 29 E
Palanan Pt. 73 17 17N 122 30 E
Palangkaraya 72 2 16S 113 56 E
Palanpur 68 24 10N 72 25 E
Palapye 92 22 30S 27 7 E
Palar → 70 12 27N 80 13 E
Palatka, U.S.A. 115 29 40N 81 40W
Palatka, U.S.S.R. 59 60 6N 150 54 E
* Palau Is. 94 7 30N 134 30 E
Palauig 73 15 26N 119 54 E
Palauk 71 13 10N 98 40 E
Palavas 20 43 32N 3 56 E
Palawan 72 9 30N 118 30 E
Palayancottai 70 8 45N 77 45 E
Palazzo San Gervásio 41 40 53N 15 58 E
Palazzolo Acreide 41 37 4N 14 54 E
Paldiski 54 59 23N 24 9 E
Pale 42 43 50N 18 38 E
Paleleh 73 1 10N 121 50 E
Palembang 72 3 0S 104 50 E
Palencia 30 42 1N 4 34W
Palencia □ 30 42 31N 4 33W
Palermo, Italy 40 38 8N 13 20 E
Palermo, U.S.A. 118 39 30N 121 37W
Palestine, Asia 62 32 0N 35 0 E
Palestine, U.S.A. 117 31 42N 95 35W
Palestrina 40 41 50N 12 52 E
Paletwa 67 21 10N 92 50 E
Palghat 70 10 46N 76 42 E
Pali 68 25 50N 73 20 E
Palinuro, C. 41 40 1N 15 14 E
Palisade 116 40 21N 101 10W
Palitana 68 21 32N 71 49 E
Palizada 120 18 18N 92 8W
Palizzi 41 37 58N 15 59 E
Palk Bay 70 9 30N 79 15 E
Palk Strait 70 10 0N 79 45 E
Palkonda 70 18 36N 83 48 E
Palkonda Ra. 70 13 50N 79 20 E
Pallanza = Verbánia 38 45 50N 8 55 E
Pallasovka 55 50 4N 47 0 E
Palleru → 70 16 45N 80 2 E
Pallisa 90 1 12N 33 43 E
Pallu 68 28 59N 74 14 E
Palm Beach 115 26 46N 80 0W
Palm Is. 97 18 40S 146 35 E
Palm Springs 119 33 51N 116 35W
Palma, Canary Is. 8 28 40N 17 50W
Palma, Mozam. 91 10 46S 40 29 E
Palma → 127 12 33S 47 52W
Palma, B. de 33 39 30N 2 39 E
Palma de Mallorca 32 39 35N 2 39 E
Palma del Río 31 37 43N 5 17W
Palma di Montechiaro 40 37 12N 13 46 E
Palma, La, Canary Is. 80 28 40N 17 50W
Palma, La, Panama 121 8 15N 78 0W
Palma, La, Spain 31 37 21N 6 38W
Palma Soriano 121 20 15N 76 0W
Palmahim 62 31 56N 34 44 E
Palmanova 39 45 54N 13 18 E
Palmares 127 8 41S 35 28W
Palmarola 40 40 57N 12 50 E
Palmas 125 26 29S 52 0W
Palmas, C. 84 4 27N 7 46W
Pálmas, G. di 40 39 0N 8 30 E
Palmdale 119 34 36N 118 7W
Palmeira dos Índios 127 9 25S 36 37W
Palmeirinhas, Pta. das 88 9 2S 12 57 E
Palmela 31 38 32N 8 57W
Palmer, Alaska, U.S.A. 104 61 35N 149 10W
Palmer, Mass., U.S.A. 113 42 9N 72 21W
Palmer →, N. Terr., Austral. 96 24 46S 133 25 E
Palmer →, Queens., Austral. 98 15 34S 142 26 E
Palmer Arch 5 64 15S 65 0W
Palmer Lake 116 39 10N 104 52W
Palmer Land 5 73 0S 60 0W
Palmerston 112 43 50N 80 51W
Palmerston, C. 97 21 32S 149 29 E
Palmerston North 101 40 21S 175 39 E
Palmerton 113 40 47N 75 36W
Palmetto 115 27 33N 82 33W
Palmi 41 38 21N 15 51 E
Palmira, Argent. 124 32 59S 68 34W
Palmira, Colomb. 126 3 32N 76 16W
Palms 112 43 37N 82 47W
Palmyra, Mo., U.S.A. 116 39 45N 91 30W
Palmyra, N.Y., U.S.A. 112 42 5N 77 18W
Palmyra = Tudmur 64 34 30N 37 17 E
Palmyra Is. 95 5 52N 162 6W
Palni 70 10 30N 77 30 E
Palni Hills 70 10 14N 77 33 E
Palo Alto 119 37 25N 122 8W
Palo del Colle 41 41 4N 16 43 E
Paloma, La 124 30 35S 71 0W
Palombara Sabina 39 42 4N 12 45 E
Palopo 73 3 0S 120 16 E
Palos, Cabo de 33 37 38N 0 40W
Palouse 118 46 59N 117 5W
Palparara 98 24 47S 141 28 E
Pålsboda 49 59 3N 15 22 E
Palu, Indon. 73 1 0S 119 52 E
Palu, Turkey 64 38 45N 40 0 E
Paluan 73 13 26N 120 29 E
Palwal 68 28 8N 77 19 E
Pama 85 11 19N 0 44 E
Pamamaroo, L. 100 32 17S 142 28 E
Pamanukan 73 6 16S 107 49 E
Pamban I. 70 9 15N 79 20 E
Pamekasan 73 7 10S 113 29 E
Pameungpeuk 73 7 38S 107 44 E
Pamiers 20 43 7N 1 39 E
Pamir 58 37 40N 73 0 E
Pamlico → 115 35 25N 76 30W
Pamlico Sd. 115 35 20N 76 0W
Pampa 117 35 35N 100 58W
Pampa de las Salinas 124 32 1S 66 58W
Pampa, La □ 124 36 50S 66 0W
Pampanua 73 4 16S 120 8 E
Pamparato 38 44 16N 7 54 E
Pampas, Argent. 124 35 0S 63 0W
Pampas, Peru 126 12 20S 74 50W
Pamplona, Colomb. 126 7 23N 72 39W
Pamplona, Spain 32 42 48N 1 38W
Pampoenpoort 92 31 3S 22 40 E
Pana 116 39 25N 89 10W
Panaca 119 37 51N 114 23W
Panagyurishte 43 42 30N 24 15 E
Panaitan 73 6 35S 105 10 E
Panaji (Panjim) 70 15 25N 73 50 E
Panamá 121 9 0N 79 25W
Panama ■ 121 8 48N 79 55W
Panama Canal 121 9 10N 79 37W
Panama City 115 30 10N 85 41W
Panamá, Golfo de 121 8 4N 79 20W
Panamint Mts. 119 36 30N 117 20W
Panão 126 9 55S 75 55W
Panarea 41 38 38N 15 3 E
Panaro → 38 44 55N 11 25 E
Panarukan 73 7 40S 113 52 E
Panay 73 11 10N 122 30 E
Panay, G. 73 11 0N 122 30 E
Pancake Ra. 119 38 30N 116 0W
Pančevo 42 44 52N 20 41 E
Panciu 46 45 54N 27 8 E
Panco 73 8 42S 118 40 E
Pancorbo, Paso 32 42 32N 3 5W
Pandan 73 11 45N 122 10 E
Pandeglang 73 6 25S 106 0 E
Pandharpur 70 17 41N 75 20 E
Pandhurna 68 21 36N 78 35 E
Pandilla 32 41 32N 3 43W
Pando 125 34 44S 56 0W
Pando, L. = Hope L. 99 28 24S 139 18 E
Panevezys 54 55 42N 24 25 E
Panfilov 58 44 10N 80 0 E
Panfilovo 55 50 25N 42 46 E
Pang-Long 67 23 11N 98 45 E
Pang-Yang 67 22 7N 98 48 E
Panga 90 1 52N 26 18 E
Pangaíon Óros 44 40 50N 24 0 E
Pangalanes, Canal des 93 22 48S 47 50 E
Pangani 90 5 25S 38 58 E
Pangani □ 90 5 25S 39 0 E
Pangani → 90 5 26S 38 58 E
Pangfou = Bengbu 77 32 56N 117 20 E
Pangil 90 3 10S 26 35 E
Pangkah, Tanjung 73 6 51S 112 33 E
Pangkalanberandan 72 4 1N 98 20 E
Pangkalanbuun 72 2 41S 111 37 E
Pangkalansusu 72 4 2N 98 13 E
Pangkoh 72 3 5S 114 8 E
Pangnirtung 105 66 8N 65 54W
Pangrango 73 6 46S 107 1 E
Panguitch 119 37 52N 112 30W
Pangutaran Group 73 6 18N 120 34 E
Panhandle 117 35 23N 101 23W
Pani Mines 68 22 29N 73 50 E
Pania-Mutombo 90 5 11S 23 51 E
Panipat 68 29 25N 77 2 E
Panjal Range 68 32 30N 76 50 E
Panjgur 66 27 0N 64 5 E
Panjim = Panaji 70 15 25N 73 50 E
Panjinad Barrage 65 29 22N 71 15 E
Pankajene 73 4 46S 119 34 E
Pankalpinang 72 2 0S 106 0 E
Pankshin 85 9 16N 9 25 E
Panna 69 24 40N 80 15 E
Panna Hills 69 24 40N 81 15 E
Pannuru 70 16 5N 80 34 E
Panorama 125 21 21S 51 51W
Panruti 70 11 46N 79 35 E
Panshan 76 41 3N 122 2 E
Panshi 76 42 58N 126 5 E
Pantano 119 32 0N 110 32W
Pantar 73 8 28S 124 10 E
Pantelleria 40 36 52N 12 0 E
Pantón 30 42 31N 7 37W
Pánuco 120 22 0N 98 15W
Panyam 85 9 27N 9 8 E
Panyu 77 22 51N 113 20 E
Páola 41 39 21N 16 2 E
Paola 116 38 36N 94 50W
Paonia 119 38 56N 107 37W
Paoting = Baoding 76 38 50N 115 28 E
Paot'ou = Baotou 76 40 32N 110 2 E
Paoua 88 7 9N 16 20 E
Papá 27 47 22N 17 30 E
Papagayo → 120 16 36N 99 43W
Papagayo, Golfo de 121 10 30N 85 50W
Papagni → 70 15 35N 77 45 E
Papakura 101 37 4S 174 59 E
Papantla 120 20 30N 97 30W
Papar 72 5 45N 116 0 E
Pápas, Ákra 45 38 13N 21 20 E
Papenburg 24 53 7N 7 25 E
Papigochic → 120 29 9N 109 40W
Paposo 124 25 0S 70 30W
Papua, Gulf of 98 9 0S 144 50 E
Papua New Guinea ■ 94 8 0S 145 0 E

* *Renamed Belau*

Papuča Penne

Papuča 39 44 22N 15 30 E
Papudo 124 32 29 S 71 27W
Papuk 42 45 30N 17 30 E
Papun 67 18 0N 97 30 E
Pará = Belém 127 1 20 S 48 30W
Pará □ 127 3 20 S 52 0W
Parábita 41 40 3N 18 8 E
Paraburdoo 96 23 14 S 117 32 E
Paracatu 127 17 10 S 46 50W
Parachilna 99 31 10 S 138 21 E
Parachinar 66 33 55N 70 5 E
Paraćin 42 43 54N 21 27 E
Paradas 31 37 18N 5 29W
Paradela 30 42 44N 7 37W
Paradip 69 20 15N 86 35 E
Paradise 118 47 27N 114 17W
Paradise → 107 53 27N 57 19W
Paradise Valley 118 41 30N 117 28W
Parado 73 8 42 S 118 30 E
Paradyz 28 51 19N 20 2 E
Paragould 117 36 5N 90 30W
Paragua → 126 6 55N 62 55W
Paragua, La 126 6 50N 63 20W
Paraguaçu → 127 12 45 S 38 54W
Paraguaçu Paulista 125 22 22 S 50 35W
Paraguaná, Pen. de 126 12 0N 70 0W
Paraguari 124 25 36 S 57 0W
Paraguarí □ 124 26 0 S 57 10W
Paraguay ■ 124 23 0 S 57 0W
Paraguay → 124 27 18 S 58 38W
Paraíba = João Pessoa 127 7 10 S 35 0W
Paraíba □ 127 7 0 S 36 0W
Paraíba do Sul → 125 21 37 S 41 3W
Parainen 51 60 18N 22 18 E
Parakhino Paddubye 54 58 26N 33 10 E
Parakou 85 9 25N 2 40 E
Parálion-Astrous 45 37 25N 22 45 E
Paramagudi 70 9 31N 78 39 E
Paramaribo 127 5 50N 55 10W
Paramithiá 44 39 30N 20 35 E
Paramushir, Ostrov 59 50 24N 156 0 E
Paran → 62 30 20N 35 10 E
Paraná 124 31 45 S 60 30W
Paranã 127 12 30 S 47 48W
Paraná □ 125 24 30 S 51 0W
Paraná → 124 33 43 S 59 15W
Paranaguá 125 25 30 S 48 30W
Paranaíba → 127 20 6 S 51 4W
Paranapanema → 125 22 40 S 53 9W
Paranapiacaba, Serra do 125 24 31 S 48 35W
Paranavaí 125 23 4 S 52 56W
Parang, Jolo, Phil. 73 5 55N 120 54 E
Parang, Mindanao, Phil. 73 7 23N 124 16 E
Parapóla 45 36 55N 23 27 E
Paraspóri, Ákra 45 35 55N 27 15 E
Paratinga 127 12 40 S 43 10W
Paratoo 99 32 42 S 139 40 E
Parattah 99 42 22 S 147 23 E
Paray-le-Monial 21 46 27N 4 7 E
Parbati → 68 25 50N 76 30 E
Parbhani 68 19 8N 76 52 E
Parchim 24 53 25N 11 50 E
Parczew 28 51 40N 22 52 E
Pardes Hanna 62 32 28N 34 57 E
Pardilla 30 41 33N 3 43W
Pardo →, Bahia, Brazil 127 15 40 S 39 0W
Pardo →, Mato Grosso, Brazil 125 21 46 S 52 9W
Pardo →, São Paulo, Brazil 127 20 10 S 48 38W
Pardubice 26 50 3N 15 45 E
Pare 73 7 43 S 112 12 E
Pare □ 90 4 10 S 38 0 E
Pare Mts. 90 4 0 S 37 45 E
Parecis, Serra dos 126 13 0 S 60 0W
Paredes de Nava 30 42 9N 4 42W
Paren 59 62 30N 163 15 E
Parent 106 47 55N 74 35W
Parent, Lac. 106 48 31N 77 1W
Parentis-en-Born 20 44 21N 1 4W
Parepare 73 4 0 S 119 40 E
Parfino 54 57 59N 31 34 E
Parfuri 93 22 28 S 31 17 E
Parguba 52 62 20N 34 27 E
Parham 113 44 39N 76 43W
Pariaguán 126 8 51N 64 34W
Pariaman 72 0 47 S 100 11 E
Paricutín, Cerro 120 19 28N 102 15W
Parigi, Java, Indon. 73 7 42 S 108 29 E
Parigi, Sulawesi, Indon. 73 0 50 S 120 5 E
Parika 126 6 50N 58 20W
Parima, Serra 126 2 30N 64 0W
Parinari 126 4 35 S 74 25W
Parincea 46 46 27N 27 9 E
Paring 46 45 20N 23 37 E
Parintins 127 2 40 S 56 50W
Pariparit Kyun 67 14 55 S 93 45 E
Paris, Can. 106 43 12N 80 25W
Paris, France 19 48 50N 2 20 E
Paris, Idaho, U.S.A. 118 42 13N 111 30W
Paris, Ky., U.S.A. 114 38 12N 84 12W
Paris, Tenn., U.S.A. 115 36 20N 88 20W
Paris, Tex., U.S.A. 117 33 40N 95 30W
Paris, Ville de □ 19 48 50N 2 20 E
Parish 113 43 24N 76 9W
Pariti 73 10 15 S 123 45 E
Park City 118 40 42N 111 35W
Park Falls 116 45 58N 90 27W
Park Range 118 40 0N 106 30W
Park Rapids 116 46 56N 95 0W
Park River 116 48 25N 97 43W
Park Rynie 93 30 25 S 30 45 E
Park View 119 36 45N 106 37W
Parker, Ariz., U.S.A. 119 34 8N 114 16W
Parker, S.D., U.S.A. 116 43 25N 97 7W
Parker Dam 119 34 13N 114 5W
Parkersburg 114 39 18N 81 31W
Parkerview 109 51 21N 103 18W
Parkes, A.C.T., Austral. 97 35 18 S 149 8 E
Parkes, N.S.W., Austral. 97 33 9 S 148 11 E
Parkside 109 53 10N 106 33W
Parkston 116 43 25N 98 0W
Parksville 108 49 20N 124 21W
Parlakimedi 70 18 45N 84 5 E
Parma, Italy 38 44 50N 10 20 E
Parma, Idaho, U.S.A. 118 43 49N 116 59W
Parma, Ohio, U.S.A. 112 41 25N 81 42W
Parma → 38 44 56N 10 26 E
Parnaguá 127 10 10 S 44 38W
Parnaíba, Piauí, Brazil 127 2 54 S 41 47W
Parnaíba, São Paulo, Brazil 127 19 34 S 51 14W
Parnaíba → 127 3 0 S 41 50W
Parnassós 45 38 35N 22 30 E
Párnis 45 38 14N 23 45 E
Párnon Óros 45 37 15N 22 45 E
Pärnu 54 58 28N 24 33 E
Parola 68 20 47N 75 7 E
Paroo → 97 31 28 S 143 32 E
Paroo Chan. 97 30 50 S 143 35 E
Páros, Greece 45 37 5N 25 9 E
Páros, Greece 45 37 5N 25 12 E
Parowan 119 37 54N 112 56W
Parpaillon 21 44 30N 6 40 E
Parral 124 36 10 S 71 52W
Parramatta 99 33 48 S 151 1 E
Parras 120 25 30N 102 20W
Parrett → 13 51 7N 2 58W
Parris I. 115 32 20N 80 30W
Parrsboro 107 45 30N 64 25W
Parry Is. 4 77 0N 110 0W
Parry Sound 106 45 20N 80 0W
Parsberg 25 49 10N 11 43 E
Parseta → 28 54 11N 15 34 E
Parshall 116 47 56N 102 11W
Parsnip → 108 55 10N 123 2W
Parsons 117 37 20N 95 17W
Partabpur 70 20 0N 80 42 E
Partanna 40 37 43N 12 51 E
Partapgarh 68 24 2N 74 40 E
Parthenay 18 46 38N 0 16W
Partinico 40 38 3N 13 6 E
Partur 70 19 40N 76 14 E
Paru → 127 1 33 S 52 38W
Parur 70 10 13N 76 14 E
Paruro 126 13 45 S 71 50W
Parván □ 65 35 0N 69 0 E
Parvatipuram 70 18 50N 83 25 E
Parys 92 26 52 S 27 29 E
Pas-de-Calais □ 19 50 30N 2 30 E
Pasadena, Calif., U.S.A. 119 34 5N 118 9W
Pasadena, Tex., U.S.A. 117 29 45N 95 14W
Pasaje 126 3 23 S 79 50W
Pasaje → 124 25 39 S 63 56W
Pascagoula 117 30 21N 88 30W
Pascagoula → 117 30 21N 88 35W
Paşcani 46 47 14N 26 45 E
Pasco 118 46 10N 119 0W
Pasco, Cerro de 126 10 45 S 76 10W
Pasewalk 24 53 30N 14 0 E
Pasfield L. 109 58 24N 105 20W
Pasha → 54 60 29N 32 55 E
Pashmakli = Smolyan 43 41 36N 24 38 E
Pasing 25 48 9N 11 27 E
Pasir Mas 71 6 2N 102 8 E
Pasir Puteh 71 5 50N 102 24 E
Pasirian 73 8 13 S 113 8 E
Pasłeka → 28 54 26N 19 46 E
Pasley, C. 96 33 52 S 123 35 E
Pašman 39 43 58N 15 20 E
Pasni 66 25 15N 63 27 E
Paso de Indios 128 43 55 S 69 0W
Paso de los Libres 124 29 44 S 57 10W
Paso de los Toros 124 32 45 S 56 30W
Paso Robles 119 35 40N 120 45W
Paspébiac 107 48 3N 65 17W
Pasrur 68 32 16N 74 43 E
Passage West 15 51 52N 8 20W
Passaic 113 40 50N 74 8W
Passau 25 48 34N 13 27 E
Passero, C. 41 36 42N 15 8 E
Passo Fundo 125 28 10 S 52 20W
Passos 127 20 45 S 46 37W
Passow 24 53 13N 14 10 E
Passy 21 45 55N 6 41 E
Pastaza → 126 4 50 S 76 52W
Pastęk 28 54 3N 19 41 E
Pasto 126 1 13N 77 17W
Pastrana 32 40 27N 2 53W
Pasuruan 73 7 40 S 112 44 E
Pasym 28 53 48N 20 49 E
Pásztó 27 47 52N 19 43 E
Patagonia, Argent. 128 45 0 S 69 0W
Patagonia, U.S.A. 119 31 35N 110 45W
Patan, Gujarat, India 70 17 22N 73 57 E
Patan, Maharashtra, India 68 23 54N 72 14 E
Patani 73 0 20N 128 50 E
Pataudi 68 28 18N 76 48 E
Patay 19 48 2N 1 40 E
Patchewollock 99 35 22 S 142 12 E
Patchogue 114 40 46N 73 1W
Patea 101 39 45 S 174 30 E
Pategi 85 8 50N 5 45 E
Patensie 92 33 46 S 24 49 E
Paternò 41 37 34N 14 53 E
Paternoster, Kepulauan 72 7 5 S 118 15 E
Pateros 118 48 4N 119 58W
Paterson, Austral. 100 32 37 S 151 39 E
Paterson, U.S.A. 114 40 55N 74 10W
Pathankot 68 32 18N 75 45 E
Pathfinder Res. 118 42 30N 107 0W
Pati 73 6 45 S 111 3 E
Patiala 68 30 23N 76 26 E
Patine Kouka 84 12 45N 13 45W
Patkai Bum 67 27 0N 95 30 E
Pátmos 45 37 21N 26 36 E
Patna 69 25 35N 85 12 E
Patonga 90 2 45N 33 15 E
Patos de Minas 127 18 35 S 46 32W
Patos, Lag. dos 125 31 20 S 51 0 E
Patosi 44 40 42N 19 38 E
Patquia 124 25 30N 102 11W
Pátrai 45 38 14N 21 47 E
Pátraikós, Kólpos 45 38 17N 21 30 E
Patrocínio 127 18 57 S 47 0W
Patta 90 2 10 S 41 0 E
Pattada 40 40 35N 9 7 E
Pattanapuram 70 9 6N 76 50 E
Pattani 71 6 48N 101 15 E
Patten 107 45 59N 68 28W
Patterson, Calif., U.S.A. 119 37 30N 121 9W
Patterson, La., U.S.A. 117 29 44N 91 20W
Patti, India 68 31 17N 74 54 E
Patti, Italy 41 38 8N 14 57 E
Pattoki 68 31 5N 73 52 E
Patton 112 40 38N 78 40W
Pattukkottai 70 10 25N 79 20 E
Patuakhali 69 22 20N 90 25 E
Patuca → 121 15 50N 84 18W
Patuca, Punta 121 15 49N 84 14W
Pátzcuaro 120 19 30N 101 40W
Pau 20 43 19N 0 25W
Pau, Gave de 20 43 33N 1 12W
Pauillac 20 45 11N 0 46W
Pauini → 126 1 42 S 62 50W
Pauk 67 21 27N 94 30 E
Paul I. 107 56 30N 61 20W
Paulhan 20 43 33N 3 28 E
Paulis = Isiro 90 2 47N 27 37 E
Paulistana 127 8 9 S 41 9W
Paullina 116 42 55N 95 40W
Paulo Afonso 127 9 21 S 38 15W
Paulpietersburg 93 27 23 S 30 50 E
Pauls Valley 117 34 40N 97 17W
Pauni 69 20 48N 79 40 E
Pavelets 55 53 49N 39 14 E
Pavia 38 45 10N 9 10 E
Pavlikeni 43 43 14N 25 20 E
Pavlodar 58 52 33N 77 0 E
Pavlograd 56 48 30N 35 52 E
Pavlovo, Gorkiy, U.S.S.R. 55 55 58N 43 5 E
Pavlovo, Yakut A.S.S.R., U.S.S.R. 59 63 5N 115 25 E
Pavlovsk 55 50 26N 40 5 E
Pavlovskaya 57 46 17N 39 47 E
Pavlovskiy-Posad 55 55 47N 38 42 E
Pavullo nel Frignano 38 44 20N 10 50 E
Pawhuska 117 36 40N 96 25W
Pawling 113 41 35N 73 37W
Pawnee 117 36 24N 96 50W
Pawnee City 116 40 8N 96 10W
Pawtucket 114 41 51N 71 22W
Paximádhia 45 35 0N 24 35 E
Paxoí 44 39 14N 20 12 E
Paxton, Ill., U.S.A. 114 40 25N 88 7W
Paxton, Nebr., U.S.A. 116 41 12N 101 27W
Paya Bakri 71 2 3N 102 44 E
Payakumbah 72 0 20 S 100 35 E
Payerne 25 46 49N 6 56 E
Payette 118 44 0N 117 0W
Paymogo 31 37 44N 7 21W
Payne L. 105 59 30N 74 30W
Paynesville, Liberia 84 6 20N 10 45W
Paynesville, U.S.A. 116 45 21N 94 44W
Pays Basque 20 43 15N 1 0W
Paysandú 124 32 19 S 58 8W
Payson, Ariz., U.S.A. 119 34 17N 111 15W
Payson, Utah, U.S.A. 118 40 8N 111 41W
Paz → 120 13 44N 90 10W
Paz, Bahía de la 120 24 15N 110 25W
Paz, La, Entre Ríos, Argent. 124 30 50 S 59 45W
Paz, La, San Luis, Argent. 124 33 30 S 67 20W
Paz, La, Boliv. 126 16 20 S 68 10W
Paz, La, Hond. 120 14 20N 87 47W
Paz, La, Mexico 120 24 10N 110 20W
Pazar 64 41 10N 40 50 E
Pazardzhik 43 42 12N 24 20 E
Pazin 39 45 14N 13 56 E
Pčinja → 42 41 50N 21 45 E
Pe Ell 118 46 30N 123 18W
Peabody 113 42 31N 70 56W
Peace → 108 59 0N 111 25W
Peace Point 108 59 7N 112 27W
Peace River 108 56 15N 117 18W
Peach Springs 119 35 36N 113 30W
Peak Downs 98 22 14 S 148 0 E
Peak Hill 99 32 47 S 148 11 E
Peak Range 97 22 50 S 148 20 E
Peak, The 12 53 24N 1 53W
Peake 99 35 25 S 140 0 E
Peale Mt. 119 38 25N 109 12W
Pearce 119 31 57N 109 56W
Pearl → 117 30 23N 89 45W
Pearl Banks 70 8 45N 79 45 E
Pearl City 110 21 24N 158 0W
Pearsall 117 28 55N 99 8W
Pearse I. 108 54 52N 130 14W
Peary Land 4 82 40N 33 0W
Pease → 117 34 12N 99 7W
Pebane 91 17 10 S 38 8 E
Pebas 126 3 10 S 71 46W
Peč 42 42 40N 20 17 E
Péccioli 38 43 32N 10 43 E
Pechea 46 45 36N 27 49 E
Pechenezhin 56 48 30N 24 48 E
Pechenga 52 69 30N 31 25 E
Pechnezhskoye Vdkhr. 55 50 0N 37 10 E
Pechora → 52 68 13N 54 15 E
Pechorskaya Guba 52 68 40N 54 0 E
Pechory 54 57 48N 27 40 E
Pecica 42 46 10N 21 3 E
Pečka 42 44 18N 19 33 E
Pécora, C. 40 39 28N 8 23 E
Pecos 117 31 25N 103 35W
Pecos → 117 29 42N 102 30W
Pécs 27 46 5N 18 15 E
Peddapalli 70 18 40N 79 24 E
Peddapuram 70 17 6N 8 13 E
Pedra Azul 127 16 2 S 41 17W
Pedreiras 127 4 32 S 44 40W
Pedrera, La 126 1 18 S 69 43W
Pedro Afonso 127 9 0 S 48 10W
Pedro Cays 121 17 5N 77 48W
Pedro de Valdivia 124 22 55 S 69 38W
Pedro Juan Caballero 125 22 30 S 55 40W
Pedro Miguel Locks 120 9 1N 79 36W
Pedro Muñoz 33 39 25N 2 56W
Pedrógão Grande 30 39 55N 8 9W
Peduyim 62 31 20N 34 37 E
Peebinga 99 34 52 S 140 57 E
Peebles 14 55 40N 3 12W
Peekskill 114 41 18N 73 57W
Peel 12 54 14N 4 40W
Peel →, Austral. 99 30 50 S 150 29 E
Peel →, Can. 104 67 0N 135 0W
Peene → 24 54 9N 13 46 E
Peera Peera Poolanna L. 99 26 30 S 138 0 E
Peers 108 53 40N 116 0W
Pegasus Bay 101 43 20 S 173 10 E
Peggau 26 47 12N 15 21 E
Pegnitz 25 49 45N 11 33 E
Pegnitz → 25 49 29N 10 59 E
Pego 33 38 51N 0 8W
Pegu Yoma 67 19 0N 96 0 E
Pehčevo 42 41 41N 22 55 E
Pehuajó 124 35 45 S 62 0W
Peine, Chile 124 23 45 S 68 8W
Peine, Ger. 24 52 19N 10 12 E
Peip'ing = Beijing 76 39 55N 116 20 E
Peiss 25 47 58N 11 47 E
Peissenberg 25 47 48N 11 4 E
Peitz 24 51 50N 14 23 E
Peixe 127 12 0 S 48 40W
Pek → 42 44 45N 21 29 E
Pekalongan 73 6 53 S 109 40 E
Pekan 71 3 30N 103 25 E
Pekin 116 40 35N 89 40W
Peking = Beijing 76 39 55N 116 20 E
Pelabuhan Ratu, Teluk 73 7 5 S 106 30 E
Pelabuhanratu 73 7 0 S 106 32 E
Pélagos 44 39 17N 24 4 E
Pelaihari 72 3 55 S 114 45 E
Pelat, Mont 21 44 16N 6 42 E
Pełczyce 28 53 3N 15 16 E
Peleaga 46 45 22N 22 55 E
Pelee I. 106 41 47N 82 40W
Pelée, Mt. 121 14 48N 61 0W
Pelee, Pt. 106 41 54N 82 31W
Pelekech, mt. 90 3 52N 35 8 E
Peleng 73 1 20 S 123 30 E
Pelham 115 31 5N 84 6W
Pelhřimov 26 49 24N 15 12 E
Pelican L. 109 52 28N 100 20W
Pelican Narrows 109 55 10N 102 56W
Pelican Portage 108 55 51N 112 35W
Pelican Rapids 109 52 45N 100 42W
Peljesac 42 42 55N 17 25 E
Pelkosenniemi 50 67 6N 27 28 E
Pella, Greece 44 40 46N 22 23 E
Pella, U.S.A. 116 41 30N 93 0W
Pélla □ 44 40 52N 22 0 E
Péllaro 41 38 1N 15 40 E
Pellworm 24 54 30N 8 40 E
Pelly → 104 62 47N 137 19W
Pelly Bay 105 68 38N 89 50W
Pelly L. 104 66 0N 102 0W
Peloponnes = Pelóponnisos □ 45 37 10N 22 0 E
Pelopónnisos □ 45 37 10N 22 0 E
Peloritani, Monti 41 38 2N 15 25 E
Peloro, C. 41 38 15N 15 40 E
Pelorus Sound 101 40 59 S 173 59 E
Pelotas 125 31 42 S 52 23W
Pelòvo 43 43 26N 24 17 E
Pelvoux, Massif de 21 44 52N 6 20 E
Pemalang 73 6 53 S 109 23 E
Pematang 72 0 12 S 102 4 E
Pematangsiantar 72 2 57N 99 5 E
Pemba, Mozam. 91 12 58 S 40 30 E
Pemba, Tanz. 90 5 0 S 39 45 E
Pemba, Zambia 91 16 30 S 27 28 E
Pemba Channel 90 5 0 S 39 37 E
Pemberton, Austral. 96 34 30 S 116 0 E
Pemberton, Can. 108 50 25N 122 50W
Pembina 109 48 58N 97 15W
Pembina → 109 49 0N 98 12W
Pembine 114 45 38N 87 59W
Pembino 116 48 58N 97 15W
Pembroke, Can. 106 45 50N 77 7W
Pembroke, U.K. 13 51 41N 4 57W
Pembroke, U.S.A. 115 32 5N 81 32W
Pen-y-Ghent 12 54 10N 2 15W
Peña de Francia, Sierra de 30 40 32N 6 10W
Peña, Sierra de la 32 42 32N 0 45W
Penafiel 30 41 12N 8 17W
Peñafiel 30 41 35N 4 7W
Peñaflor 31 37 43N 5 21W
Peñalara, Pico 30 40 51N 3 57W
Penamacôr 30 40 10N 7 10W
Penang = Pinang 71 5 25N 100 15 E
Penápolis 125 21 30 S 50 0W
Peñaranda de Bracamonte 30 40 53N 5 13W
Peñarroya-Pueblonuevo 31 38 19N 5 16W
Peñas, C. de 30 43 42N 5 52W
Peñas de San Pedro 33 38 44N 2 0W
Penas, G. de 128 47 0 S 75 0W
Peñausende 30 41 17N 5 52W
Pench'i = Benxi 76 41 20N 123 48 E
Pend Oreille → 118 49 4N 117 37W
Pend Oreille, L. 118 48 0N 116 30W
Pendálofon 44 40 14N 21 12 E
Pendelikón 45 38 10N 23 53 E
Pendembu 84 9 7N 12 14W
Pendleton 118 45 35N 118 50W
Penedo 127 10 15 S 36 36W
Penetanguishene 106 44 50N 79 55W
Pengalengan 73 7 9 S 107 30 E
Penge, Kasai Oriental, Congo 90 5 30 S 24 33 E
Penge, Kivu, Congo 90 4 27 S 28 25 E
Penglai 76 37 48N 120 42 E
Pengshui 77 29 17N 108 12 E
Penguin 99 41 8 S 146 6 E
Penhalonga 91 18 52 S 32 40 E
Peniche 31 39 19N 9 22W
Penicuik 14 55 50N 3 14W
Penida 72 8 45 S 115 30 E
Peñíscola 32 40 22N 0 24 E
Penmarch 18 47 49N 4 21W
Penmarch, Pte. de 18 47 48N 4 22W
Pennabilli 39 43 50N 12 17 E
Pennant 109 50 32N 108 14W
Penne 39 42 28N 13 56 E

Pennel Glacier **5** 69 20 S 157 27 E
Penner → **70** 14 35N 80 10 E
Pennine, Alpi **38** 46 4N 7 30 E
Pennines **12** 54 50N 2 20W
Pennino, Mte. **39** 43 6N 12 54 E
Pennsylvania □ **114** 40 50N 78 0W
Penny **108** 53 51N 121 20W
Pennyan **114** 42 39N 77 7W
Peno **54** 57 2N 32 49 E
Penola **97** 37 25 S 140 21 E
Penong **96** 31 59 S 133 5 E
Penonomé **121** 8 31N 80 21W
Penrhyn Is. **95** 9 0 S 158 30W
Penrith, Austral. **97** 33 43 S 150 38 E
Penrith, U.K. **12** 54 40N 2 45W
Pensacola **115** 30 30N 87 10W
Pensacola Mts. **5** 84 0 S 40 0W
Pense **109** 50 25N 104 59W
Penshurst **97** 37 49 S 142 20 E
Penticton **108** 49 30N 119 38W
Pentland **97** 20 32 S 145 25 E
Pentland Firth **14** 58 43N 3 10W
Pentland Hills **14** 55 48N 3 25W
Penukonda **70** 14 5N 77 38 E
Penylan L. **109** 61 50N 106 20W
Penza **55** 53 15N 45 5 E
Penzance **13** 50 7N 5 32W
Penzberg **25** 47 46N 11 23 E
Penzhino **59** 63 30N 167 55 E
Penzhinskaya Guba **59** 61 30N 163 0 E
Penzlin **24** 53 32N 13 6 E
Peoria, Ariz., U.S.A. **119** 33 40N 112 15W
Peoria, Ill., U.S.A. **116** 40 40N 89 40W
Pepperwood **118** 40 23N 124 0W
Peqini **44** 41 4N 19 44 E
Pera Hd. **98** 12 55 S 141 37 E
Perabumilih **72** 3 27 S 104 15 E
Perak → **71** 5 10N 101 4 E
Perakhóra **45** 38 2N 22 56 E
Perales de Alfambra **32** 40 38N 1 0W
Perales del Puerto **30** 40 10N 6 40W
Peralta **32** 42 21N 1 49W
Pérama **45** 35 20N 24 40 E
Perast **42** 42 31N 18 47 E
Percé **107** 48 31N 64 13W
Perche **18** 48 31N 1 1 E
Perche, Collines du **18** 48 30N 0 40 E
Percy **18** 48 55N 1 11W
Percy Is. **98** 21 39 S 150 16 E
Pereira **126** 4 49N 75 43W
Perekerten **99** 34 55 S 143 40 E
Perekop **56** 46 10N 33 42 E
Pereslavl-Zalesskiy **55** 56 45N 38 50 E
Pereyaslav Khmelnitskiy **54** 50 3N 31 28 E
Pérez, I. **120** 22 24N 89 42W
Perg **26** 48 15N 14 38 E
Pergamino **124** 33 52 S 60 30W
Pérgine Valsugano **39** 46 4N 11 15 E
Pérgola **39** 43 35N 12 50 E
Perham **116** 46 36N 95 36W
Perhentian, Kepulauan **71** 5 54N 102 42 E
Periam **42** 46 2N 20 59 E
Péribonca → **107** 48 45N 72 5W
Péribonca, L. **107** 50 1N 71 10W
Perico **124** 24 20 S 65 5W
Pericos **120** 25 3N 107 42W
Périers **18** 49 11N 1 25W
Périgord **20** 45 0N 0 40 E
Périgueux **20** 45 10N 0 42 E
Perijá, Sierra de **126** 9 30N 73 3W
Peristéra **45** 39 15N 23 58 E
Periyakulam **70** 10 5N 77 30 E
Periyar → **70** 10 15N 76 10 E
Periyar, L. **70** 9 25N 77 10 E
Perkam, Tg. **73** 1 35 S 137 50 E
Perković **39** 43 41N 16 10 E
Perlas, Arch. de las **121** 8 41N 79 7W
Perlas, Punta de **121** 12 30N 83 30W
Perleberg **24** 53 5N 11 50 E
Perlevka **55** 51 48N 38 57 E
Perlez **42** 45 11N 20 22 E
Perlis □ **71** 6 30N 100 15 E
Perm (Molotov) **52** 58 0N 57 10 E
Përmeti **44** 40 15N 20 21 E
Pernambuco = Recife **127** 8 0 S 35 0W
Pernambuco □ **127** 8 0 S 37 0W
Pernik **42** 42 35N 23 2 E
Péronne **19** 49 55N 2 57 E
Perosa Argentina **38** 44 57N 7 11 E
Perow **108** 54 35N 126 10W
Perpendicular Pt. **99** 31 37 S 152 52 E
Perpignan **20** 42 42N 2 53 E
Perros-Guirec **18** 48 49N 3 28W
Perry, Fla., U.S.A. **115** 30 9N 83 40W
Perry, Ga., U.S.A. **115** 32 25N 83 41W
Perry, Iowa, U.S.A. **116** 41 48N 94 5W
Perry, Maine, U.S.A. **115** 44 59N 67 20W
Perry, Okla., U.S.A. **117** 36 20N 97 20W
Perryton **117** 36 28N 100 48W
Perryville **117** 37 42N 89 50W
Persberg **48** 59 47N 14 15 E
Persepolis **65** 29 55N 52 50 E
Persia = Iran ■ **65** 35 0N 50 0 E
Persian Gulf **65** 27 0N 50 0 E
Perstorp **49** 56 10N 13 25 E
Perth, Austral. **96** 31 57 S 115 52 E
Perth, Can. **106** 44 55N 76 15W
Perth, U.K. **14** 56 24N 3 27W
Perth Amboy **114** 40 31N 74 16W
Perthus, Le **20** 42 30N 2 53 E
Pertuis **21** 43 42N 5 30 E
Peru, Ill., U.S.A. **116** 41 18N 89 12W
Peru, Ind., U.S.A. **114** 40 42N 86 0W
Peru ■ **126** 8 0 S 75 0W
Peru-Chile Trench **95** 20 0 S 72 0W
Perúgia **39** 43 6N 12 24 E
Perušić **39** 44 40N 15 22 E
Pervomaysk, R.S.F.S.R., U.S.S.R. **55** 54 56N 43 58 E
Pervomaysk, Ukraine S.S.R., U.S.S.R. **56** 48 10N 30 46 E
Pervouralsk **52** 56 55N 60 0 E
Pésaro **39** 43 55N 12 53 E
Pescara **39** 42 28N 14 13 E
Pescara → **39** 42 28N 14 13 E
Peschanokopskoye **57** 46 14N 41 4 E
Péscia **38** 43 54N 10 40 E
Pescina **39** 42 0N 13 39 E
Peshawar **66** 34 2N 71 37 E
* Peshawar □ **66** 33 30N 71 20 E
Peshkopia **44** 41 41N 20 25 E
Peshtera **43** 42 2N 24 18 E
Peshtigo **114** 45 4N 87 46W
Peski **55** 51 14N 42 29 E
Peskovka **55** 59 23N 52 20 E
Pêso da Régua **30** 41 10N 7 47W
Pesqueira **127** 8 20 S 36 42W
Pesqueria → **120** 25 54N 99 11W
Pessac **20** 44 48N 0 37W
Pest □ **27** 47 29N 19 5 E
Pestovo **54** 58 33N 35 42 E
Pestravka **55** 52 28N 49 57 E
Péta **45** 39 10N 21 2 E
Petah Tiqwa **62** 32 6N 34 53 E
Petalidhion **45** 36 57N 21 55 E
Petaling Jaya **71** 3 4N 101 42 E
Petaluma **118** 38 13N 122 39W
Petange **16** 49 33N 5 55 E
Petatlán **120** 17 31N 101 16W
Petauke **91** 14 14 S 31 20 E
Petawawa **106** 45 54N 77 17W
Petén Itzá, Lago **120** 16 58N 89 50W
Peter 1st, I. **5** 69 0 S 91 0W
Peter Pond L. **109** 55 55N 108 44W
Peterbell **106** 48 36N 83 21W
Peterborough, Austral. **97** 32 58 S 138 51 E
Peterborough, Can. **112** 44 20N 78 20W
Peterborough, U.K. **13** 52 35N 0 14W
Peterborough, U.S.A. **113** 42 55N 71 59W
Peterhead **14** 57 30N 1 49W
Petersburg, Alas., U.S.A. **108** 56 50N 133 0W
Petersburg, Ind., U.S.A. **114** 38 30N 87 15W
Petersburg, Va., U.S.A. **114** 37 17N 77 26W
Petersburg, W. Va., U.S.A. **114** 38 59N 79 10W
Petford **98** 17 20 S 144 58 E
Petília Policastro **41** 39 7N 16 48 E
Petit Bois I. **115** 30 16N 88 25W
Petit-Cap **107** 48 3N 64 30W
Petit Goâve **121** 18 27N 72 51W
Petit-Quevilly, Le **18** 49 26N 1 0 E
Petit Saint Bernard, Col du **38** 45 40N 6 52 E
Petitcodiac **107** 45 57N 65 11W
Petite Baleine → **106** 55 50N 77 0W
Petite Saguenay **107** 48 15N 70 4W
Petitsikapau, L. **107** 54 37N 66 25W
Petlad **68** 22 30N 72 45 E
Peto **120** 20 10N 88 53W
Petone **101** 41 13 S 174 53 E
Petoskey **106** 45 22N 84 57W
Petra, Jordan **62** 30 20N 35 22 E
Petra, Spain **32** 39 37N 3 6 E
Petra, Ostrova **4** 76 15N 118 30 E
Petralia **41** 37 49N 14 4 E
Petrel **33** 38 30N 0 46W
Petrich **43** 41 24N 23 13 E
Petrijanec **39** 46 23N 16 17 E
Petrikov **54** 52 11N 28 29 E
Petrila **46** 45 29N 23 29 E
Petrinja **39** 45 28N 16 18 E
Petrolândia **127** 9 5 S 38 20W
Petrolia **106** 42 54N 82 9W
Petrolina **127** 9 24 S 40 30W
Petromagoúla **45** 38 31N 23 0 E
Petropavlovsk **58** 54 53N 69 13 E
Petropavlovsk-Kamchatskiy **59** 53 3N 158 43 E
Petrópolis **125** 22 33 S 43 9W
Petroşeni **46** 45 28N 23 20 E
Petroskey **114** 45 22N 84 57W
Petrova Gora **39** 45 15N 15 45 E
Petrovac, Crna Gora, Yugo. **42** 42 13N 18 57 E
Petrovac, Srbija, Yugo. **42** 44 22N 21 26 E
Petrovaradin **42** 45 16N 19 55 E
Petrovsk **55** 52 22N 45 19 E
Petrovsk-Zabaykalskiy **59** 51 20N 108 55 E
Petrovskoye = Svetlograd **57** 45 25N 42 58 E
Petrozavodsk **52** 61 41N 34 20 E
Petrus Steyn **93** 27 38 S 28 8 E
Petrusburg **92** 29 4 S 25 26 E
Petukhovka **54** 53 42N 30 54 E
Peumo **124** 34 21 S 71 12W
Peureulak **72** 4 48N 97 45 E
Pevek **59** 69 41N 171 19 E
Peveragno **38** 44 20N 7 37 E
Peyrehorade **20** 43 34N 1 7W
Peyruis **21** 44 1N 5 56 E
Pézenas **20** 43 28N 3 24 E
Pezinok **27** 48 17N 17 17 E
Pfaffenhofen **25** 48 31N 11 31 E
Pfarrkirchen **25** 48 25N 12 57 E
Pfeffenhausen **25** 48 40N 11 58 E
Pforzheim **25** 48 53N 8 43 E
Pfullendorf **25** 47 55N 9 15 E
Pfungstadt **25** 49 47N 8 36 E
Phala **92** 23 45 S 26 50 E
Phalodi **68** 27 12N 72 24 E
Phalsbourg **19** 48 46N 7 15 E
Phan Rang **71** 11 34N 109 0 E
Phan Thiet **71** 11 1N 108 9 E
Phanae **45** 38 8N 25 87 E
Phangan, Ko **71** 9 45N 100 0 E
Phangnga **71** 8 28N 98 30 E
Phanh Bho Ho Chi Minh **71** 10 58N 106 40 E
Pharenda **69** 27 5N 83 17 E
Phatthalung **71** 7 39N 100 6 E
Phelps, N.Y., U.S.A. **112** 42 57N 77 5W
Phelps, Wis., U.S.A. **116** 46 2N 89 2W
Phelps L. **109** 59 15N 103 15W
Phenix City **115** 32 30N 85 0W
Phetchabun **71** 16 25N 101 8 E
Phetchabun, Thiu Khao **71** 16 0N 101 20 E
Phetchaburi **71** 13 1N 99 55 E
Phichai **71** 17 22N 100 10 E
Philadelphia, Miss., U.S.A. **117** 32 47N 89 5W
Philadelphia, N.Y., U.S.A. **113** 44 9N 75 40W
Philadelphia, Pa., U.S.A. **114** 40 0N 75 10W
Philip **116** 44 4N 101 42W
Philippeville **16** 50 12N 4 33 E
Philippi **44** 41 1N 24 16 E
Philippi L. **98** 24 20 S 138 55 E
Philippines ■ **73** 12 0N 123 0 E
Philippolis **92** 30 15 S 25 16 E
Philippopolis = Plovdiv **43** 42 8N 24 44 E
Philipsburg, Mont., U.S.A. **118** 46 20N 113 21W
Philipsburg, Pa., U.S.A. **112** 40 53N 78 10W
Philipstown **92** 30 28 S 24 30 E
Phillip **97** 38 30 S 145 12 E
Phillips, Texas, U.S.A. **117** 35 48N 101 17W
Phillips, Wis., U.S.A. **116** 45 41N 90 22W
Phillipsburg, Kans., U.S.A. **116** 39 48N 99 20W
Phillipsburg, Pa., U.S.A. **113** 40 43N 75 12W
Phillott **99** 27 53 S 145 50 E
Philmont **113** 42 14N 73 37W
Philomath **118** 44 28N 123 21W
Phitsanulok **71** 16 50N 100 12 E
Phnom Dangrek **71** 14 20N 104 0 E
Phnom Penh **71** 11 33N 104 55 E
Phnom Thbeng **71** 13 50N 104 56 E
Phoenix, Ariz., U.S.A. **119** 33 30N 112 10W
Phoenix, N.Y., U.S.A. **113** 43 13N 76 18W
Phoenix Is. **94** 3 30 S 172 0W
Phoenixville **113** 40 12N 75 29W
Phong Saly **71** 21 42N 102 9 E
Phra Chedi Sam Ong **71** 15 16N 98 23 E
Phra Nakhon Si Ayutthaya **71** 14 25N 100 30 E
Phrae **71** 18 7N 100 9 E
Phrao **71** 19 23N 99 15 E
Phu Doan **71** 21 40N 105 10 E
Phu Loi **71** 20 14N 103 14 E
Phu Ly **71** 20 35N 105 50 E
Phu Qui **71** 19 20N 105 20 E
Phuket **71** 7 52N 98 22 E
Phulera (Phalera) **68** 26 52N 75 16 E
† Phuoc Le **71** 10 30N 107 10 E
Piacenza **38** 45 2N 9 42 E
Piádena **38** 45 8N 10 22 E
Pialba **97** 25 20 S 152 45 E
Pian Cr. → **99** 30 2 S 148 12 E
Piana **21** 42 15N 8 34 E
Pianella **39** 42 24N 14 5 E
Pianoro **39** 44 20N 11 20 E
Pianosa, Puglia, Italy **39** 42 12N 15 44 E
Pianosa, Toscana, Italy **38** 42 36N 10 4 E
Piapot **109** 49 59N 109 8W
Piare → **39** 45 32N 12 44 E
Pias **31** 38 1N 7 29W
Piaseczno **28** 52 5N 21 2 E
Piaski **28** 51 8N 22 52 E
Piastów **28** 52 12N 20 48 E
Piatra **46** 43 51N 25 9 E
Piatra Neamţ **46** 46 56N 26 21 E
Piatra Olt **46** 44 22N 24 16 E
Piauí □ **127** 7 0 S 43 0W
Piave → **39** 45 32N 12 44 E
Piazza Ármerina **41** 37 21N 14 20 E
Pibor → **87** 7 35N 33 0 E
Pibor Post **87** 6 47N 33 3 E
Pica **126** 20 35 S 69 25W
Picardie **19** 50 0N 2 15 E
Picardie, Plaine de **19** 50 0N 2 0 E
Picardy = Picardie **19** 50 0N 2 15 E
Picayune **117** 30 31N 89 40W
Picerno **41** 40 40N 15 37 E
Pichilemu **124** 34 22 S 72 0W
Pickerel L. **106** 48 40N 91 25W
Pickle Lake **106** 51 30N 90 12W
Pico **8** 38 28N 28 18W
Pico Truncado **128** 46 40 S 68 0W
Picos Ancares, Sierra de **30** 42 51N 6 52W
Picquigny **19** 49 56N 2 10 E
Picton, Austral. **99** 34 12 S 150 34 E
Picton, Can. **106** 44 1N 77 9W
Picton, N.Z. **101** 41 18 S 174 3 E
Pictou **107** 45 41N 62 42W
Picture Butte **108** 49 55N 112 45W
Picún Leufú **128** 39 30 S 69 5W
Pidurutalagala **70** 7 10N 80 50 E
Piedad, La **120** 20 20N 102 1W
Piedicavallo **38** 45 41N 7 57 E
Piedmont **115** 33 55N 85 39W
Piedmont = Piemonte **38** 45 0N 7 30 E
Piedmont Plat. **115** 34 0N 81 30W
Piedmonte d'Alife **41** 41 22N 14 22 E
Piedra → **32** 41 18N 1 47W
Piedrabuena **31** 39 0N 4 10W
Piedrahita **30** 40 28N 5 23W
Piedras Blancas Pt. **119** 35 45N 121 18W
Piedras Negras **120** 28 35N 100 35W
Piedras, R. de las → **126** 12 30 S 69 15W
Piemonte □ **38** 45 0N 7 30 E
Piensk **28** 51 16N 15 2 E
Pierce **118** 46 29N 115 53W
Piercefield **113** 44 13N 74 35W
Piería □ **44** 40 13N 22 25 E
Pierre, France **19** 46 54N 5 13 E
Pierre, U.S.A. **116** 44 23N 100 20W
Pierre Benite, Barrage **21** 45 42N 4 49 E
Pierrefeu **21** 43 8N 6 9 E
Pierrefonds **19** 49 20N 3 0 E
Pierrefontaine **19** 47 14N 6 32 E
Pierrefort **20** 44 55N 2 50 E
Pierrelatte **21** 44 23N 4 43 E
Piešťany **27** 48 38N 17 55 E
Piesting → **27** 48 6N 16 40 E
Pieszyce **28** 50 43N 16 33 E
Piet Retief **93** 27 1 S 30 50 E
Pietarsaari **50** 63 40N 22 43 E
Pietermaritzburg **93** 29 35 S 30 25 E
Pietersburg **93** 23 54 S 29 25 E
Pietraperzia **41** 37 26N 14 8 E
Pietrasanta **38** 43 57N 10 12 E
Pietrosu **46** 47 12N 25 8 E
Pietrosul **46** 47 35N 24 43 E
Pieve di Cadore **39** 46 25N 12 22 E
Pieve di Teco **38** 44 3N 7 54 E
Pievepélago **38** 44 12N 10 35 E
Pigádhia **45** 35 30N 27 12 E
Pigadhítsa **44** 39 59N 21 23 E
Pigeon **114** 43 50N 83 17W
Pigeon I. **70** 14 2N 74 20 E
Piggott **117** 36 20N 90 10W
Pigna **38** 43 57N 7 40 E
Pigüe **124** 37 36 S 62 25W
Pihani **69** 27 36N 80 15 E
Pikalevo **54** 59 37N 34 0 E
Pikes Peak **116** 38 50N 105 10W
Piketberg **92** 32 55 S 18 40 E
Pikeville **114** 37 30N 82 30W
Pikwitonei **109** 55 35N 97 9W
Piła **28** 53 10N 16 48 E
Pila **33** 38 16N 1 11W
Piła □ **28** 53 0N 17 0 E
Pilaía **44** 40 32N 22 59 E
Pilani **68** 28 22N 75 33 E
Pilar, Brazil **127** 9 36 S 35 56W
Pilar, Parag. **124** 26 50 S 58 20W
Pilas **73** 6 39N 121 37 E
Pilawa **28** 51 57N 21 32 E
Pilbara **96** 21 15 S 118 16 E
Pilcomayo → **124** 25 21 S 57 42W
Pili **45** 36 50N 27 15 E
Pilibhit **69** 28 40N 79 50 E
Pilica → **28** 51 52N 21 17 E
Pilion **44** 39 27N 23 7 E
Pilis **27** 47 17N 19 35 E
Pilisvörösvár **27** 47 38N 18 56 E
Pilkhawa **68** 28 43N 77 42 E
Pilos **45** 36 55N 21 42 E
Pilot Mound **109** 49 15N 98 54W
Pilot Point **117** 33 26N 97 0W
Pilot Rock **118** 45 30N 118 50W
Pilsen = Plzen **26** 49 45N 13 22 E
Pilštanj **39** 46 8N 15 39 E
Pilzno **27** 50 0N 21 16 E
Pima **119** 32 54N 109 50W
Pimba **97** 31 18 S 136 46 E
Pimenta Bueno **126** 11 35 S 61 10W
Pimentel **126** 6 45 S 79 55W
Pina **32** 41 29N 0 33W
Pinang **71** 5 25N 100 15 E
Pinar del Río **121** 22 26N 83 40W
Pinaroo **97** 35 17 S 140 53 E
Pincehely **27** 46 41N 18 27 E
Pincher Creek **108** 49 30N 113 57W
Pinchi L. **108** 54 38N 124 30W
Pinckneyville **116** 38 5N 89 20W
Pincota **42** 46 20N 21 45 E
Pińczów **28** 50 32N 20 32 E
Pind Dadan Khan **68** 32 36N 73 7 E
Pindiga **85** 9 58N 10 53 E
Pindos Óros **44** 40 0N 21 0 E
Pindus Mts. = Pindos Óros **44** 40 0N 21 0 E
Pine **119** 34 27N 111 30W
Pine → **109** 58 50N 105 38W
Pine Bluff **117** 34 10N 92 0W
Pine, C. **107** 46 37N 53 32W
Pine City **116** 45 46N 93 0W
Pine Creek **96** 13 50 S 132 10 E
Pine Falls **109** 50 34N 96 11W
Pine, La **118** 43 40N 121 30W
Pine Pass **108** 55 25N 122 42W
Pine Point **108** 60 50N 114 28W
Pine Ridge **116** 43 0N 102 35W
Pine River, Can. **109** 51 45N 100 30W
Pine River, U.S.A. **116** 46 43N 94 24W
Pinedale **119** 34 23N 110 16W
Pinega → **52** 64 8N 46 54 E
Pinehill **98** 23 38 S 146 57 E
Pinerolo **38** 44 47N 7 21 E
Pineto **39** 42 36N 14 4 E
Pinetop **119** 34 10N 109 57W
Pinetown **93** 29 48 S 30 54 E
Pinetree **118** 43 42N 105 52W
Pineville, Ky., U.S.A. **115** 36 42N 83 42W
Pineville, La., U.S.A. **117** 31 22N 92 30W
Piney **19** 48 22N 4 21 E
Ping → **71** 15 42N 100 9 E
Pingding **76** 37 47N 113 38 E
Pingdingshan **77** 33 43N 113 27 E
Pingdong **75** 22 39N 120 30 E
Pingdu **76** 36 42N 119 59 E
Pingguo **77** 23 19N 107 36 E
Pinghe **77** 24 17N 117 21 E
Pingjiang **77** 28 45N 113 36 E
Pingle **77** 24 40N 110 40 E
Pingliang **76** 35 35N 106 31 E
Pingluo **76** 38 52N 106 30 E
Pingnan **77** 23 33N 110 22 E
Pingtan Dao **77** 25 29N 119 47 E
Pingwu **75** 32 25N 104 30 E
Pingxiang, Guangxi Zhuangzu, China **75** 22 6N 106 46 E
Pingxiang, Jiangxi, China **77** 27 43N 113 48 E
Pingyao **76** 37 12N 112 10 E
Pinhal **125** 22 10 S 46 46W
Pinhel **30** 40 50N 7 1W
Pini **72** 0 10N 98 40 E
Piniós →, Ilia, Greece **45** 37 48N 21 20 E
Piniós →, Trikkala, Greece **44** 39 55N 22 10 E
Pinjarra **96** 32 37 S 115 52 E
Pink → **109** 56 50N 103 50W
Pinkafeld **27** 47 22N 16 9 E
Pinneberg **24** 53 39N 9 48 E
Pinos **120** 22 20N 101 40W
Pinos, I. de **121** 21 40N 82 40W
Pinos Pt. **119** 36 38N 121 57W
Pinos Puente **31** 37 15N 3 45W
Pinrang **73** 3 46 S 119 41 E
Pinsk **54** 52 10N 26 1 E
Pintados **126** 20 35 S 69 40W
Pinyang **77** 27 42N 120 31 E
Pinyug **52** 60 5N 48 0 E
Pinzolo **38** 46 9N 10 45 E
Pioche **119** 38 0N 114 35W
Piombino **38** 42 54N 10 30 E
Piombino, Canale di **38** 42 50N 10 25 E
Pioner, Os. **59** 79 50N 92 0 E
Pionki **28** 51 29N 21 28 E
Piorini, L. **126** 3 15 S 62 35W

* *Now part of North West Frontier* □

† *Renamed Ba Ria*

Piotrków Trybunalski Porreras

Piotrków Trybunalski 28 51 23N 19 43 E
Piotrków Trybunalski □ 28 51 30N 19 45 E
Piove di Sacco 39 45 18N 12 1 E
Pīp 65 26 45N 60 10 E
Pipar 68 26 25N 73 31 E
Pipariya 68 22 45N 78 23 E
Pipéri 44 39 20N 24 19 E
Pipestone 116 44 0N 96 20W
Pipestone → 106 52 53N 89 23W
Pipestone Cr. → 109 49 42N 100 45W
Pipmuacan, Rés. 107 49 45N 70 30W
Pipriac 18 47 49N 1 58W
Piqua 114 40 10N 84 10W
Piquiri → 125 24 3 S 54 14W
Piracicaba 125 22 45 S 47 40W
Piracuruca 127 3 50 S 41 50W
Piræus = Piraiévs 45 37 57N 23 42 E
Piraiévs 45 37 57N 23 42 E
Piraiévs □ 45 37 0N 23 30 E
Piráino 41 38 10N 14 52 E
Pirajuí 125 21 59 S 49 29W
Piran (Pirano) 39 45 31N 13 33 E
Pirané 124 25 42 S 59 6W
Pirapora 127 17 20 S 44 56W
Pirdop 43 42 40N 24 10 E
Pirganj 69 25 51N 88 24 E
Pírgos, Ilía, Greece 45 37 40N 21 27 E
Pírgos, Messinia, Greece 45 36 50N 22 16 E
Pirgovo 43 43 44N 25 43 E
Piriac-sur-Mer 18 47 22N 2 33W
Piribebuy 124 25 26 S 57 2W
Pirin Planina 43 41 40N 23 30 E
Pirineos 32 42 40N 1 0 E
Piripiri 127 4 15 S 41 46W
Pirmasens 25 49 12N 7 30 E
Pirna 24 50 57N 13 57 E
Pirojpur 69 22 35N 90 1 E
Pirot 42 43 9N 22 39 E
Pirtleville 119 31 25N 109 35W
Piru 73 3 4 S 128 12 E
Piryatin 54 50 15N 32 25 E
Piryí 45 38 13N 25 59 E
Pisa 38 43 43N 10 23 E
Pisa → 28 53 14N 21 52 E
Pisagua 126 19 40 S 70 15W
Pisarovina 39 45 35N 15 50 E
Pisciotta 41 40 7N 15 12 E
Pisco 126 13 50 S 76 12W
Piscu 46 45 30N 27 43 E
Pisek 26 49 19N 14 10 E
Pishan 75 37 30N 78 33 E
Pising 73 5 8 S 121 53 E
Pissos 20 44 19N 0 49W
Pisticci 41 40 24N 16 33 E
Pistóia 38 43 57N 10 53 E
Pistol B. 109 62 25N 92 37W
Pisuerga → 30 41 33N 4 52W
Pisz 28 53 38N 21 49 E
Pitarpunga, L. 99 34 24 S 143 30 E
Pitcairn I. 95 25 5 S 130 5W
Pite älv → 50 65 20N 21 25 E
Piteå 50 65 20N 21 25 E
Piterka 55 50 41N 47 29 E
Piteşti 46 44 52N 24 54 E
Pithapuram 70 17 10N 82 15 E
Píthion 44 41 24N 26 40 E
Pithiviers 19 48 10N 2 13 E
Pitigliano 39 42 38N 11 40 E
Pitlochry 14 56 43N 3 43W
Pitt I. 108 53 30N 129 50W
Pittsburg, Calif., U.S.A. 118 38 1N 121 50W
Pittsburg, Kans., U.S.A. 117 37 21N 94 43W
Pittsburg, Tex., U.S.A. 117 32 59N 94 58W
Pittsburgh 114 40 25N 79 55W
Pittsfield, Ill., U.S.A. 116 39 35N 90 46W
Pittsfield, Mass., U.S.A. 114 42 28N 73 17W
Pittsfield, N.H., U.S.A. 113 43 17N 71 18W
Pittston 114 41 19N 75 50W
Pittsworth 99 27 41 S 151 37 E
Pituri → 98 22 35 S 138 30 E
Piura 126 5 15 S 80 38W
Piva → 42 43 20N 18 50 E
Piwniczna 27 49 27N 20 42 E
Piyai 44 39 17N 21 25 E
Pizzo 41 38 44N 16 10 E
Placentia 107 47 20N 54 0W
Placentia B. 107 47 0N 54 40W
Placerville 118 38 47N 120 51W
Placetas 121 22 15N 79 44W
Plačkovica 42 41 45N 22 30 E
Plain Dealing 117 32 56N 93 41W
Plainfield 114 40 37N 74 28W
Plains, Kans., U.S.A. 117 37 20N 100 35W
Plains, Mont., U.S.A. 118 47 27N 114 57W
Plains, Tex., U.S.A. 117 33 11N 102 50W
Plainview, Nebr., U.S.A. 116 42 25N 97 48W
Plainview, Tex., U.S.A. 117 34 10N 101 40W
Plainville 116 39 18N 99 19W
Plainwell 114 42 28N 85 40W
Plaisance 20 43 36N 0 3 E
Pláka 44 40 0N 25 24 E
Plakenska Planina 42 41 14N 21 2 E
Plakhino 58 67 45N 86 5 E
Planá 26 49 50N 12 44 E
Plancoët 18 48 32N 2 13W
Plandište 42 45 16N 21 10 E
Planina, Slovenija, Yugo. 39 46 10N 15 20 E
Planina, Slovenija, Yugo. 39 45 47N 14 19 E
Plankinton 116 43 45N 98 27W
Plano 117 33 0N 96 45W
Plant City 115 28 0N 82 8W
Plant, La 116 45 11N 100 40W
Plaquemine 117 30 20N 91 15W
Plasencia 30 40 3N 6 8W
Plaški 39 45 4N 15 22 E
Plassen 48 61 9N 12 30 E
Plaster Rock 107 46 53N 67 22W
Plata, La 124 35 0 S 57 55W
Plata, Río de la 124 34 45 S 57 30W
Platani → 40 37 23N 13 16 E
Plateau 5 79 55 S 40 0 E
Plateau □ 85 8 0N 8 30 E
Plateau du Coteau du Missouri 116 47 9N 101 5W
Platí, Ákra- 44 40 27N 24 0 E
Plato 126 9 47N 74 47W
Platte 116 43 28N 98 50W
Platte → 116 39 16N 94 50W
Platteville 116 40 18N 104 47W
Plattling 25 48 46N 12 53 E
Plattsburg 114 44 41N 73 30W
Plattsmouth 116 41 0N 95 50W
Plau 24 53 27N 12 16 E
Plauen 24 50 29N 12 9 E
Plav 42 42 38N 19 57 E
Plavinas 54 56 35N 25 46 E
Plavnica 42 42 20N 19 13 E
Plavsk 55 53 40N 37 18 E
Playgreen L. 109 54 0N 98 15W
Pleasant Bay 107 46 51N 60 48W
Pleasant Hill 116 38 48N 94 14W
Pleasanton 117 29 0N 98 30W
Pleasantville 114 39 25N 74 30W
Pléaux 20 45 8N 2 13 E
Pleiku (Gia Lai) 71 13 57N 108 0 E
Plélan-le-Grand 18 48 0N 2 7W
Plémet 18 48 11N 2 36W
Pléneuf-Val-André 18 48 35N 2 32W
Pleniţa 46 44 14N 23 10 E
Plenty, Bay of 101 37 45 S 177 0 E
Plentywood 116 48 45N 104 35W
Plesetsk 52 62 40N 40 10 E
Plessisville 107 46 14N 71 47W
Plestin-les-Grèves 18 48 40N 3 39W
Pleszew 28 51 53N 17 47 E
Pleternica 42 45 17N 17 48 E
Pletipi L. 107 51 44N 70 6W
Pleven 43 43 26N 24 37 E
Plevlja 42 43 21N 19 21 E
Ploče 42 43 4N 17 26 E
Płock 28 52 32N 19 40 E
Płock □ 28 52 30N 19 45 E
Plöcken Passo 39 46 37N 12 57 E
Ploëmeur 18 47 44N 3 26W
Ploërmel 18 47 55N 2 26W
Ploieşti 46 44 57N 26 5 E
Plomárion 45 38 58N 26 24 E
Plomb du Cantal 20 45 2N 2 48 E
Plombières 19 47 59N 6 27 E
Plomin 39 45 8N 14 10 E
Plön 24 54 8N 10 22 E
Plöner See 24 45 10N 10 22 E
Plonge, Lac La 109 55 8N 107 20W
Płońsk 28 52 37N 20 21 E
Płoty 28 53 48N 15 18 E
Plouaret 18 48 37N 3 28W
Plouay 18 47 55N 3 21W
Ploučnice → 26 50 46N 14 13 E
Ploudalmézeau 18 48 34N 4 41W
Plougasnou 18 48 42N 3 49W
Plouha 18 48 41N 2 57W
Plouhinec 18 48 0N 4 29W
Plovdiv 43 42 8N 24 44 E
Plum I. 113 41 10N 72 12W
Plummer 118 47 21N 116 59W
Plumtree 91 20 27 S 27 55 E
Plunge 54 55 53N 21 59 E
Pluvigner 18 47 46N 3 1W
Plymouth, U.K. 13 50 23N 4 9W
Plymouth, Ind., U.S.A. 114 41 20N 86 19W
Plymouth, Mass., U.S.A. 113 41 58N 70 40W
Plymouth, N.C., U.S.A. 115 35 54N 76 46W
Plymouth, N.H., U.S.A. 113 43 44N 71 41W
Plymouth, Pa., U.S.A. 113 41 17N 76 0W
Plymouth, Wis., U.S.A. 114 43 42N 87 58W
Plymouth Sd. 13 50 20N 4 10W
Plynlimon = Pumlumon Fawr 13 52 29N 3 47W
Plyussa 54 58 40N 29 20 E
Plyussa → 54 58 40N 29 0 E
Plzen 26 49 45N 13 22 E
Pniewy 28 52 31N 16 16 E
Pô 85 11 14N 1 5W
Po → 38 44 57N 12 4 E
Po, Foci del 39 44 55N 12 30 E
Po Hai = Bo Hai 76 39 0N 120 0 E
Pobé 85 7 0N 2 56 E
Pobeda 59 65 12N 146 12 E
Pobedino 59 49 51N 142 49 E
Pobedy Pik 58 40 45N 79 58 E
Pobiedziska 28 52 29N 17 11 E
Pobla de Lillet, La 32 42 16N 1 59 E
Pobla de Segur 32 42 15N 0 58 E
Pobladura de Valle 30 42 6N 5 44W
Pocahontas, Arkansas, U.S.A. 117 36 18N 91 0W
Pocahontas, Iowa, U.S.A. 116 42 41N 94 42W
Pocatello 118 42 50N 112 25W
Počátky 26 49 15N 15 14 E
Pochep 54 52 58N 33 29 E
Pochinki 55 54 41N 44 59 E
Pochinok 54 54 28N 32 29 E
Pöchlarn 26 48 12N 15 12 E
Pochontas 108 53 10N 117 51W
Pochutla 120 15 50N 96 31W
Pocomoke City 114 38 4N 75 32W
Poços de Caldas 125 21 50 S 46 33W
Poddebice 28 51 54N 18 58 E
Poděbrady 26 50 9N 15 8 E
Podensac 20 44 40N 0 22W
Podgorač 42 45 27N 18 13 E
Podgorica = Titograd 42 42 30N 19 19 E
Podkamennaya Tunguska → 59 61 50N 90 13 E
Podlapac 39 44 37N 15 47 E
Podmokly 26 50 48N 14 10 E
Podoleni 46 46 46N 26 39 E
Podolínec 27 49 16N 20 31 E
Podolsk 55 55 25N 37 30 E
Podor 84 16 40N 15 2W
Podporozhy 52 60 55N 34 2 E
Podravska Slatina 42 45 42N 17 45 E
Podu Turcului 46 46 11N 27 25 E
Podujevo 42 42 54N 21 10 E
Poel 24 54 0N 11 25 E
Pofadder 92 29 10 S 19 22 E
Pogamasing 106 46 55N 81 50W
Poggiardo 41 40 3N 18 21 E
Poggibonsi 39 43 27N 11 8 E
Pogoanele 46 44 55N 27 0 E
Pogorzela 28 51 50N 17 12 E
Pogradeci 44 40 57N 20 37 E
Poh 73 0 46 S 122 51 E
Pohang 76 36 1N 129 23 E
Pohorelá 27 48 50N 20 2 E
Pohořelice 27 48 59N 16 31 E
Pohorje 39 46 30N 15 20 E
Poiana Mare 46 43 57N 23 5 E
Poiana Ruscăi, Munţii 46 45 45N 22 25 E
Poinsett, C. 5 65 42 S 113 18 E
Point Edward 106 43 0N 82 30W
Point Pedro 70 9 50N 80 15 E
Point Pleasant, U.S.A. 113 40 5N 74 4W
Point Pleasant, W. Va., U.S.A. 114 38 50N 82 7W
Pointe-à-la Hache 117 29 35N 89 55W
Pointe-à-Pitre 121 16 10N 61 30W
Pointe Noire 88 4 48 S 11 53 E
Poirino 38 44 55N 7 50 E
Poissy 19 48 55N 2 0 E
Poitiers 18 46 35N 0 20 E
Poitou, Plaines et Seuil du 20 46 30N 0 1W
Poix 19 49 47N 2 0 E
Poix-Terron 19 49 38N 4 38 E
Pojoaque 119 35 55N 106 0W
Pokataroo 99 29 30 S 148 36 E
Poko, Sudan 87 5 41N 31 55 E
Poko, Zaïre 90 3 7N 26 52 E
Pokrov 55 55 55N 39 7 E
Pokrovsk 59 61 29N 126 12 E
Pol 30 43 9N 7 20W
Pola de Allande 30 43 16N 6 37W
Pola de Gordón, La 30 42 51N 5 41W
Pola de Lena 30 43 10N 5 49W
Pola de Siero 30 43 24N 5 39W
Pola de Somiedo 30 43 5N 6 15W
Polacca 119 35 52N 110 25W
Polan 65 25 30N 61 10 E
Poland ■ 28 52 0N 20 0 E
Polanów 28 54 7N 16 41 E
Polar Sub-Glacial Basin 5 85 0S 110 0 E
Polcura 124 37 17 S 71 43W
Połczyn Zdrój 28 53 47N 16 5 E
Polden Hills 13 51 7N 2 50W
Polessk 54 54 50N 21 8 E
Polevskoy 52 56 26N 60 11 E
Polewali, Sulawesi, Indon. 73 4 8 S 119 43 E
Polewali, Sulawesi, Indon. 73 3 21 S 119 23 E
Polgar 27 47 54N 21 6 E
Poli 88 8 34N 13 15 E
Poliaigos 45 36 45N 24 38 E
Policastro, Golfo di 41 39 55N 15 35 E
Police 28 53 33N 14 33 E
Polička 27 49 43N 16 15 E
Polignano a Mare 41 41 0N 17 12 E
Poligny 19 46 50N 5 42 E
Polikhnitas 45 39 4N 26 10 E
Polillo Is. 73 14 56N 122 0 E
Polístena 41 38 25N 16 4 E
Políyiros 44 40 23N 23 25 E
Polk 112 41 22N 79 57W
Polkowice 28 51 29N 16 3 E
Polla 41 40 31N 15 27 E
Pollachi 70 10 35N 77 0 E
Pollensa 32 39 54N 3 1 E
Pollensa, B. de 32 39 53N 3 8 E
Póllica 41 40 13N 15 3 E
Pollino, Mte. 41 39 54N 16 13 E
Pollock 116 45 58N 100 18W
Polna 54 58 31N 28 0 E
Polnovat 58 63 50N 65 54 E
Polo 116 42 0N 89 38W
Pologi 56 47 29N 36 15 E
Polonnoye 54 50 6N 27 30 E
Polotsk 54 55 30N 28 50 E
Polski Trŭmbesh 43 43 20N 25 38 E
Polsko Kosovo 43 43 23N 25 38 E
Polson 118 47 45N 114 12W
Poltava 56 49 35N 34 35 E
Polunochnoye 52 60 52N 60 25 E
Polur 70 12 32N 79 11 E
Polyanovgrad 43 42 39N 26 59 E
Polyarny 52 69 8N 33 20 E
Polynesia 95 10 0S 162 0W
Pomarance 38 43 18N 10 51 E
Pomarico 41 40 31N 16 33 E
Pombal, Brazil 127 6 45 S 37 50W
Pombal, Port. 30 39 55N 8 40W
Pómbia 45 35 0N 24 51 E
Pomeroy, Ohio, U.S.A. 114 39 0N 82 0W
Pomeroy, Wash., U.S.A. 118 46 30N 117 33W
Pomona 119 34 2N 117 49W
Pomorie 43 42 32N 27 41 E
Pomoshnaya 56 48 13N 31 36 E
Pompano Beach 115 26 12N 80 6W
Pompei 41 40 45N 14 30 E
Pompey 19 48 50N 6 2 E
Pompeys Pillar 118 46 0N 108 0W
Ponape 94 6 55N 158 10 E
Ponask, L. 106 54 0N 92 41W
Ponass L. 109 52 16N 103 58W
Ponca 116 42 38N 96 41W
Ponca City 117 36 40N 97 5W
Ponce 121 18 1N 66 37W
Ponchatoula 117 30 27N 90 25W
Poncheville, L. 106 50 10N 76 55W
Poncin 21 46 6N 5 25 E
Pond Inlet 105 72 40N 77 0W
Pondicherry 70 11 59N 79 50 E
Pondoland 93 31 10 S 29 30 E
Ponds, I. of 107 53 27N 55 52W
Ponferrada 30 42 32N 6 35W
Pongo, Wadi → 87 8 42N 27 40 E
Poniatowa 28 51 11N 22 3 E
Poniec 28 51 48N 16 50 E
Ponikva 39 46 16N 15 26 E
Ponnaiyar → 70 11 50N 79 45 E
Ponnani 70 10 45N 75 59 E
Ponneri 70 13 20N 80 15 E
Ponnyadaung 67 22 0N 94 10 E
Ponoi 52 67 0N 41 0 E
Ponoi → 52 66 59N 41 17 E
Ponoka 108 52 42N 113 40W
Ponorogo 73 7 52 S 111 29 E
Pons, France 20 45 35N 0 34W
Pons, Spain 32 41 55N 1 12 E
Ponsul → 31 39 40N 7 31W
Pont-à-Mousson 19 48 54N 6 1 E
Pont-Audemer 18 49 21N 0 30 E
Pont-Aven 18 47 51N 3 47W
Pont Canavese 38 45 24N 7 33 E
Pont-de-Roide 19 47 23N 6 45 E
Pont-de-Salars 20 44 18N 2 44 E
Pont-de-Vaux 19 46 26N 4 56 E
Pont-de-Veyle 21 46 17N 4 53 E
Pont-l'Abbé 18 47 52N 4 15W
Pont-l'Évêque 18 49 18N 0 11 E
Pont-St-Esprit 21 44 16N 4 40 E
Pont-sur-Yonne 19 48 18N 3 10 E
Ponta Grossa 125 25 7 S 50 10W
Ponta Pora 125 22 20 S 55 35W
Pontacq 20 43 11N 0 8W
Pontailler 19 47 18N 5 24 E
Pontarlier 19 46 54N 6 20 E
Pontassieve 39 43 47N 11 25 E
Pontaubault 18 48 40N 1 20W
Pontaumur 20 45 52N 2 40 E
Pontcharra 21 45 26N 6 1 E
Pontchartrain, L. 117 30 12N 90 0W
Pontchâteau 18 47 25N 2 5W
Ponte da Barca 30 41 48N 8 25W
Ponte de Sor 31 39 17N 7 57W
Ponte dell 'Olio 38 44 52N 9 39 E
Ponte di Legno 38 46 15N 10 30 E
Ponte do Lima 30 41 46N 8 35W
Ponte do Pungué 91 19 30 S 34 33 E
Ponte Leccia 21 42 28N 9 13 E
Ponte Macassar 73 9 30 S 123 58 E
Ponte nell' Alpi 39 46 10N 12 18 E
Ponte Nova 125 20 25 S 42 54W
Ponte San Martino 38 45 36N 7 47 E
Ponte San Pietro 38 45 42N 9 35 E
Pontebba 39 46 30N 13 17 E
Pontecorvo 40 41 28N 13 40 E
Pontedera 38 43 40N 10 37 E
Pontefract 12 53 42N 1 19W
Ponteix 109 49 46N 107 29W
Pontelandolfo 41 41 17N 14 41 E
Pontevedra 30 42 26N 8 40W
Pontevedra □ 30 42 25N 8 39W
Pontevedra, R. de → 30 42 22N 8 45W
Pontevico 38 45 16N 10 6 E
Pontiac, Ill., U.S.A. 116 40 50N 88 40W
Pontiac, Mich., U.S.A. 114 42 40N 83 20W
Pontian Kechil 71 1 29N 103 23 E
Pontianak 72 0 3 S 109 15 E
Pontine Is. = Ponziane, Isole 40 40 55N 13 0 E
Pontine Mts. = Karadeniz D. 64 41 30N 35 0 E
Pontínia 40 41 25N 13 2 E
Pontivy 18 48 5N 3 0W
Pontoise 19 49 3N 2 5 E
Ponton → 108 58 27N 116 11W
Pontorson 18 48 34N 1 30W
Pontrémoli 38 44 22N 9 52 E
Pontrieux 18 48 42N 3 10W
Ponts-de-Cé, Les 18 47 25N 0 30W
Pontypool, Can. 112 44 6N 78 38W
Pontypool, U.K. 13 51 42N 3 1W
Pontypridd 13 51 36N 3 21W
Ponza 40 40 55N 12 57 E
Ponziane, Isole 40 40 55N 13 0 E
Poole 13 50 42N 1 58W
Pooley I. 108 52 45N 128 15W
Poona = Pune 70 18 29N 73 57 E
Poonamallee 70 13 3N 80 10 E
Pooncarie 99 33 22 S 142 31 E
Poopelloe, L. 99 31 40 S 144 0 E
Poopó, Lago de 126 18 30 S 67 35W
Popayán 126 2 27N 76 36W
Poperinge 16 50 51N 2 42 E
Popigay 59 72 1N 110 39 E
Popilta, L. 99 33 10 S 141 42 E
Popina 43 44 7N 26 57 E
Popio, L. 99 33 10 S 141 52 E
Poplar 116 48 3N 105 9W
Poplar →, Man., Can. 109 53 0N 97 19W
Poplar →, N.W.T., Can. 108 61 22N 121 52W
Poplar Bluff 117 36 45N 90 22W
Poplarville 117 30 55N 89 30W
Popocatepetl 120 19 10N 98 40W
Popokabaka 88 5 41 S 16 40 E
Pópoli 39 42 12N 13 50 E
Popondetta 98 8 48 S 148 17 E
Popovača 39 45 30N 16 41 E
Popovo 43 43 21N 26 18 E
Poprád 27 49 3N 20 18 E
Poprád → 27 49 38N 20 42 E
Porbandar 68 21 44N 69 43 E
Porcher I. 108 53 50N 130 30W
Porcuna 31 37 52N 4 11W
Porcupine →, Can. 109 59 11N 104 46W
Porcupine →, U.S.A. 104 66 35N 145 15W
Pordenone 39 45 58N 12 40 E
Pordim 43 43 23N 24 51 E
Poreč 39 45 14N 13 36 E
Poretskoye 55 55 9N 46 21 E
Pori 51 61 29N 21 48 E
Pori 45 35 58N 23 13 E
Porjus 50 66 57N 19 50 E
Porkhov 54 57 45N 29 38 E
Porkkala 51 59 59N 24 26 E
Porlamar 126 10 57N 63 51W
Porlezza 38 46 2N 9 8 E
Porma → 30 42 49N 5 28W
Pornic 18 47 7N 2 5W
Poronaysk 59 49 13N 143 0 E
Póros 45 37 30N 23 30 E
Poroshiri-Dake 74 42 41N 142 52 E
Poroszló 27 47 39N 20 40 E
Poroto Mts. 91 9 0 S 33 30 E
Porquerolles, Îles de 21 43 0N 6 13 E
Porrentruy 25 47 25N 7 6 E
Porreras 32 39 31N 3 2 E

Porretta, Passo di Pripet Marshes

Porretta, Passo di **38** 44 2N 10 56 E
Porsangen **50** 70 40N 25 40 E
Porsgrunn **47** 59 10N 9 40 E
Port **19** 47 43N 6 4 E
Port Adelaide **99** 34 46 S 138 30 E
Port Alberni **108** 49 40N 124 50W
Port Albert **100** 38 42 S 146 42 E
Port Albert Victor **68** 21 0N 71 30 E
Port Alfred, Can. **107** 48 18N 70 53W
Port Alfred, S. Afr. **92** 33 36 S 26 55 E
Port Alice **108** 50 20N 127 25W
Port Allegany **114** 41 49N 78 17W
Port Allen **117** 30 30N 91 15W
Port Alma **98** 23 38 S 150 53 E
Port Angeles **118** 48 7N 123 30W
Port Antonio **121** 18 10N 76 30W
Port Aransas **117** 27 49N 97 4W
Port Arthur, Austral. **97** 43 7 S 147 50 E
Port Arthur, U.S.A. **117** 30 0N 94 0W
Port au Port B. **107** 48 40N 58 50W
Port-au-Prince **121** 18 40N 72 20W
Port Augusta **97** 32 30 S 137 50 E
Port Augusta West **97** 32 29 S 137 29 E
Port Austin **106** 44 3N 82 59W
Port Bell **90** 0 18N 32 35 E
Port Bergé Vaovao **93** 15 33 S 47 40 E
Port Blair **71** 11 40N 92 30 E
Port Blandford **107** 48 20N 54 10W
Port Bolivar **117** 29 20N 94 40W
Port Bou **32** 42 25N 3 9 E
Port Bouët **84** 5 16N 3 57W
Port Bradshaw **97** 12 30 S 137 20 E
Port Broughton **99** 33 37 S 137 56 E
Port Burwell **106** 42 40N 80 48W
Port-Cartier **107** 50 2N 66 50W
Port Chalmers **101** 45 49 S 170 30 E
Port Chester **114** 41 0N 73 41W
Port Clements **108** 53 40N 132 10W
Port Clinton **114** 41 30N 82 58W
Port Colborne **106** 42 50N 79 10W
Port Coquitlam **108** 49 15N 122 45W
Port Credit **112** 43 33N 79 35W
Port Dalhousie **112** 43 13N 79 16W
Port Darwin, Austral. **96** 12 24 S 130 45 E
Port Darwin, Falk. Is. **128** 51 50 S 59 0W
Port Davey **97** 43 16 S 145 55 E
Port-de-Bouc **21** 43 24N 4 59 E
Port-de-Paix **121** 19 50N 72 50W
Port Dickson **71** 2 30N 101 49 E
Port Douglas **98** 16 30 S 145 30 E
Port Dover **112** 42 47N 80 12W
Port Edward **108** 54 12N 130 10W
Port Elgin **106** 44 25N 81 25W
Port Elizabeth **92** 33 58 S 25 40 E
Port Ellen **14** 55 38N 6 10W
Port-en-Bessin **18** 49 21N 0 45W
Port Erin **12** 54 5N 4 45W
Port Etienne = Nouâdhibou **80** 20 54N 17 0W
Port Fairy **97** 38 22 S 142 12 E
Port Fouâd = Bûr Fuad **86** 31 15N 32 20 E
Port-Gentil **88** 0 40 S 8 50 E
Port Gibson **117** 31 57N 91 0W
Port Glasgow **14** 55 57N 4 40W
Port Harcourt **85** 4 40N 7 10 E
Port Hardy **108** 50 41N 127 30W
Port Harrison **105** 58 25N 78 15W
Port Hawkesbury **107** 45 36N 61 22W
Port Hedland **96** 20 25 S 118 35 E
Port Henry **114** 44 0N 73 30W
Port Hood **107** 46 0N 61 32W
Port Hope **106** 43 56N 78 20W
Port Huron **114** 43 0N 82 28W
Port Isabel **117** 26 4N 97 9W
Port Jackson **97** 33 50 S 151 18 E
Port Jefferson **114** 40 58N 73 5W
Port Jervis **113** 41 22N 74 42W
Port-Joinville **18** 46 45N 2 23W
Port Katon **57** 46 52N 38 46 E
Port Kelang **71** 3 0N 101 23 E
Port Kembla **99** 34 52 S 150 49 E
Port-la-Nouvelle **20** 43 1N 3 3 E
Port Laoise **15** 53 2N 7 20W
Port Lavaca **117** 28 38N 96 38W
Port-Leucate-Barcarès **20** 42 53N 3 3 E
Port Lincoln **96** 34 42 S 135 52 E
Port Loko **84** 8 48N 12 46W
Port Louis **18** 47 42N 3 22W
Port Lyautey = Kenitra **82** 34 15N 6 40W
Port Macdonnell **99** 38 0 S 140 48 E
Port Macquarie **97** 31 25 S 152 25 E
Port Maria **121** 18 25N 77 5W
Port Mellon **108** 49 32N 123 31W
Port-Menier **107** 49 51N 64 15W
Port Moresby **94** 9 24 S 147 8 E
Port Mouton **107** 43 58N 64 50W
Port Musgrave **97** 11 55 S 141 50 E
Port-Navalo **18** 47 34N 2 54W
Port Nelson **109** 57 3N 92 36W
Port Nolloth **92** 29 17 S 16 52 E
Port Nouveau-Québec (George River) **105** 58 30N 65 59W
Port O'Connor **117** 28 26N 96 24W
Port of Spain **121** 10 40N 61 20W
Port Orchard **118** 47 31N 122 38W
Port Oxford **118** 42 45N 124 28W
Port Pegasus **101** 47 12 S 167 41 E
Port Perry **106** 44 6N 78 56W
Port Phillip B. **97** 38 10 S 144 50 E
Port Pirie **97** 33 10 S 138 1 E
Port Pólnocny **28** 54 25N 18 42 E
Port Radium = Echo Bay **104** 66 10N 117 40W
Port Renfrew **108** 48 30N 124 20W
Port Rowan **106** 42 40N 80 30W
Port Safaga = Bûr Safâga **86** 26 43N 33 57 E
Port Said = Bûr Sa'îd **86** 31 16N 32 18 E
Port St. Joe **115** 29 49N 85 20W
Port St. Louis **93** 13 7 S 48 48 E
Port-St-Louis-du-Rhône **21** 43 23N 4 49 E
Port Sanilac **106** 43 26N 82 33W
Port Saunders **107** 50 40N 57 18W
Port Severn **112** 44 48N 79 43W
Port Shepstone **93** 30 44 S 30 28 E
Port Simpson **108** 54 30N 130 20W
Port Stanley **106** 42 40N 81 10W
Port Stephens **97** 32 38 S 152 12 E
Port Sudân = Bûr Sûdân **86** 19 32N 37 9 E
Port Talbot **13** 51 35N 3 48W
Port Taufiq = Bûr Taufiq **86** 29 54N 32 32 E
Port Townsend **118** 48 7N 122 50W
Port-Vendres **20** 42 32N 3 8 E
Port Vladimir **52** 69 25N 33 6 E
Port Washington **114** 43 25N 87 52W
Port Weld **71** 4 50N 100 38 E
Portachuelo **126** 17 10 S 63 20W
Portadown **15** 54 27N 6 26W
Portage **116** 43 31N 89 25W
Portage La Prairie **109** 49 58N 98 18W
Portageville **117** 36 25N 89 40W
Portalegre **31** 39 19N 7 25W
Portalegre □ **31** 39 20N 7 40W
Portales **117** 34 12N 103 25W
Portarlington **15** 53 10N 7 10W
Porte, La **114** 41 36N 86 43W
Portel **31** 38 19N 7 41W
Porter L., N.W.T., Can. **109** 61 41N 108 5W
Porter L., Sask., Can. **109** 56 20N 107 20W
Porterville, S. Afr. **92** 33 0 S 18 57 E
Porterville, U.S.A. **119** 36 5N 119 0W
Porthcawl **13** 51 28N 3 42W
Porthill **118** 49 0N 116 30W
Portile de Fier **46** 44 42N 22 30 E
Portimão **31** 37 8N 8 32W
Portland, N.S.W., Austral. **99** 33 20 S 150 0 E
Portland, Victoria, Austral. **97** 38 20 S 141 35 E
Portland, Can. **113** 44 42N 76 12W
Portland, Conn., U.S.A. **113** 41 34N 72 39W
Portland, Me., U.S.A. **107** 43 40N 70 15W
Portland, Mich., U.S.A. **114** 42 52N 84 58W
Portland, Oreg., U.S.A. **118** 45 35N 122 40W
Portland B. **99** 38 15 S 141 45 E
Portland, Bill of **13** 50 31N 2 27W
Portland, C. **97** 40 46 S 148 0 E
Portland, I. of **13** 50 32N 2 25W
Portland Prom. **105** 58 40N 78 33W
Portneuf **107** 46 43N 71 55W
Porto **30** 41 8N 8 40W
Porto □ **30** 41 8N 8 20W
Pôrto Alegre **125** 30 5 S 51 10W
Porto Alexandre **92** 15 55 S 11 55 E
Porto Amboim = Gunza **88** 10 50 S 13 50 E
Porto Argentera **38** 44 15N 7 27 E
Porto Azzurro **38** 42 46N 10 24 E
Porto Botte **40** 39 3N 8 33 E
Porto Civitanova **39** 43 19N 13 44 E
Pôrto de Móz **127** 1 41 S 52 13W
Porto Empédocle **40** 37 18N 13 30 E
Pôrto Esperança **126** 19 37 S 57 29W
Pôrto Franco **127** 6 20 S 47 24W
Porto Garibaldi **39** 44 41N 12 14 E
Porto, G. de **21** 42 17N 8 34 E
Pórto Lágo **44** 40 58N 25 6 E
Porto Mendes **125** 24 30 S 54 15W
Pôrto Murtinho **126** 21 45 S 57 55W
Pôrto Nacional **127** 10 40 S 48 30W
Porto Novo, Benin **85** 6 23N 2 42 E
Porto Novo, India **70** 11 30N 79 38 E
Porto Recanati **39** 43 26N 13 40 E
Porto San Giórgio **39** 43 11N 13 49 E
Porto Santo **80** 33 45N 16 25W
Porto Santo Stefano **38** 42 26N 11 7 E
Pôrto São José **125** 22 43 S 53 10W
Pôrto Seguro **127** 16 26 S 39 5W
Porto Tolle **39** 44 57N 12 20 E
Porto Tórres **40** 40 50N 8 23 E
Pôrto União **125** 26 10 S 51 10W
Pôrto Válter **126** 8 15 S 72 40W
Porto-Vecchio **21** 41 35N 9 16 E
Pôrto Velho **126** 8 46 S 63 54W
Portoferráio **38** 42 50N 10 20 E
Portogruaro **39** 45 47N 12 50 E
Portola **118** 39 49N 120 28W
Portomaggiore **39** 44 41N 11 47 E
Portoscuso **40** 39 12N 8 22 E
Portovénere **38** 44 2N 9 50 E
Portoviejo **126** 1 7 S 80 28W
Portpatrick **14** 54 50N 5 7W
Portree **14** 57 25N 6 11W
Portrush **15** 55 13N 6 40W
Portsall **18** 48 37N 4 45W
Portsmouth, Domin. **121** 15 34N 61 27W
Portsmouth, U.K. **13** 50 48N 1 6W
Portsmouth, N.H., U.S.A. **114** 43 5N 70 45W
Portsmouth, Ohio, U.S.A. **114** 38 45N 83 0W
Portsmouth, R.I., U.S.A. **113** 41 35N 71 15W
Portsmouth, Va., U.S.A. **114** 36 50N 76 20W
Portsoy **14** 57 41N 2 41W
Porttipahta **50** 68 5N 26 40 E
Portugal ■ **30** 40 0N 7 0W
Portugalete **32** 43 19N 3 4W
Portuguese-Guinea = Guinea-Bissau ■ **84** 12 0N 15 0W
Portuguese Timor □ = Timor **73** 8 0 S 126 30 E
Portumna **15** 53 5N 8 12W
Portville **112** 42 3N 78 21W
Porvenir **128** 53 10 S 70 16W
Porvoo **51** 60 24N 25 40 E
Porzuna **31** 39 9N 4 9W
Posada → **40** 40 40N 9 45 E
Posadas, Argent. **125** 27 30 S 55 50W
Posadas, Spain **31** 37 47N 5 11W
Poschiavo **25** 46 19N 10 4 E
Posets **32** 42 39N 0 25 E
Poshan = Boshan **76** 36 28N 117 49 E
Posidhion, Ákra **44** 39 57N 23 30 E
Posidium **45** 35 30N 27 10 E
Poso **73** 1 20 S 120 55 E
Posse **127** 14 4 S 46 18W
Possel **88** 5 5N 19 10 E
Possession I. **5** 72 4 S 172 0 E
Pössneck **24** 50 42N 11 34 E
Post **117** 33 13N 101 21W
Post Falls **118** 47 46N 116 59W
Postavy **54** 55 4N 26 50 E
Poste Maurice Cortier (Bidon 5) **82** 22 14N 1 2 E
Postmasburg **92** 28 18 S 23 5 E
Postojna **39** 45 46N 14 12 E
Potamós, Andikíthira, Greece **45** 36 18N 22 58 E
Potamós, Kíthira, Greece **45** 36 15N 22 58 E
Potchefstroom **92** 26 41 S 27 7 E
Potcoava **46** 44 30N 24 39 E
Poteau **117** 35 5N 94 37W
Poteet **117** 29 4N 98 35W
Potelu, Lacul **46** 43 44N 24 20 E
Potenza **41** 40 40N 15 50 E
Potenza → **39** 43 27N 13 38 E
Potenza Picena **39** 43 22N 13 37 E
Poteriteri, L. **101** 46 5 S 167 10 E
Potes **30** 43 15N 4 42W
Potgietersrus **93** 24 10 S 28 55 E
Poti **57** 42 10N 41 38 E
Potiskum **85** 11 39N 11 2 E
Potlogi **46** 44 34N 25 34 E
Potomac → **114** 38 0N 76 23W
Potosí **126** 19 38 S 65 50W
Pototan **73** 10 54N 122 38 E
Potrerillos **124** 26 30 S 69 30W
Potsdam, Ger. **24** 52 23N 13 4 E
Potsdam, U.S.A. **114** 44 40N 74 59W
Potsdam □ **24** 52 40N 12 50 E
Pottenstein **25** 49 46N 11 25 E
Potter **116** 41 15N 103 20W
Pottery Hill = Abu Ballas **86** 24 26N 27 36 E
Pottstown **114** 40 17N 75 40W
Pottsville **114** 40 39N 76 12W
Pouancé **18** 47 44N 1 10W
Pouce Coupé **108** 55 40N 120 10W
Poughkeepsie **114** 41 40N 73 57W
Pouilly **19** 47 18N 2 57 E
Poulaphouca Res. **15** 53 8N 6 30W
Pouldu, Le **18** 47 41N 3 36W
Poulsbo **118** 47 45N 122 39W
Pourri, Mont **21** 45 32N 6 52 E
Pouso Alegre, Mato Grosso, Brazil **127** 11 46 S 57 16W
Pouso Alegre, Minas Gerais, Brazil **125** 22 14 S 45 57W
Pouzages **20** 46 40N 0 50W
Pouzauges **18** 46 47N 0 50W
Povenets **52** 62 50N 34 50 E
Poverty Bay **101** 38 43 S 178 2 E
Povlen **42** 44 9N 19 44 E
Póvoa de Lanhosa **30** 41 33N 8 15W
Póvoa de Varzim **30** 41 25N 8 46W
Povorino **55** 51 12N 42 5 E
Powassan **106** 46 5N 79 25W
Powder → **116** 46 47N 105 12W
Powder River **118** 43 5N 107 0W
Powell **118** 44 45N 108 45W
Powell Creek **96** 18 6 S 133 46 E
Powell, L. **119** 37 25N 110 45W
Powell River **108** 49 50N 124 35W
Powers, Mich., U.S.A. **114** 45 40N 87 32W
Powers, Oreg., U.S.A. **118** 42 53N 124 2W
Powers Lake **116** 48 37N 102 38W
Powys □ **13** 52 20N 3 20W
Poyang Hu **75** 29 5N 116 20 E
Poyarkovo **59** 49 36N 128 41 E
Poysdorf **27** 48 40N 16 37 E
Poza de la Sal **32** 42 35N 3 31W
Poza Rica **120** 20 33N 97 27W
Požarevac **42** 44 35N 21 18 E
Požega **42** 43 53N 20 2 E
Poznań **28** 52 25N 16 55 E
Poznań □ **28** 52 50N 17 0 E
Pozo Alcón **33** 37 42N 2 56W
Pozo Almonte **126** 20 10 S 69 50W
Pozo Colorado **124** 23 30 S 58 45W
Pozoblanco **31** 38 23N 4 51W
Pozzallo **41** 36 44N 14 52 E
Pozzuoli **41** 40 46N 14 6 E
Pra → **85** 5 1N 1 37W
Prabuty **28** 53 47N 19 15 E
Prača **42** 43 47N 18 43 E
Prachatice **26** 49 1N 14 0 E
Prachin Buri **71** 14 0N 101 25 E
Prachuap Khiri Khan **71** 11 49N 99 48 E
Pradelles **20** 44 46N 3 52 E
Prades **20** 42 38N 2 23 E
Prado **127** 17 20 S 39 13W
Prado del Rey **31** 36 48N 5 33W
Præstø **49** 55 8N 12 2 E
Pragersko **39** 46 27N 15 42 E
Prague = Praha **26** 50 5N 14 22 E
Praha **26** 50 5N 14 22 E
Prahecq **20** 46 19N 0 26W
Prahita → **70** 19 0N 79 55 E
Prahova □ **46** 45 10N 26 0 E
Prahova → **46** 44 50N 25 50 E
Prahovo **42** 44 18N 22 39 E
Praid **46** 46 32N 25 10 E
Prainha, Amazonas, Brazil **126** 7 10 S 60 30W
Prainha, Pará, Brazil **127** 1 45 S 53 30W
Prairie **98** 20 50 S 144 35 E
Prairie → **117** 34 30N 99 23W
Prairie City **118** 44 27N 118 44W
Prairie du Chien **116** 43 1N 91 9W
Praja **72** 8 39 S 116 17 E
Pramánda **44** 39 32N 21 8 E
Prang **85** 8 1N 0 56W
Prapat **72** 2 41N 98 58 E
Praszka **28** 51 5N 18 31 E
Prata **127** 19 25 S 48 54W
Prática di Mare **40** 41 40N 12 26 E
Prato **38** 43 53N 11 5 E
Prátola Peligna **39** 42 7N 13 51 E
Pratovécchio **39** 43 44N 11 43 E
Prats-de-Mollo **20** 42 25N 2 27 E
Pratt **117** 37 40N 98 45W
Prattville **115** 32 30N 86 28W
Pravara → **70** 19 35N 74 45 E
Pravdinsk **55** 56 29N 43 28 E
Pravia **30** 43 30N 6 12W
Pré-en-Pail **18** 48 28N 0 12W
Pré St. Didier **38** 45 45N 7 0 E
Precordillera **124** 30 0 S 69 1W
Predáppio **39** 44 7N 11 58 E
Predazzo **39** 46 19N 11 37 E
Predejane **42** 42 51N 22 9 E
Preeceville **109** 51 57N 102 40W
Préfailles **18** 47 9N 2 11W
Pregrada **39** 46 11N 15 45 E
Preko **39** 44 7N 15 14 E
Prelate **109** 50 51N 109 24W
Prelog **39** 46 18N 16 32 E
Premier **108** 56 4N 129 56W
Premier Downs **96** 30 30 S 126 30 E
Premont **117** 27 19N 98 8W
Premuda **39** 44 20N 14 36 E
Prenj **42** 43 33N 17 53 E
Prenjasi **44** 41 6N 20 32 E
Prentice **116** 45 31N 90 19W
Prenzlau **24** 53 19N 13 51 E
Prepansko Jezero **44** 40 55N 21 0 E
Preparis North Channel **71** 15 12N 93 40 E
Preparis South Channel **71** 14 36N 93 40 E
Přerov **27** 49 28N 17 27 E
Presanella **38** 46 13N 10 40 E
Prescott, Can. **106** 44 45N 75 30W
Prescott, Ariz., U.S.A. **119** 34 35N 112 30W
Prescott, Ark., U.S.A. **117** 33 49N 93 22W
Preservation Inlet **101** 46 8 S 166 35 E
Preševo **42** 42 19N 21 39 E
Presho **116** 43 56N 100 4W
Presicce **41** 39 53N 18 13 E
Presidencia de la Plaza **124** 27 0 S 29 50W
Presidencia Roque Saenz Peña **124** 26 45 S 60 30W
Presidente Epitácio **127** 21 56 S 52 6W
Presidente Hayes □ **124** 24 0 S 59 0W
Presidente Hermes **126** 11 17 S 61 55W
Presidente Prudente **125** 22 5 S 51 25W
Presidio **117** 29 30N 104 20W
Preslav **43** 43 10N 26 52 E
Preslavska Planina **43** 43 10N 26 45 E
Prešov **27** 49 0N 21 15 E
Prespa **43** 41 44N 24 55 E
Prespa, L. = Prepansko Jezero **44** 40 55N 21 0 E
Presque Isle **107** 46 40N 68 0W
Presseger See **26** 46 37N 13 26 E
Prestbury **13** 51 54N 2 2W
Prestea **84** 5 22N 2 7W
Presteigne **13** 52 17N 3 0W
Přeštice **26** 49 34N 13 20 E
Preston, Can. **112** 43 23N 80 21W
Preston, U.K. **12** 53 46N 2 42W
Preston, Idaho, U.S.A. **118** 42 10N 111 55W
Preston, Minn., U.S.A. **116** 43 39N 92 3W
Preston, Nev., U.S.A. **118** 38 59N 115 2W
Preston, C. **96** 20 51 S 116 12 E
Prestonpans **14** 55 58N 3 0W
Prestwick **14** 55 30N 4 38W
Pretoria **93** 25 44 S 28 12 E
Preuilly-sur-Claise **18** 46 51N 0 56 E
Préveza **45** 38 57N 20 47 E
Préveza □ **44** 39 20N 20 40 E
Prey-Veng **71** 11 35N 105 29 E
Priazovskoye **56** 46 44N 35 40 E
Pribilof Is. **4** 56 0N 170 0W
Priboj **42** 43 35N 19 32 E
Pribram **26** 49 41N 14 2 E
Price **118** 39 40N 110 48W
Price I. **108** 52 23N 128 41W
Prichalnaya **57** 48 57N 44 33 E
Priego **32** 40 26N 2 21W
Priego de Córdoba **31** 37 27N 4 12W
Priekule **54** 57 27N 21 45 E
Prien **25** 47 52N 12 20 E
Prieska **92** 29 40 S 22 42 E
Priest L. **118** 48 30N 116 55W
Priest River **118** 48 11N 116 55W
Priestly **108** 54 8N 125 20W
Prievidza **27** 48 46N 18 36 E
Prijedor **39** 44 58N 16 41 E
Prijepolje **42** 43 27N 19 40 E
Prikaspiyskaya Nizmennost **57** 47 0N 48 0 E
Prikumsk **56** 44 50N 44 10 E
Prilep **42** 41 21N 21 37 E
Priluki **54** 50 30N 32 24 E
Primorsko **43** 42 15N 27 44 E
Primorsko-Akhtarsk **56** 46 2N 38 10 E
Primorskoye **56** 47 10N 37 38 E
Primrose L. **109** 54 55N 109 45W
Prince Albert **109** 53 15N 105 50W
Prince Albert Mts. **5** 76 0 S 161 30 E
Prince Albert Nat. Park **109** 54 0N 106 25W
Prince Albert Pen. **104** 72 30N 116 0W
Prince Albert Sd. **104** 70 25N 115 0W
Prince Alfred C. **4** 74 20N 124 40W
Prince Charles I. **105** 67 47N 76 12W
Prince Charles Mts. **5** 72 0 S 67 0 E
Prince Edward I. □ **107** 46 20N 63 20W
Prince Edward Is. **3** 45 15 S 39 0 E
Prince George **108** 53 55N 122 50W
Prince of Wales I. **104** 55 30N 133 0W
Prince of Wales Is. **97** 10 40 S 142 10 E
Prince Patrick I. **4** 77 0N 120 0W
Prince Regent Inlet **4** 73 0N 90 0W
Prince Rupert **108** 54 20N 130 20W
Princess Charlotte B. **97** 14 25 S 144 0 E
Princess Royal I. **108** 53 0N 128 40W
Princeton, Can. **108** 49 27N 120 30W
Princeton, Ill., U.S.A. **116** 41 25N 89 25W
Princeton, Ind., U.S.A. **114** 38 20N 87 35W
Princeton, Ky., U.S.A. **114** 37 6N 87 55W
Princeton, Mo., U.S.A. **116** 40 23N 93 35W
Princeton, N.J., U.S.A. **114** 40 18N 74 40W
Princeton, W. Va., U.S.A. **114** 37 21N 81 8W
Principe Chan. **108** 53 28N 130 0W
Principe da Beira **126** 12 20 S 64 30W
Principe, I. de **79** 1 37N 7 27 E
Prineville **118** 44 17N 120 50W
Prins Albert **92** 33 12 S 22 2 E
Prins Harald Kyst **5** 70 0 S 35 1 E
Prinsesse Astrid Kyst **5** 70 45 S 12 30 E
Prinsesse Ragnhild Kyst **5** 70 15 S 27 30 E
Prior, C. **30** 43 34N 8 17W
Priozersk **52** 61 2N 30 7 E
Pripet = Pripyat → **54** 51 20N 30 9 E
Pripet Marshes = Polesye **54** 52 0N 28 10 E

Pripyat Quillabamba

Pripyat →	54	51 20N	30 9 E
Prislop, Pasul	46	47 37N	25 15 E
Pristen	55	51 15N	36 44 E
Priština	42	42 40N	21 13 E
Pritchard	115	30 47N	88 5W
Pritzwalk	24	53 10N	12 11 E
Privas	21	44 45N	4 37 E
Priverno	40	41 29N	13 10 E
Privolzhsk	55	57 23N	41 16 E
Privolzhskaya Vozvyshennost	55	51 0N	46 0 E
Privolzhskiy	55	51 25N	46 3 E
Privolzhye	55	52 52N	48 33 E
Priyutnoye	57	46 12N	43 40 E
Prizren	42	42 13N	20 45 E
Prizzi	40	37 44N	13 24 E
Prnjavor	42	44 52N	17 43 E
Probolinggo	73	7 46 S	113 13 E
Prochowice	28	51 17N	16 20 E
Procida	40	40 46N	14 0 E
Proddatur	70	14 45N	78 30 E
Proença-a-Nova	31	39 45N	7 54W
Progreso	120	21 20N	89 40W
Prokhladnyy	57	43 50N	44 2 E
Prokletije	44	42 30N	19 45 E
Prokopyevsk	58	54 0N	86 45 E
Prokuplje	42	43 16N	21 36 E
Proletarskaya	57	46 42N	41 50 E
Prome = Pyè	67	18 45N	95 30 E
Prophet →	108	58 48N	122 40W
Propriá	127	10 13 S	36 51W
Propriano	21	41 41N	8 52 E
Proserpine	97	20 21 S	148 36 E
Prosna	28	51 1N	18 30 E
Prosser	118	46 11N	119 52W
Prostějov	27	49 30N	17 9 E
Prostki	28	53 42N	22 25 E
Proston	99	26 8 S	151 32 E
Proszowice	27	50 13N	20 16 E
Protection	117	37 16N	99 30W
Próti	45	37 5N	21 32 E
Provadiya	43	43 12N	27 30 E
Provence	21	43 40N	5 46 E
Providence, Ky., U.S.A.	114	37 25N	87 46W
Providence, R.I., U.S.A.	114	41 50N	71 28W
Providence Bay	106	45 41N	82 15W
Providence Mts.	119	35 0N	115 30W
Providencia, I. de	121	13 25N	81 26W
Provideniya	59	64 23N	173 18W
Provins	19	48 33N	3 15 E
Provo	118	40 16N	111 37W
Provost	109	52 25N	110 20W
Prozor	42	43 50N	17 34 E
Prud'homme	109	52 20N	105 54W
Prudnik	28	50 20N	17 38 E
Prüm	25	50 14N	6 22 E
Pruszcz Gd.	28	54 17N	18 40 E
Pruszków	28	52 9N	20 49 E
Prut →	46	46 3N	28 10 E
Pruzhany	54	52 33N	24 28 E
Prvič	39	44 55N	14 47 E
Prydz B.	5	69 0 S	74 0 E
Pryor	117	36 17N	95 20W
Przasnysz	28	53 2N	20 45 E
Przedbórz	28	51 6N	19 53 E
Przedecz	28	52 20N	18 53 E
Przemyśl	27	49 50N	22 45 E
Przeworsk	27	50 6N	22 32 E
Przewóz	28	51 28N	14 57 E
Przhevalsk	58	42 30N	78 20 E
Przysuchla	28	51 22N	20 38 E
Psakhná	45	38 34N	23 35 E
Psará	45	38 37N	25 38 E
Psathoúra	44	39 30N	24 12 E
Psel →	56	49 5N	33 20 E
Pserimos	45	36 56N	27 12 E
Pskov	54	57 50N	28 25 E
Psunj	42	45 25N	17 19 E
Pszczyna	27	49 59N	18 58 E
Pteleón	45	39 3N	22 57 E
Ptich →	54	52 9N	28 52 E
Ptolemaís	44	40 30N	21 43 E
Ptuj	39	46 28N	15 50 E
Ptujska Gora	39	46 23N	15 47 E
Puán	124	37 30 S	62 45W
Pucallpa	126	8 25 S	74 30W
Pucheng	77	27 59N	118 31 E
Pucheni	46	45 12N	25 17 E
Pučišće	39	43 22N	16 43 E
Puck	28	54 45N	18 23 E
Pucka, Zatoka	28	54 30N	18 40 E
Pudozh	52	61 48N	36 32 E
Pudukkottai	70	10 28N	78 47 E
Puebla	120	19 0N	98 10W
Puebla □	120	18 30N	98 0W
Puebla de Alcocer	31	38 59N	5 14W
Puebla de Cazalla, La	31	37 10N	5 20W
Puebla de Don Fadrique	33	37 58N	2 25W
Puebla de Don Rodrigo	31	39 5N	4 37W
Puebla de Guzmán	31	37 37N	7 15W
Puebla de los Infantes, La	31	37 47N	5 24W
Puebla de Montalbán, La	30	39 52N	4 22W
Puebla de Sanabria	30	42 4N	6 38W
Puebla de Trives	30	42 20N	7 10W
Puebla del Caramiñal	30	42 37N	8 56W
Puebla, La	32	39 46N	3 1 E
Pueblo	116	38 20N	104 40W
Pueblo Bonito	119	36 4N	107 57W
Pueblo Hundido	124	26 20 S	70 5W
Puelches	124	38 5 S	65 51W
Puelén	124	37 32 S	67 38W
Puente Alto	124	33 32 S	70 35W
Puente del Arzobispo	30	39 48N	5 10W
Puente-Genil	31	37 22N	4 47W
Puente la Reina	32	42 40N	1 49W
Puenteareas	30	42 10N	8 28W
Puentedeume	30	43 24N	8 10W
Puentes de Garcia Rodriguez	30	43 27N	7 50W
Puerco →	119	34 22N	107 50W
Puerta, La	33	38 22N	2 45W
Puerto Aisén	128	45 27 S	73 0W
Puerto Armuelles	121	8 20N	82 51W
Puerto Ayacucho	126	5 40N	67 35W
Puerto Barrios	120	15 40N	88 32W
Puerto Bermejo	124	26 55 S	58 34W
Puerto Bermúdez	126	10 20 S	75 0W
Puerto Bolívar	126	3 19 S	79 55W
Puerto Cabello	126	10 28N	68 1W
Puerto Cabezas	121	14 0N	83 30W
Puerto Capaz = Jebba	82	35 11N	4 43W
Puerto Carreño	126	6 12N	67 22W
Puerto Castilla	121	16 0N	86 0W
Puerto Chicama	126	7 45 S	79 20W
Puerto Coig	128	50 54 S	69 15W
Puerto Cortes	121	8 55N	84 0W
Puerto Cortés	120	15 51N	88 0W
Puerto Cumarebo	126	11 29N	69 30W
Puerto de Santa María	31	36 36N	6 13W
Puerto del Rosario	80	28 30N	13 52W
Puerto Deseado	128	47 55 S	66 0W
Puerto Heath	126	12 34 S	68 39W
Puerto Juárez	120	21 11N	86 49W
Puerto La Cruz	126	10 13N	64 38W
Puerto Leguízamo	126	0 12 S	74 46W
Puerto Libertad	120	29 55N	112 41W
Puerto Lobos	128	42 0 S	65 3W
Puerto Lumbreras	33	37 34N	1 48W
Puerto Madryn	128	42 48 S	65 4W
Puerto Maldonado	126	12 30 S	69 10W
Puerto Mazarrón	33	37 34N	1 15W
Puerto Montt	128	41 28 S	73 0W
Puerto Morelos	120	20 49N	86 52W
Puerto Natales	128	51 45 S	72 15W
Puerto Padre	121	21 13N	76 35W
Puerto Páez	126	6 13N	67 28W
Puerto Peñasco	120	31 20N	113 33W
Puerto Pinasco	124	22 36 S	57 50W
Puerto Pirámides	128	42 35 S	64 20W
Puerto Plata	121	19 48N	70 45W
Puerto Princesa	73	9 46N	118 45 E
Puerto Quellón	128	43 7 S	73 37W
Puerto Quepos	121	9 29N	84 6W
Puerto Real	31	36 33N	6 12W
Puerto Rico ■	121	18 15N	66 45W
Puerto Sastre	124	22 2 S	57 55W
Puerto Suárez	126	18 58 S	57 52W
Puerto Vallarta	120	20 36N	105 15W
Puerto Wilches	126	7 21N	73 54W
Puertollano	31	38 43N	4 7W
Puertomarin	30	42 48N	7 36W
Pueyrredón, L.	128	47 20 S	72 0W
Pugachev	55	52 0N	48 49 E
Puge	90	4 45 S	33 11 E
Puget Sd.	118	47 15N	122 30W
Puget-Théniers	21	43 58N	6 53 E
Púglia □	41	41 0N	16 30 E
Pugu	90	6 55 S	39 4 E
Pui	46	45 30N	23 4 E
Puiești	46	46 25N	27 33 E
Puig Mayor, Mte.	32	39 48N	2 47 E
Puigcerdá	32	42 24N	1 50 E
Puigmal	32	42 23N	2 7 E
Puisaye, Collines de	19	47 34N	3 18 E
Puiseaux	19	48 11N	2 30 E
Puka	44	42 2N	19 53 E
Pukaki L.	101	44 4 S	170 1 E
Pukatawagan	109	55 45N	101 20W
Pukekohe	101	37 12 S	174 55 E
Pukou	77	32 7N	118 38 E
Pula	40	39 0N	9 0 E
Pula (Pola)	39	44 54N	13 57 E
Pulaski, N.Y., U.S.A.	114	43 32N	76 9W
Pulaski, Tenn., U.S.A.	115	35 10N	87 0W
Pulaski, Va., U.S.A.	114	37 4N	80 49W
Pulawy	28	51 23N	21 59 E
Pulgaon	68	20 44N	78 21 E
Pulicat, L.	70	13 40N	80 15 E
Puliyangudi	70	9 11N	77 24 E
Pullman	118	46 49N	117 10W
Pulog, Mt.	73	16 40N	120 50 E
Puloraja	72	4 55N	95 24 E
Pułtusk	28	52 43N	21 6 E
Pumlumon Fawr	13	52 29N	3 47W
Puna	126	19 45 S	65 28W
Puná, I.	126	2 55 S	80 5W
Punakha	69	27 42N	89 52 E
Punalur	70	9 0N	76 56 E
Punasar	68	27 6N	73 6 E
Punata	126	17 32 S	65 50W
Punch	69	33 48N	74 4 E
Pune	70	18 29N	73 57 E
Pungue, Ponte de	91	19 0 S	34 0 E
Puning	77	23 20N	116 12 E
Punjab □	68	31 0N	76 0 E
Puno	126	15 55 S	70 3W
Punta Alta	128	38 53 S	62 4W
Punta Arenas	128	53 10 S	71 0W
Punta de Díaz	124	28 0 S	70 45W
Punta Gorda, Belize	120	16 10N	88 45W
Punta Gorda, U.S.A.	115	26 55N	82 0W
Puntarenas	121	10 0N	84 50W
Punto Fijo	126	11 50N	70 13W
Punxsutawney	114	40 56N	79 0W
Puqi	77	29 40N	113 50 E
Puquio	126	14 45 S	74 10W
Pur →	58	67 31N	77 55 E
Purace, Vol.	126	2 21N	76 23W
Puračić	42	44 33N	18 28 E
Purari →	98	7 49 S	145 0 E
Purbeck, Isle of	13	50 40N	2 5W
Purcell	117	35 0N	97 25W
Purchena Tetica	33	37 21N	2 21W
Puri	69	19 50N	85 58 E
Purli	68	18 50N	76 35 E
Purmerend	16	52 30N	4 58 E
Purna →	70	19 6N	77 2 E
Purnea	69	25 45N	87 31 E
Pursat	71	12 34N	103 50 E
Purukcahu	72	0 35 S	114 35 E
Purulia	69	23 17N	86 24 E
Purus →	126	3 42 S	61 28W
Pŭrvomay	43	42 8N	25 17 E
Purwakarta	73	6 35 S	107 29 E
Purwodadi, Jawa, Indon.	73	7 51 S	110 0 E
Purwodadi, Jawa, Indon.	73	7 7 S	110 55 E
Purwokerto	73	7 25 S	109 14 E
Purworedjo	73	7 43 S	110 2 E
Pus →	70	19 55N	77 55 E
Pusad	70	19 56N	77 36 E
Pusan	76	35 5N	129 0 E
Pushchino	59	54 10N	158 0 E
Pushkin	54	59 45N	30 25 E
Pushkino, R.S.F.S.R., U.S.S.R.	55	51 16N	47 0 E
Pushkino, R.S.F.S.R., U.S.S.R.	55	56 2N	37 49 E
Püspökladány	27	47 19N	21 6 E
Pustoshka	54	56 20N	29 30 E
Puszczykowo	28	52 18N	16 49 E
Putahow L.	109	59 54N	100 40W
Putao	67	27 28N	97 30 E
Putaruru	101	38 2 S	175 50 E
Putbus	24	54 19N	13 29 E
Puțeni	46	45 49N	27 42 E
Puthein Myit →	67	15 56N	94 18 E
Putian	77	25 23N	119 0 E
Putignano	41	40 50N	17 5 E
Puting, Tanjung	72	3 31 S	111 46 E
Putlitz	24	53 15N	12 3 E
Putna	46	47 50N	25 33 E
Putna →	46	45 42N	27 26 E
Putnam	113	41 55N	71 55W
Putnok	27	48 18N	20 26 E
Putorana, Gory	59	69 0N	95 0 E
Puttalam Lagoon	70	8 15N	79 45 E
Putten	16	52 16N	5 36 E
Puttgarden	24	54 28N	11 15 E
Puttur	70	12 46N	75 12 E
Putumayo →	126	3 7 S	67 58W
Putussibau	72	0 50N	112 56 E
Puy-de-Dôme	20	45 46N	2 57 E
Puy-de-Dôme □	20	45 47N	3 0 E
Puy-de-Sancy	20	45 32N	2 48 E
Puy-Guillaume	20	45 57N	3 29 E
Puy, Le	20	45 3N	3 52 E
Puy l'Évêque	20	44 31N	1 9 E
Puyallup	118	47 10N	122 22W
Puyang	76	35 40N	115 1 E
Puylaurens	20	43 35N	2 0 E
Puyôo	20	43 33N	0 56W
Pwani □	90	7 0 S	39 0 E
Pweto	91	8 25 S	28 51 E
Pwllheli	12	52 54N	4 26W
Pya-ozero	52	66 5N	30 58 E
Pyana →	55	55 30N	46 0 E
Pyapon	67	16 20N	95 40 E
Pyasina →	59	73 30N	87 0 E
Pyatigorsk	57	44 2N	43 6 E
Pyatikhatki	56	48 28N	33 38 E
Pydna	44	40 20N	22 34 E
Pyinmana	67	19 45N	96 12 E
Pyŏngyang	76	39 0N	125 30 E
Pyote	117	31 34N	103 5W
Pyramid L.	118	40 0N	119 30W
Pyramids	86	29 58N	31 9 E
Pyrénées	20	42 45N	0 18 E
Pyrenees = Pyrénées	20	42 45N	0 18 E
Pyrénées-Atlantiques □	20	43 15N	1 0W
Pyrénées-Orientales □	20	42 35N	2 26 E
Pyrzyce	28	53 10N	14 55 E
Pyshchug	55	58 57N	45 47 E
Pytalovo	54	57 5N	27 55 E
Pyttegga	47	62 13N	7 42 E
Pyu	67	18 30N	96 28 E
Pyzdry	28	52 11N	17 42 E

Q

Qabalān	62	32 8N	35 17 E
Qabātiyah	62	32 25N	35 16 E
Qaidam Pendi	75	37 0N	95 0 E
Qa'iya	64	24 33N	43 15 E
Qal' at Shajwa	86	25 2N	38 57 E
Qala-i-Jadid (Spin Baldak)	68	31 1N	66 25 E
Qalāt	65	32 15N	66 58 E
Qal'at al Akhḍar	64	28 0N	37 10 E
Qal'at al Mu'azzam	64	27 45N	37 31 E
Qal'at Saura	86	26 10N	38 40 E
Qal'eh-ye Now	65	35 0N	63 5 E
Qalqīlya	62	32 12N	34 58 E
Qalyûb	86	30 12N	31 11 E
Qam	62	32 36N	35 43 E
Qamar, Ghubbat al	63	16 20N	52 30 E
Qamruddin Karez	68	31 45N	68 20 E
Qāna	62	33 12N	35 17 E
Qâra	86	29 38N	26 30 E
Qarachuk	64	37 0N	42 2 E
Qārah	64	29 55N	40 3 E
Qardud	87	10 20N	29 56 E
Qarqan	75	38 5N	85 20 E
Qarqan He →	75	39 30N	88 30 E
Qarrasa	87	14 38N	32 5 E
Qasim	64	26 0N	43 0 E
Qāsim	62	32 59N	36 2 E
Qaṣr Bū Hadi	83	31 1N	16 45 E
Qaṣr-e Qand	65	26 15N	60 45 E
Qasr Farâfra	86	27 0N	28 1 E
Qatar ■	65	25 30N	51 15 E
Qattâra	86	30 12N	27 3 E
Qattâra Depression = Qattâra, Munkhafed el	86	29 30N	27 30 E
Qattâra, Munkhafed el	86	29 30N	27 30 E
Qāyen	65	33 40N	59 10 E
Qazvin	64	36 15N	50 0 E
Qena	86	26 10N	32 43 E
Qena, Wadi →	86	26 12N	32 44 E
Qeshm	65	26 55N	56 10 E
Qezi'ot	62	30 52N	34 26 E
Qian Xian	77	34 31N	108 15 E
Qianshan	77	30 37N	116 35 E
Qianxi	77	27 3N	106 3 E
Qianyang	77	27 18N	110 10 E
Qijiang	77	28 57N	106 35 E
Qila Safed	66	29 0N	61 30 E
Qila Saifulla	68	30 45N	68 17 E
Qilian Shan	75	38 30N	96 0 E
Qin Ling = Qinling Shandi	77	33 50N	108 10 E
Qin'an	77	34 48N	105 40 E
Qingdao	76	36 5N	120 20 E
Qinghai □	75	36 0N	98 0 E
Qinghai Hu	75	36 40N	100 10 E
Qingjiang, Jiangsu, China	77	33 30N	119 2 E
Qingjiang, Jiangxi, China	77	28 4N	115 29 E
Qingliu	77	26 11N	116 48 E
Qingshuihe	76	39 55N	111 35 E
Qingyang	76	36 2N	107 55 E
Qingyuan	77	23 40N	112 59 E
Qinhuangdao	76	39 56N	119 30 E
Qinling Shandi	77	33 50N	108 10 E
Qinyang	77	35 7N	112 57 E
Qinyuan	76	36 29N	112 20 E
Qinzhou	75	21 58N	108 38 E
Qiongshan	77	19 51N	110 26 E
Qiongzhou Haixia	77	20 10N	110 15 E
Qiqihar	75	47 26N	124 0 E
Qiryat 'Anavim	62	31 49N	35 7 E
Qiryat Ata	62	32 47N	35 6 E
Qiryat Bialik	62	32 50N	35 5 E
Qiryat Gat	62	31 32N	34 46 E
Qiryat Ḥayyim	62	32 49N	35 4 E
Qiryat Mal'akhi	62	31 44N	34 44 E
Qiryat Shemona	62	33 13N	35 35 E
Qiryat Yam	62	32 51N	35 4 E
Qishan	77	22 52N	120 25 E
Qishon →	62	32 49N	35 2 E
Qishrān	86	20 14N	40 2 E
Qitai	75	44 2N	89 35 E
Qiyahe	76	53 0N	120 35 E
Qiyang	77	26 35N	111 50 E
Qizan	87	16 57N	42 34 E
Qizān	63	17 0N	42 20 E
Qom	65	34 40N	51 0 E
Qomolangma Feng (Mt. Everest)	75	28 0N	86 45 E
Qondūz	65	36 50N	68 50 E
Qondūz □	65	36 50N	68 50 E
Qu Jiang →	77	30 1N	106 24 E
Qu Xian, Sichuan, China	77	30 48N	106 58 E
Qu Xian, Zhejiang, China	75	28 57N	118 54 E
Quackenbrück	24	52 40N	7 59 E
Quakertown	113	40 27N	75 20W
Quambatook	99	35 49 S	143 34 E
Quambone	99	30 57 S	147 53 E
Quan Long = Ca Mau	71	9 7N	105 8 E
Quanah	117	34 20N	99 45W
Quandialla	99	34 1 S	147 47 E
Quang Ngai	71	15 13N	108 58 E
Quang Yen	71	20 56N	106 52 E
Quantock Hills	13	51 8N	3 10W
Quanzhou, Fujian, China	75	24 55N	118 34 E
Quanzhou, Guangxi Zhuangzu, China	77	25 57N	111 5 E
Quaraí	124	30 15 S	56 20W
Quarré-les-Tombes	19	47 21N	4 0 E
Quartu Sant' Elena	40	39 15N	9 10 E
Quartzsite	119	33 44N	114 16W
Quatsino	108	50 30N	127 40W
Quatsino Sd.	108	50 25N	127 58W
Qubab = Mishmar Ayyalon	62	31 52N	34 57 E
Qūchān	65	37 10N	58 27 E
† Que Que	91	18 58 S	29 48 E
Queanbeyan	97	35 17 S	149 14 E
Québec	107	46 52N	71 13W
Québec □	107	50 0N	70 0W
Quedlinburg	24	51 47N	11 9 E
Queen Alexandra Ra.	5	85 0 S	170 0 E
Queen Charlotte	108	53 15N	132 2W
Queen Charlotte Is.	108	53 20N	132 10W
Queen Charlotte Str.	108	51 0N	128 0W
Queen Elizabeth Is.	102	76 0N	95 0W
Queen Elizabeth Nat. Park	90	0 0 S	30 0 E
Queen Mary Coast	5	70 0 S	95 0 E
Queen Maud G.	104	68 15N	102 30W
Queen Maud Ra.	5	86 0 S	160 0W
Queens Chan.	96	15 0 S	129 30 E
Queenscliff	97	38 16 S	144 39 E
Queensland □	97	22 0 S	142 0 E
Queenstown, Austral.	97	42 4 S	145 35 E
Queenstown, N.Z.	101	45 1 S	168 40 E
Queenstown, S. Afr.	92	31 52 S	26 52 E
Queguay Grande →	124	32 9 S	58 9W
Queimadas	127	11 0 S	39 38W
Quela	88	9 10 S	16 56 E
Quelimane	91	17 53 S	36 58 E
Quelpart = Cheju Do	77	33 29N	126 34 E
Quemado, N. Mex., U.S.A.	119	34 17N	108 28W
Quemado, Tex., U.S.A.	117	28 58N	100 35W
Quemú-Quemú	124	36 3 S	63 36W
Quequén	124	38 30 S	58 30W
Querétaro	120	20 40N	100 23W
Querétaro □	120	20 30N	100 0W
Querfurt	24	51 22N	11 33 E
Querqueville	18	49 40N	1 42W
Quesada	33	37 51N	3 4W
Queshan	77	32 55N	114 2 E
Quesnel	108	53 0N	122 30W
Quesnel →	108	52 58N	122 29W
Quesnel L.	108	52 30N	121 20W
Quesnoy, Le	19	50 15N	3 38 E
Questa	119	36 45N	105 35W
Questembert	18	47 40N	2 28W
Quetico Prov. Park	106	48 30N	91 45W
Quetta	66	30 15N	66 55 E
* Quetta □	66	30 15N	66 55 E
Quezaltenango	120	14 50N	91 30W
Quezon City	73	14 38N	121 0 E
Qui Nhon	71	13 40N	109 13 E
Quiaca, La	124	22 5 S	65 35W
Quibaxe	88	8 24 S	14 27 E
Quibdo	126	5 42N	76 40W
Quiberon	18	47 29N	3 9W
Quick	108	54 36N	126 54W
Quickborn	24	53 42N	9 52 E
Quiet L.	108	61 5N	133 5W
Quiindy	124	25 58 S	57 14W
Quilán, C.	128	43 15 S	74 30W
Quilengues	89	14 12 S	14 12 E
Quilimarí	124	32 5 S	71 30W
Quilino	124	30 14 S	64 29W
Quillabamba	126	12 50 S	72 50W

* *Now part of Baluchistan* □

† *Renamed Kwekwe*

Quillagua Red Rock, L.

Quillagua 124 21 40 S 69 40W
Quillaicillo 124 31 17 S 71 40W
Quillan 20 42 53N 2 10 E
Quillebeuf 18 49 28N 0 30 E
Quillota 124 32 54 S 71 16W
Quilmes 124 34 43 S 58 15W
Quilon 70 8 50N 76 38 E
Quilpie 97 26 35 S 144 11 E
Quilpué 124 33 5 S 71 33W
Quilua 91 16 17 S 39 54 E
Quimili 124 27 40 S 62 30W
Quimper 18 48 0N 4 9W
Quimperlé 18 47 53N 3 33W
Quincy, Calif., U.S.A. 118 39 56N 121 0W
Quincy, Fla., U.S.A. 115 30 34N 84 34W
Quincy, Ill., U.S.A. 116 39 55N 91 20W
Quincy, Mass., U.S.A. 114 42 14N 71 0W
Quincy, Wash., U.S.A. 118 47 22N 119 56W
Quines 124 32 13 S 65 48W
Quinga 91 15 49 S 40 15 E
Quingey 19 47 7N 5 52 E
Quintana de la Serena 31 38 45N 5 40W
Quintana Roo □ 120 19 0N 88 0W
Quintanar de la Orden 32 39 36N 3 5W
Quintanar de la Sierra 32 41 57N 2 55W
Quintanar del Rey 33 39 21N 1 56W
Quintero 124 32 45 S 71 30W
Quintin 18 48 26N 2 56W
Quinto 32 41 25N 0 32W
Quinyambie 99 30 15 S 141 0 E
Quipar → 33 38 15N 1 40W
Quirihue 124 36 15 S 72 35W
Quirindi 99 31 28 S 150 40 E
Quiroga 30 42 28N 7 18W
Quissac 21 43 55N 4 0 E
Quissanga 91 12 24 S 40 28 E
Quitilipi 124 26 50 S 60 13W
Quitman, Ga., U.S.A. 115 30 49N 83 35W
Quitman, Miss., U.S.A. 115 32 2N 88 42W
Quitman, Tex., U.S.A. 117 32 48N 95 25W
Quito 126 0 15 S 78 35W
Quixadá 127 4 55 S 39 0W
Quixaxe 91 15 17 S 40 4 E
Qul'ân, Jazâ'ir 86 24 22N 35 31 E
Qumrān 62 31 43N 35 27 E
Quneitra 62 33 7N 35 48 E
Quoin Pt. 92 34 46 S 19 37 E
Quondong 99 33 6 S 140 18 E
Quorn 97 32 25 S 138 0 E
Qurein 87 13 30N 34 50 E
Qûs 86 25 55N 32 50 E
Quseir 86 26 7N 34 16 E
Qusrah 62 32 5N 35 20 E
Quthing 93 30 25 S 27 36 E
Qytet Stalin (Kuçove) 44 40 47N 19 57 E

R

Råå 49 56 0N 12 45 E
Raab 26 48 21N 13 39 E
Raahe 50 64 40N 24 28 E
Ra'ananna 62 32 12N 34 52 E
Raasay 14 57 25N 6 4W
Raasay, Sd. of 14 57 30N 6 8W
Rab 39 44 45N 14 45 E
Raba 73 8 36 S 118 55 E
Rába → 27 47 38N 17 38 E
Raba → 27 50 8N 20 30 E
Rabaçal → 30 41 30N 7 12W
Rabah 85 13 5N 5 30 E
Rabai 90 3 50 S 39 31 E
Rabastens, Hautes-Pyrénées, France 20 43 25N 0 10 E
Rabastens, Tarn, France 20 43 50N 1 43 E
Rabat, Malta 36 35 53N 14 25 E
Rabat, Moroc. 82 34 2N 6 48W
Rabaul 94 4 24 S 152 18 E
Rabbit → 108 59 41N 127 12W
Rabbit Lake 109 53 8N 107 46W
Rabbitskin → 108 61 47N 120 42W
Rābigh 64 22 50N 39 5 E
Rabka 27 49 37N 19 59 E
Rača 42 44 14N 21 0 E
Răcale 41 39 57N 18 6 E
Racalmuto 40 37 25N 13 41 E
Răcășdia 42 44 59N 21 36 E
Racconigi 38 44 47N 7 41 E
Race, C. 107 46 40N 53 5W
Rach Gia 71 10 5N 105 5 E
Raciąż 28 52 46N 20 10 E
Racibórz 27 50 7N 18 18 E
Racine 114 42 41N 87 51W
Radama, Nosy 93 14 0 S 47 47 E
Radama, Saikanosy 93 14 16 S 47 53 E
Radan 42 42 59N 21 29 E
Rădăuţi 46 47 50N 25 59 E
Radbuza → 26 49 35N 13 5 E
Råde 47 59 21N 10 53 E
Radeburg 24 51 6N 13 55 E
Radeče 39 46 5N 15 14 E
Radekhov 54 50 25N 24 32 E
Radew → 28 54 2N 15 52 E
Radford 114 37 8N 80 32W
Radhanpur 68 23 50N 71 38 E
Radhwa, Jabal 64 24 34N 38 18 E
Radiska → 42 41 38N 20 37 E
Radisson 109 52 30N 107 20W
Radium Hill 97 32 30 S 140 42 E
Radium Hot Springs 108 50 35N 116 2W
Radja, Kepulauan 73 0 30 S 130 00 E
Radków 28 50 30N 16 24 E
Radlin 27 50 3N 18 29 E
Radna 42 46 7N 21 41 E
Radnevo 43 42 17N 25 58 E
Radnice 26 49 51N 13 35 E
Radnor Forest 13 52 17N 3 10W
Radolfzell 25 47 44N 8 58 E
Radom 28 51 23N 21 12 E
Radom □ 28 51 30N 21 0 E
Radomir 42 42 37N 23 4 E
Radomka → 28 51 31N 21 11 E
Radomsko 28 51 5N 19 28 E
Radomyshl 54 50 30N 29 12 E
Radomysl Wielki 27 50 14N 21 15 E
Radoszyce 28 51 4N 20 15 E
Radoviš 42 41 38N 22 28 E
Radovljica 39 46 22N 14 12 E
Radstadt 26 47 24N 13 28 E
Radstock 13 51 17N 2 25W
Răducăneni 46 46 58N 27 54 E
Raduša 42 42 7N 21 15 E
Radviliškis 54 55 49N 23 33 E
Radville 109 49 30N 104 15W
Radymno 27 49 59N 22 52 E
Radzanów 28 52 56N 20 8 E
Radziejów 28 52 40N 18 30 E
Radzymin 28 52 25N 21 11 E
Radzyń Chełmiński 28 53 23N 18 55 E
Radzyń Podlaski 28 51 47N 22 37 E
Rae 108 62 50N 116 3W
Rae Bareli 69 26 18N 81 20 E
Rae Isthmus 105 66 40N 87 30W
Raeren 16 50 41N 6 7 E
Raeside, L. 96 29 20 S 122 0 E
Raetihi 101 39 25 S 175 17 E
Rafaela 124 31 10 S 61 30W
Rafah 86 31 18N 34 14 E
Rafai 90 4 59N 23 58 E
Raffadali 40 37 23N 13 29 E
Rafḩā 64 29 35N 43 35 E
Rafsanjān 65 30 30N 56 5 E
Ragag 87 10 59N 24 40 E
Raglan, Austral. 98 23 42 S 150 49 E
Raglan, N.Z. 101 37 55 S 174 55 E
Ragunda 48 63 6N 16 23 E
Ragusa 41 36 56N 14 42 E
Raha 73 4 55 S 123 0 E
Rahad al Bardī 81 11 20N 23 40 E
Rahad, Nahr ed → 87 14 28N 33 31 E
Rahden 24 52 26N 8 36 E
Raheita 87 12 46N 43 4 E
Rahimyar Khan 68 28 30N 70 25 E
Raichur 70 16 10N 77 20 E
Raiganj 69 25 37N 88 10 E
Raigarh, Madhya Pradesh, India 69 21 56N 83 25 E
Raigarh, Orissa, India 70 19 51N 82 6 E
Raiis 64 23 33N 38 43 E
Raijua 73 10 37 S 121 36 E
Railton 99 41 25 S 146 28 E
Rainbow Lake 108 58 30N 119 23W
Rainier 118 46 4N 123 0W
Rainier, Mt. 118 46 50N 121 50W
Rainy L. 109 48 42N 93 10W
Rainy River 109 48 43N 94 29W
Raipur 69 21 17N 81 45 E
Raja, Kepulauan 73 0 30 S 129 40 E
Raja, Ujung 72 3 40N 96 25 E
Rajahmundry 70 17 1N 81 48 E
Rajang → 72 2 30N 112 0 E
Rajapalaiyam 70 9 25N 77 35 E
Rajasthan □ 68 26 45N 73 30 E
Rajasthan Canal 68 28 0N 72 0 E
Rajbari 69 23 47N 89 41 E
Rajgarh, Mad. P., India 68 24 2N 76 45 E
Rajgarh, Raj., India 68 28 40N 75 25 E
Rajgród 28 53 42N 22 42 E
Rajhenburg 39 46 1N 15 29 E
Rajkot 68 22 15N 70 56 E
Rajmahal Hills 69 24 30N 87 30 E
Rajnandgaon 69 21 5N 81 5 E
Rajojooseppi 50 68 25N 28 30 E
Rajpipla 68 21 50N 73 30 E
Rajpura 68 30 25N 76 32 E
Rajshahi 69 24 22N 88 39 E
Rajshahi □ 69 25 0N 89 0 E
Rakaia 101 43 45 S 172 1 E
Rakaia → 101 43 36 S 172 15 E
Rakan, Ra's 65 26 10N 51 20 E
Rakaposhi 69 36 10N 74 25 E
Rakha 86 18 25N 41 30 E
Rakhni 68 30 4N 69 56 E
Rakitovo 43 41 59N 24 5 E
Rakkestad 47 59 25N 11 21 E
Rakoniewice 28 52 10N 16 16 E
Rakops 92 21 1 S 24 28 E
Rákospalota 27 47 30N 19 5 E
Rakov 54 53 58N 26 59 E
Rakovica 39 44 59N 15 38 E
Rakovník 26 50 6N 13 42 E
Rakovski 43 42 21N 24 57 E
Rakvere 54 59 30N 26 25 E
Raleigh 115 35 47N 78 39W
Raleigh B. 115 34 50N 76 15W
Ralja 42 44 33N 20 34 E
Ralls 117 33 40N 101 20W
Ram → 108 62 1N 123 41W
Rām Allāh 62 31 55N 35 10 E
Rama 62 32 56N 35 21 E
Ramacca 41 37 24N 14 40 E
Ramachandrapuram 70 16 50N 82 4 E
Ramales de la Victoria 32 43 15N 3 28W
Ramanathapuram 70 9 25N 78 55 E
Ramanetaka, B. de 93 14 13 S 47 52 E
Ramas C. 70 15 5N 73 55 E
Ramat Gan 62 32 4N 34 48 E
Ramat HaSharon 62 32 7N 34 50 E
Ramatlhabama 92 25 37 S 25 33 E
Rambervillers 19 48 20N 6 38 E
Rambipuji 73 8 12 S 113 37 E
Rambia, La 31 37 37N 4 45W
Rambouillet 19 48 40N 1 48 E
Ramdurg 70 15 58N 75 22 E
Rame Hd. 99 37 47 S 149 30 E
Ramea 107 47 28N 57 4W
Ramechhap 69 27 25N 86 10 E
Ramelau 73 8 55 S 126 22 E
Ramenskoye 55 55 32N 38 15 E
Ramgarh, Bihar, India 69 23 40N 85 35 E
Ramgarh, Rajasthan, India 68 27 16N 75 14 E
Ramgarh, Rajasthan, India 68 27 30N 70 36 E
Rāmhormoz 64 31 15N 49 35 E
Ramla 62 31 55N 34 52 E
Ramlat Zalṭan 83 28 30N 19 30 E
Ramlu 87 13 32N 41 40 E
Ramme 49 56 30N 8 11 E
Rammūn 62 31 55N 35 17 E
Ramnad = Ramanathapuram 70 9 25N 78 55 E
Ramnäs 48 59 46N 16 12 E
Ramon 55 51 55N 39 21 E
Ramon, Har 62 30 30N 34 38 E
Ramona 119 33 1N 116 56W
Ramore 106 48 30N 80 25W
Ramos → 120 25 35N 105 3W
Ramoutsa 92 24 50 S 25 52 E
Rampart 104 65 0N 150 15W
Rampur, H.P., India 68 31 26N 77 43 E
Rampur, Mad. P., India 68 23 25N 73 53 E
Rampur, Orissa, India 69 21 48N 83 58 E
Rampur, U.P., India 68 28 50N 79 5 E
Rampura 68 24 30N 75 27 E
Rampurhat 69 24 10N 87 50 E
Ramree Kyun 67 19 0N 94 0 E
Ramsey, Can. 106 47 25N 82 20W
Ramsey, U.K. 12 54 20N 4 21W
Ramsgate 13 51 20N 1 25 E
Ramsjö 48 62 11N 15 37 E
Ramtek 69 21 20N 79 15 E
Ramu → 98 4 0 S 144 41 E
Ramvik 48 62 49N 17 51 E
Ranaghat 69 23 15N 88 35 E
Ranahu 68 25 55N 69 45 E
Ranau 72 6 2N 116 40 E
Rancagua 124 34 10 S 70 50W
Rance → 18 48 34N 1 59W
Rance, Barrage de la 18 48 30N 2 3W
Rancheria → 108 60 13N 129 7W
Ranchester 118 44 57N 107 12W
Ranchi 69 23 19N 85 27 E
Rancu 46 44 32N 24 15 E
Rand 100 35 33 S 146 32 E
Randan 20 46 2N 3 21 E
Randazzo 41 37 53N 14 56 E
Randers 49 56 29N 10 1 E
Randers Fjord 49 56 37N 10 20 E
Randfontein 93 26 8 S 27 45 E
Randolph, Mass., U.S.A. 113 42 10N 71 3W
Randolph, N.Y., U.S.A. 112 42 10N 78 59W
Randolph, Utah, U.S.A. 118 41 43N 111 10W
Randolph, Vt., U.S.A. 113 43 55N 72 39W
Randsburg 119 35 22N 117 44W
Randsfjorden 47 60 15N 10 25 E
Råne älv → 50 65 50N 22 20 E
Rangaunu B. 101 34 51 S 173 15 E
Rångedala 49 57 47N 13 9 E
Rangeley 114 44 58N 70 33W
Rangely 118 40 3N 108 53W
Ranger 117 32 30N 98 42W
Rangia 67 26 28N 91 38 E
Rangiora 101 43 19 S 172 36 E
Rangitaiki → 101 37 54 S 176 49 E
Rangitata → 101 43 45 S 171 15 E
Rangkasbitung 73 6 22 S 106 16 E
Rangon → 67 16 28N 96 40 E
Rangoon 67 16 45N 96 20 E
Ranibennur 70 14 35N 75 30 E
Raniganj 69 23 40N 87 5 E
Ranipet 70 12 56N 79 23 E
Rankin 117 31 16N 101 56W
Rankin Inlet 104 62 30N 93 0W
Rankins Springs 99 33 49 S 146 14 E
Rannoch, L. 14 56 41N 4 20W
Rannoch Moor 14 56 38N 4 48W
Ranobe, Helodranon' i 93 23 3 S 43 33 E
Ranohira 93 22 29 S 45 24 E
Ranomafana, Tamatave, Madag. 93 18 57 S 48 50 E
Ranomafana, Tuléar, Madag. 93 24 34 S 47 0 E
Ranong 71 9 56N 98 40 E
Ransiki 73 1 30 S 134 10 E
Rantau 72 2 56 S 115 9 E
Rantauprapat 72 2 15N 99 50 E
Rantemario 73 3 15 S 119 57 E
Rantīs 62 32 4N 35 3 E
Rantoul 114 40 18N 88 10W
Ranum 49 56 54N 9 14 E
Ranwanlenau 92 19 37 S 22 49 E
Raohe 76 46 47N 134 0 E
Raon l'Étape 19 48 24N 6 50 E
Raoui, Erg er 82 29 0N 2 0W
Rapa Iti 95 27 35 S 144 20W
Rapallo 38 44 21N 9 12 E
Rapang 73 3 45 S 119 55 E
Rāpch 65 25 40N 59 15 E
Rapid → 108 59 15N 129 5W
Rapid City 116 44 0N 103 0W
Rapid River 114 45 55N 87 0W
Rapides des Joachims 106 46 13N 77 43W
Rapla 54 59 1N 24 52 E
Rarotonga 95 21 30 S 160 0W
Ra's al Khaymah 65 25 50N 56 5 E
Ra's al-Unuf 83 30 25N 18 15 E
Ras Bânâs 81 23 57N 35 59 E
Ras Dashen 87 13 8N 38 26 E
Ras el Ma 82 34 26N 0 50W
Ras Mallap 86 29 18N 32 50 E
Ra's Tannūrah 64 26 40N 50 10 E
Râs Timirist 84 19 21N 16 30W
Rasa, Punta 128 40 50 S 62 15W
Raseiniai 54 55 25N 23 5 E
Rashad 87 11 55N 31 0 E
Rashīd 86 31 21N 30 22 E
Rashīd, Masabb 86 31 22N 30 17 E
Rasht 64 37 20N 49 40 E
Rasipuram 70 11 30N 78 15 E
Raška 42 43 19N 20 39 E
Rason, L. 96 28 45 S 124 25 E
Rașova 46 44 15N 27 55 E
Rasovo 43 43 42N 23 17 E
Rasra 69 25 50N 83 50 E
Rass el Oued 83 35 57N 5 2 E
Rasskazovo 55 52 35N 41 50 E
Rastatt 25 48 50N 8 12 E
Rastu 46 43 53N 23 16 E
Raszków 28 51 43N 17 40 E
Rat Buri 71 13 30N 99 54 E
Rat Is. 104 51 50N 178 15 E
Rat River 108 61 7N 112 36W
Ratangarh 68 28 5N 74 35 E
Rath 69 25 36N 79 37 E
Rath Luirc (Charleville) 15 52 21N 8 40W
Rathdrum, Ireland 15 52 57N 6 13W
Rathdrum, U.S.A. 118 47 50N 116 58W
Rathenow 24 52 38N 12 23 E
Rathkeale 15 52 32N 8 57W
Rathlin I. 15 55 18N 6 14W
Rathlin O'Birne I. 15 54 40N 8 50W
Ratibor = Racibórz 27 50 7N 18 18 E
Rätikon 26 47 0N 9 55 E
Ratlam 68 23 20N 75 0 E
Ratnagiri 70 16 57N 73 18 E
Ratnapura 70 6 40N 80 20 E
Raton 117 37 0N 104 30W
Ratten 26 47 28N 15 44 E
Rattray Hd. 14 57 38N 1 50W
Rättvik 48 60 52N 15 7 E
Ratz, Mt. 108 57 23N 132 12W
Ratzeburg 24 53 41N 10 46 E
Raub 71 3 47N 101 52 E
Rauch 124 36 45 S 59 5W
Raufarhöfn 50 66 27N 15 57W
Raufoss 47 60 44N 10 37 E
Raukumara Ra. 101 38 5 S 177 55 E
Rauland 47 59 43N 8 0 E
Rauma 51 61 10N 21 30 E
Rauma → 47 62 34N 7 43 E
Raundal 47 60 40N 6 37 E
Raung 73 8 5 S 114 4 E
Raurkela 69 22 14N 84 50 E
Rava Russkaya 54 50 15N 23 42 E
Ravanusa 40 37 16N 13 58 E
Rāvar 65 31 20N 56 51 E
Ravena 113 42 28N 73 49W
Ravenna, Italy 39 44 28N 12 15 E
Ravenna, Nebr., U.S.A. 116 41 3N 98 58W
Ravenna, Ohio, U.S.A. 112 41 11N 81 15W
Ravensburg 25 47 48N 9 38 E
Ravenshoe 97 17 37 S 145 29 E
Ravensthorpe 96 33 35 S 120 2 E
Ravenswood, Austral. 98 20 6 S 146 54 E
Ravenswood, U.S.A. 114 38 58N 81 47W
Ravi → 68 30 35N 71 49 E
Ravna Gora 39 45 24N 14 50 E
Ravna Reka 42 43 59N 21 35 E
Rawa Mazowiecka 28 51 46N 20 12 E
Rawalpindi 66 33 38N 73 8 E
Rawāndūz 64 36 40N 44 30 E
Rawang 71 3 20N 101 35 E
Rawdon 106 46 3N 73 40W
Rawene 101 35 25 S 173 32 E
Rawicz 28 51 36N 16 52 E
Rawka → 28 52 9N 20 8 E
Rawlinna 96 30 58 S 125 28 E
Rawlins 118 41 50N 107 20W
Rawlinson Range 96 24 40 S 128 30 E
Rawson 128 43 15 S 65 0W
Ray 116 48 21N 103 6W
Ray, C. 107 47 33N 59 15W
Rayachoti 70 14 4N 78 50 E
Rayadrug 70 14 40N 76 50 E
Rayagada 70 19 15N 83 20 E
Raychikhinsk 59 49 46N 129 25 E
Raymond, Can. 108 49 30N 112 35W
Raymond, U.S.A. 118 46 45N 123 48W
Raymondville 117 26 30N 97 50W
Raymore 109 51 25N 104 31W
Rayne 117 30 16N 92 16W
Rayong 71 12 40N 101 20 E
Rayville 117 32 30N 91 45W
Raz, Pte. du 18 48 2N 4 47W
Ražana 42 44 6N 19 55 E
Ražanj 42 43 40N 21 31 E
Razdelna 43 43 13N 27 41 E
Razdel'naya 56 46 50N 30 2 E
Razdolnoye 56 45 46N 33 29 E
Razelm, Lacul 46 44 50N 29 0 E
Razgrad 43 43 33N 26 34 E
Razlog 43 41 53N 23 28 E
Razmak 68 32 45N 69 50 E
Razole 70 16 36N 81 48 E
Ré, Île de 20 46 12N 1 30W
Reading, U.K. 13 51 27N 0 57W
Reading, U.S.A. 114 40 20N 75 53W
Realicó 124 35 0 S 64 15W
Réalmont 20 43 48N 2 10 E
Ream 71 10 34N 103 39 E
Rebais 19 48 50N 3 10 E
Rebi 73 6 23 S 134 7 E
Rebiana 81 24 12N 22 10 E
Rebun-Tō 74 45 23N 141 2 E
Recanati 39 43 24N 13 32 E
Recaş 42 45 46N 21 30 E
Recherche, Arch. of the 96 34 15 S 122 50 E
Rechitsa 54 52 13N 30 15 E
Recife 127 8 0 S 35 0W
Recklinghausen 24 51 36N 7 10 E
Reconquista 124 29 10 S 59 45W
Recreo 124 29 25 S 65 10W
Recz 28 53 16N 15 31 E
Red →, Can. 109 50 24N 96 48W
Red →, Minn., U.S.A. 116 48 10N 97 0W
Red →, Tex., U.S.A. 117 31 0N 91 40W
Red Bank 113 40 21N 74 4W
Red Bay 107 51 44N 56 25W
Red Bluff 118 40 11N 122 11W
Red Bluff L. 117 31 59N 103 58W
Red Cloud 116 40 8N 98 33W
Red Deer 108 52 20N 113 50W
Red Deer →, Alta., Can. 109 50 58N 110 0W
Red Deer →, Man., Can. 109 52 53N 101 1W
Red Deer L. 109 52 55N 101 20W
Red Indian L. 107 48 35N 57 0W
Red Lake 109 51 3N 93 49W
Red Lake Falls 116 47 54N 96 15W
Red Lodge 118 45 10N 109 10W
Red Oak 116 41 0N 95 10W
Red Rock 106 48 55N 88 15W
Red Rock, L. 116 41 30N 93 15W

Red Sea Röbel

Red Sea 63 25 0N 36 0 E
Red Sucker L 109 54 9N 93 40W
Red Tower Pass = Turnu Rosu P. 46 45 33N 24 17 E
Red Wing 116 44 32N 92 35W
Reda 28 54 40N 18 19 E
Redbridge 13 51 35N 0 7 E
Redcar 12 54 37N 1 4W
Redcliff 109 50 10N 110 50W
Redcliffe 99 27 12 S 153 0 E
Reddersburg 92 29 41 S 26 10 E
Redding 118 40 30N 122 25W
Redditch 13 52 18N 1 57W
Redfield 116 45 0N 98 30W
Redknife → 108 61 14N 119 22W
Redlands 119 34 0N 117 11W
Redmond 118 44 19N 121 11W
Redon 18 47 40N 2 6W
Redonda 121 16 58N 62 19W
Redondela 30 42 15N 8 38W
Redondo 31 38 39N 7 37W
Redondo Beach 119 33 52N 118 26W
Redrock Pt. 108 62 11N 115 2W
Redruth 13 50 14N 5 14W
Redvers 109 49 35N 101 40W
Redwater 108 53 55N 113 6W
Redwood 113 44 18N 75 48W
Redwood City 119 37 30N 122 15W
Redwood Falls 116 44 30N 95 2W
Ree, L. 15 53 35N 8 0W
Reed City 114 43 52N 85 30W
Reed, L 109 54 38N 100 30W
Reeder 116 46 7N 102 52W
Reedley 119 36 36N 119 27W
Reedsburg 116 43 34N 90 5W
Reedsport 118 43 45N 124 4W
Reefton 101 42 6 S 171 51 E
Reftele 49 57 11N 13 35 E
Refugio 117 28 18N 97 17W
Rega → 28 54 10N 15 18 E
Regalbuto 41 37 40N 14 38 E
Regavim 62 32 32N 35 2 E
Regen 25 48 58N 13 9 E
Regen → 25 49 2N 12 6 E
Regensburg 25 49 1N 12 7 E
Réggio di Calábria 41 38 7N 15 38 E
Réggio nell' Emilia 38 44 42N 10 38 E
Regina 109 50 27N 104 35W
Registro 125 24 29 S 47 49W
Reguengos de Monsaraz 31 38 25N 7 32W
Rehar → 69 23 55N 82 40 E
Rehoboth 92 23 15 S 17 4 E
Rehovot 62 31 54N 34 48 E
Rei-Bouba 81 8 40N 14 15 E
Reichenbach 24 50 36N 12 19 E
Reid River 98 19 40 S 146 48 E
Reidsville 115 36 21N 79 40W
Reigate 13 51 14N 0 11W
Reillo 32 39 54N 1 53W
Reims 19 49 15N 4 0 E
Reina 62 32 43N 35 18 E
Reina Adelaida, Arch. 128 52 20 S 74 0W
Reinbeck 116 42 18N 92 0W
Reindeer → 109 55 36N 103 11W
Reindeer I. 109 52 30N 98 0W
Reindeer L. 109 57 15N 102 15W
Reine, La 32 48 50N 79 30W
Reinga, C. 101 34 25 S 172 43 E
Reinosa 30 43 2N 4 15W
Reinosa, Paso 30 42 56N 4 10W
Reitz 93 27 48 S 28 29 E
Reivilo 92 27 36 S 24 8 E
Rejmyra 49 58 50N 15 55 E
Rejowiec Fabryczny 28 51 5N 23 17 E
Reka → 39 45 40N 14 0 E
Rekinniki 59 60 51N 163 40 E
Rekovac 42 43 51N 21 3 E
Reliance 109 63 0N 109 20W
Remad, Oued → 82 33 28N 1 20W
Rémalard 18 48 26N 0 47 E
Remanso 127 9 41 S 42 4W
Remarkable, Mt. 99 32 48 S 138 10 E
Rembang 73 6 42 S 111 21 E
Remchi 82 35 2N 1 26W
Remeshk 65 26 55N 58 50 E
Remetea 46 46 45N 25 29 E
Remich 16 49 32N 6 22 E
Remiremont 19 48 0N 6 36 E
Remo 87 6 48N 41 20 E
Remontnoye 57 46 34N 43 37 E
Remoulins 21 43 55N 4 35 E
Remscheid 24 51 11N 7 12 E
Rena 47 61 8N 11 20 E
Rena → 47 61 8N 11 23 E
Rende 41 39 19N 16 11 E
Rendina 45 39 4N 21 58 E
Rendsburg 24 54 18N 9 41 E
Rene 59 66 2N 179 25W
Renfrew, Can. 106 45 30N 76 40W
Renfrew, U.K. 14 55 52N 4 24W
Rengat 72 0 30 S 102 45 E
Rengo 124 34 24 S 70 50W
Renhuai 77 27 48N 106 24 E
Reni 56 45 28N 28 15 E
Renigunta 70 13 38N 79 30 E
Renk 81 11 50N 32 50 E
Renkum 16 51 58N 5 43 E
Renmark 97 34 11 S 140 43 E
Rennell Sd. 108 53 23N 132 35W
Renner Springs T.O. 96 18 20 S 133 47 E
Rennes 18 48 7N 1 41W
Rennes, Bassin de 18 48 12N 1 33W
Rennesøy 47 59 6N 5 43 E
Reno 118 39 30N 119 50W
Reno → 39 44 37N 12 17 E
Renovo 114 41 20N 77 47W
Rensselaer, Ind., U.S.A. 114 40 57N 87 10W
Rensselaer, N.Y., U.S.A. 113 42 38N 73 41W
Rentería 32 43 19N 1 54W
Renton 118 47 30N 122 9W
Réo 84 12 28N 2 35W
Réole, La 20 44 35N 0 1W
Reotipur 69 25 33N 83 45 E
Repalle 70 16 2N 80 45 E
Répcelak 27 47 24N 17 1 E
Republic, Mich., U.S.A. 114 46 25N 87 59W
Republic, Wash., U.S.A. 118 48 38N 118 42W
Republican → 116 39 3N 96 48W
Republican City 116 40 9N 99 20W
Repulse B., Antarct. 5 64 30 S 99 30 E
Repulse B., Austral. 97 20 31 S 148 45 E
Repulse Bay 105 66 30N 86 30W
Requena, Peru 126 5 5 S 73 52W
Requena, Spain 33 39 30N 1 4W
Resele 48 63 20N 17 5 E
Resen 42 41 5N 21 0 E
Reserve, Can. 109 52 28N 102 39W
Reserve, U.S.A. 119 33 50N 108 54W
Resht = Rasht 64 37 20N 49 40 E
Resistencia 124 27 30 S 59 0W
Reşiţa 42 45 18N 21 53 E
Resko 28 53 47N 15 25 E
Resolution I., Can. 105 61 30N 65 0W
Resolution I., N.Z. 101 45 40 S 166 40 E
Ressano Garcia 93 25 25 S 32 0 E
Reston 109 49 33N 101 6W
Reszel 28 54 4N 21 10 E
Retalhuleu 120 14 33N 91 46W
Reteag 46 47 10N 24 0 E
Retenue, Lac de 91 11 0 S 27 0 E
Rethel 19 49 30N 4 20 E
Rethem 24 52 47N 9 25 E
Réthimnon 45 35 18N 24 30 E
Réthimnon □ 45 35 23N 24 28 E
Rétiers 18 47 55N 1 25W
Retortillo 30 40 48N 6 21W
Rétság 27 47 58N 19 10 E
Réunion 3 22 0 S 56 0 E
Reus 32 41 10N 1 5 E
Reuss → 25 47 16N 8 24 E
Reuterstadt Stavenhagen 24 53 41N 12 54 E
Reutlingen 25 48 28N 9 13 E
Reutte 26 47 29N 10 42 E
Reval = Tallinn 54 59 29N 24 58 E
Revda 52 56 48N 59 57 E
Revel 20 43 28N 2 0 E
Revelganj 69 25 50N 84 40 E
Revelstoke 108 51 0N 118 10W
Reventazón 126 6 10 S 81 0W
Revigny 19 48 50N 5 0 E
Revilla Gigedo, Is. 95 18 40N 112 0W
Revillagigedo I. 108 55 50N 131 20W
Revin 19 49 55N 4 39 E
Revuè → 91 19 50 S 34 0 E
Rewa 69 24 33N 81 25 E
Rewari 68 28 15N 76 40 E
Rexburg 118 43 55N 111 50W
Rey Malabo 88 3 45N 8 50 E
Rey, Rio del → 85 4 30N 8 48 E
Reykjahlið 50 65 40N 16 55W
Reykjanes 50 63 48N 22 40W
Reykjavík 50 64 10N 21 57 E
Reynolds 109 49 40N 95 55W
Reynolds Ra. 96 22 30 S 133 0 E
Reynoldsville 112 41 5N 78 58W
Reynosa 120 26 5N 98 18W
Rezā'īyeh 64 37 40N 45 0 E
Rezā'īyeh, Daryācheh-ye 64 37 50N 45 30 E
Rezekne 54 56 30N 27 17 E
Rezovo 43 42 0N 28 0 E
Rgotina 42 44 1N 22 17 E
Rhamnus 45 38 12N 24 3 E
Rharis, O. → 83 26 0N 5 4 E
Rhayader 13 52 19N 3 30W
Rheden 16 52 0N 6 3 E
Rhein 109 51 25N 102 15W
Rhein → 24 51 52N 6 20 E
Rhein-Main-Donau-Kanal 25 49 1N 11 27 E
Rheinbach 24 50 38N 6 54 E
Rheine 24 52 17N 7 25 E
Rheinland-Pfalz □ 25 50 0N 7 0 E
Rheinsberg 24 53 6N 12 52 E
Rheriss, Oued → 82 30 50N 4 34W
Rheydt 24 51 10N 6 24 E
Rhin = Rhein → 24 51 52N 6 20 E
Rhinau 19 48 19N 7 43 E
Rhine = Rhein → 24 51 52N 6 20 E
Rhinelander 116 45 38N 89 29W
Rhino Camp 90 3 0N 31 22 E
Rhir, Cap 82 30 38N 9 54W
Rho 38 45 31N 9 2 E
Rhode Island □ 114 41 38N 71 37W
Rhodes = Ródhos 45 36 15N 28 10 E
Rhodes' Tomb 91 20 30 S 28 30 E
Rhodesia = Zimbabwe ■ 91 20 0 S 30 0 E
Rhodope Mts. = Rhodopi Planina 43 41 40N 24 20 E
Rhodopi Planina 43 41 40N 24 20 E
Rhondda 13 51 39N 3 30W
Rhône □ 21 45 54N 4 35 E
Rhône → 21 43 28N 4 42 E
Rhum 14 57 0N 6 20W
Rhumney 13 51 32N 3 7W
Rhyl 12 53 19N 3 29W
Ri-Aba 85 3 28N 8 40 E
Riachão 127 7 20 S 46 37W
Riaño 30 42 59N 5 0W
Rians 21 43 37N 5 44 E
Riansares → 32 39 32N 3 18W
Riasi 69 33 10N 74 50 E
Riau □ 72 0 0 102 35 E
Riau, Kepulauan 72 0 30N 104 20 E
Riaza 32 41 18N 3 30W
Riaza → 32 41 42N 3 55W
Riba de Saelices 32 40 55N 2 17W
Ribadavia 30 42 17N 8 8W
Ribadeo 30 43 35N 7 5W
Ribadesella 30 43 30N 5 7W
Ribas 32 42 19N 2 15 E
Ribble → 12 54 13N 2 20W
Ribe 49 55 19N 8 44 E
Ribeauvillé 19 48 10N 7 20 E
Ribécourt 19 49 30N 2 55 E
Ribeira 30 42 36N 8 58W
Ribeirão Prêto 125 21 10 S 47 50W
Ribemont 19 49 47N 3 27 E
Ribera 40 37 30N 13 13 E
Ribérac 20 45 15N 0 20 E
Riberalta 126 11 0 S 66 0W
Ribnica 39 45 45N 14 45 E
Ribnitz-Damgarten 24 54 14N 12 24 E
Ričany 26 50 0N 14 40 E
Riccarton 101 43 32 S 172 37 E
Riccia 41 41 30N 14 50 E
Riccione 39 44 0N 12 39 E
Rice L. 112 44 12N 78 10W
Rice Lake 116 45 30N 91 42W
Riceys, Les 19 47 59N 4 22 E
Rich 82 32 16N 4 30W
Rich Hill 117 38 5N 94 22W
Richards Bay 93 28 48 S 32 6 E
Richards L. 109 59 10N 107 10W
Richardson → 109 58 25N 111 14W
Richardton 116 46 56N 102 22W
Richelieu 18 47 0N 0 20 E
Richey 116 47 42N 105 5W
Richfield, Idaho, U.S.A. 118 43 2N 114 5W
Richfield, Utah, U.S.A. 119 38 50N 112 0W
Richford 113 45 0N 72 40W
Richibucto 107 46 42N 64 54W
Richland, Ga., U.S.A. 115 32 7N 84 40W
Richland, Oreg., U.S.A. 118 44 49N 117 9W
Richland, Wash., U.S.A. 118 46 15N 119 15W
Richland Center 116 43 21N 90 22W
Richlands 114 37 7N 81 49W
Richmond, N.S.W., Austral. 100 33 35 S 150 42 E
Richmond, Queens., Austral. 97 20 43 S 143 8 E
Richmond, N.Z. 101 41 20 S 173 12 E
Richmond, S. Afr. 93 29 51 S 30 18 E
Richmond, N. Yorks., U.K. 12 54 24N 1 43W
Richmond, Surrey, U.K. 13 51 28N 0 18W
Richmond, Calif., U.S.A. 118 37 58N 122 21W
Richmond, Ind., U.S.A. 114 39 50N 84 50W
Richmond, Ky., U.S.A. 114 37 40N 84 20W
Richmond, Mich., U.S.A. 112 42 47N 82 45W
Richmond, Mo., U.S.A. 116 39 15N 93 58W
Richmond, Tex., U.S.A. 117 29 32N 95 42W
Richmond, Utah, U.S.A. 118 41 55N 111 48W
Richmond, Va., U.S.A. 114 37 33N 77 27W
Richmond, Ra. 99 29 0 S 152 45 E
Richton 115 31 23N 88 58W
Richwood 114 38 17N 80 32W
Ricla 32 41 31N 1 24W
Riddarhyttan 48 59 49N 15 33 E
Ridgedale 109 53 0N 104 10W
Ridgeland 115 32 30N 80 58W
Ridgelands 98 23 16 S 150 17 E
Ridgetown 106 42 26N 81 52W
Ridgewood 113 40 59N 74 7W
Ridgway 114 41 25N 78 43W
Riding Mt. Nat. Park 109 50 50N 100 0W
Ried 26 48 14N 13 30 E
Riedlingen 25 48 9N 9 28 E
Rienza → 39 46 49N 11 47 E
Riesa 24 51 19N 13 19 E
Riesi 41 37 16N 14 4 E
Rieti 39 42 23N 12 50 E
Rieupeyroux 20 44 19N 2 12 E
Riez 21 43 49N 6 6 E
Rifle 118 39 40N 107 50W
Rifstangi 50 66 32N 16 12W
Rift Valley □ 90 0 20N 36 0 E
Rig Rig 81 14 13N 14 25 E
Riga 54 56 53N 24 8 E
Riga, G. of = Rīgas Jūras Līcis 54 57 40N 23 45 E
Rīgas Jūras Līcis 54 57 40N 23 45 E
Rigaud 113 45 29N 74 18W
Rigby 118 43 41N 111 58W
Rīgestān □ 65 30 15N 65 0 E
Riggins 118 45 29N 116 26W
Rignac 20 44 25N 2 16 E
Rigolet 107 54 10N 58 23W
Riihimäki 51 60 45N 24 48 E
Riiser-Larsen-halvøya 5 68 0 S 35 0 E
Rijau 85 11 8N 5 17 E
Rijeka 39 45 20N 14 21 E
Rijeka Crnojevica 42 42 24N 19 1 E
Rijn → 16 52 12N 4 21 E
Rijssen 16 52 19N 6 30 E
Rijswijk 16 52 4N 4 22 E
Rike 87 10 50N 39 53 E
Rila 43 42 7N 23 7 E
Rila Planina 42 42 10N 23 0 E
Riley 118 43 35N 119 33W
Rilly 19 49 11N 4 3 E
Rima → 85 13 4N 5 10 E
Rimah, Wadi ar → 64 26 5N 41 30 E
Rimavská Sobota 27 48 22N 20 2 E
Rimbey 108 52 35N 114 15W
Rimbo 48 59 44N 18 21 E
Rimforsa 49 58 6N 15 43 E
Rimi 85 12 58N 7 43 E
Rímini 39 44 3N 12 33 E
Rîmna → 46 45 36N 27 3 E
Rîmnicu Sărat 46 45 26N 27 3 E
Rîmnicu Vîlcea 46 45 9N 24 21 E
Rimouski 107 48 27N 68 30W
Rinca 73 8 45 S 119 35 E
Rinconada 124 22 26 S 66 10W
Rineanna 15 52 42N 8 57W
Ringarum 49 58 21N 16 26 E
Ringe 49 55 13N 10 28 E
Ringim 85 12 13N 9 10 E
Ringkøbing 49 56 5N 8 15 E
Ringling 118 46 16N 110 56W
Ringsaker 47 60 54N 10 45 E
Ringsjön 49 55 55N 13 30 E
Ringsted 49 55 25N 11 46 E
Ringvassøy 50 69 56N 19 15 E
Rinía 45 37 23N 25 13 E
Rinjani 72 8 24 S 116 28 E
Rinteln 24 52 11N 9 3 E
Rio Branco 126 9 58 S 67 49W
Río Branco 125 32 40 S 53 40W
Rio Brilhante 125 21 48 S 54 33W
Rio Claro, Brazil 125 22 19 S 47 35W
Rio Claro, Trin. 121 10 20N 61 25W
Río Colorado 128 39 0 S 64 0W
Río Cuarto 124 33 10 S 64 25W
Rio das Pedras 93 23 8 S 35 28 E
Rio de Janeiro 125 23 0 S 43 12W
Rio de Janeiro □ 125 22 50 S 43 0W
Rio do Sul 125 27 13 S 49 37W
Río Gallegos 128 51 35 S 69 15W
Río Grande 128 53 50 S 67 45W
Rio Grande 125 32 0 S 52 20W
Rio Grande → 117 25 57N 97 9W
Rio Grande City 117 26 23N 98 49W
Río Grande del Norte → 110 26 0N 97 0W
Rio Grande do Norte □ 127 5 40 S 36 0W
Rio Grande do Sul □ 125 30 0 S 53 0W
Rio Largo 127 9 28 S 35 50W
Rio Maior 31 39 19N 8 57W
Rio Marina 38 42 48N 10 25 E
Rio Mulatos 126 19 40 S 66 50W
Río Muni □ 88 1 30N 10 0 E
Rio Negro 125 26 0 S 50 0W
Rio Pardo 125 30 0 S 52 30W
Río, Punta del 33 36 49N 2 24W
Río Segundo 124 31 40 S 63 59W
Río Tercero 124 32 15 S 64 8W
Rio Tinto 30 41 11N 8 34W
Rio Verde 127 17 50 S 51 0W
Río Verde 120 21 56N 99 59W
Rio Vista 118 38 11N 121 44W
Ríobamba 126 1 50 S 78 45W
Ríohacha 126 11 33N 72 55W
Rioja, La, Argent. 124 29 20 S 67 0W
Rioja, La, Spain 32 42 20N 2 20W
Rioja, La □ 124 29 30 S 67 0W
Riom 20 45 54N 3 7 E
Riom-ès-Montagnes 20 45 17N 2 39 E
Rion-des-Landes 20 43 55N 0 56W
Rionero in Vúlture 41 40 55N 15 40 E
Rioni → 57 42 5N 41 50 E
Rios 30 41 58N 7 16W
Riosucio 126 5 30N 75 40W
Riosucio 126 7 27N 77 7W
Riou L. 109 59 7N 106 25W
Rioz 19 47 25N 6 04 E
Riparia, Dora → 38 45 7N 7 24 E
Ripatransone 39 43 0N 13 45 E
Ripley, Can. 112 44 4N 81 35W
Ripley, N.Y., U.S.A. 112 42 16N 79 44W
Ripley, Tenn., U.S.A. 117 35 43N 89 34W
Ripoll 32 42 15N 2 13 E
Ripon, U.K. 12 54 8N 1 31W
Ripon, U.S.A. 114 43 51N 88 50W
Riposto 41 37 44N 15 12 E
Risan 42 42 32N 18 42 E
Riscle 20 43 39N 0 5W
Rishiri-Tō, Japan 74 45 11N 141 15 E
Rishiri-Tō, Japan 74 45 11N 141 15 E
Rishon le Ziyyon 62 31 58N 34 48 E
Rishpon 62 32 12N 34 49 E
Risle → 18 49 26N 0 23 E
Rîsnov 46 45 35N 25 27 E
Rison 117 33 57N 92 11W
Risør 47 58 43N 9 13 E
Ritchies Archipelago 71 12 5N 94 0 E
Riti 85 7 57N 9 41 E
Rittman 112 40 57N 81 48W
Ritzville 118 47 10N 118 21W
Riva Bella 18 49 17N 0 18W
Riva del Garda 38 45 53N 10 50 E
Rivadavia, Buenos Aires, Argent. 124 35 29 S 62 59W
Rivadavia, Mendoza, Argent. 124 33 13 S 68 30W
Rivadavia, Salta, Argent. 124 24 5 S 62 54W
Rivadavia, Chile 124 29 57 S 70 35W
Rivarolo Canavese 38 45 20N 7 42 E
Rivas 121 11 30N 85 50W
Rive-de-Gier 21 45 32N 4 37 E
River Cess 84 5 30N 9 32W
Rivera 125 31 0 S 55 50W
Riverdsale 92 34 7 S 21 15 E
Riverhead 114 40 53N 72 40W
Riverhurst 109 50 55N 106 50W
Riverina 97 35 30 S 145 20 E
Rivers 109 50 2N 100 14W
Rivers □ 85 5 0N 6 30 E
Rivers Inl. 108 51 40N 127 20W
Rivers, L. of the 109 49 49N 105 44W
Riverside, Calif., U.S.A. 119 34 0N 117 22W
Riverside, Wyo., U.S.A. 118 41 12N 106 57W
Riversleigh 98 19 5 S 138 40 E
Riverton, Austral. 99 34 10 S 138 46 E
Riverton, Can. 109 51 1N 97 0W
Riverton, N.Z. 101 46 21 S 168 0 E
Riverton, U.S.A. 118 43 1N 108 27W
Rives 21 45 21N 5 31 E
Rivesaltes 20 42 47N 2 50 E
Riviera 38 44 0N 8 30 E
Riviera di Levante 36 44 23N 9 15 E
Riviera di Ponente 36 43 50N 7 58 E
Rivière-à-Pierre 107 46 59N 72 11W
Rivière-au-Renard 107 48 59N 64 23W
Rivière-du-Loup 107 47 50N 69 30W
Rivière-Pentecôte 107 49 57N 67 1W
Rívoli 38 45 3N 7 31 E
Rivoli B. 99 37 32 S 140 3 E
Riyadh = Ar Riyāḍ 64 24 41N 46 42 E
Rize 64 41 0N 40 30 E
Rizhao 77 35 25N 119 30 E
Rizzuto, C. 41 38 54N 17 5 E
Rjukan 47 59 54N 8 33 E
Rjuven 47 59 9N 7 8 E
Roa, Norway 47 60 17N 10 37 E
Roa, Spain 30 41 41N 3 56W
Roag, L. 14 58 10N 6 55W
Roanne 21 46 3N 4 4 E
Roanoke, Ala., U.S.A. 115 33 9N 85 23W
Roanoke, Va., U.S.A. 114 37 19N 79 55W
Roanoke → 115 35 56N 76 43W
Roanoke I. 115 35 55N 75 40W
Roanoke Rapids 115 36 28N 77 42W
Roatán 121 16 18N 86 35W
Robbins I. 99 40 42 S 145 0 E
Robe → 15 53 38N 9 10W
Robe, Mt. 100 31 40 S 141 20 E
Röbel 24 53 24N 12 37 E

Robert Lee Rujen

Robert Lee 117 31 55N 100 26W
Roberts 118 43 44N 112 8W
Robertsganj 69 24 44N 83 4 E
Robertson 92 33 46 S 19 50 E
Robertson I. 5 65 15 S 59 30W
Robertsport 84 6 45N 11 26W
Robertstown 99 33 58 S 139 5 E
Roberval 107 48 32N 72 15W
Robeson Ch. 4 82 0N 61 30W
Robinson Crusoe I. 95 33 38 S 78 52W
Robinson Ranges 96 25 40 S 119 0 E
Robinvale 99 34 40 S 142 45 E
Robla, La 30 42 50N 5 41W
Roblin 109 51 14N 101 21W
Roboré 126 18 10 S 59 45W
Robson, Mt. 108 53 10N 119 10W
Robstown 117 27 47N 97 40W
Roc, Pointe du 18 48 50N 1 37W
Roca, C. da 31 38 40N 9 31W
Rocas, I. 127 4 0 S 34 1W
Rocca d'Aspidé 41 40 27N 15 10 E
Rocca San Casciano 39 44 3N 11 45 E
Roccalbegna 39 42 47N 11 30 E
Roccastrada 39 43 0N 11 10 E
Roccella Iónica 41 38 20N 16 24 E
Rocha 125 34 30 S 54 25W
Rochdale 12 53 36N 2 10W
Roche-Bernard, La 18 47 31N 2 19W
Roche-Canillac, La 20 45 12N 1 57 E
Roche, La 21 46 4N 6 19 E
Roche-sur-Yon, La 18 46 40N 1 25W
Rochechouart 20 45 50N 0 49 E
Rochefort, Belg. 16 50 9N 5 12 E
Rochefort, France 20 45 56N 0 57W
Rochefort-en-Terre 18 47 42N 2 22W
Rochefoucauld, La 20 45 44N 0 24 E
Rochelle 116 41 55N 89 5W
Rochelle, La 20 46 10N 1 9W
Rocher River 108 61 23N 112 44W
Rocheservière 18 46 57N 1 30W
Rochester, Austral. 100 36 22 S 144 41 E
Rochester, Can. 108 54 22N 113 27W
Rochester, U.K. 13 51 22N 0 30 E
Rochester, Ind., U.S.A. 114 41 5N 86 15W
Rochester, Minn., U.S.A. 116 44 1N 92 28W
Rochester, N.H., U.S.A. 114 43 19N 70 57W
Rochester, N.Y., U.S.A. 114 43 10N 77 40W
Rochester, Pa., U.S.A. 112 40 41N 80 17W
Rociana 31 37 19N 6 35W
Rociu 46 44 43N 25 2 E
Rock → 108 60 7N 127 7W
Rock Hill 115 34 55N 81 2W
Rock Island 116 41 30N 90 35W
Rock Port 116 40 26N 95 30W
Rock Rapids 116 43 25N 96 10W
Rock River 118 41 49N 106 0W
Rock Sound 121 24 54N 76 12W
Rock Sprs., Ariz., U.S.A. 119 34 2N 112 11W
Rock Sprs., Mont., U.S.A. 118 46 55N 106 11W
Rock Sprs., Tex., U.S.A. 117 30 2N 100 11W
Rock Sprs., Wyo., U.S.A. 118 41 40N 109 10W
Rock Valley 116 43 10N 96 17W
Rockall 8 57 37N 13 42W
Rockdale 117 30 40N 97 0W
Rockefeller Plat. 5 80 0 S 140 0W
Rockford 116 42 20N 89 0W
Rockglen 109 49 11N 105 57W
Rockhampton 97 23 22 S 150 32 E
Rockingham B. 98 18 5 S 146 10 E
Rockingham Forest 13 52 28N 0 42W
Rocklake 116 48 50N 99 13W
Rockland, Can. 113 45 33N 75 17W
Rockland, Idaho, U.S.A. 118 42 37N 112 57W
Rockland, Me., U.S.A. 107 44 6N 69 6W
Rockland, Mich., U.S.A. 116 46 40N 89 10W
Rocklands Reservoir 100 37 15 S 142 5 E
Rockmart 115 34 1N 85 2W
Rockport 117 28 2N 97 3W
Rockville, Conn., U.S.A. 113 41 51N 72 27W
Rockville, Md., U.S.A. 114 39 7N 77 10W
Rockwall 117 32 55N 96 30W
Rockwell City 116 42 20N 94 35W
Rockwood 115 35 52N 84 40W
Rocky Ford 116 38 7N 103 45W
Rocky Lane 108 58 31N 116 22W
Rocky Mount 115 35 55N 77 48W
Rocky Mountain House 108 52 22N 114 55W
Rocky Mts. 108 55 0N 121 0W
Rocky Pt. 96 33 30 S 123 57 E
Rocky River 112 41 30N 81 40W
Rockyford 108 51 14N 113 10W
Rocroi 19 49 55N 4 30 E
Rod 66 28 10N 63 5 E
Roda, La, Albacete, Spain 33 39 13N 2 15W
Roda, La, Sevilla, Spain 31 37 12N 4 46W
Rødberg 47 60 17N 8 56 E
Rødby 49 54 41N 11 23 E
Rødbyhavn 49 54 39N 11 22 E
Roddickton 107 50 51N 56 8W
Rødding 49 55 23N 9 3 E
Rødekro 49 55 4N 9 20 E
Rødenes 47 59 35N 11 34 E
Rodenkirchen 24 53 24N 8 26 E
Roderick I. 108 52 38N 128 22W
Rodez 20 44 21N 2 33 E
Rodholívas 44 40 55N 24 0 E
Rodhópi □ 44 41 5N 25 30 E
Ródhos 45 36 15N 28 10 E
Rodi Garganico 41 41 55N 15 53 E
Rodna 46 47 25N 24 50 E
Rodnei, Munţii 46 47 35N 24 35 E
Rodney 112 42 34N 81 41W
Rodney, C. 101 36 17 S 174 50 E
Rodniki 55 57 7N 41 47 E
Rodriguez 3 19 45 S 63 20 E
Rodstock, C. 96 33 12 S 134 20 E
Roe → 15 55 10N 6 59W
Roebling 113 40 7N 74 45W
Roebourne 96 20 44 S 117 9 E
Roebuck B. 96 18 5 S 122 20 E
Roermond 16 51 12N 6 0 E
Roes Welcome Sd. 105 65 0N 87 0W
Roeselare 16 50 57N 3 7 E
Rogachev 54 53 8N 30 5 E
Rogaçica 42 44 4N 19 40 E
Rogagua, L. 126 13 43 S 66 50W
Rogaland fylke □ 47 59 12N 6 20 E
Rogaška Slatina 39 46 15N 15 42 E
Rogatec 39 46 15N 15 46 E
Rogatica 42 43 47N 19 0 E
Rogatin 54 49 24N 24 36 E
Rogers 117 36 20N 94 5W
Rogers City 114 45 25N 83 49W
Rogerson 118 42 10N 114 40W
Rogersville 115 36 27N 83 1W
Roggan 106 54 25N 79 32W
Roggeveldberge 92 32 10 S 20 10 E
Roggiano Gravina 41 39 37N 16 9 E
Rogliano, France 21 42 57N 9 30 E
Rogliano, Italy 41 39 11N 16 20 E
Rogoaguado, L. 126 13 0 S 65 30W
Rogowo 28 52 43N 17 38 E
Rogozno 28 52 45N 16 59 E
Rogue → 118 42 30N 124 0W
Rohan 18 48 4N 2 45W
Rohrbach 19 49 3N 7 15 E
Rohri 68 27 45N 68 51 E
Rohri Canal 68 26 15N 68 27 E
Rohtak 68 28 55N 76 43 E
Roi Et 71 16 4N 103 40 E
Roisel 19 49 58N 3 6 E
Rojas 124 34 10 S 60 45W
Rojo, C. 120 21 33N 97 20W
Rokan → 72 2 0N 100 50 E
Rokeby 98 13 39 S 142 40 E
Rokiskis 54 55 55N 25 35 E
Rokitno 54 50 57N 35 56 E
Rokycany 26 49 43N 13 35 E
Rolândia 125 23 18 S 51 23W
Røldal 47 59 47N 6 50 E
Rolette 116 48 42N 99 50W
Rolla, Kansas, U.S.A. 117 37 10N 101 40W
Rolla, Mo., U.S.A. 117 37 56N 91 42W
Rolla, N. Dak., U.S.A. 116 48 50N 99 36W
Rollag 47 60 2N 9 18 E
Rolleston 98 24 28 S 148 35 E
Rollingstone 98 19 2 S 146 24 E
Rom 87 9 54N 32 16 E
Roma, Austral. 97 26 32 S 148 49 E
Roma, Italy 40 41 54N 12 30 E
Roman, Bulg. 43 43 8N 23 54 E
Roman, Romania 46 46 57N 26 55 E
Roman, U.S.S.R. 59 66 4N 112 14 E
Roman-Kosh, Gora 56 44 37N 34 15 E
Romana, La 121 18 27N 68 57W
Romanche → 21 45 5N 5 43 E
Romang 73 7 30 S 127 20 E
Români 86 30 59N 32 38 E
Romania ■ 46 46 0N 25 0 E
Romanija Planina 42 43 50N 18 45 E
Romano, Cayo 121 22 0N 77 30W
Romano di Lombardia 38 45 32N 9 45 E
Romanovka = Bessarabka 56 46 21N 28 58 E
Romans 21 45 3N 5 3 E
Romanshorn 25 47 33N 9 22 E
Romblon 73 12 33N 122 17 E
Rombo □ 90 3 10 S 37 30 E
Rome, Ga., U.S.A. 115 34 20N 85 0W
Rome, N.Y., U.S.A. 114 43 14N 75 29W
Rome = Roma 40 41 54N 12 30 E
Romeleåsen 49 55 34N 13 33 E
Romenay 21 46 30N 5 1 E
Romerike 47 60 7N 11 10 E
Romilly 19 48 31N 3 44 E
Romîni 46 44 59N 24 11 E
Rommani 82 33 31N 6 40W
Romney 114 39 21N 78 45W
Romney Marsh 13 51 0N 1 0 E
Romny 54 50 48N 33 28 E
Rømø 49 55 10N 8 30 E
Romodan 54 50 0N 33 15 E
Romodanovo 55 54 26N 45 23 E
Romont 25 46 42N 6 54 E
Romorantin-Lanthenay 19 47 21N 1 45 E
Romsdalen 47 62 25N 8 0 E
Rona 14 57 33N 6 0W
Ronan 118 47 30N 114 6W
Roncador, Cayos 121 13 32N 80 4W
Roncador, Serra do 127 12 30 S 52 30W
Roncesvalles, Paso 32 43 1N 1 19W
Ronceverte 114 37 45N 80 28W
Ronciglione 39 42 18N 12 12 E
Ronco → 39 44 24N 12 12 E
Ronda 31 36 46N 5 12W
Ronda, Serranía de 31 36 44N 5 3W
Rondane 47 61 57N 9 50 E
Rondônia □ 126 11 0 S 63 0W
Rondonópolis 127 16 28 S 54 38W
Rong, Koh 71 10 45N 103 15 E
Rong Xian 77 29 23N 104 22 E
Rong'an 77 25 14N 109 22 E
Ronge, L. la 109 55 6N 105 17W
Ronge, La 109 55 5N 105 20W
Rongshui 77 25 5N 109 12 E
Ronne Land 5 83 0 S 70 0W
Ronneby 49 56 12N 15 17 E
Ronse 16 50 45N 3 35 E
Roof Butte 119 36 29N 109 5W
Roorkee 68 29 52N 77 59 E
Roosendaal 16 51 32N 4 29 E
Roosevelt, Minn., U.S.A. 116 48 51N 95 2W
Roosevelt, Utah, U.S.A. 118 40 19N 110 1W
Roosevelt I. 5 79 30 S 162 0W
Roosevelt, Mt. 108 58 26N 125 20W
Roosevelt Res. 119 33 46N 111 0W
Ropczyce 27 50 4N 21 38 E
Roper → 96 14 43 S 135 27 E
Ropesville 117 33 25N 102 10W
Roque Pérez 124 35 25 S 59 24W
Roquebrou, La 20 44 58N 2 12 E
Roquefort 20 44 2N 0 20W
Roquefort-sur-Soulzon 20 43 58N 2 59 E
Roquemaure 21 44 3N 4 48 E
Roquetas 32 40 50N 0 30 E
Roquevaire 21 43 20N 5 36 E
Roraima □ 126 2 0N 61 30W
Roraima, Mt. 126 5 10N 60 40W
Rorketon 109 51 24N 99 35W
Røros 47 62 35N 11 23 E
Rorschach 25 47 28N 9 30 E
Rosa 91 9 33 S 31 15 E
Rosa, C. 83 37 0N 8 16 E
Rosa, Monte 25 45 57N 7 53 E
Rosal 30 41 57N 8 51W
Rosal de la Frontera 31 37 59N 7 13W
Rosalia 118 47 14N 117 25W
Rosans 21 44 24N 5 29 E
Rosario 124 33 0 S 60 40W
Rosário 127 3 0 S 44 15W
Rosario, Baja Calif. N., Mexico 120 30 0N 115 50W
Rosario, Durango, Mexico 120 26 30N 105 35W
Rosario, Sinaloa, Mexico 120 23 0N 105 52W
Rosario, Parag. 124 24 30 S 57 35W
Rosario de la Frontera 124 25 50 S 65 0W
Rosario de Lerma 124 24 59 S 65 35W
Rosario del Tala 124 32 20 S 59 10W
Rosário do Sul 125 30 15 S 54 55W
Rosarno 41 38 29N 15 59 E
Rosas 32 42 19N 3 10 E
Roscoe 116 45 27N 99 20W
Roscoff 18 48 44N 4 0W
Roscommon, Ireland 15 53 38N 8 11W
Roscommon, U.S.A. 114 44 27N 84 35W
Roscommon □ 15 53 40N 8 15W
Roscrea 15 52 58N 7 50W
Rose Blanche 107 47 38N 58 45W
Rose Harbour 108 52 15N 131 10W
Rose Pt. 108 54 11N 131 39W
Rose Valley 109 52 19N 103 49W
Roseau, Domin. 121 15 20N 61 24W
Roseau, U.S.A. 116 48 51N 95 46W
Rosebery 99 41 46 S 145 33 E
Rosebud, Austral. 100 38 21 S 144 54 E
Rosebud, U.S.A. 117 31 5N 97 0W
Roseburg 118 43 10N 123 20W
Rosedale, Austral. 98 24 38 S 151 53 E
Rosedale, U.S.A. 117 33 51N 91 0W
Rosemary 108 50 46N 112 5W
Rosenberg 117 29 30N 95 48W
Rosendaël 19 51 3N 2 24 E
Rosenheim 25 47 51N 12 9 E
Roseto degli Abruzzi 39 42 40N 14 2 E
Rosetown 109 51 35N 107 59W
Rosetta = Rashîd 86 31 21N 30 22 E
Roseville 118 38 46N 121 17W
Rosewood 99 27 38 S 152 36 E
Rosh Haniqra, Kefar 62 33 5N 35 5 E
Rosh Pinna 62 32 58N 35 32 E
Rosières 19 49 49N 2 43 E
Rosignano Marittimo 38 43 23N 10 28 E
Rosignol 126 6 15N 57 30W
Roşiori de Vede 46 44 9N 25 0 E
Rositsa 43 43 57N 27 57 E
Rositsa → 43 43 10N 25 30 E
Roskilde 49 55 38N 12 3 E
Roskilde Amtskommune □ 49 55 35N 12 5 E
Roskilde Fjord 49 55 50N 12 2 E
Roslavl 54 53 57N 32 55 E
Roslyn 99 34 29 S 149 37 E
Rosmaninhal 31 39 44N 7 5W
Røsnæs 49 55 44N 10 55 E
Rosolini 41 36 49N 14 58 E
Rosporden 18 47 57N 3 50W
Ross, Austral. 99 42 2 S 147 30 E
Ross, N.Z. 101 42 53 S 170 49 E
Ross Dependency □ 5 70 0 S 170 5W
Ross I. 5 77 30 S 168 0 E
Ross Ice Shelf 5 80 0 S 180 0W
Ross L. 118 48 50N 121 5W
Ross on Wye 13 51 55N 2 34W
Ross Sea 5 74 0 S 178 0 E
Rossan Pt. 15 54 42N 8 47W
Rossano Cálabro 41 39 36N 16 39 E
Rossburn 109 50 40N 100 49W
Rosseau 112 45 16N 79 39W
Rossignol, L., N.S., Can. 107 44 12N 65 10W
Rossignol, L., Qué., Can. 106 52 43N 73 40W
Rossland 108 49 6N 117 50W
Rosslare 15 52 17N 6 23W
Rosslau 24 51 52N 12 15 E
Rosso 84 16 40N 15 45W
Rossosh 57 50 15N 39 28 E
Rossport 106 48 50N 87 30W
Rossvatnet 50 65 45N 14 5 E
Rossville 98 15 48 S 145 15 E
Rosthern 109 52 40N 106 20W
Rostock 24 54 4N 12 9 E
Rostock □ 24 54 10N 12 30 E
Rostov, Don, U.S.S.R. 57 47 15N 39 45 E
Rostov, Moskva, U.S.S.R. 55 57 14N 39 25 E
Rostrenen 18 48 14N 3 21W
Roswell 117 33 26N 104 32W
Rosyth 14 56 2N 3 26W
Rota 31 36 37N 6 20W
Rotälven → 48 61 15N 14 3 E
Rotan 117 32 52N 100 30W
Rotenburg 24 53 6N 9 24 E
Roth 25 49 15N 11 6 E
Rothaargebirge 22 51 0N 8 20 E
Rothenburg ob der Tauber 25 49 21N 10 11 E
Rother → 13 50 59N 0 40 E
Rotherham 12 53 26N 1 21W
Rothes 14 57 31N 3 12W
Rothesay, Can. 107 45 23N 66 0W
Rothesay, U.K. 14 55 50N 5 3W
Roti 73 10 50 S 123 0 E
Roto 97 33 0 S 145 30 E
Rotondella 41 40 10N 16 30 E
Rotoroa, L. 101 41 55 S 172 39 E
Rotorua 101 38 9 S 176 16 E
Rotorua, L. 101 38 5 S 176 18 E
Rott → 25 48 26N 13 26 E
Rottenburg 25 48 28N 8 56 E
Rottenmann 26 47 31N 14 22 E
Rotterdam 16 51 55N 4 30 E
Rottumeroog 16 53 33N 6 34 E
Rottweil 25 48 9N 8 38 E
Rotuma 94 12 25 S 177 5 E
Roubaix 19 50 40N 3 10 E
Roudnice 26 50 25N 14 15 E
Rouen 18 49 27N 1 4 E
Rouillac 20 45 47N 0 4W
Rouleau 109 50 10N 104 56W
Round Mt. 97 30 26 S 152 16 E
Round Mountain 118 38 46N 117 3W
Roundup 118 46 25N 108 35W
Rousay 14 59 10N 3 2W
Rouses Point 113 44 58N 73 22W
Rousse, L'Île 21 42 37N 8 57 E
Roussillon, Isère, France 21 45 24N 4 49 E
Roussillon, Pyrénées-Or., France 20 42 30N 2 35 E
Rouxville 92 30 25 S 26 50 E
Rouyn 106 48 20N 79 0W
Rovaniemi 50 66 29N 25 41 E
Rovato 38 45 34N 10 0 E
Rovenki 57 48 5N 39 21 E
Rovereto 38 45 53N 11 3 E
Rovigo 39 45 4N 11 48 E
Rovinari 46 44 56N 23 10 E
Rovinj 39 45 5N 13 40 E
Rovno 54 50 40N 26 10 E
Rovnoye 55 50 52N 46 3 E
Rovuma → 91 10 29 S 40 28 E
Rowena 99 29 48 S 148 55 E
Rowley Shoals 96 17 30 S 119 0 E
Roxa 84 11 15N 15 45W
Roxas 73 11 36N 122 49 E
Roxboro 115 36 24N 78 59W
Roxborough Downs 98 22 30 S 138 45 E
Roxburgh 101 45 33 S 169 19 E
Roxen 49 58 30N 15 40 E
Roy, Mont., U.S.A. 118 47 17N 109 0W
Roy, N. Mex., U.S.A. 117 35 57N 104 8W
Roy, Le 117 38 8N 95 35W
Roya, Peña 32 40 25N 0 40W
Royal Oak 114 42 30N 83 5W
Royan 20 45 37N 1 2W
Roye 19 49 42N 2 48 E
Røyken 47 59 45N 10 23 E
Rožaj 42 42 50N 20 15 E
Rózan 28 52 52N 21 25 E
Rozay 19 48 40N 2 56 E
Rozhishche 54 50 54N 25 15 E
Rozier, Le 20 44 13N 3 12 E
Rožnava 27 48 37N 20 35 E
Rozogi 28 53 48N 21 9 E
Rozoy-sur-Serre 19 49 40N 4 8 E
Rozwadów 28 50 37N 22 2 E
Rrësheni 44 41 47N 19 49 E
Rrogozhino 44 41 2N 19 50 E
Rtanj 42 43 45N 21 50 E
Rtishchevo 55 55 16N 43 50 E
Rúa 30 42 24N 7 6W
Ruacaná 92 17 20 S 14 12 E
Ruahine Ra. 101 39 55 S 176 2 E
Ruapehu 101 39 17 S 175 35 E
Ruapuke I. 101 46 46 S 168 31 E
Ruaus, Wadi → 83 30 26N 15 24 E
Rubeho Mts. 90 6 50 S 36 25 E
Rubezhnoye 56 49 6N 38 25 E
Rubh a' Mhail 14 55 55N 6 10W
Rubha Hunish 14 57 42N 6 20W
Rubicone → 39 44 8N 12 28 E
Rubino 84 6 4N 4 18W
Rubio 126 7 43N 72 22W
Rubtsovsk 58 51 30N 81 10 E
Ruby 104 64 40N 155 35W
Ruby L. 118 40 10N 115 28W
Ruby Mts. 118 40 30N 115 30W
Rubyvale 98 23 25 S 147 45 E
Rucava 54 56 9N 21 12 E
Ruciane-Nida 28 53 40N 21 32 E
Rud 47 60 1N 10 1 E
Ruda 49 57 6N 16 7 E
Ruda Śląska 28 50 16N 18 50 E
Ruden 24 54 13N 13 47 E
Rüdersdorf 24 52 28N 13 48 E
Rudewa 91 10 7 S 34 40 E
Rudkøbing 49 54 56N 10 41 E
Rudna 28 51 30N 16 17 E
Rudnichnyy 52 59 38N 52 26 E
Rudnik, Bulg. 43 42 36N 27 30 E
Rudnik, Poland 28 50 26N 22 15 E
Rudnik, Yugo. 42 44 8N 20 30 E
Rudnik, Yugo. 43 44 7N 20 35 E
Rudnogorsk 59 57 15N 103 42 E
Rudnya 54 54 55N 31 7 E
Rudnyy 58 52 57N 63 7 E
Rudo 42 43 41N 19 23 E
Rudolf, Ostrov 58 81 45N 58 30 E
Rudolstadt 24 50 44N 11 20 E
Rudozem 43 41 29N 24 51 E
Rudyard 114 46 14N 84 35W
Rue 19 50 15N 1 40 E
Ruelle 20 45 41N 0 14 E
Rufa'a 87 14 44N 33 22 E
Ruffec-Charente 20 46 2N 0 12 E
Rufiji □ 90 8 0 S 38 30 E
Rufiji → 90 7 50 S 39 15 E
Rufino 124 34 20 S 62 50W
Rufisque 84 14 40N 17 15W
Rufunsa 91 15 4 S 29 34 E
Rugao 77 32 23N 120 31 E
Rugby, U.K. 13 52 23N 1 16W
Rugby, U.S.A. 116 48 21N 100 0W
Rügen 24 54 22N 13 25 E
Rugles 18 48 50N 0 40 E
Ruhama 62 31 31N 34 43 E
Ruhengeri 90 1 30 S 29 36 E
Ruhla 24 50 53N 10 21 E
Ruhland 24 51 27N 13 52 E
Ruhr → 24 51 25N 6 44 E
Ruhuhu → 91 10 31 S 34 34 E
Rui'an 77 27 47N 120 40 E
Ruidosa 117 29 59N 104 39W
Ruidoso 119 33 19N 105 39W
Ruj 42 42 52N 22 42 E
Rujen 42 42 9N 22 30 E

Ruk St-Junien

Ruk 68 27 50N 68 42 E
Rukwa □ 90 7 0S 31 30 E
Rukwa L. 90 8 0S 32 20 E
Rum Cay 121 23 40N 74 58W
Rum Jungle 96 13 0S 130 59 E
Ruma 42 45 0N 19 50 E
Rumāḥ 64 25 29N 47 10 E
Rumania = Romania ■ 46 46 0N 25 0 E
Rumbêk 87 6 54N 29 37 E
Rumburk 26 50 57N 14 32 E
Rumford 114 44 30N 70 30W
Rumia 28 54 37N 18 25 E
Rumilly 21 45 53N 5 56 E
Rumoi 74 43 56N 141 39W
Rumonge 90 3 59S 29 26 E
Rumsey 108 51 51N 112 48W
Rumula 98 16 35S 145 20 E
Rumuruti 90 0 17N 36 32 E
Runan 77 33 0N 114 30 E
Runanga 101 42 25S 171 15 E
Runaway, C. 101 37 32S 178 2 E
Runcorn 12 53 20N 2 44W
Rungwa 90 6 55S 33 32 E
Rungwa → 90 7 36S 31 50 E
Rungwe 91 9 11S 33 32 E
Rungwe □ 91 9 25S 33 32 E
Runka 85 12 28N 7 20 E
Runn 48 60 30N 15 40 E
Ruoqiang 75 38 55N 88 10 E
Rupa 67 27 15N 92 21 E
Rupar 68 31 2N 76 38 E
Rupat 72 1 45N 101 40 E
Rupea 46 46 2N 25 13 E
Rupert → 106 51 29N 78 45W
Rupert House = Fort Rupert 106 51 30N 78 40W
Rupsa 69 21 44N 89 30 E
Rur → 24 51 20N 6 0 E
Rurrenabaque 126 14 30S 67 32W
Rus → 33 39 30N 2 30W
Rusambo 91 16 30S 32 4 E
Rusape 91 18 35S 32 8 E
Ruschuk = Ruse 43 43 48N 25 59 E
Ruse 43 43 48N 25 59 E
Ruşeţu 46 44 57N 27 14 E
Rushden 13 52 17N 0 37W
Rushford 116 43 48N 91 46W
Rushville, Ill., U.S.A. 116 40 6N 90 35W
Rushville, Ind., U.S.A. 114 39 38N 85 22W
Rushville, Nebr., U.S.A. 116 42 43N 102 28W
Rushworth 100 36 32S 145 1 E
Rusken 49 57 15N 14 20 E
Russas 127 4 55S 37 50W
Russell, Can. 109 50 50N 101 20W
Russell, N.Z. 101 35 16S 174 10 E
Russell, U.S.A. 116 38 56N 98 55W
Russell L., Man., Can. 109 56 15N 101 30W
Russell L., N.W.T., Can. 108 63 5N 115 44W
Russellkonda 69 19 57N 84 42 E
Russellville, Ala., U.S.A. 115 34 30N 87 44W
Russellville, Ark., U.S.A. 117 35 15N 93 8W
Russellville, Ky., U.S.A. 115 36 50N 86 50W
Russi 39 44 21N 12 1 E
Russian S.F.S.R. □ 59 62 0N 105 0 E
Russkaya Polyana 58 53 47N 73 53 E
Russkoye Ustie 4 71 0N 149 0 E
Rust 27 47 49N 16 42 E
Rustavi 57 41 30N 45 0 E
Rustenburg 92 25 41S 27 14 E
Ruston 117 32 30N 92 58W
Rutana 90 3 55S 30 0 E
Rute 31 37 19N 4 23W
Ruteng 73 8 35S 120 30 E
Ruth, Mich., U.S.A. 112 43 42N 82 45W
Ruth, Nev., U.S.A. 118 39 15N 115 1W
Rutherglen, Austral. 100 36 5S 146 29 E
Rutherglen, U.K. 14 55 50N 4 11W
Rutigliano 41 41 1N 17 0 E
Rutland I. 71 11 25N 92 40 E
Rutland Plains 98 15 38S 141 43 E
Rutledge → 109 61 4N 112 0W
Rutledge L. 109 61 33N 110 47W
Rutshuru 90 1 13S 29 25 E
Ruurlo 16 52 5N 6 24 E
Ruvo di Púglia 41 41 7N 16 27 E
Ruvu 90 6 49S 38 43 E
Ruvu → 90 6 23S 38 52 E
Ruvuma □ 91 10 20S 36 0 E
Ruwenzori 90 0 30N 29 55 E
Ruyigi 90 3 29S 30 15 E
Ruzayevka 55 54 4N 45 0 E
Rùzhevo Konare 43 42 23N 24 46 E
Ružomberok 27 49 3N 19 17 E
Rwanda ■ 90 2 0S 30 0 E
Ry 49 56 5N 9 45 E
Ryakhovo 43 44 0N 26 18 E
Ryan, L. 14 55 0N 5 2W
Ryazan 55 54 40N 39 40 E
Ryazhsk 55 53 45N 40 3 E
Rybache 58 46 40N 81 20 E
Rybachiy Poluostrov 52 69 43N 32 0 E
Rybinsk 55 58 5N 38 50 E
Rybinskoye Vdkhr. 55 58 30N 38 25 E
Rybnik 27 50 6N 18 32 E
Rybnitsa 56 47 45N 29 0 E
Rybnoye 55 54 45N 39 30 E
Rychwał 28 52 4N 18 10 E
Ryd 49 56 27N 14 42 E
Ryde 13 50 44N 1 9W
Rydöbruk 49 56 58N 13 7 E
Rydsnäs 49 57 47N 15 9 E
Rydułtowy 27 50 4N 18 23 E
Rydzyna 28 51 47N 16 39 E
Rye 13 50 57N 0 46 E
Rye → 12 54 12N 0 53W
Rye Patch Res. 118 40 38N 118 20W
Ryegate 118 46 21N 109 15W
Ryki 28 51 38N 21 56 E
Rylsk 54 51 36N 34 43 E
Rylstone 99 32 46S 149 58 E
Rymanów 27 49 35N 21 51 E
Ryn 28 53 57N 21 34 E
Rypin 28 53 3N 19 25 E
Ryūkyū Is. = Nansei-Shotō 74 26 0N 128 0 E
Rzepin 28 52 20N 14 49 E
Rzeszów 27 50 5N 21 58 E
Rzeszów □ 27 50 0N 22 0 E
Rzhev 54 56 20N 34 20 E

S

Sa Dec 71 10 20N 105 46 E
Sa'ad (Muharraqa) 62 31 28N 34 33 E
Sa'ādatābād 65 30 10N 53 5 E
Saale → 24 51 57N 11 56 E
Saaler Bodden 24 54 20N 12 25 E
Saalfeld 24 50 39N 11 21 E
Saalfelden 26 47 25N 12 51 E
Saane → 25 46 23N 7 18 E
Saar (Sarre) → 19 49 42N 6 34 E
Saarbrücken 25 49 15N 6 58 E
Saarburg 25 49 36N 6 32 E
Saaremaa 54 58 30N 22 30 E
Saariselkä 50 68 16N 28 15 E
Saarland □ 25 49 15N 7 0 E
Saarlouis 25 49 19N 6 45 E
Saba 121 17 42N 63 26W
Šabac 42 44 48N 19 42 E
Sabadell 32 41 28N 2 7 E
Sabagalet 72 1 36S 98 40 E
Sabah □ 72 6 0N 117 0 E
Sábana de la Mar 121 19 7N 69 24W
Sábanalarga 126 10 38N 74 55W
Sabang 72 5 50N 95 15 E
Sabará 127 19 55S 43 46W
Sabarania 73 2 5S 138 18 E
Sabari → 70 17 35N 81 16 E
Sabasţiyah 62 32 17N 35 12 E
Sabattis 113 44 6N 74 40W
Sabáudia 40 41 17N 13 2 E
Sabhah 83 27 9N 14 29 E
Sabhah □ 83 26 0N 14 0 E
Sabie 93 25 10S 30 48 E
Sabinal, Mexico 120 30 58N 107 25W
Sabinal, U.S.A. 117 29 20N 99 27W
Sabinal, Punta del 33 36 43N 2 44W
Sabinas 120 27 50N 101 10W
Sabinas Hidalgo 120 26 33N 100 10W
Sabine 117 29 42N 93 54W
Sabine → 117 30 0N 93 35W
Sabine L. 117 29 50N 93 50W
Sabinov 27 49 6N 21 5 E
Sabirabad 57 40 5N 48 30 E
Sabkhat Tāwurghā' 83 31 48N 15 30 E
Sablayan 73 12 50N 120 50 E
Sable, C., Can. 107 43 29N 65 38W
Sable, C., U.S.A. 121 25 13N 81 0W
Sable I. 107 44 0N 60 0W
Sablé-sur-Sarthe 18 47 50N 0 20W
Sables-d'Olonne, Les 20 46 30N 1 45W
Sabolev 59 54 20N 155 30 E
Sabor → 30 41 10N 7 7W
Sabou 84 12 1N 2 15W
Sabrātah 83 32 47N 12 29 E
Sabria 83 33 22N 8 45 E
Sabrina Coast 5 68 0S 120 0 E
Sabugal 30 40 20N 7 5W
Sabzevār 65 36 15N 57 40 E
Sabzvārān 65 28 45N 57 50 E
Sac City 116 42 26N 95 0W
Sacedón 32 40 29N 2 41W
Sachigo → 106 55 6N 88 58W
Sachigo, L. 106 53 50N 92 12W
Sachkhere 57 42 25N 43 28 E
Sacile 39 45 58N 12 30 E
Sackets Harbor 113 43 56N 76 7W
Säckingen 25 47 34N 7 56 E
Saco, Me., U.S.A. 115 43 30N 70 27W
Saco, Mont., U.S.A. 118 48 28N 107 19W
Sacramento 118 38 33N 121 30 E
Sacramento → 118 38 3N 121 56W
Sacramento Mts. 119 32 30N 105 30W
Sacratif, Cabo 33 36 42N 3 28W
Săcueni 46 47 20N 22 5 E
Sada 30 43 22N 8 15W
Sádaba 32 42 19N 1 12W
Sadani 90 5 58S 38 35 E
Sadao 71 6 38N 100 26 E
Sadasivpet 70 17 38N 77 59 E
Sadd el Aali 86 23 54N 32 54 E
Sade 85 11 22N 10 45 E
Sadimi 91 9 25S 23 32 E
Sado 74 38 0N 138 25 E
Sado → 31 38 29N 8 55W
Sado, Shima 74 38 15N 138 30 E
Sadon, Burma 67 25 28N 98 0 E
Sadon, U.S.S.R. 57 42 52N 43 58 E
Sæby 49 57 21N 10 30 E
Saegerstown 112 41 42N 80 10W
Saelices 32 39 55N 2 49W
Safaga 86 26 42N 34 0 E
Safaha 86 26 25N 39 0 E
Šafárikovo 27 48 25N 20 20 E
Säffle 48 59 8N 12 55 E
Safford 119 32 50N 109 43W
Saffron Walden 13 52 2N 0 15 E
Safi 82 32 18N 9 20W
Safīd Kūh 65 34 45N 63 0 E
Safonovo 54 55 4N 33 16 E
Safranbolu 56 41 15N 32 41 E
Sag Harbor 113 40 59N 72 17W
Saga 73 2 40S 132 55 E
Saga □ 74 33 15N 130 20 E
Sagala 84 14 9N 6 38W
Sagara 70 14 14N 75 6 E
Sagara, L. 90 5 20S 31 0 E
Saghīr, Zab al 64 35 10N 43 20 E
Sagil 75 50 15N 91 15 E
Saginaw 114 43 26N 83 55W
Saginaw B. 106 43 50N 83 40W
Sagleipie 84 7 0N 8 52W
Saglouc (Sugluk) 105 62 10N 74 40W
Sagone 21 42 7N 8 42 E
Sagone, G. de 21 42 4N 8 40 E
Sagra, La > 33 37 57N 2 35W
Sagres 31 37 0N 8 58W
Sagua la Grande 121 22 50N 80 10W
Saguache 119 38 10N 106 10W
Saguenay → 107 48 22N 71 0W
Sagunto 32 39 42N 0 18W
Sahaba 86 18 57N 30 25 E
Sahagún 30 42 18N 5 2W
Saham 62 32 42N 35 46 E
Saḥam al Jawlān 62 32 45N 35 55 E
Sahand, Kūh-e 64 37 44N 46 27 E
Sahara 82 23 0N 5 0 E
Saharanpur 68 29 58N 77 33 E
Saharien Atlas 82 33 30N 1 0 E
Sahasinaka 93 21 49S 47 49 E
Sahaswan 68 28 5N 78 45 E
Sahel, Canal du 84 14 20N 6 0W
Sahibganj 69 25 12N 87 40 E
Sahiwal 68 30 45N 73 8 E
Sahtaneh → 108 59 2N 122 28W
Sahuaripa 120 29 0N 109 13W
Sahuarita 119 31 58N 110 59W
Sahuayo 120 20 4N 102 43W
Sahy 27 48 4N 18 55 E
Saibai I. 98 9 25S 142 40 E
Sa'id Bundas 81 8 24N 24 48 E
Saïda 82 34 50N 0 11 E
Saīdābād 65 29 30N 55 45 E
Saïdia 82 35 5N 2 14W
Saidu 69 34 43N 72 24 E
Saignes 20 45 20N 2 31 E
Saigon = Phanh Bho Ho Chi Minh 71 10 46N 106 40 E
Saih-al-Malih 65 23 37N 58 31 E
Saijō 74 33 55N 133 11 E
Saikhoa Ghat 67 27 50N 95 40 E
Saiki 74 32 58N 131 51 E
Saillans 21 44 42N 5 12 E
Sailolof 73 1 7S 130 46 E
St. Abb's Head 14 55 55N 2 10W
St. Aegyd 26 47 52N 15 33 E
St-Affrique 20 43 57N 2 53 E
St-Agrève 21 45 0N 4 23 E
St-Aignan 18 47 16N 1 22 E
St. Alban's 107 47 51N 55 50W
St. Albans, U.K. 13 51 44N 0 19W
St. Albans, Vt., U.S.A. 114 44 49N 73 7W
St. Albans, W. Va., U.S.A. 114 38 21N 81 50W
St. Alban's Head 13 50 34N 2 3W
St. Albert 108 53 37N 113 32W
St-Amand 19 50 25N 3 26 E
St-Amand-en-Puisaye 19 47 32N 3 5 E
St-Amand-Mont-Rond 20 46 43N 2 30 E
St-Amarin 19 47 54N 7 0 E
St-Amour 21 46 26N 5 21 E
St-André-de-Cubzac 20 44 59N 0 26W
St-André-de-l'Eure 18 48 54N 1 16 E
St-André-les-Alpes 21 43 58N 6 30 E
St. André, Tanjona 93 16 11S 44 27 E
St. Andrew's 107 47 45N 59 15W
St. Andrews 14 56 20N 2 48W
St-Anicet 113 45 8N 74 22W
St. Ann B. 107 46 22N 60 25W
St. Anne 18 49 43N 2 11W
St. Anthony, Can. 107 51 22N 55 35W
St. Anthony, U.S.A. 118 44 0N 111 40W
St-Antonin-Noble-Val 20 44 10N 1 45 E
St. Arnaud 99 36 40S 143 16 E
St. Arthur 107 47 33N 67 46W
St. Asaph 12 53 15N 3 27W
St-Astier 20 45 8N 0 31 E
St-Aubin-du-Cormier 18 48 15N 1 26W
St. Augustin 93 23 33S 43 46 E
St-Augustin-Saguenay 107 51 13N 58 38W
St. Augustine 115 29 52N 81 20W
St. Austell 13 50 20N 4 48W
St-Avold 19 49 6N 6 43 E
St.-Barthélemy, I. 121 17 50N 62 50W
St. Bee's Hd. 12 54 30N 3 38 E
St-Benoît-du-Sault 20 46 26N 1 24 E
St. Bernard, Col du Grand 25 45 53N 7 11 E
St. Boniface 109 49 53N 97 5W
St-Bonnet 21 44 40N 6 5 E
St-Brévin-les-Pins 18 47 14N 2 10W
St-Brice-en-Coglès 18 48 25N 1 22W
St. Bride's 107 46 56N 54 10W
St. Bride's B. 13 51 48N 5 15W
St-Brieuc 18 48 30N 2 46W
St-Calais 18 47 55N 0 45 E
St-Cast 18 48 37N 2 18W
St. Catharines 106 43 10N 79 15W
St. Catherines I. 115 31 35N 81 10W
St. Catherine's Pt. 13 50 34N 1 18W
St-Céré 20 44 51N 1 54 E
St.-Cergue 25 46 27N 6 10 E
St-Cernin 20 45 5N 2 25 E
St-Chamond 21 45 28N 4 31 E
St. Charles, Ill., U.S.A. 114 41 55N 88 21W
St. Charles, Mo., U.S.A. 116 38 46N 90 30W
St-Chély-d'Apcher 20 44 48N 3 17 E
St-Chinian 20 43 25N 2 56 E
St. Christopher (St. Kitts) 121 17 20N 62 40W
St-Ciers-sur-Gironde 20 45 17N 0 37W
St. Clair, Mich, U.S.A. 112 42 47N 82 27W
St. Clair, Pa., U.S.A. 113 40 42N 76 12W
St. Clair, L. 106 42 30N 82 45W
St. Clairsville 112 40 5N 80 53W
St-Claud 20 45 54N 0 28 E
St. Claude 109 49 40N 98 20W
St-Claude 21 46 22N 5 52 E
St-Cloud 18 48 51N 2 12 E
St. Cloud, Fla., U.S.A. 115 28 15N 81 15W
St. Cloud, Minn., U.S.A. 116 45 30N 94 11W
St-Coeur de Marie 107 48 39N 71 43W
St. Croix 121 17 45N 64 45W
St. Croix → 116 44 45N 92 50W
St. Croix Falls 116 45 18N 92 22W
St-Cyprien 20 42 37N 3 0 E
St-Cyr 21 43 11N 5 43 E
St. David's, Can. 107 48 12N 58 52W
St. David's, U.K. 13 51 54N 5 16W
St. David's Head 13 51 55N 5 16W
St-Denis 19 48 56N 2 22 E
St-Denis-d'Orques 18 48 2N 0 17W
St-Dié 19 48 17N 6 56 E
St-Dizier 19 48 40N 5 0 E
St-Egrève 21 45 14N 5 41 E
St. Elias, Mt. 104 60 14N 140 50W
St Elias Mts. 108 60 33N 139 28W
St-Éloy-les-Mines 20 46 10N 2 51 E
St-Émilion 20 44 53N 0 9W
St-Étienne 21 45 27N 4 22 E
St-Étienne-de-Tinée 21 44 16N 6 56 E
St. Eugène 113 45 30N 74 28W
St. Eustatius 121 17 20N 63 0W
St-Félicien 106 48 40N 72 25W
St-Florent 21 42 41N 9 18 E
St-Florent-sur-Cher 19 46 59N 2 15 E
St-Florentin 19 48 0N 3 45 E
St-Flour 20 45 2N 3 6 E
St-Fons 21 45 42N 4 52 E
St. Francis 116 39 48N 101 47W
St. Francis → 117 34 38N 90 36W
St. Francis, C. 92 34 14S 24 49 E
St-Francis, L. 113 45 10N 74 22W
St. Francisville 117 30 48N 91 22W
St-Fulgent 18 46 50N 1 10W
St-Gabriel-de-Brandon 106 46 17N 73 24W
St-Gaudens 20 43 6N 0 44 E
St-Gengoux-le-National 21 46 37N 4 40 E
St-Geniez-d'Olt 20 44 27N 2 58 E
St. George, Austral. 97 28 1S 148 30 E
St. George, Berm. 121 32 24N 64 42W
St. George, Can. 107 45 11N 66 50W
St. George, S.C., U.S.A. 115 33 13N 80 37W
St. George, Utah, U.S.A. 119 37 10N 113 35W
St. George, C., Can. 107 48 30N 59 16W
St. George, C., U.S.A. 115 29 36N 85 2W
St-Georges 16 50 37N 5 20 E
St. George's 107 48 26N 58 31W
St. Georges 106 46 42N 72 35W
St-Georges 107 46 8N 70 40W
St. Georges 127 4 0N 52 0W
St. George's 121 12 5N 61 43W
St. George's B. 107 48 24N 58 53W
Saint George's Channel 98 4 10S 152 20 E
St. George's Channel 11 52 0N 6 0W
St-Georges-de-Didonne 20 45 36N 1 0W
St. Georges Head 100 35 12S 150 42 E
St-Germain 19 48 53N 2 5 E
St-Germain-Lembron 20 45 27N 3 14 E
St-Germain-de-Calberte 20 44 13N 3 48 E
St-Germain-des-Fossés 20 46 12N 3 26 E
St-Germain-du-Plain 19 46 42N 4 58 E
St-Germain-Laval 21 45 50N 4 1 E
St-Gers 20 45 18N 0 37W
St-Gervais, Haute Savoie, France 21 45 53N 6 42 E
St-Gervais, Puy de Dôme, France 20 46 4N 2 50 E
St-Gildas, Pte. de 18 47 8N 2 14W
St-Gilles-Croix-de-Vie 18 46 41N 1 55W
St-Gilles-du-Gard 21 43 40N 4 26 E
St-Girons 20 42 59N 1 8 E
St. Goar 25 50 12N 7 43 E
St-Gualtier 18 46 39N 1 26 E
St-Guénolé 18 47 49N 4 23W
St. Helena, Atl. Oc. 7 15 55S 5 44W
St. Helena, U.S.A. 118 38 29N 122 30W
St. Helenabaai 92 32 40S 18 10 E
St. Helens, U.K. 12 53 28N 2 44W
St. Helens, U.S.A. 118 45 55N 122 50W
St. Helier 18 49 11N 2 6W
St-Hilaire 18 48 35N 1 7W
St-Hippolyte 19 47 20N 6 50 E
St-Hippolyte-du-Fort 20 43 58N 3 52 E
St-Honoré 19 46 54N 3 50 E
St-Hubert 16 50 2N 5 23 E
St-Hyacinthe 106 45 40N 72 58W
St. Ignace 114 45 53N 84 43W
St. Ignace I. 106 48 45N 88 0W
St. Ignatius 118 47 19N 114 8W
St-Imier 25 47 9N 6 58 E
St. Ives, Cambs., U.K. 13 52 20N 0 5W
St. Ives, Cornwall, U.K. 13 50 13N 5 29W
St. James 18 48 31N 1 20W
St. James 116 43 57N 94 40W
St. Jean 106 45 20N 73 20W
St-Jean 21 45 30N 5 10 E
St-Jean → 107 50 17N 64 20W
St. Jean Baptiste 109 49 15N 97 20W
St-Jean-d'Angély 20 45 57N 0 31W
St-Jean-de-Maurienne 21 45 16N 6 21 E
St-Jean-de-Luz 20 43 23N 1 39W
St-Jean-de-Monts 18 46 47N 2 4W
St-Jean-du-Gard 20 44 7N 3 52 E
St-Jean-en-Royans 21 45 1N 5 18 E
St-Jean, L. 107 48 40N 72 0W
St-Jean-Port-Joli 107 47 15N 70 13W
St-Jérôme, Qué., Can. 106 45 47N 74 0W
St-Jérôme, Qué., Can. 107 48 26N 71 53W
St. John, Can. 107 45 20N 66 8W
St. John, Kans., U.S.A. 117 37 59N 98 45W
St. John, N.D., U.S.A. 116 48 58N 99 40W
St. John → 107 45 15N 66 4W
St. John, C. 107 50 0N 55 32W
St. John's, Antigua 121 17 6N 61 51W
St. John's, Can. 107 47 35N 52 40W
St. Johns, Ariz., U.S.A. 119 34 31N 109 26W
St. Johns, Mich., U.S.A. 114 43 0N 84 31W
St. John's → 115 30 20N 81 30W
St. Johnsbury 114 44 25N 72 1W
St. Johnsville 113 43 0N 74 43W
St. Joseph, La., U.S.A. 117 31 55N 91 15W
St. Joseph, Mich., U.S.A. 114 42 5N 86 30W
St. Joseph, Mo., U.S.A. 116 39 46N 94 50W
St. Joseph → 114 42 7N 86 30W
St. Joseph, I. 106 46 12N 83 58W
St. Joseph, L. 106 51 10N 90 35W
St-Jovite 106 46 8N 74 38W
St-Juéry 20 43 55N 2 12 E
St-Julien 21 46 8N 6 5 E
St-Julien-Chapteuil 21 45 2N 4 4 E
St-Julien-du-Sault 19 48 1N 3 17 E
St-Junien 20 45 53N 0 55 E

St-Just-en-Chaussée San Constanzo

St-Just-en-Chaussée 19 49 30N 2 25 E
St-Just-en-Chevalet 20 45 55N 3 50 E
St-Justin 20 43 59N 0 14W
St. Kilda, N.Z. 101 45 53 S 170 31 E
St. Kilda, U.K. 8 57 9N 8 34W
St. Kitts-Nevis ■ 121 17 20N 62 40W
St. Laurent 109 50 25N 97 58W
St-Laurent 127 5 29N 54 3W
St-Laurent-du-Pont 21 45 23N 5 45 E
St-Laurent-en-Grandvaux 21 46 35N 5 58 E
St. Lawrence 107 46 54N 55 23W
St. Lawrence → 107 49 30N 66 0W
St. Lawrence, Gulf of 107 48 25N 62 0W
St. Lawrence I. 104 63 0N 170 0W
St. Leonard 107 47 12N 67 58W
St-Léonard-de-Noblat 20 45 49N 1 29 E
St. Lewis → 107 52 26N 56 11W
St-Lô 18 49 7N 1 5W
St-Louis 84 16 8N 16 27W
St. Louis, Mich., U.S.A. 114 43 27N 84 38W
St. Louis, Mo., U.S.A. 116 38 40N 90 12W
St. Louis → 116 47 15N 92 45W
St-Loup-sur-Semouse 19 47 53N 6 16 E
St. Lucia ■ 121 14 0N 60 50W
St. Lucia, C. 93 28 32 S 32 29 E
St. Lucia Channel 121 14 15N 61 0W
St. Lucia, Lake 93 28 5 S 32 30 E
St. Lunaire-Griquet 107 51 31N 55 28W
St. Maarten 121 18 0N 63 5W
St-Maixent-l'École 20 46 24N 0 12W
St-Malo 18 48 39N 2 1W
St-Malo, G. de 18 48 50N 2 30W
St-Mandrier 21 43 4N 5 56 E
St-Marc 121 19 10N 72 41W
St-Marcellin 21 45 9N 5 20 E
St-Marcouf, Îs. 18 49 30N 1 10W
St. Maries 118 47 17N 116 34W
St-Martin, Charente-M., France 20 46 12N 1 22W
St-Martin, Pas-de-Calais, France 19 50 42N 1 38 E
St-Martin, I. 121 18 0N 63 0W
St. Martin L. 109 51 40N 98 30W
St-Martin-Vésubie 21 44 4N 7 15 E
St. Martins 107 45 22N 65 34W
St. Martinsville 117 30 10N 91 50W
St-Martory 20 43 9N 0 56 E
St. Mary B. 107 46 50N 53 50W
St. Mary Is. 70 13 20N 74 35 E
St. Mary Pk. 97 31 32 S 138 34 E
St. Marys, Austral. 97 41 35 S 148 11 E
St. Marys, Can. 112 43 20N 81 10W
St. Mary's, U.K. 13 49 55N 6 17W
St. Mary's, U.S.A. 114 40 33N 84 20W
St. Marys 114 41 27N 78 33W
St. Marys Bay 107 44 25N 66 10W
St. Mary's, C. 107 46 50N 54 12W
St. Mathews I. = Zadetkyi Kyun 71 10 0N 98 25 E
St-Mathieu, Pte. de 18 48 20N 4 45W
St-Maur-des-Fossés 19 48 48N 2 30 E
St-Maurice → 106 46 21N 72 31W
St-Médard-de-Guizières 20 45 1N 0 4W
St-Méen-le-Grand 18 48 11N 2 12W
St. Michaels 119 35 38N 109 5W
St. Michael's Mt. 13 50 7N 5 30W
St-Michel 21 45 15N 6 29 E
St-Mihiel 19 48 54N 5 30 E
St-Nazaire 18 47 17N 2 12W
St. Neots 13 52 14N 0 16W
St-Nicolas-de-Port 19 48 38N 6 18 E
St-Omer 19 50 45N 2 15 E
St. Ouen 19 48 50N 2 20 E
St-Ouen 19 50 2N 2 7 E
St-Pacome 107 47 24N 69 58W
St-Palais 20 45 40N 1 8W
St-Pamphile 107 46 58N 69 48W
St-Pardoux-la-Rivière 20 45 29N 0 45 E
St. Pascal 107 47 32N 69 48W
St. Paul, Can. 108 54 0N 111 17W
St. Paul, Ind. Oc. 3 30 40 S 77 34 E
St. Paul, Minn., U.S.A. 116 44 54N 93 5W
St. Paul, Nebr., U.S.A. 116 41 15N 98 30W
St-Paul-de-Fenouillet 20 42 50N 2 28 E
St. Paul, I. 107 47 12N 60 9W
St-Péray 21 44 57N 4 50 E
St-Père-en-Retz 18 47 11N 2 2W
St. Peter 116 44 21N 93 57W
St. Peter Port 18 49 27N 2 31W
St. Peters, N.S., Can. 107 45 40N 60 53W
St. Peters, P.E.I., Can. 107 46 25N 62 35W
St. Petersburg 115 27 45N 82 40W
St-Philbert-de-Grand-Lieu 18 47 2N 1 39W
St Pierre 107 46 46N 56 12W
St-Pierre-d'Oléron 20 45 57N 1 19W
St-Pierre-Église 18 49 40N 1 24W
St-Pierre-en-Port 18 49 48N 0 30 E
St-Pierre et Miquelon □ 107 46 55N 56 10W
St-Pierre, L. 106 46 12N 72 52W
St-Pierre-le-Moûtier 19 46 47N 3 7 E
St.-Pierre-sur-Dives 18 49 2N 0 1W
St.-Pol 19 50 21N 2 20 E
St-Pol-de-Léon 18 48 41N 4 0W
St-Pol-sur-Mer 19 51 1N 2 20 E
St-Pons 20 43 30N 2 45 E
St-Pourçain-sur-Sioule 20 46 18N 3 18 E
St-Quay-Portrieux 18 48 39N 2 51W
St-Quentin 19 49 50N 3 16 E
St-Rambert-d'Albon 21 45 17N 4 49 E
St-Raphaël 21 43 25N 6 46 E
St. Regis, Mont., U.S.A. 118 47 20N 115 3W
St. Regis, N.Y., U.S.A. 113 44 39N 74 34W
St-Rémy-de-Provence 21 43 48N 4 50 E
St-Renan 18 48 26N 4 37W
St-Saëns 18 49 41N 1 16 E
St-Sauveur-en-Puisaye 19 47 37N 3 12 E
St-Sauveur-le-Vicomte 18 49 23N 1 32W
St-Savin 20 46 34N 0 50 E
St-Savinien 20 45 53N 0 42W
St. Sebastien, Tanjon' i 93 12 26 S 48 44 E
St-Seine-l'Abbaye 19 47 26N 4 47 E
St-Sernin 20 43 54N 2 35 E
St-Servan-sur-Mer 18 48 38N 2 0W
St-Sever 20 43 46N 0 34W
St-Sever-Calvados 18 48 50N 1 3W
St-Siméon 107 47 51N 69 54W
St. Stephen 107 45 16N 67 17W
St-Sulpice-Laurière 20 46 3N 1 29 E
St-Sulpice-la-Pointe 20 43 46N 1 41 E
St-Thégonnec 18 48 31N 3 57W
St. Thomas, Can. 106 42 45N 81 10W
St. Thomas, W. Indies 121 18 21N 64 55W
St-Tite 106 46 45N 72 34W
St-Tropez 21 43 17N 6 38 E
St. Troud = Sint Truiden 16 50 48N 5 10 E
St-Vaast-la-Hougue 18 49 35N 1 17W
St-Valéry 19 50 10N 1 38 E
St-Valéry-en-Caux 18 49 52N 0 43 E
St-Vallier 21 45 11N 4 50 E
St-Vallier-de-Thiey 21 43 42N 6 51 E
St-Varent 18 46 53N 0 13W
St. Vincent 6 18 0N 26 1W
St. Vincent ■ 121 13 10N 61 10W
St-Vincent-de-Tyrosse 20 43 39N 1 18W
St. Vincent, G. 97 35 0 S 138 0 E
St. Vincent Passage 121 13 30N 61 0W
St. Vincent, Tanjona 93 21 58 S 43 20 E
St-Vith 16 50 17N 6 9 E
St-Yrieux-la-Perche 20 45 31N 1 12 E
Ste-Adresse 18 49 31N 0 5 E
Ste-Agathe-des-Monts 106 46 3N 74 17W
Ste Anne de Beaupré 107 47 2N 70 58W
Ste-Anne-des-Monts 107 49 8N 66 30W
Ste-Énimie 20 44 22N 3 26 E
Ste-Foy-la-Grande 20 44 50N 0 13 E
Ste. Genevieve 116 37 59N 90 2W
Ste-Hermine 20 46 32N 1 4W
Ste-Livrade-sur-Lot 20 44 24N 0 36 E
Ste-Marguerite → 107 50 9N 66 36W
Ste Marie 121 14 48N 61 1W
Ste-Marie-aux-Mines 19 48 10N 7 12 E
Ste-Marie de la Madeleine 107 46 26N 71 0W
Ste-Maure-de-Touraine 18 47 7N 0 37 E
Ste-Maxime 21 43 19N 6 39 E
Ste-Menehould 19 49 5N 4 54 E
Ste-Mère-Église 18 49 24N 1 19W
Ste-Rose 121 16 20N 61 45W
Ste.-Rose du lac 109 51 4N 99 30W
Saintes 20 45 45N 0 37W
Saintes, Île des 121 15 50N 61 35W
Saintes-Maries-de-la-Mer 21 43 26N 4 26 E
Saintonge 20 45 40N 0 50W
Sairang 67 23 50N 92 45 E
Sairecábur, Cerro 124 22 43 S 67 54W
Saitama □ 74 36 25N 139 30 E
Sajama 126 18 7 S 69 0W
Sajan 42 45 50N 20 20 E
Sajószentpéter 27 48 12N 20 44 E
Sakai 74 34 30N 135 30 E
Sakākah 64 30 0N 40 8 E
Sakami, L. 106 53 15N 77 0W
Sâkâne, 'Erg i-n 82 20 30N 1 30W
Sakania 91 12 43 S 28 30 E
Sakarya → 56 41 7N 30 39 E
Sakata 74 38 55N 139 50 E
Sakeny → 93 20 0 S 45 25 E
Sakété 85 6 40N 2 45 E
Sakhalin, Ostrov 59 51 0N 143 0 E
Sakhi Gopal 69 19 58N 85 50 E
Sakhnīn 62 32 52N 35 12 E
Saki 56 45 9N 33 34 E
Sakiai 54 54 59N 23 0 E
Sakołow Małopolski 28 50 10N 22 9 E
Sakon Nakhon 71 17 10N 104 9 E
Sakrand 68 26 10N 68 15 E
Sakri 68 21 2N 74 20 E
Sakskøbing 49 54 49N 11 39 E
Sal → 57 47 31N 40 45 E
Šal'a 27 48 10N 17 50 E
Sala 48 59 58N 16 35 E
Sala Consilina 41 40 23N 15 35 E
Sala-y-Gómez 95 26 28 S 105 28W
Salaberry-de-Valleyfield 106 45 15N 74 8W
Saladas 124 28 15 S 58 40W
Saladillo 124 35 40 S 59 55W
Salado →, Buenos Aires, Argent. 124 35 44 S 57 22W
Salado →, La Pampa, Argent. 128 37 30 S 67 0W
Salado →, Santa Fe, Argent. 124 31 40 S 60 41W
Salado →, Mexico 120 26 52N 99 19W
Salaga 85 8 31N 0 31W
Sălaj □ 46 47 15N 23 0 E
Salala, Liberia 84 6 42N 10 7W
Salala, Sudan 86 21 17N 36 16 E
Salālah 63 16 56N 53 59 E
Salamanca, Chile 124 31 46 S 70 59W
Salamanca, Spain 30 40 58N 5 39W
Salamanca, U.S.A. 114 42 10N 78 42W
Salamanca □ 30 40 57N 5 40W
Salamis 45 37 56N 23 30 E
Salar de Atacama 124 23 30 S 68 25W
Salar de Uyuni 126 20 30 S 67 45W
Sălard 46 47 12N 22 3 E
Salas 30 43 25N 6 15W
Salas de los Infantes 32 42 2N 3 17W
Salatiga 73 7 19 S 110 30 E
Salavat 52 53 21N 55 55 E
Salaverry 126 8 15 S 79 0W
Salawati 73 1 7 S 130 52 E
Salayar 73 6 7 S 120 30 E
Salazar → 32 42 40N 1 20W
Salbris 19 47 25N 2 3 E
Salcia 46 43 56N 24 55 E
Salcombe 13 50 14N 3 47W
Saldaña 30 42 32N 4 48W
Saldanha 92 33 0 S 17 58 E
Saldanhabaai 92 33 6 S 18 0 E
Saldus 54 56 38N 22 30 E
Sale 97 38 6 S 147 6 E
Salé 82 34 3N 6 48W
Sale 12 53 26N 2 19W
Salebabu 73 3 55N 126 40 E
Salekhard 58 66 30N 66 35 E
Salem, India 70 11 40N 78 11 E
Salem, Ind., U.S.A. 114 38 38N 86 6W
Salem, Mass., U.S.A. 114 42 29N 70 53W
Salem, Mo., U.S.A. 117 37 40N 91 30W
Salem, N.J., U.S.A. 114 39 34N 75 29W
Salem, Ohio, U.S.A. 114 40 52N 80 50W
Salem, Oreg., U.S.A. 118 45 0N 123 0W
Salem, S.D., U.S.A. 116 43 44N 97 23W
Salem, Va., U.S.A. 114 37 19N 80 8W
Salemi 40 37 49N 12 47 E
Salernes 21 43 34N 6 15 E
Salerno 41 40 40N 14 44 E
Salerno, G. di 41 40 35N 14 45 E
Salfīt 62 32 5N 35 11 E
Salford 12 53 30N 2 17W
Salgir → 56 45 38N 35 1 E
Salgótarján 27 48 5N 19 47 E
Salies-de-Béarn 20 43 28N 0 56W
Salina, Italy 41 38 35N 14 50 E
Salina, U.S.A. 116 38 50N 97 40W
Salina Cruz 120 16 10N 95 10W
Salinas, Brazil 127 16 10 S 42 10W
Salinas, Chile 124 23 31 S 69 29W
Salinas, Ecuador 126 2 10 S 80 58W
Salinas, U.S.A. 119 36 40N 121 41W
Salinas →, Mexico 120 16 28N 90 31W
Salinas →, U.S.A. 119 36 45N 121 48W
Salinas Ambargasta 124 29 0 S 65 0W
Salinas, B. de 121 11 4N 85 45W
Salinas, C. de 33 39 16N 3 4 E
Salinas (de Hidalgo) 120 22 30N 101 40W
Salinas Grandes 124 30 0 S 65 0W
Salinas, Pampa de las 124 31 58 S 66 42W
Saline →, Ark., U.S.A. 117 33 10N 92 8W
Saline →, Kans., U.S.A. 116 38 51N 97 30W
Salinópolis 127 0 40 S 47 20W
Salins 19 46 57N 5 53 E
Salins-les-Bains 19 46 58N 5 52 E
Salir 31 37 14N 8 2W
Salisbury, Austral. 99 34 46 S 138 40 E
Salisbury, U.K. 13 51 4N 1 48W
Salisbury, Md., U.S.A. 114 38 20N 75 38W
Salisbury, N.C., U.S.A. 115 35 20N 80 29W
• Salisbury, Zimb. 91 17 43 S 31 2 E
Salisbury Plain 13 51 13N 1 50W
Săliște 46 45 45N 23 56 E
Salka 85 10 20N 4 58 E
Salle, La 116 41 20N 89 6W
Sallent 32 41 49N 1 54 E
Salles-Curan 20 44 11N 2 48 E
Salling 49 56 40N 8 55 E
Sallisaw 117 35 26N 94 45W
Sallom Junction 86 19 17N 37 6 E
Salmerón 32 40 33N 2 29W
Salmo 108 49 10N 117 20W
Salmon 118 45 12N 113 56W
Salmon →, Can. 108 54 3N 122 40W
Salmon →, U.S.A. 118 45 51N 116 46W
Salmon Arm 108 50 40N 119 15W
Salmon Falls 118 42 48N 114 59W
Salmon Res. 107 48 05N 56 00W
Salmon River Mts. 118 45 0N 114 30W
Salo 51 60 22N 23 10 E
Salò 38 45 37N 10 32 E
Salobreña 31 36 44N 3 35W
Salome 119 33 51N 113 37W
Salon-de-Provence 21 43 39N 5 6 E
Salonica = Thessaloníki 44 40 38N 22 58 E
Salonta 46 46 49N 21 42 E
Salop = Shropshire □ 13 52 36N 2 45W
Salor → 31 39 39N 7 3W
Salou, Cabo 32 41 3N 1 10 E
Salsacate 124 31 20 S 65 5W
Salses 20 42 50N 2 55 E
Salsette I. 70 19 5N 72 50 E
Salsk 57 46 28N 41 30 E
Salso → 41 37 6N 13 55 E
Salsomaggiore 38 44 48N 9 59 E
Salt →, Can. 108 60 0N 112 25W
Salt →, U.S.A. 119 33 23N 112 18W
Salt Creek 99 36 8 S 139 38 E
Salt Fork → 117 36 37N 97 7W
Salt Lake City 118 40 45N 111 58W
Salt Range 68 32 30N 72 25 E
Salta 124 24 57 S 65 25W
Salta □ 124 24 48 S 65 30W
Saltcoats 14 55 38N 4 47W
Saltee Is. 15 52 7N 6 37W
Saltfjorden 50 67 15N 14 10 E
Saltholm 49 55 38N 12 43 E
Salthólmavík 50 65 24N 21 57W
Saltillo 120 25 30N 100 57W
Salto, Argent. 124 34 20 S 60 15W
Salto, Uruguay 124 31 27 S 57 50W
Salton Sea 119 33 20N 115 50W
Saltpond 85 5 15N 1 3W
Saltsjöbaden 49 59 15N 18 20 E
Saltspring 108 48 54N 123 37W
Saltville 114 36 53N 81 46W
Saluda → 115 34 0N 81 4W
Salûm 86 31 31N 25 7 E
Salûm, Khâlig el 86 31 30N 25 9 E
Salur 70 18 27N 83 18 E
Saluzzo 38 44 39N 7 29 E
Salvador, Brazil 127 13 0 S 38 30W
Salvador, Can. 109 52 10N 109 32W
Salvador, L. 117 29 46N 90 16W
Salvaterra de Magos 31 39 1N 8 47W
Sálvora, Isla 30 42 30N 8 58W
Salwa 65 24 45N 50 55 E
Salween → 67 16 31N 97 37 E
Salyany 53 39 10N 48 50 E
Salyersville 114 37 45N 83 4W
Salza → 26 47 40N 14 43 E
Salzach → 26 48 12N 12 56 E
Salzburg 26 47 48N 13 2 E
Salzburg □ 26 47 15N 13 0 E
Salzgitter 24 52 13N 10 22 E
Salzwedel 24 52 50N 11 11 E
Sam Neua 71 20 29N 104 0 E
Sam Ngao 71 17 18N 99 0 E
Sam Rayburn Res. 117 31 15N 94 20W
Sama 58 60 12N 60 22 E
Sama de Langreo 30 43 18N 5 40W
Samagaltai 59 50 36N 95 3 E
Samales Group 73 6 0N 122 0 E
Samalkot 70 17 3N 82 13 E
Samâlût 86 28 20N 30 42 E
Samana 68 30 10N 76 13 E
Samanga 91 8 20 S 39 13 E
Samangán □ 65 36 15N 68 3 E
Samangwa 90 4 23 S 24 10 E
Samar 73 12 0N 125 0 E
Samarai 98 10 39 S 150 41 E
Samaria = Shōmrōn 62 32 15N 35 13 E
Samarinda 72 0 30 S 117 9 E
Samarkand 58 39 40N 66 55 E
Sāmarrā'' 64 34 16N 43 55 E
Samastipur 69 25 50N 85 50 E
Samatan 20 43 29N 0 55 E
Samba 90 4 38 S 26 22 E
Sambalpur 69 21 28N 84 4 E
Sambar, Tanjung 72 2 59 S 110 19 E
Sambas 72 1 20N 109 20 E
Sambava 93 14 16 S 50 10 E
Sambawizi 91 18 24 S 26 13 E
Sambhal 68 28 35N 78 37 E
Sambhar 68 26 52N 75 6 E
Sambiase 41 38 58N 16 16 E
Sambonifacio 38 45 24N 11 16 E
Sambor, Camb. 71 12 46N 106 0 E
Sambor, U.S.S.R. 54 49 30N 23 10 E
Sambre → 16 50 27N 4 52 E
Sambuca di Sicilia 40 37 39N 13 6 E
Samburu □ 90 1 10N 37 0 E
Samchŏk 76 37 30N 129 10 E
Same 90 4 2 S 37 38 E
Samer 19 50 38N 1 44 E
Samfya 91 11 22 S 29 31 E
Sámi 45 38 15N 20 39 E
Samna 86 25 12N 37 17 E
Samnū 83 27 15N 14 55 E
Samo Alto 124 30 22 S 71 0W
Samobor 39 45 47N 15 44 E
Samoëns 21 46 5N 6 45 E
Samokov 43 42 18N 23 35 E
Samoorombón, Bahía 124 36 5 S 57 20W
Samorogouan 84 11 21N 4 57W
Sámos 45 37 45N 26 50 E
Samos 30 42 44N 7 20W
Samoš 42 45 13N 20 49 E
Samothráki 44 39 48N 19 31 E
Samothráki 44 40 28N 25 28 E
Samoylovka 55 51 12N 43 43 E
Sampa 84 8 0N 2 36W
Sampacho 124 33 20 S 64 50W
Sampang 73 7 11 S 113 13 E
Samper de Calanda 32 41 11N 0 28W
Sampit 72 2 34 S 113 0 E
Sampit, Teluk 72 3 5 S 113 3 E
Samra 64 25 35N 41 0 E
Samsø 49 55 50N 10 35 E
Samsø Bælt 49 55 45N 10 45 E
Samsun 64 41 15N 36 22 E
Samsun Dağı 45 37 45N 27 10 E
Samtredia 57 42 7N 42 24 E
Samui, Ko 71 9 30N 100 0 E
Samur → 57 41 53N 48 32 E
Samusole 91 10 2 S 24 0 E
Samut Prakan 71 13 32N 100 40 E
Samut Sakhon 71 13 31N 100 13 E
Samut Songkhram (Mekong) 71 13 24N 100 1 E
Samwari 68 28 30N 66 46 E
San 84 13 15N 4 57W
San → 27 50 45N 21 51 E
San Adrián, C. de 30 43 21N 8 50W
San Agustin, C. 73 6 20N 126 13 E
San Agustín de Valle Fértil 124 30 35 S 67 30W
San Ambrosio 95 26 28 S 79 53W
San Andreas 118 38 0N 120 39W
San Andrés, I. de 121 12 42N 81 46W
San Andres Mts. 119 33 0N 106 45W
San Andrés Tuxtla 120 18 30N 95 20W
San Angelo 117 31 30N 100 30W
San Antonio, Chile 124 33 40 S 71 40W
San Antonio, N. Mex., U.S.A. 119 33 58N 106 57W
San Antonio, Tex., U.S.A. 117 29 30N 98 30W
San Antonio → 117 28 30N 96 50W
San Antonio Abad 33 38 59N 1 19 E
San Antonio, C., Argent. 124 36 15 S 56 40W
San Antonio, C., Cuba 121 21 50N 84 57W
San Antonio, C. de 33 38 48N 0 12 E
San Antonio de los Baños 121 22 54N 82 31W
San Antonio de los Cobres 124 24 10 S 66 17W
San Antonio Oeste 128 40 40 S 65 0W
San Augustine 117 31 30N 94 7W
San Bartolomeo in Galdo 41 41 23N 15 2 E
San Benedetto 38 45 2N 10 57 E
San Benedetto del Tronto 39 42 57N 13 52 E
San Benito 117 26 5N 97 39W
San Bernardino 119 34 7N 117 18W
San Bernardino Str. 73 13 0N 125 0 E
San Bernardo 124 33 40 S 70 50W
San Bernardo, I. de 126 9 45N 75 50W
San Blas 120 26 4N 108 46W
San Blas, C. 115 29 40N 85 12W
San Borja 126 14 50 S 66 52W
San Buenaventura 120 27 5N 101 32W
San Carlos, Argent. 124 33 50 S 69 0W
San Carlos, Chile 124 36 10 S 72 0W
San Carlos, Mexico 120 29 0N 100 54W
San Carlos, Nic. 121 11 12N 84 50W
San Carlos, Phil. 73 10 29N 123 25 E
San Carlos, Uruguay 125 34 46 S 54 58W
San Carlos, U.S.A. 119 33 24N 110 27W
San Carlos, Amazonas, Venez. 126 1 55N 67 4W
San Carlos, Cojedes, Venez. 126 9 40N 68 36W
San Carlos = Butuku-Luba 85 3 29N 8 33 E
San Carlos de Bariloche 128 41 10 S 71 25W
San Carlos de la Rápita 32 40 37N 0 35 E
San Carlos del Zulia 126 9 1N 71 55W
San Carlos L. 119 33 15N 110 25W
San Cataldo 40 37 30N 13 58 E
San Celoni 32 41 42N 2 30 E
San Clemente, Chile 124 35 30 S 71 29W
San Clemente, Spain 33 39 24N 2 25W
San Clemente, U.S.A. 119 33 29N 117 36W
San Clemente I. 119 32 53N 118 30W
San Constanzo 39 43 46N 13 5 E

• Renamed Harare

San Cristóbal Santéramo in Colle

San Cristóbal, Argent. 124 30 20 S 61 10W
San Cristóbal, Dom. Rep. 121 18 25N 70 6W
San Cristóbal, Venez. 126 16 50N 92 40W
San Cristóbal de las Casas 120 16 50N 92 33W
San Damiano d'Asti 38 44 51N 8 4 E
San Daniele del Friuli 39 46 10N 13 0 E
San Demétrio Corone 41 39 34N 16 22 E
San Diego, Calif., U.S.A. 119 32 43N 117 10W
San Diego, Tex., U.S.A. 117 27 47N 98 15W
San Diego, C. 128 54 40 S 65 10W
San Donà di Piave 39 45 38N 12 34 E
San Elpídio a Mare 39 43 16N 13 41 E
San Estanislao 124 24 39 S 56 26W
San Esteban de Gormaz 32 41 34N 3 13W
San Felice sul Panaro 38 44 51N 11 9 E
San Felipe, Chile 124 32 43 S 70 42W
San Felipe, Mexico 120 31 0N 114 52W
San Felipe, Venez. 126 10 20N 68 44W
San Feliu de Guíxols 32 41 45N 3 1 E
San Feliu de Llobregat 32 41 23N 2 2 E
San Félix 95 26 23 S 80 0W
San Fernando, Chile 124 34 30 S 71 0W
San Fernando, Mexico 120 30 0N 115 10W
San Fernando, Luzon, Phil. 73 16 40N 120 23 E
San Fernando, Luzon, Phil. 73 15 5N 120 37 E
San Fernando, Spain 31 36 28N 6 17W
San Fernando, Trin. 121 10 20N 61 30W
San Fernando, U.S.A. 119 34 15N 118 29W
San Fernando ⤳ 120 24 55N 98 10W
San Fernando de Apure 126 7 54N 67 15W
San Fernando de Atabapo 126 4 3N 67 42W
San Fernando di Púglia 41 41 18N 16 5 E
San Francisco, Argent. 124 31 30 S 62 5W
San Francisco, U.S.A. 119 37 47N 122 30W
San Francisco ⤳ 119 32 59N 109 22W
San Francisco de Macorís 121 19 19N 70 15W
San Francisco del Monte de Oro 124 32 36 S 66 8W
San Francisco del Oro 120 26 52N 105 50W
San Francisco Javier 33 38 42N 1 26 E
San Francisco, Paso de 124 27 0 S 68 0W
San Fratello 41 38 1N 14 33 E
San Gavino Monreale 40 39 33N 8 47 E
San Gil 126 6 33N 73 8W
San Gimignano 38 43 28N 11 3 E
San Giórgio di Nogaro 39 45 50N 13 13 E
San Giórgio Iónico 41 40 27N 17 23 E
San Giovanni Bianco 38 45 52N 9 40 E
San Giovanni in Fiore 41 39 16N 16 42 E
San Giovanni in Persiceto 39 44 39N 11 12 E
San Giovanni Rotondo 41 41 41N 15 42 E
San Giovanni Valdarno 39 43 32N 11 30 E
San Giuliano Terme 38 43 45N 10 26 E
San Gottardo, Paso del 25 46 33N 8 33 E
San Grcángelo 40 40 14N 16 14 E
San Gregorio 125 32 37 S 55 40W
San Guiseppe Iato 40 37 57N 13 11 E
San Ignacio, Boliv. 126 16 20 S 60 55W
San Ignacio, Parag. 124 26 52 S 57 3W
San Ignacio, Laguna 120 26 50N 113 11W
San Ildefonso, C. 73 16 0N 122 1 E
San Isidro 124 34 29 S 58 31W
San Javier, Misiones, Argent. 125 27 55 S 55 5W
San Javier, Santa Fe, Argent. 124 30 40 S 59 55W
San Javier, Boliv. 126 16 18 S 62 30W
San Javier, Chile 124 35 40 S 71 45W
San Javier, Spain 33 37 49N 0 50W
San Joaquin ⤳ 119 37 4N 121 51W
San Jorge 124 31 54 S 61 50W
San Jorge, Bahía de 120 31 20N 113 20W
San Jorge, Golfo 128 46 0 S 66 0W
San Jorge, G. de 32 40 50N 0 55W
San José, Boliv. 126 17 53 S 60 50W
San José, C. Rica 121 10 0N 84 2W
San José, Guat. 120 14 0N 90 50W
San José, Mexico 120 25 0N 110 50W
San Jose, Luzon, Phil. 73 15 45N 120 55 E
San Jose, Mindoro, Phil. 73 12 27N 121 4 E
San Jose, Panay, Phil. 73 10 50N 122 5 E
San José 33 38 55N 1 18 E
San Jose, Calif., U.S.A. 119 37 20N 121 53W
San Jose, N. Mex., U.S.A. 119 35 26N 105 30W
San Jose ⤳ 119 34 58N 106 7W
San José de Feliciano 124 30 26 S 58 46W
San José de Jáchal 124 30 15 S 68 46W
San José de Mayo 124 34 27 S 56 40W
San José de Ocune 126 4 15N 70 20W
San José del Cabo 120 23 0N 109 40W
San José del Guaviare 126 2 35N 72 38W
San Juan, Argent. 124 31 30 S 68 30W
San Juan, Dom. Rep. 121 18 45N 72 45W
San Juan, Mexico 120 21 20N 102 50W
San Juan, Phil. 73 8 25N 126 20 E
San Juan, Pto. Rico 121 18 28N 66 8W
San Juan □ 124 31 9 S 69 0W
San Juan ⤳, Argent. 124 32 20 S 67 25W
San Juan ⤳, Nic. 121 10 56N 83 42W
San Juan ⤳, U.S.A. 119 37 20N 110 20W
San Juan Bautista, Parag. 124 26 37 S 57 6W
San Juan Bautista, Spain 33 39 5N 1 31 E
San Juan, C. 88 1 5N 9 20 E
San Juan Capistrano 119 33 29N 117 40W
San Juan de los Morros 126 9 55N 67 21W
San Juan del Norte, B. de 121 11 0N 83 40W
San Juan del Puerto 31 37 20N 6 50W
San Juan del Río 120 20 25N 100 0W
San Juan del Sur 121 11 20N 85 51W
San Juan Mts. 119 38 30N 108 30W
San Julián 128 49 15 S 67 45W
San Just, Sierra de 32 40 45N 0 49W
San Justo 124 30 47 S 60 30W
San Lázaro, C. 120 24 50N 112 18W
San Lázaro, Sa. de 120 23 25N 110 0W
San Leandro 119 37 40N 122 6W
San Leonardo 32 41 51N 3 5W
San Lorenzo, Argent. 124 32 45 S 60 45W
San Lorenzo, Ecuador 126 1 15N 78 50W
San Lorenzo, Parag. 124 25 20 S 57 32W
San Lorenzo ⤳ 120 24 15N 107 24W
San Lorenzo de la Parrilla 32 39 51N 2 22W
San Lorenzo de Morunys 32 42 8N 1 35 E
San Lorenzo, I., Mexico 120 28 35N 112 50W
San Lorenzo, I., Peru 126 12 7 S 77 15W
San Lorenzo, Mt. 128 47 40 S 72 20W
San Lucas, Boliv. 126 20 5 S 65 7W
San Lucas, Mexico 120 27 10N 112 14W
San Lucas, C. de 120 22 50N 110 0W
San Lúcido 41 39 18N 16 3 E
San Luis, Argent. 124 33 20 S 66 20W
San Luis, U.S.A. 119 37 3N 105 26W
San Luis □ 124 34 0 S 66 0W
San Luis de la Paz 120 21 19N 100 32W
San Luis, I. 120 29 58N 114 26W
San Luis Obispo 119 35 21N 120 38W
San Luis Potosí 120 22 9N 100 59W
San Luis Potosí □ 120 22 10N 101 0W
San Luis Río Colorado 120 32 29N 114 58W
San Luis, Sierra de 124 32 30 S 66 10W
San Marco Argentano 41 39 34N 16 8 E
San Marco dei Cavoti 41 41 20N 14 50 E
San Marco in Lámis 41 41 43N 15 38 E
San Marcos, Guat. 120 14 59N 91 52W
San Marcos, Mexico 120 27 13N 112 6W
San Marcos, U.S.A. 117 29 53N 98 0W
San Marino 39 43 56N 12 25 E
San Marino ■ 39 43 56N 12 25 E
San Martín 124 33 5 S 68 28W
San Martín de Valdeiglesias 30 40 21N 4 24W
San Martín, L. 128 48 50 S 72 50W
San Martino de Calvi 38 45 57N 9 41 E
San Mateo, Spain 32 40 28N 0 10 E
San Mateo, U.S.A. 119 37 32N 122 19W
San Matías 126 16 25 S 58 20W
San Matías, Golfo 128 41 30 S 64 0W
San Matías, G. of 122 41 30 S 64 0W
San Miguel, El Sal. 120 13 30N 88 12W
San Miguel, Spain 33 39 3N 1 26 E
San Miguel, U.S.A. 119 35 45N 120 42W
San Miguel ⤳ 126 13 52 S 63 56W
San Miguel de Salinas 33 37 59N 0 47W
San Miguel de Tucumán 124 26 50 S 65 20W
San Miguel del Monte 124 35 23 S 58 50W
San Miniato 38 43 40N 10 50 E
San Narciso 73 15 2N 120 3 E
San Nicolás de los Arroyas 124 33 25 S 60 10W
San Nicolas I. 119 33 16N 119 30W
San Pablo 124 21 43 S 66 38W
San Paolo di Civitate 41 41 44N 15 16 E
San Pedro, Buenos Aires, Argent. 125 26 30 S 54 10W
San Pedro, Jujuy, Argent. 124 24 12 S 64 55W
San-Pédro 84 4 50N 6 33W
San Pedro □ 124 24 0 S 57 0W
San Pedro ⤳, Chihuahua, Mexico 120 28 20N 106 10W
San Pedro ⤳, Nayarit, Mexico 120 21 45N 105 30W
San Pedro ⤳, U.S.A. 119 33 0N 110 50W
San Pedro de Atacama 124 22 55 S 68 15W
San Pedro de Jujuy 124 24 12 S 64 55W
San Pedro de las Colonias 120 25 50N 102 59W
San Pedro de Lloc 126 7 15 S 79 28W
San Pedro de Macorís 121 18 30N 69 18W
San Pedro del Paraná 124 26 43 S 56 13W
San Pedro del Pinatar 33 37 50N 0 50W
San Pedro Mártir, Sierra 120 31 0N 115 30W
San Pedro Mixtepec 120 16 2N 97 7W
San Pedro Ocampo = Melchor Ocampo 120 24 52N 101 40W
San Pedro, Pta. 124 25 30 S 70 38W
San Pedro, Sierra de 31 39 18N 6 40W
San Pedro Sula 120 15 30N 88 0W
San Pedro,Pta. 124 25 30 S 70 38W
San Pietro, I. 40 39 9N 8 17 E
San Pietro Vernótico 41 40 28N 18 0 E
San Quintín 73 16 1N 120 56 E
San Rafael, Argent. 124 34 40 S 68 21W
San Rafael, Calif., U.S.A. 118 37 59N 122 32W
San Rafael, N. Mex., U.S.A. 119 35 6N 107 58W
San Ramón de la Nueva Orán 124 23 10 S 64 20W
San Remo 38 43 48N 7 47 E
San Roque, Argent. 124 28 25 S 58 45W
San Roque, Spain 31 36 17N 5 21W
San Rosendo 124 37 16 S 72 43W
San Saba 117 31 12N 98 45W
San Salvador 120 13 40N 89 10W
San Salvador de Jujuy 124 24 10 S 64 48W
San Salvador I. 121 24 0N 74 32W
San Sebastián, Argent. 128 53 10 S 68 30W
San Sebastián, Spain 32 43 17N 1 58W
San Serverino Marche 39 43 13N 13 10 E
San Simon 119 32 14N 109 16W
San Stéfano di Cadore 39 46 34N 12 33 E
San Valentin, Mte. 128 46 30 S 73 30W
San Vicente de Alcántara 31 39 22N 7 8W
San Vicente de la Barquera 30 43 23N 4 29W
San Vincenzo 38 43 6N 10 29 E
San Vito 40 39 26N 9 32 E
San Vito al Tagliamento 39 45 55N 12 50 E
San Vito, C. 40 38 11N 12 41 E
San Vito Chietino 39 42 19N 14 27 E
San Vito dei Normanni 41 40 40N 17 40 E
San Ygnacio 117 27 6N 99 24W
Sana' 63 15 27N 44 12 E
Sana ⤳ 39 45 3N 16 23 E
Sanaba 84 12 25N 3 47W
Sanabria, La 30 42 0N 6 30W
Sanâfir 86 27 55N 34 37 E
Sanaga ⤳ 88 3 35N 9 38 E
Sanak I. 104 53 30N 162 30W
Sanana 73 2 5 S 125 59 E
Sanand 68 22 59N 72 25 E
Sanandaj 64 35 18N 47 1 E
Sanandita 124 21 40 S 63 45W
Sanary 21 43 7N 5 48 E
Sanawad 68 22 11N 76 5 E
Sancergues 19 47 10N 2 54 E
Sancerre 19 47 20N 2 50 E
Sancerrois, Coll. du 19 47 20N 2 40 E
Sancha He ⤳ 77 26 48N 106 7 E
Sanchor 68 24 45N 71 55 E
Sanco, Pt. 73 8 15N 126 24 E
Sancoins 19 46 47N 2 55 E
Sancti-Spíritus 121 21 52N 79 33W
Sand ⤳ 93 22 25 S 30 5 E
Sand Springs 117 36 12N 96 5W
Sandah 86 20 35N 39 32 E
Sandakan 72 5 53N 118 4 E
Sandan 71 12 46N 106 0 E
Sandanski 43 41 35N 23 16 E
Sandaré 84 14 40N 10 15W
Sanday 14 59 15N 2 30W
Sande, Möre og Romsdal, Norway 47 62 15N 5 27 E
Sande, Sogn og Fjordane, Norway 47 61 20N 5 47 E
Sandefjord 47 59 10N 10 15 E
Sandeid 47 59 33N 5 52 E
Sanders 119 35 12N 109 25W
Sanderson 117 30 5N 102 30W
Sandfly L. 109 55 43N 106 6W
Sandgate 99 27 18 S 153 3 E
Sandia 126 14 10 S 69 30W
Sandıklı 64 38 30N 30 20 E
Sandnes 47 58 50N 5 45 E
Sandness 14 60 18N 1 38W
Sandoa 88 9 41 S 23 0 E
Sandomierz 28 50 40N 21 43 E
Sandover ⤳ 97 21 43 S 136 32 E
Sandoway 67 18 20N 94 30 E
Sandpoint 118 48 20N 116 34W
Sandringham 12 52 50N 0 30 E
Sandslån 48 63 2N 17 49 E
Sandspit 108 53 14N 131 49W
Sandstone 96 27 59 S 119 16 E
Sandusky, Mich., U.S.A. 106 43 26N 82 50W
Sandusky, Ohio, U.S.A. 114 41 25N 82 40W
Sandvig 49 55 18N 14 48 E
Sandviken 48 60 38N 16 46 E
Sandwich B., Can. 107 53 40N 57 15W
Sandwich B., S. Afr. 92 23 25 S 14 20 E
Sandwich, C. 98 18 14 S 146 18 E
Sandwich Group 5 57 0 S 27 0W
Sandwip Chan. 67 22 35N 91 35 E
Sandy C., Queens., Austral. 97 24 42 S 153 15 E
Sandy C., Tas., Austral. 97 41 25 S 144 45 E
Sandy Cr. ⤳ 118 41 15N 109 47W
Sandy L. 106 53 2N 93 0W
Sandy Lake 106 53 0N 93 15W
Sandy Narrows 109 55 5N 103 4W
Sanford, Fla., U.S.A. 115 28 45N 81 20W
Sanford, Me., U.S.A. 113 43 28N 70 47W
Sanford, N.C., U.S.A. 115 35 30N 79 10W
Sanford ⤳ 96 27 22 S 115 53 E
Sanford Mt. 104 62 30N 143 0W
Sanga 91 12 22 S 35 21 E
Sanga ⤳ 88 1 5 S 17 0 E
Sanga-Tolon 59 61 50N 149 40 E
Sangamner 70 19 37N 74 15 E
Sangar 59 64 2N 127 31 E
Sangasanga 72 0 36 S 117 13 E
Sange 90 6 58 S 28 21 E
Sangeang 73 8 12 S 119 6 E
Sanger 119 36 41N 119 35W
Sangerhausen 24 51 28N 11 18 E
Sanggan He ⤳ 76 38 12N 117 15 E
Sanggau 72 0 5N 110 30 E
Sangihe, Kepulauan 73 3 0N 126 0 E
Sangihe, P. 73 3 45N 125 30 E
Sangkapura 72 5 52 S 112 40 E
Sangli 70 16 55N 74 33 E
Sangmélina 88 2 57N 12 1 E
Sangonera ⤳ 33 37 59N 1 4W
Sangre de Cristo Mts. 117 37 0N 105 0W
Sangro ⤳ 39 42 14N 14 32 E
Sangudo 108 53 50N 114 54W
Sangüesa 32 42 37N 1 17W
Sanguinaires, Îs. 21 41 51N 8 36 E
Sangzhi 77 29 25N 110 12 E
Sanhala 84 10 3N 6 51W
Sanish 116 48 0N 102 30W
Sanje 90 0 49 S 31 30 E
Sanjiang 77 25 48N 109 37 E
Sankaranayinarkovil 70 9 10N 77 35 E
Sankeshwar 70 16 23N 74 32 E
Sankt Andra 26 46 46N 14 50 E
Sankt Blasien 25 47 47N 8 7 E
Sankt Gallen 25 47 26N 9 22 E
Sankt Gallen □ 25 47 25N 9 22 E
Sankt Gotthard P. = San Gottardo, Paso del 25 46 33N 8 33 E
Sankt Ingbert 25 49 16N 7 6 E
Sankt Johann, Salzburg, Austria 26 47 22N 13 12 E
Sankt Johann, Tirol, Austria 26 47 30N 12 25 E
Sankt Moritz 25 46 30N 9 50 E
Sankt Olof 49 55 37N 14 8 E
Sankt Pölten 26 48 12N 15 38 E
Sankt Valentin 26 48 11N 14 33 E
Sankt Veit 26 46 54N 14 22 E
Sankt Wendel 25 49 27N 7 9 E
Sankt Wolfgang 26 47 43N 13 27 E
Sankuru ⤳ 88 4 17 S 20 25 E
Sanlúcar de Barrameda 31 36 46N 6 21W
Sanlúcar la Mayor 31 37 26N 6 18W
Sanluri 40 39 35N 8 55 E
Sanmenxia 77 34 47N 111 12 E
Sannaspos 92 29 6 S 26 34 E
Sannicandro Gargánico 41 41 50N 15 34 E
Sannidal 47 58 55N 9 15 E
Sannieshof 92 26 30 S 25 47 E
Sanok 27 49 35N 22 10 E
Sanquhar 14 55 21N 3 56W
Sansanding Dam 84 13 48N 6 0W
Sansepolcro 39 43 34N 12 8 E
Sanshui 75 23 10N 112 56 E
Sanski Most 39 44 46N 16 40 E
Sant' Ágata de Goti 41 41 6N 14 30 E
Sant' Ágata di Militello 41 38 2N 14 8 E
Santa Ana, Boliv. 126 13 50 S 65 40W
Santa Ana, Ecuador 126 1 16 S 80 20W
Santa Ana, El Sal. 120 14 0N 89 31W
Santa Ana, Mexico 120 30 31N 111 8W
Santa Ana, U.S.A. 119 33 48N 117 55W
Sant' Ángelo Lodigiano 38 45 14N 9 25 E
Sant' Antíoco 40 39 2N 8 30 E
Sant' Arcángelo di Romagna 39 44 4N 12 26 E
Santa Bárbara, Mexico 120 26 48N 105 50W
Santa Bárbara, Spain 32 40 42N 0 29 E
Santa Barbara 119 34 25N 119 40W
Santa Bárbara, Mt. 33 37 23N 2 50W
Santa Catalina 120 25 40N 110 50W
Santa Catalina, G. of 119 33 0N 118 0W
Santa Catalina I. 119 33 20N 118 30W
Santa Catarina □ 125 27 25 S 48 30W
Santa Catarina, I. de 125 27 30 S 48 40W
Santa Caterina Villarmosa 41 37 37N 14 1 E
Santa Cecília 125 26 56 S 50 18W
Santa Clara, Cuba 121 22 20N 80 0W
Santa Clara, Calif., U.S.A. 119 37 21N 122 0W
Santa Clara, Utah, U.S.A. 119 37 10N 113 38W
Santa Clara de Olimar 125 32 50 S 54 54W
Santa Clara Pk. 119 35 58N 106 45W
Santa Clotilde 126 2 33 S 73 45W
Santa Coloma de Farnés 32 41 50N 2 39 E
Santa Coloma de Gramanet 32 41 27N 2 13 E
Santa Comba 30 43 2N 8 49W
Santa Croce Camerina 41 36 50N 14 30 E
Santa Croce di Magliano 41 41 43N 14 59 E
Santa Cruz, Argent. 128 50 0 S 68 32W
Santa Cruz, Boliv. 126 17 43 S 63 10W
Santa Cruz, Chile 124 34 38 S 71 27W
Santa Cruz, C. Rica 121 10 15N 85 35W
Santa Cruz, Phil. 73 14 20N 121 24 E
Santa Cruz, Calif., U.S.A. 119 36 55N 122 1W
Santa Cruz, N. Mexico, U.S.A. 119 35 59N 106 1W
Santa Cruz □ 126 17 43 S 63 10W
Santa Cruz ⤳ 128 50 10 S 68 20W
Santa Cruz de Mudela 33 38 39N 3 28W
Sta. Cruz de Tenerife 80 28 28N 16 15W
Santa Cruz del Retamar 30 40 8N 4 14W
Santa Cruz del Sur 121 20 44N 78 0W
Santa Cruz do Rio Pardo 125 22 54 S 49 37W
Santa Cruz do Sul 125 29 42 S 52 25W
Santa Cruz I. 119 34 0N 119 45W
Santa Cruz, Is. 94 10 30 S 166 0 E
Santa Domingo, Cay 121 21 25N 75 15W
Santa Elena, Argent. 124 30 58 S 59 47W
Santa Elena, Ecuador 126 2 16 S 80 52W
Santa Elena, C. 121 10 54N 85 56W
Sant' Eufémia, Golfo di 41 38 50N 16 10 E
Santa Eulalia 33 38 59N 1 32 E
Santa Fe, Argent. 124 31 35 S 60 41W
Santa Fe, Spain 31 37 11N 3 43W
Santa Fe, U.S.A. 119 35 40N 106 0W
Santa Fé □ 124 31 50 S 60 55W
Santa Filomena 127 9 6 S 45 50W
Santa Genoveva 120 23 18N 109 52W
Santa Inés 31 38 32N 5 37W
Santa Inés, I. 128 54 0 S 73 0W
Santa Isabel, Argent. 124 36 10 S 66 54W
Santa Isabel, Brazil 127 11 45 S 51 30W
Santa Isabel = Rey Malabo 85 3 45N 8 50 E
Santa Isabel, Pico 85 3 36N 8 49 E
Santa Lucía, Corrientes, Argent. 124 28 58 S 59 5W
Santa Lucía, San Juan, Argent. 124 31 30 S 68 30W
Santa Lucía, Spain 33 37 35N 0 58W
Santa Lucia 124 34 27 S 56 24W
Santa Lucia Range 119 36 0N 121 20W
Santa Margarita, Argent. 124 38 28 S 61 35W
Santa Margarita, Mexico 120 24 30N 111 50W
Santa Margherita 38 44 20N 9 11 E
Santa María 124 26 40 S 66 0W
Santa Maria, Brazil 125 29 40 S 53 48W
Santa María, Spain 32 39 38N 2 47 E
Santa Maria, U.S.A. 119 34 58N 120 29W
Santa Maria, Zambia 91 11 5 S 29 58 E
Santa María ⤳ 120 31 0N 107 14W
Santa María, Bahía de 120 25 10N 108 40W
Santa Maria, Cabo de 31 36 58N 7 53W
Santa Maria Capua Vetere 41 41 3N 14 15 E
Santa Maria da Vitória 127 13 24 S 44 12W
Santa María del Oro 120 25 58N 105 20W
Santa Maria di Leuca, C. 41 39 48N 18 20 E
Santa María la Real de Nieva 30 41 4N 4 24W
Santa Marta, Colomb. 126 11 15N 74 13W
Santa Marta, Spain 31 38 37N 6 39W
Santa Marta Grande, C. 125 28 43 S 48 50W
Santa Marta, Ría de 30 43 44N 7 45W
Santa Marta, Sierra Nevada de 126 10 55N 73 50W
Santa Maura = Levkás 45 38 40N 20 43 E
Santa Monica 119 34 0N 118 30W
Santa Olalla, Huelva, Spain 31 37 54N 6 14W
Santa Olalla, Toledo, Spain 30 40 2N 4 25W
Sant' Onofrio 41 38 42N 16 10 E
Santa Paula 119 34 20N 119 2W
Santa Pola 33 38 13N 0 35W
Santa Rita 119 32 50N 108 0W
Santa Rosa, La Pampa, Argent. 124 36 40 S 64 17W
Santa Rosa, San Luis, Argent. 124 32 21 S 65 10W
Santa Rosa, Boliv. 126 10 36 S 67 20W
Santa Rosa, Brazil 125 27 52 S 54 29W
Santa Rosa, Calif., U.S.A. 118 38 26N 122 43W
Santa Rosa, N. Mexico, U.S.A. 117 34 58N 104 40W
Santa Rosa de Copán 120 14 47N 88 46W
Santa Rosa de Río Primero 124 31 8 S 63 20W
Santa Rosa I., Calif., U.S.A. 119 34 0N 120 6W
Santa Rosa I., Fla., U.S.A. 115 30 23N 87 0W
Santa Rosa Mts. 118 41 45N 117 30W
Santa Rosalía 120 27 20N 112 20W
Santa Sofia 39 43 57N 11 55 E
Santa Sylvina 124 27 50 S 61 10W
Santa Tecla = Nueva San Salvador 120 13 40N 89 25W
Santa Teresa 124 33 25 S 60 47W
Santa Teresa di Riva 41 37 58N 15 21 E
Santa Teresa Gallura 40 41 14N 9 12 E
Santa Vitória do Palmar 125 33 32 S 53 25W
Santadi 40 39 5N 8 42 E
Santai 75 31 5N 104 58 E
Santana, Coxilha de 125 30 50 S 55 35W
Santana do Livramento 125 30 55 S 55 30W
Santanayi 33 39 20N 3 5 E
Santander 30 43 27N 3 51W
Santander □ 30 43 25N 4 0W
Santander Jiménez 120 24 11N 98 29W
Santaquin 118 40 0N 111 51W
Santarém, Brazil 127 2 25 S 54 42W
Santarém, Port. 31 39 12N 8 42W
Santarém □ 31 39 10N 8 40W
Santaren Channel 121 24 0N 79 30W
Santéramo in Colle 41 40 48N 16 45 E

Santerno **Scunthorpe**

Santerno →	**39**	44 10N	11 38 E
Santhia	**38**	45 20N	8 10 E
Santiago, Brazil	**125**	29 11 S	54 52W
Santiago, Chile	**124**	33 24 S	70 40W
Santiago, Panama	**121**	8 0N	81 0W
Santiago □	**124**	33 30 S	70 50W
Santiago de Compostela	**30**	42 52N	8 37W
Santiago de Cuba	**121**	20 0N	75 49W
Santiago de los Cabelleros	**121**	19 30N	70 40W
Santiago del Estero	**124**	27 50 S	64 15W
Santiago del Estero □	**124**	27 40 S	63 15W
Santiago do Cacém	**31**	38 1N	8 42W
Santiago Ixcuintla	**120**	21 50N	105 11W
Santiago Papasquiaro	**120**	25 0N	105 20W
Santiago, Punta de	**85**	3 12N	8 40 E
Santiaguillo, L. de	**120**	24 50N	104 50W
Santillana del Mar	**30**	43 24N	4 6W
Santipur	**69**	23 17N	88 25 E
Santisteban del Puerto	**33**	38 17N	3 15W
Santo Amaro	**127**	12 30 S	38 43W
Santo Anastácio	**125**	21 58 S	51 39W
Santo André	**125**	23 39 S	46 29W
Santo Ângelo	**125**	28 15 S	54 15W
Santo Antonio	**127**	15 50 S	56 0W
Santo Corazón	**126**	18 0 S	58 45W
Santo Domingo, Dom. Rep.	**121**	18 30N	64 54W
Santo Domingo, Baja Calif. N., Mexico	**120**	30 43N	116 2W
Santo Domingo, Baja Calif. S., Mexico	**120**	25 32N	112 2W
Santo Domingo, Nic.	**121**	12 14N	84 59W
Santo Domingo de la Calzada	**32**	42 26N	2 57W
Santo Stéfano di Camastro	**41**	38 1N	14 22 E
Santo Stino di Livenza	**39**	45 45N	12 40 E
Santo Tirso	**30**	41 21N	8 28W
Santo Tomás	**126**	14 26 S	72 8W
Santo Tomé	**125**	28 40 S	56 5W
Santo Tomé de Guayana	**126**	8 22N	62 40W
Santoña	**30**	43 29N	3 27W
Santos	**125**	24 0 S	46 20W
Santos Dumont	**125**	22 55 S	43 10W
Santos, Sierra de los	**31**	38 7N	5 12W
Şanūr	**62**	32 22N	35 15 E
Sanvignes-les-Mines	**19**	46 40N	4 18 E
Sanyuan	**77**	34 35N	108 58 E
Sanza Pombo	**88**	7 18 S	15 56 E
São Anastácio	**125**	22 0 S	51 40W
São Bartolomeu de Messines	**31**	37 15N	8 17W
São Borja	**125**	28 39 S	56 0W
São Bras d'Alportel	**31**	37 8N	7 37W
São Carlos	**125**	22 0 S	47 50W
São Cristóvão	**127**	11 1 S	37 15W
São Domingos	**127**	13 25 S	46 19W
São Francisco	**127**	16 0 S	44 50W
São Francisco →	**127**	10 30 S	36 24W
São Francisco do Sul	**125**	26 15 S	48 36W
São Gabriel	**125**	30 20 S	54 20W
São Gonçalo	**125**	22 48 S	43 5W
Sao Hill	**91**	8 20 S	35 12 E
São João da Boa Vista	**125**	22 0 S	46 52W
São João da Pesqueira	**30**	41 8N	7 24W
São João del Rei	**125**	21 8 S	44 15W
São João do Araguaia	**127**	5 23 S	48 46W
São João do Piauí	**127**	8 21 S	42 15W
São José do Rio Prêto	**125**	20 50 S	49 20W
São José dos Campos	**125**	23 7 S	45 52W
São Leopoldo	**125**	29 50 S	51 10W
São Lourenço	**125**	22 7 S	45 3W
São Lourenço →	**127**	17 53 S	57 27W
São Luís Gonzaga	**125**	28 25 S	55 0W
São Luís (Maranhão)	**127**	2 39 S	44 15W
São Marcos →	**127**	18 15 S	47 37W
São Marcos, B. de	**127**	2 0 S	44 0W
São Martinho	**30**	40 18N	8 8W
São Mateus	**127**	18 44 S	39 50W
São Miguel	**8**	37 33N	25 27W
São Paulo	**125**	23 32 S	46 37W
São Paulo □	**125**	22 0 S	49 0W
Sao Paulo, I.	**6**	0 50N	31 40W
São Pedro do Sul	**30**	40 46N	8 4W
São Roque, C. de	**127**	5 30 S	35 16W
São Sebastião do Paraíso	**125**	20 54 S	46 59W
São Sebastião, I. de	**125**	23 50 S	45 18W
São Teotónio	**31**	37 30N	8 42W
São Tomé	**79**	0 10N	6 39 E
São Tomé, C. de	**125**	22 0 S	40 59W
São Vicente	**125**	23 57 S	46 23W
São Vicente, Cabo de	**31**	37 0N	9 0W
Saona, I.	**121**	18 10N	68 40W
Saône →	**19**	45 44N	4 50 E
Saône-et-Loire □	**19**	46 25N	4 50 E
Saonek	**73**	0 22 S	130 55 E
Saoura, O. →	**82**	29 0N	0 55W
Sápai	**44**	41 2N	25 43 E
Saparua	**73**	3 33 S	128 40 E
Sapele	**85**	5 50N	5 40 E
Sapelo I.	**115**	31 28N	81 15W
Sapiéntza	**45**	36 45N	21 43 E
Sapone	**85**	12 3N	1 35W
Saposoa	**126**	6 55 S	76 45W
Sapozhok	**55**	53 59N	40 41 E
Sapphire Mts.	**118**	46 20N	113 45W
Sapporo	**74**	43 0N	141 21 E
Sapri	**41**	40 5N	15 37 E
Sapudi	**73**	7 2 S	114 17 E
Sapulpa	**117**	36 0N	96 0W
Saqqez	**64**	36 15N	46 20 E
Sar-e Pol	**65**	36 10N	66 0 E
Sar Planina	**42**	42 10N	21 0 E
Sara	**84**	11 40N	3 53W
Sarāb	**64**	38 0N	47 30 E
Saragossa = Zaragoza	**32**	41 39N	0 53W
Saraguro	**126**	3 35 S	79 16W
Saraipalli	**69**	21 20N	82 59 E
Sarajevo	**42**	43 52N	18 26 E
Saralu	**46**	44 43N	28 10 E
Saran	**86**	19 35N	40 30 E
Saran, G.	**72**	0 30 S	111 25 E
Saranac Lake	**114**	44 20N	74 10W
Saranda, Alb.	**44**	39 52N	19 55 E
Saranda, Tanz.	**90**	5 45 S	34 59 E
Sarandí del Yi	**125**	33 18 S	55 38W
Sarandí Grande	**124**	33 44 S	56 20W
Sarangani B.	**73**	6 0N	125 13 E
Sarangani Is.	**73**	5 25N	125 25 E
Sarangarh	**69**	21 30N	83 5 E
Saransk	**55**	54 10N	45 10 E
Sarapul	**52**	56 28N	53 48 E
Sarasota	**115**	27 20N	82 30W
Saratoga	**118**	41 30N	106 48W
Saratoga Springs	**114**	43 5N	73 47W
Saratov	**55**	51 30N	46 2 E
Saravane	**71**	15 43N	106 25 E
Sarawak □	**72**	2 0N	113 0 E
Saraya	**84**	12 50N	11 45W
Sarbāz	**65**	26 38N	61 19 E
Sarbīsheh	**65**	32 30N	59 40 E
Sârbogârd	**27**	46 50N	18 40 E
Sarca →	**38**	45 52N	10 52 E
Sardalas	**83**	25 50N	10 34 E
Sardarshahr	**68**	28 30N	74 29 E
Sardegna	**40**	39 57N	9 0 E
Sardhana	**68**	29 9N	77 39 E
Sardinia = Sardegna	**40**	39 57N	9 0 E
Šarengrad	**42**	45 14N	19 16 E
Saréyamou	**84**	16 7N	3 10W
Sargasso Sea	**6**	27 0N	72 0W
Sargent	**116**	41 42N	99 24W
Sargodha	**68**	32 10N	72 40 E
* Sargodha □	**68**	31 50N	72 0 E
Sarh	**81**	9 5N	18 23 E
Sarhro, Djebel	**82**	31 6N	5 0W
Sārī	**65**	36 30N	53 4 E
Sária	**45**	35 54N	27 17 E
Sarida →	**62**	32 4N	34 45 E
Sarikamiş	**64**	40 22N	42 35 E
Sarikei	**72**	2 8N	111 30 E
Sarina	**97**	21 22 S	149 13 E
Sariñena	**32**	41 47N	0 10W
Sarīr Tibasti	**83**	22 50N	18 30 E
Sarita	**117**	27 14N	97 49W
Sariyer	**43**	41 10N	29 3 E
Sark	**18**	49 25N	2 20W
Sarkad	**27**	46 47N	21 23 E
Sarlat-la-Canéda	**20**	44 54N	1 13 E
Sarles	**116**	48 58N	99 0W
Sârmaşu	**46**	46 45N	24 13 E
Sarmi	**73**	1 49 S	138 44 E
Sarmiento	**128**	45 35 S	69 5W
Särna	**48**	61 41N	13 8 E
Sarnano	**39**	43 2N	13 17 E
Sarnen	**25**	46 53N	8 13 E
Sarnia	**106**	42 58N	82 23W
Sarno	**41**	40 48N	14 35 E
Sarnowa	**28**	51 39N	16 53 E
Sarny	**54**	51 17N	26 40 E
Särö	**49**	57 31N	11 57 E
Sarolangun	**72**	2 19 S	102 42 E
Saronikós Kólpos	**45**	37 45N	23 45 E
Saronno	**38**	45 38N	9 2 E
Saros Körfezi	**44**	40 30N	26 15 E
Sárospatak	**27**	48 18N	21 33 E
Sarosul Românesc	**42**	45 34N	21 43 E
Sarova	**55**	54 55N	43 19 E
Sarpsborg	**47**	59 16N	11 12 E
Sarracín	**32**	42 15N	3 45W
Sarralbe	**19**	48 55N	7 1 E
Sarre = Saar →	**19**	49 7N	7 4 E
Sarre, La	**106**	48 45N	79 15W
Sarre-Union	**19**	48 55N	7 4 E
Sarrebourg	**19**	48 43N	7 3 E
Sarreguemines	**19**	49 1N	7 4 E
Sarriá	**30**	42 49N	7 29W
Sarrión	**32**	40 9N	0 49W
Sarro	**84**	13 40N	5 15W
Sarstedt	**24**	52 13N	9 50 E
Sartène	**21**	41 38N	8 58 E
Sarthe □	**18**	47 58N	0 10 E
Sarthe →	**18**	47 33N	0 31W
Sartilly	**18**	48 45N	1 28W
Sartynya	**58**	63 22N	63 11 E
Sarum	**86**	21 11N	39 10 E
Sarūr	**65**	23 17N	58 4 E
Sárvár	**27**	47 15N	16 56 E
Sarvestān	**65**	29 20N	53 10 E
Särvfjället	**48**	62 42N	13 30 E
Sárviz →	**27**	46 24N	18 41 E
Sary-Tash	**58**	39 44N	73 15 E
Sarych, Mys.	**56**	44 25N	33 45 E
Saryshagan	**58**	46 12N	73 38 E
Sarzana	**38**	44 5N	9 59 E
Sarzeau	**18**	47 31N	2 48W
Sasa	**62**	33 2N	35 23 E
Sasabeneh	**63**	7 59N	44 43 E
Sasaram	**69**	24 57N	84 5 E
Sasca Montană	**42**	44 50N	21 45 E
Sasebo	**74**	33 10N	129 43 E
Saser Mt.	**69**	34 50N	77 50 E
Saskatchewan □	**109**	54 40N	106 0W
Saskatchewan →	**109**	53 37N	100 40W
Saskatoon	**109**	52 10N	106 38W
Saskylakh	**59**	71 55N	114 1 E
Sasnovka	**55**	56 20N	51 4 E
Sasolburg	**93**	26 46 S	27 49 E
Sasovo	**55**	54 25N	41 55 E
Sassandra	**84**	5 0N	6 8W
Sassandra →	**84**	4 58N	6 5W
Sássari	**40**	40 44N	8 33 E
Sassnitz	**24**	54 29N	13 39 E
Sasso Marconi	**39**	44 22N	11 12 E
Sassocorvaro	**39**	43 47N	12 30 E
Sassoferrato	**39**	43 26N	12 51 E
Sassuolo	**38**	44 31N	10 47 E
Sástago	**32**	41 19N	0 21W
Sastown	**84**	4 45N	8 27W
Sasumua Dam	**90**	0 45 S	36 40 E
Sasyk, Ozero	**46**	45 45N	30 0 E
Sata-Misaki	**74**	30 59N	130 40 E
Satadougou	**84**	12 25N	11 25W
Satanta	**117**	37 30N	101 0W
Satara	**70**	17 44N	73 58 E
Satilla →	**115**	30 59N	81 28W
Satka	**52**	55 3N	59 1 E
Satkhira	**69**	22 43N	89 8 E
Satmala Hills	**70**	20 15N	74 40 E
Satna	**69**	24 35N	80 50 E
Sator	**39**	44 11N	16 37 E
Sátoraljaújhely	**27**	48 25N	21 41 E
Satpura Ra.	**68**	21 25N	76 10 E
Satrup	**24**	54 39N	9 38 E
Sattenapalle	**70**	16 25N	80 6 E
Satu Mare	**46**	47 46N	22 55 E
Satui	**72**	3 50 S	115 27 E
Satumare □	**46**	47 45N	23 0 E
Satun	**71**	6 43N	100 2 E
Saturnina →	**126**	12 15 S	58 10W
Sauce	**124**	30 5 S	58 46W
Saucillo	**120**	28 1N	105 17W
Sauda	**47**	59 40N	6 20 E
Sauðarkrókur	**50**	65 45N	19 40W
Saudi Arabia ■	**64**	26 0N	44 0 E
Sauerland	**24**	51 0N	8 0 E
Saugeen →	**112**	44 30N	81 22W
Saugerties	**114**	42 4N	73 58W
Saugues	**20**	44 58N	3 32 E
Sauherad	**47**	59 25N	9 15 E
Saujon	**20**	45 41N	0 55W
Sauk Center	**116**	45 42N	94 56W
Sauk Rapids	**116**	45 35N	94 10W
Saulgau	**25**	48 4N	9 32 E
Saulieu	**19**	47 17N	4 14 E
Sault	**21**	44 6N	5 24 E
Sault Ste. Marie, Can.	**106**	46 30N	84 20W
Sault Ste. Marie, U.S.A.	**114**	46 27N	84 22W
Saumlaki	**73**	7 55 S	131 20 E
Saumur	**18**	47 15N	0 5W
Saunders C.	**101**	45 53 S	170 45 E
Saunders I.	**5**	57 48 S	26 28W
Saurbær, Borgarfjarðarsýsla, Iceland	**50**	64 24N	21 35W
Saurbær, Eyjafjarðarsýsla, Iceland	**50**	65 27N	18 13W
Sauri	**85**	11 42N	6 44 E
Saurimo	**88**	9 40 S	20 12 E
Sauveterre	**20**	43 25N	0 57W
Sauzé-Vaussais	**20**	46 8N	0 8 E
Sava	**39**	40 28N	17 32 E
Sava →	**39**	44 50N	20 26 E
Savage	**116**	47 27N	104 20W
Savai'i	**101**	13 28 S	172 24W
Savalou	**85**	7 57N	1 58 E
Savane	**91**	19 37 S	35 8 E
Savanna	**116**	42 5N	90 10W
Savanna la Mar	**121**	18 10N	78 10W
Savannah, Ga., U.S.A.	**115**	32 4N	81 4W
Savannah, Mo., U.S.A.	**116**	39 55N	94 46W
Savannah, Tenn., U.S.A.	**115**	35 12N	88 18W
Savannah →	**115**	32 2N	80 53W
Savannakhet	**71**	16 30N	104 49 E
Savant L.	**106**	50 16N	90 44W
Savant Lake	**106**	50 14N	90 40W
Savantvadi	**70**	15 55N	73 54 E
Savanur	**70**	14 59N	75 21 E
Savda	**68**	21 9N	75 56 E
Savé	**85**	8 2N	2 29 E
Save →	**20**	43 47N	1 17 E
Sāveh	**64**	35 2N	50 20 E
Savelugu	**85**	9 38N	0 54W
Savenay	**18**	47 20N	1 55W
Saverdun	**20**	43 14N	1 34 E
Saverne	**19**	48 39N	7 20 E
Savigliano	**38**	44 39N	7 40 E
Savigny-sur-Braye	**18**	47 53N	0 49 E
Saviñao	**30**	42 35N	7 38W
Savio →	**39**	44 19N	12 20 E
Šavnik	**42**	42 59N	19 10 E
Savoie □	**21**	45 26N	6 35 E
Savona	**38**	44 19N	8 29 E
Savonlinna	**52**	61 52N	28 53 E
Sävsjö	**49**	57 20N	14 40 E
Sävsjøström	**49**	57 1N	15 25 E
Sawahlunto	**72**	0 40 S	100 52 E
Sawai	**73**	3 0 S	129 5 E
Sawai Madhopur	**68**	26 0N	76 25 E
Sawara	**74**	35 55N	140 30 E
Sawatch Mts.	**119**	38 30N	106 30W
Sawdā, Jabal as	**83**	28 51N	15 12 E
Sawel, Mt.	**15**	54 48N	7 5W
Sawfajjin, W.	**83**	31 46N	14 30 E
Sawknah	**81**	29 4N	15 47 E
Sawmills	**91**	19 30 S	28 2 E
Sawu	**73**	10 35 S	121 50 E
Sawu Sea	**73**	9 30 S	121 50 E
Sawyerville	**113**	45 20N	71 34W
Saxby →	**98**	18 25 S	140 53 E
Saxony, Lower = Niedersachsen □	**24**	52 45N	9 0 E
Saxton	**112**	40 12N	78 18W
Say	**85**	13 8N	2 22 E
Saya	**85**	9 30N	3 18 E
Sayabec	**107**	48 35N	67 41W
Sayán	**126**	11 8 S	77 12W
Sayan, Vostochnyy	**59**	54 0N	96 0 E
Sayan, Zapadnyy	**59**	52 30N	94 0 E
Sayasan	**57**	42 56N	46 15 E
Saydā	**64**	33 35N	35 25 E
Şayghān	**65**	35 10N	67 55 E
Sayḫut	**63**	15 12N	51 10 E
Saynshand	**75**	44 55N	110 11 E
Sayre, Okla., U.S.A.	**117**	35 20N	99 40W
Sayre, Pa., U.S.A.	**114**	42 0N	76 30W
Sayula	**120**	19 50N	103 40W
Sayville	**113**	40 45N	73 7W
Sazan	**44**	40 30N	19 20 E
Sázava →	**26**	49 53N	14 24 E
Sazin	**69**	35 35N	73 30 E
Sazlika →	**43**	41 59N	25 50 E
Sbeïtla	**83**	35 12N	9 7 E
Scaër	**18**	48 2N	3 42W
Scafell Pikes	**12**	54 26N	3 14W
Scalea	**41**	39 49N	15 47 E
Scalpay	**14**	57 51N	6 40W
Scandia	**108**	50 20N	112 0W
Scandiano	**38**	44 36N	10 40 E
Scandinavia	**9**	64 0N	12 0 E
Scansano	**39**	42 40N	11 20 E
Scapa Flow	**14**	58 52N	3 6W
Scarborough, Trin.	**121**	11 11N	60 42W
Scarborough, U.K.	**12**	54 17N	0 24W
Scarpe →	**19**	50 31N	3 27 E
Šćedro	**39**	43 6N	16 43 E
Scenic	**116**	43 49N	102 32W
Schaal See	**24**	53 40N	10 57 E
Schaffhausen □	**25**	47 42N	8 36 E
Schagen	**16**	52 49N	4 48 E
Schärding	**26**	48 27N	13 27 E
Scharhörn	**24**	53 58N	8 24 E
Scharnitz	**26**	47 23N	11 15 E
Scheessel	**24**	53 10N	9 33 E
Schefferville	**107**	54 48N	66 50W
Scheibbs	**26**	48 1N	15 9 E
Schelde →	**16**	51 15N	4 16 E
Schenectady	**114**	42 50N	73 58W
Scherfede	**24**	51 32N	9 2 E
Schesslitz	**25**	49 59N	11 2 E
Scheveningen	**16**	52 6N	4 16 E
Schiedam	**16**	51 55N	4 25 E
Schiermonnikoog	**16**	53 30N	6 15 E
Schifferstadt	**25**	49 22N	8 23 E
Schiltigheim	**19**	48 35N	7 45 E
Schio	**39**	45 42N	11 21 E
Schirmeck	**19**	48 29N	7 12 E
Schladming	**26**	47 23N	13 41 E
Schlei →	**24**	54 45N	9 52 E
Schleiden	**24**	50 32N	6 26 E
Schleiz	**24**	50 35N	11 49 E
Schleswig	**24**	54 32N	9 34 E
Schleswig-Holstein □	**24**	54 10N	9 40 E
Schlüchtern	**25**	50 20N	9 32 E
Schmalkalden	**24**	50 43N	10 28 E
Schmölin	**24**	50 54N	12 22 E
Schmölln	**24**	53 15N	14 6 E
Schneeberg, Austria	**26**	47 47N	15 48 E
Schneeberg, Ger.	**24**	50 35N	12 39 E
Schofield	**116**	44 54N	89 39W
Schönberg, Rostock, Ger.	**24**	53 50N	10 55 E
Schönberg, Schleswig-Holstein, Ger.	**24**	54 23N	10 20 E
Schönebeck	**24**	52 2N	11 42 E
Schongau	**25**	47 49N	10 54 E
Schöningen	**24**	52 8N	10 57 E
Schortens	**24**	53 37N	7 51 E
Schouten I.	**99**	42 20 S	148 20 E
Schouten, Kepulauan	**73**	1 0 S	136 0 E
Schouwen	**16**	51 43N	3 45 E
Schramberg	**25**	48 12N	8 24 E
Schrankogl	**26**	47 3N	11 7 E
Schreiber	**106**	48 45N	87 20W
Schrobenhausen	**25**	48 33N	11 16 E
Schruns	**26**	47 5N	9 56 E
Schuler	**109**	50 20N	110 6W
Schumacher	**106**	48 30N	81 16W
Schurz	**118**	38 57N	118 48W
Schuyler	**116**	41 30N	97 3W
Schuylkill Haven	**113**	40 37N	76 11W
Schwabach	**25**	49 19N	11 3 E
Schwäbisch Gmünd	**25**	48 49N	9 48 E
Schwäbisch Hall	**25**	49 7N	9 45 E
Schwäbische Alb	**25**	48 30N	9 30 E
Schwabmünchen	**25**	48 11N	10 45 E
Schwandorf	**25**	49 20N	12 7 E
Schwarmstedt	**24**	52 41N	9 37 E
Schwarzach →	**26**	46 56N	12 35 E
Schwärze	**24**	52 50N	13 49 E
Schwarzenberg	**24**	50 31N	12 49 E
Schwarzwald	**25**	48 0N	8 0 E
Schwaz	**26**	47 20N	11 44 E
Schwedt	**24**	53 4N	14 18 E
Schweinfurt	**25**	50 3N	10 12 E
Schweizer Reneke	**92**	27 11 S	25 18 E
Schwerin	**24**	53 37N	11 22 E
Schwerin □	**24**	53 35N	11 20 E
Schweriner See	**24**	53 45N	11 26 E
Schwetzingen	**25**	49 22N	8 35 E
Schwyz	**25**	47 2N	8 39 E
Schwyz □	**25**	47 2N	8 39 E
Sciacca	**40**	37 30N	13 3 E
Scicli	**41**	36 48N	14 41 E
Scie, La	**107**	49 57N	55 36W
Scilla	**41**	38 18N	15 44 E
Scilly, Isles of	**13**	49 55N	6 15W
Šcinawa	**28**	51 25N	16 26 E
Scione	**44**	39 57N	23 36 E
Scioto →	**114**	38 44N	83 0W
Scobey	**116**	48 47N	105 30W
Scone, Austral.	**99**	32 5 S	150 52 E
Scone, U.K.	**14**	56 25N	3 26W
Scordia	**41**	37 19N	14 50 E
Scoresbysund	**4**	70 20N	23 0W
Scorno, Punta dello	**40**	41 7N	8 23 E
Scotia, Calif., U.S.A.	**118**	40 36N	124 4W
Scotia, N.Y., U.S.A.	**113**	42 50N	73 58W
Scotia Sea	**5**	56 5 S	56 0W
Scotland	**116**	43 10N	97 45W
Scotland □	**13**	57 0N	4 0W
Scotland Neck	**115**	36 6N	77 32W
Scott	**5**	77 0 S	165 0 E
Scott, C.	**5**	71 30 S	168 0 E
Scott City	**116**	38 30N	100 52W
Scott Glacier	**5**	66 15 S	100 5 E
Scott I.	**5**	67 0 S	179 0 E
Scott Inlet	**105**	71 0N	71 0W
Scott Is.	**108**	50 48N	128 40W
Scott L.	**109**	59 55N	106 18W
Scott Reef	**96**	14 0 S	121 50 E
Scottburgh	**93**	30 15 S	30 47 E
Scottdale	**112**	40 8N	79 35W
Scottsbluff	**116**	41 55N	103 35W
Scottsboro	**115**	34 40N	86 0W
Scottsburg	**114**	38 40N	85 46W
Scottsdale	**97**	41 9 S	147 31 E
Scottsville, Ky., U.S.A.	**115**	36 48N	86 10W
Scottsville, N.Y., U.S.A.	**112**	43 2N	77 47W
Scottville, Austral.	**98**	20 33 S	147 49 E
Scottville, U.S.A.	**114**	43 57N	86 18W
Scranton	**114**	41 22N	75 41W
Scugog, L.	**112**	44 10N	78 55W
Scunthorpe	**12**	53 35N	0 38W

* *Now part of Punjab* □

Scusciuban Shāhrūd

Scusciuban 63 10 18N 50 12 E
Sea Breeze 112 43 12N 77 32W
Seaford, Austral. 100 38 10S 145 11 E
Seaford, U.S.A. 114 38 37N 75 36W
Seaforth 106 43 35N 81 25W
Seagraves 117 32 56N 102 30W
Seal → 109 58 50N 97 30W
Seal Cove 107 49 57N 56 22W
Seal L. 107 54 20N 61 30W
Sealy 117 29 46N 96 9W
Searchlight 119 35 31N 114 55W
Searcy 117 35 15N 91 45W
Searles L. 119 35 47N 117 17W
Seaside 118 45 59N 123 55W
Seaspray 99 38 25S 147 15 E
Seattle 118 47 41N 122 15W
Seaview Ra. 97 18 40S 145 45 E
Sebastián Vizcaíno, Bahía 120 28 0N 114 30W
Sebastopol 118 38 24N 122 49W
Sebastopol = Sevastopol 56 44 35N 33 30 E
Sebderat 87 15 26N 36 42 E
Sebdou 82 34 38N 1 19W
Sebeş 46 45 58N 23 34 E
Sebeşului, Munţii 46 45 36N 23 40 E
Sebewaing 114 43 45N 83 27W
Sebezh 54 56 14N 28 22 E
Sébi 84 15 50N 4 12W
Şebinkarahisar 56 40 22N 38 28 E
Sebiş 46 46 23N 22 13 E
Sebkhet Te-n-Dghâmcha 84 18 30N 15 55W
Sebkra Azzel Mati 82 26 10N 0 43 E
Sebkra Mekerghene 82 26 21N 1 30 E
Sebnitz 24 50 58N 14 17 E
Sebou, Oued → 82 34 16N 6 40W
Sebring, Fla., U.S.A. 115 27 30N 81 26W
Sebring, Ohio, U.S.A. 112 40 55N 81 2W
Sebringville 112 43 24N 81 4W
Sebta = Ceuta 82 35 52N 5 19W
Sebuku 72 3 30S 116 25 E
Sebuku, Teluk 72 4 0N 118 10 E
Sečanj 42 45 25N 20 47 E
Secchia → 38 44 4N 11 0 E
Sechelt 108 49 25N 123 42W
Sechura, Desierto de 126 6 0S 80 30W
Seclin 19 50 33N 3 2 E
Secondigny 18 46 37N 0 26W
Sečovce 27 48 42N 21 40 E
Secretary I. 101 45 15S 166 56 E
Secunderabad 70 17 28N 78 30 E
Sedalia 116 38 40N 93 18W
Sedan, Austral. 99 34 34S 139 19 E
Sedan, France 19 49 43N 4 57 E
Sedan, U.S.A. 117 37 10N 96 11W
Sedano 32 42 43N 3 49W
Seddon 101 41 40S 174 7 E
Seddonville 101 41 33S 172 1 E
Sede Ya'aqov 62 32 43N 35 7 E
Sedgewick 108 52 48N 111 41W
Sedhiou 84 12 44N 15 30W
Sedičany 26 49 40N 14 25 E
Sedico 39 46 8N 12 6 E
Sedienie 43 42 16N 24 33 E
Sedley 109 50 10N 104 0W
Sedom 62 31 5N 35 20 E
Sedova, Pik 58 73 29N 54 58 E
Sedrata 83 36 7N 7 31 E
Sedro Woolley 118 48 30N 122 15W
Seduva 54 55 45N 23 45 E
Sędziszów Małapolski 27 50 5N 21 45 E
Seebad Ahlbeck 24 53 56N 14 10 E
Seefeld 26 47 19N 11 13 E
Seehausen 24 52 52N 11 43 E
Seeheim 92 26 50S 17 45 E
Seekoe → 92 30 18S 25 1 E
Seelaw 24 52 32N 14 22 E
Se'elim, Nahal 62 31 21N 35 24 E
Sées 18 48 38N 0 10 E
Seesen 24 51 53N 10 10 E
Sefadu 84 8 35N 10 58W
Séfeto 84 14 8N 9 49W
Sefrou 82 33 52N 4 52W
Sefwi Bekwai 84 6 10N 2 25W
Seg-ozero 54 63 0N 33 10 E
Segamat 71 2 30N 102 50 E
Segarcea 46 44 6N 23 43 E
Segbwema 84 8 0N 11 0W
Seget 73 1 24S 130 58 E
Segezha 52 63 44N 34 19 E
Seggueur, O. → 82 32 4N 2 4 E
Segid 87 16 55N 42 0 E
Segonzac 20 45 36N 0 14W
Segorbe 32 39 50N 0 30W
Ségou 84 13 30N 6 16W
Segovia 30 40 57N 4 10W
Segovia = Coco → 121 15 0N 83 8W
Segovia □ 30 40 55N 4 10W
Segré 18 47 40N 0 52W
Segre → 32 41 40N 0 43 E
Séguéla 84 7 55N 6 40W
Seguin 117 29 34N 97 58W
Segundo 117 37 12N 104 50W
Segundo → 124 30 53S 62 44W
Segura → 33 38 6N 0 54W
Segura, Sierra de 33 38 5N 2 45W
Sehore 68 23 10N 77 5 E
Sehwan 68 26 28N 67 53 E
Şeica Mare 46 46 1N 24 7 E
Seiland 50 70 25N 23 15 E
Seiling 117 36 10N 98 56W
Seille →, Moselle, France 19 49 7N 6 11 E
Seille →, Saône-et-Loire, France 21 46 31N 4 57 E
Sein, Î. de 18 48 2N 4 52W
Seinäjoki → 50 62 40N 22 45 E
Seine → 18 49 26N 0 26 E
Seine, B. de la 18 49 40N 0 40W
Seine-et-Marne □ 19 48 45N 3 0 E
Seine-Maritime □ 18 49 40N 1 0 E
Seine-Saint-Denis □ 19 48 58N 2 24 E
Seini 46 47 44N 23 21 E
Seistan 65 30 50N 61 0 E
Seistan-Balūchestān □ 65 27 0N 62 0 E
Sejerø 49 55 54N 11 9 E
Sejerø Bugt 49 55 53N 11 15 E
Sejny 28 54 6N 23 21 E
Seka 87 8 10N 36 52 E
Sekayu 72 2 51S 103 51 E
Seke 90 3 20S 33 31 E
Sekenke 90 4 18S 34 11 E
Sekiu 118 48 16N 124 18W
Sekken Veøy 47 62 45N 7 30 E
Sekondi-Takoradi 84 4 58N 1 45W
Sekuma 92 24 36S 23 50 E
Selah 118 46 44N 120 30W
Selama 71 5 12N 100 42 E
Selangor □ 71 3 20N 101 30 E
Selárgius 40 39 14N 9 14 E
Selaru 73 8 9S 131 0 E
Selb 25 50 9N 12 9 E
Selby, U.K. 12 53 47N 1 5W
Selby, U.S.A. 116 45 34N 100 2W
Selca 39 43 20N 16 50 E
Selden 116 39 33N 100 39W
Seldovia 104 59 30N 151 45W
Sele → 41 40 27N 14 58 E
Selemdzha → 59 51 42N 128 53 E
Selenge → 75 49 25N 103 59 E
Selenica 44 40 33N 19 39 E
Selenter See 24 54 19N 10 26 E
Sélestat 19 48 16N 7 26 E
Seletan, Tg. 72 4 10S 114 40 E
Seletin 46 47 50N 25 12 E
Selevac 42 44 28N 20 52 E
Selfridge 116 46 3N 100 57W
Sélibabi 84 15 10N 12 15W
Seliger, Oz. 54 57 15N 33 0 E
Seligman 119 35 17N 112 56W
Şelim 57 40 30N 42 46 E
Selîma, El Wâhât el 86 21 22N 29 19 E
Selinda Spillway 92 18 35S 23 10 E
Selinoús 45 37 35N 21 37 E
Selizharovo 54 56 51N 33 27 E
Selje 47 62 3N 5 22 E
Seljord 47 59 30N 8 40 E
Selkirk, Can. 109 50 10N 96 55W
Selkirk, U.K. 14 55 33N 2 50W
Selkirk I. 109 53 20N 99 6W
Selkirk Mts. 108 51 15N 117 40W
Selles-sur-Cher 19 47 16N 1 33 E
Sellières 19 46 50N 5 32 E
Sells 119 31 57N 111 57W
Sellye 27 45 52N 17 51 E
Selma, Ala., U.S.A. 115 32 30N 87 0W
Selma, Calif., U.S.A. 119 36 39N 119 39W
Selma, N.C., U.S.A. 115 35 32N 78 15W
Selmer 115 35 9N 88 36W
Selo 44 41 10N 25 53 E
Selongey 19 47 36N 5 10 E
Selowandoma Falls 91 21 15S 31 50 E
Selpele 73 0 1S 130 5 E
Selsey Bill 13 50 44N 0 47W
Seltz 19 48 48N 8 4 E
Selu 73 7 32S 130 55 E
Selukwe 91 19 40S 30 0 E
Sélune → 18 48 38N 1 22W
Selva, Argent. 124 29 50S 62 0W
Selva, Italy 39 46 33N 11 46 E
Selva, Spain 32 41 13N 1 8 E
Selva, La 32 42 0N 2 45 E
Selvas 126 6 30S 67 0W
Selwyn L. 109 60 0N 104 30W
Selwyn P.O. 97 21 32S 140 30 E
Selwyn Ra. 97 21 10S 140 0 E
Seman → 44 40 45N 19 50 E
Semara 82 26 48N 11 41W
Semarang 73 7 0S 110 26 E
Semau 73 10 13S 123 22 E
Sembabule 90 0 4S 31 25 E
Sémé 84 15 4N 13 41W
Semeih 87 12 43N 30 53 E
Semenov 55 56 43N 44 30 E
Semenovka, Ukraine S.S.R., U.S.S.R. 54 52 8N 32 36 E
Semenovka, Ukraine S.S.R., U.S.S.R. 56 49 37N 33 10 E
Semeru 73 8 4S 112 55 E
Semiluki 55 51 41N 39 2 E
Seminoe Res. 118 42 0N 107 0W
Seminole, Okla., U.S.A. 117 35 15N 96 45W
Seminole, Tex., U.S.A. 117 32 41N 102 38W
Semiozernoye 58 52 22N 64 8 E
Semipalatinsk 58 50 30N 80 10 E
Semirara Is. 73 12 0N 121 20 E
Semisopochnoi 104 52 0N 179 40W
Semitau 72 0 29N 111 57 E
Semiyarskoye 58 50 55N 78 23 E
Semmering Pass 26 47 41N 15 45 E
Semnān 65 35 55N 53 25 E
Semnān □ 65 36 0N 54 0 E
Semois → 16 49 53N 4 44 E
Semporna 73 4 30N 118 33 E
Semuda 72 2 51S 112 58 E
Semur-en-Auxois 19 47 30N 4 20 E
Sen → 71 13 45N 105 12 E
Sena 91 17 25S 35 0 E
Sena Madureira 126 9 5S 68 45W
Senador Pompeu 127 5 40S 39 20W
Senai 71 1 38N 103 38 E
Senaja 72 6 45N 117 3 E
Senanga 92 16 2S 23 14 E
Senatobia 117 34 38N 89 57W
Sendafa 87 9 11N 39 3 E
Sendai, Kagoshima, Japan 74 31 50N 130 20 E
Sendai, Miyagi, Japan 74 38 15N 140 53 E
Sendamangalam 70 11 17N 78 17 E
Sendeling's Drift 92 28 12S 16 52 E
Sendenhorst 24 51 50N 7 49 E
Sendurjana 68 21 32N 78 17 E
Senec 27 48 12N 17 23 E
Seneca, Oreg., U.S.A. 118 44 10N 119 2W
Seneca, S.C., U.S.A. 115 34 43N 82 59W
Seneca Falls 114 42 55N 76 50W
Seneca L. 114 42 40N 76 58W
Senegal ■ 84 14 30N 14 30W
Senegal → 84 15 48N 16 32W
Senekal 93 28 30S 27 36 E
Senftenberg 24 51 30N 14 1 E
Senga Hill 91 9 19S 31 11 E
Senge Khambab (Indus) → 68 28 40N 70 10 E
Sengerema □ 90 2 10S 32 20 E
Sengiley 55 53 58N 48 46 E
Sengkang 73 4 8S 120 1 E
Sengua → 91 17 7S 28 5 E
Senhor-do-Bonfim 127 10 30S 40 10W
Senica 27 48 41N 17 25 E
Senigállia 39 43 42N 13 12 E
Senio → 39 44 35N 12 15 E
Senise 40 40 6N 16 15 E
Senj 39 45 0N 14 58 E
Senja 50 69 25N 17 30 E
Senlis 19 49 13N 2 35 E
Senmonorom 71 12 27N 107 12 E
Sennâr 87 13 30N 33 35 E
Senneterre 106 48 25N 77 15W
Senniquelle 84 7 19N 8 38W
Senno 54 54 45N 29 43 E
Sennori 40 40 49N 8 36 E
Senonches 18 48 34N 1 2 E
Senorbì 40 39 33N 9 8 E
Senožeče 39 45 43N 14 3 E
Sens 19 48 11N 3 15 E
Senta 42 45 55N 20 3 E
Sentein 20 42 53N 0 58 E
Sentery 90 5 17S 25 42 E
Sentinel 119 32 45N 113 13W
Sentolo 73 7 55S 110 13 E
Senya Beraku 85 5 28N 0 31W
Seo de Urgel 32 42 22N 1 23 E
Seohara 68 29 15N 78 33 E
Seoni 69 22 5N 79 30 E
Seoriuarayan 69 21 45N 82 34 E
Seoul = Sŏul 76 37 31N 127 6 E
Separation Point 107 53 37N 57 25W
Sepik → 98 3 49S 144 30 E
Sępólno Krajeńskie 28 53 26N 17 30 E
Sepone 71 16 45N 106 13 E
Sepopa 92 18 49S 22 12 E
Sepopol 28 54 16N 21 2 E
Sept-Îles 107 50 13N 66 22W
Septemvri 43 42 13N 24 6 E
Septimus 98 21 13S 148 47 E
Sepúlveda 30 41 18N 3 45W
Sequeros 30 40 31N 6 2W
Sequim 118 48 3N 123 9W
Sequoia Nat. Park 119 36 30N 118 30W
Serafimovich 57 49 36N 42 43 E
Seraing 16 50 35N 5 32 E
Seram 73 3 10S 129 0 E
Seram Sea 73 2 30S 128 30 E
Serampore 69 22 44N 88 21 E
Serang 73 6 8S 106 10 E
Serasan 72 2 29N 109 4 E
Seravezza 38 43 59N 10 13 E
Serbia = Srbija 42 43 30N 21 0 E
Sercaia 46 45 49N 25 9 E
Serdo 87 11 56N 41 14 E
Serdobsk 55 52 28N 44 10 E
Seredka 54 58 12N 28 10 E
Seregno 38 45 40N 9 12 E
Seremban 71 2 43N 101 53 E
Serena, La, Chile 124 29 55S 71 10W
Serena, La, Spain 31 38 45N 5 40W
Serengeti □ 90 2 0S 34 30 E
Serengeti Plain 90 2 40S 35 0 E
Sereth = Siret → 46 47 58N 26 5 E
Sergach 55 55 30N 45 30 E
Serge → 32 41 54N 0 50 E
Sergino 58 62 30N 65 38 E
Sergipe □ 127 10 30S 37 30W
Seria 72 4 37N 114 23 E
Serian 72 1 10N 110 31 E
Seriate 38 45 42N 9 43 E
Seribu, Kepulauan 72 5 36S 106 33 E
Sérifontaine 19 49 20N 1 45 E
Sérifos 45 37 9N 24 30 E
Sérignan 20 43 17N 3 17 E
Sermaize-les-Bains 19 48 47N 4 54 E
Sermata 73 8 15S 128 50 E
Sèrmide 39 45 0N 11 17 E
Sernovodsk 55 53 54N 51 16 E
Serny Zavod 58 39 59N 58 50 E
Serock 28 52 31N 21 4 E
Serón 33 37 20N 2 29W
Serós 32 41 27N 0 24 E
Serov 58 59 29N 60 35 E
Serowe 92 22 25S 26 43 E
Serpa 31 37 57N 7 38 E
Serpeddi, Punta 40 39 19N 9 18 E
Serpentara 40 39 8N 9 38 E
Serpis → 33 38 59N 0 9W
Serpukhov 55 54 55N 37 28 E
Serra San Bruno 41 38 31N 16 23 E
Serracapriola 41 41 47N 15 12 E
Serradilla 30 39 50N 6 9W
Sérrai 44 41 5N 23 31 E
Sérrai □ 44 41 5N 23 37 E
Serramanna 40 39 26N 8 56 E
Serrat, C. 83 37 14N 9 10 E
Serre-Poncon, Barrage de 21 44 22N 6 20 E
Serres 21 44 26N 5 43 E
Serrezuela 124 30 40S 65 20W
Serrinha 127 11 39S 39 0W
Sersale 41 39 1N 16 44 E
Sertã 30 39 48N 8 6W
Sertânia 127 8 5S 37 20W
Sertanópolis 125 23 4S 51 2W
Serua 73 6 18S 130 1 E
Serui 73 1 53S 136 10 E
Serule 92 21 57S 27 20 E
Sérvia 44 40 9N 21 58 E
Sese Is. 90 0 20S 32 20 E
Sesepe 73 1 30S 127 59 E
Sesfontein 92 19 7S 13 39 E
Sesheke 92 17 29S 24 13 E
Sesia → 38 45 5N 8 37 E
Sesimbra 31 38 28N 9 6W
Sessa Aurunca 40 41 14N 13 55 E
Sestao 32 43 18N 3 0W
Sesto S. Giovanni 38 45 32N 9 14 E
Sestos 44 40 16N 26 23 E
Sestri Levante 38 44 17N 9 22 E
Sestrières 38 44 58N 6 56 E
Sestrunj 39 44 10N 15 0 E
Sestu 40 39 18N 9 6 E
Sète 20 43 25N 3 42 E
Sete Lagôas 127 19 27S 44 16W
Sétif 83 36 9N 5 26 E
Setonaikai 74 34 20N 133 30 E
Settat 82 33 0N 7 40W
Setté-Cama 88 2 32S 9 45 E
Séttimo Tor 38 45 9N 7 46 E
Setting L. 109 55 0N 98 38W
Settle 12 54 5N 2 18W
Settlement Pt. 115 26 40N 79 0W
Setto Calende 38 45 44N 8 37 E
Setúbal 31 38 30N 8 58W
Setúbal □ 31 38 25N 8 35W
Setúbal, B. de 31 38 40N 8 56W
Seugne → 20 45 42N 0 32W
Seul, Lac-Rés. 106 50 25N 92 30W
Seulimeum 72 5 27N 95 15 E
Sevan 57 40 33N 44 56 E
Sevan, Ozero 57 40 30N 45 20 E
Sevastopol 56 44 35N 33 30 E
Seven Sisters 108 54 56N 128 10W
Sever → 31 39 40N 7 32W
Sévérac-le-Château 20 44 20N 3 5 E
Severn →, Can. 106 56 2N 87 36W
Severn →, U.K. 13 51 35N 2 38W
Severn L. 106 53 54N 90 48W
Severnaya Zemlya 59 79 0N 100 0 E
Severnyye Uvaly 52 58 0N 48 0 E
Severo-Kurilsk 59 50 40N 156 8 E
Severo-Yeniseyskiy 59 60 22N 93 1 E
Severočeský □ 26 50 30N 14 0 E
Severodinsk 52 64 27N 39 58 E
Severodonetsk 57 48 58N 38 30 E
Severomoravský □ 27 49 38N 17 40 E
Severomorsk 52 69 5N 33 27 E
Severouralsk 52 60 9N 59 57 E
Sevier 119 38 39N 112 11W
Sevier → 119 39 10N 113 6W
Sevier L. 118 39 0N 113 20W
Sevilla 31 37 23N 6 0W
Sevilla □ 31 37 25N 5 30W
Seville = Sevilla 31 37 23N 6 0W
Sevlievo 43 43 2N 25 3 E
Sevnica 39 46 2N 15 19 E
Sèvre-Nantaise → 18 47 12N 1 33W
Sèvre Niortaise → 20 46 18N 1 8W
Sevsk 54 52 10N 34 30 E
Seward, Alaska, U.S.A. 104 60 6N 149 26W
Seward, Nebr., U.S.A. 116 40 55N 97 6W
Seward Pen. 104 65 0N 164 0W
Sewell 124 34 10S 70 23W
Sewer 73 5 53S 134 40 E
Sewickley 112 40 33N 80 12W
Sexsmith 108 55 21N 118 47W
Seychelles ■ 3 5 0S 56 0 E
Seyðisfjörður 50 65 16N 14 0W
Seym → 54 51 27N 32 34 E
Seymchan 59 62 54N 152 30 E
Seymour, Austral. 99 37 0S 145 10 E
Seymour, Conn., U.S.A. 113 41 23N 73 5W
Seymour, Ind., U.S.A. 114 39 0N 85 50W
Seymour, Tex., U.S.A. 117 33 35N 99 18W
Seymour, Wis., U.S.A. 114 44 30N 88 20W
Seyne 21 44 21N 6 22 E
Seyne-sur-Mer, La 21 43 7N 5 52 E
Seyssel 21 45 57N 5 50 E
Sežana 39 45 43N 13 41 E
Sézanne 19 48 40N 3 40 E
Sezze 40 41 30N 13 3 E
Sfax 83 34 49N 10 48 E
Sfintu Gheorghe 46 45 52N 25 48 E
Sha Xian 77 26 23N 117 45 E
Shaanxi □ 77 35 0N 109 0 E
Shaba 90 8 0S 25 0 E
† Shabani 91 20 17S 30 2 E
Shabla 43 43 31N 28 32 E
Shabunda 90 2 40S 27 16 E
Shache 75 38 20N 77 10 E
Shackleton 5 78 30S 36 1W
Shackleton Ice Shelf 5 66 0S 100 0 E
Shackleton Inlet 5 83 0S 160 0 E
Shaddad 86 21 25N 40 2 E
Shadrinsk 58 56 5N 63 32 E
Shaffa 85 10 30N 12 6 E
Shafter, Calif., U.S.A. 119 35 32N 119 14W
Shafter, Tex., U.S.A. 117 29 49N 104 18W
Shaftesbury 13 51 0N 2 12W
Shagamu 85 6 51N 3 39 E
Shah Bunder 68 24 13N 67 56 E
* Shah Faisalabad 68 31 30N 73 5 E
Shahabad, Andhra Pradesh, India 70 17 10N 76 54 E
Shahabad, Punjab, India 68 30 10N 76 55 E
Shahabad, Raj., India 68 25 15N 77 11 E
Shahabad, Ut. P., India 69 27 36N 79 56 E
Shāhābād, Kermanshāhān, Iran 64 34 10N 46 30 E
Shāhābād, Khorāsān, Iran 65 37 40N 56 50 E
Shahada 68 21 33N 74 30 E
Shahadpur 68 25 55N 68 35 E
Shahapur 70 15 50N 74 34 E
Shahdād 65 30 30N 57 40 E
Shahdadkot 68 27 50N 67 55 E
Shahganj 69 26 3N 82 44 E
Shaḥḥāt 81 32 48N 21 54 E
Shāhī 65 36 30N 52 55 E
Shahjahanpur 69 27 54N 79 57 E
Shahpur, Mad. P., India 68 22 12N 77 58 E
Shahpur, Mysore, India 70 16 40N 76 48 E
Shahpūr 64 38 12N 44 45 E
Shahpur 68 28 46N 68 27 E
Shahpura 69 23 10N 80 45 E
Shahr Kord 65 32 15N 50 55 E
Shahrezā 65 32 0N 51 55 E
Shahrig 68 30 15N 67 40 E
Shāhrūd 65 36 30N 55 0 E

* *Renamed Faisalabad*

† *Renamed Zvishavane*

Shahsād, Namakzār-e Siliguri

Shahsād, Namakzār-e 65 30 20N 58 20 E
Shahsavār 65 36 45N 51 12 E
Shaibara 86 25 26N 36 47 E
Shaikhabad 66 34 2N 68 45 E
Shajapur 68 23 27N 76 21 E
Shakargarh 68 32 17N 75 10 E
Shakawe 92 18 28 S 21 49 E
Shaker Heights 112 41 29N 81 36W
Shakhty 57 47 40N 40 16 E
Shakhunya 55 57 40N 46 46 E
Shaki 85 8 41N 3 21 E
Shakopee 116 44 45N 93 30W
Shala, L. 87 7 30N 38 30 E
Shallow Lake 112 44 36N 81 5W
Sham, J. ash 65 23 10N 57 5 E
Shamâl Dârfûr □ 87 15 0N 25 0 E
Shamâl Kordofân □ 87 15 0N 30 0 E
Shamattawa 109 55 51N 92 5W
Shamattawa → 106 55 1N 85 23W
Shambe 87 7 8N 30 46 E
Shambu 87 9 32N 37 3 E
Shamgong Dzong 69 27 13N 90 35 E
Shamīl 65 27 30N 56 55 E
Shamkhor 57 40 50N 46 0 E
Shamli 68 29 32N 77 18 E
Shammar, Jabal 64 27 40N 41 0 E
Shamo, L. 87 5 45N 37 30 E
Shamokin 114 40 47N 76 33W
Shamrock 117 35 15N 100 15W
Shan □ 67 21 30N 98 30 E
Shanan → 87 8 0N 40 20 E
Shanchengzhen 76 42 20N 125 20 E
Shandong □ 76 36 0N 118 0 E
Shang Xian 77 33 50N 109 58 E
Shangalowe 91 10 50 S 26 30 E
Shangani 91 19 41 S 29 20 E
Shangani → 91 18 41 S 27 10 E
Shangbancheng 76 40 50N 118 1 E
Shangcheng 77 31 47N 115 26 E
Shangchuan Dao 77 21 40N 112 50 E
Shangdu 76 41 30N 113 30 E
Shanggao 77 28 17N 114 55 E
Shanghai 75 31 15N 121 26 E
Shangqiu 77 34 26N 115 36 E
Shangrao 75 28 25N 117 59 E
Shangshui 77 33 42N 114 35 E
Shangsi 77 22 8N 107 58 E
Shangyou 77 25 48N 114 32 E
Shangzhi 76 45 22N 127 56 E
Shani 85 10 14N 12 2 E
Shaniko 118 45 0N 120 50W
Shannon, Greenl. 4 75 10N 18 30W
Shannon, N.Z. 101 40 33 S 175 25 E
Shannon → 15 52 35N 9 30W
Shansi = Shanxi □ 76 37 0N 112 0 E
Shantar, Ostrov Bolshoy 59 55 9N 137 40 E
Shantou 75 23 18N 116 40 E
Shantung = Shandong □ 76 36 0N 118 0 E
Shanxi □ 76 37 0N 112 0 E
Shanyang 77 33 31N 109 55 E
Shaoguan 75 24 48N 113 35 E
Shaowu 75 27 22N 117 28 E
Shaoxing 75 30 0N 120 35 E
Shaoyang 75 27 14N 111 25 E
Shapinsay 14 59 2N 2 50W
Shaqrā', Si. Arab. 64 25 15N 45 16 E
Shaqrā', Yemen, S. 63 13 22N 45 44 E
Sharafa (Ogr) 87 11 59N 27 7 E
Sharavati → 70 14 20N 74 25 E
Sharbot Lake 113 44 46N 76 41W
Shark B. 96 25 55 S 113 32 E
Sharm el Sheikh 86 27 53N 34 15 E
Sharon, Mass., U.S.A. 113 42 5N 71 11W
Sharon, Pa., U.S.A. 114 41 18N 80 30W
Sharon, Plain of = Hasharon 62 32 12N 34 49 E
Sharon Springs 116 38 54N 101 45W
Sharp Pt. 98 10 58 S 142 43 E
Sharpe L. 109 54 5N 93 40W
Sharpsville 112 41 16N 80 28W
Shary 64 27 14N 43 29 E
Sharya 55 58 22N 45 20 E
Shasha 87 6 29N 35 59 E
Shashemene 87 7 13N 38 33 E
Shashi 75 30 25N 112 14 E
Shashi → 91 21 14 S 29 20 E
Shasta, Mt. 118 41 30N 122 12W
Shasta Res. 118 40 50N 122 15W
Shatsk 55 54 0N 41 45 E
Shattuck 117 36 17N 99 55W
Shatura 55 55 34N 39 31 E
Shaumyani 57 41 22N 41 45 E
Shaunavon 109 49 35N 108 25W
Shaw → 96 20 21 S 119 17 E
Shaw I. 98 20 30 S 149 2 E
Shawan 75 44 34N 85 50 E
Shawanaga 112 45 31N 80 17W
Shawano 114 44 45N 88 38W
Shawinigan 106 46 35N 72 50W
Shawnee 117 35 15N 97 0W
Shayib el Banat, Bebel 86 26 59N 33 29 E
Shchekino 55 54 1N 37 34 E
Shcherbakov = Rybinsk 55 58 5N 38 50 E
Shchigri 55 51 55N 36 58 E
Shchors 54 51 48N 31 56 E
Shchuchiosk 58 52 56N 70 12 E
She Xian 77 29 50N 118 25 E
Shebekino 55 50 28N 36 54 E
Shebele, Wabi → 87 2 0N 44 0 E
Sheboygan 114 43 46N 87 45W
Shechem 62 32 13N 35 21 E
Shediac 107 46 14N 64 32W
Sheelin, Lough 15 53 48N 7 20W
Sheep Haven 15 55 12N 7 55W
Sheerness 13 51 26N 0 47 E
Sheet Harbour 107 44 56N 62 31W
Shefar'am 62 32 48N 35 10 E
Sheffield, U.K. 12 53 23N 1 28W
Sheffield, Ala., U.S.A. 115 34 45N 87 42W
Sheffield, Mass., U.S.A. 113 42 6N 73 23W
Sheffield, Pa., U.S.A. 112 41 42N 79 3W
Sheffield, Tex., U.S.A. 117 30 42N 101 49W
Shegaon 68 20 48N 76 47 E
Sheho 109 51 35N 103 13W
Shehojele 87 10 40N 35 9 E
Sheikhpura 69 25 9N 85 53 E
Shek Hasan 87 12 5N 35 58 E
Shekhupura 68 31 42N 73 58 E
Sheki 57 41 10N 47 5 E
Sheksna → 55 59 0N 38 30 E
Shelburne, N.S., Can. 107 43 47N 65 20W
Shelburne, Ont., Can. 106 44 4N 80 15W
Shelburne, U.S.A. 113 44 23N 73 15W
Shelburne B. 97 11 50 S 142 50 E
Shelburne Falls 113 42 36N 72 45W
Shelby, Mich., U.S.A. 114 43 34N 86 27W
Shelby, Mont., U.S.A. 118 48 30N 111 52W
Shelby, N.C., U.S.A. 115 35 18N 81 34W
Shelby, Ohio, U.S.A. 112 40 52N 82 40W
Shelbyville, Ill., U.S.A. 116 39 25N 88 45W
Shelbyville, Ind., U.S.A. 114 39 30N 85 42W
Shelbyville, Tenn., U.S.A. 115 35 30N 86 25W
Sheldon 116 43 6N 95 40W
Sheldrake 107 50 20N 64 51W
Shelikhova, Zaliv 59 59 30N 157 0 E
Shell Creek Ra. 118 39 15N 114 30W
Shell Lake 109 53 19N 107 2W
Shellbrook 109 53 13N 106 24W
Shellharbour 97 34 31 S 150 51 E
Shelling Rocks 15 51 45N 10 35W
Shelon → 54 58 10N 30 30 E
Shelton, Conn., U.S.A. 113 41 18N 73 7W
Shelton, Wash., U.S.A. 118 47 15N 123 6W
Shemakha 57 40 38N 48 37 E
Shenandoah, Iowa, U.S.A. 116 40 50N 95 25W
Shenandoah, Pa., U.S.A. 114 40 49N 76 13W
Shenandoah, Va., U.S.A. 114 38 30N 78 38W
Shenandoah → 114 39 19N 77 44W
Shenchi 76 39 8N 112 10 E
Shencottah 70 8 59N 77 18 E
Shendam 85 8 49N 9 30 E
Shendî 87 16 46N 33 22 E
Shendurni 70 20 39N 75 36 E
Sheng Xian 77 29 35N 120 50 E
Shëngjergji 44 41 17N 20 10 E
Shëngjini 44 41 50N 19 35 E
Shenmëria 44 42 7N 20 13 E
Shenmu 76 38 50N 110 29 E
Shenqiucheng 77 33 24N 115 2 E
Shensi = Shaanxi □ 77 35 0N 109 0 E
Shenyang 76 41 48N 123 27 E
Shepetovka 54 50 10N 27 10 E
Shephelah = Hashefela 62 31 30N 34 43 E
Shepparton 97 36 23 S 145 26 E
Sheqi 77 33 12N 112 57 E
Sherada 87 7 18N 36 30 E
Sherborne 13 50 56N 2 31W
Sherbro I. 84 7 30N 12 40W
Sherbrooke 107 45 28N 71 57W
Sherda 83 20 7N 16 46 E
Shereik 86 18 44N 33 47 E
Sheridan, Ark., U.S.A. 117 34 20N 92 25W
Sheridan, Col., U.S.A. 116 39 44N 105 3W
Sheridan, Wyo., U.S.A. 118 44 50N 107 0W
Sherkot 68 29 22N 78 35 E
Sherman 117 33 40N 96 35W
Sherpur 69 25 0N 90 0 E
Sherridon 109 55 8N 101 5W
Sherwood, N.D., U.S.A. 116 48 59N 101 36W
Sherwood, Tex., U.S.A. 117 31 18N 100 45W
Sherwood Forest 12 53 5N 1 5W
Sheslay 108 58 17N 131 52W
Sheslay → 108 58 48N 132 5W
Shethanei L. 109 58 48N 97 50W
Shetland □ 14 60 30N 1 30W
Shetland Is. 14 60 30N 1 30W
Shevaroy Hills 70 11 58N 78 12 E
Shewa □ 87 9 33N 38 10 E
Shewa Gimira 87 7 4N 35 51 E
Sheyenne 116 47 52N 99 8W
Sheyenne → 116 47 5N 96 50W
Shibām 63 16 0N 48 36 E
Shibîn El Kôm 86 30 31N 30 55 E
Shibîn el Qanâtir 86 30 19N 31 19 E
Shibogama L. 106 53 35N 88 15W
Shibushi 74 31 25N 131 8 E
Shidao 76 36 50N 122 25 E
Shiel, L. 14 56 48N 5 32W
Shiga □ 74 35 20N 136 0 E
Shigaib 81 15 5N 23 35 E
Shiguaigou 76 40 52N 110 15 E
Shihchiachuangi = Shijiazhuang 76 38 2N 114 28 E
Shijaku 44 41 21N 19 33 E
Shijiazhuang 76 38 2N 114 28 E
Shikarpur, India 68 28 17N 78 7 E
Shikarpur, Pak. 68 27 57N 68 39 E
Shikoku 74 33 30N 133 30 E
Shikoku □ 74 33 30N 133 30 E
Shikoku-Sanchi 74 33 30N 133 30 E
Shilabo 63 6 22N 44 32 E
Shilka 59 52 0N 115 55 E
Shilka → 59 53 20N 121 26 E
Shillelagh 15 52 46N 6 32W
Shillong 67 25 35N 91 53 E
Shilo 62 32 4N 35 18 E
Shilong 75 23 5N 113 52 E
Shilovo 55 54 25N 40 57 E
Shimabara 74 32 48N 130 20 E
Shimada 74 34 49N 138 10 E
Shimane □ 74 35 0N 132 30 E
Shimanovsk 59 52 15N 127 30 E
Shimizu 74 35 0N 138 30 E
Shimodate 74 36 20N 139 55 E
Shimoga 70 13 57N 75 32 E
Shimoni 90 4 38 S 39 20 E
Shimonoseki 74 33 58N 131 0 E
Shimpuru Rapids 92 17 45 S 19 55 E
Shimsha → 70 13 15N 77 10 E
Shimsk 54 58 15N 30 50 E
Shin, L. 14 58 7N 4 30W
Shin-Tone → 74 35 44N 140 51 E
Shinano → 74 36 50N 138 30 E
Shīndand 65 33 12N 62 8 E
Shingleton 106 46 25N 86 33W
Shingū 74 33 40N 135 55 E
Shinkafe 85 13 8N 6 29 E
Shinyanga 90 3 45 S 33 27 E
Shinyanga □ 90 3 50 S 34 0 E
Shio-no-Misaki 74 33 25N 135 45 E
Ship I. 117 30 16N 88 55W
Shipehenski Prokhod 43 42 45N 25 15 E
Shippegan 107 47 45N 64 45W
Shippensburg 114 40 4N 77 32W
Shiprock 119 36 51N 108 45W
Shiqian 77 27 32N 108 13 E
Shiqma, N. → 62 31 37N 34 30 E
Shiquan 77 33 5N 108 15 E
Shīr Kūh 65 31 39N 54 3 E
Shīrāz 65 29 42N 52 30 E
Shirbīn 86 31 11N 31 32 E
Shire → 91 17 42 S 35 19 E
Shiretoko-Misaki 74 44 21N 145 20 E
Shiringushi 55 53 51N 42 46 E
Shiriya-Zaki 74 41 25N 141 30 E
Shirol 70 16 47N 74 41 E
Shirpur 68 21 21N 74 57 E
Shīrvān 65 37 30N 57 50 E
Shishmanova 43 42 58N 23 12 E
Shisur 63 17 30N 54 0 E
Shitai 77 30 12N 117 25 E
Shivali (Sirkali) 70 11 15N 79 41 E
Shivpuri 68 25 26N 77 42 E
Shivta 62 30 53N 34 40 E
Shiwei 76 51 19N 119 55 E
Shixing 77 24 46N 114 5 E
Shiyata 86 29 25N 25 7 E
Shizuishan 76 39 15N 106 50 E
Shizuoka 74 35 0N 138 24 E
Shizuoka □ 74 35 15N 138 40 E
Shklov 54 54 16N 30 15 E
Shkoder = Shkodra 44 42 6N 19 20 E
Shkodra 44 42 6N 19 20 E
Shkodra □ 44 42 25N 19 20 E
Shkumbini → 44 41 5N 19 50 E
Shmidt, O. 59 81 0N 91 0 E
Shoal Lake 109 50 30N 100 35W
Shoalhaven → 100 34 54 S 150 42 E
Shoeburyness 13 51 31N 0 49 E
Sholapur 70 17 43N 75 56 E
Shologontsy 59 66 13N 114 0 E
Shomera 62 33 4N 35 17 E
Shōmrōn 62 32 15N 35 13 E
Shongopovi 119 35 49N 110 37W
Shoranur 70 10 46N 76 19 E
Shorapur 70 16 31N 76 48 E
Shoshone 118 43 0N 114 27W
Shoshone L. 118 44 30N 110 40W
Shoshone Mts. 118 39 30N 117 30W
Shoshong 92 22 56 S 26 31 E
Shoshoni 118 43 13N 108 5W
Shostka 54 51 57N 33 32 E
Shouyang 76 37 54N 113 8 E
Show Low 119 34 16N 110 0W
Shpola 56 49 1N 31 30 E
Shreveport 117 32 30N 93 50W
Shrewsbury 12 52 42N 2 45W
Shrivardhan 70 18 4N 73 3 E
Shropshire □ 13 52 36N 2 45W
Shuangcheng 76 45 20N 126 15 E
Shuangliao 76 43 29N 123 30 E
Shuangyashan 75 46 28N 131 5 E
Shucheng 77 31 28N 116 57 E
Shu'eib, Wadi 62 31 54N 35 38 E
Shuguri Falls 91 8 33 S 37 22 E
Shujalpur 68 23 18N 76 46 E
Shulan 76 44 28N 127 0 E
Shule 75 39 25N 76 3 E
Shumagin Is. 104 55 0N 159 0W
Shumerlya 55 55 30N 46 25 E
Shumikha 58 55 10N 63 15 E
Shunchang 77 26 54N 117 48 E
Shunde 77 22 42N 113 14 E
Shungay 57 48 30N 46 45 E
Shungnak 104 66 55N 157 10W
Shuo Xian 76 39 20N 112 33 E
Shūr → 65 28 30N 55 0 E
Shurma 55 56 58N 50 21 E
Shūsf 65 31 50N 60 5 E
Shūshtar 64 32 0N 48 50 E
Shuswap L. 108 50 55N 119 3W
Shuwaykah 62 32 20N 35 1 E
Shuya 55 56 50N 41 28 E
Shwebo 67 22 30N 95 45 E
Shwegu 67 24 15N 96 26 E
Shweli → 67 23 45N 96 45 E
Shyok 69 34 15N 78 12 E
Shyok → 69 35 13N 75 53 E
Si Kiang = Xi Jiang → 75 22 5N 113 20 E
Si Racha 71 13 10N 100 48 E
Siah 64 22 0N 47 0 E
Siahan Range 66 27 30N 64 40 E
Siaksrinderapura 72 0 51N 102 0 E
Sialkot 68 32 32N 74 30 E
Siam = Thailand ■ 71 16 0N 102 0 E
Siam, G. of 71 11 30N 101 0 E
Sian = Xi'an 77 34 15N 109 0 E
Siantan, P. 72 3 10N 106 15 E
Siāreh 65 28 5N 60 14 E
Siargao 73 9 52N 126 3 E
Siasi 73 5 34N 120 50 E
Siátista 44 40 15N 21 33 E
Siau 73 2 50N 125 25 E
Siauliai 54 55 56N 23 15 E
Siaya □ 90 0 0N 34 20 E
Siazan 57 41 3N 49 10 E
Sibâi, Gebel el 86 25 45N 34 10 E
Sibari 41 39 47N 16 27 E
Sibay 52 52 42N 58 39 E
Sibaya, L. 93 27 20 S 32 45 E
Šibenik 39 43 48N 15 54 E
Siberia 60 60 0N 100 0 E
Siberut 72 1 30 S 99 0 E
Sibi 68 29 30N 67 54 E
Sibil 73 4 59 S 140 35 E
Sibiti 88 3 38 S 13 19 E
Sibiu 46 45 45N 24 9 E
Sibiu □ 46 45 50N 24 15 E
Sibley, Iowa, U.S.A. 116 43 21N 95 43W
Sibley, La., U.S.A. 117 32 34N 93 16W
Sibolga 72 1 42N 98 45 E
Sibsagar 67 27 0N 94 36 E
Sibu 72 2 18N 111 49 E
Sibuco 73 7 20N 122 10 E
Sibuguey B. 73 7 50N 122 45 E
Sibutu 73 4 45N 119 30 E
Sibutu Passage 73 4 50N 120 0 E
Sibuyan 73 12 25N 122 40 E
Sibuyan Sea 73 12 30N 122 20 E
Sicamous 108 50 49N 119 0W
Siccus → 99 31 42 S 139 25 E
Sichuan □ 75 31 0N 104 0 E
Sicilia 41 37 30N 14 30 E
Sicilia, Canale di 40 37 25N 12 30 E
Sicilian Channel = Sicilia, Canale di 40 37 25N 12 30 E
Sicily = Sicilia 41 37 30N 14 30 E
Sicuani 126 14 21 S 71 10W
Siculiana 40 37 20N 13 23 E
Šid 42 45 8N 19 14 E
Sidamo □ 87 5 0N 37 50 E
Sidaouet 85 18 34N 8 3 E
Siddipet 70 18 0N 78 51 E
Sidéradougou 84 10 42N 4 12W
Siderno Marina 41 38 16N 16 17 E
Sidheros, Ákra 45 35 19N 26 19 E
Sidhirókastron 44 41 13N 23 24 E
Sidhpur 68 23 56N 72 25 E
Sîdi Abd el Rahmân 86 30 55N 29 44 E
Sîdi Barrâni 86 31 38N 25 58 E
Sidi-bel-Abbès 82 35 13N 0 39W
Sidi Bennour 82 32 40N 8 25W
Sidi Haneish 86 31 10N 27 35 E
Sidi Kacem 82 34 11N 5 49W
Sidi Moussa, O. → 82 26 58N 3 54 E
Sidi Omar 86 31 24N 24 57 E
Sidi Slimane 82 34 16N 5 56W
Sidi Smaïl 82 32 50N 8 31W
Sidlaw Hills 14 56 32N 3 10W
Sidley, Mt. 5 77 2 S 126 2W
Sidmouth 13 50 40N 3 13W
Sidmouth, C. 98 13 25 S 143 36 E
Sidney, Can. 108 48 39N 123 24W
Sidney, Mont., U.S.A. 116 47 42N 104 7W
Sidney, N.Y., U.S.A. 113 42 18N 75 20W
Sidney, Ohio, U.S.A. 114 40 18N 84 6W
Sidoarjo 73 7 30 S 112 46 E
Sidra, G. of = Khalīj Surt 35 31 40N 18 30 E
Siedlce 28 52 10N 22 20 E
Siedlce □ 28 52 0N 22 0 E
Sieg → 24 50 46N 7 7 E
Siegburg 24 50 48N 7 12 E
Siegen 24 50 52N 8 2 E
Siem Reap 71 13 20N 103 52 E
Siena 39 43 20N 11 20 E
Sieniawa 27 50 11N 22 38 E
Sieradź 28 51 37N 18 41 E
Sieraków 28 52 39N 16 2 E
Sierck-les-Bains 19 49 26N 6 20 E
Sierpc 28 52 55N 19 43 E
Sierra Blanca, N. Mex., U.S.A. 119 33 20N 105 54W
Sierra Blanca, Tex., U.S.A. 119 31 11N 105 17W
Sierra City 118 39 34N 120 42W
Sierra Colorada 128 40 35 S 67 50W
Sierra de Yeguas 31 37 7N 4 52W
Sierra Gorda 124 22 50 S 69 15W
Sierra Leone ■ 84 9 0N 12 0W
Sierra Mojada 120 27 19N 103 42W
Sierre 25 46 17N 7 31 E
Sif Fatima 83 31 6N 8 41 E
Sífnos 45 37 0N 24 45 E
Sifton 109 51 21N 100 8W
Sifton Pass 108 57 52N 126 15W
Sig 82 35 32N 0 12W
Sigdal 47 60 4N 9 38 E
Sigean 20 43 2N 2 58 E
Sighetul Marmatiei 46 47 57N 23 52 E
Sighişoara 46 46 12N 24 50 E
Sigli 72 5 25N 96 0 E
Siglufjörður 50 66 12N 18 55W
Sigma 73 11 29N 122 40 E
Sigmaringen 25 48 5N 9 13 E
Signakhi 57 41 40N 45 57 E
Signy I. 5 60 45 S 45 56W
Signy-l'Abbaye 19 49 40N 4 25 E
Sigsig 126 3 0 S 78 50W
Sigtuna 48 59 36N 17 44 E
Sigüenza 32 41 3N 2 40W
Siguiri 84 11 31N 9 10W
Sigulda 54 57 10N 24 55 E
Sigurd 119 38 49N 112 0W
Sihanoukville = Kompong Som 71 10 40N 103 30 E
Sihui 77 23 20N 112 40 E
Si'īr 62 31 35N 35 9 E
Siirt 64 37 57N 41 55 E
Sijarira Ra. 91 17 36 S 27 45 E
Sikar 68 27 33N 75 10 E
Sikasso 84 11 18N 5 35W
Sikeston 117 36 52N 89 35W
Sikhote Alin, Khrebet 59 46 0N 136 0 E
Sikiá 44 40 2N 23 56 E
Sikinos 45 36 40N 25 8 E
Sikkani Chief → 108 57 47N 122 15W
Sikkim □ 69 27 50N 88 30 E
Siklós 27 45 50N 18 19 E
Sil → 30 42 27N 7 43W
Sila, La 41 39 15N 16 35 E
Silandro 38 46 38N 10 48 E
Silat az Zahr 62 32 19N 35 11 E
Silba 39 44 24N 14 41 E
Silchar 67 24 49N 92 48 E
Silcox 109 57 12N 94 10W
Siler City 115 35 44N 79 30W
Sileru → 70 17 49N 81 24 E
Silesia = Slask 22 51 0N 16 30 E
Silet 82 22 44N 4 37 E
Silgarhi Doti 69 29 15N 81 0 E
Silghat 67 26 35N 93 0 E
Silifke 64 36 22N 33 58 E
Siliguri 69 26 45N 88 25 E

Siling Co Sobótka

Siling Co 75 31 50N 89 20 E
Silíqua 40 39 20N 8 49 E
Silistra 43 44 6N 27 19 E
Siljan, L. 48 60 55N 14 45 E
Silkeborg 49 56 10N 9 32 E
Sillajhuay, Cordillera 126 19 46 S 68 40W
Sillé-le-Guillaume 18 48 10N 0 8W
Siloam Springs 117 36 15N 94 31W
Silogui 72 1 10 S 9 0 E
Silsbee 117 30 20N 94 8W
Silute 54 55 21N 21 33 E
Silva Porto = Bié 89 12 22 S 16 55 E
Silver City, Panama 120 9 19N 79 53W
Silver City, N. Mex., U.S.A. 119 32 50N 108 18W
Silver City, Nev., U.S.A. 118 39 15N 119 48W
Silver Cr. → 118 43 16N 119 13W
Silver Creek 114 42 33N 79 9W
Silver Lake 118 43 9N 121 4W
Silverton, Austral. 100 31 52 S 141 10 E
Silverton, Colo., U.S.A. 119 37 51N 107 45W
Silverton, Tex., U.S.A. 117 34 30N 101 16W
Silves 31 37 11N 8 26W
Silvi 39 42 32N 14 5 E
Silvies → 118 43 22N 118 48W
Silvretta Gruppe 25 46 50N 10 6 E
Silwa Bahari 86 24 45N 32 55 E
Silwād 62 31 59N 35 15 E
Silz 26 47 16N 10 56 E
Sim, C. 82 31 26N 9 51W
Simanggang 72 1 15N 111 32 E
Simard, L. 106 47 40N 78 40W
Sîmărtin 46 46 19N 25 58 E
Simba 90 2 10 S 37 36 E
Simbach 25 48 16N 13 3 E
Simbo 90 4 51 S 29 41 E
Simcoe 106 42 50N 80 20W
Simcoe, L. 106 44 25N 79 20W
Simenga 59 62 42N 108 25 E
Simeto → 41 37 25N 15 10 E
Simeulue 72 2 45N 95 45 E
Simferopol 56 44 55N 34 3 E
Sími 45 36 35N 27 50 E
Simikot 69 30 0N 81 50 E
Simitli 42 41 52N 23 7 E
Simla 68 31 2N 77 9 E
Şimleu-Silvaniei 46 47 17N 22 50 E
Simmern 25 49 59N 7 32 E
Simmie 109 49 56N 108 6W
Simojärvi 50 66 5N 27 3 E
Simojoki → 50 65 35N 25 1 E
Simonette → 108 55 9N 118 15W
Simonstown 92 34 14 S 18 26 E
Simontornya 27 46 45N 18 33 E
Simpang, Indon. 72 1 16 S 104 5 E
Simpang, Malay. 71 4 50N 100 40 E
Simplon Pass 25 46 15N 8 0 E
Simplon Tunnel 25 46 15N 8 7 E
Simpson Des. 97 25 0 S 137 0 E
Simrishamn 49 55 33N 14 22 E
Simunjan 72 1 25N 110 45 E
Simushir, Ostrov 59 46 50N 152 30 E
Sina → 70 17 30N 75 55 E
Sinabang 72 2 30N 96 24 E
Sinadogo 63 5 50N 47 0 E
Sinai = Es Sînâ' 86 29 0N 34 0 E
Sinai, Mt. = Mûsa, G. 86 28 32N 33 59 E
Sinaia 46 45 21N 25 38 E
Sinaloa 120 25 50N 108 20W
Sinaloa □ 120 25 0N 107 30W
Sinalunga 39 43 12N 11 43 E
Sinan 77 27 56N 108 13 E
Sînandrei 46 45 52N 21 13 E
Sinâwan 83 31 0N 10 37 E
Sincelejo 126 9 18N 75 24W
Sinclair 118 41 47N 107 10W
Sinclair Mills 108 54 5N 121 40W
Sincorá, Serra do 127 13 30 S 41 0W
Sind 68 26 0N 68 30 E
Sind Sagar Doab 68 32 0N 71 30 E
Sindal 49 57 28N 10 10 E
Sindangan 73 8 10N 123 5 E
Sindangbarang 73 7 27 S 107 1 E
Sinde 91 17 28 S 25 51 E
Sinegorski 57 48 0N 40 52 E
Sinelnikovo 56 48 25N 35 30 E
Sines 31 37 56N 8 51W
Sines, Cabo de 31 37 58N 8 53W
Sineu 32 39 38N 3 1 E
Sinfra 84 6 35N 5 56W
Singa 87 13 10N 33 57 E
Singanallur 70 11 2N 77 1 E
Singaparna 73 7 23 S 108 4 E
Singapore ■ 71 1 17N 103 51 E
Singapore, Straits of 71 1 15N 104 0 E
Singaraja 72 8 6 S 115 10 E
Singen 25 47 45N 8 50 E
Singida 90 4 49 S 34 48 E
Singida □ 90 6 0 S 34 30 E
Singitikós Kólpos 44 40 6N 24 0 E
Singkaling Hkamti 67 26 0N 95 39 E
Singkawang 72 1 0N 108 57 E
Singkep 72 0 30 S 104 20 E
Singleton 97 32 33 S 151 0 E
Singleton, Mt. 96 29 27 S 117 15 E
Singö 48 60 12N 18 45 E
Singoli 68 25 0N 75 22 E
Siniátsikon, Óros 44 40 25N 21 35 E
Siniscóla 40 40 35N 9 40 E
Sinj 39 43 42N 16 39 E
Sinjai 73 5 7 S 120 20 E
Sinjajevina, Planina 42 42 57N 19 22 E
Sinjār 64 36 19N 41 52 E
Sinjil 62 32 3N 35 15 E
Sinkat 86 18 55N 36 49 E
Sinkiang Uighur = Xinjiang Uygur □ 75 42 0N 86 0 E
Sinnai 40 39 18N 9 13 E
Sinnar 70 19 48N 74 0 E
Sinni → 41 40 9N 16 42 E
Sinnicolau Maré 42 46 5N 20 39 E
Sinnuris 86 29 26N 30 31 E
Sinoe, L. 46 44 35N 28 50 E
Sinoia 91 17 20 S 30 8 E
Sinop 64 42 1N 35 11 E
Sinskoye 59 61 8N 126 48 E
Sint Maarten 121 18 0N 63 5W
Sint Niklaas 16 51 10N 4 9 E
Sint Truiden 16 50 48N 5 10 E
Sîntana 46 46 20N 21 30 E
Sintang 72 0 5N 111 35 E
Sinton 117 28 1N 97 30W
Sintra 31 38 47N 9 25W
Sinŭiju 76 40 5N 124 24 E
Sinyukha → 56 48 3N 30 51 E
Siocon 73 7 40N 122 10 E
Siófok 27 16 39 S 23 36 E
Sioma 92 16 25 S 23 28 E
Sion 25 46 14N 7 20 E
Sioux City 116 42 32N 96 25W
Sioux Falls 116 43 35N 96 40W
Sioux Lookout 106 50 10N 91 50W
Šipan 42 42 45N 17 52 E
Siping 76 43 8N 124 21 E
Sipiwesk L. 109 55 5N 97 35W
Sipora 72 2 18 S 99 40 E
Siquia → 121 12 10N 84 20W
Siquijor 73 9 12N 123 35 E
Sir Edward Pellew Group 97 15 40 S 137 10 E
Sira 70 13 41N 76 49 E
Siracusa 41 37 4N 15 17 E
Sirajganj 69 24 25N 89 47 E
Sirakoro 84 12 41N 9 14W
Sirasso 84 9 16N 6 6W
Siret 46 47 55N 26 5 E
Siret → 46 47 58N 26 5 E
Şiria 42 46 16N 21 38 E
Sirino, Monte 41 40 7N 15 50 E
Sirkali (Shivali) 70 11 15N 79 41 E
Sírna. 45 36 22N 26 42 E
Sirohi 68 24 52N 72 53 E
Široki Brijeg 42 43 21N 17 36 E
Sironj 68 24 5N 77 39 E
Síros 45 37 28N 24 57 E
Sirsa 68 29 33N 75 4 E
Sirsi 70 14 40N 74 49 E
Siruela 31 38 58N 5 3W
Sisak 39 45 30N 16 21 E
Sisaket 71 15 8N 104 23 E
Sisante 33 39 25N 2 12W
Sisargas, Islas 30 43 21N 8 50W
Sishen 92 27 47 S 22 59 E
Sishui 77 34 48N 113 15 E
Sisipuk L. 109 55 45N 101 50W
Sisophon 71 13 38N 102 59 E
Sisseton 116 45 43N 97 3W
Sissonne 19 49 34N 3 51 E
Sistema Central 30 40 40N 5 55W
Sistema Iberico 32 41 0N 2 10W
Sisteron 21 44 12N 5 57 E
Sisters 118 44 21N 121 32W
Sitamarhi 69 26 37N 85 30 E
Sitapur 69 27 38N 80 45 E
Siteki 93 26 32 S 31 58 E
Sitges 32 41 17N 1 47 E
Sithoniá 44 40 0N 23 45 E
Sitía 45 35 13N 26 6 E
Sitka 104 57 9N 135 20W
Sitoti 92 23 15 S 23 40 E
Sitra 86 28 40N 26 53 E
Sittang → 67 17 10N 96 58 E
Sittang Myit → 67 17 20N 96 45 E
Sittard 16 51 0N 5 52 E
Sittensen 24 53 17N 9 32 E
Sittona 87 14 25N 37 23 E
Situbondo 73 7 45 S 114 0 E
Sivaganga 70 9 50N 78 28 E
Sivagiri 70 9 16N 77 26 E
Sivakasi 70 9 24N 77 47 E
Sivana 68 28 37N 78 6 E
Sīvand 65 30 5N 52 55 E
Sivas 64 39 43N 36 58 E
Siverek 64 37 50N 39 19 E
Sivomaskinskiy 52 66 40N 62 35 E
Sivrihisar 64 39 30N 31 35 E
Sîwa 86 29 11N 25 31 E
Sîwa, El Wâhât es 86 29 10N 25 30 E
Siwalik Range 69 28 0N 83 0 E
Siwan 69 26 13N 84 21 E
Siyâl, Jazâ'ir 86 22 49N 3̈ 12 E
Sizewell 13 52 13N 1 38 E
Sjælland 49 55 30N 11 30 E
Sjællands Odde 49 56 0N 11 15 E
Själevad 48 63 18N 18 36 E
Sjarinska Banja 42 42 45N 21 38 E
Sjenica 42 43 16N 20 0 E
Sjoa 47 61 41N 9 33 E
Sjöbo 49 55 37N 13 45 E
Sjösa 49 58 47N 17 4 E
Skadarsko Jezero 42 42 10N 19 20 E
Skadovsk 56 46 17N 32 52 E
Skagafjörður 50 65 54N 19 35W
Skagastølstindane 47 61 28N 7 52 E
Skagen 49 57 43N 10 35 E
Skagern 48 59 0N 14 20 E
Skagerrak 49 57 30N 9 0 E
Skagway 104 59 23N 135 20W
Skaidi 50 70 26N 24 30 E
Skala Podolskaya 56 48 50N 26 15 E
Skalat 54 49 23N 25 55 E
Skalbmierz 28 50 20N 20 25 E
Skalica 27 48 50N 17 15 E
Skalni Dol = Kamenyak 43 43 24N 26 57 E
Skals 49 56 34N 9 24 E
Skanderborg 49 56 2N 9 55 E
Skånevik 47 59 43N 5 53 E
Skänninge 49 58 24N 15 5 E
Skanör 49 55 24N 12 50 E
Skantzoúra 45 39 5N 24 6 E
Skara 49 58 25N 13 30 E
Skaraborgs län □ 49 58 20N 13 30 E
Skardu 69 35 20N 75 44 E
Skarrild 49 55 58N 8 53 E
Skarszewy 28 54 4N 18 25 E
Skaryszew 28 51 19N 21 15 E
Skarzysko Kamienna 28 51 7N 20 52 E
Skattungbyn 48 61 10N 14 56 E
Skebokvarn 48 59 7N 16 45 E
Skeena → 108 54 9N 130 5W
Skeena Mts. 108 56 40N 128 30W
Skegness 12 53 9N 0 20 E
Skeldon 126 5 55N 57 20W
Skellefte älv → 50 64 45N 21 10 E
Skellefteå 50 64 45N 20 58 E
Skelleftehamn 50 64 47N 20 59 E
Skender Vakuf 42 44 29N 17 22 E
Skene 49 57 30N 12 37 E
Skerries, The 12 53 27N 4 40W
Skhíza 45 36 41N 21 40 E
Skhoinoúsa 45 36 53N 25 31 E
Skhwaner, Pegunungan 72 1 0 S 112 30 E
Ski 47 59 43N 10 52 E
Skiathos 45 39 12N 23 30 E
Skibbereen 15 51 33N 9 16W
Skiddaw 12 54 39N 3 9W
Skien 47 59 12N 9 35 E
Skierniewice 28 51 58N 20 10 E
Skierniewice □ 28 52 0N 20 10 E
Skikda 83 36 50N 6 58 E
Skillingaryd 49 57 27N 14 5 E
Skillinge 49 55 30N 14 16 E
Skillingmark 48 59 48N 12 1 E
Skinári, Ákra 45 37 56N 20 40 E
Skipton, Austral. 99 37 39 S 143 40 E
Skipton, U.K. 12 53 57N 2 1W
Skiropoúla 45 38 50N 24 21 E
Skíros 45 38 55N 24 34 E
Skivarp 49 55 26N 13 34 E
Skive 49 56 33N 9 2 E
Skjåk 47 61 52N 8 22 E
Skjálfandafljót → 50 65 59N 17 25W
Skjálfandi 50 66 5N 17 30W
Skjeberg 47 59 12N 11 12 E
Skjern 49 55 57N 8 30 E
Skoczów 27 49 49N 18 45 E
Skodje 47 62 30N 6 43 E
Škofja Loka 39 46 9N 14 19 E
Skoghall 48 59 20N 13 30 E
Skoki 28 52 40N 17 11 E
Skole 54 49 3N 23 30 E
Skópelos 45 39 9N 23 47 E
Skopin 55 53 55N 39 32 E
Skopje 42 42 1N 21 32 E
Skórcz 28 53 47N 18 30 E
Skottfoss 47 59 12N 9 30 E
Skovorodino 59 54 0N 125 0 E
Skowhegan 107 44 49N 69 40W
Skownan 109 51 58N 99 35W
Skradin 39 43 52N 15 53 E
Skreanäs 49 56 52N 12 35 E
Skrwa → 28 52 35N 19 32 E
Skull 15 51 32N 9 40W
Skultorp 49 58 24N 13 51 E
Skunk → 116 40 42N 91 7W
Skuodas 54 56 21N 21 45 E
Skurup 49 55 28N 13 30 E
Skutskär 49 60 37N 17 25 E
Skvira 56 49 44N 29 40 E
Skwierzyna 28 52 33N 15 30 E
Skye 14 57 15N 6 10W
Skykomish 118 47 43N 121 16W
Skyros = Skíros 45 38 52N 24 37 E
Slagelse 49 55 23N 11 19 E
Slamet, G. 72 7 16 S 109 8 E
Slaney → 15 52 52N 6 45W
Slangerup 49 55 50N 12 11 E
Slănic 46 45 14N 25 58 E
Slankamen 42 45 8N 20 15 E
Slano 42 42 48N 17 53 E
Slantsy 54 59 7N 28 5 E
Slany 26 50 13N 14 6 E
Slask 22 51 0N 16 30 E
Slate Is. 106 48 40N 87 0W
Slatina 46 44 28N 24 22 E
Slaton 117 33 27N 101 38W
Slave → 108 61 18N 113 39W
Slave Coast 85 6 0N 2 30 E
Slave Lake 108 55 17N 114 43W
Slave Pt. 108 61 11N 115 56W
Slavgorod 58 53 1N 78 37 E
Slavinja 42 43 9N 22 50 E
Slavkov (Austerlitz) 27 49 10N 16 52 E
Slavnoye 54 54 24N 29 15 E
Slavonska Požega 42 45 20N 17 40 E
Slavonski Brod 42 45 11N 18 0 E
Slavuta 54 50 15N 27 2 E
Slavyansk 56 48 55N 37 36 E
Slavyansk-na-Kubani 56 45 15N 38 11 E
Sława 28 51 52N 16 2 E
Sławno 28 54 20N 16 41 E
Sławoborze 28 53 55N 15 42 E
Sleaford 12 53 0N 0 22W
Sleat, Sd. of 14 57 5N 5 47W
Sleeper Is. 105 58 30N 81 0W
Sleepy Eye 116 44 15N 94 45W
Sleman 73 7 40 S 110 20 E
Slemon L. 108 63 13N 116 4W
Ślesin 28 52 22N 18 14 E
Slidell 117 30 20N 89 48W
Sliedrecht 16 51 50N 4 45 E
Slieve Aughty 15 53 4N 8 30W
Slieve Bloom 15 53 4N 7 40W
Slieve Donard 15 54 10N 5 57W
Slieve Gullion 15 54 8N 6 26W
Slieve Mish 15 52 12N 9 50W
Slievenamon 15 52 25N 7 37W
Sligo 15 54 17N 8 28W
Sligo □ 15 54 10N 8 35W
Sligo B. 15 54 20N 8 40W
Slite 51 57 42N 18 48 E
Sliven 43 42 42N 26 19 E
Slivnitsa 42 42 50N 23 0 E
Sljeme 39 45 57N 15 58 E
Sloansville 113 42 45N 74 22W
Slobodskoy 52 58 40N 50 6 E
Slobozia, Ialomiţa, Romania 43 44 34N 27 23 E
Slobozia, Valahia, Romania 46 44 30N 25 14 E
Slocan 108 49 48N 117 28W
Slochteren 16 53 12N 6 48 E
Slöinge 49 56 51N 12 42 E
Słomniki 28 50 16N 20 4 E
Slonim 54 53 4N 25 19 E
Slough 13 51 30N 0 35W
Slovakia = Slovensko 27 48 30N 19 0 E
Slovakian Ore Mts. = Slovenské Rudohorie 27 48 45N 20 0 E
Slovenia = Slovenija 39 45 58N 14 30 E
Slovenija □ 39 45 58N 14 30 E
Slovenj Gradec 39 46 31N 15 5 E
Slovenska Bistrica 39 46 24N 15 35 E
Slovenská Socialisticka Republika □ 27 48 30N 10 0 E
Slovenské Rudohorie 27 48 45N 20 0 E
Slovensko □ 27 48 30N 19 0 E
Słubice 28 52 22N 14 35 E
Sluch → 54 51 37N 26 38 E
Sluis 16 51 18N 3 23 E
Slunchev Bryag 43 42 40N 27 41 E
Slunj 39 45 6N 15 33 E
Słupca 28 52 15N 17 52 E
Słupia → 28 54 35N 16 51 E
Słupsk 28 54 30N 17 3 E
Słupsk □ 28 54 15N 17 30 E
Slurry 92 25 49 S 25 42 E
Slutsk 54 53 2N 27 31 E
Slyne Hd. 15 53 25N 10 10W
Slyudyanka 59 51 40N 103 40 E
Smålandsfarvandet 49 55 10N 11 20 E
Smalandsstenar 49 57 9N 13 24 E
Smalltree L. 109 61 0N 105 0W
Smallwood Reservoir 107 54 20N 63 10W
Smarje 39 46 15N 15 34 E
Smart Syndicate Dam 92 30 45 S 23 10 E
Smeaton 109 53 30N 104 49W
Smederevo 42 44 40N 20 57 E
Smederevska Palanka 42 44 22N 20 58 E
Smela 56 49 15N 31 58 E
Smethport 112 41 50N 78 28W
Smidovich 59 48 36N 133 49 E
Smigiel 28 52 1N 16 32 E
Smiley 109 51 38N 109 29W
Smilyan 43 41 29N 24 46 E
Smith 108 55 10N 114 0W
Smith → 108 59 34N 126 30W
Smith Arm 104 66 15N 123 0W
Smith Center 116 39 50N 98 50W
Smith Sund 4 78 30N 74 0W
Smithburne → 98 17 3 S 140 57 E
Smithers 108 54 45N 127 10W
Smithfield, Madag. 93 30 9 S 26 30 E
Smithfield, N.C., U.S.A. 115 35 31N 78 16W
Smithfield, Utah, U.S.A. 118 41 50N 111 50W
Smiths Falls 106 44 55N 76 0W
Smithton 99 40 53 S 145 6 E
Smithtown 99 30 58 S 152 48 E
Smithville, Can. 112 43 6N 79 33W
Smithville, U.S.A. 117 30 2N 97 12W
Smoky → 108 56 10N 117 21W
Smoky Falls 106 50 4N 82 10W
Smoky Hill → 116 39 3N 96 48W
Smoky Lake 108 54 10N 112 30W
Smøla 47 63 23N 8 3 E
Smolensk 54 54 45N 32 0 E
Smolikas, Óros 44 40 9N 20 58 E
Smolník 27 48 43N 20 44 E
Smolyan 43 41 36N 24 38 E
Smooth Rock Falls 106 49 17N 81 37W
Smoothstone L. 109 54 40N 106 50W
Smorgon 54 54 20N 26 24 E
Smulţi 46 45 57N 27 44 E
Smyadovo 43 43 2N 27 1 E
Smyrna = İzmir 64 38 25N 27 8 E
Snaefell 12 54 18N 4 26W
Snaefellsjökull 50 64 45N 23 46W
Snake → 118 46 12N 119 2W
Snake I. 99 38 47 S 146 33 E
Snake L. 109 55 32N 106 35W
Snake Ra. 118 39 0N 114 30W
Snake River 118 44 10N 110 42W
Snake River Plain 118 43 13N 113 0W
Snarum 47 60 1N 9 54 E
Snedsted 49 56 55N 8 32 E
Sneek 16 53 2N 5 40 E
Snejbjerg 49 56 8N 8 54 E
Snezhnoye 57 48 0N 38 58 E
Sněžka 26 50 41N 15 50 E
Snežnik 39 45 36N 14 35 E
Sniadowo 28 53 2N 22 0 E
Sniardwy, Jezioro 28 53 48N 21 50 E
Snigirevka 56 47 2N 32 49 E
Snina 27 49 0N 22 9 E
Snizort, L. 14 57 33N 6 28W
Snøhetta 47 62 19N 9 16 E
Snohomish 118 47 53N 122 6W
Snonuten 47 59 31N 6 50 E
Snow Hill 114 38 10N 75 21W
Snow Lake 109 54 52N 100 3W
Snowbird L. 109 60 45N 103 0W
Snowdon 12 53 4N 4 8W
Snowdrift 109 62 24N 110 44W
Snowdrift → 109 62 24N 110 44W
Snowflake 119 34 30N 110 4W
Snowshoe Pk. 118 48 13N 115 41W
Snowtown 99 33 46 S 138 14 E
Snowville 118 41 59N 112 47W
Snowy → 97 37 46 S 148 30 E
Snowy Mts. 99 36 30 S 148 20 E
Snyatyn 56 48 30N 25 50 E
Snyder, Okla., U.S.A. 117 34 40N 99 0W
Snyder, Tex., U.S.A. 117 32 45N 100 57W
Soahanina 93 18 42 S 44 13 E
Soalala 93 16 6 S 45 20 E
Soanierana-Ivongo 93 16 55 S 49 35 E
Soap Lake 118 47 23N 119 31W
Sobat, Nahr → 87 9 22N 31 33 E
Soběslav 26 49 16N 14 45 E
Sobhapur 68 22 47N 78 17 E
Sobinka 55 56 0N 40 0 E
Sobótka 28 50 54N 16 44 E

Sobrado Spragge

Sobrado **30** 43 2N 8 2W
Sobral **127** 3 50S 40 20W
Sobreira Formosa **31** 39 46N 7 51W
Soča → **39** 46 20N 13 40E
Sochaczew **28** 52 15N 20 13E
Soch'e = Shache **75** 38 20N 77 10E
Sochi **57** 43 35N 39 40E
Société, Is. de la **95** 17 0S 151 0W
Society Is. = Société, Is. de la **95** 17 0S 151 0W
Socompa, Portezuelo de **124** 24 27S 68 18W
Socorro, Colomb. **126** 6 29N 73 16W
Socorro, U.S.A. **119** 34 4N 106 54W
Socotra **63** 12 30N 54 0E
Socúellmos **33** 39 16N 2 47W
Soda L. **119** 35 7N 116 2W
Soda Plains **69** 35 30N 79 0E
Soda Springs **118** 42 40N 111 40W
Söderfors **48** 60 23N 17 25E
Söderhamn **48** 61 18N 17 10E
Söderköping **48** 58 31N 16 20E
Södermanlands län □ **48** 59 10N 16 30E
Södertälje **48** 59 12N 17 39E
Sodiri **81** 14 27N 29 0E
Sodo **87** 7 0N 37 41E
Södra Vi **49** 57 45N 15 45E
Sodražica **39** 45 45N 14 39E
Sodus **112** 43 13N 77 5W
Soekmekaar **93** 23 30S 29 55E
Soest, Ger. **24** 51 34N 8 7E
Soest, Neth. **16** 52 9N 5 19E
Sofádhes **44** 39 20N 22 4E
Sofara **84** 13 59N 4 9W
Sofia = Sofiya **43** 42 45N 23 20E
Sofia → **93** 15 27S 47 23E
Sofievka **56** 48 6N 33 55E
Sofiiski **59** 52 15N 133 59E
Sofikón **45** 37 47N 23 3E
Sofiya **43** 42 45N 23 20E
Sogad **73** 10 30N 125 0E
Sogakofe **85** 6 2N 0 39E
Sogamoso **126** 5 43N 72 56W
Sögel **24** 52 50N 7 32E
Sogn og Fjordane fylke □ **47** 61 40N 6 0E
Sognefjorden **47** 61 10N 5 50E
Sohâg **86** 26 33N 31 43E
Soignies **16** 50 35N 4 5E
Soira, Mt. **87** 14 45N 39 30E
Soissons **19** 49 25N 3 19E
Sōja **74** 34 40N 133 45E
Sojat **68** 25 55N 73 45E
Sok → **55** 53 24N 50 8E
Sokal **54** 50 31N 24 15E
Söke **45** 37 48N 27 28E
Sokelo **91** 9 55S 24 36E
Sokhós **44** 40 48N 23 22E
Sokki, Oued In → **82** 29 30N 3 42E
Sokna **47** 60 16N 9 50E
Soknedal **47** 62 57N 10 13E
Soko Banja **42** 43 40N 21 51E
Sokodé **85** 9 0N 1 11E
Sokol **55** 59 30N 40 5E
Sokolac **42** 43 56N 18 48E
Sokółka **28** 53 25N 23 30E
Sokolo **84** 14 53N 6 8W
Sokolov **26** 50 12N 12 40E
Sokołów Małpolski **27** 50 12N 22 7E
Sokołów Podlaski **28** 52 25N 22 15E
Sokoły **28** 52 59N 22 42E
Sokoto **85** 13 2N 5 16E
Sokoto □ **85** 12 30N 5 0E
Sokoto → **85** 11 20N 4 10E
Sol Iletsk **52** 51 10N 55 0E
Sola **47** 58 53N 5 36E
Sola → **27** 50 4N 19 15E
Solai **90** 0 2N 36 12E
Solana, La **33** 38 59N 3 14W
Solano **73** 16 31N 121 15E
Solares **30** 43 23N 3 43W
Solberga **49** 57 45N 14 43E
Solca **46** 47 40N 25 50E
Solec Kujawski **28** 53 5N 18 14E
Soledad, U.S.A. **119** 36 27N 121 16W
Soledad, Venez. **126** 8 10N 63 34W
Solent, The **13** 50 45N 1 25W
Solenzara **21** 41 53N 9 23E
Solesmes **19** 50 10N 3 30E
Solfonn **47** 60 2N 6 57E
Soligalich **55** 59 5N 42 10E
Soligorsk **54** 52 51N 27 27E
Solikamsk **58** 59 38N 56 50E
Solila **93** 21 25S 46 37E
Solimões → = Amazonas → **126** 2 15S 66 30W
Solingen **24** 51 10N 7 4E
Sollebrunn **49** 58 8N 12 32E
Sollefteå **48** 63 12N 17 20E
Sollentuna **48** 59 26N 17 56E
Sóller **32** 39 46N 2 43E
Solling **24** 51 44N 9 36E
Solna **48** 59 22N 18 1E
Solnechnogorsk **55** 56 10N 36 57E
Sologne **19** 47 40N 2 0E
Solok **72** 0 45S 100 40E
Sololá **120** 14 49N 91 10E
Solomon Is. ■ **94** 6 0S 155 0E
Solomon, N. Fork → **116** 39 29N 98 26W
Solomon Sea **98** 7 0S 150 0E
Solomon, S. Fork → **116** 39 25N 99 12W
Solomon's Pools = Birak Sulaymān **62** 31 42N 35 7E
Solon **75** 46 32N 121 10E
Solon Springs **116** 46 19N 91 47W
Solor **73** 8 27S 123 0E
Solotcha **55** 54 48N 39 53E
Solothurn **25** 47 13N 7 32E
Solothurn □ **25** 47 18N 7 40E
Solsona **32** 42 0N 1 31E
Solt **27** 46 45N 19 1E
Solta **39** 43 24N 16 15E
Soltānābād **65** 36 29N 58 5E
Soltāniyeh **64** 36 20N 48 55E
Soltau **24** 52 59N 9 50E
Soltsy **54** 58 10N 30 30E
Solund **47** 61 5N 4 50E
Solunska Glava **42** 41 44N 21 31E
Solvay **114** 43 5N 76 17W
Sölvesborg **49** 56 5N 14 35E
Solvychegodsk **52** 61 21N 46 56E
Solway Firth **12** 54 45N 3 38W
Solwezi **91** 12 11S 26 21E
Somali Rep. ■ **63** 7 0N 47 0E
Sombe Dzong **69** 27 13N 89 8E
Sombernon **19** 47 20N 4 40E
Sombor **42** 45 46N 19 9E
Sombra **112** 42 43N 82 29W
Sombrerete **120** 23 40N 103 40W
Sombrero **121** 18 37N 63 30W
Somers **118** 48 4N 114 18W
Somerset, Berm. **121** 32 16N 64 55W
Somerset, Can. **109** 49 25N 98 39W
Somerset, Colo., U.S.A. **119** 38 55N 107 30W
Somerset, Ky., U.S.A. **114** 37 5N 84 40W
Somerset, Mass., U.S.A. **113** 41 45N 71 10W
Somerset, Pa., U.S.A. **112** 40 1N 79 4W
Somerset □ **13** 51 9N 3 0W
Somerset East **92** 32 42S 25 35E
Somerset I. **104** 73 30N 93 0W
Somerset West **92** 34 8S 18 50E
Somersworth **113** 43 15N 70 51W
Somerton **119** 32 35N 114 47W
Somerville **113** 40 34N 74 36W
Someş → **46** 47 15N 23 45E
Someşul Mare → **46** 47 18N 24 30E
Somma Lombardo **38** 45 41N 8 42E
Somma Vesuviana **41** 40 52N 14 23E
Sommariva **99** 26 24S 146 36E
Sommatino **40** 37 20N 14 0E
Somme □ **19** 50 0N 2 20E
Somme, B. de la **18** 50 14N 1 33E
Sommen **49** 58 12N 15 0E
Sommen, L. **49** 58 0N 15 15E
Sommepy-Tahure **19** 49 15N 4 31E
Sömmerda **24** 51 10N 11 8E
Sommesous **19** 48 44N 4 12E
Sommières **21** 43 47N 4 6E
Somogy □ **27** 46 19N 17 30E
Somogyszob **27** 46 18N 17 20E
Sompolno **28** 52 26N 18 30E
Somport, Paso **32** 42 48N 0 31W
Somport, Puerto de **32** 42 48N 0 31W
Son, Norway **47** 59 32N 10 42E
Son, Spain **30** 42 43N 8 58W
Son La **71** 21 20N 103 50E
Sonamukhi **69** 23 18N 87 27E
Soncino **38** 45 24N 9 52E
Sondags → **92** 33 44S 25 51E
Sóndalo **38** 46 20N 10 20E
Sønder Omme **49** 55 50N 8 54E
Sønder Ternby **49** 57 31N 9 58E
Sønderborg **49** 54 55N 9 49E
Sonderjyllands Amtskommune □ **49** 55 10N 9 10E
Sondershausen **24** 51 22N 10 50E
Sóndrio **38** 46 10N 9 53E
Sone **91** 17 23S 34 55E
Sonepat **68** 29 0N 77 5E
Sonepur **69** 20 55N 83 50E
Song Cau **71** 13 27N 109 18E
Song Xian **77** 34 12N 112 8E
Songea **91** 10 40S 35 40E
Songea □ **91** 10 30S 36 0E
Songeons **19** 49 32N 1 50E
Songhua Hu **76** 43 35N 126 50E
Songhua Jiang → **75** 47 45N 132 30E
Songjiang **77** 31 1N 121 12E
Songkhla **71** 7 13N 100 37E
Songling **76** 48 2N 121 9E
Songpan **75** 32 40N 103 30E
Songtao **77** 28 11N 109 10E
Songwe **90** 3 20S 26 16E
Songwe → **91** 9 44S 33 58E
Songzi **77** 30 12N 111 45E
Sonkovo **55** 57 50N 37 5E
Sonmiani **66** 25 25N 66 40E
Sonnino **40** 41 25N 13 13E
Sono → **127** 9 58S 48 11W
Sonora, Calif., U.S.A. **119** 37 59N 120 27W
Sonora, Texas, U.S.A. **117** 30 33N 100 37W
Sonora □ **120** 29 0N 111 0W
Sonora → **120** 28 50N 111 33W
Sonora P. **118** 38 17N 119 35W
Sonsomate **120** 13 43N 89 44W
Sonthofen **25** 47 31N 10 16E
Soo Junction **114** 46 20N 85 14W
Soochow = Suzhou **75** 31 19N 120 38E
Sopi **73** 2 34N 128 28E
Sopo, Nahr → **87** 8 40N 26 30E
Sopot, Poland **28** 54 27N 18 31E
Sopot, Yugo. **42** 44 29N 20 30E
Sopotnica **42** 41 23N 21 13E
Sopron **27** 47 45N 16 32E
Sop's Arm **107** 49 46N 56 56W
Sør-Rondane **5** 72 0S 25 0E
Sør-Trøndelag fylke □ **47** 63 0N 10 0E
Sora **40** 41 45N 13 36E
Sorada **70** 19 45N 84 26E
Sorah **68** 27 13N 68 56E
Söråker **48** 62 30N 17 32E
Sorano **39** 42 40N 11 42E
Sorata **126** 15 50S 68 40W
Sorbas **33** 37 6N 2 7W
Sorel **106** 46 0N 73 10W
Sorento **99** 38 22S 144 47E
Soreq, N. → **62** 31 57N 34 43E
Soresina **38** 45 17N 9 51E
Sorgono **40** 40 01N 9 06E
Sorgues **21** 44 1N 4 53E
Soria **32** 41 43N 2 32W
Soria □ **32** 41 46N 2 28W
Soriano **124** 33 24S 58 19W
Soriano nel Cimino **39** 42 25N 12 14E
Sorkh, Kuh-e **65** 35 40N 58 30E
Sorø **49** 55 26N 11 32E
Soro **84** 10 9N 9 48W
Sorocaba **125** 23 31S 47 27W
Sorochinsk **52** 52 26N 53 10E
Soroki **56** 48 8N 28 12E
Soroksár **27** 47 24N 19 9E
Soron **68** 27 55N 78 45E
Sorong **73** 0 55S 131 15E
Soroti **90** 1 43N 33 35E
Sørøya **50** 70 40N 22 30E
Sørøyane **47** 62 25N 5 32E
Sørøysundet **50** 70 25N 23 0E
Sorraia → **31** 38 55N 8 53W
Sorrento **41** 40 38N 14 23E
Sorris Sorris **92** 21 0S 14 46E
Sorsele **50** 65 31N 17 30E
Sorso **40** 40 50N 8 34E
Sorsogon **73** 13 0N 124 0E
Sortavala **52** 61 42N 30 41E
Sortino **41** 37 9N 15 1E
Sorvizhi **55** 57 52N 48 32E
Sos **32** 42 30N 1 13W
Soscumica, L. **106** 50 15N 77 27W
Sosna → **55** 52 42N 38 55E
Sosnogorsk **52** 63 37N 53 51E
Sosnovka, R.S.F.S.R., U.S.S.R. **55** 53 13N 41 24E
Sosnovka, R.S.F.S.R., U.S.S.R. **59** 54 9N 109 35E
Sosnowiec **28** 50 20N 19 10E
Sospel **21** 43 52N 7 27E
Sostanj **39** 46 23N 15 4E
Sosva **52** 59 10N 61 50E
Soto la Marina → **120** 23 40N 97 40W
Soto y Amío **30** 42 46N 5 53W
Sotteville-lès-Rouen **18** 49 24N 1 5E
Sotuta **120** 20 29N 89 43W
Souanké **88** 2 10N 14 3E
Soúdhas, Kólpos **45** 35 25N 24 10E
Souflíon **44** 41 12N 26 18E
Souillac **20** 44 53N 1 29E
Souk-Ahras **83** 36 23N 7 57E
Souk el Arba du Rharb **82** 34 43N 5 59W
Sŏul **76** 37 31N 126 58E
Soulac-sur-Mer **20** 45 30N 1 7W
Soultz **19** 48 57N 7 52E
Soúnion, Ákra **45** 37 37N 24 1E
Sour el Ghozlane **83** 36 10N 3 45E
Sources, Mt. aux **93** 28 45S 28 50E
Sourdeval **18** 48 43N 0 55W
Soure, Brazil **127** 0 35S 48 30W
Soure, Port. **30** 40 4N 8 38W
Souris, Man., Can. **109** 49 40N 100 20W
Souris, P.E.I., Can. **107** 46 21N 62 15W
Souris → **109** 49 40N 99 34W
Soúrpi **45** 39 6N 22 54E
Sousa **127** 6 45S 38 10W
Sousel, Brazil **127** 2 38S 52 29W
Sousel, Port. **31** 38 57N 7 40W
Souss, O. → **82** 30 27N 9 31W
Sousse **83** 35 50N 10 38E
Soustons **20** 43 45N 1 19W
Souterraine, La **20** 46 15N 1 30E
South Africa, Rep. of, ■ **89** 32 0S 17 0E
South America **122** 10 0S 60 0W
South Atlantic Ocean **7** 20 0S 10 0W
South Aulatsivik I. **107** 56 45N 61 30W
South Australia □ **96** 32 0S 139 0E
South Baldy, Mt. **119** 34 6N 107 27W
South Bend, Ind., U.S.A. **114** 41 38N 86 20W
South Bend, Wash., U.S.A. **118** 46 44N 123 52W
South Boston **115** 36 42N 78 58W
South Branch **107** 47 55N 59 2W
South Brook **107** 49 26N 56 5W
South Buganda □ **90** 0 15S 31 30E
South Carolina □ **115** 33 45N 81 0W
South Charleston **114** 38 20N 81 40W
South China Sea **71** 10 0N 113 0E
South Dakota □ **116** 45 0N 100 0W
South Downs **13** 50 53N 0 10W
South East C. **97** 43 40S 146 50E
South-East Indian Rise **94** 43 0S 80 0E
South Esk → **14** 56 44N 3 3W
South Foreland **13** 51 7N 1 23E
South Fork → **118** 47 54N 113 15W
South Gamboa **120** 9 4N 79 40W
South Georgia **5** 54 30S 37 0W
South Glamorgan □ **13** 51 30N 3 20W
South Grafton **99** 29 41S 152 57E
South Haven **114** 42 22N 86 20W
South Henik, L. **109** 61 30N 97 30W
South Honshu Ridge **94** 23 0N 143 0E
South Horr **90** 2 12N 36 56E
South I., Kenya **90** 2 35N 36 35E
South I., N.Z. **101** 44 0S 170 0E
South Invercargill **101** 46 26S 168 23E
South Knife → **109** 58 55N 94 37W
South Korea ■ **76** 36 0N 128 0E
South Loup → **116** 41 4N 98 40W
South Mashonaland □ **91** 18 0S 31 30E
South Milwaukee **114** 42 50N 87 52W
South Molton **13** 51 1N 3 50W
South Nahanni → **108** 61 3N 123 21W
South Negril Pt. **121** 18 14N 78 30W
South Orkney Is. **5** 63 0S 45 0W
South Pass **118** 42 20N 108 58W
South Passage **96** 26 07S 113 09E
South Pines **115** 35 10N 79 25W
South Pittsburg **115** 35 1N 85 42W
South Platte → **116** 41 7N 100 42W
South Pole **5** 90 0S 0 0E
South Porcupine **106** 48 30N 81 12W
South River, Can. **106** 45 52N 79 23W
South River, U.S.A. **113** 40 27N 74 23W
South Ronaldsay **14** 58 46N 2 58W
South Sandwich Is. **7** 57 0S 27 0W
South Saskatchewan → **109** 53 15N 105 5W
South Seal → **109** 58 48N 98 8W
South Sentinel I. **71** 11 1N 92 16E
South Shetland Is. **5** 62 0S 59 0W
South Shields **12** 54 59N 1 26W
South Sioux City **116** 42 30N 96 24W
South Taranaki Bight **101** 39 40S 174 5E
South Thompson → **108** 50 40N 120 20W
South Twin I. **106** 53 7N 79 52W
South Tyne → **12** 54 46N 2 25W
South Uist **14** 57 20N 7 15W
South West Africa = Namibia ■ **92** 22 0S 18 9E
South West C. **99** 43 34S 146 3E
South Yemen ■ **63** 15 0N 48 0E
South Yorkshire □ **12** 53 30N 1 20W
Southampton, Can. **106** 44 30N 81 25W
Southampton, U.K. **13** 50 54N 1 23W
Southampton, U.S.A. **114** 40 54N 72 22W
Southampton I. **105** 64 30N 84 0W
Southbridge, N.Z. **101** 43 48S 172 16E
Southbridge, U.S.A. **113** 42 4N 72 2W
Southeast Pacific Basin **95** 16 30S 92 0W
Southend **109** 56 19N 103 22W
Southend-on-Sea **13** 51 32N 0 42E
Southern □, Malawi **91** 15 0S 35 0E
Southern □, S. Leone **84** 8 0N 12 30W
Southern □, Zambia **91** 16 20S 26 20E
Southern Alps **101** 43 41S 170 11E
Southern Cross **96** 31 12S 119 15E
Southern Indian L. **109** 57 10N 98 30W
Southern Ocean **5** 62 0S 60 0E
Southern Uplands **14** 55 30N 3 3W
Southington **113** 41 37N 72 53W
Southold **113** 41 4N 72 26W
Southport, Austral. **97** 27 58S 153 25E
Southport, U.K. **12** 53 38N 3 1W
Southport, U.S.A. **115** 33 55N 78 0W
Southwestern Pacific Basin **94** 42 0S 170 0W
Southwold **13** 52 19N 1 41E
Soutpansberge **93** 23 0S 29 30E
Souvigny **20** 46 33N 3 10E
Sovata **46** 46 35N 25 3E
Sovetsk, Lithuania, U.S.S.R. **54** 55 6N 21 50E
Sovetsk, R.S.F.S.R., U.S.S.R. **55** 57 38N 48 53E
Sovetskaya **57** 49 1N 42 7E
Sovetskaya Gavan **59** 48 50N 140 0E
Sovicille **39** 43 16N 11 12E
Sovra **42** 42 44N 17 34E
Sōya-Misaki **74** 45 30N 142 0E
Soyo **88** 6 13S 12 20E
Sozh → **54** 51 57N 30 48E
Sozopol **43** 42 23N 27 42E
Spa **16** 50 29N 5 53E
Spain ■ **29** 40 0N 5 0W
Spalding, Austral. **99** 33 30S 138 37E
Spalding, U.K. **12** 52 47N 0 9W
Spalding, U.S.A. **116** 41 45N 98 27W
Spangereid **47** 58 3N 7 9E
Spangler **112** 40 39N 78 48W
Spaniard's Bay **107** 47 38N 53 20W
Spanish **106** 46 12N 82 20W
Spanish Fork **118** 40 10N 111 37W
Spanish Town **121** 18 0N 76 57W
Sparks **118** 39 30N 119 45W
Sparta, Ga., U.S.A. **115** 33 18N 82 59W
Sparta, Wis., U.S.A. **116** 43 55N 90 47W
Sparta = Spárti **45** 37 5N 22 25E
Spartanburg **115** 35 0N 82 0W
Spartansburg **112** 41 48N 79 43W
Spartel, C. **82** 35 47N 5 56W
Spárti **45** 37 5N 22 25E
Spartivento, C., Calabria, Italy **41** 37 56N 16 4E
Spartivento, C., Sard., Italy **40** 38 52N 8 50E
Spas-Demensk **54** 54 20N 34 0E
Spas-Klepiki **55** 55 10N 40 10E
Spassk-Dalniy **59** 44 40N 132 48E
Spassk-Ryazanskiy **55** 54 24N 40 25E
Spátha, Ákra **45** 35 42N 23 43E
Spatsizi → **108** 57 42N 128 7W
Spearfish **116** 44 32N 103 52W
Spearman **117** 36 15N 101 10W
Speers **109** 52 43N 107 34W
Speightstown **121** 13 15N 59 39W
Speke Gulf **90** 2 20S 32 50E
Spenard **104** 61 11N 149 50W
Spence Bay **104** 69 32N 93 32W
Spencer, Idaho, U.S.A. **118** 44 18N 112 8W
Spencer, Iowa, U.S.A. **116** 43 5N 95 19W
Spencer, N.Y., U.S.A. **113** 42 14N 76 30W
Spencer, Nebr., U.S.A. **116** 42 52N 98 43W
Spencer, W. Va., U.S.A. **114** 38 47N 81 24W
Spencer B. **92** 25 30S 14 47E
Spencer, C. **97** 35 20S 136 53E
Spencer G. **97** 34 0S 137 20E
Spencerville **113** 44 51N 75 33W
Spences Bridge **108** 50 25N 121 20W
Spenser Mts. **101** 42 15S 172 45E
Sperkhiós → **45** 38 57N 22 3E
Sperrin Mts. **15** 54 50N 7 0W
Spessart **25** 50 10N 9 20E
Spétsai **45** 37 15N 23 10E
Spey → **14** 57 26N 3 25W
Speyer **25** 49 19N 8 26E
Speyer → **25** 49 19N 8 27E
Spézia, La **38** 44 8N 9 50E
Spezzano Albanese **41** 39 41N 16 19E
Spiekeroog **24** 53 45N 7 42E
Spielfeld **39** 46 43N 15 38E
Spiez **25** 46 40N 7 40E
Spíli **45** 35 13N 24 31E
Spilimbergo **39** 46 7N 12 53E
Spinazzola **41** 40 58N 16 5E
Spind **47** 58 6N 6 53E
Spineni **46** 44 43N 24 37E
Spirit Lake **118** 47 56N 116 56W
Spirit River **108** 55 45N 118 50W
Spiritwood **109** 53 24N 107 33W
Spišská Nová Ves **27** 48 58N 20 34E
Spišské Podhradie **27** 49 0N 20 48E
Spital **26** 47 42N 14 18E
Spithead **13** 50 43N 1 5W
Spittal **26** 46 48N 13 31E
Spitzbergen = Svalbard **4** 78 0N 17 0E
Split **39** 43 31N 16 26E
Split L. **109** 56 8N 96 15W
Splitski Kanal **39** 43 31N 16 20E
Splügenpass **25** 46 30N 9 20E
Spoffard **117** 29 10N 100 27W
Spokane **118** 47 45N 117 25W
Spoleto **39** 42 46N 12 47E
Spooner **116** 45 49N 91 51W
Sporádhes **45** 39 0N 24 30E
Sporyy Navolok, Mys **58** 75 50N 68 40E
Spragge **106** 46 15N 82 40W

Sprague Suceava

Sprague 118 47 18N 117 59W
Sprague River 118 42 28N 121 31W
Spratly, I. 72 8 20N 112 0 E
Spray 118 44 50N 119 46W
Spree → 24 52 32N 13 13 E
Spring City 118 39 31N 111 28W
Spring Mts. 119 36 20N 115 43W
Spring Valley, Minn., U.S.A. 116 43 40N 92 23W
Spring Valley, N.Y., U.S.A. 113 41 7N 74 4W
Springbok 92 29 42 S 17 54 E
Springburn 101 43 40 S 171 32 E
Springdale, Can. 107 49 30N 56 6W
Springdale, Ark., U.S.A. 117 36 10N 94 5W
Springdale, Wash., U.S.A. 118 48 1N 117 50W
Springe 24 52 12N 9 35 E
Springer 117 36 22N 104 36W
Springerville 119 34 10N 109 16W
Springfield, Can. 112 42 50N 80 56W
Springfield, N.Z. 101 43 19 S 171 56 E
Springfield, Colo., U.S.A. 117 37 26N 102 40W
Springfield, Ill., U.S.A. 116 39 48N 89 40W
Springfield, Mass., U.S.A. 114 42 8N 72 37W
Springfield, Mo., U.S.A. 117 37 15N 93 20W
Springfield, Ohio, U.S.A. 114 39 58N 83 48W
Springfield, Oreg., U.S.A. 118 44 2N 123 0W
Springfield, Tenn., U.S.A. 115 36 35N 86 55W
Springfield, Vt., U.S.A. 113 43 20N 72 30W
Springfontein 92 30 15 S 25 40 E
Springhill 107 45 40N 64 4W
Springhouse 108 51 56N 122 7W
Springhurst 99 36 10 S 146 31 E
Springs 93 26 13 S 28 25 E
Springsure 97 24 8 S 148 6 E
Springvale, Austral. 98 23 33 S 140 42 E
Springvale, U.S.A. 113 43 28N 70 48W
Springville, N.Y., U.S.A. 114 42 31N 78 41W
Springville, Utah, U.S.A. 118 40 14N 111 35W
Springwater 109 51 58N 108 23W
Spruce-Creek 112 40 36N 78 9W
Spur 117 33 28N 100 50W
Spurn Hd. 12 53 34N 0 8 E
Spuž 42 42 32N 19 10 E
Spuzzum 108 49 37N 121 23W
Squam L. 113 43 45N 71 32W
Squamish 108 49 45N 123 10W
Square Islands 107 52 47N 55 47W
Squillace, Golfo di 41 38 43N 16 35 E
Squinzano 41 40 27N 18 1 E
Sragen 73 7 28 S 110 59 E
Srbac 42 45 7N 17 30 E
Srbija □ 42 43 30N 21 0 E
Srbobran 42 45 32N 19 48 E
Sre Umbell 71 11 8N 103 46 E
Srebrnica 42 44 10N 19 18 E
Sredinnyy Khrebet 59 57 0N 160 0 E
Središče 39 46 24N 16 17 E
Sredna Gora 43 42 40N 24 20 E
Sredne Tambovskoye 59 50 55N 137 45 E
Srednekolymsk 59 67 27N 153 40 E
Srednevilyuysk 59 63 50N 123 5 E
Sredni Rodopi 43 41 40N 24 45 E
Śrem 28 52 6N 17 2 E
Sremska Mitrovica 42 44 59N 19 33 E
Sremski Karlovci 42 45 12N 19 56 E
Sretensk 59 52 10N 117 40 E
Sri Lanka ■ 70 7 30N 80 50 E
Sriharikota, I. 70 13 40N 80 20 E
Srikakulam 70 18 14N 83 58 E
Srinagar 66 34 5N 74 50 E
Sripur 69 24 14N 90 30 E
Srirangam 70 10 54N 78 42 E
Srirangapatnam 70 12 26N 76 43 E
Srivilliputtur 70 9 31N 77 40 E
Środa Śląska 28 51 10N 16 36 E
Środa Wielkopolski 28 52 15N 17 19 E
Srokowo 28 54 13N 21 31 E
Srpska Crnja 42 45 38N 20 44 E
Srpska Itabej 42 45 35N 20 44 E
Staaten → 98 16 24 S 141 17 E
Staberhuk 24 54 23N 11 18 E
Stade 24 53 35N 9 31 E
Staðarhólskirkja 50 65 23N 21 58W
Städjan 48 61 56N 12 52 E
Stadlandet 47 62 10N 5 10 E
Stadskanaal 16 53 4N 6 55 E
Stadthagen 24 52 20N 9 14 E
Stadtlohn 24 52 0N 6 52 E
Stadtroda 24 50 51N 11 44 E
Stafafell 50 64 25N 14 52W
Staffa 14 56 26N 6 21W
Stafford, U.K. 12 52 49N 2 9W
Stafford, U.S.A. 117 38 0N 98 35W
Stafford □ 12 52 53N 2 10W
Stafford Springs 113 41 58N 72 20W
Stagnone 40 37 50N 12 28 E
Staines 13 51 26N 0 30W
Stainz 26 46 53N 15 17 E
Stalač 42 43 43N 21 28 E
Stalingrad = Volgograd 57 48 40N 44 25 E
Staliniri = Tskhinvali 57 42 14N 44 1 E
Stalino = Donetsk 56 48 0N 37 45 E
Stalinogorsk = Novomoskovsk 55 54 5N 38 15 E
Stalowa Wola 28 50 34N 22 3 E
Stalybridge 12 53 29N 2 4W
Stamford, Austral. 98 21 15 S 143 46 E
Stamford, U.K. 13 52 39N 0 29W
Stamford, Conn., U.S.A. 114 41 5N 73 30W
Stamford, Tex., U.S.A. 117 32 58N 99 50W
Stamps 117 33 22N 93 30W
Stanberry 116 40 12N 94 32W
Standerton 93 26 55 S 29 7 E
Standish 114 43 58N 83 57W
Stanford 118 47 11N 110 10W
Stange 47 60 43N 11 5 E
Stanger 93 29 27 S 31 14 E
Stanišić 42 45 56N 19 10 E
Stanislav = Ivano-Frankovsk 54 49 0N 24 40 E
Stanisławów 28 52 18N 21 33 E
Stanke Dimitrov 42 42 17N 23 9 E
Stanley, Austral. 99 40 46 S 145 19 E
Stanley, N.B., Can. 107 46 20N 66 44W
Stanley, Sask., Can. 109 55 24N 104 22W
Stanley, Falk. Is. 128 51 40 S 59 51W
Stanley, Idaho, U.S.A. 118 44 10N 114 59W
Stanley, N.D., U.S.A. 116 48 20N 102 23W
Stanley, N.Y., U.S.A. 112 42 48N 77 6W
Stanley, Wis., U.S.A. 116 44 57N 91 0W
Stanley Res. 70 11 50N 77 40 E
Stann Creek 120 17 0N 88 13W
Stanovoy Khrebet 59 55 0N 130 0 E
Stanthorpe 97 28 36 S 151 59 E
Stanton 117 32 8N 101 45W
Staples 116 46 21N 94 48W
Stapleton 116 41 30N 100 31W
Staporków 28 51 9N 20 31 E
Star City 109 52 50N 104 20W
Stara-minskaya 57 46 33N 39 0 E
Stara Moravica 42 45 50N 19 30 E
Stara Pazova 42 45 0N 20 10 E
Stara Planina 43 43 15N 23 0 E
Stara Zagora 43 42 26N 25 39 E
Starachowice 28 51 3N 21 2 E
Starashcherbinovskaya 57 46 40N 38 53 E
Staraya Russa 54 57 58N 31 23 E
Starbuck I. 95 5 37 S 155 55W
Stargard 24 53 29N 13 19 E
Stargard Szczeciński 28 53 20N 15 0 E
Stari Bar 42 42 7N 19 13 E
Stari Trg 39 45 29N 15 7 E
Staritsa 54 56 33N 35 0 E
Starke 115 30 0N 82 10W
Starkville, Colo., U.S.A. 117 37 10N 104 31W
Starkville, Miss., U.S.A. 115 33 26N 88 48W
Starnberg 25 48 0N 11 20 E
Starnberger See 25 47 55N 11 20 E
Starobelsk 57 49 16N 39 0 E
Starodub 54 52 30N 32 50 E
Starogard 28 53 59N 18 30 E
Starokonstantinov 56 49 48N 27 10 E
Starosielce 28 53 8N 23 5 E
Start Pt. 13 50 13N 3 38W
Stary Sącz 27 49 33N 20 35 E
Staryy Biryuzyak 57 44 46N 46 50 E
Staryy Chartoriysk 54 51 15N 25 54 E
Staryy Kheydzhan 59 60 0N 144 50 E
Staryy Krym 56 45 3N 35 8 E
Staryy Oskol 55 51 19N 37 55 E
Stassfurt 24 51 51N 11 34 E
Staszów 28 50 33N 21 10 E
State College 114 40 47N 77 49W
Staten I. 113 40 35N 74 10W
Staten, I. = Los Estados, I. de 128 54 40 S 64 30W
Statesboro 115 32 26N 81 46W
Statesville 115 35 48N 80 51W
Staunton, Ill., U.S.A. 116 39 0N 89 49W
Staunton, Va., U.S.A. 114 38 7N 79 4W
Stavanger 47 58 57N 5 40 E
Stavelot 16 50 23N 5 55 E
Staveren 16 52 53N 5 22 E
Stavern 47 59 0N 10 1 E
Stavre 48 62 51N 15 19 E
Stavropol 57 45 5N 42 0 E
Stavroúpolis 44 41 12N 24 45 E
Stawell 97 37 5 S 142 47 E
Stawell → 98 20 20 S 142 55 E
Stawiski 28 53 22N 22 9 E
Stawiszyn 28 51 56N 18 4 E
Stayner 112 44 25N 80 5W
Steamboat Springs 118 40 30N 106 50W
Stębark 28 53 30N 20 10 E
Stebleva 44 41 18N 20 33 E
Steele 116 46 56N 99 52W
Steelton 114 40 17N 76 50W
Steelville 117 37 57N 91 21W
Steen River 108 59 40N 117 12W
Steenvoorde 19 50 48N 2 33 E
Steenwijk 16 52 47N 6 7 E
Steep Pt. 96 26 08 S 113 8 E
Steep Rock 109 51 30N 98 48W
Ştefăneşti 46 47 44N 27 15 E
Stefanie L. = Chew Bahir 87 4 40N 36 50 E
Stefansson Bay 5 67 20 S 59 8 E
Stege 49 55 0N 12 18 E
Steiermark □ 26 47 26N 15 0 E
Steigerwald 25 49 45N 10 30 E
Steinbach 109 49 32N 96 40W
Steinfort 16 49 39N 5 55 E
Steinheim 24 51 50N 9 6 E
Steinhuder Meer 24 52 48N 9 20 E
Steinkjer 50 63 59N 11 31 E
Stellaland 92 26 45 S 24 50 E
Stellarton 107 45 32N 62 30W
Stellenbosch 92 33 58 S 18 50 E
Stemshaug 47 63 19N 8 44 E
Stendal 24 52 36N 11 50 E
Stensele 50 65 3N 17 8 E
Stenstorp 49 58 17N 13 45 E
Stepanakert 53 39 40N 46 25 E
Stephan 116 48 30N 96 53W
Stephens Creek 99 31 50 S 141 30 E
Stephens I. 108 54 10N 130 45W
Stephenville, Can. 107 48 31N 58 35W
Stephenville, U.S.A. 117 32 12N 98 12W
Stepnica 28 53 38N 14 36 E
Stepnoi = Elista 57 46 16N 44 14 E
Stepnyak 58 52 50N 70 50 E
Steppe 60 50 0N 50 0 E
Stereá Ellas □ 45 38 50N 22 0 E
Sterkstroom 92 31 32 S 26 32 E
Sterling, Colo., U.S.A. 116 40 40N 103 15W
Sterling, Ill., U.S.A. 116 41 45N 89 45W
Sterling, Kans., U.S.A. 116 38 17N 98 13W
Sterling City 117 31 50N 100 59W
Sterling Run 112 41 25N 78 12W
Sterlitamak 52 53 40N 56 0 E
Sternberg 24 53 42N 11 48 E
Šternberk 27 49 45N 17 15 E
Stettin = Szczecin 28 53 27N 14 27 E
Stettiner Haff 24 53 50N 14 25 E
Stettler 108 52 19N 112 40W
Steubenville 114 40 21N 80 39W
Stevens Port 116 44 32N 89 34W
Stevenson L. 109 53 55N 96 0W
Stevns Klint 49 55 17N 12 28 E
Stewart, B.C., Can. 108 55 56N 129 57W
Stewart, N.W.T., Can. 104 63 19N 139 26W
Stewart, I. 128 54 50 S 71 15W
Stewart I. 101 46 58 S 167 54 E
Stewiacke 107 45 9N 63 22W
Steynsburg 92 31 15 S 25 49 E
Steyr 26 48 3N 14 25 E
Steyr → 26 48 17N 14 15 E
Steytlerville 92 33 17 S 24 19 E
Stia 39 43 48N 11 41 E
Stigler 117 35 19N 95 6W
Stigliano 41 40 24N 16 13 E
Stigsnæs 49 55 13N 11 18 E
Stigtomta 49 58 47N 16 48 E
Stikine → 104 56 40N 132 30W
Stilfontein 92 26 50 S 26 50 E
Stilis 45 38 55N 22 47 E
Stillwater, Minn., U.S.A. 116 45 3N 92 47W
Stillwater, N.Y., U.S.A. 113 42 55N 73 41W
Stillwater, Okla., U.S.A. 117 36 5N 97 3W
Stillwater Mts. 118 39 45N 118 6W
Stilwell 117 35 52N 94 36W
Stimfalías, L. 45 37 51N 22 27 E
Štip 42 41 42N 22 10 E
Stíra 45 38 9N 24 14 E
Stiring-Wendel 19 49 12N 6 57 E
Stirling, Austral. 98 17 12 S 141 35 E
Stirling, Can. 108 49 30N 112 30W
Stirling, U.K. 14 56 7N 3 57W
Stirling Ra. 96 34 23 S 118 0 E
Stittsville 113 45 15N 75 55W
Stockach 25 47 51N 9 01 E
Stockaryd 49 57 19N 14 36 E
Stockerau 27 48 24N 16 12 E
Stockett 118 47 23N 111 7W
Stockholm 48 59 20N 18 3 E
Stockholms län □ 48 59 30N 18 20 E
Stockinbingal 100 34 30 S 147 53 E
Stockport 12 53 25N 2 11W
Stockton, Austral. 100 32 50 S 151 47 E
Stockton, Calif., U.S.A. 119 38 0N 121 20W
Stockton, Kans., U.S.A. 116 39 30N 99 20W
Stockton, Mo., U.S.A. 117 37 40N 93 48W
Stockton-on-Tees 12 54 34N 1 20W
Stockvik 48 62 17N 17 23 E
Stoczek Łukowski 28 51 58N 22 0 E
Stöde 48 62 28N 16 35 E
Stogovo 42 41 31N 20 38 E
Stoke-on-Trent 12 53 1N 2 11W
Stokes Bay 106 45 0N 81 28W
Stokes Pt. 99 40 10 S 143 56 E
Stokkseyri 50 63 50N 21 2W
Stokksnes 50 64 14N 14 58W
Stolac 42 43 8N 17 59 E
Stolberg 24 50 48N 6 13 E
Stolbovaya, R.S.F.S.R., U.S.S.R. 55 55 10N 37 32 E
Stolbovaya, R.S.F.S.R., U.S.S.R. 59 64 50N 153 50 E
Stolbovoy, Ostrov 59 56 44N 163 14 E
Stolbtsy 54 53 30N 26 43 E
Stolin 54 51 53N 26 50 E
Stolnici 46 44 31N 24 48 E
Ston 42 42 51N 17 43 E
Stonehaven 14 56 58N 2 11W
Stonehenge 98 24 22 S 143 17 E
Stonewall 109 50 10N 97 19W
Stonington I. 5 68 11 S 67 0W
Stony L., Man., Can. 109 58 51N 98 40W
Stony L., Ont., Can. 112 44 30N 78 0W
Stony Rapids 109 59 16N 105 50W
Stony Tunguska = Tunguska, Nizhnyaya → 59 65 48N 88 4 E
Stopnica 28 50 27N 20 57 E
Stora Gla 48 59 30N 12 30 E
Stora Karlsö 49 57 17N 17 59 E
Stora Lulevatten 50 67 10N 19 30 E
Stora Sjöfallet 50 67 29N 18 40 E
Storavan 50 65 45N 18 10 E
Stordal 47 63 28N 10 56 E
Store Bælt 49 55 20N 11 0 E
Store Creek 99 32 54 S 149 6 E
Store Heddinge 49 55 18N 12 23 E
Støren 47 63 3N 10 18 E
Storfjorden 47 62 25N 6 30 E
Storm B. 97 43 10 S 147 30 E
Storm Lake 116 42 35N 95 11W
Stormberg 92 31 16 S 26 17 E
Stormsrivier 92 33 59 S 23 52 E
Stornoway 14 58 12N 6 23W
Storozhinets 56 48 14N 25 45 E
Storsjö 48 62 49N 13 5 E
Storsjöen, Hedmark, Norway 47 60 20N 11 40 E
Storsjöen, Hedmark, Norway 47 61 30N 11 14 E
Storsjön, Gävleborg, Sweden 48 60 35N 16 45 E
Storsjön, Jämtland, Sweden 48 62 50N 13 8 E
Storstrøms Amt. □ 49 54 50N 11 45 E
Storuman 50 65 5N 17 10 E
Storuman,sjö 50 65 13N 16 50 E
Storvik 48 60 35N 16 33 E
Stoughton 109 49 40N 103 0W
Stour →, Dorset, U.K. 13 50 48N 2 7W
Stour →, Here. & Worcs., U.K. 13 52 25N 2 13W
Stour →, Suffolk, U.K. 13 51 55N 1 5 E
Stour (Gt. Stour) → 13 51 15N 1 20 E
Stourbridge 13 52 28N 2 8W
Stout, L. 109 52 0N 94 40W
Stowmarket 13 52 11N 1 0 E
Strabane 15 54 50N 7 28W
Strabane □ 15 54 45N 7 25W
Stracin 42 42 13N 22 2 E
Stradella 38 45 4N 9 20 E
Strahan 97 42 9 S 145 20 E
Strakonice 26 49 15N 13 53 E
Straldzha 43 42 35N 26 40 E
Stralsund 24 54 17N 13 5 E
Strand, Norway 47 61 17N 11 17 E
Strand, S. Afr. 92 34 9 S 18 48 E
Stranda 47 62 19N 6 58 E
Strandebarm 47 60 17N 6 0 E
Strandvik 47 60 9N 5 41 E
Strangford, L. 15 54 30N 5 37W
Strängnäs 48 59 23N 17 2 E
Stranraer 14 54 54N 5 0W
Strasbourg, Can. 109 51 4N 104 55W
Strasbourg, France 19 48 35N 7 42 E
Strasburg, Ger. 24 53 30N 13 44 E
Strasburg, U.S.A. 116 46 12N 100 9W
Stratford, Austral. 100 37 59 S 147 7 E
Stratford, Can. 106 43 23N 81 0W
Stratford, N.Z. 101 39 20 S 174 19 E
Stratford, Calif., U.S.A. 119 36 10N 119 49W
Stratford, Conn., U.S.A. 113 41 13N 73 8W
Stratford, Tex., U.S.A. 117 36 20N 102 3W
Stratford-on-Avon 13 52 12N 1 42W
Strath Spey 14 57 15N 3 40W
Strathalbyn 99 35 13 S 138 53 E
Strathclyde □ 14 56 0N 4 50W
Strathcona Prov. Park 108 49 38N 125 40W
Strathmore, Austral. 98 17 50 S 142 35 E
Strathmore, Can. 108 51 5N 113 18W
Strathmore, U.K. 14 56 40N 3 4W
Strathnaver 108 53 20N 122 33W
Strathpeffer 14 57 35N 4 32W
Strathroy 106 42 58N 81 38W
Strathy Pt. 14 58 35N 4 0W
Stratton, U.K. 12 51 41N 1 45W
Stratton, U.S.A. 116 39 20N 102 36W
Straubing 25 48 53N 12 35 E
Straumnes 50 66 26N 23 8W
Strausberg 24 52 40N 13 52 E
Strawberry Res. 118 40 10N 111 7W
Strawn 117 32 36N 98 30W
Strážnice 27 48 54N 17 19 E
Streaky Bay 96 32 48 S 134 13 E
Streator 116 41 9N 88 52W
Středočeský □ 26 49 55N 14 30 E
Středoslovenský □ 27 48 30N 19 15 E
Streeter 116 46 39N 99 21W
Streetsville 112 43 35N 79 42W
Strehaia 46 44 37N 23 10 E
Strelcha 43 42 25N 24 19 E
Strelka 59 58 5N 93 3 E
Strésa 38 45 52N 8 28 E
Strezhevoy 58 60 42N 77 34 E
Stříbro 26 49 44N 13 0 E
Strickland → 98 7 35 S 141 36 E
Strimón → 44 40 46N 23 51 E
Strimonikós Kólpos 44 40 33N 24 0 E
Strofádhes 45 37 15N 21 0 E
Strombacka 48 61 58N 16 44 E
Strómboli 41 38 48N 15 12 E
Stromeferry 14 57 20N 5 33W
Stromness 14 58 58N 3 18W
Ströms vattudal 50 64 15N 14 55 E
Strömsnäsbruk 49 56 35N 13 45 E
Strömstad 48 58 55N 11 15 E
Strömsund 50 63 51N 15 33 E
Stróngoli 41 39 16N 17 2 E
Stronsay 14 59 8N 2 38W
Stronsburg 116 41 7N 97 36W
Stropkov 27 49 13N 21 39 E
Stroud 13 51 44N 2 12W
Stroud Road 99 32 18 S 151 57 E
Stroudsberg 113 40 59N 75 15W
Struer 49 56 30N 8 35 E
Struga 42 41 13N 20 44 E
Strugi Krasnyye 54 58 21N 29 1 E
Strumica 42 41 28N 22 41 E
Strumica → 42 41 20N 22 22 E
Struthers, Can. 106 48 41N 85 51W
Struthers, U.S.A. 114 41 6N 80 38W
Stryama 43 42 16N 24 54 E
Stryi 54 49 16N 23 48 E
Stryker 108 48 40N 114 44W
Stryków 28 51 55N 19 33 E
Strzegom 28 50 58N 16 20 E
Strzelce Krajeńskie 28 52 52N 15 33 E
Strzelce Opolskie 28 50 31N 18 18 E
Strzelecki Cr. → 97 29 37 S 139 59 E
Strzelin 28 50 46N 17 2 E
Strzelno 28 52 35N 18 9 E
Strzybnica 28 50 28N 18 48 E
Strzyżów 27 49 52N 21 47 E
Stuart, Fla., U.S.A. 115 27 11N 80 12W
Stuart, Nebr., U.S.A. 116 42 39N 99 8W
Stuart → 108 54 0N 123 35W
Stuart L. 108 54 30N 124 30W
Stuart Range 96 29 10 S 134 56 E
Stuart Town 100 32 44 S 149 4 E
Stubbekøbing 49 54 53N 12 9 E
Stuben 26 47 10N 10 8 E
Studen Kladenets, Yazovir 43 41 37N 25 30 E
Stugun 48 63 10N 15 40 E
Stühlingen 25 47 44N 8 26 E
Stull, L. 109 54 24N 92 34W
Stung Treng 71 13 31N 105 58 E
Stupart → 109 56 0N 93 25W
Stupino 55 54 57N 38 2 E
Sturgeon B. 109 52 0N 97 50W
Sturgeon Bay 114 44 52N 87 20W
Sturgeon Falls 106 46 25N 79 57W
Sturgeon L., Alta., Can. 108 55 6N 117 32W
Sturgeon L., Ont., Can. 106 50 0N 90 45W
Sturgeon L., Ont., Can. 112 44 28N 78 43W
Sturgis, Mich., U.S.A. 114 41 50N 85 25W
Sturgis, S.D., U.S.A. 116 44 25N 103 30W
Sturkö 49 56 5N 15 42 E
Štúrovo 27 47 48N 18 41 E
Sturt Cr. → 96 20 8 S 127 24 E
Stutterheim 92 32 33 S 27 28 E
Stuttgart, Ger. 25 48 46N 9 10 E
Stuttgart, U.S.A. 117 34 30N 91 33W
Stuyvesant 113 42 23N 73 45W
Stykkishólmur 50 65 2N 22 40W
Styr → 54 52 7N 26 35 E
Styria = Steiermark □ 26 47 26N 15 0 E
Su Xian 77 33 41N 116 59 E
Suakin 86 19 8N 37 20 E
Suaqui 120 29 12N 109 41W
Subang 73 6 34 S 107 45 E
Subi 72 2 58N 108 50 E
Subiaco 39 41 56N 13 5 E
Subotica 42 46 6N 19 49 E
Success 109 50 28N 108 6W
Suceava 46 47 38N 26 16 E

Suceava Tabatinga, Serra da

Suceava □	46	47 37N	25 40 E
Suceava →	46	47 38N	26 16 E
Sucha-Beskidzka	27	49 44N	19 35 E
Suchan	28	53 18N	15 18 E
Suchedniów	28	51 3N	20 49 E
Suchitoto	120	13 56N	89 0W
Suchou = Suzhou	75	31 18N	120 36 E
Süchow = Xuzhou	77	34 18N	117 10 E
Suchowola	28	53 33N	23 3 E
Suck →	15	53 17N	8 18W
Suckling, Mt.	98	9 49 S	148 53 E
Sucre	126	19 0 S	65 15W
Sućuraj	39	43 10N	17 8 E
Sud-Ouest, Pte. du	107	49 23N	63 36W
Sud, Pte.	107	49 3N	62 14W
Suda →	55	59 0N	37 40 E
Sudair	64	26 0N	45 0 E
Sudak	56	44 51N	34 57 E
Sudan	117	34 4N	102 32W
Sudan ■	81	15 0N	30 0 E
Suday	55	59 0N	43 0 E
Sudbury	106	46 30N	81 0W
Südd	87	8 20N	30 0 E
Süderbrarup	24	54 38N	9 47 E
Süderlügum	24	54 50N	8 55 E
Süderoog-Sand	24	54 27N	8 30 E
Sudetan Mts. = Sudety	27	50 20N	16 45 E
Sudety	27	50 20N	16 45 E
Sudi	91	10 11 S	39 57 E
Sudirman, Pegunungan	72	4 30 S	137 0 E
Sudiţi	46	44 35N	27 38 E
Sudogda	55	55 55N	40 50 E
Sudr	86	29 40N	32 42 E
Sudzha	54	51 14N	35 17 E
Sueca	33	39 12N	0 21W
Suedala	49	55 30N	13 15 E
Sueur, Le	116	44 25N	93 52W
Suez = El Suweis	86	28 40N	33 0 E
Suez Canal = Suweis, Qanâl es	86	31 0N	33 20 E
Sûf	62	32 19N	35 49 E
Şufaynah	64	23 6N	40 33 E
Suffield	109	50 12N	111 10W
Suffolk	114	36 47N	76 33W
Suffolk □	13	52 16N	1 0 E
Sufuk	65	23 50N	51 50 E
Şugag	46	45 47N	23 37 E
Sugar City	116	38 18N	103 38W
Sugluk = Sagloue	105	62 30N	74 15W
Suhaia, L.	46	43 45N	25 15 E
Suhār	65	24 20N	56 40 E
Suhbaatar	75	50 17N	106 10 E
Suhl	24	50 35N	10 40 E
Suhl □	24	50 37N	10 43 E
Sui Xian, Henan, China	77	34 25N	115 2 E
Sui Xian, Henan, China	77	31 42N	113 24 E
Suichang	77	28 29N	119 15 E
Suichuan	77	26 20N	114 32 E
Suide	76	37 30N	110 12 E
Suifenhe	76	44 25N	131 10 E
Suihua	75	46 32N	126 55 E
Suining, Hunan, China	77	26 35N	110 10 E
Suining, Sichuan, China	77	30 26N	105 35 E
Suiping	77	33 10N	113 59 E
Suippes	19	49 8N	4 30 E
Suir →	15	52 15N	7 10W
Suixi	77	21 19N	110 18 E
Suizhong	76	40 21N	120 20 E
Sujangarh	68	27 42N	74 31 E
Sujica	42	43 52N	17 11 E
Sukabumi	73	6 56 S	106 50 E
Sukadana, Kalimantan, Indon.	72	1 10 S	110 0 E
Sukadana, Sumatera, Indon.	72	5 5 S	105 33 E
Sukaradja	72	2 28 S	110 25 E
Sukarnapura = Jayapura	73	2 37 S	140 38 E
Sukhindol	43	43 11N	25 10 E
Sukhinichi	54	54 8N	35 10 E
Sukhona →	52	60 30N	45 0 E
Sukhumi	57	43 0N	41 0 E
Sukkur	68	27 42N	68 54 E
Sukkur Barrage	68	27 40N	68 50 E
Sukma	70	18 24N	81 45 E
Sukovo	42	43 4N	22 37 E
Sukunka →	108	55 45N	121 15W
Sula →	54	49 40N	32 41 E
Sula, Kepulauan	73	1 45 S	125 0 E
Sulaiman Range	68	30 30N	69 50 E
Sulak →	57	43 20N	47 34 E
Sulam Tsor	62	33 4N	35 6 E
Sulawesi □	73	2 0 S	120 0 E
Sulechów	28	52 5N	15 40 E
Sulęcin	28	52 26N	15 10 E
Sulejów	28	51 26N	19 53 E
Sulejówek	28	52 13N	21 17 E
Sulima	84	6 58N	11 32W
Sulina	46	45 10N	29 40 E
Sulingen	24	52 41N	8 47 E
Suliţa	46	47 39N	26 59 E
Sulitälma	50	67 17N	17 28 E
Sulitjelma	50	67 9N	16 3 E
Sułkowice	27	49 50N	19 49 E
Sullana	126	4 52 S	80 39W
Sullivan, Ill., U.S.A.	116	39 40N	88 40W
Sullivan, Ind., U.S.A.	114	39 5N	87 26W
Sullivan, Mo., U.S.A.	116	38 10N	91 10W
Sullivan Bay	108	50 55N	126 50W
Sully-sur-Loire	19	47 45N	2 20 E
Sulmierzyce	28	51 37N	17 32 E
Sulmona	39	42 3N	13 55 E
Sulphur, La., U.S.A.	117	30 13N	93 22W
Sulphur, Okla., U.S.A.	117	34 35N	97 0W
Sulphur Pt.	108	60 56N	114 48W
Sulphur Springs	117	33 5N	95 36W
Sulphur Springs, Cr. →	117	32 12N	101 36W
Sultan	106	47 36N	82 47W
Sultanpur	69	26 18N	82 4 E
Sultsa	52	63 27N	46 2 E
Sulu Arch.	73	6 0N	121 0 E
Sulu Sea	73	8 0N	120 0 E
Sululta	87	9 10N	38 43 E
Suluq	83	31 44N	20 14 E
Sulzbach	25	49 18N	7 4 E
Sulzbach-Rosenberg	25	49 30N	11 46 E
Sumalata	73	1 0N	122 31 E
Sumampa	124	29 25 S	63 29W
Sumatera □	72	0 40N	100 20 E
Sumatera Barat □	72	1 0 S	100 0 E
Sumatera Selatan □	72	3 30 S	104 0 E
Sumatera Utara □	72	2 0N	99 0 E
Sumatra	118	46 38N	107 31W
Sumatra = Sumatera □	72	0 40N	100 20 E
Sumba	73	9 45 S	119 35 E
Sumba, Selat	73	9 0 S	118 40 E
Sumbawa	72	8 26 S	117 30 E
Sumbawa Besar	72	8 30 S	117 26 E
Sumbawanga □	90	8 0 S	31 30 E
Sumbing	73	7 19 S	110 3 E
Sumburgh Hd.	14	59 52N	1 17W
Sumedang	73	6 49 S	107 56 E
Sümeg	27	46 59N	17 20 E
Sumenep	73	7 3 S	113 51 E
Sumgait	57	40 34N	49 38 E
Summer L.	118	42 50N	120 50W
Summerland	108	49 32N	119 41W
Summerside	107	46 24N	63 47W
Summerville, Ga., U.S.A.	115	34 30N	85 20W
Summerville, S.C., U.S.A.	115	33 2N	80 11W
Summit Lake	108	54 20N	122 40W
Summit Pk.	119	37 20N	106 48W
Sumner	116	42 49N	92 7W
Sumperk	27	49 59N	17 0 E
Sumter	115	33 55N	80 22W
Sumy	54	50 57N	34 50 E
Sunart, L.	14	56 42N	5 43W
Sunburst	118	48 56N	111 59W
Sunbury, Austral.	99	37 35 S	144 44 E
Sunbury, U.S.A.	114	40 50N	76 46W
Sunchales	124	30 58 S	61 35W
Suncho Corral	124	27 55 S	63 27W
Sunchon	77	34 52N	127 31 E
Suncook	113	43 8N	71 27W
Sunda Is.	94	5 0 S	105 0 E
Sunda Kecil, Kepulauan	72	7 30 S	117 0 E
Sunda, Selat	72	6 20 S	105 30 E
Sundance	116	44 27N	104 27W
Sundarbans, The	69	22 0N	89 0 E
Sundargarh	69	22 4N	84 5 E
Sundays = Sondags →	92	33 44 S	25 51 E
Sundbyberg	48	59 22N	17 58 E
Sunderland, Can.	112	44 16N	79 4W
Sunderland, U.K.	12	54 54N	1 22W
Sunderland, U.S.A.	113	42 27N	72 36W
Sundre	108	51 49N	114 38W
Sundridge	106	45 45N	79 25W
Sunds	49	56 13N	9 1 E
Sundsjö	48	62 59N	15 9 E
Sundsvall	48	62 23N	17 17 E
Sungaigerong	72	2 59 S	104 52 E
Sungailiat	72	1 51 S	106 8 E
Sungaipakning	72	1 19N	102 0 E
Sungaipenuh	72	2 1 S	101 20 E
Sungaitiram	72	0 45 S	117 8 E
Sungari = Songhua Jiang →	76	47 45N	132 30 E
Sungei Patani	71	5 38N	100 29 E
Sungei Siput	71	4 51N	101 6 E
Sungguminasa	73	5 17 S	119 30 E
Sunghua Chiang = Songhua Jiang →	76	47 45N	132 30 E
Sungikai	87	12 20N	29 51 E
Sungtao Hu	77	19 20N	109 35 E
Sungurlu	56	40 12N	34 21 E
Sunja	39	45 21N	16 35 E
Sunndalsøra	47	62 40N	8 33 E
Sunne	48	59 52N	13 5 E
Sunnfjord	47	61 25N	5 18 E
Sunnyside, Utah, U.S.A.	118	39 34N	110 24W
Sunnyside, Wash., U.S.A.	118	46 24N	120 2W
Sunray	117	36 1N	101 47W
Sunshine	100	37 48 S	144 52 E
Suntar	59	62 15N	117 30 E
Sunyani	84	7 21N	2 22W
Suoyarvi	52	62 12N	32 23 E
Supai	119	36 14N	112 44W
Supaul	69	26 10N	86 40 E
Superior, Ariz., U.S.A.	119	33 19N	111 9W
Superior, Mont., U.S.A.	118	47 15N	114 57W
Superior, Nebr., U.S.A.	116	40 3N	98 2W
Superior, Wis., U.S.A.	116	46 45N	92 5W
Superior, L.	111	47 40N	87 0W
Supetar	39	43 25N	16 32 E
Suphan Buri	71	14 14N	100 10 E
Suphan Daği	64	38 54N	42 48 E
Supraśl	28	53 13N	23 19 E
Suq al Jum'ah	83	32 58N	13 12 E
Sūq ash Shūyukh	64	30 53N	46 28 E
Suqian	77	33 54N	118 8 E
Sūr, Leb.	62	33 19N	35 16 E
Sūr, Oman	65	22 34N	59 32 E
Sur, Pt.	119	36 18N	121 54W
Sura →	55	56 6N	46 0 E
Surabaja = Surabaya	73	7 17 S	112 45 E
Surabaya	73	7 17 S	112 45 E
Surahammar	48	59 43N	16 13 E
Suraia	46	45 40N	27 25 E
Surakarta	73	7 35 S	110 48 E
Surakhany	57	40 25N	50 1 E
Surandai	70	8 58N	77 26 E
Šurany	27	48 6N	18 10 E
Surat, Austral.	99	27 10 S	149 6 E
Surat, India	68	21 12N	72 55 E
Surat Thani	71	9 6N	99 20 E
Suratgarh	68	29 18N	73 55 E
Suraz	28	52 57N	22 57 E
Surazh, Byelorussia, U.S.S.R.	54	55 25N	30 44 E
Surazh, R.S.F.S.R., U.S.S.R.	54	53 5N	32 27 E
Surduc	46	47 15N	23 25 E
Surduc Pasul	46	45 21N	23 23 E
Surdulica	42	42 41N	22 11 E
Sûre →	16	49 44N	6 31 E
Surendranagar	68	22 45N	71 40 E
Surgères	20	46 7N	0 47W
Surgut	58	61 14N	73 20 E
Suri	69	23 50N	87 34 E
Surianu	46	45 33N	23 31 E
Suriapet	70	17 10N	79 40 E
Şūrīf	62	31 40N	35 4 E
Surigao	73	9 47N	125 29 E
Surin	71	14 50N	103 34 E
Surinam ■	127	4 0N	56 0W
Suriname →	127	5 50N	55 15W
Surmene	57	41 0N	40 1 E
Surovikino	57	48 32N	42 55 E
Surprise L.	108	59 40N	133 15W
Surrey □	13	51 16N	0 30W
Sursee	25	47 11N	8 6 E
Sursk	55	53 3N	45 40 E
Surt	83	31 11N	16 39 E
Surt, Al Hammadah al	83	30 0N	17 50 E
Surt, Khalīj	83	31 40N	18 30 E
Surtsey	50	63 20N	20 30W
Suruga-Wan	74	34 45N	138 30 E
Susa	38	45 8N	7 3 E
Susâ →	49	55 20N	11 42 E
Sušac	39	42 46N	16 30 E
Susak	39	44 30N	14 18 E
Süsangerd	64	31 35N	48 6 E
Susanino	59	52 50N	140 14 E
Susanville	118	40 28N	120 40W
Sušice	26	49 17N	13 30 E
Susquehanna →	114	39 33N	76 5W
Susquehanna Depot	113	41 55N	75 36W
Susques	124	23 35 S	66 25W
Sussex, Can.	107	45 45N	65 37W
Sussex, U.S.A.	113	41 12N	74 38W
Sussex, E. □	13	51 0N	0 20 E
Sussex, W. □	13	51 0N	0 30W
Sustut →	108	56 20N	127 30W
Susuman	59	62 47N	148 10 E
Susunu	73	3 20 S	133 25 E
Susz	28	53 44N	19 20 E
Şuteşti	46	45 13N	27 27 E
Sutherland, S. Afr.	92	32 33 S	20 40 E
Sutherland, U.S.A.	116	41 12N	101 11W
Sutherland Falls	101	44 48 S	167 46 E
Sutherland Pt.	97	28 15 S	153 35 E
Sutherlin	118	43 28N	123 16W
Sutivan	39	43 23N	16 30 E
Sutlej →	68	29 23N	71 3 E
Sutton, Can.	113	45 6N	72 37W
Sutton, U.S.A.	116	40 40N	97 50W
Sutton →	106	55 15N	83 45W
Sutton-in-Ashfield	12	53 7N	1 20W
Suttor →	98	21 36 S	147 2 E
Suva	94	18 6 S	178 30 E
Suva Gora	42	41 45N	21 3 E
Suva Planina	42	43 10N	22 5 E
Suva Reka	42	42 21N	20 50 E
Suvo Rudište	42	43 17N	20 49 E
Suvorov	55	54 7N	36 30 E
Suvorov Is. = Suwarrow Is.	95	13 15 S	163 30W
Suvorovo	43	43 20N	27 35 E
Suwałki	28	54 8N	22 59 E
Suwałki □	28	54 0N	22 30 E
Suwannee →	115	29 18N	83 9W
Suwanose Jima	74	29 26N	129 30 E
Suwarrow Is.	95	15 0 S	163 0W
Suweis, Khalîg el	86	28 40N	33 0 E
Suweis, Qanâl es	86	31 0N	32 20 E
Suwŏn	76	37 17N	127 1 E
Suzdal	55	56 29N	40 26 E
Suze, La	18	47 54N	0 2 E
Suzhou	75	31 19N	120 38 E
Suzu-Misaki	74	37 31N	137 21 E
Suzuka	74	34 55N	136 36 E
Suzzara	38	45 0N	10 45 E
Svalbard	4	78 0N	17 0 E
Svalbarð	50	66 12N	15 43W
Svalöv	49	55 57N	13 8 E
Svanvik	50	69 25N	30 3 E
Svappavaara	50	67 40N	21 03 E
Svarstad	47	59 27N	9 56 E
Svartisen	50	66 40N	13 50 E
Svartvik	48	62 19N	17 24 E
Svatovo	56	49 35N	38 11 E
Svay Rieng	71	11 9N	105 45 E
Sveio	47	59 33N	5 23 E
Svendborg	49	55 4N	10 35 E
Svene	47	59 45N	9 31 E
Svenljunga	49	57 29N	13 5 E
Svenstrup	49	56 58N	9 50 E
Sverdlovsk, R.S.F.S.R., U.S.S.R.	52	56 50N	60 30 E
Sverdlovsk, Ukraine S.S.R., U.S.S.R.	57	48 5N	39 37 E
Sverdrup Is.	4	79 0N	97 0W
Svetac	39	43 3N	15 43 E
Sveti Ivan Zelina	39	45 57N	16 16 E
Sveti Jurij	39	46 14N	15 24 E
Sveti Lenart	39	46 36N	15 48 E
Sveti Nikola, Prokhad	42	43 27N	22 6 E
Sveti Nikole	42	41 51N	21 56 E
Sveti Rok	39	40 1N	9 6 E
Sveti Trojica	39	46 37N	15 50 E
Svetlogorsk	54	52 38N	29 46 E
Svetlograd	57	45 25N	42 58 E
Svetlovodsk	54	49 2N	33 13 E
Svetozarevo	42	44 5N	21 15 E
Svidník	27	49 20N	21 37 E
Svilaja Pl.	39	43 49N	16 31 E
Svilajnac	42	44 15N	21 11 E
Svilengrad	43	41 49N	26 12 E
Svir →	52	60 30N	32 48 E
Svishtov	43	43 36N	25 23 E
Svisloch	54	53 3N	24 2 E
Svitava →	27	49 30N	16 37 E
Svitavy	27	49 47N	16 28 E
Svobodnyy	59	51 20N	128 0 E
Svoge	43	42 59N	23 23 E
Svolvær	50	68 15N	14 34 E
Svratka →	27	49 11N	16 38 E
Svrljig	42	43 25N	22 6 E
Swabian Alps = Schäbischer Alb	25	48 30N	9 30 E
Swain Reefs	97	21 45 S	152 20 E
Swainsboro	115	32 38N	82 22W
Swakopmund	92	22 37 S	14 30 E
Swale →	12	54 5N	1 20W
Swan →	96	32 3 S	115 45 E
Swan Hill	97	35 20 S	143 33 E
Swan Hills	108	54 42N	115 24W
Swan Islands	121	17 22N	83 57W
Swan L.	109	52 30N	100 40W
Swan River	109	52 10N	101 16W
Swanage	13	50 36N	1 59W
Swansea, Austral.	99	33 3 S	151 35 E
Swansea, U.K.	13	51 37N	3 57W
Swartberge	92	33 20 S	22 0 E
Swartruggens	92	25 39 S	26 42 E
Swarzędz	28	52 25N	17 4 E
Swastika	106	48 7N	80 6W
Swatow = Shantou	76	23 18N	116 40 E
Swaziland ■	93	26 30 S	31 30 E
Sweden ■	50	67 0N	15 0 E
Swedru	85	5 32N	0 41W
Sweet Home	118	44 26N	122 25W
Sweetwater	117	32 30N	100 28W
Sweetwater →	118	42 31N	107 2W
Swellendam	92	34 1 S	20 26 E
Swider →	28	52 6N	21 14 E
Świdnica	28	50 50N	16 30 E
Świdnik	28	51 13N	22 39 E
Świdwin	28	53 47N	15 49 E
Świebodzice	28	50 51N	16 20 E
Świebodzin	28	52 15N	15 31 E
Świecie	28	53 25N	18 30 E
Świętokrzyskie, Góry	28	51 0N	20 30 E
Swift Current	109	50 20N	107 45W
Swiftcurrent →	109	50 38N	107 44W
Swilly, L.	15	55 12N	7 35W
Swindle, I.	108	52 30N	128 35W
Swindon	13	51 33N	1 47W
Swinemünde = Świnoujście	28	53 54N	14 16 E
Świnoujście	28	53 54N	14 16 E
Switzerland ■	25	46 30N	8 0 E
Swords	15	53 27N	6 15W
Syasstroy	54	60 5N	32 15 E
Sychevka	54	55 59N	34 16 E
Syców	28	51 19N	17 40 E
Sydney, Austral.	97	33 53 S	151 10 E
Sydney, Can.	107	46 7N	60 7W
Sydney, U.S.A.	116	41 12N	103 0W
Sydney Mines	107	46 18N	60 15W
Sydprøven	4	60 30N	45 35W
Sydra G. of = Surt, Khalīj	35	31 40N	18 30 E
Syke	24	52 55N	8 50 E
Syktyvkar	52	61 45N	50 40 E
Sylacauga	115	33 10N	86 15W
Sylarna	50	63 2N	12 13 E
Sylhet	67	24 54N	91 52 E
Sylt	24	54 50N	8 20 E
Sylvan Lake	108	52 20N	114 03W
Sylvania	115	32 45N	81 37W
Sylvester	115	31 31N	83 50W
Sym	58	60 20N	88 18 E
Syracuse, Kans., U.S.A.	117	38 0N	101 46W
Syracuse, N.Y., U.S.A.	114	43 4N	76 11W
Syrdarya →	58	46 3N	61 0 E
Syria ■	64	35 0N	38 0 E
Syriam	69	16 44N	96 19 E
Syrian Desert	60	31 0N	40 0 E
Syul'dzhyukyor	59	63 14N	113 32 E
Syutkya	43	41 50N	24 16 E
Syzran	55	53 12N	48 30 E
Szabolcs-Szatmár □	27	48 2N	21 45 E
Szamocin	28	53 2N	17 7 E
Szamos →	27	48 7N	22 20 E
Szaraz →	27	46 28N	20 44 E
Szarvas	27	46 50N	20 38 E
Százhalombatta	27	47 20N	18 58 E
Szczawnica	27	49 26N	20 30 E
Szczebrzeszyn	28	50 42N	22 59 E
Szczecin	28	53 27N	14 27 E
Szczecin □	28	53 25N	14 32 E
Szczecinek	28	53 43N	16 41 E
Szczekocimy	28	50 38N	19 48 E
Szczucin	28	50 18N	21 4 E
Szczuczyn	28	53 36N	22 19 E
Szczytno	28	53 33N	21 0 E
Szechwan = Sichuan □	75	31 0N	104 0 E
Szécsény	27	48 7N	19 30 E
Szeged	27	46 16N	20 10 E
Szeghalom	27	47 1N	21 10 E
Székesfehérvár	27	47 15N	18 25 E
Szekszárd	27	46 22N	18 42 E
Szendrö	27	48 24N	20 41 E
Szentendre	27	47 39N	19 4 E
Szentes	27	46 39N	20 21 E
Szentgotthárd	27	46 58N	16 19 E
Szentlörinc	27	46 3N	18 1 E
Szerencs	27	48 10N	21 12 E
Szigetvár	27	46 3N	17 46 E
Szikszó	27	48 12N	20 56 E
Szkwa →	28	53 11N	21 43 E
Szlichtyngowa	28	51 42N	16 15 E
Szob	27	47 48N	18 53 E
Szolnok	27	47 10N	20 15 E
Szolnok □	27	47 15N	20 30 E
Szombathely	27	47 14N	16 38 E
Szprotawa	28	51 33N	15 35 E
Sztum	28	53 55N	19 1 E
Sztutowo	28	54 20N	19 15 E
Szubin	28	53 1N	17 45 E
Szydłowiec	28	51 15N	20 51 E
Szypliszki	28	54 17N	23 2 E

T

Tabacal	124	23 15 S	64 15W
Tabaco	73	13 22N	123 44 E
Tabagné	84	7 59N	3 4W
Ţābah	64	26 55N	42 38 E
Tabar Is.	98	2 50 S	152 0 E
Tabarca, Isla de	33	38 17N	0 30W
Tabarka	83	36 56N	8 46 E
Ţabas, Khorāsān, Iran	65	33 35N	56 55 E
Ţabas, Khorāsān, Iran	65	32 48N	60 12 E
Tabasará, Serranía de	121	8 35N	81 40W
Tabasco □	120	17 45N	93 30W
Tabatinga, Serra da	127	10 30 S	44 0W

Tabelbala, Kahal de Tarp

Tabelbala, Kahal de **82** 28 47N 2 0W
Tabelkaza **80** 29 50N 0 55 E
Taber **108** 49 47N 112 8W
Tabernas **33** 37 4N 2 26W
Tabernes de Valldigna **33** 39 5N 0 13W
Tablas **73** 12 25N 122 2 E
Table B. **107** 53 40N 56 25W
Table Mt. **92** 34 0 S 18 22 E
Table Top, Mt. **98** 23 24 S 147 11 E
Tábor **26** 49 25N 14 39 E
Tabor **62** 32 42N 35 24 E
Tabora **90** 5 2 S 32 50 E
Tabora □ **90** 5 0 S 33 0 E
Tabou **84** 4 30N 7 20W
Tabrīz **64** 38 7N 46 20 E
Tabuenca **32** 41 42N 1 33W
Tabūk **64** 28 23N 36 36 E
Tacheng **75** 46 40N 82 58 E
Tach'ing Shan = Daqing Shan **76** 40 40N 111 0 E
Tachov **26** 49 47N 12 39 E
Tácina → **41** 38 57N 16 55 E
Tacloban **73** 11 15N 124 58 E
Tacna **126** 18 0 S 70 20W
Tacoma **118** 47 15N 122 30W
Tacuarembó **125** 31 45 S 56 0W
Tademaït, Plateau du **82** 28 30N 2 30 E
Tadent, O. → **83** 22 25N 6 40 E
Tadjerdjeri, O. → **83** 26 0N 8 0W
Tadjerouna **82** 33 31N 2 3 E
Tadjettaret, O. → **83** 21 20N 7 22 E
Tadjmout, Atlas, Alg. **82** 33 52N 2 30 E
Tadjmout, Sahara, Alg. **82** 25 37N 3 48 E
Tadjoura **87** 11 50N 42 55 E
Tadjoura, Golfe de **87** 11 50N 43 0 E
Tadmor **101** 41 27 S 172 45 E
Tadoule, L. **109** 58 36N 98 20W
Tadoussac **107** 48 11N 69 42W
Tadzhik S.S.R. □ **58** 35 30N 70 0 E
Taegu **76** 35 50N 128 37 E
Taejŏn **76** 36 20N 127 28 E
Tafalla **32** 42 30N 1 41W
Tafar **87** 6 52N 28 15 E
Ţafas **62** 32 44N 36 5 E
Tafassasset, O. → **83** 22 0N 9 57 E
Tafelbaai **92** 33 35 S 18 25 E
Tafelney, C. **82** 31 3N 9 51W
Tafermaar **73** 6 47 S 134 10 E
Taffermit **82** 29 37N 9 15W
Tafí Viejo **124** 26 43 S 65 17W
Tafiré **84** 9 4N 5 4W
Tafnidilt **82** 28 47N 10 58W
Tafraoute **82** 29 50N 8 58W
Taft, Phil. **73** 11 57N 125 30 E
Taft, Calif., U.S.A. **119** 35 9N 119 28W
Taft, Tex., U.S.A. **117** 27 58N 97 23W
Taga Dzong **69** 27 5N 89 55 E
Taganrog **57** 47 12N 38 50 E
Taganrogskiy Zaliv **56** 47 0N 38 30 E
Tagânt **84** 18 20N 11 0W
Tagbilaran **73** 9 39N 123 51 E
Tággia **38** 43 52N 7 50 E
Taghrīfat **83** 29 5N 17 26 E
Taghzout **82** 33 30N 4 49W
Tagish **108** 60 19N 134 16W
Tagish L. **104** 60 10N 134 20W
Tagliacozzo **39** 42 4N 13 13 E
Tagliamento → **39** 45 38N 13 5 E
Táglio di Po **39** 45 0N 12 12 E
Tagomago, I. de **33** 39 2N 1 39 E
Taguatinga **127** 12 16 S 42 26W
Tagula I. **98** 11 30 S 153 30 E
Tagum (Hijo) **73** 7 33N 125 53 E
Tagus = Tajo → **29** 39 44N 5 50W
Tahakopa **101** 46 30 S 169 23 E
Tahala **82** 34 0N 4 28W
Tahan, Gunong **71** 4 34N 102 17 E
Tahat **83** 23 18N 5 33 E
Tāherī **65** 27 43N 52 20 E
Tahiti **95** 17 37 S 149 27W
Tahoe City **118** 39 12N 120 9W
Tahoe, L. **118** 39 0N 120 9W
Tahoua **85** 14 57N 5 16 E
Tahta **86** 26 44N 31 32 E
Tahulandang **73** 2 27N 125 23 E
Tahuna **73** 3 38N 125 30 E
Taï **84** 5 55N 7 30W
Tai Hu **75** 31 5N 120 10 E
Tai Shan **76** 36 25N 117 20 E
Tai'an **76** 36 12N 117 8 E
Taibei **75** 25 4N 121 29 E
Taibus Qi **76** 41 54N 115 22 E
T'aichung = Taizhong **75** 24 10N 120 38 E
Taidong **75** 22 43N 121 9 E
Taieri → **101** 46 3 S 170 12 E
Taiga Madema **83** 23 46N 15 25 E
Taigu **76** 37 28N 112 30 E
Taihang Shan **76** 36 0N 113 30 E
Taihape **101** 39 41 S 175 48 E
Taihe **77** 26 47N 114 52 E
Taihu **77** 30 22N 116 20 E
Taijiang **77** 26 39N 108 21 E
Taikang, Heilongjiang, China **76** 46 50N 124 25 E
Taikang, Henan, China **77** 34 5N 114 50 E
Taikkyi **69** 17 20N 96 0 E
Tailai **76** 46 23N 123 24 E
Tailem Bend **99** 35 12 S 139 29 E
Tailfingen **25** 48 15N 9 1 E
Taimyr = Taymyr **59** 75 0N 100 0 E
Taimyr, Oz. **59** 74 20N 102 0 E
Tain **14** 57 49N 4 4W
Tainan **77** 23 17N 120 18 E
Taínaron, Ákra **45** 36 22N 22 27 E
Taining **77** 26 54N 117 9 E
T'aipei = Taibei **75** 25 4N 121 29 E
Taiping **71** 4 51N 100 44 E
Taishan **77** 22 14N 112 41 E
Taishun **77** 27 30N 119 42 E
Taita □ **90** 4 0 S 38 30 E
Taita Hills **90** 3 25 S 38 15 E
Taitao, Pen. de **128** 46 30 S 75 0W
Taivalkoski **50** 65 33N 28 12 E
Taiwan ■ **75** 24 0N 121 0 E
Taïyetos Óros **45** 37 0N 22 23 E
Taiyib → **62** 31 55N 35 17 E
Taiyiba **62** 32 36N 35 27 E
Taiyuan **76** 37 52N 112 33 E
Taizhong **77** 24 12N 120 35 E
Taizhou **77** 32 28N 119 55 E
Ta'izz **63** 13 35N 44 2 E
Tajarḥī **83** 24 21N 14 28 E
Tajo → **31** 38 40N 9 24W
Tajumulco, Volcán de **120** 15 2N 91 50W
Tājūrā **83** 32 51N 13 21 E
Tak **71** 16 52N 99 8 E
Takada **74** 37 7N 138 15 E
Takaka **101** 40 51 S 172 50 E
Takamatsu **74** 34 20N 134 5 E
Takanabe **74** 32 8N 131 30 E
Takaoka **74** 36 47N 137 0 E
Takapuna **101** 36 47 S 174 47 E
Takasaki **74** 36 20N 139 0 E
Takatsuki **74** 34 51N 135 37 E
Takaungu **90** 3 38 S 39 52 E
Takayama **74** 36 18N 137 11 E
Takefu **74** 35 50N 136 10 E
Takengeun **72** 4 45N 96 50 E
Takeo **71** 10 59N 104 47 E
Tåkern **49** 58 22N 14 45 E
Tākestān **64** 36 0N 49 40 E
Takhar □ **65** 36 40N 70 0 E
Takla L. **108** 55 15N 125 45W
Takla Landing **108** 55 30N 125 50W
Takla Makan **60** 39 0N 83 0 E
Takla Makan = Taklimakan Shamo **75** 38 0N 83 0 E
Taklimakan Shamo **75** 38 0N 83 0 E
Taku → **108** 58 30N 133 50W
Takua Pa **71** 7 18N 9 59 E
Takum **85** 7 18N 9 36 E
Tala **125** 34 21 S 55 46W
Talagante **124** 33 40 S 70 50W
Talaïnt **82** 29 41N 9 40W
Talak **85** 18 0N 5 0 E
Talamanca, Cordillera de **121** 9 20N 83 20W
Talara **126** 4 38 S 81 18 E
Talas **58** 42 30N 72 13 E
Talasea **98** 5 20 S 150 2 E
Talata Mafara **85** 12 38N 6 4 E
Talaud, Kepulauan **73** 4 30N 127 10 E
Talavera de la Reina **30** 39 55N 4 46W
Talayan **73** 6 52N 124 24 E
Talbert, Sillon de **18** 48 53N 3 5W
Talbot, C. **96** 13 48 S 126 43 E
Talbragar → **99** 32 12 S 148 37 E
Talca **124** 35 28 S 71 40W
Talca □ **124** 35 20 S 71 46W
Talcahuano **124** 36 40 S 73 10W
Talcher **69** 21 0N 85 18 E
Talcho **85** 14 44N 3 28 E
Taldy Kurgan **58** 45 10N 78 45 E
Ţalesh, Kūhhā-ye **64** 39 0N 48 30 E
Talfit **62** 32 5N 35 17 E
Talguharai **86** 18 19N 35 56 E
Tali Post **87** 5 55N 30 44 E
Taliabu **73** 1 45 S 125 0 E
Talibon **73** 10 9N 124 20 E
Talihina **117** 34 45N 95 1W
Talikoti **70** 16 29N 76 17 E
Taling Sung **71** 15 5N 99 11 E
Taliwang **72** 8 50 S 116 55 E
Talkeetna **104** 62 20N 150 9W
Tall **62** 33 0N 35 6 E
Tall 'Afar **64** 36 22N 42 27 E
Tall 'Asūr **62** 31 59N 35 17 E
Talla **86** 28 5N 30 43 E
Talladega **115** 33 28N 86 2W
Tallahassee **115** 30 25N 84 15W
Tallangatta **99** 36 15 S 147 19 E
Tallarook **99** 37 5 S 145 6 E
Tällberg **48** 60 51N 15 2 E
Tallering Pk. **96** 28 6 S 115 37 E
Tallinn **54** 59 22N 24 48 E
Tallulah **117** 32 25N 91 12W
Ţallūzā **62** 32 17N 35 18 E
Tălmaciu **46** 45 38N 24 19 E
Talmest **82** 31 48N 9 21W
Talmont **20** 46 27N 1 37W
Talnoye **56** 48 50N 30 44 E
Taloda **68** 21 34N 74 11 E
Talodi **87** 10 35N 30 22 E
Talovaya **55** 51 6N 40 45 E
Talsi **54** 57 10N 22 30 E
Talsinnt **82** 32 33N 3 27W
Taltal **124** 25 23 S 70 33W
Taltson → **108** 61 24N 112 46W
Taltson L. **109** 61 30N 110 15W
Talwood **99** 28 29 S 149 29 E
Talyawalka Cr. → **99** 32 28 S 142 22 E
Tama **116** 41 56N 92 37W
Tamale **85** 9 22N 0 50W
Taman **56** 45 14N 36 41 E
Tamanar **82** 31 1N 9 46W
Tamano **74** 34 29N 133 59 E
Tamanrasset **83** 22 50N 5 30 E
Tamanrasset, O. → **82** 22 0N 2 0 E
Tamaqua **113** 40 46N 75 58W
Tamar → **13** 50 33N 4 15W
Tamarite de Litera **32** 41 52N 0 25 E
Tamási **27** 46 40N 18 18 E
Tamaské **85** 14 49N 5 43 E
Tamaulipas □ **120** 24 0N 99 0W
Tamaulipas, Sierra de **120** 23 30N 98 20W
Tamazula **120** 24 55N 106 58W
Tamba-Dabatou **84** 11 50N 10 40W
Tambacounda **84** 13 45N 13 40W
Tambelan, Kepulauan **72** 1 0N 107 30 E
Tambo **98** 24 54 S 146 14 E
Tambo de Mora **126** 13 30 S 76 8W
Tambohorano **93** 17 30 S 43 58 E
Tambora **72** 8 12 S 118 5 E
Tambov **55** 52 45N 41 28 E
Tambre → **30** 42 49N 8 53W
Tambuku **73** 7 8 S 113 40 E
Tamburâ **87** 5 40N 27 25 E
Tâmchekket **84** 17 25N 10 40W
Tamega → **30** 41 5N 8 21W
Tamelelt **82** 31 50N 7 32W
Tamenglong **67** 25 0N 93 35 E
Tamerza **83** 34 23N 7 58 E
Tamgak, Mts. **80** 19 12N 8 35 E
Tamiahua, Laguna de **120** 21 30N 97 30W
Tamil Nadu □ **70** 11 0N 77 0 E
Tamluk **69** 22 18N 87 58 E
Tammerfors = Tampere **51** 61 30N 23 50 E
Tammisaari **51** 60 0N 23 26 E
Ţammūn **62** 32 18N 35 23 E
Tämnaren **48** 60 10N 17 25 E
Tamo Abu, Pegunungan **72** 3 10N 115 0 E
Tampa **115** 27 57N 82 38W
Tampa B. **115** 27 40N 82 40W
Tampere **51** 61 30N 23 50 E
Tampico **120** 22 20N 97 50W
Tampin **71** 2 28N 102 13 E
Tamri **82** 30 49N 9 50W
Tamrida = Hadibu **63** 12 35N 54 2 E
Tamsagbulag **75** 47 14N 117 21 E
Tamsalu **54** 59 11N 26 8 E
Tamsweg **26** 47 7N 13 49 E
Tamu **67** 24 13N 94 12 E
Tamuja → **31** 39 38N 6 29W
Tamworth, Austral. **97** 31 7 S 150 58 E
Tamworth, U.K. **13** 52 38N 1 41W
Tan-tan **82** 28 29N 11 1W
Tana **50** 70 26N 28 14 E
Tana →, Kenya **90** 2 32 S 40 31 E
Tana →, Norway **50** 70 30N 28 23 E
Tana, L. **87** 13 5N 37 30 E
Tana River **90** 2 0 S 39 30 E
Tanafjorden **50** 70 45N 28 25 E
Tanagro → **41** 40 35N 15 25 E
Tanahbala **72** 0 30 S 98 30 E
Tanahgrogot **72** 1 55 S 116 15 E
Tanahjampea **73** 7 10 S 120 35 E
Tanahmasa **72** 0 12 S 98 39 E
Tanahmerah **73** 6 5 S 140 16 E
Tanakura **74** 37 10N 140 20 E
Tanami Des. **96** 18 50 S 132 0 E
Tanana **104** 65 10N 152 15W
Tanana → **104** 65 9N 151 55W
Tananarive = Antananarivo **93** 18 55 S 47 35 E
Tanannt **82** 31 54N 6 56W
Tánaro → **38** 45 1N 8 47 E
Tanaunella **40** 40 42N 9 45 E
Tancarville **18** 49 29N 0 28 E
Tanchŏn **76** 40 27N 128 54 E
Tanda, U.P., India **68** 28 57N 78 56 E
Tanda, U.P., India **69** 26 33N 82 35 E
Tanda, Ivory C. **84** 7 48N 3 10W
Tandag **73** 9 4N 126 9 E
Tandaia **91** 9 25 S 34 15 E
Tăndărei **46** 44 39N 27 40 E
Tandaué **92** 16 58 S 18 5 E
Tandil **124** 37 15 S 59 6W
Tandil, Sa. del **124** 37 30 S 59 0W
Tandlianwala **68** 31 3N 73 9 E
Tando Adam **68** 25 45N 68 40 E
Tandou L. **99** 32 40 S 142 5 E
Tandsbyn **48** 63 0N 14 45 E
Tandur **70** 19 11N 79 30 E
Tane-ga-Shima **74** 30 30N 131 0 E
Taneatua **101** 38 4 S 177 1 E
Tanen Tong Dan **67** 16 30N 98 30 E
Tanew → **28** 50 29N 22 16 E
Tanezrouft **82** 23 9N 0 11 E
Tanga **88** 5 5 S 39 2 E
Tanga □ **90** 5 20 S 38 0 E
Tanga Is. **98** 3 20 S 153 15 E
Tangail **69** 24 15N 89 55 E
Tanganyika, L. **90** 6 40 S 30 0 E
Tanger **82** 35 50N 5 49W
Tangerang **73** 6 12 S 106 39 E
Tangerhütte **24** 52 26N 11 50 E
Tangermünde **24** 52 32N 11 57 E
Tanggu **76** 39 2N 117 40 E
Tanggula Shan **75** 32 40N 92 10 E
Tanghe **77** 32 47N 112 50 E
Tangier = Tanger **82** 35 50N 5 49W
Tangkak **71** 2 18N 102 34 E
Tangorin P.O. **98** 21 47 S 144 12 E
Tangshan **76** 39 38N 118 10 E
Tanguiéta **85** 10 35N 1 21 E
Tanimbar, Kepulauan **73** 7 30 S 131 30 E
Taninges **21** 46 7N 6 36 E
Tanjay **73** 9 30N 123 5 E
Tanjore = Thanjavur **70** 10 48N 79 12 E
Tanjung **72** 2 10 S 115 25 E
Tanjungbalai **72** 2 55N 99 44 E
Tanjungbatu **72** 2 23N 118 3 E
Tanjungkarang **72** 5 20 S 105 10 E
Tanjungpandan **72** 2 43 S 107 38 E
Tanjungpinang **72** 1 5N 104 30 E
Tanjungpriok **73** 6 8 S 106 55 E
Tanjungredeb **72** 2 9N 117 29 E
Tanjungselor **72** 2 55N 117 25 E
Tank **68** 32 14N 70 25 E
Tänndalen **48** 62 33N 12 18 E
Tannis Bugt **49** 57 40N 10 15 E
Tannu-Ola **59** 51 0N 94 0 E
Tano → **84** 5 7N 2 56W
Tanout **85** 14 50N 8 55 E
Tanta **86** 30 45N 30 57 E
Tantoyuca **120** 21 21N 98 10W
Tantung = Dandong **76** 40 10N 124 20 E
Tantūra = Dor **62** 32 37N 34 55 E
Tanuku **70** 16 45N 81 44 E
Tanumshede **49** 58 42N 11 20 E
Tanunda **99** 34 30 S 139 0 E
Tanur **70** 11 1N 75 52 E
Tanus **20** 44 8N 2 19 E
Tanzania ■ **90** 6 40 S 34 0 E
Tanzilla → **108** 58 8N 130 43W
Tao'an **76** 45 22N 122 40 E
Taormina **41** 37 52N 15 16 E
Taos **119** 36 28N 105 35W
Taoudenni **82** 22 40N 3 55W
Taoudrart, Adrar **82** 24 25N 2 24 E
Taounate **82** 34 25N 4 41W
Taourirt, Alg. **82** 26 37N 0 20 E
Taourirt, Moroc. **82** 34 25N 2 53W
Taouz **82** 30 53N 4 0W
Taoyuan, China **77** 28 55N 111 16 E
Taoyuan, Taiwan **77** 25 0N 121 13 E
Tapa **54** 59 15N 25 50 E
Tapa Shan = Daba Shan **75** 31 50N 109 20 E
Tapachula **120** 14 54N 92 17W
Tapah **71** 4 12N 101 15 E
Tapajós → **127** 2 24 S 54 41W
Tapaktuan **72** 3 15N 97 10 E
Tapanui **101** 45 56 S 169 18 E
Tapauá → **126** 5 40 S 64 21W
Tapeta **84** 6 29N 8 52W
Tapia **30** 43 34N 6 56W
Tápiószele **27** 47 25N 19 55 E
Tapirapecó, Serra **126** 1 10N 65 0W
Tapolca **27** 46 53N 17 29 E
Tappahannock **114** 37 56N 76 50W
Tapti → **68** 21 8N 72 41 E
Tapuaenuku, Mt. **101** 42 0 S 173 39 E
Tapul Group **73** 5 35N 120 50 E
Taquara **125** 29 36 S 50 46W
Taquari → **126** 19 15 S 57 17W
Tar Island **108** 57 03N 111 40W
Tara, Austral. **99** 27 17 S 150 31 E
Tara, Can. **112** 44 28N 81 9W
Tara, U.S.S.R. **58** 56 55N 74 24 E
Tara, Zambia **91** 16 58 S 26 45 E
Tara →, U.S.S.R. **58** 56 42N 74 36 E
Tara →, Yugo. **42** 43 21N 18 51 E
Tarabagatay, Khrebet **58** 48 0N 83 0 E
Tarābulus, Leb. **64** 34 31N 35 50 E
Tarābulus, Libya **83** 32 49N 13 7 E
Tarahouahout **83** 22 41N 5 59 E
Tarakan **72** 3 20N 117 35 E
Tarakit, Mt. **90** 2 2N 35 10 E
Taralga **99** 34 26 S 149 52 E
Taranagar **68** 28 43N 74 50 E
Taranaki □ **101** 39 5 S 174 51 E
Tarancón **32** 40 1N 3 1W
Taranga **68** 23 56N 72 43 E
Taranga Hill **68** 24 0N 72 40 E
Táranto **41** 40 30N 17 11 E
Táranto, G. di **41** 40 0N 17 15 E
Tarapacá **126** 2 56 S 69 46W
Tarapacá □ **124** 20 45 S 69 30W
Tarare **21** 45 54N 4 26 E
Tararua Range **101** 40 45 S 175 25 E
Tarascon, Ariège, France **20** 42 50N 1 37 E
Tarascon, Bouches-du-Rhône, France **21** 43 48N 4 39 E
Tarashcha **56** 49 30N 30 31 E
Tarat **80** 25 55N 9 3 E
Tarat, Bj. **83** 26 13N 9 18 E
Tarauacá **126** 8 6 S 70 48W
Tarauacá → **126** 6 42 S 69 48W
Taravo → **21** 41 42N 8 49 E
Tarawera **101** 39 2 S 176 36 E
Tarawera L. **101** 38 13 S 176 27 E
Tarazona **32** 41 55N 1 43W
Tarazona de la Mancha **33** 39 16N 1 55W
Tarbat Ness **14** 57 52N 3 48W
Tarbert, Strathclyde, U.K. **14** 55 55N 5 25W
Tarbert, W. Isles, U.K. **14** 57 54N 6 49W
Tarbes **20** 43 15N 0 3 E
Tarboro **115** 35 55N 77 30W
Tarbrax **98** 21 7 S 142 26 E
Tarbū **83** 26 0N 15 5 E
Tarcento **39** 46 12N 13 12 E
Tarcoola **96** 30 44 S 134 36 E
Tarcoon **99** 30 15 S 146 43 E
Tardets-Sorholus **20** 43 8N 0 52W
Tardoire → **20** 45 52N 0 14 E
Taree **97** 31 50 S 152 30 E
Tarentaise **21** 45 30N 6 35 E
Tarf, Ras **82** 35 40N 5 11W
Tarf Shaqq al Abd **86** 26 50N 36 6 E
Tarfa, Wadi el → **86** 28 25N 30 50 E
Tarfaya **80** 27 55N 12 55W
Targon **20** 44 44N 0 16W
Targuist **82** 34 59N 4 14W
Târhăus **46** 46 40N 26 8 E
Târhăus, Munţii **46** 46 39N 26 7 E
Tarhbalt **82** 30 39N 5 20W
Tarhit **82** 30 58N 2 0W
Tarhūnah **83** 32 27N 13 36 E
Tarib, Wadi → **86** 18 30N 43 23 E
Tarifa **31** 36 1N 5 36W
Tarija **124** 21 30 S 64 40W
Tarija □ **124** 21 30 S 63 30W
Tariku → **73** 2 55 S 138 26 E
Tarim He → **75** 39 30N 88 30 E
Tarim Pendi **75** 40 0N 84 0 E
Tarime □ **90** 1 15 S 34 0 E
Taritatu → **73** 2 54 S 138 27 E
Tarka → **92** 32 10 S 26 0 E
Tarkastad **92** 32 0 S 26 16 E
Tarkhankut, Mys **56** 45 25N 32 30 E
Tarko Sale **58** 64 55N 77 50 E
Tarkwa **84** 5 20N 2 0W
Tarlac **73** 15 29N 120 35 E
Tarm **49** 55 56N 8 31 E
Tarma **126** 11 25 S 75 45W
Tarn □ **20** 43 49N 2 8 E
Tarn → **20** 44 5N 1 6 E
Tarn-et-Garonne □ **20** 44 8N 1 20 E
Tarna → **27** 47 31N 19 59 E
Tårnby **49** 55 37N 12 36 E
Tarnica **27** 49 4N 22 44 E
Tarnobrzeg **28** 50 35N 21 41 E
Tarnobrzeg □ **28** 50 40N 22 0 E
Tarnogród **28** 50 22N 22 45 E
Tarnów **27** 50 3N 21 0 E
Tarnów □ **27** 50 0N 21 0 E
Tarnowskie Góry **28** 50 27N 18 54 E
Táro → **38** 45 0N 10 15 E
Tarong **99** 26 47 S 151 51 E
Taroom **97** 25 36 S 149 48 E
Taroudannt **82** 30 30N 8 52W
Tarp **24** 54 40N 9 25 E

Tarpon Springs Thaon

Tarpon Springs 115 28 8N 82 42W
Tarquinia 39 42 15N 11 45 E
Tarqūmiyah 62 31 35N 35 1 E
Tarragona 32 41 5N 1 17 E
Tarragona □ 32 41 0N 1 0 E
Tarrasa 32 41 34N 2 1 E
Tárrega 32 41 39N 1 9 E
Tarrytown 113 41 5N 73 52W
Tarshiha = Me'ona 62 33 1N 35 15 E
Tarso Emissi 83 21 27N 18 36 E
Tarso Ourari 83 21 27N 17 27 E
Tarsus 64 36 58N 34 55 E
Tartagal 124 22 30 S 63 50W
Tartas 20 43 50N 0 49W
Tartna Point 99 32 54 S 142 24 E
Tartu 54 58 20N 26 44 E
Tarṭūs 64 34 55N 35 55 E
Tarussa 55 54 44N 37 10 E
Tarutao, Ko 71 6 33N 99 40 E
Tarutung 72 2 0N 98 54 E
Tarvisio 39 46 31N 13 35 E
Tarz Ulli 83 25 32N 10 8 E
Tasāwah 83 26 0N 13 30 E
Taschereau 106 48 40N 78 40W
Taseko → 108 52 4N 123 9W
Tasgaon 70 17 2N 74 39 E
Tash-Kumyr 58 41 40N 72 10 E
Ta'shan 87 16 31N 42 33 E
Tashauz 58 41 49N 59 58 E
Tashi Chho Dzong = Thimphu 69 27 31N 89 45 E
Tashkent 58 41 20N 69 10 E
Tashtagol 58 52 47N 87 53 E
Tasikmalaya 73 7 18 S 108 12 E
Tåsjön 50 64 15N 16 0 E
Taskan 59 62 59N 150 20 E
Taskopru 56 41 30N 34 15 E
Tasman B. 101 40 59 S 173 25 E
Tasman Mts. 101 41 3 S 172 25 E
Tasman Pen. 97 43 10 S 148 0 E
Tasman Sea 94 36 0 S 160 0 E
Tasmania □ 97 42 0 S 146 30 E
Tăşnad 46 47 30N 22 33 E
Tassil Tin-Rerhoh 82 20 5N 3 55 E
Tassili n-Ajjer 83 25 47N 8 1 E
Tassili-Oua-n-Ahaggar 83 20 41N 5 30 E
Tasu Sd. 108 52 47N 132 2W
Tata, Hung. 27 47 37N 18 19 E
Tata, Moroc. 82 29 46N 7 56W
Tatabánya 27 47 32N 18 25 E
Tatahouine 83 32 57N 10 29 E
Tatar A.S.S.R. □ 52 55 30N 51 30 E
Tatarbunary 56 45 50N 29 39 E
Tatarsk 58 55 14N 76 0 E
• Tatarskiy Proliv 59 54 0N 141 0 E
Tateyama 74 35 0N 139 50 E
Tathlina L. 108 60 33N 117 39W
Tathra 99 36 44 S 149 59 E
Tatinnai L. 109 60 55N 97 40W
Tatnam, C. 109 57 16N 91 0W
Tatra = Tatry 27 49 20N 20 0 E
Tatry 27 49 20N 20 0 E
Tatta 68 24 42N 67 55 E
Tatuí 125 23 25 S 47 53W
Tatum 117 33 16N 103 16W
Tat'ung = Datong 76 40 6N 113 12 E
Tatura 100 36 29 S 145 16 E
Tatvan 64 38 31N 42 15 E
Taubaté 125 23 0 S 45 36W
Tauberbischofsheim 25 49 37N 9 40 E
Taucha 24 51 22N 12 31 E
Tauern 26 47 15N 12 40 E
Tauern-tunnel 26 47 0N 13 12 E
Taufikia 87 9 24N 31 37 E
Taumarunui 101 38 53 S 175 15 E
Taumaturgo 126 8 54 S 72 51W
Taung 92 27 33 S 24 47 E
Taungdwingyi 67 20 1N 95 40 E
Taunggyi 67 20 50N 97 0 E
Taungup 67 18 51N 94 14 E
Taungup Pass 67 18 40N 94 45 E
Taunsa Barrage 68 30 42N 70 50 E
Taunton, U.K. 13 51 1N 3 7W
Taunton, U.S.A. 114 41 54N 71 6W
Taunus 25 50 15N 8 20 E
Taupo 101 38 41 S 176 7 E
Taupo, L. 101 38 46 S 175 55 E
Taurage 54 55 14N 22 16 E
Tauranga 101 37 42 S 176 11 E
Tauranga Harb. 101 37 30 S 176 5 E
Taurianova 41 38 22N 16 1 E
Taurus Mts. = Toros Dağlari 64 37 0N 35 0 E
Tauste 32 41 58N 1 18W
Tauz 57 41 0N 45 40 E
Tavda 58 58 7N 65 8 E
Tavda → 58 59 20N 63 28 E
Taverny 19 49 2N 2 13 E
Taveta 90 3 23 S 37 37 E
Taveuni 101 16 51 S 179 58W
Tavignano → 21 42 7N 9 33 E
Tavira 31 37 8N 7 40W
Tavistock, Can. 112 43 19N 80 50W
Tavistock, U.K. 13 50 33N 4 9W
Tavolara 40 40 55N 9 40 E
Távora → 30 41 8N 7 35W
Tavoy 71 14 2N 98 12 E
Taw → 13 17 37 S 177 55 E
Tawas City 114 44 16N 83 31W
Tawau 72 4 20N 117 55 E
Tawitawi 73 5 10N 120 0 E
Tāwurgha' 83 32 1N 15 2 E
Tay → 14 56 37N 3 38W
Tay, Firth of 14 56 25N 3 8W
Tay, L. 14 56 30N 4 10W
Tay Ninh 71 11 20N 106 5 E
Tayabamba 126 8 15 S 77 16W
Taylakovy 58 59 13N 74 0 E
Taylor, Can. 108 56 13N 120 40W
Taylor, Ariz., U.S.A. 119 34 28N 110 5W
Taylor, Nebr., U.S.A. 116 41 46N 99 23W
Taylor, Pa., U.S.A. 113 41 23N 75 43W
Taylor, Tex., U.S.A. 117 30 30N 97 30W
Taylor Mt. 119 35 16N 107 36W
Taylorville 116 39 32N 89 20W
Taymā' 64 27 35N 38 45 E
Taymyr, P-ov. 59 75 0N 100 0 E
Tayport 14 56 27N 2 52W
Ṭayr Zibnā 62 33 14N 35 23 E
Tayshet 59 55 58N 98 1 E
Tayside □ 14 56 25N 3 30W
Taytay 73 10 45N 119 30 E
Taz → 58 67 32N 78 40 E
Taza 82 34 16N 4 6W
Tazenakht 82 30 35N 7 12W
Tazin → 109 60 26N 110 45W
Tazin L. 109 59 44N 108 42W
Tazoult 83 35 29N 6 11 E
Tazovskiy 58 67 30N 78 44 E
Tbilisi (Tiflis) 57 41 43N 44 50 E
Tchad (Chad) ■ 81 12 30N 17 15 E
Tchad, L. 81 13 30N 14 30 E
Tch'ang-k'ing = Changqing 75 29 35N 106 35 E
Tchaourou 85 8 58N 2 40 E
Tch'eng-tou = Chengdu 75 30 38N 104 2 E
Tchentlo L. 108 55 15N 125 0W
Tchibanga 88 2 45 S 11 0 E
Tchin Tabaraden 85 15 58N 5 56 E
Tczew 28 54 8N 18 50 E
Te Anau, L. 101 45 15 S 167 45 E
Te Aroha 101 37 32 S 175 44 E
Te Awamutu 101 38 1 S 175 20 E
Te Kuiti 101 38 20 S 175 11 E
Te Puke 101 37 46 S 176 22 E
Te Waewae B. 101 46 13 S 167 33 E
Teaca 46 46 55N 24 30 E
Teague 117 31 40N 96 20W
Teano 41 41 15N 14 1 E
Teapa 120 18 35N 92 56W
Teba 31 36 59N 4 55W
Tebakang 72 1 6N 110 30 E
Teberda 57 43 30N 41 46 E
Tébessa 83 35 22N 8 8 E
Tebicuary → 124 26 36 S 58 16W
Tebingtinggi, Bengkulu, Indon. 72 3 38 S 103 9 E
Tebingtinggi, Sumatera Utara, Indon. 72 3 20N 99 9 E
Tébourba 83 36 49N 9 51 E
Téboursouk 83 36 29N 9 10 E
Tebulos 57 42 36N 45 17 E
Tech → 20 42 36N 3 3 E
Techiman 84 7 35N 1 58W
Techirghiol 46 44 4N 28 32 E
Tecuala 120 22 23N 105 27W
Tecuci 46 45 51N 27 27 E
Tecumseh 114 42 1N 83 59W
Tedzhen 58 37 23N 60 31 E
Tees → 12 54 36N 1 25W
Teesside 12 54 37N 1 13W
Teeswater 112 43 59N 81 17W
Tefé 126 3 25 S 64 50W
Tegal 73 6 52 S 109 8 E
Tegelen 16 51 20N 6 9 E
Tegernsee 25 47 43N 11 46 E
Teggiano 41 40 24N 15 32 E
Teghra 69 25 30N 85 34 E
Tegid, L. 12 52 53N 3 38W
Tegina 85 10 5N 6 11 E
Tegucigalpa 121 14 5N 87 14W
Tehachapi 119 35 11N 118 29W
Tehachapi Mts. 119 35 0N 118 40W
Tehamiyam 86 18 20N 36 32 E
Tehilla 86 17 42N 36 6 E
Téhini 84 9 39N 3 40W
Tehrān 65 35 44N 51 30 E
Tehrān □ 65 35 0N 49 30 E
Tehuacán 120 18 30N 97 30W
Tehuantepec 120 16 21N 95 13W
Tehuantepec, Golfo de 120 15 50N 95 0W
Tehuantepec, Istmo de 120 17 0N 94 30W
Teich, Le 20 44 38N 0 59W
Teifi → 13 52 4N 4 14W
Teign → 13 50 41N 3 42W
Teignmouth 13 50 33N 3 30W
Teil, Le 21 44 33N 4 40 E
Teilleul, Le 18 48 32N 0 53W
Teiuş 46 46 12N 23 40 E
Teixeira Pinto 84 12 3N 16 0W
Tejo → 31 38 40N 9 24W
Tekamah 116 41 48N 96 22W
Tekapo, L. 101 43 53 S 170 33 E
Tekax 120 20 11N 89 18W
Tekeli 58 44 50N 79 0 E
Tekeze → 87 14 20N 35 50 E
Tekija 42 44 42N 22 26 E
Tekirdağ 64 40 58N 27 30 E
Tekkali 70 18 37N 84 15 E
Tekoa 118 47 19N 117 4W
Tekouiât, O. → 82 22 25N 2 35 E
Tel Adashim 62 32 30N 35 17 E
Tel Aviv-Yafo 62 32 4N 34 48 E
Tel Lakhish 62 31 34N 34 51 E
Tel Megiddo 62 32 35N 35 11 E
Tel Mond 62 32 15N 34 56 E
Tela 120 15 40N 87 28W
Télagh 82 34 51N 0 32W
Telanaipura = Jambi 72 1 38 S 103 37 E
Telavi 57 42 0N 45 30 E
Telciu 46 47 25N 24 24 E
Telegraph Cr. 108 58 0N 131 10W
Telekhany 54 52 30N 25 46 E
Telemark fylke □ 47 59 25N 8 30 E
Telén 124 36 15 S 65 31W
Teleneshty 46 47 35N 28 24 E
Teleño 30 42 23N 6 22W
Teleorman □ 46 44 0N 25 0 E
Teleorman → 46 44 15N 25 20 E
Teles Pires → 126 7 21 S 58 3W
Telescope Peak 119 36 6N 117 7W
Teletaye 85 16 31N 1 30 E
Telford 12 52 42N 2 31W
Telfs 26 47 19N 11 4 E
Telgte 24 51 59N 7 46 E
Télimélé 84 10 54N 13 2W
Telkwa 108 54 41N 127 5W
Tell City 114 38 0N 86 44W
Tellicherry 70 11 45N 75 30 E
Telluride 119 37 58N 107 48W
Telok Anson 71 4 3N 101 0 E
Telom → 71 4 20N 101 46 E
Telpos Iz 52 63 35N 57 30 E
Telsen 128 42 30 S 66 50W
Telšiai 54 55 59N 22 14 E
Teltow 24 52 24N 13 15 E
Telukbetung 72 5 29 S 105 17 E
Telukbutun 72 4 13N 108 12 E
Telukdalem 72 0 33N 97 50 E
Tema 85 5 41N 0 0 E
Temanggung 73 7 18 S 110 10 E
Temax 120 21 10N 88 50W
Tembe 90 0 16 S 28 14 E
Tembeling → 71 4 20N 102 23 E
Tembleque 32 39 41N 3 30W
Tembuland 93 31 35 S 28 0 E
Teme → 13 52 23N 2 15W
Temecula 119 33 26N 117 6W
Temerloh 71 3 27N 102 25 E
Temir 58 49 21N 57 3 E
Temirtau, Kazakh, U.S.S.R. 58 50 5N 72 56 E
Temirtau, R.S.F.S.R., U.S.S.R. 58 53 10N 87 30 E
Témiscaming 106 46 44N 79 5W
Temma 99 41 12 S 144 48 E
Temnikov 55 54 40N 43 11 E
Temo → 40 40 20N 8 30 E
Temora 99 34 30 S 147 30 E
Temosachic 120 28 58N 107 50W
Tempe 119 33 26N 111 59W
Tempino 72 1 42 S 103 30 E
Témpio Pausania 40 40 53N 9 6 E
Temple 117 31 5N 97 22W
Temple B. 97 12 15 S 143 3 E
Templemore 15 52 48N 7 50W
Templeton → 98 21 0 S 138 40 E
Templin 24 53 8N 13 31 E
Temryuk 56 45 15N 37 24 E
Temska → 42 43 17N 22 33 E
Temuco 128 38 45 S 72 40W
Temuka 101 44 14 S 171 17 E
Tenabo 120 20 2N 90 12W
Tenaha 117 31 57N 94 25W
Tenali 70 16 15N 80 35 E
Tenancingo 120 19 0N 99 33W
Tenango 120 19 7N 99 33W
Tenasserim 71 12 6N 99 3 E
Tenasserim □ 71 14 0N 98 30 E
Tenay 21 45 55N 5 30 E
Tenby 13 51 40N 4 42W
Tendaho 87 11 48N 40 54 E
Tende 21 44 5N 7 35 E
Tende, Col de 21 44 9N 7 32 E
Tendelti 87 13 1N 31 55 E
Tendjedi, Adrar 83 23 41N 7 32 E
Tendrara 82 33 3N 1 58W
Teneida 86 25 30N 29 19 E
Ténéré 85 19 0N 10 30 E
Tenerife 80 28 15N 16 35W
Ténès 82 36 31N 1 14 E
Teng → 71 20 30N 98 10 E
Teng Xian, Guangxi Zhuangzu, China 77 23 21N 110 56 E
Teng Xian, Shandong, China 77 35 5N 117 10 E
Tengah □ 73 2 0 S 122 0 E
Tengah Kepulauan 72 7 5 S 118 15 E
Tengchong 75 25 0N 98 28 E
Tenggara □ 73 3 0 S 122 0 E
Tenggarong 72 0 24 S 116 58 E
Tengiz, Ozero 58 50 30N 69 0 E
Tenille 115 32 58N 82 50W
Tenkasi 70 8 55N 77 20 E
Tenke, Congo 91 11 22 S 26 40 E
Tenke, Zaïre 91 10 32 S 26 7 E
Tenkodogo 85 11 54N 0 19W
Tenna → 39 43 12N 13 47 E
Tennant Creek 96 19 30 S 134 15 E
Tennessee □ 111 36 0N 86 30W
Tennessee → 114 34 30N 86 20W
Tennsift, Oued → 82 32 3N 9 28W
Tenom 72 5 4N 115 57 E
Tenosique 120 17 30N 91 24W
Tenryū-Gawa → 74 35 39N 137 48 E
Tent L. 109 62 25N 107 54W
Tenterfield 97 29 0 S 152 0 E
Teófilo Otoni 127 17 50 S 41 30W
Teotihuacán 120 19 44N 98 50W
Tepa 73 7 52 S 129 31 E
Tepalcatepec → 120 18 35N 101 59W
Tepelena 44 40 17N 20 2 E
Tepic 120 21 30N 104 54W
Teplice 26 50 40N 13 48 E
Tepoca, C. 120 30 20N 112 25W
Tequila 120 20 54N 103 47W
Ter → 32 42 0N 3 12 E
Ter Apel 16 52 53N 7 5 E
Téra 85 14 0N 0 45 E
Tera → 30 41 54N 5 44W
Téramo 39 42 40N 13 40 E
Terang 99 38 15 S 142 55 E
Terazit, Massif de 83 20 2N 8 30 E
Terceira 8 38 43N 27 13W
Tercero → 124 32 58 S 61 47W
Terdal 70 16 33N 75 3 E
Terebovlya 54 49 18N 25 44 E
Teregova 46 45 10N 22 16 E
Terek →, U.S.S.R. 56 43 55N 47 30 E
Terek →, U.S.S.R. 57 44 0N 47 30 E
Terembone Cr. → 99 30 25 S 148 50 E
Terengganu □ 71 4 55N 103 0 E
Tereshka → 55 51 48N 46 26 E
Teresina 127 5 9 S 42 45W
Terespol 28 52 5N 23 37 E
Terewah L. 99 29 52 S 147 35 E
Terges → 31 37 49N 7 41W
Tergnier 19 49 40N 3 17 E
Terhazza 82 23 38N 5 22W
Terlizzi 41 41 8N 16 32 E
Terme 56 41 11N 37 0 E
Termez 58 37 15N 67 15 E
Términi Imerese 40 37 58N 13 42 E
Términos, Laguna de 120 18 35N 91 30W
Térmoli 39 42 0N 15 0 E
Ternate 73 0 45N 127 25 E
Terneuzen 16 51 20N 3 50 E
Terney 59 45 3N 136 37 E
Terni 39 42 34N 12 38 E
Ternitz 26 47 43N 16 2 E
Ternopol 54 49 30N 25 40 E
Terra Nova B. 5 74 50 S 164 40 E
Terrace 108 54 30N 128 35W
Terrace Bay 106 48 47N 87 5W
Terracina 40 41 17N 13 12 E
Terralba 40 39 42N 8 38 E
Terranuova Bracciolini 39 43 31N 11 35 E
Terrasini Favarotta 40 38 10N 13 4 E
Terrasson 20 45 7N 1 19 E
Terre Haute 114 39 28N 87 24W
Terrebonne B. 117 29 15N 90 28W
Terrecht 82 20 10N 0 10W
Terrell 117 32 44N 96 19W
Terrenceville 107 47 40N 54 44W
Terrick Terrick 98 24 44 S 145 5 E
Terry 116 46 47N 105 20W
Terschelling 16 53 25N 5 20 E
Terter → 57 40 35N 47 22 E
Teruel 32 40 22N 1 8W
Teruel □ 32 40 48N 1 0W
Tervel 43 43 45N 27 28 E
Tervola 50 66 6N 24 49 E
Teryaweyna L. 99 32 18 S 143 22 E
Tešanj 42 44 38N 17 59 E
Teseney 87 15 5N 36 42 E
Tesha → 55 55 38N 42 9 E
Teshio-Gawa → 74 44 53N 141 45 E
Tešica 42 43 27N 21 45 E
Tesiyn Gol → 75 50 40N 93 20 E
Teslić 42 44 37N 17 54 E
Teslin 104 60 10N 132 43W
Teslin → 108 61 34N 134 35W
Teslin L. 108 60 15N 132 57W
Tessalit 85 20 12N 1 0 E
Tessaoua 85 13 47N 7 56 E
Tessin 24 54 2N 12 28 E
Tessit 85 15 13N 0 18 E
Test → 13 51 7N 1 30W
Testa del Gargano 41 41 50N 16 10 E
Teste, La 20 44 37N 1 8W
Tét 27 47 30N 17 33 E
Têt → 20 42 44N 3 2 E
Tetachuck L. 108 53 18N 125 55W
Tetas, Pta. 124 23 31 S 70 38W
Tete 91 16 13 S 33 33 E
Tete □ 91 15 15 S 32 40 E
Teterev → 54 51 1N 30 5 E
Teterow 24 53 45N 12 34 E
Teteven 43 42 58N 24 17 E
Tethul → 108 60 35N 112 12W
Tetiyev 56 49 22N 29 38 E
Teton → 118 47 58N 111 0W
Tétouan 82 35 35N 5 21W
Tetovo 42 42 1N 21 2 E
Tetuán = Tétouan 82 35 30N 5 25W
Tetyushi 55 54 55N 48 49 E
Teuco → 124 25 35 S 60 11W
Teulada 40 38 59N 8 47 E
Teulon 109 50 23N 97 16W
Teun 73 6 59 S 129 8 E
Teutoburger Wald 22 52 5N 8 20 E
Tevere → 39 41 44N 12 14 E
Teverya 62 32 47N 35 32 E
Teviot → 14 55 21N 2 51W
Tewantin 99 26 27 S 153 3 E
Tewkesbury 13 51 59N 2 8W
Texada I. 108 49 40N 124 25W
Texarkana, Ark., U.S.A. 117 33 25N 94 0W
Texarkana, Tex., U.S.A. 117 33 25N 94 3W
Texas 99 28 49 S 151 9 E
Texas □ 117 31 40N 98 30W
Texas City 117 29 20N 94 55W
Texel 16 53 5N 4 50 E
Texhoma 117 36 32N 101 47W
Texline 117 36 26N 103 0W
Texoma L. 117 34 0N 96 38W
Teykovo 55 56 55N 40 30 E
Teyvareh 65 33 30N 64 24 E
Teza → 55 56 32N 41 53 E
Teziutlán 120 19 50N 97 22W
Tezpur 67 26 40N 92 45 E
Tezzeron L. 108 54 43N 124 30W
Tha-anne → 109 60 31N 94 37W
Tha Nun 71 8 12N 98 17 E
Thaba Putsoa 93 29 45 S 28 0 E
Thabana Ntlenyana 93 29 30 S 29 16 E
Thabazimbi 93 24 40 S 27 21 E
Thabor, Mt. 21 45 7N 6 34 E
Thai Nguyen 71 21 35N 105 55 E
Thailand (Siam) ■ 71 16 0N 102 0 E
Thakhek 71 17 25N 104 45 E
Thal 66 33 28N 70 33 E
Thal Desert 68 31 10N 71 30 E
Thala 83 35 35N 8 40 E
Thala La 67 28 25N 97 23 E
Thallon 99 28 39 S 148 49 E
Thalwil 25 47 17N 8 35 E
Thame → 13 51 35N 1 8W
Thames 101 37 7 S 175 34 E
Thames →, Can. 106 42 20N 82 25W
Thames →, U.K. 13 51 30N 0 35 E
Thames →, U.S.A. 113 41 18N 72 9W
Thamesford 112 43 4N 81 0W
Thamesville 112 42 33N 81 59W
Thâmit, W. 83 30 51N 16 14 E
Thana 70 19 12N 72 59 E
Thanesar 68 30 1N 76 52 E
Thanet, I. of 13 51 21N 1 20 E
Thang Binh 71 15 50N 108 20 E
Thangool 98 24 38 S 150 42 E
Thanh Hoa 71 19 48N 105 46 E
Thanjavur (Tanjore) 70 10 48N 79 12 E
Thanlwin Myit → 67 20 0N 98 0 E
Thann 19 47 48N 7 5 E
Thaon 19 48 15N 6 25 E

• *Renamed Sakhalinskiy Zaliv*

Thar Tocina

Thar (Great Indian) Desert	**68**	28 0N	72 0 E
Tharad	**68**	24 30N	71 44 E
Thargomindah	**97**	27 58 S	143 46 E
Tharrawaddy	**67**	17 38N	95 48 E
Thasopoúla	**44**	40 49N	24 45 E
Thásos, Greece	**44**	40 50N	24 42 E
Thásos, Greece	**44**	40 40N	24 40 E
Thatcher, Ariz., U.S.A.	**119**	32 54N	109 46W
Thatcher, Colo., U.S.A.	**117**	37 38N	104 6W
Thaton	**67**	16 55N	97 22 E
Thau, Étang de	**20**	43 23N	3 36 E
Thaungdut	**67**	24 30N	94 40 E
Thayer	**117**	36 34N	91 34W
Thayetmyo	**67**	19 20N	95 10 E
Thazi	**67**	21 0N	96 5 E
The Bight	**121**	24 19N	75 24W
The Dalles	**118**	45 40N	121 11W
The English Company's Is.	**97**	11 50 S	136 32 E
The Flatts	**121**	32 16N	64 45W
The Frome →	**99**	29 8 S	137 54 E
The Granites	**96**	20 35 S	130 21 E
The Grenadines, Is.	**121**	12 40N	61 20W
The Hague = s'-Gravenhage	**16**	52 7N	4 14 E
The Hamilton →	**96**	26 40 S	135 19 E
The Johnston Lakes	**96**	32 25 S	120 30 E
The Macumba →	**97**	27 52 S	137 12 E
The Pas	**109**	53 45N	101 15W
The Range	**91**	19 2 S	31 2 E
The Rock	**99**	35 15 S	147 2 E
The Salt Lake	**99**	30 6 S	142 8 E
The Warburton →	**99**	28 4 S	137 28 E
Thebes	**86**	25 40N	32 35 E
Thebes = Thívai	**45**	38 19N	23 19 E
Thedford, Can.	**112**	43 9N	81 51W
Thedford, U.S.A.	**116**	41 59N	100 31W
Theebine	**99**	25 57 S	152 34 E
Theil, Le	**18**	48 16N	0 42 E
Thekulthili L.	**109**	61 3N	110 0W
Thelon →	**109**	62 35N	104 3W
Thénezay	**18**	46 44N	0 2W
Thenia	**83**	36 44N	3 33 E
Thenon	**20**	45 9N	1 4 E
Theodore	**97**	24 55 S	150 3 E
Thérain →	**19**	49 15N	2 27 E
Theresa	**113**	44 13N	75 50W
Thermaïkos Kólpos	**44**	40 15N	22 45 E
Thermopolis	**118**	43 35N	108 10W
Thermopylae P.	**45**	38 48N	22 35 E
Thesprotía □	**44**	39 27N	20 22 E
Thessalía □	**44**	39 30N	22 0 E
Thessalon	**106**	46 20N	83 30W
Thessaloníki	**44**	40 38N	22 58 E
Thessaloníki □	**44**	40 45N	23 0 E
Thessaly = Thessalía	**44**	39 30N	22 0 E
Thetford	**13**	52 25N	0 44 E
Thetford Mines	**107**	46 8N	71 18W
Theunissen	**92**	28 26 S	26 43 E
Thiámis →	**44**	39 15N	20 6 E
Thiberville	**18**	49 8N	0 27 E
Thibodaux	**117**	29 48N	90 49W
Thicket Portage	**109**	55 19N	97 42W
Thief River Falls	**116**	48 15N	96 48W
Thiel Mts.	**5**	85 15 S	91 0W
Thiene	**39**	45 42N	11 29 E
Thiérache	**19**	49 51N	3 45 E
Thiers	**20**	45 52N	3 33 E
Thies	**84**	14 50N	16 51W
Thiet	**87**	7 37N	28 49 E
Thika	**90**	1 1 S	37 5 E
Thikombia	**101**	15 44 S	179 55W
Thille-Boubacar	**84**	16 31N	15 5W
Thillot, Le	**19**	47 53N	6 46 E
Thimphu (Tashi Chho Dzong)	**69**	27 31N	89 45 E
Þingvallavatn	**50**	64 11N	21 9W
Thionville	**19**	49 20N	6 10 E
Thíra	**45**	36 23N	25 27 E
Thirasía	**45**	36 26N	25 21 E
Thirsk	**12**	54 15N	1 20W
Thistle I.	**96**	35 0 S	136 8 E
Thívai	**45**	38 19N	23 19 E
Thiviers	**20**	45 25N	0 54 E
Thizy	**21**	46 2N	4 18 E
Þjórsá →	**50**	63 47N	20 48W
Thlewiaza →, Man., Can.	**109**	59 43N	100 5W
Thlewiaza →, N.W.T., Can.	**109**	60 29N	94 40W
Thoa →	**109**	60 31N	109 47W
Thoissey	**21**	46 12N	4 48 E
Thomas, Okla., U.S.A.	**117**	35 48N	98 48W
Thomas, W. Va., U.S.A.	**114**	39 10N	79 30W
Thomas, L.	**99**	26 4 S	137 58 E
Thomaston	**115**	32 54N	84 20W
Thomasville, Ala., U.S.A.	**115**	31 55N	87 42W
Thomasville, Ga., U.S.A.	**115**	30 50N	84 0W
Thomasville, N.C., U.S.A.	**115**	35 55N	80 4W
Thompson	**109**	55 45N	97 52W
Thompson →, Can.	**108**	50 15N	121 24W
Thompson →, U.S.A.	**116**	39 46N	93 37W
Thompson Falls	**118**	47 37N	115 20W
Thompson Landing	**109**	62 56N	110 40W
Thompson Pk.	**118**	41 0N	123 3W
Thompsons	**119**	39 0N	109 50W
Thompsonville	**113**	42 0N	72 37W
Thomson →	**97**	25 11 S	142 53 E
Thomson's Falls = Nyahururu	**90**	0 2N	36 27 E
Thon Buri	**71**	13 43N	100 29 E
Thônes	**21**	45 54N	6 18 E
Thonon-les-Bains	**21**	46 22N	6 29 E
Thorez	**57**	48 4N	38 34 E
Þórisvatn	**50**	64 20N	18 55W
Þorlákshöfn	**50**	63 51N	21 22W
Thornaby on Tees	**12**	54 36N	1 19W
Thornbury	**112**	44 34N	80 26W
Thorne Glacier	**5**	87 30 S	150 0W
Thorold	**112**	43 7N	79 12W
Þórshöfn	**50**	66 12N	15 20W
Thouarcé	**18**	47 17N	0 30W
Thouars	**18**	46 58N	0 15W
Thrace = Thráki □	**44**	41 10N	25 30 E
Thráki □	**44**	41 9N	25 30 E
Thrakikón Pélagos	**44**	40 30N	25 0 E
Three Forks	**118**	45 55N	111 32W
Three Hills	**108**	51 43N	113 15W
Three Hummock I.	**99**	40 25 S	144 55 E
Three Lakes	**116**	45 48N	89 10W
Three Points, C.	**84**	4 42N	2 6W
Three Rivers	**117**	28 30N	98 10W
Three Sisters, Mt.	**118**	44 10N	121 46W
Throssell Ra.	**96**	22 3 S	121 43 E
Thrun Pass	**26**	47 20N	12 25 E
Thubun Lakes	**109**	61 30N	112 0W
Thuddungra	**100**	34 8 S	148 8 E
Thueyts	**21**	44 41N	4 9 E
Thuin	**16**	50 20N	4 17 E
Thuir	**20**	42 38N	2 45 E
Thule, Antarct.	**5**	59 27 S	27 19W
Thule, Greenl.	**4**	77 40N	69 0W
Thun	**25**	46 45N	7 38 E
Thunder B.	**114**	45 0N	83 20W
Thunder Bay	**106**	48 20N	89 15W
Thunersee	**25**	46 43N	7 39 E
Thung Song	**71**	8 10N	99 40 E
Thunkar	**69**	27 55N	91 0 E
Thur →	**25**	47 32N	9 10 E
Thurgau □	**25**	47 34N	9 10 E
Thüringer Wald	**24**	50 35N	11 0 E
Thurles	**15**	52 40N	7 53W
Thurloo Downs	**99**	29 15 S	143 30 E
Thurn P.	**25**	47 20N	12 25 E
Thursday I.	**97**	10 30 S	142 3 E
Thurso, Can.	**106**	45 36N	75 15W
Thurso, U.K.	**14**	58 34N	3 31W
Thurston I.	**5**	72 0 S	100 0W
Thury-Harcourt	**18**	49 0N	0 30W
Thutade L.	**108**	57 0N	126 55W
Thyborøn	**49**	56 42N	8 12 E
Thylungra	**99**	26 4 S	143 28 E
Thyolo	**91**	16 7 S	35 5 E
Thysville = Mbanza Ngungu	**88**	5 12 S	14 53 E
Ti-n-Barraouene, O. →	**85**	18 40N	4 5 E
Ti-n-Medjerdam, O. →	**82**	25 45N	1 30 E
Ti-n-Tarabine, O. →	**83**	21 0N	7 25 E
Ti-n-Zaouaténe	**82**	20 0N	2 55 E
Tia	**99**	31 10 S	150 34 E
Tian Shan	**75**	43 0N	84 0 E
Tiandu	**77**	18 18N	109 36 E
Tian'e	**77**	25 1N	107 9 E
Tianhe	**77**	24 48N	108 40 E
Tianjin	**76**	39 8N	117 10 E
Tiankoura	**84**	10 47N	3 17W
Tianshui	**77**	34 32N	105 40 E
Tianyang	**77**	23 42N	106 53 E
Tianzhen	**76**	40 24N	114 5 E
Tiaret	**82**	35 20N	1 21 E
Tiassalé	**84**	5 58N	4 57W
Tibagi	**125**	24 30 S	50 24W
Tibagi →	**125**	22 47 S	51 1W
Tibati	**85**	6 22N	12 30 E
Tiber = Tevere →	**39**	41 44N	12 14 E
Tiber Res.	**118**	48 20N	111 15W
Tiberias, L. = Kinneret, Yam	**62**	32 45N	35 35 E
Tibesti	**83**	21 0N	17 30 E
Tibet = Xizang □	**75**	32 0N	88 0 E
Tibiri	**85**	13 34N	7 4 E
Ţibleş	**46**	47 32N	24 15 E
Tibnīn	**62**	33 12N	35 24 E
Tibooburra	**97**	29 26 S	142 1 E
Tibro	**49**	58 28N	14 10 E
Tiburón	**120**	29 0N	112 30W
Tîchît	**84**	18 21N	9 29W
Ticho	**87**	7 50N	39 32 E
Ticino □	**25**	46 20N	8 45 E
Ticino →	**38**	45 9N	9 14 E
Ticonderoga	**114**	43 50N	73 28W
Ticul	**120**	20 20N	89 31W
Tidaholm	**49**	58 12N	13 55 E
Tiddim	**67**	23 28N	93 45 E
Tideridjaouine, Adrar	**82**	23 0N	2 15 E
Tidikelt	**82**	26 58N	1 30 E
Tidjikja	**84**	18 29N	11 35W
Tidore	**73**	0 40N	127 25 E
Tiébissou	**84**	7 9N	5 10W
Tiéboro	**83**	21 20N	17 7 E
Tiel, Neth.	**16**	51 53N	5 26 E
Tiel, Senegal	**84**	14 55N	15 5W
Tieling	**76**	42 20N	123 55 E
Tielt	**16**	51 0N	3 20 E
Tien Shan = Tian Shan	**65**	42 0N	80 0 E
Tien-tsin = Tianjin	**75**	39 8N	117 10 E
T'ienching = Tianjin	**76**	39 8N	117 10 E
Tienen	**16**	50 48N	4 57 E
Tiénigbé	**84**	8 11N	5 43W
Tientsin = Tianjin	**76**	39 8N	117 10 E
Tierp	**48**	60 20N	17 30 E
Tierra Amarilla, Chile	**124**	27 28 S	70 18W
Tierra Amarilla, U.S.A.	**119**	36 42N	106 33W
Tierra de Barros	**31**	38 40N	6 30W
Tierra de Campos	**30**	42 10N	4 50W
Tierra del Fuego, I. Gr. de	**128**	54 0 S	69 0W
Tiétar →	**30**	39 50N	6 1W
Tieté →	**125**	20 40 S	51 35W
Tifarit	**82**	26 9N	10 33W
Tiffin	**114**	41 8N	83 10W
Tiflèt	**82**	33 54N	6 20W
Tiflis = Tbilisi	**57**	41 43N	44 50 E
Tifrah	**62**	31 19N	34 42 E
Tifton	**115**	31 28N	83 32W
Tifu	**73**	3 39 S	126 24 E
Tigil	**59**	57 49N	158 40 E
Tignish	**107**	46 58N	64 2W
Tigre □	**87**	13 35N	39 15 E
Tigre →	**126**	4 30 S	74 10W
Tigris = Dijlah, Nahr →	**64**	31 0N	47 25 E
Tiguentourine	**83**	27 52N	9 8 E
Tigveni	**46**	45 10N	24 31 E
Tigyaing	**67**	23 45N	96 10 E
Tigzerte, O. →	**82**	28 10N	9 37W
Tîh, Gebel el	**86**	29 32N	33 26 E
Tihama	**64**	22 0N	39 0 E
Tihodaine, Dunes de	**83**	25 15N	7 15 E
Tijesno	**39**	43 48N	15 39 E
Tījī	**83**	32 0N	11 18 E
Tijuana	**120**	32 30N	117 10W
Tikal	**120**	17 13N	89 24W
Tikamgarh	**68**	24 44N	78 50 E
Tikhoretsk	**57**	45 56N	40 5 E
Tikhvin	**54**	59 35N	33 30 E
Tikkadouine, Adrar	**82**	24 28N	1 30 E
Tiko	**85**	4 4N	9 20 E
Tikrīt	**64**	34 35N	43 37 E
Tiksi	**59**	71 40N	128 45 E
Tilamuta	**73**	0 32N	122 23 E
Tilburg	**16**	51 31N	5 6 E
Tilbury, Can.	**106**	42 17N	82 23W
Tilbury, U.K.	**13**	51 27N	0 24 E
Tilcara	**124**	23 36 S	65 23W
Tilden, Nebr., U.S.A.	**116**	42 3N	97 45W
Tilden, Tex., U.S.A.	**117**	28 28N	98 33W
Tilemses	**85**	15 37N	4 44 E
Tilemsi, Vallée du	**85**	17 42N	0 15 E
Tilhar	**69**	28 0N	79 45 E
Tilia, O. →	**82**	27 32N	0 55 E
Tilichiki	**59**	60 27N	166 5 E
Tiligul →	**56**	47 4N	30 57 E
Tililane	**82**	27 49N	0 6W
Tílissos	**45**	35 2N	25 0 E
Till →	**12**	55 35N	2 3W
Tillabéri	**85**	14 28N	1 28 E
Tillamook	**118**	45 29N	123 55W
Tillberga	**48**	59 52N	16 39 E
Tillia	**85**	16 8N	4 47 E
Tillsonburg	**106**	42 53N	80 44W
Tílos	**45**	36 27N	27 27 E
Tilpa	**99**	30 57 S	144 24 E
Tilrhemt	**82**	33 9N	3 22 E
Tilsit = Sovetsk	**54**	55 6N	21 50 E
Tilt →	**14**	56 50N	3 50W
Tilton	**113**	43 25N	71 36W
Timagami L.	**106**	47 0N	80 10W
Timanskiy Kryazh	**52**	65 58N	50 5 E
Timaru	**101**	44 23 S	171 14 E
Timashevsk	**57**	45 35N	39 0 E
Timau, Italy	**39**	46 35N	13 0 E
Timau, Kenya	**90**	0 4N	37 15 E
Timbákion	**45**	35 4N	24 45 E
Timbedgha	**84**	16 17N	8 16W
Timber Lake	**116**	45 29N	101 6W
Timboon	**99**	38 30 S	142 58 E
Timbuktu = Tombouctou	**84**	16 50N	3 0W
Timdjaouine	**82**	21 37N	4 30 E
Timellouline	**83**	29 22N	8 55 E
Timétrine Montagnes	**85**	19 25N	1 0W
Timfi Óros	**44**	39 59N	20 45 E
Timfristós, Óros	**45**	38 57N	21 50 E
Timhadit	**82**	33 15N	5 4W
Tîmia	**85**	18 4N	8 40 E
Timimoun	**82**	29 14N	0 16 E
Timimoun, Sebkha de	**82**	28 50N	0 46 E
Timiş □	**42**	45 40N	21 30 E
Timiş →	**46**	45 30N	21 0 E
Timişoara	**42**	45 43N	21 15 E
Timmins	**106**	48 28N	81 25W
Timok →	**42**	44 10N	22 40 E
Timon	**127**	5 8 S	42 52W
Timor	**73**	9 0 S	125 0 E
Timor □	**73**	9 0 S	125 0 E
Timor Sea	**97**	10 0 S	127 0 E
Tin Alkoum	**83**	24 42N	10 17 E
Tin Gornai	**85**	16 38N	0 38W
Tin Gornaï →	**85**	20 30N	4 35 E
Tîna, Khalîg el	**86**	31 20N	32 42 E
Tinaca Pt.	**73**	5 30N	125 25 E
Tinafak, O. →	**83**	27 10N	7 0 E
Tinca	**46**	46 46N	21 58 E
Tinchebray	**18**	48 47N	0 45W
Tindivanam	**70**	12 15N	79 41 E
Tindouf	**82**	27 42N	8 10W
Tinee →	**21**	43 55N	7 11 E
Tineo	**30**	43 21N	6 27W
Tinerhir	**82**	31 29N	5 31W
Tinfouchi	**82**	28 52N	5 49W
Tinglev	**49**	54 57N	9 13 E
Tingo Maria	**126**	9 10 S	75 54W
Tingsryd	**49**	56 31N	15 0 E
Tinjoub	**82**	29 45N	5 40W
Tinnoset	**47**	59 55N	9 3 E
Tinnsjø	**47**	59 55N	8 54 E
Tinogasta	**124**	28 5 S	67 32W
Tínos	**45**	37 33N	25 8 E
Tiñoso, C.	**33**	37 32N	1 6W
Tintina	**124**	27 2 S	62 45W
Tintinara	**99**	35 48 S	140 2 E
Tinto →	**31**	37 12N	6 55W
Tioga	**112**	41 54N	77 9W
Tioman, Pulau	**71**	2 50N	104 10 E
Tione di Trento	**38**	46 3N	10 44 E
Tionesta	**112**	41 29N	79 28W
Tior	**87**	6 26N	31 11 E
Tioulilin	**82**	27 1N	0 2W
Tipongpani	**67**	27 20N	95 55 E
Tipperary	**15**	52 28N	8 10W
Tipperary □	**15**	52 37N	7 55W
Tipton, U.K.	**13**	52 32N	2 4W
Tipton, Calif., U.S.A.	**119**	36 3N	119 19W
Tipton, Ind., U.S.A.	**114**	40 17N	86 0W
Tipton, Iowa, U.S.A.	**116**	41 45N	91 12W
Tiptonville	**117**	36 22N	89 30W
Tiptur	**70**	13 15N	76 26 E
Tirahart, O.	**82**	23 45N	3 10 E
Tīrān	**65**	32 45N	51 8 E
Tirân	**86**	27 56N	34 45 E
Tirana	**44**	41 18N	19 49 E
Tirana-Durrësi □	**44**	41 35N	20 0 E
Tirano	**38**	46 13N	10 11 E
Tiraspol	**56**	46 55N	29 35 E
Tirat Karmel	**62**	32 46N	34 58 E
Tirat Yehuda	**62**	32 1N	34 56 E
Tirat Zevi	**62**	32 26N	35 31 E
Tiratimine	**82**	25 56N	3 37 E
Tirdout	**85**	16 7N	1 5W
Tire	**64**	38 5N	27 50 E
Tirebolu	**64**	40 58N	38 45 E
Tiree	**14**	56 31N	6 55W
Tîrgovişte	**46**	44 55N	25 27 E
Tîrgu Frumos	**46**	47 12N	27 2 E
Tîrgu-Jiu	**46**	45 5N	23 19 E
Tîrgu Mureş	**46**	46 31N	24 38 E
Tîrgu Neamţ	**46**	47 12N	26 25 E
Tîrgu Ocna	**46**	46 16N	26 39 E
Tîrgu Secuiesc	**46**	46 0N	26 10 E
Tirich Mir	**66**	36 15N	71 55 E
Tiriola	**41**	38 57N	16 32 E
Tirna →	**70**	18 4N	76 57 E
Tîrnava Mare →	**46**	46 15N	24 30 E
Tîrnava Mică →	**46**	46 17N	24 30 E
Tîrnăveni	**46**	46 19N	24 13 E
Tírnavos	**44**	39 45N	22 18 E
Tîrnova	**46**	45 23N	22 1 E
Tirodi	**69**	21 40N	79 44 E
Tirol □	**26**	47 3N	10 43 E
Tirschenreuth	**25**	49 51N	12 20 E
Tirso →	**40**	39 52N	8 33 E
Tirso, L. del	**40**	40 8N	8 56 E
Tiruchchirappalli	**70**	10 45N	78 45 E
Tiruchendur	**70**	8 30N	78 11 E
Tiruchengodu	**70**	11 23N	77 56 E
Tirumangalam	**70**	9 49N	77 58 E
Tirunelveli (Tinnevelly)	**70**	8 45N	77 45 E
Tirupati	**70**	13 39N	79 25 E
Tiruppattur	**70**	12 30N	78 30 E
Tiruppur	**70**	11 5N	77 22 E
Tiruturaipundi	**70**	10 32N	79 41 E
Tiruvadaimarudur	**70**	11 2N	79 27 E
Tiruvallar	**70**	13 9N	79 57 E
Tiruvannamalai	**70**	12 15N	79 5 E
Tiruvarur	**70**	10 46N	79 38 E
Tiruvatipuram	**70**	12 39N	79 33 E
Tiruvottiyur	**70**	13 10N	80 22 E
Tisa →	**42**	45 15N	20 17 E
Tisdale	**109**	52 50N	104 0W
Tishomingo	**117**	34 14N	96 38W
Tisjön	**48**	60 56N	13 0 E
Tisnaren	**48**	58 58N	15 56 E
Tišnov	**27**	49 21N	16 25 E
Tisovec	**27**	48 41N	19 56 E
Tissemsilt	**82**	35 35N	1 50 E
Tissint	**82**	29 57N	7 16W
Tissø	**49**	55 35N	11 18 E
Tista →	**69**	25 23N	89 43 E
Tisza →	**27**	46 8N	20 2 E
Tiszaföldvár	**27**	47 0N	20 14 E
Tiszafüred	**27**	47 38N	20 50 E
Tiszalök	**27**	48 0N	21 10 E
Tiszavasvári	**27**	47 58N	21 18 E
Tit, Ahaggar, Alg.	**83**	23 0N	5 10 E
Tit, Tademait, Alg.	**82**	27 0N	1 29 E
Tit-Ary	**59**	71 55N	127 2 E
Titaguas	**32**	39 53N	1 6W
Titel	**42**	45 10N	20 18 E
Titicaca, L.	**126**	15 30 S	69 30W
Titilagarh	**70**	20 15N	83 11 E
Titiwa	**85**	12 14N	12 53 E
Titograd	**42**	42 30N	19 19 E
Titov Veles	**42**	41 46N	21 47 E
Titova Korenica	**39**	44 45N	15 41 E
Titovo Užice	**42**	43 55N	19 50 E
Titule	**90**	3 15N	25 31 E
Titusville, Fla., U.S.A.	**115**	28 37N	80 49W
Titusville, Pa., U.S.A.	**114**	41 35N	79 39W
Tivaouane	**84**	14 56N	16 45W
Tivat	**42**	42 28N	18 43 E
Tiveden	**49**	58 50N	14 30 E
Tiverton	**13**	50 54N	3 30W
Tívoli	**39**	41 58N	12 45 E
Tiwī	**65**	22 45N	59 12 E
Tiyo	**87**	14 41N	40 15 E
Tizga	**82**	32 1N	5 9W
Ti'zi N'Isli	**82**	32 28N	5 47W
Tizi-Ouzou	**83**	36 42N	4 3 E
Tizimín	**120**	21 0N	88 1W
Tiznit	**82**	29 48N	9 45W
Tjeggelvas	**50**	66 37N	17 45 E
Tjirebon = Cirebon	**73**	6 45 S	108 32 E
Tjöme	**47**	59 8N	10 26 E
Tjörn	**49**	58 0N	11 35 E
Tkibuli	**57**	42 26N	43 0 E
Tkvarcheli	**57**	42 47N	41 42 E
Tlahualilo	**120**	26 20N	103 30W
Tlaxcala	**120**	19 20N	98 14W
Tlaxcala □	**120**	19 30N	98 20W
Tlaxiaco	**120**	17 18N	97 40W
Tlell	**108**	53 34N	131 56W
Tlemcen	**82**	34 52N	1 21W
Tleta Sidi Bouguedra	**82**	32 16N	9 59W
Tlumach, U.S.S.R.	**54**	48 46N	25 0 E
Tlumach, U.S.S.R.	**56**	48 51N	25 0 E
Tłuszcz	**28**	52 25N	21 25 E
Tlyarata	**57**	42 9N	46 26 E
Tmassah	**83**	26 19N	15 51 E
Tnine d'Anglou	**82**	29 50N	9 50W
Toad →	**108**	59 25N	124 57W
Toala	**73**	1 30 S	121 40 E
Toamasina	**93**	18 10 S	49 25 E
Toamasina □	**93**	18 0 S	49 0 E
Toay	**124**	36 43 S	64 38W
Toba	**74**	34 30N	136 51 E
Toba, Danau	**72**	2 40N	98 50 E
Toba Kakar	**68**	31 30N	69 0 E
Toba Tek Singh	**68**	30 55N	72 25 E
Tobago	**121**	11 10N	60 30W
Tobarra	**33**	38 37N	1 44W
Tobelo	**73**	1 45N	127 56 E
Tobermorey	**98**	22 12 S	137 51 E
Tobermory, Can.	**106**	45 12N	81 40W
Tobermory, U.K.	**14**	56 37N	6 4W
Tobin L.	**109**	53 35N	103 30W
Toboali	**72**	3 0 S	106 25 E
Tobol	**58**	52 40N	62 39 E
Toboli	**73**	0 38 S	120 5 E
Tobolsk	**58**	58 15N	68 10 E
Tobruk = Tubruq	**81**	32 7N	23 55 E
Tobyhanna	**113**	41 10N	75 25W
Tocantinópolis	**127**	6 20 S	47 25W
Tocantins →	**127**	1 45 S	49 10W
Toccoa	**115**	34 32N	83 17W
Toce →	**38**	45 56N	8 29 E
Tochigi	**74**	36 25N	139 45 E
Tochigi □	**74**	36 45N	139 45 E
Tocina	**31**	37 37N	5 44W

Tocopilla Treuenbrietzen

Tocopilla 124 22 5S 70 10W
Tocumwal 99 35 51S 145 31 E
Tocuyo → 126 11 3N 68 23W
Todeli 73 1 38S 124 34 E
Todenyang 90 4 35N 35 56 E
Todi 39 42 47N 12 24 E
Todos os Santos, Baía de 127 12 48S 38 38W
Todos Santos 120 23 27N 110 13W
Todtnau 25 47 50N 7 56 E
Toecé 85 11 50N 1 16W
Tofield 108 53 25N 112 40W
Tofino 108 49 11N 125 55W
Töfsingdalens nationalpark 48 62 15N 12 44 E
Toftlund 49 55 11N 9 2 E
Tofua 101 19 45S 175 05W
Togba 84 17 26N 10 12W
Togian, Kepulauan 73 0 20S 121 50 E
Togliatti 55 53 32N 49 24 E
Togo ■ 85 6 15N 1 35 E
Togtoh 76 40 15N 111 10 E
Toinya 87 6 17N 29 46 E
Tojo 73 1 20S 121 15 E
Tokaj 27 48 8N 21 27 E
Tōkamachi 74 37 8N 138 43 E
Tokanui 101 46 34S 168 56 E
Tokar 81 18 27N 37 56 E
Tokara Kaikyō 74 30 0N 130 0 E
Tokarahi 101 44 56S 170 39 E
Tokat 64 40 22N 36 35 E
Tokelau Is. ■ 94 9 0S 171 45W
Tokmak 58 42 49N 75 15 E
Toko Ra. 98 23 5S 138 20 E
Tokong 71 5 27N 100 23 E
Tokushima 74 34 4N 134 34 E
Tokushima □ 74 34 15N 134 0 E
Tokuyama 74 34 3N 131 50 E
Tōkyō 74 35 45N 139 45 E
Tōkyō □ 74 35 40N 139 30 E
Tolbukhin 43 43 37N 27 49 E
Toledo, Spain 30 39 50N 4 2W
Toledo, Ohio, U.S.A. 114 41 37N 83 33W
Toledo, Oreg., U.S.A. 118 44 40N 123 59W
Toledo, Wash., U.S.A. 118 46 29N 122 51W
Toledo, Montes de 31 39 33N 4 20W
Tolentino 39 43 12N 13 17 E
Tolga, Alg. 83 34 40N 5 22 E
Tolga, Norway 47 62 26N 11 1 E
Toliara 93 23 21S 43 40 E
Toliara □ 93 21 0S 45 0 E
Tolima, Vol. 126 4 40N 75 19W
Tolitoli 73 1 5N 120 50 E
Tolkmicko 28 54 19N 19 31 E
Tollarp 49 55 55N 13 58 E
Tolleson 119 33 29N 112 10W
Tolmachevo 54 58 56N 29 51 E
Tolmezzo 39 46 23N 13 0 E
Tolmin 39 46 11N 13 45 E
Tolna 27 46 25N 18 48 E
Tolna □ 27 46 30N 18 30 E
Tolo 88 2 55S 18 34 E
Tolo, Teluk 73 2 20S 122 10 E
Tolochin 54 54 25N 29 42 E
Tolosa 32 43 8N 2 5W
Tolox 31 36 41N 4 54W
Toluca 120 19 20N 99 40W
Tom Burke 93 23 5S 28 4 E
Tom Price 96 22 40S 117 48 E
Tomah 116 43 59N 90 30W
Tomahawk 116 45 28N 89 40W
Tomar 31 39 36N 8 25W
Tómaros Óros 44 39 29N 20 48 E
Tomaszów Mazowiecki 28 51 30N 19 57 E
Tombé 87 5 53N 31 40 E
Tombigbee → 115 31 4N 87 58W
Tombouctou 84 16 50N 3 0W
Tombstone 119 31 40N 110 4W
Tomé 124 36 36S 72 57W
Tomelilla 49 55 33N 13 58 E
Tomelloso 33 39 10N 3 2W
Tomingley 99 32 6S 148 16 E
Tomini 73 0 30N 120 30 E
Tomini, Teluk 73 0 10S 122 0 E
Tominian 84 13 17N 4 35W
Tomiño 30 41 59N 8 46W
Tommot 59 59 4N 126 20 E
Tomnavoulin 14 57 19N 3 18W
Toms River 113 39 59N 74 12W
Tomsk 58 56 30N 85 5 E
Tomtabacken 49 57 30N 14 30 E
Tonalá 120 16 8N 93 41W
Tonale, Passo del 38 46 15N 10 34 E
Tonalea 119 36 17N 110 58W
Tonantins 126 2 45S 67 45W
Tonasket 118 48 45N 119 30W
Tonawanda 114 43 0N 78 54W
Tonbridge 13 51 12N 0 18 E
Tondano 73 1 35N 124 54 E
Tondela 30 40 31N 8 5W
Tønder 49 54 58N 8 50 E
Tondi 70 9 45N 79 4 E
Tondi Kiwindi 85 14 28N 2 02 E
Tondibi 85 16 39N 0 14W
Tong Xian 76 39 55N 116 35 E
Tonga ■ 101 19 50S 174 30W
Tonga Trench 94 18 0S 175 0W
Tongaat 93 29 33S 31 9 E
Tongaland 93 27 0S 32 0 E
Tongareva 95 9 0S 158 0W
Tongatapu 101 21 10S 174 0W
Tongcheng 77 31 4N 116 56 E
Tongchuan 77 35 6N 109 3 E
Tongdao 77 26 10N 109 42 E
Tongeren 16 50 47N 5 28 E
Tongguan 77 34 40N 110 25 E
Tonghua 76 41 42N 125 58 E
Tongio 99 37 14S 147 44 E
Tongjiang, Heilongjiang, China 75 47 40N 132 27 E
Tongjiang, Sichuan, China 77 31 58N 107 11 E
Tongking = Tonkin, G. of 71 20 0N 108 0 E
Tongliao 76 43 38N 122 18 E
Tongling 77 30 55N 117 48 E
Tonglu 77 29 45N 119 37 E
Tongnan 77 30 9N 105 50 E
Tongobory 93 23 32S 44 20 E
Tongoy 124 30 16S 71 31W
Tongren 75 27 43N 109 11 E
Tongres = Tongeren 16 50 47N 5 28 E
Tongue 14 58 29N 4 25W
Tongue → 116 46 24N 105 52W
Tongyu 76 44 45N 123 4 E
Tongzi 77 28 9N 106 49 E
Tonj 87 7 20N 28 44 E
Tonk 68 26 6N 75 54 E
Tonkawa 117 36 44N 97 22W
Tonkin = Bac-Phan 71 22 0N 105 0 E
Tonlé Sap 71 13 0N 104 0 E
Tonnay-Charente 20 45 56N 0 55W
Tonneins 20 44 23N 0 19 E
Tonnerre 19 47 51N 3 59 E
Tönning 24 54 18N 8 57 E
Tonopah 119 38 4N 117 12W
Tønsberg 47 59 19N 10 25 E
Tonstad 47 58 40N 6 45 E
Tonto Basin 119 33 56N 111 27W
Tooele 118 40 30N 112 20W
Toompine 99 27 15S 144 19 E
Toonpan 98 19 28S 146 48 E
Toora 99 38 39S 146 23 E
Toora-Khem 59 52 28N 96 17 E
Toowoomba 97 27 32S 151 56 E
Top-ozero 52 65 35N 32 0 E
Topalu 46 44 31N 28 3 E
Topeka 116 39 3N 95 40W
Topki 58 55 20N 85 35 E
Topl'a → 27 48 45N 21 45 E
Topley 108 54 49N 126 18W
Toplica → 42 43 15N 21 49 E
Toplița 46 46 55N 25 20 E
Topocalma, Pta. 124 34 10S 72 2W
Topock 119 34 46N 114 29W
Topola 42 44 17N 20 41 E
Topolčani 42 41 14N 21 56 E
Topoľčany 27 48 35N 18 12 E
Topoli 57 47 59N 51 38 E
Topolnitsa → 43 42 11N 24 18 E
Topolobampo 120 25 40N 109 4W
Topolovgrad 43 42 5N 26 20 E
Topolvătu Mare 42 45 46N 21 41 E
Toppenish 118 46 27N 120 16W
Topusko 39 45 18N 15 59 E
Tor Bay 96 35 5S 117 50 E
Torá 32 41 49N 1 25 E
Tora Kit 87 11 2N 32 36 E
Toraka Vestale 93 16 20S 43 58 E
Torata 126 17 23S 70 1W
Torbat-e Ḩeydārīyeh 65 35 15N 59 12 E
Torbat-e Jām 65 35 16N 60 35 E
Torbay, Can. 107 47 40N 52 42W
Torbay, U.K. 13 50 26N 3 31W
Tørdal 47 59 10N 8 45 E
Tordesillas 30 41 30N 5 0W
Tordoya 30 43 6N 8 36W
Töreboda 49 58 41N 14 7 E
Torey 59 50 33N 104 50 E
Torfajökull 50 63 54N 19 0W
Torgau 24 51 32N 13 0 E
Torgelow 24 53 40N 13 59 E
Torhout 16 51 5N 3 7 E
Tori 87 7 53N 33 35 E
Torigni-sur-Vire 18 49 3N 0 58W
Torija 32 40 44N 3 2W
Torin 120 27 33N 110 15W
Toriñana, C. 30 43 3N 9 17W
Torino 38 45 4N 7 40 E
Torit 87 4 27N 32 31 E
Torkovichi 54 58 51N 30 21 E
Tormac 42 45 30N 21 30 E
Tormentine 107 46 6N 63 46W
Tormes → 30 41 18N 6 29W
Tornado Mt. 108 49 55N 114 40W
Torne älv → 50 65 50N 24 12 E
Torneträsk 50 68 24N 19 15 E
Tornio 50 65 50N 24 12 E
Tornionjoki → 50 65 50N 24 12 E
Tornquist 124 38 8S 62 15W
Toro 30 41 35N 5 24W
Torö 49 58 48N 17 50 E
Toro, Cerro del 124 29 10S 69 50W
Toro, Pta. 120 9 22N 79 57W
Törökszentmiklós 27 47 11N 20 27 E
Toroníios Kólpos 44 40 5N 23 30 E
Toronto, Austral. 99 33 0S 151 30 E
Toronto, Can. 106 43 39N 79 20W
Toronto, U.S.A. 114 40 27N 80 36W
Toronto, L. 120 27 40N 105 30W
Toropets 54 56 30N 31 40 E
Tororo 90 0 45N 34 12 E
Toros Dağlari 64 37 0N 35 0 E
Torpshammar 48 62 29N 16 20 E
Torquay, Can. 109 49 9N 103 30W
Torquay, U.K. 13 50 27N 3 31W
Torquemada 30 42 2N 4 19W
Torralba de Calatrava 31 39 1N 3 44W
Torrão 31 38 16N 8 11W
Torre Annunziata 41 40 45N 14 26 E
Tôrre de Moncorvo 30 41 12N 7 8W
Torre del Greco 41 40 47N 14 22 E
Torre del Mar 31 36 44N 4 6W
Torre-Pacheco 33 37 44N 0 57W
Torre Pellice 38 44 49N 7 13 E
Torreblanca 32 40 14N 0 12 E
Torrecampo 31 38 29N 4 41W
Torrecilla en Cameros 32 42 15N 2 38W
Torredembarra 32 41 9N 1 24 E
Torredonjimeno 31 37 46N 3 57W
Torrejoncillo 30 39 54N 6 28W
Torrelaguna 32 40 50N 3 38W
Torrelavega 30 43 20N 4 5W
Torremaggiore 41 41 42N 15 17 E
Torremolinos 31 36 38N 4 30W
Torrens Cr. → 98 22 23S 145 9 E
Torrens Creek 98 20 48S 145 3 E
Torrens, L. 97 31 0S 137 50 E
Torrente 33 39 27N 0 28W
Torrenueva 33 38 38N 3 22W
Torréon 120 25 33N 103 25W
Torreperogil 33 38 2N 3 17W
Torres 120 28 46N 110 47W
Torres Novas 31 39 27N 8 33W
Torres Strait 97 9 50S 142 20 E
Torres Vedras 31 39 5N 9 15W
Torrevieja 33 37 59N 0 42W
Torrey 119 38 18N 111 25W
Torridge → 13 50 51N 4 10W
Torridon, L. 14 57 35N 5 50W
Torrijos 30 39 59N 4 18W
Torrington, Conn., U.S.A. 114 41 50N 73 9W
Torrington, Wyo., U.S.A. 116 42 5N 104 8W
Torroella de Montgri 32 42 2N 3 8 E
Torrox 31 36 46N 3 57W
Torsås 49 56 24N 16 0 E
Torsby 48 60 7N 13 0 E
Torsö 49 58 48N 13 45 E
Tortola 121 18 19N 65 0W
Tórtoles de Esgueva 30 41 49N 4 2W
Tortona 38 44 53N 8 54 E
Tortoreto 39 42 50N 13 55 E
Tortorici 41 38 2N 14 48 E
Tortosa 32 40 49N 0 31 E
Tortosa, C. 32 40 41N 0 52 E
Tortosendo 30 40 15N 7 31W
Tortue, Î. de la 121 20 5N 72 57W
Tortuga, La 126 11 0N 65 22W
Ţorūd 65 35 25N 55 5 E
Toruń 28 53 0N 18 39 E
Toruń □ 28 53 20N 19 0 E
Torup, Denmark 49 57 5N 9 5 E
Torup, Sweden 49 56 57N 13 5 E
Tory I. 15 55 17N 8 12W
Torysa → 27 48 39N 21 21 E
Torzhok 54 57 5N 34 55 E
Tosa-Wan 74 33 15N 133 30 E
Toscana 38 43 30N 11 5 E
Toscano, Arcipelago 38 42 30N 10 30 E
Tosno 54 59 38N 30 46 E
Tossa 32 41 43N 2 56 E
Tostado 124 29 15S 61 50W
Tostedt 24 53 17N 9 42 E
Tosya 64 41 1N 34 2 E
Toszek 28 50 27N 18 32 E
Totak 47 59 40N 7 45 E
Totana 33 37 45N 1 30W
Toten 47 60 37N 10 53 E
Toteng 92 20 22S 22 58 E
Tôtes 18 49 41N 1 3 E
Tótkomlós 27 46 24N 20 45 E
Totma 55 60 0N 42 40 E
Totnes 13 50 26N 3 41W
Totonicapán 120 14 58N 91 12W
Totten Glacier 5 66 45S 116 10 E
Tottenham, Austral. 99 32 14S 147 21 E
Tottenham, Can. 112 44 1N 79 49W
Tottori 74 35 30N 134 15 E
Tottori □ 74 35 30N 134 12 E
Touat 82 27 27N 0 30 E
Touba 84 8 22N 7 40W
Toubkal, Djebel 82 31 0N 8 0W
Toucy 19 47 44N 3 15 E
Tougan 84 13 11N 2 58W
Touggourt 83 33 10N 6 0 E
Tougué 84 11 25N 11 50W
Toukmatine 83 24 49N 7 11 E
Toul 19 48 40N 5 53 E
Toulepleu 84 6 32N 8 24W
Toulon 21 43 10N 5 55 E
Toulouse 20 43 37N 1 27 E
Toummo 83 22 45N 14 8 E
Toummo Dhoba 83 22 30N 14 31 E
Toumodi 84 6 32N 5 4W
Tounassine, Hamada 82 28 48N 5 0W
Toungoo 67 19 0N 96 30 E
Touques → 18 49 22N 0 8 E
Touquet-Paris-Plage, Le 19 50 30N 1 36 E
Tour-du-Pin, La 21 45 33N 5 27 E
Touraine 18 47 20N 0 30 E
Tourcoing 19 50 42N 3 10 E
Tournai 16 50 35N 3 25 E
Tournan-en-Brie 19 48 44N 2 46 E
Tournay 20 43 13N 0 13 E
Tournon 21 45 4N 4 50 E
Tournon-St-Martin 18 46 45N 0 58 E
Tournus 21 46 35N 4 54 E
Tours 18 47 22N 0 40 E
Touside, Pic 83 21 1N 16 29 E
Touwsrivier 92 33 20S 20 0 E
Tovarkovskiy 55 53 40N 38 14 E
Tovdal 47 58 47N 8 10 E
Tovdalselva → 47 58 15N 8 5 E
Towamba 99 37 6S 149 43 E
Towanda 114 41 46N 76 30W
Towang 67 27 37N 91 50 E
Tower 116 47 49N 92 17W
Towerhill Cr. → 98 22 28S 144 35 E
Towner 116 48 25N 100 26W
Townsend 118 46 25N 111 32W
Townshend, C. 97 22 18S 150 30 E
Townshend I. 97 22 10S 150 31 E
Townsville 97 19 15S 146 45 E
Towson 114 39 26N 76 34W
Towyn 13 52 36N 4 5W
Toyah 117 31 20N 103 48W
Toyahvale 117 30 58N 103 45W
Toyama 74 36 40N 137 15 E
Toyama □ 74 36 45N 137 30 E
Toyama-Wan 74 37 0N 137 30 E
Toyohashi 74 34 45N 137 25 E
Toyokawa 74 34 48N 137 27 E
Toyonaka 74 34 50N 135 28 E
Toyooka 74 35 35N 134 48 E
Toyota 74 35 3N 137 7 E
Tozeur 83 33 56N 8 8 E
Trabancos → 30 41 36N 5 15W
Traben Trarbach 25 49 57N 7 7 E
Trabzon 64 41 0N 39 45 E
Tracadie 107 47 30N 64 55W
Tracy, Calif., U.S.A. 119 37 46N 121 27W
Tracy, Minn., U.S.A. 116 44 12N 95 38W
Tradate 38 45 43N 8 54 E
Trafalgar 100 38 14S 146 12 E
Trafalgar, C. 31 36 10N 6 2W
Trāghān 83 26 0N 14 30 E
Traian 46 45 2N 28 15 E
Trail 108 49 5N 117 40W
Trainor L. 108 60 24N 120 17W
Tralee 15 52 16N 9 42W
Tralee B. 15 52 17N 9 55W
Tramore 15 52 10N 7 10W
Tran Ninh, Cao Nguyen 71 19 30N 103 10 E
Tranås 49 58 3N 14 59 E
Trancas 124 26 11S 65 20W
Tranche, La 20 46 20N 1 26W
Tranche-sur-Mer, La 18 46 20N 1 27W
Trancoso 30 40 49N 7 21W
Tranebjerg 49 55 51N 10 36 E
Tranemo 49 57 30N 13 20 E
Trang 71 7 33N 99 38 E
Trangahy 93 19 7S 44 31 E
Trangan 73 6 40S 134 20 E
Trangie 99 32 4S 148 0 E
Trångsviken 48 63 19N 14 0 E
Trani 41 41 17N 16 24 E
Tranoroa 93 24 42S 45 4 E
Tranquebar 70 11 1N 79 54 E
Tranqueras 125 31 13S 55 45W
Trans Nzoia □ 90 1 0N 35 0 E
Transcona 109 49 55N 97 0W
Transilvania 46 46 19N 25 0 E
Transkei □ 93 32 15S 28 15 E
Transtrand 48 61 6N 13 20 E
Transvaal □ 92 25 0S 29 0 E
Transylvania = Transilvania 46 46 19N 25 0 E
Transylvanian Alps 46 45 30N 25 0 E
Trápani 40 38 1N 12 30 E
Trapper Peak 118 45 56N 114 29W
Traralgon 97 38 12S 146 34 E
Traryd 49 56 35N 13 45 E
Trarza □ 84 17 30N 15 0W
Trasacco 39 41 58N 13 30 E
Trăscău, Munţii 46 46 14N 23 14 E
Trasimeno, L. 39 43 10N 12 5 E
Trat 71 12 14N 102 33 E
Traun 26 48 14N 14 15 E
Traunsee 26 47 55N 13 50 E
Traunstein 25 47 52N 12 40 E
Tråvad 49 58 15N 13 5 E
Traveller's L. 99 33 20S 142 0 E
Travemünde 24 53 58N 10 52 E
Travers, Mt. 101 42 1S 172 45 E
Traverse City 114 44 45N 85 39W
Traverse Is. 5 57 0S 28 0W
Travnik 42 44 17N 17 39 E
Trazo 30 43 0N 8 30W
Trbovlje 39 46 12N 15 5 E
Trébbia → 38 45 4N 9 41 E
Trebel → 24 53 55N 13 1 E
Třebíč 26 49 14N 15 55 E
Trebinje 42 42 44N 18 22 E
Trebisacce 41 39 52N 16 32 E
Trebišnica → 42 42 47N 18 8 E
Trebišov 27 48 38N 21 41 E
Trebižat → 42 43 15N 17 30 E
Trebnje 39 45 54N 15 1 E
Třeboň 26 48 59N 14 48 E
Trebujena 31 36 52N 6 11W
Trecate 38 45 26N 8 42 E
Tredegar 13 51 47N 3 16W
Tregaron 13 52 14N 3 56W
Trégastel-Plage 18 48 49N 3 31W
Tregnago 39 45 31N 11 10 E
Tréguier 18 48 47N 3 16W
Trégune 18 47 51N 3 51W
Treherne 109 49 38N 98 42W
Tréia 39 43 20N 13 20 E
Treignac 20 45 32N 1 48 E
Treinta y Tres 125 33 16S 54 17W
Treis 25 50 9N 7 19 E
Treklyano 42 42 33N 22 36 E
Trekveld 92 30 35S 19 45 E
Trelde Næs 49 55 38N 9 53 E
Trelew 128 43 10S 65 20W
Trelissac 20 45 11N 0 47 E
Trelleborg 49 55 20N 13 10 E
Trélon 19 50 5N 4 6 E
Tremblade, La 20 45 46N 1 8W
Tremiti 39 42 8N 15 30 E
Tremonton 118 41 45N 112 10W
Tremp 32 42 10N 0 52 E
Trenary 114 46 12N 86 59W
Trenche → 106 47 46N 72 53W
Trenčín 27 48 52N 18 4 E
Trenggalek 73 8 5S 111 38 E
Trenque Lauquen 124 36 5S 62 45W
Trent → 12 53 33N 0 44W
Trentino-Alto Adige □ 38 46 30N 11 0 E
Trento 38 46 5N 11 8 E
Trenton, Can. 106 44 10N 77 34W
Trenton, Mo., U.S.A. 116 40 5N 93 37W
Trenton, N.J., U.S.A. 114 40 15N 74 41W
Trenton, Nebr., U.S.A. 116 40 14N 101 4W
Trenton, Tenn., U.S.A. 117 35 58N 88 57W
Trepassey 107 46 43N 53 25W
Tréport, Le 18 50 3N 1 20 E
Trepuzzi 41 40 26N 18 4 E
Tres Arroyos 124 38 26S 60 20W
Três Corações 125 21 44S 45 15W
Três Lagoas 127 20 50S 51 43W
Tres Marías 120 21 25N 106 28W
Tres Montes, C. 128 46 50S 75 30W
Três Pontas 125 21 23S 45 29W
Tres Puentes 124 27 50S 70 15W
Tres Puntas, C. 128 47 0S 66 0W
Três Rios 125 22 6S 43 15W
Treska → 42 42 0N 21 20 E
Treskavika Planina 42 43 40N 18 20 E
Trespaderne 32 42 47N 3 24W
Trets 21 43 27N 5 41 E
Treuchtlingen 25 48 58N 10 55 E
Treuenbrietzen 24 52 6N 12 51 E

Treviglio Tyldal

Treviglio 38 45 31N 9 35 E
Trevinca, Peña 30 42 15N 6 46W
Treviso 39 45 40N 12 15 E
Trévoux 21 45 57N 4 47 E
Treysa 24 50 55N 9 12 E
Trgovište 42 42 20N 22 10 E
Triabunna 99 42 30 S 147 55 E
Triánda 45 36 25N 28 10 E
Triaucourt-en-Argonne 19 48 59N 5 2 E
Tribsees 24 54 4N 12 46 E
Tribulation, C. 97 16 5 S 145 29 E
Tribune 116 38 30N 101 45W
Tricárico 41 40 37N 16 9 E
Tricase 41 39 56N 18 20 E
Trichinopoly = Tiruchchirappalli 70 10 45N 78 45 E
Trichur 70 10 30N 76 18 E
Trida 99 33 1 S 145 1 E
Trier 25 49 45N 6 37 E
Trieste 39 45 39N 13 45 E
Trieste, G. di 39 45 37N 13 40 E
Trieux → 18 48 50N 3 3W
Triggiano 41 41 4N 16 58 E
Triglav 39 46 21N 13 50 E
Trigno → 39 42 4N 14 48 E
Trigueros 31 37 24N 6 50W
Tríkeri 45 39 6N 23 5 E
Trikhonis, Límni 45 38 34N 21 30 E
Tríkkala 44 39 34N 21 47 E
Tríkkala □ 44 39 41N 21 30 E
Trikora, Puncak 73 4 15 S 138 45 E
Trilj 39 43 38N 16 42 E
Trillo 32 40 42N 2 35W
Trim 15 53 34N 6 48W
Trincomalee 70 8 38N 81 15 E
Trindade, I. 7 20 20 S 29 50W
Trinidad, Boliv. 126 14 46 S 64 50W
Trinidad, Colomb. 126 5 25N 71 40W
Trinidad, Cuba 121 21 48N 80 0W
Trinidad, Uruguay 124 33 30 S 56 50W
Trinidad, U.S.A. 117 37 15N 104 30W
Trinidad, W. Indies 121 10 30N 61 15W
Trinidad & Tobago ■ 121 10 30N 61 20W
Trinidad → 120 17 49N 95 9W
Trinidad, I. 128 39 10 S 62 0W
Trinitápoli 41 41 22N 16 5 E
Trinity, Can. 107 48 59N 53 55W
Trinity, U.S.A. 117 30 59N 95 25W
Trinity →, Calif., U.S.A. 118 41 11N 123 42W
Trinity →, Tex., U.S.A. 117 30 30N 95 0W
Trinity B., Austral. 97 16 30 S 146 0 E
Trinity B., Can. 107 48 20N 53 10W
Trinity Mts. 118 40 20N 118 50W
Trinkitat 81 18 45N 37 51 E
Trino 38 45 10N 8 18 E
Trion 115 34 35N 85 18W
Trionto C. 41 39 38N 16 47 E
Triora 38 44 0N 7 46 E
Tripoli = Tarābulus, Leb. 64 34 31N 35 50 E
Tripoli = Tarābulus, Libya 83 32 58N 13 12 E
Trípolis 45 37 31N 22 25 E
Tripp 116 43 16N 97 58W
Tripura □ 67 24 0N 92 0 E
Trischen 24 54 3N 8 32 E
Tristan da Cunha 7 37 6 S 12 20W
Trivandrum 70 8 41N 77 0 E
Trivento 41 41 48N 14 31 E
Trnava 27 48 23N 17 35 E
Trobriand Is. 98 8 30 S 151 0 E
Trochu 108 51 50N 113 13W
Trodely I. 106 52 15N 79 26W
Troezen 45 37 25N 23 15 E
Trogir 39 43 32N 16 15 E
Troglav 39 43 56N 16 36 E
Trøgstad 47 59 37N 11 16 E
Tróia 41 41 22N 15 19 E
Troilus, L. 106 50 50N 74 35W
Troina 41 37 47N 14 34 E
Trois Fourches, Cap des 82 35 26N 2 58W
Trois-Pistoles 107 48 5N 69 10W
Trois-Rivières 106 46 25N 72 34W
Troitsk 58 54 10N 61 35 E
Troitsko Pechorsk 52 62 40N 56 10 E
Trölladyngja 50 64 54N 17 16W
Trollhättan 49 58 17N 12 20 E
Trollheimen 47 62 46N 9 1 E
Troms fylke □ 50 68 56N 19 0 E
Tromsø 50 69 40N 18 56 E
Tronador 128 41 10 S 71 50W
Trondheim 47 63 36N 10 25 E
Trondheimsfjorden 47 63 35N 10 30 E
Trönninge 49 56 37N 12 51 E
Trönö 48 61 22N 16 54 E
Tronto → 39 42 54N 13 55 E
Troon 14 55 33N 4 40W
Tropea 41 38 40N 15 53 E
Tropic 119 37 36N 112 4W
Tropoja 44 42 23N 20 10 E
Trossachs, The 14 56 14N 4 24W
Trostan 15 55 4N 6 10W
Trostberg 25 48 2N 12 33 E
Trostyanets 54 50 33N 34 59 E
Trotternish 14 57 32N 6 15W
Troup 117 32 10N 95 3W
Trout → 108 61 19N 119 51W
Trout L., N.W.T., Can. 108 60 40N 121 40W
Trout L., Ont., Can. 109 51 20N 93 15W
Trout Lake 106 46 10N 85 2W
Trout River 107 49 29N 58 8W
Trouville 18 49 21N 0 5 E
Trowbridge 13 51 18N 2 12W
Troy, Turkey 44 39 57N 26 12 E
Troy, Turkey 64 39 55N 26 20 E
Troy, Ala., U.S.A. 115 31 50N 85 58W
Troy, Idaho, U.S.A. 118 46 44N 116 46W
Troy, Kans., U.S.A. 116 39 47N 95 2W
Troy, Mo., U.S.A. 116 38 56N 90 59W
Troy, Montana, U.S.A. 118 48 30N 115 58W
Troy, N.Y., U.S.A. 114 42 45N 73 39W
Troy, Ohio, U.S.A. 114 40 0N 84 10W
Troyan 43 42 57N 24 43 E
Troyes 19 48 19N 4 3 E
Trpanj 42 43 1N 17 15 E
Trstena 27 49 21N 19 37 E
Trstenik 42 43 36N 21 0 E
Trubchevsk 54 52 33N 33 47 E
Trucial States = United Arab Emirates ■ 65 24 0N 54 30 E
Truckee 118 39 20N 120 11W
Trujillo, Hond. 121 16 0N 86 0W
Trujillo, Peru 126 8 6 S 79 0W
Trujillo, Spain 31 39 28N 5 55W
Trujillo, U.S.A. 117 35 34N 104 44W
Trujillo, Venez. 126 9 22N 70 38W
Truk 94 7 25N 151 46 E
Trumann 117 35 42N 90 32W
Trumbull, Mt. 119 36 25N 113 8W
Trun 42 42 51N 22 38 E
Trun 18 48 50N 0 2 E
Trundle 99 32 53 S 147 35 E
Trung-Phan 72 16 0N 108 0 E
Truro, Can. 107 45 21N 63 14W
Truro, U.K. 13 50 17N 5 2W
Trustrup 49 56 20N 10 46 E
Truth or Consequences 119 33 9N 107 16W
Trutnov 26 50 37N 15 54 E
Truyère → 20 44 38N 2 34 E
Tryavna 43 42 54N 25 25 E
Tryon 115 35 15N 82 16W
Tryonville 112 41 42N 79 48W
Trzcianka 28 53 3N 16 25 E
Trzciel 28 52 23N 15 50 E
Trzcińsko Zdrój 28 52 58N 14 35 E
Trzebiatów 28 54 3N 15 18 E
Trzebiez 28 53 38N 14 31 E
Trzebinia-Siersza 27 50 11N 19 18 E
Trzebnica 28 51 20N 17 1 E
Trzemeszno 28 52 33N 17 48 E
Tržič 39 46 22N 14 18 E
Tsageri 57 42 39N 42 46 E
Tsamandás 44 39 46N 20 21 E
Tsaratanana 93 16 47 S 47 39 E
Tsaratanana, Mt. de 93 14 0 S 49 0 E
Tsarevo = Michurin 43 42 9N 27 51 E
Tsarichanka 56 48 55N 34 30 E
Tsaritsáni 44 39 53N 22 14 E
Tsau 92 20 8 S 22 22 E
Tsebrikovo 56 47 9N 30 10 E
Tselinograd 58 51 10N 71 30 E
Tsetserleg 75 47 36N 101 32 E
Tshabong 92 26 2 S 22 29 E
Tshane 92 24 5 S 21 54 E
Tshela 88 4 57 S 13 4 E
Tshesebe 93 21 51 S 27 32 E
Tshibeke 90 2 40 S 28 35 E
Tshibinda 90 2 23 S 28 43 E
Tshikapa 88 6 28 S 20 48 E
Tshilenge 90 6 17 S 23 48 E
Tshinsenda 91 12 20 S 28 0 E
Tshofa 90 5 13 S 25 16 E
Tshwane 92 22 24 S 22 1 E
Tsigara 92 20 22 S 25 54 E
Tsihombe 93 25 18 S 45 29 E
Tsimlyansk 57 47 40N 42 6 E
Tsimlyanskoye Vdkhr. 57 48 0N 43 0 E
Tsinan = Jinan 76 36 38N 117 1 E
Tsineng 92 27 05 S 23 05 E
Tsinga 44 41 23N 24 44 E
Tsinghai = Qinghai □ 75 36 0N 98 0 E
Tsingtao = Qingdao 76 36 5N 120 20 E
Tsinjomitondraka 93 15 40 S 47 8 E
Tsiroanomandidy 93 18 46 S 46 2 E
Tsivilsk 55 55 50N 47 25 E
Tsivory 93 24 4 S 46 5 E
Tskhinali 53 42 22N 43 52 E
Tskhinvali 57 42 14N 44 1 E
Tsna → 55 54 55N 41 58 E
Tsodilo Hill 92 18 49 S 21 43 E
Tsu 74 34 45N 136 25 E
Tsu L. 108 60 40N 111 52W
Tsuchiura 74 36 5N 140 15 E
Tsugaru-Kaikyō 74 41 35N 141 0 E
Tsumeb 92 19 9 S 17 44 E
Tsumis 92 23 39 S 17 29 E
Tsuruga 74 35 45N 136 2 E
Tsushima 74 34 20N 129 20 E
Tsvetkovo 56 49 8N 31 33 E
Tua → 30 41 13N 7 26W
Tual 73 5 38 S 132 44 E
Tuam 15 53 30N 8 50W
Tuamotu Arch. 95 17 0 S 144 0W
Tuamotu Ridge 95 20 0 S 138 0W
Tuao 73 17 55N 122 22 E
Tuapse 57 44 5N 39 10 E
Tuatapere 101 46 8 S 167 41 E
Tuba City 119 36 8N 111 18W
Tubac 119 31 37N 111 20W
Tuban 73 6 54 S 112 3 E
Tubarão 125 28 30 S 49 0W
Tūbās 62 32 20N 35 22 E
Tubau 72 3 10N 113 40 E
Tübingen 25 48 31N 9 4 E
Tubja, W. → 86 25 27N 38 45 E
Ţubruq 81 32 7N 23 55 E
Tubuai Is. 95 25 0 S 150 0W
Tucacas 126 10 48N 68 19W
Tuchodi → 108 58 17N 123 42W
Tuchola 28 53 33N 17 52 E
Tuchów 27 49 54N 21 1 E
Tucker's Town 121 32 17N 64 43W
Tucson 119 32 14N 110 59W
Tucumán □ 124 26 48 S 66 2W
Tucumcari 117 35 12N 103 45W
Tucupita 126 9 2N 62 3W
Tucuruí 127 3 42 S 49 44W
Tuczno 28 53 13N 16 10 E
Tudela 32 42 4N 1 39W
Tudela de Duero 30 41 37N 4 39W
Tudmur 64 34 36N 38 15 E
Tudor, Lac 107 55 50N 65 25W
Tudora 46 47 31N 26 45 E
Tuella → 30 41 30N 7 12W
Tufi 98 9 8 S 149 19 E
Tuguegarao 73 17 35N 121 42 E
Tugur 59 53 44N 136 45 E
Tukangbesi, Kepulauan 73 6 0 S 124 0 E
Tukarak I. 106 56 15N 78 45W
Tûkh 86 30 21N 31 12 E
Tukobo 84 5 1N 2 47W
Tūkrah 83 32 30N 20 37 E
Tuktoyaktuk 104 69 27N 133 2W
Tukums 54 57 2N 23 10 E
Tukuyu 91 9 17 S 33 35 E
Tula, Hidalgo, Mexico 120 20 0N 99 20W
Tula, Tamaulipas, Mexico 120 23 0N 99 40W
Tula, Nigeria 85 9 51N 11 27 E
Tula, U.S.S.R. 55 54 13N 37 38 E
Tulak 65 33 55N 63 40 E
Tulancingo 120 20 5N 99 22W
Tulare 119 36 15N 119 26W
Tulare Lake 119 36 0N 119 53W
Tularosa 119 33 4N 106 1W
Tulbagh 92 33 16 S 19 6 E
Tulcán 126 0 48N 77 43W
Tulcea 46 45 13N 28 46 E
Tulcea □ 46 45 0N 29 0 E
Tulchin 56 48 41N 28 49 E
Tulemalu L. 109 62 58N 99 25W
Tulgheş 46 46 58N 25 45 E
Tuli, Indon. 73 1 24 S 122 26 E
Tuli, Zimb. 91 21 58 S 29 13 E
Ţūlkarm 62 32 19N 35 2 E
Tulla 117 34 35N 101 44W
Tullahoma 115 35 23N 86 12W
Tullamore, Austral. 99 32 39 S 147 36 E
Tullamore, Ireland 15 53 17N 7 30W
Tulle 20 45 16N 1 46 E
Tullibigeal 99 33 25 S 146 44 E
Tullins 21 45 18N 5 29 E
Tulln 26 48 20N 16 4 E
Tullow 15 52 48N 6 45W
Tullus 87 11 7N 24 31 E
Tully 98 17 56 S 145 55 E
Ţulmaythah 81 32 40N 20 55 E
Tulmur 98 22 40 S 142 20 E
Tulnici 46 45 51N 26 38 E
Tulovo 43 42 33N 25 32 E
Tulsa 117 36 10N 96 0W
Tulsequah 108 58 39N 133 35W
Tulu Milki 87 9 55N 38 20 E
Tulu Welel 87 8 56N 34 47 E
Tulua 126 4 6N 76 11W
Tulun 59 54 32N 100 35 E
Tulungagung 72 8 5 S 111 54 E
Tum 73 3 36 S 130 21 E
Tuma 55 55 10N 40 30 E
Tuma → 121 13 6N 84 35W
Tumaco 126 1 50N 78 45W
Tumatumari 126 5 20N 58 55W
Tumba 48 59 12N 17 48 E
Tumba, L. 88 0 50 S 18 0 E
Tumbarumba 99 35 44 S 148 0 E
Tumbaya 124 23 50 S 65 26W
Túmbes 126 3 37 S 80 27W
Tumbwe 91 11 25 S 27 15 E
Tumen 76 43 0N 129 50 E
Tumen Jiang → 76 42 20N 130 35 E
Tumeremo 126 7 18N 61 30W
Tumkur 70 13 18N 77 6 E
Tummel, L. 14 56 43N 3 55W
Tump 66 26 7N 62 16 E
Tumpat 71 6 11N 102 10 E
Tumsar 69 21 26N 79 45 E
Tumu 84 10 56N 1 56W
Tumucumaque, Serra 127 2 0N 55 0W
Tumut 97 35 16 S 148 13 E
Tumwater 118 47 0N 122 58W
Tunas de Zaza 121 21 39N 79 34W
Tunbridge Wells 13 51 7N 0 16 E
Tuncurry 99 32 17 S 152 29 E
Tunduru 91 11 8 S 37 25 E
Tunduru □ 91 11 5 S 37 22 E
Tundzha → 43 41 40N 26 35 E
Tune 47 59 16N 11 2 E
Tunga → 70 15 0N 75 50 E
Tunga Pass 67 29 0N 94 14 E
Tungabhadra → 70 15 57N 78 15 E
Tungabhadra Dam 70 15 0N 75 50 E
Tungaru 81 10 9N 30 52 E
Tungla 121 13 24N 84 21W
Tungnafellsjökull 50 64 45N 17 55W
Tungsten, Can. 108 61 57N 128 16W
Tungsten, U.S.A. 118 40 50N 118 10W
Tunguska, Nizhnyaya → 59 65 48N 88 4 E
Tunguska, Podkamennaya → 59 61 36N 90 18 E
Tuni 70 17 22N 82 36 E
Tunica 117 34 43N 90 23W
Tunis 83 36 50N 10 11 E
Tunis, Golfe de 83 37 0N 10 30 E
Tunisia ■ 83 33 30N 9 10 E
Tunja 126 5 33N 73 25W
Tunkhannock 113 41 32N 75 46W
Tunliu 76 36 13N 112 52 E
Tunnsjøen 50 64 45N 13 25 E
Tunungayualok I. 107 56 0N 61 0W
Tunuyán 124 33 35 S 69 0W
Tunuyán → 124 33 33 S 67 30W
Tunxi 75 29 42N 118 25 E
Tuolumne 119 37 59N 120 16W
Tuoy-Khaya 59 62 32N 111 25 E
Tupã 125 21 57 S 50 28W
Tupelo 115 34 15N 88 42W
Tupik, U.S.S.R. 54 55 42N 33 22 E
Tupik, U.S.S.R. 59 54 26N 119 57 E
Tupinambaranas 126 3 0 S 58 0W
Tupiza 124 21 30 S 65 40W
Tupižnica 42 43 43N 22 10 E
Tupper 108 55 32N 120 1W
Tupper L. 114 44 18N 74 30W
Tupungato, Cerro 124 33 15 S 69 50W
Tuquan 76 45 18N 121 38 E
Tuque, La 106 47 30N 72 50W
Túquerres 126 1 5N 77 37W
Tura, India 69 25 30N 90 16 E
Tura, U.S.S.R. 59 64 20N 100 17 E
Turaba, Wadi → 86 21 15N 41 32 E
Turabah 64 28 20N 43 15 E
Turaiyur 70 11 9N 78 38 E
Tūrān 65 35 39N 56 42 E
Turan 59 51 55N 95 0 E
Turayf 64 31 41N 38 39 E
Turbacz 27 49 30N 20 8 E
Turbe 42 44 15N 17 35 E
Turda 46 46 34N 23 47 E
Turégano 30 41 9N 4 1W
Turek 28 52 3N 18 30 E
Turfan = Turpan 75 43 58N 89 10 E
Turfan Depression = Turpan Hami 75 42 40N 89 25 E
Tŭrgovishte 43 43 17N 26 38 E
Turgutlu 64 38 30N 27 48 E
Turhal 56 40 24N 36 5 E
Turia → 33 39 27N 0 19W
Turiaçu 127 1 40 S 45 19W
Turiaçu → 127 1 36 S 45 19W
Turiec → 27 49 07N 18 55 E
Turin 108 49 47N 112 24W
Turin = Torino 38 45 3N 7 40 E
Turka 54 49 10N 23 2 E
Turkana □ 90 3 0N 35 30 E
Turkana, L. 90 3 30N 36 5 E
Turkestan 58 43 17N 68 16 E
Túrkeve 27 47 6N 20 44 E
Turkey ■ 64 39 0N 36 0 E
Turki 55 52 0N 43 15 E
Turkmen S.S.R. □ 58 39 0N 59 0 E
Turks Is. 121 21 20N 71 20W
Turks Island Passage 121 21 30N 71 30W
Turku 51 60 30N 22 19 E
Turkwe → 90 3 6N 36 6 E
Turlock 119 37 30N 120 55W
Turnagain → 108 59 12N 127 35W
Turnagain, C. 101 40 28 S 176 38 E
Turneffe Is. 120 17 20N 87 50W
Turner 118 48 52N 108 25W
Turner Valley 108 50 40N 114 17W
Turners Falls 113 42 36N 72 34W
Turnhout 16 51 19N 4 57 E
Türnitz 26 47 55N 15 29 E
Turnor L. 109 56 35N 108 35W
Turnov 26 50 34N 15 10 E
Tŭrnovo 43 43 5N 25 41 E
Turnovo 43 43 5N 25 41 E
Turnu Măgurele 46 43 46N 24 56 E
Turnu Rosu Pasul 46 45 33N 24 17 E
Turnu-Severin 46 44 39N 22 41 E
Turobin 28 50 50N 22 44 E
Turon 117 37 48N 98 27W
Turpan 75 43 58N 89 10 E
Turpan Hami 75 42 40N 89 25 E
Turrës, Kalaja e 44 41 10N 19 28 E
Turriff 14 57 32N 2 28W
Tursha 55 56 55N 47 36 E
Tursi 41 40 15N 16 27 E
Turtle Hd. I. 98 10 56 S 142 37 E
Turtle L., Can. 109 53 36N 108 38W
Turtle L., U.S.A. 116 45 22N 92 10W
Turtle Lake 116 47 30N 100 55W
Turtleford 109 53 23N 108 57W
Turukhansk 59 65 21N 88 5 E
Turun ja Porin lääni □ 51 60 27N 22 15 E
Turzovka 27 49 25N 18 35 E
Tuscaloosa 115 33 13N 87 31W
Tuscánia 39 42 25N 11 53 E
Tuscany = Toscana 38 43 28N 11 15 E
Tuscola, Ill., U.S.A. 114 39 48N 88 15W
Tuscola, Tex., U.S.A. 117 32 15N 99 48W
Tuscumbia 115 34 42N 87 42W
Tuskar Rock 15 52 12N 6 10W
Tuskegee 115 32 24N 85 39W
Tustna 47 63 10N 8 5 E
Tuszyn 28 51 36N 19 33 E
Tutayev 55 57 53N 39 32 E
Tuticorin 70 8 50N 78 12 E
Tutin 42 43 0N 20 20 E
Tutóia 127 2 45 S 42 20W
Tutong 72 4 47N 114 40 E
Tutova → 46 46 20N 27 30 E
Tutrakan 43 44 2N 26 40 E
Tutshi L. 108 59 56N 134 30W
Tuttle 116 47 9N 100 00W
Tuttlingen 25 47 59N 8 50 E
Tutuala 73 8 25 S 127 15 E
Tutuila 101 14 19 S 170 50W
Tuva A.S.S.R. □ 59 51 30N 95 0 E
Tuvalu ■ 94 8 0 S 178 0 E
Tuxpan 120 20 58N 97 23W
Tuxtla Gutiérrez 120 16 50N 93 10W
Tuy 30 42 3N 8 39W
Tuy Hoa 71 13 5N 109 10 E
Tuya L. 108 59 7N 130 35W
Tuyen Hoa 71 17 50N 106 10 E
Tuz Gölü 64 38 45N 33 30 E
Ţūz Khurmātū 64 34 56N 44 38 E
Tuzla 42 44 34N 18 41 E
Tuzlov → 57 47 28N 39 45 E
Tvååker 49 57 4N 12 25 E
Tvedestrand 47 58 38N 8 58 E
Tvŭrditsa 43 42 42N 25 53 E
Twardogóra 28 51 23N 17 28 E
Tweed 112 44 29N 77 19W
Tweed → 14 55 42N 2 10W
Tweedsmuir Prov. Park 108 53 0N 126 20W
Twentynine Palms 119 34 10N 116 4W
Twillingate 107 49 42N 54 45W
Twin Bridges 118 45 33N 112 23W
Twin Falls 118 42 30N 114 30W
Twin Valley 116 47 18N 96 15W
Twisp 118 48 21N 120 5W
Twistringen 24 52 48N 8 38 E
Two Harbors 116 47 1N 91 40W
Two Hills 108 53 43N 111 52W
Two Rivers 114 44 10N 87 31W
Twofold B. 97 37 8 S 149 59 E
Tychy 27 50 9N 18 59 E
Tyczyn 27 49 58N 22 2 E
Tydal 47 63 4N 11 34 E
Tykocin 28 53 13N 22 46 E
Tyldal 47 62 8N 10 48 E

Tyler Uvira

Tyler, Minn., U.S.A. 116 44 18N 96 8W
Tyler, Tex., U.S.A. 117 32 18N 95 18W
Týn nad Vltavou 26 49 13N 14 26 E
Tynda 59 55 10N 124 43 E
Tyne & Wear □ 12 54 55N 1 35W
Tyne → 12 54 58N 1 28W
Tynemouth 12 55 1N 1 27W
Tynset 47 62 17N 10 47 E
Tyre = Sūr 62 33 12N 35 11 E
Tyrifjorden 47 60 2N 10 8 E
Tyringe 49 56 9N 13 35 E
Tyristrand 47 60 5N 10 5 E
Tyrnyauz 57 43 21N 42 45 E
Tyrol = Tirol 26 47 3N 10 43 E
Tyrone 112 40 39N 78 10W
Tyrrell → 100 35 26 S 142 51 E
Tyrrell Arm 109 62 27N 97 30W
Tyrrell, L. 99 35 20 S 142 50 E
Tyrrell L. 109 63 7N 105 27W
Tyrrhenian Sea 34 40 0N 12 30 E
Tysfjorden 50 68 7N 16 25 E
Tysnes 47 60 1N 5 30 E
Tysnesøy 47 60 0N 5 35 E
Tyssedal 47 60 7N 6 35 E
Tystberga 49 58 51N 17 15 E
Tyub Karagan, M. 57 44 40N 50 19 E
Tyuleniy 57 44 28N 47 30 E
Tyulgan 52 52 22N 56 12 E
Tyumen 58 57 11N 65 29 E
Tywi → 13 51 48N 4 20W
Tzaneen 93 23 47 S 30 9 E
Tzermiadhes Neápolis 46 35 11N 25 29 E
Tzoumérka, Óros 44 39 30N 21 26 E
Tzukong = Zigong 75 29 15N 104 48 E

U

Uad Erni, O. → 82 26 45N 10 47W
Uanda 98 21 37 S 144 55 E
Uarsciek 63 2 28N 45 55 E
Uasin □ 90 0 30N 35 20 E
Uato-Udo 73 9 7 S 125 36 E
Uatumã → 126 2 26 S 57 37W
Uaupés 126 0 8 S 67 5W
Ub 42 44 28N 20 6 E
Ubá 125 21 8 S 43 0W
Ubaitaba 127 14 18 S 39 20W
Ubangi = Oubangi → 88 1 0N 17 50 E
Ubauro 68 28 15N 69 45 E
Ubaye → 21 44 28N 6 18 E
Ube 74 33 56N 131 15 E
Ubeda 33 38 3N 3 23W
Uberaba 127 19 50 S 47 55W
Uberlândia 127 19 0 S 48 20W
Überlingen 25 47 46N 9 10 E
Ubiaja 85 6 41N 6 22 E
Ubombo 93 27 31 S 32 4 E
Ubon Ratchathani 71 15 15N 104 50 E
Ubondo 90 0 55 S 25 42 E
Ubort → 54 52 6N 28 30 E
Ubrique 31 36 41N 5 27W
Ubundu 90 0 22 S 25 30 E
Ucayali → 126 4 30 S 73 30W
Uchi Lake 109 51 5N 92 35W
Uchiura-Wan 74 42 25N 140 40 E
Uchte 24 52 29N 8 52 E
Uchur → 59 58 48N 130 35 E
Ucluelet 108 48 57N 125 32W
Ucuriş 46 46 41N 21 58 E
Uda → 59 54 42N 135 14 E
Udaipur 68 24 36N 73 44 E
Udaipur Garhi 69 27 0N 86 35 E
Udamalpet 70 10 35N 77 15 E
Udbina 39 44 31N 15 47 E
Uddeholm 48 60 1N 13 38 E
Uddevalla 49 58 21N 11 55 E
Uddjaur 50 65 25N 21 15 E
Udgir 70 18 25N 77 5 E
Udi 85 6 23N 7 21 E
Udine 39 46 5N 13 10 E
Udipi 70 13 25N 74 42 E
Udmurt A.S.S.R. □ 52 57 30N 52 30 E
Udon Thani 71 17 29N 102 46 E
Udvoy Balkan 43 42 50N 26 50 E
Udzungwa Range 91 9 30 S 35 10 E
Ueckermünde 24 53 45N 14 1 E
Ueda 74 36 24N 138 16 E
Uedineniya, Os. 4 78 0N 85 0 E
Uelen 59 66 10N 170 0W
Uelzen 24 53 0N 10 33 E
Uere → 88 3 45N 24 45 E
Ufa 52 54 45N 55 55 E
Ufa → 52 54 40N 56 0 E
Uffenheim 25 49 32N 10 15 E
Ugalla → 90 5 8 S 30 42 E
Uganda ■ 90 2 0N 32 0 E
Ugento 41 39 55N 18 10 E
Ugep 85 5 53N 8 2 E
Ugie 93 31 10 S 28 13 E
Ugijar 33 36 58N 3 7W
Ugine 21 45 45N 6 25 E
Ugla 86 25 40N 37 42 E
Uglegorsk 59 49 5N 142 2 E
Uglich 55 57 33N 38 20 E
Ugljane 39 43 35N 16 46 E
Ugolyak 59 64 33N 120 30 E
Ugra → 54 54 30N 36 7 E
Ugûrchin 43 43 6N 24 26 E
Uh → 27 48 7N 21 25 E
Uherske Hradiště 27 49 4N 17 30 E
Uhersky Brod 27 49 1N 17 40 E
Úhlava → 26 49 45N 13 24 E
Uhrichsville 114 40 23N 81 22W
Uige 88 7 30 S 14 40 E
Uiju 76 40 15N 124 35 E
Uinta Mts. 118 40 45N 110 30W
Uitenhage 92 33 40 S 25 28 E
Uithuizen 16 53 24N 6 41 E
Újfehértó 27 47 49N 21 41 E
Ujhani 68 28 0N 79 6 E
Ujjain 68 23 9N 75 43 E
Újpest 27 47 32N 19 6 E
Újszász 27 47 19N 20 7 E
Ujung Pandang 73 5 10 S 119 20 E
Uka 59 57 50N 162 0 E
Ukara I. 90 1 50 S 33 0 E
Ukerewe □ 90 2 0 S 32 30 E
Ukerewe I. 90 2 0 S 33 0 E
Ukholovo 55 53 47N 40 30 E
Ukhrul 67 25 10N 94 25 E
Ukhta 52 63 55N 54 0 E
Ukiah 118 39 10N 123 9W
Ukmerge 54 55 15N 24 45 E
Ukrainian S.S.R. □ 56 49 0N 32 0 E
Ukwi 92 23 29 S 20 30 E
Ulaanbaatar 75 47 54N 106 52 E
Ulaangom 75 50 0N 92 10 E
Ulamba 91 9 3 S 23 38 E
Ulan Bator = Ulaanbaatar 75 47 54N 106 52 E
Ulan Ude 59 51 45N 107 40 E
Ulanga □ 91 8 40 S 36 50 E
Ulanów 28 50 30N 22 16 E
Ulaya, Morogoro, Tanz. 90 7 3 S 36 55 E
Ulaya, Tabora, Tanz. 90 4 25 S 33 30 E
Ulcinj 42 41 58N 19 10 E
Ulco 92 28 21 S 24 15 E
Ulefoss 47 59 17N 9 16 E
Uleza 44 41 46N 19 57 E
Ulfborg 49 56 16N 8 20 E
Ulhasnagar 70 19 15N 73 10 E
Uljma 42 45 2N 21 10 E
Ulla → 30 42 39N 8 44W
Ulladulla 99 35 21 S 150 29 E
Ullånger 48 62 58N 18 10 E
Ullapool 14 57 54N 5 10W
Ullared 49 57 8N 12 42 E
Ulldecona 32 40 36N 0 20 E
Ullswater 12 54 35N 2 52W
Ullung-do 76 37 30N 130 30 E
Ulm 25 48 23N 10 0 E
Ulmarra 99 29 37 S 153 4 E
Ulmeni 46 45 4N 26 40 E
Ulricehamn 49 57 46N 13 26 E
Ulsberg 47 62 45N 9 59 E
Ulsteinvik 47 62 21N 5 53 E
Ulster □ 15 54 35N 6 30W
Ulstrem 43 42 1N 26 27 E
Ulubaria 69 22 31N 88 4 E
Uluguru Mts. 90 7 15 S 37 40 E
Ulungur He 75 47 1N 87 24 E
Ulutau 58 48 39N 67 1 E
Ulverston 12 54 13N 3 7W
Ulverstone 97 41 11 S 146 11 E
Ulvik 47 60 35N 6 54 E
Ulya 59 59 10N 142 0 E
Ulyanovsk 55 54 20N 48 25 E
Ulyasutay (Javhlant) 75 47 56N 97 28 E
Ulysses 117 37 39N 101 25W
Umag 39 45 26N 13 31 E
Umala 126 17 25 S 68 5W
Uman 56 48 40N 30 12 E
Umarkhed 70 19 37N 77 46 E
Umatilla 118 45 58N 119 17W
Umba 52 66 50N 34 20 E
Umbertide 39 43 18N 12 20 E
Umboi I. 98 5 40 S 148 0 E
Umbrella Mts. 101 45 35 S 169 5 E
Umbria □ 39 42 53N 12 30 E
Ume älv → 50 63 45N 20 20 E
Umeå 50 63 45N 20 20 E
Umera 73 0 12 S 129 37 E
Umfuli → 91 17 30 S 29 23 E
Umgusa 91 19 29 S 27 52 E
Umka 42 44 40N 20 19 E
Umkomaas 93 30 13 S 30 48 E
Umm al Arānib 83 26 10N 14 43 E
Umm al Qaywayn 65 25 30N 55 35 E
Umm Arda 87 15 17N 32 31 E
Umm az Zamul 65 22 42N 55 18 E
Umm Bel 87 13 35N 28 0 E
Umm Dubban 87 15 23N 32 52 E
Umm el Fahm 62 32 31N 35 9 E
Umm Koweika 87 13 10N 32 16 E
Umm Lajj 64 25 0N 37 23 E
Umm Merwa 86 18 4N 32 30 E
Umm Qays 62 32 40N 35 41 E
Umm Rumah 86 25 50N 36 30 E
Umm Ruwaba 87 12 50N 31 20 E
Umm Sidr 87 14 29N 25 10 E
Ummanz 24 54 29N 13 9 E
Umnak 104 53 20N 168 20W
Umniati → 91 16 49 S 28 45 E
Umpang 71 16 3N 98 54 E
Umpqua → 118 43 42N 124 3W
Umrer 68 20 51N 79 18 E
Umreth 68 22 41N 73 4 E
Umshandige Dam 91 20 10 S 30 40 E
* Umtali 91 18 58 S 32 38 E
Umtata 93 31 36 S 28 49 E
Umuahia 85 5 33N 7 29 E
Umvukwe Ra. 91 16 45 S 30 45 E
Umvukwes 91 17 0 S 30 57 E
Umvuma 91 19 16 S 30 30 E
Umzimvubu 93 31 38 S 29 33 E
Umzingwane → 91 22 12 S 29 56 E
Umzinto 93 30 15 S 30 45 E
Una 68 20 46N 71 8 E
Una → 39 45 16N 16 55 E
Unac → 39 44 30N 16 9 E
Unadilla 113 42 20N 75 17W
Unalaska 104 53 40N 166 40W
Uncastillo 32 42 21N 1 8W
Uncía 126 18 25 S 66 40W
Uncompahgre Pk. 119 38 5N 107 32W
Unden 49 58 45N 14 25 E
Underbool 99 35 10 S 141 51 E
Undersaker 48 63 19N 13 21 E
Undersvik 48 61 36N 16 20 E
Undredal 47 60 57N 7 6 E
Unecha 54 52 50N 32 37 E
Ungarie 99 33 38 S 146 56 E
Ungava B. 105 59 30N 67 30W
Ungeny 56 47 11N 27 51 E
Unggi 76 42 16N 130 28 E
Ungwatiri 87 16 52N 36 10 E
Uni 55 56 44N 51 47 E
União da Vitória 125 26 13 S 51 5W
Uniejów 28 51 59N 18 46 E
Unije 39 44 40N 14 15 E
Unimak 104 55 0N 164 0W
Unimak Pass. 104 53 30N 165 15W
Union, Miss., U.S.A. 117 32 34N 89 14W
Union, Mo., U.S.A. 116 38 25N 91 0W
Union, S.C., U.S.A. 115 34 43N 81 39W
Union City, N.J., U.S.A. 113 40 47N 74 5W
Union City, Ohio, U.S.A. 114 40 11N 84 49W
Union City, Pa., U.S.A. 114 41 53N 79 50W
Union City, Tenn., U.S.A. 117 36 25N 89 0W
Union Gap 118 46 38N 120 29W
Unión, La, Chile 128 40 10 S 73 0W
Unión, La, El Sal. 120 13 20N 87 50W
Unión, La, Spain 33 37 38N 0 53W
Union, Mt. 119 34 34N 112 21W
Union of Soviet Socialist Republics ■ 59 60 0N 100 0 E
Union Springs 115 32 9N 85 44W
Uniondale 92 33 39 S 23 7 E
Uniontown 114 39 54N 79 45W
Unionville 116 40 29N 93 1W
Unirea 46 44 15N 27 35 E
United Arab Emirates ■ 65 23 50N 54 0 E
United Kingdom ■ 11 55 0N 3 0W
United States of America ■ 111 37 0N 96 0W
United States Trust Terr. of the Pacific Is. 94 10 0N 160 0 E
Unity 109 52 30N 109 5W
Universales, Mtes. 32 40 18N 1 33W
Unjha 68 23 46N 72 24 E
Unnao 69 26 35N 80 30 E
Uno, Ilha 84 11 15N 16 13W
Unst 14 60 50N 0 55W
Unstrut → 24 51 10N 11 48 E
Unuk → 108 56 5N 131 3W
Ünye 56 41 5N 37 15 E
Unzha 55 58 0N 44 0 E
Unzha → 55 57 30N 43 40 E
Upa → 27 50 35N 16 15 E
Upata 126 8 1N 62 24W
Upemba, L. 91 8 30 S 26 20 E
Upernavik 4 72 49N 56 20W
Upington 92 28 25 S 21 15 E
Upleta 68 21 46N 70 16 E
Upolu 101 13 58 S 172 0W
Upper Alkali Lake 118 41 47N 120 8W
Upper Arrow L. 108 50 30N 117 50W
Upper Austria = Oberösterreich 26 48 10N 14 0 E
Upper Foster L. 109 56 47N 105 20W
Upper Hutt 101 41 8 S 175 5 E
Upper Klamath L. 118 42 16N 121 55W
Upper L. Erne 15 54 14N 7 22W
Upper Lake 118 39 10N 122 55W
Upper Musquodoboit 107 45 10N 62 58W
Upper Red L. 116 48 0N 95 0W
Upper Sandusky 114 40 50N 83 17W
Upper Taimyr → 59 74 15N 99 48 E
Upper Volta ■ 84 12 0N 1 0W
Upphärad 49 58 9N 12 19 E
Uppsala 48 59 53N 17 38 E
Uppsala län □ 48 60 0N 17 30 E
Upstart, C. 98 19 41 S 147 45 E
Upton 116 44 8N 104 35W
Ur 64 30 55N 46 25 E
Uracara 126 2 20 S 57 50W
Urach 25 48 29N 9 25 E
Urad Qianqi 76 40 40N 108 30 E
Ural → 58 47 0N 51 48 E
Ural, Mt. 99 33 21 S 146 12 E
Ural Mts. = Uralskie Gory 52 60 0N 59 0 E
Uralla 99 30 37 S 151 29 E
Uralsk 52 51 20N 51 20 E
Uralskie Gory 52 60 0N 59 0 E
Urambo 90 5 4 S 32 0 E
Urambo □ 90 5 0 S 32 0 E
Urana 100 35 15 S 146 21 E
Urandangie 97 21 32 S 138 14 E
Uranium City 109 59 34N 108 37W
Uravakonda 70 14 57N 77 12 E
Urawa 74 35 50N 139 40 E
Uray 58 60 5N 65 15 E
Urbana, Ill., U.S.A. 114 40 7N 88 12W
Urbana, Ohio, U.S.A. 114 40 9N 83 44W
Urbana, La 126 7 8N 66 56W
Urbánia 39 43 40N 12 31 E
Urbel → 32 42 21N 3 40W
Urbino 39 43 43N 12 38 E
Urbión, Picos de 32 42 1N 2 52W
Urcos 126 13 40 S 71 38W
Urda, Spain 31 39 25N 3 43W
Urda, U.S.S.R. 57 48 52N 47 23 E
Urdinarrain 124 32 37 S 58 52W
Urdos 20 42 51N 0 35W
Urdzhar 58 47 5N 81 38 E
Ure → 12 54 20N 1 25W
Uren 55 57 35N 45 55 E
Urengoy 58 65 58N 28 25 E
Ures 120 29 30N 110 30W
Urfa 64 37 12N 38 50 E
Urfahr 26 48 19N 14 17 E
Urgench 58 41 40N 60 41 E
Uri □ 25 46 43N 8 35 E
Uribia 126 11 43N 72 16W
Urim 62 31 18N 34 32 E
Uriondo 124 21 41 S 64 41W
Urique → 120 26 29N 107 58W
Urk 16 52 39N 5 36 E
Urla 64 38 20N 26 47 E
Urlati 46 44 59N 26 15 E
Urmia = Rezā'īyeh 64 37 40N 45 0 E
Urmia, L. = Rezā'īyeh, Daryācheh-ye 64 37 30N 45 30 E
Uroševac 42 42 23N 21 10 E
Urshult 49 56 31N 14 50 E
Ursus 28 52 12N 20 53 E
Uruana 127 15 30 S 49 41W
Uruapan 120 19 30N 102 0W
Urubamba 126 13 20 S 72 10W
Urubamba → 126 10 43 S 73 48W
Uruçuí 127 7 20 S 44 28W
Uruguai → 125 26 0 S 53 30W
Uruguaiana 124 29 50 S 57 0W
Uruguay ■ 124 32 30 S 56 30W
Uruguay → 124 34 12 S 58 18W
Urumchi = Ürümqi 75 43 45N 87 45 E
Ürümqi 75 43 45N 87 45 E
Urup → 57 46 0N 41 10 E
Urup, Os. 59 46 0N 151 0 E
Uryung-Khaya 59 72 48N 113 23 E
Uryupinsk 55 50 45N 41 58 E
Urzhum 55 57 10N 49 56 E
Urziceni 46 44 40N 26 42 E
Usa → 52 65 67N 56 55 E
Uşak 64 38 43N 29 28 E
Usakos 92 22 0 S 15 31 E
Ušće 42 43 30N 20 39 E
Usedom 24 53 50N 13 55 E
Usfan 86 21 58N 39 27 E
Ush-Tobe 58 45 16N 78 0 E
Ushakova, O. 4 82 0N 80 0 E
Ushant = Ouessant, Île d' 18 48 25N 5 5W
Ushashi 90 1 59 S 33 57 E
Ushat 87 7 59N 29 28 E
Ushuaia 128 54 50 S 68 23W
Ushumun 59 52 47N 126 32 E
Usk → 13 51 37N 2 56W
Uskedal 47 59 56N 5 53 E
Üsküdar 64 41 0N 29 5 E
Uslar 24 51 39N 9 39 E
Usman 55 52 5N 39 48 E
Usoke 90 5 7 S 32 19 E
Usolye Sibirskoye 59 52 48N 103 40 E
Usoro 85 5 33N 6 11 E
Uspallata, P. de 124 32 37 S 69 22W
Uspenskiy 58 48 41N 72 43 E
Ussel 20 45 32N 2 18 E
Ussuriysk 59 43 48N 131 59 E
Ust-Aldan = Batamay 59 63 30N 129 15 E
Ust Amginskoye = Khandyga 59 62 42N 135 0 E
Ust-Bolsheretsk 59 52 50N 156 15 E
Ust Buzulukskaya 55 50 8N 42 11 E
Ust chaun 59 68 47N 170 30 E
Ust-Donetskiy 57 47 35N 40 55 E
Ust'-Ilga 59 55 5N 104 55 E
Ust Ilimpeya = Yukti 59 63 20N 105 0 E
Ust-Ilimsk 59 58 3N 102 39 E
Ust Ishim 58 57 45N 71 10 E
Ust-Kamchatsk 59 56 10N 162 28 E
Ust-Kamenogorsk 58 50 0N 82 36 E
Ust-Karenga 59 54 25N 116 30 E
Ust Khayryuzova 59 57 15N 156 45 E
Ust-Kut 59 56 50N 105 42 E
Ust Kuyga 59 70 1N 135 43 E
Ust-Labinsk 57 45 15N 39 41 E
Ust Luga 54 59 35N 28 20 E
Ust Maya 59 60 30N 134 28 E
Ust-Mil 59 59 40N 133 11 E
Ust-Nera 59 64 35N 143 15 E
Ust-Nyukzha 59 56 34N 121 37 E
Ust Olenek 59 73 0N 119 48 E
Ust-Omchug 59 61 9N 149 38 E
Ust Port 58 69 40N 84 26 E
Ust Tsilma 52 65 25N 52 0 E
Ust-Tungir 59 55 25N 120 36 E
Ust Urt = Ustyurt, Plato 58 44 0N 55 0 E
Ust Usa 52 66 0N 56 30 E
Ust Vorkuta 58 67 24N 64 0 E
Ustaoset 47 60 30N 8 2 E
Ustaritz 20 43 24N 1 27W
Uste 55 59 35N 39 40 E
Ústi nad Labem 26 50 41N 14 3 E
Ústi nad Orlicí 27 49 58N 16 24 E
Ustica 40 38 42N 13 10 E
Ustka 28 54 35N 16 55 E
Ustroń 27 49 43N 18 48 E
Ustrzyki Dolne 27 49 27N 22 40 E
Ustye 59 57 46N 94 37 E
Ustyurt, Plato 58 44 0N 55 0 E
Ustyuzhna 55 58 50N 36 32 E
Usu 75 44 27N 84 40 E
Usuki 74 33 8N 131 49 E
Usulután 120 13 25N 88 28W
Usumacinta → 120 17 0N 91 0W
Usure 90 4 40 S 34 22 E
Uta 73 4 33 S 136 0 E
Utah □ 118 39 30N 111 30W
Utah, L. 118 40 10N 111 58W
Ute Cr. 117 35 21N 103 45W
Utena 54 55 27N 25 40 E
Ütersen 24 53 40N 9 40 E
Utete 90 8 0 S 38 45 E
Uthai Thani 71 15 22N 100 3 E
Utiariti 126 13 0 S 58 10W
Utica, N.Y., U.S.A. 114 43 5N 75 18W
Utica, Ohio, U.S.A. 112 40 13N 82 26W
Utiel 32 39 37N 1 11W
Utik L. 109 55 15N 96 0W
Utikuma L. 108 55 50N 115 30W
Utrecht, Neth. 16 52 5N 5 8 E
Utrecht, S. Afr. 93 27 38 S 30 20 E
Utrecht □ 16 52 6N 5 7 E
Utrera 31 37 12N 5 48W
Utsjoki 50 69 51N 26 59 E
Utsunomiya 74 36 30N 139 50 E
Uttar Pradesh □ 69 27 0N 80 0 E
Uttaradit 71 17 36N 100 5 E
Uttoxeter 12 52 53N 1 50W
Ütze 24 52 28N 10 11 E
Uusikaarlepyy 50 63 32N 22 31 E
Uusikaupunki 51 60 47N 21 25 E
Uva 52 56 59N 52 13 E
Uvac → 42 43 35N 19 40 E
Uvalde 117 29 15N 99 48W
Uvarovo 55 51 59N 42 14 E
Uvat 58 59 5N 68 49 E
Uvinza 90 5 5 S 30 24 E
Uvira 90 3 22 S 29 3 E

* Renamed Mutare

Uvs Nuur Verdigre

Uvs Nuur 75 50 20N 92 30 E
Uwajima 74 33 10N 132 35 E
Uweinat, Jebel 86 21 54N 24 58 E
Uxbridge 112 44 6N 79 7W
Uxin Qi 76 38 50N 109 5 E
Uxmal 120 20 22N 89 46W
Uyandi 59 69 19N 141 0 E
Uyo 85 5 1N 7 53 E
Uyuni 126 20 28 S 66 47W
Uzbek S.S.R. □ 58 41 30N 65 0 E
Uzen 53 43 27N 53 10 E
Uzen, Bol. → 55 50 0N 49 30 E
Uzen, Mal. → 55 50 0N 48 30 E
Uzerche 20 45 25N 1 34 E
Uzès 21 44 1N 4 26 E
Uzh → 54 51 15N 30 12 E
Uzhgorod 54 48 36N 22 18 E
Uzlovaya 55 54 0N 38 5 E
Uzunköprü 43 41 16N 26 43 E

V

Vaal → 92 29 4 S 23 38 E
Vaaldam 93 27 0 S 28 14 E
Vaalwater 93 24 15 S 28 8 E
Vaasa 50 63 6N 21 38 E
Vaasan lääni □ 50 63 2N 22 50 E
Vabre 20 43 42N 2 24 E
Vác 27 47 49N 19 10 E
Vacaria 125 28 31 S 50 52W
Vacaville 118 38 21N 122 0W
Vaccarès, Étang de 21 43 32N 4 34 E
Vach → 58 60 45N 76 45 E
Vache, Î.-à- 121 18 2N 73 35W
Väddö 48 59 55N 18 50 E
Vadnagar 68 23 47N 72 40 E
Vado Ligure 38 44 16N 8 26 E
Vadodara 68 22 20N 73 10 E
Vadsø 50 70 3N 29 50 E
Vadstena 49 58 28N 14 54 E
Vaduz 25 47 8N 9 31 E
Værøy 50 67 40N 12 40 E
Vagney 19 48 1N 6 43 E
Vagnhärad 48 58 57N 17 33 E
Vagos 30 40 33N 8 42W
Váh → 27 47 55N 18 0 E
Vahsel B. 5 75 0 S 35 0W
Vaigach 58 70 10N 59 0 E
Vaigai → 70 9 15N 79 10 E
Vaiges 18 48 2N 0 30W
Vaihingen 25 48 55N 8 58 E
Vaijapur 70 19 58N 74 45 E
Vaikam 70 9 45N 76 25 E
Vailly Aisne 19 49 25N 3 30 E
Vaippar → 70 9 0N 78 25 E
Vaison 21 44 14N 5 4 E
Vajpur 68 21 24N 73 17 E
Vakarel 43 42 35N 23 40 E
Vaksdal 47 60 29N 5 45 E
Vál 27 47 22N 18 40 E
Val-d'Ajol, Le 19 47 55N 6 30 E
Val-de-Marne □ 19 48 45N 2 28 E
Val-d'Oise □ 19 49 5N 2 10 E
Val d'Or 106 48 7N 77 47W
Val Marie 109 49 15N 107 45W
Valadares 30 41 5N 8 38W
Valahia 46 44 35N 25 0 E
Valais □ 25 46 12N 7 45 E
Valandovo 42 41 19N 22 34 E
Valašské Meziříčí 27 49 29N 17 59 E
Valáxa 45 38 50N 24 29 E
Vălcani 42 46 0N 20 26 E
Valcheta 128 40 40 S 66 8W
Valdagno 39 45 38N 11 18 E
Valdahon, Le 19 47 8N 6 20 E
Valday 54 57 58N 33 9 E
Valdayskaya Vozvyshennost 54 57 0N 33 30 E
Valdeazogues → 31 38 45N 4 55W
Valdemarsvik 49 58 14N 16 40 E
Valdepeñas, Ciudad Real, Spain 31 38 43N 3 25W
Valdepeñas, Jaén, Spain 31 37 33N 3 47W
Valderaduey → 30 41 31N 5 42W
Valderrobres 32 40 53N 0 9 E
Valdés, Pen. 128 42 30 S 63 45W
Valdez 104 61 14N 76 17W
Valdivia 128 39 50 S 73 14W
Valdobbiádene 39 45 53N 12 0 E
Valdosta 115 30 50N 83 20W
Valdoviño 30 43 36N 8 8W
Valdres 47 60 55N 9 28 E
Vale, U.S.A. 118 44 0N 117 15W
Vale, U.S.S.R. 57 41 30N 42 58 E
Valea lui Mihai 46 47 32N 22 11 E
Valença, Brazil 127 13 20 S 39 5W
Valença, Port. 30 42 1N 8 34W
Valença do Piauí 127 6 20 S 41 45W
Valençay 19 47 9N 1 34 E
Valence 21 44 57N 4 54 E
Valence-d'Agen 20 44 8N 0 54 E
Valencia, Spain 33 39 27N 0 23W
Valencia, Venez. 126 10 11N 68 0W
Valencia □ 33 39 20N 0 40W
Valencia, Albufera de 33 39 20N 0 27W
Valencia de Alcántara 31 39 25N 7 14W
Valencia de Don Juan 30 42 17N 5 31W
Valencia del Ventoso 31 38 15N 6 29W
Valencia, G. de 33 39 30N 0 20 E
Valenciennes 19 50 20N 3 34 E
Văleni 46 44 15N 24 45 E
Valensole 21 43 50N 5 59 E
Valentia Hr. 15 51 56N 10 17W
Valentia I. 15 51 54N 10 22W
Valentim, Sa. do 127 6 0 S 43 30W
Valentine, Nebr., U.S.A. 116 42 50N 100 35W
Valentine, Tex., U.S.A. 117 30 36N 104 28W
Valenza 38 45 2N 8 39 E
Våler 47 60 41N 11 50 E
Valera 126 9 19N 70 37W
Valga 54 57 44N 26 0 E
Valguarnera Caropepe 41 37 30N 14 22 E
Valier 118 48 25N 112 9W
Valinco, G. de 21 41 40N 8 52 E
Valjevo 42 44 18N 19 53 E
Valkenswaard 16 51 21N 5 29 E
Vall de Uxó 32 39 49N 0 15W
Valla 48 59 2N 16 20 E
Valladolid, Mexico 120 20 40N 88 11W
Valladolid, Spain 30 41 38N 4 43W
Valladolid □ 30 41 38N 4 43W
Vallata 41 41 3N 15 16 E
Valldemosa 32 39 43N 2 37 E
Valle 47 59 13N 7 33 E
Valle d'Aosta □ 38 45 45N 7 22 E
Valle de Arán 32 42 50N 0 55 E
Valle de Cabuérniga 30 43 14N 4 18W
Valle de la Pascua 126 9 13N 66 0W
Valle de Santiago 120 20 25N 101 15W
Valle Fértil, Sierra del 124 30 20 S 68 0W
Valle Hermoso 120 25 35N 97 40W
Vallecas 30 40 23N 3 41W
Vallejo 118 38 12N 122 15W
Vallenar 124 28 30 S 70 50W
Valleraugue 20 44 6N 3 39 E
Vallet 18 47 10N 1 15W
Valletta 36 35 54N 14 30 E
Valley City 116 46 57N 98 0W
Valley Falls 118 42 33N 120 16W
Valleyview 108 55 5N 117 17W
Valli di Comácchio 39 44 40N 12 15 E
Vallimanca, Arroyo 124 35 40 S 59 10W
Vallo della Lucánia 41 40 14N 15 16 E
Vallon 21 44 25N 4 23 E
Vallorbe 25 46 42N 6 20 E
Valls 32 41 18N 1 15 E
Vallsta 48 61 31N 16 22 E
Valmaseda 32 43 11N 3 12W
Valmiera 54 57 37N 25 29 E
Valmont 18 49 45N 0 30 E
Valmontone 40 41 48N 12 55 E
Valmy 19 49 5N 4 45 E
Valnera, Mte. 32 43 9N 3 40W
Valognes 18 49 30N 1 28W
Valona = Vlóra 42 40 32N 19 28 E
Valongo 30 41 8N 8 30W
Valpaços 30 41 36N 7 17W
Valparaíso, Chile 124 33 2 S 71 40W
Valparaíso, Mexico 120 22 50N 103 32W
Valparaiso 114 41 27N 87 2W
Valparaíso □ 124 33 2 S 71 40W
Valpovo 42 45 39N 18 25 E
Valréas 21 44 24N 5 0 E
Vals 25 46 39N 9 11 E
Vals → 92 27 23 S 26 30 E
Vals-les-Bains 21 44 42N 4 24 E
Vals, Tanjung 73 8 26 S 137 25 E
Valsbaai 92 34 15 S 18 40 E
Valskog 48 59 27N 15 57 E
Válta 44 40 3N 23 25 E
Valtellina 38 46 9N 9 55 E
Valuyki 55 50 10N 38 5 E
Valverde del Camino 31 37 35N 6 47W
Valverde del Fresno 30 40 15N 6 51W
Vama 46 47 34N 25 42 E
Vámos 45 35 24N 24 13 E
Vamsadhara → 70 18 21N 84 8 E
Van 64 38 30N 43 20 E
Van Alstyne 117 33 25N 96 36W
Van Bruyssel 107 47 56N 72 9W
Van Buren, Can. 107 47 10N 67 55W
Van Buren, Ark., U.S.A. 117 35 28N 94 18W
Van Buren, Me., U.S.A. 115 47 10N 68 1W
Van Buren, Mo., U.S.A. 117 37 0N 91 0W
Van der Kloof Dam 92 30 04 S 24 40 E
Van Diemen, C. 97 16 30 S 139 46 E
Van Diemen G. 96 11 45 S 132 0 E
Van Gölü 64 38 30N 43 0 E
Van Horn 117 31 3N 104 55W
Van Reenen P. 93 28 22 S 29 27 E
Van Rees, Pegunungan 73 2 35 S 138 15 E
Van Tassell 116 42 40N 104 3W
Van Tivu 70 8 51N 78 15 E
Van Wert 114 40 52N 84 31W
Vanavara 59 60 22N 102 16 E
Vancouver, Can. 108 49 15N 123 10W
Vancouver, U.S.A. 118 45 44N 122 41W
Vancouver I. 108 49 50N 126 0W
Vandalia, Ill., U.S.A. 116 38 57N 89 4W
Vandalia, Mo., U.S.A. 116 39 18N 91 30W
Vandeloos Bay 70 8 0N 81 45 E
Vanderbijlpark 93 26 42 S 27 54 E
Vandergrift 114 40 36N 79 33W
Vanderhoof 108 54 0N 124 0W
Vanderlin I. 97 15 44 S 137 2 E
Vandyke 98 24 10 S 147 51 E
Vänern 49 58 47N 13 30 E
Vänersborg 49 58 26N 12 19 E
Vang Vieng 71 18 58N 102 32 E
Vanga 90 4 35 S 39 12 E
Vangaindrano 93 23 21 S 47 36 E
Vanguard 109 49 55N 107 20W
Vanier 106 45 27N 75 40W
Vanimo 98 2 42 S 141 21 E
Vanivilasa Sagara 70 13 45N 76 30 E
Vaniyambadi 70 12 46N 78 44 E
Vankarem 59 67 51N 175 50 E
Vankleek Hill 106 45 32N 74 40W
Vanna 50 70 6N 19 50 E
Vännäs 50 63 58N 19 48 E
Vannes 18 47 40N 2 47W
Vanoise, Massif de la 21 45 25N 6 40 E
Vanrhynsdorp 92 31 36 S 18 44 E
Vanrook 98 16 57 S 141 57 E
Vans, Les 21 44 25N 4 7 E
Vansbro 48 60 32N 14 15 E
Vanse 47 58 6N 6 41 E
Vansittart B. 96 14 3 S 126 17 E
Vanthli 68 21 28N 70 25 E
Vanua Levu 101 16 33 S 179 15 E
Vanua Mbalavu 101 17 40 S 178 57W
Vanwyksvlei 92 30 18 S 21 49 E
Vanylven 47 62 5N 5 33 E
Vapnyarka 56 48 32N 28 45 E
Var □ 21 43 27N 6 18 E
Var → 21 43 39N 7 12 E
Vara 49 58 16N 12 55 E
Varada → 70 15 0N 75 40 E
Varades 18 47 25N 1 1W
Varaita → 38 44 49N 7 36 E
Varaldsøy 47 60 6N 5 59 E
Varallo 38 45 50N 8 13 E
Varanasi (Benares) 69 25 22N 83 0 E
Varangerfjorden 50 70 3N 29 25 E
Varazdin 39 46 20N 16 20 E
Varazze 38 44 21N 8 36 E
Varberg 49 57 6N 12 20 E
Vardar → 42 40 35N 22 50 E
Varde 49 55 38N 8 29 E
Varde Å 49 55 35N 8 19 E
Varel 24 53 23N 8 9 E
Varena 54 54 12N 24 30 E
Varennes-sur-Allier 20 46 19N 3 24 E
Vareš 42 44 12N 18 23 E
Varese 38 45 49N 8 50 E
Varese Ligure 38 44 22N 9 33 E
Vårgårda 49 58 2N 12 49 E
Varginha 125 21 33 S 45 25W
Vargön 49 58 22N 12 20 E
Varhaug 47 58 37N 5 41 E
Variadero 117 35 43N 104 17W
Varillas 124 24 0 S 70 10W
Väring 49 58 30N 14 0 E
Värmeln 48 59 35N 12 54 E
Värmlands län □ 48 60 0N 13 20 E
Varna 43 43 13N 27 56 E
Varna → 70 16 48N 74 32 E
Värnamo 49 57 10N 14 3 E
Varnsdorf 26 50 55N 14 35 E
Värö 49 57 16N 12 11 E
Vars 113 45 21N 75 21W
Varteig 47 59 23N 11 12 E
Varvarin 42 43 43N 21 20 E
Varzaneh 65 32 25N 52 40 E
Varzi 38 44 50N 9 12 E
Varzo 38 46 12N 8 15 E
Varzy 19 47 22N 3 20 E
Vas □ 27 47 10N 16 55 E
Vasa 50 63 6N 21 38 E
Vasa Barris → 127 11 10 S 37 10W
Vásárosnamény 27 48 9N 22 19 E
Vascão → 31 37 31N 7 31W
Vaşcău 46 46 28N 22 30 E
Vascongadas 32 42 50N 2 45W
Väse 48 59 23N 13 52 E
Vasht = Khāsh 65 28 14N 61 14 E
Vasilevichi 54 52 15N 29 50 E
Vasilikón 45 38 25N 23 40 E
Vasilkov 54 50 7N 30 15 E
Vaslui 46 46 38N 27 42 E
Vaslui □ 46 46 30N 27 45 E
Väsman 48 60 9N 15 5 E
Vassar, Can. 109 49 10N 95 55W
Vassar, U.S.A. 114 43 23N 83 33W
Västerås 49 59 37N 16 38 E
Västerbottens län □ 50 64 58N 18 0 E
Västernorrlands län □ 48 63 30N 17 30 E
Västervik 49 57 43N 16 43 E
Västmanlands län □ 48 59 45N 16 20 E
Vasto 39 42 8N 14 40 E
Vasvár 27 47 3N 16 47 E
Vatan 19 47 4N 1 50 E
Vathí, Itháki, Greece 45 38 18N 20 40 E
Vathí, Sámos, Greece 45 37 46N 27 1 E
Váthia 45 36 29N 22 29 E
Vatican City ■ 39 41 54N 12 27 E
Vaticano, C. 40 38 40N 15 48 E
Vatin 42 45 12N 21 20 E
Vatnajökull 50 64 30N 16 48W
Vatnås 47 59 58N 9 37 E
Vatne 47 62 33N 6 38 E
Vatneyri 50 65 35N 24 0W
Vatoa 101 19 50 S 178 13W
Vatoloha, Mt. 93 17 52 S 47 48 E
Vatomandry 93 19 20 S 48 59 E
Vatra-Dornei 46 47 22N 25 22 E
Vättern 49 58 25N 14 30 E
Vaucluse □ 21 44 3N 5 10 E
Vaucouleurs 19 48 37N 5 40 E
Vaud □ 25 46 35N 6 30 E
Vaughan 119 34 37N 105 12W
Vaughn 118 47 37N 111 36W
Vaupés → 126 0 2N 67 16W
Vauvert 21 43 42N 4 17 E
Vauxhall 108 50 5N 112 9W
Vava'u 101 18 36 S 174 0W
Vavincourt 19 48 49N 5 12 E
Vavoua 84 7 23N 6 29W
Vaxholm 48 59 25N 18 20 E
Växjö 49 56 52N 14 50 E
Vaygach, Ostrov 58 70 0N 60 0 E
Vazovgrad 43 42 39N 24 45 E
Vechta 24 52 47N 8 18 E
Vechte → 16 52 34N 6 6 E
Vecilla, La 30 42 51N 5 27W
Vecsés 27 47 26N 19 19 E
Vedaraniam 70 10 25N 79 50 E
Veddige 49 57 17N 12 20 E
Vedea → 46 44 0N 25 20 E
Vedia 124 34 30 S 61 31W
Vedra, I. del 33 38 52N 1 12 E
Veendam 16 53 5N 6 52 E
Veenendaal 16 52 2N 5 34 E
Vefsna → 50 65 48N 13 10 E
Vega, Norway 50 65 40N 11 55 E
Vega, U.S.A. 117 35 18N 102 26W
Vega, La 121 19 20N 70 30W
Vegadeo 30 43 27N 7 4W
Vegafjorden 50 65 37N 12 0 E
Vegesack 24 53 10N 8 38 E
Veggli 47 60 3N 9 9 E
Veghel 16 51 37N 5 32 E
Vegorritis, Límni 44 40 45N 21 45 E
Vegreville 108 53 30N 112 5W
Vegusdal 47 58 32N 8 10 E
Veii 39 42 0N 12 24 E
Vejen 49 55 30N 9 9 E
Vejer de la Frontera 31 36 15N 5 59W
Vejle 49 55 43N 9 30 E
Vejle Fjord 49 55 40N 9 50 E
Vela Luka 39 42 59N 16 44 E
Velanai I. 70 9 45N 79 45 E
Velarde 119 36 11N 106 1W
Velasco 117 29 0N 95 20W
Velasco, Sierra de. 124 29 20 S 67 10W
Velay, Mts. du 20 45 0N 3 40 E
Velddrif 92 32 42 S 18 11 E
Velebit Planina 39 44 50N 15 20 E
Velebitski Kanal 39 44 45N 14 55 E
Veleka → 43 42 4N 27 58 E
Velenje 39 46 23N 15 8 E
Velestínon 44 39 23N 22 43 E
Veleta, La 31 37 1N 3 22W
Vélez 126 6 1N 73 41W
Velež 42 43 19N 18 2 E
Vélez Blanco 33 37 41N 2 5W
Vélez Málaga 31 36 48N 4 5W
Vélez Rubio 33 37 41N 2 5W
Velhas → 127 17 13 S 44 49W
Velika 42 45 27N 17 40 E
Velika Gorica 39 45 44N 16 5 E
Velika Gradište 42 44 46N 21 29 E
Velika Kapela 39 45 10N 15 5 E
Velika Kladuša 39 45 11N 15 48 E
Velika Morava → 42 44 43N 21 3 E
Velika Plana 42 44 20N 21 1 E
Velikaya → 54 57 48N 28 20 E
Velikaya Lepetikha 56 47 2N 33 58 E
Veliké Kapušany 27 48 34N 22 5 E
Velike Lašče 39 45 49N 14 45 E
Veliki Backa Kanal 42 45 45N 19 15 E
Veliki Jastrebac 42 43 25N 21 30 E
Veliki Popović 42 44 8N 21 18 E
Veliki Ustyug 52 60 47N 46 20 E
Velikiye Luki 54 56 25N 30 32 E
Velikonda Range 70 14 45N 79 10 E
Velikoye, Oz. 55 55 15N 40 10 E
Velingrad 43 42 4N 23 58 E
Velino, Mte. 39 42 10N 13 20 E
Velizh 54 55 36N 31 11 E
Velké Karlovice 27 49 20N 18 17 E
Velke Meziřici 26 49 21N 16 1 E
Vel'ký ostrov Žitný 27 48 5N 17 20 E
Vellar → 70 11 30N 79 36 E
Velletri 40 41 43N 12 43 E
Vellinge 49 55 29N 13 0 E
Vellore 70 12 57N 79 10 E
Velsen-Noord 16 52 27N 4 40 E
Velsk 52 61 10N 42 5 E
Velten 24 52 40N 13 11 E
Velva 116 48 6N 100 56W
Velvendós 44 40 15N 22 6 E
Vembanad Lake 70 9 36N 76 15 E
Veme 47 60 14N 10 7 E
Ven 49 55 55N 12 45 E
Vena 49 57 31N 16 0 E
Venado 120 22 56N 101 10W
Venado Tuerto 124 33 50 S 62 0W
Venafro 41 41 28N 14 3 E
Venarey-les-Laumes 19 47 32N 4 26 E
Venaria 38 45 6N 7 39 E
Venčane 42 44 24N 20 28 E
Vence 21 43 43N 7 6 E
Vendas Novas 31 38 39N 8 27W
Vendée □ 18 46 50N 1 35W
Vendée → 18 46 20N 1 10W
Vendée, Collines de 18 46 35N 0 45W
Vendeuvre-sur-Barse 19 48 14N 4 28 E
Vendôme 18 47 47N 1 3 E
Vendrell 32 41 10N 1 30 E
Vendsyssel 49 57 22N 10 0 E
Véneta, Laguna 39 45 23N 12 25 E
Véneto □ 39 45 40N 12 0 E
Venev 55 54 22N 38 17 E
Venézia 39 45 27N 12 20 E
Venézia, Golfo di 39 45 20N 13 0 E
Venezuela ■ 126 8 0N 65 0W
Venezuela, Golfo de 126 11 30N 71 0W
Vengurla 70 15 53N 73 45 E
Vengurla Rocks 70 15 55N 73 22 E
Venice = Venézia 39 45 27N 12 20 E
Vénissieux 21 45 43N 4 53 E
Venkatagiri 70 14 0N 79 35 E
Venkatapuram 70 18 20N 80 30 E
Venlo 16 51 22N 6 11 E
Vennesla 47 58 15N 8 0 E
Venraij 16 51 31N 6 0 E
Venta de Cardeña 31 38 16N 4 20W
Venta de San Rafael 30 40 42N 4 12W
Ventana, Punta de la 120 24 4N 109 48W
Ventana, Sa. de la 124 38 0 S 62 30W
Ventersburg 92 28 7 S 27 9 E
Ventimíglia 38 43 50N 7 39 E
Ventnor 13 50 35N 1 12W
Ventotene 40 40 48N 13 25 E
Ventoux 21 44 10N 5 17 E
Ventspils 54 57 25N 21 32 E
Ventuarí → 126 3 58N 67 2W
Ventura 119 34 16N 119 18W
Vera, Argent. 124 29 30 S 60 20W
Vera, Spain 33 37 15N 1 51W
Veracruz 120 19 10N 96 10W
Veracruz □ 120 19 0N 96 15W
Veraval 68 20 53N 70 27 E
Verbánia 38 45 56N 8 43 E
Verbicaro 41 39 46N 15 54 E
Vercelli 38 45 19N 8 25 E
Verchovchevo 56 48 32N 34 10 E
Verdalsøra 50 63 48N 11 30 E
Verde →, Argent. 128 41 56 S 65 5W
Verde →, Chihuahua, Mexico 120 26 29N 107 58W
Verde →, Oaxaca, Mexico 120 15 59N 97 50W
Verde →, Veracruz, Mexico 120 21 10N 102 50W
Verde →, Parag. 124 23 9 S 57 37W
Verde, Cay 121 23 0N 75 5W
Verden 24 52 58N 9 18 E
Verdhikoúsa 44 39 47N 21 59 E
Verdigre 116 42 38N 98 0W

Verdon Visoko

Verdon → 21 43 43N 5 46 E
Verdon-sur-Mer, Le 20 45 33N 1 4W
Verdun 19 49 12N 5 24 E
Verdun-sur-le Doubs 19 46 54N 5 0 E
Vereeniging 93 26 38 S 27 57 E
Vérendrye, Parc Prov. de la 106 47 20N 76 40W
Verga, C. 84 10 30N 14 10W
Vergara 32 43 9N 2 28W
Vergato 38 44 18N 11 8 E
Vergemont 98 23 33 S 143 1 E
Vergemont Cr. → 98 24 16 S 143 16 E
Vergennes 113 44 9N 73 15W
Vergt 20 45 2N 0 43 E
Verín 30 41 57N 7 27W
Veriña 30 43 32N 5 43W
Verkhnedvinsk 54 55 45N 27 58 E
Verkhnevilyuysk 59 63 27N 120 18 E
Verkhneye Kalinino 59 59 54N 108 8 E
Verkhniy Baskunchak 57 48 14N 46 44 E
Verkhovye 55 52 55N 37 15 E
Verkhoyansk 59 67 35N 133 25 E
Verkhoyanskiy Khrebet 59 66 0N 129 0 E
Verlo 109 50 19N 108 35W
Verma 47 62 21N 8 3 E
Vermenton 19 47 40N 3 42 E
Vermilion 109 53 20N 110 50W
Vermilion →, Alta., Can. 109 53 22N 110 51W
Vermilion →, Qué., Can. 106 47 38N 72 56W
Vermilion, B. 117 29 45N 91 55W
Vermilion Bay 109 49 51N 93 34W
Vermilion Chutes 108 58 22N 114 51W
Vermilion L. 116 47 53N 92 25W
Vermillion 116 42 50N 96 56W
Vermont □ 114 43 40N 72 50W
Vernal 118 40 28N 109 35W
Verner 106 46 25N 80 8W
Verneuil-sur-Avre 18 48 45N 0 55 E
Vernon, Can. 108 50 20N 119 15W
Vernon, France 18 49 5N 1 30 E
Vernon, U.S.A. 117 34 10N 99 20W
Vero Beach 115 27 39N 80 23W
Véroia 44 40 34N 22 12 E
Verolanuova 38 45 20N 10 5 E
Véroli 40 41 43N 13 24 E
Verona 38 45 27N 11 0 E
Veropol 59 65 15N 168 40 E
Versailles 19 48 48N 2 8 E
Vert, C. 84 14 45N 17 30W
Vertou 18 47 10N 1 28W
Vertus 19 48 54N 4 0 E
Verulam 93 29 38 S 31 2 E
Verviers 16 50 37N 5 52 E
Vervins 19 49 50N 3 53 E
Verwood 109 49 30N 105 40W
Verzej 39 46 34N 16 13 E
Veseli nad Lužnicí 26 49 12N 14 43 E
Veseliye 43 42 18N 27 38 E
Veselovskoye Vdkhr. 57 47 0N 41 0 E
Veshenskaya 57 49 35N 41 44 E
Vesle → 19 49 23N 3 38 E
Vesoul 19 47 40N 6 11 E
Vessigebro 49 56 58N 12 40 E
Vest-Agder fylke □ 47 58 30N 7 15 E
Vestby 47 59 37N 10 45 E
Vestfjorden 50 67 55N 14 0 E
Vestfold fylke □ 47 59 15N 10 0 E
Vestmannaeyjar 50 63 27N 20 15W
Vestmarka 47 59 56N 11 59 E
Vestnes 47 62 39N 7 5 E
Vestone 38 45 43N 10 25 E
Vestsjællands Amtskommune □ 49 55 30N 11 20 E
Vestspitsbergen 4 78 40N 17 0 E
Vestvågøy 50 68 18N 13 50 E
Vesuvio 41 40 50N 14 22 E
Vesuvius, Mt. = Vesuvio 41 40 50N 14 22 E
Vesyegonsk 55 58 40N 37 16 E
Veszprém 27 47 8N 17 57 E
Veszprém □ 27 47 5N 17 55 E
Vésztő 27 46 55N 21 16 E
Vetapalem 70 15 47N 80 18 E
Vetlanda 49 57 24N 15 3 E
Vetluga 55 57 53N 45 45 E
Vetluzhskiy 55 57 17N 45 12 E
Vetovo 43 43 42N 26 16 E
Vetralia 39 42 20N 12 2 E
Vetren 43 42 15N 24 3 E
Vettore, Monte 39 42 49N 13 16 E
Veurne 16 51 5N 2 40 E
Vevey 25 46 28N 6 51 E
Vévi 44 40 47N 21 38 E
Veynes 21 44 32N 5 49 E
Veys 64 31 30N 49 0 E
Vézelise 19 48 30N 6 5 E
Vézère → 20 44 53N 0 53 E
Vezhen 43 42 50N 24 20 E
Viacha 126 16 39 S 68 18W
Viadana 38 44 55N 10 30 E
Viana, Brazil 127 3 13 S 45 0W
Viana, Spain 32 42 31N 2 22W
Viana del Bollo 30 42 11N 7 6W
Viana do Alentejo 31 38 17N 7 59W
Viana do Castelo 30 41 42N 8 50W
Vianna do Castelo □ 30 41 50N 8 30W
Vianópolis 127 16 40 S 48 35W
Viar → 31 37 36N 5 50W
Viaréggio 38 43 52N 10 13 E
Viaur → 20 44 8N 1 58 E
Vibank 109 50 20N 103 56W
Vibo Valéntia 41 38 40N 16 5 E
Viborg 49 56 27N 9 23 E
Vibraye 18 48 3N 0 44 E
Vic-en-Bigorre 20 43 24N 0 3 E
Vic-Fézensac 20 43 47N 0 19 E
Vic-sur-Cère 20 44 59N 2 38 E
Vic-sur-Seille 19 48 45N 6 33 E
Vicenza 39 45 32N 11 31 E
Vich 32 41 58N 2 19 E
Vichuga 55 57 12N 41 55 E
Vichy 20 46 9N 3 26 E
Vicksburg, Mich., U.S.A. 114 42 10N 85 30W
Vicksburg, Miss., U.S.A. 117 32 22N 90 56W
Vico del Gargaro 41 41 54N 15 57 E
Vico, L. di 39 42 20N 12 10 E
Viçosa 127 9 28 S 36 14W
Victor, Colo., U.S.A. 116 38 43N 105 7W
Victor, N.Y., U.S.A. 112 42 58N 77 24W
Victor Harbour 97 35 30 S 138 37 E
Victoria, Argent. 124 32 40 S 60 10W
Victoria, Camer. 88 4 1N 9 10 E
Victoria, Can. 108 48 30N 123 25W
Victoria, Chile 128 38 13 S 72 20W
* Victoria, Guin. 84 10 50N 14 32W
Victoria, H. K. 75 22 16N 114 15 E
Victoria, Malay. 72 5 20N 115 14 E
Victoria, Kans., U.S.A. 116 38 52N 99 8W
Victoria, Tex., U.S.A. 117 28 50N 97 0W
Victoria □, Austral. 97 37 0 S 144 0 E
Victoria □, Zimb. 91 21 0 S 31 30 E
Victoria → 96 15 10 S 129 40 E
Victoria Beach 109 50 40N 96 35W
Victoria de las Tunas 121 20 58N 76 59W
Victoria Falls 91 17 58 S 25 52 E
Victoria, Grand L. 106 47 31N 77 30W
Victoria Harbour 106 44 45N 79 45W
Victoria I. 104 71 0N 111 0W
Victoria, L. 90 1 0 S 33 0 E
Victoria Ld. 5 75 0 S 160 0 E
Victoria, Mt. 98 8 55 S 147 32 E
Victoria Nile → 90 2 14N 31 26 E
Victoria Res. 107 48 20N 57 27W
Victoria River Downs 96 16 25 S 131 0 E
Victoria Taungdeik 67 21 15N 93 55 E
Victoria West 92 31 25 S 23 4 E
Victoriaville 107 46 4N 71 56W
Victorica 124 36 20 S 65 30W
Victorville 119 34 32N 117 18W
Vicuña 124 30 0 S 70 50W
Vicuña Mackenna 124 33 53 S 64 25W
Vidalia 115 32 13N 82 25W
Vidauban 21 43 25N 6 27 E
Vidigueira 31 38 12N 7 48W
Vidin 42 43 59N 22 50 E
Vidio, Cabo 30 43 35N 6 14W
Vidisha (Bhilsa) 68 23 28N 77 53 E
Vidöstern 49 57 5N 14 0 E
Vidra 46 45 56N 26 55 E
Viduša 42 42 55N 18 21 E
Vidzy 54 55 23N 26 37 E
Viechtach 25 49 5N 12 53 E
Viedma 128 40 50 S 63 0W
Viedma, L. 128 49 30 S 72 30W
Vieira 30 41 38N 8 8W
Viella 32 42 43N 0 44 E
Vien Pou Kha 71 20 45N 101 5 E
Vienenburg 24 51 57N 10 35 E
Vienna 117 37 29N 88 54W
Vienna = Wien 27 48 12N 16 22 E
Vienne 21 45 31N 4 53 E
Vienne □ 20 46 30N 0 42 E
Vienne → 18 47 13N 0 5 E
Vientiane 71 17 58N 102 36 E
Vientos, Paso de los 121 20 0N 74 0W
Viersen 24 51 15N 6 23 E
Vierwaldstättersee 25 47 0N 8 30 E
Vierzon 19 47 13N 2 5 E
Vieste 40 41 52N 16 14 E
Vietnam ■ 71 19 0N 106 0 E
Vieux-Boucau-les-Bains 20 43 48N 1 23W
Vif 21 45 5N 5 41 E
Vigan 73 17 35N 120 28 E
Vigan, Le 20 44 0N 3 36 E
Vigévano 38 45 18N 8 50 E
Vigia 127 0 50 S 48 5W
Vignacourt 19 50 1N 2 15 E
Vignemale, Pic du 20 42 47N 0 10W
Vigneulles 19 48 59N 5 40 E
Vignola 38 44 29N 11 0 E
Vigo 30 42 12N 8 41W
Vigo, Ría de 30 42 15N 8 45W
Vihiers 18 47 10N 0 30W
Vijayadurg 70 16 30N 73 25 E
Vijayawada (Bezwada) 70 16 31N 80 39 E
Vikedal 47 59 30N 5 55 E
Viken 49 58 39N 14 20 E
Vikersund 47 59 58N 10 2 E
Viking 108 53 7N 111 50W
Vikna 50 64 55N 10 58 E
Vikramasingapuram 70 8 40N 76 47 E
Viksjö 48 62 45N 17 26 E
Vikulovo 58 56 50N 70 40 E
Vila Aiferes Chamusca 93 24 27 S 33 0 E
Vila Caldas Xavier 91 14 28 S 33 0 E
Vila Coutinho 91 14 37 S 34 19 E
Vila da Maganja 91 17 18 S 37 30 E
Vila de João Belo = Xai-Xai 93 25 6 S 33 31 E
Vila de Junqueiro 91 15 25 S 36 58 E
Vila de Manica 91 18 58 S 32 59 E
Vila de Rei 31 39 41N 8 9W
Vila do Bispo 31 37 5N 8 53W
Vila do Chibuto 93 24 40 S 33 33 E
Vila do Conde 30 41 21N 8 45W
Vila Fontes 91 17 51 S 35 24 E
Vila Franca de Xira 31 38 57N 8 59W
Vila Gamito 91 14 12 S 33 0 E
Vila Gomes da Costa 93 24 20 S 33 37 E
Vila Luisa 93 25 45 S 32 35 E
Vila Machado 91 19 15 S 34 14 E
Vila Mouzinho 91 14 48 S 34 25 E
Vila Nova de Foscôa 30 41 5N 7 9W
Vila Nova de Ourém 31 39 40N 8 35W
Vila Novo de Gaia 30 41 4N 8 40W
Vila Paiva de Andrada 91 18 44 S 34 2 E
Vila Pouca de Aguiar 30 41 30N 7 38W
Vila Real 30 41 17N 7 48W
Vila Real de Santo António 31 37 10N 7 28W
Vila Vasco da Gama 91 14 54 S 32 14 E
Vila Velha 125 20 20 S 40 17W
Vila Veríssimo Sarmento 88 8 7 S 20 38 E
Vila Viçosa 31 38 45N 7 27W
Vilaboa 30 42 21N 8 39W
Vilaine → 18 47 30N 2 27W
Vilanculos 93 22 1 S 35 17 E
Vilar Formosa 30 40 38N 6 45W
Vilareal □ 30 41 36N 7 35W
Vilaseca-Salou 32 41 7N 1 9 E
Vîlcea □ 46 45 0N 24 10 E
Vileyka 54 54 30N 26 53 E
Vilhelmina 50 64 35N 16 39 E
Vilhena 126 12 40 S 60 5W
Viliga 59 61 36N 156 56 E
Viliya → 54 55 54N 23 53 E
Viljandi 54 58 28N 25 30 E
Vilkovo 56 45 28N 29 32 E
Villa Abecia 124 21 0 S 68 18W
Villa Ahumada 120 30 38N 106 30W
Villa Ana 124 28 28 S 59 40W
Villa Ángela 124 27 34 S 60 45W
Villa Bella 126 10 25 S 65 22W
Villa Bens = Tarfaya 80 27 55N 12 55W
Villa Cañás 124 34 0 S 61 35W
Villa Cisneros = Dakhla 80 23 50N 15 53W
Villa Colón 124 31 38 S 68 20W
Villa Constitución 124 33 15 S 60 20W
Villa de María 124 29 55 S 63 43W
Villa Dolores 124 31 58 S 65 15W
Villa Guillermina 124 28 15 S 59 29W
Villa Hayes 124 25 0 S 57 20W
Villa Iris 124 38 12 S 63 12W
Villa María 124 32 20 S 63 10W
Villa Mazán 124 28 40 S 66 30W
Villa Minozzo 38 44 21N 10 30 E
Villa Montes 124 21 10 S 63 30W
Villa Ocampo 124 28 30 S 59 20W
Villa Ojo de Agua 124 29 30 S 63 44W
Villa San Giovanni 41 38 13N 15 38 E
Villa San José 124 32 12 S 58 15W
Villa San Martín 124 28 15 S 64 9W
Villa Santina 39 46 25N 12 55 E
Villablino 30 42 57N 6 19W
Villacañas 32 39 38N 3 20W
Villacarlos 32 39 53N 4 17 E
Villacarriedo 32 43 14N 3 48W
Villacarrillo 33 38 7N 3 3W
Villacastín 30 40 46N 4 25W
Villach 26 46 37N 13 51 E
Villaciado 40 39 27N 8 45 E
Villada 30 42 15N 4 59W
Villadiego 30 42 31N 4 1W
Villadóssola 38 46 4N 8 16 E
Villafeliche 32 41 10N 1 30W
Villafranca 32 42 17N 1 46W
Villafranca de los Barros 31 38 35N 6 18W
Villafranca de los Caballeros 33 39 26N 3 21W
Villafranca del Bierzo 30 42 38N 6 50W
Villafranca del Cid 32 40 26N 0 16W
Villafranca del Panadés 32 41 21N 1 40 E
Villafranca di Verona 38 45 20N 10 51 E
Villagarcía de Arosa 30 42 34N 8 46W
Villagrán 120 24 29N 99 29W
Villaguay 124 32 0 S 59 0W
Villaharta 31 38 9N 4 54W
Villahermosa, Mexico 120 18 0N 92 50W
Villahermosa, Spain 33 38 46N 2 52W
Villaines-la-Juhel 18 48 21N 0 20W
Villajoyosa 33 38 30N 0 12W
Villalba 30 43 26N 7 40W
Villalba de Guardo 30 42 42N 4 49W
Villalcampo, Pantano de 30 41 31N 6 0W
Villalón de Campos 30 42 5N 5 4W
Villalpando 30 41 51N 5 25W
Villaluenga 30 40 2N 3 54W
Villamanán 30 42 19N 5 35W
Villamartín 31 36 52N 5 38W
Villamayor 32 39 50N 2 59W
Villamblard 20 45 2N 0 32 E
Villanova Monteleone 40 40 30N 8 28 E
Villanueva 119 35 16N 105 23W
Villanueva de Castellón 33 39 5N 0 31W
Villanueva de Córdoba 31 38 20N 4 38W
Villanueva de la Fuente 33 38 42N 2 42W
Villanueva de la Serena 31 38 59N 5 50W
Villanueva de la Sierra 30 40 12N 6 24W
Villanueva de los Castillejos 31 37 30N 7 15W
Villanueva del Arzobispo 33 38 10N 3 0W
Villanueva del Duque 31 38 20N 5 0W
Villanueva del Fresno 31 38 23N 7 10W
Villanueva y Geltrú 32 41 13N 1 40 E
Villaodrid 30 43 20N 7 11W
Villaputzu 40 39 28N 9 33 E
Villar del Arzobispo 32 39 44N 0 50W
Villar del Rey 31 39 7N 6 50W
Villarcayo 32 42 56N 3 34W
Villard-Bonnet 21 45 14N 5 53 E
Villard-de-Lans 21 45 3N 5 33 E
Villarino de los Aires 30 41 18N 6 23W
Villarosa 41 37 36N 14 9 E
Villarramiel 30 42 2N 4 55W
Villarreal 32 39 55N 0 3W
Villarrica, Chile 128 39 15 S 72 15W
Villarrica, Parag. 124 25 40 S 56 30W
Villarrobledo 33 39 18N 2 36W
Villarroya de la Sierra 32 41 27N 1 46W
Villarrubia de los Ojos 33 39 14N 3 36W
Villars 21 46 0N 5 2 E
Villarta de San Juan 33 39 15N 3 25W
Villasayas 32 41 24N 2 39W
Villaseca de los Gamitos 30 41 2N 6 7W
Villastar 32 40 17N 1 9W
Villatobas 32 39 54N 3 20W
Villavicencio, Argent. 124 32 28 S 69 0W
Villavicencio, Colomb. 126 4 9N 73 37W
Villaviciosa 30 43 32N 5 27W
Villazón 124 22 0 S 65 35W
Ville-Marie 106 47 20N 79 30W
Ville Platte 117 30 45N 92 17W
Villedieu 18 48 50N 1 12W
Villefort 20 44 28N 3 56 E
Villefranche 19 47 19N 1 46 E
Villefranche-de-Lauragais 20 43 25N 1 44 E
Villefranche-de-Rouergue 20 44 21N 2 2 E
Villefranche-du-Périgord 20 44 38N 1 5 E
Villefranche-sur-Saône 21 45 59N 4 43 E
Villel 32 40 14N 1 12W
Villemaur 19 48 14N 3 40 E
Villemur-sur-Tarn 20 43 51N 1 31 E
Villena 33 38 39N 0 52W
Villenauxe 19 48 36N 3 30 E
Villenave 20 44 46N 0 33W
Villeneuve, France 19 48 42N 2 25 E
Villeneuve, Italy 38 45 40N 7 10 E
Villeneuve-l'Archevêque 19 48 14N 3 32 E
Villeneuve-lès-Avignon 21 43 57N 4 49 E
Villeneuve-sur-Allier 20 46 40N 3 13 E
Villeneuve-sur-Lot 20 44 24N 0 42 E
Villeréal 20 44 38N 0 45 E
Villers-Bocage 18 49 3N 0 40W
Villers-Bretonneux 19 49 50N 2 30 E
Villers-Cotterêts 19 49 15N 3 4 E
Villers-Outreaux 19 50 2N 3 18 E
Villers-sur-Mer 18 49 21N 0 2W
Villersexel 19 47 33N 6 26 E
Villerupt 19 49 28N 5 55 E
Villerville 18 49 26N 0 5 E
Villiers 93 27 2 S 28 36 E
Villingen 25 48 4N 8 28 E
Villingen-Schwenningen 25 48 3N 8 29 E
Villisca 116 40 55N 94 59W
Villupuram 70 11 59N 79 31 E
Vilna 108 54 7N 111 55W
Vilnius 54 54 38N 25 19 E
Vils 26 47 33N 10 37 E
Vils → 25 48 38N 13 11 E
Vilsbiburg 25 48 27N 12 23 E
Vilshofen 25 48 38N 13 11 E
Vilskutskogo, Proliv 59 78 0N 103 0 E
Vilusi 42 42 44N 18 34 E
Vilvoorde 16 50 56N 4 26 E
Vilyuy → 59 64 24N 126 26 E
Vilyuysk 59 63 40N 121 35 E
Vimercate 38 45 38N 9 25 E
Vimiosa 30 41 35N 6 31W
Vimmerby 49 57 40N 15 55 E
Vimoutiers 18 48 57N 0 10 E
Vimperk 26 49 3N 13 46 E
Viña del Mar 124 33 0 S 71 30W
Vinaroz 32 40 30N 0 27 E
Vincennes 114 38 42N 87 29W
Vinchina 124 28 45 S 68 15W
Vindel älven → 50 63 55N 19 50 E
Vindeln 50 64 12N 19 43 E
Vinderup 49 56 29N 8 45 E
Vindhya Ra. 68 22 50N 77 0 E
Vineland 114 39 30N 75 0W
Vinga 42 46 0N 21 14 E
Vingnes 47 61 7N 10 26 E
Vinh 71 18 45N 105 38 E
Vinhais 30 41 50N 7 0W
Vinica, Hrvatska, Yugo. 39 46 20N 16 9 E
Vinica, Slovenija, Yugo. 39 45 28N 15 16 E
Vinita 117 36 40N 95 12W
Vinkovci 42 45 19N 18 48 E
Vinnitsa 56 49 15N 28 30 E
Vinson Massif 5 78 35 S 85 25W
Vinstra 47 61 37N 9 44 E
Vinton, Iowa, U.S.A. 116 42 8N 92 1W
Vinton, La., U.S.A. 117 30 13N 93 35W
Vinţu de Jos 46 46 0N 23 30 E
Viöl 24 54 32N 9 12 E
Vipava 39 45 51N 13 58 E
Vipiteno 39 46 55N 11 25 E
Viqueque 73 8 52 S 126 23 E
Vir 39 44 17N 15 3 E
Virac 73 13 30N 124 20 E
Virago Sd. 108 54 0N 132 30W
Virajpet 70 12 10N 75 50 E
Viramgam 68 23 5N 72 0 E
Viranşehir 64 37 13N 39 45 E
Virarajendrapet = Virajpet 70 12 10N 75 50 E
Viravanallur 70 8 40N 77 30 E
Virden 109 49 50N 100 56W
Vire 18 48 50N 0 53W
Vire → 18 49 20N 1 7W
Virgenes, C. 128 52 19 S 68 21W
Virgin →, Can. 109 57 2N 108 17W
Virgin →, U.S.A. 119 36 50N 114 10W
Virgin Gorda 121 18 30N 64 26W
Virgin Is. 121 18 40N 64 30W
Virginia, S. Afr. 92 28 8 S 26 55 E
Virginia, U.S.A. 116 47 30N 92 32W
Virginia □ 114 37 45N 78 0W
Virginia Beach 114 36 54N 75 58W
Virginia City, Mont., U.S.A. 118 45 18N 111 58W
Virginia City, Nev., U.S.A. 118 39 19N 119 39W
Virginia Falls 108 61 38N 125 42W
Virginiatown 106 48 9N 79 36W
Virieu-le-Grand 21 45 51N 5 39 E
Virje 42 46 4N 16 59 E
Viroqua 116 43 33N 90 57W
Virovitica 42 45 51N 17 21 E
Virpazar 42 42 14N 19 6 E
Virserum 49 57 20N 15 35 E
Virton 16 49 35N 5 32 E
Virtsu 54 58 32N 23 33 E
Virudunagar 70 9 30N 78 0 E
Vis 39 43 0N 16 10 E
Vis Kanal 39 43 4N 16 5 E
Visalia 119 36 25N 119 18W
Visayan Sea 73 11 30N 123 30 E
Visby 49 57 37N 18 18 E
Viscount Melville Sd. 4 74 10N 108 0W
Visé 16 50 44N 5 41 E
Višegrad 42 43 47N 19 17 E
Viseu, Brazil 127 1 10 S 46 5W
Viseu, Port. 30 40 40N 7 55W
Viseu □ 30 40 40N 7 55W
Vişeu de Sus 46 47 45N 24 25 E
Vishakhapatnam 70 17 45N 83 20 E
Vishnupur 69 23 8N 87 20 E
Visikoi I. 5 56 43 S 27 15W
Visingsö 49 58 2N 14 20 E
Viskafors 49 57 37N 12 50 E
Vislanda 49 56 46N 14 30 E
Vislinskil Zaliv (Zalew Wislany) 28 54 20N 19 50 E
Visnagar 68 23 45N 72 32 E
Višnja Gora 39 45 58N 14 45 E
Viso del Marqués 33 38 32N 3 34W
Viso, Mte. 38 44 38N 7 5 E
Visoko 42 43 58N 18 10 E

* Renamed Limbe

Visp Wangdu

Visp 25 46 17N 7 52 E
Visselhövede 24 52 59N 9 36 E
Vistonikos, Ormos 44 41 0N 25 7 E
Vistula = Wisła → 28 54 22N 18 55 E
Vit → 43 43 30N 24 30 E
Vitanje 39 46 25N 15 18 E
Vitebsk 54 55 10N 30 15 E
Viterbo 39 42 25N 12 8 E
Viti Levu 101 17 30 S 177 30 E
Vitiaz Str. 98 5 40 S 147 10 E
Vitigudino 30 41 1N 6 26W
Vitim 59 59 28N 112 35 E
Vitim → 59 59 26N 112 34 E
Vitina 45 37 40N 22 10 E
Vitina 42 43 17N 17 29 E
Vitória 127 20 20 S 40 22W
Vitoria 32 42 50N 2 41W
Vitória da Conquista 127 14 51 S 40 51W
Vitória de São Antão 127 8 10 S 35 20W
Vitré 18 48 8N 1 12W
Vitry-le-François 19 48 43N 4 33 E
Vitsi, Óros 44 40 40N 21 25 E
Vitteaux 19 47 24N 4 30 E
Vittel 19 48 12N 5 57 E
Vittória 41 36 58N 14 30 E
Vittório Véneto 39 45 59N 12 18 E
Vitu Is. 98 4 50 S 149 25 E
Viver 32 39 55N 0 36W
Vivero 30 43 39N 7 38W
Viviers 21 44 30N 4 40 E
Vivonne 20 46 25N 0 15 E
Vizcaíno, Desierto de 120 27 40N 113 50W
Vizcaíno, Sierra 120 27 30N 114 0W
Vizcaya □ 32 43 15N 2 45W
Vizianagaram 70 18 6N 83 30 E
Vizille 21 45 5N 5 46 E
Vizinada 39 45 20N 13 46 E
Viziru 46 45 0N 27 43 E
Vizovice 27 49 12N 17 56 E
Vizzini 41 37 9N 14 43 E
Vjosa → 44 40 37N 19 42 E
Vlaardingen 16 51 55N 4 21 E
Vlădeasa 46 46 47N 22 50 E
Vladicin Han 42 42 42N 22 1 E
Vladimir 55 56 15N 40 30 E
Vladimir Volynskiy 54 50 50N 24 18 E
Vladimirci 42 44 36N 19 45 E
Vladimirovac 42 45 1N 20 53 E
Vladimirovka, R.S.F.S.R., U.S.S.R. 57 48 27N 46 10 E
Vladimirovka, R.S.F.S.R., U.S.S.R. 57 44 45N 44 41 E
Vladimirovo 43 43 32N 23 22 E
Vladislavovka 56 45 15N 35 15 E
Vladivostok 59 43 10N 131 53 E
Vlasenica 42 44 11N 18 59 E
Vlašić 42 44 19N 17 37 E
Vlašim 26 49 40N 14 53 E
Vlasinsko Jezero 42 42 44N 22 22 E
Vlasotinci 42 42 59N 22 7 E
Vlieland 16 53 16N 4 55 E
Vlissingen 16 51 26N 3 34 E
Vlóra 44 40 32N 19 28 E
Vlóra □ 44 40 12N 20 0 E
Vlorës, Gjiri i 44 40 29N 19 27 E
Vltava → 26 50 21N 14 30 E
Vobarno 38 45 38N 10 30 E
Vočin 42 45 37N 17 33 E
Vöcklabruck 26 48 1N 13 39 E
Vodice 39 43 47N 15 47 E
Vodňany 26 49 9N 14 11 E
Vodnjan 39 44 59N 13 52 E
Vogelkop = Doberai, Jazirah 73 1 25 S 133 0 E
Vogelsberg 24 50 37N 9 15 E
Voghera 38 44 59N 9 1 E
Vohibinany 93 18 49 S 49 4 E
Vohimarina 93 13 25 S 50 0 E
Vohimena, Tanjon' i 93 25 36 S 45 8 E
Vohipeno 93 22 22 S 47 51 E
Voi 90 3 25 S 38 32 E
Void 19 48 40N 5 36 E
Voineşti, Iaşi, Romania 46 47 5N 27 27 E
Voineşti, Prahova, Romania 46 45 5N 25 14 E
Voiotia □ 45 38 20N 23 0 E
Voiron 21 45 22N 5 35 E
Voisey B. 107 56 15N 61 50W
Voitsberg 26 47 3N 15 9 E
Voiviïs Límni 44 39 30N 22 45 E
Vojens 49 55 16N 9 18 E
Vojmsjön 50 64 55N 16 40 E
Vojnik 38 46 18N 15 19 E
Vojnió 39 45 19N 15 43 E
Vojvodina, Auton. Pokrajina □ 42 45 20N 20 0 E
Vokhma 55 59 0N 46 45 E
Vokhma → 55 56 20N 46 20 E
Vokhtoga 55 58 46N 41 8 E
Volary 26 48 54N 13 52 E
Volborg 116 45 50N 105 44W
Volcano Is. 94 25 0N 141 0 E
Volchansk 55 50 17N 36 58 E
Volchayevka 59 48 40N 134 30 E
Volchya → 56 48 0N 37 0 E
Volda 47 62 9N 6 5 E
Volga 55 57 58N 38 16 E
Volga → 57 48 30N 46 0 E
Volga Hts. = Privolzhskaya V. S. 53 51 0N 46 0 E
Volgodonsk 57 47 33N 42 5 E
Volgograd 57 48 40N 44 25 E
Volgogradskoye Vdkhr. 55 50 0N 45 20 E
Volgorechensk 55 57 28N 41 14 E
Volissós 45 38 29N 25 54 E
Volkach 25 49 52N 10 14 E
Völkermarkt 26 46 39N 14 39 E
Volkhov 54 59 55N 32 15 E
Volkhov → 54 60 8N 32 20 E
Völklingen 25 49 15N 6 50 E
Volkovysk 54 53 9N 24 30 E
Volksrust 93 27 24 S 29 53 E
Vollenhove 16 52 40N 5 58 E
Vol'n'ansk 56 47 55N 35 29 E
Volnovakha 56 47 35N 37 30 E
Volochanka 59 71 0N 94 28 E
Volodarsk 55 56 12N 43 15 E
Vologda 55 59 10N 40 0 E
Volokolamsk 55 56 5N 35 57 E
Volokonovka 55 50 33N 37 52 E
Vólos 44 39 24N 22 59 E
Volosovo 54 59 27N 29 32 E
Volozhin 54 54 3N 26 30 E
Volsk 55 52 5N 47 22 E
Volta → 85 5 46N 0 41 E
Volta, L. 85 7 30N 0 15 E
Volta Redonda 125 22 31 S 44 5W
Volterra 38 43 24N 10 50 E
Voltri 38 44 25N 8 43 E
Volturara Áppula 41 41 30N 15 2 E
Volturno → 41 41 1N 13 55 E
Volubilis 82 34 2N 5 33W
Volujak 42 43 53N 17 47 E
Vólvi, L. 44 40 40N 23 34 E
Volzhsk 55 55 57N 48 23 E
Volzhskiy 57 48 56N 44 46 E
Vondrozo 93 22 49 S 47 20 E
Vónitsa 45 38 53N 20 58 E
Voorburg 16 52 5N 4 24 E
Vopnafjörður 50 65 45N 14 40W
Vorarlberg □ 26 47 20N 10 0 E
Vóras Óros 44 40 57N 21 45 E
Vorbasse 49 55 39N 9 6 E
Vorderrhein → 25 46 49N 9 25 E
Vordingborg 49 55 0N 11 54 E
Voreppe 21 45 18N 5 39 E
Voríai Sporádhes 45 39 15N 23 30 E
Vórios Evvoïkos Kólpos 45 38 45N 23 15 E
Vorkuta 52 67 48N 64 20 E
Vorma → 47 60 9N 11 27 E
Vorona → 55 51 22N 42 3 E
Voronezh, R.S.F.S.R., U.S.S.R. 55 51 40N 39 10 E
Voronezh, Ukraine, U.S.S.R. 54 51 47N 33 28 E
Voronezh → 55 51 56N 37 17 E
Vorontsovo-Aleksandrovskoye = Zelenokumsk 57 44 30N 44 1 E
Voroshilovgrad 57 48 38N 39 15 E
Vorovskoye 59 54 30N 155 50 E
Vorskla → 56 48 50N 34 10 E
Võru 54 57 48N 26 54 E
Vorupør 49 56 58N 8 22 E
Vosges 19 48 20N 7 10 E
Vosges □ 19 48 12N 6 20 E
Voskopoja 44 40 40N 20 33 E
Voskresensk 55 55 19N 38 43 E
Voskresenskoye 55 56 51N 45 30 E
Voss 47 60 38N 6 26 E
Vostochnyy Sayan 59 54 0N 96 0 E
Vostok I. 95 10 5 S 152 23W
Votice 26 49 38N 14 39 E
Votkinsk 52 57 0N 53 55 E
Votkinskoye Vdkhr. 52 57 30N 55 0 E
Vouga → 30 40 41N 8 40W
Vouillé 18 46 38N 0 10 E
Voulte-sur-Rhône, La 21 44 48N 4 46 E
Vouvray 18 47 25N 0 48 E
Voúxa, Ákra 45 35 37N 23 32 E
Vouzela 30 40 43N 8 7W
Vouziers 19 49 22N 4 40 E
Voves 19 48 15N 1 38 E
Voxna 48 61 20N 15 40 E
Vozhe Oz. 52 60 45N 39 0 E
Vozhgaly 55 58 9N 50 11 E
Voznesenka 59 56 40N 95 3 E
Voznesensk 56 47 35N 31 21 E
Voznesenye 52 61 0N 35 45 E
Vráble 27 48 15N 18 16 E
Vraćevšnica 42 44 2N 20 34 E
Vrådal 47 59 20N 8 25 E
Vraka 44 42 8N 19 28 E
Vrakhnéïka 45 38 10N 21 40 E
Vrancea □ 46 45 50N 26 45 E
Vrancei, Munții 46 46 0N 26 30 E
Vrangelya, Ostrov 59 71 0N 180 0 E
Vranica 42 43 55N 17 50 E
Vranje 42 42 34N 21 54 E
Vranjska Banja 42 42 34N 22 1 E
Vranov 27 48 53N 21 40 E
Vransko 39 46 17N 14 58 E
Vratsa 43 43 13N 23 30 E
Vrbas 42 45 40N 19 40 E
Vrbas → 42 45 8N 17 29 E
Vrbnik 39 45 4N 14 40 E
Vrbovec 39 45 53N 16 28 E
Vrbovsko 39 45 24N 15 5 E
Vrchlabí 26 50 38N 15 37 E
Vrede 93 27 24 S 29 6 E
Vredefort 92 27 0 S 26 22 E
Vredenburg 92 32 51 S 18 0 E
Vredendal 92 31 41 S 18 35 E
Vrena 49 58 54N 16 41 E
Vrgorac 42 43 12N 17 20 E
Vrhnika 39 45 58N 14 15 E
Vriddhachalam 70 11 30N 79 20 E
Vrïdi 84 5 15N 4 3W
Vrindaban 68 27 37N 77 40 E
Vrnograč 39 45 10N 15 57 E
Vrondádhes 45 38 25N 26 7 E
Vrpolje 42 45 13N 18 24 E
Vršac 42 45 8N 21 18 E
Vrsacki Kanal 42 45 15N 21 0 E
Vryburg 92 26 55 S 24 45 E
Vryheid 93 27 45 S 30 47 E
Vsetín 27 49 20N 18 0 E
Vucha → 43 42 10N 24 26 E
Vučitrn 42 42 49N 20 59 E
Vught 16 51 38N 5 20 E
Vukovar 42 45 21N 18 59 E
Vulcan, Can. 108 50 25N 113 15W
Vulcan, Romania 46 45 23N 23 17 E
Vulcan, U.S.A. 114 45 46N 87 51W
Vulcano 41 38 25N 14 58 E
Vŭlchedruma 43 43 42N 23 27 E
Vulci 39 42 23N 11 37 E
Vulkaneshty 56 45 35N 28 30 E
Vunduzi → 91 18 56 S 34 1 E
Vung Tau 71 10 21N 107 4 E
Vŭrbitsa 43 42 59N 26 40 E
Vurshets 43 43 15N 23 23 E
Vutcani 46 46 26N 27 59 E
Vuyyuru 70 16 28N 80 50 E
Vyara 68 21 8N 73 28 E
Vyasniki 55 56 10N 42 10 E
Vyatka → 52 56 30N 51 0 E
Vyatskiye Polyany 52 56 5N 51 0 E
Vyazemskiy 59 47 32N 134 45 E
Vyazma 54 55 10N 34 15 E
Vyborg 52 60 43N 28 47 E
Vychegda → 52 61 18N 46 36 E
Vychodné Beskydy 27 49 30N 22 0 E
Východočeský □ 26 50 20N 15 45 E
Východoslovenský □ 27 48 50N 21 0 E
Vyg-ozero 52 63 30N 34 0 E
Vyksa 55 55 19N 42 11 E
Vypin 70 10 10N 76 15 E
Vyrnwy, L. 12 52 48N 3 30W
Vyshniy Volochek 54 57 30N 34 30 E
Vyškov 27 49 17N 17 0 E
Vysoké Mýto 27 49 58N 10 10 E
Vysokovsk 55 56 22N 36 30 E
Vysotsk 54 51 43N 26 32 E
Vyšší Brod 26 48 37N 14 19 E
Vytegra 52 61 0N 36 27 E

W

W.A.C. Bennett Dam 108 56 2N 122 6W
Wa 84 10 7N 2 25W
Waal → 16 51 59N 4 30 E
Wabakimi L. 106 50 38N 89 45W
Wabana 107 47 40N 53 0W
Wabasca 108 55 57N 113 56W
Wabash 114 40 48N 85 46W
Wabash → 114 37 46N 88 2W
Wabeno 114 45 25N 88 40W
Wabi → 87 7 45N 40 50 E
Wabigoon L. 109 49 44N 92 44W
Wabowden 109 54 55N 98 38W
Wąbrzeźno 28 53 16N 18 57 E
Wabuk Pt. 106 55 20N 85 5W
Wabush 107 52 55N 66 52W
Wabuska 118 39 9N 119 13W
Wächtersbach 25 50 16N 9 18 E
Waco 117 31 33N 97 5W
Waconichi, L. 106 50 8N 74 0W
Wad Ban Naqa 87 16 32N 33 9 E
Wad Banda 87 13 10N 27 56 E
Wad el Haddad 87 13 50N 33 30 E
Wad en Nau 87 14 10N 33 34 E
Wad Hamid 87 16 30N 32 45 E
Wâd Medanî 87 14 28N 33 30 E
Waddān 83 29 9N 16 10 E
Waddān, Jabal 83 29 0N 16 15 E
Waddeneilanden 16 53 25N 5 10 E
Waddenzee 16 53 6N 5 10 E
Waddington 113 44 51N 75 12W
Waddington, Mt. 108 51 23N 125 15W
Waddy Pt. 99 24 58 S 153 21 E
Wadena, Can. 109 51 57N 103 47W
Wadena, U.S.A. 116 46 25N 95 8W
Wädenswil 25 47 14N 8 40 E
Wadesboro 115 35 2N 80 2W
Wadhams 108 51 30N 127 30W
Wādī ash Shāţi' 83 27 30N 15 0 E
Wādī Banī Walīd 83 31 49N 14 0 E
Wadi Gemâl 86 24 35N 35 10 E
Wadi Halfa 86 21 53N 31 19 E
Wadi Masila 63 16 30N 49 0 E
Wadi Şabāḩ 64 23 50N 48 30 E
Wadlew 28 51 31N 19 23 E
Wadowice 27 49 52N 19 30 E
Wadsworth 118 39 38N 119 22W
Wafrah 64 28 33N 47 56 E
Wageningen 16 51 58N 5 40 E
Wager B. 105 65 26N 88 40W
Wager Bay 105 65 56N 90 49W
Wagga Wagga 97 35 7 S 147 24 E
Waghete 73 4 10 S 135 50 E
Wagin 96 33 17 S 117 25 E
Wagon Mound 117 36 1N 104 44W
Wagoner 117 36 0N 95 20W
Wągrowiec 28 52 48N 17 11 E
Wahai 73 2 48 S 129 35 E
Wahiawa 110 21 30N 158 2W
Wahoo 116 41 15N 96 35W
Wahpeton 116 46 20N 96 35W
Wai 70 17 56N 73 57 E
Waiau → 101 42 47 S 173 22 E
Waiawe Ganga → 70 6 15N 81 0 E
Waibeem 73 0 30 S 132 59 E
Waiblingen 25 48 49N 9 20 E
Waidhofen, Niederösterreich, Austria 26 48 49N 15 17 E
Waidhofen, Niederösterreich, Austria 26 47 57N 14 46 E
Waigeo 73 0 20 S 130 40 E
Waihi 101 37 23 S 175 52 E
Waihou → 101 37 15 S 175 40 E
Waika 90 2 22 S 25 42 E
Waikabubak 73 9 45 S 119 25 E
Waikaremoana 101 38 42 S 177 12 E
Waikari 101 42 58 S 172 41 E
Waikato → 101 37 23 S 174 43 E
Waikerie 99 34 9 S 140 0 E
Waikokopu 101 39 3 S 177 52 E
Waikouaiti 101 45 36 S 170 41 E
Waimate 101 44 45 S 171 3 E
Wainganga → 69 18 50N 79 55 E
Waingapu 73 9 35 S 120 11 E
Wainwright, Can. 109 52 50N 110 50W
Wainwright, U.S.A. 104 70 39N 160 1W
Waiouru 101 39 28 S 175 41 E
Waipara 101 43 3 S 172 46 E
Waipawa 101 39 56 S 176 38 E
Waipiro 101 38 2 S 178 22 E
Waipu 101 35 59 S 174 29 E
Waipukurau 101 40 1 S 176 33 E
Wairakei 101 38 37 S 176 6 E
Wairarapa, L. 101 41 14 S 175 15 E
Wairoa 101 39 3 S 177 25 E
Waitaki → 101 44 56 S 171 7 E
Waitara 101 38 59 S 174 15 E
Waitsburg 118 46 15N 118 0W
Waiuku 101 37 15 S 174 45 E
Wajima 74 37 30N 137 0 E
Wajir 90 1 42N 40 5 E
Wajir □ 90 1 42N 40 20 E
Wakasa-Wan 74 35 40N 135 30 E
Wakatipu, L. 101 45 5 S 168 33 E
Wakaw 109 52 39N 105 44W
Wakayama 74 34 15N 135 15 E
Wakayama-ken □ 74 33 50N 135 30 E
Wake Forest 115 35 58N 78 30W
Wake I. 94 19 18N 166 36 E
Wakefield, N.Z. 101 41 24 S 173 5 E
Wakefield, U.K. 12 53 41N 1 31W
Wakefield, Mass., U.S.A. 113 42 30N 71 3W
Wakefield, Mich., U.S.A. 116 46 28N 89 53W
Wakema 67 16 30N 95 11 E
Wakkanai 74 45 28N 141 35 E
Wakkerstroom 93 27 24 S 30 10 E
Wakool 99 35 28 S 144 23 E
Wakool → 99 35 5 S 143 33 E
Wakre 73 0 19 S 131 5 E
Wakuach L. 107 55 34N 67 32W
Walamba 91 13 30 S 28 42 E
Wałbrzych 28 50 45N 16 18 E
Walbury Hill 13 51 22N 1 28W
Walcha 99 30 55 S 151 31 E
Walcheren 16 51 30N 3 35 E
Walcott 118 41 50N 106 55W
Wałcz 28 53 17N 16 27 E
Wald 25 47 17N 8 56 E
Waldbröl 24 50 52N 7 36 E
Waldeck 24 51 12N 9 4 E
Walden, Colo., U.S.A. 118 40 47N 106 20W
Walden, N.Y., U.S.A. 113 41 32N 74 13W
Waldport 118 44 30N 124 2W
Waldron, Can. 109 50 53N 102 35W
Waldron, U.S.A. 117 34 52N 94 4W
Waldshut 25 47 37N 8 12 E
Walembele 84 10 30N 1 58W
Wales □ 11 52 30N 3 30W
Walewale 85 10 21N 0 50W
Walgett 97 30 0 S 148 5 E
Walgreen Coast 5 75 15 S 105 0W
Walhalla, Austral. 99 37 56 S 146 29 E
Walhalla, U.S.A. 109 48 55N 97 55W
Walker 116 47 4N 94 35W
Walker L., Man., Can. 109 54 42N 95 57W
Walker L., Qué., Can. 107 50 20N 67 11W
Walker L., U.S.A. 118 38 56N 118 46W
Walkerston 98 21 11 S 149 8 E
Walkerton 112 44 10N 81 10W
Wall 116 44 0N 102 14W
Walla Walla 118 46 3N 118 25W
Wallabadah 98 17 57 S 142 15 E
Wallace, Idaho, U.S.A. 118 47 30N 116 0W
Wallace, N.C., U.S.A. 115 34 44N 77 59W
Wallace, Nebr., U.S.A. 116 40 51N 101 12W
Wallaceburg 106 42 34N 82 23W
Wallachia = Valahia 46 44 35N 25 0 E
Wallal 99 26 32 S 146 7 E
Wallaroo 97 33 56 S 137 39 E
Wallasey 12 53 26N 3 2W
Walldürn 25 49 34N 9 23 E
Wallerawang 99 33 25 S 150 4 E
Wallingford, U.K. 12 51 40N 1 15W
Wallingford, U.S.A. 113 41 27N 72 50W
Wallis Arch. 94 13 18 S 176 10W
Wallowa 118 45 40N 117 35W
Wallowa, Mts. 118 45 20N 117 30W
Wallsend, Austral. 99 32 55 S 151 40 E
Wallsend, U.K. 12 54 59N 1 30W
Wallula 118 46 3N 118 59W
Wallumbilla 99 26 33 S 149 9 E
Walmer 92 33 57 S 25 35 E
Walmsley, L. 109 63 25N 108 36W
Walney, Isle of 12 54 5N 3 15W
Walnut Ridge 117 36 7N 90 58W
Walsall 13 52 36N 1 59W
Walsenburg 117 37 42N 104 45W
Walsh 117 37 28N 102 15W
Walsh → 98 16 31 S 143 42 E
Walsh P.O. 98 16 40 S 144 0 E
Walsrode 24 52 51N 9 37 E
Waltair 70 17 44N 83 23 E
Walterboro 115 32 53N 80 40W
Walters 117 34 25N 98 20W
Waltershausen 24 50 53N 10 33 E
Waltham 113 42 22N 71 12W
Waltham Sta. 106 45 57N 76 57W
Waltman 118 43 8N 107 15W
Walton 113 42 12N 75 9W
Walvisbaai 92 23 0 S 14 28 E
Wamba, Kenya 90 0 58N 37 19 E
Wamba, Zaïre 90 2 10N 27 57 E
Wamego 116 39 14N 96 22W
Wamena 73 4 4 S 138 57 E
Wampsville 113 43 4N 75 42W
Wamsasi 73 3 27 S 126 7 E
Wana 68 32 20N 69 32 E
Wanaaring 99 29 38 S 144 9 E
Wanaka L. 101 44 33 S 169 7 E
Wan'an 77 26 26N 114 49 E
Wanapiri 73 4 30 S 135 59 E
Wanapitei L. 106 46 45N 80 40W
Wanbi 99 34 46 S 140 17 E
Wanda Shan 76 46 0N 132 0 E
Wanderer 91 19 36 S 30 1 E
Wandiwash 70 12 30N 79 30 E
Wandoan 97 26 5 S 149 55 E
Wang Kai (Ghâbat el Arab) 87 9 3N 29 23 E
Wang Saphung 71 17 18N 101 46 E
Wanga 90 2 58N 29 12 E
Wangal 73 6 8 S 134 9 E
Wanganella 99 35 6 S 144 49 E
Wanganui 101 39 56 S 175 3 E
Wangaratta 97 36 21 S 146 19 E
Wangdu 76 38 40N 115 7 E

Wangerooge Wetzlar

Wangerooge	24	53 47N	7 52 E
Wangi	90	1 58 S	40 58 E
Wangiwangi	73	5 22 S	123 37 E
Wangjiang	77	30 10N	116 42 E
Wangqing	76	43 12N	129 42 E
Wankaner	68	22 35N	71 0 E
* Wankie	91	18 18 S	26 30 E
* Wankie Nat. Park	92	19 0 S	26 30 E
Wanless	109	54 11N	101 21W
Wanning	77	18 48N	110 22 E
Wannon →	100	37 38 S	141 25 E
Wanquan	76	40 50N	114 40 E
Wanxian	75	30 42N	108 20 E
Wanyuan	77	32 4N	108 3 E
Wanzai	77	28 7N	114 30 E
Wapakoneta	114	40 35N	84 10W
Wapato	118	46 30N	120 25W
Wapawekka L.	109	54 55N	104 40W
Wappingers Falls	113	41 35N	73 56W
Wapsipinicon →	116	41 44N	90 19W
Waranga Res.	100	36 32 S	145 5 E
Warangal	70	17 58N	79 35 E
Waratah	99	41 30 S	145 30 E
Waratah B.	99	38 54 S	146 5 E
Warburg	24	51 29N	9 10 E
Warburton	99	37 47 S	145 42 E
Warburton →	97	28 4 S	137 28 E
Ward	101	41 49 S	174 11 E
Ward →	99	26 28 S	146 6 E
Ward Cove	108	55 25N	132 43W
Ward Hunt, C.	98	8 2 S	148 10 E
Wardak □	65	34 0N	68 0 E
Warden	93	27 50 S	29 0 E
Wardha	68	20 45N	78 39 E
Wardlow	108	50 56N	111 31W
Ware, Can.	108	57 26N	125 41W
Ware, U.S.A.	113	42 16N	72 15W
Wareham	113	41 45N	70 44W
Waren	24	53 30N	12 41 E
Warendorf	24	51 57N	8 0 E
Warialda	97	29 29 S	150 33 E
Wariap	73	1 30 S	134 5 E
Warka	28	51 47N	21 12 E
Warkopi	73	1 12 S	134 9 E
Warley	13	52 30N	2 0W
Warm Springs, Mont., U.S.A.	118	46 11N	112 48W
Warm Springs, Nev., U.S.A.	119	38 16N	116 32W
Warman	109	52 19N	106 30W
Warmbad, Namibia	92	28 25 S	18 42 E
Warmbad, S. Afr.	93	24 51 S	28 19 E
Warmeriville	19	49 20N	4 13 E
Warnambool Downs	98	22 48 S	142 52 E
Warnemünde	24	54 9N	12 5 E
Warner	108	49 17N	112 12W
Warner Range, Mts.	118	41 30 S	120 20W
Warner Robins	115	32 41N	83 36W
Warnow →	24	54 6N	12 9 E
Warora	70	20 14N	79 1 E
Warracknabeal	100	36 9 S	142 26 E
Warragul	99	38 10 S	145 58 E
Warrego →	97	30 24 S	145 21 E
Warrego Ra.	97	24 58 S	146 0 E
Warren, Austral.	99	31 42 S	147 51 E
Warren, Ark., U.S.A.	117	33 35N	92 3W
Warren, Minn., U.S.A.	116	48 12N	96 46W
Warren, Ohio, U.S.A.	114	41 18N	80 52W
Warren, Pa., U.S.A.	114	41 52N	79 10W
Warrenpoint	15	54 7N	6 15W
Warrensburg	116	38 45N	93 45W
Warrenton, S. Afr.	92	28 9 S	24 47 E
Warrenton, U.S.A.	118	46 11N	123 59W
Warrenville	99	25 48 S	147 22 E
Warri	85	5 30N	5 41 E
Warrina	96	28 12 S	135 50 E
Warrington, U.K.	12	53 25N	2 38W
Warrington, U.S.A.	115	30 22N	87 16W
Warrnambool	97	38 25 S	142 30 E
Warroad	116	48 54N	95 19W
Warsa	73	0 47 S	135 55 E
Warsaw, Ind., U.S.A.	114	41 14N	85 50W
Warsaw, N.Y., U.S.A.	112	42 46N	78 10W
Warsaw, Ohio, U.S.A.	112	40 20N	82 0W
Warsaw = Warszawa	28	52 13N	21 0 E
Warstein	24	51 26N	8 20 E
Warszawa	28	52 13N	21 0 E
Warszawa □	28	52 30N	21 0 E
Warta	28	51 43N	18 38 E
Warta →	28	52 35N	14 39 E
Waru	73	3 30 S	130 36 E
Warud	68	21 30N	78 16 E
Warwick, Austral.	97	28 10 S	152 1 E
Warwick, U.K.	13	52 17N	1 36W
Warwick, U.S.A.	114	41 43N	71 25W
Warwick □	13	52 20N	1 30W
Wasa	108	49 45N	115 50W
Wasaga Beach	112	44 31N	80 1W
Wasatch, Ra.	118	40 30N	111 15W
Wasbank	93	28 15 S	30 9 E
Wasco, Calif., U.S.A.	119	35 37N	119 16W
Wasco, Oreg., U.S.A.	118	45 36N	120 46W
Waseca	116	44 3N	93 31W
Wasekamio L.	109	56 45N	108 45W
Wash, The	12	52 58N	0 20 E
Washago	112	44 45N	79 20W
Washburn, N.D., U.S.A.	116	47 17N	101 0W
Washburn, Wis., U.S.A.	116	46 38N	90 55W
Washington, D.C., U.S.A.	114	38 52N	77 0W
Washington, Ga., U.S.A.	115	33 45N	82 45W
Washington, Ind., U.S.A.	114	38 40N	87 8W
Washington, Iowa, U.S.A.	116	41 20N	91 45W
Washington, Mo, U.S.A.	116	38 35N	91 1W
Washington, N.C., U.S.A.	115	35 35N	77 1W
Washington, N.J., U.S.A.	113	40 45N	74 59W
Washington, Pa., U.S.A.	114	40 10N	80 20W
Washington, Utah, U.S.A.	119	37 10N	113 30W
Washington □	118	47 45N	120 30W
† Washington I., Pac. Oc.	95	4 43N	160 25W
Washington I., U.S.A.	114	45 24N	86 54W
Washington Mt.	114	44 15N	71 18W
Wasian	73	1 47 S	133 19 E
Wasilków	28	53 12N	23 13 E
Wasior	73	2 43 S	134 30 E
Waskaiowaka, L.	109	56 33N	96 23W
Waskesiu Lake	109	53 55N	106 5W
Wasm	86	18 2N	41 32 E
Wassenaar	16	52 8N	4 24 E
Wasserburg	25	48 4N	12 15 E
Wasserkuppe	24	50 30N	9 56 E
Wassy	19	48 30N	4 58 E
Waswanipi	106	49 40N	76 29W
Waswanipi, L.	106	49 35N	76 40W
Watangpon	73	4 29 S	120 25 E
Water Park Pt.	98	22 56 S	150 47 E
Water Valley	117	34 9N	89 38W
Waterberg, Namibia	92	20 30 S	17 18 E
Waterberg, S. Afr.	93	24 14 S	28 0 E
Waterbury, Conn., U.S.A.	114	41 32N	73 0W
Waterbury, Vt., U.S.A.	113	44 22N	72 44W
Waterbury L.	109	58 10N	104 22W
Waterdown	112	43 20N	79 53W
Waterford, Can.	112	42 56N	80 17W
Waterford, Ireland	15	52 16N	7 8W
Waterford □	15	52 10N	7 40W
Waterford Harb.	15	52 10N	6 58W
Waterhen L., Man., Can.	109	52 10N	99 40W
Waterhen L., Sask., Can.	109	54 28N	108 25W
Waterloo, Belg.	16	50 43N	4 25 E
Waterloo, Ont., Can.	106	43 30N	80 32W
Waterloo, Qué., Can.	113	45 22N	72 32W
Waterloo, S. Leone	84	8 26N	13 8W
Waterloo, Ill., U.S.A.	116	38 22N	90 6W
Waterloo, Iowa, U.S.A.	116	42 27N	92 20W
Waterloo, N.Y., U.S.A.	112	42 54N	76 53W
Watersmeet	116	46 15N	89 12W
Waterton Lakes Nat. Park	108	49 5N	114 15W
Watertown, Conn., U.S.A.	113	41 36N	73 7W
Watertown, N.Y., U.S.A.	114	43 58N	75 57W
Watertown, S.D., U.S.A.	116	44 57N	97 5W
Watertown, Wis., U.S.A.	116	43 15N	88 45W
Waterval-Boven	93	25 40 S	30 18 E
Waterville, Can.	113	45 16N	71 54W
Waterville, Me., U.S.A.	107	44 35N	69 40W
Waterville, N.Y., U.S.A.	113	42 56N	75 23W
Waterville, Pa., U.S.A.	112	41 19N	77 21W
Waterville, Wash., U.S.A.	118	47 38N	120 1W
Watervliet	114	42 46N	73 43W
Wates	73	7 53 S	110 6 E
Watford, Can.	112	42 57N	81 53W
Watford, U.K.	13	51 38N	0 23W
Watford City	116	47 50N	103 23W
Wathaman →	109	57 16N	102 59W
Watkins Glen	113	42 25N	76 55W
Watling I. = San Salvador	121	24 0N	74 40W
Watonga	117	35 51N	98 24W
Watrous, Can.	109	51 40N	105 25W
Watrous, U.S.A.	117	35 50N	104 55W
Watsa	90	3 4N	29 30 E
Watseka	114	40 45N	87 45W
Watson	109	52 10N	104 30W
Watson Lake	104	60 6N	128 49W
Watsonville	119	36 55N	121 49W
Wattwil	25	47 18N	9 6 E
Watuata = Batuata	73	6 12 S	122 42 E
Watubela, Kepulauan	73	4 28 S	131 35 E
Wau	98	7 21 S	146 47 E
Waubamik	112	45 27N	80 1W
Waubay	116	45 22N	97 17W
Waubra	99	37 21 S	143 39 E
Wauchope	99	31 28 S	152 45 E
Wauchula	115	27 35N	81 50W
Waugh	109	49 40N	95 20W
Waukegan	114	42 22N	87 54W
Waukesha	114	43 0N	88 15W
Waukon	116	43 14N	91 33W
Wauneta	116	40 27N	101 25W
Waupaca	116	44 22N	89 8W
Waupun	116	43 38N	88 44W
Waurika	117	34 12N	98 0W
Wausau	116	44 57N	89 40W
Wautoma	116	44 3N	89 20W
Wauwatosa	114	43 6N	87 59W
Wave Hill	96	17 32 S	131 0 E
Waveney →	13	52 24N	1 20 E
Waverley	101	39 46 S	174 37 E
Waverly, Iowa, U.S.A.	116	42 40N	92 30W
Waverly, N.Y., U.S.A.	114	42 0N	76 33W
Wavre	16	50 43N	4 38 E
Wâw	87	7 45N	28 1 E
Waw al Kabir	81	25 20N	17 20 E
Wāw al Kabīr	83	25 20N	16 43 E
Wāw an Nāmūs	83	24 55N	17 46 E
Wawa, Can.	106	47 59N	84 47W
Wawa, Nigeria	85	9 54N	4 27 E
Wawa, Sudan	86	20 30N	30 22 E
Wawanesa	109	49 36N	99 40W
Wawoi →	98	7 48 S	143 16 E
Waxahachie	117	32 22N	96 53W
Waxweiler	25	50 6N	6 22 E
Wayabula Rau	73	2 29N	128 17 E
Wayatinah	99	42 19 S	146 27 E
Waycross	115	31 12N	82 25W
Wayi	87	5 8N	30 10 E
Wayne, Nebr., U.S.A.	116	42 16N	97 0W
Wayne, W. Va., U.S.A.	114	38 15N	82 27W
Waynesboro, Ga., U.S.A.	115	33 6N	82 1W
Waynesboro, Miss., U.S.A.	115	31 40N	88 39W
Waynesboro, Pa., U.S.A.	114	39 46N	77 32W
Waynesboro, Va., U.S.A.	114	38 4N	78 57W
Waynesburg	114	39 54N	80 12W
Waynesville	115	35 31N	83 0W
Waynoka	117	36 38N	98 53W
Wāzin	83	31 58N	10 40 E
Wazirabad	68	32 30N	74 8 E
Wda →	28	53 25N	18 29 E
We	72	5 51N	95 18 E
Weald, The	13	51 7N	0 9 E
Wear →	12	54 55N	1 22W
Weatherford, Okla., U.S.A.	117	35 30N	98 45W
Weatherford, Tex., U.S.A.	117	32 45N	97 48W
Weaverville	118	40 44N	122 56W
Webb City	117	37 9N	94 30W
Webster, Mass., U.S.A.	113	42 4N	71 54W
Webster, N.Y., U.S.A.	112	43 11N	77 27W
Webster, S.D., U.S.A.	116	45 24N	97 33W
Webster, Wis., U.S.A.	116	45 53N	92 25W
Webster City	116	42 30N	93 50W
Webster Green	116	38 38N	90 20W
Webster Springs	114	38 30N	80 25W
Weda	73	0 21N	127 50 E
Weda, Teluk	73	0 30N	127 50 E
Weddell I.	128	51 50 S	61 0W
Weddell Sea	5	72 30 S	40 0W
Wedderburn	99	36 26 S	143 33 E
Wedge I.	96	30 50 S	115 11 E
Wedgeport	107	43 44N	65 59W
Wedza	91	18 40 S	31 33 E
Wee Waa	99	30 11 S	149 26 E
Weed	118	41 29N	122 22W
Weedsport	113	43 3N	76 35W
Weedville	112	41 17N	78 28W
Weemelah	99	29 2 S	149 15 E
Weenen	93	28 48 S	30 7 E
Weener	24	53 10N	7 23 E
Weert	16	51 15N	5 43 E
Wegierska-Gorka	27	49 36N	19 7 E
Wegliniec	28	51 18N	15 10 E
Węgorzewo	28	54 13N	21 43 E
Węgrów	28	52 24N	22 0 E
Wei He →, Hebei, China	76	36 10N	115 45 E
Wei He →, Shaanxi, China	77	34 38N	110 15 E
Weida	24	50 47N	12 3 E
Weiden	25	49 40N	12 10 E
Weifang	76	36 44N	119 7 E
Weihai	76	37 30N	122 6 E
Weilburg	24	50 28N	8 17 E
Weilheim	25	47 50N	11 9 E
Weimar	24	51 0N	11 20 E
Weinan	77	34 31N	109 29 E
Weingarten	25	47 49N	9 39 E
Weinheim	25	49 33N	8 40 E
Weipa	97	12 40 S	141 50 E
Weir →, Austral.	99	28 20 S	149 50 E
Weir →, Can.	109	56 54N	93 21W
Weir River	109	56 49N	94 6W
Weirton	112	40 23N	80 35W
Weiser	118	44 10N	117 0W
Weishan	77	34 47N	117 5 E
Weissenburg	25	49 2N	10 58 E
Weissenfels	24	51 11N	12 0 E
Weisswasser	24	51 30N	14 36 E
Weitra	26	48 41N	14 54 E
Weiyuan	76	35 7N	104 10 E
Weiz	26	47 13N	15 39 E
Weizhou Dao	77	21 0N	109 5 E
Wejherowo	28	54 35N	18 12 E
Wekusko	109	54 30N	99 45W
Wekusko L.	109	54 40N	99 50W
Welby	109	50 33N	101 29W
Welch	114	37 29N	81 36W
Weldya	87	11 50N	39 34 E
Welega □	87	9 25N	34 20 E
Welkite	87	8 15N	37 42 E
Welkom	92	28 0 S	26 50 E
Welland	106	43 0N	79 15W
Welland →	12	52 43N	0 10W
Wellesley Is.	97	16 42 S	139 30 E
Wellin	16	50 5N	5 6 E
Wellingborough	13	52 18N	0 41W
Wellington, Austral.	97	32 35 S	148 59 E
Wellington, Can.	106	43 57N	77 20W
Wellington, N.Z.	101	41 19 S	174 46 E
Wellington, S. Afr.	92	33 38 S	18 57 E
Wellington, U.K.	13	50 58N	3 13W
Wellington, Col., U.S.A.	116	40 43N	105 0W
Wellington, Kans., U.S.A.	117	37 15N	97 25W
Wellington, Nev., U.S.A.	118	38 47N	119 28W
Wellington, Ohio, U.S.A.	112	41 9N	82 12W
Wellington, Tex., U.S.A.	117	34 55N	100 13W
Wellington □	101	40 8 S	175 36 E
Wellington, I.	128	49 30 S	75 0W
Wellington, L.	99	38 6 S	147 20 E
Wellington (Telford)	12	52 42N	2 31W
Wells, Norfolk, U.K.	12	52 57N	0 51 E
Wells, Somerset, U.K.	13	51 12N	2 39W
Wells, Me., U.S.A.	113	43 18N	70 35W
Wells, Minn., U.S.A.	116	43 44N	93 45W
Wells, Nev., U.S.A.	118	41 8N	115 0W
Wells Gray Prov. Park	108	52 30N	120 15W
Wells L.	96	26 44 S	123 15 E
Wells River	113	44 9N	72 4W
Wellsboro	114	41 45N	77 20W
Wellsburg	112	40 15N	80 36W
Wellsville, Mo., U.S.A.	116	39 4N	91 30W
Wellsville, N.Y., U.S.A.	114	42 9N	77 53W
Wellsville, Ohio, U.S.A.	114	40 36N	80 40W
Wellsville, Utah, U.S.A.	118	41 35N	111 59W
Wellton	119	32 39N	114 6W
Welmel, Wabi →	87	5 38N	40 47 E
Welna →	28	52 46N	17 32 E
Welo □	87	11 50N	39 48 E
Wels	26	48 9N	14 1 E
Welshpool	13	52 40N	3 9W
Welwyn	109	50 20N	101 30W
Wem	12	52 52N	2 45W
Wembere →	90	4 10 S	34 15 E
Wen Xian	77	32 43N	104 36 E
Wenatchee	118	47 30N	120 17W
Wenchang	77	19 38N	110 42 E
Wenchi	84	7 46N	2 8W
Wenchow = Wenzhou	75	28 0N	120 38 E
Wendell	118	42 50N	114 42W
Wendeng	76	37 15N	122 5 E
Wendesi	73	2 30 S	134 17 E
Wendo	87	6 40N	38 27 E
Wendover	118	40 49N	114 1W
Wengcheng	77	24 22N	113 50 E
Wenlock	98	13 6 S	142 58 E
Wenlock →	97	12 2 S	141 55 E
Wensu	75	41 15N	80 10 E
Wentworth	97	34 2 S	141 54 E
Wenut	73	3 11 S	133 19 E
Wenxi	77	35 20N	111 10 E
Wenzhou	75	28 0N	120 38 E
Weott	118	40 19N	123 56W
Wepener	92	29 42 S	27 3 E
Werda	92	25 24 S	23 15 E
Werdau	24	50 45N	12 20 E
Werder, Ethiopia	63	6 58N	45 1 E
Werder, Ger.	24	52 23N	12 56 E
Werdohl	24	51 15N	7 47 E
Wereilu	87	10 40N	39 28 E
Weri	73	3 10 S	132 38 E
Werne	24	51 38N	7 38 E
Werneck	25	49 59N	10 6 E
Wernigerode	24	51 49N	10 45 E
Werra →	24	51 26N	9 39 E
Werribee	99	37 54 S	144 40 E
Werrimull	99	34 25 S	141 38 E
Werris Creek	99	31 18 S	150 38 E
Wersar	73	1 30 S	131 55 E
Wertach →	25	48 24N	10 53 E
Wertheim	25	49 44N	9 32 E
Wertingen	25	48 33N	10 41 E
Wesel	24	51 39N	6 34 E
Weser →	24	53 33N	8 30 E
Wesiri	73	7 30 S	126 30 E
Wesleyville, Can.	107	49 8N	53 36W
Wesleyville, U.S.A.	112	42 9N	80 1W
Wessel Is.	97	11 10 S	136 45 E
Wesselburen	24	54 11N	8 53 E
Wessington	116	44 30N	98 40W
Wessington Springs	116	44 10N	98 35W
West	117	31 50N	97 5W
West B.	117	29 5N	89 27W
West Bend	114	43 25N	88 10W
West Bengal □	69	23 0N	88 0 E
West Branch	114	44 16N	84 13W
West Bromwich	13	52 32N	2 1W
West Chazy	113	44 49N	73 28W
West Chester	114	39 58N	75 36W
West Columbia	117	29 10N	95 38W
West Des Moines	116	41 30N	93 45W
West Falkland	128	51 40 S	60 0W
West Frankfurt	116	37 56N	89 0W
West Germany ■	24	52 0N	9 0 E
West Glamorgan □	13	51 40N	3 55W
West Hartford	113	41 45N	72 45W
West Haven	113	41 18N	72 57W
West Helena	117	34 30N	90 40W
West Ice Shelf	5	67 0 S	85 0 E
West Indies	121	15 0N	70 0W
West Looe	13	50 21N	4 29W
West Lorne	112	42 36N	81 36W
West Lunga →	91	13 6 S	24 39 E
West Magpie →	107	51 2N	64 42W
West Memphis	117	35 5N	90 11W
West Midlands □	13	52 30N	1 55W
West Monroe	117	32 32N	92 7W
West Moors	12	50 49N	1 50W
West Newton	112	40 14N	79 46W
West Nicholson	91	21 2 S	29 20 E
West Palm Beach	115	26 44N	80 3W
West Pittston	113	41 19N	75 49W
West Plains	117	36 45N	91 50W
West Point, Ga., U.S.A.	115	32 54N	85 10W
West Point, Miss., U.S.A.	115	33 36N	88 38W
West Point, Nebr., U.S.A.	116	41 50N	96 43W
West Point, Va., U.S.A.	114	37 35N	76 47W
West Pokot □	90	1 30N	35 15 E
West Road →	108	53 18N	122 53W
West Rutland	114	43 38N	73 0W
West Schelde → = Westerschelde	16	51 25N	3 25 E
West Siberian Plain	60	62 0N	75 0 E
West Sussex □	13	50 55N	0 30W
West-Terschelling	16	53 22N	5 13 E
West Virginia □	114	39 0N	81 0W
West-Vlaanderen □	16	51 0N	3 0 E
West Wyalong	100	33 56 S	147 10 E
West Yellowstone	118	44 47N	111 4W
West Yorkshire □	12	53 45N	1 40W
Westbrook, Maine, U.S.A.	115	43 40N	70 22W
Westbrook, Tex., U.S.A.	117	32 25N	101 0W
Westbury	99	41 30 S	146 51 E
Westby	116	48 52N	104 3W
Westerland	24	54 51N	8 20 E
Western □, Kenya	90	0 30N	34 30 E
Western □, Uganda	90	1 45N	31 30 E
Western □, Zambia	91	15 15 S	24 30 E
Western Australia □	96	25 0 S	118 0 E
Western Ghats	70	14 0N	75 0 E
Western Isles □	14	57 30N	7 10W
Western Samoa ■	101	14 0 S	172 0W
Westernport	114	39 30N	79 5W
Westerschelde →	16	51 25N	3 25 E
Westerstede	24	53 15N	7 55 E
Westerwald	24	50 39N	8 0 E
Westfield, Mass., U.S.A.	113	42 9N	72 49W
Westfield, N.Y., U.S.A.	112	42 20N	79 38W
Westfield, Pa., U.S.A.	112	41 54N	77 32W
Westhope	116	48 55N	101 0W
Westland □	101	43 33 S	169 59 E
Westland Bight	101	42 55 S	170 5 E
Westlock	108	54 9N	113 55W
Westmeath □	15	53 30N	7 30W
Westminster	114	39 34N	77 1W
Westmorland	119	33 2N	115 42W
Weston, Malay.	72	5 10N	115 35 E
Weston, Oreg., U.S.A.	118	45 50N	118 30W
Weston, W. Va., U.S.A.	114	39 3N	80 29W
Weston I.	106	52 33N	79 36W
Weston-super-Mare	13	51 20N	2 59W
Westport, Can.	113	44 40N	76 25W
Westport, Ireland	15	53 44N	9 31W
Westport, N.Z.	101	41 46 S	171 37 E
Westport, U.S.A.	118	46 48N	124 4W
Westray, Can.	109	53 36N	101 24W
Westray, U.K.	14	59 18N	3 0W
Westree	106	47 26N	81 34W
Westview	108	49 50N	124 31W
Westville, Ill., U.S.A.	114	40 3N	87 36W
Westville, Okla., U.S.A.	117	36 0N	94 33W
Westwood	118	40 26N	121 0W
Wetar	73	7 30 S	126 30 E
Wetaskiwin	108	52 55N	113 24W
Wethersfield	113	41 43N	72 40W
Wetteren	16	51 0N	3 53 E
Wetzlar	24	50 33N	8 30 E

* Renamed Hwange

† Renamed Teraina

Wewak Workington

Wewak 98 3 38 S 143 41 E
Wewaka 117 35 10N 96 35W
Wexford 15 52 20N 6 28W
Wexford □ 15 52 20N 6 25W
Wexford Harb. 15 52 20N 6 25W
Weyburn 109 49 40N 103 50W
Weyburn L. 108 63 0N 117 59W
Weyer 26 47 51N 14 40 E
Weyib → 87 7 15N 40 15 E
Weymouth, Can. 107 44 30N 66 1W
Weymouth, U.K. 13 50 36N 2 28W
Weymouth, U.S.A. 113 42 13N 70 53W
Weymouth, C. 97 12 37 S 143 27 E
Whakatane 101 37 57 S 177 1 E
Whale → 107 58 15N 67 40W
Whale Cove 104 62 11N 92 36W
Whales, B. of 5 78 0 S 165 0W
Whalsay 14 60 22N 1 0W
Whangamomona 101 39 8 S 174 44 E
Whangarei 101 35 43 S 174 21 E
Whangarei Harbour 101 35 45 S 174 28 E
Wharfe → 12 53 55N 1 30W
Wharfedale 12 54 7N 2 4W
Wharton, N.J., U.S.A. 113 40 53N 74 36W
Wharton, Pa., U.S.A. 112 41 31N 78 1W
Wharton, Tex., U.S.A. 117 29 20N 96 6W
Wheatland 116 42 4N 104 58W
Wheatley 112 42 6N 82 27W
Wheaton 116 45 50N 96 29W
Wheeler, Oreg., U.S.A. 118 45 50N 123 57W
Wheeler, Tex., U.S.A. 117 35 29N 100 15W
Wheeler → 109 57 25N 105 30W
Wheeler Pk., N. Mex., U.S.A. 119 36 34N 105 25W
Wheeler Pk., Nev., U.S.A. 119 38 57N 114 15W
Wheeling 114 40 2N 80 41W
Whernside 12 54 14N 2 24W
Whidbey I. 108 48 15N 122 40W
Whidbey Is. 96 34 30 S 135 3 E
Whiskey Gap 108 49 0N 113 3W
Whiskey Jack L. 109 58 23N 101 55W
Whistler 115 30 50N 88 10W
Whitby, Can. 112 43 52N 78 56W
Whitby, U.K. 12 54 29N 0 37W
White →, Ark., U.S.A. 117 33 53N 91 3W
White →, Colo., U.S.A. 118 40 8N 109 41W
White →, Ind., U.S.A. 114 38 25N 87 44W
White →, S.D., U.S.A. 116 43 45N 99 30W
White B. 107 50 0N 56 35W
White Bear Res. 107 48 10N 57 5W
White Bird 118 45 46N 116 21W
White Butte 116 46 23N 103 19W
White City 116 38 50N 96 45W
White Cliffs 99 30 50 S 143 10 E
White Deer 117 35 30N 101 8W
White Hall 116 39 25N 90 27W
White Haven 113 41 3N 75 47W
White I. 101 37 30 S 177 13 E
White L., Can. 113 45 18N 76 31W
White L., U.S.A. 117 29 45N 92 30W
White Mts., Calif., U.S.A. 119 37 30N 118 15W
White Mts., N.H., U.S.A. 113 44 15N 71 15W
White Nile = Nîl el Abyad → 87 15 38N 32 31 E
White Nile Dam 87 15 24N 32 30 E
White Otter L. 106 49 5N 91 55W
White Pass 104 59 40N 135 3W
White Plains 113 41 2N 73 44W
White River, Can. 106 48 35N 85 20W
White River, S. Afr. 93 25 20 S 31 00 E
White River, U.S.A. 116 43 34N 100 45W
White River Junc. 113 43 38N 72 20W
White Russia = Byelorussian S.S.R. □ 54 53 30N 27 0 E
White Sea = Beloye More 52 66 30N 38 0 E
White Sulphur Springs, Mont., U.S.A. 118 46 35N 110 54W
White Sulphur Springs, W. Va., U.S.A. 114 37 50N 80 16W
White Volta (Volta Blanche) → 85 9 10N 1 15W
Whitecliffs 101 43 26 S 171 55 E
Whitecourt 108 54 10N 115 45W
Whiteface 117 33 35N 102 40W
Whitefield 113 44 23N 71 37W
Whitefish 118 48 25N 114 22W
Whitefish L. 109 62 41N 106 48W
Whitefish Pt. 114 46 45N 85 0W
Whitegull, L. 107 55 27N 64 17W
Whitehall, Mich., U.S.A. 114 43 21N 86 20W
Whitehall, Mont., U.S.A. 118 45 52N 112 4W
Whitehall, N.Y., U.S.A. 114 43 32N 73 28W
Whitehall, Wis., U.S.A. 116 44 20N 91 19W
Whitehaven 12 54 33N 3 35W
Whitehorse 104 60 43N 135 3W
Whitehorse, Vale of 13 51 37N 1 30W
Whiteman Ra. 98 5 55 S 150 0 E
Whitemark 99 40 7 S 148 3 E
Whitemouth 109 49 57N 95 58W
Whiteplains 84 6 28N 10 40W
Whitesail, L. 108 53 35N 127 45W
Whitesboro, N.Y., U.S.A. 113 43 8N 75 20W
Whitesboro, Tex., U.S.A. 117 33 40N 96 58W
Whiteshell Prov. Park 109 50 0N 95 40W
Whitetail 116 48 54N 105 15W
Whiteville 115 34 20N 78 40W
Whitewater 114 42 50N 88 45W
Whitewater Baldy, Mt. 119 33 20N 108 44W
Whitewater L. 106 50 50N 89 10W
Whitewood, Austral. 98 21 28 S 143 30 E
Whitewood, Can. 109 50 20N 102 20W
Whitfield 99 36 42 S 146 24 E
Whithorn 14 54 44N 4 25W
Whitianga 101 36 47 S 175 41 E
Whitman 113 42 4N 70 55W
Whitmire 115 34 33N 81 40W
Whitney 106 45 31N 78 14W
Whitney, Mt. 119 36 35N 118 14W
Whitney Pt. 113 42 19N 75 59W
Whitstable 13 51 21N 1 2 E
Whitsunday I. 97 20 15 S 149 4 E
Whittier 104 60 46N 148 48W
Whittlesea 99 37 27 S 145 9 E
Whitwell 115 35 15N 85 30W
Wholdaia L. 109 60 43N 104 20W
Whyalla 97 33 2 S 137 30 E
Whyjonta 99 29 41 S 142 28 E
Wiarton 106 44 40N 81 10W
Wiawso 84 6 10N 2 25W
Wiazów 28 50 50N 17 10 E
Wibaux 116 47 0N 104 13W
Wichita 117 37 40N 97 20W
Wichita Falls 117 33 57N 98 30W
Wick 14 58 26N 3 5W
Wickenburg 119 33 58N 112 45W
Wickett 117 31 37N 102 58W
Wickham, C. 99 39 35 S 143 57 E
Wickliffe 112 41 36N 81 29W
Wicklow 15 53 0N 6 2W
Wicklow □ 15 52 59N 6 25W
Wicklow Hd. 15 52 59N 6 3W
Wicklow Mts. 15 53 0N 6 30W
Widawa 28 51 27N 18 51 E
Widawka 28 51 7N 19 36 E
Widnes 12 53 22N 2 44W
Więcbork 28 53 21N 17 30 E
Wiedenbrück 24 51 52N 8 15 E
Wiek 24 54 37N 13 17 E
Wielbark 28 53 24N 20 55 E
Wieleń 28 52 53N 16 9 E
Wieliczka 27 50 0N 20 5 E
Wieluń 28 51 15N 18 34 E
Wien 27 48 12N 16 22 E
Wiener Neustadt 27 47 49N 16 16 E
Wieprz →, Koszalin, Poland 28 54 26N 16 35 E
Wieprz →, Lublin, Poland 28 51 34N 21 49 E
Wierden 16 52 22N 6 35 E
Wieruszów 28 51 19N 18 9 E
Wiesbaden 25 50 7N 8 17 E
Wiesental 25 49 15N 8 30 E
Wigan 12 53 33N 2 38W
Wiggins, Colo., U.S.A. 116 40 16N 104 3W
Wiggins, Miss., U.S.A. 117 30 53N 89 9W
Wight, I. of 13 50 40N 1 20W
Wigry, Jezioro 28 54 2N 23 8 E
Wigtown 14 54 52N 4 27W
Wigtown B. 14 54 46N 4 15W
Wil 25 47 28N 9 3 E
Wilamowice 27 49 55N 19 9 E
Wilber 116 40 34N 96 59W
Wilberforce 112 45 2N 78 13W
Wilberforce, C. 97 11 54 S 136 35 E
Wilburton 117 34 55N 95 15W
Wilcannia 97 31 30 S 143 26 E
Wilcox 112 41 34N 78 43W
Wildbad 25 48 44N 8 32 E
Wildeshausen 24 52 54N 8 25 E
Wildon 26 46 52N 15 31 E
Wildrose 116 48 36N 103 11W
Wildspitze 26 46 53N 10 53 E
Wildwood 114 38 59N 74 46W
Wilga → 28 51 52N 21 18 E
Wilhelm II Coast 5 68 0 S 90 0 E
Wilhelm Mt. 98 5 50 S 145 1 E
Wilhelm-Pieck-Stadt Guben 24 51 59N 14 48 E
Wilhelmsburg, Austria 26 48 6N 15 36 E
Wilhelmsburg, Ger. 24 53 28N 10 1 E
Wilhelmshaven 24 53 30N 8 9 E
Wilhelmstal 92 21 58 S 16 21 E
Wilkes Barre 114 41 15N 75 52W
Wilkes Land 5 69 0 S 120 0 E
Wilkes Sub-Glacial Basin 5 75 0 S 130 0 E
Wilkesboro 115 36 10N 81 9W
Wilkie 109 52 27N 108 42W
Wilkinsburg 112 40 26N 79 50W
Willamina 118 45 9N 123 32W
Willandra Billabong Creek → 99 33 22 S 145 52 E
Willapa, B. 118 46 44N 124 0W
Willard, N. Mex., U.S.A. 119 34 35N 106 1W
Willard, Utah, U.S.A. 118 41 28N 112 1W
Willcox 119 32 13N 109 53W
Willemstad 121 12 5N 69 0W
William → 109 59 8N 109 19W
Williams 119 35 16N 112 11W
Williams Lake 108 52 10N 122 10W
Williamsburg, Ky., U.S.A. 115 36 45N 84 10W
Williamsburg, Pa., U.S.A. 112 40 27N 78 14W
Williamsburg, Va., U.S.A. 114 37 17N 76 44W
Williamson, N.Y., U.S.A. 112 43 14N 77 15W
Williamson, W. Va., U.S.A. 114 37 46N 82 17W
Williamsport 114 41 18N 77 1W
Williamston 115 35 50N 77 5W
Williamstown, Austral. 99 37 51 S 144 52 E
Williamstown, Mass., U.S.A. 113 42 41N 73 12W
Williamstown, N.Y., U.S.A. 113 43 25N 75 54W
Williamsville 117 37 0N 90 33W
Willimantic 113 41 45N 72 12W
Williston, S. Afr. 92 31 20 S 20 53 E
Williston, Fla., U.S.A. 115 29 25N 82 28W
Williston, N.D., U.S.A. 116 48 10N 103 35W
Williston L. 108 56 0N 124 0W
Willits 118 39 28N 123 17W
Willmar 116 45 5N 95 0W
Willoughby 112 41 38N 81 26W
Willow Bunch 109 49 20N 105 35W
Willow L. 108 62 10N 119 8W
Willow Lake 116 44 40N 97 40W
Willow River 108 54 6N 122 28W
Willow Springs 117 37 0N 92 0W
Willowlake → 108 62 42N 123 8W
Willowmore 92 33 15 S 23 30 E
Willows, Austral. 98 23 39 S 147 25 E
Willows, U.S.A. 118 39 30N 122 10W
Wills Cr. → 98 22 43 S 140 2 E
Wills Pt. 117 32 42N 95 57W
Willunga 99 35 15 S 138 30 E
Wilmette 114 42 6N 87 44W
Wilmington, Austral. 99 32 39 S 138 7 E
Wilmington, Del., U.S.A. 114 39 45N 75 32W
Wilmington, Ill., U.S.A. 114 41 19N 88 10W
Wilmington, N.C., U.S.A. 115 34 14N 77 54W
Wilmington, Ohio, U.S.A. 114 39 27N 83 50W
Wilpena Cr. → 99 31 25 S 139 29 E
Wilsall 118 45 59N 110 40W
Wilson 115 35 44N 77 54W
Wilson → 99 27 38 S 141 24 E
Wilson, Mt. 119 37 55N 108 3W
Wilson's Promontory 97 38 55 S 146 25 E
Wilster 24 53 55N 9 23 E
Wilton, U.K. 13 51 5N 1 52W
Wilton, U.S.A. 116 47 12N 100 47W
Wiltshire □ 13 51 20N 2 0W
Wiltz 16 49 57N 5 55 E
Wiluna 96 26 36 S 120 14 E
Wimereux 19 50 45N 1 37 E
Wimmera 97 36 30 S 142 0 E
Wimmera → 99 36 8 S 141 56 E
Winam G. 90 0 20 S 34 15 E
Winburg 92 28 30 S 27 2 E
Winchendon 113 42 40N 72 3W
Winchester, U.K. 13 51 4N 1 19W
Winchester, Conn., U.S.A. 113 41 53N 73 9W
Winchester, Idaho, U.S.A. 118 46 11N 116 32W
Winchester, Ind., U.S.A. 114 40 10N 84 56W
Winchester, Ky., U.S.A. 114 38 0N 84 8W
Winchester, Mass., U.S.A. 113 42 28N 71 10W
Winchester, N.H., U.S.A. 113 42 47N 72 22W
Winchester, Tenn., U.S.A. 115 35 11N 86 8W
Winchester, Va., U.S.A. 114 39 14N 78 8W
Wind → 118 43 8N 108 12W
Wind River Range 118 43 0N 109 30W
Windber 114 40 14N 78 50W
Windermere, L. 12 54 20N 2 57W
Windfall 108 54 12N 116 13W
Windflower L. 108 62 52N 118 30W
Windhoek 92 22 35 S 17 4 E
Windischgarsten 26 47 42N 14 21 E
Windom 116 43 48N 95 3W
Windorah 97 25 24 S 142 36 E
Window Rock 119 35 47N 109 4W
Windrush → 13 51 48N 1 35W
Windsor, Austral. 99 33 37 S 150 50 E
Windsor, N.S., Can. 107 44 59N 64 5W
Windsor, Newf., Can. 107 48 57N 55 40W
Windsor, Ont., Can. 106 42 18N 83 0W
Windsor, U.K. 13 51 28N 0 36W
Windsor, Col., U.S.A. 116 40 33N 104 45W
Windsor, Conn., U.S.A. 113 41 50N 72 40W
Windsor, Mo., U.S.A. 116 38 32N 93 31W
Windsor, N.Y., U.S.A. 113 42 5N 75 37W
Windsor, Vt., U.S.A. 114 43 30N 72 25W
Windsorton 92 28 16 S 24 44 E
Windward Is., Atl. Oc. 121 13 0N 63 0W
Windward Is., Pac. Oc. 95 18 0 S 149 0W
Windward Passage = Vientos, Paso de los 121 20 0N 74 0W
Windy L. 109 60 20N 100 2W
Winefred L. 109 55 30N 110 30W
Winejok 87 9 1N 27 30 E
Winfield 117 37 15N 97 0W
Wingen 99 31 54 S 150 54 E
Wingham, Austral. 99 31 48 S 152 22 E
Wingham, Can. 106 43 55N 81 20W
Winifred 118 47 30N 109 28W
Winisk 106 55 20N 85 15W
Winisk → 106 55 17N 85 5W
Winisk L. 106 52 55N 87 22W
Wink 117 31 49N 103 9W
Winkler 109 49 10N 97 56W
Winklern 26 46 52N 12 52 E
Winlock 118 46 29N 122 56W
Winneba 85 5 25N 0 36W
Winnebago 116 43 43N 94 8W
Winnebago L. 114 44 0N 88 20W
Winnemucca 118 41 0N 117 45W
Winnemucca, L. 118 40 25N 119 21W
Winner 116 43 23N 99 52W
Winnetka 114 42 8N 87 46W
Winnett 118 47 2N 108 21W
Winnfield 117 31 57N 92 38W
Winnibigoshish L. 116 47 25N 94 12W
Winnipeg 109 49 54N 97 9W
Winnipeg → 109 50 38N 96 19W
Winnipeg Beach 109 50 30N 96 58W
Winnipeg, L. 109 52 0N 97 0W
Winnipegosis 109 51 39N 99 55W
Winnipegosis L. 109 52 30N 100 0W
Winnipesaukee, L. 113 43 38N 71 21W
Winnsboro, La., U.S.A. 117 32 10N 91 41W
Winnsboro, S.C., U.S.A. 115 34 23N 81 5W
Winnsboro, Tex., U.S.A. 117 32 56N 95 15W
Winokapau, L. 107 53 15N 62 50W
Winona, Miss., U.S.A. 117 33 30N 89 42W
Winona, Wis., U.S.A. 116 44 2N 91 39W
Winooski 114 44 31N 73 11W
Winschoten 16 53 9N 7 3 E
Winsen 24 53 21N 10 11 E
Winslow 119 35 2N 110 41W
Winsted 113 41 55N 73 5W
Winston-Salem 115 36 7N 80 15W
Winter Garden 115 28 33N 81 35W
Winter Haven 115 28 0N 81 42W
Winter Park 115 28 34N 81 19W
Winterberg 24 51 12N 8 30 E
Winters 117 31 58N 99 58W
Winterset 116 41 18N 94 0W
Wintersville 112 40 22N 80 38W
Winterswijk 16 51 58N 6 43 E
Winterthur 25 47 30N 8 44 E
Winthrop, Minn., U.S.A. 116 44 31N 94 25W
Winthrop, Wash., U.S.A. 118 48 27N 120 6W
Winton, Austral. 97 22 24 S 143 3 E
Winton, N.Z. 101 46 8 S 168 20 E
Winton, N.C., U.S.A. 115 36 25N 76 58W
Winton, Pa., U.S.A. 113 41 27N 75 33W
Wintzenheim 19 48 4N 7 17 E
Wipper → 24 51 17N 11 10 E
Wirral 12 53 25N 3 0W
Wisbech 12 52 39N 0 10 E
Wisconsin □ 116 44 30N 90 0W
Wisconsin → 116 43 0N 91 15W
Wisconsin Dells 116 43 38N 89 45W
Wisconsin Rapids 116 44 25N 89 50W
Wisdom 118 45 37N 113 27W
Wishaw 14 55 46N 3 55W
Wishek 116 46 20N 99 35W
Wisła 27 49 38N 18 53 E
Wisła → 28 54 22N 18 55 E
Wisłok → 27 50 13N 22 32 E
Wisłoka → 27 50 27N 21 23 E
Wismar 24 53 53N 11 23 E
Wisner 116 42 0N 96 46W
Wissant 19 50 52N 1 40 E
Wissembourg 19 49 2N 7 57 E
Wistoka → 27 49 50N 21 28 E
Wisznice 28 51 48N 23 13 E
Witbank 93 25 51 S 29 14 E
Witdraai 92 26 58 S 20 48 E
Witham → 12 53 3N 0 8W
Withernsea 12 53 43N 0 2 E
Witkowo 28 52 26N 17 45 E
Witney 13 51 47N 1 29W
Witnossob → 92 26 55 S 20 37 E
Wittdün 24 54 38N 8 23 E
Witten 24 51 26N 7 19 E
Wittenberg 24 51 51N 12 39 E
Wittenberge 24 53 0N 11 44 E
Wittenburg 24 53 30N 11 4 E
Wittenoom 96 22 15 S 118 20 E
Wittingen 24 52 43N 10 43 E
Wittlich 25 50 0N 6 54 E
Wittmund 24 53 39N 7 45 E
Wittow 24 54 37N 13 21 E
Wittstock 24 53 10N 12 30 E
Witzenhausen 24 51 20N 9 50 E
Wkra → 28 52 27N 20 44 E
Władysławowo 28 54 48N 18 25 E
Wlen 28 51 0N 15 39 E
Wlingi 73 8 5 S 112 25 E
Włocławe □ 28 52 50N 19 10 E
Włocławek 28 52 40N 19 3 E
Włodawa 28 51 33N 23 31 E
Włoszczowa 28 50 50N 19 55 E
Woburn 113 42 31N 71 7W
Wodonga 99 36 5 S 146 50 E
Wodzisław Śląski 27 50 1N 18 26 E
Woerth 19 48 57N 7 45 E
Woëvre, Plaine de la 19 49 15N 5 45 E
Wokam 73 5 45 S 134 28 E
Woking 108 55 35N 118 50W
Wolbrom 28 50 24N 19 45 E
Wołczyn 28 51 1N 18 3 E
Woldegk 24 53 27N 13 35 E
Wolf → 108 60 17N 132 33W
Wolf Creek 118 47 1N 112 2W
Wolf L. 108 60 24N 131 40W
Wolf Point 116 48 6N 105 40W
Wolfe I. 106 44 7N 76 20W
Wolfenbüttel 24 52 10N 10 33 E
Wolfenden 108 52 0N 119 25W
Wolfsberg 26 46 50N 14 52 E
Wolfsburg 24 52 27N 10 49 E
Wolgast 24 54 3N 13 46 E
Wolhusen 25 47 4N 8 4 E
Wolin, Poland 28 53 50N 14 37 E
Wolin, Poland 28 54 0N 14 40 E
Wollaston, Islas 128 55 40 S 67 30W
Wollaston L. 109 58 7N 103 10W
Wollaston Pen. 104 69 30N 115 0W
Wollondilly → 100 34 12 S 150 18 E
Wollongong 97 34 25 S 150 54 E
Wolmaransstad 92 27 12 S 26 13 E
Wolmirstedt 24 52 15N 11 35 E
Wołomin 28 52 19N 21 15 E
Wołów 28 51 20N 16 38 E
Wolseley, Austral. 99 36 23 S 140 54 E
Wolseley, Can. 109 50 25N 103 15W
Wolseley, S. Afr. 92 33 26 S 19 7 E
Wolstenholme Fjord 4 76 0N 70 0W
Wolsztyn 28 52 8N 16 5 E
Wolvega 16 52 52N 6 0 E
Wolverhampton 13 52 35N 2 6W
Wondai 97 26 20 S 151 49 E
Wonder Gorge 91 14 40 S 29 0 E
Wongalarroo L. 99 31 32 S 144 0 E
Wŏnju 76 37 22N 127 58 E
Wonosari 73 7 58 S 110 36 E
Wŏnsan 76 39 11N 127 27 E
Wonthaggi 97 38 37 S 145 37 E
Woocalla 99 31 42 S 137 12 E
Wood Buffalo Nat. Park 108 59 0N 113 41W
Wood L. 109 55 17N 103 17W
Wood Lake 116 42 38N 100 14W
Woodbridge 112 43 47N 79 36W
Woodburn 99 29 6 S 153 23 E
Woodend 99 37 20 S 144 33 E
Woodland 118 38 40N 121 50W
Woodlark I. 98 9 10 S 152 50 E
Woodpecker 108 53 30N 122 40W
Woodridge 109 49 20N 96 9W
Woodroffe, Mt. 96 26 20 S 131 45 E
Woodruff, Ariz., U.S.A. 119 34 51N 110 1W
Woodruff, Utah, U.S.A. 118 41 30N 111 4W
Woods, L., Austral. 96 17 50 S 133 30 E
Woods, L., Can. 107 54 30N 65 13W
Woods, L. of the 109 49 15N 94 45W
Woodside 100 38 31 S 146 52 E
Woodstock, Austral. 98 19 35 S 146 50 E
Woodstock, N.B., Can. 107 46 11N 67 37W
Woodstock, Ont., Can. 106 43 10N 80 45W
Woodstock, U.K. 13 51 51N 1 20W
Woodstock, Ill., U.S.A. 116 42 17N 88 30W
Woodstock, Vt., U.S.A. 113 43 37N 72 31W
Woodsville 114 44 10N 72 0W
Woodville, N.Z. 101 40 20 S 175 53 E
Woodville, U.S.A. 117 30 45N 94 25W
Woodward 117 36 24N 99 28W
Woolamai, C. 99 38 30 S 145 23 E
Woombye 99 26 40 S 152 55 E
Woomera 97 31 30 S 137 10 E
Woonona 100 34 21 S 150 54 E
Woonsocket 114 42 0N 71 30W
Woonsockett 116 44 5N 98 15W
Wooramel → 96 25 47 S 114 10 E
Wooster 114 40 48N 81 55W
Worcester, S. Afr. 92 33 39 S 19 27 E
Worcester, U.K. 13 52 12N 2 12W
Worcester, Mass., U.S.A. 114 42 14N 71 49W
Worcester, N.Y., U.S.A. 113 42 35N 74 45W
Wörgl 26 47 29N 12 3 E
Workington 12 54 39N 3 34W

Worksop Yining

Worksop 12 53 19N 1 9W
Workum 16 52 59N 5 26 E
Worland 118 44 0N 107 59W
Wormhoudt 19 50 52N 2 28 E
Worms 25 49 37N 8 21 E
Wörth 25 49 1N 12 24 E
Wortham 117 31 48N 96 27W
Wörther See 26 46 37N 14 10 E
Worthing 13 50 49N 0 21W
Worthington 116 43 35N 95 36W
Wosi 73 0 15 S 128 0 E
Wou-han = Wuhan 75 30 31N 114 18 E
Wour 83 21 14N 16 0 E
Wowoni 73 4 5 S 123 5 E
Wozniki 28 50 35N 19 4 E
Wrangell 104 56 30N 132 25W
Wrangell, I. 108 56 20N 132 10W
Wrangell Mts. 104 61 40N 143 30W
Wrath, C. 14 58 38N 5 0W
Wray 116 40 8N 102 18W
Wrekin, The 12 52 41N 2 35W
Wrens 115 33 13N 82 23W
Wrexham 12 53 5N 3 0W
Wriezen 24 52 43N 14 9 E
Wright, Can. 108 51 52N 121 40W
Wright, Phil. 73 11 42N 125 2 E
Wrightson, Mt. 119 31 43N 110 56W
Wrigley 104 63 16N 123 37W
Wrocław 28 51 5N 17 5 E
Wrocław □ 28 51 0N 17 0 E
Wronki 28 52 41N 16 21 E
Września 28 52 21N 17 36 E
Wschowa 28 51 48N 16 20 E
Wu Jiang → 75 29 40N 107 20 E
Wuchang 76 44 55N 127 5 E
Wuchuan 77 28 25N 108 3 E
Wuding He → 76 37 2N 110 23 E
Wugang 77 26 44N 110 35 E
Wugong Shan 77 27 30N 114 0 E
Wuhan 75 30 31N 114 18 E
Wuhsi = Wuxi 75 31 33N 120 18 E
Wuhu 75 31 22N 118 21 E
Wukari 85 7 51N 9 42 E
Wulehe 85 8 39N 0 0
Wuliaru 73 7 27 S 131 0 E
Wulumuchi = Ürümqi 75 43 45N 87 45 E
Wum 85 6 24N 10 2 E
Wuning 77 29 17N 115 5 E
Wunnummin L. 106 52 55N 89 10W
Wunsiedel 25 50 2N 12 0 E
Wunstorf 24 52 26N 9 29 E
Wuntho 67 23 55N 95 45 E
Wuping 77 25 5N 116 5 E
Wuppertal, Ger. 24 51 15N 7 8 E
Wuppertal, S. Afr. 92 32 13 S 19 12 E
Wuqing 76 39 23N 117 4 E
Wurung 98 19 13 S 140 38 E
Würzburg 25 49 46N 9 55 E
Wurzen 24 51 21N 12 45 E
Wushan 77 31 7N 109 54 E
Wustrow 24 54 4N 11 33 E
Wutach → 25 47 37N 8 15 E
Wutongqiao 75 29 22N 103 50 E
Wuwei, Anhui, China 77 31 18N 117 54 E
Wuwei, Gansu, China 75 37 57N 102 34 E
Wuxi, Jiangsu, China 75 31 33N 120 18 E
Wuxi, Sichuan, China 77 31 23N 109 35 E
Wuxing 77 30 51N 120 8 E
Wuyi, Hebei, China 76 37 46N 115 56 E
Wuyi, Zhejiang, China 77 28 52N 119 50 E
Wuyi Shan 75 27 0N 117 0 E
Wuying 76 47 53N 129 56 E
Wuyo 85 10 23N 11 50 E
Wuyuan 76 41 2N 108 20 E
Wuzhai 76 38 54N 111 48 E
Wuzhi Shan 75 18 45N 109 45 E
Wuzhong 76 38 2N 106 12 E
Wuzhou 75 23 30N 111 18 E
Wyaaba Cr. → 98 16 27 S 141 35 E
Wyalusing 113 41 40N 76 16W
Wyandotte 114 42 14N 83 13W
Wyandra 97 27 12 S 145 56 E
Wyangala Res. 100 33 54 S 149 0 E
Wyara, L. 99 28 42 S 144 14 E
Wycheproof 99 36 0 S 143 17 E
Wye → 13 51 36N 2 40W
Wyk 24 54 41N 8 33 E
Wymondham 13 52 45N 0 42W
Wymore 116 40 10N 96 40W
Wynberg 92 34 2 S 18 28 E
Wyndham, Austral. 96 15 33 S 128 3 E
Wyndham, N.Z. 101 46 20 S 168 51 E
Wyndmere 116 46 23N 97 7W
Wynne 117 35 15N 90 50W
Wynnum 99 27 27 S 153 9 E
Wynyard 109 51 45N 104 10W
Wyoming □ 110 42 48N 109 0W
Wyong 99 33 14 S 151 24 E
Wyrzysk 28 53 10N 17 17 E
Wysoka 28 53 13N 17 2 E
Wysokie 28 50 55N 22 40 E
Wysokie Mazowieckie 28 52 55N 22 30 E
Wyszków 28 52 36N 21 25 E
Wyszogród 28 52 23N 20 9 E
Wytheville 114 37 0N 81 3W

X

Xai-Xai 93 25 6 S 33 31 E
Xainza 75 30 58N 88 35 E
Xangongo 92 16 45 S 15 0 E
Xanten 24 51 40N 6 27 E
Xánthi 44 41 10N 24 58 E
Xánthi □ 44 41 10N 24 58 E
Xapuri 126 10 35 S 68 35W
Xau, L. 92 21 15 S 24 44 E
Xavantina 125 21 15 S 52 48W
Xenia 114 39 42N 83 57W
Xi Jiang → 75 22 5N 113 20 E
Xi Xian 76 36 41N 110 58 E
Xiachengzi 76 44 40N 130 18 E
Xiachuan Dao 77 21 40N 112 40 E
Xiaguan 75 25 32N 100 16 E
Xiajiang 77 27 30N 115 10 E
Xiamen 75 24 25N 118 4 E
Xi'an 77 34 15N 109 0 E
Xianfeng 77 29 40N 109 8 E
Xiang Jiang → 75 28 55N 112 50 E
Xiangfan 75 32 2N 112 8 E
Xiangning 76 35 58N 110 50 E
Xiangtan 75 27 51N 112 54 E
Xiangxiang 77 27 43N 112 28 E
Xiangyang 75 32 1N 112 8 E
Xiangyin 77 28 38N 112 54 E
Xiangzhou 77 23 58N 109 40 E
Xianju 77 28 51N 120 44 E
Xianyang 77 34 20N 108 40 E
Xiao Hinggan Ling 75 49 0N 127 0 E
Xiaogan 77 30 52N 113 55 E
Xiapu 75 26 54N 119 59 E
Xichang 75 27 51N 102 19 E
Xichuan 77 33 0N 111 30 E
Xieng Khouang 71 19 17N 103 25 E
Xifeng 77 27 7N 106 42 E
Xigazê 75 29 5N 88 45 E
Xihe 77 34 2N 105 20 E
Xiliao He → 76 43 32N 123 35 E
Xilin 77 24 30N 105 6 E
Xilókastron 45 38 4N 22 43 E
Xin Xian 76 38 22N 112 46 E
Xinavane 93 25 2 S 32 47 E
Xinbin 76 41 40N 125 2 E
Xincheng 77 24 5N 108 39 E
Xinfeng 77 25 27N 114 58 E
Xing'an 75 25 38N 110 40 E
Xingan 77 27 46N 115 20 E
Xingcheng 76 40 40N 120 45 E
Xingguo 77 26 21N 115 21 E
Xinghua 77 32 58N 119 48 E
Xinghua Wan 77 25 15N 119 20 E
Xingning 77 24 3N 115 42 E
Xingren 75 25 24N 105 11 E
Xingshan 77 31 15N 110 45 E
Xingtai 76 37 3N 114 32 E
Xingu → 127 1 30 S 51 53W
Xingyang 77 34 45N 112 52 E
Xinhua 77 27 42N 111 13 E
Xiniás, L. 45 39 2N 22 12 E
Xining 75 36 34N 101 40 E
Xinjiang 76 35 34N 111 11 E
Xinjiang Uygur Zizhiqu □ 75 42 0N 86 0 E
Xinjin 76 39 25N 121 58 E
Xinle 76 38 25N 114 40 E
Xinmin 76 41 59N 122 50 E
Xinning 77 26 28N 110 50 E
Xinxiang 77 35 18N 113 50 E
Xinyang 75 32 6N 114 3 E
Xinzheng 77 34 20N 113 45 E
Xinzhou 77 19 43N 109 17 E
Xinzhu 75 24 49N 120 57 E
Xiongyuecheng 76 40 12N 122 5 E
Xiping 77 33 22N 114 0 E
Xique-Xique 127 10 50 S 42 40W
Xiuyan 76 40 18N 123 11 E
Xixabangma Feng 67 28 20N 85 40 E
Xixiang 77 33 0N 107 44 E
Xizang □ 75 32 0N 88 0 E
Xuancheng 77 30 56N 118 43 E
Xuan'en 77 30 0N 109 30 E
Xuanhan 77 31 18N 107 38 E
Xuanhua 76 40 40N 115 2 E
Xuchang 77 34 2N 113 48 E
Xuguit Qi 76 49 17N 120 44 E
Xunke 76 49 35N 128 27 E
Xupu 77 27 53N 110 32 E
Xuwen 77 20 20N 110 10 E
Xuyong 77 28 10N 105 22 E
Xuzhou 77 34 18N 117 10 E

Y

Ya 'Bad 62 32 27N 35 10 E
Yaamba 98 23 8 S 150 22 E
Ya'an 75 29 58N 103 5 E
Yaapeet 99 35 45 S 142 3 E
Yabassi 85 4 30N 9 57 E
Yabelo 87 4 50N 38 8 E
Yablanitsa 43 43 2N 24 5 E
Yablonovy Khrebet 59 53 0N 114 0 E
Yabrīn 64 23 17N 48 58 E
Yacheng 77 18 22N 109 6 E
Yacuiba 124 22 0 S 63 43W
Yadgir 70 16 45N 77 5 E
Yadkin → 115 35 23N 80 3W
Yadrin 55 55 57N 46 12 E
Yagaba 85 10 14N 1 20W
Yagodnoye 59 62 33N 149 40 E
Yagoua 88 10 20N 15 13 E
Yagur 62 32 45N 35 4 E
Yahila 90 0 13N 24 28 E
Yahk 108 49 6N 116 10W
Yahuma 88 1 0N 23 10 E
Yajua 85 11 27N 12 49 E
Yakima 118 46 42N 120 30W
Yakima → 118 47 0N 120 30W
Yako 84 12 59N 2 15W
Yakoruda 43 42 1N 23 29 E
Yakut A.S.S.R. □ 59 62 0N 130 0 E
Yakutat 104 59 29N 139 44W
Yakutsk 59 62 5N 129 50 E
Yala 71 6 33N 101 18 E
Yalabusha → 117 33 30N 90 12W
Yalboroo 98 20 50 S 148 40 E
Yale 112 43 9N 82 47W
Yalgoo 96 28 16 S 116 39 E
Yalinga 88 6 33N 23 10 E
Yalkubul, Punta 120 21 32N 88 37W
Yalleroi 98 24 3 S 145 42 E
Yallourn 97 38 10 S 146 18 E
Yalong Jiang → 75 26 40N 101 55 E
Yalpukh, Oz. 46 45 30N 28 41 E
Yalta 56 44 30N 34 10 E
Yalu Chiang → 76 41 30N 126 30 E
Yalu He → 76 46 56N 123 30 E
Yalu Jiang → 76 40 0N 124 22 E
Yalutorovsk 58 56 41N 66 12 E
Yam Kinneret 62 32 45N 35 35 E
Yamagata 74 38 15N 140 15 E
Yamagata □ 74 38 30N 140 0 E
Yamaguchi 74 34 10N 131 32 E
Yamaguchi □ 74 34 20N 131 40 E
Yamal, Poluostrov 58 71 0N 70 0 E
Yamama 64 24 5N 47 30 E
Yamanashi □ 74 35 40N 138 40 E
Yamantau 52 54 20N 57 40 E
Yamantau, Gora 52 54 15N 58 6 E
Yamba 99 29 26 S 153 23 E
Yâmbiô 87 4 35N 28 16 E
Yambol 43 42 30N 26 36 E
Yamdena 73 7 45 S 131 20 E
Yamil 85 12 53N 8 4 E
Yamma-Yamma, L. 97 26 16 S 141 20 E
Yampa → 118 40 37N 108 59W
Yampi Sd. 96 16 8 S 123 38 E
Yampol 56 48 15N 28 15 E
Yamrat 85 10 11N 9 55 E
Yamrukchal 43 42 44N 24 52 E
Yamuna (Jumna) → 68 25 30N 81 53 E
Yamzho Yumco 75 28 48N 90 35 E
Yan 85 10 5N 12 11 E
Yan → 70 9 0N 81 10 E
Yana → 59 71 30N 136 0 E
Yanac 99 36 8 S 141 25 E
Yanai 74 33 58N 132 7 E
Yanam 70 16 47N 82 15 E
Yan'an 76 36 35N 109 26 E
Yanaul 52 56 25N 55 0 E
Yanbu 'al Baḥr 64 24 0N 38 5 E
Yancannia 99 30 12 S 142 35 E
Yanchang 76 36 43N 110 1 E
Yancheng, Henan, China 77 33 35N 114 0 E
Yancheng, Jiangsu, China 77 33 23N 120 8 E
Yanchi 76 37 48N 107 20 E
Yanchuan 76 36 51N 110 10 E
Yanco 100 34 38 S 146 27 E
Yandaran 98 24 43 S 152 6 E
Yanfolila 84 11 11N 8 9W
Yangambi 90 0 47N 24 20 E
Yangch'ü = Taiyuan 76 37 52N 112 33 E
Yangchun 75 22 11N 111 48 E
Yanggao 76 40 21N 113 55 E
Yangi-Yer 58 40 17N 68 48 E
Yangjiang 75 21 50N 110 59 E
Yangquan 76 37 58N 113 31 E
Yangshan 77 24 30N 112 40 E
Yangshuo 77 24 48N 110 29 E
Yangtze Kiang = Chang Jiang → 75 31 20N 121 52 E
Yangxin 77 29 50N 115 12 E
Yangzhou 77 32 21N 119 26 E
Yanhee Res. 71 17 30N 98 45 E
Yanji 76 42 59N 129 30 E
Yankton 116 42 55N 97 25W
Yanna 99 26 58 S 146 0 E
Yanonge 90 0 35N 24 38 E
Yanqi 75 42 5N 86 35 E
Yanqing 76 40 30N 115 58 E
Yanshan 77 28 15N 117 41 E
Yantabulla 99 29 21 S 145 0 E
Yantai 76 37 34N 121 22 E
Yanting 77 31 11N 105 24 E
Yantra → 43 43 40N 25 37 E
Yanzhou 76 35 35N 116 49 E
Yao 81 12 56N 17 33 E
Yaoundé 88 3 50N 11 35 E
Yap 94 9 31N 138 6 E
Yapen 73 1 50 S 136 0 E
Yapen, Selat 73 1 20 S 136 10 E
Yappar → 98 18 22 S 141 16 E
Yaqui → 120 27 37N 110 39W
Yar 55 58 14N 52 5 E
Yar-Sale 58 66 50N 70 50 E
Yaraka 97 24 53 S 144 3 E
Yarangüme 64 37 35N 29 8 E
Yaransk 55 57 22N 47 49 E
Yaratishky 54 54 3N 26 0 E
Yare → 13 52 36N 1 28 E
Yarensk 52 61 10N 49 8 E
Yarfa 86 24 40N 38 35 E
Yari → 126 0 20 S 72 20W
Yarkand = Shache 75 38 20N 77 10 E
Yarker 113 44 23N 76 46W
Yarkhun → 69 36 17N 72 30 E
Yarmouth 107 43 50N 66 7W
Yarmuk → 62 32 38N 35 34 E
Yarmūk → 62 32 42N 35 40 E
Yaroslavl 55 57 35N 39 55 E
Yarra → 100 37 50 S 144 53 E
Yarram 99 38 29 S 146 9 E
Yarraman 99 26 50 S 152 0 E
Yarranvale 99 26 50 S 145 20 E
Yarras 99 31 25 S 152 20 E
Yarrawonga 100 36 0 S 146 0 E
Yartsevo, R.S.F.S.R., U.S.S.R. 54 55 6N 32 43 E
Yartsevo, R.S.F.S.R., U.S.S.R. 59 60 20N 90 0 E
Yasawa Group 101 17 00 S 177 23 E
Yaselda → 54 52 7N 26 28 E
Yashi 85 12 23N 7 54 E
Yasinovataya 56 48 7N 37 57 E
Yasinski, L. 106 53 16N 77 35W
Yasothon 71 15 50N 104 10 E
Yass 97 34 49 S 148 54 E
Yas'ur 62 32 54N 35 10 E
Yatağn 45 37 20N 28 10 E
Yates Center 117 37 53N 95 45W
Yathkyed L. 109 62 40N 98 0W
Yatsushiro 74 32 30N 130 40 E
Yatta Plateau 90 2 0 S 38 0 E
Yaṭṭah 62 31 27N 35 6 E
Yauyos 126 12 19 S 75 50W
Yaval 68 21 10N 75 42 E
Yavari → 126 4 21 S 70 2W
Yavne 62 31 52N 34 45 E
Yavorov 54 49 55N 23 20 E
Yawatahama 74 33 27N 132 24 E
Yawri B. 84 8 22N 13 0W
Yazd (Yezd) 65 31 55N 54 27 E
Yazdān 65 33 30N 60 50 E
Yazoo → 117 32 35N 90 50W
Yazoo City 117 32 48N 90 28W
Ybbs 26 48 12N 15 4 E
Ye Xian 76 37 8N 119 57 E
Yebbi-Souma 83 21 7N 17 54 E
Yebyu 67 14 15N 98 13 E
Yecla 33 38 35N 1 5W
Yedintsy 56 48 9N 27 18 E
Yefremov 55 53 8N 38 3 E
Yegorlyk → 57 46 33N 41 40 E
Yegorlykskaya 57 46 35N 40 35 E
Yegoryevsk 55 55 27N 38 55 E
Yegros 124 26 20 S 56 25W
Yehuda, Midbar 62 31 35N 35 15 E
Yei 87 4 9N 30 40 E
Yei, Nahr → 87 6 15N 30 13 E
Yelabuga 52 55 45N 52 4 E
Yelan 55 50 55N 43 43 E
Yelan-Kolenovski 55 51 16N 41 4 E
Yelandur 70 12 6N 77 0 E
Yelanskoye 59 61 25N 128 0 E
Yelarbon 99 28 33 S 150 38 E
Yelatma 55 55 0N 41 45 E
Yelets 55 52 40N 38 30 E
Yélimané 84 15 9N 10 34W
Yell 14 60 35N 1 5W
Yell Sd. 14 60 33N 1 15W
Yellamanchilli (Elamanchili) 70 17 33N 82 50 E
Yellow Mt. 100 32 31 S 146 52 E
Yellow Sea 76 35 0N 123 0 E
Yellowhead P. 108 52 53N 118 25W
Yellowknife 108 62 27N 114 29W
Yellowknife → 104 62 31N 114 19W
Yellowstone → 116 47 58N 103 59W
Yellowstone L. 118 44 30N 110 20W
Yellowstone National Park 118 44 35N 110 0W
Yellowtail Res. 118 45 6N 108 8W
Yelnya 54 54 35N 33 15 E
Yelsk 54 51 50N 29 10 E
Yelvertoft 98 20 13 S 138 45 E
Yelwa 85 10 49N 4 41 E
Yemen ■ 63 15 0N 44 0 E
Yenakiyevo 56 48 15N 38 15 E
Yenangyaung 67 20 30N 95 0 E
Yenda 99 34 13 S 146 14 E
Yendéré 84 10 12N 4 59W
Yendi 85 9 29N 0 1W
Yenisaía 44 41 1N 24 57 E
Yenisey → 58 71 50N 82 40 E
Yeniseysk 59 58 27N 92 13 E
Yeniseyskiy Zaliv 58 72 20N 81 0 E
Yenne 21 45 43N 5 44 E
Yenotayevka 57 47 15N 47 0 E
Yenyuka 59 57 57N 121 15 E
Yeo, L. 96 28 0 S 124 30 E
Yeola 70 20 0N 74 30 E
Yeotmal 70 20 20N 78 15 E
Yeovil 13 50 57N 2 38W
Yepes 32 39 55N 3 39W
Yeppoon 97 23 5 S 150 47 E
Yeráki 45 37 0N 22 42 E
Yerbent 58 39 30N 58 50 E
Yerbogachen 59 61 16N 108 0 E
Yerevan 57 40 10N 44 31 E
Yerla → 70 16 50N 74 30 E
Yermak 58 52 2N 76 55 E
Yermakovo 59 52 25N 126 20 E
Yermo 119 34 58N 116 50W
Yerofey Pavlovich 59 54 0N 122 0 E
Yershov 55 51 22N 48 16 E
Yerushalayim 62 31 47N 35 10 E
Yerville 18 49 40N 0 53 E
Yes Tor 13 50 41N 3 59W
Yesnogorsk 55 54 32N 37 38 E
Yeso 117 34 29N 104 37W
Yessentuki 57 44 0N 42 53 E
Yessey 59 68 29N 102 10 E
Yeste 33 38 22N 2 19W
Yeu, I. d' 18 46 42N 2 20W
Yevlakh 57 40 39N 47 7 E
Yevpatoriya 56 45 15N 33 20 E
Yevstratovskiy 55 50 11N 39 45 E
Yeya → 57 46 40N 38 40 E
Yeysk 56 46 40N 38 12 E
Yhati 124 25 45 S 56 35W
Yhú 125 25 0 S 56 0W
Yi → 124 33 7 S 57 8W
Yi Xian 76 41 30N 121 22 E
Yiali 45 36 41N 27 11 E
Yi'allaq, G. 86 30 21N 33 31 E
Yiáltra 45 38 51N 22 59 E
Yianisádhes 45 35 20N 26 10 E
Yiannitsa 44 40 46N 22 24 E
Yibin 75 28 45N 104 32 E
Yichang 75 30 40N 111 20 E
Yicheng 76 35 42N 111 40 E
Yichuan 76 36 2N 110 10 E
Yichun, Heilongjiang, China 75 47 44N 128 52 E
Yichun, Jiangxi, China 77 27 48N 114 22 E
Yidhá 44 40 35N 22 53 E
Yidu 76 36 43N 118 28 E
Yihuang 77 27 30N 116 12 E
Yijun 76 35 28N 109 8 E
Yilan, China 76 46 19N 129 34 E
Yilan, Taiwan 75 24 51N 121 44 E
Yilehuli Shan 76 51 20N 124 20 E
Yimianpo 76 45 7N 128 2 E
Yinchuan 76 38 30N 106 15 E
Ying He → 77 32 30N 116 30 E
Ying Xian 76 39 32N 113 10 E
Yingcheng 77 30 56N 113 35 E
Yingde 77 24 10N 113 25 E
Yingkou 76 40 37N 122 18 E
Yingshan 77 30 41N 115 32 E
Yingshang 77 32 38N 116 12 E
Yingtan 75 28 12N 117 0 E
Yining 75 43 58N 81 10 E

Yinjiang Zikhron Ya'Aqov

Name	Page	Lat.	Long.
Yinjiang	77	28 1N	108 21 E
Yinkanie	99	34 22 S	140 17 E
Yinnietharra	96	24 39 S	116 12 E
Yioúra, Greece	44	39 23N	24 10 E
Yioúra, Greece	45	37 32N	24 40 E
Yipinglang	75	25 10N	101 52 E
Yirga Alem	87	6 48N	38 22 E
Yirshi	76	47 18N	119 49 E
Yishan	75	24 28N	108 38 E
Yíthion	45	36 46N	22 34 E
Yitong	76	43 13N	125 20 E
Yitulihe	76	50 38N	121 34 E
Yixing	77	31 21N	119 48 E
Yiyang, Henan, China	77	34 27N	112 10 E
Yiyang, Hunan, China	75	28 35N	112 18 E
Yizhang	77	25 27N	112 57 E
Yizre'el	62	32 34N	35 19 E
Ylitornio	50	66 19N	23 39 E
Ylivieska	50	64 4N	24 28 E
Yngaren	49	58 50N	16 35 E
Ynykchanskiy	59	60 15N	137 35 E
Yoakum	117	29 20N	97 20W
Yog Pt.	73	14 6N	124 12 E
Yogan	85	6 23N	1 30 E
Yogyakarta	73	7 49 S	110 22 E
Yoho Nat. Park	108	51 25N	116 30W
Yojoa, L. de	120	14 53N	88 0W
Yokadouma	88	3 26N	15 6 E
Yokkaichi	74	35 0N	136 38 E
Yoko	85	5 32N	12 20 E
Yokohama	74	35 27N	139 28 E
Yokosuka	74	35 20N	139 40 E
Yola	85	9 10N	12 29 E
Yolaina, Cordillera de	121	11 30N	84 0W
Yonago	74	35 25N	133 19 E
Yong Peng	71	2 0N	103 3 E
Yong'an	77	25 59N	117 25 E
Yongchun	77	25 16N	118 20 E
Yongding	77	24 43N	116 45 E
Yongfeng	77	27 20N	115 22 E
Yongfu	77	24 59N	109 59 E
Yonghe	76	36 46N	110 38 E
Yongji	77	34 52N	110 28 E
Yongshun	77	29 2N	109 51 E
Yongxin	77	26 58N	114 15 E
Yongxing	77	26 9N	113 8 E
Yongxiu	77	29 2N	115 42 E
Yonibana	84	8 30N	12 19W
Yonkers	114	40 57N	73 51W
Yonne □	19	47 50N	3 40 E
Yonne →	19	48 23N	2 58 E
Yoqne'am	62	32 40N	35 6 E
York, Austral.	96	31 52 S	116 47 E
York, U.K.	12	53 58N	1 7W
York, Ala., U.S.A.	115	32 30N	88 18W
York, Nebr., U.S.A.	116	40 55N	97 35W
York, Pa., U.S.A.	114	39 57N	76 43W
York, C.	97	10 42 S	142 31 E
York, Kap	4	75 55N	66 25W
York Sd.	96	14 50 S	125 5 E
Yorke Pen.	97	34 50 S	137 40 E
Yorkshire Wolds	12	54 0N	0 30W
Yorkton	109	51 11N	102 28W
Yorktown	117	29 0N	97 29W
Yosemite National Park	119	38 0N	119 30W
Yoshkar Ola	55	56 38N	47 55 E
Yŏsu	77	34 47N	127 45 E
Yotvata	62	29 55N	35 2 E
You Jiang →	75	23 22N	110 3 E
Youbou	108	48 53N	124 13W
Youghal	15	51 58N	7 51W
Youghal B.	15	51 55N	7 50W
Youkounkoun	84	12 35N	13 11W
Young, Austral.	97	34 19 S	148 18 E
Young, Can.	109	51 47N	105 45W
Young, Uruguay	124	32 44 S	57 36W
Young, U.S.A.	119	34 9N	110 56W
Younghusband Pen.	99	36 0 S	139 25 E
Youngstown, Can.	109	51 35N	111 10W
Youngstown, N.Y., U.S.A.	112	43 16N	79 2W
Youngstown, Ohio, U.S.A.	114	41 7N	80 41W
Youngsville	112	41 51N	79 21W
Youssoufia	82	32 16N	8 31W
Youyang	77	28 47N	108 42 E
Youyu	76	40 10N	112 20 E
Yozgat	64	39 51N	34 47 E
Ypané →	124	23 29 S	57 19W
Yport	18	49 45N	0 15 E
Ypres = Ieper	16	50 51N	2 53 E
Ypsilanti	114	42 18N	83 40W
Yreka	118	41 44N	122 40W
Ysleta	119	31 45N	106 24W
Yssingeaux	21	45 9N	4 8 E
Ystad	49	55 26N	13 50 E
Ythan →	14	57 26N	2 12W
Ytterhogdal	48	62 12N	14 56 E
Ytyk-Kel	59	62 30N	133 45 E
Yu Shan	75	23 30N	120 58 E
Yu Xian, Hebei, China	76	39 50N	114 35 E
Yu Xian, Henan, China	77	34 10N	113 28 E
Yuan Jiang →	75	28 55N	111 50 E
Yuanling	75	28 29N	110 22 E
Yuanyang	75	23 10N	102 43 E
Yuba City	118	39 12N	121 37W
Yucatán □	120	21 30N	86 30W
Yucatán, Canal de	121	22 0N	86 30W
Yucca	119	34 56N	114 6W
Yucheng	76	36 55N	116 32 E
Yuci	76	37 42N	112 46 E
Yudino, R.S.F.S.R., U.S.S.R.	55	55 51N	48 55 E
Yudino, R.S.F.S.R., U.S.S.R.	58	55 10N	67 55 E
Yudu	77	25 59N	115 30 E
Yueqing	77	28 9N	120 59 E
Yueyang	77	29 21N	113 5 E
Yugan	77	28 43N	116 37 E
Yugoslavia ■	37	44 0N	20 0 E
Yuhuan	77	28 9N	121 12 E
Yujiang	77	28 10N	116 43 E
Yukhnov	54	54 44N	35 15 E
Yukon Territory □	104	63 0N	135 0W
Yukti	59	63 26N	105 42 E
Yule →	96	20 41 S	118 17 E
Yuli	85	9 44N	10 12 E
Yülin	77	18 10N	109 31 E
Yulin, Guangxi Zhuangzu, China	77	22 40N	110 8 E
Yulin, Shaanxi, China	76	38 20N	109 30 E
Yuma, Ariz., U.S.A.	119	32 45N	114 37W
Yuma, Colo., U.S.A.	116	40 10N	102 43W
Yuma, B. de	121	18 20N	68 35W
Yumbe	90	3 28N	31 15 E
Yumbi	90	1 12 S	26 15 E
Yumen	75	39 50N	97 30 E
Yun Xian	75	32 50N	110 46 E
Yungas	126	17 0 S	66 0W
Yungay	124	37 10 S	72 5W
Yunhe	77	28 8N	119 33 E
Yunlin	77	23 42N	120 30 E
Yunnan □	75	25 0N	102 0 E
Yunquera de Henares	32	40 47N	3 11W
Yunta	99	32 34 S	139 36 E
Yunxiao	77	23 59N	117 18 E
Yur	59	59 52N	137 41 E
Yurgao	58	55 42N	84 51 E
Yuribei	58	71 8N	76 58 E
Yurimaguas	126	5 55 S	76 7W
Yurya	55	59 1N	49 13 E
Yuryev-Polskiy	55	56 30N	39 40 E
Yuryevets	55	57 25N	43 2 E
Yuscarán	121	13 58N	86 45W
Yushu, Jilin, China	76	44 43N	126 38 E
Yushu, Qinghai, China	75	33 5N	96 55 E
Yuyao	77	30 3N	121 10 E
Yuzha	55	56 34N	42 1 E
Yuzhno-Sakhalinsk	59	46 58N	142 45 E
Yvelines □	19	48 40N	1 45 E
Yverdon	25	46 47N	6 39 E
Yvetot	18	49 37N	0 44 E
Z			
Zaandam	16	52 26N	4 49 E
Zab, Monts du	83	34 55N	5 0 E
Žabalj	42	45 21N	20 5 E
Žabari	42	44 22N	21 15 E
Zabarjad	86	23 40N	36 12 E
Zabaykalskiy	59	49 40N	117 25 E
Zabid	63	14 0N	43 10 E
Ząbkowice Śląskie	28	50 35N	16 50 E
Žabljak	42	43 18N	19 7 E
Zabłudów	28	53 0N	23 19 E
Žabno	27	50 9N	20 53 E
Zābol	65	31 0N	61 32 E
Zābolī	65	27 10N	61 35 E
Zabré	85	11 12N	0 36W
Zabrze	28	50 18N	18 50 E
Zabul □	65	32 0N	67 0 E
Zacapa	120	14 59N	89 31W
Zacatecas	120	22 49N	102 34W
Zacatecas □	120	23 30N	103 0W
Zacatecoluca	120	13 29N	88 51W
Zacoalco	120	20 14N	103 33W
Zadar	39	44 8N	15 14 E
Zadawa	85	11 33N	10 19 E
Zadetkyi Kyun	72	10 0N	98 25 E
Zadonsk	55	52 25N	38 56 E
Zafora	45	36 5N	26 24 E
Zafra	31	38 26N	6 30W
Zafriya	62	31 59N	34 51 E
Żagań	28	51 39N	15 22 E
Zagazig	86	30 40N	31 30 E
Zaghouan	83	36 23N	10 10 E
Zaglivérion	44	40 36N	23 15 E
Zaglou	82	27 17N	0 3W
Zagnanado	85	7 18N	2 28 E
Zagorá	44	39 27N	23 6 E
Zagora	82	30 22N	5 51W
Zagórów	28	52 10N	17 54 E
Zagorsk	55	56 20N	38 10 E
Zagórz	27	49 30N	22 14 E
Zagreb	39	45 50N	16 0 E
Zāgros, Kudhā-ye	65	33 45N	47 0 E
Žagubica	42	44 15N	21 47 E
Zaguinaso	84	10 1N	6 14W
Zagyva →	27	47 5N	20 4 E
Zāhedān	65	29 30N	60 50 E
Zahirabad	70	17 43N	77 37 E
Zahlah	64	33 52N	35 50 E
Zahna	24	51 54N	12 47 E
Zahrez Chergui	82	35 0N	3 30 E
Zahrez Rharbi	82	34 50N	2 55 E
Zaïr	82	29 47N	5 51W
Zaïre →	88	6 4 S	12 24 E
Zaïre, Rep. of ■	88	3 0 S	23 0 E
Zaječar	42	43 53N	22 18 E
Zakamensk	59	50 23N	103 17 E
Zakataly	57	41 38N	46 35 E
Zakavkazye	57	42 0N	44 0 E
Zākhū	64	37 10N	42 50 E
Zákinthos	45	37 47N	20 57 E
Zaklików	28	50 46N	22 7 E
Zakopane	27	49 18N	19 57 E
Zakroczym	28	52 26N	20 38 E
Zala □	27	46 42N	16 50 E
Zala →	27	46 43N	17 16 E
Zalaegerszeg	27	46 53N	16 47 E
Zalakomár	27	46 33N	17 10 E
Zalalövö	27	46 51N	16 35 E
Zalamea de la Serena	31	38 40N	5 38W
Zalamea la Real	31	37 41N	6 38W
Zalău	46	47 12N	23 3 E
Zalazna	55	58 39N	52 31 E
Žalec	39	46 16N	15 10 E
Zaleshchiki	56	48 45N	25 45 E
Zalewo	28	53 50N	19 41 E
Zalingei	81	12 51N	23 29 E
Zaltan, Jabal	83	28 46N	19 45 E
Zambeke	90	2 8N	25 17 E
Zambeze →	91	18 55 S	36 4 E
Zambezi	89	13 30 S	23 15 E
Zambezi = Zambeze →	91	18 55 S	36 4 E
Zambezia □	91	16 15 S	37 30 E
Zambia ■	89	15 0 S	28 0 E
Zamboanga	73	6 59N	122 3 E
Zambrów	28	52 59N	22 14 E
Zametchino	55	53 30N	42 30 E
Zamora, Mexico	120	20 0N	102 21W
Zamora, Spain	30	41 30N	5 45W
Zamora □	30	41 30N	5 46W
Zamość	28	50 43N	23 15 E
Zamość □	28	50 40N	23 10 E
Zamzam, W.	83	31 0N	14 30 E
Zan	85	9 26N	0 17W
Zanaga	88	2 48 S	13 48 E
Záncara →	33	39 18N	3 18W
Zandvoort	16	52 22N	4 32 E
Zanesville	114	39 56N	82 2W
Zangue →	91	17 50 S	35 21 E
Zanjan	64	36 40N	48 35 E
Zannone	40	40 58N	13 2 E
Zante = Zákinthos	45	37 47N	20 54 E
Zanthus	96	31 2 S	123 34 E
Zanzibar	90	6 12 S	39 12 E
Zanzūr	83	32 55N	13 1 E
Zaouiet El-Kala = Bordj Omar Driss	83	28 4N	6 40 E
Zaouiet Reggane	82	26 32N	0 3 E
Zapadna Morava →	42	43 38N	21 30 E
Zapadnaya Dvina	54	56 15N	32 3 E
Zapadnaya Dvina →	54	57 4N	24 3 E
Západné Beskydy	27	49 30N	19 0 E
Zapadni Rodopi	43	41 50N	24 0 E
Západočeský □	26	49 35N	13 0 E
Západoslovenský □	27	48 30N	17 30 E
Zapala	128	39 0 S	70 5W
Zapaleri, Cerro	124	22 49 S	67 11W
Zapata	117	26 56N	99 17W
Zapatón →	31	39 0N	6 49W
Zapodnyy Sayan	59	52 30N	94 0 E
Zapolyarnyy	52	69 26N	30 51 E
Zaporozhye	56	47 50N	35 10 E
Zapponeta	41	41 27N	15 57 E
Zara	64	39 58N	37 43 E
Zaragoza, Coahuila, Mexico	120	28 30N	101 0W
Zaragoza, Nuevo León, Mexico	120	24 0N	99 46W
Zaragoza, Spain	32	41 39N	0 53W
Zaragoza □	32	41 35N	1 0W
Zarand	65	30 46N	56 34 E
Zărandului, Munţii	46	46 14N	22 7 E
Zaranj	65	30 55N	61 55 E
Zarasai	54	55 40N	26 20 E
Zarate	124	34 7 S	59 0W
Zaraysk	55	54 48N	38 53 E
Zarembo I.	108	56 20N	132 50W
Zaria	85	11 0N	7 40 E
Zarisberge	92	24 30 S	16 15 E
Zárkon	44	39 38N	22 6 E
Żarów	28	50 56N	16 29 E
Zarqā' →	62	32 10N	35 37 E
Zaruma	126	3 40 S	79 38W
Żary	28	51 37N	15 10 E
Zarza de Alange	31	38 49N	6 13W
Zarza de Granadilla	30	40 14N	6 3W
Zarza, La	31	37 42N	6 51W
Zarzaïtine	83	28 15N	9 34 E
Zarzis	83	33 31N	11 2 E
Zas	30	43 4N	8 53W
Zashiversk	59	67 25N	142 40 E
Zaskar Mountains	69	33 15N	77 30 E
Zastron	92	30 18 S	27 7 E
Žatec	26	50 20N	13 32 E
Zator	27	49 59N	19 28 E
Zavala	42	42 50N	17 59 E
Zavarāh	65	33 29N	52 28 E
Zavetnoye	57	47 13N	43 50 E
Zavidovići	42	44 27N	18 13 E
Zavitinsk	59	50 10N	129 20 E
Zavodoski	5	56 0 S	27 45W
Zavolzhsk	55	57 30N	42 10 E
Zavolzhye	55	56 37N	43 26 E
Zawadzkie	28	50 37N	18 28 E
Zawichost	28	50 48N	21 51 E
Zawidów	28	51 1N	15 1 E
Zawiercie	28	50 30N	19 24 E
Zāwiyat al Bayḍā	81	32 30N	21 40 E
Zawyet Shammâs	86	31 30N	26 37 E
Zâwyet Um el Rakham	86	31 18N	27 1 E
Zâwyet Ungeîla	86	31 23N	26 42 E
Zāyandeh →	65	32 35N	52 0 E
Zayarsk	59	56 12N	102 55 E
Zaysan	58	47 28N	84 52 E
Zaysan, Oz.	58	48 0N	83 0 E
Zaytā	62	32 23N	35 2 E
Zāzamt, W.	83	30 29N	14 30 E
Zazir, O. →	83	22 0N	5 40 E
Zázrivá	27	49 16N	19 7 E
Zbarazh	54	49 43N	25 44 E
Zbąszyń	28	52 14N	15 56 E
Zbąszynek	28	52 16N	15 51 E
Zblewo	28	53 56N	18 19 E
Zdolbunov	54	50 30N	26 15 E
Ždrelo	42	44 16N	21 28 E
Zduńska Wola	28	51 37N	18 59 E
Zduny	28	51 39N	17 21 E
Zeballos	108	49 59N	126 50W
Zebediela	93	24 20 S	19 7 E
Zeebrugge	16	51 19N	3 12 E
Zeehan	97	41 52 S	145 25 E
Zeeland □	16	51 30N	3 50 E
Ze'elim	62	31 13N	34 32 E
Zeerust	92	25 31 S	26 4 E
Zefat	62	32 58N	35 29 E
Zegdou	82	29 51N	4 45W
Zege	87	11 43N	37 18 E
Zégoua	84	10 32N	5 35W
Zehdenick	24	52 59N	13 20 E
Zeila	63	11 21N	43 30 E
Zeist	16	52 5N	5 15 E
Zeitz	24	51 3N	12 9 E
Żelechów	28	51 49N	21 54 E
Zelengora	42	43 22N	18 30 E
Zelenika	42	42 27N	18 37 E
Zelenodolsk	55	55 55N	48 30 E
Zelenogradsk	54	54 53N	20 29 E
Zelenokumsk	57	44 24N	43 53 E
Zelënyy	57	48 6N	50 45 E
Zeleznik	42	44 43N	20 23 E
Zell, Baden, Ger.	25	47 42N	7 50 E
Zell, Rhld-Pfz., Ger.	25	50 2N	7 11 E
Zell am See	26	47 19N	12 47 E
Zella Mehlis	24	50 40N	10 41 E
Zelów	28	51 28N	19 14 E
Zelzate	16	51 13N	3 47 E
Zembra, I.	83	37 5N	10 56 E
Zémio	90	5 2N	25 5 E
Zemlya Frantsa Iosifa	4	81 0N	55 0 E
Zemmora	82	35 44N	0 51 E
Zemoul, O. →	82	29 15N	7 0W
Zemun	42	44 51N	20 25 E
Zengbe	85	5 46N	13 4 E
Zenica	42	44 10N	17 57 E
Zenina	82	34 30N	2 37 E
Žepče	42	44 28N	18 2 E
Zeraf, Bahr ez →	87	9 42N	30 52 E
Zerbst	24	51 59N	12 8 E
Zerhamra	82	29 58N	2 30W
Żerków	28	52 4N	17 32 E
Zermatt	25	46 2N	7 46 E
Zernez	25	46 42N	10 7 E
Zernograd	57	46 52N	40 19 E
Zerqani	44	41 30N	20 20 E
Zestafoni	57	42 6N	43 0 E
Zetel	24	53 25N	7 57 E
Zeulenroda	24	50 39N	12 0 E
Zeven	24	53 17N	9 19 E
Zévio	38	45 23N	11 10 E
Zeya	59	53 48N	127 14 E
Zeya →	59	53 13N	127 35 E
Zêzere →	31	39 28N	8 20W
Zgierz	28	51 50N	19 27 E
Zgorzelec	28	51 10N	15 0 E
Zhabinka	54	52 13N	24 2 E
Zhailma	58	51 37N	61 33 E
Zhangguangcai Ling	76	45 0N	129 0 E
Zhanghua	75	24 6N	120 29 E
Zhangjiakou	76	40 48N	114 55 E
Zhangping	77	25 17N	117 23 E
Zhangpu	77	24 8N	117 35 E
Zhangwu	76	42 43N	123 52 E
Zhangye	75	38 50N	100 23 E
Zhangzhou	75	24 30N	117 35 E
Zhanhua	76	37 40N	118 8 E
Zhanjiang	75	21 15N	110 20 E
Zhanyi	75	25 38N	103 48 E
Zhanyu	76	44 30N	122 30 E
Zhao Xian	76	37 43N	114 45 E
Zhao'an	77	23 41N	117 10 E
Zhaoping	77	24 11N	110 48 E
Zhaoqing	77	23 0N	112 20 E
Zhaotong	75	27 20N	103 44 E
Zhaoyuan	76	37 20N	120 23 E
Zharkovskiy	54	55 56N	32 19 E
Zhashkov	56	49 15N	30 5 E
Zhdanov	56	47 5N	37 31 E
Zhecheng	77	34 7N	115 20 E
Zhejiang □	75	29 0N	120 0 E
Zheleznodorozhny	52	62 35N	50 55 E
Zheleznogorsk	54	52 22N	35 23 E
Zheleznogorsk-Ilimskiy	59	56 34N	104 8 E
Zheltyye Vody	56	48 21N	33 31 E
Zhen'an	77	33 27N	109 9 E
Zhenfeng	77	25 22N	105 40 E
Zheng'an	77	28 32N	107 27 E
Zhengding	76	38 8N	114 32 E
Zhenghe	77	27 20N	118 50 E
Zhengyang	77	32 37N	114 22 E
Zhengyangguan	77	32 30N	116 29 E
Zhengzhou	77	34 45N	113 34 E
Zhenjiang	75	32 11N	119 26 E
Zhenlai	76	45 50N	123 5 E
Zhenning	77	26 4N	105 45 E
Zhenyuan, Gansu, China	76	35 35N	107 30 E
Zhenyuan, Guizhou, China	75	27 4N	108 21 E
Zherdevka	55	51 56N	41 29 E
Zhigansk	59	66 48N	123 27 E
Zhigulevsk	55	53 28N	49 30 E
Zhijiang	75	27 27N	109 42 E
Zhirnovsk	55	50 57N	44 49 E
Zhitomir	54	50 20N	28 40 E
Zhizdra	54	53 45N	34 40 E
Zhlobin	54	52 55N	30 0 E
Zhmerinka	56	49 2N	28 2 E
Zhodino	54	54 5N	28 17 E
Zhokhova, Ostrov	59	76 4N	152 40 E
Zhong Xian	77	30 21N	108 1 E
Zhongdian	75	27 48N	99 42 E
Zhongshan	77	22 26N	113 20 E
Zhongwei	76	37 30N	105 12 E
Zhongxiang	77	31 12N	112 34 E
Zhoushan Dao	77	28 5N	122 10 E
Zhouzhi	77	34 10N	108 12 E
Zhovtnevoye	56	46 54N	32 3 E
Zhuanghe	76	39 40N	123 0 E
Zhucheng	76	36 0N	119 27 E
Zhugqu	77	33 40N	104 30 E
Zhuji	77	29 40N	120 10 E
Zhukovka	54	53 35N	33 50 E
Zhumadian	75	32 59N	114 2 E
Zhuo Xian	76	39 28N	115 58 E
Zhupanovo	59	53 40N	159 52 E
Zhushan	77	32 15N	110 13 E
Zhuxi	77	32 25N	109 40 E
Zhuzhou	75	27 49N	113 12 E
Ziarat	68	30 25N	67 49 E
Zibo	76	36 47N	118 3 E
Zidarovo	43	42 20N	27 24 E
Ziębice	28	50 37N	17 2 E
Zielona Góra	28	51 57N	15 31 E
Zielona Góra □	28	51 57N	15 30 E
Zierikzee	16	51 40N	3 55 E
Ziesar	24	52 16N	12 19 E
Zifta	86	30 43N	31 14 E
Zigey	81	14 43N	15 50 E
Zigong	75	29 15N	104 48 E
Zigui	75	31 0N	110 40 E
Ziguinchor	84	12 35N	16 20W
Zikhron Ya'Aqov	62	32 34N	34 56 E

Zile	64 40 15N 35 52 E	Ziz, Oued →	82 31 40N 4 15W	Zorra Island	120 9 18N 79 52W	Zunyi	75 27 42N 106 53 E
Žilina	27 49 12N 18 42 E	Zizhong	77 29 48N 104 47 E	Zorritos	126 3 43 S 80 40W	Żupanja	42 45 4N 18 43 E
Zillah	83 28 30N 17 33 E	Zlarin	39 43 42N 15 49 E	Zory	27 50 3N 18 44 E	Zuqar	87 14 0N 42 40 E
Zillertaler Alpen	26 47 6N 11 45 E	Zlatar, Hrvatska, Yugo.	39 46 5N 16 3 E	Zorzor	84 7 46N 9 28W	Żur	42 42 13N 20 34 E
Zima	59 54 0N 102 5 E	Zlatar, Srbija, Yugo.	42 43 25N 19 47 E	Zossen	24 52 13N 13 28 E	Zürich	25 47 22N 8 32 E
Zimane, Adrar in	82 22 10N 4 30 E	Zlataritsa	43 43 2N 25 55 E	Zou Xiang	77 35 30N 116 58 E	Zürich □	25 47 26N 8 40 E
Zimapán	120 20 54N 99 20W	Zlatibor	42 43 45N 19 43 E	Zouar	83 20 30N 16 32 E	Zürichsee	25 47 18N 8 40 E
Zimba	91 17 20 S 26 11 E	Zlatitsa	43 42 41N 24 7 E	Zouérate	80 22 44N 12 21W	Zuromin	28 53 4N 19 51 E
Zimbabwe	91 20 16 S 30 54 E	Zlatna	46 46 8N 23 11 E	Zousfana, O. →	82 31 28N 2 17W	Zuru	85 11 20N 5 11 E
Zimbabwe ■	91 20 0 S 30 0 E	Zlatograd	43 41 22N 25 7 E	Zoutkamp	16 53 20N 6 18 E	Żut	39 43 52N 15 17 E
Zimnicea	46 43 40N 25 22 E	Zlatoust	52 55 10N 59 40 E	Zrenjanin	42 45 22N 20 23 E	Zutphen	16 52 9N 6 12 E
Zimovniki	57 47 10N 42 25 E	Zletovo	42 41 59N 22 17 E	Zuarungu	85 10 49N 0 46W	Zuwārah	83 32 58N 12 1 E
Zinder	85 13 48N 9 0 E	Žlitan	83 32 32N 14 35 E	Zuba	85 9 11N 7 12 E	Zuyevka	55 58 25N 51 10 E
Zinga	91 9 16 S 38 49 E	Złocieniec	28 53 30N 16 1 E	Zubair, Jazāir	87 15 0N 42 10 E	Žužemberk	39 45 52N 14 56 E
Zingst	24 54 24N 12 48 E	Złoczew	28 51 24N 18 35 E	Zubia	31 37 8N 3 33W	Zvenigorodka	56 49 4N 30 56 E
Ziniaré	85 12 35N 1 18W	Zlot	42 44 1N 22 0 E	Zubtsov	54 56 10N 34 34 E	Zverinogolovskoye	58 54 23N 64 40 E
Zinjibār	63 13 5N 45 23 E	Złotoryja	28 51 8N 15 55 E	Zuénoula	84 7 34N 6 3W	Zvezdets	43 42 6N 27 26 E
Zinkgruvan	49 58 50N 15 6 E	Złotów	28 53 22N 17 2 E	Zuera	32 41 51N 0 49W	Zvolen	27 48 33N 19 10 E
Zinnowitz	24 54 5N 13 54 E	Złoty Stok	28 50 27N 16 53 E	Zuetina	83 30 58N 20 7 E	Zvonce	42 42 57N 22 34 E
Zion Nat. Park	119 37 25N 112 50W	Zmeinogorsk	58 51 10N 82 13 E	Zufar	63 17 40N 54 0 E	Zvornik	42 44 26N 19 7 E
Zipaquirá	126 5 0N 74 0W	Żmigród	28 51 28N 16 53 E	Zug	25 47 10N 8 31 E	Zwedru (Tchien)	84 5 59N 8 15W
Zippori	62 32 45N 35 16 E	Zmiyev	56 49 39N 36 27 E	Zugdidi	57 42 30N 41 55 E	Zweibrücken	25 49 15N 7 20 E
Zirc	27 47 17N 17 42 E	Znamenka	56 48 45N 32 30 E	Zugersee	25 47 7N 8 35 E	Zwenkau	24 51 13N 12 19 E
Žiri	39 46 5N 14 5 E	Znamensk	54 54 37N 21 17 E	Zugspitze	25 47 25N 10 59 E	Zwettl	26 48 35N 15 9 E
Žirje	39 43 39N 15 42 E	Żnin	28 52 51N 17 44 E	Zuid-Holland □	16 52 0N 4 35 E	Zwickau	24 50 43N 12 30 E
Zirko	65 25 0N 53 40 E	Znojmo	26 48 50N 16 2 E	Zuidhorn	16 53 15N 6 23 E	Zwiesel	25 49 1N 13 14 E
Zirl	26 47 17N 11 14 E	Zoar	92 33 30 S 21 26 E	Zújar	33 37 34N 2 50W	Zwischenahn	24 53 12N 8 1 E
Zisterdorf	27 48 33N 16 45 E	Zobia	90 3 0N 25 59 E	Zújar →	31 39 1N 5 47W	Zwoleń	28 51 21N 21 36 E
Zitácuaro	120 19 28N 100 21W	Zogno	38 45 49N 9 41 E	Zújar, Pantano del	31 38 55N 5 35W	Zwolle, Neth.	16 52 31N 6 6 E
Zitava →	27 48 14N 18 21 E	Zolochev	54 49 45N 24 51 E	Zula	87 15 17N 39 40 E	Zwolle, U.S.A.	117 31 38N 93 38W
Žitište	42 45 30N 20 32 E	Zolotonosha	56 49 39N 32 5 E	Zulpich	24 50 41N 6 38 E	Żychlin	28 52 15N 19 37 E
Žitsa	44 39 47N 20 40 E	Zomba	91 15 22 S 35 19 E	Zululand	93 43 19N 2 15 E	Zymoetz →	108 54 33N 128 31W
Zittau	24 50 54N 14 47 E	Zongo	88 4 20N 18 35 E	Zumaya	32 43 19N 2 15W	Żyrardów	28 52 3N 20 28 E
Zitundo	93 26 48 S 32 47 E	Zonguldak	56 41 28N 31 50 E	Zumbo	91 15 35 S 30 26 E	Zyrya	57 40 20N 50 15 E
Živinice	42 44 27N 18 36 E	Zorgo	85 12 15N 0 35W	Zummo	85 9 51N 12 59 E	Zyryanka	59 65 45N 150 51 E
Ziway, L.	87 8 0N 38 50 E	Zorita	31 39 17N 5 39W	Zungeru	85 9 48N 6 8 E	Zyryanovsk	58 49 43N 84 20 E
Zixi	77 27 45N 117 4 E	Zorleni	46 46 14N 27 44 E	Zunhua	76 40 18N 117 58 E	Żywiec	27 49 42N 19 10 E
Ziyang	77 32 32N 108 31 E	Zornitsa	43 42 23N 26 58 E	Zuni	119 35 7N 108 57W		

Recent Place Name Changes

The following place name changes have recently occurred.
The new names are on the maps but the former names are in the index.

India

Former name	New name
Ambarnath	Amarnath
Arrah	Ara
Aruppukottai	Aruppukkottai
Barrackpur	Barakpur
Berhampore	Baharampur
Bokharo Steel City	Bokaro
Budge Budge	Baj Baj
Burdwam	Barddhaman
Chapra	Chhapra
Cooch Behar	Koch Bihar
Dohad	Dahod
Dhulia	Dhule
English Bazar	Ingraj Bazar
Farrukhabad-cum-Fatehgarh	Fategarh
Ferozepore	Firozpur
Gadag-Batgeri	Gadag
Gudiyatam	Gudiyattam
Hardwar	Haridwar
Hooghly-Chinsura	Chunchura
Howrah	Haora
Hubli-Dharwar	Dharwad
Kadayanallur	Kadaiyanallur
Manaar, Gulf of	Mannar, Gulf of
Maunath Bhanjan	Mau
Mehsana	Mahesana
Midnapore	Medinipur
Monghyr	Munger
Morvi	Morbi
Nabadwip	Navadwip
Nander	Nanded
Palayancottai	Palayankottai
Purnea	Purnia
Rajnandgaon	Raj Nandgaon
Santipur	Shantipur
Serampore	Shrirampur
Siliguri	Siliguri
Sonepat	Sonipat
South Suburban	Behala

Iran

Former name	New name
Bandar-e Pahlavi	Bandar-e Anzalī
Bandar-e Shāh	Bandar-e Torkeman
Bandar-e Shahpur	Bandar-e Khomeynī
Dezh Shāhpūr	Marīvan
Gach Sārān	Gachsārān
Herowābād	Khalkhāl
Kermānshāh	Qahremānshahr
Naft-e Shāh	Naftshahr
Rezā īyeh	Orūmīyeh
Rezā īyeh, Daryācheh-ye	Orūmīyeh, Daryācheh-ye
Shāhābād	Āshkhāneh
Shāhābād	Eslāmābad-e Gharb
Shāhī	Qā 'emshahr
Shahrezā	Qomsheh
Shāhrud	Emāmrūd
Shahsavār	Tonekābon
Solṭāniyeh	Sa'īdīyeh

Mozambique

Former name	New name
Augusto Cardosa	Metangula
Entre Rios	Malema
Malvérnia	Chicualacuala
Miranda	Macalogue
Olivença	Lupilichi
Vila Alferes Chamusca	Guijá
Vila Caldas Xavier	Muende
Vila Coutinho	Ulonguè
Vila Fontes	Caia
Vila de Junqueiro	Gurué
Vila Luísa	Marracuene
Vila Paiva de Andrada	Gorongoza

Zimbabwe

Former name	New name
Balla Balla	Mbalabala
Belingwe	Mberengwa
Chipinga	Chipinge
Dett	Dete
Enkeldoorn	Chivhu
Essexvale	Esigodini
Fort Victoria	Masvingo
Gwelo	Gweru
Hartley	Chegutu
Gatooma	Kadoma
Inyazura	Nyazura
Marandellas	Marondera
Mashaba	Mashava
Melsetter	Chimanimani
Mrewa	Murewa
Mtoko	Mutoko
Nuanetsi	Mwenezi
Que Que	Kwekwe
Salisbury	Harare
Selukwe	Shurugwi
Shabani	Zvishavane
Sinoia	Chinhoyi
Somabula	Somabhula
Tjolotjo	Tsholotsho
Umvuma	Mvuma
Umtali	Mutare
Wankie	Hwange

Maps, Illustrations and Index printed in Great Britain by George Philip Printers Ltd., London